Praise for
Choosing the Right College

"*Choosing the Right College* is by far the best college guide in America. It covers subjects not even mentioned in other college guides, but which are urgently important for parents and students to know about. This is especially so at a time when choosing the wrong college can lead not merely to disappointment but to disaster."

—**Thomas Sowell**, Hoover Institution, Stanford University

"*Choosing the Right College* is aimed at exposing the political biases of academe, the prevalence of permissive sex and the lack of core curriculums to prospective students and their parents."

—*New York Times*

"In choosing among schools, it pays to have connections to people who know them firsthand. That is what this book provides, in abundance. I will recommend it to parents and young people looking for that increasingly rare thing, an education."

—**Richard John Neuhaus**, editor in chief,
First Things: A Monthly Journal of Religion and Public Life

"American parents (and students) have long needed a reliable 'review' of our nation's universities so they can be sure they will not be supporting the systematic destruction of the values, faith, and worldview they have spent so many years building up. *Choosing the Right College* is the right book for them. It exposes the bad ones and confirms the good ones. My only regret is that it wasn't available as early as the sixties. Think of the administration buildings that might have been spared occupation!"

—**Cal Thomas**, syndicated columnist

"This guide to colleges is by far the most factually based of any I have seen. The editors have made a serious attempt to gain objective information on the colleges about which they report. This review is in striking contrast to the subjective opinions recorded by *U.S. News and World Report*."

—**John Silber**, Chancellor, Boston University

"[P]rovides as comprehensive a catalogue of the academic skies as is anywhere available. . . . Given the encyclopedic scope of this guide, one can only stand in awe of the consistency with which its editors have been able to grasp what makes each campus tick."

—**Stephen H. Balch**, President,
National Association of Scholars

"What is remarkable about ISI's offering is that it captures the tone of the academic, political, and social life of each school, as well as that school's attitude toward the traditional liberal arts."

—*Crisis*

"I've got children approaching college age, so I'll be consulting this useful book. I'll even do my best to get the kids to read it."

—**William Kristol**, editor and publisher,
Weekly Standard, and Fox News analyst

"At last, parents and prospective students can get an honest, in-depth account of what really awaits them at America's top colleges. This book does not mince words. It provides exacting, no-nonsense assessments of academic life in both its intellectual and moral dimensions. In my opinion, *Choosing the Right College* is an indispensable guide for anyone who wants to make an informed and intelligent choice about one of the most important—and expensive—decisions most of us will ever make."

—**Roger Kimball**, author of *Tenured Radicals:
How Politics Has Corrupted Our Higher Education*

"What more can I say? I am using *Choosing the Right College*—actively and appreciatively—as our high school senior son contemplates colleges and universities. To parents like me, this wise and informative book is a rich blessing."

—**William Murchison**, syndicated columnist

"[F]or us, [*Choosing the Right College*] was a godsend, its lengthy and meticulously researched entries confirming our impressions of certain schools we'd seen, giving us a new insight into others. Though brutal to certain 'hot' schools . . . it can be just as generous when it finds rigor and real respect for learning."

—from *How I Accidently Joined the Vast Right-Wing Conspiracy,* by Harry Stein

Choosing the Right College

Project Director
Jeffrey O. Nelson

Editor in Chief
John Zmirak

Senior Editors
Jeremy Beer, Jeremy Nafziger

Contributing Editors
Amanda Beer, Richard Cowden, Paul Chu, Charles A. Coulombe, Alexandra Gilman, Claudia Henrie, Erica Kane, Anne Larson, Katherine Dillon Luppi, James McCoy, Colleen O'Connor, Frank Purcell, Jennifer Roche, Cathy Ryan, Laura Vanderkam

Core Curriculum Consultant
Mark C. Henrie

Choosing the Right College

2006

The Whole Truth about America's Top Schools

Produced by the Intercollegiate Studies Institute (ISI)
T. Kenneth Cribb Jr., President

Choosing the Right College 2006 was supported by grants from Menlo F. Smith and Arthur E. Rasmussen. The Intercollegiate Studies Institute gratefully acknowledges this support.

This is the fifth edition of *Choosing the Right College*.

ISBN: 1-932236-60-0

ISSN: 1548-4068

Published by: ISI Books
Intercollegiate Studies Institute
P.O. Box 4431
Wilmington, DE 19807-0431

Book design by Kara Beer and Sam Torode

CONTENTS

Middle Atlantic

South

Midwest

West

INTRODUCTION

William J. Bennett

When the first edition of *Choosing the Right College* appeared in 1998, it struck a surprisingly responsive chord. Despite a minimal publicity and advertising budget, *Choosing the Right College* became the bestselling essay-style college guide in America. Readers appreciated its honesty, its independence, and its narrative structure. No other guide evaluated the adequacy of institutions' core curricula for the provision of a liberal arts education worthy of the name; no other guide concerned itself with the level of political correctness on campus; no other guide pointed out the worst departments and the best professors; no other guide spoke to the level of crime on or around campus; no other guide evaluated the extent to which institutions had abandoned the last vestiges of their former *in loco parentis* obligations.

In other words, no other guide brought to its task the educational vision explicitly advocated by the ISI guide: to wit, that a core curriculum that introduces students to the best that has been thought and said—especially the best that has been thought and said by those Western thinkers whose ideas have formed our political, religious, and cultural landscapes—is what best serves students, even in this age of multiculturalism and globalization. In ISI's view, classic texts and the fundamental questions they raise should, as far as possible, be approached on their own terms. Rather than insisting that the disciplines be approached from the narrow perspectives of race, gender, or ethnicity (or whatever), a genuine liberal arts education should attempt to liberate students from the prison houses of such provincialities. And the ends of education are best served when there is a campus atmosphere marked by intellectual freedom, a healthy sense of community and tradition, and relative safety.

As it turns out, this unfashionable educational vision still appeals to a sizable public. Not only have students, parents, and grandparents purchased tens of thousands of copies of the first four editions of *Choosing the Right College,* but the critics have loved it as well. Hundreds of articles, reviews, and columns devoted to *Choosing the Right College* have appeared in magazines and newspapers of all sizes across the country. Dr. Laura Schlessinger, Michael Medved, Walter Williams, Thomas Sowell, John Leo, John Silber, Richard John Neuhaus, William Kristol, Christina Hoff Sommers, Midge Decter, Cal Thomas—they all have praised it. The *Chicago Sun-Times, Charlotte Observer, Arizona Republic, Houston Chronicle, Denver Post* and *Rocky Mountain News, Detroit News* and *Free Press,* even the *New York Times,* heralded its publication. It is heartening to see just how widely appealing *Choosing the Right College*'s commitment to a nonideological liberal arts ideal is.

A few things have changed since I contributed the introduction to the first edition of this guide. For one thing, with success has come imitation. Other guides now also claim to steer students toward the "best professors" and "best courses." And other guides now also venture to comment on each campus's "political atmosphere." But since these guides are not informed by a coherent educational philosophy—they often read as though they were written by the schools' admissions offices themselves—their evaluations are not particularly trustworthy.

More importantly, the atmosphere of higher education itself has shifted subtly during the last six years. When the ISI staff put together the first edition of this guide, extreme political correctness—as manifested in speech codes, secret and unconstitutional tribunals, the refusal to grant the right of due process to students and faculty with unpopular views—still seemed to be spreading unchecked. Today, although extreme manifestations of political correctness still occur, they are at least a matter of public ridicule. Having been made aware of the draconian measures being taken in the academy to promote a tendentious ideological vision, observers of all political stripes—including cartoonists, pundits, lawyers, comedians, speechwriters, politicians, editorialists, even journalists—are quick to make fun of academic nonsense. And why not? When an instructor calls the victims of 9/11 "little Eichmanns" (see the University of Colorado at Boulder entry), or when a university administrator offers counseling sessions to students at a purportedly Catholic school because they may have been traumatized by their exposure to Catholic doctrine (see Georgetown University)—well, it certainly makes for sensational copy.

During the last few years, student and faculty victims of politically motivated retribution and censorship have found a ready ally in organizations like the Foundation for Individual Rights in Education and the Student Press Law Center. Religious student groups have had their rights reaffirmed by the Supreme Court.

But what hasn't changed is the politicization of the curriculum under the guise of those ubiquitous headings, multiculturalism and diversity. Though the majority of colleges and universities cannot rouse themselves to require of their students a grounding in Western civilization or American history, these same schools are adding "cultural diversity" course requirements at a dazzling pace. They also continue to use "diversity" as an excuse to water down standards in the traditional disciplines. For example, a recent study of the English departments at twenty-five prestigious liberal arts schools by the National Association of Scholars (NAS) found that between 1964 and 1997, the number of English electives offered in these departments had increased 74 percent. Many of these additional courses focus on racial, ethnic, sexual, or other nonliterary themes, so that the proportion of foundational courses offered has dropped from 58 percent to 35 percent. While in 1964, 48 percent of departments had required a course on Shakespeare, in 1997 only 16 percent did. And just four departments still required survey courses in English and American literature; in 1964, more than half had such requirements.

Nor has there been any detectible trend toward the restoration of genuine core curricula. Yet there is some evidence that such a curriculum measurably contributes to the quality of a student's education. A recent study conducted by Alexander W. Astin, director of the Higher Education Research Institute at UCLA, reports that "[a]ttending an institution with a true core curriculum (that is, one that requires all students to take exactly the same courses in order to satisfy general education requirements) has positive effects on several satisfaction measures." On the other hand, general education distribution requirements have little discernible direct impact on such measures. "Only a true core curriculum," writes Astin, "seems to have distinctive effects on student development: high satisfaction, and positive effects on leadership in particular." Astin concludes with what the alumni of liberal arts schools with strong, integrated cores already know: "having students take exactly the same general education courses provides a common experience that can stimulate student discussion outside of class and facilitate the formation of strong bonds among student peers."

Finally, our college graduates continue to display a dismal lack of cultural literacy and a troubling grasp of ethics. Here again, polls commissioned by NAS have provided some devastating data. Item 1: Today's college graduates fare little or no better than a sample of 1955 *high school* graduates on questions covering literature, music, science, geography, and history (a subject on which they appear to know considerably *less* than the high schoolers of half a century ago). Item 2: Graduating seniors from Arizona's public universities failed to average a passing score in seven of eleven subject areas. Only 14 percent knew that James Madison was the U.S. Constitution's principal author. Item 3: 73 percent of college seniors reported that their professors taught them that "what is right and wrong depends on differences in individual values and cultural diversity." Only 25 percent said that they had been taught that "there are clear and uniform standards of right and wrong by which everyone should be judged."

If students wish to obtain a genuinely liberating education—one that provides the inward freedom that only develops by having wrestled with the great minds, ideas, and questions, and by having had dedicated teachers who could help make sense of it all—they must know what they are getting into. This guide attempts to provide the foreknowledge that will allow students to make good choices and become truly educated citizens.

You hold in your hands the 2006 edition of *Choosing the Right College,* now published annually. Compiled under the direction of Jeffrey O. Nelson, this edition includes revised and updated entries on 134 schools. Essays on the importance of the humanities and on the relationship between the core curriculum and the liberal arts have been contributed by Robert Royal, president of the Faith and Reason Institute, and Mark C. Henrie, author of *A Student's Guide to the Core Curriculum,* respectively. John Zmirak, editor in chief of *Choosing the Right College 2006,* discusses the volume's guiding philosophy and its contents, including a unique feature, first introduced in the 2004 edition, in which students are told what specific courses they can take in order to create their own core curricula at colleges that do not provide one. Finally, a helpful appendix titled *Asking the Right Questions* advises parents and prospective students on what questions to consider when making a decision on where to go to school. All parents and college-bound students will want to review these questions before making campus visits.

Forming a citizenry educated for liberty has been the mission of the Intercollegiate Studies Institute for fifty years now. ISI has more than 50,000 student and faculty members, an influential and growing book imprint—ISI Books—and a nationwide educational program that includes hundreds of lectures, seminars, and conferences on college and university campuses throughout the country each year. Few organizations are as well positioned to analyze and interpret trends in higher education, and even fewer are as equipped to help students and parents choose the right college. I invite you to learn more about ISI and the state of higher education today at this guide's companion Web site, www.collegeguide.org.

William J. Bennett, a Distinguished Fellow at the Heritage Foundation and the Washington Fellow of the Claremont Institute, is one of the nation's most tenacious advocates of bold education reform. He served as the secretary of education and chairman of the National Endowment for the Humanities under President Ronald Reagan and director of the Office of National Drug Control Policy under President George H. W. Bush. The author of the bestselling The Book of Virtues *among many other volumes, his current book is* Why We Fight: Moral Clarity and the War on Terrorism.

The Importance of the Humanities

Robert Royal

Nearly everyone who has gone to college, or is thinking about going, has experienced the excitement of entering a larger world. That feeling is a clue to something quite important. It is a natural reaction to the prospect of broader social life and intellectual vistas, usually at an age when we are just reaching adulthood. But at whatever age a person decides to pursue serious study, the excitement stems from a sense that personally, socially, and intellectually, institutions of higher learning are places where, if we are fortunate, we may come into living contact with what being more fully human is all about.

The humanities are about being human. In a technological age such as our own, we may decide to study at a college or university so that we can pursue a career in the sciences or get a good job. There is nothing wrong—and much that is right—in these goals. But specialized technical schools or even educational programs sponsored by private companies can do those things for us, and they will probably become the common route for that kind of education in the future. The humanities, however, have always aimed at something quite different, something that many people feel is particularly lacking in twenty-first-century America. *Choosing the Right College* is written to show where you can still find this knowledge on America's campuses.

As Plato, one of the great sources of the Western humanistic tradition, once put it:

> It is not the life of knowledge, not even if it includes all the sciences, that creates happiness and well-being, but a single branch of knowledge—the science of the good life. If you exclude this from the other branches, medicine will remain equally able to give us health, and shoemaking shoes, and weaving clothes; seamanship will continue to save life at sea, and strategy to win battles; but without the knowledge of good and evil the use and excellence of these sciences will be found to have failed us.

Plato's goal here is not to make a highbrow argument about the need to study ethics or pursue abstruse philosophical investigations, though ethics will inevitably come into the humanities, as will hard thinking. As Plato shows by comparing it with other kinds of knowledge, the science of the good life is valuable for its own sake as well as for its practical value. It aims at discovering the truths that tell us both who we are and what we need to know if we want to use our other knowledge to make us more fully human. Put briefly and in a modern idiom: at their best, the humanities can teach us how to live.

Human beings are in a unique condition compared with other living things. The higher animals may teach their young a few survival techniques. But we have to teach and learn about many things in order to flourish. No other being that we know of has the intellectual capacity and relative freedom that we humans possess. These two powers make it impossible for us to live by instinct, as most animals do. We have entire ranges of understanding and action that go far beyond anything in the rest of nature. Consequently, both our minds and wills need to be properly formed if we are going to live up to everything that is in us. *Choosing the Right College* will help you find the resources you need to develop your talents fully.

Most talk about freedom today suggests that freedom means liberation from constraints. The older humanistic tradition agrees that we need to be freed from certain external constraints, but even more from internal constraints like unfocused passivity and a slavery to ignorance, habit, emotion, or impulse—our natural condition prior to education. Indeed, without freedom from inner bondage, mere freedom from outward limitations is likely to turn into utter disaster. We need to understand and train ourselves to pursue not only *freedom from* evils and limitations but also *freedom for* what is good. The kinds of human beings most of us typically admire combine a lively spontaneity with well-formed habits of rationality and self-mastery that make it easy for them to both know and do what is good for themselves and others.

How do we make ourselves into the kinds of people we admire? Such things are not achieved without good external guidance and firm internal discipline. Even the very finest university can only offer a beginning to what is, by its very nature, a lifelong pursuit. A good college experience may open us up to the prospect of unlimited opportunities and intellectual stimulation; a bad one may condemn us to perpetual frustration and narrowness. The difference is not merely a matter of individual psychology, but the result of a successful or unsuccessful attempt to encounter, and to get some understanding of, the fundamental questions about human existence. Human societies always exist in a state of no little confusion about basic truths. That is one of the reasons why higher learning, which is also a clarification, is necessary. Getting down to basics has never been easy, but in our time it is further complicated by the fact that even many colleges and universities have become confused about what an education in the humanities means. Any student who wants what humanistic studies can give today has to search carefully for guides and work hard with them when they are found. This college guide points the way to a genuine education in the humanities on 125 of America's best campuses.

Contrary to the impression given by most course catalogs, the subjects students need to confront are not very numerous, though they may be approached from many different perspectives and in no little detail. Historically, they have centered around questions about God and man, virtue and vice, heroism and cowardice, tyranny and freedom, truth and untruth. Study of those questions was intended to produce a similarly small number of exemplary human types: the saint, the philosopher, the hero, the statesman, the artist, the scholar, and the scientist.

The basic humanistic subjects—and they must be very basic now because elementary and secondary education today hardly prepare us for them—at any given institution are crucial to whether we will preserve the old authentic thrill of learning to be human beings, or will find ourselves in backwaters of mere information. Most students of the humanities today will have to encounter the essential subject matter in disciplines such as literature, history, politics, and languages. (Philosophy and theology are also crucial subjects. But like mathematics, relatively few people can do the kind of abstract thinking they require to any great extent.) Wherever we choose to begin, however, each of the humanistic disciplines deals with the multiple values a thinking person will encounter over the whole course of his or her life. Hence, they are subjects that can never finally be outdated, superseded, or finished.

Literature provides us with an imaginative re-creation of life that enables us to see things, thanks to the author, that we would be unable to see on our own. A novel like *Moby-Dick*, for example, contains a good deal of sea lore and local color. For many readers, that in itself will open their eyes to a larger world. But few people, even those who did whaling in the period in which that novel is set, ever thought as deeply as Herman Melville did about the human struggle with God and nature, good and evil, and what it means for all of us, even landlubbers. After we return from that voyage, we stand on very different ground.

History provides a similar expansion of horizons but has the added advantage of leading us to reflect on what has actually happened in the human past. Human beings change over the course of their lives, and the human race has changed as well. But there are some basic human features that we can observe in the most distant regions of the earth among peoples far remote from us in time. Knowledge about those permanent human things gives us a better perspective on who we are. History also allows us to understand that our own age is not merely the natural order of things. It took great human efforts to build up our civilization, efforts involving intellectual discoveries, backbreaking physical labor, and, often enough, the heroic sacrifice of life itself.

For example, every schoolchild has heard the words from the Declaration of Independence: "We hold these Truths to be self-evident, that all Men are created equal, that they are endowed by their Creator with certain unalienable Rights, that among these are Life, Liberty, and the Pursuit of Happiness—That to secure these Rights, Governments are instituted among Men. . . ." Like any of the truths of the humanities, these principles can be lazily passed over as truisms only useful for Memorial Day speeches and other ceremonial occasions. But if we begin to look at them carefully, a number of questions of central importance to human life jump out at us. Do we need to refer to a God to understand beings who have rights? What kind of God would that be? Does liberty mean I am free to do whatever I want or, as the Founding Fathers warned, do we need to distinguish sharply between liberty and license? What is this Happiness that we are to pursue? Such questions are the culmination of centuries of struggle to understand individuals in society and to build up a civilized order that makes our relations with one another as productive of the common good as possible.

Just to begin listing such questions helps us to realize how quickly even the most common sentiments lead us out into deep waters. The kind of learning the humanities convey to us is not a matter of knowing a little bit about this and that so that we can take part in polite dinner-table conversations. The range of subjects we encounter in every serious humanistic pursuit goes to the heart of the question of whether we will live well and in good societies, or, like most of the human race for most of history, we will not. As such, these subjects are not a matter of annoying "distribution requirements" or of whimsical "electives" that we can choose at will. Each of us has aptitudes and interests that will lead us to focus on one or more particular areas in the humanities. But to understand even our own favorite areas well, we need very broad views of human beings—and we need to acquire them by looking hard for how and where to get them.

Some people who recognize this have a partly mistaken impression of the problem on campuses today. The most notorious cases have even appeared in newspapers: an English department that no longer requires students majoring in English to read Shakespeare, or a university with few or no requirements for graduation. An even more difficult problem is the *way* the great humanist thinkers are often taught, even when they are present in the curriculum. The great texts of our culture have endured because they have repeatedly revealed their value to all kinds of people over centuries in very different cultural settings. There is a presumption in favor of ideas with that kind of life in them. But often today they are approached—when they are not merely dismissed— as instances of past prejudices of various kinds. These are alarming signs and the parent or student who wants a concrete evaluation of what such signs mean will want to read the following pages very closely.

Like ourselves, even the greatest figures of the past were imperfect human beings and their prejudices ought to be corrected. But we need to be cautious that our desire to counteract prejudice does not turn into a narrowness and prejudice of its own. One of the ways that often happens today is through a movement called multiculturalism. Spurred by the alleged biases in Western thinking against women, the marginalized, and non-white races, multiculturalism offers non-Western cultures as an antidote. On the surface, this appears utterly benign and even necessary. Who could possibly object to a wider acquaintance with the world or to correctives to our Western ideas from the outside? Properly pursued, these are part and parcel of a true humanism.

Unfortunately, they are not often properly pursued. To understand another culture we have to study its languages, history, great people and events, and then come to a proper appraisal of them, just as we might some earlier period of Western culture such as Ancient Greece. Too often, however, multiculturalism stops at the surface, presenting a few selected dimensions of another culture as a weapon with which to attack our own ways and the long social and intellectual traditions on which they are based. Furthermore, on closer inspection, these claims usually prove to be Western values pushed to extremes without proper attention to other truths. Most multicultural approaches to the humanities challenge very little of the culture with which students arrive on contemporary campuses: in fact, they are usually used to enforce ideas already present without opening up any new vistas at all. As such, they should not be allowed to obscure one of the West's great cultural achievements.

So if you want an education in the humanities today it will require work—and vigilance. One reason that the initial excitement of going to college soon dies down for most people is that it seems so difficult to find institutions, departments, or individual teachers that can help in orienting us to the tasks at hand. More typically, our desire for humane learning is thwarted by educational institutions themselves that cannot seem to make up their minds what a humanistic—and human—education should be. The great value of the present guide is that, without concerning itself with any question other than which institutions best provide an education in the humanities or which professors or departments do so in otherwise inhospitable institutions, it provides some practical suggestions for entering the perpetually exciting world of discovering how we may be free, responsible, and ever more human beings.

Robert Royal, who holds a PhD in comparative literature from the Catholic University of America, is the president of the Faith & Reason Institute in Washington, D.C. Among his many books are 1492 and All That: Political Manipulations of History *and* Dante Alighieri.

FINDING AND FOLLOWING THE CORE

Mark C. Henrie

Faithfully following the strictures of the contemporary ideology of multicultural diversity, American university curricula today resemble a dazzling cafeteria indifferently presided over by an amiable and indulgent nutritionist. There are succulent offerings to suit every taste, and the intellectual gourmand can only regret that he has but four years to sample the fare. Never in history have there existed institutions providing such an array of fields of study—from Sanskrit to quantum mechanics, from neoclassical microeconomic theory to Jungian psychology, from the study of medieval folklore to the study of 1950s billboards. Everything which can repay study is studied, however small the dividend. The only constraint on the diversity of offerings is a financial one, which, given the truly astonishing wealth of American universities, is hardly a constraint at all.

But as every parent knows, children seldom choose to eat what's good for them. They seem irresistibly drawn to high-fat foods and sugary desserts. Or, sometimes, they develop a fixation upon one particular dish and will eat no others. Parents do what they can to ensure a balanced diet, and in years past, the university, standing *in loco parentis*, likewise made sure that the bill of fare, the courses required for graduation, were also "balanced." Various dimensions of intellectual virtue were each given their due: the basic cultural knowledge by which an educated man situates himself in history, a broad exposure to various methods of inquiry, the mastery and command that are the fruit of disciplinary specialization. Programmatically, this balance was achieved by a core curriculum in the literary, philosophical, and artistic monuments of Western civilization; a diverse set of requirements in general education; and a carefully structured course of studies in a major.

Things are rather different today, for we live in an era when the idea of a university—and therefore the university's institutional expression—has been transformed by the cultural currents that erupted in the 1960s. Commentators make much of the "tenured radicals" who have "destroyed" the traditional curriculum, and after reading so much about these depredations, we are apt to approach such views with skepticism: Can it really be *that* bad? How can we reconcile such doom-saying with the fact that American universities are the envy of the world, drawing the most talented students and faculty from around the globe? Are not American universities at the forefront of research in virtually every field? Are academia's critics perhaps pining nostalgically for a world that never was?

Such skepticism is not unwarranted, especially with regard to the most extreme claims of the critics: the American university is not on the point of collapse, and it is still possible to acquire a genuinely fine liberal arts education. Nonetheless, we can trace quite clearly the effect that the 1960s generation has had on the American university. That generation rebelled against their parents, and so, against the very idea of anyone or anything standing *in loco parentis*. Enthusiasts for various forms of Marxist and post-Marxist critique, they understood themselves not as inquirers standing on the shoulders of giants but rather as change-agents striving to overcome an inheritance of injustice. Like Thrasymachus in Plato's *Republic*, their sense of outraged injustice drove them to the moral relativism we now call postmodernism. But this very relativism led only to the dead end of self-contradiction, for it required them to deny that there could be any *true* standard of justice by which injustice could be admitted. Famously, they enjoined themselves to trust no one over thirty: obviously, the great works of the Western tradition, hundreds and thousands of years old, could not be trusted. They were instead to be deconstructed. Locked into an indiscriminate stance of questioning authority, they found themselves at length well over thirty and in the awkward position of being university authorities. What have been the effects on the curriculum?

The Major. The system of majors still flourishes, reflecting the still high prestige of the disciplinary model of the natural sciences—reflecting, as well, the guild-like structure of the PhD system, which credentials faculty and serves as the basis for their institutional authority within the university. Yet outside the natural sciences, the structured sequencing of courses within the major—one course building upon another and probing to a deeper level—has been largely abandoned. For reasons associated with careerism, professors today are often more committed to their research than to their teaching obligations, and so they resist or reject a "rigid" curricular plan that would make frequent and irregular sabbaticals difficult. Moreover, faculty themselves have fundamental disagreements about the very nature of their disciplines and so find it impossible to reach a consensus about the "end" toward which a course of studies should be directed. The faculty's solution has been to avoid direction.

Students in a major are thus largely free to pick and choose as they please, and as the current course offerings allow. Consequently, many students experience their major in a rather aimless way: the major does not "progress" or "culminate" in anything. Graduating students often do not understand themselves to have achieved even preliminary mastery of a discipline. Whereas "critical" methods of teaching and learning have been "pushed forward" to earlier and earlier years of study in the past generation, mastery of a discipline (in fields outside the natural sciences) has been "pushed back" to the MA years of graduate school.

General Education and Distribution Requirements. A system of distribution and other general education requirements also persists. Commonly, students will find that they are required to reach a certain proficiency in a foreign language, that they will need to demonstrate command of written English, and that they will be required to take a prescribed number of courses in a range of fields of study. Sometimes these last, "distribution," requirements are vague: for example, they might prescribe twelve credits each from the sciences, humanities, and social sciences. Sometimes, the distribution requirements are more specific: e.g., two courses in math, one in the physical sciences and one in the life sciences, a course in history, a course in a non-Western subject, etc.

The theoretical justification for requirements in general education is *broad* exposure to various bodies of knowledge and approaches to understanding. There is an echo here of John Henry Newman's argument in his famous book *The Idea of a University* that a university is "a place of teaching universal knowledge," and that failure to take the measure of all areas of inquiry results in a kind of deformity of the intellect. Some students may grumble at these requirements, which take them away from pursuing their major subject with single-mindedness: in the university cafeteria, they want nothing but the lime Jell-o. Frequently, faculty members sympathize with such complaints. After all, the professors have themselves undertaken graduate studies in increasingly narrow fields; their liberal education is many years in the past, and their self-esteem depends on their standing in their particular disciplines, not on their reputation for the synthetic skills of the generalist. But Newman's argument about the humane value of broad learning remains compelling. Students should approach their general education requirements as a serious opportunity for intellectual growth.

Consider, for example, the requirement of mastery in a foreign language. Americans are notoriously bad at foreign languages; ambitious students may fear that their GPAs will suffer in language courses. But it really is true that some thoughts are better expressed in one language than another. Acquiring a foreign language can open up whole new *worlds*, and when kept up, a foreign language is a possession for life. Similarly, it is only through distribution requirements that the "two cultures" of science and the humanities are forced to engage each other in the modern university. Without this encounter, the student of the sciences risks falling into a value-free technological imperialism. Without this encounter, the student of the humanities risks falling into an antiquarian idyll, cut off from one of the major currents of the modern world.

There is also a simply practical advantage to distribution requirements. Today, about two-thirds of all students will change their major during their college career: many will change more than once. What students will "be" in life is almost certainly not what they thought they would "be" when they set off for college. Distribution requirements offer an opportunity to view the world from different intellectual perspectives. Who knows but that an unexpected horizon may prove to correspond to the heart's deepest desires?

The Core Curriculum. It is the core curriculum, a survey of the great works of Western civilization, which has fared the worst in the curricular reforms of the past generation. With few exceptions, the core curriculum has been simply eliminated from American higher education. Those of a suspecting cast of mind may speculate that this change has occurred for structural reasons. Following the model of the natural sciences, PhDs in the humanities are awarded for original "contributions to knowledge." But the great works of Western culture have been studied for centuries. What genuinely "new" insights can be gleaned there? Have aspiring PhDs perhaps turned, in desperation, to other subjects in which there is still something "original" to be said? If so, how can they be expected to teach the great books, which were not their subject of study? But then, the elimination of the core is also surely the result of a moral rejection: the generation of the 1960s, which admired the Viet Cong and cheered U.S. defeat in Southeast Asia, viewed their own civilizational tradition as a legacy not to be honored but to be overcome. The "privileging" of the great books of the West therefore had to end.

A more positive justification for the demise of the core is frequently given, however. In order to prepare students for the Multicultural World of Tomorrow, it is said, students must be exposed to the *diversity* of world cultures. A merely Western curriculum would be parochial, a failure of liberal learning. Moreover, since our modern or postmodern technological civilization is characterized by rapid change, it is more important to be exposed to "approaches to knowledge," to "learn how to learn," than it is to acquire any particular body of knowledge. Education then becomes nothing but the cultivation of abstract instrumental rationality, divorced from any content and divorced from any end. Consistent with these arguments, many universities now call their *distribution requirements* a "core curriculum." They claim to have undergone curricular development rather than curricular demise.

As a practical matter, this multicultural transformation of the curriculum can have two curious results. In the worst cases, what passes for a multicultural curriculum is nothing but a peculiar kind of Western echo chamber. Students are given over to studying Marxist critics in contemporary Algeria and neo-Marxist critics in contemporary Brazil and post-Marxist critics in contemporary France. All that is really learned are variations on the "critique of ideologies"—a legacy of one great Western mind, that of Karl Marx. In other cases, however, students really are exposed to the high cultures and great works of non-Western societies; but their encounter with Western high culture remains slight. We thus are presented with the spectacle of many students today who habitually associate high ideals, profound insight, and wisdom with every culture but their own.

What, then, is the abiding justification for the traditional core curriculum in Western civilization? Why is it a major premise of this guide that a university lacking a core curriculum is educationally deficient—even as we stand at the dawn of the Multicultural World of Tomorrow? The purpose of the core is *not* to inculcate any kind of Western chauvinism, certainly not any ethnocentrism that would prevent a student from exploring and learning from non-Western cultures. Indeed, one expects that it will be precisely those who have delved most thoughtfully into the wisdom of the Occident who will then be in a position to learn the most from the wisdom of the Orient—rather like

Matteo Ricci and the other Jesuits who encountered Chinese civilization with such sympathetic results in the sixteenth century. Lacking a foundation in the depths of our own civilization, a student can approach another as little more than a tourist.

There are really two arguments for the traditional core. They concern the importance of high culture and the importance of history.

High Culture. A not uncommon sight on a university campus during freshman week is a group of students sitting on the grass in the evening, one with a guitar, singing together the theme songs of vintage television sitcoms. In a society as diverse as America at the dawn of the twenty-first century, this is to be expected: television is one of the few things that young people from all walks of life have in common. But what are we to think when the same scene is repeated at senior week, four years later? Has higher education done its job when the only common references of those with a baccalaureate degree remain those of merely popular culture?

The core curriculum is the place in university studies where one encounters what Matthew Arnold called "the best that has been thought and said." Such a view of education is hierarchical, discriminating, judgmental: it reflects the fact that the high can be distinguished from the low, and the further understanding that the high can comprehend the low whereas the low can never take the measure of the high. By spending time with the best, with the highest expressions and reflections of a culture, the mind of the student is equipped for its own ascent. Without such an effort, the student remains trapped in the unreflective everyday presumptions of the current culture: the student remains trapped in clichés. The high culture of the traditional core curriculum is therefore *liberating*, as befits the liberal arts.

Throughout history there have been countless thinkers, poets, writers, and artists; the vast majority of all their labor has been lost, and most of them have been entirely forgotten. What survives are the truly great works that have been held in consistently high esteem through the changing circumstances of time and place. Thus, the traditional canon of great books—the common possession of educated men and women across the centuries of Western history—is not an arbitrary list, nor does the canon reflect relations of "power"; rather, as Louise Cowan has observed, the classics of a civilization "select themselves" by virtue of their superior insight. The presumptions and presuppositions of our lives, which lie so deep in us that we can scarcely recognize them, are in the great works made available for inspection and inquiry. High culture is a matter not of snobbish refinement but of superior understanding.

It is here that the core curriculum is indispensable. For every student brings to college a preliminary "enculturation"—we have all by the age of eighteen absorbed certain perspectives, insights, narratives, stereotypes, and values that communicate themselves to us in the prevailing popular culture. This enculturation is the common possession of a generation, whatever the diversity of their family backgrounds by class or ethnicity. But the artifacts of popular culture are always mere reflections of the possibilities glimpsed and made possible by works of high culture. The traditional core curriculum provides a student with access to that high culture; its *higher* "enculturation" provides a student with a vantage point from which he can grasp the meaning and implications of his everyday cultural presumptions. And he begins to hold something in common with the educated men and women of past ages; they become his peers.

One of the peculiar presumptions of our time is that novelty is good: social and technological transformations have given us a prejudice against tradition and in favor of "originality." But it is the great works of the traditional canon that constitute the record of true originality: that is why they have survived. Only by becoming familiar with them are we enabled to recognize just how derivative is much of that which now passes as original insight. A university that does not orient its students to high culture effectively commits itself to a project of deculturation, and thereby traps its students in a kind of permanent adolescence.

History. George Santayana famously asserted that those who do not remember the past are condemned to repeat it. Centuries earlier, Cicero observed that to know nothing of the world before one's birth is to remain always a child. These cautionary aphorisms are perfectly and pointedly true, and in the first instance they constitute one justification for the historical studies undertaken in a core curriculum. Practically speaking, there is wisdom to be found in experience. This wisdom is never more fully appreciated than when we experience the consequences of our actions at first-hand. But because human affairs exhibit certain recurring patterns, knowledge of history provides a stock of experiences at second-hand from which more general "lessons" may be drawn as well—at least, by those with ears to hear and eyes to see.

Nevertheless, these admonitions of Santayana and Cicero do not constitute the truly decisive historical reason for embarking on the traditional core curriculum. After all, insofar as human affairs exhibit patterns, and insofar as we approach history merely in search of the generally applicable "laws" or "rules" of human interaction, one may as well find one's stock of lessons in any given civilization as in any other. Anyone's history would be as good as anyone else's. It is because the contemporary academic mind views the matter in just this social-scientific way that it is necessarily driven to understand the traditional core curriculum's Western focus as nothing but the result of chauvinism or laziness.

But the core curriculum's particular emphasis on Western history is not the result either of ethnocentrism or of sloth. There is something far deeper going on here. Indeed, when history is approached merely as the raw material of social science, historical study in itself loses any *intrinsic* value; all that really matters in such a scheme are the "laws" that are abstracted from the pool of historical "examples." The core curriculum, however, does mean to value history *in itself*. How so?

All of us are born into a natural world governed by laws not of our making. Some of these laws are the laws of human nature and of human interaction, laws that apply in every time and place. But all of us are also born into the historical world at a particular time, and there is a certain *unrepeatable* (and unpredictable) quality to each historical moment, the result of free human choices. What is more, the historical moment we inhabit *now* is the outcome, in part, of the contingent history of our particular community, both recently and more remotely. In order to answer the first question of every true inquirer—*What is going on here?*—it is necessary to uncover the historical narrative of the present: that is, it is necessary to answer the question, What is going on *now?* To answer this question in any profound sense, it is necessary to understand the historical narrative of one's own civilization—to understand, as well, what was going on *then.* Consequently, the traditional core curriculum is not simply the study of the great books of the Western world isolated from their historical contexts; rather, that study proceeds side-by-side with an inquiry that locates those works in history. While the great works articulate the great human possibilities, not all human possibilities are equally available to us today. In effect, to understand the meaning of that relative availability (and unavailability) is to understand one's place in the stream of history, and this is the second argument for undertaking a core curriculum.

Typically, when a core curriculum has been poorly constructed, it reads history in a Whiggish way, or "progressively." In the Whig narrative, Western history tells the simple tale of how the world has progressed ever upward until it reaches its highpoint, the present (and in particular, me). Moreover, such a facile historical sense anticipates a future that is a straight-line extrapolation of the present. When the core is structured well, however, it leaves open the question of whether the present is the outcome of progress or decline. (The truth, it has been said, is that things are always getting both better and worse, at the same time.) A student who has learned the deep historical lessons of a core curriculum is as alert to the possibilities of historical transformation just ahead as he is to the possibility of continuity.

Today, it is extremely common for a college student to reach the end of four years of study with all requirements met but with a profound sense of disorientation and confusion, even disappointment. What's it all about? Usually, there will have been no sense of progression in the student's plan of study, no sense of mastery, no perspective touching deeply upon many connected subjects that might serve as the basis for ever-deeper inquiry with the passing of the years. There will have been no ascent to a truly higher culture, and no cultivation of historical consciousness.

What a lost opportunity!

The bad news is that it is most unlikely that we will see a return of the core curriculum in the next generation, and certainly not in time to benefit most of the readers of this guide. The good news is that much of the substance of the old core is still available, scattered across various courses in the departments. The eight courses that may constitute a "core of one's own" are here listed for each of the universities covered in this guide (excepting only those schools which still offer a true core); the rationale for these eight courses—what each contributes to the comprehensive perspective of the core—is given in my monograph, *A Student's Guide to the Core Curriculum* (ISI Books, 2000). Thanks to the elective system, the benefits of the core are not entirely beyond reach. The very best dishes are still available in the contemporary university-cafeteria: you simply have to choose them. Alas, that may entail occasionally passing on the chocolate cheesecake.

A curriculum is a "course"—like the course that is run by a river. A curriculum should take you somewhere. After four years of college, a graduating senior should be a different and better person than his former self, the matriculating freshman. Instead, most students today find themselves merely lost at sea, swamped by the roiling waters of various intellectual enthusiasms. Undertaking the *discipline* of a "voluntary" core curriculum today offers the prospect for the most profound of transformations—and the most delightful of journeys.

Mark C. Henrie holds degrees from Dartmouth, Cambridge, and Harvard. He is editor of the Intercollegiate Review *and senior editor of* Modern Age, *both published by ISI. He recently contributed the introduction to a new edition of* The Politics of Prudence, *by Russell Kirk.*

How to Use This Guide

John Zmirak

This is not your average college guide. If you're looking for a collection of the nation's "party schools," you won't find it here (except by way of warning). Nor do we tell you how to write a crack admissions essay, win scholarships, or score additional financial aid—though we do report which schools are generous with grants and loans, so that needy, worthy students aren't scared off by high ticket prices. (You might be surprised to learn, for instance, that smart blue-collar students will pay less at Princeton than at many state universities. And Princeton could use them!) Our book won't bombard you with statistics and factoids about thousands of colleges, covering everything from the number of computers available to the number of companies recruiting on campus. We don't even rank schools, since we know that different colleges are suited to different students. Many highly selective colleges are presented here—check the average SAT scores and percentage of applicants admitted—alongside many excellent schools that admit a wide range of students. Then, too, some state schools with virtually open admissions harbor excellent honors programs that rival any experience one might have at the Ivies.

There are plenty of reference books out there that do all of these tasks which we decided not to fool with, and do them well. The one thing these guides don't really help with is . . . well, picking the best college *for you*. This is probably the toughest choice you've had to make so far in your life, and it may well make a huge difference in how the rest of it turns out. Colleges can form your character—or twist it. They can challenge, enrich, and deepen your treasured beliefs—or trash them and leave you with nothing. They can help you find lifelong friendships, professional contacts, and intellectual mentors—or drop you back into the world with not much more than a degree and a load of debt. It all depends on which one you choose, which in turn depends on who you are. We don't assume that there's just one college (or even a list of 10 or 20) which is right for everyone. The truth is that there's a wide range of schools with strengths and weaknesses that might complement your own, schools with vastly different atmospheres and codes, some of which would suit you well but might tend to stifle others, and vice versa.

It's our job to tell you which is which. Reading through these essays, you'll see, side-by-side, comments by current students, professors, and graduates, selections from research studies and investigative journalism, analyses of curricula, fond reminiscences and horror stories. Each essay has been compiled by a team of reporters who consulted a wide range of sources to give you the most candid, comprehensive, and up-to-date description of what life is really like on campus, what you'd learn there, where are the treasure troves and where the pitfalls. You'll find in these pages entries devoted to the elite Ivies and other prestigious liberal arts institutions, where world-famous scholars deliver lectures to hundreds of ambitious activists, essays on tiny religious colleges that study the great books and the Bible, and write-ups on workaday state universities, each of which has at least a few excellent programs—and a lot of programs to avoid. You'll learn which colleges have strong sports teams, vital, faith-filled chaplaincies, and good systems for providing academic advice. And also which ones have coed bathrooms, by the way.

Unlike some other guides, this one is independently researched, written, and funded. Believe it or not, some books make schools pay in order to be included. Others let schools write their own profiles. How helpful is that? If you want to know what a school says about itself, check out its Web site. Or call its public relations department. (They sometimes call us, complaining about our candor.)

We're also upfront about our point of view. We have an agenda, and it's laid out right here in these introductory pages. That agenda is determined by our view of what constitutes a good education. There are many different views out there on this topic—many more than when John Henry Newman wrote his classic *The Idea of a University*—and most of them are partial or just plain wrong. Is a "good education" one that gives students the best chance to land a high-paying job? One that gives them entrée to the highest circles of cultural power? One that drenches them in "diversity" ideology, introduces them mainly to foreign and marginalized cultures, and teaches them to undermine the "status quo"? And how should a truly good education be structured? Like a Shonee's breakfast, where students pick and choose every item on their plate? Or like a thoughtfully constructed prix-fix menu at a fine restaurant—with a careful balance of meaty and flavorful, fresh ingredients prepared in a classic style? We think that once you think about it a bit, the answer is obvious.

In fact, while it may seem un-American to say it, we don't believe in the absolute virtue of choice. Not every high school kid comes into college knowing what he needs to learn, or even prepared to learn it. It's a sad fact that U.S. secondary education does not compare to what is offered in Europe or Japan. The mass-egalitarian ideology that pervades our secondary schools has dumbed most of us down. To expect every American teenager to take responsibility for planning every detail of his or her education is to guarantee that most of them will fail. They will emerge with a few specialties, a grab-bag of information, a pile of fashionable prejudices, and little else. This is what happens when we treat the fragile, multifarious fruit of thousands of years of human culture as a pile of consumer goods to be handled, sniffed, and accepted or rejected, according to whim.

If you think that a college education is just a ticket you have to get punched before you find a cozy cubicle, there is no reason to purchase this guide—or any other, really. For a high-paying job, get a technological or research-oriented degree, preferably at a prestigious university; to get access to power, go to one of the top 20 or so liberal arts schools in the *U.S. News and World Report* rankings; for soft relativism, thoroughgoing multiculturalism, and the "freedom" to pick your own courses at random, go virtually anywhere.

But if you want to get a little more out of the four most expensive years of your life, if you're inclined to grow as a person and tap into the wisdom of the ages, sages, and saints, then please read on. And be forewarned: the *New York Times,* with its usual perceptiveness, has called this guide "biased." What they mean is that we don't pretend to neutrality about what constitutes a serious education for an adult in Western society. We agree with what Newman wrote in 1852 when he described the ideal university in this way:

> An assemblage of learned men, zealous for their own sciences, and rivals of each other, are brought, by familiar intercourse and for the sake of intellectual peace, to adjust together the claims and relations of their respective subjects of investigation. They learn to respect, to consult, to aid each other. Thus is created a pure and clear atmosphere of thought, which the student also breathes, though in his own case he only pursues a few sciences out of the multitude. He profits by an intellectual tradition, which is independent of particular teachers, which guides him in his choice of subjects, and duly interprets for him those which he chooses. He apprehends the great outline of knowledge, the principles on which it rests, the scale of its parts, its lights and its shades, its great points and its little, as he otherwise cannot apprehend them. Hence it is that this education is called "Liberal."
>
> One good test of a college is whether it teaches all its graduates— not just its English or philosophy majors—how to read and comprehend such a paragraph. Another is whether its curriculum partakes in this broadly traditional vision of the mission of education as something that forms the self, trains the mind, disciplines habits, and connects the student as one more link in the chain of civilized liberty that ties us to the ancient citizens of Athens, the prophets of Israel, the fathers of the church, and the founders of our nation.

The philosophy of education that informs this college guide is further explained by William J. Bennett, Robert Royal, and Mark C. Henrie in our introductory essays. In short, we agree with Newman's contemporary John Ruskin that there is "an education which, in itself, is advancement in Life." A genuine education, like sanity, holiness, happiness, love, or good health, is an end in itself. While it may well enhance one's opportunities to advance in the world—to become productive and prosperous, to pursue a rewarding career—it does even more than that. An education teaches us how to decide what we want from life, how to weigh all the many trade-offs and face the moral challenges that will confront us throughout our lives. It teaches us how to be more fully human.

Now, it is widely argued, especially among conservatives, that American higher education is being held hostage by tenured radicals, professors blinded by unexamined, unchallenged ideologies of the left who transform their courses into catechism sessions propounding politics and imparting a corrosive, anti-Western view of the world that treats with reverence every civilization but our own. This view travels under the name of "multiculturalism," and the buzzword used to promote is "diversity." These words are cleverly chosen, since for most well-meaning people they suggest a broad range of views, imparted in a tolerant spirit, to students from a wide variety of ethnic and social backgrounds. If that were what these terms signified in practice, only bigots would oppose the agenda of the academic left. But in practice, as you will see if you read further, these terms too often refer to something quite different—to a systematic training in prejudice against the achievements of the West and a romanticized, neo-Marxist embrace of favored "victim" groups. These groups' cultures are rarely viewed with critical respect and objectivity. Instead, they are used as cudgels with which to abuse a teacher's least favorite aspect of our intellectual, political, or religious heritage. One great writer spoke of the past as a "far country." If that is true, then the professors who view it with moralistic condescension, and the students who never bother to learn about it, are xenophobes and chauvinists. They desperately need the broadening experience of travel—but they believe, with the father depicted by Nancy Mitford, that "abroad is bloody, and foreigners are fiends." We disagree.

Tragically, many schools are afflicted with the attitude described above. In the following pages, the reader will be warned at which schools current students warn Christians or conservatives to keep a low profile if they wish to receive fair grades or make any friends. But there are other problems as well in academia, problems that cannot be blamed on the left. Too many who are not in the grip of radical ideologies are simply pragmatists who view an education simply as a form of technical or preprofessional training, so that a school's success could essentially be judged by looking at the incomes of its graduates. If this were true, then universities would not be essentially different from schools that teach students the skills of a court stenographer or refrigerator repair man. We would not lavish them will billions of dollars of private philanthropy and taxpayer subsidies. Few of their alumni would gather at intervals of 10 and 20 years or speak of their schools as "alma maters," nourishing mothers.

The place that colleges still hold in our culture tells us that we remember, albeit dimly, that they are meant to do something more—to form the free citizen, prepare the future parent, and fortify the soul. Universities train us to think and argue for ourselves, but also to listen to older and wiser authorities, to question but also to take seriously the wisdom of other periods and peoples, to learn from our contemporaries and serve as mentors to the young. Most of us carry with us memories of one or two faculty members who stand in our minds as models of how to teach, how to counsel, how to correct, memories that guide us when we have children or students of our own. Schools also teach how to wisely spend our time, how to choose among the myriad political, cultural, and social options that a free society offers. That—and not keeping the kids entertained—is the secret function of a university's extracurricular activities.

Of course, colleges ought also to train us in particular disciplines and instruct those of us who intend further study in one of the arts or sciences. The workload imposed should be sufficient to engage the bright and awaken the lazy. A university must challenge us to succeed and prod us to get up again when we fail. Our institutions of higher education ought to be, in every sense, schools of life. It is by these criteria that this book judges a college.

Needless to say, we are often disappointed.

But after one recovers from the initial shock of seeing how far many schools have strayed from their founding missions—be they religious or classically humanist—it is possible to adopt another view. Once one admits that the great edifice of traditional education has crumbled, that the Roman aqueducts and Gothic arches are broken, it is possible to look for what one poet called "love among the ruins." Few schools still fully embody a vision of liberal (that is, liberating) education that Newman would recognize. (Any such schools that we could find we have included and commended them to your attention.) But in many colleges and universities, there are still significant remnants, even some recent growths, of excellence—brilliant scholars, dedicated and fair-minded teachers, extraordinary libraries and museums, and intellectually motivated fellow students. Some places more than others have clung to their traditions (see Hampden-Sydney, Providence College, and the University of Chicago, for instance); some have even begun to remember the deeper reasons why they were founded (see Seton Hall, Baylor, and Villanova); still others have sprung up to fill the void created by the great catastrophes of the 1960s and 1970s (see Christendom and Thomas More colleges). And even on many of the campuses that saw the most—and most destructive—changes in that great period of anti-intellectualism, one can piece together a first-rate education by choosing carefully among professors and programs. In fact, there are very few prominent schools in America at which this is not possible.

An old joke tells of a traveler through the South who asks directions, only to be told, "You can't get there from here." The news here isn't that bad. The far country of intellectual adulthood, civilized discourse, and a liberated intellect is certainly within reach—and you can get there by many different routes. However, there is plenty of rough and dangerous terrain ahead. Think of this volume as a sort of travel guide, one that identifies the major landmarks, watering holes, and pitfalls of 134 distinct regions, telling the traveler what to expect while there, what (and whom) to seek out, and what to avoid.

In selecting the 134 schools to be profiled in this guide, we have been careful to include those institutions generally considered to be "America's top schools." Thus, we have included the top 40 most selective national universities and the top 35 most selective liberal arts colleges according to the objective selectivity rankings used by *U.S. News and World Report.* We have then chosen 59 more schools from different regions of the country, institutions that have special emphases, unique virtues, or distinctive missions. This edition, for the first time, includes the three U.S. service academies, which offer excellent educational opportunities for those willing to risk life and limb in defense of their country. We have also added several more small colleges renowned for their intimate social interaction and intellectual seriousness, as well as some lesser-known schools with serious curricula.

We couldn't fit every school—even every worthwhile school—in a single book and hope to do any one of them justice. So if you're considering a place not included in this volume, do your own research using the sort of criteria we lay down here. (See the appendix of this guide for a list of specific questions to ask when visiting a college or university.) We also encourage readers to keep an eye on www.collegeguide.org, where we will be posting, as opportunity allows, shorter essays on schools not covered here.

Each institutional profile is divided into two sections: "Academic Life" and "Student Life." In writing and editing these profiles, we have examined school literature and Web sites, researched magazine and newspaper articles, and most importantly, talked to thousands of administrators, professors, and students. Each essay has been updated and revised to reflect the latest changes at each college covered.

In the Academic Life section, our team of researchers and contributing editors gathered information pertaining to the following questions: What is the school's academic reputation? Is a genuine core curriculum in place? If not, how good a job do the general education requirements do in ensuring students graduate having received a broad liberal arts education and having taken foundational courses? Who are the best professors and which are the best departments or programs? Which programs or departments are the weakest or most politicized? What kind of academic advising do students receive? How strong are the relationships between faculty and students? How large are classes, typically? To what extent are graduate students relied on for teaching and grading? How bad is grade inflation?

A word is in order here about what we are attempting to do when we recommend professors. When we list an institution's "top professors," we are certainly not pretending to present an exhaustive list, nor are we applying a political test. Some of these professors are known to be conservatives, others liberals, and some radicals, but we have no idea where most of them stand politically. Rather, these are those individuals who were most often nominated by their colleagues and students as being fair, nonpoliticized, and pedagogically committed and talented.

An exclusive feature of *Choosing the Right College* is the inclusion, in each institutional profile, of an inset box that tells students how to build their own core curriculum. In this box we highlight eight specific courses that cover the eight areas we believe together make for a decent substitute for a traditional integrated core. These areas are:

1. Classical literature (in translation)
2. Ancient philosophy
3. The Bible
4. Christian thought before 1500
5. Modern political theory

6. Shakespeare
7. U.S. history before 1865
8. Nineteenth-century European intellectual history

The rationale behind this vision of the core curriculum is explained in detail in Mark Henrie's book, *A Student's Guide to the Core Curriculum* (which, by the way, may be purchased at www.isibooks.org or downloaded for free at www.collegeguide.org). In essence, this grouping of courses reflects the input of dozens of distinguished professors from a wide variety of disciplines as to what a brief but genuine core curriculum ought to cover. If taught well—and especially if taught using primary texts—these courses will help students obtain a broad and sophisticated understanding of the West—that is, an understanding of the narratives, beliefs, events, thinkers, and institutions that have shaped the world around them and the core beliefs encoded in our culture and Constitution. And if you don't understand your own culture, you'll make a poor student of anyone else's. (As Socrates famously insisted, "Know thyself.")

If students take the eight courses we recommend, and especially if they can contrive to take them from professors we recommend, they should graduate with at least a semblance of a true liberal arts education. That means they will have minds that are free to go on learning all through life from a vast variety of sources, minds supported by hard-won skills and guided by a sure intellectual compass.

The Student Life section tries to give readers an idea of what it's like to go to each school. Here is where we go into detail about each institution's residential life: Are all dorms coed? If so, are there coed rooms? Coed bathrooms? Does the school guarantee housing for all four years? Would you want to live in the dorms in any case? (Some are Gothic gems, others Stalinist monoliths.) In this section we also try to give some idea of how students spend their time outside the classroom. Is this a service-oriented school? Do the kids party five nights a week or are they a studious, intellectual bunch? In addition, we discuss whether campus crime is a problem, the extent to which athletics, particularly intercollegiate athletics, shapes the campus atmosphere, and whether school traditions still create a spirit of cohesion. There is much else in this section besides, depending on the character of the institution, including everything from controversial mascots to quaint customs, school songs, and curious but telling facts. (Did you know, for instance, that in the chapel of Washington and Lee, General Robert E. Lee is actually buried under the main altar? That Louisiana State University keeps a live tiger on campus? That Caltech freshmen are encouraged to try to vandalize the dorm rooms of seniors—who fortify them like bunkers to weather the siege?)

Finally, we provide some "vital stats" that we believe help bring into focus the character of each institution. These statistics reflect the best and most up-to-date information available as we went to press. Beware: the costs of tuition and room and board reflect 2004–5 rates; the reader ought to expect each number to be a bit higher for subsequent years. Also note that the precise metrics provided by schools for some statistical categories are not always the same—this is especially the case in schools' reported standardized test scores and average class sizes.

As Mark Twain once quipped, "There are lies, damned lies, and statistics." We agree. Statistics can be spun like sugar into almost any shape. Take the "courses taught by graduate TAs" question, for example. While this number—which many schools are unwilling to give or even calculate, by the way, most probably because they would be embarrassed by it—provides a rough idea of how much TAs are being used, it is almost always deceptively low. Typically, it does not include the discussion sections attached to large lecture courses, which are usually taught by TAs. Nor does it accurately reflect the percentage of students taught by TAs over the course of a semester, a statistic that we have never seen reported. Not that all TAs are necessarily bad teachers. But it's important to realize that you will probably spend a lot more of your time at some schools talking to harried graduate students than to the Nobel Prize winners featured on the front of the college viewbook.

Our hope is that *Choosing the Right College 2006* will do a better job than ever of informing students, parents, grandparents, teachers, and guidance counselors about the state of higher education at 134 of our nation's top schools. We offer it with our sincere belief that it is the most incisive and compelling critical college guide on the market.

John Zmirak took his doctorate in English literature from Louisiana State University and his BA from Yale. He has worked as a journalist for over 10 years at periodicals such as Investor's Business Daily. *He is the author of* Wilhelm Röpke: Swiss Localist, Global Economist *and* The Bad Catholic's Guide to Good Living *and serves as a contributing editor at the* American Conservative.

NEW ENGLAND

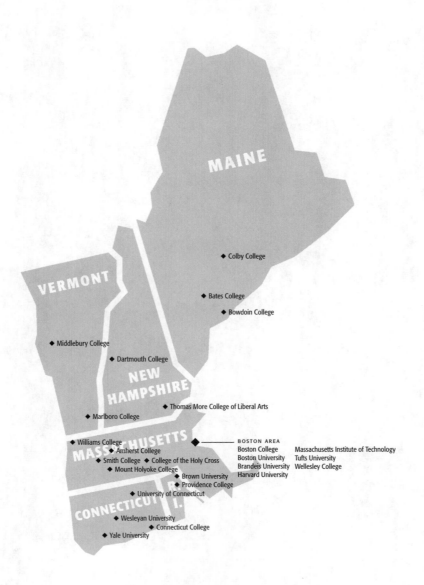

MAINE

◆ Colby College

◆ Bates College

◆ Bowdoin College

VERMONT

◆ Middlebury College

◆ Dartmouth College

NEW HAMPSHIRE

◆ Thomas More College of Liberal Arts

◆ Marlboro College

◆ Williams College

MASSACHUSETTS

◆ Amherst College

◆ Smith College ◆ College of the Holy Cross

◆ Mount Holyoke College

◆ Brown University

◆ Providence College

◆ University of Connecticut

R. I.

CONNECTICUT

◆ Wesleyan University

◆ Connecticut College

◆ Yale University

BOSTON AREA
Boston College   Massachusetts Institute of Technology
Boston University   Tufts University
Brandeis University   Wellesley College
Harvard University

AMHERST COLLEGE

AMHERST, MASSACHUSETTS • WWW.AMHERST.EDU

Silencing Cal

In 1891, while Amherst College was celebrating its 70th anniversary, Calvin Coolidge arrived on campus for the first
time. Most of the young men gathered in this small town in
western Massachusetts sought to become teachers or ministers, but this student had come to prepare for a career in
the law. Later, when he was asked to remember his time at
Amherst, Coolidge praised "the strength of its faculty,"
whose "great distinguishing mark" was "that they were men
of character."

Things at Amherst have changed considerably since
Coolidge's day. For one thing, during the time he was at
Amherst, Coolidge was in the conservative majority. Today,
the school is one of the more famously (some say overwhelmingly) left-leaning in the nation, and in some ways it
actively discourages diversity of thought. Of course, there
are still "men of character" on the faculty—women, too, for
that matter. But the college has abandoned a concerted effort to instill character through a well-defined program in
the liberal arts; Amherst now has no core curriculum or
distribution requirements at all. While there is no denying
the excellence and intellectual seriousness of many of the
students and faculty at Amherst, we wonder what Silent
Cal would say if he returned to the college today. (Not much,
it's a safe bet.)

Academic Life: Could I but ride indefinite

In its recruiting literature, Amherst calls itself the "premier
liberal arts college in the nation," and looking only at its rankings in various magazines,
one would be hard pressed to disagree. Widely respected for its history and tradition,
the college has enjoyed the benefits of its lofty reputation. Amherst's good name was
largely built on the school's so-called "New Curriculum," which required two years of
basic coursework in the sciences, history, and English. But that curriculum was abolished in 1967; these days the school employs a much less stringent academic program.
Today, there are no core requirements and not even any distribution requirements. The

VITAL STATISTICS
Religious affiliation: none
Total enrollment: 1,623
Total undergraduates: 1,623
ACT midrange: 30–33
Applicants: 5,631
Applicants accepted: 18%
Accepted applicants who enrolled: 41%
Tuition: $29,170
Room and board: $7,740
Freshman retention rate: 97%
Graduation rate: 88% (4 yrs.), 96% (6 yrs.)
Average class size: 15
Student-faculty ratio: 8:1
Courses taught by graduate TAs: none
Most popular majors: social sciences, English, foreign languages
Students living on campus: 98%
Guaranteed housing for four years? yes
Students in fraternities or sororities: none

administration claims that this laxity "ensures that each student in every classroom is there by choice."

The only academic regulation that dictates a student's curriculum is the major field of study. Most majors at Amherst require eight courses, usually built around the fundamental topics of the discipline. Yet different majors have drastically different requirements. For example, the economics department requires students to complete nine courses, five of which every major must complete: "Introduction to Economics," "Microeconomics," "Macroeconomics," and "Introduction to Econometrics," plus a mathematics course, "Introduction to the Calculus." In addition, economics majors must pass a comprehensive examination before they can receive their degrees. English majors complete 10 courses for the major, but in this department students are completely free to choose the courses they take. Upon declaring the major, each English student completes a "concentration statement" with the help of his advisor, and before graduating majors must submit a five-page "concentration essay" summarizing what they have learned. In other words, the English department requires no coursework in the history of the language, Shakespeare, or even British or American literature. Students may opt for courses in film studies, cultural studies, or gender studies instead. In the 1960s, the English department, like the economics program, required a comprehensive examination; today, however, that requirement has been cast aside. The history department, which does insist upon a culminating research project, requires nine courses distributed across at least three geographic areas—but none of those areas need be the United States. The department of political science requires only one introductory course and no culminating essay or examination.

In short, Amherst's curriculum provides tremendous freedom to students—a good thing only if one knows how to use it (and perhaps many Amherst students do). Given the autonomy Amherst gives to uneducated and inexperienced collegians, one would expect the college to offer a strong advising program, and Amherst provides it. Each first-year student is assigned a faculty advisor who serves no more than five freshmen. After declaring majors, usually as sophomores, students move to the care of major advisors in their chosen fields of study. Through this system, the college encourages—but does not require—all students to explore certain knowledge areas. All students are urged to study another language and culture, to deconstruct their own culture, to employ abstract reasoning, to work with the scientific method, to "engage in creative action," and to "interpret, evaluate, and explore the life of the imagination," according to the course catalog.

In addition to its fine advising program, the school boasts a student-faculty ratio of eight to one, and the average Amherst class has only 15 students. According to college statistics, only 7 percent of all courses enroll more than 50 students. In such an environment, teacher-student interaction is, happily, inevitable.

The dominant political ideology at Amherst is clearly evident in the classroom and in every department, although bias varies by class and professor. "In many classes, the professors let their political thoughts be known, but still respect and cover the variety of opinions," one student says. "Overall, I would say that ideology definitely has a presence in the classes." A class titled "Representing Domestic Violence" questions "how domestic violence challenges the normative cultural definitions of home as safe or love as enabling"; this course is offered in the English department, of all places. Left-wing perspectives on themes like globalization and Marxism are pervasive. But although the politics at Amherst are decidedly skewed, one sophomore says this does not necessarily make for an oppressive environment: "As a white, Protestant moderate with conservative tendencies, I must say that I do not at all feel ostracized or silenced. The political views, especially of the administration, have thoroughly impressed me for their intelligence and honesty. I cannot say the same for all the students, who fall under a spectrum of political views, some highly radical, some more moderate, some intelligent, some simply regurgitating propaganda."

ACADEMIC REQUIREMENTS

According to Amherst's "Open Curriculum," the first-year seminar is the only requirement students must satisfy outside the mandates of their major. Students may choose from a wide variety of topics, including "Women and Politics in Africa," "The Arts of Spain," "The Art of Mathematical Thinking," and "Sociology of Conflict and Conflict Resolution."

Outstanding professors at Amherst include Hadley Arkes, Uday Mehta, William Taubman, and Ronald Tiersky in political science; Richard Fink and David Hansen in chemistry; Robert Hilborn in physics; Walter Nicholson, Frank Westhoff, and Geoffrey Woglom in economics; Allen Guttmann, William Pritchard, and David Sofield in English; N. Gordon Levin Jr. in history; Frederick Griffiths and Rebecca Sinos in classics; and Antonio Benítez-Rojo, James Maraniss, and Ilán Stavans in Spanish. Comparatively outstanding departments include classics, economics, fine arts, philosophy, political science, and all of the natural science departments, particularly physics.

Amherst is certainly one of the nation's top private colleges, and the academics are correspondingly rigorous. One physics major says that he and his classmates spend between four to six hours per night studying, but he also claims that "although the workload is demanding, it is not usually burdensome. Most of the work is engaging and interesting." This perspective is a typical one at Amherst, where a genuine love of learning seems to prevail. Students attend Amherst because they want to learn from the best and eventually *be* the best, not because it will give them cushy jobs (although it may). Through the Five College Consortium, Amherst students also may take courses for credit at Smith, Mount Holyoke, Hampshire, and the University of Massachusetts.

Thankfully, some on campus have begun to question the school's watered-down requirements. One alumnus who has become active in reforming Amherst told the student weekly newspaper, "The college has become decidedly unbalanced and has produced a dumbed-down curriculum over the last 20 years or so. What you've got is a pale imitation of a college." This charge is too strong, but the concern is entirely valid (and perhaps applies best to the once highly esteemed English department). Some students will revel in the freedom Amherst offers and will excel as a result, but what Amherst offers is decidedly not a model of the traditional liberal arts education—but rather a romp through the groves of academe, with fruits plucked here, there, and anywhere.

Student Life: Industrious angels? Afternoons to play

Amherst offers students a choice of 33 residential housing options. While all buildings are coed, some dorms do offer single-sex floors. On coed floors with only one bathroom, students vote on whether the bathroom will also be coed or whether one sex will have to use bathrooms on another floor. Students may not only find themselves sharing a bathroom area with members of the opposite sex, but also rooms. Ostensibly because some gay and lesbian students find it awkward to live in rooms with members of the same sex, members of opposite sexes are allowed to share rooms at Amherst. Some space is also allocated for "theme housing" in which like-minded students live together to explore a foreign language and culture, black culture, or health and wellness.

Off-campus living is the exception, not the rule; 98 percent of Amherst students live at the college, whose policy permits only 50 students to live off campus per semester. Priority is given to upperclassmen and students with significant personal or financial reasons for wanting the exception. All freshmen must live on campus. Housing is decided by a lottery system, using class-based rankings, and is guaranteed for each student's four years.

Students do not have the option of living in a fraternity or sorority house because the college prohibits the Greek system on campus. This policy, however, has not discouraged students from exploring their inner Bacchus. Amherst's students are hardly shy when it comes to partying. Wild parties have in fact long been a tradition at Amherst. Theme parties like "Pimps and Hos" are well known for the sexual abandon that characterizes them. These parties, which one student describes as "meat markets," are organized by the student-run Social Committee. Such decadence, obviously not uncommon on American campuses, is at Amherst a significant part of campus life. But one student claims that while there are a number of raucous events held each year on campus, Amherst has less binge drinking and riotous partying than some other schools have. "I am decidedly a non-partier, non-drinker, and I have found a very positive social life within my dorm and the campus. There is a tremendous amount of non-partying to do on campus—usually so many things that one feels almost overwhelmed by the choices." These include an "almost continuous stream of talks, shows, movies, performances, lectures, club meetings, and activities." Amherst College also sponsors a weekly alcohol-free shindig called The Amherst Party (TAP for short), which is usually well attended. Amherst has a thriving and highly visible Democratic club; the Republican population is miniscule, but does exist. Additionally, the *Amherst Spectator,* a conservative newspaper, has gained strength and support at the college and is a viable outlet for conservative students. The Foundation for Classical Studies in Statecraft was founded in 2000 by political science professor Hadley Arkes in order to offer lectures and colloquia to balance the political and intellectual diversity on campus, and perhaps someday, to help bring more faculty with conservative views to Amherst. The largest student organizations on campus are the *Amherst Student* (the weekly student newspaper), Amherst Student Government, the Amherst College Outing Club, Amherst College Diversity Coalition, and numerous musical groups.

Students at Amherst will find that their classmates are not only smart, but also usually athletic. Amherst offers 27 Division III sports programs. The college is a member of the New England Small College Athletic Conference with 10 other schools, including Bowdoin College and Tufts University. Around 30 percent of Amherst students participate in varsity sports and more than 80 percent participate in club and intramural sports. Named after Lord Jeffrey Amherst, the teams' mascot is "Lord Jeff," and hence Amherst teams are called the Jeffs. The archaic nickname seems appropriate for the school, which boasts the oldest collegiate athletic program in the nation. (Amherst participated in the first intercollegiate basketball game in history, defeating Williams in 1859.) Since the Sears Cup, a measure of overall athletic success, has been keeping track of Division III programs, Amherst has never finished lower than 12th in the nation. The Amherst–Williams football game is one of the college's most valued and long-standing traditions. In a less serious tradition, the ski teams run the last race of each season dressed in costume; recent garb has included bikinis and duct tape.

> ### SUGGESTED CORE
> 1. European Studies 21, Readings in the European Tradition I
> 2. Philosophy 17, Ancient Philosophy
> 3. Religion 21, Ancient Israel *and* Religion 204, Introduction: The New Testament
> 4. Religion 45, History of Christianity
> 5. Political Science 28, Modern Political Philosophy
> 6. English 36, Shakespeare
> 7. History 38, Era of the American Revolution
> 8. No suitable course

About a third of the students in the Amherst class of 2006 identify themselves as "students of color." Women make up a little more than half of the student body. Students come from 48 states, but New York, Massachusetts, and California are the most common home states in the class of 2006. Additionally, more than 40 countries are represented among the student population. Most students enter with the hope of studying the humanities or the social sciences, with a third planning to pursue the hard sciences or mathematics.

The Amherst campus spreads over 1,000 acres. Campus facilities include the Robert Frost Library, with more than 900,000 volumes. Students have access to more than eight million books through the Five College Consortium program that includes Hampshire, Mount Holyoke, Smith, and the University of Massachusetts at Amherst. The newly renovated Mead Art Museum houses more than 15,000 works. The school also has a newly completed 50,000-square-foot Life Sciences building dedicated to biological research.

Amherst, Massachusetts, a town of 35,000 people, lies in the western part of the state, some 90 minutes west of Boston and three hours north of New York City. Amherst is a small, New England farming town, but the 30,000 college students in the area enjoy all the resources that the town provides. The town of Amherst "has a historic downtown that is well-lit, well-kept, and has a good collection of shops and restaurants," says one student. "There is not [that much] to do in the town, but for people interested in going to college in the country, yet who do not want to be cut off from the world, Amherst is a pretty good compromise." A bus system, the Pioneer Valley Transit Authority, provides regular and free transportation between the surrounding towns. The tree-lined Freshman Quad, dominated on one end by Johnson Chapel and including several dormitories, forms the heart of the campus and exudes a peaceful college atmosphere. Stearns Church, built in 1873, once served as the campus chapel, but it was torn down in 1948 to make room for a modern arts building and was replaced with the college's present chapel. Today only the steeple of Stearns Church survives, and it dominates the school's skyline. Surrounded by small traditional New England houses and sharing the town with several other schools, including UMass and Hampshire College, Amherst College has retained the form, if not the content, of an old-fashioned liberal arts school.

The crime figures for Amherst are unremarkable. The most common form of crime on campus is larceny, specifically the theft of college property, a typical problem for college dorms. There were 10 forcible sex offenses, 2 aggravated assaults, 1 stolen car, and 25 burglaries on campus in 2003. Crimes that are on the rise at Amherst, according to police statistics, are liquor and drug violations, referrals for which went from 80 in the year 2000 to 191 in 2003. The school does run its own police department and constantly works to improve campus lighting and to increase crime awareness. All Amherst residential halls are secured with digital combination locks. Of course, the small Massachusetts town in which the school is located is largely responsible for the college's relatively low crime rates. One student says that although overall the campus is safe, certain areas of Amherst are "not completely desirable." For instance, the University of Massachusetts's Frat Row, right down the street from the college, is not a safe place for walking alone at night.

Amherst is one of the priciest schools in this book, with a comprehensive fee (tuition, room and board) of $38,940. However, the school practices need-blind admissions, and provides aid to some 48 percent of students, meeting the need of most admitted students. The average student loan burden of recent graduates is a relatively modest $10,787.

BATES COLLEGE

LEWISTON, MAINE • WWW.BATES.EDU

But they still tolerate the liberal arts

The first nonsegregated, coeducational institution in the East, Bates College was founded just before the Civil War on the principle of tolerance—a bit ironic, considering the pervasive political correctness that characterizes the school today. Bates, perhaps more than most other elite eastern liberal arts schools, is an uncomfortable place for students who hold dissident beliefs.

If you can live with the politics of the school and love the Maine outdoors scene, however, you are bound to do very well at Bates. The college is well known as one of the country's top liberal arts colleges and has a reputation that has been rising steadily over the past 20 years. Thanks to intense student-faculty interaction and classmates who truly enjoy learning, the wary Bates student can receive a sound liberal education.

Academic Life: Short term and long term

More than one-third of the courses Bates students take during their four years are mandated by the college's general education requirements. Sounds promising—but given the loose parameters, it doesn't amount to much. Bates does not guarantee that students will graduate with a broad and integrated liberal arts foundation. The distribution requirements basically push science students to take a handful of courses outside of the sciences, and humanities students to take a couple classes in the sciences. Students have a vast array of courses from which to choose; indeed, both students and administrators are proud of the curriculum's flexibility. But Bates students can conceivably graduate without ever having taken a course in philosophy, English, history, or a foreign language—and several students report that they have done exactly that. One economics student says the general education requirements are "very easy to take care of." An environmental studies major says that science students who don't enjoy reading or writing can take humanities courses geared toward them, while humanities students can take plenty of math-for-poets style courses. None-

VITAL STATISTICS	
Religious affiliation: none	
Total enrollment: 1,743	
Total undergraduates: 1,743	
SAT midranges: V: 630–710, M: 640–710	
Applicants: 4,098	
Applicants accepted: 30%	
Accepted applicants who enrolled: 38%	
Tuition: $34,100 (includes room and board)	
Freshman retention rate: 96%	
Graduation rate: 78% (4 yrs.), 85% (6 yrs.)	
Courses with fewer than 20 students: 64%	
Student-faculty ratio: 10:1	
Courses taught by graduate TAs: none	
Most popular majors: social sciences, psychology, English	
Students living on campus: 90%	
Guaranteed housing for four years? yes	
Students in fraternities or sororities: none	

theless, students are self-directed enough that most leave Bates having sampled a broad array of subjects.

One of the features of Bates academic life is a short term in May. During this term, most students take one intense course four days a week for five weeks. (Each student must take two such short-term class during his time at Bates.) The course choices are manifold; examples include "Experimental Biology," set at the Mount Desert Island Biological Laboratory, and "Math Camp," otherwise known as "Introduction to Abstraction," a course required for all math majors. For many students, short-term courses are the most challenging ones they take at Bates. But some students spend short term enjoying springtime in Maine while taking courses like "The Japanese Tea Bowl." The short term also gives students the chance for internships in museums, hospitals, schools, newspapers, or state and federal government.

It would be impossible to graduate from Bates without having taken a number of challenging courses. As one biology major says, "The stereotypical jock taking easy, no-brainer classes doesn't exist on the Bates campus." Naturally, some courses are more rigorous than others. Bates is particularly strong in the sciences, and even the brightest students majoring in math, chemistry, biology, or physics are bound to feel challenged. A chemistry major says that when she tells people her course of study, their "first reaction is to cringe." The Bates science program has distinguished itself from those at other small liberal arts colleges in New England and brings in millions of dollars in research grants. Very few schools without graduate programs are able to provide graduate-level research opportunities to their undergraduates, but Bates students inclined to the sciences participate in research during the summers and throughout the school year. One way the college has proven its excellence in the sciences is in its success in preparing its students for medical school: acceptance rates for seniors who apply to medical school are consistently higher than the national average.

Besides the sciences, particularly strong departments at Bates include English, history, political science, and psychology. While the philosophy course list is characterized by a number of serious offerings, students say that the religion portion of the philosophy and religion department has the most fluff courses. Many are presented in a seminar style and deal with peripheral issues (e.g., "Women's Journey: Still Waters Run Deep," a course that proposes to show how women "actively define the world around them and pursue their own relationship with the divine, their environment, and the search for perfection"). The history department is fragmented and overspecialized—unless you really believe that undergraduates need an entire course on "Shanghai 1927–1937" or, for that matter, a course devoted wholly to the history of the Vikings. Sociology is another relatively weak department.

Bates is one of the few liberal arts colleges that still requires a senior thesis, and the admissions department claims that it is one of the most distinctive features of a Bates education. Most seniors spend their final semester, or even their entire senior year, working on the thesis, either conducting new research or preparing for a performance or other service, then writing a substantial paper explaining the project. The senior thesis requires self-discipline and academic focus, and Bates is to be credited for holding on to this important tradition. As one student told the school newspaper, "It gave my major a real meaning. It was a nice finale to my Bates education." For other students, completing such an impressive academic project as undergraduates makes a career or graduate school all the less intimidating. Ninety percent of 2003 seniors reported being satisfied with the senior thesis program.

With a student body of around 1,700, Bates has all the advantages of a small, teaching-centered institution. The college has only 10 students for every faculty member, and the average class size is a comfortable 14 students. Even the largest lecture halls are intimate enough to encourage questions from the audience. With no graduate program, there are no teaching assistants leading undergraduate courses. Qualified upperclassmen, however, sometimes assist faculty in lower-level laboratory sections in the sciences. Professors devote a great deal of their attention to teaching and most are very accessible to their students. Even faculty members in the sciences put students as their highest priority; any research they conduct complements coursework and is rarely at the expense of students. One student says that every professor posts office hours and that even outside these hours, professors are usually happy to have walk-ins. A sophomore says that when she was having trouble with her organic chemistry class, her professor went to tremendous lengths to make sure she not only passed the class, but remembered the material for future courses. "Professors are so accessible to students that you might wonder when they find the time to accomplish any work," another student says. "They genuinely care about the academic and social well-being of the students."

Professors are well integrated into the Bates community, and it is not uncommon for a student to have dinner with a professor or to become a personal friend of his family. "I was on a first-name basis with all my professors and got to know them well," a foreign language major says. Any faculty member who teaches a First-Year Seminar also serves as the academic advisor for the 15 or fewer students who enroll in his course. Since 90 percent of first-year students take such a seminar, almost every freshman has frequent interaction with his advisor. It is not unusual for these relationships to last a lifetime. Once a student declares a major, he is assigned—or can choose—a faculty advisor within the major department. Students report that advisors are helpful; one student says hers "provided not only academic advice, but also advice

ACADEMIC REQUIREMENTS

On top of the demands of a major, Bates students must meet the following distribution requirements:

- Three courses in the hard sciences. Introductory courses range from "Musical Acoustics" (which promises that "no background in physics or mathematics beyond algebra is assumed") and "Planetarium Production" to "Cellular and Molecular Biology."
- Three courses in the social sciences (which include anthropology, economics, education, political science, psychology, and sociology). Eligible courses include "Principles of Microeconomics" and "African-American Culture through Sports."
- One math course. Choices include "Working with Data," "Great Ideas in Mathematics," and "Calculus I."
- Five courses in the humanities (in at least three different departments). These could include "Introduction to the Ancient World" or "Ballroom Dance."

on my future decisions and other interests in my life that weren't necessarily academic." Independent study courses are quite popular, and students often work closely with professors either to explore a subject not offered in a traditional course or to perform new research.

The typical Bates student seems more concerned with acquiring a thorough education than with life after school. Some students are career-oriented—economics and political science majors are said to be the most interested in padding their résumés— but most students agree that career types are not the norm at Bates. And while the curriculum might not force students to take a terribly broad selection of courses, students typically do anyway. According to one humanities student, "Most students are open to taking courses in other areas outside their major." Another says, "Most people enjoy college now, and think about a career later." This attitude is not atypical at New England liberal arts colleges, says a vice president quoted in the *Chronicle of Higher Education*: "By and large, New England has not moved to job-oriented curriculums. If a student wants to major in advertising and marketing, we don't offer it."

As at Bowdoin and Colby, two other highly regarded liberal arts schools in Maine, study abroad is extraordinarily popular at Bates; 70 percent of the student body participates in such a program, usually during the junior year. The college itself sponsors fall semester programs in countries like Germany, Austria, China, and Russia. Through the Colby-Bates-Bowdoin Off-Campus Study Consortium, students can study for a semester in Ecuador, South Africa, or the United Kingdom. Bates also jointly sponsors programs in Japan, India, and Sri Lanka, and it allows students to avail themselves of a host of other international options sponsored by other colleges.

Professors praised for their teaching include Matthew J. Côté and Thomas J. Wenzel in chemistry; Will Ambrose, Joe Pelliccia, and Rebecca Sommer in biology; James W. Hughes and Michael P. Murray in economics; John H. Corrie in music; John Rhodes in math; Richard C. Williamson in French; Mark Okrent in philosophy; and John Cole in history and classical and medieval studies.

Student Life: Outing club

Bates College is the lone intellectual hotspot in the working-class New England mill town of Lewiston, Maine, which made headlines in 2002 when its mayor pleaded with Somali refugees to stop moving there (more than 2,000 Somalis have settled in Lewiston since February 2001). The campus is the undisputed center of student life. The college guarantees housing for all four years and requires students to live on campus, except by special permission.

Most of the dormitories are coed, but some have single-sex floors. Bates does not offer coed dorm rooms, but in some coed suites, students of opposite sexes might share a common bathroom. Students have to specifically select suites, so no student will be forced to use a coed bathroom. Students also have an alcohol-free living option, and studious underclassmen or seniors focusing completely on their theses may wish to live in a designated quiet house or hall where they won't be bothered by late-night parties. First-year students all live together in doubles, triples, or quads, with every 15 or so students matched with a junior advisor. Bates has only one dining hall, Memorial Commons, which compares favorably to that of almost any other school in this guide. While some students may complain about the lack of dining options—though there is now one Somali restaurant, the Red Sea, in Lewiston—a senior claims that the dining hall helps everyone keep in touch: "I never have to wonder where so and so is. He'll be at dinner." Everything at Bates emphasizes the school's close-knit community atmosphere.

That community becomes even closer on typical weekend nights, when most students resort to drinking. "There's not much else to do," says one student. Other students say there is plenty to do if one knows where to look. "There are also activities for people who don't like the party scene—movies, dances, or shows," a sophomore says. The college provides activities throughout the week and on the weekend to keep students occupied. The Chase Hall Committee, a student-run activities group, along with the Student Activities office, has brought big-name bands to campus, including Counting Crows, Gin Blossoms, and Guster. The Bates Museum of Art specializes in Maine artists, and in April and May, studio art majors showcase their works. The annual Gala is a college-wide formal featuring a live orchestra or band. Bates brings in a number of lecturers each year.

SUGGESTED CORE
1. Classical and Medieval Studies 106, Greek Civilization
2. Philosophy 271, Greek Philosophy
3. Religion 235, Ancient Israel: History, Religion, and Literature *and* Religion 236, Introduction to the New Testament
4. Religion 241, History of Christian Thought I
5. Political Science 191, Western Political Theory
6. English 213/214, Shakespeare
7. History 140, Origins of the New Nation, 1500–1820 *and* History 141, America in the Nineteenth Century
8. Philosophy 273, Philosophy in the Nineteenth Century

Bates students of all political persuasions agree on one thing, and that is that the campus leans decidedly to the left. But the Bates student body is largely uninterested in politics. A handful of student activists and a small group of faculty members are primarily responsible for the school's left-liberal image. Many of the political issues on campus revolve around one central theme: an overwhelming feeling of white privilege. Bates' student body is only 2 percent black, the price tag for tuition, room, and board is a hefty $34,100 per year, and Bates students are hardly denied the creature comforts during their time on campus. After hearing professors dwell on the sins of the West in almost every history class, it's no wonder that students begin to feel guilty about their backgrounds. Activist types often jump in their cars to go protest the working conditions in L.L. Bean's overseas factories or environmental pollution in New England or to "march against hate" in Lewiston, Boston, or Washington, D.C.

Bates's highly visible Multicultural Center is typical of the genre, sponsoring lectures by Grace Lee Boggs, Sonia Sanchez, bell hooks, and Sistah Souljah; showing a "Coming Out Day" film called *Living with Pride*; providing information on social justice internships; and hosting an entire month dedicated to Native American events—though only 0.3 percent of the Bates student population is Native American. The Multicultural

Center also oversees a number of political, religious, and cultural organizations, including Amandla!, a group that plans to promote "better understanding of the many communities of the African diaspora"; the gay/lesbian/transgender club, OUTfront; and the Women's Action Coalition, the main campus feminist group.

These activist groups rarely face opposition. A once thriving libertarian student newspaper recently went defunct. A number of conservatives have taken editorial posts on the *Bates Student*, the weekly student newspaper, though to no great effect on the overall political bent of the publication. The College Republicans hold meetings but have little influence on campus politics.

Of course, one cannot spend four years in Maine and not take advantage of the great outdoors. The Bates Outing Club is the most popular extracurricular organization; in fact, students are automatically registered as members when they arrive on campus. The club allows students to borrow backpacks, bikes, and tents for free, and it sponsors outings to the beach, mountains, and Maine ski resorts several times each semester. The annual Lobster Bake is a huge feast at the beach, with all-you-can-eat lobster and clams. Student organizations sometimes sponsor trips to Portland and Freeport, the latter town a bargain shopper's paradise.

Bates is a very athletic campus, with around 60 percent of the student body participating in intramural sports. One-third of Bates students are varsity members of one of the Bobcats' 30 intercollegiate teams. The college has excellent athletic facilities for a school of its size, including an indoor track and an ice arena.

Religion isn't a major priority for Bates students—most would prefer to study or ski. But as one student says, "There are ways to grow in your faith if you're looking for it." Bates Christian Fellowship holds Bible studies and prayer services each week. The school also hosts a Hillel and a Newman Club. For those who like their religion laced with strong doses of feminist and liberation theology, the Bates chaplain and chapel are happy to oblige.

At one point, Bates College was surrounded by razor wire to keep out undesirable Lewistonians. The school's previous president tore down the fences to promote better college-community interaction. It might be time to put them back up. Bates has suffered a handful of violent crimes in recent years, including a rape that happened in a major academic building and a murder a block away from the school. One upperclassman believes that "college and town relations are at an all-time low." Two young women report that they no longer walk across campus alone because they don't feel safe doing so. Bates public safety department does offer a free security ride and escort service, and the most recent crime numbers do not reflect an unsafe environment; in 2003 Bates reported one forcible sex offense, 22 burglaries, one stolen car, and two arsons on campus.

At almost $35,000 a year, Bates ain't cheap. Thirty-eight percent of students receive financial aid, however, and the school practices need-blind admission, meeting 100 percent of students' demonstrated need. The average recent graduate owed a modest $14,401 in student loans.

BOSTON COLLEGE

CHESTNUT HILL, MASSACHUSETTS • WWW.BC.EDU

Pillars of the throne

Inscribed on the facade of a building in Boston College's main quadrangle is a Bible verse that would raise some skeptical, if not hostile, eyebrows on most campuses: "You will come to know the truth and the truth will set you free." Equally suspicious to some are the quotations that flank it: "Right and justice are the pillars of Thy Throne," and "Fear of the Lord is true wisdom and true learning."

Like many institutions with a religious heritage, Boston College is involved in a tug-of-war between tradition and what passes for progress in mainstream academia. But there are encouraging signs that the university is, at least in part, pulling for tradition. The current administration has proclaimed its wish to preserve the school's Jesuit tradition and has stood surprisingly firm on the side of academic standards when faced with accusations, for instance, that the curriculum is not "diverse" or "specialized" enough. Boston College is one of the nation's finest Catholic educational institutions and wants to remain so.

Academic Life: Four years BC

Boston College is nationally recognized for fostering some of the best classroom discussion environments in the United States. "Professors here have teaching as their prime motivating factor," a student says. "Very few are here for just research and publishing. Faculty members jump at the chance to interact with students." Another student says, "All of my professors have very personal relations with students. They go out of their way to help, but you do have to take a bit of an initiative."

The health of student-faculty relations is supported by the serious academic environment. For an institution of its size, BC does a decent job of ensuring that every undergraduate receives some exposure to the great texts of our culture. Trendy courses and courses taught by professors using fashionable methods of analysis are outnumbered by courses of traditional and truly useful content and form. Opportunities for an excellent undergraduate experience abound, if the student knows where to look.

VITAL STATISTICS
Religious affiliation: Roman Catholic
Total enrollment: 14,419
Total undergraduates: 9,830
SAT midrange: 1250–1400
Applicants: 22,451
Applicants accepted: 32%
Accepted applicants who enrolled: 32%
Tuition: $28,940
Room and board: $9,620
Freshman retention rate: 95%
Graduation rate: 86% (6 yrs.)
Average class size: 25
Student-faculty ratio: 13:1
Courses taught by graduate TAs: not provided
Most popular majors: communications, English, finance
Students living on campus: 78%
Guaranteed housing for four years? no
Students in fraternities or sororities: none

NEW ENGLAND

15

The formal advising program maintained by BC requires students to run their schedules past a faculty member every semester. Not all students can actually be troubled to meet with their advisors and rely instead on e-mail to obtain an approval. But students who show interest find that professors are happy to meet with them and offer guidance. The school's collegiality and low student-teacher ratio (13 to 1) make such collaboration more likely for those who seek it out.

Some of the strongest departments at BC are the disciplines that constitute the foundation of any good liberal education. One such department is philosophy, which promises to provide the "opportunity for open-ended inquiry and reflection on the most fundamental questions about ourselves, our world, and our destiny." The department offers a broad selection of courses in Western philosophy along with several courses in topics like ancient Chinese philosophy—an academically worthy way to satisfy the cultural diversity requirement. The university's Catholic heritage is of paramount importance in this department, perhaps even more so than in the theology department. "Philosophy takes its Catholic character seriously and this informs its hiring and its course offerings," such as courses in Catholic apologetics, says one professor. Noteworthy faculty members include Richard Cobb-Stevens, Joseph Flanagan, S.J., Jorge and Laura Garcia, Richard Kearney, Peter Kreeft, and Ronald Tacelli, S.J.

Another outstanding department at BC is political science, where, according to one professor, students will find "a seriousness about the study of politics in its broader theoretical and historical context, and a very strong commitment to undergraduate and graduate teaching." Although political science does not require specific courses, its distribution requirements—courses in American politics, comparative politics, international politics, and political theory—are solid, and all students must take two introductory classes. The department is proud of its heavy workload and emphasizes that "clarity of thought and writing are two sides of the same skill," according to its Web page. The distinguished political science faculty includes Alice and Nasser Behnegar, Christopher Bruell, Robert Faulkner, Christopher Kelly, Marc Landy, Susan Shell, and Alan Wolfe.

Boston College's theology department, especially when compared to philosophy and political science, is disappointing, students report. "The theology department has placed a lot of emphasis on interreligious dialogue," a former student familiar with the program says. While allowing that the discussions are engaging, this student warns that any young scholar on his way to Boston College, especially to study theology, needs to "assume that his experience is going to be liberal." Indeed, at times "interreligious dialogue" seems to be a cover for "political correctness," as in courses like "Suffering, Politics, and Liberation" and "Race, Religion, and Social Justice." Still, students of theology must take two year-long introductory courses, either "Biblical Heritage" or "The Religious Quest," and either "Introduction to Christian Theology" or "Exploring Catholicism: Tradition and Transformation." All of these courses expose students to the fundamentals of Christianity; "The Religious Quest" focuses more on non-Christian religions than do the others and also satisfies the cultural diversity requirement. One real bonus for theology students is BC's membership in the Boston Theological Institute, which allows advanced students to take classes at and use the resources of Harvard Divinity School, Weston Jesuit School of Theology, and other schools. Stephen F. Brown, David Hollenbach, S.J., Matthew Lamb, S.J., Frederick Lawrence, and Thomas E. Wangler are all faculty of distinction in theology.

Students recommend Michael J. Connolly in Slavic and Eastern languages; Thomas Epstein in the Honors Program; Thomas C. Chiles in biology; J. Robert Barth, S.J., in English; and Avner Ash, Gerard E. Keough, and Mark Reeder in mathematics. Overall, besides philosophy and political science, the school's best departments are economics, biology, chemistry, physics, history, and English, which one professor says is a generally strong department with "significant weaknesses." Particularly poor departments are sociology—"This department is at the center of leftist activism on campus, and should be avoided by all students seeking the otherwise well-rounded and top quality education offered by Boston College," says a student—and communications, "which should not be a major department, and wasn't until recently," according to one professor.

BC's Honors Program invites "presidential scholars," the top 60 or so students, to embark on the kind of educational journey that college students used to take when real core curricula were the educational norm at liberal arts colleges. Freshmen and sophomores in the program take a six-credit course called "The Western Cultural Tradition," in which they read primary texts beginning with ancient Greek literature and philosophy, continuing through the works of the Roman Empire, early Christianity, the medieval age, and the Renaissance, and ending with major cultural, historical, and philosophical works of modernity. As juniors, students take an advanced seminar called "The Twentieth Century and the Tradition," a course perhaps too little concerned with the tradition and too much concerned with a few thinkers of the last century. The first semester of this course explores modernism and the second semester, postmodernism. Here students explore "feminism, deconstructionism, the communications revolution, changing views of non-Western cultures, and new perspectives centering on race, ethnicity, and gender," according to the course description. Seniors end their BC years by writing a senior thesis or by participating in an integrative seminar, in which they study in more depth texts they encountered earlier in their college years.

ACADEMIC REQUIREMENTS

Every student enrolled in one of the five BC colleges serving undergraduates—the College of Arts and Sciences, the Carroll School of Management, the Lynch School of Education, the Connell School of Nursing, and the Woods College of Advancing Studies—must complete what is called the University Core, really a set of distribution requirements:

- Students must take two courses each in philosophy, theology, history, social science, and natural science. BC students choose among 15 philosophy courses, including "Western Cultural Tradition," "Philosophy of the Person," "Person and Social Responsibility," and "Philosophy of Human Existence." The history requirement can be completed by choosing from a list of around 15 courses per semester—all fair, fundamental courses.
- Courses in writing, literature, the arts, mathematics, and cultural diversity are also mandatory.

The Perspectives program in the College of Arts and Sciences is a four-year interdisciplinary program that often gives students credits in more than one subject area. The series includes "Perspectives on Western Culture," "Modernism in the Arts," "Horizons of the New Social Sciences," and "New Scientific Visions." PULSE, a program administrated by the philosophy department, operates in a similar manner to Perspectives and uses some of the same texts but focuses more on ethics and politics. This service-oriented program, now in its 36th year, represents a serious effort to combine philosophical learning with social service or advocacy.

The Society of Jesus founded Boston College in 1863, and 130 Jesuits live on campus, where about half are active professors, graduate students, and administrators. Under President William Leahy, S.J., the administration has reaffirmed BC's tradition by hiring more Jesuits and by focusing on the fundamentals of liberal education. Since the arrival of President Leahy in 1996, BC has seen a tentative but progressive reidentification with the school's Catholic identity, says one alumnus. Not that BC has an unblemished record in this regard: Four years ago, the school took down all the crucifixes in its classrooms. More troublingly, BC has chosen not to implement the Vatican directive, *Ex Corde Ecclesiae*, which insists that all theology professors receive a mandate from the local bishop certifying their Catholic orthodoxy.

As for politics in the classroom, apart from the "cultural diversity" requirement, BC offers some interdisciplinary minors such as "faith, peace, and justice," black studies, and women's studies. History students are free to waste their time in courses like "Introduction to Feminisms" and "Lesbian/Gay/Bisexual/Straight."

Student Life: Mass. acquisitions

Boston, one of the most culturally rich cities in the nation, has no dearth of activities for the thousands of college students in the area. From the 116-acre main BC campus in the suburb of Chestnut Hill, an affluent residential neighborhood, it is a six-mile (30-minute) trolley ride downtown. Boston College, with its large Gothic-style buildings, is "very Cambridge-like," says one student. Space is precious here, and BC is more condensed than other universities of its size; however, it will soon have more breathing room. In a recent historical land acquisition, the college acquired for $99.4 million the former residence of the Boston archbishop, four additional archdiocese buildings, and the surrounding 43 acres, with an option to buy the neighboring 13.5-acre St. John's Seminary property. For $16.5 million, BC also acquired the rustic 78-acre St. Stephen Priory on the Charles River in Dover, Mass.

The BC campus is located on three hills. Lower Campus has the theater, some residence halls for upperclassmen, the football stadium, athletic buildings, and a dining hall. Main Campus includes the main library, most classroom buildings, and the student union. Upper Campus has most of the underclassmen residence halls. The university has no college-town atmosphere in the immediate area, but its proximity to the numerous Boston-area colleges makes those activities readily available to BC students. "As with any school," says one student, "there are parties here. And you don't have to go very far to find an Irish bar in Boston." Strong drink is readily available and joyously consumed at BC, but the administration has lately been cracking down on alcohol abuse, making it harder for underage students to obtain illicit drink, says one student.

Although it's hard to characterize the typical student at a school of Boston College's size, there are certain trends. The admissions office reports that more than half of the undergraduate population comes from the Northeast. For the most part, BC students "are intellectually focused and serious about their studies," says one student. "At the same time, studies do not dominate their lives; they know how to let loose and have an active social life." Another student says, "I think the typical BC student is smart, hardworking, enterprising, and fun-loving."

Among the more than 200 registered student organizations at BC, students should have no trouble finding a club to fit their interests. Besides multicultural groups, there are the typical political organizations, sports clubs, and professional societies, including the Political Science Association and the Accounting Academy. BC has no social fraternities or sororities.

SUGGESTED CORE
1. Classics 217, Heroic Poetry: Homer, Virgil, and Beyond
2. and 3. Theology 90/ Philosophy 90, Perspectives on Western Culture I
4. and 5. Theology 91/ Philosophy 91, Perspectives on Western Culture II
6. English 310, Shakespeare
7. History 181, American Civilization I
8. History 469, Intellectual History of Modern Europe

The university does not officially recognize the Lesbian, Gay, and Bisexual Community student group, but it does let it meet and maintain an office on university property. Recently sanctioned by the administration is the student group "Allies," which is committed to building toleration and understanding of homosexuals, according to a university Web page. In 2004, as in years past, the student government promoted on-campus events for National Coming Out Week.

BC recently settled a dispute with the student-run newspaper the *Heights*. According to the *Chronicle of Higher Education,* BC had sought direct administrative oversight of the paper and a ban on alcohol and tobacco advertising in return for continuing to grant it virtually free office space. In a compromise, the paper agreed to pay a higher rent and to refuse advertising from pro-abortion groups such as Planned Parenthood.

About 70 percent of Boston College students are Catholic, but their degree of involvement in religious activities varies. Opportunities abound for student participation, including daily liturgies and student clubs. In some on-campus residences, Jesuit priests say mass, counsel students, and sponsor floor retreats. Students recommend the daily mass at St. Mary's Chapel in St. Mary's Hall, home to BC's Jesuit community. The Campus Ministry has a Multifaith Chapel and offers ecumenical as well as Catholic worship services.

Catholic students who cherish official church teaching should seek out the St. Thomas More Society, an orthodox Catholic student group, and the *Observer*, a student publication that is a visible defender of the Catholic faith and conservative politics on campus. When the St. Thomas More Society sponsored a presentation by Dr. Paul

Cameron of the Family Research Institute titled "The Case Against Gay Marriage," a flyer was distributed criticizing the speaker and some students walked out of the speech. However, in an atmosphere of balanced, fairly tolerant debate, both conservatives and liberals feel fairly at home at BC, and there even seems to be a centripetal force toward political moderation. As one student says, "Both sides are comfortable, but there is some trepidation about speakers who are either very strong conservatives or very strong liberals. Most people get a bit nervous."

On campus, there are living arrangements to accommodate the needs of nearly every undergraduate and to guarantee at least three years in campus housing. There are 29 dormitories, with freshmen housed on the school's Newton Campus (a one-and-a-half-mile bus ride from the main campus) or the Upper Campus. More than 70 percent of undergraduates live in university housing. Opportunities for special-interest housing include the Greycliff Honors House, as well as multicultural, "social activism," and substance-free floors. Residence halls separate men and women by floor. There are no single-sex dorms available, and while the housing office says that members of the opposite sex cannot stay in residence halls overnight, that rule is not strictly enforced.

An escape from coursework for BC students is provided by the school's sports programs. The university fields 13 Division I varsity teams for men and 16 for women. Boston College is particularly strong in basketball, football, and hockey. BC jilted the Big East for the Atlantic Coast Conference in 2005—a money grab that left BC's former conference mates none too pleased and cost BC a $1 million exit fee. In sports not offered by the ACC—notably, men's and women's ice hockey, fencing, skiing, sailing—BC teams will stay in the same leagues and associations.

Boston College's urban setting makes it a prime target for criminals. In 2003, the university reported 10 forcible sex offenses, two robberies, five aggravated assaults, 58 burglaries, two stolen cars and two arsons. The campus police department has worked to curb crime, and most incidents can be prevented by taking reasonable precautions. The university also offers crime prevention workshops and sponsors a van and walking safety/escort service at night.

Around 60 percent of the student body receives financial aid. The university pledges to meet 100 percent of a student's financial need.

BOSTON UNIVERSITY

BOSTON, MASSACHUSETTS • WWW.BU.EDU

Safe at home

Boston University is inextricably entwined with the city of Boston, and not just because of its name. The integration of the university into the city gives BU an atmosphere different from that of any other American college. Speckled with brownstones and towering buildings, Boston University is located on the Charles River next to the city's historic Back Bay district. Boston is not so much a college town as a town full of colleges. To study and live in a city so rich in American history and culture is an education in itself. For almost three decades, BU's political and academic culture was shaped by the presidency of John Silber, a no-nonsense Democrat who ran for governor of Massachusetts in 1990 (and nearly won), then served until 2003 as the school's chancellor. Silber was a staunch opponent of academic postmodernism and relativism, bravely preserving the integrity of the humanities at BU. After Silber's resignation, the university hired former NASA administrator Daniel Goldin as president, but then withdrew the offer for undisclosed reasons. BU is currently under the leadership of interim president Aram V. Chobanian, former dean of the School of Medicine and a BU faculty member for more than 40 years. In addition to its interim president, BU has seven deans ad interim and an ad interim provost—while the longest serving trustees (Silber's allies) are being urged to retire. In other words, there is underway an administrative battle to seize the helm. As a result, BU finds itself at a critical crossroads. It is not yet clear for how long Silber's legacy will maintain the school's commitment to being something more than "that *other* school in Boston"—the one that's not Harvard, or MIT, or even Boston College. That *other* one.

VITAL STATISTICS
Religious affiliation: none
Total enrollment: 29,596
Total undergraduates: 17,740
SAT/ACT midranges: SAT V: 600–690, M: 620–700; ACT: 26–30
Applicants: 28,240
Applicants accepted: 55%
Accepted applicants who enrolled: 28%
Tuition: $29,988
Room and board: $9,288
Freshman retention rate: 89%
Graduation rate: 62% (4 yrs.), 75% (6 yrs.)
Courses with fewer than 20 students: 57%
Student-faculty ratio: 15:1
Courses taught by graduate TAs: 6%
Most popular majors: social sciences, communications, business
Students living on campus: 74%
Guaranteed housing for four years? yes
Students in fraternities: 3% sororities: 5%

Academic Life: Buried treasures

With almost 18,000 undergraduates and 12,000 graduate students, Boston University is the nation's fourth-largest private institution of higher education. As such, the univer-

Boston University's liberal arts division imposes serious and worthy requirements for graduation—making its diploma more intrinsically meaningful than some others available in town. Students must:

- Take a two-course sequence focused on writing, reading, thinking, and research skills (a requirement recently beefed up from just one semester).
- Show proficiency in a foreign language at the advanced level, either through placement tests or coursework.
- Show competency in math. Most students test out of taking any courses, however—good SAT scores are enough, and they shouldn't be.

On top of these skills requirements, BU has general education requirements, which can be met through completion of the excellent Core Curriculum, or through fulfilling distributional mandates.

The Core Curriculum consists of eight integrated courses in classic works, humanities, and natural and social sciences. Students in the program take two prescribed courses each semester during their

sity cannot easily be categorized: it is neither a large state university, nor a small liberal arts college. Although it is overshadowed by neighbors Harvard and MIT, Boston University has earned national respect. Many BU students comment that they experience a heavier workload than their counterparts across town, in courses with equally distinguished professors.

The best news of all about Boston University is this: the school actually offers a true core curriculum, providing undergraduates who seek it with the foundations of a liberal arts education. The BU Core Curriculum is designed for students who want to enjoy the traditional liberal arts experience within a larger university. Sadly, it is not mandatory (Silber was a prophet, not a wizard), and students eager to specialize or squirm out of learning the humanities can instead choose to fulfill the somewhat weaker general education requirements. One student who participated in the core says the program is "really impressive because it covers all aspects—not just what a professor happens to be interested in at that moment."

Boston University offers more than 250 majors and minors from 17 schools and colleges, including arts and sciences, arts, education, communication, general studies, and engineering. Most general studies students are at Boston University on something like a probationary basis. They must spend four semesters studying the humanities, social science, natural science, and mathematics in 16 prescribed courses. After the second year, they transfer to the school of their choice to complete coursework in their majors. Some students enroll in general studies simply so they can later be accepted into one of the university's more competitive colleges. The College of Communication, for instance, is very selective, and the general studies path allows students who might not otherwise get in to earn a place there.

After completing the general education requirements, the BU student goes on to complete a major. The English department requires 11 courses, including one in American literature, one period class, and one author-specific course. The department does not require a survey of English literature, courses in British literature, or a Shakespeare class. Outside of the three required areas of study, students may pursue their own interests. The good news, however, is that most of the department's courses center around important writers and their works (not something to be taken for granted these days). But the history major hardly ensures a breadth of knowledge. Students in the general program are required to take a course focusing on Africa, East Asia, Latin America, or the Middle East, and must take at least one course in either European or American history. The program also calls for a methodological seminar and two colloquia. Political science majors must take 12 courses, including an introduction to the subject, an introduction to political analysis, elementary statistics, and a choice of three introductory-level courses in American politics, public policy, comparative politics, international relations, and political theory.

Students finding their way through this labyrinth of academic options can turn to their advisors for guidance. Each freshman receives an advisor and is able to choose a new advisor upon declaration of his major. Students must consult with their advisors before registering for the next semester's courses, but for many students the program ends there. "The advising program here is what you make of it," one senior says. "Some of my friends can't stand their advisors and never talk to them. But I've switched my advisor to one I like and respect, and he has helped me choose courses and is aware of all my career plans." The university also offers prelaw and premed advising.

Boston University only requires each student to take four courses each semester (that's 32 in four years), which means that a full third of a student's coursework goes toward the major. At least eight courses contribute to general area requirements, leaving the rest free for electives. As a large university thinking small, 60 percent of Boston University's classes have fewer than 20 students and the student-teacher ratio is 15 to 1. Only about 10 percent of courses have more than 50 students. One political science major says that "except for a few bad seeds," most BU professors are incredibly accessible. "I think that's the best thing about BU. All of my professors have Web sites and send e-mails throughout the week, keeping us interested in the course. They make themselves very available." Graduate students teach some introductory courses each year, and lead almost all discussion and laboratory sections. But "by your junior year, nearly all interaction is with professors," says one student.

BU has an impressive array of well-known scholars and writers among its faculty.

REQUIREMENTS (CONT'D)

first two years. Covering the history and major texts of the ancient world through the Renaissance and into modernity, the core provides students with a thorough and broad understanding of the intellectual tradition to which they are the heirs.

The Division Studies Program, an alternative to the Core, requires two courses in each of the academic areas outside the student's area of concentration. These areas are:

- Humanities. Choices include "Readings in Shakespeare" and "Self and Society in Modern Japanese Literature."
- Mathematics and computer science. Options include "Calculus I" and "Introduction to Computers."
- Natural sciences. Choices include "The Solar System" and "Earthquakes, Volcanoes, and Other Natural Disasters."
- Social sciences. Options here range from "Introduction to Archeology" to "Women and Men: Cultural Expectations and Gender Experiences."

Students name the following faculty members as among the university's best teachers: presidential historian Robert Dallek, William R. Keylor, Igor Lukes, and Nina Silber (no relation to John) in history; Roye Wates in music; Stephen Geller in film and television; religious poet Geoffrey Hill, poet laureate Robert Pinsky, Rosanna Warren, and author Elie Weisel in English; Walter Clemens, Walter D. Connor, and Sofía Pérez in political science; David Eckel in religion; and David Hempton in the School of Theology. Faculty members who teach courses in the core curriculum are known for being fair and even-handed in their approach to controversial topics. One student characterizes them as "scholarly, academic, and not biased at all." Students and professors say that overall, the best departments are economics, literature, and the School of Theology, the oldest and founding school of the university. BU is one of the few American universities with a department of international relations. With top-notch faculty, it is one of the fastest growing majors at BU.

The most politicized departments are psychology/sociology, women's studies, and African American studies; students say these are also the weakest majors, whose professors do not distinguish scholarship from activism. According to the BU administration, the College of Communications is not up to snuff, either. The dean of the college and the head of the film and television department were both forced to resign at the end of the 2003 academic year. "Administrators have . . . criticized the direction of the college's journalism department, which they believe should put more emphasis on the liberal arts and less on the nuts-and-bolts of daily journalism," reports the *Chronicle of Higher Education*. The new dean, John Schultz, encourages "strong writing and speaking skills and a solid grounding in liberal arts education as the essential first building blocks to success." A hopeful sign.

The University Professors Program allows BU's best students to learn from distinguished faculty members "who have built their own intellectual bridges between various disciplines of the humanities, arts, and sciences." Students take a set of eight courses, with titles like "Ethics and Politics" and "Interrogating the Universe," plus a weekly seminar in which faculty members in the program present "the fruits of their own scholarship for examination and discussion," according to the program Web page. Students complete their participation in the program with a senior thesis.

The politics of ethnicity are not entirely absent from BU's classrooms. But even if courses like "Economics and Politics of Racial Inequality," "The Afro-Russian Experience in Russia," "Blacks in Modern Europe," and "History of Racial Thought" are a bit politicized, things could be much, much worse. One conservative student says that liberal professors usually present both sides equally and fairly and welcome debate in class, although a few sometimes present the opposing viewpoint "so terribly that it looks pathetic." In general, the students at BU seem more interested in the trappings of political activism and protest than do the faculty. "Students are much more liberal than the faculty," says one student. But as one faculty member says, the student body is "less politicized and less politically active than seems to be the case elsewhere."

Lately, the most controversial issues have been administrative. During his tenure, Silber rejected a proposed women's studies program and refused to designate homosexuals as a protected class. This policy was reversed in December 2004. One professor says, "After years of taking flak from leftist academics and the liberal *Boston Globe*, the university's board of trustees seems to aspire to the quiet life . . . focusing on noncontroversial issues such as completing new athletic facilities, neglecting more difficult academic issues such as appointing strong faculty." Nor does

BU want to appoint another Silber any time soon. According to the *Chronicle of Higher Education*, BU's trustees have voted to limit future presidents to a term of 14 years.

If the virus of political correctness has not yet infected teachers at BU, some other viruses have. The *Chronicle* reports that three biomedical researchers at BU fell ill in 2004 after working with a "potentially lethal bacterium." The school claimed that the researchers had failed to follow university-mandated precautions. Nevertheless, the controversy which erupted over the infections has thrown into question BU's ambitious plans to build a new, U.S. government–funded, $120 million lab that would study, um, infectious diseases. Stay tuned. And keep taking your echinacea.

Student Life: The house that Ruth . . . lived in

Boston University guarantees four years of on-campus housing to students, unless they move off campus and then decide to move back. Most freshmen live in large dormitories and can choose to live on single-sex floors or wings. The university also has an all-female dormitory. BU has no coed dorm rooms or coed bathrooms.

Upperclassmen may opt for smaller residences, including one of more than 100 brownstones, some of which overlook the Charles River. Many of these residences are used as specialty houses where students with common academic or social interests—a foreign language, philosophy, environmental awareness, or engineering, for example—can live together. Students in the Wellness House agree to forgo drugs, alcohol, and smoking. Another of the school's dormitories, a former hotel, is so close to Fenway Park that Babe Ruth once lived there.

Boston's large metropolitan area gives students plenty of housing options off campus. The university maintains lists of local realtors and available apartments and rooms. Of course, living off campus comes with a hefty price tag: in 2001, the National Housing Conference voted Boston the 15th-most "unaffordable city in the country." The city simply has far more demand for housing than it has supply. As a consequence, in recent years record numbers of Boston University students have sought on-campus housing, making competition for the most popular residences even fiercer. In order to keep its pledge to provide housing for every student who asks for it, the university has forced many sophomores and juniors to live in traditionally freshman dormitories. To rectify the situation, the university is rushing to build more student housing, some of it in a 10-acre Student Village featuring three new residence halls slated to open in 2005.

One of the most controversial aspects of student life has been the university's dormitory visitation policy, which requires guests to be out of the dorm by 1 a.m. on weekdays and 2 a.m. on weekends. When many of the university's more liberated students complained about the policy, President Silber stood firm. In one interview, he explained that the university was not "in the business of providing weekend love nests for our students." In fact, many students welcome the policy. "I think it's great," one student says. "There's none of the awkwardness of having a third roommate—your roommate's boyfriend." However, it remains to be seen whether the visitation policy will continue now that Silber's tenure is over.

No matter where students end up living, they will have plenty of recreational opportunities on campus and in Boston. The university hosts an annual World Fair complete with cultural shows, music performances, lectures, an outdoor Culturefest, and an International Ball.

The campus is close to Fenway Park, home of the World Series–winning (at last) Red Sox, and Boston's many musical, artistic, and cultural events keep students occupied. Anyone living in Boston should make sure to visit the Isabella Stewart Gardner Museum, a palatial former private home that houses the art acquisitions of a famous collector in their original, Victorian context. Its Venetian courtyard serves as an ideal place to read and reflect. With easy access to Boston's rail-based mass transit system, "the T," the entire city is available for exploration. And most BU students do take advantage of the university's setting.

With such a wealth of attractions off campus, it is not surprising that Boston University has a limited Greek presence. Only about 4 percent of the student body participates in Greek life. Although most fraternities have houses, sororities do not.

One college tradition absent from BU is a football team. Five years ago, after 91 years of competition, the university put the Terriers to sleep. The athletic director blamed student apathy (only about 2,000 students showed up for the average game), budget pressures, and the constraints of Title IX—a piece of federal egalitarian sex management, which demands that for every dollar spent on a wildly popular men's wrestling or women's field hockey team, an equal amount must be spent on obscure pastimes like women's boxing or coed dodgeball. (We exaggerate, but only slightly.) The university still fields 23 varsity sports teams, most of which compete in the Colonial Athletic Conference. Students can also participate in intramurals, choosing from sports ranging from sailing to ice broomball.

In 2005, BU opened a new $90 million Fitness and Recreation Center, right beside the school's new sports arena. According to the *Chronicle of Higher Education*, the center "takes up half a city block and, at 280,000 square feet, may well be the biggest fitness center ever built on an urban campus." The facility includes a 35-foot climbing wall, an elevated indoor running track, a full array of fitness machines, hot tubs, and a roller hockey rink—providing "33 times as much usable activity space as the institution had before" reports the *Chronicle*.

The Boathouse, one of the country's best rowing centers, is located along the banks of the Charles River. Interstate 90 runs on the other side of campus. The university owns most of tree-lined Bay Street, including its historic brownstone residences. The Castle, built in the Gothic style in 1905, is the campus's most architecturally significant building. The building was once a private residence but today serves as the center of student life. It includes a bar, The Pub, and even hosts wedding receptions and other events. Marsh Chapel, according to one professor, "is not only the geographical, but in many ways, the intellectual-moral center of the university," Marsh houses some dozen chaplains of various faiths and multiple weekly religious services are held there.

To protect students, the administration has initiated several safety measures: 50 trained police officers, emergency call boxes, and a student escort service. Recently, the community adopted a campus crime watch, which employs community members in the same way as a traditional neighborhood watch program. Crime statistics vary depending on how you calculate them. The administration claims that BU is one of the safest schools in the nation, but they reach that conclusion by excluding crime in areas adjacent to campus. Burglaries are the most common on-campus crime: there were 80 (over half of them in residence halls) in 2003. Other crimes were much less frequent: in that year, the school reported six forcible sex offenses, three aggravated assaults, six stolen cars, and one arson.

Tuition at BU is $29,988 plus another $9,288 for room and board. Admissions are need-blind, though the school does not guarantee it will cover all demonstrated financial need to all applicants. Some 50 percent of students receive financial aid and the average debt load of a 2004 graduate was $17,186.

BOWDOIN COLLEGE

BRUNSWICK, MAINE • WWW.BOWDOIN.EDU

No kidding

This fabled New England liberal arts college—whose classics professor Joshua Chamberlain probably saved the Union at Gettysburg—does a pretty good job of living up to its legend. At Bowdoin, students *really* do discuss ideas with their professors and classmates. Some *really* do climb Maine's Mount Katahdin. And the campus *really* is gorgeous in any season. The biggest problem at Bowdoin is that its administrators have gotten confused over which areas of a student's experience they should exert influence—asserting too much control of student life, while meekly relinquishing the task of shaping students' curricula. Bowdoin's literature says that "the great mission of the college is to instill in students the love, the ways, and the habit of learning." But it offers them precious little guidance along these paths.

Still, academic life is the highest priority at Bowdoin, whose students by and large graduate as well-informed and well-read citizens of the republic. And that's saying a lot.

Academic Life: Remember Maine

Bowdoin's most salient virtue is its commitment to teaching. As one student says, "It's the reason we shell out so much money to go here." While research and publishing may pull in grant money and attract attention, Bowdoin prefers to focus first on the close interaction between professors and students. Hence, Bowdoin encourages its faculty members to spend a majority of their time in the classroom, and students almost universally report that faculty are extraordinarily accessible and possess a true concern for each of them. If a student is having trouble in class, odds are that the Bowdoin professor will invite him to office hours. "All professors keep at least four to five office hours a week. My advisor practically lives in his office," says one student. Another reports that professors "want to see students achieve, succeed, and learn. And they're interested in just talking, discussing the subject, helping with papers, almost anything." Says another, "I have tea with my professors." To stimulate this interest in the classroom, Bowdoin limits professors' loads to just two courses per semester. The student-faculty ratio is an excellent 10 to 1, which allows for very intimate classroom settings. "I have a friend with three people in her class, and [the college] didn't cut the course," says a government major. For the past five years, Bowdoin's median class size has hovered around 16. Introductory classes are considered large at 50, and the largest classes at Bowdoin have just 85 students.

Many more courses are presented in cozy seminars. A significant amount of students participate in at least one independent study course, working closely with a professor. Freshman seminars, meant to help newcomers hone their academic skills, are required; students may choose from topics like the Korean War, Hawthorne's writings, and "Science Fiction, Science Fact." There are no graduate students at Bowdoin, thus, no graduate teaching assistants. Upperclassmen—mostly native speakers—sometimes lead discussion classes in foreign languages once a week and also run the language lab.

As for the curriculum, a Bowdoin insider says, "The kids who want a conservative education can find it. There are enough good courses. But it's navigating through a system that doesn't provide much guidance." We discern the outline of an (alas, voluntary) core curriculum in the freshman one-year cluster program. For instance, in 2004, freshmen could select a year-long cluster of courses including philosophy, English, and government, centered around the theme "Modernity and Its Discontents." The philosophy, English, and government professors teach from the same syllabus, and texts range from Descartes to Shakespeare to "serious contemporary works," including Melville, Nabokov, Marx, Nietzsche, Arendt, Woolf, and Freud. As one professor says, "The kinds of issues that they're exposed to in the books they read might help them pick their way towards similar courses down the road."

This is all part of Bowdoin's first major curriculum reform in more than two decades. Students are still required to take courses in natural sciences, mathematics, social sciences, humanities, and fine arts—and the new regulations are more rigorous, insiders report. Two new requirements obliquely relate to the old "non-Eurocentric" requirement. "Exploring Social Differences" is designed to expose students to courses that examine "diversity" issues such as ethnicity and gender. The "International Perspectives" requirement is far better. It prescribes study of any culture or society other than American—which means a student can focus on Greece, China, or medieval Europe. One professor says, "This was a step in the right direction because it doesn't just explore the third-world exotic places."

Students say that advisors play a greater role at Bowdoin than they do at similar schools. Each advisor—usually a full-time professor—handles no more than six students. As a freshman, each student is assigned an advisor with similar academic interests; once he declares a major, the student may switch to a faculty member in his department. One student says that it is at this point that Bowdoin's advising is particularly strong. "Generally, the [initial] advisors just sign off on what the student is taking.

VITAL STATISTICS
Religious affiliation: none
Total enrollment: 1,677
Total undergraduates: 1,677
SAT midranges: V: 640–740, M: 650–720
Applicants: 4,853
Applicants accepted: 24%
Accepted applicants who enrolled: 40%
Tuition: $30,944
Room and board: $8,054
Freshman retention rate: 99%
Graduation rate: 83% (4 yrs.), 89% (6 yrs.)
Courses with fewer than 20 students: 63%
Student-faculty ratio: 10:1
Courses taught by graduate TAs: none
Most popular majors: social sciences, foreign languages, biology
Students living on campus: 93%
Guaranteed housing for four years? yes
Students in fraternities or sororities: none

While it has no core curriculum, Bowdoin does impose some distribution requirements:

- One first-year seminar. These are small, intensive learning settings designed to support the development of intellectual capabilities such as clear writing, analytic thinking, argumentation, information seeking and assessment, and oral presentation.
- One course on "Inquiry in the Natural Sciences" in which students expand their scientific literacy, conduct active investigations of scientific problems, and perform work in laboratories and in the field. This can be filled by a course in biology, chemistry, or physics. Some psychology courses also count.
- One course in mathematical, computational, or statistical reasoning in which students of subjects as wide-ranging as economics, psychology, mathematics, and computer science use mathematical and quantitative models to understand the world "around them." This requirement could be fulfilled, for example, by a political science course

But after that, when students have declared majors and have chosen their major advisors, the system improves a bit. It depends on how involved the professor is and how much the students want to hear from the professor." In other words, help is there for students who seek it.

And seek it they should: Despite the recent curricular reforms, students could theoretically graduate by taking mostly courses like "Science, Magic, and Religion" and "The History of South Africa," pretty much skipping American or Western history, art, and literature altogether. Very few students choose to do that, but as one government major says, "Students regretfully can graduate with a limited area of knowledge. . . . The unfortunate thing is that most students feel that 'Western' requirements are a realm for high school, and the college acquiesces. As soon as you say it's required, the kids don't want it."

The faculty at Bowdoin is predominantly liberal. "There's a handful of conservative faculty on campus and that's not enough," one person says. "There are students who say they feel they've never heard an intelligent conservative point of view." However, students are not penalized for dissenting views; two avowedly conservative students won the prestigious Keasbey Scholarship last year. Such "students can certainly shine and hold their own here," says one student. Another student says, "I don't have problems with liberal professors, if they can teach in an appropriate and disinterested manner." And another reports, "The faculty try to hide their personal political orientation, at least in the government department . . . everyone tries to be neutral."

Reportedly, the anthropology and sociology departments are heavily politicized. And one student who was considering a history major or minor decided against it. Once he eliminated all the "social construction/victimology courses," there simply wasn't enough left that interested him. But things may be looking up for such students. The college's president, Barry Mills, is "not hostile towards conservatives and is dismayed by univocal political issues," says one professor. However, a recent push to diversify Bowdoin's professor base was focused entirely on hiring more professors of color and fails to speak to the ideological homogeneity inflicted upon students. One Bowdoin professor says that in hiring the new faculty, the president's feet were being "held to the fire."

On the whole, courses at Bowdoin are rigorous, and students report that earning good grades demands a genuine commitment to learning. However, there are some notoriously easy courses that some students take only to fulfill distribution requirements, and in some departments grades are inflated. For instance, students receive higher marks in foreign language and various social science courses than they receive in the hard sciences, after expending the equivalent amount of effort.

The best departments at Bowdoin are government, economics, and some of the hard sciences—and these are also said to be the toughest-grading disciplines. In government, students can find courses like "Classical Political Philosophy" and "Liberalism and Its Critics." Solid economics classes include "European Economic History." One would expect a strong English department at a college that graduated Nathaniel Hawthorne, Harriet Beecher Stowe, and Henry Wadsworth Longfellow. And here Bowdoin does not disappoint. Its English faculty offer some trendy courses in feminist and ethnic literature, but also serve up more traditional fare. English majors are required to take 10 courses, at least three of which must focus on pre-1800 British or Irish literature and two on "literature of the Americas." Courses like "Shakespeare's History Plays" and "Early American Literature" both qualify.

Bowdoin does not offer English composition courses, but the college does make an effort—a successful one, most students say—to continue its strong writing tradition with the Bowdoin Writing Project, a peer tutoring program that links qualified students with those who would like to improve their writing.

Even if high grades are a bit easier to obtain in them, the foreign language programs at Bowdoin are impressive. That a college the size of Bowdoin can offer solid instruction in nine languages—Chinese, French, German, ancient Greek, Italian, Latin, Japanese, Russian, and Spanish—is impressive. The study-abroad programs are also solid and quite popular; more than half of the student body chooses to study off campus. Students can also select from any number of programs sponsored by other colleges, such as a Hamilton College program in France or a Duke University program in Rome.

Almost all humanities departments have some very fine faculty. Keep in mind that, in general, "the religion department has nothing to do with religion," and the

REQUIREMENTS (CONT'D)

that incorporates statistical analysis.

- One course in the arts in which students expand their understanding of the artistic process and expression through creation, performance, and analysis of artistic work in the areas of dance, film, music, theater, or visual art.

- One course in "Exploring Social Differences" drawing from courses spanning multiple disciplines, including sociology, history, Asian studies, environmental science, women's studies, and economics. The requirement is designed to expose students to courses that examine differences such as class, environmental conditions, ethnicity, gender, race, religion, and sexual orientation.

- One course in "International Perspectives" that will challenge students to understand societies different from their own— that is, study of a culture or society other than that of the United States.

philosophy department "is focused mainly on analytic philosophy. . . . It's John Rawls at a junior level," says one Bowdoin professor. Faculty most often lauded by Bowdoin students are: Lance Guo, Richard E. Morgan, Christian P. Potholm II, and Allen L. Springer in government; Thomas Baumgarte in physics; Guillermo Herrera and B. Zorina Khan in economics; John C. Holt in religion; Steven R. Cerf in German; William C. VanderWolk in French; and Sarah F. McMahon and Patrick J. Rael in history. Robert K. Greenlee is a "genius" in music, while Paul N. Franco and Jean M. Yarbrough are mentioned again and again as excellent political theory professors in the government department.

Student Life: Outward bound

Although not all Bowdoin campus buildings are of the same architectural style, many have been around for over 200 years, and those that are relatively new are typically fine structures in themselves. For instance, the handsome Kanbar Hall, which opened in 2004, serves as the new home for several departments. The ever-popular Bowdoin Outing Club got its own new building in 2003—the $1.25 million, 5,500-square-foot Schwartz Outdoor Leadership Center.

Around 90 percent of the student body chooses to live in one of the college's residential spaces, which include singles, doubles, and suites in houses and dormitories. First-year students live together in separate dorms with upperclassmen residential advisors on each floor. Bowdoin offers no single-sex dormitories, and many students may find that members of the opposite sex live right next door; however in the freshmen "bricks," four out of the six floors are single sex. There are no coed rooms, but bathrooms can be coed, if so ordered by house vote. There are also several chemical-free (no alcohol) dormitories available on campus. Bowdoin consistently ranks among the top five colleges in the nation for student satisfaction in dining, and the school accommodates the vegetarians and vegans in the student body; PETA recently ranked Bowdoin among the nation's top 10 most vegetarian-friendly campuses. Appealingly, there's even a Bowdoin organic farm. "The dining is tremendously wonderful," raves one student.

A few years back, most of the weekend activities on campus revolved around fraternities. Then in 2000, the Bowdoin administration decided to assert its control over the campus social scene, abolishing fraternities and replacing them with a "college house" system. Some students saw this action as an infringement on their right of free association. But a professor says, "The fraternity system was already on its last legs. The kids were out of control." The college now assigns each freshman to a college house, each with its own set of residence halls, parties, and other social events.

The college controls all the alcohol within the houses. With more than half of partygoers under 21, the administration has chosen to shift legal risks onto students themselves, requiring that a student "host" sign for every keg at a party; if any alcohol-related injuries occur, he is held responsible. One person on campus reports that "the administration was just trying to protect itself legally before a student kills himself or anyone else." Says one nervous student, "Though nobody has gotten into serious legal trouble yet, I fear the system is a ticking time bomb, and I don't want to be holding it when it goes off."

Even though Bowdoin is a small college in a small town, "it's hard to be bored here," says one student. Of the three elite Maine liberal arts colleges (Bates and Colby are the others), Bowdoin probably has the most social options available. One student says that Bowdoin "is challenging academically, but it also really has a culture of do what you want to do and take advantage of it while you're here." Many activities center around sports teams. Most students at the school are involved in sports, varsity or intramural. The Bowdoin Polar Bears are Division III in every sport except for ice hockey, skiing, and squash, in which they're Division I and highly competitive. Bowdoin's women's basketball team was a top finisher in Division III finals last year, attracting national attention. However, the football team has won only three games in the past four years. According to one true-blue professor, "We will continue with the football team because it's just part of what you do on Saturdays—you go to the game and get your heart broken."

The Bowdoin chapel, a beautiful old Congregational style church, has finally reopened after renovation. Catholics celebrate a well-attended mass in the Bowdoin Chapel sanctuary. "There are a number of religious students who take their faiths very seriously," says one professor. Another notes the presence of a "fairly intense evangelical fellowship" on campus. President Mills, the college's first Jewish president, is active in the Jewish high holy days and welcomes expressions of religious faith. There is still an opening prayer at commencement.

The college as a whole does a terrific job of providing intellectual and artistic stimuli on campus outside of the classroom, hosting frequent lectures, many political speakers, and a number of cultural events. Memorial Hall, built in the 1880s, and the more modern Pickard Theater are often the venues. The Walker Art Building includes one of the top college art museums in the country, housing original portraits of Thomas Jefferson and James Madison. Extracurricular clubs occupy a good chunk of students' time, and options abound in theater, dance, politics, culture, and sports. By far the most popular organization is the Outing Club, which gives students the chance to explore the great state of Maine and northern New England. From mountain biking trips to sea kayaking on Casco Bay, there's something for every adventurous Bowdoin student.

Outside of the classroom, perhaps the most obvious left-wing presence comes from the Women's Resource Center. The center offers exclusively feminist fare, including "information for students interested in internships with Planned Parenthood." Other groups include environmental organizations and the Bowdoin Queer/Straight Alliance,

SUGGESTED CORE
1. Classics 102, Introduction to Ancient Greek Culture
2. Philosophy 111, Ancient Philosophy
3. Religion 215/216, The Hebrew Bible / The New Testament
4. Religion 210, Early Christian Literature (*closest match*)
5. Government 241, Modern Political Philosophy
6. English 210/211/212, Shakespeare
7. History 233, American Society in the New Nation (*closest match*)
8. Government 117, Questioning the Modern

which sponsors events like the annual Drag Ball. Campus election polls continue to reveal an overwhelming dominance of the left, but outside the classroom the college has seen an emergence of a more balanced debate on campus.

By and large, the students are more intellectually diverse than the faculty. The Bowdoin College Republicans have established chapters all over Maine and the former chair of the group was the chief page at the Republican National Convention in 2004. For the most part, students of various political stripes feel secure enough to voice their opinions. "People are very interested in making everyone feel comfortable," says one student.

In Brunswick, home to 21,000, Bowdoin has a true college town. A short walk from campus on Maine Street are coffeehouses, a local movie theater, a performing arts theater, 38 restaurants, bookstores, a local theater, and plenty of shops. The most popular off-campus hangouts are Jack Magee's Pub (a campus bar), Joshua's, and the Sea Dog. On Thursday nights, students go bowling in town. The Big Top is a favorite weekend breakfast locale. "There are plenty of places to escape to . . . Portland, Freeport, ski mountains, the beach, and Boston's two hours away," a student says. The students are studious enough that they usually sacrifice at least one weekend day to study, write papers, or read for class.

Bowdoin's rural location provides, not surprisingly, for a very safe environment. A faculty member said, "It's really small-town Maine; I don't lock my car." Statistics show that the occurrence of violent crime on or around campus is truly rare. In 2003, Bowdoin reported two forcible sex offenses, one aggravated assault, seven burglaries, one stolen car, and two arsons. A 2004 graduate says, "I used to leave my wallet and laptop in the library; nothing happened. I lived in a house full of women and we never locked our doors."

One year's education at Bowdoin costs approximately $40,000. This includes tuition, room rent, health fees, and activity fees. Books only inflate the cost. Happily, Bowdoin is a need-blind school and fulfills 100 percent of a student's calculated financial need. Including grants and loans, 46 to 48 percent of students receive financial aid at Bowdoin. The average indebtedness upon graduation is $16,000 to $17,000.

BRANDEIS UNIVERSITY

New and improved

Brandeis is a relatively new university, founded on what was formerly the property of Middlesex College in 1948, but it has accomplished a great deal in a little more than a half century. Not only are its 3,000 undergraduates exposed to excellent teaching in the humanities, sciences, and the liberal arts in general, but the university is well regarded as a research institution serving not only its undergraduates, but also about 1,300 graduate students. A $400 million endowment supports the enterprise. Though originally sponsored by the American Jewish community in the wake of World War II, Brandeis began as and remains a nonsectarian institution, and students on campus generally describe an open community reinforced by its diversity rather than one obsessed with attempts to artificially enhance it.

Brandeis is named for Louis Dembitz Brandeis (1856–1941), the first Jewish associate justice on the Supreme Court of the United States, and the school's literature states that "the university that carries the name of the justice who stood for the rights of individuals must be distinguished by academic excellence, by truth pursued wherever it may lead, and by awareness of the power and responsibilities that come with knowledge." The university's pursuit of these goals seems, for the most part, to be successful.

Academic Life: The right to be left alone

Like most schools these days, Brandeis eschews a real core curriculum, and merely asks its students to select a few courses from a few broad categories. According to the university, "Courses can double for the core curriculum, distribution, and concentration requirements. This allows for at least one-third of all courses taken to be elective courses."

Brandeis's distribution requirements may well push students toward a well-rounded liberal arts program, but it does not make that a necessity in exchange for a diploma. "If someone really wants to avoid a subject, it's far from impossible," says a

VITAL STATISTICS
Religious affiliation: nonsectarian, Jewish-sponsored
Total enrollment: 4,397
Total undergraduates: 3,051
SAT/ACT midranges: SAT V: 630–720, M: 630–720; ACT: 28–33
Applicants: 5,831
Applicants accepted: 40%
Accepted applicants who enrolled: 33%
Tuition: $31,072
Room and board: $ 8,836
Freshman retention rate: 93%
Graduation rate: 84% (4 yrs.), 89% (6 yrs.)
Average class size: 17
Student-faculty ratio: 9:1
Courses taught by graduate TAs: none
Most popular majors: computer science, social sciences, political science
Students living on campus: 84%
Guaranteed housing for four years? no
Students in fraternities or sororities: none

The basic curriculum in the College of Arts and Sciences, the primary undergraduate unit of the university, imposes some distributional mandates. Students must take one among selected introductory courses from each of the four schools of the college:

- Humanities. For instance, "The Dynamics of Religious Experience" or "Introduction to East Asian Civilization."
- Social science. Choices include "The History of the Family" and "Race and Ethnicity in American Politics."
- Science. "Introduction to Physics" or "Chemistry and Art" would both work.
- Creative arts, with classes such as "The Theater in History" and "Introduction to Drawing."

student. Another student says, "Brandeis will not tell you what you should think. It will not tell you what your major should be. And it will most definitely not choose your courses for you. Self-devised majors are not abnormal." According to one professor, "The curriculum here is well structured so that students take a good mixture of courses that are necessary fundamentals and fun electives, as well as being exposed to new ideas in their fields of study." The university in this regard subscribes to its namesake's famous formulation of the "right to be left alone."

The University Seminars in Humanistic Inquiries (USEMs) probably come the closest to traditional introductory courses in the liberal arts at Brandeis, though students do get to choose which one they take. "The primary goal is to provide a small seminar environment where students, under the close guidance of regular faculty, can engage major texts from ancient time to the present," according to the school. The interdisciplinary courses for first-year students "all address important questions, normally have a multi-century historical framework, and draw upon a wide range of texts . . . [in] attempt[ing] to address fundamental, enduring questions of the human experience."

The idea is good, and some of the courses may actually get at the aforementioned fundamental questions, but one wonders at the route some of the seminars elect to take. The majority of the courses, while comprehensive in scope, focus on feminism, race, or deconstruction. "Slavery, Religion, and Women," for instance, is described as a course to help students "learn to think in a complex fashion about inter-sectionality (in this case, of gender, religion, race, and legal status), and to see how religion can function as a force for good and for evil." It notes that students will have the opportunity to participate in a "feminist sexual ethics project." The reading list consists almost entirely of female authors.

Similarly, a host of courses count toward the intensive writing requirement, including some solid ones and some not-so-traditional ones. Students can take, for example, a course centered on "finding your writing voice," or one devoted to "what makes writing good," drawing its inspiration from the four lines of William Carlos William's poem about a red wheelbarrow. (It could be said that much depends upon the student.) Quantitative reasoning courses leave less to chance: "Cell Structure and Function," "Basic Chemistry," "Introduction to Economics," and "Statistics" are typical offerings in this category. But even though Albert Einstein was one of the school's founders, there are also some ways to slide by without getting too deep into hard science topics.

If you intend to study science, one student warns that the department is "overly focused on premed students." Regardless of department, though, don't expect to get by without studying. "The classes here are challenging in any discipline you study," says one student. "The tests will ask you to think, not simply list facts. And you will get to know the library pretty well."

Though Brandeis doesn't require students to take a course in Western history, it does require a single "non-Western and comparative studies" course. There are a fair amount of politicized courses here, but even though a number of the classes in the long list of options appear to consist of solid economics, literature, or historical studies, one wonders how students are expected to compare other traditions to their own—when they haven't necessarily studied the West at all.

For anyone who would like to even things out—and then some—Brandeis offers an excellent interdisciplinary major in European cultural studies (ECS). "In the tradition of the liberal arts, Brandeis's ECS concentration integrates and unifies many discrete aspects of European culture," the program's Web page says. "It recognizes that Europe is the cradle of Western thought and values, and that these do not belong to any single discipline. Consequently, the ECS curriculum cuts across boundaries in order more fully to achieve a well-rounded view of the literature, art, history, politics, and philosophy of Europe since the Middle Ages." The program requires an introductory seminar in ECS, followed by a course called "The Western Canon," three classes in European literature, and three courses selected by the student from the departments of fine arts, history, music, philosophy, politics, sociology, and theater arts. Clearly, for the Brandeis student seeking the best liberal arts education possible, ECS is the way to go.

In all, Brandeis offers 34 majors and 19 interdisciplinary programs, along with 22 minors. Students list these departments as among the strongest at Brandeis: Near Eastern and Judaic studies (said by some to be the best in the country); English and American literature; classical studies; the sciences (the faculty includes nine members of the National Academy of Sciences); history; and politics. Among the best professors are William Flesch and Caren Irr in English and American literature; Jacob Cohen in American studies; Gordon A. Fellman in sociology; Ray Jackendoff in linguistics and cognitive science; and Robert J. Art in international relations. University faculty have received MacArthur Foundation "genius" grants in each of the last three years. Indeed, academic excellence and research start at the top of the organization chart: The president, Dr. Jehuda Reinharz, is an accomplished scholar of Jewish history.

Brandeis's library system includes more than a million volumes and many other

REQUIREMENTS (CONT'D)

Students must also pass:
- Three writing-intensive courses.
- One class in quantitative reasoning.
- One course in non-Western or comparative studies.
- Two semesters of physical education.
- One "University Seminar in Humanistic Inquiries."

Note that one class can fulfill both the first and the second sets of requirements. Brandeis also requires students to attain third-semester proficiency in a language other than English, either through coursework or testing.

resources including microforms, and 35,000 video and audio titles. The archives of Soviet dissident Andrei Sakharov and his wife, Yelena Bonner, are held in a special collection.

Each freshman is assigned an advisor (a faculty member or administrator) upon arrival on campus and must consult with him before registering for classes. The student gets a new faculty advisor when he selects a major but isn't required to meet with that person. "Most people I know honestly saw no need for their advisors," one student says. Twenty-year-olds who think they're above accepting counsel from famous scholars . . . well, they really are in need of advice.

Brandeis has an enviable student-faculty ratio of nine to one. Students report no problems with registering for classes or with their access to teachers "during office hours and beyond," in the words of one. In larger courses, professors deliver lectures, leaving teaching assistants to conduct discussion sections occasionally. One faculty member says, "Students are very highly motivated and curious. They often come by to discuss their ideas, follow up on interesting discussions in class, and talk about ways of furthering their education outside the classroom." Another professor says, "[M]y classes have a large percentage of students engaged intellectually. I am never bored by the seminars I teach, and that is a good sign." And with more than 20 National Merit Scholars entering as freshmen each year, one would expect no less. "The number one priority at Brandeis is academics," says one student matter-of-factly.

Brandeis has done a good job of keeping politics out of most classrooms and promoting solid teaching along with research, but some departments and courses are weaker than others. A new program called social justice and social policy is "basically a bunch of really liberal sociology classes and the like," a student says. The foundation course in the program is called "Crisis of the Welfare State." The sociology and politics departments are also noteworthy for their politicization.

Student Life: World religions

Waltham, Massachusetts, home of Brandeis University, is but nine miles west of Boston. That city, of course, offers many things for the thousands of area college students to do and visit, from historical attractions to sports and concerts to restaurants and bars. But suburban Waltham, a city of 56,000 on the Charles River, is not without its charms; the university says its variety of restaurants, interesting old buildings, and independent theater are enough to keep many people close to campus. But students have mixed opinions. "It's definitely not a party school," says one. "Don't be fooled by the school's proximity to Boston," says another. "Most students spend nights and weekends studying. If you do get out, it will probably be only as far as the highly suburbanized Harvard Square." But a third student says, "Brandeis is what you make of it. The school pours money into hundreds of student clubs and organizations that are constantly organizing events, dances, concerts, etc. I guarantee you that there is not a single weekend during the school year when the event calendar is completely empty." Students who do find time to get off campus will not find themselves wanting for transportation either: round-trip bus fares from Waltham to Boston are included in room and board fees for on-campus students.

Brandeis's Jewish base and the relative youth of the institution make it unique among top-flight American colleges. "I was particularly attracted to Brandeis because everyone is a bit different, sometimes a bit odd and eccentric," a student says. "Some of the kids are really annoying or overbearing, but they're interesting. A lot of students care about issues. It's not your run-of-the-mill school where everyone wears Abercrombie and Fitch. Fortunately, jocks and preps are not the majority here. . . . It's not another generic Harvard wanna-be." On the other hand, one student laments that "Brandeis seems to be the place to go if you are rejected from your Ivy League schools and are still bitter." "A lot of students spend their four years here trying to get the grades they need to get into Harvard Law, Med, or Business School," says another.

Although some students and faculty do complain of bias in the classroom and around campus, most students say political life at Brandeis is fair and evenhanded. Recent speakers have addressed political topics from a number of different viewpoints. They have included Charlton Heston, Noam Chomsky, Dinesh D'Souza, Christopher Hitchens, Rep. Barney Frank, and former senator Bill Bradley, among others. One professor says, "I have a range of opinion in my classes and we have vigorous debates." But there are issues of which to be aware. One student says, "There is tension between Jewish students and minority students about whether the university should maintain its Jewish roots or become a truly diverse university." Another says, "You will find a myriad of cultures interacting with one another, if not integrating." Politically, says another student, "There is a lot more tolerance [at] Brandeis than I have noticed elsewhere, but the school is still overwhelmingly close-minded. If you are openly conservative or libertarian, you basically box yourself into a social corner where no one wants to befriend you."

University higher-ups occasionally discuss "diversifying" the campus, meaning in most cases that they would like to hire more professors "of color." But at least these discussions are usually set in the greater context of the university's academic mission. "You weigh so many things [in hiring faculty], and so race is hardly ever the factor," an associate dean told a campus publication. "I've never seen it as the main factor that distinguishes one person from another." Added the campus provost: "Qualifications are qualifications." The real push on campus for multiculturalism and the like comes from students rather than from the administration. One student admits that while they are very serious about their work and quite intense academically, his peers "lack a certain open-mindedness" to opposing viewpoints. Besides activist groups representing ethnic minorities—many of which are primarily social networks—there are a num-

SUGGESTED CORE
1. and 3. Humanities 10, The Western Canon
2. Philosophy 122, ClassicalPolitical Theory (*closest match*)
4. Philosophy 71, MedievalPhilosophy
5. Politics 184, Utopia and Power in Modern Political Thought
6. English 33, Shakespeare
7. History 51a, History of the United States (1607–1865)
8. History 132, EuropeanThought and Culture since Darwin

ber of leftist student political groups, including Students for a Just Society ("I'd put 'Just' in quotation marks," says one student) and the Activist Resource Center. There are no conservative groups of similar size or stature; the College Republicans are essentially a social organization. The student newspaper, the *Justice*, is a generally well-written publication that recognizes the separation between the news and features and the editorial page. There is also a good conservative publication called *Concord Bridge*.

Students across the board comment on the remarkable religious tolerance that prevails at the school. There are several chaplains—Jewish, Catholic, Protestant, and Muslim—and Brandeis takes pains to see that all students are accommodated. The Hillel group is the largest on campus, since every student is automatically enrolled unless he opts out, but there are also active fellowships for other religions. A look through the university Web site reveals a school trying very hard to be nonsectarian: There is little information on religious activities, other than that given in campus calendars (the school is closed for most Jewish holidays). The campus chapel, designed by Eero Saarinen, is really three chapels—Jewish, Catholic, and Protestant—set together in such a way that the shadow from each one never falls on the other two. The university also hosts "awareness" weeks for Christians and Muslims, although the former was somewhat marred in 2002 by the theft of two crosses erected to mark the event. (Organizers chained the remaining crosses to fixed objects to keep them in place, which may or may not be symbolic of something.) As one organizer told the *Justice*, "It's great to be Christian at Brandeis because you've got a lot of exposure to lots of theologies that maybe you would not otherwise receive."

Statistics on religious affiliation are also absent from the university Web site, and if it's that unimportant to the school, then perhaps it should be to us as well. Instead, the university lists other demographic information, such as the fact that students come from 46 states and more than 100 countries. International students make up 11 percent of the student body (graduate and undergraduate), and 54 percent of all students are female. Says a student: "There is a broad mix. Some are frat boys who got in to play basketball. Some are bioresearchers who got in because they won a Westinghouse [research fellowship]. Most of us fall somewhere in between."

Freshmen and sophomores are guaranteed spots in campus dorms, which are said to be adequate but not luxurious. The university is building more dormitories to make up for a housing shortage that has forced some upperclassmen off campus when they would have preferred to stay on. One student complains that the housing selection process ("which is revised every year because it is so inefficient") is routinely circumvented by students who know anyone of influence involved in coordinating it. Another complains that the newly finished campus center project has taken priority over desperately needed upgrades to classrooms, labs, and dorms. Brandeis has both single-sex dorms and coed dorms (with single-sex floors). All but two dorms are officially dry, and students say resident advisors will intervene to stop excessive noise. The school's alcohol policy is pretty lenient, according to students; the "wet" dorms allow alcohol for people of drinking age. There is a bar on campus.

The new dorm, along with a few other construction projects, might help out the mostly run-of-the-mill campus architectural scene. While the campus grounds themselves are quite nice, "the buildings are a bit of a mix and match," says one student. "Some are weird, some are very ugly, some are good looking."

There are more than 175 student-led groups on campus, including religious groups (Hillel, as well as the Catholic Student Organization and the Muslim Students Association); publications; political groups like Amnesty International, the Brandeis American Civil Liberties Union, Brandeis Zionist Association, Students for Peace in Israel and Palestine, and Students for the Second Amendment; ethnic student groups; hobby groups for pottery, foosball, scuba diving, and belly dancing; and wacky clubs like Muggles United for Wizardry (a Harry Potter thing—for the uninitiated), the Jehuda Reinharz Fan Club (how many university presidents have one of those?), and the festively named Vagina Club, whose "purpose is to educate the Brandeis community about violence against women and how to prevent it through fun and informative events. . . ." Funding for student organizations is controlled by the Student Union, said by many to be very liberal.

There are also a variety of intramural and club sports for both men and women (including basketball, equestrian, volleyball, and tennis) to fill in the gaps in Brandeis's intercollegiate athletic program, which includes eight varsity teams for men and nine for women. The Judges, as the school's teams are known, compete in NCAA Division III. Athletic facilities for all students include a pool, racket sports courts, a gymnasium, and a track. Athletics, however, plays little role in forming the campus ethos. "Athletes in general are considered a minority and sometimes feel marginalized," says one student. "Most kids simply don't have the time to invest in sports. They read books and write papers."

Notable school traditions include the annual fall Bronstein Weekend, a celebration with parties, dinners, performances, and other events. Louis, Louis Weekend and Community Service Day are fixtures on the school calendar. There is also an event called "Screw Your Roommate"—meant, thankfully, in the figurative sense. The university describes it as "Brandeis's annual semi-formal, set-your-roommate-up-with-some-one-special, fantastical gala!"

Brandeis posts its crime statistics on its own Web site, and it should be proud of them. Given its proximity to a large city, crime is rare on the Brandeis campus. In 2003, the university reported two forcible sexual assaults, one aggravated assault, 47 burglaries, and one stolen car on campus. Overall, students say they feel safe at Brandeis.

Brandeis is pricey but generous. Tuition for 2004-5 was $31,072, and room and board $8,836. However, Brandeis admissions decisions are need-blind, meaning a student's financial situation does not influence his admission to the school. While the school does not guarantee to meet the full financial need of all admitted students, it provides gift aid to some 75 percent of those who apply.

NEW ENGLAND

BROWN UNIVERSITY

PROVIDENCE, RHODE ISLAND • WWW.BROWN.EDU

Amateur architects

Brown University likes to think of itself as an Ivy-sized liberal arts college, a school that emphasizes undergraduate education more than its graduate programs. Unfortunately, it accomplishes this in part by treating all students like grad students. By placing a premium on choice and diversity at the cost of structure and direction, Brown provides a fascinating environment for someone who has already had an excellent liberal education—for instance, in a European *Gymnasium*. For those recovering from a typically chaotic American high school, it offers more temptations than tutelage.

Brown students, says the school's literature, are "architects of their own educational experience." But who wants to live in a house designed by an 18-year-old who never studied math or engineering?

Academic Life: Trusting Providence

Its protean curriculum is just one reason that Brown enjoys a reputation as the most progressive of the Ivies. Frequent protests also prop up the school's reputation for leftism and rampant political correctness. Thankfully, Brown doesn't quite live up to its name: as one graduate teaching assistant remarks, one or two students per discussion section of 25 might be conservatives, three or four leftist social crusaders, and the rest mildly liberal. "In my observation, academic freedom in the classroom is respected," says one professor.

There are also some good things happening at the school. In 2001, Brown inaugurated Ruth Simmons as its new president. Simmons, the first black American to head an Ivy League institution, is an old-fashioned liberal: she believes in free speech. In her opening convocation address in 2002, Simmons said, "If you've come to this place for comfort, I urge you to rise, walk through yonder gate, and don't look back. . . . Welcome to this quarrelsome enterprise that we call a university. Enjoy."

Simmons has so far managed to garner praise from students of all political stripes. "She is encouraging a campus climate where students feel free to speak out on any issue and to bring their concerns to the administration," says one conservative student. Says another, "I think she is an inspirational president who clearly sees the need for intellectual diversity and academic freedom. Unfortunately, it seems that she faces a lot of opposition from leftist faculty."

Students are also helping to change the climate. A few years ago, Brown was little but a deep-pink echo chamber. Now, several right-of-center groups such as Students for Liberty and the College Republicans have taken their place in Brown's marketplace of ideas. The student newspaper, the *Brown Daily Herald*, has made an effort to solicit conservative columnists to present a philosophically balanced point of view. Simmons has increased the number of faculty and placed a high priority on student-faculty ratios. While Brown academics still suffer from a race-gender-class myopia, things are improving. "I think that Simmons is the best president that Brown has had in years, and I think that her policies will improve Brown's academic reputation," a student says.

As one faculty member puts it, at Brown "a student can get a good liberal arts education, but he must be able to avoid the academic fads . . . that some departments at Brown embrace." That word "fad" comes up a lot in discussions of Brown. Courses appear and disappear based on whim, and have included such gems as "Black Lavender: A Study of Black Gay and Lesbian Plays and Dramatic Constructions in the American Theatre" and "Policing the Crisis: A History of Sex Panics in the U.S." Says a professor, "To get a good liberal arts education at Brown, a student should choose courses with an eye to the classics" and not dabble in anything with the words "feminism/poststructuralism/materialism" in the title. Good advice at any school, but especially at Brown.

And choices are all a student has—Brown has no core curriculum or distribution requirements of any kind. The bottom line is that students must pass 30 courses before graduating and prove their competency in writing. Students can take anything they feel like taking; theoretically, they can even take all of their courses on a pass/fail basis. This extreme academic flexibility is all part of the curriculum reform instituted at Brown in the 1960s and was meant to encourage students to try a little of everything. Parents—and employers, for that matter—should know that students can graduate with a Brown diploma without ever having taken American or world history, a foreign language, English, economics, philosophy, or even one science course. "Intellectual curiosity is very high, if somewhat lacking in direction," says a faculty member. "Students are encouraged to pursue all avenues of inquiry, but aren't always given the proper tools. It is in this regard that the lack of a university-mandated core curriculum is detrimental."

The school claims that its system works for the thoughtful and intellectually mature. Indeed, students interested in a traditional curriculum may appreciate the lack of a structure that keeps them from it. Says one, "Although I see how the lack of a core curriculum is problematic, I have always said that this allows me to avoid all of the bad

VITAL STATISTICS

Religious affiliation: none
Total enrollment: 8,004
Total undergraduates: 6,014
SAT/ACT midranges: SAT V: 650–760, M: 660–760; ACT: 27–32
Applicants: 15,286
Applicants accepted: 17%
Accepted applicants who enrolled: 58%
Tuition: $30,672
Room and board: $8,474
Freshman retention rate: 97%
Graduation rate: 83% (4 yrs.), 96% (6 yrs.)
Courses with fewer than 20 students: 65%
Student-faculty ratio: 9:1
Courses taught by graduate TAs: 2%
Most popular majors: history, international relations, biology
Students living on campus: 80%
Guaranteed housing for four years? yes
Students in fraternities: 9% sororities: 3%

43

left-wing courses. So ironically I have had a very conservative education here at Brown." And there remain, of course, some powerful utilitarian reasons for choosing one's courses wisely. A sarcastic joke on campus—"So did you hear about the guy who took all his classes pass/fail but got into Harvard Med?"—makes it clear, for instance, why the pass/fail option is not used as often as one might think. Students have ambitions, graduate schools (and occasionally even employers) want to see good marks and certain classes on one's transcript, and the administration frowns on too many pass/fail grades.

Whatever academic structure there is at Brown is provided by individual departments and concentrations, which often require students to take a handful of core courses. English majors, for instance, must take three courses on the history of English literature: "Introduction to Medieval and Early Modern Literatures and Cultures," "Introduction to the Enlightenment and the Rise of National Literatures and Cultures," and "Introduction to Modern and Contemporary Literatures and Cultures." They must also complete eight electives in English.

The classics department at Brown is considered to be very strong. Those concentrating in the classics can choose from five different tracks: classics, Greek, Latin, a combined Greek and Latin program, or classics and Sanskrit. The strictly classics major is required to take eight courses, including one advanced Greek or Latin class, two semesters of ancient history, and five other electives. Comparative literature and geology get strong marks for teaching, as do applied math and international relations. Philosophy bucks the trend toward, well, trendiness, with a sober, classical approach to Continental philosophy. The sciences in general are serious and highly regarded.

Students report that history is always a popular concentration; history majors and history buffs should seek out Joe Pucci's classics lectures on late antiquity and the early medieval world, a course on the American Revolution by Gordon Wood (or "anything by Gordon Wood," says a student—but act quickly; Wood is said to be on the verge of retirement), and a Civil War course taught by Michael Vorenberg. A concentration in history requires eight courses, but students are allowed to choose a focus to the program, defined by geography and period, or comparative and topical (like comparative intellectual history), and then take at least four courses in the focus. The only department-wide requirement is a seminar, for which many choices are offered each year, including, in recent times, "Portugal and the Discovery of the World," "The City as Modernity: Popular Culture, Mass Consumption, and Urban Entertainment in Nineteenth-Century Paris," and "Social History of Sports in America." Other good teachers at Brown include Kurt Raaflaub in classics and history, Michael Putnam in classics, and Bernard Reginster in philosophy.

The English department houses a number of quality teachers, but one professor cautions that the department has vocal Marxist faculty members who freely share their political views in class. Graduate students in the department have a reputation for abrasive interactions with other faculty and undergraduate students and for offering "unique" interpretations of English literature. Students are advised to ask around to find the more serious courses.

Several other departments are also infected by academic trend-sniffing. One professor reports that in the American civilization department and modern culture and the media (MCM) department, faculty members tend to approach their disciplines via "narratives of processes of domination." As a consequence, most American civilization courses deal with race, gender, or sexual orientation.

On the positive side, Brown professors are accessible, students say, and the laid-back atmosphere means competition isn't quite as cutthroat as it is at some of the other Ivies. "Brown places a greater emphasis on community-building activity than many other colleges do," one student says. A professor says: "There is a generally casual academic culture on campus, and not the overall academic intensity that Chicago, MIT, and Caltech are known for." Notes one student, "For a student who wants the freedom to shape her own education and the chance to develop a close relationship with professors and other students in a friendly, relatively laid-back environment, Brown might be the ideal choice."

Another key feature of a Brown education is the uncommonly long two-week "shopping period," during which students can judge for themselves the pedagogical skills and atmosphere evident in various classes before registering and committing to a set of classes for the term.

One disadvantage at Brown is the small size of its academic departments, which offer fewer course choices than one finds at other schools. Course enrollments are strictly limited and the university rarely opens up new sections. Thus, a student might not be able to get into the most popular classes until his senior year, if then—which is a constant source of student frustration. Brown's library is also small for an Ivy League school, partly due to the school's relatively modest endowment.

As freshmen, Brown students are assigned an "advising partner," usually a faculty member, who guides the student through first-year courses and premajor choices. Brown calls them "partners" because students are half of the program, and the university expects students to "be prepared to articulate the reasons for [their] academic choices, and remain open to suggestions and new ideas." Once students have declared concentrations, they work with faculty advisors in their departments.

Faculty report that hiring and tenure decisions are based on "merit plus"—that is, the person's skill and accomplishments, surely, but with an eye also to diversity, balancing women and men faculty, and so forth. "Some of the postdoctoral appointments have raised a few eyebrows; it may be that merit is being treated as simply one factor among others," says one. Self-appointed watchdog organizations on campus try to ensure that the expansion of the faculty includes the appropriate proportion of all protected minority groups. "Being ideologically proper is extremely important," another professor says. "In social sciences and humanities, open, even conspicuous, allegiance to leftist causes is *de rigueur*." The problem is most pronounced among younger faculty and grad students, who drink the academic brew of postmodernism, critical theory, and Marxism. Older professors tend to be more traditional liberal types who are not as openly ideological. A 2002 *American Enterprise* magazine article showed that in sheer numbers, Brown's faculty—at least in certain departments—is overwhelmingly liberal. For example, all 17 of the history department's faculty members were registered in a political party of the left.

The Simmons administration has been somewhat cagey about concrete steps to promote intellectual diversity. Simmons appointed Associate Provost Brenda Allen as the new director of institutional diversity. Allen told the *Brown Spectator* that "intellectual diversity will play a role in freshman seminars," and that of the proposed 100 new faculty hires, 25 have been set aside for "points of view that may be underrepresented." Whether this will include conservative points of view is anyone's guess; as Allen pointed out, "not all liberals think alike."

Finally, grade inflation is an issue at Brown, just as it is at most schools these days. The problem is not as pronounced at Brown as it is at Harvard, say, but it certainly exists. Much of the blame can be placed on the university's unique grading system. Explains one faculty member: "Part of the problem at Brown results from the fact that there are no pluses or minuses added to grades. So a hard-earned B-plus is indistinguishable on the transcript from a B. The tendency, as a result, is to round up a B-plus to an A in order to distinguish it from the B (which could be a rounded-up C-plus)." Brown has no plans to change this system. Another faculty member blames grade inflation on the fact that no student expects a grade lower than B. "Their ability to bargain for grades is truly extraordinary," he says. Eventually, many professors give in, not wanting to spend all of their office hours defending grade decisions. This expectation of getting everything is part of the "Brown personality." Some find it refreshing, others find it infuriating.

Student Life: Politics, sports, shin guards

As the school's Web site boasts, Brown's "mosaic of campus life" consists of "closely connected neighborhoods" situated around the central College Green. Indeed, Brown offers an arm's-length experience of city life, compared to fellow urban Ivies such as Harvard, Yale, Penn, or Columbia.

The university guarantees housing for all four years and requires that students live on campus for at least three years. Around 80 percent of the student body lives on campus. Students who wish to live off campus can petition the residential life office and pay a $468 "nonresident fee." The campus is divided into five main areas. The largest is East Campus, but Pembroke Quad—once the home of Pembroke College, a women's college that merged with Brown in 1971—houses the most students. Residence halls are located no more than a six- or seven-minute walk from classes. The university does offer at least one hall exclusively for women each year. There are several coed bathrooms on campus, but a housing official says this is a mere "practicality," since in some coed suites, it makes sense to share a bathroom rather than forcing one sex to use the one on the other end of the hall. Brown also recently set aside one dormitory for coed suites, where students can elect to live with a member of the opposite sex, although the university never randomly assigns men to room with women, or vice versa.

A recent campus controversy involved whether transgender first-year students could avoid specifying a gender on their housing forms—stay tuned for how this one turns out. The Greek organizations are also single sex and occupy dormitory space. The university offers virtually every type of living option, including suites and apartments, theme houses, and traditional dormitories.

Brown is reputed to be more of a party school than the other Ivies. Marijuana is easy to get, as are some of the "higher-class drugs" popular with some wealthy students. Brown students also enjoy the standard college drinking scene, found mainly at private parties rather than fraternities; the Greek scene is largely peripheral, with about 10 percent of the student body participating. Brown students view fraternities and sororities as representatives of old-school conformity—and they prefer a newer, hipper conformity. According to a survey of Ivy League schools, Brown also has a higher percentage of sexually active students than its counterparts.

Brown's reputation as the Ivy with the most lefty politics is not unfounded; the joke goes: "How many Brown students does it take to change a light bulb? The whole campus—to protest for the rights of the bulb." Nonetheless, many students across the political spectrum steer clear of the protest culture altogether. "This is not Berkeley, and students who have come to Brown with the expectation that their college life will consist of continual protests have been disappointed," a student says. Students discuss politics in the cafeteria, the *Brown Daily Herald* is a decent paper for news coverage, and on the opinion side there is usually at least one conservative columnist. True, liberal, blue-state insularity means that discourse is not always at the highest level. The *Daily Herald* quoted a Brown sophomore saying, "I really had no idea that entire states were against gay marriage. I thought it was just small, radical groups." One of the *Herald*'s conservative columnists, Robert Kaufman, reported that he was physically attacked just after the 2004 election, seemingly by a band of enraged pacifists.

One of Brown's greatest concerns is that women and minority students be comfortable. All students living in the dorms are aided by residential advisors, but women also get "women's peer counselors," and minority students also get their own counselors. For female minorities, this can prove an embarrassment of riches. The Sarah Doyle Women's Center promotes the views of leftist, pro-choice women. One recent event included the "bring a non-feminist to the women's center" dinner. Brown also offers a special orientation, the Third-World Transition Program, for designated freshmen. One student who participated in the program writes on the Noindoctrination.org Web site

SUGGESTED CORE
1. Classics 1, The Greeks
2. Philosophy 35, Ancient Philosophy
3. Jewish Studies 47, The Hebrew Bible and the History of Ancient Israel *and* Religious Studies 71, The New Testament and the Beginnings of Christianity
4. Religious Studies 72, Christianity in Late Antiquity (*closest match*)
5. Political Science 103, Modern Political Thought
6. English 30, Introduction to Shakespeare
7. History 51, American History to 1877
8. History 121, European Intellectual History: Discovering the Modern

that the orientation program advised students which groups to avoid because they were "against minorities" or "biased" and were "given advice on how to 'deal' with a white roommate."

Stereotypically, sports at Brown take a back seat compared to the other Ivies, especially basketball-friendly Princeton and Penn. Actually, Brown's teams have improved markedly in recent years, though one student refers to his classmates as "fair-weather fans." Brown does field 35 varsity teams, and the university also has around 20 club sports and an intramural program featuring flag football, ultimate Frisbee, tennis, ice hockey, and other pursuits.

The arts, more so than sports, play a large part in student life at Brown. The school is a short drive from the Rhode Island School of Design (RISD, pronounced "ris-dee"), where students can register for art classes and receive course credit. Musical groups emerge at night like earthworms after a storm, and the campus dance groups perform frequently. And there are many artistic and cultural groups among the approximately 300 student organizations, including student theater, a popular student-run radio station, and a wide variety of community and social outreach programs.

The attractions of Providence, Rhode Island, population 160,000, are within walking distance of campus. The town touts itself as a "Renaissance City," and is "a real delight for students who are willing to walk down College Hill," says a student. The town is an odd mixture of liberal artsy types and working-class ethnic Catholics. Its corrupt politics are fascinating to follow. Rhode Island is so small that it is essentially a "city-state," and so students can get involved in state politics if they wish. As for restaurants, "the dining scene here is the best in New England," says a student. The town has plenty of interesting food joints, including a plethora of ethnic restaurants. The area surrounding the campus caters to students and their eccentricities. One student describes how an Egyptian restaurant displayed a flier for a Young Socialists meeting. Judging by the restaurant's bustling business, the immigrant owner seemed to think his capitalist enterprise had more to gain than to lose by posting the flier.

Crime on campus isn't that bad for an urban school: in 2003, the school reported one forcible sex offense, two robberies, two aggravated assaults, 49 burglaries, and seven stolen cars. Providence isn't a huge city, but it isn't the safest. Students should take caution, particularly on the eastern perimeter of the campus. Brown's Department of Public Safety is an accredited law enforcement agency with more than 80 employees. It sponsors escort and safety van services as well as crime prevention workshops. At present, a move to arm DPS officers with handguns seems inevitable; though it faces some opposition from the left on campus, several recent assaults on campus and the wishes of President Simmons seem likely to carry the day.

Along with the rest of the Ivies, Brown is astronomically expensive. Tuition for 2004–5 was $30,672, and room and board ran to $8,474. For many years Brown could not afford to institute need-blind admissions or guarantee full aid to needy students. In 2004, businessman Sidney Frank, who himself struggled with poverty during his own education at Brown in the late 1930s and early 1940s, donated $100 million in undergraduate scholarship funds for the neediest of students. Those who qualify should, in combination with financial aid, be able to graduate from Brown with minimal debt. (This was Mr. Frank's second major contribution to college life in the United States. The first was the introduction of Jägermeister to the United States.) Currently, 43 percent of the undergraduate student body receives need-based financial aid.

Brown was the last Ivy League institution to institute a policy of need-blind admissions, meaning that some current students were accepted partly on their ability to afford the school's heavy tuition costs. The university has raised tuition in order to support need-blind admissions—a move that was unpopular in many quarters. It remains to be seen whether Mr. Frank's largesse will "trickle up" in the form of lower tuition costs, but at this point it seems unlikely.

COLBY COLLEGE

WATERVILLE, MAINE • WWW.COLBY.EDU

The diversity one

Maine has three top-tier liberal arts colleges—Bowdoin, Bates, and Colby—and even the admissions officers at the three schools have trouble making their own schools stand out from the others. Each has similar benefits: small classes and close faculty-student interaction, strong study-abroad programs, a considerate community atmosphere, and all the best of the Maine outdoors. Students at all three colleges tend to be intellectually driven rather than motivated by a future career, but each college has watered down its curriculum so much that if a student does graduate with a broad and integrated liberal arts education, the fault is all his own.

Of the three, Colby is probably the most addicted to the shibboleths of multiculturalism, and the one where politics most overshadows academics and campus life. The school's new president, William D. Adams, at one point headed Stanford University's Great Works in Western Culture program. Sadly, he doesn't seem to have brought much of that background to bear on his new job. Colby's weak distribution requirements have seen just one change since Adams came to Colby in 2000: The college now requires students to take *two* courses—instead of one—focusing on "prejudice, privilege, oppression, inequality, and injustice." For sadistic students who enjoy gloating about the past, this sounds like tons of fun.

Joking aside, students do have to search a little to locate the great works of Western culture at Colby. With courage, drive, and intellectual focus, however, a Colby student can receive an excellent education. One of the best aspects of the college is the intense commitment to teaching of Colby professors, with whom students have the opportunity to forge lasting intellectual relationships.

Academic Life: See you at the buffet

The Colby Plan, adopted in 1989, contains the college's requirements for a liberal arts education—and they aren't much. "Flexibility" in choosing courses is something of a buzzword on campuses these days, and Colby is no exception. A campus tour guide's advice is to "take courses you're interested in, and you'll have no problem fulfilling the requirements." You may emerge from Colby with little or no understanding of American history, philosophy, or literature—that is, if you prefer to entertain yourself with obscure courses like "Women in Japanese Cinema and Literature," which would fulfill one distribution requirement. A humanities major says that students majoring in the sciences often choose "some easier options specifically for those who need to fill the requirements." However, one faculty member says, "Students generally embrace the liberal arts philosophy and take a range of courses, willingly. The ones that don't are either slackers or those beautiful few who are one kind of geek or another—verbal or mathematical, but not both." Reassuring news, if true.

Colby has a history of sacrificing traditional education to feed its flesh-eating sacred cows. For instance, the women's studies program enjoys tremendous favor with the administration but is known to be academically weak compared to other departments. When it was revealed that the women's studies program awarded the highest percentage of As at the college, chivalrous administrators fought off any criticism. The religious studies department is largely staffed by women with primary interests in feminism. It lists few courses focusing on Christianity, of which only one, "Introduction to Christian Scriptures," is offered regularly. There are several courses dealing with Asian religions as well as others on women and feminism, film, and the radical feminist theologian Mary Daly. One course is "The Goddess: A Hermeneutics in Theology," and another, "Contemporary Wicca: Formalists, Feminists, and Free Spirits." The anthropology department is as weak as such departments tend to be at small liberal arts schools, offering a number of narrow or partisan courses. The interdisciplinary majors tend to be the most politicized: American studies, indigenous peoples of the Americas (a minor in the anthropology department), African and African American studies, and women's, gender, and sexuality studies.

To be fair, some departments have retained some traditional requirements. For instance, English majors still have to take three courses in English literature before 1800, and history majors take two courses each in United States and European history, as well as two in non-Western history.

Also, on the positive side, students wax effusive about professors' dedication, asserting that faculty members put their time and thought into teaching, rather than publishing. One economics major says that she chose Colby precisely because of its commitment to pedagogy and the close relationships that exist between professors and students. "When I visited Colby as a prospective student, an economics professor gave me her name and e-mail address," she says. "Now I'm majoring in economics and I know every faculty member in the department. I come to office hours frequently, have dinner with them, and even babysit their kids." Another student says that professors often share books with their students, attend campus events, and "are very willing to use their contacts and knowledge to steer you into programs." A professor to whom she'd never spoken before gave her valuable advice about where to study abroad.

As at many small colleges, Colby students have a good deal of one-on-one time with their professors. The college encourages this by offering teachers free lunch in the dining halls if they bring along a student. A senior writes in the student newspaper that he "interviews" his professors over a meal before enrolling in their classes. The result: "I can honestly say that I have never in my four years at Colby had a class that I didn't both enjoy and learn a great deal from." A faculty member says, "Colby obsessively emphasizes good teaching, so one could quite easily have only great professors."

First-year students are assigned faculty advisors to help them plan their courses for the first couple of semesters. Once a student has declared a major, he may select another advisor. Students are required to get approval from their advisors before making any academic choices—like choosing courses, adding a minor, or switching majors.

Colby is one of those rare colleges that attracts bright overachievers who are cooperative rather than competitive, who treat education as an experience to be shared with their classmates. The Farnham Writers' Center is staffed by students eager to help classmates with papers. During exam time, the center is open 24 hours a day for those pulling the inevitable all-nighter.

A recent article in the student newspaper, the *Colby Echo*, revealed that grade inflation is increasingly a problem at the college. A task force composed of faculty members is studying whether grade inflation exists—about half the faculty seems to believe it does—and if it does, what solutions are available. While conclusions have not yet been released, data available show that the cumulative GPA for the senior class has risen from 2.38 in 1967 to 3.01 in recent years. In a recent survey, over half the professors reported that there is a relationship between evaluations given by students and the grades they receive in their classes. Some professors insist that since Colby students are above average, their grades should be too; the classics department chair told the paper, "To get into Colby is unbelievably competitive. Should we be surprised students get

VITAL STATISTICS

Religious affiliation: none
Total enrollment: 1,821
Total undergraduates: 1,821
SAT/ACT midranges: SAT V: 640–720, M: 640–710; ACT: 27–31
Applicants: 4,065
Applicants accepted: 37%
Accepted applicants who enrolled: 34%
Tuition: $39,800 (includes room and board)
Freshman retention rate: 92%
Graduation rate: 85% (4 yrs.), 88% (6 yrs.)
Courses with fewer than 20 students: 62%
Student-faculty ratio: 10:1
Courses taught by graduate TAs: none
Most popular majors: social sciences, ethnic studies, English
Students living on campus: 93%
Guaranteed housing for four years? yes
Students in fraternities or sororities: none

NEW ENGLAND

NEW ENGLAND

ACADEMIC REQUIREMENTS

Distributional mandates at Colby are as follows:

- Two courses in the natural sciences, at least one with a lab component.
- English 115, a freshman writing-intensive class based on readings that vary according to section and professor.
- Competence at the intermediate level of a foreign language, demonstrated either through classes, testing, or study abroad.
- Two classes dealing with "political and cultural change directed against . . . prejudice, privilege, oppression, inequality, and injustice." One must deal with the United States, one with a foreign country.

As?" Some departments were reported as being more generous than others; interdisciplinary departments were the most lavish, with women's studies most of all.

The strongest departments at Colby are biology, English, and government, although students must take care in choosing courses. Under the guidance of an advisor, students are welcome to pursue an independent major concentrating on a certain theme by taking courses in a variety of departments. Colby also offers some majors that combine studies in two departments, like economics-mathematics, classical civilization–English, and philosophy-mathematics—a program in which students take several logic courses, some core philosophy courses, calculus, and other abstract mathematics courses. Students mention the following faculty members as among the best at Colby: Joseph Reisert in government, Andrea Tilden in biology, Catherine Besteman in anthropology, George Welch in math, Peter Harris in English, and Bevin Engman in art.

More than two-thirds of the student body chooses to study abroad for a semester or two, and Colby's international programs are particularly strong. Granted, some students may participate simply because they've become stir crazy in Waterville, but one student who plans to study in Sri Lanka and Japan says that others "use it to challenge themselves in an entirely different way than you can in the United States." Colby sponsors programs in Salamanca, Dijon, Cork, and St. Petersburg. In addition to programs jointly sponsored with Bowdoin and Bates in London, Cape Town, and Quito, students have dozens of other international opportunities.

In 1962, Colby became the first school in the nation to institute a four-one-four calendar (two four-month semesters separated by a January term), giving students the opportunity to take shorter, more intense courses during the winter. Many students choose to extend their winter breaks away from Colby by participating in internships or independent projects, but the college also offers some 50 courses on campus. Among them are courses on emergency medical training, winter ecology, geology courses on volcanoes and volcanology, and literature courses focusing on individual authors.

Student Life: Waterville and wine

While the 714-acre Colby campus is surrounded by lush scenery, the faculty and students are what make the campus "green." Colby College is one of only two colleges that recently committed to becoming 100 percent eco-friendly. The school will soon make a substantial purchase of "green" electricity, generated by geothermal wells. Colby expects that soon these wells will provide all heating and cooling needs for its new buildings.

It's not just trees that earn a hug. After Colby's board of trustees passed its 10-year strategic plan, students rallied for an end to "institutional racism and heterosexism" and presented a list of demands, including the addition of a multicultural residence house, a college-funded "queer studies" program, and the guarantee that three of the 10 new faculty members to be hired as part of the plan would be part of ethnic or queer studies programs. Students also claimed that there weren't enough Native American students at Colby. While students were not able to win concessions to all their demands, university president William Adams commissioned a task force on gay, lesbian, bisexual, and transgender issues—which promptly renamed itself the Queer Task Force. Various academic departments have hired individuals who have an expertise in queer studies, and new courses are including ever queerer material.

Perhaps more than any other college in this guide, Colby is obsessed with diversity. At Colby, "diversity" includes ethnicity, sexuality, race, and culture—but not, of course, politics. Incessantly, the lead "news" article in the *Colby Echo* will spotlight some instance or breach of multiculturalism, and at least one editorial will plead for bringing more ethnics to campus. The mandatory Colby Outdoor Orientation Trip (COOT) for freshmen now includes a diversity workshop that, according to an article in the *Echo*, proposes to "concentrate on helping first-year students embrace the Colby community by emphasizing diversity's importance within the student body." Topics include "the reasons people feel marginalized [and] the ways in which people characterize gender"; activities "address emotionally charged issues such as sexual assault, racial prejudice, and homophobia." In 2003 the first round of "Diversity Reports" were compiled. These reports, mandatory for all academic departments, are self-assessments to address issues of race, gender, and sexual orientation. Each department is responsible for updating its progress on a yearly basis.

At Colby, debate too often means two or more people speaking on the same side of an issue. A rare conservative student interviewed in the Colby alumni magazine says, "The vocal majority is definitely very, very left. . . . If you don't agree with them, you're wrong. You don't understand. It's some sort of white privilege or *something* privilege." There may be a number of more or less conservative students at Colby, but very few feel comfortable enough to speak up. One student who says she is not politically involved says that one cannot help but notice that "conservative viewpoints often get ridiculed, or at least openly disapproved."

Religion occasionally rears its head on campus. A Catholic mass is held in the

REQUIREMENTS (CONT'D)

- Attendance (first-year students only) at five of seven "supper seminars" that focus on "mental, emotional, social, physical, and spiritual fitness." Recent choices have included "Vagina Monologues," "Four Stages of Drinking," "AIDS, Love, and the Secret of College Students," and "But That's Different" (an educational dialogue on "heterosexism").

  Students must also take one course each in:
- The arts (either history, theory, or practice).
- Historical studies.
- Literature.
- Quantitative reasoning.
- Social sciences.

chapel twice a week, along with an interdenominational service each Sunday evening. Chaplains seem eager enough to promote spirituality, although the college does not. "Personally, I feel comfortable being a Christian on campus, but it can be hard," a student says. "There is a pervasive attitude, especially among intellectuals, that there is no such thing as an absolute truth, which contradicts Christianity, so it's a more subtle wearing away rather than outright objections. It's a very liberal place, and religion can be brushed aside as meaningless." The Colby Christian Fellowship, with approximately 50 active members, hosts small prayer and Bible discussion groups and participates in volunteer activities. The campus also has a Newman Council (Catholic), Hillel (Jewish), and various other religious groups.

When Colby abolished fraternities on campus in 1984, it provoked an uproar among the student body, since the Greek system had been a central part of student life. Colby's housing and social life is now focused on three traditional commons, each of which consists of several dorms, its own dining hall, and meeting spaces. Students are free to move from one common to another each year, so they end up meeting a wide variety of students. Each weekend, one of the commons is responsible for a major social event, usually a dance or other party. However, students admit that these events are not well attended.

Colby not only guarantees housing for all four years; with a few exceptions it requires it. Ninety-three percent of the student body lives on campus. The college goes to great lengths to prevent cliquishness. Students are integrated into residences proportionately by class, so that freshmen live with upperclassmen and can have them as advisors and friends. All of the campus residences are centrally located dormitories, except for one apartment complex in which about 100 seniors live. The campus is in the midst of a $45 million renovation in which all of the dormitories will be completely redone within the next few years. Colby offers no single-sex dormitories—or even single-sex floors—and students are bound to find themselves living next door to a member of the opposite sex. However, there are no coed dorm rooms or coed bathrooms in the residence halls. Housing authorities designate the bathroom on a coed floor for a particular sex and then switch the next semester. Men and women, however, are permitted to share apartments as seniors. One living option is a quiet dorm, where residents and visitors must adhere to a 21-hour-a-day quiet rule. All dorms on campus are non-smoking, and there are also alcohol-free and chemical-free residences available.

As for social life in general, "drinking is too popular," says one student. "It's the overwhelming majority's choice of social activity, and the rules about it are fairly lax." Colby has its own on-campus pub, which serves alcohol, and many students spend weekends drinking together in dorm rooms. The college attempts to provide alternatives to alcohol, and there is a rule that at least 50 percent of all social programming money must go into funding alcohol-free events. College-sponsored dances are usually not well attended, but other more popular events include performances by hypnotists, comedians, and musicians. The Student Government Association also sponsors a movie each weekend. The Coffeehouse, a student-run business on campus, brings in small-name bands every few weeks, and math professors lead a folk night each week. At the

Spa, located in the Cotter Student Union, students can hang out, play video games or pool, or enjoy student productions.

Many students occupy their free time with activities in small niche clubs like pottery or photography, politically oriented groups, or sports. Colby is a fairly athletic campus, fielding 32 varsity teams in the New England Small College Athletic Conference. There are also a number of intramural options. When Colby's athletic center was damaged by fire 10 years ago, it was rebuilt to include nearly everything the athletic heart desires: training facilities, competition courts in almost every sport, saunas, a climbing wall, and a swimming pool. The college's central Maine location encourages students to explore the outdoors—and not surprisingly, the Outing Club is the most active student organization on campus, organizing hiking, boating, skiing, and camping trips in the Waterville area, along the Maine coast, and ever further from campus.

The campus, though not historic, is quaint and charming, with red brick buildings separated by lush, green lawns. Completion draws near for the Colby Green, a new section of campus built in the style of a New England village green. Downtown Waterville is only a 15-minute walk away and boasts several good restaurants, a bowling alley, a movie theater, and other attractions; however, some students complain that outside of the usual fare of food and movies, the town offers very little. "Cars are useful," says one student.

Except for a handful of burglaries, crime is virtually nonexistent at Colby. The latest crime statistics (from 2003) show just a single incident—a forcible sex offense. The college is fairly secluded from the town of Waterville, so any miscreant townsfolk would have to make a special effort to come to campus. Colby has a security force that patrols the campus regularly and also offers a campus escort service and a safety shuttle to and from various Waterville locations.

Students consider the higher costs of Colby worth the investment and are quick to remark that financial aid is not difficult to get. The college awards more than $14 million annually in grants, loans, and campus employment to approximately 65 percent of the full-time student population. The average financial assistance to an incoming freshman is $26,000. A good thing, too: the 2004 academic year at Colby cost $39,800. Colby has a federal work-study program, and all students may work on campus regardless of being admitted into a work-study program. The average debt of a 2002 grad who received financial aid was $17,270.

SUGGESTED CORE
1. Classics 137, Literature of Greece and Rome
2. Philosophy 175, Ancient Greek Thought
3. Religion 233/234, Introduction to Hebrew Scriptures / Introduction to the Second Testament
4. History 216, Church History and Theology in Medieval Europe
5. Government 272, Modern Political Theory
6. English 411, Shakespeare I
7. History 131, Survey of the United States to 1865
8. History 223, European Politics, Culture, and Thought, 1789–1914

CONNECTICUT COLLEGE

NEW LONDON, CONNECTICUT • WWW.CONNCOLL.EDU

New Athenians?

In 1910, Wesleyan University changed its charter to admit only men, leaving Connecticut women no place to earn a bachelor of arts degree. The next year, a group of Wesleyan alumnae founded Connecticut College for Women. And while this commitment to education for women may have been the wave of the future, the education itself was profoundly steeped in the values of the past.

Old curricular guides indicate that Connecticut College's first students—overwhelmingly upper-class and conservative—were exposed, tirelessly, to the intellectual foundations of Western civilization, and the school itself adopted in 1922 as its Honor Code a version of the Athenian Oath (to which the young of the ancient polis committed themselves at age 17):

> We will never, by any selfish or other unworthy act, dishonor this our college; individually and collectively we will foster her ideals and do our utmost to instill a respect in those among us who fail in their responsibility; unceasingly we will strive to quicken a general realization of our common duty and obligation to our college. And thus in manifold service we will render our alma mater greater, worthier, and more beautiful.

This Honor Code, which also provided for a student-run judicial system and self-proctored exams, maximizes student flexibility and reduces end-of-term stress. It is buttressed by the Matriculation Pledge, signed by every incoming freshman, which reads:

> I accept membership into Connecticut College, a community committed to cultural and intellectual diversity. I understand my obligation to this community under the Honor Code and pledge to uphold standards of behavior governed by honor. I pledge to take responsibility for my beliefs, and to conduct myself with integrity, civility, and the utmost respect for the dignity of all human beings. I pledge that my actions will be thoughtful and ethical and that I will do my best to instill a sense of responsibility in those among us who falter.

Today, the Honor Code and Matriculation Pledge are still very much in force—and students take them seriously. "Some students even go to the point of ratting on classmates," one junior says.

However, the administration seems to grant much more weight to another, more controversial code, expressed in the school's "diversity statement:"

While inviting openness to all types of diversity, the college pays special attention to historically disadvantaged groups such as: African Americans, Hispanics, Asians, Native Americans, women, gay, lesbian, bisexual, and transgender people, and the differently-abled. . . . [I]t is important that we attempt to redress historical wrongs by opening doors that were previously closed to members of these groups. Thus it is a goal of Connecticut College to have a student body, faculty and staff that are diverse in terms of race, gender and ethnic background, in numbers representative of the general population.

Quite a nice paean to quotas based on race, sex, orientation, and (if one dares peel back the euphemism) handicap. This is no surprise, coming as it does from a modern educational institution. But trying to reconcile ideals such as "intellectual diversity" with this kind of political correctness provokes a head-splitting predicament.

For those willing to traverse these thickets of scruple, Connecticut College is not a stifling environment. Most students, who despite the siren song of diversity still tend to come from privileged backgrounds, find life at CC pleasant. Faculty are committed to teaching, and students are intent on learning. Both conservative and liberal students say they feel comfortable speaking their minds in class, and those who call the gorgeous hilltop campus home enjoy its small-college atmosphere and quirky traditions—such as "lobster night," when students compete to eat the most crustaceans. But CC students are no longer required to learn the best of the West.

VITAL STATISTICS
Religious affiliation: none
Total enrollment: 1,894
Total undergraduates: 1,894
SAT/ACT medians: SAT V: 700, M: 690; ACT: 29
Applicants: 4,503
Applicants accepted: 34%
Accepted applicants who enrolled: 32%
Tuition: $39,975 (includes room and board)
Freshman retention rate: 92%
Graduation rate: 82% (4 yrs.), 85% (6 yrs.)
Average class size: 20
Student-faculty ratio: 11:1
Courses taught by graduate TAs: none
Most popular majors: social sciences, political science, visual and performing arts
Students living on campus: 99%
Guaranteed housing for four years? yes
Students in fraternities or sororities: none

Academic Life: Black and white and gray all over

In plain black and white, Connecticut College declares in its catalog that it is "dedicated to providing [students] with as fine a liberal arts education as is possible in the conviction that this is more empowering and more enriching than technical or specialized education." And while studying the liberal arts may "prepare [students] for the rigors of the finest graduate and professional schools and leadership in numerous careers," it is the "pursuit of wisdom and self-knowledge" that is the overarching goal.

After that declaration, the catalog shifts from black and white to gray. CC's general education requirements are a little stricter than those of many liberal arts colleges, where administrators are abandoning core and even distribution requirements in order to give students more "flexibility." Even so, "It's really easy to fulfill [the general education requirements]," a campus tour guide assures us. "You can knock out the

ACADEMIC REQUIREMENTS

Connecticut College has no core curriculum, but rather a series of distribution requirements. In addition to the requirements for a major, students must take one "foundation course" in each of seven areas:

- Physical and biological sciences.
- Mathematics and logic.
- Social sciences.
- Critical studies in literature and the arts.
- Creative arts.
- Philosophical and religious studies.
- Historical studies.

The catalog says that foundation courses "are those courses which offer a basic introduction to the central issues or major texts of a discipline, or the skills and methodologies needed to pursue a given discipline at the intermediate or advanced levels." But the college makes little judgment as to which topics—especially in the humanities—students should study. Courses like "Hispanic Writers in the United States" and "History of Dance" satisfy the literature requirement just as fully as a course in Shakespeare.

requirements without even knowing you've completed them." How's that for an overarching goal?

One's social science requirement could be fulfilled by "Introduction to Gender and Women's Studies: A Transnational Feminist Approach." In that course, students and instructor examine "colonization, imperialism, and immigration; the making of a gendered global economy and of sexual citizens; body politics; women and the gendered processes of militarization; work, sex work, wages, and welfare; sexuality and the politics of desire; education, schooling, and the reproduction of inequality; and the organization of global feminist struggles." All in one class! Even the sciences are not wholly immune; CC has a flourishing environmental studies program, combining a natural science orientation with a definite left-wing social science slant.

In general, "political bias creeps into the classroom most obviously through pedagogical decisions made by the administration," says one history major. "The college is willing to embrace alternative approaches to the liberal arts, sometimes selecting courses with controversial themes like homosexuality." For instance, the gender and women's studies department has approximately 35 associated faculty members who teach courses cross-listed with their departments. A classics professor, for instance, teaches "Greek Sexual Mythology: Male and Female in Western Thought." A course called "Bodies for Sale: Prostitution in Early Modern and Modern Europe" falls under the comparative studies in culture department. And so on.

However, an attentive student could avoid most of these bizarre courses and design a curriculum composed of foundational courses, such as "History of Ancient Philosophy," "Introduction to European History," and "Classical Epic."

Students report that faculty members at CC are teachers first, researchers and writers a distant second. One student says, "You will know your professor and he or she will know you." Another says, "If there is one thing to stress about professors . . . it is their commitment to students. They don't come to New London to hide in the library—they come to share their ideas with us. It makes for quite an academic journey." With a student-faculty ratio of around 11 to 1, classes are generally small. The largest ones—introductory courses in biology, English, and psychology—

are capped at 100 students, but even these have weekly discussion sections or laboratory sections of 10 to 15 students, taught by the professors themselves. (There are no graduate students at Connecticut College.) Smaller seminars, says one student, are student-led, so "you never want to miss class because you feel like you're going to add something to the discussion and you'll learn from your classmates." Most students, says a sophomore, form tight relationships with their instructors, often eating dinner together, minding their children, and discussing ideas outside of class. But closeness with professors depends on the student. "There's some outreach on the part of the professor, but you have to be motivated," a student says.

REQUIREMENTS (CONT'D)

Students also must take:
- A foreign language, either one course at the intermediate level or two courses in a language the student has not previously studied.
- Two courses designated as "writing-intensive" or "writing-enriched."
- At least eight courses in their major, but no more than 13 courses in a single department.

Those who need help navigating the required writing-intensive courses can visit the Roth Writing Center, where student tutors help with essays. One student says that seeking such help "makes you look really good in your professor's eyes."

A conservative student reports that, in the Connecticut College classroom, at least, many professors are fair and tolerant. "In the government department, for example, you'll find professors who are flamingly liberal but you couldn't tell in class," a student says. "Others are only moderately liberal, but they let everybody know it. The good thing though, is that you'd never be graded down for your views; professors are respectful." It's true that one professor quoted in the alumni magazine *CC* proclaimed that her primary educational mission was to "emancipate from the *status quo*" and fight "systems of privilege, sexism, racism, heterosexism, classism," et cetera. But another progressive professor said, "I don't want to make my students think like me, but I want to give them the skills and tools to understand other perspectives. If they are liberals, conservatives or radicals, my job is to demonstrate the historical origin and impact of each position on American society."

The best instructors, according to students, are Edward Brodkin and Bruce Kirmmse in history; William Frasure in government; Donald Peppard in economics; J. Melvin Woody in philosophy; Robert E. Proctor in Italian; Catherine Spencer in French; Perry Susskind in mathematics; John S. Gordon and George Willauer in English; and Jacqueline McCormick in dance.

The advising program is strong. Upon entry, every student is assigned a faculty advisor and required to meet with him five or six times in his first two years. Student advisors also help newcomers adjust to college life. After a student declares a major, he is assigned (or chooses) a faculty advisor within his major.

Connecticut College has only around 1,900 students, but the school offers 47 single-discipline majors and seven interdisciplinary majors: Africana studies, American studies, architectural studies, comparative studies in culture, environmental studies, medieval studies, and neuroscience/psychology. Four interdisciplinary centers help students connect learning and life. The most unusual of the four is the Toor Cummings

Center for International Studies and the Liberal Arts (CISLA), where students can learn a language, intern in a foreign country, and then produce an original project that pulls it all together. A zoology major studied Japanese, interned at a field station in Japan, and researched the "cultural and ecological considerations of the Japanese snow monkey." A philosophy/ international relations major recently interned in Russia and wrote "a critique of philosopher Karl Popper's concept of an open society." One Japanese/ sociology major interned in Japan through an organization interested in helping Latino immigrants to that country. He says that "CISLA is really a great way to internationalize your major." Other interdisciplinary programs include the Ammerman Center for Arts and Technology, the Goodwin-Niering Center for Conservation Biology and Environmental Studies, and the Holleran Center for Community Action and Public Policy.

More than half the student body spends at least one semester in a foreign country. The college's Study Abroad/Teach Abroad program sends a group of 15 to 30 students abroad to take courses with Connecticut College professors and local faculty. Recent programs have been held in Greece, Tanzania, Egypt, Italy, and the Czech Republic. CC is affiliated with many other universities, so students can study virtually anywhere in the world.

Students say Connecticut College is strongest in the arts, especially music, theater, and dance. Palmer Auditorium performance hall can seat most of the student body. Cummings Arts Center, which houses the art, art history, and music departments, holds three art galleries, studios, practice rooms, and a music library. The government, philosophy, and economics departments are also described as solid. Government majors are required to take at least one course in each of four areas: political theory, comparative politics, United States politics, and international politics. The botany and biology departments are also reported to be strong; professors and students take advantage of the school's lush surroundings for research.

Shain Library houses half a million books and periodicals. Connecticut College's partnership with Trinity College and Wesleyan University allows students from each of these institutions to check out books from all three schools.

Student Life: No reason to walk

Add Connecticut College to the long list of gorgeous New England schools. The relatively new campus (the oldest building dates to 1915) of gray granite hearkens to the country clubs that hosted the elite which built the school. From the Blaustein Humanities Center in Palmer Library, one can see the town of New London, Long Island Sound, and—on clear days—Long Island itself. The campus is designated as an arboretum, giving the CC community space to study, research, and enjoy the outdoors.

Connecticut College guarantees housing for all four years, and 99 percent of students live on campus. One student says that the result is "a strong, close-knit community." Some might find it a little too close knit—all dormitories are coed, and all the bathrooms on coed floors are also coed, though dorm rooms are not. If that makes you squeamish, there are a few single-sex floors available.

Before moving onto campus, freshmen go through a rigorous roommate selection process, and as a result, students tend to become close to their roommates throughout the remaining three years. Connecticut has a high percentage of single rooms, so if a student misses the mad scramble to make friends during his freshman year, he may find himself happily or unhappily alone for the rest of his time at CC. A few areas are designated as specialty residences; students can live with students of like interests in the Earth House, the Multicultural/Unity House, and student-chosen theme houses like Hip Hop Culture and Women's Health. Students living in the Language House can practice their skills by immersing themselves in a foreign language at dinner and in dorm activities. The campus also offers a quiet house, apartments, co-op living, and substance-free options. Students are free to eat at any of seven dining halls on campus.

Because Connecticut College has no fraternities or sororities, many activities are organized around dorm life. Each hall adopts a faculty or staff member to participate in dorm events with residents. The annual Camelympics is a favorite competition between dorms; Dessert and Dialogue allows students to discuss topics like "Representation of American Culture and the Super Bowl" with an invited faculty or staff member. Despite the college's small size, students should have no trouble finding clubs that interest them, whether academic, service, or issue-driven. There are seven singing groups at CC, a film society, a comedy club, a jazz band, and an orchestra. Around 90 percent of the student body participates in some form of organized sport. The Camels compete on 19 teams at the NCAA Division III level in the New England Small College Athletic Conference against schools like Bowdoin, Middlebury, and Williams. Since women outnumber men on campus almost three to two, Title IX requires that female athletes outnumber male athletes in a proportionate fashion.

Harkness Chapel is a quaint New England–style church that seems to be used just as often for secular activities as for services. The college has on staff a Catholic priest, a Protestant minister, and a rabbi for services and counseling. There are a few religious organizations like Hillel, Baptist Campus Ministry, and the InterVarsity Christian Fellowship, but these do not play a terribly prominent role in campus life.

If there is an established creed at CC, it is "diversity." In 2004, a single crank phone call directed at a black student prompted administrators to shut down the campus for a day and summon the entire student body to an emergency "diversity forum," according to the *Chronicle of Higher Education*. "Diverse" sexual practices, of course, are celebrated. Among the most active student organizations is Sexual Orientations United

SUGGESTED CORE
1. Classics 203, Classical Epic
2. Philosophy 201, History of Ancient Philosophy
3. Religious Studies 113/ 114, Hebrew Bible: Old Testament / New Testament
4. Religious Studies 203, The Christian Tradition
5. Government 214, Modern Political Thought
6. English 209, Shakespeare: The Early Plays *or* English 210, Shakespeare: The Late Plays
7. History 105, An Introduction to the History of the U.S.
8. History 307/308, Intellectual and Cultural History of Nineteenth-Century Europe

NEW ENGLAND

for Liberation (SOUL). The financial support that SOUL receives from the college helps sponsor the annual "Fabulous Drag Ball" and political lobbying.

However, CC has seen some resistance to radical trends on campus lately. The College Republicans began in 2002 with just two members; within the year, there were 60. "There's really been no opposition," says the organization's president. "I think CC has welcomed this political diversity." The College Republicans have brought speakers to campus, sent care packages to U.S. troops, and passed around a petition to acknowledge support of the troops; CC president Norman Fainstein, a vocal liberal, signed it.

New London doesn't add much to the college—the large town is too far for students to walk to, and they wouldn't find much anyway, save for beaches, a few restaurants, and one bar, the Oasis. Almost all evening and weekend activities occur on campus, including performances, lectures, and drinking. New London lies halfway between New York and Boston, and the Amtrak station is just a few minutes from the college. Students occasionally take the train to visit friends over weekends. A student shuttle service, the Camel Van, will take students as far as Mystic, Connecticut, which students say is a little more exciting than New London. The Coast Guard Academy is virtually just across the street from the college, and while the two institutions have lately tried to forge a relationship by exchanging professors and sharing facilities, the school personalities do not mesh well; Connecticut students sniff at Coast Guard recruits as right-wing flag-wavers; Academy students jeer at CC students as rich, conceited liberals.

Connecticut College is secluded enough that the crime rate is miniscule. During 2003, there was one forcible sex offense, one robbery, and one burglary on campus. Students need a PIN to enter residence halls, and although a safety walk service is offered, it is rarely used; students say they feel safe walking on campus, even late at night.

The school's tuition is similar to that of Ivy League institutions; tuition, room, and board (the school computes them all together) for 2004–5 was $39,975. Admission is not entirely need-blind, but the college meets the full need of each student who does get in. Forty-three percent of students receive need-based financial aid.

UNIVERSITY OF CONNECTICUT

STORRS, CONNECTICUT • WWW.UCONN.EDU

No slam dunk

The University of Connecticut began as the Storrs Agricultural School (named after $5,000-donors Charles and Augustus Storrs) in 1881. A dozen years after its founding, the Connecticut General Assembly admitted women and designated the university as the state's land-grant college. The school grew significantly after the world wars, when vast numbers of American servicemen entered public universities.

Throughout most of the country, the University of Connecticut—UConn—figures in the common mind more as a basketball team than as an educational institution. Rather, as two basketball teams: The cute-nickname Huskies (UConn? Yukon? Get it?) of both sexes lead the list of NCAA hoop powerhouses, having managed a first-ever men's-women's sweep in 2004. Apart from stats like this, when it comes to UConn, most outside New England tend to draw a blank.

So does the school, to some extent. With four name changes, a late start in the land-grant sweepstakes, and the brutal competitive position of a state university in college-rich New England—there are well over 100 colleges within a 100-mile radius—UConn has struggled to find its niche in higher education. While it holds a respectable position alongside the Universities of Massachusetts and Vermont in New England, the university desperately wants to raise its national profile. Through its Twenty-First Century UConn building initiative, begun in 1995, Connecticut poured $1.3 billion into the expansion of the quality and quantity of its facilities. The school claims that the project has improved residence halls (through the creation of new "living and learning" communities), made the main campus more pedestrian-friendly, and allowed it to build new lecture halls and research laboratories. Together, all this has helped recruit faculty members who are "among the most talented and diverse in the university's history." The endowment has certainly benefited, soaring from $50 million in 1995 to $210 million today.

VITAL STATISTICS
Religious affiliation: none
Total enrollment: 22,694
Total undergraduates: 15,751
SAT/ACT midranges: SAT: 1080–1260; ACT: 22–27
Applicants: 17,666
Applicants accepted: 53%
Accepted applicants who enrolled: 35%
Tuition: $5,720 (in state), $17,448 (out of state)
Room and board: $7,300
Freshman retention rate: 88%
Graduation rate: 45% (4 yrs.), 70% (6 yrs.)
Average class size: 35
Student-faculty ratio: 18:1
Courses taught by graduate TAs: 22%
Most popular majors: business, social sciences, liberal arts
Students living on campus: 75%
Guaranteed housing for four years? no
Students in fraternities: 8% sororities: 6%

NEW ENGLAND

63

In the absence of a core curriculum, all students at UConn must complete certain distribution requirements:

- Two courses in the humanities, with choices ranging from "Greek Civilization" and "Introduction to Shakespeare" to "Magicians, Witches, and Wizards: Parallel Belief and Popular Culture in France" and "Feminisms and the Arts."
- Three math skills courses.
- Two classes in the social sciences, such as "Principles of Economics," "Introduction to the American Political Process," "Race, Class and Gender," or "Gender in a Global Perspective"
- Two courses in the hard sciences, with choices such as "Honors General Chemistry," "Introductory Astronomy," "Chemistry for an Informed Electorate," and "The Science of Food."
- Two "diversity"-related courses, with options ranging from the worthysounding—"World Religions" and "Introduction to Comparative Politics"—to the witless: "White Racism" and "Sociology of Sexualities."

Despite these capital improvements, however, UConn's student body is still not of the caliber of the top national public universities, though it has grown stronger over the last few years. Over 50 percent of all applicants are accepted, and the midrange of these students' SAT scores is between 1080 and 1260—a shade above UMass's 1030–1240 or Vermont's 1060–1250, but hardly in line with the 1230–1430 found at Virginia or the 1200–1410 at Michigan. While the New England setting is a tough competitive position, the fact remains that many UConn students are not well prepared for college, and only 70 percent graduate within six years.

Although it may not attract as many beautiful minds as Virginia or Michigan, UConn has had an advantage over such schools in that its general education curriculum has done a better job in ensuring that students take at least one fundamental course in each of several fields of inquiry. This legacy, however, is under assault.

Academic Life: The (U) Conn is on

The heart of the University of Connecticut's academic program has long been its general education curriculum, a set of requirements that all students must meet. However, in fall 2005, these requirements were downgraded.

Up to then, every UConn student—whether in the College of Liberal Arts or in one of the 11 other schools offering undergraduate degrees—received some exposure to seven areas of knowledge. By agglomerating four of these areas (arts, literature, history, and philosophy) and requiring only two courses in the Arts and Humanities concentration that replaced them, the new general education requirement cuts the required courses from eight to seven, while leaving room for one additional course each in social science and diversity. The traditional Western Civ course, previously mandatory for all students, is now optional.

It could have been worse. The College of Liberal Arts, to which 61 percent of undergraduates belong, still requires coursework in four basic fields (arts, literature, history and philosophy)—although, as in general education, the Western Civ class now must compete for students with 11 other courses. The new program renders it possible (though difficult) to graduate from UConn with no "Eurocentric" courses at all.

Even now, each student must take an introductory writing seminar—either "Academic Writing" or "Writing through Literature"—and two courses (in any department) that call for extensive writing. Most introductory writing courses are taught by graduate students from various disciplines. One instructor, an English graduate student, says there is no university-wide curriculum for these courses, "so we can pretty much teach what we want—nice, although open to abuses, I am sure, though I don't know of any in particular."

Thus, even with the new modifications, UConn's liberal arts curriculum requires basic academic work in the most important academic fields, though it demands little depth. And the requirements listed above can only be satisfied by a limited number of courses—though the number, predictably, is expanding somewhat in the new core. For instance, the catalog had listed only nine courses that could fulfill the philosophical or ethical analysis requirement, mostly introductory-level classes like the linguistics course "Language and Mind," and the philosophy courses "Philosophical Classics," "Philosophy and Logic," and "Philosophy and Religion." The new catalog allows for 12 choices—a change, not likely for the better, but also none too dramatic. Similar evolutionary, frog-boiling changes are found in other disciplines. Under the old program, as one student says, "it [was] not possible to construct your schedule so you only have easy courses." What the new program will engender remains to be seen.

REQUIREMENTS (CONT'D)

- A two-semester sequence in a foreign language. Students who took at least three years of foreign language in high school are exempt.

  BA students in the College of Liberal Arts face more serious requirements. They need to take two expository writing classes, three writing-intensive courses in any department, at least one class in literature, one in fine arts, one of two basic history courses, one class each in Western and non-Western cultures, one course in philosophy and ethical analysis, three classes in the social sciences, and two in the hard sciences.

That said, the requirements for major fields of study at UConn are, on the whole, commendable. English majors, for instance, are required to take a number of specific courses, including survey courses in Shakespeare, English-language poetry, British literature, and American literature. In addition to these, students must take a course focusing on a major author and one in multicultural literature (like "Literature and Culture of the Third World" or "Advanced Study: Lesbian, Gay, Bisexual, and Transgendered Literature"). History majors must take one course in ancient, medieval, and early modern history, one in modern Europe, one in United States history, and two courses selected from African, Asian, Latin American, and Middle Eastern history. In addition, majors must take a course on historical methodology and complete a thesis seminar that requires extensive writing and original research.

Students and faculty say the English department is one of the school's best. It often hosts visiting professors from top schools in England and the United States. The business school and the sciences are also very strong, with excellent facilities and faculty. A political science major also praises his department, noting that majors face de-

NEW ENGLAND

partmental requirements that ensure a broad understanding of the discipline. These requirements call for introductory courses in three of four divisions—theory and methodology, comparative politics, international relations, and American politics—in addition to upper-level courses in these areas as well as in public policy and law. Most of the courses that the political science department offers are straightforward, like "Constitutional Law" and "Classical and Medieval Political Theory." There are a few courses of the ilk of "Black Feminist Politics," but only a few. Students say that Richard Vengroff and David A. Yalof in political science, Sam Pickering in English, and Peter Kaminsky in music are among the best undergraduate teachers.

UConn's Honors Scholar Program does not have separate requirements or a special curriculum; rather, honors students follow the same requirements as do regular students, but they can select more challenging courses open only to those in the program. The university Web site notes that honors classes are "smaller in size, more interactive, and enroll a high-caliber student." In addition, honors students can "get advice from nationally known faculty members in many disciplines."

New liberal arts students are assigned to professional advisors—not faculty members—through the Academic Center for Entering Students. From these staffers they get help planning courses and choosing majors. When students declare majors they are assigned to faculty advisors in their department. Close faculty-student relationships, it seems, are uncommon. When one student says, "I don't believe in asking an advisor for help, since all the information that I would need I can usually find on my own," he is more or less expressing the view of a majority of students. Another student says that the effectiveness of the advising program depends on which major a student chooses.

UConn's size—more than 15,000 undergraduates—means that some classes are apt to be large. Enrollments for large, freshman-level survey courses can reach the hundreds. The average class size is a hefty 35. One small consolation of the new program requirements: with broader core choices, more classes are likely to be offered, driving down the enrollment in such freshman mega-magnets as History 100/101.

Student Life: Little in Storrs

Storrs, Connecticut, is home to approximately 10,000 permanent residents. Located about a half-hour east of Hartford, Storrs offers little besides the university, a drugstore, a flower shop, and a few bars. That may change, as Storrs attempts to become "a vibrant, economic center—not a pass-through, but a destination," says the chairman of the town's revitalization project, as quoted by UConn's *Advance* newspaper. But for now, students spend most of their social lives on campus—or at least someplace other than the town of Storrs.

The campus itself has improved significantly over the past few years. The center is no longer accessible to automobile traffic and parking has been pushed to the perimeter. The architectural highlight of the campus is the Wilbur Cross Building, which was constructed 70 years ago as the school's library but now houses all of the school's student services. UConn has no shortage of rolling green hills and shady paths—it even has two lakes, Swann and Mirror—in addition to ugly academic buildings, modern high-rise dormitories, and oceanic parking lots.

One of the primary focal points of campus life is the Harry A. Gampel Pavilion, home to the aforementioned 2004 national champion men's and women's basketball teams. With 22 varsity teams, UConn competes in the Big East Athletic Conference against schools like Pitt, Syracuse, and West Virginia. UConn sports are a definite growth industry; football, which joined the Big East in 2004, clinched a minor bowl berth in its first season. For the more recreational athlete, Connecticut also offers close to 50 club sports—from cycling to skydiving—and many intramural options. UConn's mascot is a husky, named Jonathan in honor of Revolutionary War hero Jonathan Trumbull. Today's mascot, cared for by a university fraternity, is the 12th dog to serve in this honorable capacity.

Some 75 percent of UConn students live on campus. They have a number of housing options from which to choose. The university's 13 residential complexes range from new and modern facilities to older, more stately buildings. UConn offers single-sex dormitories for both men and women, and in some of the coed halls, men and women are separated by floor. There are no coed bathrooms or dorm rooms. Students can choose to live in alcohol-free dormitories, and all buildings are smoke free. The university has faced a bit of a housing crunch in the past few years, as enrollment has risen and the number of dorm rooms has not kept pace. Back in fall 2001, the residential life department was forced to give 300 entering students temporary beds in dorm lounges and elsewhere. Due to limited space, the university only guarantees housing for freshmen. However, the situation is improving. The school's building initiative added a number of suite-style housing complexes for students, including academic clusters in which students can live with classmates. One new residence hall houses honors students.

The Greek system is not as popular at UConn as it is at many other large schools. The university has 20 fraternities and nine sororities, but only 7 percent of university men and women are members. Greek houses are considered on-campus housing.

While extracurricular life at UConn provides ample opportunity for political expression, political life on campus may best be described as apathetic. The Animal Rights Club does give students a forum to "collectively and peacefully organize public protests and information tables." A few years ago, the UConn Student Labor Action Coalition led a series of protests against the university's refusal to raise the wages of janitors. With slogans like "Hey, hey, ho, ho, this UConn greed has got to go," the organization launched rallies, marches, and demonstrations. After a three-day sit-in by some students, the university agreed to meet their demands. One student says, however, that

SUGGESTED CORE
1. Classics 241, Greek and Roman Epic
2. Philosophy 221, Ancient Philosophy
3. Interdepartmental 294, The Bible
4. History 257, The Early Church and Christian Thought
5. Political Science 202, Modern Political Theory
6. English 230/231, Shakespeare I/II
7. History 231, American History to 1877: A Survey
8. History 258, Intellectual and Social History of Europe in the Nineteenth Century

NEW ENGLAND

most activist groups on campus make big commotions with only a few participants: "There have been several antiwar demonstrations on campus, but they are sparsely attended. A peace vigil in front of the Congregational Church never draws more than a handful of people."

UConn provides a wealth of cultural opportunities for both students and locals. The Jorgensen Center for the Performing Arts provides a diverse program of artistic entertainment, hosting opera, ballet, symphony orchestras from around the world, comedians such as Jerry Seinfeld, and pop music acts such as Ben Folds. The Puppet Festival is held on campus each year—perhaps not a student favorite, but certainly an event you can't find anywhere else. (UConn actually offers a major in puppetry.) A favorite activity on the UConn calendar is Spring Weekend—"a hedonistic nightmare," says one student—which offers a carnival-like atmosphere replete with music, food, and alcohol and draws tens of thousands of students from UConn and other colleges in the region. To discourage the bacchanalia traditionally associated with this last weekend in April, administrators have lately promoted more wholesome aspects of the celebration, including concerts, intramural tournaments, laser light shows, and dances.

One student says the typical UConn student has "more of a love for alcohol, sex, and music" than he does for "intelligence, respect, integrity, and success. Apathy overwhelms this campus everywhere except for the party scene." The campus cops would probably agree. A spokesman for the university police department told the *Daily Campus*, "Alcohol fuels much of the crime at UConn, especially property damage in dorms, intimidation, simple assaults, and disorderly conduct." The university has recently become stricter in the enforcement of underage drinking laws, even going so far as converting one of the campus's most notoriously wild dormitories, known as "The Jungle," into an alcohol-free residence. One UConn official, quoted in the *Daily Campus,* said that students' "extreme drinking . . . has an incredibly negative effect on the quality of campus life." Statistics show that the number of alcohol-related arrests has declined in recent years, but the university police chief says that student alcohol use has increased—the lower number of arrests simply reflects the thinning of police resources.

Police were distracted in 2003 by three UConn undergrads who staged a fake kidnapping, alarming passersby by leaving one of their friends blindfolded and bound in a car, shouting "They're going to kill me! They're going to kill me!" The *Chronicle of Higher Education* reported that when the students were arrested, they claimed they'd been conducting a "psychological experiment." Since they were laughing hysterically as they ran from the scene, the scientific usefulness of the study seems doubtful. "Nothing in our courses would allow or encourage this sort of thing," a UConn psychology professor told the *Chronicle*. "My guess is that it was a jackass-type prank."

Real violent crimes are comparatively rare. The latest statistics (2003) show 11 forcible sex offenses, seven robberies, five aggravated assaults, 108 burglaries, six stolen cars, and six arsons. Although one in every three students says he has personally witnessed a crime on campus, most students (probably the other two-thirds) say they feel safe. To prevent crime on campus, the university runs several safety programs. All exterior residence hall doors are locked at night, usually at 10 p.m., and can only be opened by students. Connecticut also provides a walking escort service until 3 a.m. and a shuttle service until 12:30 a.m.

UConn is a real bargain for in-state students at only $5,720 tuition; outsiders pay $17,448. Both also pay fees of $1,714, and room and board of $7,300. Admissions are need-blind, and the school guarantees to meet the need of students who get in. More than 70 percent of students receive some form of financial aid.

DARTMOUTH COLLEGE

HANOVER, NEW HAMPSHIRE • WWW.DARTMOUTH.EDU

Being charitable

Dartmouth College was founded in 1754 as More's Indian Charity School by the Reverend Eleazar Wheelock. Its original mission was to educate Native American youth along with English children for the ministry. The school was later renamed for William Legge, the Earl of Dartmouth, who financially supported the school.

As one of the "ancient eight" institutions in the Ivy League, Dartmouth has a rich and prestigious history of overcoming severe obstacles. Wheelock had great difficulty finding initial resources and a charter. Later, in 1819, the college narrowly escaped a state takeover. Its decision to admit women and expand in 1975 proved to be a difficult adjustment for the school and generated some lingering hard feelings—as have the administration's attempts to impose political correctness on a traditionally conservative New England college.

Traditions run deep at Dartmouth, and those who studied here have a strong allegiance to them. This leads many alumni to assist conservative undergraduates who resent the administration's efforts to reshape Dartmouth—for instance, by persecuting the fraternities while supporting women's studies and gay programs, suppressing the long-abolished mascot (an Indian, like the school's first students), and de-emphasizing the football program. Their complaints are familiar—and for good reason. This school was the first to spawn its own conservative newspaper, the *Dartmouth Review*, whose founders went public with their criticism of the school's policies—inspiring like-minded students and alums at dozens of other colleges.

But despite the administration's misplaced priorities, Dartmouth remains an institution beloved by its students and alumni, known for its rowdy Greek social life and close interaction between world-class faculty and students.

NEW ENGLAND

69

Academic Life: Parental guidance suggested

Dartmouth uses a unique academic schedule called the D-Plan (Dartmouth Plan), a quarter-term calendar of 10 weeks per term originally implemented when the school went coed to allow for the most efficient use of its resources. Students customize the plan to their own needs and schedules, spending their terms on campus, off campus in Dartmouth programs abroad or at other institutions, or on vacation. If it does nothing else, the plan enables students to travel abroad extensively. Indeed, 62 percent of Dartmouth's undergraduates study abroad during their time at the college, making it number one nationally for study abroad, according to the Institute for International Education. The D-Plan also gives students the chance to travel within the United States via popular programs in Washington, D.C., and throughout the American West. Sophomores attend "sophomore summer" at the college—a rollicking 10 weeks of New England beauty and strong class bonding. The terms that students then take off because of summer attendance ensure that Dartmouth students have a leg up on their competition for internships in the off season. Despite all its benefits, some students complain that the D-Plan also forces them away from the college and friends they love.

The college offers 38 traditional majors, as well as interdisciplinary majors in African and African American studies, environmental studies, Native American studies, and women's studies. Students may also choose to work toward a double major or to create their own fields of study.

The distribution requirements leave students a great deal of flexibility—more than what might be prudent for some students. According to one junior, some students "manipulate their course selections to boost GPAs." Compounding the problem is that courses that should be mandatory are placed alongside others of marginal importance. For example, a student can fulfill a Social Analysis requirement with either "Roman History: The Republic" or "Roots of Feminism: Texts and Contexts." The course description for the latter describes the content as a survey of writings that are deemed misogynist and a review of the ways in which women resisted. The readings focus on various characters to round out the analysis, including a sixteenth-century Spanish cross-dresser and an anarchist. More traditional subject matter is still taught at Dartmouth, and taught very well by distinguished scholars. You just have to seek them out.

However, those courses are not always graded accurately. According to a 2003 report by the American Council of Trustees and Alumni, Dartmouth is one of the elite schools suffering from grade inflation. The group warns that colleges across the board are lowering standards and devaluing the worth of an education. Dartmouth in particular has seen its average GPA go from 2.2 in 1958 to 3.3 in 2001, even as distribution requirements have slackened.

Students aren't required to seek guidance in choosing courses, even though the flexible requirements would seem to make it a necessity. The college assigns advisors to freshmen, and students may choose new major-specific professors to advise them later. "Many students seek informal advising from various professors and peers," a student says. But another student says, "The interaction between accomplished professors and undergraduates at Dartmouth is unmatched by any of its peer institutions."

Many students also use the online Student Assembly Professor/Course Review to help select courses. This tool allows students to anonymously comment on, and rate their experiences in, specific courses and professors. The site, which one student says offers "some of the best course advice," allows students to review each course they've taken. Students should take the ratings with a grain of salt; some professors' scores are (at least partly) influenced by the grades they give out. More help comes from the *Dartmouth Review*, which offers candid, sometimes biting assessments. (Most of the 4,000 students read the paper and more than 10,000 alumni subscribe.) The *Review* publishes and distributes a "freshman issue" that includes articles on "worst and best professors" and "courses of note."

The most traditional and rigorous departments at Dartmouth, according to students and professors, are classics, economics, history, and religion. Students majoring in these areas will graduate with a thorough understanding of their discipline if they resist the temptation to cut corners and opt instead for classes with heft.

Departments considered highly politicized and academically weak include English, Latin American studies, and women's and gender studies. English majors must pass courses from required periods and regions, but they can also graduate without reading any Shakespeare or Milton. The women's and gender studies department is full of courses like "Here and Queer: Placing Sexuality" and "Animals and Women in Western Literature: Nags, Bitches, and Shrews."

Among the many excellent professors at Dartmouth are Edward M. Bradley and William C. Scott in classics; Shakespeare scholar Peter Saccio, Jeffery Hart (emeritus), and Barbara Will in English; John Rassias in French (in fact, all foreign language classes at Dartmouth use the now-famous Rassias method); Allan Koop, David Lagomarsino, and Michael Mastanduno in history; Colin Calloway in history and Native American studies; Ehud Benor and Charles H. Stinson in religion; and Jim A. Kuypers in speech.

The Ernest Martin Hopkins Institute, an official alumni organization, seeks to preserve traditional study at Dartmouth and functions as a watchdog for the more ridiculous attempts of the school to regiment student life. It works with likeminded student organizations to bring speakers to campus and also provides some scholarships. "Dartmouth students are no longer required to read Shakespeare, Dante, Plato, or even to know the basic facts of American history," says one alumnus associated with

VITAL STATISTICS
Religious affiliation: none
Total enrollment: 5,704
Total undergraduates: 4,079
SAT/ACT midranges: SAT V: 670–770, M: 690–780; ACT: 28–34
Applicants: 11,734
Applicants accepted: 19%
Accepted applicants who enrolled: 50%
Tuition: $30,279
Room and board: $9,124
Freshman retention rate: 98%
Graduation rate: 86% (4 yrs.), 95% (6 yrs.)
Courses with fewer than 20 students: 60%
Student-faculty ratio: 9:1
Courses taught by graduate TAs: none
Most popular majors: social sciences, history, biology
Students living on campus: 83%
Guaranteed housing for four years? no
Students in fraternities: 40% sororities: 34%

71

Dartmouth has no core curriculum. Students must satisfy a set of general education requirements. Students must pass:

- An English composition course in their freshman year (unless AP scores exempt them) and one of more than 70 first-year writing seminars offered by various departments. Choices here range from "Medieval Manuscript Illumination" to "Beatniks, Hot Rods, and The Feminine Mystique."
- One course each on European, North American, and non-Western cultures.
- Three semesters of a foreign language, or otherwise demonstrate proficiency.

  Each student must pass ten other courses, as follows:
- One in the arts. Choices here range from "Gothic Art and Architecture" to "Gender, Race and Politics in Eighteenth-Century Visual Culture."
- One in literature. Options include "The English Renaissance" and "Danger: Primates at Work."
- One in philosophical or historical analysis or religion. This could be fulfilled with "Ancient Philosophy" or "Feminism and Philosophy";

the group. "The school isn't easily influenced by outside groups, but the speaker's program has been very successful."

Professors' accessibility is uniformly and enthusiastically praised by students. With the popular Take Your Professor to Lunch program, students and professors use vouchers to enjoy a free lunch together at a local inn. Student-professor communication is also carried on through e-mail, especially in large classes. Professors, not teaching assistants, teach all courses—a major benefit which should not be taken for granted; it isn't true at every Ivy.

Student Life: Sheepskin vs. pigskin

Dartmouth lies in the New Hampshire town of Hanover, located in the upper valley of the Connecticut River. The 200-acre campus, surrounded by woodland and mountains, offers students a beautiful setting for study. Philadelphia and La Guardia can be reached by smaller planes from the Hanover/Lebanon airport. Concord, New Hampshire, is about an hour away by car, and Boston is a two-hour drive.

Dartmouth has male, female, and coed leagues for 17 club and 24 intramural sports. Dartmouth also fields 34 NCAA Division I intercollegiate teams. Opportunities for outdoor recreation, especially of the winter variety, abound near campus. The Moosilauke Ravine Lodge offers accommodations and more than 30 miles of trails for hiking or skiing. The Dartmouth Skiway and the Silver Fox Ski Touring Center host skating and skiing, the Hanover Country Club has excellent golf facilities, and students can ride horses at the Morton Farm Riding Center. The Dartmouth Programs Office makes canoeing, riding, skiing, and gardening available to students, and the venerable Outing Club also has several affiliated organizations and clubs, including the Ledyard Canoe Club, Bait & Bullet, Boots & Saddles, Cabin & Trail, Mountaineering Club, Women in the Wilderness, and Ski Patrol.

In the fall of 2004, the school's head football coach, John Lyons, was fired; poor performance was cited. In the wake of this event, a letter was made public which was written by Karl Furstenberg, dean of admissions and financial aid at Dartmouth, to the president of Swarthmore College in 2000. At the time the letter was written, Swarthmore had just eliminated its football program. Furstenberg wrote to express his support and his wish that the same thing would happen at Dartmouth. He asserted that football undermined the academic quality and diversity of entering first-year classes, calling football programs "a national problem" to which he was happy to see Swarthmore taking the lead on a "solution." Happily, Furstenberg doesn't seem to have taken concrete steps to advance his vision.

On the other hand, it's not hard to notice the Dartmouth administration's ministries on behalf of the god called diversity. A writer for the *Review* covered the 10-day-long orientation program for the class of 2008 and revealed that during a mandatory session students were required to stand and recite the Pledge of Allegiance to the rainbow gay pride flag. One student who works in the official school organization that distributes student activity money complains to us that the kinds of events student activity fees help fund are downright discouraging. Two weeks after a front-page articlein the *New York Times* (in November 2002) applauded the school for the millions it was spending on diversity training, the administration had to eliminate the swim team. Then a major budget crunch ensued.

The long-flourishing Greek scene attracts more than a third of the college population to join one of 28 fraternity and sorority houses—despite the best efforts of the school to "henpeck them into submission through regulation," according to the *Review*. Under the auspices of Dartmouth president James Wright's ambitious (or nefarious, depending on one's perspective) Student Life Initiative, Greek houses were folded into the school's formal organization. This requires the houses to adhere to diversity requirements and enables the school to keep a tight rein on all alcohol-related activity. Despite this pressure, the groups are not without their victories. In April 2004, a dean announced that a previously imposed increase in age for new members would be softened. The new rush period was moved forward to the fifth week of the sophomore year (from winter term of the sophomore year). The dean announced that "the war is over" between the Greeks and the school. We think at best that this marks a truce.

A review of the student newspapers reveals a litany of complaints about the school's attempts to turn the campus into a politically correct playroom. The annual Bonfire event has not been com-

REQUIREMENTS (CONT'D)

"America's Founders and the World They Made" or "Historical Materialism: The Marxist Theory of the Past"; "Reason and Religious Belief" or "Beyond God the Father: An Introduction to Gender and Religion."

- One in international or comparative study. Options range from "Introduction to Chinese Culture" to "Gender Politics in Latin America."
- Two in social analysis. Choices include "International Trade" and "From Pole to Pole: An Introduction to the Earth's Cold Regions."
- One in quantitative and deductive sciences. Options include "Calculus with Algebra" and "Logic and Language."
- Two in the natural sciences. Choices include "History of Modern Biology" and "Understanding the Universe."
- One in technology or applied science. Options range from "Principles of Human Brain Mapping with fMRI" to "The Technology of Sailing."
- One of the courses in the natural science or technology categories must have a laboratory, field, or experimental component.

NEW ENGLAND

pletely eliminated, but it's now "bring your own binoculars" since the students aren't allowed anywhere near the fire. Students note that the school tries to compete with the Greek parties by throwing lavish-but-dry parties—which few attend.

In December 2003, Dartmouth Alumni for Open Governance, an alumni organization that often finds itself at odds with the current administration, rallied support against a major constitutional change at the college that would have eroded alumni influence. As Student Assembly members protested this power grab by the administration, alumni streamed in to cast their votes on the proposed amendments. The proposed changes, which required a three-fourths majority to gain approval, lost by a razor-thin margin. "To give some sense of the dramatics, when the vote tally was announced, you could have heard a pin drop," said a key organizer of the opposition. "There was stunned silence. [The administration] never imagined they would lose." The battle for Dartmouth's soul continues.

One trustee who was elected to Dartmouth's board after a populist uprising by disgruntled alumni told the *Review* that he thought the greatest problem facing the school was "the degradation of freedom of speech and the freedom of assembly. . . . To me, any time that you lose the ability to be with whom you want, or to say what you want, then other bad things can happen. They happen by edict in the dead of night; they happen without announcement. You're in a precarious state when the freedom of speech is not robust."

Dartmouth sustains a lively political feud. Vocal conservatives have had some success in publicizing the gradual encroachment of political correctness into the college's academic and student life. The *Review*, with its constant calls for free speech, plays a large part in bringing unsavory issues to light, and the school administration does not always appreciate the favor. Some history of the administration's attempts to stifle the paper can be found in Charles Sykes's *The Hollow Men: Politics and Corruption in Higher Education* and Benjamin Hart's *Poisoned Ivy*. Reporters from the *Review* have been arrested, suspended (this was later overruled), denied public records, and even bitten by an angry professor. Then, too, the paper has occasionally published juvenile, genuinely offensive things. Still, the *Review* has had a positive impact on the campus as a strident conservative voice and appears to be resurgent after a short period of decline. In fact, the demand for conservative news must be increasing; in late 2004, rival journalists started the *Dartmouth Beacon,* billing it as the "compassionate conservative" voice on campus.

The Young Democrats and the College Republicans are both active, and the Green Party has recently become strong as well. New Hampshire's first-in-the-nation primary status gives Dartmouth students unprecedented access to aspiring presidential nominees. The 2004 election cycle brought Howard Dean, Wesley Clark, Joe Lieberman, and other hopefuls to speak and meet with students on campus. Other student-operated papers include the far-left *Dartmouth Free Press* and the *Dartmouth* (the official school newspaper).

One *Dartmouth Review* contributor recounts a sociology professor telling his class that even his young children "know who the enemy is": the Republican Party. A government professor's syllabus includes a list of terms students should know, such as, "Left—favoring a greater degree of equality (social, economic, political). Right—favoring a greater degree of inequality, believing that a select few should have power based on birth or merit." One religion professor even sent an e-mail to her students and fellow professors urging them to add their names to an antiwar petition. (We would think this an inappropriate use of student information regardless of the cause.) And in 2003, the Spanish and Portuguese department joined the sociology department to subsidize a student trip to an antiwar protest with department funds.

Traditional residence halls and smaller social houses make up the 41 residences that are home to almost 4,100 undergraduates. Nearly a third of the rooms are singles, most of which are assigned to upperclassmen, and many of the rooms have private or semiprivate bathrooms. There are a few single-sex floors but no single-sex dorms. Around 400 upperclassmen live in college-owned and affiliated coed, fraternity, sorority, and undergraduate society houses. Substance-free housing is also available to students who don't wish to be exposed to drinking or smoking. In addition, there are houses called, inexplicably, "academic affinity programs," which include both the offices of ethnic clubs and societies and theme houses for minority students. There isn't much about the membership criteria that meets the "academic" part of the title: Cutter/Shabazz is the African American house, La Casa houses interested Hispanic students, and a Native American house is also offered.

Dozens of independent student organizations round out campus life: the Afro-American Society, the Dartmouth Rainbow Alliance, and La Alianza Latina, among many others. Some, such as the Dartmouth Coalition for Life, Students for Choice, and Animal Advocacy are only sporadically active. More than 20 percent of Dartmouth students volunteer through the Tucker Foundation for community service. Religious groups abound; more than 25 are represented in the directory. The Aquinas House offers a daily mass, the Muslim prayer room in Rollins holds daily prayers, and various Jewish groups sponsor services. There is an active evangelical Alpha Omega student group, and the Society of Friends has weekly meetings and monthly speakers.

The Collis Center is a popular hangout for food, beverages, and billiards. Both the Programming Board and the Hopkins Center bring live entertainment to campus. But when students free themselves from coursework they usually socialize in the dorms or social houses. One student claims that "'pong' is the most popular social activity on campus," referring to a drinking game that involves tossing ping-pong balls into cups of beer, which must then be consumed.

SUGGESTED CORE

1. Classical Studies 5, The Heroic Vision: Epics of Greece and Rome
2. Philosophy 11, Introduction to Ancient Philosophy
3. Religion 4/5, The Hebrew Bible / The New Testament
4. Religion 15, The Christian Tradition *or* History 43, European Intellectual and Cultural History, 400–1300
5. Government 64, Modern Political Theory
6. English 24, Shakespeare I
7. History 1, U.S. History 1763–1877 *or* History 20, American Thought and Culture to 1865
8. History 51, Eighteenth- and Nineteenth-Century European Intellectual History

NEW ENGLAND

Student interest groups are especially strong in the performing arts and debate. Radio fans, too, find much to engage them at Dartmouth: WDCR and its sister station, WFRD, are the only completely student-run commercial broadcast stations in the United States. More than 100 students carry out their operation, and the stations feature both rock music and political debate and discourse from across the spectrum.

The campus is very safe, according to students and official records. Crime reports from 2003 reveal seven forcible sex offenses (up from two in 2002), one robbery, and 36 burglaries. The campus includes 25 emergency phones, constant patrol by 30 full-time security officers, car and bike patrols, and 10 night security guards.

Dartmouth is an expensive but generous school. Tuition last year came in at $30,279, while room and board was $9,124. Admissions are need-blind, and the college guarantees to meet the full need of accepted students. Some 60 percent of a recently admitted class qualified for at least partial assistance.

HARVARD UNIVERSITY

CAMBRIDGE, MASSACHUSETTS • WWW.HARVARD.EDU

First

You've probably heard of this one. Harvard University was founded by Protestant divines in 1636, and it is the oldest university in the United States (though not in North America—Spaniards founded the College of Santa Cruz in Tlaltelolco, Mexico, in 1534). Harvard has gone through many permutations, and its evolution continues. As the Congregationalism of its founders waned into Unitarianism, then Transcendentalism, Harvard ceased to be a center of theology but remained America's intellectual touchstone and the training ground for her ruling elite. Graduates of the school still emerge with a sense that they have been anointed for national leadership. Opinions differ, of course, about the direction in which they're leading.

One of Harvard's "golden ages" took place from 1953 to 1971 under President Nathan Marsh Pusey. He raised the curricular standards, increased the number of undergraduates, tripled the size of the faculty, and accepted excellent students from public schools. This broadened the social base of the university, admitting an influx of achievement-oriented Jewish and other "ethnic" students to what had long been a preserve of Protestant New England Americanism. Pusey also hired the Divinity School's first Catholic professor. As Brian Domitrovic has noted in *Modern Age,* "Pusey's Harvard was the school's first real era of meritocracy."

Pusey left behind a school that in every way deserved the eminent reputation it had achieved. In most ways, the school still does. However, subsequent administrations have set about dismantling the edifice Pusey built, including Harvard's impressive core curriculum, and have remade Harvard as the model of the modern research university—afflicted by specialization, premature professionalism, and political correctness. Indeed, it was Harvard's abandonment of broad-based liberal education that set the trend followed by almost every major university in the country.

Nevertheless, with a massive ($22.1 *billion*) endowment, unmatched library facilities, a faculty which consists of the cream skimmed off the best universities in the world, and students who have survived a highly selective admissions process, Harvard will remain a powerhouse of intellectual life for the foreseeable future—despite its destructive love affair with leftist politics, curricular laxity, and the anti-Western cult of "diversity."

Harvard inaugurated former Clinton treasury secretary Lawrence Summers as its president in July 2001. On several occasions, Summers has displayed significant political courage, rectifying some of the excesses of leftism on campus. He has confronted questionable faculty members and given a cautious welcome to long-banished ROTC programs. In 2005, he ignited a firestorm among feminists by offering, during a seminar, the opinion that male/female cognitive differences might be innate—and might partly account for masculine predominance in the "hard" sciences. One female professor, overcome with emotion, stormed out of the meeting. Instead of standing firm for freedom of inquiry, Summers spent the next several weeks apologizing to any women who would listen, setting up panels and commissions to placate enraged feminists, and warmly denying that any differences among people—including those relating to sex—could possibly, *possibly* have any relationship to their genetic differences. His critics, having tasted blood, seem unlikely to relent, and Summers's future at Harvard is in doubt. Perhaps he should have sent Godiva.

Academic Life: Genius observed

One Harvard professor says, wryly: "Of course we have a core curriculum. It contains over 350 courses!" Actually, Harvard's core consists of a modest set of distribution requirements directing students to mostly excellent courses—many of which, however, are rather narrow and specialized. As a result, "Harvard provides absolutely no guarantee

VITAL STATISTICS
Religious affiliation: none
Total enrollment: 19,731
Total undergraduates: 6,562
SAT/ACT midranges: SAT: 1400–1590; ACT: 30–34
Applicants: 19,605
Applicants accepted: 10%
Accepted applicants who enrolled: 79%
Tuition: $30,620
Room and board: $8,868
Freshman retention rate: 96%
Graduation rate: 83% (4 yrs.), 92% (6 yrs.)
Average class size: 17
Student-faculty ratio: 8:1
Courses taught by graduate TAs: not provided
Most popular majors: economics, political science, psychology
Students living on campus: 96%
Guaranteed housing for four years? yes
Students in fraternities or sororities: none

The Harvard "core" curriculum will soon change, but students arriving at Harvard College in 2006 will still face the old system, which features the requirements below. In most cases, more than a dozen choices are available with which to mark each checkbox. Students need not take survey courses introducing a discipline or imparting general knowledge, but can take narrow classes focused on special topics. They need to take:

- One course in foreign cultures. Choices run from "Sources of Indian Civilization" to "Nazi Cinema."
- Two courses in historical studies. Choices range from "Reason and Faith in the West" to "Gendered Communities: Women, Islam, and Nationalism."
- One course in literature. Options include everything from "Classics in Christian Literature" to "American Protest Literature from Tom Paine to Tupac."

that a student will emerge with a broad liberal education," says a student. "You can get away without learning a scrap of European or U.S. history." That said, the Harvard catalog "is an astonishing document," says one graduate. "I don't know if any university in the world offers such an amazing array of courses on everything under the sun, most of them taught by serious, often outstanding scholars."

Guiding the current system, explains a student, is "the theory that learning about 'how to do history' is somehow more valuable than, say, learning about actual events—and it has created a student body filled with people who know *neither* how historians think, nor what they think about." This is not entirely Harvard's fault; the school expects too much of its students, assuming that they have had an adequate high school education and that therefore survey courses giving the raw outlines of American history, English literature, or political science would be superfluous. This might have been true 40 years ago. It no longer is. One student recommends that beginning students at Harvard take the initiative to read broad survey texts on their own (such as, excuse the plug, ISI's own Student Guides to the Major Disciplines).

It may be good news, then, that Harvard has decided to dismantle its current, unsatisfactory core and craft a new one—which will not be finished and in place until at least 2007, sources say. But we're not so sure an improvement is in the offing. The preliminary report issued by the faculty committee is not encouraging. It states:

> [W]e seek to broaden the scope of a liberal education and to expand choices for Harvard College students, crafting an undergraduate curriculum that is defined less by the requirements that it places on students and more by the commitments that the Faculty makes to undergraduate education in the liberal tradition.

The document goes on to speak of "greater freedom of choice" for students, tempered mostly by the suggestions of faculty advisors. To replace the current core classes, the report suggests developing a set of "Harvard College Courses." For instance,

> A Harvard College Course on world histories might be built around 'cultures and contacts,' introducing students to significant moments,

from multiple centuries and continents, in which civilizations interacted in cooperative or competitive ways; it might introduce students to episodes of international trade, war, conquest, and international organization. A world literature course might look at cultural representation in different places and periods, and cultural flows across traditional national boundaries and among hierarchies of culture. A social science course could focus on poverty, bringing together historical, political, sociological, economic, public health, and normative perspectives.

Not promising.

Spurred by internal critics, Harvard president Summers has acknowledged that the school has a problem with grade inflation. This phenomenon is especially rampant in the humanities and social sciences—whereas "disciplines like economics and physics are places where the professoriate still believes in the value of concepts like 'truth,' and so are more likely to apply strict standards," a student says. Another undergrad complains that Harvard's reputation for inflated grades "just hurts people who choose to take hard classes. Students inflate their grades by the choice of classes." However, one teacher says, "In the five years I've taught here, I've never had someone breathing down my neck about a low grade I've assigned a student, and if they did, I would defend my decision. If senior professors cannot do that, I wonder why they are senior professors. I honestly haven't encountered this problem in my work here."

Upon entering the university, each student is assigned a freshman-year advisor—a faculty member, university administrator, or graduate student—who helps the student choose courses and eventually declare a concentration. Later on, the student is assigned a concentration advisor (a faculty member or graduate student). "Advising is as varied as the advisors," says one student. "Most undergrads find that graduate student advisors know more than the faculty advisors, but it's very dependent on the person." One student called her interaction with advisors "an extremely strengthening experience. Once I started talking to professors and concentration advisors, I found doors to many hitherto unknown opportunities and resources opening in front of me. I think seeking out help and solving problems on your own is how you come to mature at Harvard. It's a very, very rewarding lesson in independence and initiative."

REQUIREMENTS(CONT'D)

- One course in fine arts, where the options include "The Gothic Cathedral" and "Sayin' Something: Jazz as Sound, Sensibility, and Social Dialogue."
- One course in cultural criticism, ranging from "Concepts of the Hero in Greek Civilization" to "The German Colonial Imagination."
- One in moral reasoning, with choices such as "If There Is No God, All Is Permitted" and "Slavery in Western Political Thought."
- One class in quantitative reasoning. Options range from "Deductive Logic" to "Medical Detectives."
- Two science courses, such as "The Einstein Revolution" or "Energy, Environment, and Industrial Development."
- One course in social analysis, such as "Principles of Economics" or "Psychological Trauma."
- One year of foreign language study.

Graduate teaching assistants (called "teaching fellows") have a lot of interaction with undergraduates—more than many faculty do. A history major says he finds Harvard professors to be generally inaccessible unless one is determined to track them down. "Professors here must publish to keep their jobs," he says, "but they will spend time with you if you are aggressive." TAs usually lead the weekly discussion sections that supplement lecture courses. "In certain classes, graduate students actually do most of the teaching," another student says.

Harvard undergrads are eager to praise challenging courses and professors. Student favorites include Lino Pertile in romance languages and literature; Robert Levin in music; Daniel Albright, Daniel Donoghue, Robert Kiely, and Louis Menand in English; James McCarthy in earth and planetary sciences; Thomas Scanlon in philosophy; Jon Levenson of the Divinity School; Peter Hall, Stanley Hoffman, Samuel Huntington, Harvey Mansfield, Michael Sandel, and Steve Rosen in government; Robert J. Barro and Martin S. Feldstein in economics; and Ann Blair, James Hankins, Mark Kishlansky, Ernest May, and Stephan Thernstrom in history.

The leftward tilt of Harvard's faculty is partly balanced by the presence of several stellar thinkers in the center or on the right, who help "sober the academic discourse and attitudes on campus," in the words of a student. Of course, dozens more Harvard professors are stars in their fields, and for that reason are worth seeking out—although some are better teachers than others.

Graduates report that one of the finest departments at Harvard is government. One student says that "the closest thing Harvard gets to great books are the courses Government 1060 and 1061, which cover ancient and modern political philosophy and are typically taught by the eminent Harvey Mansfield." Said one student, "Even if you don't want to become a political theorist, it's the type of curriculum that could change your intellectual outlook for life." He also recommended the "Government Sophomore Tutorial" as "an excellent survey class on American political thought."

The social studies program presents "the history of social thought, from Hume and Adam Smith, through Weber to Foucault." One graduate calls this "a great books program of the left, with some exceptions such as Burke and Tocqueville." A professor says that social studies "indoctrinates the best of the students with multiculturalism." At least one student agrees, saying, "Major historical events are assumed to arise out of economic and social conditions. The independent role of ideas and philosophy in shaping history is underestimated."

One alumnus calls the classics department "ideologically obsessed and useless." But a current student says it is possible to avoid the politicized classes that apply "structuralism to Herodotus and Thucydides" in favor of the more rigorous composition courses. She notes that one professor teaches in the great Germanic tradition of philology, demanding of his students not just correct grammar but Ciceronian style. The department also offers—unlike most seminaries—a course in ecclesiastical Latin, and another in medieval/Byzantine Greek.

Harvard's music, history, physics, mathematics, earth and planetary sciences, and other science departments are among the world's finest. Virtually all students agree that Harvard's research facilities and other such resources are second to none, and that the university's biological science programs are as rigorous as any in existence. "Undergraduates have numerous opportunities to do cutting-edge research in the labs on both the medical campus and the School of Public Health campus," says a former biology instructor. "You can't take short cuts around research." Unfortunately, one of those areas of research now involves embryonic stem cells; in a widely publicized move, Harvard has decided to lavishly fund an institute devoted entirely to finding "therapeutic" uses for embryonic humans—whom ethically challenged researchers at Harvard and elsewhere hope to clone and use as spare parts for treating various diseases. However, there is some hope that the state of Massachusetts may step in and rein in the mad scientists of Cambridge.

Opportunities for study abroad abound at Harvard, which sends students to 10 countries in Africa, 16 in Latin America and the Caribbean, 12 in Asia, 20 in Europe, and three in the Middle East, as well as Australia and New Zealand.

It's better to get your multiculturalism abroad than in Cambridge, it seems. The religion and multicultural studies departments (e.g., African studies, women's studies), as well as social studies and language departments, are said to be heavily politicized. One senior professor says that "many departments, especially in the humanities, are very politicized. There are a number of egregiously bad courses." However, for a student with his ear to the ground, such classes are easy to avoid. Furthermore, conservative students report that they have benefited greatly from having to defend their beliefs in class—and none have reported classroom harassment or punitive grading. As one alum says, Harvard "retains a largeness of outlook that eclipses the more parochial liberalism of some people. Much of what I learned here, I would not have learned elsewhere. For that I am both grateful to and proud of my school. I don't think anyone should flinch from Harvard's so-called liberalism, because it might even turn him into a better conservative."

She continues: "The professors who have taught me and with whom I now work are some of the finest thinkers I've ever met. We don't necessarily agree about faith or politics, but in my opinion that makes our relationship even more fruitful—we learn from each other."

Student Life: Harvard men and women

Campus life is centered around Harvard Yard during the freshman year and a series of residential houses thereafter. Though students reside in same-sex suites, house floors

SUGGESTED CORE
1. Literature & Arts C-14, Concept of the Hero in Greek Civilization
2. Philosophy 101, Plato *or* Government 1060, History of Ancient and Medieval Political Philosophy
3. Religion 42, The Christian Bible and Its Interpretation
4. Religion 1434, History of Western Christianity, 300–1100 (*closest match*)
5. Government 1061, Modern Political Philosophy
6. English 120, Introduction to Shakespeare
7. History 71a, America: Colonial Times to the Civil War
8. History 1470a, European Intellectual History Part I

(but not bathrooms) can be coed. Each of Harvard's residences once had its own distinctive character—to the point where they resembled fraternity or special-interest houses—but students voted to change the system in the late 1980s. No longer, a graduate says, does "Eliot House exclude someone because he isn't on the lacrosse team, or North House choose only science majors." However, "the houses have still, by and large, maintained their respective interests and reputations; you just can't say that 'all the rich kids live in Adams' anymore," this graduate says.

Harvard students do not have a reputation for bacchanalian excess, but alcohol and drug use are far from unknown, in the houses and elsewhere. Most Harvard students are too ambitious to jeopardize their futures with reckless carousing.

Instead, many take to prayer. "A lot of students seem to become more religious at Harvard," one student says. "The Catholic Students Association runs a tight ship." Groups and support services exist for members of many creeds, of course. "There are active and vibrant Christian groups here and I've grown in my faith," says a Protestant student. A February 2004 *Boston Globe* article quotes Peter Gomes, the university's longest-serving Plummer Professor of Christian Morals, as saying, "there are probably more evangelicals [at Harvard] than at any time since the 17th century." On the other hand, Harvard graduate Ross Douthat, author of *Privilege: Harvard and the Education of the Ruling Class,* complained in the *Harvard Salient* that the appointment of homosexual clergy at Harvard's chapel "was intended to establish Mem Church as a place where those with orthodox religious views would not be welcomed. . . . Tolerance for gays, it is now clear, means intolerance for others, namely those who cling to what the administration obviously regards as outdated nonsense—the idea that not all sexual behavior is morally equivalent."

That doctrine is just one of the heterodox notions that Harvard makes its own and promotes to students. Undergraduates face a gamut of gender-neutral language requirements, sexual harassment policies, humorless affirmative action and sex tutorials, and sensitivity training sessions. Resident assistants organize meetings between incoming freshmen and "peer contraceptive counselors," who distribute condoms and dental dams and demonstrate their proper use. However, a student insists, "Harvard is certainly not a school distinguished by a high level of casual sexual activity. The condom dispersion and sex awareness lectures are quite strange and somewhat unnecessary. They only add to the already excessive pressure toward politically correct language and attitudes."

Some students also consider Harvard's affirmative action policies downright divisive. "It creates a definite tension," says one source. "If you're a designated 'minority,' you spend your years as an undergraduate trying to prove to everyone else that you were one of the kids who got in based on merit."

Students say the most active Harvard political groups include labor union and peace activists; gay/lesbian/transsexual organizations; a handful of pro-Palestinian groups; feminist clubs; and public service fraternities. The *Harvard Salient* is a smart, well-edited alternative paper that takes staunch socially conservative positions. Some say that public advocacy of traditionalist ideas is a quick ticket to social isolation. But one undergrad insists that "between student and student, one still can still discuss controversies with an open mind. Yes, I've met people who, against the rules of the university, tore down the pro-life posters I put up, but I was also fortunate to have had generous roommates who, in spite of their professed liberalism, handed me those posters intact. I think students value people more than any political ideology."

In February 2004, a Harvard faculty committee approved plans for a student magazine called *H Bomb,* which is now in business, featuring windy sex advice and naked undergrads—and others in uncomfortable-looking leather outfits—along with the usual agitprop about tolerance, lifestyle diversity, and condoms. The magazine— described rather gleefully by the student newspaper as a "porn magazine"—receives funding from the student government.

Harvard caters to nearly as many extracurricular as intellectual interests—and does so with a distinctive style. As one student says, "I'm not inclined to think that any other school, let alone your average community college, offers quite the same élan as this place does." Harvard University athletics, intramurals, newspapers, and literary societies offer an unmatched variety of creative outlets and comfortable niches for students seeking a release from their studies. The most prestigious of these organizations are the *Harvard Crimson,* the justly famous *Harvard Lampoon,* Harvard's world-famous men's Glee Club, and the Hasty Pudding Club. "I sing madrigals, play sports, spend long hours in the dining hall," says one student. Other charming customs include fall foliage and apple-picking tours in the gorgeous New England countryside.

Harvard's football team hasn't won a national championship since 1919, but it and other varsity sports still attract the attention of the student body. The school fields 41 varsity teams, giving it the largest Division I program in the U.S, according to the university. Harvard has excellent facilities for recreational sports such as tennis, squash, and the like. There are numerous intramural teams, most of which are formed around the residential houses. The university's literature says that about two-thirds of the student body participates at some level in athletic activities.

Cambridge offers many entertainment and dining options, from pizza to excellent restaurants, and some fine booksellers—although bookstores have been closing under the pressure of high local rent. Harvard Square is a quirky, pseudo-bohemian hangout for all manner of people and activity, including almost continual chess matches, and Boston is one of the nation's last truly livable large cities, with a vibrant downtown comprising beautiful architecture and countless stores and shops.

Though Harvard's Cambridge campus is relatively safe, students should not forget that they live in a large city. Forcible sex offenses on campus have fallen from 25 incidents in 2002 to 16 in 2003. In the same year the school reported six aggravated assaults, six arsons, and a stunning 451 burglaries. Bicycles, wallets, and electronics— especially laptop computers—are the articles most frequently stolen.

Harvard's tuition matches its reputation. For 2004–5, it was $30,620, with room and board at $8,868. However, the school's aid program is one of the nation's most generous. Admission is need-blind, students are guaranteed all the aid they need, and, in a new initiative, families with incomes of less than $40,000 are no longer expected to

NEW ENGLAND

83

contribute to the cost of their child's education. Harvard has also reduced the contributions expected of families with incomes between $40,000 and $60,000.

COLLEGE OF THE HOLY CROSS

WORCESTER, MASSACHUSETTS • WWW.HOLYCROSS.EDU

Crossing the street

The Jesuit liberal arts College of the Holy Cross in Worcester, Massachusetts, founded in 1843, is the oldest Catholic college in New England. Originally all male, Holy Cross went coed in the 1970s. The college is committed to undergraduate teaching and has resisted the profitable temptation to spawn graduate and professional schools. However, Holy Cross has succumbed to other snares—mainly at the expense of its religious heritage. In his *Ex Corde Ecclesiae*, Pope John Paul II writes that a Catholic university is a "primary and privileged place for a fruitful dialogue between the Gospel and culture." Unfortunately, Holy Cross has followed those academic trends which have secularized and standardized so many religious schools—although significant pockets of both excellence and orthodoxy are to be found there.

Academic Life: Missing statement

Since St. Ignatius Loyola founded the Society of Jesus in the sixteenth century, a Jesuit education has had a certain cachet and hewed to certain principles. Holy Cross invokes these in its mission statement, where it promises "to exemplify the long-standing dedication of the Society of Jesus to the intellectual life and its commitment to the service of faith and promotion of justice." Jesuits have been praised even by their detractors for their rigorous liberal arts curricula, which paid special attention to philosophy, rhetoric, and theology. Not long ago, typical Jesuit colleges required all their undergraduates, regardless of major, to obtain a minor in philosophy. Sadly, the academic program at Holy Cross requires very little mandatory liberal arts coursework—especially in philosophy, language, and religion, the very courses that once distinguished a Jesuit education.

When Holy Cross president Michael McFarland, S.J., took charge in 2000, some expected him to strengthen the college's diluted distribution requirements or even to create an actual core curriculum. According to our sources, Holy Cross has not moved in that direction.

The aim of the college's distribution requirements is for students "to develop a reflective attitude with regard to different ways of knowing and the bodies of knowledge associated with them," according to the course catalog. But since students can choose from a number of courses to fulfill each of the distribution requirements, students may not be exposed to—much less master—a core body of knowledge. A student may satisfy his historical studies requirement by taking a course such as "Colonial Latin America"—and nothing else. "Only a knowledgeable and energetic student can get a true liberal arts education, and he has to work to find it," a student says. "Students get a random sampling of different areas, but few find any unity to what they learn."

When, several years ago, Holy Cross added a cross-cultural studies requirement and weakened its foreign language requirement, the school demonstrated the direction in which its curriculum was going. What better path into an unknown culture than through its language, which many consider the very house of culture? Cross-cultural study, on the other hand, often has political rather than pedagogical objectives. The catalog says that the requirement "provides an opportunity to understand more fully—and perhaps to transcend—one's own cultural presuppositions." Not such a bad idea, except that one can't transcend, in a single college course, what one does not know. And Holy Cross does not require that students engage the basic thinkers and texts of their own culture.

Furthermore, Holy Cross's distribution requirements include none that would necessarily acquaint students with the Jesuit tradition, Catholicism, or even Christianity. Holy Cross students may choose to study Islam, Buddhism, Hinduism, Confucianism, or Taoism instead. In sum, the liberal arts requirements at Holy Cross turn out to be little more than course suggestions, snacks instead of balanced meals. Some instructors at Holy Cross say distribution requirements have "tightened up," but admit that students would have been better served by a return to an authentic core curriculum.

Many Holy Cross students—20 percent—seek the structure that the school's regular curriculum lacks through the college's First-Year Program (FYP). The program is billed as "an exciting, innovative program for first-year students interested in exploring the connections between learning and living." Students in the program enroll in a year-long seminar in addition to their three regular college courses and live together in one dorm, where they attend special discussions and other cocurricular events. The FYP courses are shaped around a question and a set of common readings. For the 2004–5

VITAL STATISTICS
Religious affiliation: Roman Catholic
Total enrollment: 2,745
Total undergraduates: 2,745
SAT midranges: V: 580–670, M: 580–680
Applicants: 4,969
Applicants accepted: 44%
Accepted applicants who enrolled: 32%
Tuition: $29,220
Room and board: $8,860
Freshman retention rate: 93%
Graduation rate: 86% (4 yrs.), 90% (6 yrs.)
Courses with fewer than 20 students: 52%
Student-faculty ratio: 11:1
Courses taught by graduate TAs: none
Most popular majors: social sciences, psychology, English
Students living on campus: 88%
Guaranteed housing for four years? yes
Students in fraternities or sororities: none

While Holy Cross has no core curriculum, students do face certain distribution requirements. Students must take one class each in

- Fine arts. Options range from "Survey of Art: Renaissance to Modern Art" to "Music of Bali-Gamelan."
- Literature. Course choices are extensive, including everything from "Cicero's Philosophical Works" to "Introduction to Postcolonial Theory."
- Religious studies. Choices range from "Reformation and Counter Reformation" to "Feminist Perspectives in Theology."
- Philosophical studies. Options include "Medieval Philosophy" and "Ethics and the Natural World."
- Historical studies. Any place or period will do, ranging from "The Rise of the Christian West to A.D. 1000" to "Latino History."

academic year, the theme was: "Confronted by suffering, how then shall we live?" The reading list included six works, both classic and contemporary works of nonfiction and fiction. Studied were the book of Job, *Journal of the Plague Year* by Daniel Defoe, and Tolstoy's *The Death of Ivan Illych*. The contemporary works included a Holocaust survivor memoir; *Wit*, a play about cancer; and the classic antiwar novel, *All Quiet on the Western Front*.

The Honors Program is another bright spot at Holy Cross. In this intellectually serious program, students explore themes in small classes of six to 12 undergraduates. Sophomores begin by taking a team-taught course on "human nature"; throughout the semester, a number of professors teach on various aspects of that theme in the sciences, social sciences, humanities, and the arts. As juniors, students select another honors-level seminar (past topics have included "Music and Literature," "Reason and Faith," "Human Rights, Citizenship, and Democracy," and "The Berlin Wall"). Every senior writes a thesis, and the results of the research are published in-house and presented in a conference at the end of the year. Qualified students are selected for the program in their second year at the college, and admission is limited to 36 entrants from each class. According to Holy Cross, the program will appeal to students who "seek an especially challenging multidisciplinary experience."

The college's list of programs includes a mix of the trendy and the traditional. The Center for Interdisciplinary and Special Studies, "which seeks to be a catalyst for innovation and experimentation in the curriculum," offers students "experimental" degrees in such disciplines as women's studies, peace and conflict studies, environmental studies, and Africana studies. Courses include "The Tomahawk and the Cross: Peace and Conflict in Indian America," "Black Political and Social Thought," "Balinese Dance," "Theology of Homosexuality," "Deaf Literature," and "Queer Theory." The center allows students to participate in academic internships in the Washington, D.C., area. Refreshingly, the internships have often proved to be academically legitimate and rigorous, according to one professor; a senior says "this was probably my favorite experience at the Cross." One may obtain an "aging internship" through the gerontology studies program, or take a semester abroad, for example. Students can also create their own courses of study.

In the Multidisciplinary Studies Program, the catalog says students "may design their minor from scratch," or they may use a faculty-designed template as a basis for their coursework. Recent examples have included "Africana Studies," "Film Making," "Environmental Studies," and "Middle Eastern Studies."

The Holy Cross classics program is often ranked as one of the largest and most active in the country. As one professor says, "students fall in love with the classics." A major calls the department "first rate." The classics department even hosts a chariot race on campus each year for local high school students. Enhancing the study of the ancients is a very modern study program called the Perseus Project, a digital library focusing primarily on ancient Greece, of which students may avail themselves in the college's new St. Isidore of Seville Computer Lab. The best professors in the department include John D. B. Hamilton, Thomas R. Martin, Blaise Nagy, and William J. Ziobro. Over the years, the political science department has distinguished itself as one of the finest in the country, taking a serious and traditional approach to the discipline. Majors must take introductory courses in the following areas: American government, political philosophy, comparative politics, and international relations, in addition to at least six upper-division courses in specific areas. The department boasts a number of outstanding faculty, including Donald R. Brand, Loren R. Cass, Caren G. Dubnoff, Daniel Klinghard, Stephen Kocs, Vickie Langlohr, B. Jeffrey Reno, David L. Schaefer, Denise Schaeffer, and Ward J. Thomas. In other departments, students and faculty name the following as excellent teachers: Frederick J. Murphy in religious studies; Jeffrey Bernstein, Jeffrey Bloechl, Lawrence E. Cahoone, Christopher A. Dustin, and Joseph P. Lawrence in philosophy; Robert K. Cording, James M. Kee, and Lee Oser in English; Nicholas Sanchez and David Schap in economics; Noel Cary in history; Jessica Waldoff in music; Virginia Raguin in visual arts; and John F. Axelson, Mark Freeman, Charles M. Locurto, and Amy Wolfson in psychology.

Students say that classes in many departments are taught with a political bent, usually from the left. However, says one, "my professors respect my views so long as I back them up." Students are encouraged to organize panel debates. The most recent was a faculty-student debate surrounding the documentary *Fahrenheit 9/11*. While the most politicized department is sociology, the history, religious studies, and English departments also offer a slate of courses taught from a leftist perspective. Of the English department, a professor says that "while it has a few very strong faculty, it has unfortunately tended to replace teachers who were devoted to literary classics with others who are interested in race/class/gender." The religious studies department of-

REQUIREMENTS (CONT'D)

- Cross-cultural studies. Options range from "East Asian Development" to "Slaves, Peasants, Farmers in Central American and the Caribbean."

Students must take two courses each in

- Social sciences. Choices include "Economic History of the United States" and "Drugs of Abuse."
- Natural sciences. Options here include "Atoms and Molecules" and "General Physics in Daily Life."
- Mathematics. Choices range from "Probability and Statistics" to "Topics in Mathematics."

While the curriculum once required students to become proficient in both a classical and modern language, today that requirement has been changed to two courses in any foreign language.

fers such courses as "Theology and Ecology," "Feminist Perspectives in Theology," "Latin American Liberation Theology," and "North American Theologies of Liberation," in which, according to the catalog, there will be "special attention given to black, U.S. Hispanic, and gay/lesbian theological works."

Faculty advisors meet with students at the beginning of each semester to help them select courses, although many students end up just visiting their advisors to have them sign off on their course lists. The advisors are readily accessible, however, to students who seek further advice during the year. The school's premedical, law, and science advising programs are "very successful" at preparing students for entry into graduate schools, says one professor.

Student Life: Worcester sauce

Worcester, Massachusetts, is a college town with more than 15 colleges, universities, and academic societies, including Assumption College, Clark University, and Worcester Polytechnic Institute. Holy Cross belongs to the Colleges of Worcester Consortium, an intercollegiate organization that allows students to take classes at member schools. With more than 36,000 college students in the area, Worcester is an appealing city. Students report that they generally enjoy the area because it offers plenty of cultural activities not always found in cities of its size. And if Worcester isn't happening enough, Boston is less than an hour away; New York City is a three-hour drive.

The College of the Holy Cross is located on a 174-acre wooded hill overlooking the city. The campus is divided into several quads with paths, manicured lawns, and walkways connecting the various groups of classical and modern buildings; there is a historic Jesuit cemetery and an arboretum. Students say the campus is pleasant and generally peaceful. Approximately 88 percent of the 2,700-member student body lives in the college's 10 residence halls, the availability of which is guaranteed for 4 years. Though the sexes are separated by floor, all dormitories are coed. Each room offers a high-speed Internet connection.

A professor observes about the students at the school, "Like most schools at its level, Holy Cross has a mix of some students genuinely motivated by intellectual curiosity and others just here for the fun and the degree. Certainly we have a significant number of intellectual, serious, motivated students. But there is a large party crowd as well."

Holy Cross undergrads have more than 100 student organizations, ranging from a ballroom dancing society to academic clubs like the Biology Society—and activist groups like the Allies, a homosexual and bisexual advocacy group that collected, to give to legislators, signatures on petitions supporting the 2003 same-sex marriage ruling by Massachusetts' highest court. The Allies' rainbow stickers are posted throughout the campus as signs of support for the group.

Holy Cross encourages students to be of service to the community (the school's motto is "men and women for others"). Student Programs for Urban Development (SPUD), sponsored by the Chaplain's Office, is the largest student organization and serves more than 25 agencies in Worcester. Approximately 450 students (mostly female) volunteer annually.

Programming organized by the administration has exhibited a decidedly partisan, left-wing tilt, students complain. Since 2002, Holy Cross and the Women's Forum have hosted—despite considerable public, faculty, and student opposition—yearly performances of *The Vagina Monologues* in order "to raise awareness of the violence against women," according to the college president. If that's the reason, this play is a curious choice, given that one scene celebrates the lesbian rape of a teenage girl. This event has been the subject of protest both on and off campus by many who argue that the show betrays the college's Catholic mission. One student says, "Father McFarland himself defended the play by turning to moral relativism and emotivism, despite other attempts to appeal to Catholic moral teachings and objective truth."

In 2003, the women's studies department invited Francis Kissling, president of the pro-abortion Catholics for a Free Choice, to speak on campus. Kissling is a former abortion clinic administrator who was quoted (in 1991) as saying, "I spent 20 years looking for a government that I could overthrow without being thrown in jail. I finally found one in the Catholic Church." President McFarland would

SUGGESTED CORE
1. Classics 103, Greek and Roman Epic
2. Philosophy 225, Ancient Philosophy
3. Religious Studies 118, Introduction to the New Testament *and* Religious Studies 126, Introduction to the Old Testament
4. Religious Studies 117, History of Christianity I: The Rise of the Christian West
5. Political Science 228, Modern Political Philosophy
6. English 329, Shakespeare
7. History 202, Age of the American Revolution
8. Philosophy 241, Modern Philosophy (*closest match*)

not use university money for her $500 speaking fee, but he allowed Kissling to speak on campus. One conservative student says the campus Women's Forum flogged McFarland's lame stance "by publicly complaining that the president was not allowing 'academic freedom.'" Controversy also arose that year when television talk show host Chris Matthews, an alumnus of the college and an abortion-rights advocate, was allowed to be the school's commencement speaker and an honorary award recipient. The invitation sparked a group of Holy Cross alumni to speak out against the administration, garnering media attention. According to the *Boston Globe,* the bishop of Worcester boycotted the commencement.

In connection with Black History Month, the college has sponsored such speakers as Jesse Jackson and Chuck D (the race-obsessed rapper from the band Public Enemy). In 2004, McFarland sent an e-mail to the entire campus in which he denounced the "incivility" of those students who had asked sharply critical questions of Jesse Jackson at his lecture. Students and professors contrasted the e-mail with McFarland's silence after demonstrators disrupted a lecture during the previous year by Daniel Pipes on Islamist terrorism.

But the good news, says one student, is that "while from the top down things do not look good for the college's Catholic identity, there is a small group of committed Catholic students who are determined to spread the faith by witnessing to their peers, hoping that one day there will be enough students who want more of an authentic Catholic education to really make an impact on the college." There is support to be found for traditional Catholic moral teachings on campus, as demonstrated by the Students for Life organization and Compass, a club for faithful Catholics. The *Fenwick Review*, a student newspaper geared for conservatives, publishes four or five issues each year. While a mix of viewpoints can be found in the articles and editorials on the pages of the student weekly, the *Crusader,* readers should be prepared to also find faculty defending public policy contrary to the teachings of the Catholic Church. In the fall, in response to an article by a student defending traditional marriage, a religious studies professor wrote a letter condoning same-sex unions and criticizing "our society" and "many churches" that "still try to silence gay people."

The College Republicans club, which one instructor described as "much larger and more active than the College Dem[ocrat]s," sponsors political events on campus regularly. The student-run Hanify-Howland Memorial Lecture in recent years has brought a number of significant figures to campus, including Harvard law professor Mary Ann Glendon, Supreme Court Justice Clarence Thomas (a Holy Cross alum), and conservative commentator Linda Chavez. A professor says that at these lectures "there is an opportunity for motivated students to hear all sides." Furthermore, under the new leadership of Dr. William Shea, a theological scholar, the College's Center for Religion, Ethics, and Culture has displayed an interest in programming reflective of a wide variety of political and intellectual points of view.

At Holy Cross there are daily masses at the St. Joseph Memorial Chapel and two other chapels. To accommodate students of other religions, the college also has Protestant and nondenominational services each Sunday and provides a Muslim prayer room.

One-quarter of students compete as varsity athletes. The college's athletic programs are housed in the expansive Hart Recreation Center, which boasts a fitness center in addition to a 3,600-seat basketball arena, an ice rink, and an Olympic-size swimming pool. In addition to 13 clubs and eight intramural sports, Holy Cross supports 15 teams for men and 12 teams for women in its intercollegiate athletic program. The Crusaders compete in the Patriot League in 24 sports. Holy Cross has one of the highest student-athlete graduation rates of any NCAA Division I school.

Like many colleges, Holy Cross has had trouble with student drinking. But the college has instituted a tough, zero-tolerance policy that it strictly enforces. On the whole, the campus is safe, though in 2003 Holy Cross reported 12 forcible sex assaults, one robbery, two aggravated assaults, and three burglaries on campus. The college's public safety department supports several programs that promote campus security: a student escort service that helps late-night study bugs and partiers back to their dormitories, crime prevention workshops, and 24-hour patrols. The Colleges of Worcester Consortium also sponsors a van service that transports students from campus to campus.

About 58 percent of the student body receives financial aid. Admissions are need-blind, and the school offers to meet 100 percent of a student's financial need. The average recent graduate of Holy Cross bears a student loan debt of $16,063, according to *Kiplinger's Personal Finance*.

MARLBORO COLLEGE

Itsy bitsy, teeny weeny

Nearly every small liberal arts school featured in this guide recruits its students the same way, declaring that its classes are small, its faculty are dedicated, its campus is quaint, and its student body is talented and unique. Marlboro College in Marlboro, Vermont, makes all these claims, but it also acknowledges that it is set apart from the rest; admissions materials, in a welcome departure from their kind, even confess that Marlboro is not for everyone. This is clear from the freshman retention rate (a not-so-high 83 percent) and graduation rate (a quite low four-year rate of 31 percent). But for those who do belong here, Marlboro provides a powerful learning experience.

That a tiny school of 324 students can still make the lists in major college guides is testament itself to Marlboro's uniqueness. In 2004, at her inauguration as president of the college, Ellen McCulloch-Lovell described the Marlboro student as a "thinking, feeling, acting, creating, social, political person, seeing a connection between what they learn themselves and alongside faculty and how they participate in the community. The individual and the community are not different here." Marlboro exists as this close-knit community, she says, "not a cloister from the raucous world, but a haven for the self in community."

Marlboro was founded in 1947 by Walter Hendricks, a friend and student of Robert Frost who wanted to offer a strong academic program for returning World War II veterans. Since its founding, the college has grown significantly in prestige, but little in size, and its size is really what makes Marlboro unique, allowing students plenty of attention in academics and social life.

VITAL STATISTICS
Religious affiliation: none
Total enrollment: 324
Total undergraduates: 324
SAT median: 1210
Applicants: 367
Applicants accepted: 85%
Accepted applicants who enrolled: 40%
Tuition: $26,940
Room and board: $8,190
Freshman retention rate: 83%
Graduation rate: 31% (4 yrs.), 67% (6 yrs.)
Average class size: 10
Student-faculty ratio: 8:1
Courses taught by graduate TAs: none
Most popular majors: social sciences, English, visual arts
Students living on campus: 80%
Guaranteed housing for four years? yes
Students in fraternities or sororities: none

Academic life: Marlboro country

Marlboro's small size affects every aspect of academic life. With an average of eight students for every faculty member, students get to know their professors professionally and often personally as well. Students attend Marlboro to learn, and faculty members are there to facilitate learning. "The faculty is great," says one freshman. "I have been profoundly affected by each of the professors I've had the privilege of working with. The faculty, in class, have an amazing way of drawing the students into the material that I've never witnessed before. They are passionate about what they do, and it shows." This passion allows Marlboro faculty to offer much more to its students than their numbers—just 41 teachers—would suggest. The school offers degrees in 33 areas—in the arts, humanities, natural sciences, and social sciences, as well as in multidisciplinary areas. For upperclassmen, one-on-one tutorials are common, and students are able to work closely with faculty in academic areas that interest both. In the history department, for example, topics for past tutorials have included "Caste and Communism in India," "Readings in the History of the Vikings," "English Hegemony and Ethnic Radicalism in the Celtic Fringes," and "Post-War Images of Soviet Women."

While students and faculty usually enjoy this close interaction, Marlboro courses can occasionally be academically stifling, and students should be aware that there are views besides the ones that their professors offer. For instance, the religion department consists of one professor, and the department's course offerings reflect his expertise and interests. The department offers four main introductory courses: "World Religions I: Judaism, Christianity, and Islam," "World Religions II: Hinduism, Buddhism, Confucianism, and Taoism," "North American Indians," and "Topics in Human Understanding." He also teaches intermediate-level courses in Eastern religions, according to student demand. The philosophy department consists of one full-time faculty member, who teaches, on a three-year cycle, courses in the following areas: ancient Greek philosophy (Plato, Aristotle, and the Presocratics), Descartes and Hume, Kant, existentialism and phenomenology, Schopenhauer and Nietzsche, and Husserl and Heidegger, and occasionally upper-level courses in the "Ethics of Everyday Life" and "Geometry for Philosophers." Note the curious absence of medieval philosophy—as if reflective thought had simply stopped around 200 B.C., then picked up again in 1600. Alas, such an omission is all too common on campus. However, at Marlboro the gap may be filled by a worthy course, "Medieval Political Theology," which sets students reading Augustine, Anselm, and Aquinas.

Given its size, Marlboro simply can't offer a great deal of variety; it's pretty much "one professor per discipline," an alumnus says. "That means that if the teacher who represents your area of interest isn't to your taste—or takes an approach with which you don't agree—you might have trouble pursuing your interests here. You can get a very solid grounding and strong education, but you have to know how to pick the right professors. Freshman and sophomore year are spent taking broader courses, across the curriculum. That's how you find the professors you want to be your mentors."

One refreshing aspect of life at Marlboro is the fair-mindedness, a graduate reports. While most students and professors do lean toward left-wing secularism, this religious "moderate conservative" found the atmosphere free and invigorating: "Teachers make a clear distinction between their own beliefs and what they're teaching. Most teachers don't try to move you to their point of view. If you want to argue against feminism, the teacher will ask you to read feminist works so that you can have a grounding in what you're critiquing—not in order to move you to his position."

Many of the teachers get high marks from students. "Faculty are always busy working directly with students, surrounded by seminal texts," one said. "Marlboro is the kind of place which helps you find what you're really interested in, then sets you free. One of my professors made me go back and read the classics in my field, and I'm grateful he did so. For instance, I'm interested in the sea change between digital and print culture. So he directed me to study the last transformation of this scale—the development of printing. It really opened my eyes."

Some of the better faculty include Max Weber scholar Gerald Levy in sociology; Kathryn Ratcliff in American studies; Neal Weiner in philosophy; Dana Howell in cultural history; Robert Engel in environmental science; Jennifer Ramstetter in biology; author Laura Stevenson in writing and literature; and J. Birjepatil in English literature. A highly recommended course is "Articulation of Thought," which one grad called "the most transformative course for me. My advisors looked specifically at what I needed to learn—how to articulate a syllogistic argument at a length of 30 to 40 pages—and advised that I take that one," he says. The result? "I wrote a 150-page paper as my final project, and published work in professional journals. The ability to do that is something impressive to develop in an undergraduate."

In 2005, *The Princeton Review* ranked Marlboro among the top 20 colleges in the United States in 18 academic categories. The school ranked first in "Professors Bring Material to Life," and second in "Best Overall Academic Experience," "Class Discussions Encouraged," and "Professors Make Themselves Accessible."

Students majoring in literature are required to take a two-semester sequence in "Religion, Literature, and Philosophy," a literature criticism course, and a sequence in dramatic literature, the English novel, or poetry. The department also offers courses in Shakespeare, African American literature, "Fiction of the American South," the Russian novel, "Buddhism and Poetry," a seminar on Sylvia Plath, and Romantic and Victorian poetry. Choices depend on the interests of the professors and on the demands of students, which don't always match up.

One popular option for Marlboro students is the World Studies Program, which

ACADEMIC REQUIREMENTS

Marlboro has no core curriculum or specific distribution requirements. However, its highly individualized, advisor-based system of course selection appears to succeed at giving students broad educations, as well as depth in the fields they choose. Students must:

- Demonstrate sufficient writing skills. Students meet this requirement by presenting a 20-page portfolio of clear, concise, grammatical expository writing to the faculty within two semesters of matriculation.
- Complete the requirements of the area of study (major) they have chosen, and the plans of concentration upon which they agree with supervising faculty members of their choice. Typically, these programs of study are rigorous and interdisciplinary, and include the study of mathematics, foreign languages, and (where appropriate) natural sciences, in addition to liberal arts classes.

allows students to internationalize any major through foreign study. Students on this path must take three general foundation courses—"Twentieth-Century World," "Topics in Human Understanding," and the weekly "World Studies Colloquium," a one-credit course; at least one internship support course; a graduate-level course through the School for International Training, an intensive world studies school 15 miles from Marlboro; reach advanced level proficiency in at least one foreign language; and participate in a six- to eight-month work- or independent study abroad.

Marlboro attracts the type of student who is looking for independence, and the school offers that in the form of its curriculum—basically, there isn't any, and students need only to satisfy a few requirements in order to graduate. To start with, the "clear writing" requirement ensures that students become proficient in academic and expository writing, and students must submit a 20-page portfolio of clear writing within two semesters of matriculation at Marlboro. In the subsequent semesters, students must take at least one course each semester that requires substantial writing. "The school tests you on your way in, to check your writing skills," a student says. "Then you're evaluated in two years, and if you don't know how to write, you can't move on. Period."

The structure of a Marlboro education is based on a student's required "plan of concentration," a project of classes, writing, and independent study. After taking two years of introductory courses, each sophomore submits a proposed plan during the spring semester, selecting a topic for the thesis or project and choosing faculty advisors from Marlboro and an outside expert in the academic field who will evaluate the student's work.

Plans have varied greatly in past years. A student majoring in dance and psychology focused on "Dance Movement Therapy," studying the "use of movement in helping children with developmental disabilities with a focus on autism spectrum disorders." Another student, majoring in photography and writing, produced a photography exhibit exploring Tibetan refugee life, Indian culture, and particularly Thangkas, a form of Tibetan religious painting. A philosophy student studied "ways in which literature can resolve conflicting philosophical theories, using the moral philosophies of Kant and Nietzsche as illustrations," while a music student analyzed "the compositional process in Beethoven's late piano sonatas." This system does have its dangers, one graduate says: "If you're not good at being a self-directed student, you can choose two professors as advisors who don't understand each other's work. You'd end up wasting much of your time just ping-ponging between what the two professors like, which is not cohesive. But that's a worst-case scenario, for students who aren't suited to it."

Students are virtually forced to have close relationships with their advisors. Upon entering the school, each student is assigned to an advising group, which includes a faculty member and members from each academic year. The advising group meets every Wednesday at the "Dedicated Hour," a school tradition, in order to discuss academic or community issues. The handbook makes clear that "the advisor is not only an experienced guide to the curriculum and the institution, but is active in helping the student to set educational goals and to work toward meeting them." Later, every student must work closely with the professors who help him draw up and execute his plan.

"The teachers guide you through what you need by helping you build a foundation that's in many ways very core and classical," an alumnus says.

Marlboro students may vary in their academic interests, but there is a love of learning among students and faculty that is rare on many other college campuses, where pre-professionalism reigns supreme. "The challenge of Marlboro is what most appeals to me because it is not only an intellectual one, but a personal one," says one freshman. "It asks not only how far are you willing to push your work, but also how far are you willing to push yourself to grow." Academic ideas are discussed frequently outside the classroom. "I've had more philosophical discussions the four months up on that hill than I have had in 18 years of my life," says the student. "There is this sense of exploration that is encouraged not only from faculty to student but also from student to student."

SUGGESTED CORE
1. Humanities 1082, Homer's Iliad
2. Humanities 225, Greek Philosophy: Plato
3. Humanities 742, "Reading" the Bible
4. Humanities 1134, Medieval Political Theory (*closest match*)
5. Humanities 1107, Introduction to Political Theory (*closest match*)
6. Art 518, Shakespeare: Text and Performance
7. and 8. No suitable course

Student Life: The different-ness difference

Everything at Marlboro College is what a Scot might call "wee." One student says the small community is both the greatest benefit and the worst drawback of attending Marlboro: "There is a real sense of 'home' here. Since the school is so far from any major city, campus events are mostly community events, and there is rarely a feeling of exclusion for any student." What's the downside? A feeling of "isolation and limited social interaction," the student says. "I think that the biggest adjustment for me to make was to come to the realization that, yep, I'm on a hill with 370-some other people . . . and that's it."

The school does provide some outside-the-classroom amusement. For instance, Monday-night lectures by outside speakers are common; past topics have included "Teaching Whiteness," a talk on "what it means to teach and learn whiteness in the context of a small liberal arts college"; and "Citizenship and Scientific Literacy," which discussed why "science and technology are vital to the ideal citizen." But for real entertainment, students have to get creative. In their (limited) spare time, says one student, "Marlboro students do what most college students do: procrastinate, party, dance, sled down the library hill on dining hall trays, work, watch movies, play Twister. When students finish their work, they know how to play. For example, about halfway through the semester, I found myself playing musical chairs in the Campus Center, something I hadn't done since I was in elementary school. Why? Why not?"

To outdoor enthusiasts, Marlboro would seem the ideal locale. The school boasts 17 miles of ski trails, enjoyed especially during the campus-wide Wendell Cup cross-country ski race, now in its 40th year. The Green Mountain National Forest, only a half-hour away, provides many lakes, rivers, and hiking trails to the stir-crazy student.

The college outdoor program sponsors regular sea kayaking and whitewater rafting trips, hiking, backpacking, and rock-climbing trips, and loans out equipment at no cost to students.

When President McCulloch-Lovell became president, she made clear that Marlboro "is a haven for different-ness . . . where we make no assumptions that we all think the same or hold the same beliefs; where we are free to express them, and free to change our minds." Politically speaking, students aren't particularly diverse; one liberal student says, "Personally, I discovered that once I came here it was very overwhelming to be around so many people who shared my beliefs." However, the leftish consensus at Marlboro isn't stifling, according to one alumnus. "Being the resident conservative, I got a lot out of having students who disagreed with me; we could bounce ideas off each other. And they recognized it was valuable to have me to debate with." Given the tales of campus intolerance we've heard from across the country, this atmosphere of liberty at Marlboro deserves recognition.

Students are not as much activists as they might be at other schools—largely because there is little audience for the protests. There is a Political Action Group, but as one student says, it has not made much impact on the student body. One thing is for sure—if you attend Marlboro, you will get to know the other people there very well, and they will learn about you and your beliefs. They'll also challenge them, in the context of small-group discussions and intimate seminars. If you're up for that challenge, this might be the place for you.

One fascinating aspect of life at Marlboro is drawn from its roots in rural Vermont: the town meeting. According to the school, "All students, faculty and staff members may participate, each with an equal vote. The monthly assembly governs community life and serves as a forum for college-wide issues. Community sentiment figures heavily into administrative decisions, and town meeting representatives serve on a number of faculty and administrative committees, and represent the students at trustee meetings. Town meeting distributes thousands of dollars to committee projects and student initiatives." Recalling the primitive roots of Western democracy in ancient Athens and medieval Swiss villages, the town meeting makes a fascinating forum in which to learn skills of rhetoric, negotiation, and leadership.

The small town of Marlboro is two miles from campus and offers the bare necessities—a post office, an inn, and the town hall. Brattleboro, population 12,000, is 15 minutes away. It boasts some movie theaters and a few cultural attractions. "There is really no religious community present," says one graduate, "so if you're looking for that, this might not be the place for you. There are various Christian churches, but they are filled with a graying population, where students don't feel very welcome." The nearby towns are an interesting sociological mix of the old Vermont and the new; longtime New England farmers rub shoulders, not always happily, with aging hippies who used to live on communes in the area and visiting skiers in SUVs.

Some of the best cultural attractions on campus arise directly from academic work; students as part of their plans often invite famous writers, performers, or other artists to campus to evaluate their work. While they're up the hill, they usually agree to some sort of reading, recital, or talk—allowing the whole community to benefit from a single student's interests. "By junior and senior year students are so intent on their plans, they live, eat, sleep their plan," a graduate says. "Basically we sat around on weekends bouncing our ideas back and forth—so we learned from each other. You dig at each other to see if what you need will come out of the other person's mouth."

The Marlboro campus was once an assortment of barns and houses that became academic and living facilities. The school still makes use of these facilities, but has since added a few small dormitories. The dorms are by no means uniform—some have kitchens; one is "chem-free" (no alcohol or smoking), and another is a converted inn. There are also a small number of semi-independent accommodations—mostly cabins and small houses—for upperclassmen who don't mind cooking for themselves.

Crime on campus is virtually nonexistent, as the only incidents reported for the past three years (2001–3) were seven burglaries—three in 2001, and four in 2002.

Tuition is mid-range for a private school at $26,940, with room and board at $8,190. The school practices need-blind admissions, though it does not guarantee to meet a student's full need. However, more than 80 percent of students receive some need-based aid.

MASSACHUSETTS INSTITUTE OF TECHNOLOGY

CAMBRIDGE, MASSACHUSETTS • WEB.MIT.EDU

From those to whom much is given

The Massachusetts Institute of Technology was founded with 15 students during the last year of the Civil War. Even at its inauspicious beginning, the school stressed the importance in education of research; we've probably all benefited in some way from something discovered or invented by an MIT scientist. Virtually no one goes to MIT to major in the liberal arts, of course, but besides being a vital research center and a strong teaching school, MIT also requires its students to become more well rounded than a number of highly ranked liberal arts institutions. It deserves its reputation as one of the very best schools in the nation. The main drawback to an MIT education is the amount of work it takes to get one, and the pressure it causes students—who occasionally crack under the strain.

Academic Life: Precision bearings

MIT comprises the following schools: Science; Engineering; Architecture and Planning; Humanities, Arts, and Social Sciences; the Sloan School of Management; and the Whitaker College of Health Sciences and Technology. All but the last accept undergraduates. MIT is home to about 4,000 undergrads and 6,000 graduate students. The Engineering School awards the most undergraduate degrees (about half the total, in recent years) and houses the most popular fields of study: computer science and engineering, electrical engineering and computer science, and mechanical engineering. Science is the next largest school, graduating about half as many students as Engineering, the biggest groups coming from biology and mathematics. Humanities, Arts, and Social Sciences graduates less than 100 students each year, with economics the most popular concentration by far—although the school offers 11 other majors in addition to foreign languages. Architecture and Planning awards roughly 25 degrees to undergraduates each year.

As many colleges used to do—and as the best science colleges still seem to do—MIT explicitly structures the better part of each freshman's schedule. Students take five of their science core courses—in calculus, physics, chemistry, and biology—as well as two humanities courses and the communications requirement during their first year on campus. Students usually complete all general requirements by the end of their second year, the year during which they begin the pursuits of their majors (confusingly called capital-C "Courses" at MIT). Each undergraduate is awarded an SB (really a Bachelor of Science) degree. Students have a small amount of choice within the science requirements—if one considers "Calculus with Theory" much of an alternative to "Calculus with Applications" or just plain "Calculus." But whichever course a student picks, it can be assumed, according to those on campus, that it is solid and essential to future studies at MIT.

MIT offers five alternative freshman programs. In these, "students make progress comparable to other freshmen, but the manner in which individual institute requirements are met varies from program to program and among students within each program," according to the university. The Concourse Program, begun in 1971 and run by the engineering department, combines formal courses with informal activities; "in structure and atmosphere, Concourse resembles a small school rather than a large institution," the catalog says.

The interdisciplinary Experimental Study Group has "small, discussion-oriented classes, and seminars, study groups, hands-on labs, and independent study." The 50 freshmen in that group, along with 15 sophomores, 10 staff members, and 20 "upper-class instructors" (alumni of the program) also plan and teach labs and seminars like "The Art of Color," "Robotics," and "Introduction to Photography."

MIT's famous Media Lab is home to the Media Arts and Sciences Freshman Program, part of the School of Architecture and Planning. Only two dozen students are allowed into this program, in which "instructors connect research topics in the Media Laboratory to core physics and chemistry subjects, and students learn first hand how research is carried out." Another program, the newest learning community, is Terrascope. Here students learn the foundations of basic science and engineering "and are encouraged to apply those concepts in creative ways to understand the interdependent physical and biological processes that shape our planet, and to design strategies to ensure a sustainable environment for the future."

Seminar XL is an academic enrichment program in calculus, physics, chemistry, and biology that is open to all first-year students. In addition to the freshman programs, students may participate in the Independent Activities Period (IAP), a four-week period in January during which students may pursue their own interests and programs. Many students stay on campus and participate in workshops, seminars, research projects, lectures, field trips, or other programs that don't easily fit into a traditional academic schedule. Students may take up to 12 units of credit per IAP. MIT is one of the few

VITAL STATISTICS

Religious affiliation: none
Total enrollment: 10,320
Total undergraduates: 4,136
SAT/ACT midranges: SAT V: 680–760, M: 730–800; ACT: 31–34
Applicants: 10,466
Applicants accepted: 16%
Accepted applicants who enrolled: 65%
Tuition: $30,800
Room and board: $9,100
Freshman retention rate: 98%
Graduation rate: 81% (4 yrs.), 92% (6 yrs.)
Courses with fewer than 20 students: 61%
Student-faculty ratio: 7:1
Courses taught by graduate TAs: 1%
Most popular majors: engineering, computer science, biology
Students living on campus: 93%
Guaranteed housing for four years? yes
Students in fraternities: 48% sororities: 26%

As you might expect, MIT imposes a core curriculum, but it has nothing to do with the liberal arts. All students must take:

- Two courses in calculus.
- Two classes in physics.
- One chemistry course.
- One biology class.
- Two science electives.

At least two of these courses must "emphasize work of a project type (rather than routine experimental exercises), which gives students the opportunity to exercise the same type of initiative and resourcefulness as a professional would."

Students also take four communications courses, one in each of four years; the first course is based on the student's level of ability, while the final two usually fall within the student's major. Students must also satisfy an additional writing skills requirement (two-thirds of which can be completed before the student even starts coursework).

In addition, students do take some courses in the humanities, arts, and social sciences. Students take eight courses in these subjects, with choices

remaining campuses that offers ROTC programs in all three branches of the military: Army, Navy/Marine Corps, and Air Force.

MIT is a work-intensive, challenging environment, especially for freshmen. University publications note that until all incoming students get through the science basics, it is difficult to hold them to the highest university standards. Thus, MIT gives first-semester freshmen only pass/fail grades. During the second semester, freshmen earn A's, B's, or C's; if they get a D or F, it will not appear on their transcripts. Even so, very little grade inflation is reported at MIT.

As students move into their Courses (majors), they are subjected to standard grading processes and the options for research open up even further. MIT's Undergraduate Research Opportunities Program is used by about 80 percent of undergrads at some point in their careers; it offers hundreds of chances for students to assist with ongoing faculty research projects. Participants spend six to ten hours a week working for credit or for pay—but, as the commercial has it, the experience is priceless. MIT conducted more than $470 million of sponsored research in 2003 (involving both graduate and undergraduate students).

Everyone knows that MIT has an accomplished faculty; saying so is like saying the Norton Anthology of Literature includes an accomplished set of writers. MIT has 10 Nobel winners on the faculty; in the institution's history, 59 "present or former members of the MIT community have won the Nobel Prize," according to the university Web site. The current faculty also includes 15 MacArthur Fellows and four winners of the Kyoto Prize. To its credit, MIT does not bother with glossy admissions talk about how you're sure to be invited for tea to the home of Wolfgang Ketterle (Nobel in physics, 2001) or go bowling with Robert Solow (Nobel in economics, 1987). You won't. But you might contribute to one of their research projects and start to make a name in your field.

MIT has about 975 faculty members, supplemented by almost 800 graduate students employed as teachers and teaching assistants. Students are likely to be taught by (or at least assisted by) a graduate student in some introductory courses—you won't get Noam Chomsky as your "Introduction to Linguistics" instructor. MIT puts its full-time professor-student ratio at seven to one, an amazingly low ratio, and claims that "most [faculty] do teach undergraduates." According to the institution, "Discussion sections of lecture classes are limited to 20 students, and other classes average 30 to 50 students." But MIT fails to mention the size of the lecture classes themselves, which can enroll hundreds of students.

For help understanding the curriculum, MIT assigns a faculty or staff member to each freshman to serve as his freshman advisor. Students meet their advisors during orientation and weekly as part of the class schedule in certain freshman seminars. When a student selects a major, an upperclassman in that department becomes his advisor. But the advising Web page suggests that students need to take responsibility for keeping in contact with professors who can help them when their four years are up: "If you go through MIT with straight As but have a hard time finding someone who knows you well enough to write a recommendation, then you've probably missed one of the most important experiences at MIT: informal intellectual and social interactions with MIT faculty members." Students say that faculty are busy but willing to talk if you can find them at the right time. Still, one would think that a better advising system would help more MIT students keep their wits about them and alert the university when something is going desperately wrong—but more on this below.

Former University President Charles M. Vest boosted MIT's endowment from $1.4 billion to $5.1 billion in his thirteen years at the university, according to the *Chronicle of Higher Education*. The Campaign for MIT raised $2 billion. About $1.1 billion is earmarked for academic programs, "awarding innovation," salary raises, and student assistance. Another $300 million is for building new facilities, something MIT has been doing a lot of lately. Recent projects include the new 350-bed undergraduate dorm (Simmons Hall), the Frank Gehry–designed Stata Center for Computer, Information, and Intelligence Sciences, an expansion of the Media Lab, a new sport and fitness center, and a number of renovations to existing buildings.

Besides raising a heck of a lot of money, Vest promoted multiculturalism and an increase in the number of women students and professors at MIT. Susan Hockfield, former Yale provost and noted neuroscientist, was elected the first

REQUIREMENTS (CONT'D)

coming from at least three of five areas:

- Literary and textual studies.
- Language, thought, and value.
- Visual and performing arts.
- Cultural and social studies.
- Historical studies.

Students must compile three or four courses among these electives to form a "concentration." Concentrations can be as straightforward as economics or philosophy, or as interdisciplinary as black studies, labor in industrial society, and urban studies. These courses vary by department. For example, in the literary and textual studies department, a student can take either "Shakespeare" or "International Women's Voices" and get the same credit. In visual and performing arts, choices include "Introduction to Western Music," "Harmony and Counterpoint," and "Jazz."

Students also need eight points of physical education credit, and must pass a swimming test by the end of sophomore year.

NEW ENGLAND

101

woman president of MIT in August 2004, replacing Vest. According to an article in the the *Chronicle of Higher Education*, Hockfield "plans to continue efforts to improve opportunities for female and minority students and professors."

MIT does not have many political extremists among its students or faculty (except for the fascinating but infuriating linguist and leftist Noam Chomsky). Students surely have a wide disparity of political ideas, but they don't spend time promoting them, rallying others to the cause, or demonstrating for them. They have too much else to do. Political speakers are far outnumbered by scientific ones discussing topics you have never heard of. Trust us. Campus news is delivered by the student paper, the *Tech*, which was first published in 1881 and claims to have been the first newspaper available on the Internet (starting in 1993). The newspaper seems to approximate the moderate political atmosphere of MIT; it perhaps leans a little toward the progressive side, but it is also open to many viewpoints.

Student Life: Catastrophe theory

MIT students have two things working for them and against them. The first is Boston and all the things to do there, from sporting events to concerts, museums, historical sites, and restaurants and bars of every kind. This is both a distraction and a great release. The second is the academic load they all face—the benefits are obvious and the camaraderie of being in the same boat is helpful, but one has to wonder whether that boat is seaworthy for all students. Since the death of a student from alcohol poisoning and the suicide in 2000 of a sophomore who set herself on fire, MIT has devoted considerable energy to improving its student mental health services and other support organizations. Still, student tragedies are disturbingly common. In 2001, a student ordered cyanide through the mail, ingested it, and died; there have been several other suicides in recent years. "The number of students taking medical leaves has grown to well over 100 per year; most of these leaves are mental health leaves," said MIT's Chief of Mental Health, Alan Siegel. MIT has recently added to the mental health staff, is training faculty to recognize students who need help, and made other changes intended "to provide better access, greater responsiveness and improved communications among medical staff."

MIT has been trying to create a more cohesive community among its freshmen and sophomores for a few years now, believing that it would help all students better adjust to campus life. In fall 2002, the institution began requiring unmarried freshmen to live in on-campus residence halls. Institute housing, as the dorms are called, is coed (except for the all-female McCormick Hall), though most dorms have "single-gender living areas," according to the school. After their freshman year, students may live in fraternities or sororities (MIT has 37) or in cooperative housing. Living off campus is an option, but rent in and around Boston is atrocious; MIT says fewer than 500 undergraduates elect to live off campus each year.

With a workload such as MIT students face, more than a few turn to liquor as a sedative. The Campus Alcohol Advisory Board hosts "Frank Talks About Alcohol" in the dorms, trying to diminish underage tippling. MIT is trying to develop a policy that meets the state's drinking laws but still allows students to get anonymous medical help. "Given the potential for disciplinary or even legal sanctions due to underage drinking, students who need medical assistance due to alcohol consumption have historically been reluctant to call for help," says a story in the *Tech*. The "risk manager" of the Intrafraternity Council at MIT is quoted as saying that every weekend there are "five or six students [who] do not go to Medical when they should because of fear of getting in trouble." MIT has changed its policy so that first offenses no longer earn an MIT alcohol citation, but fraternities can still face problems with the Cambridge Licensing Commission, which can suspend residence permits for underage drinking.

Not every social activity involves alcohol; there's an abundance of extracurricular activities at MIT; the school hosts more than 500 exhibits, performances, and concerts each year, plus a number of its own performing groups. The university is home to 30 religious groups of all stripes, including 15 groups for evangelical Christians alone, according to the *Boston Globe*, which quotes a senior as saying, "When I came to MIT, I was expecting it to be full of nerds—people who don't really put together science and religion. I was really surprised—and still am—by the volume of Christian fellowship here." There are also pro-life and pro-choice groups, Democrats, Republicans, and Greens, and literally hundreds of other organizations—scientific, cultural, and otherwise. Technical mischief is a favorite MIT pastime and MIT's signature Great Dome on Building 10 is a preferred target for elaborate practical jokes. In celebration of the 100th anniversary of human flight, a replica of the Wright brother's biplane "Flyer" was recently erected on the top of the Great Dome. Back in 2001, on the eve of the opening of the movie "Fellowship of the Ring," the dome was crowned with a golden ring; complete with an elvish inscription.

The inventive students at this science school sometimes apply their skills to improving their lives on campus. In 2005, MIT opened a new eating facility, the Steam Café, which was designed by two architecture students. It serves organic and vegetarian meals, soliciting feedback and recipes online from students who eat there, according to the *Chronicle of Higher Education*.

MIT students come from all 50 states and more than 100 foreign nations. Despite the effort required to get through MIT, the university reports that more than 90 percent who enroll as freshmen graduate within six years.

Students live in the cityscape of Cambridge, which stretches along the Charles River. Killian Court is among the oldest sections of campus, but the more striking

SUGGESTED CORE
1. Literature 21L.001, Foundations of Western Culture I: Homer to Dante (*closest match*)
2. Linguistics and Philosophy 24.200, Ancient Philosophy
3. Literature 21L.458, The Bible
4. History 21H.411, History of Western Thought, 500–1300 (*closest match*)
5. Political Science 17.03, Introduction to Political Thought
6. Literature 21L.009, Shakespeare
7. History 21H.101, American History to 1865
8. History 21H.433, The Age of Reason: Europe in the Eighteenth and Nineteenth Centuries (*closest match*)

NEW ENGLAND

103

architecture is provided by the modernist designs of I. M. Pei, Eero Saarinen, and Alvar Aalto's Baker House dormitory.

About 20 percent of MIT undergrads participate in intercollegiate athletics, while 65 percent play intramurals. The school has 41 varsity teams, a big number anywhere. MIT competes in the NCAA Division III, which emphasizes a student's academic experience. "For student-athletes at MIT, admission standards never waver, special financial aid incentives are not supported and separate curriculums are unavailable," says the college Web site. Nevertheless, MIT has produced 14 Academic All-Americans, the third largest number for any division and the highest for Division III. In 2003, MIT won two national championships; one in men's water polo and one in men's tennis.

MIT's natural local rival, socially and academically, is Harvard. Recently, a student wore the Tim the Beaver (MIT's mascot) costume to Harvard Square to take pictures with the statue of John Harvard—in what poses, exactly, we do not know. When the student took off the beaver's hands and feet to climb onto the statue, an enterprising Harvard student stole a foot from the costume and escaped into a Harvard dorm. "None of the MIT students were able to stop the thief or get a good look at him," the *Tech* reported. Explained one student, "I was too busy holding up the beaver."

The campus is fairly safe, though crime has increased in recent years. Larceny is the most common crime at MIT, as at most other schools, and laptop computers are a common target. In 2003, MIT reported six forcible sex offenses, compared to one in each of the previous two years. Burglaries jumped from 34 in 2002 to 101 in 2003. There were 10 motor vehicle thefts.

Tuition and fees for 2004–5 was $30,800, with another $9,100 or so needed for room and board. Admissions are need-blind, however, and the school guarantees that it will cover all demonstrated financial need. Some 60 percent of undergraduates receive some kind of need-based aid, and the average student loan debt of a 2004 graduate was $19,472.

MIDDLEBURY COLLEGE

Strong language

Any college blessed with the gorgeous campus and small-town charm of Middlebury College ought to be able to attract some of the nation's best students. With its Old Stone Row and Old Chapel, Middlebury has been called, with just cause, New England's most beautiful campus. The quaint village of Middlebury is the ideal small college town, and from its "college on the hill" one has a view of Vermont's Green Mountains to the east and New York's Adirondack Mountains to the west.

The historical architecture and natural wonder are indeed remarkable, but Middlebury is one of the nation's most selective liberal arts colleges not because of these attributes but because its academic life is rigorous and its faculty members deeply concerned with their students' intellectual paths. While Middlebury is best known for its fantastic language programs, the school is also strong in many other areas, including English and the sciences.

There is a catch, however. As one professor says, "The left on this campus sees its views as moderate, reasonable, and humane, while it considers those on the right to be extremist, stupid, and not worthy of respect." Naturally, a student who holds alternative viewpoints must have courage and a strong backbone to flourish at Middlebury. But it can be done, and it is well worth the effort.

Academic Life: Nothing is a sure thing

When Middlebury College was founded in 1800, students were expected "to read, translate, and parse Tully, Virgil, and the Greek Testament, and to write true Latin in prose, and [to] have also learned the rules of Vulgar Arithmetic," according to the college catalog. Needless to say, there are no such expectations today. Middlebury is a liberal arts college, but students choose which particular liberal arts to study, as the college makes no stipulations as to which texts or ideas students should engage. Middlebury gives its

VITAL STATISTICS
Religious affiliation: none
Total enrollment: 2,357
Total undergraduates: 2,357
SAT/ACT midranges: SAT V: 690–750, M: 690–750; ACT: 28–32
Applicants: 5,122
Applicants accepted: 26%
Accepted applicants who enrolled: 44%
Tuition: $40,400 (includes room and board)
Freshman retention rate: 96%
Graduation rate: 84% (4 yrs.), 90% (6 yrs.)
Courses with fewer than 20 students: 68%
Student-faculty ratio: 11:1
Courses taught by graduate TAs: none
Most popular majors: economics, history, literature
Students living on campus: 97%
Guaranteed housing for four years? yes
Students in fraternities or sororities: none

To fulfill Middlebury's distribution requirements, students must satisfy a number of conditions:

- Take one freshman seminar. Recent examples have included: "Beyond Cowboys: The Literary West," "Modern Age of Science," "Contemporary Ireland through Fiction and Film," and "The Age of Crusades."
- Complete two college writing courses, such as "The Writing Workshop" I and II, "Writing Across Differences," or "Writing to Heal."
- Take three courses: one on the cultures and civilizations of the United States, one on European culture and civilizations, and one dealing with a non-Western or Latin American civilization. These requirements are quite loose: to fulfill the U.S. requirement a student could take "The History of Photography."

Students must also complete at least one course in seven of the following eight areas:

- Literature. A Shakespeare course would count. So would "Chinese Cinema" (in translation).

students a great deal of flexibility in designing their curricula and consequently cannot guarantee that students will have a decent handle on the Western tradition before graduating—though they certainly are offered the resources to learn that tradition, if they choose. Middlebury does offer a sampling of obscure and trivial courses which can fulfill requirements. As one English professor says, gaps in students' educations are certainly possible, but they are not the norm. "A student who was extremely adept and savvy could probably avoid most of the 'fundamental' courses, but my experience is that they do not try to do that. The curriculum offers in general many vibrant courses taught by people passionate about their subjects, but to get all the fundamental courses of a good liberal arts education, the student has to select his courses deliberately with that end in view." Another professor agrees that Middlebury students are more inclined to take solid classes than not. While some faculty are disposed towards a St. John's College curriculum, he says, "We know, however, that the best way to have something like that is to offer attractive fundamental courses. If such courses are offered at Middlebury, students will come to them."

In a student newspaper article, one sophomore writes about overhearing one student asking another, "What are you going to do with a theater major?" He writes, "The value of a liberal arts education is that a degree from Middlebury College should be strong enough proof that a student has the discipline and skills needed to start any career." True enough, and for the most part the college steers clear of the emphasis on professional preparation that one finds at larger colleges or research universities. Middlebury offers only the bachelor of arts degree, even for science majors. According to the catalog, among the college's goals are that the student graduate as "a person who can think logically; who can write and speak with accuracy, clarity, style, and an individual voice . . . who can make intelligent value judgments . . . [and] who can read critically and imaginatively." By and large, the Middlebury graduate is this person.

One of the main factors responsible for developing this well-rounded student is the close and frequent faculty-student interaction that occurs at Middlebury. "I know my teachers very well," a senior says, "With very few exceptions, there are such great interactions and the profs are completely approachable. Sometimes you'll even get 'call me at home' on a syllabus—so long as you don't call at 11 when they're putting their two-year-old to bed." Middlebury is the kind of school where students and faculty form intellectual relationships that last for years. As one economics and geography major says of the teachers, "Because they give so much, they expect a lot too. Without doubt they are the most demanding and rewarding part of my life at Middlebury, particularly because of the intimacy of the relationships that I have with them, giving me no excuse for bad work and always a reason to do more and better work."

From the beginning, in fact, Middlebury students are encouraged to foster academic relationships with their professors. Freshmen are required to take one of several first-year seminars, which are "intimately sized, thematic courses designed to explore an area of intellectual inquiry from a perspective that makes connections among a number of traditional academic disciplines." Some of the more recent seminar course offerings have been "The Lessons of History: Herodotus and Thucydides," "Physical Immortality: Hope and Dangers," "The Art and Language of the Civil War," "*The Silmarillion* and *The Lord of the Rings*," and "The Economics of Social Issues." Seminar instructors also serve as advisors for students until they declare majors. After completing the first-year seminar, each student completes a college writing course, which can be chosen from among a number of academic fields.

Many Middlebury professors do conduct research, but teaching is by far the highest priority among faculty. "Professors rarely speak of their outside research and are generally interested in benefiting each and every student," an English major says. "They are almost always infectiously excited about their specialization." One upperclassman highlights the opportunities created for students in faculty research and recounts his experience during a recent summer: "What at first sounded like a number-crunching job turned out to be one with much more responsibility. I co-authored two papers, one of which we presented at a conference in Montreal, and had a huge amount of say in the direction of the project and the editing and rewriting process." A physics major says that in the sciences most faculty research is centered around senior thesis projects, and conversely, these projects tend to be informed by faculty interests. Professors—not teaching assistants—teach every course.

REQUIREMENTS (CONT'D)

- The arts. One could choose "Form and Structure in Sculpture"—or "Anime: Japanese Animation."
- Philosophical and religious studies. Choices range from "Introduction to the Philosophical Tradition" to "Philosophy and Feminism."
- Historical studies. These courses range from "The Making of Europe" to "Nomads of Eurasia."
- Physical and life sciences. Choices here all seem sound, with plenty of offerings for nonspecialists such as "Conservation Ecology" and "The Ocean Floor."
- Deductive reasoning and analytical processes. This lets students choose either mathematics classes such as "Introduction to Statistical Science" or certain philosophy courses like "Introduction to Modern Logic."
- Social analysis. Courses range across many departments, including "Introduction to the World Economy," "Anthropology through the Arts," and "Introduction to Gay and Lesbian Studies."
- Foreign language.

NEW ENGLAND

Students name the best professors at Middlebury as John Bertolini, John Elder, Robert Hill, Don Mitchell, Jay Parini, David Price, and Marion A. Wells in English; Gregg Humphrey in teacher education; Richard Wolfson in physics; Charles Nunley and Nancy O'Connor in French; Stephen C. Trombulak in biology; Murray Dry, Paul Nelson, and Allison Stanger in political science; Patricia Manley in geology; and Travis Jacobs in history.

Middlebury is internationally known for its total-immersion foreign language programs, which bring in hundreds of students each summer. Middlebury offers majors in Arabic, Chinese, classics, French, German, Italian, Japanese, Portuguese, Russian, and Spanish, and the school provides a number of courses in foreign literature in translation. The international studies major allows students to specialize in the language and culture of East Asia, Europe, Latin America, or Russia and Eastern Europe, and also accepts individual proposals for African studies. The department sponsors lectures and symposiums frequently. Sixty percent of each junior class studies abroad each year. One student suggests that many students enroll in study-abroad programs as a break from Middlebury's rigorous academic life, as many of the programs require less work than those on campus.

Besides the language programs, another respected Middlebury program is the Bread Loaf School of English in nearby Ripton, Vermont, which offers courses in literature and writing. The school holds its famous Bread Loaf Writers' Conference each August, when some of the nation's most distinguished writers gather to lead a series of seminars and workshops. The college's Center for Northern Studies is located about an hour and a half northeast of campus in Wolcott, Vermont. Students who live there for a semester explore different aspects of the region, from "Polar Biota" to "The Political Economy of Resource Management" to "Northern Archaeology." Middlebury's Environmental Studies program is well known in the field.

President John M. McCardell Jr. left in 2004 after serving for 13 years as the college's president. McCardell was certainly successful as a fundraiser and presided over a spate of new construction projects. Among these, Bicentennial Hall, a $47 million, 108,000-square-foot science facility, pushed the school toward a greater focus on the natural sciences along with its traditional academic emphasis on the liberal arts and languages. Other additions have included the Center for the Arts, four new student social houses, and a $40 million library/learning center, scheduled to open soon. As one of his last acts, McCardell announced the largest gift in the college's history—an anonymous $50 million "challenge grant." Some $10 million came in almost immediately to get the ball rolling.

McCardell's successor, Russian history scholar Ron Liebowitz, has spent the past 20 years at Middlebury and served as provost and executive vice president of the college, so his appointment promises continuity rather than change. In his first remarks to the school after accepting the post, Liebowitz said he would emphasize improvements in science education, foreign languages, and strategic collaboration with larger institutions.

It should come as no surprise that this small northeastern liberal arts college in a notably liberal state leans left. While the campus boasts tolerance for various viewpoints, as one student says, "It is more difficult to be a Republican on campus than it is to be a Democrat, especially given the context of the liberal town and state." The course offerings at the school reflect this bias. Middlebury offers more women's and gender studies courses than economics courses, for instance, and since the women's studies department is interdisciplinary, many of these courses can, regrettably, fulfill several of the distribution requirements—including literature, social sciences, art, and history, as well as the cultures and civilizations requirements.

Fortunately, Middlebury's English department has largely resisted the ideological fashions that have ruined once-proud departments elsewhere. It is one of the few English departments that still requires that its majors, who constitute a lofty 10 percent of the student body, take a course in Shakespeare. A recent National Association of Scholars study of liberal arts colleges' English departments concluded that "Middlebury offers a relatively well-structured major containing a high proportion of foundational courses" and that "it has largely resisted the postmodernist tide, changing less in many respects than the other majors we examined."

SUGGESTED CORE
1. Classics 150, Ancient Epic Poetry
2. Philosophy 201, Ancient Greek Philosophy
3. Religion 180, An Introduction to Biblical Literature
4. Religion 233, Medieval Christendom and Its Reformations
5. Political Science 318, Modern Political Philosophy
6. English 330, Shakespeare
7. History 203, United States History: 1492–1861
8. Philosophy 225, Nineteenth-Century European Philosophy

Middlebury's strong tradition in English is likely to change soon, however. In February 2004, both the English department and the American literature and civilizations department voted to move forward with a plan to merge into the "English and American literature" department and major. American studies, which includes "African American studies, ethnic studies, American popular culture studies, and the study of American culture in a global perspective, among others," according to a February 2004 Middlebury *Campus* newspaper article, could weaken Middlebury's English department. One professor says the combined major would eliminate the four-course sequence on American literature that English majors are currently required to take.

Student Life: Uncommon commons

Middlebury College abolished all-male fraternities in 1990, in part because the administration felt that the school was becoming too cliquish and exclusionary. Today, upon entering the college each student is assigned to one of five commons, which—the administration hopes—will serve as the center of the student's academic, social, and residential life. Every commons has its own faculty head, dean, coordinator, and residential advisors. The campus is overwhelmingly residential: 97 percent of students live on campus. First-year students can choose to live on either a single-sex or a coed floor, but floors for upperclassmen are all coed. (There are no coed dorm rooms or bathrooms; in fact, a housing official laughed out loud when we asked.) The college also has substance-free floors available for those who request them.

Within the commons system, students have additional choices regarding living arrangements. Academic-interest houses encourage learning outside the libraries and classrooms. These include total immersion language houses in Chinese, German, Italian, Spanish, Russian, Japanese, and French; the latter house's residents live in Le Château, a grand hall modeled on the Pavillon Henri IV of the Chateau de Fontainebleau. Other academic houses include the Environmental House and the Pan-African-Latino-Asian-Native American (PALANA) Center, a residence hall and cultural center for minority students. Such houses "are fairly popular and also sponsor events," one student says. "If the Spanish house sponsors a party, there'll be sangria, awesome music, and people will come in hordes."

To replace Greek life, the college also offers six coed "social houses," which host parties, concerts, and other events. Binge drinking was another of the administration's reasons for eliminating fraternities, and in that area, they have had little success. Now, apparently, as one upperclassman says, "a lot of events are off campus—which is fine if you've got a car and a dependable driver. The people who are on campus are too spread out to be a cohesive social group, so the social-house scene suffers." Ex-president McCardell came out in 2004 in the *New York Times* for a lowered drinking age, to reflect the realities on college campuses. Characterizing weekend life at Middlebury, students say again and again that they "work hard and play hard." Middlebury students compartmentalize their activities so that they not only binge drink once or twice a week, but they also binge study. "Social life at Middlebury often revolves around alcohol and partying," a student says. "On weekends, students like to hang out and possibly study on Saturday, with lots of partying on both Friday and Saturday nights. Sunday is a big work day."

Middlebury gives special preference to such cultural groups as the African American Alliance and Arabesque (the Arab Heritage Club). Other student groups are denied their own autonomy. A Christian group at Middlebury recently faced a controversy similar to more publicized ones at Tufts and Rutgers. To wit, when a member of the group announced that he was homosexual, he was denied a leadership position. As a response, the administration proposed adding a line in the student handbook to the effect that "no student may be eliminated from being considered for leadership of any campus group because of beliefs or identity." If this change is made, Jewish students could presumably no longer be denied leadership roles in the Islamic Society, or vice versa. All very curious, since a course in logical reasoning is required for graduation.

One student says that many Middlebury students are "very anti-religion." But religious student groups, Bible discussions, and prayer meetings are available for students who want them. One leader of the Middlebury InterVarsity Christian Fellowship says, "The college definitely encourages spirituality," and the Web page for "diversity" resources includes a link to the Christian groups on campus.

Things may be looking up for the conservative minority at Middlebury. One member of the College Republicans, who says she "would be hard-pressed to name more than three Republicans in the entire faculty," nonetheless notes various opportunities for her group and points to increased enthusiasm in the club: "We bring speakers to campus, write for the paper, assist in local charity, organize rallies to support the troops, hold screenings, and attend weekly meetings as our major events. . . . We are also working on increasing membership and becoming more active." Still, Middlebury is not as tolerant as campus literature claims. In March 2004, the student constitution committee denied a new pro-life student organization official college recognition.

Many Middlebury students are involved in leftist activist groups and their various protests. One Middlebury Democrats member says, "The campus is very liberal and very active in social causes from Tibet to environmentalism." At a recruitment event for the CIA (which probably should have expected something like this), student activists staged a "die-in," lying on the ground with fake blood on their clothes and heckling the recruiter. The Middlebury ROTC chapter was abolished in 1976; a recent suggestion to revive it was met with more protests. Interested students are welcome to participate at the University of Vermont.

Around half the student body participates in sports—varsity, club, or intramural. The Middlebury Panthers compete on 30 varsity teams in the NCAA Division III. The college encourages fitness through a physical education requirement. The college's location in western Vermont gives students other athletic outlets as well; skiing is as popular in the winter as hiking, biking, and camping are in the other seasons. Otter Creek runs right through town. The Rikert Ski Touring Center, the Middlebury College Snow Bowl, and the Ralph Myre Golf Course are all operated by the college. According to students, the college's January term provides ample opportunities for skiing and other sports. This is perhaps one reason the students fought so hard in 2004 against a professor-supported proposal to replace J-term with longer fall and spring semesters.

"One of the first things I noticed when I got here was how in-shape people are," one student wrote in the school newspaper. "Very few people are overweight." Students agree that they and their classmates are very concerned with image. To stereotype, the typical Middlebury student wears "somewhat worn-out clothing, with an expensive North Face fleece on, drinking out of a Nalgene bottle, reading in a Crazy Creek on the field," says a student. After revisiting Middlebury, one nostalgic alumna remarked in a magazine article that "[t]he student body has cleaned up considerably since the first semester of my freshman year. They're much more polite and respectful—some would say politically correct. Outbursts and outrageousness at Middlebury have gone the way of fraternities and downtown drug dealing."

The town of Middlebury is only a five-minute walk from campus. Students enjoy an abundance of restaurants and shops—many more than one would expect in a town of only 8,000. Along with Middlebury's natural surroundings and the plentiful campus events, the presence of the town means that students rarely if ever have good reason to be bored.

Middlebury lays claim to one of the great advantages of small-town New England: safety. Students can live and study on campus without worrying too much about how to get home from the library or a friend's dorm room. In 2003, the college reported one forcible sex offense, two stolen cars, and 12 burglaries on campus. The Midd Ride Program and Safety Escorts transport students to and from various on-campus locations, and red emergency phones around campus can be used to contact police immediately.

Middlebury is a connoisseur's college, at a premium price. The "comprehensive" fee (including tuition, room and board, health and other fees) for 2004–5 was $40,400. But the school admits students regardless of need and guarantees that it will meet every student's demonstrated financial requirements.

MOUNT HOLYOKE COLLEGE

SOUTH HADLEY, MASSACHUSETTS • WWW.MTHOLYOKE.EDU

Designing women

Mount Holyoke is a small, highly selective, nondenominational college for women enrolling approximately 2,150 students from across the United States and more than 80 countries. Founded in 1837 by progressive educator and chemist Mary Lyon, the school's identity is shaped by a commitment to "the search for knowledge and the compassionate understanding of humanity and the world." Mt. Holyoke was the first of the Seven Sisters (the female consort of the once-male Ivy League). Mount Holyoke boasts that it graduates "independent critical thinkers who speak and write powerfully," while being "technologically savvy, and . . . distinguished by their ability to lead in a complex, pluralistic world."

Mount Holyoke women are known for their love of learning and intellectual drive. There are plenty of solid course offerings and faculty members who genuinely care about their students' academic progress. Most students graduate with a true liberal arts education. Still, it is wise to avoid courses that the college calls "innovative" and "experimental," since they are likely to be steeped in leftist politics—even more so than the rest of the college, which is saying something.

Academic Life: Girls who wear glasses

Mount Holyoke is widely recognized for, in its own words, its "rigorous and innovative academic program, its global community, its legacy of women leaders, and its commitment to connecting the work of the academy to the concerns of the world." These are not idle claims: The college's academics are indeed rigorous and certainly innovative, its focus is strenuously global, its graduates often go on to do great things, and its commitment to social action is evident in much of the curricular and extracurricular activities of its students. "If college was just about academics," says one sciences major, "I would be satisfied with my decision to be at Mount Holyoke." An atmosphere of serious study characterizes the campus, where the library is active every night of the week. "Everyone at MHC loves to learn, and that fact makes classes so engaging," says one student. "Professors have utmost respect for their students, not to mention high expectations.

The 200 faculty members of Mount Holyoke are impressive teachers dedicated to their students. They have also proven themselves to be busy scholars, research scientists, and artists. Half are women, and 96 percent of the faculty have their doctoral degrees. Students rave about the excellence of the instruction they receive, the one-on-one support from professors, and the fairness in grading. In the 2003 graduating class, 93 percent of the graduates were working or in graduate school six months later. Of those students, 20 percent were attending graduate or professional schools and another 25 percent will enroll within five years. Alumnae attend graduate school at places like Harvard, Yale, Stanford, and Georgetown, and the college employs among its ranks Fulbright fellows and other award-winning scholars.

VITAL STATISTICS
Religious affiliation: none
Total enrollment: 2,145
Total undergraduates: 2,143
SAT/ACT midranges: SAT V: 610–700, M: 580–680; ACT: 26–30
Applicants: 2,912
Applicants accepted: 56%
Accepted applicants who enrolled: 35%
Tuition: $30,770
Room and board: $9,060
Freshman retention rate: 92%
Graduation rate: 75% (4 yrs.), 78% (6 yrs.)
Average class size: 12
Student-faculty ratio: 9:1
Courses taught by graduate TAs: none
Most popular majors: social sciences, psychology, English
Students living on campus: 93%
Guaranteed housing for four years? yes
Students in sororities: none

Students at MHC choose from 45 disciplinary and interdisciplinary majors. Around a third of Mount Holyoke students choose interdisciplinary majors, and many opt to design their own. In addition to the standard programs such as physics and French, newer fields of study include interdisciplinary offerings like African American and African studies, Asian studies, Latin American studies, and women's studies. "I always wanted to suggest a men's studies program, but I'm sure it wouldn't fly," one student says.

Students are assigned faculty advisors in their first year and may later change advisors when they settle on majors. Advising is "whatever you want to make of it," a student says. "If you really need your advisor he or she will be there—and if all you want is a signature on your registration, then that is possible too."

Mount Holyoke has long prided itself on its small class sizes and student-professor ratio of nine to one. Students are enthusiastic about the attention they receive: "I've never known a professor who is not quick in responding to e-mails, and many even

While Mount Holyoke falls far short of imposing a uniform core curriculum, it does maintain some general education requirements. A student must complete courses in seven different categories, distributed among the following three curricular divisions:

- Three courses in the humanities. A student can fulfill her arts and literature requirement with "Modern Drama," "Shakespeare," or the more politically correct "Ethnic Expressions in America." The history/philosophy/religion requirement can be satisfied by "Ancient Greece and Rome" or the trendier "History of Global Inequality." Other interesting electives such as "Martyrdom as Social Protest: Resistance and Honor in Antiquity and the Middle Ages" can also fulfill requirements.

- Two courses from two different disciplines in science and mathematics, including at least one laboratory course in a natural or physical science.

send along additional pieces of interest in their e-mails outside of class to students" says one. Another says, "I've been able to build close relationships with some of my professors. This will be extremely beneficial when I need recommendations for jobs or graduate school." Professors teach all courses, although assistants sometimes lead laboratory sections. Lately, however, enrollment has been up and a large number of professors have been on sabbatical; these two factors have contributed to overextending the faculty, according to an article in the *Mount Holyoke News*. "Seniors and juniors who want to do independent work have been turned away by professors who simply do not have the time for another advisee," the paper noted. One student has noticed the change: "I know people in the humanities that have struggled with large classes recently. We've had an increase in enrollment over the past four years and this has created this problem." A science student reports that she hasn't noticed overburdened faculty, but adds that perhaps it is more of an issue in the humanities. Another says that "if a class is overenrolled, the professors will try to be fair if they must cap the class, but usually they tend to take more than they wanted to."

Mount Holyoke has few "easy-A" classes. Students repeatedly stress that they work very hard for the grades they get. One student says, "Most students come in with straight A's from high school and find that they are no longer getting the same results, but have to work much harder to stand out." Says another, "Grading is done by the teachers and they are usually very helpful in comments about the marks or questions on the grading. The teachers don't want to see their students fail, but good marks are not just given out like candy." Another student, who is designing her own major in physics, astronomy, and geology, says, "Classes here are very rigorous; I really have to work. . . . The hardest class I have had didn't have traditional homework, but required a lot of independent proofs for problems with collaborative work that was done over time." Grade inflation, in short, does not appear to be a problem at Mount Holyoke.

However, curricular politics is. With the exception of the sciences, students can easily select classes that approach their topics almost exclusively through the goggles of race, gender, and sexuality, since these interpretive tropes are popular in every discipline at the school. The school's foundational goals—a comprehensive knowledge of Western history, music, and arts—have suffered here as elsewhere under the assault of trendy academic theories and practice.

The most popular majors at MHC include departments in the social sciences, psychology, and English. The history department is particularly strong, with a number of scholars studying traditional areas to balance those in feminist theory and ethnic studies. The classics and ancient studies department is also strong. The African and African American studies and the women's studies departments are filled with more politicized courses. Professors at Mount Holyoke noted for their teaching include Terese Freedman in dance, Mary A. Renda in women's studies and history, Eleanor R. Townsley in sociology, James Hartley in economics, and John Grayson in religion. The incendiary leftist Chris Pyle's politics classes are "so popular they're almost impossible to get into," according to a student. In the science departments, which one student calls "some of the best in the country," Darren G. Hamilton (organic chemistry) and W. Donald Cotter (inorganic chemistry) stand out.

During Mount Holyoke's January Term, students participate in some form of internship or self-study. This program is academically lightweight—"more fun than serious," one student says. "The formal academic aspect of it has faded," says a professor, who adds that because most faculty are preoccupied with administrative duties (hiring, for example) during that time of year, "they don't have time to teach January term."

Three years ago, Mount Holyoke chose to make SATs optional for prospective students, thus initiating an experiment intended to gauge whether such scores are necessary to predict student success. However, a majority of students still do submit these scores—which have risen slightly among Mt. Holyoke applicants, suggesting that students who did well in high school but not so well on the tests may simply be withholding their scores. Some preliminary analysis of the data shows that nearly 20 percent of the top-rated students chose not to submit SAT scores. The admissions office also asserts that a number of "exceptional and highly motivated students who may have hesitated to apply to MHC in the past" have begun to matriculate. Extensive articles have been published in the *College Street Journal*, the *Journal of Blacks in Higher Education*, and in the *Alumnae Quarterly* addressing the

REQUIREMENTS (CONT'D)

- Two courses from two different disciplines in social sciences. The options here range from the rigorous to the trendy.

Students also must complete one course in "multicultural perspectives" devoted primarily to the study of "Africa, Asia, Latin America, the Middle East, or the nonwhite peoples of North America." Among the more than 200 classes that fulfill the requirement are "Chocolate Cities and Vanilla Suburbs," "Gender and Sexuality: Hindu Religious Perspectives," and "Feminist Anthropology."

Students complete a language requirement by taking two elementary semesters in a new foreign language, one intermediate course, one literature course taught in a foreign language, or (for nonnative English speakers), passing a test.

Students also need six physical education units, which do not count toward 128 semester credits required to graduate.

NEW ENGLAND

115

effects—both pro and con—of this experiment, which so far is inconclusive.

As part of the Five College Consortium, MHC students are welcome to attend classes and events at Amherst, Hampshire, Smith, and the University of Massachusetts; there is even free transportation between the schools. But right at MHC students have many worthy academic programs available to them, despite the school's small size. Among them are the Junior Year Abroad program; the Weissman Center for Leadership; the Speaking, Arguing, and Writing Program; the Center for Environmental Literacy; and a variety of internships. Moving off campus, students can take part in the Twelve College Exchange, which allows students to spend a semester or two at another northeastern school like Bowdoin, Wellesley, or the Thayer School of Engineering at Dartmouth College; the Johns Hopkins University Nursing Program (students spend three years at MHC and two years at Johns Hopkins, earning a bachelor of arts degree and a bachelor's degree in nursing); a dual-degree public health program with the University of Massachusetts; and dual-degree engineering programs with the University of Massachusetts, Dartmouth College, and the California Institute of Technology.

In the *Plan for 2010* issued by college president Joanne Creighton, the college promises to stand against the dominant trends in higher education toward large, public, urban, and coed institutions. The document also acknowledges that the college's endowment remains much smaller than many of its peer institutions. However, the college does secure significant funding, which in 2004 included a $1.2 million Howard Hughes Medical Institute grant and a $325,000 grant from the Andrew W. Mellon Foundation that will fund a new fiber-optic network for students and faculty.

Student Life: South Hadley country club

With its red-brick, ivy-covered buildings, large oak and maple trees, and peaceful surroundings, Mount Holyoke is generally regarded as one of the loveliest campuses in the country. About 95 percent of students live on campus in 17 residence halls built in several different styles, from Victorian to Tudor to Modern Institutional Ugly. Almost all residence halls house freshmen through seniors, nicely mixing the classes and encouraging mentor relationships. Each hall has a common area with a piano and grandfather clock, as well as a dining room in which breakfast and dinner are served daily. The college recently introduced a kosher/halal dining facility, one of only a few of its kind on American college campuses. Seven of the residence halls also serve lunch and weekend meals. Milk and crackers (affectionately known as "M and C's") are served in each residence hall during the evenings on Sunday through Thursday. Kitchenettes can be found in all the residences, and all residence halls are smoke free.

One student describes the campus as a very close community. She tells the story of how the student body went into an uproar over proposed changes to the meal plan, including the closure of certain popular dining halls. Students mobilized to protest, and the administration met every one of the students' demands.

As a result of the increased enrollment, Mount Holyoke has experienced a housing crunch. The college plans to construct an additional hall and to renovate others to alleviate the problem, but in the meantime some first-year students may find themselves in less comfortable accommodations. Parking is also difficult.

Approximately 18 percent of Mount Holyoke's 2,100 students are black, Hispanic, Asian American, Native American, or multiracial. Some 15 percent are foreign students. The college's faculty is similarly diverse, with more than 20 percent "individuals of color or international scholars." The college believes that its diversity "reflects the increasing globalization taking place in the world" and is a "valuable educational asset"; some students see it that way, too. "The high number of international students is visible when considering the work ethic. They work very hard and raise the standard for everyone else to do so," says one. But another student sees the constant focus on diversity in a different light: "I do think that by increasing multiculturalism we also make our school more segregated. Women from the same countries . . . automatically associate with each other."

"Mount Holyoke is a very politically liberal-leftist campus and seems to like to shy away from anything that has to do with traditional WASPism," says one MHC student. That pretty much sums up the political climate on campus. In February 2004, a presidential diversity commission concluded that "a diversified student body not only enhances the education of all students and helps prepare them to live in a multicultural world, but also helps build a more equitable society."

One might wish that political, philosophical, and intellectual diversity were valued as highly at Mt. Holyoke (and elsewhere) as crude, demographic differences among elite students and scholars. But a glance at the political groups active on campus at MHC suggests that the school is far from achieving that kind of diversity. Students at MHC are faced with a large number of radical campus social and political groups, precious few of them right-leaning. AIDS Awareness Coalition; Lesbian, Bisexual and Questioning Women of Color; Sisters of Hinduism Reaching Inward; and True Colors (a lesbian and bisexual support group) are among the many that populate the campus scene. There is a small but visible group of College Republicans that brings in speakers and hosts a Conservative Awareness Week in the spring. In April 2001 the group hosted, amid great controversy, the CEO of the National Rifle Association. The College Democrats are less active, "but they really don't need to push their views; they are already widely accepted on campus," says one student. The Green Party is beginning to make its presence felt at the college. "A lot of students see themselves in leadership roles," says a professor. "There is a long tradition of political involvement here."

Despite MHC's very public commitment to diversity, campus tolerance toward dis-

SUGGESTED CORE

1. Classics 106f, Homer's *Iliad*: A Big Fat Ancient Greek War? (*closest match*)
2. Philosophy 201, Philosophical Foundations of Western Thought: The Greek Period
3. Religion 203, Introduction to the Hebrew Bible *and* Religion 204, Introduction to the New Testament
4. History 121, The Middle Ages, 312–1300
5. Politics 212, Modern Political Thought
6. English 211, Shakespeare
7. History 170, The American People, 1500–1865
8. Philosophy 352, Nineteenth-Century Continental Philosophy: Hegel and Marx (*closest match*)

senting views is said to be low. One student says, "The political scene on campus is very left-wing, and there is often a tone of accepted discrimination shared with staff and students alike against anyone who believes differently." Another says, "I think the college tries to hire people and speakers who support its ideologies, of course—and the college is very liberal. Most of the professors and speakers also share this viewpoint.... They forget that there is another point of view, and even if they at least acknowledge that fact, they are hesitant to give any credit to it." We haven't heard reports of bias in the classroom—which is refreshing. But conservative first-year students who are open about their beliefs do face difficulty from their peers. "Students are always free to express their views. The majority of the faculty encourages and welcomes it. However, minority views—particularly of the political right or evangelical Christians—are not always welcomed and are often misunderstood," says one conservative student. Concerning the campus ambiance, another student believes that "there is a broad internationalism on campus. If I were to characterize the political atmosphere on campus, I would definitely say that it is liberal. But conservatives on campus are definitely visible."

Mount Holyoke provides religious advisors and worship space for students of all faiths. In the residence halls, an intergroup dialogue project funded by the Mellon Foundation urges students to connect along "lines of difference through conversations about topics ranging from race to anti-Semitism to homophobia." From the dominance of lesbian and transgender groups on campus, it would appear that "homophobia," at least, is relatively uncommon. In fact, no one need fear a witch hunt at Holyoke. As the school boasts on its Web site: "Mount Holyoke . . . is one of the few liberal arts colleges in the country to serve nine active faith groups—Baha'i, Buddhist, Catholic, Hindu, Jewish, Muslim, Protestant, Unitarian Universalist, and Wiccan." So on a given weekend, one might celebrate Sunday, Sabbath, or Sabbat.

Time outside the classroom is rarely spent idly. Flyers and posters for forthcoming activities, including concerts and parties, are posted around campus by different clubs. "There is always something happening on campus," says one student. "One of the many student groups is usually hosting something, and the Speaking, Writing, and Arguing [Program] hosts a speaker most every week to discuss some current topic. There are always performances or speakers at the other colleges, too." If students don't feel like listening, across the street from campus is the college-owned Village Commons, which includes a small theater, restaurants, and shops. The popular coffeeshop, the Thirsty Mind, sometimes hosts live acoustic music. About 15 minutes away, Northampton is popular for shopping and dining, while Amherst, 15 minutes in the other direction, is the choice for bars and pubs.

Mount Holyoke students have enviable choices when it comes to extracurricular activities, many of which have a definite country-club character. The college maintains the nation's third-largest equestrian center, considered the "finest East Coast facility" by *Town and Country*, where students may board their horses and participate in the college's dressage team, which recently won a regional championship. The center also offers beginning and advanced riding lessons for students, sponsors clinics and a riding club, stables 60 horses, and hosts intercollegiate horse shows. The college manages The

Orchards, an 18-hole championship golf course designed by Donald Ross, which hosted the 2004 U.S. Women's Open. Within walking distance of the golf course is the state-of-the-art athletic and dance complex, which houses a 25-meter, eight-lane pool, indoor track, numerous tennis, racquetball, volleyball, basketball, and squash courts, and weight training and cardiovascular fitness areas. Intercollegiate athletics include NCAA Division III teams in basketball, crew, cross-country running, field hockey, golf, lacrosse, riding, soccer, squash, swimming and diving, tennis, indoor and outdoor track and field, and volleyball. Participation in extracurricular arts such as dancing and singing is equally popular.

Mount Holyoke seems particularly concerned about security. The Department of Public Safety patrols the campus 24 hours a day. The campus is well lit and campus phones are always nearby. Few crimes of consequence are reported. One aggravated assault and 18 burglaries were reported on campus in 2003. Students report feeling very safe on campus.

If Mount Holyoke is an oasis of learning, its prices mirror those of a resort. Tuition in 2004–5 was $30,770, room and board, $9,060. However, 70 percent of students receive financial aid, and some receive merit scholarships. According to *Kiplinger.com,* Mount Holyoke appears to meet 100 percent of needy students' financial requirements. Recent graduates carry an average student loan debt of $14,200.

PROVIDENCE COLLEGE

PROVIDENCE, RHODE ISLAND • WWW.PROVIDENCE.EDU

Providence, the one in Rhode Island

Providence College is one of the younger schools in this guide. Founded in 1917 by the Dominican order of the Roman Catholic Church, Providence's academic reputation is consistently strong. *U.S. News and World Report* has ranked it first or second among 165 universities in the North for eight consecutive years. Despite a few anti-Catholic professors and an administration that does little to silence them, Providence also boasts a dedicated band of real teachers and believing Catholic priests. These keep alive a regard for Providence's original mission and try to defend its Catholic identity against the forces of disintegration that have neutered so many once-religious schools. And they have at least preserved a strong core curriculum that focuses on Western civilization—a rare achievement, nowadays. Although Providence students are not especially known

NEW ENGLAND

for their piety, they are forced to consider certain ultimate realities in class. As one professor says, "Though we're not Steubenville, we're not Georgetown, either."

Academic Life: Western Civ lives

Virtually every liberal arts school in this guide proclaims its commitment to the humanities. Yet some of the most famous schools in the nation give 18-year-olds free rein to chart their own educational courses and to emerge, four years later, with scant knowledge of American history, Western philosophy, or the great books, and a scattered intellectual training.

This can't happen at Providence. Its core curriculum guides students through the liberal arts, moving chronologically through the Western tradition from Greece and Israel, through the Middle Ages, the Renaissance, the Enlightenment, and the nineteenth century, up to a final course that appraises "the time when European hegemony over the planet seems complete, but Nietzsche is proclaiming the anti-Gospel that God is dead." These core classes are held five days a week and are taught by a team of professors from the art, English, languages, history, theology, and philosophy departments. Each week, smaller groups of students meet with one of the professors for discussion.

A professor who once taught the four-semester core sequence says that while "the pace is obviously fairly fast and we aim at coverage and a coherent metanarrative rather than depth," recently professors have begun to meet as teams before and during semesters "to determine what important ideas or questions will organize our presentation of the material." This professor says that the core sequence "has become . . . a powerful course in the history of ideas." One junior says, "Western Civ was one of the best parts of my academic life. You'd be surprised how much actually is useful in these classes. It's also a great backbone course because everything else builds on these core courses."

Upon completing the sequence, however, a student critic complained in the student newspaper, the *Cowl*, that the courses were a "rushed Cliff Notes revisit of high school" and a "skewed version of history." He was especially critical of the philosophy portion of the course, which he charged with being overburdened by "unknown quasi-philosophers that . . . leave most confused and befuddled as to their relationship in civilization's development." One of the more prominent professors at Providence disputes this, arguing that "the philosophers covered include no second-rank figures." Whether or not the Providence curriculum could be stronger, it's heartening—no, inspiring—to see students arguing seriously with professors about the intellectual significance of particular thinkers assigned as part of a serious core curriculum. If only every school faced just such a controversy.

Perhaps a weakness at Providence is the absence of writing courses. Outside the Western civilization core, students can avoid writing-intensive courses entirely. Students so inclined may visit the Writing Center where fellow students will provide advice. In other academic matters, the Tutorial Center offers peer help from capable students.

Departmental requirements for majors are impressive. The English department requires 10 courses: "Introduction to Literature," four courses in literature before 1800, four in literature after 1800, and one elective. The history major requires three specific U.S. history courses (one on history up to 1815, one from 1815 to 1900, and one that covers 1900 to the present), three European history courses ("The Renaissance," "Medieval Europe," "The Ancient World," and several other general European history classes will do), and four history electives. Theology demands seven specific courses and one class in sacred scripture, one in historical theology, a special elective, and an upper-level major seminar. The required courses are "Old Testament Literature and Theology," "New Testament Literature and Theology," "Mystery of God," "Principles of Moral Decision," "Christ, Word and Redeemer," "The Church," and "Sacraments." One professor reports that "there is a solid group of committed Catholics on the faculty who maintain a serious [Catholic] identity through their teaching and through the witness of their lives. Our theology department is, *mirabile dictu!*, a stronghold of orthodoxy."

Another professor notes that the education, business, and sociology departments are the least rigorous at Providence. However, the major in public and community service is the only one of its kind in the country. Students who opt for it spend time in the community as well as in the classroom, where they take courses like "Community Service in American Culture," "Catholic Social Thought," "Ethics, Moral Leadership, and the Common Good," and one cultural diversity course such as "Race and Politics in the Americas," or "Sociology of Women and Men." Black studies, Latin American studies, and women's studies are offered only as minors, their class offerings often cross-listed with other departments. Many students combine other majors with courses in the education department, earning teaching certificates for elementary/special education, secondary education, or music education.

Except for a few introductory courses, Providence classes are small enough that students often develop enduring relationships with their professors. "Professors know you. . . . They know everything about you," says one student. "Some even give you their home phone numbers on the first day of class. I've heard of one professor-priest who noticed that one of his students was missing from class. He called the student up, found that he had overslept, and marched the whole class to his dorm room to hold class there. That's commitment." Another student adds that "the professors here truly are caring and attentive." There are no teaching assistants at Providence College, so faculty members teach all courses. All advisors—premajor advisors and advisors within the major—are also faculty members.

VITAL STATISTICS

Religious affiliation:
  Roman Catholic
Total enrollment: 5,367
Total undergraduates: 3,770
SAT median: 1199
Applicants: 7,827
Applicants accepted: 55%
*Accepted applicants who
  enrolled*: 24%
Tuition: $23,180
Room and board: $8,445
Freshman retention rate: 92%
Graduation rate: 85% (6 yrs.)
Average class size: 19
Student-faculty ratio: 13:1
*Courses taught by graduate
  TAs*: none
Most popular majors:
  education, management,
  marketing
Students living on campus:
  75%
*Guaranteed housing for four
  years?* no
*Students in fraternities or
  sororities*: none

NEW ENGLAND

ACADEMIC REQUIREMENTS

Providence requires all freshmen and sophomores to take "Development of Western Civilization," a sequence of courses spread out over four semesters. It covers:

- First semester: Classical Greece and Rome and ancient Israel.
- Second semester: The Middle Ages and the Renaissance.
- Third semester: The Enlightenment to the nineteenth century.
- Fourth semester: The late nineteenth through early twenty-first centuries.

On top of this respectable core sequence, Providence expects students to meet serious distribution requirements, while providing some flexibility in choosing courses "from a variety of . . . designated electives," according to the school's catalog:

- Social sciences, two courses. Options range from "Principles of Economics: Micro" to "Introduction to Women's Studies."
- Natural sciences, two courses, with choices such as "Contemporary Biology" and "Genes and Gender."

Providence's best qualities are highlighted in the college's Liberal Arts Honors Program. Honors students can choose from a list of smaller and more demanding courses only open to them. They must complete at least six honors classes, average no lower than a B, and complete a semester-long colloquium during their junior or senior years.

With some 300,000 volumes, the library is rather small, but as part of the Higher Education Library Information Network consortium, Providence has access to roughly six million volumes from any of the eight Rhode Island academic libraries. "You really can't ever use the excuse 'I couldn't find the book,'" a junior says.

Providence's best teachers, students say, include Brian Barbour, Rodney Delasanta, Anthony Esolen, and Steven Lynch in English; Mario DiNunzio, Richard Grace, John Lawless, Fr. Thomas McGonigle, and Raymond Sickinger in history; Matthew Cuddeback and Vance Morgan in philosophy; Joseph Cammarano in political science; and Paul Gondreau, James Keating, and Fr. David Stokes in theology.

Hostility to the Catholic faith is notoriously evident, however, in the case of one professor, Jim Moorhead, whose "Sociology of the Family" and other courses have provoked complaints on campus and in the *Cowl*. Students note that what Moorhead calls his "sex classes" extol divorce and adultery, denounce "that whole bull—t idea of love," and pepper such wisdom with obscene discussions of sexual intimacy and accompanying foul language. Students also note that Professor Moorhead thinks it important they understand that religion generally, and Catholicism in particular, is "patriarchal bull—t," and he does not welcome outside scrutiny of such perspectives; a *Cowl* piece noted his refusal to allow their reporters to attend his classes, and the *Chronicle of Higher Education* reported college pressure on the *Cowl* not to publish several letters about the classes until, with a touch of irony, after Family Day, when prospective students and their families visit the college.

In 2003, Providence also allowed the presentation of *The Vagina Monologues*. Arguably mirroring the vigilance once practiced by a certain cardinal in Boston, the administration officially disapproved—while permitting the production to be held on campus property under the sponsorship of eight academic departments. The "administration's behavior with regard to *Monologues* has been cowardly," was the consensus of many of the college's professors, one told us. One respected priest added: "As for Moorhead, he is an absolute disgrace. . . . Why he was not sacked immediately when this information came out is beyond me. Sure, he would have sued, but we would have won, and made a very important point. Now we're just waiting until he dies or retires," but "once there is a precedent set for that . . . it gets easier." Despite these inexcusable episodes, the Catholics on the faculty, and the students we spoke to, were uniform in holding that these controversies are exceptions. The most influential professors, one observed, are "the core" of some 30 solid believers who hold the fort. Perhaps tellingly, the former editor of *Latin Mass Magazine* sends his son to Providence.

College president Philip Smith, O.P., will be retiring at the end of this school year. His successor, who has not yet been chosen, will help determine whether Providence hews to its roots or drifts away.

Student Life: Providential upbringing

Not counting international students, more than 90 percent of the student body at Providence is white. Worried about this unwelcome statistic, the college has been trying to make the school more racially diverse, offering a number of scholarships only to students who are members of preferred minority groups. There are, meanwhile, 12 student-run multicultural groups, from the campus chapter of the NAACP and the Amigos Unidos to the Gaelic Society and the Hellenic Society.

Roughly 60 percent of the Providence student body is female, and since Title IX requires proportionate support for male and female athletic programs, the school has been forced to make some unpopular decisions, including cutting men's golf, tennis, and baseball from varsity-level play. Several years later, many students and staff still grieve the losses.

There are few political clubs for students, except for the College Republicans and a floundering College Democrats chapter. Some professors and a number of students complain of student apathy. One student notes favorably the recent founding of an Evangelization Committee,

REQUIREMENTS (CONT'D)

- Philosophy, two courses, one of them in ethics. Options include "Introduction to the Philosophy of St. Thomas" and "Twentieth-Century Women Philosophers."
- Theology, two courses. Choices range from "Theology of the New Testament" to "Ecology, Creation, Redemption."
- Mathematics, one course.
- Fine arts, one course. Choices range from "Baroque and Rococo Art" to "History of Jazz."
- Nondepartmental electives, three courses outside one's major department or program.
- English, one course or proficiency. Students are deemed proficient if they enter Providence with an AP English score of four or better; have scored above 540 on their verbal SAT and complete an approved English literature course during their first semester; successfully complete a writing seminar by the end of their sophomore year; or pass the English Proficiency Exam. Two attempts to pass the test are allowed during one semester. A student who fails the test twice is required to take English 101 in a subsequent semester.

"whose mission is essentially to get the lapsed Catholics to become practicing Catholics again," and an apologetics newsletter in which "quite a few [students] . . . have shown great interest."

When the Providence College campus was built in 1919, Harkins Hall was its only building. Students ate, slept, and attended class there. Today, Providence's campus encompasses more than 100 acres, and since the school has tried to keep the architecture somewhat coherent, most of the buildings are of dark red brick. Besides Harkins Hall and the new chapel, the buildings aren't especially remarkable, but the pedestrian-friendly campus has a pleasant feel, with no roads running through the grounds. In 2001, the college began a 10-year Master Space Plan that will continue to improve the campus both practically and aesthetically. Renovations to the library, the student union, athletic facilities, and a dining hall are already complete; the Smith Center for the Arts, complete with classroom space, studios, practice rooms, a music library, and 275-seat auditorium, opened in 2004.

The college is surrounded by residential neighborhoods; Brown University and the Rhode Island School of Art and Design are a couple miles closer to the historic downtown area of the city. Classroom buildings are scattered throughout the campus, so some students may roll out of bed and attend class downstairs in the dormitory, while others might have to walk for 15 minutes.

Three-quarters of Providence students live on campus; freshmen and sophomores, with rare exceptions, are required to do so. Students can choose from either traditional dormitories (with singles, doubles, triples, or quads) or on-campus apartments, which are especially popular with seniors. The most coveted spots are in the centrally located three dorms on "the quad"; Suites Hall, a 348-bed suite-style residence, opened in 2004. Of the nine residence halls, three are for men, three are for women, and three are coed, with men and women separated by floor. Men are allowed to be in the rooms of women and vice versa, but on school nights they must be out by midnight, and on weekends by 2 a.m. Providence students do not have to head to the library to find a quiet place to study because every dormitory features a large study lounge. (The study room in Aquinas Hall was donated by Judy Garland in 1938.) The college adds $42 to the cost of room and board to make laundry "free."

Providence is not only a home to students; 50 to 60 Dominican friars and sisters live on campus. Twenty-five of them are full-time professors, and many serve as mentors and advisors to students. "Pasta with Padres," says one student, "is a fun evening not to be missed. Students and friars get together to have a pasta dinner in the basement of the chapel, and they both get to know each other better and learn more about each other. It is a nice way to bond with other students as well as the friars here." St. Dominic Chapel seats around 600 people and offers three masses daily, one on Saturday evening, and three on Sunday. The Pastoral Services Organization manages spiritual life on campus, sponsoring retreats, service work, and other events for interested students, but, as one student says, "You can get involved as much as you want or as little as you want. Nobody forces Catholicism down your throat." Approximately 80 percent of Providence students say they are Catholic. For others, Pastoral Services will identify other churches or religious centers in the area.

Providence College is a member of the Big East Athletic Conference—so naturally, sports are a huge part of student life. The college viewbook boasts that the school has more postseason tournament wins and more former players in the pros than any other school in New England. Students get courtside seats at the downtown Dunkin Donuts Center, which contributes to Providence's reputation as a difficult place for visiting teams to play. Nonvarsity sports are popular as well, with around 70 percent of students participating in either club or intramural teams.

The city of Providence offers plenty of attractions to students—restaurants (Little Italy especially), artistic performances and exhibits (at the Rhode Island School of Art and Design, for example), and shopping, to name a few. The college provides shuttles downtown until 3 a.m., and a cab ride is only about four dollars. Newport's beaches are only a half hour away, Boston is an hour, and New York City is about three and a half hours distant. On campus, students can attend lectures, performances by the famous Blackfriars theater group, movies on the lawn, college-wide dances, or the meetings and activities of 100 student clubs. Then there is alcohol. One student says, "There is a lot of drinking that goes on here, both on and off campus, but for those who do not want to be involved in that, there are plenty of other options and ways to meet people and have fun. . . . Not everyone goes out and parties all night." Two favorite traditions of Providence students are associated with the Western civilization core courses: Each semester on the midnight before the course exam, freshmen and sophomores participate in the Civ Scream, yelling at the top of their lungs to let out their stress. And at the end of the first two years, sophomores celebrate at the Done with Civ Barbecue.

The college is surrounded by a stone wall, and a security guard watches the main entrance 24 hours a day. Crime is relatively infrequent, with a three-year average of 32 burglaries a year and five aggravated assaults. In 2003, the last year for which statistics were available, there were 11 aggravated assaults, one robbery, 14 burglaries, six stolen cars and four arsons. Residence halls are probably the safest places on campus. Female students feel safe walking around campus at night, their well-being buttressed by dozens of emergency call boxes. A student escort is waiting at the library during evening hours to convey late-night travelers home.

Providence cannot promise to meet every student's full financial aid needs. But admissions are need-blind, and about 70 percent of students receive some need-based financial aid. One must maintain a respectable grade point average to have such aid renewed. Tuition for the 2004–5 academic year was $23,180. Room plus special fees ranged from $4,645 for residence halls to $7,030 for campus apartment rentals. Meal plans ran from $2,200 to $4,250. The average indebtedness of Providence graduates is $16,000 to $17,000.

SMITH COLLEGE

I am Smith, hear me roar

Founded in 1875, Smith College is the largest private women's college in the United States and perhaps the most famous. It is also considered one of the top liberal arts schools in the nation. The college is named after Sophia Smith, who provided funding for the school's land and first buildings. Smith stated in her will that the college was established "with the design to furnish for my own sex means and facilities for education equal to those which are afforded now in our colleges to young men." And indeed, the college produces independent and ambitious women competent in their chosen professions. However, this independence appears to many to be compromised by the school's thoroughgoing commitment to radical feminism. At Smith, some students complain, the feminist perspective pervades most courses and activities outside the classroom. The constant theme of female self-empowerment is spread across Smith's promotional materials with inspirational images of women labeled—with a touch of bathos—"I am Smith."

Academic Life: Sylvia Plath, Gloria Steinem, and Barbara Bush go into a college . . .

Liberal arts have been a priority at Smith since its founding, but today the college places more emphasis on technology and the sciences, as well as majors such as education. Smith students are intelligent, hard working, and socially active. The college assumes that its graduates will take on leadership roles in society, and its commitment to the liberal arts, particularly the humanities, has helped Smithies do just that. The Alumnae Association of Smith College is one of the largest and most active in the country. Notable Smith graduates include Sylvia Plath, Gloria Steinem, Betty Friedan, world-famous television chef and former OSS operative Julia Child, feminist legal scholar Catharine MacKinnon, columnist Molly Ivins, and former first ladies Nancy Reagan and Barbara Bush. Among its alumnae, the college proudly boasts a list of firsts, including the first woman to be ordained an Episcopal priest.

At this all-women school, nearly every subject tends to be approached from the perspective of feminist ideology. Coupled with the school's emphasis on multiculturalism and diversity, Smith can be disappointingly homogeneous, according to some students. Each fall, on Otelia Cromwell Day (named for the first African American to graduate from Smith), classes are canceled and students are expected to attend lectures, performances, and workshops dealing with issues of diversity, racism, and oppression. Smith also has a special orientation program for "students of color," designed, it says, for such students "to gain a further appreciation of their own and others' cultures."

The school's president since 2002, Carol Christ, said recently that one of her main focuses is diversity and that she intends to explore how the campus can be even further "diversified" via admissions. She wants more community-wide discussions and debates on issues of race, class, gender, and sexual identification. The school paper quotes her as saying, "At every college and university, building a diverse community is a continuing challenge, [and at Smith] we haven't achieved the kind of equity that we hope to achieve." But, hey, things aren't as bad as they used to be. In 2002, Smith received twice as many applications from black students as it did the two previous years, and "an increase of 72 percent in applications from under-represented minorities in comparison to 2000 and 58 percent in comparison to 2001," according to President Christ.

Since 1970, Smith has had no general education requirements. None. The only mandatory courses are those in a student's major, plus 64 credits outside it, and one writing-intensive course. This blank space, to be filled with the personal preferences of 17- to 21-year-olds, has replaced Smith's once impressive curriculum.

Smith students must carefully structure their own programs to have any hope of an authentic liberal education. The bulletin advises students to select from among seven fields of knowledge: literature, historical studies, social science, natural science, the arts, foreign language, and mathematics and analytical philosophy. Advice is always nice; but Smith does nothing to require students graduating from this elite school to learn a thing about Greek philosophy, English literature, or even American history. Its course catalog is filled with the sort of courses one would expect at an institution committed to latter-day academic feminism. The women's studies department, for instance, includes courses like "Overseas Filipina Workers," "Sexualities and the State," "Global Women, Feminized Work," "The Politics of Sexual Representation," "Afro-Caribbean Women Writers," and "Sexual Histories, Lesbian Stories." Smith offers a minor in third-world development studies, with courses like "Native South Americans: Conquest and Resistance" and "The Anthropology of Food." Still, at least one Smith professor assures us that while the school's system "doesn't guarantee distribution, [it] tends nevertheless to accomplish that objective."

Academics at Smith are described as competitive, and class discussions are said to be characterized by a high degree of student participation. "They are an ambitious lot," says one faculty member. About 15 percent of students pursue degrees in the hard

VITAL STATISTICS
Religious affiliation: none
Total enrollment: 3,165
Total undergraduates: 2,692
SAT/ACT midranges: SAT V: 590–700, M: 570–670; ACT: 25–30
Applicants: 2,993
Applicants accepted: 57%
Accepted applicants who enrolled: 41%
Tuition: $29,156
Room and board: $9,730
Freshman retention rate: 91%
Graduation rate: 78% (4 yrs.), 84% (6 yrs.)
Courses with fewer than 20 students: 68%
Student-faculty ratio: 9:1
Courses taught by graduate TAs: none
Most popular majors: social sciences, fine art, languages
Students living on campus: 87%
Guaranteed housing for four years? yes
Students in sororities: none

sciences. The most popular departments at Smith include government, economics, psychology, biology, English, and art. A student may also design her own major if she can get it approved by the administration.

Requirements for the majors provide some structure, but not much. English majors, for instance, are required to take one core course called "Methods of Literary Study," two courses on literature before 1832, a seminar, courses on two of three major literary figures (Chaucer, Shakespeare, and Milton), and six electives within the department. One may also take classes like "Love and the Literary Imagination," which is "a study of the way literary convention shapes and interprets the experience of love."

History majors are required to take an "Introduction to History" course and five courses in a field of concentration. They are also supposed to achieve "geographical breadth" by taking courses in three of the following areas: Africa, East Asia and Central Asia, Europe, Latin America, Middle East and South Asia, and North America. Thus, a history major can conceivably graduate without ever learning anything about ancient or medieval history, the American Revolution, or the Civil War, spending her time instead on courses such as "Of Women Delivered: Midwifery in Historical and Cross-Cultural Perspective" and "Women Writing Resistance: U.S. History through Women's Testimony." But as conventional wisdom goes, not all is so bad. The department also offers compelling electives such as "Authority and Legitimacy in the Age of More and Shakespeare," which carefully examines the texts and historical context of Shakespeare's *Richard II, Henry IV* (parts I and II), *Henry V, Richard III, King Lear,* and Thomas More's *Utopia.*

Rigorous interdepartmental majors and minors in medieval studies and ancient studies are also offered at Smith. While ancient studies has almost been swallowed up by the languages and literature department and is only available as a minor, medieval studies—offered as a major and a minor—is described as a "vibrant program" by one professor. In fact, medieval studies may be the program at Smith that comes the closest to a traditional liberal arts education. All students enrolled in the major are required to have a working knowledge of Latin and to gain in-depth knowledge of the history, religion, and art of European civilization. A major in classical studies is also offered; students do not have to complete a specified core, but Greek and Latin are strongly recommended.

Smith became the first women's college to award diplomas in engineering in May 2004. The program has a typical Smithian twist. According to the *Chronicle of Higher Education*: "Instead of piling equations and formulas on first-year students, [the Smith program] offered them introductory classes that explore ways in which engineers can improve society." (One way, we'd suggest, would be for them to learn those equations and formulas.)

With no structured curriculum, it is fortunate that Smith students have access to a strong advising program. Upon entering Smith as a freshman, a student is assigned a faculty advisor who helps direct her path until she declares a major, usually during her sophomore year. Then she chooses her own advisor within her department.

The student-faculty ratio at Smith is an excellent nine to one, and student-faculty relationships are reportedly strong. Classes are usually small, and although there is a small population of graduate students on campus, professors teach all the classes and grade all exams. Students rate the accessibility of Smith's faculty as one of the school's finest points.

Almost 50 percent of students participate in a study-abroad program at some point during their time at Smith. The college has junior-year-abroad programs in Florence, Hamburg, Geneva, and Paris. The college maintains a formal affiliation with programs in Japan, China, Rome, Spain, southern India, and Russia. And if those aren't enough, more than 100 other study-abroad programs have been pre-approved by the school.

Another way to study off campus is through the Twelve College Exchange. This program allows students to spend their junior year at another college, such as Amherst, Bowdoin, Connecticut College, Dartmouth, Mount Holyoke, Trinity, Vassar, Wellesley, Wesleyan, Wheaton (the one in Massachusetts), or Williams. There is also a one-to-one student exchange program with Pomona College in Claremont, California. Two semester-long internship programs in Washington, D.C., are available, and students may also opt to study for a year at a historically black college such as Howard University or the all-women Spelman College.

Smith's extensive internship program, "Praxis: The Liberal Arts at Work," gives every student the opportunity to take part in a summer internship funded by the school. Many students take advantage of the program, obtaining positions at the White House, medical research facilities, or legal aid programs.

Recommended faculty at Smith include Donald C. Baumer and J. Patrick Coby in government; Richard Lim, Lester Little, Howard Nenner, and Joachim W. Stieber in history; Henri Cole, Dean Flower, and Douglas Lane Patey in English language and literature; and Carol G. Zaleski in religion and biblical literature.

With an endowment of nearly $1 billion—to be augmented by its current $425 million fundraising campaign, reportedly the largest ever undertaken by a liberal arts college—Smith has plenty of resources. A career development office helps students decide what occupation to pursue and helps locate job opportunities. The Jacobson Center provides students with writing assistance, tutoring, and various skills workshops. The Clark Science Center has laboratories with state-of-the-art equipment, including a nuclear magnetic resonance spectrometer. Smith's special Center for Foreign Languages

ACADEMIC REQUIREMENTS

One intensive writing course is required for each student during her first or second semester at Smith.

Apart from that, no specific courses are required for the bachelor of arts degree, and no distribution requirements are in place. The college does require that students complete a major and take at least half their courses outside the department or program of their major. The curricular requirements for the bachelor of science degree in engineering are extensive, including many classes in mathematics and physics as well as engineering, and several liberal arts electives.

One course (usually four credits) in each of seven major fields is required for students who want to earn Latin Honors at graduation.

and Cultures houses a computer-based multimedia facility that uses interactive digital video and audio at individual workstations, allowing students to study at their own pace. According to the school's Web site, the college provides one computer for every 5 Smith students, but 85 percent of students choose to bring their own. Smith's library is stocked with more than 1.4 million volumes, and students also have access to the libraries of the other schools in the Five College Consortium.

Student Life: It's paid for

Smith is a curious place—definitely not your mother's women's college (even if she went to Smith). In April 2003, by a campus-wide vote, Smith students decided to eliminate the words "she" and "her" from their student government's constitution, according to the *Chronicle of Higher Education.* Why? To avoid offending those Smith students who *don't identify as women.* Apparently, a small contingent of students consider themselves "transgender." To provide them "a more welcoming and comfortable environment," the student government decided to replace female pronouns with "gender-neutral terms." (No word on whether Smith wishes to be referred to henceforth as an "all-whatever college.")

In response to similar initiatives, Smith College administrators have hired a part-time gender specialist "to provide counseling services and consultation to the college to support transgender students." Smith's Campus Diversity Board works closely with the administration's Office of Institutional Diversity and the diversity committees associated with each campus residence. The board is working to change the student handbook; it wants additional diversity training for residential life staff and counselors to deal with transgender and sexuality issues. Already, each year faculty and staff must sit through three full days of a diversity training session called "Understanding Ourselves, Understanding Each Other." Residential life staff members also are required to participate in diversity sessions before the school year starts and in follow-up sessions throughout the year. Probably motivated by a desire to understand the other, one Democrat student reported that she had attended the College Republican meeting. She says, "I found that I was welcomed by the board despite my political affiliation, and I found members who were proud to be Republican."

Smith has an active lesbian community that is loud and proud. The group has its own student organization, not to mention special committees for lesbians of color, bisexuals, and transgendered people. Smith also offers health insurance benefits to domestic partners. Some students claim that a number of Smithies are merely "LUGs"— lesbians until graduation. The truth of this can be tested, we suppose, by attending class reunions.

The college collects a student fee that is used to help fund campus organizations. Smith has more than 100 student clubs of all types (arts, social and political action, cultural heritage, career-related, language, and support groups) to choose from. Students have a weekly paper, the *Sophian,* and a campus radio station. A new $23 million, 60,000-square-foot campus center was dedicated in 2003.

Nearly every religious group is represented at Smith; there are even clubs called the Association of Smith Pagans and the Radical Catholic and Feminist Organization at Smith. The university has chaplains or advisors for many different faiths, and services in several religious traditions are available. There are a handful of more conservative groups on campus, including a College Republican Club and a pro-life group, both of which are active. One student says that "going to Smith as a conservative would be difficult." Yet despite its liberal political tenor, Smith is "a very civil place," notes one professor. Another professor says, "People treat each other well, and the college takes academic freedom very seriously."

Smithies come from throughout the nation (75 percent hail from out of state) and many different countries. Most (88 percent) live in the residential house system, which has been in place since the beginning of the college. The campus has 35 of these houses and apartment buildings, and students are expected to stay in the same residence for all four years (although some students change after their freshman year). A limited number of seniors are allowed to live off campus, but this is decided by lottery or as the result of special permission given in exceptional circumstances. A house is home to between 12 and 100 residents, with a mix of students from each academic year. The houses are self-governing, meaning that students make and enforce the rules. Naturally, a student's house is the center of her social life while at Smith, and each house has unique traditions and styles. Some traditions are campus-wide, such as the family-style candlelight dinners served every Thursday night and the Friday afternoon teas to which special guests are sometimes invited.

The college holds a formal convocation ceremony each year with an opening address by the school president and a performance by the Glee Club. And each fall, the president surprises the campus by declaring "Mountain Day," canceling all classes on short notice and providing food, activities, and the opportunity for students to enjoy the outdoors. On the day before commencement, alumnae escort graduating seniors, who, wearing white dresses, parade around campus and then plant ivy to symbolize the connection between the school and its graduates. That night the entire campus is lit with colored paper lanterns, providing a soft glow to the grounds that is perfect for reminiscing about bygone days and long-lost LUGs.

Smithies should have no complaints regarding the accoutrements of the houses, as each has its own kitchen, dining room, piano, and house cook. Each bedroom has high-speed Internet access. Special-interest housing includes a French house, a senior house, and a vegetarian co-op.

SUGGESTED CORE
1. Classics 190, The Trojan Wars
2. Philosophy 124, History of Ancient and Medieval Philosophy
3. Religion and Biblical Literature 210/215, Introduction to the Bible I/II
4. Religion and Biblical Literature 208, The Catholic Philosophical Tradition
5. Government 262, Early Modern Political Theory, 1500–1800
6. English 213, Introduction to Shakespeare
7. History 265/266, North America in an Age of Empires *and* The Age of the American Civil War
8. History 250, Europe in the Nineteenth Century (*closest match*)

First-year students are well cared for. Before a student arrives on campus, one of the "heads of new students" contacts her to explain various campus details. Once at Smith, she helps the student during orientation. A Big Sister–Little Sister program puts new students in contact with alumnae who send letters and the occasional care package. First-year students are offered a variety of seminars that emphasize writing, public speaking, group work, and library and quantitative skills.

Sports are a big part of life at Smith. The school even offers an exercise and sports studies major. Smith's 14 varsity teams compete in the NCAA Division III in basketball, crew, cross country, equestrian, field hockey, lacrosse, skiing, soccer, softball, squash, swimming and diving, tennis, track and field, and volleyball. Intercollegiate club sports include croquet, badminton, fencing, rugby, sailing, and ultimate Frisbee. Intramurals and individual instruction are offered in more than 30 activities. The college opened a new three-level, $4 million fitness center in January 2004. Outdoor recreational facilities include 25 acres of playing fields; a 400-meter, eight-lane, all-weather track; 5,000-meter cross-country course; crew facilities and boat houses; lighted tennis courts; indoor and outdoor riding rings, a five-acre hunt course, and turnout paddocks and horse trails.

The quality of social life at Smith is varied. Though there aren't any sororities, keg parties still find a place on campus. Plenty of young men from nearby colleges stay the weekend at Smith, and a 24-hour free bus system makes access to coeducational colleges in the area rather easy. Smith has a large counseling department to help students deal with such issues as depression and eating disorders. According to the school's Web site, about 25 percent of the student body avails itself of these services in some form or another. Smoking is banned in every building at Smith; those wishing to light up must stand at least 20 feet away from any Smith facility.

Smith has one of the finest art museums in the country, with a permanent collection of more than 25,000 items that includes works by Eakins, Rodin, Copley, Picasso, Degas, and Matisse. Art, dance, music, and theater are all majors offered by the college and there are several theatrical, writing, and performance groups of various types. Noon concerts are held weekly in the Sage Hall for Performing Arts. The arts are well funded at Smith and the college's museum and fine arts center is currently undergoing a $35 million expansion and renovation.

Smith's location in Northampton, Massachusetts, a college town with a population of about 30,000, provides students with a small-town environment that has the cultural benefits of a metropolitan center. Indeed, not long ago Northampton received the top ranking in the book *The 100 Best Small Art Towns in America*. Students may visit a farmers' market in town, then shop at Thorne's Marketplace, a 30-store indoor shopping center. Northampton also has used bookstores, coffeeshops, a variety of artistic enterprises, and two art-house movie theaters.

Northampton is located right outside Smith's gates, but the school's semi-rural setting means students are only a five-minute walk from the countryside. Nearby is the Mill River, where students go for picnics and relaxation. Boston is only two hours away; New York is less than three. Normally, though, students prefer to stay on campus or on the campuses of nearby colleges, since academic and extracurricular life occupies most of their time. Most students ride bikes or walk to get around the area.

While Smith is extraordinarily safe compared to other schools, crime does exist. Most crimes are committed by other students, ranging from theft to harassment. The 2003 crime statistics listed one forcible sex offense, five burglaries and three motor vehicle thefts on campus. Of greater concern is the number of disciplinary actions/ judicial referrals that have been issued for drugs (20) and liquor violations (31). The school maintains a 24-hour campus security force and 40 emergency telephones throughout the campus, but emphasizes personal responsibility when it comes to safety; residents of each house are to monitor their own buildings each evening during "house watch."

Smith is a pricey experience, at $29,156 tuition and another $9,730 for room and board. But the school's financial aid is generous. Almost 70 percent of students receive some need-based aid, with Smith grants ranging from $521 to $38,354. The average is $20,555. Smith guarantees to meet the full financial need, as calculated by the college, of all admitted students who meet the published admission and financial aid deadlines. The average Smithie, upon graduation, owes $20,570.

THOMAS MORE COLLEGE OF LIBERAL ARTS

MERRIMACK, NEW HAMPSHIRE • WWW.THOMASMORECOLLEGE.EDU

More is small, small is more

"An absolutely new idea is one of the rarest things known to man," wrote the sixteenth-century Catholic humanist St. Thomas More. That maxim suggests that one should be a little suspicious of notions branded or marketed as "new"—and receptive to those with long pedigrees and centuries of practice behind them, refurbished for modern use. Of course, this is not the guiding principle at most American schools, which follow the scent of the "new" like a pack of hungry dogs. But a prudent embrace of the best of the past did guide the small band of Catholic educators who came together in 1978 to found Thomas More. Located 40 miles north of Boston in Merrimack, New Hampshire, Thomas More College of Liberal Arts provides an intimate setting for a most unusual school—an academy the size of an extended family, focused tightly on the intellectual heritage of the Christian West. Says the Thomas More guidebook: "The education [at Thomas More] is conceived as being not so much the acquisition of information or the aggregation of skills as a gradual transformation in which students of a wide range of abilities come to understand the major ideas and modes of thought of our civilization, to examine situations and make judgments, and to proceed to original thinking."

Such a mission, embraced by a school with only 90 students and eight professors, out in the woods, makes for a heady microbrew. But the reports of Thomas More students and alumni indicate that the school is largely successful in its mission. The most obvious consequence of Thomas More's small size is that students get to know their classmates and instructors almost as well as their own siblings. (If that kind of intimacy doesn't appeal to you—and it's not for everyone—look elsewhere.) Faculty members care deeply about their students' academic progress and overall well-being; students are cooperative rather than competitive, and intensely intellectually curious. Many alumni go on to graduate school and academic careers—and not a few into seminaries. In other words, Thomas More may be the closest thing now existing to the tiny "colleges" which grew up at Paris and Oxford in the Middle Ages and nourished such thinkers as Thomas Aquinas and Ignatius Loyola.

Academic Life: No way around it

The Thomas More academic experience is inseparable from its core curriculum. As one student says, "There is no way to get around the core requirements, which come from virtually every department in the school."

The core goes by the name of the Cowan Program of Liberal Arts, named after benefactors Donald and Louise Cowan. Every student, regardless of his major, takes one six-hour core course every semester during his four years at Thomas More, so that the entire school ends up taking one course together each semester. According to the school's Web site, "this mingling of age groups reminds the upper-classmen of their connection to the world outside through their necessary, continuing contact with new students fresh from that outside world. . . . This fact stands them in good stead after graduation, for throughout their four years they have always had to 'translate' their most complex ideas into language that can be understood by new students." The core courses focus on the philosophy, literature, culture, history, and politics of a specific period. Students say that the program is carefully constructed and provides them with a truly broad liberal arts education that covers the entire span of civilized history in the West.

One student says that the core is "the primary focus of the institution: four years of active engagement with the greatest thinkers and perennial issues that have shaped and continue to shape our world. In some respects, this education is a retreat from the workaday world, but in no sense should it be understood as a form of escapism, an excuse to indulge in aimless reverie. Rather the whole structure and focus of the college seeks to cultivate a love of learning and a community of scholars, with each student sharing in the other's education through their rigorous study in the program of liberal arts." In other words, don't come here to major in marketing.

Indeed, this is perhaps the furthest thing from a preprofessional school. Instead, it is meant for students devoted to learning for its own sake. As one faculty member has written about the core's importance: "Nowadays, of course, we tend to worry primarily about jobs and economic questions. And while these are necessary concerns, practical affairs ought not determine who we are. At our peril we risk losing the knowledge of what it means to live a truly human life."

Perhaps the most delightful aspect of the Thomas More experience is the semester students spend on the college's campus in Rome. This aspect of the program has been in place since 1983, when the college arranged to have students reside in a convent located in Rome's Trastevere section. All Thomas More sophomores must study in Rome. (Twist my *other* arm!) Faculty members accompany the class to Italy, and while in Rome, students do as their schoolmates in New Hampshire do, following the same humanities and writing curriculum. Except, of course, they are in Rome: participants take one course in theology and one in the art and architecture of Rome, which in-

VITAL STATISTICS
Religious affiliation: Roman Catholic
Total enrollment: 90
Total undergraduates: 90
SAT midrange: 1150–1250
Applicants: 40
Applicants accepted: 84%
Accepted applicants who enrolled: 72%
Tuition: $10,600
Room and board: $8,000
Freshman retention rate: 85%
Graduation rate: 88% (4 yrs.), 88% (6 yrs.)
Average class size: 17
Student-faculty ratio: 9:1
Courses taught by graduate TAs: none
Most popular majors: literature, philosophy, political science
Students living on campus: 92%
Guaranteed housing for four years? yes
Students in fraternities or sororities: none

NEW ENGLAND

135

In addition to the requirements of a major, each Thomas More student must complete the college's core, which consists of the following courses:

- Humanities I—"The Ancient World: Ancient Literature, Politics, and Philosophy."
- Humanities II—"The Ancient World: Ancient Literature, Philosophy, and Politics."
- Humanities III—"Rome and the Early Middle Ages: Early Medieval Theology and Literature."
- Humanities IV—"The High Middle Ages: Medieval Philosophy, Medieval Literature."
- Humanities V—"The Renaissance and Reformation: Renaissance Philosophy, Renaissance Literature."
- Humanities VI—"Early Modern Studies: Modern Philosophy, Literature, Politics."
- Humanities VII— "American Studies: American Politics, American Literature."

cludes walking tours around the city, guided by a chatty, urbane professor. "It gives you a chance to explore your place in the world and in the Western tradition," a student says. "[On the trip], you feel very connected to the tradition and to the truth."

The school's eight professors obviously play a crucial part in a student's life at Thomas More. "The faculty culture here is unique," a student says. "There's a simple, unspoken rule: If the office door is closed, the professor must not be on campus." Another student says professors "usually don't have office hours per se, but are often willing to set aside time to talk with students per their request. Some spend a lot of time on campus and most eat in common with the students and engage in discussion with them outside of the classroom."

Another student says, "All of the professors who teach the majors classes are first-rate. They are very dedicated to their teaching and have developed unique insights and interpretations of the works they lecture on. All of them really go above and beyond to help students with problems and ensure that the standards for academic achievement remain challenging." The faculty includes the college's founding president, Peter Sampo, who teaches most of the politics courses. However, Dr. Sampo is scheduled to retire in 2006, both from teaching and administration. The school is currently engaged in an energetic search for a worthy successor—who will not only man the helm, but also constitute some 12.5 percent of the teaching faculty.

Students have just four choices for majors—literature, philosophy, political science, and biology. The curricula for these majors are as structured as the core. Philosophy majors, for instance take courses in the philosophy of history, epistemology, metaphysics, the philosophy of science, ethics, formal logic, and political philosophy, plus one elective. The biology major is a recent addition to the Thomas More curriculum, and the college obviously does not have the laboratory resources of larger institutions. This department does have its advantages, however. "Because very few students select this major, they benefit greatly from the direct personal attention from the professor," a student says.

Another challenge faced by Thomas More students is the school's tiny staff. One upperclassman applying to graduate schools said, "I spoke to my friends at larger universities, and they told me that the development department helps them find internships, with résumés, etc. Thomas More does not have all of these resources. At first I found this very frustrating. However, I had to learn how to engage in these endeavors on my own. It is part of the education to learn how to engage in practical activities of the world—on your own."

For the required junior project, a literature major might study a poet and take an oral exam wherein faculty members make sure the student has attained a thorough understanding of the thinker and his works, perhaps asking him to recite key poems. Seniors must complete a thesis and formal presentation—given before the entire school—and pass a comprehensive examination. Like the junior project, the senior thesis is done as independent study, and students rely for advice or help on a professor of their choice. In all courses students read mainly primary texts, as in great books programs; however, various secondary sources are also used to illuminate the primary readings and spark discussion.

Each department has its own unique focus. A student describes them in this way, "The literature department strongly focuses on the Southern Agrarians, Faulkner, and Russian literature. The political science department focuses on thinkers like Eric Voegelin, Leo Strauss, F. A. Hayek, Lewis Mumford, and Milton Friedman. The philosophy department is very committed to the history of philosophy, offering a thorough study of the major philosophers as diverse as the pre-Socratics, medievals, rationalists, empiricists, logical positivists, and contemporary continental thinkers." The approach of all departments, however, is characterized by a degree of genuine openness that is often lacking in higher education, both at other religious institutions and especially at many secular schools. No writers or texts are ruled out of bounds if they are of historical importance or have made significant contributions to their fields. "The majors seem to be able to appreciate the various interpretative frameworks arising in their fields (e.g., feminist, Marxist, etc.)," says one student, "while at the same time not allowing the departments to become enslaved to any of these 'isms.'"

All aspects of life at Thomas More are suffused with the school's commitment to faithful Catholicism. As one student says, "The college is frank about this point of view so that every student will know that the context in which they are being taught takes its orientation from the Catholic tradition." The student says, "The college has certain broad principles that shape the interpretation of the material: man as body and soul, history as enveloping both secular and salvation history, life as a dramatic struggle between good and evil, a sacramental vision of the world, and the Incarnation as the

REQUIREMENTS (CONT'D)

- Humanities VIII—"The Late- and Post-Modern Era: Contemporary Philosophy, Twentieth-Century Literature."
- "Writing Workshop" I, II, III, and IV.
- Theology I—"Christology and Ecclesiology."
- Theology II—"Sacraments."
- Fine Arts—"The Art and Architecture of Rome."
- "Introductory Latin" I and II and "Intermediate Latin" or "Introductory Greek" I and II and "Intermediate Greek."
- "General Biology."
- "General Chemistry."
- "Mathematics" I and II.

Every student, regardless of major, must complete a junior project focused on a major author in the student's discipline as well as a senior thesis.

central event in history." The student cautions that these broad principles might organize the Thomas More curriculum, but they do not dictate the curriculum's particulars.

This sometimes bothers pious students. One complains that the "biology and chemistry programs need serious revamping," claiming that the textbooks used "overtly teach birth control methods for women and men, sex ed, female empowerment, and other controversial topics from a worldly and, frankly, immoral standpoint." The student suggests that the books be replaced, or the offending sections skipped or "supplemented with solid Catholic doctrine." That's the kind of student protest one might sometimes, but not often, encounter at Thomas More.

Most students are Catholic, but according to one graduate, "It's not in-your-face all the time. Students believe the teachings of the Catholic Church and try to be virtuous and moral, but it's a place where non-Catholics usually feel very comfortable, too. They don't feel persecuted." Students and faculty say Thomas More is a Catholic liberal arts college, with the emphasis on the liberal arts, while schools like Christendom College and Thomas Aquinas College emphasize Catholicism first.

A professor sums up Thomas More's political scene: "Issues of multiculturalism and diversity have not posed a difficulty at the college either in curricular or social concerns. The college does not seek to promote in either its curriculum or its social climate a narrow view of what Western culture is or a narrow view of the person. In a feature which arises out of its catholicity, the college believes in recruiting students from diverse backgrounds and in allowing the students to realize their own personal gifts and destiny." Questions of ethnicity are less important at Thomas More than the divide between students who were home-schooled and those who weren't.

Most students at Thomas More come from a conservative Catholic background and are drawn to the rigorous, traditionalist core curriculum. The Western heritage governs course topics and choices, and as one student says, "The type of education offered at TMC tends to weed out those very much opposed to this tradition."

But Thomas More deliberately fosters a sort of detachment from contemporary politics that helps students engage texts without always worrying about their "relevance." And so while the atmosphere is certainly more or less conservative, it is far from partisan, and overt politics among either the students or faculty is rare. "With the emphasis on the academic life being so strong," says one student, "few on campus have the time or energy to devote much time to political groups, other than responsible voting when the time comes and casual debate on political issues in conversation." One alumna says, "Nobody really talks about day-to-day politics. They do, however discuss political theory quite often." In other words, as another student puts it: "TMC is not exactly a politically charged campus. . . . The approach of the college is rather inimical to ideologies. Most stereotypical conservative or liberal students attending TMC will often find their ideas challenged, and through the high academic standards of the college, are prompted to reexamine their opinions and encouraged to develop more informed opinions or defend themselves through more logical argument. Most students completing the four-year program will have few of their unreflective assumptions remaining unchallenged."

Student Life: More, with less

Thomas More's campus is situated in Merrimack, New Hampshire, and includes just five buildings: a colonial house and barn from the 1600s, two dormitories, and a library. However, the school this year broke ground for its Chapel

of the North American Martyrs. Designed by renowned ecclesial architect Duncan Stroik, the chapel will be the center of campus religious life. This should help rectify one student's complaint that "there are no opportunities for daily mass, unless you have a car and don't mind missing lunch three days a week to drive into town. There are no retreats or any liturgical or religious events outside mass three days a week."

Like almost everything else at the school, residential life at Thomas More is distinctive. Men and women are separated by dormitory, and ordinarily there are no visitation opportunities for members of the opposite sex. The buildings have plenty of common space, and students usually leave doors unlocked—or wide open when they are at home. Students usually study in the library, choosing a carrel at the beginning of the year and keeping it all year long. One student says, "There is generally enough room on campus for you to have a comfortable study area."

Thomas More is a Catholic institution with an ecumenical outlook. As one person puts it, the goal of Thomas More College is to provide "a Catholic education for all." But Thomas More is not a seminary—the social life here is not so different from what you would find on many other liberal arts campuses, only with far fewer students and a narrower range of things to do. As the college puts it, "Because the college recognizes the academic festivity that occurs in the classroom as the center of its life, all its other activities, formal and informal, have the true basis for a spirit of celebration." A student says, "It's hard to separate social life from academic life. We—faculty and students—are all engaged in the pursuit of truth. At meals, for instance, we're always discussing what we're reading, what we're learning in our classes."

Social life at the college centers around the school's lecture series, wherein guest speakers visit campus on Friday evenings for talks and discussions. The guest speaker often spends the night on campus, continuing the dialogue with students during breakfast the next morning. With such a small student body, the school hardly needs any sort of student government. Nevertheless, a student Social Council assumes responsibility for planning activities. The New England setting allows for day trips to Boston or outdoor activities in the surrounding area; often the school sponsors trips to area attractions. Students occasionally organize other social activities like a dating game show on Valentine's Day and a silent movie night followed by a discussion. Or more often, they study. "There's so much work that you feel like you're always catching up on something," says one student.

There are no varsity sports at Thomas More—just as there are no fraternities or sororities—but students organize spontaneous sporting events year round. A YMCA near campus includes a pool, weight room, jogging track, and tennis, basketball, volleyball, and racquetball courts. However, some students complain that membership is "expensive and not included in tuition." Indeed, students' main gripe about the campus is its lack of facilities for extracurricular activities.

One student says that the college "enforces rules of conduct that would perhaps be viewed as highly restrictive at contemporary colleges, but all such rules are instituted to help keep the student focused upon the real reason they are in college: to become educated." Examples of such rules include no alcohol on campus, taking meals in common on a set schedule, and the segregation of dormitories according to sex. However, TMC students often have, shall we say, an earthy sort of piety. Off-campus drinking is common, and many students smoke in lieu of other vices. Puritanical attitudes are rare.

Crime is all but nonexistent at the college; official statistics from 2003 show a spotless record in all criminal categories. When one student was robbed of a laptop, digital camera, and Discman, it shocked the campus. Says the student, "The response of the community was tremendous. Without my knowing it, the students raised for me over $300 to buy a new camera and then presented me with the remainder of the money at our big Christmas dinner celebration."

The school's small size gives students the opportunity to form lasting relationships with faculty members and students. Alumni keep in close contact after graduation, and many come back to TMC for the annual reunion. Sometimes, of course, there are problems on campus, and in such an intimate atmosphere, gossip and talk are only accentuated. "Close quarters make it hard sometimes. A friend of mine was dating another student, and when they broke up, they still had to face each other all the time," a student says. Thomas More's freshman retention rate, 85 percent, illustrates that Thomas More is not necessarily for everybody. But then again, it doesn't have to be. There will always be at least 90 students in the United States who seek this kind of education. Those who remain on campus for four years usually come to love the quirks of their little liberal arts school—not to mention the superior education they have received.

At $10,600, Thomas More's tuition is drastically lower than it is at most liberal arts colleges (room and board costs an additional $8,000). One reason is that the college saves money by putting students to work. The college does have a cook during the week, but on the weekends and for breakfast on weekdays, students take turns setting up the dining hall, washing the dishes, and doing the cooking. And three times a week, students are assigned a clean-up task—sometimes cleaning a bathroom, sometimes vacuuming the floor. Student proctors oversee these jobs as well as residential life in general. Admissions are need-blind, and the school promises to meet at least 70 percent of one's financial need. Some 71 percent of students receive such aid, and the average student loan debt of recent grads is $19,363.

TUFTS UNIVERSITY

MEDFORD, MASSACHUSETTS • WWW.TUFTS.EDU

Acting globally

The 150-year history of Tufts University has seen the institution grow from a small college associated with the Universalist Church to a leading research university for both undergraduate and graduate students. Today, the science and engineering departments, along with numerous preprofessional programs, are Tufts' particular strengths. The school's location near Boston is also an asset for urban-minded students.

When Lawrence Bacow became the president of Tufts in 2002, he reaffirmed that the school's foremost academic mission was to "educate the first generation of leaders for a truly global world." Many of the university's features derive from this goal, including its foreign language and cultural course requirements, its solid study-abroad programs, and its many on-campus cultural events. But alas, Tufts' conception of a "truly global world," itself a tired cliché, entails the acceptance of the dogmas of multi-culturalism, an anti-Western ideology that suffuses campus life at this as at many other schools. Aggressive affirmative action directs hiring and admissions decisions. But somewhere in the midst of all that hides the opportunity for the discerning to find a genuine education.

Academic Life: Tuft enough

Tufts puts a high priority on teaching. Professors, not teaching assistants, teach nearly all classes. However, the mandatory freshman writing courses are taught by graduate students from various departments. Otherwise, graduate students are mainly used to lead weekly recitation or discussion groups in large lecture courses. Apart from its effect on undergraduate education, this has led to labor troubles; in September 2004, the *Chronicle of Higher Education* reported that Tufts' grad students were battling to unionize.

Most courses have fewer than 20 students, so students eventually get the opportunity to form relationships with professors. In general, according to students, profes-

VITAL STATISTICS

Religious affiliation: none
Total enrollment: 8,624
Total undergraduates: 4,843
SAT/ACT midranges: SAT
    V: 660–750, M: 680–760;
    ACT: 27–32
Applicants: 14,729
Applicants accepted: 27%
*Accepted applicants who
    enrolled*: 32%
Tuition: $30,969
Room and board: $9,030
Freshman retention rate: 96%
Graduation rate: 84% (4 yrs.),
    91% (6 yrs.)
*Courses with fewer than 20
    students*: 70%
Student-faculty ratio: 8:1
*Courses taught by graduate
    TAs*: 3%
Most popular majors: social
    sciences, engineering,
    international relations
Students living on campus:
    75%
*Guaranteed housing for four
    years?* yes
*Students in fraternities or
    sororities*: 15%

NEW ENGLAND

In lieu of a core curriculum, Tufts imposes some distribution requirements. Students must take:

- Two courses in humanities, such as "Greek, Roman, and Near Eastern History" or "Films about Love, Sex, and Society."
- Two classes in the arts, like "Introduction to Classical Archaeology" or "Kathak Dance."
- Two courses in the social sciences, with choices such as "Principles of Economics" and "Introduction to Peace and Justice Studies."
- Two natural sciences classes, chosen from options like "Radio Astronomy" and "Biology and the American Social Contract."

sors are much more accessible than they are at larger research institutions. Professors in the sciences often use student assistants on research projects. One student says, "The teaching is fantastic, they know everything about everything." A history and political science double major says, "Some professors are phenomenal."

When it comes to advising, students have a number of options. Some Tufts advisors can be excellent, "but you have to be careful about the advisor you choose," a student says. Freshmen can enroll in small-group seminars in which their professors will serve as their advisors. One student says, "This program was worthwhile because I met people in an academic setting so I was guaranteed to get to know them better through the class." Another student says, "It was fun but the advising wasn't helpful at all." Freshman who don't use these seminars are appointed a faculty advisor and two upperclassmen as peer advisors, any of which they are free to change. However, one student says, "you have to be careful in the advisor you choose. Finding an advisor is very much something you have to do on your own—people have ended up having to do a fifth year at school because their advisor was a professor who didn't know the requirements of his major." Another student says that "the advisors are fantastic; they take a keen interest in the student's well-being and welfare."

Tufts University's commitment to an international outlook begins in the classroom; as the college Web site explains, the "foundation of a Tufts liberal arts education rests on the ability to write well and the ability to use a foreign language." One student says that "good research and writing skills are expected of all students, and professors make certain that students employ them."

Tufts strongly encourages study abroad, and from 40 to 50 percent of all undergraduates do so, usually during their junior year. One student calls the program "a defining Tufts experience." Another says that "for most people, a semester in London, Madrid, or Paris does little beyond helping their language skills and getting them far away from their parents. For others, however, who travel to Japan, Chile, China, Ghana, or spend a semester at sea, the experience is unlike anything they have ever experienced in the past or are likely to in the future." Tufts also offers a summer study-abroad option in Talloires, France, that is highly praised by students who have participated; one student calls the program in the Alps "a jewel."

Tufts has no core curriculum but does maintain a set of distribution requirements. Many of the courses that fulfill them are foundational introductory classes. But a student could fulfill a number of these requirements with less serious choices. "Undoubtedly, students can get away with it," one senior says. "With primary majors in women's studies, American studies, peace and justice studies, and the like, the arts and sciences curriculum can be easily manipulated so that a student might not ever take anything more difficult than introductory math and 'Women in Native American Culture.'"

Beyond these basic classes, students face further requirements in their majors. However, the amount and difficulty of these requirements vary: one student says that "in trying to offer students so much flexibility in course selection, they actually weaken the academic depth of some majors." Another decried "a relative paucity of major requirements."

On the other hand, certain majors are quite demanding, such as international relations. In addition to a language requirement, majors take 13 courses, including an introduction to international relations; "Principles of Economics"; "International Economics"; a course in United States foreign policy; and one course in the arts or literature of the language that the student used to fulfill the language requirement. IR majors are also required to take four courses in a specific thematic cluster, such as "Regional and Comparative Analysis" or "Global Conflict, Cooperation, and Justice." However, one professor says that the quality of this program depends on "what [students] make of it," since "there are so many ways to fulfill the requirements."

REQUIREMENTS (CONT'D)

- Two classes in mathematical sciences, such as "Introduction to Calculus" and "Mathematics and Social Choice."
- One world civilizations class; two of the dozens of choices include "Qur'an and Islamic Tradition" and "Introduction to Women's Studies."
- A mathematics class in the fall semester of their first year. Students with a mathematics SAT score of 560 or better are exempt.
- Two freshman-year writing courses or demonstrated competency through standardized writing exam scores.
- Three foreign language courses (or equivalent test scores).

The nearly 800-student College of Engineering, separate from the College of Liberal Arts, is held in high esteem on campus. A professor in a liberal arts department says he is "impressed with the engineering students—they are among the best I have had." A student says of engineering majors, "I'm living with two engineers and they are always working, they have to work so hard, but when they come out they have so many job opportunities—they're set, they are ready for anything. One engineering student went on to Georgetown Law School."

In September 2004, the Cummings Foundation announced it would give $50 million to Tufts' School of Veterinary Medicine—the largest donation in the university's history. The vet school is very competitive, with about 750 applicants for a class of 80.

The best departments at Tufts are international relations, history, biology, chemistry, and philosophy. English is excellent, a major says, if you stick with the more traditional courses. Outstanding professors at Tufts include Judith Haber, Nan Levinson, Neil Miller, and Christina Sharpe in English; Robert Devigne and Vickie Sullivan in political science; Peggy Hutaff and Joseph Walser in comparative religion; David Denby in philosophy; George J. Marcopoulos in history; E. Todd Quinto in mathematics; and Chris Morse in chemistry.

Tufts offers majors in practically everything a student could want, but if he craves more options, the "plan of study" major is available. This major allows a student to create his own major under the guidance of an academic advisor. Past topics have included human–computer interaction, ethnomusicology, and urban studies.

Through the school's Experimental College, Tufts offers an additional 30 undergraduate courses in nontraditional topics of study—most of which are taught by outside professionals in the fields of law, education, government, media, or business. Past classes have included a class in baseball led by an announcer for the Red Sox; "Introduction to Forensic Science and Criminal Investigation," taught by a police inspector in the Connecticut State Attorney's office; and "Cuba: Its Music, Art, and Culture," taught by an opera singer. Students cannot major in the Ex-College, but one staff person in the department says that some students have managed to take five or six of their electives there. A majority of Tufts students take at least one Ex-College course during their time at the school.

As one might imagine, Tufts is especially attractive to career-oriented students. One student says that although there are a "good number of intellectually active students, . . . the line is very clear between those who are and those who aren't."

One student reports that among English classes for freshmen some are leftist, politicized wastes of time—for instance, "Love and Sexuality," a seminar which assigned students to watch a porn movie. The student says, "I'm surprised they didn't ask them to actually *make* a porn film."

The courses that fulfill the world civilizations requirement are also notoriously politicized. As a writer for the conservative journal on campus says, "Among the more worthy requirements for liberal arts majors, like foreign language and a foundation in science, lies a requirement that many students dread: the world civilizations requirement. A hodgepodge of classes that seek to expose students to the diversity of cultures across the globe, this requirement often serves no purpose greater than boosting the student's GPA." Courses that illustrate the point are: "West African Dance and Drumming," "Race, Class, and Power in South Africa," and "Women in Migration."

The more politicized departments are the interdisciplinary ones, such as Latin American studies, Africa and the New World, and urban studies. In peace and justice studies, students can concentrate in one of four areas: war and peace, social movements, conflict resolution, or peace cultures. Better cross-disciplinary options include medieval studies and engineering science.

At Tufts, professors' political views are often obvious; many post political cartoons and slogans on their office doors. Their opinions often permeate classroom discussion as well. One philosophy and political science major says, "They do more than seep into the discussion—they *are* the discussion." This is not universally true, however. One student praised a philosophy professor who "takes a vote on what students think on a certain issue in class. One time, a student asked him what his thoughts were on the issue. He said, 'Wait to ask me until after the semester.'"

An English major says, "In one of my literature survey courses, the professor insisted on calling attention to the inherent racism and sexism in every single work. Never once did she discuss the historical context of such attitudes." A student complains of politicized classes in the political science department. During the 2004 presidential campaign, one professor let his anti-Bush bias be widely known by distributing articles and making remarks such as, "The guy can't say 'hi' or tie his shoe," and "John Kerry was a decorated war hero and Bush skipped out on the last year of his service." When the student—hardly an avid Bush supporter himself—complained, the professor "did not take criticism well."

Student Life:
The elephant (ashes) in the corner

Most Tufts students live in university residence halls, and Tufts offers an abundance of options in that area. Special-interest houses allow students to base their residential life on a particular theme, including Africana, Asian American culture, Jewish culture, Islam, arts, crafts, and foreign languages. The Rainbow House is a "gay-friendly" residence hall that sponsors regular social and political events on related themes. Many of these interest houses are actually apartments.

Tufts undergraduate housing is not separated by class year, but freshmen can choose to live in an all-freshmen dorm that features a live-in faculty member and four upperclassman tutors in addition to the regular resident assistants. Tufts offers a single-sex dorm for women, but for men fraternities are the only single-sex option. Most dorms have young men and women living as next-door neighbors, although some separate the sexes by floor. A few halls have coed bathrooms, but they are single-use with lockable doors. Dormitories usually offer substance-free and "healthy living" floors. Dorm food is "pretty good," according to a student, and is rated as among the best in the nation, although, the same student says, "They rip you off with the meal plan." Tufts has established contracts with some local restaurants, where students can use their meal cards as payment—even on take-out. Some fraternities have their own chefs.

The Tufts campus is located in the Boston suburbs of Somerville and Medford, neither of which can be described as a college town. For that sort of environment, students must take the subway to Cambridge. Davis Square, a shopping and cultural center with small stores and a movie theater, is a short walk from campus.

Weekend social life for Tufts students revolves around Boston and its many colleges rather than around the campus. Tufts' Greek system, which might be expected to help keep students around campus on the weekends, recently suffered some setbacks when police began closing down parties early and cracking down on underage drink-

SUGGESTED CORE
1. Classics 31, Classics of Greece *or* Classics 65S, The Journey of the Hero
2. Philosophy 151, Ancient Philosophy
3. Comparative Religion 115, The English Bible
4. Comparative Religion 35, Intellectual History of Christianity
5. Political Science 46, Western Political Thought II
6. English 67/68, Shakespeare
7. History 83, Revolutionary and Early National America, 1763–1815 *and* History 84, Antebellum and Civil War America, 1803-1877
8. Philosophy 55, The Making of the Modern Mind

ing—leading the university to severely discipline three Greek houses in 2003. About 15 percent of Tufts students join fraternities or sororities, which don't "seem like much of a huge presence except for parties," according to a student. "The university has us by the neck. They will threaten criminal or disciplinary charges if they think you're abetting underage drinking. Regulations are very strict and Greek houses get shut down or go on probation all the time." However, another student reports that "pledges have gone up significantly."

Overall, the Tufts campus has become much less raucous, mostly due to President Larry Bachauer's more stringent drug and alcohol rules. One student complains, "It used to be crazy parties with lines around the block. Now you're lucky to get 50 people without a hassle." Further changes have been implemented in the drug policy. According to one student, "They used to knock on your door if they smelled pot and ask you to stop. Now they call the police."

Town-gown relations are reportedly very strained. Tufts students who live off campus have complained that residents resent the college kids who live in apartments in their communities. One student says, "A lot of neighbors are really obnoxious to the students. There was a noise complaint because students were merely talking in their apartment. The community loves going after Tufts students." All this in spite of the fact that according to the *Chronicle of Higher Education*, Tufts has joined the ranks of wealthy universities such as Harvard and Yale that "make payments to their cities instead of taxes."

Tufts is a challenging place for conservative students. A student sums up the political atmosphere at Tufts by saying, "We're a northeast, liberal campus. That's no secret." Another says, "I can see how it would be difficult to be conservative here, because most people are liberal. If you're actively conservative people will actively dislike you and will try to engage you in an antagonistic dialogue." Another student says, "For the average student who just wants to have his own opinion without being assailed for it—I feel bad for that kid."

The campus has become more activist over the years. For instance, in 2004, Voices for Choice, a division of Planned Parenthood, turned the Tufts Campus Center into a sexual relations carnival at the first annual Sex Fair. Some of the items ostensibly illustrating the issue of "choice" were vagina-shaped cookies and lollypops, posters prominently displaying the "c" word, a lubricant taste testing, male/female genitalia masks in which you could have your photo taken, and the ever-popular free condoms. "They could present themselves in a mature way but they choose to be juvenile," one student says. "They want to see how much they can shock you, not educate you."

Several years ago, I. Melvin Bernstein, then Tufts' vice president of arts, sciences, and technology, appropriated $500,000 per year for diversity programming. This has meant increased funding for the university's "Group of Six": the Asian American Center; the Africana Center; the International Center; the Latino Center; the Lesbian, Gay, Bisexual, and Transgender (LGBT) Center; and the Women's Center.

Alongside these left-leaning student groups lie several right-leaning organizations such as the Tufts Republicans and the *Primary Source,* "the journal of conservative and libertarian thought at Tufts University. Both are very active. In addition, a number of recently founded organizations cater to more conservative students—for example, the brand new Tufts Right to Arms. Tufts Right to Arms addresses "gun rights, education, and training." It has been the target (no pun intended) of scathing articles and editorials in virtually every Tufts publication except the *Primary Source*.

One student reports that "religious students feel really comfortable at Tufts, although the majority of students aren't religious." The Granoff Family Hillel Center is reportedly one of the most welcoming buildings on campus. A student says that "the Jewish population is pretty active, more so than other religious groups." A rainbow of faiths is represented at Tufts, including Buddhism and Islam. Tufts Christian Fellowship, Protestant Christian Fellowship, and Catholic Community at Tufts are some of the Christian organizations. The chaplaincy office sponsors a series of discussions that involves all faiths. In fall 2004 the theme was "Religion and the Arts," which brought discussions like "Buddhist Meditations and Creative Expression" and "Gospel, The Good News Message in Music."

Tufts boasts some rich campus traditions. It seems that the famous circus owner P. T. Barnum donated $50,000 to Tufts in the late 1800s and threw in the stuffed hide of his most famous elephant, Jumbo, as a bonus. The animal was destroyed in a fire in 1975, but some of his ashes are kept in a jar, which Tufts athletes rub before games for luck. The appropriately monikered Tufts Jumbos compete on 30 varsity teams in all three NCAA divisions. A number of club and intramural teams are also available and popular. Tufts students say that school spirit is not especially intense, however. As one student puts it, "Athletics are not a spectator sport here." Teams with strong records in recent years include men's cross country, men's lacrosse, and sailing. The Gantcher Family Sports and Convocation Center, opened in 1999, houses an indoor track and four indoor tennis courts.

One popular campus event is the Naked Quad Run, which takes place on the first night of reading period in the fall semester. Students congregate in one particular dorm, "party, drink heavily, strip down, and run around the Residential Quad in the buff (and often in the bitter cold). Throngs of clothed students line the course to cheer their nude counterparts on," according to a student. Last year, there was an added bonus: "They made snow angels naked," a student says.

The campus is comparatively safe; the school reported 11 forcible sex offenses, 55 burglaries, and two motor vehicle thefts in 2003. Safety phones are located all over the well-lit grounds, and campus police assist with student shuttle and escort services. A female student says, "They're very nice about that."

Costs at Tufts total a hefty $40,00 for residential students and nearly $31,000 for students who commute. About half the students get some form of financial aid and about 35 percent get grant money. Tufts is not need blind in its decision making process, but once a student is accepted, Tufts will meet 100 percent of his need. The average indebtedness of a 2004 graduate was about $17,000.

WELLESLEY COLLEGE

WELLESLEY, MASSACHUSETTS • WWW.WELLESLEY.EDU

Traditions exist, but an identity?

Wellesley College was founded in 1870 as a private, all-female institution by Henry and Pauline Fowle Durant to provide educational opportunities for women. Since then, it has earned a glowing academic reputation. Today it is widely considered to be the crown jewel of the "Seven Sisters," the most prestigious women's colleges in America. Admission to the college is selective; last year 4,094 prospective students applied and 41 percent were accepted. The college is financially sound, with an endowment of $1 billion, and its proximity to Boston—just 13 miles west—gives Wellesley women access to numerous academic, political, and social resources. The college sits on 500 idyllic acres and is often heralded for its pastoral beauty. Most of the campus, in fact, was designed by Frederick Law Olmsted Jr.

Wellesley's motto: *non ministrari sed ministrare*—"not to be ministered unto but to minister," indicates the college's intention to have a marked influential in the world. In the past, Wellesley prided itself on the well-rounded liberal arts education it provided its students. Today, Wellesley's curriculum, while still grounded in the liberal arts, is presented in the contemporary idioms of diversity and multi-culturalism. While the overall quality of a Wellesley education won't likely be utterly destroyed by sociopolitical agendas any time soon, such agendas haven't gone unnoticed, especially among some of the more traditional students. As one student wonders, "Wellesley has a rich tradition, but does it have an identity?" A few Wellesley parents we spoke to have similar concerns: they fear the school is abandoning its heritage in order to remain the quintessentially "hip" women's college.

Academic Life: Deep Wellesley

The humanities are considered to be one of Wellesley's strong suits—especially the English and classics programs. With the exception of a few sexual politics classes, most courses' syllabi are quite promising. And according to one student, in many cases even nontraditional courses are taught well. Professor Mary R. Lefkowitz's class, "Women's Life in Greece and Rome," is presented without the usual feminist assumptions. As one student says, "It was an inquisitive class in history, not sentiment." Lefkowitz is the author of *Not out of Africa: How Afrocentrism Became an Excuse to Teach Myth as History*, and she has spent much of her academic career debunking various myths promulgated by members of academia—from the "blackness" of Aristotle and Cleopatra to the notion that the Iroquois Confederacy inspired the U.S. Constitution. Lefkowitz's work has ruffled many feathers, particularly on campus.

There have been a number of political firestorms in Wellesley's recent history, and there are certainly more than a few professors who have made themselves political lightning rods. The majority of recent controversies have had to do, one way or another, with multiculturalism and the administration's pledge to increase it. But these disagreements have also, for the most part, played out through rational argumentation rather than censorship.

One exception might be the case of Wellesley professor Tony Martin, who recently published—and used for one of his classes—*The Secret Relationship Between Blacks and Jews: Volume One*, a book that is widely considered to be anti-Semitic—not to mention inaccurate. But that was only the beginning. Martin has claimed that he received hate mail and death threats and that Jewish organizations were pressuring Wellesley to fire him—especially after he published *The Jewish Onslaught: Dispatches from the Wellesley Battlefront*, and after Wellesley opted not to give him a merit raise. Martin sued, claiming that the decision was racially motivated, as evidenced by the fact that he was the only black professor eligible for the raise, and he was the only one among his 30 eligible colleagues who didn't get one. He lost.

Inside the classroom, students say they generally feel comfortable sharing their own ideas and opinions, regardless of whether their thoughts align with those of their professors. "I knew my professors were generally very liberal, but I never felt looked down upon for my views," says one conservative student. "Wellesley's near-worship of tolerance has, for the most part, also been afforded to conservative students both in and out of the classroom," a conservative student says. "When I quoted the Bible in an English class to emphasize a literary point about Dante, it was praised and not ostracized. After disagreeing strongly with a professor in my final essay about *Roe v. Wade*, where I preferred using 'baby' and she preferred 'fetus,' she gave the paper an A, writing that I was to be applauded for maintaining my conservative beliefs on a campus like Wellesley." Another student disagrees, saying that " it is virtually impossible for a free marketplace of ideas to exist at the college, especially within the administration." She adds, "There is definite pressure to conform to political correctness here at every level. Certainly the faculty is asked to join the party line. Students should know this about Wellesley before deciding to come here." Asked about the political climate on campus, one student says, "It is pretty oppressive. . . . An American flag was placed on a door in the administrative building following 9/11. Later the door was severely vandalized, the flag gouged out and the door ruined by some sharp instrument."

VITAL STATISTICS	
Religious affiliation: none	
Total enrollment: 2,291	
Total undergraduates: 2,291	
SAT/ACT midranges: SAT: 1260–1450; ACT: 27–31	
Applicants: 4,094	
Applicants accepted: 41%	
Accepted applicants who enrolled: 37%	
Tuition: $29,176	
Room and board: $9,202	
Freshman retention rate: 95%	
Graduation rate: 85% (4 yrs.), 90% (6 yrs.)	
Average class size: 18–21	
Student-faculty ratio: 9:1	
Courses taught by graduate TAs: none	
Most popular majors: economics, psychology, English	
Students living on campus: 94%	
Guaranteed housing for four years? yes	
Students in sororities: none	

At Wellesley, nine of the 32 units required for graduation are drawn from eight substantive and skill-based categories. Students must complete:

- One writing-intensive course.
- A quantitative reasoning requirement. This is satisfied in two phases: Students must first pass a basic math course or demonstrate mastery by passing an exam. Then students take one course that emphasizes statistical analysis or data interpretation, such as "Basic Astronomical Techniques" or "Organismal Biology."
- One course with a multicultural focus addressing African, Asian, Middle Eastern, Caribbean, Latin American, Native American, or Pacific Island peoples, cultures, or societies; and/or a minority American culture. Students must write a 250-word statement on *why* they have chosen the course and how it relates to their overall field of study.
- One or more courses leading to intermediate-level proficiency in a foreign language. Students with sufficient AP scores in a foreign language can be exempted from this requirement.

There are nearly 900 courses offered at Wellesley—and in that mix are a fair number of classes like "History of Sexuality: Queer Theory" and "Representations of Women, Natives, and Others: Race, Class, and Gender," both offered by the women's studies department. The extra-departmental course, "Introduction to Reproductive Issues," is taught by a professor who is a former board member of the National Abortion Rights Action League. She also teaches a course called "Multidisciplinary Approaches to Abortion." Courses in Africana studies often have leftist overtones. But those students who are sensitive to politics in the classroom know how to avoid it. As one student says, "I don't expect a course in feminism or sexuality to be conservative, so I'm generally not fazed by their radicalism." The sociology department is much better than what one might expect, listing several good courses, including "Classical Sociology Theory" and "The Sociology of Conservatism," both taught by department chair Jonathan Imber. Some new courses offered in 2004–5—for better or worse—reflect the increasing importance of popular culture at Wellesley. These include "Disneyland and American Culture" and "Sex and the City in the Victorian Novel."

Whatever you're discussing at Wellesley, you're probably doing it in an intimate seminar: the average class size is between 18 and 21 students. Some introductory courses enroll more than 100, but these classes divide into small discussion groups. Seminars usually have 15 to 18 students and a professor to examine comprehensively certain choice topics. Due to the small student body, there are also opportunities for honor students to engage in independent research projects with faculty. Students agree that Wellesley is very good in supplying its students with the support systems they need. Rarely do students fall through the cracks; there is constant interaction between students and faculty both in and out of the classroom. The student-faculty ratio is a very comfortable nine to one.

Wellesley is also proud of its science program; its facilities were once considered the second best in the nation, after MIT's. In September 2004, Wellesley announced that it will share in a $200,000 grant from the National Science Foundation (NSF) to support new undergraduate research. The grant will allow Wellesley astronomers to continue their work with student research projects for the next two years.

In the Science Center students have access to state-of-the-art instrumentation, including a confocal microscope, two NMR spectrometers, microcalorimeters, and a high-power pulsed tunable laser. There is also an observatory with sophisticated telescopes. The greenhouses and botanical gardens are used for study and are open to the public.

Wellesley students can now register for courses at MIT, so science-minded students should have no problem finding classes they need. There are a number of exchange programs in which students may cross-register at Brandeis University and MIT. A double-degree program also exists with MIT that can lead to a five-year BA/SB degree (an SB is the same as a BS). Through the Twelve College Exchange Program, students may opt to study for a total of two semesters at one of the participating schools, such as Amherst, Bowdoin, Dartmouth, Vassar, Smith, or Mt. Holyoke.

Students and faculty agree that after science and English and classics, the best departments at Wellesley are biology, political science (a program that hatched both Madeleine Albright and Hillary Clinton), philosophy, and economics. Notable Wellesley professors include Mary Lefkowitz in classics; Marion R. Just and Edward A. Stettner in political science; Thomas Cushman and Jonathan B. Imber in sociology; Karl "Chip" Case in economics; Larry Rosenwald in English; Andrew C. Webb in biological sciences; and Kenneth P. Winkler in philosophy.

Every new student chooses a faculty advisor to help her choose courses and a major. After selecting a major, the student can change advisors or keep the one she has. Fortunately, advisors at Wellesley really are *advisors,* professors who actually guide students through college and aren't just there to make sure students satisfy course requirements. The First-Year Mentoring Program pairs 15 freshmen with a junior or senior who lives in the same dormitory complex. There are also a number of peer tutoring resources available for students who need academic help. Since Wellesley does not have graduate students, professors—not teaching assistants—conduct all courses.

Wellesley has two major assets that enhance its academic programs: a distinguished alumnae network that is nonpareil among American colleges, and access to seemingly unlimited funding sources, both internal and external. Among the many programs for students is the Wash-

REQUIREMENTS (CONT'D)

- A physical education requirement. This is satisfied by taking the equivalent of two semester courses in an athletic activity.

    Students must also take 18 courses to complete distribution requirements. These must come from at least two departments, and at least four must be at the advanced level. Three courses must come from each of three areas:

- Group A, which includes the arts and humanities. Students need at least one course in language and literature and one in "visual arts, music, theatre, film, [or] video."

- Group B, the social sciences. Students must take at least one course in social and behavioral analysis and two more courses from two of the following three areas: epistemology and cognition; religion, ethics, and moral philosophy; and historical studies.

- Group C, the hard sciences and mathematics. Students are required to take at least one course in natural and physical science and another in "mathematical modeling and problem solving." One of the three courses in this group must be a lab science course.

NEW ENGLAND

151

ington Public Service Summer Internship Program for juniors, which offers "ten-week internships, including a living expense stipend and housing in local university dormitories." These internships often lead to first jobs and any number of networking opportunities. The Stone Center for Women, Hestia Institute in Wellesley, and the Wellesley Center for Research on Women also increase opportunities for students to engage in research and networking.

Students looking for ways to participate in community service and paid jobs can visit the Center for Work and Service. The college also offers service opportunity grants so that students can afford to spend summers volunteering.

Student Life: Don't settle for second

Wellesley College is located in the affluent Boston suburb of Wellesley, Massachusetts. The most beautiful spot on campus is the Academic Quad, defined by large red-brick buildings, but other facilities like the Davis Museum and Cultural Center and the Clapp Library (with more than one million volumes) make significant contributions to the physical environment of this small school. Lake Waban, part of the campus, offers outdoor activities and recreation for students.

Wellesley's proximity to Boston means that there are plenty of opportunities for students to socialize with students from other schools—both on and off the campus grounds. The college funds two forms of transportation: the Exchange Bus and the Senate Bus. The commuter rail runs within easy walking distance of campus. Wellesley itself has more than 200 campus organizations, including the Body and Soul vocal jazz ensemble, a college orchestra, speech and debating societies, a few literary groups, and even an air rifle club. Wellesley participates in NCAA Division III athletics on 13 teams, including basketball, field hockey, and tennis. The school is most competitive in crew, in which it regularly wins conference titles. The crew team practices on the Charles River.

In 2001, Wellesley blushed when *Rolling Stone* published a story titled "The Highly Charged Erotic Life of the Wellesley Girl." The story depicted the sexual exploits of various students and faculty, describing campus life as "a climate of sexual experimentation where no woman, or man—including professors, kitchen staff, and campus police officers—is off limits." This claim met with outrage across campus, especially among members of the Wellesley administration; the school's president proclaimed the article "an example of irresponsible and sensationalist journalism." *Rolling Stone* claims to possess the interview tapes that corroborate its story.

Wellesley maintains an Office of Religious and Spiritual Life for students. It is probably one of the most ecumenical religious life offices of the East Coast schools, including Unitarians, Protestants, Catholics, Jews, Native Americans, Sikhs, Hindus, Buddhists, Muslims, Baha'is, Zoroastrians, and pagans.

In general, the tenor of the political environment at Wellesley is comparatively subdued. And while Wellesley has long had a reputation for being overwhelmingly liberal, conservative students still find several outlets for their views. The weekly student newspaper, the *Wellesley News,* is a more balanced publication than most colleges can claim, and its opinion pages often include both liberal and conservative viewpoints. The college even occasionally sponsors conservative or libertarian lectures on campus, though a visit from Phyllis Schlafly in 2003 "elicited a strong reaction on campus" according to the *Wellesley News.* "Following her lecture, a question and answer period allowed for attendees to both question and challenge Schlafly's viewpoints," the paper reported. "The emotional session required the assistance of policemen to calm down the crowd." There are rumored to be quite a few moderate-to-conservative professors and students at Wellesley. "Sure, I could speak my mind," says one alumna, "and most of the time people respected me, though I would sometimes detect a hint of condescension during discussions." There is a thriving College Republicans chapter and the Wellesley Alliance for Life, a pro-life organization. Influential liberal groups on campus include Wellesley Lesbians, Bisexuals, Transgenders, and Friends (WLBTF), Women for Choice, and a number of cultural organizations.

SUGGESTED CORE
1. Classical Civilization 120b, Troy and the Poets
2. Philosophy 201, Ancient Greek Philosophy
3. Religion 104/105, Study of the Hebrew Bible: Old Testament / Study of the New Testament
4. Religion 216, Christian Thought, 100–1600
5. Political Science 241, Modern Political Theory
6. English 112, Introduction to Shakespeare
7. History 203, History of the United States, 1607–1877
8. Philosophy 230, Nineteenth-Century Philosophy

Besides these activities, the college provides social and extracurricular options for weeknights and weekends. The society houses are a persistent but compelling feature of extracurricular life. These buildings are not residences, but have dining facilities and social spaces where groups sponsor lectures and gatherings. Shakespeare House, fittingly enough, is for students interested in Elizabethan drama. Three others focus on art and music, literature, and "intelligent interest in cultural and public affairs." Students may join society houses as early as the second semester of their freshman year. These organizations do not receive funding from the college.

Wellesley is almost entirely a residential school—94 percent of students choose to live on campus. A small-community atmosphere is preserved through the residence halls, with first-year students sharing both dorms (if not rooms) and meals with members of other classes. Most housing options are traditional dormitories, but five apartment buildings are available for juniors and seniors. Students living in the feminist co-op, "INSTEAD," cook and clean for themselves—but in a highly liberated fashion, we presume. On foreign language floors (Chinese, German, Japanese, and Russian), students pledge to speak only their chosen languages.

Wellesley has a number of time-honored traditions that date back to its founding. But these traditions have been modified over the years to accommodate politically correct sensibilities. Flower Sunday, originally a religious tradition, has evolved into a "day of sisterhood and celebration of the new school year. Held annually in early September, it features a multicultural and multi-faith pageantry of song, music, and dance," according to the college Web site. Hoop Rolling Day, once a May Day tradition but now held on a separate day, has changed as well. Seniors race in rolling hoops down Tupelo Lane, and the winner gets thrown into Lake Waban. In a transformation that speaks volumes about the evolving social definition of female "success," while it used to be said that the winner was fated to be the first to get married, she later became destined to become a CEO. Today, the hoop rolling winner is going to be the "first person in her class who will achieve success, however she defines it," says the college Web site, lamely.

Despite the fact that the college is single sex, Wellesley women maintain an extensive social life with men from the many colleges around Boston, and men are welcome visitors on campus. One faculty member says, almost incredulously, "There's no drinking problem. It's the most sober campus." There were disciplinary actions filed for only five liquor-law violations—and zero drug arrests—in 2003. Wellesley has comparatively little crime. In 2003 the school reported two forcible sex offenses, 36 burglaries, and one aggravated assault on campus. The college's police force promotes campus safety by providing blue-light emergency phones all over campus and an escort service for students walking late at night.

Wellesley is a pricey pleasure, with tuition at $29,176 and room and board, $9,202. However some 57 percent of undergraduates receive financial aid, graduating with an average student loan debt of only $11,913.

WESLEYAN UNIVERSITY

MIDDLETOWN, CONNECTICUT • WWW.WESLEYAN.EDU

Double dare

Wesleyan University was founded in 1831 by the Methodist Church to educate ministers. Since then, Wesleyan has assiduously abandoned most of its traditions. The school severed its ties with Methodism way back in 1910, and even the school's namesake, John Wesley, the founder of Methodism, is now referred to in college literature only as "the greatest Englishman of his time" or as a "daring humanitarian." "Daring" is a word much in vogue at Wesleyan: the school sometimes seems to believe it has a corner on audacity. But rather than bucking current trends, Wesleyan simply rides them to their illogical conclusions. What could be more craven?

Wesleyan is rich in physical and intellectual resources; classes are usually small and professors care about their students. The school is one of the top three liberal arts colleges in terms of sending students on to complete PhDs. But there is almost no intellectual or political diversity in the classroom or elsewhere. And reading about certain current practices at Wesleyan may make you want to take a shower (with the door closed—see below). In many ways, Wesleyan manages to concentrate on its small campus the worst features of contemporary "elite" liberal arts schools. And it does so with a certain amount of flamboyance.

Academic Life: As you like it

Wesleyan University's student body consists of approximately 2,700 full-time undergraduate students, as well as about 150 graduate students in the natural sciences, mathematics, and ethnomusicology, and another 600 students in the graduate liberal studies program. The university's most popular majors are English, government, psychology, and economics.

Wesleyan does not have any core requirements, and the set of "general education expectations" it "strongly encourages" are weak, allowing many students to graduate without any exposure to several major disciplines. "I suppose students (if they really tried) could graduate through 'puff' courses, but people come to Wesleyan to learn,"

VITAL STATISTICS
Religious affiliation: none
Total enrollment: 2,850
Total undergraduates: 2,700
SAT/ACT midranges: SAT: 1310–1490; ACT: 28–32
Applicants: 6,568
Applicants accepted: 28%
Accepted applicants who enrolled: 40%
Tuition: $31,650
Room and board: $8,474
Freshman retention rate: 92%
Graduation rate: 83% (4 yrs.), 92% (6 yrs.)
Average class size: 22
Student-faculty ratio: 9:1
Courses taught by graduate TAs: none
Most popular majors: social sciences, area and ethnic studies, economics
Students living on campus: 92%
Guaranteed housing for four years? yes
Students in fraternities or sororities: not reported

one student says. "Taking easy courses at a school like Wesleyan seems like a waste of money." The problem, of course, is that what some 18-year-olds see as intellectually valuable *is* actually a waste of money. Like "Signs of Imagination: Constructions of Gender and Race in Popular Culture," an English course. And there's more where that came from.

In the First-Year Initiative Program (FYI), freshmen take special classes designed to improve their writing and rhetorical skills. Taught in small seminars, usually fewer than 20 students, FYIs are "entirely optional," although "students are advised to consider taking at least one of these courses during their first year," according to the catalog. There is no English composition requirement, since, the school asserts, "writing skills are emphasized and developed throughout the curriculum."

Wesleyan justifies its unstructured approach by claiming that the school allows students to bring "order to their own college program, rather than have that order imposed upon them from outside." Wesleyan argues that students need the experience of structuring their own education from the moment they set foot on campus. While many liberal arts schools believe that, ideally, students slowly acquire the knowledge and wisdom necessary to direct their further studies, Wesleyan expects students to be able to assess the relative importance of a wide swath of subject matter before they have even been exposed to any of it.

Requirements within the majors have weakened considerably over the decades. In 1964, all English majors were required to complete a senior thesis and a comprehensive exam meant to ensure that they had a grasp of the major figures, genres, and eras of English literature. English majors also had to complete a two-semester survey of English literature from the fourteenth through the twentieth century. While a thesis seminar is still required, today's Wesleyan students no longer have to take the English exam. Instead, majors must take a seminar, English 201, which "introduces close-reading skills and familiarizes students with the idea of literature as a part of history and culture." There are different sections available for this course, and what students learn and discuss depends primarily on the professor. However, students in all sections will read lyric poems, a play by Shakespeare, and essays "about critical terms and concepts that are used in the study of literature," according to the course catalog. Two courses on pre-1800 literature are also required, as is a course on literary theory.

History majors at Wesleyan are not required to take any broad survey courses in history (though they do need a historiography course), and there is no United States or European history course requirement. The department only calls for six courses within an area of concentration—Africa, Asia, and Latin America; European; gender and history; intellectual history; religion and history; or United States—and two courses outside of the concentration. Students must also complete three seminars and a final research project.

Politics is omnipresent at Wesleyan, inside and outside the classroom, so it's hard to name the most politicized courses or professors—the competition is too stiff. "Most teachers here have extreme liberal biases [that] often reinforce students' own biases, and most classes have their curricula structured with liberal tenets," a student says. "In any psychology, sociology, or gender studies class, you will learn that the white man is responsible for everyone's problems. Books written by conservatives have literally been held up . . . to be laughed at in sociology classes." The university offers majors in African American studies, Latin American studies, and women's studies. The African American studies department offers dozens of courses with names like "Political Independence and Literary Dependence in Nineteenth-Century Franco-Caribbean Literatures," which sound more like the titles of obscure (and dull) dissertations than explorations of significant subjects. Another program, ethnic studies, does not have its own department but is instead part of the American studies program. When students petitioned the university to expand the program, the university decided it would cost too much money. One supporter of expansion responded by whining that "the most progressive [fields] of contemporary academia" had failed to take root at Wesleyan. Multiculturalism of this sort is obviously insatiable—though it might be placated by demolishing the school brick by brick and replacing it with, say, a sweat lodge.

In fact, Wesleyan offers a vast array of controversial and academically questionable courses. Most of these classes even meet the distribution guidelines—for example, "Rereading Gendered Agency: Black Women's Experience of Slavery," "Comparative Emancipation," "The Nature of Prejudice," "Everyday Forms of Resistance," "Questions of Queer Travel," "Problems and Methods in Queer Historiography," and the catch-all "Multiculturalism and Oppression."

There are some bright spots at Wesleyan, of course. Some of the more worthwhile departments include history, medieval studies, art history and architectural history, theater, classics, molecular biology and biochemistry, biology, and physics. Wesleyan also has a strong literary tradition, reflected in the presence of its own university press and a series of prestigious summer workshops for writers. Standout faculty members include Andrew Szegedy-Maszak in classics; Martha Crenshaw, Marc Allen Eisner, and John E. Finn in government; John Bonin in economics; and Joseph Reed and Richard Slotkin in English. Peter Rutland, who teaches Russian and Eastern European studies in the government department, is a notable scholar of Soviet economics.

ACADEMIC REQUIREMENTS

Wesleyan has no core curriculum or distribution requirements. However, it maintains a set of general education "expectations." On top of the demands of their major, by the end of their second year students are *advised* to take:

- Two classes in humanities and the arts. Choices range from "Weimar Cinema, 1918–1933" and "Reading Sonic Black Iconography" to "Shakespeare," and "History and the Humanities."
- Two classes in the social and behavioral sciences. These include any courses in anthropology, economics, government, history, philosophy, religion, and sociology.
- Two classes in the natural sciences and mathematics, such as astronomy, biology, chemistry, computer science, earth and environment, mathematics, molecular biology and biochemistry, neuroscience and behavior, physics, and psychology.

  Students are warmly encouraged to take one more course in each of these three subject areas before graduation.

Students receive faculty advisors upon entering the university and different ones after declaring their majors. Because the school does not require a core curriculum, students will lose out immeasurably if they do not receive adequate support when designing their "individualized programs." The success of the system is said to hinge mostly on students being active and involved. As one student says, "The quality of advising is heavily dependent on the advisor; some students love and praise their advisors," while others find that their advisors offer little of use.

Wesleyan can justly boast of its strong student-faculty relationships. Approximately 60 percent of all classes contain fewer than 20 students, and only 6 percent contain more than 50. The student-faculty ratio is nine to one. Students enjoy ample opportunities to interact with their peers and professors in and out of class. Graduate teaching assistants do not teach undergraduates; the school's focus is squarely on undergraduate education. One student says professors are easily accessible, and students often go to office hours to speak to their instructors.

Student Life: Handle with latex gloves

Middletown, Connecticut, is aptly named, sitting in the middle of the state on the banks of the Connecticut River. Wesleyan's 290-acre campus lies in the center of this midsized, blue-collar town. Main Street, with its restaurants and shops, is within easy walking distance, but otherwise the town doesn't offer much to students. Wesleyan's architectural style varies widely from building to building. The school's oldest buildings are brownstones constructed in the middle part of the nineteenth century. Today, the campus is a mix of the old and the new. The Van Vleck Observatory was designed by Henry Bacon, architect of the Lincoln Memorial. The Olin Memorial Library's design was influenced by Bacon, and was originally built as a Greek revival, symmetrical building. But in the 1980s, it was remodeled and expanded to add a modern flavor. Recently renovated for $22 million were the Petriceli '92 Theater and the neighboring Wesleyan Memorial Chapel, which features a 3,000-pipe organ and stained glass windows depicting biblical scenes—and serves as a teaching and assembly space. Wesleyan recently exchanged eight acres of land for the building of the African Methodist Episcopal Zion Church; Wesleyan will use the church building to house its archaeological collection, and Zion will construct a new, larger church on the former Wesleyan property.

Wesleyan is definitely a residential school, with about 92 percent of the undergraduate student body living on campus; the administration has plans to house even more. "Interest houses of any kind," says a professor, "are about to vanish from the landscape, as the university is building blocks of dormitories with the idea of phasing out all student off-campus houses." A recent graduate recommends Clark Hall for freshmen. It is a newly renovated residence that offers doubles, provides kitchen amenities and is well situated in the middle of campus.

The nature of residential life probably contributes most to the "progressive" character of the Wesleyan experience. While the current university policy assigns first-year students roommates of the same sex, upperclassmen can choose coed dorm rooms and coed bathrooms. It is not unusual for students in these coed bathrooms to shower with the doors open. A housing official says, "The hall makes the decision [whether to have coed bathrooms] at the beginning of the school year, after they get to know one another." (A tip of the hat to modesty there!) The Wesleyan Student Assembly is pressing the administration to implement gender-neutral housing for all students. A WSA resolution states that since "gender and biological sex are separate and distinct concepts" and "the historical rationale for same-sex roommate assignments is based upon antiquated heterosexist assumptions and obsolete concerns," incoming freshmen should not be excluded from the right "to define their own gender and make housing decisions, irrespective of that definition." As if defining their own college curriculum weren't enough.

There are a handful of single-sex residences for those who request them. Substance-free options are also available. Housing is guaranteed for four years; upperclassmen who wish to live off campus have to petition for permission.

In an effort to cater to diverse student tastes, Wesleyan currently still offers a number of special-interest houses. In the Earth House, students can "minimize our negative impact on the environment by composting, recycling, conserving energy and water, and educating ourselves and the Wesleyan community about environmental issues." The Womanist House is for students "who are committed to the issues of Wesleyan women, regardless of race, class, sexual orientation, or cultural background," while the Open House is "a safe space for lesbian, gay, bisexual, transgender, transsexual, queer, questioning, flexual, asexual, genderf**k, polyamorous, bondage/disciple, dominance/submission, sadism/masochism (LGBTTQQFAGPBDSM) communities and for people of sexually or gender dissident communities." Yep, they use all the letters. The Malcolm X House is for students who share an interest in the "cultural heritage of the African Diaspora both for themselves and for the larger Wesleyan community."

Other students may opt to live in a limited selection of Greek housing; Wesleyan has four fraternities and six sororities. There are no houses for sororities. Douglas Bennett, the president of Wesleyan since 1995, is encountering resistance from students as well as alumni as he attempts to force fraternities to become coed. An alumnus wrote in the student newspaper, the *Wesleyan Argus*, "Since Wesleyan endorses single-gender dorm floors, gender-based and ethnic and race-based houses, clubs, studies, publications, sororities, gender-based sports, race-based and sexual orientation-based

SUGGESTED CORE
1. Classical Civilization 112, Three Great Myths: Prometheus, Persephone and Dionysus (*closest match*)
2. Philosophy 201, Philosophical Classics I: Ancient Western Philosophy
3. Religion 201/212, Old Testament: Hebrew Bible / New Testament: An Introduction
4. Religion 275, Romans and Christians: The World of Late Antiquity
5. Government 338, Modern Political Theory
6. English 205, Shakespeare
7. History 237, Early America: The Seventeenth and Eighteenth Centuries
8. History 216, European Intellectual History since the Renaissance

alumni groups/networking, and partnerships with Smith College (which discriminates against men), then it has no legitimacy to hypocritically force fraternities to go coed."

As you might guess, Wesleyan has gone to enormous lengths to promote multiculturalism and ethnic diversity on campus. The university offers several academic programs to encourage minority students to pursue graduate degrees. The admissions department vigorously recruits minority students, sponsors a Students of Color Weekend, and on another weekend, flies in minority students from outside the Northeast to visit Wesleyan. In a newsletter for "students of color," Wesleyan promotes minority scholarships, career opportunities, and political events. The Queer Resource Center serves an active and noisy homosexual student population; in its library, students can check out videos like *Goat Boy and the Potato Chip Ritual, Dress Up for Daddy, Female Misbehavior, Party: A Safer Sex Videotape for Black Gay Men, Macho Dancer, Stop the Church,* and *Two in Twenty: A Lesbian Soap Opera.* In addition to pornography, the Queer Resource Center library serves up a number of juicy books along with "free condoms, lube, and dental dam instructions."

In a restaurant review in the *Argus* in 2004, a student wrote that the typical student at Wesleyan is "probably vegan or vegetarian" and "since you're a Wesleyan student you're probably also Jewish." Wesleyan students tend to think of themselves as outsiders, members of the old counterculture. At least geographically, many of them are in fact outsiders: almost 80 percent of students come from outside New England. All told, students at Wesleyan represent 48 states and 45 countries.

Among the student organizations at Wesleyan are the Black Women's Collective, the Wesleyan Christian Fellowship, Step One ("a confidential resource for students questioning their sexuality), several a cappella groups, Wesleyan Film Series, Clinic Escorts (which provides escorts for women heading to abortion clinics), Scrabble Club, Wesleyan Democrats, Woodrow Wilson Debate Team, and Wheatgrass Co-op. Second Stage is a student-run group overseeing Wesleyan's student theater. The company produces dance and theater shows that are entirely designed, directed, teched, and performed by Wesleyan students.

The Center for the Arts, which focuses on contemporary and world arts, is a vibrant element of campus life at Wesleyan, with its concert, dance, theater, and family series; exhibitions; and special events. The complex of studios, classrooms, galleries, performance spaces, and departments provides ample opportunities for students to engage in the arts.

Wesleyan regularly ranks near the top of *The Princeton Review*'s list of schools "where students ignore God on a regular basis." However, there are religious resources on campus for those students interested in them. Recently, a Muslim chaplain was added to the staff of Jewish, Catholic, and Protestant chaplains already on campus. In addition to religious-themed program houses, the university also sponsors several faith-based student groups.

Wesleyan students are no slouches when it comes to leftist activism. Among the more politically oriented student organizations are the Environmental Organizer's Network, Ethnic Studies Committee, Trans/Gender Group, Wesleyan Satan's Advocates, the African American student group Ujamaa, Wesleyan Feminist Network, Students for a Sensible Drug Policy, Amnesty International, a pair of ACLU groups, Students for a Free Palestine, Students for Democratic Action, and the Wesleyan Animal Rights Network.

Then there is the "C**t Club." The club is about "celebrating vaginas," and came under attack from community members when it sold a button reading "Vagina Friendly" to a first-grader attending a student activity fair. That club is getting a run for its money in the bad taste department from PERVS (Promoting the Enjoyment of Radically Variant Sex), whose weekly meetings are open to "anyone who is interested in exploring issues of polyamory, bondage/disciple, dominance/submission, sadism/masochism, and public sex," according to its Web page, available from Wesleyan's site.

This sort of crassness may not be as shocking to Wesleyan students as it is to outside observers. Wesleyan has earned, as its student newspaper notes, a reputation for public nudity. Students often streak university libraries, classrooms, parties, and public spaces. The December 2004 issue of the *Argus* had a special way of illuminating the holiday season. Named a "joke issue," it skewered (or soiled) everything from Christmas trees in its "Ecumenical Group Installs Holiday Tree" article to performance art, with its mock review of an improv show where simulated sex acts, a circumcision, sex toys, and a child molester were woven into the skits.

In 2002, *Mother Jones* magazine ranked Wesleyan University the most activist campus in the nation. Says a recent graduate, "There are not very many Republicans on campus, but they do have a presence. There is a football team and fraternities, after all." A student writes that some conservative articles posted on a dorm bulletin board were promptly torn down by angry students. "Wesleyan students are supposed to be open-minded, tolerant, and respectful of different ideas and people," he says. One politically moderate student says, however, that although "political biases can be felt in class," they "do not generally affect" grading and that sort of thing. "Conservatives (at times) may feel uncomfortable but not overly so." Hard to believe.

Underage drinking is pervasive at Wesleyan. It is permitted openly, along with liberal drug usage, during the annual outdoor music festivals: Zonker Harris Day (named after the hippie character in the Doonesbury cartoon), Duke Day, Buttstock, and the Spring Fling.

Wesleyan sports teams compete in the NCAA Division III New England Small College Athletic Conference (NESCAC). Committed primarily to academics, the conference does not permit member schools to recruit off campus, to hold out-of-season practices, or to grant athletic scholarships. In other words, among the 29 available intercollegiate sports, interested students should find ample opportunities to compete. Wesleyan varsity teams once competed as the "Methodists," but today, Wesleyan athletes are known as "Cardinals." (What *would* John Wesley think?) The Freeman Athletic Center features ice skating, swimming, track, and basketball facilities; a fitness and strength-training center; and an exercise room. A recent addition to the center includes a gymnasium with seating for 1,000, a 7,500-square-foot fitness center, and eight squash courts.

One Wesleyan tradition remains, although in altered form. The Douglas cannon is an artillery piece dating back at least to the Civil War. After the war, freshmen would try to fire the gun as sophomores struggled to stop them. This "cannon scrap" is no longer practiced—the gun is wisely rendered inoperable now—but students again began stealing the cannon in 1957. Since then, students have cunningly stowed the gun away in dorm rooms, presented it to Russian UN representatives as a "symbol of peace, brotherhood, and friendship," given it to President Nixon in protest of the Vietnam War, and even baked it into a sesquicentennial birthday cake. A professor says that the cannon "made a transcontinental car trip two summers ago and is rumored to be in hiding in Los Angeles."

In 2003, the last year for which statistics were available, the university reported two forcible sex offenses, one robbery, 70 burglaries, and one arson. Community safety is promoted and maintained by a public safety patrol, which although it is not a university police force, gives out free whistles to use in case of emergency and patrols the campus by foot, bicycle, and automobile. The school offers a shuttle service that stops at designated pick-up/drop-off points at night, and students walking around campus late at night can call for an escort. The campus is equipped with emergency response phones.

Going to Wesleyan is a costly excursion into parts unknown; tuition in 2004–5 was $31,650, with room and board at $8,474. However, the school is expert at fundraising—having just collected some $281 million from alumni—so it can afford to be generous with financial aid. It offers need-blind admission and commits to meeting 100 percent of a student's demonstrated financial need. Approximately 50 percent of the freshmen who applied for financial aid for the 2004–5 academic year received a need-based award.

WILLIAMS COLLEGE

If every college were thus located

It is hard to question the distinguished tradition of Williams College, a richly endowed liberal arts school in the gorgeous Berkshires of western Massachusetts that attracts topnotch students who are willing to work hard. Even its athletic program is superior to most any other school of similar size.

Colonel Ephraim Williams wrote his last will and testament in 1755, leaving $9,000 and change to found a school. There were conditions: the school had to be named for him, the town it sat in had to be named for him, and it had to be in Massachusetts. He died a few months later fighting in the French and Indian Wars. Thus was Williams College founded in 1793, in newly renamed Williamstown, Massachusetts—a town that now has around 8,000 residents but whose beautiful surroundings and cultural attractions bring one million visitors a year. If visitors come only for the scenery, they will miss out on three top-flight art museums—the Clark Art Institute, with a fine French Impressionist collection among its holdings; the Williams College Museum of Art, perhaps the best college art museum in the land; and the nearby Massachusetts Museum of Contemporary Art. Williamstown is also home to the Chapin Rare Books Library and the summer Williamstown Theatre Festival, whose performers include Hollywood and Broadway stars.

The college is currently undertaking several major building projects. It is expanding the Stetson and Sawyer library buildings and the student union and renovating the Adams Memorial Theater. The new theater, the '62 Center for Theatre and Dance, is a $20 million endeavor which opened in spring 2005. The recently renovated Thompson Chapel celebrated its centennial in 2005. Although the college has never had an official religious affiliation, prior to World War II, daily chapel was a mandatory fixture of a Williams education. Until the late 1950s, Williams required Sunday evening chapel in which students were required to sit alphabetically by last names. This placed two notable Williams alumni, George Steinbrenner ('52) and

VITAL STATISTICS
Religious affiliation: none
Total enrollment: 2,050
Total undergraduates: 1,991
SAT midranges: V: 660–760, M: 660–750
Applicants: 5,705
Applicants accepted: 19%
Accepted applicants who enrolled: 52%
Tuition: $29,786
Room and board: $8,110
Freshman retention rate: 98%
Graduation rate: 91% (4 yrs.), 96% (6 yrs.)
Courses with fewer than 20 students: 71%
Student-faculty ratio: 8:1
Courses taught by graduate TAs: none
Most popular majors: social sciences, psychology, foreign languages
Students living on campus: 93%
Guaranteed housing for four years? yes
Students in fraternities or sororities: none

Stephen Sondheim ('50), next to each other in church.

Henry David Thoreau looked at the college and the Berkshires that surround it and wrote: "It would be no small advantage if every college were thus located at the base of a mountain." He calculated that the scenery was worth at least the equivalent of one endowed professorship. Another Thoreau quote may be just as apt, however: "Read the best books first or you may not have a chance to read them all."

Past generations of Williams scholars faced a curriculum that covered the most important texts of Western civilization. The college Web site claims that "a survey of the college curriculum in 1925 showed that Williams had combined the principles of prescription and election, the goals of concentration and distribution, in such a way as to be the only major American college without any absolutely required courses and without any uncontrolled wide-option electives." The contemporary Williams scholar continues to study without the guidance of a serious core curriculum, but the buffet table from which they feast includes more salad than meat and potatoes.

Academic Life: In dark woods, the right road lost

Williams has not gone wild with the number of majors it offers; students select from a list of 33, with psychology, history, and English the most popular choices. Approximately one-quarter of students complete two majors, and yet 91 percent of students manage to graduate within four years. There are about 2,000 undergraduates, and the student-faculty ratio is an excellent eight to one.

Williams has several unusual academic programs available to all students. One notable example is the Williams–Mystic Program in Maritime Studies, in which students spend a semester at the Mystic (Connecticut) Seaport Museum. Another excellent opportunity is the Williams–Oxford Programme, run at Oxford University's Exeter College. One source described it as "superb" and added that many devout students enter it in order to study theology. The cost is the same as a year at Williams, but students take the full Oxford course of study, including five tutorials, each of which involves eight papers on assigned readings and the requisite discussion. Williams's own on-campus tutorial program is modeled after this one.

Williams puts a great deal of emphasis on tutorials, recently increasing the number it offers and even making them available to sophomores rather than just seniors. A tutorial typically enrolls 10 students grouped into five pairs. The pairs meet for an hour each week in the presence of the professor, who attempts to say little while one student presents a short paper that is then critiqued by the other. Students and professors alike speak very highly of the tutorials. One faculty member told the *Chronicle of Higher Education* that his tutorials were, "without a doubt, the single best teaching experience I ever had." Even President Morton O. Schapiro, an economics professor, has taught tutorials—and found the approach difficult, as he told the *Chronicle*: "The students run the damn thing. I'm not trained to give up all that control." About 40 percent of graduating seniors have taken at least one tutorial, and that number is growing.

Outside of tutorials, students who seek attention from professors will readily receive it. Students can expect good teachers committed to their educational and intellectual development. "The key is finding and working with the best professors," says one student. "They're out there, and you can usually build a strong major around one or two of them." Another student says, "Professors are definitely accessible to students. Every professor provides plenty of office hours, and many give you their home phone numbers to call them any time. . . . Many professors I've had enjoy meeting outside the classroom for coffee or a meal." Class sizes are miniscule compared to those at larger institutions.

Students are assigned departmental faculty advisors after they declare a major; this normally occurs after their sophomore year. Before that, freshmen get advisors from the general faculty. Through the senior advisor program, seniors mentor freshmen and sophomores.

Williams operates on a two-semester schedule, with a four-week Winter Study Program between semesters. During this month, students take a single course pass-fail. Some topics look interesting and useful (like teaching practica, senior thesis work, research opportunities, and courses like "Living by Words: Surviving and Thriving in the Art and Sport of Rhetoric"), while many look like a quasiacademic excuse for winter vacation, though not necessarily less interesting. In this latter category one might sign up for marble carving, visits to regional museums, "The Science of Chocolate," "The Art and History of Knitting," or "How to Buy a Car."

Williams's students can easily graduate without having studied what most people regard as the basic texts of Western civilization, although those who choose to study them will find fine professors in almost every department to help. But it's up to these young scholars to find their way through the thickets of learning and thistles of ideology.

Williams did add two requirements starting with the class of 2006: one course in quantitative or formal reasoning and two courses designated as writing-intensive. Both are improvements, but there are a variety of ways to meet them, some rather diluted. True, some students say they appreciate the flexibility in the curriculum. "It allows the student to take courses in areas that interest him or her while exposing the student to different departments," a history major says. "Someone who majors in a science will

ACADEMIC REQUIREMENTS

Williams students need three courses—pretty much anything from any related department—in each of three areas:

- Languages and the arts. Choices range from "Arthurian Literature" to "Representing Sexualities."
- Social studies, including everything from "Augustine's *City of God*" to "Food, Taste, and the Sociology of Production."
- Science and mathematics, with options ranging from "Quantum Physics" to "Mathematical Politics: Voting, Power, and Conflict."

Students are also required to take:

- Two courses that are designated as writing intensive, with some available in almost every department.
- One class that emphasizes quantitative and formal reasoning. Choices range from "Introduction to Astrophysics" to "Understanding the Web."
- One "diversity" class dealing with nonwhite Americans. Courses that could be taken here include "Latino Cityscapes" and "Fictions of Race."

take some history courses and vice versa, but requirements aren't overbearing." But the risk remains that a student could easily miss fundamental areas outside his major.

And perhaps inside them. While the requirements for particular departments are by no means trivial, they are sometimes too loose to be useful. For instance, an English major need take only two courses set before 1700; in other words, Shakespeare is optional (you could focus on Chaucer and Milton instead). Likewise, the otherwise rigorous history major requires only one class in U.S. history—which need not focus on the founding, but could instead consist of "Latinas in the Global Economy." Of course, one could argue that any major who chose this as his sole American history class deserves what he gets. But we believe that schools should protect the young in the wisdom of their folly.

A recent article in the *Williams Record*, a student newspaper, indicates that there is some frustration with the current obsession with diversity and the effect it has on the curriculum. The author notes that many courses have been eliminated to make room for more politically correct material, resulting in choices that have become very homogenous. He bemoans the proliferation of "classes about minorities" over "classes about stuff deemed important for the last hundred years." Or the last couple thousand, for that matter.

"The study of Western civilization is given no special place in the curriculum," says a student. "Sure, the courses in history, literature, and philosophy are often there— or at least seem to be, but it is entirely possible to leave here without reading any really great books or learning any history beyond that of race and gender."

Though there is no Western culture or Western civilization requirement, students do have to take at least one course to fulfill a peoples and culture requirement. According to the catalog, courses in this area are "intended to help students to begin to understand the cultural diversity of American society and the world at large, so that, as citizens of an increasingly interconnected world, they may become better able to respond sensitively and intelligently to peoples of varied social backgrounds and cultural frameworks." Eligible classes must deal with either "the peoples and cultures of North America that trace their origins to Africa, Asia, Latin America, Oceania, or the Caribbean or Native American peoples and cultures." According to one student, the requirement is "basically a joke. I fulfilled mine through 'American Economic History' (I guess because we studied slaves and immigrants) and countless other courses fulfill it too."

One thing that is no joke at Williams is its honor code. Because students broadly adhere to it, faculty feel safe in leaving exams unproctored, and even allowing students to "self-schedule" tests as take-homes.

Disappointingly, Williams imposes no foreign language requirement. However, it offers a foreign language major with concentrations in German, Russian, French, Spanish, Italian, Chinese, Japanese, and self-study courses with native speakers of Arabic, Hebrew, Hindi, Korean, and Swahili.

The best departments at Williams are in the sciences—especially biology, chemistry, physics, geology, computer science, mathematics, and neuroscience. In addition, the international relations component of the political science department has an excellent program. Most humanities and social science departments have some very good professors, including Eugene J. Johnson, Michael J. Lewis, and Sheafe Satterthwaite in art; Stephen Fix in English; Jim B. Wood and Charles B. Dew in history; Joe Cruz in philosophy, James McAllister in political science; and Robert Jackall and James L. Nolan Jr. in sociology. The Chinese and Japanese departments are strong, and the art history program is said to be extraordinary. Students can take advantage of the Clark Institute of Art and the Williams College Museum of Art, the former nearby, the latter on campus. As at most every other university on this planet, students should avoid the women's and gender studies department—which at Williams helpfully announces its orientation on its Web site with an image from a lesbian pulp novel.

Faculty members at Williams, though usually liberal, seem to be fair. "I have yet to take a class where I thought the professor's ideology influenced the course or my evaluation in it," a student says. "If anything, the course I took that had the strongest ideological tilt (a very slight one at that) was from a conservative professor in a course on American imperialism. . . . I even had one professor regularly ask me if I thought the course was leaning to the left, as he knew I was a conservative student."

Student Life: Amherst *delenda est*

Williams is located 145 miles from Boston and 165 miles from New York City, making its location either "bucolic" or "remote," depending on one's perspective. The campus itself adds much to the landscape, with the older buildings designed in traditional academic style. Each member of the graduating classes, since 1862 at least, has planted a sprig of ivy next to some building or wall, giving the campus a classic look.

Almost all students live on campus, and more than 90 percent of upperclassmen have single rooms, either in dorms or in one of 36 self-governed houses. In addition to frats and sororities, Williams has also banned special-interest housing in the interest of maintaining a less segmented (that is, less segregated) student body. This does not strike us as a bad idea.

Upperclassmen can live in mansions confiscated from campus fraternities in 1962. The six freshman dorms were all built before 1930 (though they have been renovated since); Morgan Hall (1882) is a medieval-looking place, complete with a gargoyle or two. The dorms are coed (Williams began admitting women in 1971, long after it had apparently decided to stop building freshmen dorms), and some of the bathrooms are

SUGGESTED CORE
1. Classics 101/102, Greek Literature / Roman Literature
2. Philosophy 221, Greek Philosophy
3. Religion 201/210, Reading the Hebrew Bible / Reading Jesus, Writing Gospels: Christian Origins in Context
4. Religion 212, The Development of Christianity: 30–600 (*closest match*)
5. Political Science 232, Modern Political Thought
6. English 201, Shakespeare's Major Plays
7. History 252a, British Colonial America and the United States to 1877
8. History 227, Europe's Long Nineteenth Century

167

coed—a Web description of Williams and Sage halls, for example, says the bathrooms are *"usually* single sex and are shared by [four to six] people" (our emphasis). Williams is the school that inspired Wendy Shalit's brilliant manifesto *A Return to Modesty*, which the Williams grad published when she was only 23.

Much of students' out-of-class activity takes place on campus, with many involved in sports, student organizations, and social events. The campus proper is 450 acres, but the college also owns the 2,200-acre Hopkins Memorial Forest. The athletic program is one of the strongest in the nation in the NCAA Division III; the school almost always wins the division's Sears Directors' Cup, a national award based on the aggregate success of a school's teams. "A lot of people compare it [the sports program] to a fraternity and sorority system. . . . It's their prime affiliation, and it seems like it's stronger than other kinds of student groups," Mark Robertson, editor of the *Record*, told the *Chronicle*. The school mascot is a purple cow. About 40 percent of students participate in intercollegiate athletics, 34 percent in varsity athletics. By comparison, 9 percent of students participate in the college's 25 performing arts groups.

Since 1821, when the Williams president nearly depopulated the college by taking a group of faculty and students to start Amherst College, a favorite Williams obsession has been beating Amherst in anything and everything. Williams generally stomps Amherst in the annual bowl-game-like football contest. Williams also played Amherst College in 1859 in the first ever intercollegiate baseball game, which was actually "a doubleheader—a baseball game and a chess match," according to the Williams Web site—which doesn't mention that Amherst won the baseball game, 73-32 (in 26 innings!). "The Mountains," written at Williams in 1859, was the first school song in the nation. In other traditional activities, the graduating class drops a perfectly good watch 80 feet from the tower of the college chapel. If it takes that licking and keeps on ticking, the class will supposedly be lucky. Incidentally, Williams's graduates were the first in the United States (in 1887) to don caps and gowns, a tradition that evolved to hide the disparity between the garb of rich and poor students, according to the college. Massachusetts, New York, and California send the greatest number of students to Williams. The student body contains members from 46 states and more than 50 foreign countries. The group as a whole might be a little bit on the privileged side: fewer than 60 percent of students come from public high schools.

The Princeton Review recently dropped Williams from its list of the nation's top 20 "Birkenstock-wearing, tree-hugging, clove-smoking vegetarian" schools, but the campus still veers toward the port side, culturally. Because students tend to be very good writers, well read, and aware of rhetorical tropes, discussions are at least conducted—if the pages of the *Record* are any guide—in the high-minded, some might say self-important tone of prodigies who are smart before they're all that wise.

While the default position is liberal, debaters write and speak in complete sentences, and the insults are at least disguised in a somewhat mannerly fashion. That doesn't mean it is easy to disagree with prevailing views. In a column in a January 2002 edition of the *Record*, the paper's former opinion page editor confessed: "I've been afraid to speak up; to speak up about anything controversial or worthy of debate."

Nevertheless, it seems to be a more intellectual and talkative—rather than demonstrative and noisy—sort of politics that prevails at Williams. Students who dissent from the left-liberal line may find the atmosphere a bit stifling—but then again, the college did recently host a debate between Pat Buchanan and ACLU president Nadine Strosser. The school has also hosted the infamous Ward Churchill, the faux-Indian academic from the University of Colorado–Boulder who compared the victims of September 11, 2001, with Adolf Eichmann. One conservative student says that Williams "has not proven to be the liberal hippie bastion that I was told it would be, though it has its share of leftist activism. In the long run, attending a school like Williams known for both its academic rigor and liberal political leanings will better serve conservative students than seeking out a college with like-minded students."

Most of the political student groups listed on Williams's Web site are leftist, including Amnesty International, Williams Feminist Alliance, and the Williams Purple Druids, who promote anti-sweatshop campaigns, fair trade coffee, and the like. The Queer Student Union (QSU) holds two big events a year: Coming Out Days and Pride Days. These include chalking campus property with redeeming messages like "Do you enjoy anal sex as much as I do?" The school does try to erase such chalkings—to loud complaints and with limited success. Williams also hosts a Garfield Republican Club (named for the president, an alumnus). One student described the club as "vibrant" and says that the club has been the largest political group on campus in recent years. One highly visible student group is the Williams "streaking" team, which recently doffed its clothes and "strode through a dining hall, pausing to chug their unsuspecting spectators' drinks," according to the *Chronicle of Higher Education*.

The college does have a multicultural center that hosts a number of speakers and events per year. It offers an orientation program for minority students prior to the regular college orientation, intended to create a "network of support" for incoming minority students through a variety of social events and forums. The college reports its "U.S. minority enrollment" as 23 percent. Spirituality persists amidst the uplifting natural vistas of Williams, which hosts a Catholic, Jewish, Muslim, and several Protestant chaplains.

Williams is a mostly safe campus, with burglary being the most commonly reported offense (65 incidents in 2003). However, forcible sex offenses did double from three in 2002 to six in 2003. The security patrol works with local law enforcement in cases of violent crime or arrests and works to prevent crime through a Rape Aggression Program and a student escort service for the evening hours.

Williams is costly, with tuition at $29,786 and another $8,110 due for room and board. However, because it is also rich—Williams has one of the highest endowment-to-student ratios in the world, sitting as it does on almost $1.4 *billion* in assets—it can afford to be generous. Admissions are need-blind, and the college promises to meet 100 percent of demonstrated need for every student. Some 42 percent of students receive aid.

YALE UNIVERSITY

New Haven, Connecticut • www.yale.edu

Despite all this

It used to be true that at elite American colleges, every student got a balanced exposure to the liberal arts as part of a core curriculum. Except at a few schools (see Columbia and the University of Chicago), this is no longer true. Most of the other leading schools boast weak core requirements, obnoxious classroom politics, and degraded campus atmospheres. Despite all this, at some of these schools one can still find a superb education. That's especially true at Yale, which is at once highly political and academically extraordinary. It's a matter of knowing where to look.

Based in a battered but recovering New England town, Yale boasts one of the most beautiful, architecturally eclectic campuses in the country. Students arriving at Yale will discover a vibrant intellectual life, the best political clubs in the nation, a vast array of artistic opportunities, and a high-mindedness befitting one of the world's most respected educational institutions.

Academic Life: First a college

While Yale's commitment to undergraduate education is stronger than many schools', it nevertheless leaves students to define their education and pick which courses to take. Yale merely "urges each undergraduate to design a program of study suited to his or her own particular needs and interests from the multitude of courses available to college students in a university," according to the school.

This means that Yale cedes the responsibility for answering a complex question— "What should an educated person know?"—to largely ignorant, if bright, 18-year-olds. Yale's distribution requirements make sure that students are exposed to the methods used in a wide variety of disciplines, but they don't require that students learn *anything in particular*—not even the core texts of Western culture, English literature, or the American republic. At this, your average Yalie might roll his eyes and reply that one should have studied those things in high school. To which we'd reply, "Did you?" Chances are, even at Yale, that arriving undergrads have not, with any depth. On the positive side, however, these requirements give one the freedom to avoid the most politicized courses and teachers.

There are few if any genuinely mediocre professors at Yale, where tenured chairs are the academic equivalent of a seat in Britain's House of Lords—although considerably harder to obtain. But some are better at teaching than others, while a few have trouble keeping their personal politics out of the classroom. Hence, students reading

Yale's "Blue Book" should seek out the professors and programs recommended by this guide, trusted faculty advisors, and sensible peers.

Among the many fine scholars at Yale, the following stand out as teachers: Ian Shapiro and Steven Smith in political science; Joanne Freeman, John Lewis Gaddis, Donald Kagan, Paul Kennedy, Jonathan Spence, Frank Turner, and Henry Turner in history; Nigel Alderman, Harold Bloom, Matthew Giancarlo, Traugott Lawler, David Quint, Alexander Welsh, and Ruth Bernard Yeazell in English language and literature; Charles Hill in international studies; Minh Luong in ethics, politics, and economics (EPE); the Dante scholar Giuseppe Mazzotta in Italian; Troy Cross and Karsten Harries in philosophy; Serge Lang in mathematics; Eric Denardo in operations research; Maria Rosa Menocal in Spanish; Cyrus Hamlin in German; Walter Cahn (emeritus), George Hersey (emeritus), and Vincent Scully in art history; Carlos M. N. Eire, Bentley Layton, and Harry Stout in religious studies; Vladimir Alexandrov in Slavic languages and literature; and Sidney Altman and Stephen Stearns in biology.

Students and faculty list the following departments as particularly strong: history, art history, biology, biochemistry, genetics, mathematics, music, neuroscience, physiology, and religious studies.

All students admitted to Yale should look into the directed studies program—essentially a writing-intensive, seminar-driven great books program, and one of the best educational options at Yale. Those wishing to take part must apply the summer after they are accepted at Yale. The program accepts 125 students each year, up from 80 just three years ago. (More than 200 students apply out of the freshman class of approximately 1,100.) Students in the program spend their first year taking three two-semester courses in literature, philosophy, and historical and political thought; the curriculum consists of the close reading of primary sources of the West, from the Greeks to the modern world, in classes of 18 students or fewer.

"Directed studies is a good choice because it is the only chance these students have at Yale to immerse themselves in a coherent syllabus," one professor says. "It is a truly outstanding program—there is no matching its quality. Professors can pick out these students later because they are better writers and speakers." On the down side, according to one student in the program, it is "very hard to make friends during one's freshman year when you're reading or writing for six hours every night." It's also difficult to get started on any math or science major if you do directed studies, another

VITAL STATISTICS

Religious affiliation: none
Total enrollment: 11,441
Total undergraduates: 5,319
SAT/ACT midranges: SAT V: 700–780, M: 700–780; ACT: 30–34
Applicants: 19,682
Applicants accepted: 10%
Accepted applicants who enrolled: 66%
Tuition: $29,820
Room and board: $9,030
Freshman retention rate: 98%
Graduation rate: 90% (4 yrs.), 96% (6 yrs.)
Courses with fewer than 20 students: 74%
Student-faculty ratio: 6:1
Courses taught by graduate TAs: 7%
Most popular majors: history, political science, economics
Students living on campus: 87%
Guaranteed housing for four years? no
Students in fraternities: 10% sororities: 11%

In the absence of a core curriculum, Yale imposes distribution requirements that force students to complete at least three courses in each of the groups below that fall outside their majors. For students whose major lies outside Group IV, at least two of the three course credits in Group IV must be earned in the natural sciences. The groups are as follows:

- Group I (languages and literature). Courses that count include introductions to foreign languages, literature surveys, and courses in women's fiction, gay fiction, and other politicized topics.
- Group II, which includes, according to the *Yale Herald*, "American studies, architecture, film studies, African American studies, women's and gender studies, theater studies, art, history of art, history, and philosophy." So one could choose to study medieval architecture and Renaissance painting—or mambo dancing and suburbia.

student says; there simply isn't time in the day to do the work of a numbers-crunching course in addition to these reading-heavy classes, which take up the whole of freshman year.

Directed studies stands in contrast to the handful of politicized departments at Yale, such as women's studies; African American studies; and ethnicity, race, and migration, or ERM. One professor calls the latter program "pure leftist propaganda." Another professor calls American studies Yale's "worst department," and "notoriously easy. Students there don't have to know anything" to get good grades; they need only "swallow a very big political pill" to move along. Although the history department contains several excellent scholar-teachers, another professor notes that it also has "people who under the guise of social history are really teaching ethnic and feminist studies." According to one undergrad, "the political science department, so revered here as the second-most popular major, has fallen prey to scientism and the construction of sterile, contrived models to explain and dissect society in order to mold it. Unfortunately, the departments of anthropology and sociology are largely already in that trap." Another student says that the philosophy department is "falling apart" due to a faculty shortage.

But even less-than-stellar departments do not detract much from the good choices Yale offers. "For those students who wish to find Old Yale in the course catalog, it's there," a student says. Yale as a university is more dedicated to educating undergraduates than most rival Ivies. "I had visited Harvard and others and found them more focused on the graduate level," says a student. "These [other] schools, following the German *Wissenschaft* model, sought to produce specialists receiving MAs." Says one student, "Yale is first a college, then a university."

Faculty at Yale are said to be mostly quite accessible, happy to work with students and to meet with them during office hours. Grade inflation, a national problem particularly pronounced at the Ivies, is found in some courses, but less so in seminars. Each entering freshman is assigned a faculty member or administrator to serve as a first-year advisor. Once the student has declared a major, he selects a faculty advisor within that department.

Yale does use teaching assistants in its larger introductory courses, but students report that many of their TAs are excellent teachers and first-rate scholars. Some of them, it should be noted, are also turning into hard-nosed, left-wing labor organizers, intent on forming a graduate student union; in fact, they launched a week-long strike at semester's end in 2005. At Yale, as at most universities, teaching assistants are more likely to be radical in their politics and pedagogy than the faculty. "Less judicious and more politicized TAs would attempt to quash the conservative viewpoint [of students]," a student says. "Yet the seasoned professor is willing to hear all sides, regardless of his own persuasion. . . . Being the lone conservative student in a seminar of 12 students, my conservative beliefs were often discarded by my peers. The professor, though himself a man of the far left, was always willing to call on me [and] complimented my willingness to be iconoclastic in that environment." Yale professors, secure in the most coveted academic positions available, are famously magnanimous. One student (actually, one of this guide's editors) recalls that as a callow 17-year-old freshman—on his very first day of class, first semester—he interrupted the lecture of world-famous scripture scholar Bentley Layton to question him for off-handedly challenging an important Christian doctrine. Layton generously conceded the point, apologized, and thanked the student for his intervention. That's the kind of place Yale is.

Students for Academic Freedom, a right-leaning student group, recently surveyed Yale students about their experiences of bias in the lecture hall and seminar room. Many students agreed with the respondent who wrote: "To a large degree, in all of my classes, my professors have shown a great effort to be as impartial as possible, and to ensure that their political beliefs do not influence their students."

Others, however, reported a broad array of political digressions from the course material—almost all of them slanted to the left. Said one: "My teacher came into class the day after the [2004 presidential] election proclaiming, 'That's it. This is the death of America.' The rest of the class was eager to agree, and 20 minutes of Bush-bashing ensued." Another recalled, "In my German class, the teacher was expressing her political views and said, 'They [people who vote for Bush] are sheep! They're blind sheep!' When someone protested her comment, she said in front of the class, 'How could you vote for him?! He's so scary!' The following assignments were translating German articles that bashed G[eorge] W." More disturbingly, another student wrote, "One of my professors has consistently expressed the opinion that 'conservatives want people to die' rather than provide any drug addiction or AIDS treatment." Another student spoke to a broader problem: "It's not so much that I feel indoctrinated as I feel intimidated. In a small English class of 15, current political issues and figures are often discussed,

REQUIREMENTS (CONT'D)

- Group III, which encompasses such majors as sociology, political science, economics, psychology, international studies, and other "soft" sciences. Choices here range from "The Moral Foundations of Politics" to "Women and Gender in a Transnational Context."
- Group IV, which contains the "hard sciences." Options here range from "Calculus of Functions of One Variable" to "Chemistry in Popular Novels."

In addition, a student must fulfill a foreign language requirement by demonstrating competence in a foreign language at the intermediate level either through coursework or testing.

with one side being ridiculed by the prof and students. I am the only one who doesn't share those views, but won't say so."

Still, all in all, the survey was fairly encouraging, according to the conservative student who organized it. She says of the biased teachers cited by respondents, "I think these are the rare but unfortunate exceptions, and with a little work a conservative student can avoid them."

Unfortunately, when this rather even-handed, not-especially-alarming survey was published in the *Yale Free Press*, a conservative campus paper, every single copy was stolen before students could read it. According to Students for Academic Freedom, some "2,400 missing issues, estimated to have been worth $600, were taken over the Thanksgiving holiday in what appears to be an organized and ideologically motivated theft." Refreshingly, the university denounced the theft; the group, undaunted, reprinted and redistributed the papers.

Student Life: There are even groups for nonjoiners

Student life at Yale College centers around the residential college system, a hallmark of life at Yale since 1932, which was designed in imitation of the (much more extensive) college system at Oxford and Cambridge. According to the catalog: "Each college has its own dining hall, where the students eat together, as well as its own library, common rooms, and athletic teams; each college offers courses for which academic credit is given; and each college celebrates the progress of the academic year with various festivities, concerts, and dramatic presentations."

Every college, headed by a residential master and a dean, has developed its own personality over the decades, and graduates are almost as loyal to their college as to their school. Most freshmen live together on the Old Campus and move into their residential colleges their sophomore year. All freshmen and sophomores must live on campus, and most undergraduates choose to live in their colleges throughout their four years at Yale; only 13 percent live off campus. Most of the colleges are quite beautiful, varying in style from Georgian, to meticulously "aged" Gothic replicas of Oxford colleges, to starkly modern residences that recall surrealist landscapes by Giorgio di Chirico. Students get no choice about which residence they'll inhabit, though it's possible to transfer.

The residential colleges create tighter circles within an otherwise daunting 11,000-student university. A professor notes that the level of civility in the colleges is higher than in most school dorms. A student calls the residential college system "a high point of the Yale life." The residential colleges provide some shelter from the stresses of college existence by allowing students the luxury of "a long dinner or relaxing in a common room." The menu offerings are diverse, plentiful, and usually good. One college offers healthy, "sustainable food" grown organically by local farmers. One graduate, decades later, still speaks fondly of his favorite table in one of the Gothic dining halls, where the smell of magnolia trees would waft in through the open stained glass windows.

Privacy isn't to be expected, however. A student notes that "Yale students live in suites of up to 10 people, so they gather with many people in the common room or can be alone in their rooms." Even the most private room there is—the bathroom—isn't private. "In fact," says a student, "many bathrooms are coed. Frankly, I do find the prospect a bit repulsive." It's possible to request a single-sex bathroom, if one is willing to make other trade-offs in the housing lottery. Most freshman bathrooms are single-sex, however.

As for drug and alcohol use, a student says that "there is definitely the presence of alcohol on campus. . . . Alcohol [is used in] a very traditional, social form." Students say there is the regular measure of frat-house drinking, but that no one is pressured to drink if he wishes to abstain. As for drugs, "There is a very small (almost nonexistent) group of drug users who largely keep to themselves," a student says. One college dean says, "Generally the demands of the courses are such that you can't do a lot of drinking and smoking weed. Most people realize that the demands are too great, after a brief period of experimentation."

Substances like these definitely don't get in the way of what is perhaps the most vigorous undergraduate political scene in the nation. "Conservatives and libertarians have highly active parties and publications available to them and are perhaps the most lively and self-confident political groups at Yale," a professor says. "The brightest new students, even leftists, are attracted to these parties because that's where the brightest upperclassmen seem to have gravitated." Says a recent graduate: "There's a lot of free-wheeling debate there. You can say almost anything"—if you're willing to stand up for what you believe and can withstand the peer pressure to conform.

A current student concurs: "It is quite amazing to see the extent to which conservative students have an outlet for activity on this dominantly liberal campus." Activity more than activism: the conservative groups are "centers of debate, discussion, and friendship that complement coursework and the rest of the Yale experience," the student says. Prominent organizations worth investigating are the newspapers *Light and Truth* and the *Yale Free Press,* the Party of the Right, the Tory Party, and the Conservative Party (all part of the broader Yale Political Union). Among these rightist groups, students will find serious discussions (in coat and tie) of medieval culture, the pros and cons of democracy, the existence and benevolence of God. The old days of "political correctness" (a term once used at Yale without a trace of

SUGGESTED CORE

1. Classical Civilization 111b, Homer, Virgil, Dante
2. Philosophy 116a, Introduction to Ancient Philosophy
3. Religious Studies 145a/ 152b, Introduction to the Old Testament (Hebrew Bible) / Introduction to the New Testament: History and Literature
4. Religious Studies 158a, History of Christianity in the Ancient World: Jesus to Augustine *and* 164b, History, Hope, and the Self: Modern Christian Thought
5. Political Science 114a, Introduction to Political Philosophy
6. Humanities 258a, Shakespeare and the Canon: Histories, Comedies, and Poems
7. History 002a, Revolutionary America (*closest match*)
8. History 271a, European Thought and Culture: Rousseau to Nietzsche

irony) seem to be long gone. "It's trite to say, but Yale really is a welcoming place. It's both a warm community and a genuine home," said an editor of the *Yale Free Press*.

It's still true that Yale is a left-leaning campus, reflecting the prejudices of America's elites. Students from religious households are likely to be shocked by many of the events they encounter on campus—for instance, "Sex Week at Yale." Using Yale student fees and Yale facilities, this 2004 event was cosponsored by an adult film company, which also provided one of the keynote speakers, a porn star. But if tradition-minded students are self-confident enough and seek out the company of like-minded people, or steep themselves in the practice of their faith through one of the many campus ministries, they should do just fine. "Some of the larger and more active student groups are the evangelical Yale Christian Fellowship and Yale Students for Christ. Jewish students, too, have a remarkable variety of more and less Orthodox options through the Slifka Center for Jewish Life at Yale, Yale Friends of Israel, and such," says a student. More traditional Catholic students usually avoid the stark, trendy Thomas More chapel in favor of St. Mary's Church on Hillhouse Avenue, where liturgies feature an exquisite Gregorian chant and polyphonic choir.

Several students volunteered that the most appealing aspect of campus life is the abundance and variety of extracurricular groups. Among them are the Whiffenpoofs (a musical group), the Yale College Entrepreneurial Society, the Yale Bach Society, and publications like the *Yale Free Press*, the *Yale Record* (a humor monthly), and the *Yale Daily News*, Yale's student daily. A student calls the *Daily News* "notoriously left-wing, but a fine Yale tradition." The paper is said to be looking for conservative writers to balance its editorial page.

Yale fields intercollegiate teams in all the major sports. Like other Ivy League schools, it requires that its athletes maintain high academic standards and does not award athletic scholarships. This often results in hilariously lopsided contests against more athletically inclined schools, with Yalies cheering on their hopeless warriors with chants such as "It's all right, / it's okay. / You'll be working for us someday." Some consolation is provided at football games by the cheerfully obscene Yale Precision Marching Band. Among the many intramural sports, organized by residential college, are golf, soccer, football, tennis, basketball, swimming, squash, softball, and billiards.

Yale brims with cultural institutions, including the Center for British Art; the University Art Gallery; the Peabody Museum of Natural History; and the huge library system. Centered in the Sterling Memorial Library, Yale's collection of more than ten million volumes is second in size only to Harvard's and is one of the great collections in the world. Designed to look like a cathedral, Sterling boasts catalogs in side chapels, phone booths in the shape of confessionals, and a vast image of "Lady Learning" over its main circulation desk—which looks so much like a high altar that annually (legend tells) some Catholic freshman gets confused and genuflects.

A campaign to repair and update Yale's beautiful campus is partially complete. Fifteen architectural firms were retained to help renovate 100 of the 224 buildings—a project that will take $2.6 billion to finish, according to the *Chronicle of Higher Education*. Yale has traditionally been known for its humanities and social science departments, but that balance of power could shift as it prepares to spend half a billion dollars on a new medical school and an equal sum on new science buildings.

Traditional haunts for Yalies include the venerable "tables down at Mory's" Bar; Naples Pizza, home of impecunious grad students marking blue books; the Yankee Doodle, which a student magazine describes as serving "world-class burgers and other excellent food" faster than McDonald's; and J. Press, originator of the Ivy League look now popular among non-grungy young people everywhere. New York City, the shore, and the New England countryside are all within easy reach by train or car.

New Haven was once regarded by Yalies as a fearsome ghetto, with crime kept at bay by the moats, wrought-iron gates, and crenellated walls of campus. But things are changing for the better, with gentrification well under way. Within walking distance of campus students will find trendy shops, chic restaurants, and interesting night spots. Boarded-up rowhouses a few blocks from campus are gradually being bought up, renovated, and rented to wealthy students. However, crime is still a concern, and new students should learn their way around before straying too far. By far the most common crime on campus is burglary, with 63 reported in 2003, up from 42 the previous year. The school also reported five forcible sexual assaults, eight robberies, and seven stolen cars in 2003. "I feel very safe in New Haven, which really is no worse than any other city," a student says.

Yale doesn't come cheap. The tuition for 2004–5 was $29,820, and $9,030 for room and board. However, Yale admissions are need blind, and the school guarantees to meet the full demonstrated financial need of admitted undergraduates. All financial aid is need-based; in 2004–5, about 41 percent of undergraduates received aid from Yale. The average student loan debt upon graduation for the class of 2004 was $14,880. Like several other Ivies, Yale does not expect any financial contribution from families with annual incomes of less than $45,000. In addition, Yale provides undergraduates on financial aid with grant support for summer study and unpaid internships abroad.

MIDDLE ATLANTIC

NEW YORK

- ◆ Hamilton College
- ◆ Colgate University
- ◆ Bard College
- ◆ Cornell University
- ◆ Vassar College
- ◆ SUNY – Binghamton
- ◆ U.S. Military Academy

PENNSYLVANIA

N. J.

◆ — NEW YORK CITY AREA
Barnard College   New York University
Columbia University   Rutgers University
Cooper Union   Seton Hall University

- ◆ Grove City College
- ◆ Bucknell University
- ◆ Lafayette College
- ◆ Pennsylvania State University
- ◆ Princeton University
- ◆ Carnegie Mellon University

◆ — PHILADELPHIA AREA
Bryn Mawr College
Haverford College
Swarthmore College
University of Pennsylvania
Villanova University

MARYLAND

- ◆ Johns Hopkins University
- ◆ St. John's College
- ◆ U.S. Naval Academy

WASHINGTON, DC
Catholic University of America
Georgetown University

BARD COLLEGE

ANNANDALE-ON-HUDSON, NEW YORK • WWW.BARD.EDU

Not a four-letter word

Founded in 1860 as St. Stephen's College by John Bard and the New York City leadership of the Episcopal Church, Bard College began as a men's college with a strong classical curriculum. From 1928 to 1944, the school was an undergraduate college of Columbia University. It was guided through the '20s by conservative philosopher Bernard Iddings Bell— later a friend of Russell Kirk's—who resigned when the school abolished the custom of students standing as professors entered the room. The college has changed radically over the years, most notably in the 1930s and '40s. It was then that it became a coeducational haven for European intellectual émigrés in flight from fascism—and transformed itself into a self-consciously "progressive" institution. The school changed its name to Bard, then severed its ties with Columbia University and the Episcopal Church. As one student says, "Bard is a cultural anomaly, a throwback to when socialism wasn't a 'four-letter' word, when intellectualism was taken very seriously."

In the decades since independence, the college has expanded, adding several institutes, affiliations with colleges in other countries for study-abroad programs, and a number of facilities to complement its curriculum. Throughout all these changes Bard has retained a commitment to academic rigor and a structured curriculum. Further changes are on the way. In December 2001, Bard's trustees pitched in to give the institution a gift of $120 million, more than doubling the $115 million endowment. The college is about to add a new science building and expand its funding for student activity clubs and scholarships.

VITAL STATISTICS

Religious affiliation: none
Total enrollment: 2,600
Total undergraduates: 1,458
SAT median: 1320
Applicants: 3,367
Applicants accepted: 36%
Accepted applicants who enrolled: 31%
Tuition: $29,910
Room and board: $8,908
Freshman retention rate: 90%
Graduation rate: 59% (4 yrs.), 69% (6 yrs.)
Average class size: 15
Student-faculty ratio: 9:1
Courses taught by graduate TAs: none
Most popular majors: English language and literature, social sciences, fine arts
Students living on campus: 81%
Guaranteed housing for four years? no
Students in fraternities or sororities: none

Academic Life: Instant admission, painstaking study

One thing that sets Bard apart academically is its unique option for admissions. The school initiated the "instant admissions" system in the late 1970s. Each fall up to 200 applicants sign up to visit the college, submitting applications in advance. On their

ACADEMIC REQUIREMENTS

Bard's academic breadth requirements are respectable, given the high quality of most of its courses:

- The First-Year Seminar. This two-semester course focuses on some of the great books—among others. The fall 2004 reading list included Plato, Confucius, Pascal, Descartes, Locke, and Jane Austen. Spring subjects included Rousseau, Kant, Darwin, Mary Shelley, Dostoevsky, Nietzsche, Marx—and Chinua Achebe, who teaches at Bard.
- One laboratory course in the physical or life sciences.
- A course in mathematics, computing, statistics or logic; students must also pass a "quantitative test."
- A history course. Options range from "Europe from 1815 to Present" to "Negotiation and Conquest as Native American History."
- A course in the empirical social sciences. Choices include "Religion and Politics" and "Race as a Variable in History: The African American Case."
- A course analyzing primary texts in philosophy, religion, or social thought. Options range from "The Bible as

visit, they discuss readings with professors, meet with the admissions staff—and, before they return home, find out whether they have earned a spot at Bard. Bard's Web site says it receives 10 applications for each place in a first-year class.

Bard's undergraduate academic system is set up a bit differently than those of other small liberal arts colleges. In 1934, then-dean Donald Tewksbury adopted an innovative curriculum based partly on the Oxford and Cambridge tutorial systems. The basic characteristics of that system—including an emphasis on seminars, the process of "moderation," and the senior project—are still integral to Bard's curriculum. However, it has been adapted over time to allow for a great deal of student choice.

To graduate from Bard with a bachelor of arts degree, students must complete a two-part first-year seminar, earn promotion to the Upper College, complete the requirements of a major, complete Bard's distribution requirements, accumulate 124 semester hours of academic credit (40 of which must be outside their major), and complete a senior project.

First-year students arrive on campus three weeks before the fall term in order to participate in orientation and the workshop on Language and Thinking (L&T). What they are given to read is telling about Bard's intellectual orientation. The 2004 L&T syllabus was heavily weighted toward modern and contemporary works, and though it included a number of serious and important writers from the Western canon—Francis Bacon, Proust, Freud, Wallace Stevens—it featured far more of our overrated contemporaries. In general, the list includes more criticism and theory than is digestible by American high school graduates, however bright. In this way, L&T prepares Bard students to fit right in among today's academics. But at least it's serious—as it should be.

First-years (as freshmen are called at Bard) enroll in the "First-Year Seminar," a two-semester course that introduces students to "worldwide intellectual, artistic, and cultural traditions and to methods of studying those traditions." The seminar is designed to train students in close reading, critical thinking, and analytical writing.

First-years are free to choose electives (three per semester) as well. They get guidance from assigned academic advisors, with whom they must meet several times each semester. Later, each student chooses a faculty member to serve as an advisor for the rest of his or her education. If their interests change, students may switch advisors.

Students at Bard major in a "program" or course of study—and most of its programs are straightforward, many downright traditional. For instance, classical (and medieval, and Victorian) studies, biology, and sociology. But Bard's interdivisional programs are more inventive: one finds there Africana studies, Irish and Celtic studies, and Latin American and Iberian studies, among many, many others. In the arts, a photography program exists next to a history of photography program. Bard seems to be trying to keep some sort of balance, then, in its academic offerings, between respect for tradition and embrace of the experimental.

The senior project is considered by the college to be the capstone of a Bard education. Students begin preparing during their junior year, consulting with advisors, doing coursework, and participating in tutorials. Depending on the major, the senior project can be a research paper, a close textual analysis, a report of findings from field work, a photographic essay, a series of original experiments, an analysis of published research findings, a contribution to theory, an exhibition of original artwork, a film, or a musical or dance composition or performance. If students do not pass, they do not graduate, no matter how many credits they have. Knowing this fuels a certain "edgy and energetic" feeling among students, in the words of one. "The senior project is an opportunity to work one-on-one with a faculty member that is rare among the U.S. academic world today," one professor says, "and the personal relationship and the pressure of this situation brings out the most creativity and brilliance a student is capable of at that point in his life."

An impressively high proportion of Bard's professors are famous and award-winning intellectuals and writers: Chinua Achebe and John Ashbery are on the regular faculty of the Division of Languages and Literature, and in 2004 Luc Sante served as a visiting professor. Bradford Morrow, professor of literature, won a 2003 O. Henry Prize for short story. For their teaching skills, students praise William Mullen in classics, Benjamin La Farge and Mark Lambert in literature, Peter Skiff in physics, William Griffith in philosophy, and Robert Martin in music.

REQUIREMENTS (CONT'D)

Literature" to "Philosophy of Wittgenstein."

- A foreign language course.
- An English literature or literature in translation course. Choices are many, including "Goethe's Faust: Sympathy for the Devil?" and "Rewriting Conquest: Latin America and the Anglo-American Imagination."
- A course in visual or performing arts or creative writing. Some of the many options include "Cybergraphics," "First Poetry Workshop," and "Photographic Seeing."
- A course in the analysis of nonverbal art. Choices include "The Gothic Cathedral and the Gothic Revival" and "Women Artists of the Surrealist Movement."
- A "Rethinking Difference" course. These focus on "globalization, nationalism, and social justice, as well as differences of race, religion, ethnicity, class, gender, and/or sexuality." Some of the more appealing options here are "Japanimation and Culture in Post-War Japan," and "Jews in the Modern World, 1492–1948."

MIDDLE ATLANTIC

A rare conservative on the faculty is Rabbi Jacob Neusner, an outspoken pro-life scholar of religion.

Most of the academic divisions offer an impressive selection of subjects and courses. The foreign languages, cultures, and literatures division features the usual offerings and then some: ancient Greek, Latin, Sanskrit, Hebrew, Russian, Arabic, and Chinese. The Division of Languages and Literature is loaded with the kind of intensive, traditional courses that other left-leaning liberal arts colleges are phasing out: classes on medieval, Victorian, and Romantic literature, single courses on Dante, Dickens, Tolstoy, the German masters, and Joyce, even (rare at any college nowadays) on prosody, as in "Writing Metrical Verse." Of course there are also more trendy offerings—"Ideology and Political Commitment in Modern Literature," "Race, Gender, and Modernism," etc.—but who can complain, when there is an entire course on *Finnegan's Wake*?

Particularly strong departments include literature, photography, film, history, psychology, and biology. Economics students enjoy the resources of the Jerome Levy Economics Institute; one student says he took a course with the founder of Oppenheimer Funds through this program. The political science department encourages and helps students to find internships that pertain to the major. The drama and dance departments have a reputation for being rigid in their avant-gardism. Interdivisional programs and multidisciplinary studies tend to be the weakest and most politicized. Two of these are gender studies and multiethnic studies. Others have the potential to be either very strong or terribly weak, since students form the curricula themselves. For instance, those concentrating in American studies can choose legitimate history or literature courses—or the trendier classes available in the social sciences.

Professors teach all courses, and students report that "even the celebrity profs are incredibly helpful and make themselves available." One economics major says, "Students have a very direct relationship with their professors." A German studies major says, "The professors I've had so far are interesting, concerned people who are active academically and also dedicated to their jobs as teachers. . . . Bard is a small enough place where if a professor is bad, everyone knows about it right away, and he or she is not retained." Class sizes average around 15; the student-faculty ratio is nine to one.

Students or professors to the right of center are vastly outnumbered. The few conservative faculty members on campus fiercely and publicly disagree with what they deem to be Bard president Leon Botstein's liberal orientation. Still, Botstein reportedly understands the purpose of higher education is to be open to "various sides of discourse." And student publications (the *Bard Free Press* and the *Bard Observer*, both left-leaning) feel free to criticize the college's administration, often intelligently. "The students and faculty tend to be left wing, but there is a minority of students and faculty who are conservative," says one student. "Because of the liberal majority, classes tend to reflect the same type of thinking." One professor says conservative students are beginning to feel more comfortable and vocal, and that student religious groups are becoming better attended. However, when student funding was up for review, a certain group of students wanted to deny all funding to a student Republican group. Other students voted them down. It seems Bard students value free discourse. One conservative student chose to come to Bard over West Point because he wanted to be in "the trenches" of liberalism. Another student says of the conservative minority on campus, "The right-wing kids come out intellectually stronger because they've had their ideas challenged for four years."

Bard is pervaded by an informed liberalism, rather than a knee-jerk one. Students know what's going on in the world. All those solid historical courses may have something to do with it—although a student says, "The leftist lean might influence classes, since the professors often share the views of the students and vice versa." Students do say that professors try their best not to politicize their lessons, utilizing the different viewpoints that may be present in a classroom for honest intellectual exchange.

None of this is to say that Bard is anything but quite far left. The chair of the social studies department at Bard, Joel Kovez, whose chair is named for Alger Hiss, has written a book that describes anticommunism as a psychiatric condition. (For those whose memories of the Cold War era are dim, Hiss was the Communist spy outed by Whittaker Chambers and long lionized by lefties.) Courses like "Victorian Bodies" and "Topics in Sexual Identity" are bound to be politicized. An upper-level student observes too that the "Bard type" is "a student who is politically progressive, intelligent, critical, outgoing, and observant."

Student Life: Catskill collegiate

Bard College lies in Annandale-on-Hudson, a small town of 2,400 located an hour south of Albany. The college accommodates its 1,400 students on more than 500 acres along the Hudson River. Students can see the Catskill Mountains from their dorm rooms, and the area provides plenty of opportunities for outdoor activities. There is a waterfall in the woods and a pond where students can swim. Breathtaking trails through the woods surrounding Bard are marked for hiking, and canoeing and kayaking on the tributaries to the Hudson are great opportunities for outdoor adventure.

The campus comprises nearly 75 buildings of different architectural styles, including the original stone buildings and a number of mansions on the river. Some students find the rural atmosphere dull, but the college tries to spice up student life by offering free trips each hour to local towns and, each weekend, shuttles to New York City. But there's usually a lot happening on campus. A glance at two weeks in the student activities calendars reveals dozens of choices open to all students: a free chamber music concert; a poetry reading; a film; a seminar on Rubens; a women's soccer match;

SUGGESTED CORE
1. Classics 155, Roman Civilization *and* Greek 202, Greek Tragedy
2. Philosophy 106, Introduction to Philosophy: Reality, Knowledge and Value (*closest match*)
3. Theology 201, Working Theologies: Biblical Literatures *and* Religion 324, St. Paul: From Antioch to Rome (*closest matches*)
4. Religion 123, Religious Foundations of Western Civilization
5. Political Studies 211, Western Political Theory: Ancient and Modern
6. Literature 2501/2502, Shakespeare's Comedies / Shakespeare's Tragedies
7. History 104, American Bedrock
8. Philosophy 213, Nineteenth-Century Continental Philosophy

a luncheon lecture series on "Mystical Practices of Jesus and Paul"; a Shostakovich concert; a math table; Hebrew, Spanish, German, and Russian tables; a Buddhist meditation group; and a photography critique.

Clearly, the visual and performing arts are integral to life at Bard. The Colorado String Quartet, oddly enough, resides at the school, and its music program brings in other critically acclaimed chamber, orchestral, period music, and jazz musicians regularly. The popular and praised Bard Music Festival is held in August on campus and at New York's Lincoln Center. About a dozen student organizations perform or bring bands or theater productions to the campus. They perform in the 110,000-square-foot Richard B. Fisher Center for the Performing Arts designed by Frank Gehry, which houses two theaters and four rehearsal studios. But while performing arts are a major occupation of most Bard students, studies are not neglected. The Stevenson Library contains 275,000 books and 1,400 periodicals and newspapers.

The wackier side of student protests is encapsulated in the demonstration that occurred on the opening night of the Fisher Center. Students rode their bicycles through the lobby—naked. Students say alcohol rules have become stricter on campus since the "Drag Race," a drag queen ball, was shut down due to numerous cases of alcohol poisoning. However, students can still walk through the center of campus with an open can of beer or a dacquiri.

"Housing is a problem here," one Bard insider says. The school can't seem to keep up with the growing size of the Bard population. One faculty member wonders aloud "why they just can't seem to get it right." Some students returned to campus in fall 2004 only to be housed in hastily erected prefab dorms and double-wide trailers. But there are plans to fix all that. The school intends to add more than 200 suite-style rooms. More than 30 residence halls of variable size and style house about 81 percent of Bard students. The larger residences have kitchens and laundry facilities. Resident directors manage the dorms, and peer counselors manage the halls. Students praise peer counselors for being well trained, accessible, and "nonjudgmental." All residence halls are coed except for one women-only dormitory. A housing officer says that the college also countenances a number of coed bathrooms, "mostly out of necessity," since men and women live next door to each other. A guest policy which mandates that visitors check in with security is loosely enforced. And, if parents and students request it, students can live with members of the opposite sex.

In the fall of 2004, Bard was feeling growing pains not only in its housing but its facilities as well. The "old gym"—till then the main indoor facility on campus—was shut down due to structural failures. The building was near and dear to students' hearts as a place they could cut loose at parties, spray paint the walls, and practice with their rock bands at deafening volumes. It is still unclear how the administration and students of Bard will handle the demise of the beloved "old gym," but it is rumored that he administration will build a new venue to replace it.

The old stone Episcopalian church on the Bard campus is "breathtakingly beautiful" one student says. There are five college chaplains: Episcopal, Anglican, Catholic, Muslim, and Jewish. The school has Jewish and Muslim student organizations, a Christian Students Fellowship, a Buddhist Meditation Group, and a Catholic community. Evensong is observed on Sundays in the Chapel of the Holy Innocents. A Christian evangelical group is somewhat active on campus, as are the Buddhists. One student says, however, of life at Bard, "It's very secular . . . [even] straightforwardly atheistic. In my first-year seminar, the professor asked those who believed in God to raise their hands. I was the only one in the room. But everyone was respectful and curious about my beliefs." Maybe this is why the religion department has increased its faculty from one fulltime teacher in 1988 to eight in 2004. In another quirk, Jewish and Muslim students share a sacred space and a kitchen. This fits the mission of the school's chaplaincy, which promises to "help students of different faiths learn about each other."

When students aren't hitting the books—which they do a lot—they may attend the meetings or events of more than 50 student organizations and clubs. Arts and music clubs include Audio Co-op, the Surrealist Training Circus, and the Contradance Club, among many others. Service and community-based clubs include Best Buddies, which reaches out to the mentally impaired community; the well-known Bard Prison Initiative, in which students volunteer to teach inmates; Bard Co-opcycle; the Dime Store, whose sole purpose is to sell inexpensive condoms; Care Bears (bringing soup and cheer to sick students); the Migrant Labor Project (within the Hudson Valley); and the WXBC radio station. Ethnically and culturally based groups include the (Indian) Sweat Lodge, the feminist Ladies Misbehavior Society, the Queer Alliance, and organizations for various ethnic groups. Other organizations celebrate knitting, beer brewing, cooking, digital media, martial arts, and boat building and sailing.

Some groups are better than others. The *Bard Free Press* printed a porn movie review in the fall of 2004. In the same year, two new magazines sprung up: the *Moderator*, a "sexual lifestyles" magazine; and *Verse Noire*, an erotically charged literary review. Recently, the *Moderator* held its first erotic photo shoot. Photographers took shots of the models in college dorms. Throughout the night participants reached various stages of undress. A related poster series should soon be up around campus. "I am on the whole disappointed by the level of student publications," says one professor wryly.

Sports play a smallish role at Bard, according to one student. The college does, however, make room for them, sponsoring 13 men's and women's NCAA Division III teams, as well as intramural and club sports. The "Raptors" rugby, volleyball and tennis games are well attended, and, especially when it's Bard vs. Vassar, the rivalry is vigorously tongue-in-cheek. The Stevenson Gymnasium complex contains a six-lane, 25-yard swimming pool, a fitness center, squash courts, locker rooms with saunas, an aerobics studio, an athletic training room, and a main gymnasium that houses basketball, volleyball, and badminton courts. Next to the building are six lighted tennis courts, athletic fields, and miles of groomed cross-country running and Nordic skiing trails.

Bard's campus, isolated as it is, is quite safe, and students seem to feel secure. The Bard Department of Safety and Security patrols the campus, but they don't often find much action. Still, to make students feel more comfortable, new illumination and security talk-boxes have been added all over campus. A professor says, "The top security alert is bike theft." Occasional acts of vandalism are perpetrated on campus by locals who don't attend Bard. In fall 2004, there were four burglaries, very unusual for Bard. One student blamed it partially on Bard students feeling completely secure and leaving their doors and windows unlocked. Those were the only on-campus crimes reported that year.

Tuition for 2004–5 was $29,910, and room and board $8,908. However, Bard admissions are need-blind, and about 70 percent of students receive some aid. The average 2004 graduate of Bard owes $18,000 in student loans.

BARNARD COLLEGE

NEW YORK, NEW YORK • WWW.BARNARD.EDU

Columbia's little sister

The institution now known as Barnard College began in 1889, when 36 students and six faculty members met in a brownstone on Madison Avenue in New York City. Columbia University's president, Frederick A. P. Barnard, wanted to offer women a broad liberal arts education, which Columbia at the time only offered to men. Today, Barnard College is recognized as one of the top liberal arts colleges in the country.

While Columbia, located just across the street, has been coed for two decades, Barnard remains single-sex and financially independent from Columbia (Barnard's endowment totals almost $128 million). Barnard students can take from Columbia University as much or as little as they want. One Barnard student says, "Most semesters, the majority of my classes are across the street. I study in Butler [Columbia's history and humanities library] every day, and most of my friends are Columbia students. . . . Columbia is a really good resource and is one of the major reasons I don't go crazy at Barnard."

Despite Barnard's close ties to Columbia, most college guides treat them separately, and the women's college, about 2,300 students strong, is intent on keeping Barnard's identity distinct from Columbia's. Barnard has its own unique curriculum, its own strong professors, and several Barnard-only student activities.

Academic Life: Crossing the street

Academically, Barnard College benefits a great deal from its affiliation with Columbia. Barnard students can easily sign up for most Columbia College classes, while Columbia students are less successful in gaining entry to one of Barnard's intimate seminars, although students report that there are "Columbia boys" in almost all Barnard classes. New York also offers many opportunities for research, internships, and transfer credit from area colleges and universities. For instance, students can major in music by taking courses from Barnard as well as Juilliard or the Manhattan School of Music.

To start with, each incoming student takes a first-year seminar, in which she learns writing and speaking skills in a small-group environment. Each seminar enrolls around 16 students and emphasizes reading and writing. Students considering serious studies in math or the sciences at Barnard should be forewarned that most of their classes will take place at Columbia; Barnard offers few math or physics courses, for instance. In foreign languages, Barnard offers instruction in French, German, Spanish, Russian, Italian, Latin, and ancient Greek—others must be studied at Columbia.

The Barnard advising system, by all accounts, is superb. The student-faculty ratio is 10 to 1. Each student is assigned a professor from the department of her proposed major as an advisor, advocate, and friend. Most of these professors have volunteered for the job; they have an interest in the student's success and a high level of expertise in their fields—and are often helpful with last-minute advice on papers. All students must visit their advisors at least once a semester, since he or she must approve the advisee's courseload, no exceptions. Few if any students see this as a bother, especially as freshmen, when the 2,000 or so courses in the catalog run together in a blur.

Barnard students should count on half their classes being seminars (with five to 15 students) and half being lectures (most with 50 or fewer students). Some of the best professors, according to students, are Sharon Harrison, Rajiv Sethi, and Mark Skousen in economics; Anne Prescott in English; Joel Kaye and Robert McCaughey in history; Alan Gabbey in philosophy; and Jeffrey Friedman, Kimberly Zisk Marten, and Richard Pious in political science.

Barnard most clearly excels in English, political science, and psychology. The Barnard English major cannot help but learn a good deal about our literary past; in addition to a class called "Critical Writing," she must take two courses in pre-nineteenth-century literature as well as "The English Colloquium," a two-semester introduction to literature of the Renaissance and the Enlightenment. (Students may substitute appropriate courses—for instance, one on Shakespeare.) English majors also must choose three other advanced electives and two senior seminars. Allowing for the expected doses of feminism, the courses seem mostly solid and interesting.

VITAL STATISTICS

Religious affiliation: none
Total enrollment: 2,287
Total undergraduates: 2,287
SAT/ACT midranges: SAT V: 650–730, M: 620–700; ACT: 28–31
Applicants: 4,380
Applicants accepted: 27%
Accepted applicants who enrolled: 45%
Tuition: $27,064
Room and board: $10,800
Freshman retention rate: 96%
Graduation rate: 72% (4 yrs.), 84% (6 yrs.)
Average class size: 14
Student-faculty ratio: 10:1
Courses taught by graduate TAs: none
Most popular majors: social sciences, psychology, English
Students living on campus: 90%
Guaranteed housing for four years? yes
Students in sororities: none

ACADEMIC REQUIREMENTS

Unlike its brother school Columbia, Barnard has no set core curriculum. However, it maintains respectable requirements:

- "First-Year English: Reinventing Literary History." Topics in this one-semester writing course vary widely from section to section. Students can choose one of three clusters: "Legacy of the Mediterranean," which covers "key intellectual moments that have shaped Western culture," "The Americas," and "Women and Culture," which offers "revisionist responses to the constraints of canonicity," according to the catalog.
- First-Year Seminar. This small seminar introduces students to college work—and some of its several choices sound quite worthwhile. For instance, "Reacting to the Past," a class in which students are assigned roles and act out significant historical events. In a "succession dispute between Wan-li Emperor and his Confucian bureaucrats," students read the *Analects* of Confucius.

   Students must take two courses in laboratory science, which abounds in solid, challenging courses.

All students must prepare a semester- or year-long project or thesis within their major. Across the curriculum, and especially in the humanities, instructors emphasize good writing and communication skills. The economics department is well regarded, but one student says, "They're all Marxists and are famous for their politicized bent." As is usually the case, the hotshot professors rarely make the best teachers, but Barnard is blessed with excellent faculty, many of whom actually interact with students. To pick one name out of many: novelist Mary Gordon, whose books are often on college syllabi, usually offers an auditorium-sized lecture course on the modern English novel, as well as an intimate round-table creative writing seminar. Students agree that her teaching is superb.

Other faculty members are not as well known, but perhaps deserve to be. Alan Segal, professor of religion and Jewish studies, is an expert on Judaism in the time of Jesus and served on the advisory council for work on *The Gospel of John,* a three-hour film of . . . well, the Gospel of John (no screenwriter really needed—it's word for word). Students say that one of Barnard's best attributes is that students can develop lasting relationships with professors. And they are real professors—graduate teaching assistants do not teach at Barnard. One student says, "The professors actually care about what you're learning and are always willing to talk about assignments in class or related to class, or about their field in general. They are very accessible and helpful." Another says, "The professors here are some of the best in the country, and the environment is challenging, creative, and fun."

It is not, however, an environment in which conservatives feel comfortable. Said one student, "My current English professor sometimes takes a break from Auden or Yeats to rail against 'thuggish' capitalists and people with a 'corporate mentality.' I can think of two undergrad professors in all of campus who aren't Democrats; they're both libertarians." Such dissidents also "aren't particularly vocal about going against the prevailing leftist wisdom here. One of these libertarians actually swore me to secrecy about his personal views. 'I could lose my job,' he whispered."

Another highly touted department is the women's studies department, a department Columbia College lacks. As at most schools, Barnard's women's studies classes are less concerned with actual women than with an ever-growing collection of feminist texts, most of which emphasize sexist oppression throughout history. In this environment, "debate" takes place within very specific parameters; great thinkers who have the temerity to admit to sexist or "antifeminist" leanings are laughed at as buffoons. As one student notes, in her women's studies class "the teacher doesn't even read the texts correctly. Whenever the word is 'mankind,' she just reads the word 'humankind' out loud. The text doesn't matter. Just her opinion." A less popular major, though potentially as politicized, is human rights studies, an interdisciplinary program.

Barnard's Center for Research on Women "promotes a dialogue between feminist scholarship and activism," according to the center's Web page. The center sponsors an annual conference called "The Scholar and the Feminist" and publishes an online journal by that name. In its summer 2004 issue, entitled "Young Feminists Take on the Family," the magazine featured an article by writer Lisa Johnson in which she defended her decision to carry on an affair with a married man, describing herself not as an adulteress, but as "a social agent bent on queering heterosexuality—valuing intimacy outside marriage, separating sex from reproduction, recognizing pleasure as a worthwhile end in itself, and resisting the categorization of women as 'wives' and 'mistresses' according to the state regulation of sexuality—rather than consenting to it whole cloth." We're sure the guy's wife bought that one.

The political milieu at Barnard, then, is unremittingly leftist. One student says, "Undeniably, this school has major problems with political correctness and blatant bias toward liberal—even communist—positions. I tried majoring in political science and then in history, but grew frustrated with these 100 percent leftist departments. The English courses I've taken were just as bad: Marxist, feminist, raceconscious—you name it. We actually read *The Communist Manifesto* in 'First-Year English.' When I tried to defend capitalism in class, the professor called me into her office for a private meeting. 'Surely, you have to admit that capitalism is a brutal system,' she insisted. I refused, and we argued at length. I ended up with a low grade in the class."

Notable Barnard alumnae include Zora Neale Hurston, Margaret Mead, Martha Stewart, Jeanne

---

REQUIREMENTS (CONT'D)

Students must complete the fourth semester in a foreign language.

Other requirements are arranged in categories. Students must take one course each in:

- Reason and Value, offering 56 classes from which to choose, ranging from "What Is Philosophy, Anyway?" to "Gender and Sexuality in Ancient Greece"
- Social analysis, which offers a wide variety of options—most of them politicized, like "Gendered Controversies: Women's Bodies and Global Conflicts."
- Historical studies, which includes many solid choices such as "Introduction to Art History."
- Cultures in comparison, ranging from courses like "Queer Diasporas: Race, Sexuality, and Migration" to "Classical and Biblical Historiography."
- Quantitative and deductive reasoning, which includes math and logic courses.
- Literature, for which both "Shakespeare in Performance" and "Reading for Difference: Lesbian and Gay Themes in Hispanic Literature and Film" qualify, among others.
- Visual and performing arts.

Kirkpatrick, musician Laurie Anderson, actress Cynthia Nixon, and Dr. Carol Berkowitz, 2004–5 president of the American Academy of Pediatrics.

Student Life: They say the neon lights are bright

Most of Barnard's pedestrian-friendly campus is clustered between Broadway and Claremont Avenues. Space, of course, is tight, and Barnard has no room to expand. Architectural styles vary from building to building, but the main structures are Milbank Hall, which houses several administrative offices and academic departments, and Barnard Hall, with more classrooms, a gym, and a swimming pool. Most students consider the Barnard campus quite appealing; it served as the set for a 2003 filming of an episode of *Law and Order: Criminal Intent.* McIntosh Center is the main locus of student life and includes a dining hall and coffeeshop, as well as plenty of space for student activities and clubs. The Quad, a group of four residence halls with a courtyard in the center, is where most first-year students live. Students need only cross Broadway to get to Columbia. A series of underground tunnels connect buildings and halls around the Barnard campus, rendering umbrellas and snow boots almost unnecessary.

Barnard's social scene is centered around New York City. Not surprisingly, students say the city is one of the best advantages of attending the school. The Upper West Side has a number of lively bars, from the beer-reeking frat hangout, The West End, to the more mellow 1020. Students report that these bars strictly enforce underage drinking laws, and the drinking scene, compared to other colleges, is mild. With some exceptions, there isn't much partying on the Barnard campus, because when it comes down to it, nothing compares to the city scene. In fact, smoking is prohibited not just in university buildings, but even outdoors on the campus—except for two specially designated exterior smoker pens.

The college sponsors annual student events, including spring and winter festivals and Founder's Day. There are more than 100 student clubs and organizations on campus, including Asian Women's Coalition, Literary Society, Caribbean Students Organization, Campus Crusade for Christ, Postscrypt Arts, a gospel choir, a marching band, a radio station, Student Theatre, Women's Collective, Student Political Action Group, and the Undergraduate Law Society.

Barnard and Columbia students spend many of their free nights and weekends downtown in Soho or the West Village, hanging out with students from New York's other schools. On weekends, students enjoy nightclubs, often complete with fishnet stockings and platform shoes, but they also frequent coffeehouses to study or read for pleasure. Unfortunately, students' freedom to explore the city and hobnob with students from other area schools has detracted from the sense of community that Barnard might have hoped for. Barnard does not have the close-knit atmosphere that other all-women colleges like Bryn Mawr and Mount Holyoke can boast. In fact, Barnard's "all-women" status makes little practical difference, in the end. One student says that 90 percent of her classes are coed, as are her extracurricular activities—and so are some of the dorms (at Columbia, where Barnard students are allowed to live). "I wouldn't say the fact that Barnard is a women's school has too much effect on my social life, although I do wish that there were more guys around sometimes," she says. "Girls can be catty!"

Barnard prides itself on being an extraordinarily tolerant place where women of every race, creed, etc. are invited to bring their various backgrounds to bear on the issues that affect them and others. One notable example of Barnard's diversity is the mix of religious backgrounds that is present at the school: adherents of more conservative religious persuasions are drawn to this all-female environment. There is, for example, a thriving Orthodox Jewish community on campus, and the cafeteria offers kosher food. It also offers special dining hours during Ramadan. Such diversity can make for some fascinating theological conversations, students say. The same holds true racially, though to a lesser degree. The Barnard student body is more than 20 percent Asian, around 5 percent black, and 5 percent Hispanic. Barnard has fewer international students (only 3 percent of its population) than do most schools because it has little financial aid to offer them, but an admissions counselor says Barnard has a huge immigrant population. The college is geographically diverse, too, representing all 50 states; 48 percent of students come from the mid-Atlantic region.

But then there is this well-known paradox: The more tolerant a student body claims to be, the less tolerant it will become. The Barnard community is very accepting of students, whatever their race, economic class, sexuality, or even sex (some Barnard students have chosen to define themselves as "men," despite their biology). But don't try sporting that pro-life button, if you want to make many friends. Lesbianism is amply celebrated, and gay students tend to be more outspoken than their straight classmates. One student says, "I think conservatives are definitely marginalized on campus politically. There are a lot of social conservatives because of the large Orthodox Jewish, Indian, and East Asian communities here, but they don't tend to give voice to their conservatism." A more liberal student says, "If there are any conservatives here, they stay nice and quiet so as to avoid the wrath of the open-minded Barnard girls who will soon shut them up for good." Another student says, "While there are conservative students on campus, they tend to be silenced by a prominent lesbian community." Still another says, "I'd imagine that being right-wing is difficult on most campuses these days. It's especially hard, though, at places like Columbia and Barnard, where the administration has no sympathy for students like us."

The Office of Multicultural Affairs oversees the Committee on Race, Religion, Identity, and Ethnicity (CORRIE), a college-wide program that sponsors and supports

SUGGESTED CORE

1. Classical Literature W4300y, The Classical Tradition
2. Philosophy V 2101x, History of Philosophy I
3. Religion V3501x/V3120x, Introduction to the Hebrew Bible / Introduction to Christianity
4. Religion V 2610y, Christianity *or* Religion V 3402x, Early Christianity
5. Political Science BC 1014y, Political Theory II
6. English BC 3163x, 3164y, Shakespeare
7. History BC 1401x, Survey of American Civilization to the Civil War
8. Philosophy V 3270x, Nineteenth-Century Philosophy: Hegel to Nietzsche

MIDDLE ATLANTIC

193

activities like Latina Heritage Month, Queer Awareness Month, Celebration of Black Womanhood, and the Rennert Women in Judaism Forum.

Students say there is more of a conservative presence at Columbia, and Barnard students sometimes attend College Republicans meetings there. When the college held a "bipartisan" conference to coincide with the 2004 Republican National Convention in New York, the keynote speaker representing that party was Anne Stone, chair of Republicans for Choice.

Barnard students' very enthusiasm, their dedication to their studies, and their generally congenial dispositions reveal an honest desire to make sense of their world. A more conservative first-year student will certainly feel a bit out of the loop at this school where "queer" means cool. But she will probably be able to find intelligent and interesting friends among her quieter peers.

The dorms themselves are neither luxurious nor uncomfortable, considering how tight space is in Manhattan. Barnard supports 10 residence halls (including both suite-style and traditional corridor-style halls), along with four halls at Columbia College, where some students live in coed dorms with Columbia students. A housing official says that these are suite-style residences where men and women could potentially share bathrooms. The college also owns a few apartments in brownstones located in the immediate area. First-year students are housed together in freshmen-only dormitories or floors. Barnard guarantees housing for all four years, no small feat in Manhattan. Only 10 percent of students brave the local rents off campus.

Although sports are not terribly popular among Barnard students, there are several options available for those who are interested. Students at Barnard and Columbia play together on 14 NCAA Division I–level varsity teams, and also team up in more than 30 club sports. Barnard offers intramural teams in basketball, floor hockey, indoor soccer, equestrian, tennis, and volleyball, and students can also play on coed intramural teams at Columbia.

Barnard is intent on preventing crime, and security becomes stronger every day. "I feel totally comfortable here," says one Barnard student. "It's a very safe environment to walk around in, even at night." Burglary is the most common complaint, with just 12 incidents reported in 2003. Considering the school's location in the heart of New York City, the low crime rate is a remarkable tribute to the school's diligent security system. There are guardposts every block, with guards keeping watch 24 hours a day. A Columbia University van shuttles students between the campuses at all hours of the night and pledges to arrive within 10 minutes of a call. In order to enter a campus dormitory, students and visitors must show identification to a patrolman—at any hour. There has been a raging debate in the last few years over whether Columbia College students should be allowed into Barnard dorms without having to be signed in, and vice versa, but for now, Columbia students—men and women—need permission before entering a Barnard dorm. Barnard has updated and doubled the number of emergency call boxes campus-wide, installing a new "blue light" system that is highly visible and incorporates new technology that will speed up the response time to any emergency.

Barnard is as pricey as any of the Seven Sisters, with 2004–5 tuition at $27,064.

Room and board were listed at $10,800. However, its financial aid is generous; admissions are need-blind, and the school guarantees to meet a student's full financial need. Some 38 percent of students get grants and the average loan debt of a freshly minted Barnard grad is $17,577.

BRYN MAWR COLLEGE

BRYN MAWR, PENNSYLVANIA • WWW.BRYNMAWR.EDU

The smart sister on the high hill

Among the women's colleges of the Northeast known as the "Seven Sisters," Bryn Mawr has long been known as the "smart sister." Bryn Mawr College was founded in 1885 by Dr. Joseph Taylor, a Quaker physician who wanted to establish a college dedicated to the education of lady Friends. At that time, an education in Greek, mathematics, philosophy, and the like was open only to men. Bryn Mawr was the first women's school to offer graduate programs, and remains the only one to offer a wide range of advanced degrees. The school teaches 1,334 undergraduates, among whom the most popular majors are political science, English, biology, math, and psychology. Located about 11 miles west of Philadelphia, the college sits in the village of Bryn Mawr—which, in case you're wondering, is Welsh for "high hill."

Academic Life: Friends of truth

In many ways, the school's approach is lofty. Bryn Mawr prescribes a full slate of rigorous courses for almost all its majors and boasts a distinguished faculty. The typical student is serious about her studies; many opt to spend weekends in the library. "The courseload is very rigorous," one student says. "It's hard to take more than four classes, and completely impossible to take more than five. Almost all the classes are very challenging. Still, the work is not impossible, and classes are not designed to weed out students."

In past years, Bryn Mawr had a higher proportion of its women go on to receive doctorates than any other college in the country. Of all women awarded PhDs in physics, more began their educations at Bryn Mawr than at any other liberal arts school. Here students in the sciences work closely with professors on research projects, gaining valuable experience and strengthening academic relationships with faculty members.

And science departments offer another advantage—an escape from the feminist ideology that saturates the humanities departments and most aspects of campus life at Bryn Mawr.

The school's mission is to give students "a rigorous education and to encourage the pursuit of knowledge as preparation for life and work." But while its individual courses are mostly strong, the college's curriculum is frail and sickly. Bryn Mawr's distribution requirements do not demand a true breadth of study. One faculty member says, "A colleague of mine recently suggested that we do away with all requirements, but I think he's wrong. Bryn Mawr expects its students to want to learn, and our requirements simply map the curricular terrain for them." Bryn Mawr has far fewer general education requirements than other liberal arts colleges, even in this age of curricular laissez-faire. With enough Advanced Placement coursework, students can even avoid three of these six required courses. As one student maintains, "the point of going to college is to study something a bit more specific." She didn't think it was necessary to continue study beyond high school in all the traditional liberal arts or to require all students to do so. At Bryn Mawr, she won't have to.

Bryn Mawr students can choose from a full list of traditional majors, and it is encouraging that trendy departments are offered as only minors or concentrations. These include peace and conflict, feminism and gender, and Africana studies. Students who feel constricted by the small college's offerings can even create an independent major with the direction of an advisor. Past independent majors have included American studies, linguistics, creative writing, and theater.

One of the main features of Bryn Mawr academic life—one that is lamentably absent at most schools—is the strength of the relationships that develop between faculty members and students, sometimes by working together on research projects. The Mellon Foundation recently awarded the college $1.5 million in support of such research in the humanities. In 2002–3, Bryn Mawr students teamed with faculty to complete more than 500 independent study projects.

Such relationships also grow naturally, thanks to the school's small size and low faculty-student ratio (eight to one). Class sizes range from around 30 for introductory courses to just three for senior-level topical seminars. Many students say that professors treat them as younger colleagues, gifted with the ability and the curiosity to learn. Students visit their professors regularly, often discussing subjects unrelated to class. Faculty members view teaching as their main responsibility—not publishing or research. They invite students to their homes and eat lunch with them on weekdays. One student who had trouble in her introductory calculus class said her professor did everything possible to help her learn the material, calling her at home, meeting with her during office hours, and arranging a peer tutor for further assistance. Two years later, they remain close. Another student says, "I have a few former professors who I actually consider to be friends, and it's not uncommon for a professor to invite a small class to his or her home for an end-of-semester dinner party." There are graduate students at Bryn Mawr; they teach no courses, but sometimes lead laboratory sections. Upon entry to Bryn Mawr, students are assigned a college dean as an advisor. After the student declares a major, she chooses a faculty advisor from her department.

Some of the many excellent professors at Bryn Mawr are Robert Dostal in philosophy; Julia Gaisser and Richard Hamilton in Greek, Latin, and classical studies; Peter Briggs in English; and political science professor Stephen Salkever, who one student says is "one of the most unbiased professors" she has ever had.

The history of art department is one of the strongest programs at Bryn Mawr, providing an emphasis on Western art from the early Christian through the modern era. Many majors in this department choose to study abroad in Florence, Paris, or other art centers of the Western world. International study is an especially popular choice among Bryn Mawr juniors, who can select programs in any number of countries. One in three students goes abroad for a semester.

English is a popular major at Bryn Mawr, but many of the courses in the department focus more on politics than on traditional scholarship. The same is true for the comparative literature department. In each department, some students end up reading more secondary than primary sources.

The relationship between Bryn Mawr and its Philadelphia Main Line neighbor, Haverford College, is essential to academic life at both schools. Bryn Mawr students are free to take courses at either college, and can even major in a discipline at Haverford not offered at Bryn Mawr. And if a desired course is not offered at either campus, a student can enroll at Swarthmore College or the University of Pennsylvania. A limited number of courses at Villanova University are also available to Bryn Mawr students. Bryn Mawr's proximity and close connection to these colleges allow students to seek greater depth in their studies and to encounter views that may not be discussed at their own college. For example, Bryn Mawr's philosophy department employs just three tenured professors. By taking philosophy courses at Haverford and the other area schools, a student can gain a broader base of knowledge in the discipline. And through these close ties to other elite colleges, Bryn Mawr students can take courses in the same discipline from several different professors instead of just one or two. The Bryn Mawr, Haverford, and Swarthmore libraries allow loans between colleges, and together this collection amounts to more than one million titles. Frequent shuttle vans run between campuses, and students who request a book typically receive it the next day.

At Bryn Mawr, no line is drawn between academic and political life. Political opinions permeate course offerings, content, and classroom discussion. The politics is, of

VITAL STATISTICS
Religious affiliation: none
Total enrollment: 1,781
Total undergraduates: 1,334
SAT/ACT medians: SAT V: 670, M: 630; ACT: 28
Applicants: 1,743
Applicants accepted: 50%
Accepted applicants who enrolled: 35%
Tuition: $27,900
Room and board: $9,700
Freshman retention rate: 92%
Graduation rate: 76% (4 yrs.), 83% (6 yrs.)
Average class size: 16
Student-faculty ratio: 9:1
Courses taught by graduate TAs: none
Most popular majors: political science, English, biology
Students living on campus: 98%
Guaranteed housing for four years? yes
Students in sororities: none

course, almost exclusively of the left. If a student would be put off or intimidated by such near-monolithic liberalism, she should look elsewhere. Many of the humanities course offerings are dedicated to the exploration of feminist issues or the politics of victimhood. Options range from the English department's "Here and Queer: Placing Sexuality" and "Writing Indians: Sidekicking the American Canon," to the classics course "Cleopatra: Images of Female Power." Faculty members and students alike generally assume that modern feminism is an unqualified good and that no one at Bryn Mawr ought to question such a view. And so one gets sociology courses like "Public Problems, Public Policy: Focus on Gender," which "focus[es] on how issues pertaining to gender are negotiated at the policy level. . . . Some of the particular policy areas we will examine include reproductive rights and reproductive health, welfare, childcare, and sexual harassment." Each department has its share of radicalized courses, mostly aligned along the axis of sexual politics.

Students report that in such courses and in others, professors often make no attempts to conceal their political opinions—and that they are not above proselytizing. Office doors have political cartoons and leftist bumper stickers, making visits awkward for students of minority views. "Professors do not hesitate to make fun of Republicans and Christians (in the abstract) during class, and some will even tease specific students," one says. Students and professors naturally assume their interlocutors are conventionally liberal, and thus are surprised to find any students who are not. But one student says, "I don't think there's a great deal of outright hatred of conservatives and libertarians, just a lack of familiarity with the idea that any educated person could think that way."

Bryn Mawr admissions policies put a high priority on having a racially diverse student body; about 25 percent of recent classes have come from minority groups, mostly Asian American. Once students are admitted, a panoply of ethnic-based programming awaits them. "Voices of Color," an orientation event held each April, is a "multicultural experience" during which admitted students learn that—surprise!—Bryn Mawr is a diverse and welcoming place for racial minorities. As if to make that point, students of African or Hispanic descent are given the chance to live . . . in separate residence halls.

In its mission statement, the Office of Institutional Diversity pledges to pursue "a policy of affirmative action in recruitment and employment." It oversees several campus organizations including the Association of International Students, the Asian Students Association, Bryn Mawr Caribbean and African Students Organization, Half and Half (a group for students of mixed race), Sisterhood (a black women's group), and others. These organizations help the college to forward the notion that "community doesn't mean uniformity." (Except, perhaps, when it comes to political ideas.) Eleven percent of Bryn Mawr's undergraduates are international students.

A program at Bryn Mawr that piques interest for those seeking "real world" career preparation is the community-based learning program called Praxis. Organized around the college's strong tradition of civic engagement, Praxis is intensive academic study integrated with rigorous, relevant fieldwork.

The college's Honor Code and self-governance system are crucial to the school's identity; the college Web site says Bryn Mawr was the first college in the United States to "give students responsibility not only for enforcing rules of behavior upon themselves, but also for deciding what those rules should be." Faculty and peers trust that Bryn Mawr students are committed to honesty, and as a result students can schedule their own final exams and may take tests home. The Honor Code is an extension of the prevailing enthusiasm for learning, which is mostly free of the competition one finds at other top-notch schools.

Student Life: The untold benefits of clean bathrooms

A trip to Bryn Mawr's magnificent campus will impress the most jaded visitor. Its 135-acre suburban campus was designed by landscape-architecture pioneers Frederick Law Olmsted and Calvert Vaux, the creators of New York City's Central Park. When it was built in 1885, Bryn Mawr introduced the "collegiate Gothic" architectural style to the United States. With its yellow-gray stone buildings, lush green lawns, and tree-lined terraces, Bryn Mawr is truly one of the country's most beautiful campuses. One particularly charming area is the Cloisters, a grassy outdoor square surrounded by stone buildings; professors often bring their classes there when the weather is warm enough. Thomas Great Hall, a large room with high ceilings and dark wood, is a popular place to study. The room is also home to a statue of the goddess Athena, to whom Bryn Mawr women offer cigarettes, beer, ornaments—and notes asking her for help on exams.

Ninety-eight percent of Bryn Mawr students live on campus, and the school offers many comfortable dorm rooms for its students. Each room has its own charm—some have fireplaces, window seats, and high ceilings—and every residence hall includes common space for studying, socializing, and holding dorm events. *The Princeton Review* judged Bryn Mawr's dormitories best in the United States. First-year students live together in their own halls, but upperclassmen are housed close by. The administration has taken great pains to make the campus a comfortable place to live and study. The Campus Center is a popular hangout between classes and in the evening, offering a late night cafe, post office, the Career Development Center, and offices for other student services.

ACADEMIC REQUIREMENTS

In the absence of a core curriculum, Bryn Mawr imposes certain requirements for the A.B. (bachelor's) degree, on top of those for each major:

- Two "college seminars," small, writing-intensive classes that introduce young women to academic life.
- One mathematics ("quantitative methods") course, or sufficient test scores or A.P. credit.
- Two intermediate or advanced courses in a foreign language—or a 690+ Achievement Test score in that tongue.
- Two courses in social science.
- Two courses in laboratory science and/or mathematics (one must include a lab).
- Two courses from the humanities (one may be in the performing or studio arts).

Of the 32 courses required, 24 must be taken at Bryn Mawr.

Bryn Mawr women enjoy athletics—participating in competition, not necessarily watching it. The college viewbook spotlights serious athletes who manage to balance a rigorous academic schedule with sports training. A charter member of the Centennial Conference and the only women's college in the conference, Bryn Mawr sponsors almost a dozen varsity intercollegiate sports: badminton, basketball, cross country, crew, field hockey, lacrosse, soccer, swimming, tennis, track and field, and volleyball. The college also sponsors varsity club rugby, and students at Bryn Mawr and Haverford have formed bi-college equestrian and ultimate Frisbee clubs that are supported by a combination of Self-Government Association fees and members' contributions.

One of the most vocal groups on campus is the Rainbow Alliance, a homosexual group whose membership has been declining steadily since the 1998–99 school year, when—as one student claims—almost half the student body belonged to it. The most popular political causes on campus concern feminism and the environment. The school's political activists often participate in Philadelphia's many protests and rallies. Recent years have seen the advent of some ideological diversity on campus, including the creation of a Campus Republicans group, the Pro-Life Club, and a publication called *Unpopular Opinions*, which prints them. But such views are not always welcomed. A leader of the publication says, "After I published *Unpopular Opinions*, I and the other editors had to endure personal insults printed in a letter to the editor of the campus newspaper, but we weren't treated differently by any of the people we encountered in our daily lives on campus." At the other end of the spectrum is *College News,* which in spring 2004 was replete with phrases like "Death to the Patriarchy," "Dykes to Watch Out For," and an explicit sex tips column called "Lady Oracle Finds Your Spot." She may be an oracle, but she's no lady.

One characteristic of all-women's colleges is that the private is often made public. At Bryn Mawr, this means that the crude and vulgar must be endured by all. Many of the events on campus deal with body image and ways in which women can purportedly become more comfortable with their own. For instance, a decades-old tradition of dancing around the May pole in white dresses now has its intentionally non-phallic feminist counterpart: the May Hole Dance.

Speaking of heathen rites, in addition to the ordinary line of religious organizations—Catholic, Protestant, Jewish, Muslim, and Quaker—Bryn Mawr features Athena's Circle, "a student Pagan group" for "Wiccans, Greco-Roman and Egyptian reconstructionists, Goddess-worshippers, Buddhists, and other magical people" who "worship during full moons, dark moons, solstices, equinoxes, and the other Wiccan Sabbats."

Bryn Mawr's close-knit community cherishes a number of more innocuous traditions. One is Parade Night, when freshmen officially walk under the arches of Bryn Mawr College while sophomores pummel them with water balloons, juniors welcome them, and seniors sit back with an air of cool nonchalance. On Lantern Night, students receive lanterns to welcome them to their new academic class. Tradition is that the first one to have her lantern go out will be the first to be married; the last student holding a lit lantern will be the first to receive her PhD. Walking on the Senior Steps before a student is a senior will jinx her from graduating. Bryn Mawr, with its own inside jokes and decades-old traditions, is a college that recognizes its differences from other schools and wears them with flair.

Bryn Mawr is an all-women's school, but with men on campus for classes, frequent buses to and from Haverford and Swarthmore, and countless opportunities to interact with men (Bryn Mawr students can even live in coed dormitories at Haverford) many students don't even notice the difference. One student says that while she sees men all the time in classes at Haverford, and she and many of her friends have boyfriends at area colleges, Bryn Mawr is an escape from testosterone. "Attending an all-women's college lets you concentrate on your work without having to worry about men," she says. "There's no intimidation." Another student says, "Most of the time I don't actually notice that I'm at a women's college. I don't see any huge benefits to myself from attending a women's college, except perhaps that the bathrooms stay cleaner."

On weekends, Bryn Mawr students often take the Main Line train into Philadelphia to visit museums, night clubs, frat parties at the University of Pennsylvania, sporting events, and performances. Many students participate in volunteer work in the city. But plenty of entertainment options are available at home in Bryn Mawr and at Haverford. Students often stay on campus for speakers or other events, parties at Haverford, or casual socializing in the dorms. A weekend spent in the library is quite common, and sometimes even expected. As one student puts it, "Bryn Mawr students don't study all the time to the exclusion of everything else, certainly, but this is a college for people who are serious about academics."

The college and the affluent suburb that is its home have almost no crime problems. During 2003, there were two burglaries and one forcible sex offense on campus. Nevertheless, the campus is patrolled 24 hours a day. Crime may have dropped, but drinking abuse rose from two arrests for liquor violations in 2002 to eight in 2003. Also, while no disciplinary actions were filed on campus for drugs in 2002, there were four issued in 2003.

Bryn Mawr is as expensive as one might expect: Tuition and fees in 2004–5 were $27,900, and room and board was $9,700. Some 58 percent of the Bryn Mawr student body receives aid from the college. Admissions used to be need-blind, but the school recently changed that policy. The average financial aid package was $25,024 in 2002–3, and almost 75 percent of that package was gift aid.

SUGGESTED CORE
1. Classical Studies 270, Classical Heroes and Heroines
2. Philosophy 101, A Historical Introduction to Philosophy
3. Religion 122, Introduction to the New Testament (*at Haverford*) *and* Religion 118, Hebrew Bible: Literary Text and Historical Context
4. Religion 206, History and Literature of Early Christianity (*at Haverford*)
5. Political Science 231, Introduction to Political Philosophy: Modern
6. English 225/226: Shakespeare
7. History 201, American History, 1600 to the Present
8. History 318 and 319, Topics in Modern European History (*varies from year to year*)

BUCKNELL UNIVERSITY

LEWISBURG, PENNSYLVANIA • WWW.BUCKNELL.EDU

Safety school?

Bucknell University was founded by Baptists in 1846 as the University at Lewisburg. It later shed its Baptist roots and was renamed for William Bucknell, a Philadelphia benefactor who helped get the university off the ground. By the turn of the century, the liberal arts college had begun to include courses in engineering and business. The goal of the university today is "to provide a broad curriculum which includes the humanities, social sciences, natural sciences, and professional studies in engineering, education and management." Bucknell bills itself as both a professional university and a liberal arts college, claiming to offer the best of both institutional models.

The university's recently appointed president, Brian C. Mitchell, former president of Washington and Jefferson College, is charged with bridging this "liberal" and "professional" education divide. He inherits a university with excellent credentials: strong academic programs, faculty members who enjoy teaching, and plenty of opportunities to get involved in research or study abroad. At Washington and Jefferson, located in Washington, Pennsylvania, Mitchell managed to turn a combative relationship between town and gown into "a model for collaboration," according to the *Chronicle of Higher Education*. Bucknell hopes he will have similar luck working with the town of Lewisburg—which has witnessed friction between students and residents—and that this will help attract more top students. Mitchell plans to initiate a capital campaign in his first year.

However, it remains to be seen if the school under a Mitchell administration will continue to seem stuck—at least in the minds of its applicants—just below the top tier of private schools. In the past few decades, Bucknell has had a reputation as a safety school for those applying to Ivy League colleges. As at those schools, students can earn a solid liberal arts education at Bucknell but they'll have to be intent on attaining one, since the university's curriculum does not guarantee it.

Academic Life: Small classes and a monkey house

Bucknell University's two colleges, Arts and Sciences and Engineering, enroll 3,484 undergraduates. About 80 percent of undergraduates study in the college of Arts and Sciences, which offers more than 50 majors and 60 minors. The College of Engineering is much smaller, enrolling about 650 students, and offers a more research-based curriculum in computer science and the engineering fields.

Like many universities these days, Bucknell seems to think that to be a university is somehow more serious than to be a college. In truth, there is not much university to

Bucknell. And the university's utilitarian approach to education obscures the true focus of a traditional liberal arts education.

Bucknell's graduate program is still very small (around 200 students), and it does not even award doctorates. However, Bucknell compensates in the number of students it sends to graduate school. In the last decade, Bucknell ranked twelfth in the country in the number of graduates who went on to receive doctoral degrees. The College of Engineering sent more students to PhD programs (not just in engineering) than did any other college surveyed. Moreover it is ranked as the eighth-best undergraduate engineering program among non-PhD-granting schools.

Bucknell has no core curriculum, requiring instead that students in the Arts and Sciences college complete the Common Learning Agenda (CLA). The CLA hopes that students will become "critical and complex thinkers, lifelong learners, and free and original decision makers who have learned compassion, civility, and a concern for social justice as part of their educational maturation." It isn't a particularly well-founded hope. A student must complete only six CLA requirements and is free to experiment with specialty and trendy courses instead of courses embracing a common core of knowledge and skills.

Because of its amorphous nature, Bucknell's curriculum allows loopholes, and unfortunately it's up to the student to find and avoid them, since the university's advising program is only what students make of it. Faculty members are there to help, and the university has instituted a policy requiring the signature of a student's faculty advisor before the student can register for classes—a move which may be to the student's advantage so long as the advisor's advice is not political. The student-to-faculty ratio is a reasonable 12 to 1, and only half the classes have enrollments of more than 20. Professors are generally lauded for their accessibility outside of class. Though Bucknell is larger than most traditional liberal arts colleges, it works hard to retain close interpersonal contact between students and professors. Professors teach all courses—not graduate students.

For first-year students, Bucknell's six residential colleges help "immerse new students in theme-centered courses and activities." Students enrolled in the theme houses live together, attend a course together, and participate in a common hour discussion each week. Some houses go on field trips together to further explore their theme, typically a topic in the arts, the environment, global issues, the humanities, social justice, and society and technology. Around a third of first-year students enroll in this living-learning program each year, which encourages intellectual discussion outside the class-

VITAL STATISTICS
Religious affiliation: none
Total enrollment: 3,678
Total undergraduates: 3,484
SAT/ACT midranges: SAT: 1230–1370; ACT: 27–31
Applicants: 7,706
Applicants accepted: 47%
Accepted applicants who enrolled: 49%
Tuition: $30,534
Room and board: $6,579
Freshman retention rate: 94%
Graduation rate: 84% (4 yrs.), 89% (6 yrs.)
Courses with fewer than 20 students: 50%
Student-faculty ratio: 12:1
Courses taught by graduate TAs: none
Most popular majors: social sciences, business, engineering
Students living on campus: 89%
Guaranteed housing for four years? yes
Students in fraternities: 38% sororities: 38%

Bucknell maintains no core curriculum but does impose certain requirements. The mandates for liberal arts (as opposed to engineering) students are divided as follows.

First, students must complete six courses in the "Common Learning Agenda." These include:

- A "foundation seminar," capped at about 15 students, on any of a wide variety of topics. Students can choose among such topics as "Ideologues, Tyrants, and Thieves: Modern Authoritarian Politics," and "Our Technological World: Utopia or Dystopia?"
- Four courses in the humanities, with no two from the same department. Choices here range from traditional offerings (such as courses on Shakespeare and Milton) to "Popular Culture and Prints" and "The Japanese Warrior in Literature" to "Jazz, Rock, and the Avant-garde" and "Scene Design."
- Two courses in "Broadened Perspectives for the Twenty-First Century." One must address "human diversity, either within or across national

room—but also contributes to politicization of the campus. The Social Justice and Global Colleges are the most partisan at the university. For instance, the Social Justice College examines, in the contexts of minority rights, capital punishment, and public education, "the degree to which our society is providing 'justice for all.'" The instructor who teaches the course is heavily involved in leftist politics. Global College students will encounter a vision of global progress that focuses on "the role of racial, ethnic, gender, lower class and weak state 'others' in the world system and their efforts to liberate themselves from diverse forms of oppression."

On a brighter note, Bucknell has plenty of monkeys. That's right, one of Bucknell's unique features is the psychology department's primate laboratory; created in the 1960s and dubbed the "Monkey House" by students, it houses colonies of *Hamadryas* baboons, macaques, squirrel monkeys, and capuchin monkeys. Undergraduate and graduate students observe the animals for research and some courses include regular field trips to the center.

The university's best departments are computer science, economics, physics, English, chemistry, and engineering. Of Bucknell's 310 full-time and part-time faculty members, students say the best teachers include Alexander (Tristan) Riley in sociology; Thomas T. Shawe, Robert A. Stockland Jr. and Eric Tillman in chemistry; Richard Ellis and Kenneth Field in biology; John Enyeart and John D. Kirkland in history; Scott Meinke and Susan Tabrizi in political science; Richard Fleming and Peter Groff in philosophy; Mary Beth Gray in geology; Christopher S. Magee and Nancy E. White in economics; and Michael P. Coyne and William R. Gruver in management. As for weak areas, one faculty member says, "Most of the departments in the humanities and social sciences are a mixed bag of solid courses and professors, fad courses, and some ideologically driven professors."

Student Life: It's Greek to them

Rated fifteenth in *The 100 Best Small Towns in America*, Lewisburg, Pennsylvania, offers students a pleasing balance between peaceful beauty and university culture. This Susquehanna Valley town, located 50 miles north of Harrisburg, Pennsylvania, is home to 10,000 residents, a federal maximum-security penitentiary, and about 3,500 Bucknell students. The town's main drag, Market Street, is a quaint tree-lined avenue replete with more than 40 boutiques, restaurants, and bars. But for Bucknell's largely urbane student body, the town is smaller than it appears. Nearly 40 percent of the student body studies abroad; perhaps some do so as an escape from small-town life. Town-gown relations are strained. Lewisburg residents call Bucknell students spoiled brats for overwhelming bars and siphoning off cheap housing, while Bucknell students, many of whom graduated from elite Northeastern private schools, complain about the town's provincialism.

Bucknell University is located on a hill overlooking the Susquehanna River. There are more than 100 buildings on the 450-acre campus. A significant new addition is the Breakiron Engineering building, which was built for $8 million to provide extra classroom, lab, and office space for the College of Engineering. Approximately 89 percent of the 3,500-member student body lives in the school's residence halls, apartments, special-interest, theme, and fraternity houses. Though men can live in fraternity houses, sorority members are housed in Hunt Hall, an all-women dormitory. Most other residence halls are coed by room, meaning that men often live right next door to women. There are no coed rooms or bathrooms, except in apartments and special-interest houses. Recent theme houses have included the African American, scholars program, substance-free, and international studies houses. Bucknell guarantees housing for all four years for undergraduates who desire to live on campus.

Student life at Bucknell is dominated by the Greek system. Phi Kappa Psi founded the first fraternity at Bucknell in 1855, followed by the first national sorority in 1895. About 40 percent of Bucknell undergraduates are members of one of the university's 11 fraternities or seven sororities. (Bucknell was ranked as having the thirteenth-largest Greek scene in America by *The Princeton Review* in 2003.) The university recently adopted the Plan for Prominence, which defines responsibilities, expectations, and guidelines for Greek student life. Consequently, the university began instituting higher standards for Greek admission, including higher GPAs, more educational programming, required community service hours, and an external review process.

REQUIREMENTS (CONT'D)

borders." Choices include "Sexuality and Culture," "Witchcraft and Politics," and "Religion, Magic and Healing"—as well as foreign language courses, various history classes, or a semester spent studying abroad. The other requirement here, "Perspectives on the Natural and Fabricated Worlds," offers options ranging from "Global Environmental Change" and "Human Impact on the Environment" to "Archeology of Greece" and "Behavior and Ecology of Birds and Mammals."

- Two social sciences courses. Choices range from "Economic Principles and Problems" to "Gender, Race, Ethnicity, and National Identity."
- Two laboratory sciences and one other course in natural sciences, mathematics, or computer science.
- One writing course, and two writing-intensive classes in any department.
- A capstone experience—a final, typically interdisciplinary seminar in which students are meant to integrate what they have learned from various courses and their majors.

Social venues on campus without alcohol are the nightclub Uptown and the Seventh Street Cafe, a popular place to relax. The cafe is open every day and schedules music on the weekends. Bucknell hosts a number of activities each year. In 2003, the Ataris, Jason Mraz, and Mitch Albom, author of *Tuesdays with Morrie,* were featured guests. The "Chrysalis Ball," an annual campus event, has in the past featured George Clinton and Parliament Funkadelic.

Students have at least 150 student-run clubs to choose from—65 of which are academically oriented. Arts groups include slam poetry, comedy improv, singing and theater. CALVIN & HOBBES provides the campus with substance-free activities. K.R.A.I.D., a high-tech videogame club, invites students to skip parties, play videogames, and socialize late at night on the weekends. The campus also offers ROTC, appropriately named the "Bison Battalion."

A full-time Protestant chaplain, Catholic priest, and Jewish rabbi provide weekly religious services and masses on campus. In addition to these worship services, students also can participate in weekly Episcopal and Orthodox services, weekly Buddhist meditation, and daily Muslim prayers.

Because of increasing student activism, the school's traditional apathy—which once earned the campus the nickname of "Bucknell Bubble"—seems to have burst. Political groups on campus include the left-leaning Bucknell Caucus for Economic Justice, which includes several professors from the economics department and concentrates on issues like the living wage. It collectively publishes the *Catalyst* with P.U.L.S.E (Partnership for Unveiling Labor and Sweatshop Exploitation). Another group, the V-Day club, is headed by the director of the Women's Studies Program (which provides buses to take students to pro-choice rallies). V-Day brings *The Vagina Monologues* to Bucknell each year on St. Valentine's Day.

The Bucknell University Conservatives Club, which constantly calls for free speech and more intellectual and political diversity, tirelessly advances the cause of conservatism at Bucknell. "It seems like a lot of the liberal student groups activities solely consist of complaining about the conservatives club," says one student. The BUCC and its leader, Charles Mitchell, were featured in the cover story, "Armies of the Right: The Young Hipublicans" in a 2003 edition of the *New York Times Magazine*. The article focused on a perceived shift to the right on campuses nationwide. "In less than two years, the [BUCC] established itself as one of the most visible and influential student groups on campus," the article stated. The club presents its ideas to students through its popular monthly magazine, the *Counterweight*. The magazine's most recent articles provide biting commentary on issues such as the school's speech code and alcohol policy. A recent free speech controversy surrounded an orientation performance by a student improv group that poked fun at one of the orientation's leaders, a motivational speaker–type who is also a lesbian. Deans accused the group of "ruining diversity on campus" and threatened to take away the group's university recognition status, according to an article in the *Counterweight*.

The *Bucknell Guide about Bias-Related Harassment and Violence* states, "Bias-related behavior includes any action that discriminates against, ridicules, humiliates, or otherwise creates a hostile environment for another individual or group because of race, religion, ethnic identity, sexual orientation, gender, language, or beliefs." Students say that the speech code is selectively enforced against certain people. If applied universally, it would prohibit virtually all political discussion on campus. The recent short documentary film *Brainwashing 101* brought national attention to the school's onerous speech code.

Programming organized by the administration has exhibited a decidedly partisan, left-wing tilt. According to a *Counterweight* article, in fall 2004 administrators at Bucknell refused the BUCC's request to invite Republican congressman and Senate candidate Pat Toomey to give a speech, arguing that his visit would violate a school policy against campaigning on campus. Meanwhile, Bucknell did not enforce its own rule when it paid presidential candidate Ralph Nader to give the school's commencement address. (In the spring, Rep. Toomey was allowed to speak on campus in commemoration of National Right to Life month). Past speakers hosted by the administration include Howard Zinn, Janet Reno, and Bobby Seale. BUCC's activism, however, has resulted in a wider spectrum of speakers visiting the campus, including John Stossel, Ben Stein, Reginald Jones, Dinesh D'Souza, and David Horowitz.

SUGGESTED CORE
1. Classics 221, Tales of Heroes: The Epic
2. Philosophy 205, Greek Philosophy
3. Religion 105, Introduction to the Bible
4. Religion 212, Christianity (*closest match*)
5. Political Science 251, History of Western Political Thought II: Machiavelli to Bentham
6. English 257, Shakespeare
7. History 117, Survey of American History to 1860
8. History 268, European Intellectual History II

At Bucknell, where baseball legend Christy Mathewson is among the school's alums, athletics is a priority. In addition to 16 clubs and 14 intramural sports (including corecreational), Bucknell supports 12 teams for men and 13 teams for women in its Division I athletic program. The Bucknell Bison compete in the Patriot League. Bucknell has the highest graduation rate (100 percent) among student-athletes nationwide, according to a recent NCAA study. Christy Mathewson Memorial Stadium is home to the football and lacrosse teams and has an all-weather track. The 2003 Kenneth Langone Athletics and Recreation Center boasts a fitness center, 3,600-seat basketball arena, strength training center, tennis and racquetball courts, and an Olympic-size swimming pool.

The bacchanalian parties hosted by fraternities and sororities have attracted persistent attention from the liability-conscious administration over the past few years. Campus crime statistics in 2003 revealed that there were more than 280 liquor-law violations reported by the Department of Public Safety—one-quarter occurring off-campus. That year, in an effort to stem the tide of reckless drinking (alcohol poisoning, acts of violence, and DUI) by students at the school and downtown, an emergency alcohol policy was implemented. The policy, based on a disciplinary point system, banned hard liquor. "It was widely despised for its lack of student input," complains one student. Student protests included a BUCC-hosted "rootbeer kegger" outside the student union. The policy was modified early in 2004 and now distinguishes between violations involving beer and wine and those for hard liquor. It provides the severest sanctions—including a semester leave—for those who become extremely intoxicated, are stopped for DUI, or become violent. The university also initiated a mandatory alcohol education program for incoming freshmen—"Alcohol 101"—taught by professors and staff.

The university's Department of Public Safety operates an escort service, patrols the campus on bicycles, maintains call boxes all over campus, and hosts regular crime prevention workshops for students. Overall, the school is extremely safe: in 2003, Bucknell reported four sexual assaults, one aggravated assault, one burglary, and one arson on campus.

Bucknell tuition for 2004–5 was $30,534, with an average cost of $6,579 for room and board. Sixty-five percent of the students going to Bucknell receive some form of need-based financial aid.

CARNEGIE MELLON UNIVERSITY

PITTSBURGH, PENNSYLVANIA • WWW.CARNEGIEMELLON.EDU

Nerves of steel

Carnegie Mellon University, located in the Oakland neighborhood of Pittsburgh and five miles from downtown, comes from a tradition of pragmatic thinking, learning, and research. The school has changed names a few times, and the succession of monikers reflects the path it has taken since 1900, when industrialist and philanthropist Andrew Carnegie first announced to the city of Pittsburgh his intention to build a "first-class technical school" for the sons of local steel mill workers. Founded as the Carnegie Technical Schools, it was called the Carnegie Institute of Technology from 1912 until 1967, when it merged with the Mellon Institute and became the institution now known as Carnegie Mellon University.

Along the way, Carnegie Mellon has at times struggled to find its academic niche. Providing a liberal education has never been Carnegie Mellon's primary purpose, but it excels at its specialties. Its technical school roots and its steel-town setting may have formerly hindered its efforts to earn a reputation as a leader in high-tech education and research. But although Carnegie Mellon is not the most prestigious science-oriented university (a list topped by Caltech and MIT), CMU has certainly become a highly regarded institution of that type. In 2003, *U.S. News and World Report* rated the school number two nationwide in management information systems, production/operations management, and quantitative analysis/methods. Andrew Carnegie would have been proud.

The school has had a major presence in the digital revolution and is widely recognized as a leader in computer science, robotics, and engineering. In 2004, *Newsweek* dubbed the school the "Most Tech-Savvy" in the United States. Carnegie Mellon's students enjoy some of the most advanced applications of computing in education, including "Andrew," the campus computing network, and the most comprehensive wireless network for an institution worldwide. The school has even installed a system called "E-Suds," designed to notify students via e-mail when there are open washing machines and when their laundry is done. The school's pragmatism pays off for career-oriented students; the university reports that 82 percent of students accept a job offer upon graduation.

Academic Life: How do you get to Carnegie Hall?

Carnegie Mellon comprises four undergraduate colleges and three graduate schools. The engineering school in the Carnegie Institute of Technology (CIT), the College of Fine Arts (CFA), the College of Humanities and Social Sciences (H&SS), and the Mellon College of Science (MCS) enroll undergraduates, while the David A. Tepper School of Business, the School of Computer Science, and the H. John Heinz III School of Public Policy and Management are for graduate students. Undergraduates are almost evenly distributed among the four undergraduate colleges.

Engineering students in the Carnegie Institute of Technology boast that they learn not just by reading engineering textbooks but also by doing the "fun stuff"— wiring robots, designing Ferris wheels, and building steam engines. True to the pragmatism of its founder, Carnegie Mellon goes further than other engineering schools by introducing students to such "industrial experiences" so they may learn about customer needs, competitive markets, and manufacturing. One professor said that what makes a Carnegie Mellon education distinctive is "a mixture of creativity, practical problem solving, and innovation."

In the Mellon College of Science, students take what one might call a science core in the fundamentals, including two semesters each of calculus and physics and one semester each of biology, chemistry, and computer science. Students in both CIT and MCS declare their majors at the end of their freshmen year, after finishing these courses.

VITAL STATISTICS
Religious affiliation: none
Total enrollment: 9,803
Total undergraduates: 5,389
SAT/ACT midranges: SAT V: 610–710, M: 680–770; ACT: 27–32
Applicants: 14,113
Applicants accepted: 42%
Accepted applicants who enrolled: 24%
Tuition: $30,650
Room and board: $8,554
Freshman retention rate: 95%
Graduation rate: 65% (4 yrs.), 85% (6 yrs.)
Average class size: 25
Student-faculty ratio: 10:1
Courses taught by graduate TAs: 1%
Most popular majors: engineering, computer science, mathematics
Students living on campus: 62%
Guaranteed housing for four years? yes
Students in fraternities: 10% sororities: 6%

Beginning in 2004, students in the College of Humanities and Social Science were presented with a more rigorous set of distribution requirements than had existed before:

- Three common courses: "World Cultures," "Writing and Expression," and "Statistical Reasoning."
- One course in writing: "Interpretation and Argument."
- "Computing Skills Workshop," completed in the first semester of freshman year.
- 18 credits in "Communicating: Language and Interpretations," including the required course "Interpretation and Argument." Other courses here include "Talking Across Differences," "Communicating in the Global Marketplace," and foreign language classes.
- 18 credits in "Reflecting: Societies and Cultures," including the required "Introduction to World History." This category is the broadest, including everything from "Renaissance Literary and Cultural Studies" and "God in the West" to "Gender Studies."
- 27 credits in "Modeling: Mathematics and Experiments," including nine from mathematics and

Mellon's common undergraduate writing course, "Interpretation and Argument," is supposed to "give students a comprehensive grounding in communication processes" by "reading and understanding the important issues and arguments regarding those issues advanced by a variety of texts, both fiction and nonfiction." Unfortunately, the university does not have a common reading list for all sections of this course, and the content consequently varies by section—meaning that some classes can end up focusing on the teacher's narrow political interests. Choose wisely.

The College of Fine Arts is organized into five schools: architecture, art, design, drama, and music. These schools offer multidisciplinary programs among the arts while integrating engineering and technical features into the design and architecture programs. Besides the courses required by their particular schools, students in fine arts must take a few courses outside of the college. Students pursuing a major in the School of Art, for instance, take one course in each of the following three areas: culture (humanities or languages), technical subjects (math, science, or engineering), and the social sciences (history, psychology, or economics), plus three more courses in one of these areas. Many options are available to complete the requirements, so there is no guarantee that fine arts students graduate with anything remotely resembling a liberal education.

Carnegie Mellon is nationally recognized as a premier institution for the study of chemical and electrical engineering, but its drama and music departments also have outstanding reputations. Nevertheless, while CMU promotes an unusual blend of science and performing arts, the humanistic disciplines seem to get lost somewhere in the shuffle. Within H&SS are a limited number of departments: economics, English, history, modern languages, philosophy, psychology, social and decision sciences, and statistics. "The majority of the departments on campus are excellent," one student says. "In fact, the only programs that are a bit weak are the English and history programs due to CMU being such a technical and artistic school." Another architecture student admires the students in his department: "We work hard here, and students are like professionals in that they compete rigorously." In keeping with its focus on the applied, analytic dimension of education, the college offers two tracks of majors in most areas: a more traditional "disciplinary" major (economics, philosophy, or political science, for instance) and a more specialized "professional" major (usually a compound name, like managerial economics, computational linguistics, or policy and management).

Incoming H&SS freshmen are assigned to one of just four academic advisors at the Academic Advisory Center, which functions as a student's home department until he declares a major. Once a student declares a major, he is assigned a faculty advisor from his department. Students are encouraged to make appointments to see their advisors, although walk-in appointments are usually available. However, since many students do not declare majors until the middle of the sophomore year, having four advisors for the entire college is wholly inadequate. Students complain of receiving little in the way of individual academic advising before they have settled into a department.

As its impersonal advising and the varying requirements of its colleges suggest, Carnegie Mellon is not the best option for students seeking to use their college years as a period of soul searching. It is a much better choice for students who know with a high level of certainty what they want to study, especially if they seek a career in science or the arts. Carnegie Mellon does not allow students to experiment or dabble much in different disciplines before choosing majors; transfers between colleges can be difficult, and changing majors may delay graduation.

What it lacks in advising quality CMU attempts to make up for in strong faculty-student relationships. Professors at CMU teach nearly all classes—the school reports that just 1 percent of courses are taught by graduate students—and students express satisfaction with the quality of teaching they receive. One student says, "I've never had a lecture taught by a TA, but during my freshman and sophomore years, once or twice a week the TAs would hold 'recitation' classes reviewing the lectures and going over practice problems." Another student says that "professors assign thoughtful projects that integrate and synthesize old and new knowledge." For the university as a whole, the student-faculty ratio is about 10 to 1; in the engineering school, it's 12 to 1. As at any university where faculty members are pressured with research responsibilities on top of their teaching duties, there are the occasional complaints that

---

REQUIREMENTS (CONT'D)

nine from natural science.

- 18 credits in "Deciding: Social Sciences and Values," including the required "Statistical Reasoning," an admirable requirement for today's innumerate student. Other courses here include "Principles of Economics," "Religion in American Society," and "Abnormal Psychology."

- 18 credits in "Creating: Designs and Productions." Here we find courses such as "Introduction to Architectural Drawing," "Letterpress and Bookbinding," various dance, playwriting, and theater classes, and the university's Shakespeare courses—which can be skipped entirely in favor of "Introduction to Lighting Design" or "Theatre Management."

- Freshman Seminar. These small classes range from the sublime ("Mysticism") to the meticulous ("An Economist's Perspective on Public Policy"). Many of the choices center on ethnic or sexual politics.

In addition to these requirements and those of his major, a liberal arts student must take 18 additional credits from any of the above categories.

certain faculty members are inaccessible. But most students indicate that professors are, on the whole, genuinely interested in getting to know their students.

Students of all disciplines participate in the university's strong study-abroad program. Carnegie Mellon sponsors six university-wide exchange programs (in Chile, Mexico, Switzerland, Singapore, Japan, and at a branch campus, opened in 2004, in Qatar), and individual departments have exchanges overseas. The university has a host of international job, internship, and volunteer opportunities for interested students.

Among the best professors at CMU are Daniel P. Resnick and Kiron Skinner in history; Bob Dalton and Bob Dammon in economics; Bruce Armitage and Garry Warnock in chemistry; and noted art critic David S. Carrier and Alex John London in philosophy. Finn E. Kydland, professor of economics in CMU's Tepper School of Business, was awarded the Nobel Prize in Economics in 2004.

Student Life: Finding time

To a large extent, the character of student life at Carnegie Mellon derives from the school's demanding curriculum and particular set of strengths. Which is to say, the vast majority of students are very serious about their work, put in long hours outside of class, and learn to operate on little sleep. Add to this the fact that the typical CMU student is a career-focused, practical type, and one starts to understand why there is comparatively little interest in social and political issues on campus.

The school has a reputation for having a student body of "nerds" and "geeks," which is not entirely fair, but it does indicate that there exists a certain interest in ideas among students—sometimes to the detriment of social life. Socializing certainly doesn't occur while following the school's athletics teams. The student body is rather indifferent to intercollegiate athletics, and some students complain that there is virtually no school spirit at CMU. The Tartans (a nickname that honors the school's Scottish founder) field 17 varsity athletic teams in the NCAA Division III. The relatively new athletic and physical education complex is a big hit among students and faculty.

First-year students are required to live on campus and have a meal plan unless granted an exception through the Dean of Student Affairs. Almost all freshmen—99 percent—live on campus in college-affiliated housing, typically in standard double or triple rooms. Most dormitories are coed, but the university also offers some single-sex dorms as well as plenty of smoke-free buildings and floors. There is also New House, a "green" dormitory designed to conserve energy. There are no coed bathrooms or dorm rooms in the residence halls.

While campus housing and meal plans are optional for upperclassmen, the majority of students return to campus housing their sophomore year. Most students and professors carp about the abominable quality of food on campus. To remedy this, many health-conscience or food connoisseurs should plan to spend Saturday mornings in the Strip District downtown, where one can purchase gourmet foods, fresh breads, and farmers' market items at very good prices. Some 38 percent of undergraduates live off campus. Public transportation consists of the city's inadequate downtown subway and poor bus system, which has recently suffered unfortunate cutbacks in routes and availability, making the campus shuttle or a car the preferred mode of transport for most students.

Students continue to complain about the school's imbalance of men to women, particularly in the engineering and science schools. The university as a whole hovers at about 60 percent male, while the engineering school is almost 75 percent male. An admissions counselor tells us that the university looks more kindly on women in engineering during the admissions process, since Carnegie Mellon would prefer to even the balance of the sexes. Although students hail from all 50 states, around one-fourth are local kids from the state of Pennsylvania. Minority and international students make up about 40 percent of the student population, with Asian/Pacific Island students the largest minority group at 23 percent.

The most important annual tradition at CMU is the Spring Carnival, for which students usually turn their genius to creating elaborate house-front themes at the many fraternities across the street from the university. Both alumni and current students gather for this three-day festival, which features game booths put together by student organizations, musicians, rides, and the very popular buggy races, and which draws many students from the area, including Chatham College, a nearby all-female school.

During the rest of the year students frequent fraternity and sorority parties. A healthy Greek system exists at CMU; approximately 8 percent of students enter fraternities or sororities. They can also join a vast number of student organizations—including political groups from all across the spectrum. While controversial author/filmmaker Michael Moore did appear on campus in 2004, funded by student fees, most CMU people we consulted agreed that theirs is a largely apolitical campus.

As one would expect, given the number of minority students enrolled at CMU, many of the student organizations center on ethnicity, including the Asian Student Association, Hong Kong Student Association, Persian Student Association, Society of Hispanic Professional Engineers, Japanese Cultural Club, South Asian Student Association, and Taiwanese Activism Organization. The school also has many religiously oriented clubs, including organizations for Baptist, Methodist, Mormon, Episcopal, Jewish, Lutheran, Orthodox, and Catholic students. One student says, "I think it's a good idea to get involved with at least one organization because it's a good way to help people, meet new people, take a break from academic life, and in some cases learn more about the field you are interested in."

SUGGESTED CORE
1. No suitable course
2. Philosophy 250, Ancient Philosophy
3. Philosophy 151, God in the West (*closest match*)
4. History 220, Early Christianity
5. Philosophy 135, Introduction to Political Philosophy *or* Political Science 235, Political Philosophy (*closest matches*)
6. English 245A, Shakespeare: Histories and Early Comedies *or* English 245B, Shakespeare and the Genres: Comedies and Romance
7. History 238, From Independence to Civil War: U.S. History, 1776–1865
8. Philosophy 253, Continental Philosophy (*closest match*)

Pittsburgh offers students a wealth of activities at very reasonable prices, if students can find the time. The city has plenty of good museums, including the unique single-artist collection on the North Shore featuring the city's own Andy Warhol. Carnegie Museum's famous dinosaurs are a few minutes' walk down the street from CMU. Other cultural venues, such as the stellar Pittsburgh Symphony Orchestra and Pittsburgh Ballet and Opera, are a 10-minute drive downtown. For numerous outdoor activities, there is sprawling Shenley Park, just a stone's throw from the university. Frick Park is also nearby. An hour outside of the city, one can take off for whitewater rafting in the Laurel Highland Mountains and also visit two Frank Lloyd Wright homes, Fallingwater and Kentuck Knob. In addition to CMU's new art center, students with a visual art slant can also escape to the top floor of Hunt Library, where the Hunt Botanical Center surprises most visitors with wonderful exhibitions of botanical art and illustration. The center also has a fine botanical research library.

Sports fans will note that Pittsburgh hosts three major franchises: the Penguins, Pirates, and Steelers. The city is often listed by Rand McNally among the nation's "most livable." Housing is generally quite affordable and many students opt to live off campus and do their shopping in the trendy Shady Side area or in residential Squirrel Hill.

Despite the major building projects of recent years, most students agree that Carnegie Mellon is not an attractive campus; but at least it is a relatively safe one. Crime statistics (one forcible sex offense, two aggravated assaults, three arsons and 18 burglaries in 2003, the last year for which statistics were available) illustrate that serious crime is rather rare, and few students express any major qualms about safety on campus. The majority of on-campus arrests were for liquor-law violations.

The cost of tuition, room, and board at Carnegie-Mellon tops $39,000. However, the school practices need-blind admissions and doles out aid to some 52 percent of students. Recent graduates have an average loan burden of $22,902.

CATHOLIC UNIVERSITY OF AMERICA

WASHINGTON, D.C. • WWW.CUA.EDU

The real thing

Founded by the bishops of the United States and chartered by Pope Leo XIII in 1887, the Catholic University of America is this country's only pontifically sponsored institute of higher education. To this day, the archbishop of Washington, D.C., Theodore Cardinal McCarrick, serves *ex officio* as the university's chancellor. Catholic parishes across the country take up collections for the school each year. Many Catholics consider CUA to be *the* place for devout parents to send their children when they want them to acquire an authentic liberal education within the Catholic tradition. It is located in the northeast quadrant of the nation's capital.

Academic Life: The canon is law

"Our greatest strength is our Catholic identity, for it gives form and substance, shape and direction to all we do as a university," university president Rev. David O'Connell said a few years ago in his inaugural address. Not everyone at CUA expected (or, in some cases, wanted) to see these words backed up with deeds; doubters, however, have found themselves sorely mistaken.

    For instance, in the fall of 2004, Father O'Connell ruled that the university should rescind an invitation to actor Stanley Tucci to speak on Italian cinema at a university film festival—once it was revealed that Tucci is a board member of Planned Parenthood. Some saw this as petty; others regarded it as denying the abortion enterprise a major symbolic victory. (Should a board member of David Duke's white supremacist organization be invited to speak at historically black Morehouse College—even on the subject of Italian cinema?) While this decision was much reviled in the press, internal critics of the president's move, especially faculty, were almost unanimous in reaffirming Catholic teachings on abortion; this wouldn't be true at any number of other Catholic universities in the United States (including that posh Jesuit acad-

VITAL STATISTICS

Religious affiliation:
  Roman Catholic
Total enrollment: 5,981
Total undergraduates: 2,910
SAT/ACT midranges: SAT
  V: 520–640, M: 510–620;
  ACT: 21–27
Applicants: 2,744
Applicants accepted: 82%
*Accepted applicants who
  enrolled*: 32%
Tuition: $23,600
Room and board: $9,498
Freshman retention rate: 85%
Graduation rate: 63% (4 yrs.),
  73% (6 yrs.)
*Courses with fewer than 20
  students*: 56%
Student-faculty ratio: 9:1
*Courses taught by graduate
  TAs*: not provided
Most popular majors:
  architecture, politics,
  business
Students living on campus:
  68%
*Guaranteed housing for four
  years?* yes
Students in fraternities: 1%
  sororities: 1%

While it doesn't offer a core curriculum, Catholic University offers stronger distribution requirements than many schools. For the School of Arts and Sciences, students must complete:

- An introductory English composition course.
- Four courses in philosophy, including two introductory courses and two others: "Logic, Morality, and Action" and "Nature, Knowledge, and God."
- Four courses in religion. More than 400 courses fulfill this requirement—the overwhelming majority of them sound and useful classes in Catholic history and doctrine, such as "Introduction to Christianity," though one could waste some time studying "Theologies of Liberation."
- Four courses in social/ behavioral sciences, from some 200 mostly worthy choices, such as introductions to psychology or sociology.
- Four courses in mathematics or natural sciences, such as anthropology, biology, chemistry, computer science, environmental studies, math, and physics; however, one of the courses must be math. Choices include "Analytic

emy across town). Indeed, the university as a whole is overwhelmingly pro-life; as one graduate student says, "Nobody publicly advocates legalized abortion." A recent outside survey found that 78 percent of the CUA student body considered abortion morally wrong.

According to another student, the atmosphere at CUA "has definitely shifted to the right" since Father O'Connell took over in 1998; Attorney General John Ashcroft was one of the commencement speakers in 2002. Another student adds that CUA has never pushed a "feminist thing" on campus. Most students with opposing political inclinations pursue their interests off campus, participating in national protests on the Mall or snagging one of the many media and political internships available on Capitol Hill.

All in all, CUA makes for a prime destination for students seeking authentically Catholic learning. One student says, "For Catholics looking for a great education that does not require them to compromise their faith, Catholic is one of the best educations possible, and for non-Catholics looking for a classical education, a small campus, a great location, and lots of opportunities, Catholic has much to offer."

Catholic University was founded as a graduate research institution; it wasn't until 1894 that undergraduates arrived on campus. Even today, undergraduates account for less than half the student body. CUA offers a multitude of master's and doctoral programs, first professional degrees in architecture, law, and theology, and joint master's programs of study. Although students see tension between the undergraduate and graduate programs, Catholic has recently focused on improving the former.

Despite CUA's emphasis on graduate education, the university offers 83 bachelor's degree programs in six schools: Arts and Sciences, Architecture and Planning, Engineering, Music, Nursing (ranked as one of the best in the country), and Philosophy. Although CUA is not a "great books" school, a student can find such courses there. Moreover, the college does have an Honors Program, which "strives to provide a structured interdisciplinary program to interested and bright undergrads," says one professor. Another calls it "one of the most attractive parts of the entire undergraduate curriculum." It offers five different study sequences, some more traditional than others: "An Aristotelian Studium," "The Christian Tradition," "Critical Exploration of Social Reality," "The Environment, Energy, and Policy," and "Media, Technology, and Culture."

While Catholic cannot be said to have a true core curriculum, it does have a much stronger set of distribution requirements than most schools. On the other hand, a student claims that some of these requirements are actually weaker than they appear: "It's possible, and even kind of easy, to skimp on both religion and philosophy," he says. The religion requirement, says another, can be met "without ever having to do anything more substantial than a few 'reflection' papers—the sort of thing that begins with the words 'I feel.'"

CUA students take at least 20 courses to fulfill distribution requirements, and while there is considerable flexibility in their options—especially outside of philosophy and religion—CUA discourages students from taking these courses from a single area. In fact, the school does not allow a student to take more than 14 in the field of his major.

A reorganization of the School of Religious Studies and Theology has distributed undergraduate teaching responsibilities (which had been concentrated exclusively in the faculty of religion and religious education) over four faculties: theology, biblical studies, church history, and religion and religious education. Now, religion majors can concentrate in biblical studies, Roman Catholic studies, religious development and religious education, or religion and culture. For each of these concentrations, the curriculum is carefully structured and serious. Students interested in religion can earn an arts and sciences degree in the discipline or an undergraduate certificate in pastoral ministry.

CUA recently pulled out of the Association of American Universities, a group of graduate research universities, because its professors had not published enough, nor had it raised enough funds. While some at the university view CUA's break with the association as a defeat, others hope it will refocus CUA on undergraduates and their needs.

Although architecture is the largest undergraduate major, politics is considered the strongest department for undergraduates and is particularly solid in political theory. The best faculty members in the department, students say, are John Kromkowski, James O'Leary, Claes Ryn, and David Walsh. The academic pride and flagship school of CUA is

REQUIREMENTS (CONT'D)

Geometry" and "Calculus I," along with the less demanding "In Search of Extraterrestrial Life," a lecture course with major components devoted to "UFO-logy" and interstellar travel.

- Three courses in humanities, out of hundreds such as "The Medieval World, "Comparative Colonial Systems, 1500–1800," and the intriguing "Long-Haired Kings and Barbarians."

- Two courses in literature. Again, a long list of courses qualify—most of them solid subjects like "Chaucer and His Age" or "Epic Tradition from Homer to Joyce." Unfortunately, the extreme freedom granted students would allow someone to graduate having skipped Shakespeare and Milton in favor of "Poetry and Rock in the Age of Dickey and Dylan."

- Two courses in a foreign language at the intermediate level. Students may be exempted by presenting sufficient standardized test scores in a language.

- A "comprehensive requirement," consisting of either a comprehensive exam or comparable project, is satisfied during the senior year and is determined by the student's major department.

MIDDLE ATLANTIC

its School of Philosophy, which is highly regarded nationwide for its programs in classical and medieval philosophy. Professors V. Bradley Lewis, Fr. Kurt Pritzl, Fr. Brian Shanley, and Kevin White are named as some of the best in the school, along with Msgr. Robert Sokolowski, who specializes in phenomenology, and Msgr. John F. Wippel in metaphysics. Some standout faculty members in Theology and Religious Studies include Joseph Capizzi in moral theology and ethics, Fr. Francis Danella in Christian and Salesian spirituality; Gösta Hallonsten in ecumenical theology and the history of theology; and William Loewe in Christology. Other notable professors in the university include Michael Mack, famous on campus for his Shakespeare class, as well as Ernest Suarez, Christopher Wheatley, Rosemary Winslow, and Stephen Wright in English; Virgil Nemoianu in comparative literature and philosophy; and Katherine L. Jansen and Jerry Z. Muller in history.

Recently, Harold Bloom, the renowned literary scholar and critic, listed Catholic University's English department among the few English departments in the country that have maintained exceptionally high standards of teaching and scholarship, according to the department Web site. Music and drama are also especially strong programs.

Most students say that the CUA faculty is committed to teaching as its first priority. Four out of five professors teach at the undergraduate level. Graduate students occasionally teach introductory courses, especially in the social sciences, but the university says it closely monitors them for quality control. The university requires teaching assistants to take a pedagogy class before teaching their first course. One student says that his introductory anthropology class was "primarily taught by the TA, with almost no involvement from the listed instructor." In addition, some of the professors who are minor celebrities in their fields are said to have little time for teaching and to care more about publishing and research.

Class sizes—once you get past the introductory courses—are usually small, at fewer than 20 students. Small classes encourage discussion and faculty-student interaction. Class participation is often part of a student's grade, especially in seminars.

The university does offer academic advising, but students decide how and to what extent to take advantage of it. Since most advising takes place within departments, students are encouraged to make an early, tentative choice of major, and then the university selects a faculty advisor for each within that program. Students who remain undecided are appointed general-purpose advisors. As at most universities, advisors don't necessarily search out their advisees. Students must take the initiative; once they do, faculty members are willing to help. Advisors are all full-time faculty members, not graduate students, and students can change advisors at any time. One student says, "Despite all the counsel I've received from my advisors, I've found that my friends usually offer better advice on which professors and courses to take."

Science majors sometimes complain that the chemistry and biology departments lack adequate, modern facilities. Students and faculty alike say that modern language is the weakest department at the university. The university's Mullen Library needs improvement, too, especially in staffing and resources; missing or stolen books are constant problems. However, CUA is part of the Washington Research Library Consortium, so students have access to 15 other local university libraries—as well as various government resources such as the Library of Congress, the National Institutes of Health, the National Archives, and various federal libraries. Things have been changing and CUA is addressing this problem; the library has just begun a multimillion- dollar renovation.

CUA is also a member of the Consortium of Universities of the Washington Metropolitan Area, which allows students to take courses at 11 other area schools, including Georgetown, American, George Washington, and Howard.

Student Life: In the city, but not of it

CUA students—largely East Coast, Catholic, parochial-schooled, and middle to upper-middle class—tend to take their college careers seriously. Nevertheless, they find time to take part in the life of the nation's capital.

Unless they commute from home, students are required to live on campus for the first two years of school. The university has sufficient space to provide housing for those who wish to live on campus past the sophomore year. Most dorms are coed, but men are usually separated from women by floors or wings. There are no coed bathrooms or dorm rooms in the residence halls. The university also offers a couple of all-female dorms. In the "wellness" dorm, students pledge to go without alcohol. Students are not allowed to have overnight guests of the opposite sex, but this rule is often disregarded—and students are consequently punished. Dormitories also have noise regulations with special hours during finals, but whether resident advisors enforce these rules depends on the dorm.

Smoking is not allowed inside any building on campus and drugs aren't as popular at Catholic as they are at many colleges in the metropolitan area. CUA's drug policy is tough—students caught using drugs are normally suspended for the rest of the semester, even for a first offense. Alcohol is more of a problem; many students leave campus to drink in order to avoid penalties, and some students have expressed concerns, one writing in the *Tower* student newspaper of "hope[s] that a reasonable compromise can be found between the administration's sweet dreams of a puritanical, dry campus and their nightmare of *National Lampoon's Animal House*." The university no longer has a bar or pub on campus that serves alcoholic beverages.

Freshman orientation is a three-day marathon designed to acclimate new students to college life. One student complains that the main purpose of the orientation programs is "to indoctrinate students into thinking that the administration is abso-

SUGGESTED CORE
1. Classics 312, Greek Literature in Translation *or* English 345, The Epic Tradition from Homer to Joyce
2. Philosophy 353, History of Ancient Philosophy *or* 201, The Classical Mind
3. Theology and Religious Studies 200/210, Theologies of the Old Testament / Introduction to the New Testament
4. Theology and Religious Studies 220, Church through the Ages: Paul to Luther
5. Politics 360, Modern Political Thought
6. English 461/462, Plays of Shakespeare I/II
7. History 257, American History Survey I
8. History 341, Modern European Intellectual History II

MIDDLE ATLANTIC

lutely wonderful and any voices of dissent are simply wrong." But most students say the program is effective; one even calls it "the best three days of my life." Orientation gives students tips on how to succeed academically, how to be safe, and how to make the most of the nation's capital. Before orientation, students register for classes, and during the program they plot out the courses required to graduate in time in small advising sessions with the dean or undergraduate coordinator of the program. According to one student, with the exception of orientation lectures on the dangers associated with alcohol, drug use, and promiscuity, "moral formation seems to be left to the student rather than entrusted to the school."

Among the most active student organizations are the political ones—not surprisingly, given the school's location. The College Republicans have presented lectures by Oliver North, Robert Novak, Edwin Meese, and Ben Stein. The College Democrats are less active, and a gay rights group that used to exist last received funding in 2001. Both Republicans and Democrats are particularly proud to have had graduates of their future alma mater, Ed Gillespie and Terry McAuliffe, recently chairing the Republican and Democratic National Committees; the two debated on campus in 2002. Formal political discussion at CUA was quelled somewhat in 2004 by a moratorium on political speakers during the presidential campaign.

The university does have a variety of multicultural student organizations like the African Students Union, Chinese Students and Scholars Association, Filipino Organization of Catholic University Students (FOCUS), Muslim Students and Islam Awareness Association, National Society of Black Engineers, and an umbrella organization called Minority Voices. There is a chapter on campus for Amnesty International, two international affairs organizations, and numerous service organizations, fraternities, and professional societies. A recent attempt to start a chapter of the NAACP was almost squelched, in response to the NAACP national organization's pro-abortion stance; to get a place on campus, the national group had to exempt its CUA chapter from taking a stance favoring legal abortion.

Students are very active in campus ministry at CUA. Organizations like Habitat for Humanity, the House, Knights of Columbus, and Students for Life bring students together for spiritual and charitable purposes, emphasizing the university's Catholic tradition. The Campus Ministry sponsors devotional events for students and a community service program through which students visit convalescent homes and read to children. Swing dancing and ballroom dancing lessons are available and popular with students, in addition to a wide variety of outdoor activities.

The immense, impressive National Shrine of the Immaculate Conception stands adjacent to campus. Students also have access to Saint Vincent's Chapel on the west campus. Caldwell Chapel—always open—sits on the east campus.

CUA competes in the NCAA Division III and has an excellent men's basketball team that won the national championship in 2001. The university also has 20 other varsity sports teams, as well as intramural sports, including golf, ice hockey, men's and women's rugby, and a popular group sport known on campus as CUltimate Frisbee.

A new student center, the Pryzbyla Center, opened in 2003. The center houses the student organizations, two cafeterias, student lounge areas, and the Office of University Center, Student Programs and Events, which manages the facility. Catholic recently bought 49 acres from the Armed Forces Retirement Home. This purchase will increase the size of the university's campus by more than 30 percent and permit expansion across CUA's western edge. The area, bordered by Harewood Road, Michigan Avenue, and North Capitol Street, is the largest tract of open land in D.C. According to Father O'Connell, the purchase "allows [us] to maximize our assets for the university's future growth [and] also will ensure that we continue to provide for our students, faculty, staff, and visitors a traditional campus and a beautiful green oasis in the heart of the nation's capital." A Metro stop at one corner of the campus provides easy access to the rest of the Washington area.

Washington is not the safest place in the world; though crime rates have fallen in recent years, students should be cautious when they leave the confines of the school. The closest bar to campus (one notable for good relations between students and townies) was the scene of a triple homicide in 2002, and car theft is frequent. But then, a triple homicide occurred at a Starbucks in Georgetown a few years ago—proving that no part of the District is a safe haven. The campus provides lighted emergency phone boxes all over campus, and security personnel patrol the university grounds 24 hours a day. Again, students should use common sense when venturing off campus at night through the area's neighborhoods. Escort services provided by Public Safety and the Saferides program take students home at night from late-night study sessions and parties. Students must swipe identification cards to gain entrance to residence halls.

Catholic University's tuition in 2004–5 was $23,600, with room and board at $9,498. The school offers both merit- and need-based aid, but it does not practice need-blind admission or guarantee to meet a student's full financial need. Still, 84 percent of students receive some need-based aid, with the average need-based aid gift to freshmen at $10,231.

COLGATE UNIVERSITY

HAMILTON, NEW YORK • WWW.COLGATE.EDU

The way we were

Colgate University has historically placed teaching as its highest priority. With a very good student-faculty ratio, no teaching assistants, professors who care about whether and how their students learn, and a faculty full of experienced scholars, at Colgate "the students are the faculty's main priorities, and advising them is a close second," says a student. A visitor to the campus today, a remote but beautiful location (designed with input from Frederick Law Olmstead), would likely notice the wholesome, traditional nature of the students. These kids, as one professor put it, are "boys with big necks and girls with small waists that really like each other." In general, Colgate students are animated by surprisingly traditional moral values and are well rounded, both athletic and smart. They tend to go on to be CEOs, not PhDs.

This may not exactly conform to the "idea of a university" treasured by traditional educators, but it's a respectable heritage for a middle-rank school in a middle-class country. However, the status quo at Colgate has proven intolerable to its administrators, who are wielding their institutional power to reengineer the school, its curriculum, and its student body. Colgate's president since 2002, Rebecca Chopp, has generated controversy thanks to her grand visions of transforming the sleepy university into a progressivist training academy. Chopp's background and primary research interests are in feminism and theology; she was once director of the Institute of Women's Studies at Emory University. Fittingly, perhaps, she has adopted the role of moral matriarch, seemingly intent upon infusing the school and its students with a new, postmodern ethos. Working with a politicized minority in the ranks of the administration and faculty, she has begun to change the curriculum and atmosphere at Colgate in ways that are all too familiar to veterans of the PC wars. The success of this unhappy endeavor depends on how successful the administration is at recruiting new students with likeminded goals. According to an insider, the admissions process has been changed to include more oversight and to ensure that incoming students possess an "angular" disposition—whatever that means. A report issued in 2003 by the Task Force on Campus Culture recommended "that diversity be made a hallmark of the Colgate experience." And they don't mean diversity of viewpoint.

Academic Life: Out with the old

The heart of a university, regardless of its politics, lies in its curriculum and its teaching. And at least in the first department, Colgate is limping. According to the American Council of Trustees and Alumni (ACTA), Colgate's core curriculum leaves major gaps in the education it requires of undergraduates. In fact, Colgate earned an F in ACTA's recent ranking of liberal art programs. (So did a number of elite schools, alas; perhaps Colgate is racing them to the bottom.)

For instance, one goal of a liberal arts education is to provide a student with the historical perspective that will allow him to judge current events and exercise responsible citizenship. Those who crafted Colgate's current curriculum seem oblivious to this concern. Almost without exception, first-year courses approach matters from a twenty-first-century perspective. Most challenge the student to consider—before he has studied such foundational subjects as religion, philosophy, or Western history—such hot-button issues as global warming, stem-cell research, alternative energy, modern medicine, and AIDS. In other words, all the staples of the editorial pages. Why should parents pony up $31,440 a year so that their children can learn what's already published in the *New York Times*?

Freshmen participate in a first-year seminar, which, according to the catalog, aims to help students understand "the nature of the learning process, the exploration of individual needs and strengths, learning from classmates, and learning from the multiplicity of resources beyond the classroom." Students must also complete a two-semester track in "Continuity and Change in the West." That might sound promising, but the course descriptions show an unwholesome tendency to view events of world history exclusively through the jaundiced lens of contemporary controversy.

VITAL STATISTICS
Religious affiliation: none
Total enrollment: 2,859
Total undergraduates: 2,796
SAT/ACT midranges: SAT: 1240–1400; ACT: 28–32
Applicants: 5,870
Applicants accepted: 42%
Accepted applicants who enrolled: 30%
Tuition: $31,440
Room and board: $7,620
Freshman retention rate: 97%
Graduation rate: 85% (4 yrs.), 91% (6 yrs.)
Average class size: 19
Student-faculty ratio: 10:1
Courses taught by graduate TAs: none
Most popular majors: biology, economics, English
Students living on campus: 84%
Guaranteed housing for four years? yes
Students in fraternities: 35% sororities: 32%

Finally, for the last of the "core" requirements, students must take a course on "Cultures of Africa, Asia, and the Americas," choosing from a list of 39 courses on China, Japan, the Iroquois, Nigeria, or the Black Diaspora, to name a few. Through whatever course they choose, students are supposed to develop an "appreciation of the individual culture for its own sake," according to the catalog. "These courses are designed to expand students' awareness and understanding of the world's cultural diversity."

Until recently, the ideological bias present in some Colgate courses seemed mostly localized in the usual places—departments such as women's, Africana, and Latin American studies. However, the political virus is said to be infecting some traditional departments like philosophy and religion. For example, students may fulfill one of their scant humanities requirements with "Philosophy of Feminisms," in which they study feminist, "womanist," and *mujerista* interpretations of politics; specifically, how politics have impacted "marginalized people." The course focuses on the "interconnections among oppressions," the (allegedly unique) political characteristics of violence against women, and the "barriers separating women and embodiment." Another option is "Queer Studies Meets Religious Studies," the title of which pretty much speaks for itself. One could take care of a social science requirement with "Gender in the Economy." However, such courses can be avoided by the savvy student.

Colgate's advising system does seem to do a fine job of guiding students through the rigors of college. Even before entering Colgate, students can ask for help from "prematriculation advisors," who help students choose their courses for the first semester. As freshmen, students turn to their first-year seminar instructors for guidance. These professors serve as advisors until students choose their concentrations, at which time they select faculty advisors from their major departments.

Teaching also seems strong at Colgate. The average class size at Colgate is 19. Of all the university's undergraduate courses, almost 60 percent have fewer than 20 students. The university has a very good student-faculty ratio of 10 to 1. Graduate students do not teach courses at Colgate. Faculty members hold regular office hours, and most students take advantage of these. "Office hours are the best way to get to know your professor on a different level while still having all of your academic questions answered," a political science major says. Another student says, "Most students take advantage of the professors' office hours as professors know all of their students, so it is not uncomfortable in any way." Professors are interested in teaching, but they are also scholars. "[Members of the] faculty are still active researchers, and, as a result, undergraduates get unusual opportunities and greater responsibilities," a professor says. "Students get a lot more one-on-one attention at Colgate than they would get elsewhere."

Opinions differ about the relationship between students and faculty. One professor says, "Colgate has a professorial culture where if you are not highly regarded by students it will, of course, affect tenure—but, more interestingly, it results in demerits even for tenured faculty." Another professor says, "It is hard to know exactly why the faculty continues to care as much about teaching, after tenure, as they do. . . . Colgate succeeds remarkably well at maintaining a balance between teaching and research." Surprisingly, a strong sense of distrust prevails between the students and the faculty, as noted by the school's Task Force on Campus Culture, which published its findings in 2003. In response, the school began a Residential Education program which incorporates faculty members into the student residences.

Colgate does boast some excellent departments, according to professors. "The best . . . in the humanities are English and a small but very serious classics department," one says. "In the natural sciences, the best are chemistry, geology, and a highly rigorous department of psychology. And in the social sciences, the economics and political science departments are both excellent, with a number of relatively conservative faculty." One professor in the political science department says that the department often has hundreds of students on the waiting list for its courses.

Students name the following faculty members as among the best at Colgate: Michael Johnston, Robert Kraynak, and Barry Alan Shain in political science; Kay Johnston in educational studies; Margaret Maurer in English; Karen Harpp, Amy

Leventer, and Paul Pinet in geology; Robert Turner in economics; Doug Johnson in psychology; and Thomas Balonek in physics and astronomy.

Unlike most colleges and universities, Colgate expects its students to take only four courses per semester. They may take five with special permission, but are not allowed to enroll in more than that. The idea is to give students the chance to focus more closely on the courses they do take. Besides satisfying general education requirements, students must also choose a concentration, where they will generally receive more structure. For instance, the English department requires its majors to take a broad range of courses. Unfortunately, its curriculum has been watered down in recent years and no longer includes a survey course that exposes students to the canonical works of English literature, such as Chaucer, Shakespeare, and Milton. In this area, too, Colgate appears to be blindly following trends set by more prestigious schools.

Student Life: Freedom is slavery

The most notable thing about campus life at Colgate today is the degree to which the administration is seeking to subject it to Orwellian control. Colgate has 13 Greek organizations, and about a third of students are members. Such groups have existed on campus since 1856, and the fact that they own their own properties has given them some independence from the university. It has also offered students significant freedom of association—too much freedom, according to the bureaucrats who now run Colgate. In July 2003 the school decreed that all Greek houses must be sold to the school or their chapters would lose recognition. Any student who belongs to an unrecognized fraternity can face suspension or expulsion. (Try to imagine what would happen to a university that threatened such sanctions against students who belonged to gay, pro-choice, or other "progressive" organizations.) It appears that President Chopp took away from her study of theology mainly a nostalgia for the Inquisition.

Once they have been confiscated, the Greek houses face an uncertain future. According to Students and Alumni for Colgate—a group leading the resistance to this power (and land) grab by the administration—the school "anticipates that university-owned Greek-letter houses will . . . serve as 'theme' houses. Current theme houses are

---

ACADEMIC REQUIREMENTS

Colgate has no core curriculum and rather lax requirements for breadth of study. There are four courses that students must take, but they don't constitute a "core" in any meaningful sense:

- "Scientific Perspectives on the World."
- "Continuity and Change in the West."
- "Challenge of Modernity."
- "Cultures of Africa, Asia, and the Americas."

Students must also take two courses from each of the following areas:

- Humanities. "Plato and his Predecessors" will count. So will "Queer Studies Meets Religious Studies."
- Natural sciences and mathematics. Choices range from "Astronomical Techniques" to "Evolution, Ecology, and Diversity" and "Prejudice and Racism."
- Social sciences. Options include "American History to 1877" and "The Emergence of Modern Woman."

MIDDLE ATLANTIC

225

designed as residences for students who want to live with others who share a common background or interest—Asian, African American, Latino, homosexuality, creative arts, environmental activism, and peace studies." Any student considering Colgate should first visit the alumni resistance Web site at *www.sa4c.com* to see what he's getting into.

Hamilton is a small town named after Alexander Hamilton that lies about a half-hour southeast of Syracuse and a half-hour southwest of Utica. Since these cities provide relatively few cultural opportunities, most students stay on campus on weekends. With only 3,800 full-time residents, Hamilton's population almost doubles during the academic year. The Colgate community enjoys a comfortable relationship with the town of Hamilton; many town residents attend university events, and students support local businesses. Students can easily walk to local shops or restaurants or to the village green at the center of town, where the university hosts a college-town picnic at the start of each new year. One of the most popular attractions in town is the Palace Theater, which now serves as a dance club.

Colgate's 512-acre campus includes Taylor Lake, a favorite spot for watching local wildlife. Although most of the school's original structures remain, many of the university's larger buildings, such as the library and the student center, were constructed more recently to accommodate a rise in enrollment.

Colgate is largely a residential school, with 84 percent of students living in university-owned housing. The university guarantees housing for all four years. Students can choose single-sex or coed dormitory floors (no single-sex dorms are available), substance-free dorms, and smoke-free housing. There are no coed dorm rooms or bathrooms in the residence halls yet, but some observers have predicted that this will soon change. Colgate offers a number of theme houses for first-year students and upperclassmen. Some of the choices include Outdoor Connections, a hall for environmentally conscious students interested in outdoor education, and the Harlem Renaissance Center, which is dedicated to the "culture and heritage of Africans and African Americans," according to the housing Web page. Others are the Asia Interest House, the Creative Arts House, and the French/Italian House.

One house in particular speaks volumes about the administrative agenda. While most of the college houses are lovely, the finest is The Class of 1934 House. This is what the school calls a "rotating theme" house. Each year, 12 seniors are allowed to live there after competing for "a theme." The most developed theme wins and gets to play foosball and swim in the built-in pool. The winning theme for 2004–5 was "Safe House," and thus this house became, allegedly, a place where gays, lesbians, et. al., can feel safe—safer, at least, than students who belong to dissenting fraternities or sororities.

Seniors wishing to live off campus must obtain written approval from the director of residential life. This isn't usually hard to get, but the number of students allowed to live off campus is capped at 250; if more apply, the college holds a lottery to determine who lives where. Colgate obviously recognizes the benefits of having a primarily residential school and works to make sure the campus remains one.

Colgate's new Residential Education program will dramatically change the student housing experience. President Chopp has made this opportunity to reach a "captive audience" the cornerstone of her reform program. The program is a comprehensive redefinition of housing and its purpose. Students are placed in housing specified by year and are required to participate in scheduled programs intended to produce a student body that is "forward thinking" and "progressive." Beginning in fall 2004, sophomores were required to participate in "The Sophomore Experience in the Art of Democracy." This program is billed as an opportunity for students to practice democratic principles while developing into future citizens. Apparently, "democracy" as defined by the Colgate authorities does not include freedom of thought, action, or association.

Devout students will find religious houses on campus. There is a Jewish Union, a Christian Fellowship, a Muslim group, and a Newman Center. More traditional Catholics may enjoy attending St. Mary's in Hamilton.

For students interested in debate, the school has recently hired Miranda Weigler to head up a team which had been on ice since 2001. Thanks to a generous donor, the entire team went to Malaysia to participate in an intercollegiate debate in December 2004. Whether the debate team will gather any steam remains to be seen. According to one published report, the debate held at the Palace (the popular night spot in Hamilton) during fall 2004 was less than edifying. The topic required students to argue whether the pope, after having a vision and realizing that the Catholic faith was a fraud, should lie or publicly come clean.

SUGGESTED CORE
1. Classics 221, The Epic Voice and Its Echoes
2. Philosophy 301, Plato and His Predecessors
3. Religion 209, The New Testament *and* Religion 208, The Hebrew Bible
4. Religion 301, The Christian Tradition
5. Political Science 464, Freedom and Authority in Modern Political Philosophy
6. English 321 and 322, Shakespeare
7. History 103, American History to 1877
8. History 339, Traditions of European Intellectual History *or* Political Science 385, Modernity and Its Conservative Critics

Students hungry for extracurricular liberalism may choose from an array of student organizations. Colgate's political organizations include vaguely named groups like Students for a Better World, Colgate Students for Change, Sisters of the Round Table, and Students for Social Justice. Those who find these causes too general may choose from organizations such as Students for Environmental Awareness, Rainbow Alliance (the campus "lesbian, gay, bisexual, transgender, and questioning" group), Feminist Majority Leadership Alliance, Colgate Greens, or Colgate Democrats. Colgate offers plenty of opportunities to become involved in social tinkering.

Some political groups receive considerable support from the university. When the Feminist Majority Leadership Alliance needed help organizing and funding its National Young Women's Day of Action, the student group turned to the university's Women's Studies Center. The day's festivities included the promotion of abortion rights and purportedly educational activities focusing on issues like "domestic violence, sweatshops, abortion, [and] welfare."

The Colgate student activities programming group often sponsors concerts, comedy shows, and free movies. The university also hosts five student singing groups that perform regularly on campus.

In the area surrounding the university, outdoor activities abound. The Outdoor Education Web page says that 600 students participated in their programs last year. Outdoor Education lets students rent backpacks, tents, and other outdoor equipment and conducts a Wilderness Adventure Program for freshmen.

More than two-thirds of the student body participates in the university's intramurals program, which holds more than 50 tournaments each semester. In addition to these activities, Colgate maintains its own boathouse, shooting range, bowling alley, and climbing wall. The university offers its students about 30 club sports, in which about 16 percent of the student body participate. For more serious athletes, or at least better ones, the university's 25 varsity teams compete in the Patriot League (NCAA Division I) against schools like Army, Navy, and American University.

The Colgate campus is equipped with emergency call boxes and all dorms are secured with a keypad lock. A security force patrols the campus around the clock and a volunteer foot patrol monitors the area at night. The university has also organized a walking escort service to help students home after dark. There is very little reported crime. In 2003, there were two forcible sex offenses on campus, along with eight burglaries. Colgate's administration says that the theft of compact discs is by far the most common offense. Students should have few safety concerns, as Hamilton is a small town with little criminal activity.

The folks in the financial aid office are friendly and helpful. They ought to be; in 2004–5, Colgate's tuition was a hefty $31,440, with room and board at $7,620. More than 40 percent of the students receive some form of financial aid. Admissions are not quite need-blind, but the school does meet the full financial need of those who get in. The schools admits students, and offers aid, on a first-come, first-served basis. After the money runs out, Colgate stops admitting students who require financial assistance.

COLUMBIA UNIVERSITY

NEW YORK, NEW YORK • WWW.COLUMBIA.EDU

God save the King's College

Columbia University in New York City is a fascinating para-dox. It was founded in 1754 as King's College, and many of the school's faculty—along with much of New York State—remained loyal to King George at the time of the War of Independence. Leading teachers fled the victorious Ameri-can revolutionaries to Canada. In Windsor, Nova Scotia, they founded another excellent liberal arts institution, the Uni-versity of King's College (now in Halifax). The campus of King's College was handed over to the newly formed Co-lumbia University in 1784. The school became a center of humane letters in the United States, which it has remained ever since. But in the 1960s, Columbia also served as the locus for some of the worst excesses of the radical antiwar movement—as students enjoying draft deferments organized violent protests against U.S. involvement in Vietnam, even-tually occupying more than a dozen campus buildings. Af-ter a weeklong standoff between the administration and several hundred students, the police attempted to put an end to the siege. Instead, violence broke out and hundreds of students were arrested. The university president resigned a few months later, and the school has never quite shaken its leftist reputation.

It seems worthy of note that Columbia presented a revised university symbol in March 2004. The three crosses that once accompanied a crown, a reminder of Columbia's Anglican heritage, are now gone. "Predictably," wrote Rich-ard John Neuhaus, "some conservatives lamented the change. Others, however, took comfort in the fact that the university, while no longer Christian, is still monarchist."

Through all this, by some apparent miracle, Columbia has preserved one of the elements of a traditional liberal arts education: a genuine core curriculum that tries to impart to each student the broad outlines of Western civilization and American his-tory. Recently installed Columbia president Lee Bollinger faces quite a task trying to maintain this curriculum—Columbia's single greatest strength—in the face of a strongly,

VITAL STATISTICS	
Religious affiliation: none	
Total enrollment: 23,650	
Total undergraduates: 7,114	
SAT/ACT midranges: SAT: 1320–1520; ACT: 27–32	
Applicants: 14,665	
Applicants accepted: 11%	
Accepted applicants who enrolled: 62%	
Tuition: $31,472	
Room and board: $9,066	
Freshman retention rate: 61%	
Graduation rate: 86% (4 yrs.), 94% (6 yrs.)	
Average class size: 20	
Student-faculty ratio: 7:1	
Courses taught by graduate TAs: not provided	
Most popular majors: English, history, political science	
Students living on campus: 95%	
Guaranteed housing for four years? yes	
Students in fraternities or sororities: 10–15%	

Admirably, amid the general collapse of curricula across the country, Columbia has maintained a serious, rewarding core, along with several other requirements. The Columbia Core consists of the following:

- "Masterpieces of Western Literature and Philosophy" (two semesters). In small-group seminars, students read original works.
- "Contemporary Civilization" (two semesters). Another small-group discussion course, this class most recently studied classic texts ranging from Rousseau, and Kant to Freud and Hannah Arendt.
- "University Writing," an English composition course. The only text is the students' own writing. Each section has no more than 12 students, which alone makes this course preferable to the cattle calls that freshman comp classes have become at many other schools.
- "Art Humanities," which is an "analytical study of a limited number of major monuments and images in Western art."
- "Music Humanities." This class teaches students to appreciate and understand music, emphasizing

if not quite monolithically, leftist student body and faculty. His success or failure will determine whether Columbia retains its distinctive excellence—or casts it aside, becoming little more than a "safety school" for students intent on gaining entry to the Ivy League.

Academic Life: Gem of the . . . nation

With some of the most respected scholars in the country on its faculty, Columbia's elite reputation is well deserved. This reputation is further justified by the university's requirement that all undergraduates take a number of courses focused on the Western canon; this core dominates the course load for freshmen and sophomores and is popular among students of different political stripes—who knew what they were getting into before they enrolled. "These were all books I wanted to read," says one English major. "Very few institutions offer a type of program like this, and there aren't a lot of people walking around saying, 'This is ethnocentric. Why are we learning the canon?'" A faculty member says, "In the core, the requirements are very specific, and there is little latitude for individual choice."

However, according to one graduate student, "the quality of the core curriculum is very inconsistent and depends on the individual instructor. It is telling that from 2003 to 2004, *The Federalist Papers* were erased from the Contemporary Civilization syllabus, while *The Marx/Engels Reader* remains a permanent fixture." We should add, however, that students in this class are assigned Edmund Burke as an antidote to the ravings of the Jacobins, and offered Hannah Arendt as an alternative to Foucault. Indeed, at how many schools do freshmen even read *The City of God* and the *Nicomachean Ethics*? Brown University should face such problems.

Columbia has a number of very strong departments, but among the Ivies it is most renowned for its history department. Among the department's faculty are Eric Foner, former president of the American Historical Association; Alan Brinkley, a popular historian; and Kenneth Jackson, head of the New York Historical Society. Columbia history majors must take at least one course in each of four areas: history before 1750; modern Europe; the Americas; and Africa, Asia, or the Middle East. Of the 10 courses required in the major, about half must be within a "specialization"; students can specialize in fields such as United States history, modern western European history, ancient history, and African history.

The English and comparative literature department has in recent years been at the center of one of academia's most acrimonious controversies. Because the department was split between postmodernist ideologues and remarkably stalwart traditionalists, until recently many vacant positions in the department simply went unfilled—the warring factions could not agree on a candidate. The university even went so far as to appoint an independent panel including faculty from other universities to conduct interviews with potential professors. But with the recent hiring of several tenure-track faculty, the bitterest fighting may now lie in the past.

Speaking of conflict, the Middle Eastern and Asian languages and cultures department bears the stamp of the late leftist scholar Edward Said—a strong advocate of Palestinian rights whom some labeled the "professor of terror" for his support of armed resistance to the Israeli occupation of the West Bank. Jewish students have made repeated complaints that faculty in this department are biased toward Arab perspectives, and that this has led to classroom incidents of anti-Semitism. According to a recent documentary produced by pro-Israel Columbia students, one professor "was teaching the class about the Jenin incidents [during the Palestinian intifada] and a girl raised her hand and tried to bring up an alternative point of view and before she could get her point across, he quickly . . . shouted at her, 'I will not have anyone sit through this class and deny Israeli atrocities.' Which pretty much limited the students' ability to even question him, or bring up an alternative point of view." A U.S. congressman, Anthony Wiener, wrote to President Bollinger calling on the professor to be fired because of reports that he had "likened Israel to Nazi Germany, said that Israel doesn't have the right to exist as a Jewish state, . . . [and] asked an Israeli student, 'How many Palestinians have you killed?' and then refused to allow the student to ask questions," according to the *Chronicle of Higher Education*.

Supporters of the department dispute these incidents and accuse their critics of trying to silence criticism of Likud

REQUIREMENTS (CONT'D)

the evolution in artistic style over time.

- "Major Cultures," the only element of the Columbia core that deviates from the curriculum's focus on Western civilization. This can be fulfilled with some excellent courses, such as "Ancient History of Mesopotamia and Anatolia," "Jazz," and "Egyptian Archeology"—or by any of the standard-issue "white guilt" classes.

- "Frontiers of Science." This is a weekly science class that involves lectures by leading Columbia scientists and seminar sections with researchers (all with PhDs) that include lab experiments.

Other general education requirements are:

- Foreign language. Students must complete the second term of an intermediate language sequence, or test out.

- Two additional science courses in any natural science department. Columbia offers two-term sequences designed for non-science majors in astronomy, biology, engineering, and mathematics—including one called "Physics for Poets."

- Physical education. Students must take a P.E. course and pass a swimming test or take beginning swimming.

Party policies and America's support for them. Columnist Nat Henthoff wrote of this controversy in the *Village Voice*: "The answer to this dilemma is for Lee Bollinger to provide an actually diversified Middle East studies department. It's not about bringing in pro-Israel professors, but scholars who teach—not inculcate." President Bollinger appointed a committee to investigate this controversy, though some have called its report a whitewash—noting that the committee included public supporters (but not opponents) of an academic "boycott" of Israel, as well as friends of the accused.

Another political incident, to which there were 3,000 witnesses, was the speech made on the eve of the Iraq invasion by Nicholas De Genova, an assistant professor of anthropology and Latino studies, who "said he hoped Iraq would defeat the United States and that he wished there would be 'a million Mogadishus,' a reference to the 1993 killing of 18 U.S. soldiers in Somalia," according to the *Chronicle*. This has left De Genova beleaguered and isolated, with few defenders on campus.

Columbia has worked hard in the last few years to expand its economics department, and it still offers renowned experts such as R. Glenn Hubbard and globetrotting development specialist Jeffrey Sachs. One major recent addition, Nobel Prize–winner and former Stanford professor Joseph Stiglitz, came as some consolation to Columbia after Harvard economist Robert Barro reneged on an agreement to join the faculty a couple years ago.

Besides the aforementioned faculty, excellent teachers at Columbia include Richard Bushman (emeritus), Caroline Walker Bynum, Carol N. Gluck, and Simon Schama in history; Elaine Combs-Schilling in anthropology; Andrew Delbanco, Joan M. Ferrante, Austin Quigley, Michael A. Seidel, and James Shapiro in English; David Sidorsky in philosophy; Brian Barry in political science; Vijay Modi in mechanical engineering; James H. Beck, Richard Brilliant, David Freedberg, Stephen Murray, and David Rosand in art history; Samuel Danishefsky in chemistry; James E. G. Zetzel in classics; and Robert Mundell in economics. One of the most rewarding courses, students report, is Kenneth Jackson's "History of the City of New York," which culminates in an exhilarating all-night bike ride, on which the professor leads the whole class through the city. Since Columbia students are eligible to take classes at its sister school across the street, also see this book's essay on Barnard College for other worthy teachers.

Columbia makes a wide—if not overwhelming—variety of courses available. But a common complaint among students is that the advising system is, at best, harmlessly inadequate. Students may ask their class deans whether they have met requirements, but advising systems vary by department, and most do not assign students to specific faculty advisors. Several departments require students to meet with faculty members periodically, but these meetings usually are formalities during which students have professors sign off on plans of study developed wholly by the students. In any event, Columbia's mediocre advising system has long been a part of the university's tradition. While the core classes are celebrated for their small class sizes and personalized attention, students have to actively seek out advisors.

Usually, the more famous the professor, the less likely it is that he will grade any of a student's work over the course of a semester. Classes with well-known professors are often lecture courses of up to 400 students, so while the university touts the fame of many of its professors, students may have trouble getting to know them. While all professors have office hours twice a week, unless students take the initiative faculty members will rarely learn their names. Grade inflation varies by department. It is most common in the newer and less rigorous disciplines like women's studies.

Though professors conduct almost all classes, graduate students do teach—particularly the small "recitation" sections of 15 to 20 students that usually accompany large lecture courses, where assistants are responsible for the grading. Their quality is said to vary. One of these assistants says, "In many cases, foreign language teaching assistants don't know the language they claim to teach. I myself was told that I'm 'not here to teach grammar.' We use an expensive ($165) book that has more pictures than actual text. So much for the old logocentric approach."

When TAs aren't teaching, it's because they're on strike. Aided by the AFL-CIO, a campus leftist group has organized graduate students in a campaign to unionize as "knowledge workers." President Bollinger has resisted these efforts, saying that graduate students are not employees but rather students and apprentices. Labor groups took Columbia to court over this issue, and in 2004 graduate students went on a widely publicized strike, forcing the cancellation of numerous entry-level classes. A ruling by the National Labor Relations Board against unionized grad students at another school suggests that the students are unlikely to prevail in court; however, the unionizers aren't giving up; a majority of 1,900 graduate employees at Columbia University in New York City have reportedly signed cards requesting representation by the United Auto Workers, of all groups, which has called on Columbia to voluntarily recognize the union. The threat of classroom disruption will likely be present for semesters to come.

President Bollinger is an outspoken proponent of affirmative action—indeed his name graces the recent Supreme Court decision upholding racial preferences in education, since he was the litigant defending admissions quotas (at the University of Michigan). In 2004, when Columbia College Conservative Club students held an "affirmative action bake sale," dramatizing the impact of racial preferences by selling food at lower prices to members of "protected" minority groups, a campus furor erupted. (It didn't help that a campus paper published a racially insensitive cartoon at the same time.) The brouhaha prompted Bollinger—whose biography on the Columbia Web site describes his "primary teaching and scholarly interests" as "focused on free speech and

SUGGESTED CORE

1. Classical Literature W4300y, The Classical Tradition
2. Philosophy V2101, The History of Philosophy: Pre-Socratics through Augustine
3. Religion V3501x/V3120x, Introduction to the Hebrew Bible / Introduction to Christianity
4. Religion V3402, Early Christianity *or* Religion V2610, Christianity
5. Political Science BC 1014y, Political Theory II
6. English W3335, Shakespeare I *or* English W3336, Shakespeare II
7. History W1401, Survey of American Civilization to the Civil War
8. Philosophy V3270, Nineteenth-Century Philosophy: Hegel to Nietzsche

First Amendment issues"—to e-mail every student at Columbia about the danger of offensive speech, asserting "this university's commitment to a spirit of tolerance and mutual respect, to the value of diversity within our community, and to the importance of affirmative action in the pursuit of both these goals."

At Columbia, a tolerant and open-minded brand of liberalism is more or less regnant among the faculty. And most Columbia professors remain traditionalists when it comes to how and what they teach and how they approach their scholarship. The propagandistic African American studies, Middle East languages and cultures, and women's and gender studies departments are the exceptions. However, claims one graduate student, "Columbia employs professors who make an issue of their sexuality in the classroom. In one case, a professor incorporates his homosexual lifestyle into his lesson plans (perhaps in the name of 'sensitivity training'). This is particularly insensitive to religious people."

Student Life: Roll on

Housing in New York City is notoriously expensive and hard to find. It's not surprising, then, that 95 percent of the Columbia student body lives on campus. Columbia guarantees housing to its undergraduates for all four years. Dormitories are coed, but the university sets aside a few floors solely for men or women. Women students can also live at Barnard, which offers all-women residence halls. Columbia does have a few coed bathrooms, but students can easily avoid them. "Columbia is generally pretty accommodating about bathrooms, and if someone has a request based on religion, I would be very surprised if they didn't accommodate," a student says. Special-interest housing allows groups of students to live together in one of several townhouses.

Quiet hours and noise regulations govern almost every dormitory. Sensitive students may have trouble getting these policies enforced, but generally, students on campus do not view noise as a major problem. Though it is up to the discretion of the residence advisor, most floors offer some sort of "condom box," making contraception widely available to students. Likewise, some floors have signs that provide information on the morning-after pill and other "health"-related services.

Columbia students have plenty of opportunities to engage in extracurricular activities—it's New York, after all. Within the immediate area of Columbia are a huge number of coffeehouses, bars, bookstores, and restaurants, and all of Manhattan's resources and attractions are within easy reach. A Columbia University ID card will give students free admission to almost any museum. Students can enjoy movies not likely to be screened elsewhere in the country in art house theaters throughout the city. Discounted tickets for some theaters are even sold at Undergraduate Class Centers, so students can avoid paying the full $10.50 ticket price common throughout Manhattan.

As part of orientation week, the university sponsors a number of tours to familiarize students with the city. Other activities during freshman orientation are more controversial. Informational sessions on the dangers of date rape are mandatory for all students and focus less on safety and more on the problem with men. Selected freshmen also attend receptions segregated by race or interest, including the Black Students Reception and the Gay, Lesbian, and Transgender Students Reception.

The politically active population on campus comprises only a minority of students, but it is an outspoken group with strong allies in student government and the faculty. The Columbia community has hundreds of student organizations covering a broad spectrum of interests, including the Columbia College Republicans, College Democrats, College Libertarians, academic societies like the Columbia Barnard Economics Society and the Political Science Students Association, journalism outlets, and a number of arts and music groups.

Some popular activist groups include a local chapter of the International Socialist Organization, International Deconstruction Workers United, the Campaign to End the Death Penalty, Students for Economic and Environmental Justice, *Conversio Virium*: "Columbia University's Student BDSM Discussion Organization," and Students Active for Ending Rape. Most of these groups belong to the Columbia Student Solidarity Network (CSSN), the self-described "umbrella organization for all left and progressive groups on campus." The Columbia College Conservative Club exists as a kind of support group for lonely right-wing students, sometimes hosting speakers from the Intercollegiate Studies Institute, the publisher of this guide.

Devout students will find chaplains representing most common (and many uncommon) faiths. The Catholic chaplain, Fr. Jacek Buda, an approachable young philosopher-friar from Poland, hosts the highbrow Augustine Club, which features doctrinal discussions and lectures. The school also hosts a Hillel, a chapter of Campus Crusade for Christ, an Orthodox Christian Fellowship, a Muslim Students Association, a Ba'hai and a Buddhist organization, among many others. Episcopalian students—and fans of exquisite architecture—should check out the nearby Cathedral of St. John the Divine, the largest (and perhaps the laxest) Gothic church in the world.

Perhaps the only lifestyle that has not been embraced by the campus community is the athletic one. The Columbia Lions, who compete—if that is the word—in the Ivy League, are known for record losing streaks. The urban setting of the campus does not lend itself well to intramural or varsity sports teams, and though a state-of-the-art gym is only a couple of blocks from most dormitories, the football field and other sports arenas are located some distance from campus.

Columbia has several unique traditions. An annual Yule Log Ceremony brings the Columbia community out to enjoy hot apple cider and to watch the lighting of the Christmas trees. Perhaps the most widely celebrated tradition surrounds the annual festivities conducted by the Columbia Marching Band on "Orgo Night," the day before the dreaded organic chemistry final exam. The band enters the Columbia library and blares music while chemistry and premed students cram ferociously. The wider Columbia community sometimes follows the band through the library and outside for a few more numbers in honor of those studying for the semester's last final.

Many prospective students and their parents still worry about New York's crime rate. Students, of course, should take every precaution, but the campus is safer than one would think. Says one student, "I feel extremely safe. I have no problem walking home with my laptop at two o'clock in the morning." Columbia has its own security squad and the New York Police Department contributes its resources if a crime occurs on campus. In 2003, Columbia reported six forcible sex offenses, eight robberies, one aggravated assault, and 28 burglaries on campus.

Columbia students pay for the privilege: tuition in 2004–5 was $31,472, and room and board $9,066. However, admissions are need-blind, and Columbia promises to meet the full need of any student who gets in. Some 49 percent of students receive need-based aid, and the average student loan debt of a recent graduate is around $16,000.

COOPER UNION FOR THE ADVANCEMENT OF SCIENCE AND ART

NEW YORK, NEW YORK • WWW.COOPER.EDU

Free as air and water

Cooper Union was founded in 1859 by entrepreneur and philanthropist Peter Cooper as a "unique educational and charitable institution" for "the advancement of science and art" in New York City. Cooper famously stated that education should be as "free as air and water" to deserving poor students "of good character." Located in a historic brownstone building in Astor Place, near St. Mark's Place, the "gateway" to the East Village, Cooper as an institution has historically had a high profile in American public life. The Great Hall was the site of Lincoln's "right makes might" speech and other famous speeches connected to many causes considered "progressive" in America from the Civil War period through World War I, including the national women's suffrage movement and the foundation of the American Red Cross. Speakers at its podium have included, apart from several U.S. presidents and presidential candidates (most recently Sen. John Kerry), Mark Twain, Henry Ward Beecher, William Jennings Bryan, W. H. Auden, and Orson Welles.

The first fact that leaps out about this venerable New York institution is the fact that Cooper Union is free; the select few that gain admission receive full tuition scholarships. This makes the school very attractive and allows it to be extremely selective—its acceptance rate is lower than many Ivy League colleges. But it will also cost you: Cooper Union's work regimen is more demanding (some say "grueling") than almost any other in the country.

Despite Cooper's intense and demanding focus on its specialty disciplines, it shows a surprising degree of commitment to its efforts to provide a substantive liberal arts education. A highly motivated student committed to pursuing one of the fields in which it specializes should place Cooper Union high on his list of schools to consider.

Academic Life:
The union of all the liberal arts

Cooper is composed of the Irwin S. Chanin School of Architecture, the School of Art, and the Albert Nerken School of Engineering. Education in each of the three schools is generally described as stellar, although art students we spoke to seemed less enthusiastic about the school than others.

Professors have a reputation for being very engaged. They can often be seen on school grounds during the weekends, and it's not unheard of for them to respond to e-mail or even phone inquiries regarding coursework during the weekends as well. Professors work hard to be innovative and to avoid dryness in presentation, and they can be quite creative in designing some assignments to incorporate the experience of immersion in the ever-tense, bustling, electrified environment of New York City. Class size is generally capped at around 30. A family atmosphere seems to prevail. Students, because of the frequently collaborative requirements of the study sessions and projects, tend to forge close friendships and lasting relationships.

The engineering school has in recent years moved from specialized majors in such areas as chemical engineering, electrical engineering, mechanical engineering, and civil engineering toward a cross-disciplinary model stressing the overarching importance of cultivating general design principles.

The architecture bachelor's program takes at least five years to complete—and frequently longer. The architectural school's self-description has a positively Renaissance flavor: "The philosophical foundation of the school is committed to the complex symbiotic relationships of education, research, theory, practice, and a broad spectrum of creative endeavors relevant to significant architectural development. . . . Fundamental to the school is the maintenance of a long-established creative environment where freedom of thought and intuitive exploration are given a place to flourish, where

VITAL STATISTICS

Religious affiliation: none
Total enrollment: 955
Total undergraduates: 918
SAT median: 1370
Applicants: 2,414
Applicants accepted: not reported
Accepted applicants who enrolled: 70%
Tuition: $0
Room and board: $9,000–$11,065
Freshman retention rate: 92%
Graduation rate: 60% (4 yrs.), 78% (6 yrs.)
Average class size: not reported
Student-faculty ratio: 7:1
Courses taught by graduate TAs: none
Most popular majors: art, architecture, engineering
Students living on campus: 20%
Guaranteed housing for four years? no
Students in fraternities: 10% sororities: 5%

Although it is mainly a studio arts and technical school, Cooper Union gives its students an abbreviated core curriculum and solid distribution requirements that put most liberal arts schools to shame. In addition to the demanding requirements of their major, art students must take the following:

- "Literary Forms and Expressions."
- "Texts and Contexts: Old Worlds and New."
- "The Making of Modern Society."
- "The Modern Context: Figures and Topics."
- Three credits of science electives.
- Twelve credits of electives chosen from among courses in art history, foreign languages, history of architecture, humanities, social sciences, and sciences.

the intangible chemistry of personal and public interactions stimulate an intensity of purpose and dedication, where the gifted mind and spirit can seek the means of expression and the mastery of form, and where a sense of the vast and joyous realm of creation can reveal an unending path for gratifying human endeavor." And students at the school include quite a few Renaissance men and women; you're likely to find them using their free time doing things like studying esoteric Asian martial arts or discussing philosophy over chess.

The art school offers a generalist curriculum that covers all of the fine arts and promotes an integrated perspective. The school's literature states that "students are taught to become socially aware, creative practitioners, and historically grounded, perceptive, and critical analysts of the world of contemporary communications, art, and the culture at large." More than two-thirds of a student's class time is spent in studio courses. The art school's facilities include painting studios, sculpture and printmaking shops, photography studios and darkrooms, and film and video facilities.

Instead of departments such as English or political science, Cooper has a single "faculty of humanities and social sciences." The department requires a set of core liberal arts classes for each student regardless of school, a program that was enacted in the late 1990s. The core humanities courses in the first year are devoted to language and literature; the second year's, to history and political science in the "making of the modern world." There's generally freedom to pursue humanities electives only in the third and fourth years. Although classes required for one's major are guaranteed, lines for enrollment in choice electives can start in the wee hours of the morning—and you can't use the argument, "I'm paying good money for this course."

All the bachelor's programs in the engineering school and architecture school require a minimum of 24 credit hours in the humanities and social sciences (inclusive of the 12 credits in the core program). Art students must complete 38 liberal arts credits.

A graduate who transferred from Cornell University at the start of the second year says that, especially considering the Western culture and literature humanities material, "the curriculum is far more demanding and comprehensive than the required curriculum at Cornell." He reports reading Plato, Aristotle, and Descartes, along with such works as Erasmus's *In Praise of Folly*, Goethe's *Sorrows of Young Werther*, Milton's *Paradise Lost* and *Paradise Regained*, Martin Luther's *The Freedom of a Christian Man*, and even the *Spiritual Exercises of St. Ignatius Loyola*. The reading of classics and of short stories is said to expand in the second year. Another student reports reading a full array of selections from Enlightenment and modern Western philosophers. A freshman says he has already read the *Odyssey*, the *Aeneid, Medea, Inferno, The Tempest*, and *The Autobiography of Ben Franklin*. It's enough to make you wish that more liberal arts colleges would declare themselves technical schools.

The sophomore year's survey of the roots of geopolitical modernity goes unflinchingly to the sources: students read the actual words of Marx, Lenin, Mussolini, and Hitler. The fall 2003 semester's segment titled "Rise of Fascism and the Holocaust" included not only a reading of Elie Wiesel's *Night* but also a partial viewing and discussion of Leni Riefenstahl's notorious classic, *The Triumph of the Will*. Professor Kaplan's segment, "Fall of Communism," included a review of *The Black Book of Communism: Crimes, Terror, Repression*—another book we wish were required reading at every university.

An ongoing struggle at Cooper is the school's effort to balance a thorough humanities education against students' limited time and the heavy demands of their technical fields of study. The administration seems to be in a process of evaluation regarding just how much students can handle. "I feel that the actual material we study in [humanities classes] . . . is often rushed through," a freshman says. "Sometimes we have seven books to cover for the course and end up spending like two days on one book, or just enough time for us to write an essay on one." But the school struggles mightily to make humanities courses more engaging, to keep the interest of students tempted to complain that they didn't come to Cooper to study the great books. "There has been a lot more of a focus on dialogue and presentation [lately]," a student says. "We are required to do presentation and receive anonymous commentary from fellow classmates."

Distinguished humanities professors include the widely published political writer Fred Siegel. In art history, classicist Mary Stieber is highly respected and popular. Students also recommend historian Peter Buckley's classes in English literature. (The humanities faculty, while excellent, is small and not permitted to specialize.)

Despite the relative seriousness of Cooper regarding the Western heritage material in its core curriculum, as elsewhere, New Left critical theory and ideology does have its sway at the school. Of electives that were offered in spring 2005, the most respectable seemed to be "Shakespeare in Performance," which explores the Bard's work

---

REQUIREMENTS (CONT'D)

On top of their heavy load of science and mathematics courses, architecture students must take:

- "Literary Forms and Expressions" I & II.
- "The Making of Modern Society" I & II.
- 26 credits in general studies, chosen from electives in humanities and social sciences, visual arts, mathematics and sciences, and languages.

In addition to their demanding math and science curriculum, engineering students must take:

- "Studies in Literature" I & II.
- "The Making of the Modern World" I & II.
- 12 credits in general studies selected from art history, foreign language, humanities, or social sciences.

as a "barometer of culture." Even this offering, however, while allowing for an in-depth study of eight plays, introduces "literary-critical concepts" (not to mention new words) such as "authenticity, genre, and performativity . . . and historical-cultural pressures such as nationalism, religion, and gender" into its analyses. The fall 2004 elective "Women and Men: Power and Politics" purveyed typical post-French deconstructionist clichés regarding alleged societal "gender constructs," referred to "classics" within subversive quotation marks, and incorporated "queer theory." A recent elective offering, "Eros in Antiquity," asked students to "seek in both the words and images of the ancients ways to understand the wide variety of their opinions about love," and had them read works by Euripides, Aristophanes, Plato, Virgil, Horace, Propertius, and Ovid in the light of politicized "issues of sexuality."

Student Life: Cooped up

A graduate of Cooper's engineering school says that students here "are known for having very little social life" because of the demanding curriculum, which is designed to give students a master's level of coursework in their field by graduation. This graduate says that most social activities at Cooper "center around the standard nerd celebrations: science fiction, videogaming, study groups, and the like." Students admit that their reputation for eccentricity is not entirely unfair and tend to view it positively as a source of charm; still, any jokes about pocket protectors might make you unpopular. "A lot of the socializing" at Cooper, according to another student, "takes place at exhibitions, events where wine and cheese are provided, and at the very few school-sponsored events. Otherwise most students party in their studios, or somewhere in the school while they are working." The current predominance of hipsters and yuppies in the once-Bohemian neighborhood has made bars and markets a bit pricey. However, for those who can get away from the study carrels, the environs of the school are still almost unparalleled for live music, quirky bookstores, and countless reasonably priced restaurants of every possible variety. Within a 10-minute walk you can find affordable Afghan food, Tibetan clothes, live jazz and blues, herbal medicines, Ukrainian crafts, or Belgian beer served by waiters dressed as Franciscan friars to the tune of Gregorian chant (this at a student hangout called "Burp Castle").

Although Cooper is right in the middle of New York and all its attractions, some students say they hardly notice because of the heavy workload. Some insist that only about a fourth of students have what could be described as a really active social life. On the bright side, this means that drugs are fairly unpopular on campus. It's said that those who do drugs don't last long, and one can hardly imagine how they could, given the rigorous study demands. "I would say that Cooper Union has definitely become more uptight [in terms of trying to be] a dry campus than it was, say, three years ago," says one student. A current freshman comments that Cooper students tend to make a ritual out of consuming large quantities of alcohol in small groups in which the principal topic of conversation is how tough the school can be.

There's no need to soft-pedal the political climate at Cooper; it's a very liberal place. The campus newspaper has featured pieces fiercely denouncing the war in Iraq as a corporate enrichment conspiracy. A fringe left element can sometimes assert itself, but not much more than in most contemporary urban college settings. One graduate remembers some art students standing up in protest in the middle of a commencement speech by then-mayor Rudolf Giuliani. Veteran gay activist Larry Kramer gave a speech in the Great Hall in 2004 to a massive turnout.

At the same time, political stridency of any sort is not really the norm at Cooper: "The political climate on the surface level appears to be unquestionably liberal, though there are no big expressions of this topic generally," an art student says. "Most of the staff appear to be liberal, but our student body is quite diverse. Most political views I've expressed [within the art school] haven't been for one particular side, but rather a commentary on the current events of both. I am a liberal and I have had discussions with right-wing students attending my school." The most conservative students are said to be in the engineering school. No one reported feeling any sense of oppressive political correctness, either among faculty or fellow students.

In the end, everyone at Cooper is so weighed down with the rigor and volume of studies and coursework that to devote one's free time as well to weighty and divisive issues might send one over the edge. There was a Republican club in the late '90s, but it now seems to be inactive. A Democratic club is said to exist but has no Web site or even e-mail contact; no list of current activities for the group could be found. Ethnic cultural groups, in contrast, hold popular events: Kesher-Hillel, the Jewish student association, is quite active, and the South Asia society is also popular, with its Diwali (Indian New Year) celebration and other activities. Surprisingly, there is a large Campus Crusade for Christ organization at Cooper. Beyond this group, the environment is quite secular. However, New York is replete with busy houses of worship. A devout student will find synagogues and Protestant churches of every denomination within walking distance; the nearby New York University is said to have a very active and worthwhile Catholic chaplaincy. A magnificent Ukrainian Catholic cathedral stands right across the street from Cooper's main building, offering reverent services in an exotic tongue.

Dorm housing is apartment-style with three-, four-, and five-person apartments, but these are only guaranteed for freshmen. The administration frequently worries about how to mitigate the stress of transition to second year by making more housing available, but there simply isn't space. Currently almost all sophomores from out of town are cast out to fend for themselves in New York's very pricey and sparse rental market. Student also complain that Cooper's facilities are old and dirty, and they sometimes regret the lack of amenities such as a gym. Nevertheless, there are both intercollegiate and intramural sports, with five intercollegiate men's teams, two women's teams, and 12 intramural coed teams. Cooper's teams are pretty good given the lack of both

---

SUGGESTED CORE

1.–5. and 8. From the Core Curriculum course offerings, Humanities/Social Sciences I, II, and III are recommended.
6. H110, Shakespeare in Performance
7. H360, American Intellectual History

facilities and funding for sports. A dirt-cheap, surprisingly good city gym, Asser Levy, is a long walk or short bus ride away at 14th Street and Avenue D.

Believe it or not, New York City is one of the safest metropolises in the country, and Cooper Union has an impressive campus security record; no crimes of any kind were reported between 2001 and 2003.

The school is an amazing educational bargain to those who can get it. In accordance with the wishes of its founder—a son of the working class who wished to share his self-made wealth—the school offers a free tuition scholarship to anyone admitted. Housing on campus costs between $9,000 and $11,065, while local rents thereafter can be pricey. The school does offer financial aid to help students with that expense.

CORNELL UNIVERSITY

ITHACA, NEW YORK • WWW.CORNELL.EDU

Better than Ezra?

Cornell University is New York's land-grant institution, into which philanthropist Ezra Cornell embedded a liberal arts college. In 1865 Cornell wrote, "I would found an institution where any person can find instruction in any study." Through its size and scope, the university has certainly made itself such a place—where students may receive an Ivy League education at a state university price (as long as they plan to major in one of a narrow range of state-subsidized subjects).

Cornell places heavy emphasis on research; the university stands in the top 15 institutions nationwide in research spending (nearly a half a billion dollars a year), over half of that in federal grants and contracts. Its endowment is around $3 billion, and more than 25 Nobel Prize winners have spent time as students or faculty at this school in remote upstate New York.

Liberal arts and social science students are a distinct minority on campus. Other undergraduates outnumber Arts and Sciences students two to one—and in Arts and Sciences, the hard sciences have pride of place. In addition, three decades of student protest and administrative capitulation have weakened the morale of the university—for instance, inspiring the revulsion of the late Allan Bloom, who left Cornell for the University of Chicago. There he meditated on his Cornell experience—and wrote *The Closing of the American Mind*. Still, with so many good classes, professors, and programs, the university offers the chance for a stellar undergraduate experience, if you look in the right places and keep your head down.

Academic Life: Seven colleges, no waiting

Undergraduate Cornell is divided into seven colleges: the College of Agriculture and Life Sciences; the College of Architecture, Art, and Planning; the College of Engineering; the School of Hotel Administration; the College of Human Ecology; the School of Industrial and Labor Relations; and the College of Arts and Sciences. There are also six graduate and professional schools. In a rare kind of partnership, two of the colleges—Agriculture and Human Ecology—are sponsored by the state of New York. The rest are private colleges whose funds come from Cornell. For our purposes, the College of Arts and Sciences is the most important, though several of the others are well regarded, especially Engineering, Architecture, and Hotel Administration.

The College of Arts and Sciences is home to departments in the humanities, the arts, basic sciences, and social sciences—50 departments in all, serving 4,400 undergraduates (out of some 13,625 undergrads on campus). Here is where one finds the English, psychology, history, and other programs associated with a liberal arts school. What one does not find is something that used to be associated with a liberal arts school: a core curriculum. Students must fulfill a set of distribution requirements, but no courses are required by name—a fact of which the university boasts, while one faculty member calls Cornell's requirements "meaningless and arbitrary."

There is one worthy vestige of the old curricular ideal that students share a base of knowledge: the entire freshman class reads a common book before arriving on campus. The class of 2007, for example, read *Antigone*. They discussed the implications of her actions for our understanding of the state, the family, and religion—in small groups at orientation, in freshman writing seminars, and at other events, including screenings of film adaptations.

The two required freshman writing seminars, with just 15 to 20 students per section, draw the most praise. "There are 500 to choose from, so whatever your interest, you'll find a cool class," says a student. "You will become a better writer by default. You'll be writing papers on a regular basis."

Since the distribution courses and electives (five courses are required outside the student's major, apart from the distribution requirements) can come from any under-

VITAL STATISTICS
Religious affiliation: none
Total enrollment: 19,518
Total undergraduates: 13,625
SAT/ACT midranges: SAT V: 630–730, M: 660–760; ACT: 28–32
Applicants: 20,822
Applicants accepted: 30%
Accepted applicants who enrolled: 50%
Tuition: $30,167
Room and board: $9,883
Freshman retention rate: 96%
Graduation rate: 85% (4 yrs.), 92% (6 yrs.)
Courses with fewer than 20 students: 44%
Student-faculty ratio: 9:1
Courses taught by graduate TAs: not provided
Most popular majors: agriculture, business, engineering
Students living on campus: 42%
Guaranteed housing for four years? yes
Students in fraternities: 27% sororities: 24%

ACADEMIC REQUIREMENTS

In lieu of a core curriculum, the Cornell University College of Arts and Sciences imposes certain (mostly distribution) requirements. Students must pass five courses in the humanities and social sciences, representing at least four different categories, with no more than three in the same department. The categories are:

- Cultural analysis, with classes like "Greek Art and Archaeology" and "Introduction to Feminist, Gender, and Sexuality Studies."
- Historical analysis, with choices including "Introduction to American History" and "Riot and Revolution in Nineteenth-Century Africa."
- Knowledge, cognition, and moral reasoning. Options include "Ancient Philosophy" and "Minds, Machines, and Intelligence."
- Literature and the arts. Many courses will do, including "Shakespeare and Europe" and "Race, Technology, and Visuality."
- Social and behavioral analysis. Choices range from "Civil Liberties in the United States" to "Domestic Television."

graduate college, there are literally a thousand options at a student's disposal. The trick is whether a student can put together a coherent program of study that addresses fundamental intellectual skills and areas of knowledge—much less one that provides a grasp of Western civilization. The university itself has not taken on this responsibility, and given the insularity of its technologists and the trendy leftism of its humanists, that may be just as well.

A fascinating section in the Cornell parents' guide is titled "The Canon—Where Is It?"; the answer is apparently addressed to parents who look at the basic College of Arts and Science curriculum and worry about the same things we do. "When people talk about the canon and decry its loss, they usually assume the existence of a permanently defined body of Western civilization's great literature, philosophy, and history," says the guide, written by an academic dean. "This set of works is thought to have once served, and should still serve, as the base of undergraduate education in the liberal arts and sciences." The canon was, the entry explains, "one of the creations of nineteenth-century Anglo-American classical education for clergymen and the aristocrats who were expected to become public leaders." This statement betrays a breathtaking ignorance of intellectual history. The entry's stunning conclusion is that, "At Cornell, we believe trying to teach some uniform subset of Great Books to all students would be intellectually limiting. We all yearn for some list of books that once studied would render us educated. But that yearning is unrealistic in any rigorous and honest intellectual endeavor." The bankruptcy of this educational philosophy is evidenced by the dean's apparent need to imply that anyone who disagrees with him is either ignorant, careless, or dishonest. His mode of argument would be laughed out of any serious scholarly forum, but Cornell thinks it good enough for students and parents. The academic advising page of the university Web site finally admits that "no subject is considered inherently more intellectually important than others." Perhaps the Hotel Management students would be flattered to hear that their courses in efficient checkout procedures rate as high in Cornell's eyes as their electives in moral philosophy. But we think they will remain skeptical.

On the positive side, Cornell's practice is rather better than its agitprop. There are thousands of solid courses at Cornell and a remarkably small number of frivolous ones. What is more, most of the latter do not fulfill distribution requirements. The school's faculty is top-notch and devoted to teaching. "Many of the faculty are world renowned in their fields, have published the authoritative works in their fields, are heads of international institutions, have done groundbreaking research, and these are the people teaching the intro courses to freshmen," a student says. "The best professors are the ones teaching the freshmen," says another. That may be because many faculty members who teach upper-level courses are more involved in research and publishing than they are in teaching. It is publications, not teaching skills, according to a full professor, that are given almost exclusive consideration in decisions regarding tenure.

It is very rare for a teaching assistant to be the only instructor of a class at Cornell, and students say that the TAs who deliver the occasional lecture and supervise sectional discussions are first-rate. Those sectional meetings can be important in survey courses that enroll up to 500 students. Cornell has one course, Psychology 101, which, according to the school's Web site, is the world's largest lecture at 1,600 students. The instructor in that class, James Maas, told Cornell's *Daily Sun* that the administration has not increased support funds for large classes (including money for equipment and staff) in two decades; he called for greater "support for course coordinators, better teaching facilities, and greater involvement of outstanding TAs."

With an amazing number of course choices, students clearly need guidance. Students select their own faculty academic advisors from their major departments, but, warns one, advisors "can be great or completely ignorant, depending on the person. Do not trust your advisor with your academic career. Seek multiple sources of advice and information. . . . Advising is what you make of it." The university has a Peer Advisor Program that pairs upperclassmen with new students; advice includes "anything from campus resources to social life to dining options," according to the *Daily Sun*. The university also has a strong and well-advertised Career Office for both academic counseling and finding a job after graduation. Students say that some courses can be hard to get in to—such as the infamous and wildly popular wine appreciation course offered by the School of

REQUIREMENTS (CONT'D)

Students must also complete:

- Two first-year writing seminars.
- One foreign language course at the non-introductory level or above, or at least 11 credits in one language (one to three courses).
- One science class chosen from a short list including "Fundamentals of Physics" and "Earthquake!" and one other science course from any school of the university.
- One course in applied mathematics from a list including introductions to econometrics and cryptology.
- A further course in mathematics or science.
- One Arts and Sciences course on an area or a people other than those of the United States, Canada, or Europe.
- One course on an historical period before the twentieth century, such as "Major Works of Goethe" or "Tantric Traditions."
- Four or five elective courses (at least 15 credits) not used to fulfill other requirements and not in the major field.
- A swimming test and two one-credit, nonacademic courses in physical education.

MIDDLE ATLANTIC

Hotel Management. It's infamous not for its subject matter, but because it is the toughest, most frequently failed course at Cornell, according to a student. However, even the most popular courses usually become available at some point in one's undergraduate career; it just takes persistence.

Many departments have outstanding teachers, and most Cornell faculty members are committed to undergraduate instruction and available during office hours. Students we interviewed praised the government and history departments, especially Isaac Kramnick, the Vice Provost for Undergraduate Education, Theodore J. Lowi, Jeremy Rabkin, and Elizabeth Sanders in government; and John Najemy and Richard Polenberg in history. Other notable professors include Gail Fine in philosophy and Patricia Carden in Russian literature, who is also Director of Undergraduate Studies. The hard sciences, especially physics, chemistry, and biology, are the stars of the College of Arts and Sciences, and the School of Agriculture and Life Sciences is very well regarded on campus and nationally. The ethnic studies departments and the feminist, gender, and sexuality studies department are notoriously weak. Even the economics department has allowed politics to get in the way of substance, as has anthropology, students report.

Cornell has some highly politicized departments, including Africana studies and feminist, gender, and sexuality studies, the latter of which "seeks to deepen our understanding of how gender and sexuality are ubiquitously intertwined with structures of power and inequality," according to its Web page. That program changed its name from "Women's Studies" in 2002; the old name "quickly became controversial [after the department's founding in 1972], not only because it suggested that the objects of study, as well as those undertaking the studies, were exclusively women, but also because it did nothing to discourage the common assumption that the women in question were white, middle-class, and heterosexual." Heaven forfend.

One worthy initiative at Cornell we can't resist mentioning: the Small Farms Program, designed to help New York state family farmers stay in business. It publishes a journal, the *Small Farms Quarterly,* which should interest agrarian-minded students.

Grade inflation at Cornell appears to be no worse than at any other college; the university states that the average undergraduate grade is between a B and a B-plus. "Cornell does not inflate grades," one student says. "Cornell fails students every semester. . . . If you get an A at Cornell, you had to work for it, no matter what the course."

Student Life: Sailing in Ithaca

The winter weather is lousy—let's admit that up front. But students and visitors alike speak highly of the natural beauty of Ithaca, New York, and surrounding Tompkins County. The Finger Lakes area is full of parks, waterfalls, and woods, while "Ithaca itself is a thriving small city with great opportunities, nightlife, and restaurants," a student says. "You name it, it's available." A university Web page claims the county has more restaurants per capita than any other in the United States.

The Cornell campus features a mix of traditional buildings, such as the McGraw

Tower with the Cornell Chimes, and modern ones, including an art museum designed by I. M. Pei and a spectacular Center for the Theatre Arts. You can see Cayuga Lake from various parts of the campus, and waterfalls border the grounds. A 3,600-acre preserve and botanical garden, Cornell Plantations, is part of the university campus.

At a university the size of Cornell, students can find plenty to fill up time outside the classroom. Students and their primary interests run the gamut, as one would expect. "You can't label the students," one says. "I knew brains, stoners, athletes, artists, well-rounded and balanced students, drug addicts, alcoholics—they were all in the mix. On the whole, however, most students practiced the 'work hard, play hard' motto at Cornell. During the week, they studied, and then on the weekend they partied."

With about 500 student groups, Cornell students have no room to complain. The university has a number of liberal political groups and a handful of conservative ones, "large in membership and very vocal and mobilized," according to a student. The left has the hysterical stridency of an embattled minority—though it is generally supported by the administration—while the conservative majority is sullen and silent, apart from the *Cornell Review,* a vigorous neoconservative newspaper.

Other organizations skew to social or cultural themes; more than a dozen chaplaincies on campus support different religious persuasions. A good way to experience the natural surroundings of the college is through Cornell Outdoor Education, a group that sponsors backpacking and kayaking trips and maintains "the largest indoor natural rock climbing wall in North America," according to its Web page. With 25 percent of the student body pledged, the Greek system is "the center of the social scene on campus," says the *Daily Sun.* But according to a student, "There is a huge underground drug culture that pervades the Greek system."

Cornell regularly attracts big-name speakers to campus—and we do mean big. The 2003–4 school year brought Bill Clinton, physicist/theologian Rev. John Polkinghorne, former Rep. Jim Hightower, former French leader Lionel Jospin, John Updike, former Rep. Cynthia McKinney, former attorney general Janet Reno, Bill Cosby, author Jamaica Kincaid, and alumnus Bill Nye (TV's "Science Guy"), among others. The university also has a number of student publications. Best known is the *Daily Sun,* whose staff has included E. B. White, Dick Schaap, Kurt Vonnegut Jr., and Frank Gannett. The *Sun* became the first collegiate member of the Associated Press in 1912. The university also has a slew of departmental publications and literary magazines.

Undergraduates choose their housing from dormitories, program houses, cooperative programs, and fraternities and sororities. Most "freshmen stay in North Campus [housing], which has brand-new dorms and the best food in the nation," a student

---

SUGGESTED CORE

1. Classics 222, Ancient Fiction
2. Philosophy 211, Ancient Philosophy
3. Religious Studies 223, Introduction to the Bible
4. Religious Studies 295, Introduction to Christianity
5. Government 362, Modern Political Philosophy
6. English 227, Shakespeare
7. History 153, Introduction to American History
8. History 363, European Cultural History, 1870–1945 *or* Comparative Literature 425, Marx, Nietzsche, Freud

says. Freshmen can still choose program houses, so long as they are on North Campus. Ethnic options include the black activist Ujaama House; other less politicized houses include the Risley Residential College for the Creative and Performing Arts, a lovely old building with its own small stage, gallery, rehearsal space, art studios, and a darkroom and video editing facility. Residence halls are usually coed, but the university has a few single-sex dorms, even for those not in fraternities. There are no coed bathrooms or dorm rooms in the residence halls, but neither do they have restricted visiting hours. "We're not a Christian school and this isn't the 1950s," one student sniffs. "General rules of respect and order are enforced by the [resident advisor], but it depends on the RA. Some might not care about drinking or drugs in the dorm, some might."

Orientation at Cornell is just that: a week of orientation on where things are, how to get there, and what to do. "It's a fun week and a great way to start college," a student says. The student body is a mixture of different types, but "the majority are rich white kids from Long Island and New York and the rest of the Northeast. . . . Most people are very competitive, ambitious, driven, and have connections from their parents. Most are well off and many went to private school before Cornell," says a student. University statistics show that about two in five come from the state of New York and that 8 percent are international students.

Cornell's athletes compete on 36 sports teams—18 for men, 18 for women—at the NCAA Division I level under the name "Big Red." Students who are not varsity material can still play sports through the largest intramural program in the Ivy League.

Campus police periodically man DWI checkpoints, but the University Police Department's Web page announces their locations and hours a few days ahead. The department says it considers the checkpoints to be as much about education as enforcement. "Unfortunately, we are still experiencing alcohol-related problems, particularly on weekends and after large sporting events," a department spokesman told the *Daily Sun.*

Speaking of alcohol, Cornell made some minor changes a couple years ago to its rules for Slope Day, a massive party held on a campus hill called Libe Slope on the last day of classes. The drinking and partying lasts from 8 a.m. to 6 p.m., at the Slope at least, and one student claims it is the biggest college party on the East Coast. It originally began in the 1970s as "the Great Feast," a huge spread prepared by the college dining service and available to all. The drinking came shortly thereafter. In 2002, however, the university banned hard liquor and allowed students of drinking age to bring no more than a six-pack of beer or hard lemonade with them. Of course, the area isn't completely fenced off, so we suspect more gets in than that. In fact, they should probably change the name to "Libation" Slope.

Those who live at Cornell consider the campus typically safe. However, there seems to have been a crime wave in 2003 (the most recent year reported). The school saw 10 forcible sexual assaults, two robberies, 16 aggravated assaults, 68 burglaries, one stolen car, and one arson on campus.

Cornell's tuition system is unique. For a narrow range of students—those hailing from New York State who wish to study in the colleges of Agriculture and Life Sciences,

Human Ecology, or Industrial and Labor Relations—tuition is only $16,037 per year. Out-of-state students who want to study those subjects pay $28,567. For those at other Cornell colleges—for instance, Arts and Sciences—tuition is a more typical $30,167. Room and board runs $9,883 for everyone. Admission is need-blind, and the school promises to meet the full need of admitted students; it provides need-based aid to some 70 percent of enrollees.

Georgetown University

Ignatius wept

Georgetown tour guides will be quick to tell you that the university has been tolerant and welcoming of opposing views since its founding in 1789. Fr. John Carroll, a Jesuit and the first head of the Roman Catholic Church in America, wanted his academy to be "the mainsheet anchor" of Catholics in the new country. But Georgetown has long since abandoned its post as the "anchor" of U.S. Catholicism, becoming more like a kite tossed about by the winds of elite opinion. Many Catholic colleges have abandoned their religious missions in pursuit of mainstream respectability—as if the church that founded the Sorbonne, Oxford, and Salamanca had been exposed as a shameful, obscurantist sect. But this movement has been led by Jesuit universities since that highly centralized order was captured by religious modernists during the 1960s. Novelist Walker Percy once felt constrained to write an open letter to Pope John Paul II, straining for arguments as to why the order should not simply be suppressed. (Not everyone was convinced.)

Georgetown, an elite university that huddles close to the centers of secular power in the nation's capital, embodies much of what has changed in Catholic education since Vatican II. Except for a handful of traditionally minded faculty members, Georgetown tries hard to evade its Catholic identity. Leftists at the university don't just dissent from doctrine; now they openly attack it. Cardinal Francis Arinze—the highest-ranking African prelate in the church, long considered *papabile*—gave a commencement address in 2003 in which he chose to reiterate the church's teaching on sexual ethics, condemning the "anti-life mentality" displayed "in contraception, abortion, infanticide and euthanasia . . . pornography . . . fornication and adultery, homosexuality . . . irregular unions, [and] divorce."

MIDDLE ATLANTIC

249

According to the *Atlanta Journal-Constitution,* the cardinal's boilerplate Catholic message prompted a theology professor and other faculty and students to leave the stage in protest. Within a week, about 70 faculty members had signed a letter to the dean of the school criticizing the cardinal's "highly inappropriate" remarks. The dean then sent an e-mail to all students of the college in which she "apologized for any offense and offered counseling sessions to those who suffered psychological trauma as a result of the speech," one insider reported. President John J. DeGioia, named Georgetown's first lay president in 2001, refused to defend the cardinal, issuing statements reaffirming Georgetown's commitment to students of all sexual orientations. Ironically, Dr. David Satcher, President Clinton's surgeon general and a supporter of legal partial-birth abortion, addressed School of Nursing and Health Studies graduates a year later—encountering no protests. That about sums up Georgetown. Still, for highly ambitious students with no particular interest in orthodox Catholicism and eager to attend a prestigious college near the Beltway, this school just might fit the bill.

Academic Life: Doctrine is an option

Georgetown University encompasses four undergraduate schools that enroll roughly 6,300 students—Georgetown College, the McDonough School of Business, the Walsh School of Foreign Service, and the School of Nursing and Health Studies—plus graduate programs and the law and medical schools. Georgetown College, enrolling half of the undergraduates, offers more than 30 majors and 40 minors, including the core liberal arts areas: fine arts, humanities, sciences, mathematics, and languages.

Georgetown's curriculum is certainly more carefully arranged than are most schools'. "One of the things that I found—both as an undergraduate student and as a professor—is that the existence of the core requirements creates a common base for intellectual and moral discourse," a professor says. Perhaps, but students can fulfill the literature requirement by taking nearly any writing-intensive course in the English department or a course in literature in translation from the foreign language departments. Thus, courses like "The Latina Novel," "Avant Garde Film," and "East Asia: Texts and Contexts" all satisfy the requirement, as do several medieval or Renaissance courses and "British Enlightenment."

The history requirement is a sequence of two semester-long courses, chosen from "European Civilization I and II," "History of the Atlantic World," "History of the Pacific World," and "World History I and II." There are also several regional history survey courses, including ones in Middle Eastern civilization and the history of China. The social sciences requirement can be fulfilled with courses as diverse as "Principles of Microeconomics," "Sport and Society," and "Globalization and Social Change." Students complete the philosophy requirement by taking an introductory philosophy course and an ethics course (like "Ethics and Bioethics," "The Right and the Good," or "Introduction to Catholic Ethics"). Be aware that one of the ethics teachers at Georgetown, Thomas Beauchamp, is an advocate of physician-assisted suicide and a member of the board of directors of the Compassion in Dying Federation.

The theology requirement need not be satisfied by taking a course in Catholic doctrine, although that is an option. One of the courses must be either "The Problem of God," which examines faith and atheism, or "Introduction to Biblical Literature," a course that explores the parts of the Bible, historical periods, and literary expression.

One professor boasts that "Georgetown does not impose a philosophy on any student. Ultimately, he will have to choose what he believes. But what Georgetown does require is that students grapple with . . . fundamental philosophical and theological issues during their time here." That judgment is questioned, or at least qualified, by others. "You can spend your four years here without really feeling the Catholic nature of the school," says one student.

While it is true that Georgetown provides a vast number of solid courses, an important exception would be those listed in the women's studies department, where students can drown themselves in feminist politics and theory. Courses in the department include "Women in American History: Movement Rebels," "Athletics and Gender," and "Questioning Inequalities: Gender, Race, Class, and Sexuality."

There are a number of other departments, luckily, that are more balanced. Georgetown's best-known, and just plain best, department may be government, which makes room for conservative ideas in large part thanks to the teaching and scholarship of professors George Carey and Fr. James Schall, S.J. However, one graduate student says, "[The conservative climate] is rapidly changing; when Schall and Carey retire, I hear rumors that their positions will be combined into one theory professorship that will probably not be filled by a conservative of their character." All government majors must take introductory courses in international relations, United States political systems, political theory, and comparative politics. They can also take advantage of the dozens of government and public policy departments just a Metro ride away. Many students undertake part-time internships at the think tanks and federal agencies that proliferate in D.C., laying the groundwork for careers in government.

Philosophy is another of the better academic departments at Georgetown; indeed, it is one of the better departments in the country. Every philosophy major must take "History of Ancient and Medieval Philosophy," "History of Modern Philosophy," a seminar that studies a philosophy text closely, and a course in logic. Almost all of the department's offerings are excellent. Georgetown is also especially strong in foreign languages—the university offers study in the classics, Chinese, Japanese, Korean, Greek,

VITAL STATISTICS
Religious affiliation: Roman Catholic
Total enrollment: 10,319
Total undergraduates: 6,282
SAT/ACT midranges: SAT: 1280–1470; ACT: 27–32
Applicants: 15,420
Applicants accepted: 22%
Accepted applicants who enrolled: 47%
Tuition: $29,808
Room and board: $9,642
Freshman retention rate: 97%
Graduation rate: 89% (4 yrs.), 93% (6 yrs.)
Average class size: not reported
Student-faculty ratio: 11:1
Courses taught by graduate TAs: none
Most popular majors: finance, business, English
Students living on campus: 78%
Guaranteed housing for four years? no
Students in fraternities or sororities: none

Hebrew, Turkish, French, German, Italian, Portuguese, Polish, Russian, Ukrainian, and Spanish. Study-abroad programs are popular; more than half the student body studies internationally at some point. Georgetown College is the university's largest college, but the School of Foreign Service is perhaps the most renowned, in part because of its famous alumni, which include former president Bill Clinton, who makes frequent visits to the campus.

Many Georgetown students use college as a stepping stone to graduate or professional school or to a job on Capitol Hill, but they are not entirely on the make. "The students are extremely intellectually curious," a government professor says. "It is not unusual to spend hours talking with students about a variety of issues. I almost always have a large group during office hours." Students say they often visit professors during office hours. "I'd say I know about 85 percent of my professors personally," says a senior.

The best professors, says one student, are the Jesuits. "When you have a Jesuit for a professor, everybody says you lucked out. They are the most committed teachers at the university." Excellent Georgetown professors include Anthony Arend, Michael Bailey, George Carey, Patrick Deneen, Herbert Howe, Robert Lieber, Joshua Mitchell, James Schall, S.J., and W. Clyde Wilcox in government; Paul F. Betz, Joan M. Holmer, Alvaro F. V. Ribeiro, S.J., and Jeffrey Shulman in English; Wayne Davis, Alfonso Gomez-Lobo, and Wilfried Ver Eecke in philosophy; Marius Schwartz and George J. Viksnins in economics; Marcus Maloof and T. Clay Shields in computer science; and Stephen M. Fields, S.J., John Pilch, and Thomas King, S.J., in theology.

The advising program pairs each student with a faculty advisor and a peer advisor once the student declares a major; before the student has chosen a major, he is assigned to a faculty member in the university at large. Courses are taught by faculty members, not graduate students, with the exception of once-a-week discussion sections attached to large introductory lecture courses. Class sizes can vary from a couple hundred students in "Introduction to Biology" to just five or six students in upper-level courses. Language classes are capped at 12 students; English classes are limited to around 18 students.

Student Life: Getting off your Foggy Bottom

Situated on a hill overlooking the rest of Washington, D.C., Georgetown's main campus (approximately 100 acres) boasts one of the most impressive college settings in the country. Its neo-Gothic buildings tower over students, as if to force them to recognize the magnitude of the school and its influence. From the steps of the oldest building on campus, Old North Hall, 13 U.S. presidents have spoken. In 2003, the Southwest Quadrangle was completed—a one-million-square-foot complex on the main campus accommodating residence halls, a dining facility, a Jesuit residence, and underground parking. Slated for completion in 2005 is the Royden B. Davis, S.J., Performing Arts Center, which will bring a 300-seat theater, studio spaces, classrooms, and faculty offices. Long-term plans for a new business school, science building, and multi-sports facility are on the table. Georgetown just finished a Third Century Campaign started in 1998 that raised $1.16 billion, but these funds did not significantly boost the size of the school's endowment. According to a report in the *Chronicle of Higher Education*, Georgetown's debt is approaching $700 million and its $650 million endowment is "substantially below peers." The school is expected to have operating losses exceeding $20 million in 2004. President DeGioia told alumni at a reunion in June 2004 "the most significant [challenges] we face are financial."

How much advantage one takes of the school's location in Washington, D.C., depends on the student. "I'm sure some people spend all four years right here [on campus] . . . but there is so much to do in Washington that it seems a waste not to use it," says a student. The museums on the National Mall are popular especially for those new to the city, and the Dupont Circle and Adams Morgan areas offer nightlife. In the tony Georgetown neighborhood, students can visit dozens of shops, bars, and restaurants. There is no Metro stop in Georgetown (it is said that the wealthy residents wanted it that way to keep out the riff-raff), but the university provides a free shuttle bus to the Rosslyn stop, which is just across the Key Bridge on the other side of the Potomac, in Virginia.

About 78 percent of students live on campus each year, and although the university doesn't guarantee housing for all four years, there is no shortage of space. Housing is one of Georgetown's best attributes, students say. After living in traditional dormitories as freshmen, most students move into suites, apartments, or townhouses on campus. All residence halls are coed, although there are two all-female floors that students can specially request. Special-interest housing includes substance-free floors, Hindu or Muslim interest communities, and a Justice in Action Living-Learning community. Georgetown is a very compact campus; no dorm requires much of a hike to class. Gaining the "freshman 15" is encouraged through an all-you-can-eat meal plan—but upperclassmen, especially those with private kitchens, eat less (and pay less). For roughly 30 years Georgetown students have run the largest student business in the country, the Corp, a business which oversees a grocery store, cafes, a one-hour photo store, and other services. Every position, from cashier to manager to accountant, is staffed by a student. An on-campus bank is also student-run.

ACADEMIC REQUIREMENTS

For Georgetown College, the university's liberal arts division, students must complete the following mandates in addition to the requirements for their majors:

- Two courses in philosophy, including either general philosophy or ethics.
- Theology—either the introductory "Problem of God" course or "Introduction to Biblical Literature," plus one elective.
- Two literature and writing courses. Nearly any writing-intensive course in English literature or writing in translation suffices.
- History. Students take one sequence of two semester-long courses, chosen from "European Civilization I and II," "History of the Atlantic World," "History of the Pacific World," "World History I and II," and several regional history surveys.
- Two math/science courses.
- Two social science courses.
  Each student must also reach the intermediate level in a foreign language.

Georgetown's location in the nation's capital generally attracts politically aware students. But while protests and demonstrations occur on campus frequently, hot issues are more often discussed in lecture halls, the editorial pages of student newspapers, and debating societies. "At GU, we settle our political scores through op-eds in the campus newspapers or tastefully done protests, and then we all go have a beer afterwards," says a recent graduate. Student news publications include the twice-weekly *Georgetown Hoya* and the biweekly *Georgetown Independent*. The *Georgetown Voice* is a liberal weekly newsmagazine. The *Georgetown Academy*, a publication run by conservative students, has recently become defunct. Prominent on campus is the Philodemic Debate Society; a recent debate was titled "Resolved: That the birth of Christ is the most important event in Western history." The Georgetown International Relations Association participates in and hosts model UN events for high school and college-aged students. The College Republicans and the College Democrats are the most active political groups on the hilltop, often sponsoring national politicians' visits to campus. "Georgetown has a very open environment," says a government professor. "We have frank and engaging exchanges from all sides of the political, ideological, and religious spectrum. I believe that individuals feel comfortable sharing their views."

For the most part, Georgetown students are an energetic lot. On campus alone there are countless activities. Georgetown has more than 100 student groups, including Groove Theory (a hip-hop dance group), GU Knights of Columbus, GUTV, the Native American Student Association, GU Right to Life, and several academic honor societies. Georgetown is strong in the arts, not particularly in its academic departments, but in extracurricular groups like the Mask & Bauble, which is the oldest continually operating student theatrical society in the country. The Georgetown Orchestra, Jazz Band, and several other groups are also good. Although the university has no fraternities or sororities, Georgetown students have no trouble finding, or staging, parties. The Georgetown University Program Board sponsors movies, concerts, comedy shows, and other events each weekend. Georgetown brings dozens of speakers to campus each year, including, most recently, George Tenet, José Maria Aznar, former secretary of state Colin Powell, and James D. Wolfensohn.

Approximately half of Georgetown students say they're Catholic, but students say the school's Catholic identity is of the cafeteria variety. If you seek it, says one student, it is possible to "find a very supportive environment for developing your spiritual life." On the main campus Catholic students can attend daily and Sunday masses at Dahlgren Chapel of the Sacred Heart and St. Williams Chapel—though more traditional students might do well to take the Metro to Chinatown to hear the mass in Latin at Old St. Mary's, a church frequented by Pat Buchanan and Justice Antonin Scalia. Georgetown attends to the religious needs of non-Catholics as well. On staff are Jewish, Muslim, and Protestant chaplains. The Campus Ministry department also sponsors retreats, study groups, and faith-based student organizations.

Still and all, Georgetown is clearly worried by complaints that the school is not particularly . . . Catholic. In response to student-initiated movements and vocal alumni, a variety of crucifixes have been installed in classrooms where they were missing over the years, and the distribution of condoms by Peer Education has been discontinued. In a document titled "Georgetown's Catholic and Jesuit Identity," the university lists several ways in which it "expresses and affirms its Catholic identity." It mentions that it employs prominent Catholic scholars and contributes to the Catholic intellectual tradition, that many of its students say they are Catholic, that there are Jesuits teaching on campus, and so on. There is no mention, anywhere, of how the school attempts to imbue its students with anything more than "the spirit" of Catholicism, or how it attempts to uphold Catholic moral teaching on campus.

But technically, Georgetown *is* a Catholic institution and adheres—usually begrudgingly—to at least some of the church's teachings. A hopeful new initiative by faculty members is participation in a pregnancy outreach program in conjunction with the pro-life Northwest Pregnancy Center. However, no prospective student or parent should expect the school's religious identity to shape much of the atmosphere at the school. Even though one self-described feminist student says that "compared to other Catholic schools, we're one of the most progressive, but compared to secular universities, we still have a long way to go," the camel sticks its nose further and further into the tent each year. When Georgetown is forced to put its foot down in matters dictated by the Roman Catholic Church, dissenters always find ways of getting around the issue. For instance, a Women's Center staff member, who acknowledges that the center has serious issues with Catholic views, says, "Georgetown's status as a Catholic university does present a few problems, especially practically speaking." She continues, "We'd be kicked off campus if we suggested abortion to a student. But thankfully, we can send students to other resources like Planned Parenthood, where at least they can get both sides of the issues." Thus runs the Georgetown way of the cross.

Homosexual acts are condemned by the Catholic Church, but the administration works to destigmatize the sexual activities of lesbian, gay, bisexual, and transgender people at Georgetown. "Safe Zones" were officially established where LGBT people could find acceptance and "come out" in campus offices and dorms. GU Pride is an officially recognized student group that "provides educational and support services to the [LGBT] communities" and offers "support and referral services to those exploring their sexual orientation and/or gender identity," according to its Web site. The group's activities include an annual "drag race," films on gay issues, socials, barbecues, and lectures. In 2003, the administration established a coordinator of LGTB, the first such position at a Catholic institution. The interim coordinator told the *Hoya* that he felt that National Coming Out Week and related events worked effectively to "normalize" the status of sexual dissenters at Georgetown. The article stated that it is the goal of the coordinator to make gay issues more of a routine aspect of life at Georgetown partly by working to bring more speakers to campus and hosting more visible events. GU Pride has been pushing for a special LGBT resource center for several years. It is not clear if the university will continue to deny this request.

MIDDLE ATLANTIC

The Georgetown Hoyas participate in the NCAA Division I and are members of the Big East Conference. Intercollegiate men's and women's sports include basketball, track and field, lacrosse, cross country, crew, golf, sailing, soccer, tennis, and swimming. In addition, women participate in volleyball and field hockey and men compete in football and baseball. Following a few uninspired men's basketball seasons, a new head coach has been appointed—John Thompson III, son of the legendary Georgetown coach John Thompson Jr. On some Hoyas' wish lists is a new basketball arena. "Our men's team has to play at MCI Arena, which is hard to get to and which we can never fill," says a recent graduate. Other facilities include Kehoe Field, an all-weather playing surface located on the roof of the underground Yates Fitness Center. Yates provides fitness equipment and a full range of intramural and instructional activities.

Although Georgetown's relative inaccessibility is sometimes a nuisance, it does separate the university from the rest of the city—and from Washington's frightening crime rate. During 2003, Georgetown reported 16 forcible sex offenses, five stolen cars, and 26 burglaries. The Saferide escort service takes students anywhere on campus late at night and to various off-campus locations, and a shuttle van service is provided by a fraternity. Emergency phones stand everywhere on campus.

Georgetown maintains an elite reputation and charges a commensurate price, with tuition at $29,808, and room and board at $9,642. The school practices need-blind admissions and guarantees to meet a student's complete financial need. Some 55 percent of students receive some form or scholarship or need-based aid.

GROVE CITY COLLEGE

GROVE CITY, PENNSYLVANIA • WWW.GCC.EDU

Right thinking

"We must first have faith in God before we can enjoy the blessings of liberty, for God is the author of liberty." Perhaps these words spoken by past board chairman J. Howard Pew best describe the mission of Grove City College. Grove City usually finds itself grouped with Hillsdale College as a "conservative" school, in large part because each forbids its students to accept federal funds and loans—and the onerous micromanagement which comes with them.

Founded in 1876, Grove City College is historically associated and still loosely affiliated with the Presbyterian Church (USA). The college's mission statement says that the school is "committed to Christian principles" and that it "seeks to provide liberal and professional education of the highest quality that is within the reach of families with modest means who desire a college that will strengthen their children's spiritual and moral character."

Grove City seems to be living up to this mission, which raises the question: Is it also providing a free environment for liberal education—or mirroring leftist schools by subordinating intellectual inquiry and education to dogma? Happily, few at Grove City make such a complaint. As a student says, the school "is rigorous academically and intellectually, and not engaged in indoctrination." Some 92 percent of freshmen return for the sophomore year. By its sheer existence, Grove City College provides real diversity within the blandly homogeneous landscape of American higher education—and a window into the worldview that gave this country birth.

Academic Life: A continuing heritage

The direction and character of Grove City have much to do with the legacy of two famous Pews—Joseph Newton and J. Howard—whose combined service as presidents of the college's board of trustees totaled 75 years, between 1895 and 1971. J. Howard—Joseph's son—was himself an alumnus of the college, completing his degree at the age of

Grove City's core curriculum, unlike most, is worthy of the name. Students face slightly different requirements, depending on whether they enroll in the Arts and Letters or the Science and Engineering school. But all students take the Humanities Core, which consists of the following courses:

- "Civilization," which examines "foundational questions, worldviews, major movements, and decisive developments in the history of civilization."
- "Civilization and the Biblical Revelation," a study of "Christian revelation and how it influenced the course of Western civilization." (Students can replace this class with two semesters of Christian history.)
- "Civilization and the Speculative Mind," a course in philosophy and apologetics that studies modern, secular worldviews as well.
- "Civilization and Literature," a survey course of major literary works from two millennia, focused on "the nature of God and humanity . . . good and evil, the meaning of moral choice, the purpose of life,

18. Both Pews also served as presidents of the Sun Oil Company.

In 2003, John H. Moore retired after seven years as president of Grove City. The new president is Richard Jewell, a Pittsburgh lawyer and businessman and a 1967 Grove City graduate. (No, not the Richard Jewell falsely charged with blowing up the Centennial Olympic Park in Atlanta—just in case you were wondering.) Jewell also holds faculty rank as a professor of business law and public policy.

Grove City has two schools: Arts and Letters, and Science and Engineering. Most students at Grove City major in the liberal arts and sciences (especially education), but the engineering, business administration, and preprofessional programs are also popular. No matter which of the colleges a student chooses, he will face a serious core curriculum that guarantees him an approximation of an old-fashioned liberal education (without, perhaps, a fluency in Latin and Greek).

Like everything at Grove City, the core courses are quite consciously designed to "emphasize America's religious, political, and economic heritage of individual freedom and responsibility and their part in the development of Western civilization," even while they also "examine many different points of view and consider other nations and cultures." The core "is a recognition that some prescription on the part of the university is needed," says a professor. "One needs to be an educated person by coming in close contact with some of the best that has been thought and written." Teachers differ as to the effectiveness of the core; some suggest that it prevents professors from teaching in their major fields. "All faculty in history, political science, and religion must also teach in the humanities core, which means that they do not have adequate time to teach courses in their major fields, shortchanging students in their respective majors," one says. Another weakness, says a teacher, is the absence of a required writing course; however, students who write poorly may be required to take such a class on the recommendation of a professor.

With a couple of exceptions, the various sections of the civilization courses cover pretty much the same material. Unfortunately, these core courses are not really great books courses, since most of them use readers that include fairly short snippets from primary sources. Thus, there is no sustained, in-depth confrontation of fundamental texts (the Bible excepted), but rather a survey of canonical thinkers. One exception is "Civilization and Literature," in which students read, for example, *Hamlet* and "a good chunk of Dante," according to a professor.

The course descriptions at Grove City are refreshingly and uniformly sane. And at this intensely Christian school there are courses one would find almost nowhere else, including "C. S. Lewis: Christian Apologist," where the "primary subject of study is Lewis's unique contributions to apologetics, including his epistemology, view of myth, and defense of supernaturalism. Various examples of Lewis's writings are examined from selected essays and theological articles and the space trilogy."

Highly competitive majors—to which students must apply when they enter the school—are biology, engineering, and education. Yes, *education*: At Grove City, this is one of the most serious disciplines, requiring students who would teach high school or above to double major, studying also the field they intend to teach. Other strong departments include English, economics, and business. The old religion major has been renamed Christian thought, and it offers courses on both Protestant and Catholic theologians. There are many excellent faculty throughout the school; a partial list includes James G. Dixon III and Eric Potter in English and communication; Michael Coulter, Marvin J. Folkertsma Jr., and Paul G. Kengor in political science; Gillis Harp in history; Timothy C. Homan in chemistry; Gary S. Smith in history; Linda Christie, John A. Sparks, and Andrew Markley in business; Jeffrey M. Herbener in economics; Roger Mackey and John Stephens in education; and T. David Gordon, Paul Kemeny, and Paul R. Schaefer in Christian thought. Some students may be interested in Grove City's new entrepreneurship major, offered by the business department. Indeed, there are many business-oriented majors—and as a bonus to budding economists, Grove City hosts one of the major archives of Ludwig von Mises' papers. (The other is at Auburn's Mises Institute.) The famous Walter Williams (who serves on Grove City's board) often guest lectures.

However, there are some glaring lacunae in the liberal arts. Nowhere to be found are majors in classics, art history, or in any foreign language other than Spanish and French. A few courses are offered in German and New Testament Greek, but none in

REQUIREMENTS (CONT'D)

and the meaning of salvation."
- "Civilization and the Arts," a music and visual arts survey focused on religious themes.
- "Modern Civilization in International Perspective," a class that examines modern political philosophy and movements "since the American and French revolutions."

Students must also complete distribution and other requirements. All choices offered seem sane and serious:
- Two courses in social sciences/international studies.
- Two courses in quantitative/logical reasoning.
- Two courses (with labs) in natural sciences. One unique option here is "Medical Missions," which "involves clinical experience supervised by a faculty member and assisted by medical staff at a medically underserved domestic or foreign location."
- Four semesters of foreign language study. (Students may test out of these, and BS science students are exempt).
- Two semesters of twice-weekly physical education classes (segregated by sex).

MIDDLE ATLANTIC

259

Latin. Some students complain that with the loss of an important professor last year, "the political science department is weak."

"There is no secret," says one (perhaps overworked) professor, as to how Grove City can afford to charge such low tuition: Every professor, even department chairs, teaches four courses per term. (There are no graduate teaching assistants.) The student-faculty ratio is fairly high at 16 to 1, and thus each professor teaches an inordinately large number of students each semester—often 150 or more. Furthermore, one insider notes, the student-faculty ratios vary widely among departments— "from 18 to 1 in education, to 40 to 1 in others, such as political science and religion."

The board of trustees only recently approved a sabbatical program—to the cheers of the faculty—but there are no plans to lighten the workload. This means that teachers can do little research or publishing. "GCC likes it when faculty engage in research, provided that the research does not interfere with teaching responsibilities. Teaching is clearly paramount," says a professor. "There is some support for research, but it is limited to the use of a student assistant a few hours each week and financial support for attending conferences. There are no research grants provided by the institution." Another says, "It is very difficult to expect much in the way of scholarship." One Grove City veteran considers this a major drawback, asking: "Should not a reputable teacher also write? . . . Why should a faculty member write a doctoral dissertation and then never publish anything during the rest of his career? Frankly the 'teaching college' influence at GCC seriously inhibits faculty from becoming nationally known, precludes graduates from getting references from nationally known faculty, and reduces the 'cutting-edge' potential of GCC's classrooms. An outstanding professor should run on all cylinders—teaching, advising, and scholarship."

However, Grove City faculty do raise their voices in the public square. The college started The Center for Vision and Values in 2004 "to develop research and commentary to be used in the classroom and in the media to address major policy and social issues. In 2004, faculty-authored opinion editorials appeared in more than 180 newspapers in 41 states, including the *New York Times,* the *Washington Times* and the *San Francisco Chronicle.* Faculty did more than 60 radio and 30 television interviews, according to a teacher. In other words, expect more op-eds than monographs.

Publishing isn't needed for tenure; in fact, tenure does not exist. Every employee is hired on a year-to-year contract. This doesn't create a high turnover, however. "The college has a very low attrition rate among the faculty," says one professor. "We don't dismiss someone for transient reasons. If I ceased to teach they would first try to rehabilitate me, but they wouldn't put up with me indefinitely. There is a great deal of trust here. You don't worry about it if you do a good job." Another professor reports that one of the primary consequences of the lack of tenure is that faculty members tend to avoid voicing strong criticisms of administration policy. "There is very little faculty participation in institutional governance," he says. A different faculty member warns that the heavy workload is in fact causing faculty attrition—noting that three highly regarded professors chose to leave last year: "How can a faculty member teach 150 to 250 students in four classes during a semester, as some do, and devote adequate time to advising large numbers of majors and also do scholarly writing?" The professor said that some colleagues teach four different subjects each semester, imposing a crushing load of class preparation.

Somehow, professors make time to become involved in the life of the college. "Faculty here are really, truly interested in their students," says one professor, who claims that faculty often advise students about jobs and like to see their old students at homecoming. Most professors live within 20 minutes of campus, which makes it all the easier for them to pop in on football games and the like. On a formal level, each student is assigned a faculty advisor. "Some faculty members are more assiduous" about advising than others, says a professor. Students have to meet with their advisors before they can schedule their classes, but beyond that the extent of the relationship is up to the student.

One professor boasts that the school has "no politicized departments whatsoever." Teachers are recruited not only for their academic and pedagogical abilities, but for the way in which their teaching and personal philosophies fit with the stated purpose of the school. "There are no pockets of opposition," says another professor. "There are many fine faculty out there with good PhDs. We let them know we're committed to Christian values and we check their references. We don't get bamboozled." Another professor agrees: "Because we have a clear statement of purpose and a mission, we attract like-minded people and we're able to concentrate on the intellectual development of our students. People who come here to teach can actually do what they're most interested in."

Finding people who match the college's requirements and philosophy, however, is getting more difficult, says another faculty member. "It's especially difficult in literature and theology.... We say right up front that we're evangelical and are committed to personal and economic liberty." Another suggests that Grove City has "a bias in favor of hiring—where possible—faculty who are southerners, libertarians, and Calvinists." Since that describes a good number of America's founding fathers, we suppose there are worse things in the world.

SUGGESTED CORE
1. English 302, Classical Literature in Translation
2. Philosophy 334, Plato and Aristotle
3. Religion 211, Old Testament *and* Religion 212, New Testament Literature and History
4. Religion 341, Church History I
5. Political Science 256, Modern Political Thought
6. English 351/352, Shakespeare
7. History 271, Colonial and Revolutionary America
8. Political Science 354, Marxism (*closest match*)

Student Life: Clean-scrubbed Presbyterians

Grove City's commitment to Christian values is apparent in its student life policies. Students are required to live in single-sex campus housing (and 90 percent do) unless they are commuters living with their families. All students must attend chapel or convocations at least 16 times per semester. Similarly, students are warned that certain types of behavior on campus will result in disciplinary action, perhaps even dismissal. Among these are the use of drugs and alcohol, premarital or homosexual sex or "any other conduct which violates historic Christian standards." The penalty for getting caught with alcohol on campus is a week at home. (Unlike, say, Wheaton College students, Grove City students who are of age can drink off campus.)

The college catalog frankly describes what students will find here: "Members of the Grove City College campus community are expected to observe Christian moral standards, as they have been understood by most of the Christian community historically." Grove City has had no trouble finding students who welcome such an environment. Tom Wolfe's Charlotte Simmons would have thrived here.

Sitting 60 miles north of cosmopolitan, artsy Pittsburgh, the town of Grove City has a population of about 8,000. To visit Grove City is "like going back into the 1950s," says a professor. "It's just a traditional American small town," with a movie theater and a few stores and restaurants—and very little crime (indeed, statistics reported by the college indicate that serious crime, at least on campus, is almost unheard of). The college's relationship with the town is said to have improved over the last couple of decades, and the college actively encourages students to become involved in local churches and organizations.

Grove City College's 150-acre campus, separated physically from the town proper, houses students from 46 states; however, a high percentage typically hail from Pennsylvania. The school is built in traditional collegiate Gothic style—no Bauhaus prison-style monoliths blight this campus. In summer 2005, the college was scheduled to start building apartments to house an additional 200 students.

Political controversy at Grove City is substantially absent, because the faculty and students who choose to come to campus are a self-selected group. Indeed, there's a look of healthy, wholesome, Presbyterian clean-scrubbedness to the college's materials and people. "Sometimes students complain that all the speakers are Republican or free-market economists," says one professor. But generally, he reports, students are surprisingly apolitical; many of them are "hardworking suburban kids who just want to get a business degree." One student says of the atmosphere, "I love it. This college has the ideal atmosphere for learning. The people are wonderful and very homogeneous, which is a great perk. Everyone is conservative and Christian."

Grove City students have the option of participating in one of more than 120 student organizations. None of these, says a student, are "diversity nonsense clubs for gays or ethnic groups." At least 20 organizations are religiously oriented, including groups for Protestants and Catholics (the latter are said to feel somewhat uncomfortable on campus). Two of the more popular groups are Salt Company, a Bible study group, and Warriors for Christ, a prayer and study club. Many theatrical and musical performances are offered throughout the year. Grove City also boasts an excellent marching band that is 200 members strong, making it one of the nation's largest for a school of Grove City's size. There are 19 honor societies and as many departmental and professional clubs. Six sororities and eight fraternities fill out the social scene, but going Greek is not especially common. Off campus, students "go to Pittsburgh a lot more than they used to," reports one alumnus. The college newspaper often highlights things to do and places to eat both in Pittsburgh and Youngstown, Ohio.

Grove City students compete in 20 intercollegiate sports at the NCAA Division III level; their teams last year won eight President's Athletic Conference championships. There are also five club teams. The Physical Learning Center contains two swimming pools—one for recreation, one for competition—as well as fitness and weight rooms, four full-size basketball courts, a dance studio, a bowling alley, and racquetball courts. A recent article in the *Washington Times* highlighted the vigor of Grove City's sports program. In fact, athletics and the demands of Title IX were originally the cause over which Grove City refused federal support. Now, according to the article, more than "two-thirds of the college's 2,300 students—equally divided between young men and women—participate in intramural and varsity sports—playing everything from bowling to rugby football on the exquisitely manicured 500-acre campus." The *Times* also noted that the men's swim team has had 53 consecutive winning seasons, 20 conference championships, and placed second in the conference 14 times since 1951. However, the school's athletes are also scholars; Grove City has led its athletic conference academically for the past four semesters, keeping a consistent 78 percent graduation rate among its sportsmen.

Grove City is completing a capital campaign, nearing its $60 million goal. The fruits of the campaign can be seen in the new Hall of Arts and Letters (done in the usual collegiate Gothic manner, but with wireless Internet access). Campaign money has also been used to increase the student scholarship fund.

Despite its modest endowment, the college has remained affordable. Tuition, as the college is proud to claim, is less than half the national average for private liberal arts colleges. Amazingly, tuition plus room and board, as well as a laptop and a printer (for students to keep upon graduation), is $15,100 a year. For this reason the school is often ranked as one of the nation's best values. This is especially impressive in light of Grove City's decision not to accept federal aid: its students cannot receive Pell grants or Stafford/PLUS loans because the school wishes to remain as free as possible from federal regulation. Grove City's private programs are more generous than most federal assistance, offering loans of up to $7,500 a year, or $45,000 over four years, at a 3.55 percent interest rate, which is comparable to the federal rate, according to the college's financial aid office. It reports that 38 percent of the student body took loans for the 2003–4 academic year, The college raises private donations for its own generous $3.5 million yearly financial aid program, reports the *Washington Times*.

HAMILTON COLLEGE

CLINTON, NEW YORK • WWW.HAMILTON.EDU

Prepared for a master, and deserves one

"I've always wanted to come here," said former president Bill Clinton in 2004 at Hamilton College in Clinton, New York. "Some of your alums are friends of mine, including the great Sol Linowitz, who negotiated the Panama Canal Treaty . . . the legendary civil rights leader, Bob Moses, Ezra Pound, and my friends, the governor and first lady of Iowa. . . . I love the legacy that you have given to America." Most people don't realize that Ezra Pound, after two years at Penn, finally finished up at Hamilton—or that the poet served as an inspiration to Mr. Clinton.

Hamilton College came into being more than 200 years ago, when Samuel Kirkland, a missionary to the Oneida Indians, wanted to establish a school for the natives and nearby white settlers. When Alexander Hamilton offered his support, the Hamilton-Oneida Academy was born. After a shaky start, the school was chartered as Hamilton College in 1812. Students entered the all-male institution—Hamilton would merge with the nearby all-female Kirkland College to become coed only in the 1970s— already well schooled in Greek and Latin, and Hamilton's rigorous curriculum obliged these young men to continue their studies in those ancient languages, as well as in mathematics, religion, history, philosophy, and the humanities.

Today, the college "urges" and "suggests" certain courses, but it does not demand any course in particular. "Experimental education" and "interdisciplinary perspectives" are the lingua franca now, and Greek and Latin is left to the inscriptions. One professor complains that Hamilton's "curricular freedom," as the school likes to call it, makes it "likely that students will learn more about condoms than the Constitution." And with little ideological diversity on campus, he says, students are "more likely to be exposed to a transvestite performance artist than to a conservative speaker"—for instance, someone who shares the views of Alexander Hamilton.

Hamilton president Eugene Tobin resigned in October 2002 after admitting to plagiarizing portions of his speeches over a period of years. Joan Stewart, the former dean of liberal arts at the University of South Carolina, was inaugurated as the college's nineteenth president a year later. Stewart, a specialist in eighteenth-century French literature, has spoken of her strong commitment to the liberal arts. Her presidency will prove crucial to the future of the college, says one professor: "Hamilton has the potential, under the right leadership, to be a truly great liberal arts school."

If Hamilton deserves inclusion in this guide, it is because a fair number of the faculty share Stewart's commitment to the liberal arts and kept their spirit alive even as Tobin's administration trashed the curriculum. Indeed, classics professor Barbara Gold was recently named the first female editor of the *American Journal of Philology*, and for the first time in its 120-year history, this prestigious publication is headquartered in a liberal arts college rather than a research university. The student who wants a real liberal education can still find one here—if he hunts down the best advice.

Academic Life: Why has government been instituted at all?

A few years after Tobin's inauguration in 1993, he and his faculty made several significant changes to the college's curriculum. Hamilton was beginning to be known as just another small liberal arts college in the Northeast, and Tobin wanted to make the school stand out. And so he revealed his Hamilton Plan for a Liberal Education in time for the 2001–2 academic year. The goal of the plan was to provide "highly motivated students with both the freedom and responsibility to make the educational choices that emphasize breadth and depth." Instead of requiring specific courses—or even study within specific disciplinary areas—Hamilton gives its students guidelines to follow and goals to achieve. An administrator in the dean of faculty's office says that students are no longer restricted by specifics: "With the old curriculum, students were talking with their advisors only to find the mechanisms for satisfying distribution requirements. Now advisors help students construct a broad outline of their education, and how they can attain it." A government professor says, "I was skeptical at first, but I now think that this will be a much more effective way of getting students to get—and maintain—a broad and integrated liberal arts education, before they go on to specialize somewhat on their major." A student says that "this new system allows each student to have the freedom of choice and puts the burden of widening our minds on us."

We think that for $30,000-plus a year students deserve a little more—for instance, some firm guidance so they don't waste the four most critical years of their lives.

Nothing in the Hamilton Plan requires educational breadth. Students can conceivably graduate without ever taking a course in history, philosophy, English, or a foreign language. Hamilton "urges all students to develop proficiency in at least one foreign language," but it does not require them to do so. Another effect of Hamilton's curriculum is that many students choose to double major, and since each major imposes its own unique requirements, some students graduate having taken most of their courses in just two disciplines.

VITAL STATISTICS
Religious affiliation: **none**
Total enrollment: 1,792
Total undergraduates: 1,750
SAT midranges: V: 620–710, M: 640–710
Applicants: 4,445
Applicants accepted: 34%
Accepted applicants who enrolled: 30%
Tuition: $31,700
Room and board: $7,825
Freshman retention rate: 91%
Graduation rate: 80% (4 yrs.), 86% (6 yrs.)
Courses with fewer than 20 students: 74%
Student-faculty ratio: 9:1
Courses taught by graduate TAs: none
Most popular majors: economics, political science, psychology
Students living on campus: 95%
Guaranteed housing for four years? yes
Students in fraternities: 34% sororities: 20%

There are still a few general education requirements, however. Hamilton students must take four small-group seminars, three writing-intensive courses, and another interdisciplinary sophomore-level seminar. These sophomore seminars can deal with ephemeral or faddish topics, depending on the professor. Nearly half the 24 courses that satisfied the requirement for the 2003–4 year dealt with globalizing something or other: "Globalization and the Politics of Identity," "Remapping Identities: Globalization and the Chinese Visual Culture," "Globalization and Religion," "Cultural Diversity, Conflict, and Pluralism," and "The Global Economy," for example. Other choices have included "Students in Revolt," "Theatre in Your Face," and "Pop Culture in the Age of Sex, Drugs, and Rock 'n Roll."

Each Hamilton student also must pass a quantitative literacy requirement, either through a course or an exam. Finally, each fourth-year student participates in the Senior Program, which requires students to demonstrate a "synthesis of knowledge." To meet this provision, students can teach a seminar to peers, conduct a research project, or pass a series of comprehensive exams in their major.

Advisors play a greater role at Hamilton than they do at most colleges, since the curriculum itself is little help. "We've got a more intense and systematic advising system set up to make this all work, and the incoming classes seem more intellectually engaged than before," a social science professor says. Each student is assigned a faculty advisor who, according to college literature, "will help [the student] adjust to the intellectual demands of the college." After the student has declared a major, he is assigned to another faculty advisor within his department. The college claims that students "will find [their] advisor concerned about the balance of [their] curriculum as defined by the educational goals" of the school. Most advisors do genuinely guide students in course choices, but others let students follow their whims. And even if professors do provide some direction, as one faculty member in the humanities says, "The problem is there's no enforcement. Students don't have to take these courses if they don't want to."

One of the advantages of the Hamilton Plan—and one of the administration's intentions in instituting it—has been that it has brought students and faculty closer together by strongly encouraging students to seek advice from their professors. Classes at Hamilton are small, with 74 percent of all classes having 20 or fewer students, and the student-faculty ratio a good nine to one. And students enjoy that close interaction. "[Professors] have always been more than accessible and always willing to listen when I needed time," a student says. One professor says that he has never had a student come in to question a grade. Instead, "they come in to figure out what they could do better."

Hamilton has a fairly strong focus on writing. Besides the writing-intensive course requirements, students can improve their writing skills by visiting the Writing Center, which is open until 11 p.m. every day except Friday and Saturday. At the center, peer writing tutors help students choose essay topics or revise essays. Professors and students alike report that the Writing Center is very good at what it does.

History is "regarded as perhaps the most demanding department on campus," according to one professor in the department. The government department is also strong, as is geology, which has a reputation for both good teaching and research. The philosophy department has almost 40 majors—a lot, given Hamilton's small size. One philosophy professor says that these "are excellent students, and many are quite involved in moral and social issues."

Hamilton offers majors in Africana studies, Asian studies, and women's studies, and a minor in Latin American studies. The American studies department offers plenty of politically correct courses like "The Latino/a Experience." Hamilton's interdisciplinary studies departments, along with the Spanish department and comparative literature, are said to be the most politicized. One faculty member says that instructors in these departments are "more activists than scholars." A student echoes the sentiment, charging that many faculty members in these departments "use the classroom as a forum to preach political ideology and their personal beliefs."

When Hamilton dropped most of its general education requirements, it also eliminated its cultural diversity requirement, although courses with a "diversity" focus are still strongly encouraged. In fact, in most departments it would be hard to avoid them. In the religious studies department, for example, students could choose to take courses such as "Cosmology and Ritual in Native American Religion," "The Dao and the Buddha-Mind," and "Seminar on Gender, Sexuality, and Body in Asia." To be fair, the department also offers seminars on the New Testament, Biblical parables, and one called "Jesus and the Gospels."

Through a number of strong cooperative programs, students can earn joint degrees in engineering, law, medicine, or other professional programs by taking courses at other colleges and universities in the area. Hamilton offers two well-known study abroad programs—the Hamilton Junior Year in France and the Junior Year in Spain—but students can also transfer credit from other university programs in other foreign countries. Forty percent of each junior class studies abroad, studies at another school, or undertakes an internship.

One of President Tobin's objectives for Hamilton College was to increase funding for diversity programming and to make multiculturalism (surprise!) a primary focus for the entire college. Tobin accomplished the financial part of his goal when he obtained a three-year, $150,000 grant

ACADEMIC REQUIREMENTS

The minimal mandates imposed by Hamilton on its students are called the "Hamilton Plan for Liberal Education." Students must take:

- Four "proseminars," courses with enrollments of no more than 16 offering "intensive interaction among students and between students and instructors, through emphasis on writing, speaking and discussion, and other approaches to inquiry and expression." A recent year's options ranged from "Elementary Greek" to "Introduction to Disability Studies."

- Three writing-intensive courses, each taken in a different semester during the first two years of study. Choices range from "Seminar in Classics and Government: Cicero, Hamilton, and Jefferson" to "Spanish Immersion."

- A sophomore seminar emphasizing inter- or multidisciplinary learning, culminating in an integrative project with a public presentation. Recent choices included "The Historical and Intellectual Foundations of Property and Its Relationship to Freedom in Modern States" and "1968: Students in Revolt."

MIDDLE ATLANTIC

from the Hewlett Foundation as part of the foundation's Pluralism and Unity Program. A college news article reported that "the grant will support a new curricular initiative for discussing issues of diversity, difference, and social justice in and out of the classroom." Tobin said that the grant would help the school foster "greater inclusion, acceptance, and understanding, which continue to be among the college's top priorities." It's true: Diversity programming dominates academic and extracurricular life. The Office of Multicultural Affairs has its own dean. The college sponsors events such as Men and Women of Color Conferences, Celebrate Sexuality Week, and Womyn's Energy Week. Many academic departments and campus centers join forces to sponsor events such as these; one faculty member says that many professors "actively deny the distinction between advocacy and scholarship."

One of the college's programs in this area is the Kirkland Project, named after the women's college with which Hamilton College merged. "The Kirkland Project is the best example of an institutional fix of liberalism that does not even entertain any other ideology than liberal thought, even though they are funded by the college," a student says. The project has introduced courses into the curriculum like "Coming of Age in America, Narratives of Difference," a first-year seminar in which "discussions focus on differences of culture, race, class, gender, and sexual orientation." In past years, the project's regular Brown Bag Lunch discussions have featured such topics as "Industrial Porn; Or, The Politics of Mass Pro(se)duction in the Work of Busby Berkeley," "Will the 'Real' Mother Please Stand Up? Lesbian Couples Transition to Shared Motherhood," "Masculinity and the Medieval Clergy: Reform, Gender Ambiguity, and the Rise of Misogyny in Western Europe," "Quilting as a Woman's Voice," and "Meditation on Chalk Graffiti: 'Alexander Hamilton Was a Gay, Black Man?'" The project's research associates participate in "projects about race, multiculturalism, and gender" and are paid a stipend for the semester's work.

A few genuinely atrocious examples of campus leftism put Hamilton briefly in the headlines in 2005. The school tried to hire a former terrorist, 1960s bomb-thrower Susan Rosenberg, to teach creative writing—a skill she learned in prison. She was invited by Nancy Sorkin Rabinowitz, the same comparative literature professor who tried to bring in as a speaker Colorado professor Ward Churchill. You might remember him as the make-believe American Indian who famously described the victims of Sept. 11, 2001, as "Little Eichmanns" who had no right to expect immunity from violence provoked by American imperialism, etc. In each case, explosive publicity and controversy among alumni and the general public forced the school to back down from implementing Rabinowitz's bright ideas.

Some of the better teachers and scholars at Hamilton are Douglas Ambrose, Alfred Kelly, and Robert Paquette in history; Daniel Chambliss in sociology; Barbara Tewksbury in geology; James Bradfield and Derek Jones in economics; Bonnie Urciuoli in anthropology; and Philip Pearle in physics.

It is strange that Hamilton has bought into the Blackboard electronic course management system, which may be more appropriate for high school than higher education, especially since other and better systems can be had for free. This may indicate that college administrators pay more attention to slick corporate salesmen than to their own faculty and students, a syndrome by no means unique to Hamilton.

Student Life: Debt, if it is not excessive

Despite everything, Hamilton students seem to love their alma mater, and their fond memories of college days usually turn into dollars for the school. Hamilton is one of the top 10 colleges in the nation for alumni support; each year, around 60 percent of alumni donate to Hamilton. The college also boasts a substantial endowment for a school of its size—about $450 million. "The resources here are amazing," says one professor. "Hamilton is very, very well endowed." Other resources are just as important. As one student says, "The typical Hamilton student will use his or her connections made here with alums or others to get himself a good job after graduating."

Hamilton's campus has two parts: the older Hamilton part is known for its ivy-covered stone architecture, while what was once Kirkland College is more modern. Twenty-three residence halls house Hamilton's small student body. Hamilton has no single-sex dormitories, although it does offer single-sex housing by floor. Some halls have coed bathrooms, but only if everybody on the floor approves. The college does offer coed apartments—with separate bedrooms, a housing official says. Smoke-free, substance-free, and noise-free areas are available for those who request them. Students take meals at either of the college's two large dining halls, at the school's diner, or at the campus pub.

A few years ago, the college trustees launched a kind of urban renewal in the campus, attempting to bulldoze the school's Greek system. It seized the residence spaces from campus fraternities, reluctantly allowing them to continue as student organizations. Until 1978, when Hamilton merged with Kirkland College, about 90 percent of the student body belonged to a fraternity, according to the *Chronicle of Higher Education*. In order to convert the school from a residential fraternity campus, Hamilton has spent about $20 million to restructure the campus's residential life. A *Christian Science Monitor* article says that fraternities were banned in 1995 to produce a "civilizing effect," or in other words, "to equalize housing and improve what many perceived as a male-dominated social scene." Hamilton also wanted to "attract better academically qualified women." The university couldn't quash all Greek life, however; today, roughly 34 percent of men and 20 percent of women participate.

The student body is mostly white, wealthy, and preppy. Although the largest chunk of students comes from the Northeast, Hamilton is attended by students from through-

SUGGESTED CORE

1. Classics 250, Heroism, Ancient and Modern (*closest match*)
2. Philosophy 201, History of Ancient Western Philosophy
3. Religious Studies 111, Ancient Jewish Wisdom: Introduction to the Bible *and* Religious Studies 257, The New Testament
4. Religious Studies 412, Seminar in Early Christianity (*closest match*)
5. Government 276, Enlightenment and Counter-Enlightenment
6. English 225, Shakespeare
7. History 241, American Colonial History
8. History 226, Modern European Intellectual History: 1830 to the Present

out the United States and by a number of international students.

One professor insists that the Hamilton community welcomes students of all political beliefs: "I think the political climate on campus is quite good. Liberals and conservatives don't shy away from disagreeing and seem to do so in intelligent (as opposed to knee-jerk) sort of ways." In comparing Hamilton to a similar school of similar size with a noticeable liberal climate, he says, "Hamilton seems to be more open to all sides."

Others assess the campus political situation differently. Only one faculty member at Hamilton seems to be outspokenly conservative, and there is no conservative student organization—the College Republicans club has a membership in the single digits and "does very little," according to a professor. One student says, "In terms of political/ideological diversity on campus, there is little to none. This campus is governed and has a faculty that is very liberal-minded and one-sided on all issues." Even though many students are moderate to conservative, says this student, they are afraid to speak up in class or in outside activities.

One student says that "the administration puts the burden of social programming on students, but does not supply us with the proper amount of funding to fully entertain all options. Our location makes the need for social options even greater, yet the school is very tight with money to student organizations." Indeed, the small town of Clinton, New York, doesn't offer much for entertainment. Utica is a 10-minute drive away and offers a few more options. There are a few things to do on campus, though. In addition to its permanent collection, Emerson Gallery offers lectures, films, and workshops in the arts. The theater and dance department sponsors concerts and student performances regularly, and the music department is also quite strong.

Hamilton does bring in a pretty wide range of lecturers. Recent speakers have included Colin Powell, Desmond Tutu, Ralph Reed, Oliver North, Jimmy Carter, Cornel West, Julian Bond, and Rudy Giuliani. However, when distinguished economist Walter Williams came to campus to speak on the "Hypocrisy of Affirmative Action," faculty members called him a racist (Williams is black). Some even sent out an all-campus e-mail demanding that the college cancel the speech. The president had to hire extra security for Williams's talk.

The Hamilton Continentals field 28 NCAA Division III teams. First- and second-year students can play on junior varsity teams. In a typical year, 40 percent of the Hamilton student body participates in varsity or JV sports. Students can also play intramural and club sports.

A popular organization is the Hamilton Action Volunteers Outreach Coalition, a group that organizes community service opportunities like tutoring in city schools, soup kitchens, and nursing home visits. A $10 membership fee in the Outing Club allows students to use camping and ski equipment. The club also sponsors hiking, rock climbing, and other outdoor activities throughout the school year. For relaxation, students have easy access to the Root Glen, a 7.5-acre wooded garden on campus.

The isolated location usually helps keep the campus and its environs safe, although Hamilton's latest crime statistics (2003) include seven forcible sex offenses, up from five each year in 2001 and 2002. The only other crimes reported on campus were burglaries—13 of them.

For a place with such left-leaning sympathies, Hamilton is hardly welcoming to students from outside the upper class. Tuition in 2004–5 was $ 31,700, and room and board cost $7,825. Admissions are not need-blind, nor does the school guarantee full financial aid to needy students. Some 55 percent of students do get need-based aid, and the average student loan debt of recent graduates is around $16,000.

HAVERFORD COLLEGE

HAVERFORD, PENNSYLVANIA • WWW.HAVERFORD.EDU

Fast Friends

Haverford is a coeducational private institution founded by the Religious Society of Friends (Quakers) in 1833. Haverford is not "officially" Quaker, but you hear a lot about the Quaker mindset and principles at the college. In a 2003 newsletter, Haverford's "Quaker resource person" asked students how Quaker ideals manifest themselves in campus life. Students listed the following: "accessibility of the administration, the inclusion of students in college-wide decision making processes, the use of silence at the beginning of meetings, the trust in student-teacher relations, the noncompetitive academic climate, the Quaker resources in the library, the Quakerism course, the influence of particular Friends, the tradition of Collection, the Quaker activities for students, and the architecture of the campus." One of the most noticeable expressions of Quaker principles is the honor code, the main point of which is trust in one's professors, in one's classmates, in oneself. One student says, "It really works! You are guaranteed to come out of here valuing honesty as the highest of virtues."

Academic Life: Leeway or the highway

"Liberal education requires a sense of the breadth of human inquiry and creativity," asserts Haverford. "Every student is encouraged to engage a full range of disciplines—fine arts, the written word, empirical investigation, economy, and society—in order to become a broadly educated person." Encouraged, but not required: the college's distribution requirements impose no real constraints on students—72 different courses in the English department alone satisfy the humanities requirement, while 29 courses in political science could stand in for social sciences.

Haverford's curriculum requirements do little to guarantee that students will be broadly educated. The college attracts intellectually curious students, most of whom are eager to take a wide variety of courses. (And it is highly selective: only 29 percent of students get in.) Unfortunately, students have the option to choose courses like "Sex, Gender, and Representation: An Introduction to Theories of Sexuality" and "Native American Music and Belief" to fulfill the basic humanities requirements. Even the natural sciences offer questionable courses: one's sole science course could be "Disease and Discrimination," which "analyzes the nature of discrimination against individuals and groups with . . . diseases."

Haverford requires students to take one writing-intensive course in their first year. At the college's Writing Center, student advisors help other students choose topics, proofread, and polish assignments every evening, Sunday though Thursday.

Academic life at Haverford is not as politicized as at other schools. As a 2003 study by the Independent Women's Forum points out, Haverford still offers traditional courses. Haverford is one of only three top-ten liberal arts colleges to offer comprehensive introductory courses in English, history, and political science, as well as a history course in Western civilization. The history department offers courses in each of the discipline's fundamental areas, and the philosophy, religion, and English departments are similarly balanced. The most popular majors at Haverford are biology, economics, English, and history.

Academic life at Haverford is intense, say professors. One points to "many students here who are adventurous and do take courses merely to learn and not simply to get a good grade." Students expect to work every night during the week and during the day on weekends. "Everybody is studying during the week," says a student. "We're very academically focused." Every student must complete a senior thesis; students say that the work this requirement entails makes for a worthy capstone to their education.

Haverford benefits from a close relationship with its sister school, Bryn Mawr College, and nearby Swarthmore. Haverford students can take courses at the other two schools, even choose to major in a discipline offered only there—for instance, linguistics at Swarthmore. Haverford students can major in psychology at Bryn Mawr, where the focus is clinical, or at their home campus, where the department is more biological. Some 90 percent of Haverford students take at least one course at Bryn Mawr during their four years in college. Haverford students can also take courses at and use the library of the University of Pennsylvania, but this rather distant option is used less frequently. Haverford's McGill Library has 500,000 volumes, but add in Bryn Mawr's and Swarthmore's, and that number is almost tripled. Borrowing from these two schools is convenient and speedy.

Haverford is strongest in the sciences, particularly biology and chemistry, and the school says it is one of only two undergraduate colleges in the country (along with Pomona College) that guarantees research opportunities for students in the sciences, the humanities, or the social sciences. Among the fine professors at Haverford are Linda

Gerstein in history; Kimberly Benston, C. Stephen Finley, and Laura McGrane in English; and Richard J. Ball and Vernon J. Dixon in economics.

The Cantor Fitzgerald Gallery provides the college with an elegant space to host smart exhibitions. In 2004, the gallery staged a French masterpieces show that included works by Gaugin, Matisse, Renoir, Picasso, and Rodin. The gallery is a state-of-the-art facility with self-healing fabric to correct the post-installation nail holes. The John B. Hurford '60 Humanities Center offers unique alternatives to learning in the classroom, "fostering challenging exchanges among faculty, students, and diverse communities of writers, artists, performers, thinkers, activists, and innovators."

Faculty-student relationships at Haverford are about as close as one sees anywhere—as it should be, with a student to faculty ratio of just eight to one. A professor says that one of the school's greatest strengths is its "dedicated teachers across the board, who spend a lot of time with students." Without a graduate program and without the accompanying pressure to secure large grants, Haverford teachers can actually afford to invest time and energy in, well, teaching. One student says, "Professors aren't going to be your best buddies, but there is always a close academic relationship." Faculty members are, for the most part, eager to help. As for the formal advising program, each freshman is assigned both a faculty advisor and an upperclassman "peer advisor."

Haverford's academic honor code further strengthens relationships between students and teachers. Students say they are amazed at the amount of trust faculty members place in them. "Cheating, plagiarism, and other dishonesty in the classroom are incredibly rare because students are not willing to break that trust," one said. Students can usually take exams home and complete them on their own time. One student reports that when he brought an exam home, his time ran out mid-sentence; he turned it in just like that. The honor code is student-written and student-run. Students who violate it are judged by their peers on the honor council; the most serious consequence of breaking the code is "separation," which is essentially a one-semester expulsion, akin to ostracism in ancient Athens. One junior political science major explains that the honor code treats students as adults; its authority stems primarily from the students themselves, not the administration.

VITAL STATISTICS

Religious affiliation: none
Total enrollment: 1,172
Total undergraduates: 1,172
SAT midranges: V: 640–740, M: 640–720
Applicants: 3,035
Applicants accepted: 29%
Accepted applicants who enrolled: 37%
Tuition: $29,990
Room and board: $9,420
Freshman retention rate: 90%
Graduation rate: 86% (4 yrs.), 90% (6 yrs.)
Average class size: 12
Student-faculty ratio: 8:1
Courses taught by graduate TAs: none
Most popular majors: biology, economics, English
Students living on campus: 99%
Guaranteed housing for four years? yes
Students in fraternities or sororities: none

MIDDLE ATLANTIC

ACADEMIC REQUIREMENTS

Haverford's rather laissez-faire curricular requirements include:

- One semester of a writing-intensive seminar, chosen from any of the college's academic departments. Among the 2004–5 courses qualifying were "My Blog, Myself," "Satire and Irony," "The Art of Persuasion," and "College Sports World."

- One course credit in social justice, meaning any class that analyzes either "the structures, workings, and consequences of prejudice, inequality, and injustice" or "efforts at political and cultural change directed against, and achievements that overcome prejudice, inequality, and injustice."

    Students must also take three courses in each of the three divisions of the curriculum:

- Humanities. Choices range from "Introduction to Literature Analysis" to "Sex, Gender, Representation: An Introduction to Theories of Sexualities."

- Social sciences. Options include "Introduction to Western History" and "Gender and Feminist Theory: Cross-National Perspectives."

Student Life: Let there be peace

One of the greatest of Quaker ideals and goals is peace, and peace is what you'll find in the architecture and grounds of Haverford College. The campus once consisted solely of one long stone building, Founders' Hall, where students studied, attended classes, ate, and slept. While Haverford has expanded considerably since then, the college wisely continues to build in an architectural style that is consistent with its past. Nearly every building is of gray stone, though architectural styles vary. One of Haverford's newest buildings, the 50,000-square-foot Campus Center, meshes nicely with its older neighbors. Between the classrooms and dormitories are lush expanses of green lawn and centuries-old trees originally landscaped by the English gardener William Carvill. The 216-acre campus includes more than 400 species of trees and shrubs and features a duck pond. A two-mile nature trail surrounds the school, offering a place for quiet contemplation. Peace pervades all.

This serenity is further strengthened through the honor system and the kind of community it creates. Students leave their backpacks in the dining hall lobby while they eat and leave their mailboxes wide open. Students make eye contact. There is a trust that one doesn't find at most other schools. In place of residential advisors, Haverford appoints CPs ("custom people") to show the first-year students the ropes and catechize them about the school's traditions. This arrangement dates back to the mid-1800s.

Haverford's Quaker principles shape much of its atmosphere. The emphasis on honesty extends well beyond the classroom, and can be seen perhaps most concretely in political life. Haverford encourages confrontation through nonviolent discussion and dialogue, and it promotes reaching agreement by consensus. When a problem arises, as minor as a hallmate playing music too loud or as major as whether the nation should go to war, students' first reaction is to confront the opposition and discuss the issue. In fall 2003, for example, students met to discuss whether an on-campus cafe should allow smoking. The final consensus was that the eatery would allow smoking, but if the smoking bothered another student, he could ask an employee to move the smoker to a special "nook," separate from nonsmokers, according to a *Bi-College News* article. This approach was deemed the "most Haverfordian." Haverford students generally are less inclined to hold a march or a demonstration than they are to hold a discussion.

As one ought to expect of a small, elite, Quaker, liberal arts college, Haverford offers a haven for students and faculty of leftish principles, but the politics here are mostly tolerant. "Hardy, smart students of conservative views should not avoid Haverford," says one professor. "Years ago, one would be hard-pressed to find a student of conservative political views. That has changed. While liberal views tend to dominate, there is a strong conservative minority active in political matters on campus today. Students are comfortable expressing different views, although the liberal consensus views of the 1970s [and] 1980s tend to be the 'default' view."

Conservatives are rarely shouted down or ridiculed for their views at Haverford. But it is tacitly assumed that all students share similar political views or that some opinions are universally accepted among all college-educated people. For instance, the Haverford Women's Center links to the student groups Voice for Choice and Planned Parenthood Escorts on its Web site. Haverford also offers its support to homosexual students through student groups like "InQUEERy," a "political active [sic] organization that creates awareness of issues of sexual orientation through campus-wide postings, mailings, meetings, and activism," according to a brochure. There are also the Bisexual, Gay, and Lesbian Alliance (BGALA), which has its own lounge, and the Coming Out Support Group. Haverford College joins with Bryn Mawr and Swarthmore for gay-themed parties and political events each year. The curriculum includes courses like "The Politics of Sexual Marginalization," "Gay and Lesbian Literature," and "Sex and Gender on Film."

The undergraduate population comprises 1,172 students (48 percent male and 52 percent female). A little more than a quarter of Haverford students are members of a minority group (including international students), and the college is intent on admitting and retaining a more racially diverse student body. But one student complains that while "Haverford is sufficiently diverse racially and ethnically, and students are accepting of other cultures . . . we're not really diverse socioeconomically—we're all privileged and upper class." Haverford sponsors, along with Bryn Mawr and

- **Natural sciences.** Choices include "Classical and Modern Physics" and "Perspectives in Biology: How Do I Know Who I Am?"

  At least one of these courses must meet the school's "quantitative requirement." Suitable courses focus on statistical reasoning; a widely applicable type of mathematical reasoning; working with, manipulating, and judging the reliability of quantitative data; generating and understanding graphical relationships; or using mathematics to obtain concrete numerical predictions about natural or social systems.

- **Foreign language.** This requirement can be met in any of several ways: scoring four or five on an Advanced Placement test; scoring 600 or higher on a language achievement test; taking one full year of language study; or studying a language in a summer program abroad or semester abroad.

  Haverford also requires students to participate in some area of the physical education program during their first two years at the college.

Swarthmore, a summer orientation program for incoming minority freshmen. Haverford's Minority Scholars Program offers a bonanza of support services for minority students. And despite its size, Haverford has a plethora of minority student groups, among them Alliance of Latino American Students, Asian Students Association, Sexuality and Gender Alliance, Students for Diversity and Unity, and Girlz 2 Women, a Haverford student-run mentoring program to instill "self-respect" in area teenage girls. The school still has a ways to go towards attaining ideological diversity; for now, the Republican Club is the token conservative group on campus.

Haverford students confess that their school is not exactly an athletic powerhouse in the NCAA Division III Centennial Conference, where it competes with Swarthmore, Bryn Mawr, Franklin and Marshall, and Johns Hopkins, among others. Academics come first, and classes are scheduled so that students have no conflicts with practice. "We're not spectacular, but we always have a lot of fun," says one student, who ran for the track and cross-country teams even without any previous experience. "On every team, there is an incredible range of abilities." Around 40 percent of students are varsity athletes. There are 21 varsity squads (but no football team). Haverford fields the only varsity cricket team in the nation; their competition comes from adult cricket leagues and club teams at area universities. The college also has a physical education requirement, which consists of six half-semester courses during a student's first two years at Haverford. Students are a physically fit lot. "At four o'clock every day, the library clears out and everybody is outside doing something. Haverford students are incredibly active," says a senior. Athletic facilities at the moment are rather limited—an atrocious metal-siding field house contains the main gym—but the college is building the $20 million Douglas B. Gardner Memorial Athletic Center, named for an athlete alum who died along with many other Cantor Fitzgerald employees in the World Trade Center on September 11, 2001.

Haverford's multitude of options—traditional dormitories, single rooms in suite-style arrangements, on-campus apartments, and even living at Bryn Mawr—leaves students with virtually no reason to live off campus, and only 1 percent do. At the beginning of each school year, students decide whether to make the bathrooms single-sex or coed, and for some reason, students usually choose the coed route. In addition to a couple of on-campus cafes, Haverford offers one dining center, reputed to be the worst in the tri-college system.

As small as Haverford College is, there is still plenty to do. Regular buses to Bryn Mawr and Swarthmore colleges expand options even further. One student says that, in general, "Haverford students tend to think of 'Mawrtyrs' as weird—either gay or [promiscuous]. Swatties [Swarthmore students] are just weird and snobby." The party atmosphere is muted, with many students content to hang out with friends, play board games in Lunt Café, or attend the lectures and concerts held on campus every week. Fords Against Boredom (FAB) sponsors free social events like midnight bowling, trips to Phillies games, and a weekly film series. Philadelphia's Center City is only a 10-mile, cheap train ride away. The city offers numerous restaurants, nightclubs, and other attractions for the work-weary student. The Philadelphia Museum of Art is the largest of many cultural institutions visited by students, and historic sites dating from before the founding of the nation are within easy reach. Students can often score special rates for tickets to events at the Kimmel Center for the Performing Arts. The New Jersey and Delaware beaches are an easy drive, as are ski resorts in the Poconos. Closer to home, Haverford, Bryn Mawr, and other neighboring upscale towns along the Main Line offer a large assortment of restaurants and other centers of shopping and entertainment.

In 2003 campus crime was rare, but still troubling: The school reported four forcible sex offenses, two robberies, one aggravated assault, two arsons, one auto theft, and 18 burglaries in residence halls, along with 32 liquor-law violations. Violent crime is prevented in part through blue-light emergency phones situated all over campus.

A year at Haverford costs a stiff $29,990 in tuition, plus $9,420 for room and $board. Some 43 percent of undergraduates receive financial aid, and the average student loan debt upon graduation is $15,362.

SUGGESTED CORE

1. Classics 210, The Epic
2. Philosophy 101, Historical Introduction to Philosophy: Greek Philosophy (*offered at Bryn Mawr*)
3. Religion 118, Hebrew Bible: Literary Text and Historical Context
4. Religion 206b, History and Literature of Early Christianity
5. Political Science 231, Western Political Theory (*offered at Bryn Mawr*)
6. English 225/226, Shakespeare (*offered at Bryn Mawr*)
7. History 203a, The Age of Jefferson and Jackson, 1789–1850 (*closest match*)
8. History 225a, Europe in the Nineteenth Century

MIDDLE ATLANTIC

JOHNS HOPKINS UNIVERSITY

BALTIMORE, MARYLAND • WWW.JHU.EDU

Research shows

When Johns Hopkins University inaugurated Daniel Coit Gilman as president in 1876, Gilman asked, "What are we aiming at? The encouragement of research . . . and the advancement of individual scholars, who by their excellence will advance the sciences they pursue and the society where they dwell." Gilman's vision lives on at Johns Hopkins University, the first research university of its kind and still one of the world's finest. Unfortunately, the success of Hopkins has come at a cost. The school's emphasis on research and faculty publication results, predictably, in undergraduates often being left behind. Still, many faculty members use their research to complement their teaching, especially in the sciences and engineering, and 80 percent of undergraduates supplement their coursework by participating in faculty research projects.

Hopkins is for serious students who don't mind putting their social lives on hold for a few years so that they can work with the best scholars in their fields. As one student says, "If one wishes to come to Hopkins, prepare to spend four years studying, not making friends."

Academic Life: Competing interests

Hopkins has made it clear from the beginning that it is primarily a research university, not a liberal arts college. Even today, the administration makes few attempts to pass itself off as one. There are eight schools at the university: Arts and Sciences, Engineering, Medicine, Hygiene and Public Health, Nursing, the Peabody Conservatory of Music, the School of Advanced International Studies, and the School of Continuing Studies. Students, particularly in the sciences, tend not to take courses outside their areas of study; few come to Hopkins to explore a variety of disciplines. Some students see the courses outside their (often highly technical) majors as ways to boost their grade point averages. But one senior insists there is "absolutely no grade inflation [at Hopkins] save for in the writing seminars department." There's not much room for padding here—or educational breadth. The chemistry department, for instance, recommends the following program for majors in the first two years:

- Freshman/fall term: introductory chemistry, introductory chemistry lab, calculus, and a language

- Freshman/spring term: introductory organic chemistry, organic chemistry lab, calculus, and a language

- Sophomore/fall term: intermediate organic chemistry, intermediate organic chemistry lab, general physics, and general physics lab

- Sophomore/spring term: intermediate chemistry, advanced inorganic lab, general physics, and general physics lab

Each field also has its own course requirements, of course. An English major, for example, must take two introductory courses outside the English department (for example, "Philosophic Classics," "History of the Ancient World," or "Introduction to American Politics"); one year of a foreign language at the intermediate level; and 10 courses in English, which must meet certain conditions. Many departments do require majors to take fundamental courses—and most require a proficiency in a foreign language—but in general, courses are required only if they directly pertain to the major.

Besides the required two to four semesters of writing-intensive courses, students—especially those in the sciences—have little flexibility to pursue a broad liberal arts degree, since their semesters are filled with the requirements of their majors. A student who found himself at Johns Hopkins with a hunger for a liberal education could take advantage of the school's flexible curriculum to design his own major in humanistic studies—taking eight core courses divided between two departments (history and philosophy, for example), six more courses not necessarily in the humanities, a foreign language through the sophomore level, and the university-wide writing requirement.

If Hopkins students aren't always well rounded or even particularly interested in ideas, they are at least set to become experts in their fields. Undergraduates are intelligent and ambitious, sometimes to the degree of being antisocial, cutthroat competitors. One student says that premedical students are so competitive that they spend more hours than necessary on assignments simply to try to earn the best grade in the class. In a physics lab, one alumnus says, some of the most overachieving students spent hours collecting iron filings, not because they needed so many samples, but only because they wanted to outdo their classmates. Another student says that professors lock organic chemistry labs to prevent students from sabotaging classmates' experiments.

If a student can survive this competition with his sanity intact, a Johns Hopkins diploma is surely valuable. Alumni graduate and professional school acceptance rates

Johns Hopkins has no university-wide curriculum. The only requirement that every undergraduate must satisfy is a series of writing-intensive courses—four semesters for arts and sciences students, two semesters for engineering. This requirement can be fulfilled by any number of options and does not guarantee breadth to students' usually science-intensive curricula. For example, a physics major can take "Undergraduate Workshop in Science Writing," a course in which students interview scientists and write short articles, or "Stories from Contemporary Science," a course modeled on the scientific press conference.

are well above the national average: 90 percent for medical school and 95 percent for law school, for example.

Students may learn some of their competitive habits from their professors, many of whom are top researchers vying for grants and awards. But persistent students should be able to find professors who are willing and eager to help with coursework and to offer advice. "Every professor has office hours and almost all of them are friendly and helpful when students talk to them," a student says. "I had one professor who announced his office hours every lecture and told us that there was no need to do poorly in his class. . . . All we had to do was come in and talk to him." But as another student says, "Students must show some initiative . . . as the professors really will not waste their time unless you make them. Once they come to know you, they are generally most helpful." Professors teach almost all classes, but teaching assistants play a slightly greater role in engineering courses than they do in the humanities.

The extent to which faculty members advise students varies. One student calls the freshman advising program "atrocious," since students can avoid personal relationships with professors by using the professional Office of Academic Advising. But after the first year, each student is assigned a faculty advisor based on his academic interests. One student says her advisor is "always aware of what classes I'm taking and gives lots of good advice on what courses to take when [and] which professors to take them with."

Students name the following as among the university's best undergraduate teachers in the liberal arts: Jeffrey Brooks, John Marshall, David Nirenberg, and William Rowe in history; and William Connolly, Daniel H. Deudney, and Richard Flathman in political science. The science and engineering departments have many good professors, as well.

A good way to foster strong academic relationships with faculty members is by taking advantage of one of many research opportunities, especially in the sciences. For most research projects, students can even earn academic credit while preparing themselves for graduate school or a science-related career.

Hopkins is best known for its science and engineering departments. The biology program was the nation's first; biology, biomedical engineering, neuroscience, and public health are some of the university's best. But the university also maintains other excellent departments. The Romance language departments are all highly regarded, as is German, history of art, and international relations. The political science department, one of the first in the country, continues to be respected in the field, especially in the area of political theory. Students interested in a variety of disciplines can choose so-called "area majors," which are "multidisciplinary programs tailored to their own academic concerns," i.e., create-your-own majors that allow students enormous flexibility in their curricula. Past "area majors" have chosen American history, literature, and philosophy; religion and philosophy; science and philosophy; and comparative literature. A counterpart major in the natural sciences allows students to create majors that bridge two or more academic disciplines—for example, biology and chemistry or physics and chemistry. In both area majors, students work closely with advisors to structure a four-year curriculum.

Art students at Johns Hopkins can take advantage of a pilot program available at fewer than 40 campuses in the world: ArtSTOR, an online repository of nearly 300,000 images drawn from major university collections, which high-tech observers cited by the *Chronicle of Higher Education* think might someday replace the art history textbook—or at least the classroom slide projector.

Hopkins students had better enjoy the art at home, since few of them will see it in the flesh; only about 15 percent of undergraduates study abroad. Johns Hopkins does support campuses in Bologna, Italy, and Nanjing, China, as well as an art history facility in Florence.

Hopkins tries to alleviate at least a bit of student stress by making students take the courses in their first semester as freshmen on a pass/fail basis. There is also a January term that students can use as an extra-long vacation or to take an intensive interim course, thereby easing the strain in future semesters.

Student Life: Life on the street

What do America's future doctors and engineers do with their free time? They study, of course. Johns Hopkins attracts some of the most academically focused students in the nation, and therefore the school lacks most of the community atmosphere and social options one finds at other colleges. One biology major says, "Social life is what you make of it. Many people go to the library and practically live there. I'm in a very hard major, but I still find time to enjoy at least part of my Friday and Saturday. Maybe go see a movie or go out to eat." The university does little to promote community life. Johns Hopkins has plans to guarantee on-campus housing for all four undergraduate years, but currently on-campus housing is assured only for the first two years, and only a small fraction of upperclassmen choose Hopkins housing over off-campus apartments. All dormitories are coed, but there are no coed bathrooms or dorm rooms on campus. Many students say that they met most of their friends during their freshman year, when all freshmen live in dormitories on one residential quad. Freshman-year student life is

---

REQUIREMENTS (CONT'D)

Depending on the major, a Hopkins undergraduate takes eight to 10 courses outside his major:

- For science, math, or engineering majors, roughly six of the courses must be in the humanities or social sciences.
- A humanities or social sciences major must take about four courses in the natural sciences, math, or engineering areas.

like that of most colleges in the sense that students leave their doors open and hallmates often drop by to say hello. Most sophomores, however, live in university-owned apartments, and social life suffers accordingly. The more intense students emerge from their dorm rooms only to attend class or visit the library.

With most of the student body focused on schoolwork and making the grade, the average Hopkins student has little time left for political activism. And even if he did have the time, he would probably not be interested. Students are typically either apolitical or apathetic; a student tour guide claims that she doesn't know whether the school is balanced politically and can't name any political issues that roil the campus. One student says that while the campus has a slight liberal tendency because of the large number of students from Washington, D.C., and the northeastern states, politics just isn't a priority at Hopkins. "There are liberals and conservatives, but neither really are very active on campus. This is a place where people are more concerned with things like research, and political talk is usually minimal." One conservative student says that Hopkins has "committed leftists here and there, but they are quite obvious and can easily be avoided."

Hopkins has more than 200 student organizations, many of which are preprofessional societies or academic interest groups; others revolve around culture, political action, community service, media, sports, religion, arts, and various hobbies. About one-fifth of Hopkins students are involved in fraternities and sororities. One student says of the Greek system, "You can take it or leave it, and students can attend any of the campus fraternity parties." As for alcohol, one student says, "I think it's a lot less prevalent than in many other places, but it's here if you want it. There's a lot of stuff to do here, so there's no need to drink, thinking it's the only thing to do." But another humanities major says that since the school has no social life, "most students drink themselves to oblivion at one of the many frat parties. Most students still try to have a life when there is really no possibility of having one, and for this reason they are by and large miserable."

The main Homewood campus is composed primarily of Georgian-style red-brick buildings with white marble columns. A recent donation allowed the school to dig up the campus's asphalt pathways and replace them with more harmonious brick ones. Gilman Hall, the oldest and most photographed building on campus, is named after the university's founder and first president, Daniel Coit Gilman. The seal of the college, in the foyer of the building, is so hallowed that it has curses tied to it: Prospective students who step on it will not be admitted, current students who step on it will not graduate, parents who step on it will not receive financial aid, and faculty who tread on the seal will not receive tenure. So just don't do it, whoever you are. The Milton S. Eisenhower Library, a fantastic resource, is built five stories underground so as not to be as tall as the revered Gilman Hall. Students say each floor becomes progressively quieter as you move downstairs; those studying on D level should expect annoyed stares at the slightest cough or crinkle of paper. "The Beach" is a green lawn behind the Eisenhower Library and bordering Charles Street, where students sunbathe and play soccer or Frisbee when the weather is pleasant. The Mattin Student Arts Center opened in January 2001 and features a black box theater, practice rooms, and arts and dance studios. The university is in the planning stages for a new student union and dining hall.

Varsity athletics do not play a significant role in life at Hopkins—after all, who goes to Hopkins for sports?—and almost all varsity teams are Division III. One exception is lacrosse, the school's only Division I sport and a national power. "Everybody goes to [their games]," says one student. "Lacrosse is huge." The admissions department says that 75 percent of students participate in sports—varsity, club, or intramural. The newly built Ralph S. O'Connor Recreation Center is used frequently by undergraduates.

Historic Baltimore has its bright spots. The Baltimore Museum of Art is free for students and is only a short walk from campus, as is the Walters Art Museum. Johns Hopkins's own Peabody Conservatory of Music is a prime cultural venue. Charles Village, next to campus, has a number of pubs, restaurants, and shops, as does Fells Point, further away. The Inner Harbor, a touristy area with bookstores, shops, restaurants, historical attractions, and the National Aquarium, not to mention nearby stadiums for the Orioles and Ravens, is a popular escape. Washington, D.C., and its array of attractions is a five-dollar train ride away on the MARC, Maryland's commuter train.

Hopkins's urban setting is a major turn-off for many students. Crime, ranging from petty theft to rape, is a concern for students, especially at night. The campus is not at all separated from area neighborhoods, and some of Baltimore's finest can—and do—wander onto campus. The university has taken steps to curb crime, including the provision of evening shuttle services around campus. On-campus crime statistics for 2003 include two forcible sex offenses, three robberies (down from 11 in 2001), one aggravated assault, seven burglaries, six stolen cars, and two arsons.

Elite schools such as Johns Hopkins come at a premium price: Tuition for 2004–5 was $30,140; room and board was an additional $9,516. However, admission is need-blind, and some 59 percent of students receive some financial aid or merit scholarship.

SUGGESTED CORE

1. Classics 040.111, Greek Civilization
2. Philosophy 150.201, Introduction to Greek Philosophy
3. English 060.121, Bible as Scripture
4. No suitable course
5. Philosophy 150.240, Introduction to Political Philosophy
6. English 060.151-152, Shakespeare
7. History 100.109, Introduction to U.S. History: Slavery and Freedom, 1776–1876
8. Philosophy 150.406, History of Modern Philosophy: Kant to the Twentieth Century

MIDDLE ATLANTIC

LAFAYETTE COLLEGE

EASTON, PENNSYLVANIA • WWW.LAFAYETTE.EDU

Windows illuminated

The centerpiece of Lafayette's new Skillman Library is a magnificent 1898 stained glass window of Charlemagne and Alcuin of York by Lewis Comfort Tiffany. The window shows the father of the West with his arm resting on the shoulder of the British monk who brought classical learning back to the Continent at the end of the dark ages; Alcuin is reading an astronomy book. The window, which has narrowly escaped destruction more than once over the decades, has been lovingly restored, and its history is emblematic of the story of civilization in Western Europe and of liberal education in the United States.

The flame that Alcuin lit and Charlemagne tended still burns at Lafayette College in Pennsylvania's Lehigh Valley, which offered its first classes in 1832. While the general education requirements are nothing extraordinary, interaction between faculty and students is frequent and highly valued, professors kindle a love for learning in their students, and teaching, not research, is the top priority. And the college's beautiful hilltop campus in Easton, Pennsylvania, makes Lafayette a pleasant place to spend four years.

Academic Life: On the marquee

For all its devotion to teaching, Lafayette has followed the nearly universal trend toward a lax curriculum. The school's graduation requirements give students enough leeway that they can ignore whole academic disciplines, should they choose to do so.

All students take a first-year seminar followed by an English course, "College Writing." Another seminar in "values and science/ technology" encourages students to think about ethical issues in daily life. Along with these interdisciplinary courses, Lafayette students must also fulfill a few distribution requirements—the main goal of which, it seems, is to prevent students from taking all of their courses in just one area. Every course in the catalog will satisfy at least one of the distribution requirements, but nothing forces or even encourages students to choose classes that contribute centrally to a broad liberal arts education. "To get the depth of knowledge envisioned for a liberal arts college, the burden falls on the student," says one.

Lafayette students do share some of that burden with their professors, who are almost always willing to help guide students in their educations. With no graduate students at the school, faculty members are able to focus their attention on undergraduates. "Lafayette, more than any other school I've seen, has professors who genuinely care if their students are learning the material," says a student. "I've never been turned away by a professor if I was seeking out help. My professors' doors are always open." A student majoring in history says, "Professors are so accessible. Most of them even give you their home phone numbers and encourage you to call with questions. When I raise my hand in class, my professor knows my name." And the faculty is becoming more impressive. One professor says that when the college hires teachers, it usually gets its first or second choice. "Per person, the faculty is extraordinary," the professor says. "As a whole, the faculty works very, very hard, partly because Lafayette is small enough that everyone would notice if you didn't."

Classes are small—seminars are capped at 15 students, while most other classes have fewer than 20. The advising program pairs each freshman with a faculty member; once the student declares a major, he can choose another advisor. One student majoring in government and law says, "The advising program is what you make of it. . . . I am a very self-sufficient person, so I only need my advisor to help pick courses and to keep me abreast of research/work opportunities in the department." A faculty member says that while faculty members are still very committed to their students, the college has gradually become slightly less student-centered than it was, say, 30 years ago, because of the administration's increased focus on research and publishing. However, the strongest student-faculty relationships are fostered in the course of academic research and independent study. The EXCEL Scholars program allows students to gain valuable research experience while getting paid for it; around 160 students participate each year. Lafayette's is one of the best undergraduate research programs in the country.

Lafayette was one of the first colleges in the country to offer an engineering program, and the department remains Lafayette's best known. Besides engineering, Lafayette's strengths lie in its economics and business department, but there has been recent improvement in the natural sciences as well, especially biology, chemistry, and physics.

Apart from the impressive engineering programs, Lafayette's course offerings are limited and fairly traditional. The English department, for instance, offers good classes in Shakespeare and British and American literature. It has a strong drama and theater focus, and many of its courses are dedicated to this area. The philosophy department has just four faculty members, but it offers courses in logic, ethics, metaphysics, existentialism, ancient and modern philosophy, and the philosophy of mind. "Lafayette is a small college with a relatively large endowment, so we can do a lot more than other

---

VITAL STATISTICS

Religious affiliation: Presbyterian
Total enrollment: 2,279
Total undergraduates: 2,279
SAT/ACT midranges: SAT V: 610–700, M: 640–720; ACT: 25–29
Applicants: 5,504
Applicants accepted: 36%
Accepted applicants who enrolled: 29%
Tuition: $24,921
Room and board: $9,000
Freshman retention rate: 94%
Graduation rate: 82% (4 yrs.), 87% (6 yrs.)
Average class size: 18
Student-faculty ratio: 11:1
Courses taught by graduate TAs: none
Most popular majors: economics, business, engineering
Students living on campus: 88%
Guaranteed housing for four years? yes
Students in fraternities: 35% sororities: 40%

Lafayette has replaced the core curriculum with a modest set of distribution requirements, which run as follows:

- First-year seminar, a small class "designed to introduce students to intellectual inquiry through engaging them as thinkers, speakers, and writers." Students may choose among many options, ranging from "Why Poetry Matters" to "Of Males and Men: Myths of Masculinity."
- One common course, "College Writing."
- A values and science/technology seminar. Among the 50 or so courses that fulfill the requirement are "Artificial Minds," "The 3 Cs: Conception, Contraception, and Carrying Capacity," and "Gothic Architecture."
- One course in humanities, with choices ranging from "Literary History" to "Post-Colonial Literature," from "Italian Renaissance Art" to "Protest Art."
- One course in social sciences, such as "Principles of Economics" or "Alienation."

colleges our size," says a professor. "But we're stretched. We all want to hire more faculty members." In addition to what is offered on campus, Lafayette students have access to courses at Muhlenberg, Moravian, De Sales, and Cedar Crest colleges, and at Lehigh University, all members of the Lehigh Valley Association of Independent Colleges.

For those who want them, politicized courses and majors exist. Africana studies offers courses like "African Cultural Institutions," "The Black Experience" (both required for majors), and "Global Africa: Comparative Black Experience." An English course called "Rhetorics of Race" examines "theories of race and racism in the literatures and cultures of the Americas from the nineteenth century to the present." In the course, students are called to answer questions like, "[H]ow do the antecedents to the *mestizo* or hybrid identities celebrated by Chicana author Gloria Anzaldúa call into question her reconceptualization of racial identity? To what extent can nineteenth-century black nationalism be equated to racial separatism (the early Malcolm X) and to what extent does it embrace other cultures (the later Malcolm X)?"

Lafayette faculty members are encouraged to abide by a style manual prescribing nonsexist language—in other words, they are supposed to use "first-year student" instead of "freshman" and "humanity" instead of "mankind." Even so, the Lafayette administration is rather moderate. President Arthur Rothkopf, who just retired, served in the first Bush administration as deputy secretary of transportation. His successor is Daniel Weiss, previously dean of the Krieger School of Arts and Sciences at Johns Hopkins University. Weiss's academic background is in art history.

Among Lafayette's best teachers are Wendy L. Hill in psychology; Gary P. Gordon, Elizabeth W. McMahon, Clifford A. Reiter, Robert J. Root, and Derek Smith in mathematics; Paul D. Barclay and Robert I. Weiner in history; William J. Carpenter and Ian Smith in English; George E. Panichas in philosophy; Howard J. Marblestone in foreign languages and literatures; John T. McCartney, Joshua I. Miller, Bruce Allen Murphy, Ilan Peleg, and Helena Silverstein in government and law; Susan L. Averett, Rose Marie L. Bukics, Edward N. Gamber, and Sheila Handy in economics and business; John F. Greco and Ismail I. Jouny in electrical and computer engineering; and Steven M. Nesbit in mechanical engineering.

Among the top 30 liberal arts colleges in the country, Lafayette has the fifth-highest rate of participation in study-abroad programs, according to *U.S. News and World Report*. Many students choose to go abroad during the interim session (three weeks in January) with Lafayette faculty members. In 2004, faculty traveled overseas with students to teach such courses as "Modern Sub-Saharan Africa: Kenya and Tanzania," "Medieval Architecture in Northern Europe: Belgium, Germany, and the Netherlands," and "The Geologic Evolution of the Hawaiian Islands." Lafayette offers majors in French, German, and Spanish, and additional courses in ancient Greek, Hebrew, Japanese, Latin, and Russian. More languages are available at the other Lehigh Valley colleges. However, there is no foreign language requirement for graduates, even for liberal arts students.

Lafayette faculty show the usual liberal tendencies, but seem unusually tolerant of disagreement. "Students with strong conservative beliefs are more likely to have to defend themselves in class," says a student. But for the most part, faculty members are said to be willing to give them a hearing. "The faculty is liberal in its outlook, but I have never seen or heard of bias in the classroom," says another student. "Our professors believe that both sides of an issue deserve a hearing."

Student Life: The view from College Hill

More Lafayette students come from across the Delaware River in New Jersey than from the college's home state of Pennsylvania. A solid majority of students hail from these and surrounding northeastern states, but they tend to stay on campus once they get there. Students say they usually head home only on official breaks, not weekends, and the college provides plenty of reasons for students to stick around.

On-campus housing is guaranteed for four years and required for students not commuting from home. Seniors who wish to live off campus must obtain special permission. Most residences are arranged in traditional corridor halls, but there are suite-style and townhouse options as well. Dormitories are coed except for two all-female residences. Soles Hall, an all-women suite-style residence, has a fitness center in its basement for residents. Many students choose living units whose residents share an interest in a particular theme; for 2003–4, these included the French/German House, Dry Surfers (for students interested in technology), El Mundo (for international and diversity interests), community service, and a few substance-free residences.

REQUIREMENTS (CONT'D)

- An additional course in either humanities or social science, including anything from "Classical Mythology" to "Deviance."
- Two laboratory courses in biology, chemistry, geology, physics, or psychology.
- A mathematics course or "Logic" or "Principles of Computer Science."
- Two upper-level writing-intensive courses, chosen from a long list that includes everything from "British History" to "Feminist Philosophy."

Liberal arts students must also complete a "foreign culture cluster," either by studying abroad, reaching intermediate proficiency in a foreign language, or by taking three related courses on another (non-English-speaking) culture.

The student body is almost 90 percent white and only 4 percent black, and the administration would like to see those numbers more in line with national demographics. Since 1970, the college has supported the Portlock Black Cultural Center, which hosts lectures on multicultural topics, and it has sponsored student groups like the Association of Black Collegians and the Brothers of Lafayette. It hosted a Paul Robeson Conference in April 2005. Other cultural groups include the Arab Club, *Aya* (a black literary magazine), and a French club. A brochure called "Intercultural Experience: Bringing Cultures Together" highlights all that Lafayette does to create a more culturally diverse atmosphere. The college has a director of intercultural development, a visitation weekend for black and Hispanic prospective students, and annual festivals that celebrate Kwanzaa, Hispanic heritage, and international food. But Lafayette remains overwhelmingly white, and minority students are said to often segregate themselves. A social club for black men called Brothers of Lafayette has its own living space in Keefe Residence Hall.

More than one-third of Lafayette students are members of fraternities or sororities, but students insist that the Greek organizations are not exclusive. "The Greek system is not cliquey," says a sorority member. "Lots of my friends are in different sororities than my own." Students cannot rush fraternities or sororities until their sophomore year, a rule that allows students to make friends with hallmates and classmates before settling into Greek organizations, should they choose to do so. The college offers dozens of other social, political, and academic organizations. Among them are the *Lafayette* newspaper, musical groups, the Forensics Society, and student government. The college's Landis Community Outreach Center promotes volunteer activities like Habitat for Humanity, Prison Tutors, Alternative Spring Break, and visits to nursing homes, schools, and hospitals. Lafayette also has religious groups for several different faiths, but one student says, "Lafayette as a whole can be a hostile environment to grow in your faith." Another says, "I've received slight verbal persecution for my beliefs, but I think I am stronger for it." This student is a member of Lafayette Christian Fellowship, a group that organizes regular morning prayer groups, Bible studies, and a one-on-one "discipleship program."

Politics aren't terribly important to campus life at Lafayette, and there are few voices on the right. "Overall, the student population swings to the left/middle," says a student. "If there is a conservative, nonreligious group on campus, I haven't heard of any." (Actually, the College Republicans would presumably fall into that category, but they do little to contribute to the intellectual life of the school.) Groups such as Students for Social Justice and QuEST (Questioning Established Sexual Taboos) are the most outspoken among the student political groups, often sponsoring panel discussions on topics in which they are interested. QuEST also sponsors National Coming Out Day activities on campus each year as well as other events and protests, but students say that these and similar events draw little student interest.

One of Lafayette's few campus controversies broke out a couple of years ago when a group of students built a 12-foot replica of male genitalia out of beer cans and displayed it prominently on Junior Visiting Day, an event for prospective students and their parents. The project was part of a performing arts class assignment that was meant to spark reactions from fellow students. It worked. The *Lafayette* quoted the students' instructor as saying, "I didn't know they were planning on doing it on Junior Visiting Day, but I applaud it. Maybe it will attract students other than the conformists we get." The incident was reported to the dean of students, but no disciplinary action was taken.

The city of Easton, best known nationally as the home of Crayola crayons, adds little to the school environment. Lafayette looks down on the town from what is known as College Hill. "Easton is at the bottom of the hill," says one student, "and no one comes up. . . . People go there just to get cash and food, but the area of Easton that's at the foot of the hill really isn't that great." Another student says there isn't much in Easton to interest students unless they are of drinking age. On campus, alcohol is present too, but students say it plays less of a role in campus life each year and is easily avoided, even at parties. One parent says drinking and other violations are prevalent and accepted at Lafayette—contrary to what the college says about cracking down on these sorts of incidents. "Our tour guide delighted in telling the assembled group of how many things students can 'get away with' in the dorms, compared to what they could do at home or at other schools such as Muhlenberg where the RAs were 'ridiculous' and 'uptight,'" says the parent. "He spoke expansively on the topic of how RAs at Lafayette look the other way—literally."

Lafayette's sports program has never been a huge money-maker for the school, and support for athletics relies heavily on tuition dollars. In 1999, faced with the choice of cutting sports teams, dropping down a division (Lafayette is an NCAA Division I school), or raising outside money, Lafayette chose to seek additional funding. The college has struggled to maintain a balance between sports and academics. Lafayette athletes are eligible only for ordinary need-based aid—not sports scholarships—and are said to be admitted under the same academic criteria as other students. As things stand, the Lafayette Leopards compete in the Patriot League in 23 varsity sports—a large number for a school of Lafayette's small size. Lafayette's archrival is nearby Lehigh University. "We hate Lehigh," says a student. "That's our only real tradition at the school." Among the club teams are crew, skiing, ultimate Frisbee, volleyball, ice hockey, and equestrianism. Intramural sports are popular as well. The college's Kirby Sports Center, which was completed in 2000, is an excellent facility for nonvarsity athletes, with a 40-foot indoor climbing wall, racquetball and squash courts, a gym, and a fitness center. Informal group exercise classes like cardio-kickboxing, spin cycling, and Jazzercise help keep Lafayette students in tip-top shape.

SUGGESTED CORE
1. Foreign Languages and Literatures 121/125, Greek Literature in English / Latin Literature in English
2. Philosophy 107, The First Philosophers
3. Religion 202, Christian Scriptures
4. Religion 214, Christianity: From Jesus to the Third Millennium
5. Government 244, Modern Political Theory
6. English 301, Shakespeare
7. History 108, Survey of American History from the Colonial Period through Reconstruction
8. History 254, European Thought, Society, and Culture II

MIDDLE ATLANTIC

289

Lafayette's geographic separation from Easton, no doubt, helps keep campus crime relatively infrequent. According to one student, crime is "not at all" a problem. "I always can walk around at night," he says, "it's very well lit, and security is prevalent." Lafayette reported six forcible sex offenses, one stolen car, two arsons, and 20 burglaries for 2003, the last year for which statistics were available.

The school is not cheap in absolute terms, but it *is* less expensive than most other elite liberal arts schools. Tuition in 2004–5 was $24,921, with room and board around $9,000. Admission is need-blind, but the school does not guarantee to meet a student's full financial need. Some 56 percent of students receive some need-based aid.

NEW YORK UNIVERSITY

NEW YORK, NEW YORK • WWW.NYU.EDU

It takes the Village

New York University was founded in 1831 with the hope—as the university's first president, Albert Gallatin, put it—of providing "a rational and practical education for all." From the start, NYU offered courses in the practical sciences and arts, such as business, law, and medicine, instead of just in the liberal arts. The school continues to emphasize the practical, and many students participate in internships in the city as well as hands-on research at the school.

If going to a college nestled between gay bars and drug dealers bothers you, New York University is not your school. As one student warns, "NYU is not for the faint of heart." Located in the middle of Greenwich Village at Washington Square, NYU's setting is also its strongest drawing point, and the university's administration sometimes seems to use the school's site as a crutch; they know that people will and do put up with anything to live in New York City. (The school reports that it received some 30,101 undergraduate freshman applications for fall 2004, more than any other private university in the nation.) As one student says of the school, "The city saves it. I wouldn't go here if it wasn't for that."

Certainly the NYU curriculum is nothing special; as at many schools, it's possible to graduate with an education that is either narrow or scattered. But there are a number of academic gems to be mined at the school, and the university is intent on improving its reputation. Unlike other universities that invested their endowments in high-flying stocks in the 1990s, NYU followed a boring bond strategy—and so instead of losing money in the crash, NYU now has cash to spend on new hires and buildings. A $150 million donation received in 2002 was earmarked for creating 150 endowed chairs over the next 25 years, particularly in science and technology (NYU's weakest areas).

By going to NYU, students sacrifice many traditional college experiences—tailgating and football, for instance, or a bucolic and undisturbed central campus green (Washington Square Park doesn't count). What students gain is four years spent in one of the world's great cities, which is an education in itself.

Academic Life: Morse for "core"

NYU has 13 divisions, including schools of medicine, business, social work, dentistry, and law. Undergraduates interested in the liberal arts enroll in the College of the Arts and Sciences or the Gallatin School of Individualized Study. Arts and Sciences students must meet the requirements of the Morse Academic Plan (named for Samuel Morse, inventor of the telegraph and a one-time professor at NYU), a curriculum aimed at providing students with a well-rounded education. This set of distribution requirements is more respectable than those at many more overtly prestigious schools. In theory, the courses could provide a real humanities education; however, in practice, they are sometimes conducted by professors more intent on their own research than on undergraduate teaching, faculty say. "The undergraduate courses are large and anonymous," one professor says. "The undergraduate curriculum does not meet the standards of higher education," says another.

VITAL STATISTICS
Religious affiliation: none
Total enrollment: 39,408
Total undergraduates: 20,212
SAT/ACT midranges: SAT V: 610–700, M: 610–710; ACT: 27–31
Applicants: 34,457
Applicants accepted: 35%
Accepted applicants who enrolled: 38%
Tuition: $31,690
Room and board: $8,010
Freshman retention rate: 92%
Graduation rate: 72% (4 yrs.), 80% (6 yrs.)
Courses with fewer than 20 students: 58%
Student-faculty ratio: 12:1
Courses taught by graduate TAs: not provided
Most popular majors: business, social sciences, visual and performing arts
Students living on campus: 54%
Guaranteed housing for four years? no
Students in fraternities: 5% sororities: 3%

An alternative for students looking for smaller classes and a different curriculum is the Gallatin School of Individualized Study, home to about 900 undergraduate students. Gallatin describes itself as "a school for people who want to push the boundaries of college education." It encourages individual exploration, often through internships and private lessons in the arts. Most notably, the Gallatin School offers students the opportunity to study the seminal works of the Western tradition, since most courses focus on influential primary texts from the ancient and modern worlds (though this isn't a classic great books program, either). Only self-motivated students should consider Gallatin; some students warn that undirected dilettantes have given the school a bad name, and that "the degree is laughed at." NYU assures us otherwise, but Gallatin students should take care that their transcripts and résumés show seriousness before pursuing jobs or grad school.

NYU does not have a traditional core curriculum, but its distribution requirements go quite a way towards making sure students receive a broad, if not comprehensive, exposure to the humanities. Students must take:

- One class out of four offerings grouped as "Conversations of the West." This class comes in four flavors, focusing on "Antiquity and the Middle Ages," "Antiquity and the Renaissance," "Antiquity and the Enlightenment," or "Antiquity and the Nineteenth Century." Texts for the sections vary slightly, but in all of them students read classics, not interpretations or commentaries.
- One world cultures course focusing on Muslim Europe, "Russia between East and West," ancient Israel, China, India, or Japan, or pre-Columbian America.
- One social science course. Choices range from standard introductions to economics or political science to "Interdisciplinary Perspectives on Gender and Power."

The best courses at the Gallatin School are the interdisciplinary seminars, which cover great works by authors such as Shakespeare, Plato, Homer, and Nietzsche, as well as modern works by Toni Morrison, Elie Wiesel, and others. Though NYU has a fairly weak advising system for its College of Arts and Sciences, Gallatin places a great deal of emphasis on its advisors, who help students develop their academic plans. About 200 faculty members serve as Gallatin advisors.

Choosing a major at the College of the Arts and Sciences (or a concentration at Gallatin) requires some care, because departments vary wildly. The politics department is said by students to house good and fair teachers, but its best courses fill up quickly. Since students register for classes in descending order by seniority, students might have to wait until they are upperclassmen to get the classes they want.

Advisors are available for students who ask for help, but as is typical of NYU, students have to take the initiative. NYU types, though, don't necessarily regard this as a bad thing. "I think one of the things that makes NYU such a great school is that there is not a lot of hand-holding or babysitting by the advisors or professors," says one student. "In my experience they have all generally been accessible and approachable, but leave it largely up to the students to approach them." But even for those who do want good advice, help isn't always there. One alumna who is now a graduate student at NYU says, "At the undergraduate level, the advisors are generally pretty clueless, and at the graduate level they just don't seem to care. That's something that could definitely use some work."

Even though NYU is a rather large school, classes are remarkably small—at least in the humanities. In the sciences, one student says, most courses are "huge lectures with professors," and graduate teaching assistants actually do more of the teaching. (This situation, in part, led to adjunct faculty unionizing through, amazingly, the United Auto Workers). TAs also teach lower-level foreign languages and the mandatory freshman writing course, as well as many of the weekly discussion sessions for the larger introductory courses. Upper-level courses generally have fewer than 20 students. Shuffling between classes can be a problem: the university snatches up buildings whenever it can, and consequently, NYU sprawls out far beyond Washington Square. However, campus transportation is good—and there's always the bus or subway.

The amount of grade inflation at NYU depends on the professor and the department. One grad student reports a massive tilt toward the A-minus range. An undergrad, however, says that "for the most part you get what you deserve, but I've had a couple professors fear the inflation bogeymen so they try to grade as hard as possible. 'I said Helvetica font! C+!'"

The philosophy department is ranked first in the country by the educators who publish the *Philosophical Gourmet Report*. And with good reason; philosophy majors must complete a strict core that ensures students will graduate with a broad knowledge of the discipline. Courses in this curriculum include logic, ancient philosophy, modern philosophy, ethics or political philosophy, metaphysics, the philosophy of mind or language, and upper-level seminars. Few philosophy programs in the country provide students with such a structured curriculum. And there are very few "philosophy of feminism," "eco-ethics," or other such courses at NYU. The one weak spot has been the history of philosophy. To rectify the situation, the university recently hired Don Garrett from the University of North Carolina to focus on rationalists and empiricists, and Princeton's Beatrice Longuenesse, an expert on nineteenth-century German philosophy.

The Judaic studies, Middle Eastern studies, and math departments are strong, as are the English and Spanish departments, although one student advises that in these last two, students should "choose their professors with care." He adds, "History, classics, and others may not be rated too highly, but in general, most of what there is at NYU is either fairly good or well rated."

The university offers courses in more than 20 languages, including ancient Greek, Swahili, Turkish, and Japanese. And through an agreement with Columbia University, NYU students can take language courses not offered at their own school, including Hungarian, Finnish, modern Tibetan, and Sanskrit. NYU's own foreign language programs are a particular strength. The university also encourages students to study abroad for at least a semester. NYU hosts programs in Buenos Aires, Florence, London, Madrid, Paris, and Prague and allows students to study elsewhere through other universities' programs.

Given its location, it is no surprise that NYU is widely recognized for its film and television, theater, and business schools. Generally these are the best-funded and best-

REQUIREMENTS (CONT'D)

- One arts course, chosen from a list including "Expressive Culture: Words," "Images— Painting and Sculpture in New York Field Study," and "Performance," a course that involves students attending a wide variety of live acts, from Broadway to gospel concerts.
- Three courses in the "foundations of scientific inquiry," including a quantitative reasoning course—satisfied by any number of math or statistics courses or by having taken AP calculus in high school—and two courses in the natural sciences.
- "Expository Writing," a one-course writing requirement that emphasizes formal and argumentative writing.
- Students must also demonstrate proficiency to the intermediate level in a foreign language, either through courses or testing.

run divisions at the university, schools in which the city is the student's classroom. Creative writing courses in subjects such as screenwriting are especially strong. Those studying television can see a Midtown taping of an NBC program. Theater students might apprentice themselves in off-Broadway theaters down the street. Internships in other areas abound; many business students, for instance, work on Wall Street, earning course credit and work experience at the same time. NYU's weakest departments are in the sciences and fields like sociology, women's studies, psychology, and Africana studies.

Some of the best teachers at NYU, according to students, are Larissa Bonfante in classics; Luis Cabral (in the School of Business), Israel M. Kirzner, and Mario J. Rizzo (both in the College of Arts and Sciences) in economics; Anthony Low and Haruko Momma in English; John Costello in linguistics; Marilyn Horowitz in creative writing; Evelyn Birge Vitz in French; Angela Dillard in the Gallatin division; Alfred L. Ivry and Lawrence H. Schiffman in Hebrew and Judaic studies; Walter Johnson and Stewart A. Stehlin in history; Steven Brams, David Denoon, and Lawrence Mead in politics; Paul Vitz (emeritus) in psychology; Wolf Heydebrand in sociology; Anne Lounsbery in Russian and Slavic studies; and Kenneth L. Krabbenhoft in Spanish and Portuguese languages and literatures.

One communications major warns that her department is inefficiently run and that she has "had many professors who made their political preferences very clear, and some were even known for allowing differences of political opinion to influence students' grades." The journalism department is said to have become more politicized over the past few years, while the teaching and learning (i.e., education) department is perhaps the worst in this regard. One student tells of an education professor who calls Republicans "Nazis" and another who informs students that "the Republican agenda is to destroy public education." Students should ask older students for advice on classes. A conservative student says she received a good education in the department of teaching and learning by avoiding the bad apples.

Classroom politics at NYU is usually implicit, however, and therefore tolerable. "Most professors, at least all I encountered, were liberal but reasonable. There is a sort of assumption that everyone is liberal so no one asks," says one student. "I did have to put up with hearing a lot of gobbledygook liberal claptrap, but it wasn't forced on me in the way I hear it is at other schools."

Student Life: The center of the world

As one student puts it, NYU students consider themselves Manhattan residents who just happen to be attending classes. And since New York is the city that never sleeps, students never lack for things to do (although they might lack the money). One recent graduate says NYU students do "the same things everyone else does for fun in New York: go to restaurants, shows, museums, and bars. No football games or keg parties." Several museums, such as the Metropolitan Museum of Art, are always "pay what you wish." Soho's trendy galleries—free to enter—are a short walk away, as are the best art house movie theaters in America; hundreds of inexpensive, excellent ethnic restaurants;

dozens of new and used bookstores; several premium jazz, blues, and folk venues; charming old-world cafes; landmark houses of worship, including a Ukrainian Catholic *and* a Russian Orthodox cathedral—you name it. NYU sits squarely in the most interesting part of America's most cosmopolitan city.

Says one student, "There's so much to do in New York City that one would be ridiculous to spend [one's] entire college career getting hammered in someone's dorm room." Likewise, fraternities and sororities are not a big part of student life—only 5 percent of men are in fraternities, and only 3 percent of women belong to sororities.

Nonetheless, NYU is sensitive to criticism that it lacks a genuine "collegiate atmosphere." One student says, "There is basically no communal feel to NYU, which is in large part I think due to the urban environment and lack of a centralized campus." Another student says, "There are a lot of student clubs and organizations. And the dormitories, especially freshman dorms, do their best to plan activities and encourage students to get to know each other. At times there is a sense of 'real college'—for example, when NYU has events such as Bobcat Day, Strawberry Festival, Autumn Fest, Grad Alley, [and] Violet Ball." Says another: "The administration is always trying to foster school spirit, but it's a tough thing to do. What makes NYU NYU is that it is a completely urban university, with all that entails."

SUGGESTED CORE
1. Classics 303, Civilization of Greece and Rome
2. Philosophy 020, History of Ancient Philosophy
3. Hebrew and Judaic Studies 126, Modern Perspectives on the Bible *and* Religious Studies 844, Jesus and the Gospel Writings (*closest matches*)
4. Religious Studies 60, Philosophy in the Middle Ages
5. Politics 120, Modern Political Thought: 1500 to Present
6. English 410/411, Shakespeare I/II
7. History 009, The United States to 1865
8. History 153, European Thought and Culture, 1750–1870

In the past few years, the vast, modernist Bobst Library has witnessed the extremes of student life—and death. Two desperate students committed suicide in the most public way possible, leaping down its cavernous central stairwell to perish on the marble before dozens of their schoolmates. In response, the school beefed up counseling services—and glassed in the stairwell. A few months later, an impoverished undergraduate whose financial aid wouldn't cover his dorm room was found to be living in the library.

Tight housing comes with the downtown territory. While students in Columbia University apartments uptown tend to get their own private rooms, such luxuries are scarce at NYU. Still, students get a bed, sometimes a kitchen and a living room, and "all student rooms have their own bathrooms, which is a huge plus," one student says. The university has five traditional dormitories—one of which is exclusively for freshmen—plus a number of row houses, apartments, and suite-style residence halls. Although all halls are coed, this arrangement isn't such a problem at NYU because of the bathroom situation. There are also a few substance-free options (no smoking and no alcohol allowed) for those who ask for them. Some of the dorms are rather far from campus, but transportation is reliable. The university attempts to buy and renovate Washington

Square buildings as they become available, though the school occasionally has to fend off lawsuits from neighbors who resent the changing neighborhood.

Speaking of campus growth, NYU is breaking ground on an expansive new science center, reports the *Chronicle of Higher Education*. The planned facility will house labs, classrooms, and offices for the life sciences, expanding their elbow room by almost one-third. It will be the first new NYU science building to be opened since 1971. The school has also embarked on an ambitious fundraising campaign, again according to the *Chronicle*. NYU parent Billy Joel kicked off the initiative with a concert for high-rolling donors in 2004; the university hopes to raise $2.5 billion "to support financial aid, recruit new faculty, expand academic programs, and develop facilities."

No question about it, NYU is a left-leaning campus. A recent "man-on-the-street" section in the student-run *Washington Square News* asked students their favorite restaurants—and the first two interviewees listed vegan establishments. The university's unionized (and politicized) adjunct faculty mull the occasional strike. As in any environment where most people are crowded into a narrow part of the political spectrum, people try to outdo each other by being ever more radical.

But the lefty politics need not stifle anyone's intellectual curiosity. "As long as you can defend your beliefs and carry on an intelligent, rational conversation, most people, while disagreeing, can still generally respect others' opinions," says one student. Indeed, "with such a diverse student body, one has to generally be accepting of all cultures and beliefs, political or otherwise," says another. And a third student says, "One of the good things about New York is that people do tend to be pretty tolerant, whether you are a gay activist or a Republican." With eight million people in the city, you are bound to find others who share your causes, however small or pedestrian they may be. The school also boasts a strong, active College Republicans chapter that brought English conservative philosopher (and eloquent defender of fox hunting) Roger Scruton to campus in 2005. There is also a (somewhat beleaguered) group called Students for Life. The school maintains vibrant chaplaincies, and the Catholic Student Center is said to be especially active (although the chapel is mind-bendingly hideous). There are also dozens of churches of every denomination—and historic synagogues—within walking distance.

Some students have complained about a lack of free speech on campus, but Director of Student Activities Robert Butler says the university has instituted a protest policy that is "structured to protect free speech," even in this heavily populated urban area. When university groups decide to host a lecture or program, they decide whether it is closed—meaning only members of a private group are invited—or open—meaning any member of the NYU community can attend. If an open meeting is held inside a campus building, protesters are allowed to oppose the speaker or program, as long as it is done peacefully. Butler says, "We don't allow protesters to prevent the speaker from speaking."

Athletic facilities exist at NYU, and sports teams as well, although no one seems to care about them except when there is the occasional high-profile victory. For instance, the women's volleyball team made the Final Four in 2003, prompting the *Wash-*

ington Square News to editorialize about how exciting that accomplishment was in a "school not known for its athletic prowess." NYU fields 10 men's teams and eight women's varsity teams. Intramural sports include bowling, volleyball, basketball, tennis, football, home run derby, and something called Quickball.

As for the students, NYU attracts all types. For one thing, there is much genuine diversity. "It's NYU and NYC—you will never see anyone from your same exact background," says a student. Once you're there, New York City becomes the center of the world. Many NYU students are in preprofessional programs, and their ambition leads them to work extraordinarily hard. Students also tend to be ferociously independent. Says one student, "Everyone knows that freshman year of college can be overwhelming, but New York City can be entirely overwhelming, even scary. Independence and self-confidence are absolutely essential to avoid feeling overwhelmed and intimidated." The college can be a bit impersonal, and sometimes overwhelming, but most students report that the freedom and fun they find there are absolutely exhilarating.

Crime can be a problem, as at any urban university, but New York City grew appreciably safer under former mayor Giuliani, and the crack wars that raged in the early 1990s have died down. New York has far fewer murders per capita than cities such as Washington, D.C. The Village is busy at all hours of the day or night, and it is generally well patrolled. While you may have to step over homeless people or strung-out addicts to get to class, they're usually harmless. Some students report being offered drugs; one says that during an orientation break, "immediately after I settled myself on the bench (in Washington Square Park) a young man came and sat down next to me, saying 'Hi, I'm Angel, I sell coke, E, and weed.'" As in any city, students must be aware of their surroundings, never leave belongings unattended, walk briskly, and avoid eye contact or calling attention to themselves. But surprisingly, the university reports few criminal incidents on the NYU campus. In 2003 there were four forcible sex offenses and nine burglaries.

NYU, like everything in New York, is expensive, with a 2004–5 tuition of $31,690, and a room and board price tag of $8,010. But the school practices need-blind admissions and provides aid to approximately 56 percent of students. The average loan burden of recent graduates is $27,639.

STATE UNIVERSITY OF NEW YORK – BINGHAMTON

VESTAL, NEW YORK • WWW.BINGHAMTON.EDU

Disrespecting the Bing

The *Chronicle of Higher Education* recently asked the president of SUNY–Binghamton, Lois B. DeFleur, what she would do for the school with an extra billion dollars. Her suggestions ranged from strengthening undergraduate mentoring and implementing more study-abroad opportunities and cross-disciplinary programs to big-picture projects that would bring the university and outside community closer together.

The president has a point. Since it would take more than a billion dollars to transform the school into a Williams or a UVA, it makes sense to use the money to get students out of Binghamton and into programs around the globe. Of course, we figure you could also develop a pretty decent liberal arts curriculum for 10 digits' worth of cash, were you so inclined.

Make no mistake, this is a campus that uses the Wal-Mart business model; it is big and cheap. For a certain type of student, this place can be a home run, but don't even think about attending until you have visited the campus. If a student is planning to study science, can create his own fun (or doesn't require any), and is willing to proactively seek out exposure to some great research projects, then this school could be a cost-effective academic opportunity. This also assumes the student is a New York resident and will either enjoy—or ignore—the strong reaction that results from confining 6,000 kids from Long Island in a small, grey space. For students in need of more guidance, seeking a classical education, or looking for small class sizes, this may not be a safe choice.

Academic Life: Cross-listed, crossed up

Binghamton has noble academic goals for its students, including the desire that its students gain "knowledge about various intellectual traditions" during their time at the school. How this is supposed to occur and precisely what traditions are involved is a bit of a mystery, since the university's curriculum does little to define that. Binghamton students must satisfy several university-wide general education requirements, but these requirements are loose enough that students can meet them with any of hundreds of courses. For instance, a student could bypass a basic course in Western literature by enrolling in the literature course "Cyberspace and Globality," or he could choose "World Environmental History" over an introductory American history course.

Since many courses are cross-listed among disciplines, students often graduate without taking many classes outside their academic areas, says one student. Furthermore, even in basic foundation courses like "Foundations of Western Civilization," professors have a "great deal of autonomy as far as course material is concerned, which can be a blessing or a curse," a student wrote in one of the campus newspapers. He proposed that the university set guidelines for basic freshman courses: "Many assume that freshman philosophy classes begin with a study of the ideas of Aristotle, St. Thomas Aquinas, and John Locke, but that is not always the case." Some departments do have additional course requirements that impart some structure to a student's education. The curriculum for English majors, for instance, must include two British literature courses, "American History before 1920," a course in Shakespeare, and "Introduction to Literature Theory/Criticism," plus six more elective courses in literature, rhetoric, or creative writing above the introductory level. Students are advised to choose their professors wisely, though, as two members of the English department are listed on the school's Web site as "witchcraft experts." Though at least with two such specialists on staff, students won't complete their education with only a narrow perspective on the topic.

Despite the fact that Binghamton trumpets itself as the "Ivy League of the SUNYs," some students are disappointed with the level of academic rigor at the school. One recent alumnus says that coursework is not demanding and that "professors tend to give decent grades for the most minimal effort." In the political science department, for instance, students report that they can receive a B for almost no work. "Skip the readings, make an uninformed comment in class once or twice a month, and write your final paper the night before, and you are guaranteed at least a B," says a student who worked in the campus tutorial center and believes that the other social science departments operate in much the same way. "Just scribble some words on a page, turn it in, and you will get a passing grade. You hardly even need to write in coherent sentences, much less proofread." Another student says that many Binghamton students just ask upperclassmen which courses and professors are easiest and base their course selection on that information.

Bright students who wish to surround themselves with other bright students can participate in the Binghamton Scholars Program. The four-year honors program allows the top 120 students at Binghamton to take smaller, more rigorous courses, often using collaborative and experiential learning. One faculty member says that the honors students at Binghamton are "equaled by few and surpassed by none." The program

VITAL STATISTICS
Religious affiliation: none
Total enrollment: 13,860
Total undergraduates: 11,034
SAT/ACT midranges: SAT V: 570–650, M: 600–690; ACT: 24–28
Applicants: 20,116
Applicants accepted: 44%
Accepted applicants who enrolled: 24%
Tuition: $4,350 (in state), $10,610 (out of state)
Room and board: $7,710
Freshman retention rate: 92%
Graduation rate: 69% (4yrs.), 81% (6 yrs.)
Courses with fewer than 20 students: 40%
Student-faculty ratio: 22:1
Courses taught by graduate TAs: not provided
Most popular majors: social sciences, business, psychology
Students living on campus: 58%
Guaranteed housing for four years? no
Students in fraternities: 8% sororities: 7%

Binghamton has no core curriculum, but it does maintain some distribution requirements—most of which can be met by either straightforward, useful courses, or trendy wastes of time. The choice is yours. (Which rather defeats their purpose, doesn't it?) Students must take:

- One course in English composition. Themed options range from "Exploring Jules Verne" to "Witches, Scapegoats, and Disorders."
- One course in oral communication. Choices include "Argumentative Theory" and "Theorizing Race Queerly."
- Three semesters (or equivalent test scores) in a foreign language. Choices range from Yiddish to Latin.
- One course in "pluralism in the U.S." Choices include "Philosophy in Literature" and "Pop, Rock, and Soul Music."
- One class dealing with "Global Interdependencies." Options run from "Introduction to Geography" to "Human Rights in a Global Context."

consists of one class per semester, taken along with the student's regular work. The program fulfills the general education requirements, and that frees up the student's schedule a bit.

Freshmen in the Binghamton Scholars Program complete "Worlds of Inquiry and Discovery," a project-based course in which students record in portfolios what they have learned. The risk here is that topics for this course change each year and are entirely up to the faculty member involved. Juniors take "Worlds of Experience," an internship program in which they work closely with faculty advisors.

The courses in the Binghamton Scholars Program have no set curriculum and no set readings. The student is required to navigate the program with the help of the faculty researchers. A successful student should be able to discern the various opportunities and be able to select an appropriate program. The core courses "take you into the intellectual world of your professors, may range as far and wide as suburbia in the 1930s or Stonehenge in prehistoric Britain, and may ask you to critique American economic policy from the perspective of a foreign government or hurl you forward in time and space to discover new forms of literacy in the landscape of the Internet." So students sign up for courses not knowing what, exactly, they will be learning. Apart from this program, every academic department also has a slate of honors courses that are supposed to be more challenging than the regular ones.

Graduate teaching assistants are used at Binghamton in the same way they are used at most research universities: Professors teach larger lecture courses, and TAs lead weekly discussion sessions. Some lower-level seminars are also led by graduate students rather than full-time faculty members. Professors normally keep weekly office hours, but how accessible or how willing they are to help undergraduates depends on the professor. "Some of them . . . are great teachers and they care about the students' well-being," a biological science major says. "Others are cold and care only about themselves and their research. It's all in the luck of the draw." Many students seem to seek help from their instructors only if they are in danger of failing. Harpur College (a liberal arts division of the university) does have a formal advising program, but otherwise, advising is "virtually nonexistent," says one student—since the only advice professors are instructed to give is on how students can fulfill the university's distribution requirements. Even in that, the student says, "most professors aren't even aware what is going on outside of their classrooms or offices, much less of graduation requirements and so forth."

Students say the best professors are Nancy Tittler in German, Russian, and East Asian languages; Steven Scalet in philosophy and economics; Martin C. Dillon in philosophy; Melvin C. Shefftz in history; Scott T. Handy in chemistry; and David S. Wilson in biological sciences.

Binghamton's best departments are biology and economics, while special-interest majors (like Caribbean studies, Africana studies, and women's studies) are notoriously weak. The philosophy, politics, and law (PPL) major is popular, especially among those who wish to go to law school. One professor says, "The coursework in this major hammers away at traditional problems in ethics, political philosophy, history, and political science. PPL comes closer than most to the idea of a basic liberal arts education and staffs its core courses with tenured faculty who have earned a reputation for good teaching." This is in striking contrast to several other departments. According to one self-described liberal professor, most of the soft sciences are suspect, but the departments most marked by left-leaning identity politics are comparative literature, sociology, and women and gender studies.

Binghamton is often handicapped by the budget issues that are part and parcel of being a state university. One consequence of this fact, coupled with the poor management of funds, is that the university does not have enough instructors to teach certain courses required for graduation. Since writing courses tend to be smaller classes in which faculty members delve more deeply into the subject matter, the university has had difficulty providing enough instructors for students' needs. Some students enroll in summer school in order to graduate on time.

The school did experiment with a Winter Schedule program this past January. The program offered about 15 classes that could be completed over the three-week semester break. It was hailed as a success and may help some students graduate on time, but not if they needed a serious course. Most of the courses offered looked like this sampling: "Golf," "Advanced Auditing," "Reds and Jews," and "Hockey." If graduation statistics are any indication, the average student isn't in much of a rush to get out; only 69 percent emerge within four years.

REQUIREMENTS (CONT'D)

- One class in a laboratory science. Choices include "Physical Geography" and "Weather and Climate."
- One social sciences class. Options are many, including "The High Middle Ages: 900–1350" and "Bollywood Cinema Worldwide."
- One mathematics/reasoning course. Choices include "Elementary Logic" and "Statistics."
- One class in "aesthetics." Options include everything from "Beginning Photography" to "Weimar and Nazi Cinema."
- One course in humanities. Choices range from "Chaucer" to "Introduction to Race, Gender, and Equality."
- One course in physical education. Options include "Golf" and "Yoga for Actors."
- One course in wellness. Choices here range from "Nutrition" to "Love Thyself."

MIDDLE ATLANTIC

Student Life: I Love NY

If the Binghamton campus were based on a theme, it would have to be *One Day in the Life of Ivan Denisovich*; most of the 13,000 students share five residence halls. Mostly built in the 1960s, the campus comprises mainly red-brick prison-style buildings separated by more pleasant lawns of green. A clock tower in the center of campus is a modern contraption that looks like scaffolding. Demand for on-campus housing at Binghamton is strong, and the university is facing a housing crunch caused by poor planning. Thus, the typically small college dorm room has gotten a little smaller, as many doubles have been converted to triples. Some students are being housed in a nearby Holiday Inn. The newest dormitory, Mountainview College, opened in 2003 with room for 606 students. More typical is the College in the Woods "compound," which is made up of six units housing a total of 1,800 students. Ouch. The most notorious dorm seems to be Newing College; it appears repeatedly on various college blogs and the reviews are not good. It seems that unless you are a serious partier from Long Island, you may not get much sleep. Each dorm has its own cafeteria, but one student suggested The Kosher Kitchen, which is on campus and open for every meal, as a tasty alternative to the regular routine.

There are no single-sex dormitories at the university, but students do have the option of living on single-sex or coed floors. The school does not have any coed bathrooms in campus residences, and the university abolished coed dorm rooms a few years ago, according to a housing representative. Binghamton also offers a few special-interest dormitories, in which students live with others of similar interests and work on projects and activities throughout the year. Some recent groups have included fitness, community service, alternative lifestyle, robotics, and engineering. The Off-Campus College program provides lists of available apartments and houses in the Binghamton area.

The university banned alcohol on campus a few years ago, but as one student reports, "That doesn't mean the campus is completely dry. Lots of students drink in their dorm rooms. It's just a matter of not getting caught." Another student says, "Binghamton students go to bars, go to house parties, frat parties, drink, and hook up. There is a lot to do on campus, but very few students participate in those weekend events." Around 8 percent of Binghamton students participate in Greek life, but fraternities are housed off campus and sororities are not residential. Many of the fraternity parties tend to consist of smaller groups of friends, not the raucous *Animal House* scene students might have in mind.

Students at Binghamton agree that their classmates are quite apolitical. "Out of about 11,000 undergraduates, I don't think there are ever more than a few hundred hard-core activist/political types," one student says. "And these few do not get taken seriously by the majority of students." While every year brings a few leftist rallies, teach-ins, and other political events, only a few students—around 20 is typical—attend them, and each event seems to have the same organizers. Even the *Binghamton Review*, a conservative student newspaper, seems to have gone to sleep. The last issue was printed in 2003, and no sign of life has been detected since the previous editor graduated. The school has the usual gamut of progressive organizations that haunt any given college campus. The school sponsors the Womyn's Center and the Rainbow Pride Union, alongside more traditional activities such as Ultimate Frisbee and Hillel. The school does have a Newman Center right on campus, located just steps away from the previously mentioned Newing College dorm of ill repute. The school also has a strong Jewish community, which appears to harbor a group of conservative students.

As students at a SUNY school, Binghamton students also have the opportunity to belong to the state-wide SASU alliance. This group is a politically active, progressive, grassroots organization that fights for the usual egalitarian ideals; this means plenty of long, earnest bus trips to Albany. In addition, every Binghamton student is required to contribute five dollars each year—through student fees— to the New York Public Interest Research Group (NYPIRG), a liberal political action committee.

Prospective students should remember that Binghamton is a *state* university. Approximately 89 percent of the freshman class of 2008 comes from the state of New York, and about 57 percent from New York City, Long Island, or Westchester County. Clearly, as one student puts it, "If you like New Yorkers, this is your school. If not, don't apply here." Since the majority of students live so close to home, many are away on weekends, but Binghamton is by no means a suitcase school. The area is surrounded by natural beauty, for students who are willing to pull themselves away from books and beer. The Pocono Mountains, only an hour south in northern Pennsylvania, are great for hiking, skiing, snowboarding, and other outdoor activities.

SUNY–Binghamton is actually located in Vestal, New York, outside the municipal limits of Binghamton proper, a small city with which the university and its students have a lukewarm relationship. Students enjoy a few off-campus hangouts like The Sports Bar and The Ratt. Two nearby malls, Town Square and Oakdale, are popular venues for students. Since many students live off campus and commute to classes each day, there is not a strong community feel at the university. Local sports teams include a minor-league baseball team, the Binghamton Mets, and the Binghamton Senators hockey team. The area also has a few theaters, a community symphony, an art museum, an opera company, and an astronomical observatory. Many of these can be reached by a public bus system.

The Binghamton Bearcats (formerly the less politically correct Colonials) compete in 21 varsity sports in NCAA Division I. Students can also participate in intercollegiate and intramural sports. The football and men's basketball teams get publicity disproportional to their accomplishments due to regular mentions on alumnus Tony Kornheiser's TV and radio shows.

If you need a break from the local color, the school offers an impressive array of

SUGGESTED CORE

1. Classical and Near Eastern Studies 214, Greek Drama
2. Philosophy 201, Plato and Aristotle
3. History 241, Biblical History: Hebrew Origins to the Exile
4. History 481J, Medieval Christianity
5. Political Science 115, Introduction to the Ideas of Politics (*closest match*)
6. English 270, Shakespeare
7. History 103, Foundations of American Civilization
8. Philosophy 408, Nineteenth-Century Philosophy

overseas programs, and students have access to any of the other overseas programs offered by any of the New York state universities. Programs can be either a semester long or span the entire academic year. Each October, the school holds an Overseas Program Fair that gives students a chance to review all the programs at once.

The university also has an excellent performing arts center in the Anderson Center for the Arts, which includes a 1,200-seat theater and a wall that retracts for lawn seating. This venue hosts a variety of world-class performances such as the St. Petersburg Ballet and the Luxembourg Philharmonic Orchestra. The newest addition to campus is the $33 million Events Center, a sports arena with room for more. It has received mixed reviews, the way any large sporting expense does in a tight budgetary environment.

For those not on a team roster, the school offers 130 student organizations that, taken as a whole, suggest that most any student could find a niche, even if he doesn't like New Yorkers. The school has a student-run newspaper (*Pipe Dream*), a television studio, a radio station, and an enormous greenhouse that is used for research but is open to students. Harpur's Ferry is a student-run volunteer ambulance service that provides free, advanced life-support emergency service to the campus. No training is required to apply; the group will provide all the necessary training for certification.

Crime is not perceived as a big problem at Binghamton; there were five forcible sex-offenses, one robbery, nine burglaries and two arsons on campus in 2003. A recent student council meeting was well attended due to a protest over security cameras being installed in the dorms. The school did not inform the students that they would be installing the cameras and the students felt this was a violation of their privacy. The school posts a register of local sex offenders on its Web site, and the university police work to prevent campus crime by offering a walking escort and van service for students who are uneasy late at night. In addition to emergency phones and panic buttons, the university also has a gate surrounding the main campus that is locked each night from midnight until 5 a.m.

Other college guides often tout Binghamton as an affordable alternative to an Ivy education, yet the tuition has increased quite a bit from $2,175 in 2003. In-state students pay $4,350, nonresidents pay $10,610, and everyone pays $7,710 for room and board and $1,380 in mandatory fees. Admission is need-blind. The school itself doesn't give out much direct aid; the Binghamton University Foundation distributed only half a million dollars in aid last year. The school's financial aid office, not well liked by the students, functions as the direct marketing arm of government loan programs. In other words, they simply assist students with the paperwork to access public funds. According to *U.S. News and World Report*, the average Binghamton graduate walks away with a debt of $12,367.

UNIVERSITY OF PENNSYLVANIA

PHILADELPHIA, PENNSYLVANIA • WWW.UPENN.EDU

All about the Benjamins

The University of Pennsylvania is known as one of America's top universities. The school's Web site describes it as "a historic Ivy League school with highly selective admissions and a history of innovative interdisciplinary education and scholarship" on "a picturesque campus amidst a dynamic city." During the past decade, under the leadership of Judith Rodin, Penn has risen significantly in national standing, nearly doubled its research funding, and tripled both its annual fundraising and the size of its endowment, according to a university self-study. (In 2005 *U.S. News and World Report* ranked the university fourth among national research universities.)

Penn was started by Benjamin Franklin more than 250 years ago to teach both the practical and theoretical arts, and Franklin features prominently in the admissions literature and on the main campus quad. Says the university's Web site, "Penn carries on the principles and spirit of its founder, Benjamin Franklin: entrepreneurship, innovation, invention, outreach, and a pragmatic love of knowledge. Franklin's practical outlook has remained a driving force in the university's development." Some fret that the practical trumps the intellectual at Penn, particularly in the famous professional programs of the Wharton School. Still, there is no doubt that Penn is the inheritor of a profound Quaker intellectual tradition that blends both classical and useful learning. Despite tragicomic episodes of political correctness in past years, and uncertainty about where recently selected president Amy Gutmann will lead the school, the University of Pennsylvania has much to recommend it.

VITAL STATISTICS
Religious affiliation: none
Total enrollment: 23,305
Total undergraduates: 10,047
SAT median: 1431
ACT midrange: 28–33
Applicants: 18,282
Applicants accepted: 21%
Accepted applicants who enrolled: 63%
Tuition: $30,716
Room and board: $8,918
Freshman retention rate: 98%
Graduation rate: 86% (4 yrs.), 93% (6 yrs.)
Average class size: 16
Student-faculty ratio: 6:1
Courses taught by graduate TAs: not provided
Most popular majors: business, engineering, economics
Students living on campus: 64%
Guaranteed housing for four years? no
Students in fraternities: 28% sororities: 18%

Academic Life: Penn is mightier than the word

About 10,050 Penn undergraduates are enrolled in one of its four schools: "The College," which includes majors in the arts and sciences; the School of Engineering and Applied Science; the School of Nursing; and the Wharton School, for business students.

MIDDLE ATLANTIC

305

The liberal arts College of the University of Pennsylvania has the strongest distributional mandates at the school. Students can fulfill them by selecting courses from a list of around 50 in each category from a number of departments. Students must take:

- Two "society" courses, such as economics, sociology, political science, cultural anthropology, demography, social psychology, or moral and political philosophy.
- Two "history and tradition" classes from the various fields of history, such as social, political, and cultural history, or folklore, religion, and philosophy.
- Two "arts and letters" courses exploring paintings, films, poetry, fiction, theatre, dance, or music.
- A "formal reasoning and analysis" course, such as mathematics, computer science, formal linguistics, symbolic logic, statistics, or decision theory.

Approximately 65 percent of the undergraduate student body enrolls in the College. Undergraduates can take classes in any of these four schools, but students choose one from the beginning to be their home area. Penn also has 12 graduate and professional schools that enroll about 13,000 students.

As is true of most modern colleges—even elite ones—the University of Pennsylvania has given up on the idea of a core curriculum and instead imposes a series of distribution requirements. Penn's are better than many, but they still leave plenty of room for students enrolled even in the liberal arts-oriented College to graduate with enormous gaps in their knowledge of Western culture—particularly those students who have come to Philly merely to snag an Ivy League diploma before marching into the business world or law school. Happily, most Penn students demonstrate significant intellectual curiosity and often take the initiative to study the great books and ideas themselves. But that's no argument for leaving the classics to happy accident.

On the positive side, Penn imposes no diversity requirement—typically a catechesis in white male guilt. While nearly every department has a few politicized courses, students can sidestep these pretty easily or choose their biases as they wish. Says a student, "Most professors avoid politics. Of the ones who don't there are some departments that are often conservative (e.g., economics, Wharton) and some that are often liberal (e.g., linguistics, English)." The English department is one of the most politicized departments at Penn; one professor calls the curriculum there "politicized, self-indulgent, and intolerant," while a student says the department's take on literary criticism resides "on the cutting edge of wackiness." But the department also includes several solid course offerings and a few traditionally oriented professors—and many who win awards for their undergraduate teaching.

Most Penn majors ensure that students have at least some exposure to the main areas of the discipline. For instance, history majors have to take courses in world, European, and American history; two courses that deal with events before 1800; and two departmental seminars. English majors must fulfill a language and literature requirement and take courses on the medieval through Renaissance period, English poetry from Pope to Eliot, the history of the novel, and early American literature.

Penn's variety of courses is one of the school's major selling points, with classes ranging from Iranian literature to nursing. In 2004 the university became the first Ivy League institution to add a criminology department to its arts and sciences offerings. Highly recommended departments include history (particularly diplomatic and military), classics, ancient languages, and chemistry.

The university offers an alternative Pilot Curriculum, which students can select instead of the general requirements. The Pilot Curriculum attempts to create an interdisciplinary and research-oriented education. Requirements include four general education areas—"Structure and Values in Human Societies," "Science, Culture, and Society," "Earth, Space, and Life," and "Imagination, Representation, and Reality"—all of which can be satisfied by choosing from only a handful of courses. For spring 2005, approved courses for the science, culture, and society category included "The Origins and Evolution of Scientific Thought," "Human Sexuality," and "Technology and Society" (among others). The earth, space, and life category offered "What Every Lawyer, Businessman, and Citizen Needs to Know about Molecular Biology" alongside "Environmental Chemistry." Pilot Curriculum students also must satisfy a foreign language requirement and take courses in writing and math. Pilot students enter their major, the school promises, "with significant research experience."

At Penn, as at many big-name schools, students shouldn't be fooled by promotional literature that touts the names of big-shot professors, since most of them will be of little actual use to students. "Many of the professors are at the forefronts of their fields. Unfortunately, getting to know them is the most difficult part," says a student. Some faculty members are more accessible, though. A sophomore history major says that in all but two of his classes "the professors have encouraged us to use office hours, sometimes getting upset if we didn't."

On the humanities side, Alan Charles Kors, a professor of history who also heads the Foundation for Individual Rights in Education, is a devoted proponent of free discussion on campus. One Penn law student reports that if he could do it all over again, he'd be sure to take a class with Robert A. Kraft in religious studies. Other good professors include Martin Seligman in psychology; John J. DiIulio Jr. (late of the Bush administration) and Stephen Gale in political science; Al Filreis in English; Thomas Childers, Walter McDougall, Ann Moyer, Edward Peters, and Arthur Waldron in history; and Zoltan

REQUIREMENTS (CONT'D)

- A "living world" class dealing with the evolution, development, structure, and/or function of living systems.
- A "physical world" course in physics, chemistry, geology and environmental studies, or astronomy.
- A "science studies" course focusing on scientific thought and practice in cultural, historical, and philosophical context, or another "formal reasoning and analysis," "living world," or "physical world" class.
- A writing seminar from those offered by departments such as English, anthropology, history, music, or philosophy—or two "Writing Across the University" classes.
- A quantitative data analysis course that uses mathematical or statistical analysis of quantitative data as a method for understanding a subject.

  Students must also demonstrate competency, either through coursework or testing, in a foreign language.

Domotor, Gary Hatfield, and James F. Ross in philosophy. The classics department at Penn is highly regarded, and Professor Jeremy McInerney is especially recommended.

Faculty report that tenure and hiring decisions are made largely on the basis of merit. "Recent hiring decisions have been very good," says one professor. "I think we have perhaps the finest junior faculty in the country, and they have every prospect of promotion"—even if they're not writing about lesbian literary theory. "Conservative opinion is represented, though as anywhere else, the dominant worldview is a rather archaic and romantic liberalism," that professor continues. "Penn is not complacent: it is on the move, upward, and wants to maintain that momentum. So it looks for the talent."

Says one professor, "Penn is a big university. Some students work very hard and do very well. They become known to the faculty and have plenty of access. But others just drift along." Drifting along is entirely possible, students report—saying that no one would really notice unless you started failing classes. Advising is described by students as somewhat anonymous; in the words of one, it consists of "random professors who don't necessarily know anything even about the major requirements." Before declaring a major, underclassmen are assigned premajor advisors (not necessarily faculty members), but after choosing a major students are given faculty advisors within their departments.

When President Rodin stepped down as president in 2004, Amy Gutmann, a former Princeton provost and a political philosopher known for addressing such issues as affirmative action and identity group politics, was named as her replacement. How President Gutmann's ideas will be translated into the governance of Penn and how they will influence the liberal arts education at the school remain to be seen.

Student Life: Penn's station

Despite its location in the center of the Washington–New York corridor, Philadelphia is a surprisingly provincial town with quirks that make it unfailingly interesting. Besides world-class museums and concert facilities, there are distinctive accents and phrases ("Have a goot one," "What can I getchyouzguys?"), lots of unhealthy cheesesteak-and-hoagie shops, water ice stands, pro sports teams whose fortunes are passionately followed and bemoaned (especially the Eagles, who finally made the Super Bowl after losing the previous three NFC championship games), and plenty of bars and restaurants, if you can afford them. "A lot of people take advantage of the many events in the city, which is fairly accessible from campus," says one student. (Note: This "accessible" claim is debated by others, who say they take taxis to travel safely from campus.)

The 262-acre campus includes attractions such as Houston Hall, the nation's first student union; the University of Pennsylvania Museum (considered one of the finest university archeology and anthropology museums in the country); and Franklin Field, the oldest collegiate football field still in use and the country's first double-decked college stadium. Victorian buildings are intermingled with modern structures on campus. Locust Walk, once a city street but now open only to non-motorized traffic, is perhaps the most beautiful part of campus. "During the day, Locust Walk hosts an ongoing ballet of people coming in and out of class," says a recent graduate. In 2004, the university bought a 24-acre waterfront site from the U.S. Postal Service, expanding the campus to the east. Development of the property into research facilities and playing fields will occur after 2007.

The University of Pennsylvania is primarily a residential campus; about 64 percent of Penn's undergraduates live on campus, and those who don't usually live nearby. Freshmen who send in their housing applications on time are guaranteed campus housing. Most students live on campus for two or three years, then move to one of the rental houses around campus, which, according to students, seem to be owned and managed by a near-monopoly called Campus Apartments. According to some students, this company buys up all housing close to campus, does some renovation, and then jacks up the rent. But students moving to non–Campus Apartments buildings to save money often find the housing run down and unsafe. "It is very hard to find safe, affordable housing in University City," says one student. Some students live across the Schuylkill River in Center City, the heart of Philadelphia, but rentals there are pricey, too.

SUGGESTED CORE
1. Classical Studies 360, The Epic Tradition
2. Philosophy 3, History of Ancient Philosophy
3. Religious Studies 15, The English Bible
4. Religious Studies 433/ 434, Christian Thought from 200–1000 / 1000–1800
5. Political Science 181, Modern Political Thought
6. English 36/37, Shakespeare
7. History 20, History of the United States to 1877
8. History 343, Nineteenth-Century European Intellectual History

Those students who stay on campus face limited choices. Says one student, "The [university-owned] high rises aren't the best places to live. They're just not in the best condition, the rooms are not that great, the guards aren't very friendly, and the fire alarms go off at all times at all hours because people are always pulling them. Plus, they're way overpriced." The *Daily Pennsylvanian,* a student-run newspaper, reported that the most recent alarm woes are causing some students to refuse to leave their rooms in Stouffer Hall. The new alarms, which are louder than their predecessors, have been triggered by such causes as construction and burned popcorn. This problem triggered the formation of a protest group called People Who Absolutely Hate Stouffer Fire Alarms.

In the dorms, there are no coed rooms but there are a number of coed bathrooms—though residents can vote on this. The university knows it has a housing problem, and ongoing dorm renovations should alleviate the most common complaints ("slow elevators and old smelly carpets"), even if the sounds of construction are currently disturbing some students. Harrison College House is the latest residential campus high rise to get a makeover. Completed in the summer of 2004, the $26.5 million renovation includes larger, energy efficient windows, updated heating and ventilation, and new furniture. Harnwell College House is slated for renovation in 2005.

The university offers race-based housing for separatists, such as the African American Resource Center, the Pan-Asian American Community House, and La Casa Latina,

MIDDLE ATLANTIC

as well as special ethnic dormitories. The Dubois College House, for instance, "provides a vibrant, supportive living environment for the pursuit of African American scholarship," according to the house's Web page. The house is also meant to increase retention among black students.

The real color of Penn, however, is green: The students, regardless of race, are rather rich. "While I have met people from all over the world, of all different nationalities, most people were relatively well off," one student says. "So I guess from a socioeconomic perspective, I wouldn't say the student body was that diverse."

Students unanimously affirm that Penn is challenging; students have that typical Ivy League competitive streak. They compete not just for the best grades in class, but also in the number of extracurricular activities in which they are engaged, the "how much work I have to do" conversation, and in their social lives. "When students were studying, they were studying hard, but when they were doing other things, they were also very engaged in their other activities," a recent graduate says.

Penn has more than 200 student groups—about half of them academic-oriented. The Philomathean Society, Penn's student literary society established in 1813, sponsors informal Friday afternoon teas with professors, lectures, dramatic performances, and an annual recitation. A popular news publication on campus is the previously mentioned *Daily Pennsylvanian*, which does not receive funding from the university. Penn is noted for its arts scene, which includes award-winning a capella groups ranging from the traditional Counterparts to groups like Penn Masala, the world's premier Hindi group. Another lively group is the "Wiggers"—which isn't what you might think, but rather a 115-year-old comedy group more accurately known as the "Mark and Wig Club." The student government's Social Planning and Events group sponsors speakers, crafts fairs, a jazz music series, arts programs, concerts, dance parties, and other special events. Spring Fling is the largest college festival on the East Coast; Haitian-born rapper Wyclef Jean was featured there in 2004. Speakers visiting the campus in 2004 included sports broadcaster Bob Costas and Jesse Jackson. Before the 2004 election, Penn sponsored a debate between Patrick Buchanan and Howard Dean—no doubt the most interesting exchange of the whole campaign.

Penn's sports teams are called the Quakers. They participate in the NCAA Division I (Division I-AA for football). Penn students take pride in cheering for the basketball team and throwing toast on the field at football games. (Get it? A "toast" to the team.) In recent decades, both teams have often been league champions, though only—it must be said—of the *Ivy* League. The Quakers play basketball at the Palestra, Philadelpia's historic arena, and the football team plays on campus at Franklin Field. The David S. Pottruck Health and Fitness Center includes 17,000 square feet of fitness space and an Olympic-sized pool.

Penn has a large Jewish student population, and cultural activities sponsored by Penn Hillel and other Jewish organizations are common. Other faiths are represented by the campus Newman Center and Protestant, nondenominational Christian, Muslim, and Hindu groups.

In 2004, many students were engaged in political activities, participating in various voter registration efforts and talking about the election. At Penn, "there is a lot of room to express your opinion," says one student. Another student characterizes the environment as "very centrist, perhaps slightly rightward leaning. I think a lot of the typical liberal college types are countered by the generally conservative Wharton types." While this moderation may usually be the norm, some conservative-leaning students felt silenced in classes during the election season when their professors made their political affiliations known. The students say they feared that their grades would suffer if they spoke up. After the election "people were passing around a printed-out e-mail in class about the stupidity of the red states," says one student.

Penn is notorious for certain examples of political correctness. According to Alan Charles Kors and Harvey Silverglate's book *The Shadow University*, the current director of the Women's Center, Elena DiLapi, once barred a black woman from a meeting of White Women Against Racism, apparently completely blind to the irony. The campus Women's Center hosts groups such as Penn for Choice and PEARL—"Penn's Eagerly Awaited Radical LesBiTrans Women."

Freshman orientation at many schools often turns out to be the university's chance to indoctrinate students. At Penn, it seems relatively harmless; no one really remembers much about its politics. Most students recall meeting friends, which is what freshman orientation is supposed to facilitate anyway. Incoming students read a book over the summer to discuss during orientation, and it's usually a pretty good one. In 2004, students read a fascinating study of human behavior titled *The Tipping Point,* by Malcolm Gladwell. In 2003, they read Graham Greene's *The Quiet American.* Past books have included *Things Fall Apart* by Chinua Achebe, Voltaire's *Candide,* Kafka's *Metamorphosis,* and Hemingway's *A Moveable Feast.*

Penn's party scene relies on traditional campus elements, such as the Greek system, which dominates campus events—frat parties are the favorite activity for those too young to hit the bars. Drinking on campus is much more prevalent than drugs. "Sometimes it seemed like there was nothing else to do but go out and drink," one student says, as implausible as that may seem. Following the two-story fall and resulting critical injury of a junior who drank 21 shots on his twenty-first birthday in 2004, the school is considering revisions to its alcohol policy. The Alcohol Response Team is slated to release the details in 2005.

Crime is a problem in West Philadelphia. In order to improve campus safety, Penn has installed more than 400 surveillance cameras on or near campus, which are monitored by Penn Police. Blue light safety phones have also been placed at major intersections. During 2003, the last year for which statistics were available, Penn reported six forcible sex offenses, six aggravated assaults, two motor vehicle thefts, and 61 burglaries. Town-gown relations are somewhat strained. Students are frequently guilty of vandalism and rowdiness, and the university's tax-exempt status means that other citizens have to carry the financial weight—and they're not happy about it. Some students in off-campus housing report good relationships with their neighbors, but other neighbors complain about late-night partying, trash disposal (or the lack thereof), and other problems associated with residents who stay a year and move on.

Despite the aforementioned complaints about socioeconomic homogeneity, Penn does try to attract bright kids from poor backgrounds, offering need-blind admission and the promise that it will meet 100 percent of a student's need. A hefty 78 percent of the freshmen who applied for financial aid for 2004–5 received need-based awards.

PENNSYLVANIA STATE UNIVERSITY

STATE COLLEGE, PENNSYLVANIA • WWW.PSU.EDU

State-related

Pennsylvania State University became Pennsylvania's official land-grant college in 1863. Its goal was to incorporate scientific principles into farming, which stood as a dramatic departure from the traditional curriculum steeped in mathematics, rhetoric, and classical languages. Evidence of its agricultural past stands in the form of the University Creamery, which serves up all manner of cheese, yogurt, butter, and ice cream—a popular source of campus desserts.

Although it remains a "state-related" university rather than an entirely public one, the university receives about $300 million of state money each year, so it may as well be public. University Park campus, Penn State's administrative and research hub, is located at the center of the state in a town called State College, and is one of 24 Penn State campuses around the state. But the University Park campus is more popularly known by its location, Happy Valley.

Penn State is a strong research institution with a wide range of programs for its 35,000 undergraduates (at University Park alone). It recently completed an extravagantly named and sized $1.3 billion "Grand Destiny" fundraising campaign to boost the university endowment. The larger endowment should serve the school well, as the 24 Penn State campuses sing to the tune of $2.8 billion annually and employ overall about 36,000 faculty and staff.

As with most large schools, the best results come to those students who know what they want to study and can find it in the maze they surely will encounter. Unlike students at some other massive state universities, Penn State students aren't constantly up in arms about issues, and the campus politics are usually kept to a dim roar. The university football team and the wholly atypical rough time it's going through appear to inspire the most conversations on campus. And with no major cities nearby, Penn

State provides a big-school atmosphere in a small-town environment.

Academic Life: Down in the valley

Penn State offers about 160 majors through the 12 colleges at University Park. The largest colleges for undergraduates are Engineering (about 7,000 students), followed by Liberal Arts (6,000), and Business (5,400). Only two colleges enroll fewer than 1,000 students, so whatever course of study he chooses, a student should expect to join a crowd. One student warns that the class sizes can be overwhelming; she reports that two of her introductory-level business classes had more than 400 students. Another student complains that some professors are not receptive to student requests for assistance: "The professor comes to teach the class and then leaves. There is little interaction."

The choices for study at Penn State are vast, but the general education requirements are scant. The university admits "successful, satisfying lives require a range of skills and knowledge," but the university does little to ensure that its students will acquire them. The college categorizes many of the core requirements as "knowledge domains," and they have embarrassingly self-evident explanations such as "developing the skill to communicate by means of the written word is extremely important." It isn't hard to find a course that meets one of these requirements; dozens will do. More than 200 courses meet the humanities requirement, ranging from "The Life and Thought of Malcolm X" to "The Culture of Stalinism and Nazism" to "Shakespeare." Students should get advice from other students and the professors listed below and use common sense. If it sounds politicized, it probably is.

One way to improve one's general education is to enter the Schreyer Honors College. Freshmen apply for admission to this college, which includes a scholarship of up to $3,000, special honors sections that satisfy the general requirements, and independent study and research. Another worthy option is the Penn State Washington D.C. Program, which offers internships in the nation's capital at places such as the Nature Conservancy, CNN, and Sen. Arlen Specter's office. The university also offers a long list of options for study abroad. An interdisciplinary program called classics and ancient Mediterranean studies (CAMS) is solid and emphasizes primary texts.

Courses outside of the sciences vary widely in terms of how politicized they can be. One PSU student says, "Obviously, classes are ideologically polarized, if not politicized. For example, in a political theory class on property, we spent three weeks on

VITAL STATISTICS

Religious affiliation: none
Total enrollment: 41,289
Total undergraduates: 34,824
SAT midranges: V: 530–630, M: 560–660
Applicants: 30,122
Applicants accepted: 58%
Accepted applicants who enrolled: 34%
Tuition: $9,374 (in state), $19,286 (out of state)
Room and board: $6,230
Freshman retention rate: 93%
Graduation rate: 48% (4 yrs.), 83% (6 yrs.)
Courses with fewer than 20 students: 30%
Student-faculty ratio: 17:1
Courses taught by graduate TAs: not provided
Most popular majors: business, engineering, social sciences
Students living on campus: 38%
Guaranteed housing for four years? no
Students in fraternities: 13% sororities: 10%

Distributional demands at Penn State are modest. In addition to the various requirements of one's major and college, a student must take:

- A course to develop quantitative and communication skills, like "General View of Mathematics," "Computer Programming for Engineers Using FORTRAN," or "Symbolic Logic."
- Studies in the "Knowledge Domains" of the arts (options include "Analysis of Human Settlements: Villages" and "An Introduction to Western Music"); humanities (like "The Life and Thought of Martin Luther King Jr." and "The Life and Thought of Malcolm X"); and the sciences (areas including the health sciences, natural sciences, and the social and behavioral sciences).
- One of the first-year seminars, which help introduce students to the scholarly community of the university. Each baccalaureate student must complete at least one credit of the first-year

Marx, three weeks on Rousseau, two days on eco-feminist thought, but only two weeks on Locke and only one day on Friedman, not to mention no time on F. A. Hayek. In another political theory class, we read extremist feminist authors, John Rawls, and Foucault, and this is considered a good cross section of contemporary theory." His experience is not necessarily universal—PSU is a big, diverse place. That means you'll find an amazing variety of courses available, catering to many interests. But your experience is likely to be uneven.

One history professor says naming good departments at Penn State is like telling somebody about the weather in the United States: "You can't generalize. It's warm in Arizona, and cold in Maine. Penn State is huge, and even within each department there is tremendous variety." Even so, one can say that the business and engineering programs at University Park are well regarded both on campus and nationally. "[The engineering program] is very developed and provides great opportunities for its students," says a student. "The faculty is intelligent and established." The geography department is also among the university's best, offering a balanced combination of hard science and social science courses. The William Randolph Hearst Foundation gives high ratings to several journalism programs at the school.

The philosophy department is considered to be very good and offers a wide array of courses. Within the department, students can choose from six options for majors—general philosophy, humanities and arts, philosophy of science and mathematics, social sciences, professional studies, and value studies. Except for a course in basic logic, which is required, the course requirements vary depending on a student's concentration. Students pursuing the general philosophy option, for instance, should graduate with a broad understanding of the discipline; they must fulfill course requirements in ancient philosophy and modern philosophy and choose two of the following three courses: "Medieval Philosophy," "Nineteenth-Century Philosophy," and "Twentieth-Century Philosophy." The professional studies option has students choose from courses such as "Philosophy of Law," "Business Ethics," and "Ethics of Science and Engineering." Better teachers in the department include Douglas R. Anderson, John P. Christman, Richard A. Lee Jr., and Stanley H. Rosen.

Other excellent professors among the Penn State faculty include D. Douglas Miller in music and Philip Jenkins in history and religious studies.

Students who want to perform research at Penn State have many opportunities, even as undergraduates. The university is consistently among the top recipients in the nation of research funding. Some tenants of the university's Innovation Park research complex also take Penn State interns.

The library system at Penn State is very good; according to the Association of Research Libraries, it is ranked twelfth among public research libraries. It includes about 4.6 million volumes and almost 50,000 current serials housed in two central buildings and six branches.

Penn State reports that 85 percent of first-year classes have fewer than 50 students. That, of course, means that 15 percent of first-year classes have more than that, and university figures show that 10 percent of first-year classes have more than 100 students. So do almost as many upper-level courses. In a guide for parents of students considering Penn State, the university claims: "A Penn State education is personalized! Take a look at our latest class size statistics to see first-hand what the Penn State classroom experience offers." Apparently, the PR folks are banking on parents being mathematically illiterate.

With 2,516 faculty members serving 35,000 undergraduates and more than 6,000 graduate students, students can expect to find teaching assistants leading at least the discussion sections of large classes—although professors do teach most classes, and mostly teach well, students say. Even those professors wrapped up in their research tend to pay attention to their undergraduate loads. One faculty member says that some students, especially in the humanities, genuinely enjoy learning and visit professors during office hours—not just to contest a bad grade, but to talk about ideas in the discipline. As for teaching assistants, the university offers courses and publications to prepare TAs for their duties, and these courses include instruction on how to evaluate student homework, participation, and exams. Lamentably, Penn State has a fairly weak advising system. Degree students are assigned an advisor through the advising center of the student's college. Since many students are assigned to each advisor, it is difficult for students to establish personal relationships with professors, and unless students take the initiative, they may never know a professor personally.

Just because there are hundreds of ways to get lost in the crowd doesn't mean

REQUIREMENTS (CONT'D)

seminar. These are usually small sections, sometimes paired with a larger course, and vary from college to college. Students say that these seminars tend to involve a lot of work. Samples among many include "Be a Master Student," "First-Year Seminar in American Studies," "Revisiting Jefferson's Washington: Research/Writing/Presentation," and "Health and Disease."

- One writing-intensive course within the student's major or college of enrollment.
- One course in "Intercultural and International Competence." These courses are intended to increase students' understanding of the relationship between cultures and widen their international perspective. Options include "Diversity, Pedagogy, and Visual Culture" and "Gender Dynamics in Africa."

Many of the PSU colleges also require two years of foreign language study or the equivalent, but this depends on one's major.

that the courses are easy. Students claim that there is little grade inflation. But "you do your work, and you'll be all right," a student says. "It's a big school," says another student, "and, like all big schools, it is what you make it. You can either become a number in the system, or take advantage of its benefits."

Penn State president Graham B. Spanier is a sociologist and family therapist who has held his post since 1995. He has worked in a variety of professional and academic positions, but seems to especially enjoy working with students. He has made appearances with the marching band, glee club, and musical theater and also occasionally serves as the school mascot during football games. He is also, literally, a magician; he has opened for Penn and Teller and is the faculty advisor for the Penn State Performing Magicians. He even ran with the bulls in Pamplona not long ago.

Running with the bulls was a picnic compared to some events in the spring of 2001 at Penn State. In April of that year, the leader of a black student group received a chilling typewritten death threat that claimed the body of a young black man could be found in a wooded area near campus. (This turned out to be false.) Other black students had received hate e-mail in the previous few months.

After months of controversy and protests, the university acceded to a long list of demands made by minority activists. President Spanier committed the university to establishing an Africana Studies Research Center at a cost of at least $900,000 over five years; to increasing the African American studies faculty from six to 10 members (at a cost of nearly $400,000); and to creating five new scholarships for African American studies majors who also major in another field ($350,000 over five years). In addition, the university installed a pre-freshman seminar "designed to acquaint incoming students with issues related to racism and diversity." Each budgetary unit of the university is now required to submit a progress report on its work toward the five-year diversity plan; the university's vice provost for educational equity has been added to the President's Council and other academic committees; the university is paying for an independent review of its diversity programs; and so on. Posted on the college's Web site is a plan that details Penn State's "Framework to Foster Diversity." This document includes strategic initiatives, benchmarks for implementing these goals, and measures for "success of behaviorally anchored outcomes."

The politicized departments at Penn State are those that one would expect: African and African American studies, and women's studies. The two departments cross-list some courses, like "The African American Woman" and "Women of Color: A Cross-Cultural Perspective." It suffices to say that the college brags far more about its diversity programs than about its core curriculum. On a cheerful note, students say they typically don't feel pressure to conform to professors' points of view. One student says that "there is a clear bias from many against conservative ideas, but most would rather keep their bias latent in the subject matter of the syllabus rather than beat their students over the head."

Student Life: They don't call it Happy Valley for nothing

Happy Valley is isolated and surrounded by mountains—scenic, but not exactly cosmopolitan. Students lament the lack of movie theaters but say there are good restaurants and bars and a decent program of on-campus events and concerts. In related news, Penn State was recently rated as the number 19 party school in the land by *The Princeton Review*. (This was good news at Penn State, which ranked fourth the year before and whose recruiting materials actually advertise that 20 percent of its students *don't* drink.) Penn State also cracked the *Review*'s top 20 in the "Frat and Sorority Scene" category.

The university has made concerted efforts to counter the notion that there is nothing to do at Penn State. Some of them involve, um, leaving the state: Offerings such as a three-credit physical education course called "Hiking in the Alps," during which students attend lectures with a trip to the Mont Blanc region in France, Switzerland, and Italy, are intended to help to gloss over its very rural setting. Worth noting on campus is the Palmer Museum of Art, which house a diverse and compelling collection and plays host to a number of interesting lectures, foreign films, and special events—a recent one was an afternoon recital of classical Italian arias. The strength of the permanent collection is American art, from eighteenth- and nineteenth-century portraiture and landscape painting to modern abstraction and contemporary art. The university also boasts more than 600 clubs and organizations across all its campuses.

The university requires freshmen to live on campus, but only about 20 percent choose to stay after that; Penn State only has room for 13,000 of its 41,000-plus students. Residence halls are clustered in six groups. Most are coed by floor (each floor is single sex), and students must use their ID cards to open outer building doors. Students say housing is in high demand, and more is being built, mainly for upperclassmen and graduate students. Off-campus students live in nearby apartments in the town of State College. Penn State offers a number of special living options. These include Arts and Architecture, Business and Society, International Languages, Women in Science and Engineering, and Martin Luther King Jr. houses. Another is dedicated to freshmen science and engineering students. Residential fraternities also play a large role in the social life of the school.

The *Collegian* has been run by students for 112 years. It has a very liberal editorial page that can sometimes get vicious, according to a student. The paper turned down an advertisement for David Horowitz's 2002 book *Uncivil Wars*, the writer reported. Speak-

SUGGESTED CORE

1. Classical and Ancient Mediterranean Studies 001, Greek and Roman Literature
2. Philosophy 200, Ancient Philosophy
3. Religious Studies 110, The Hebrew Bible *and* Religious Studies 120, New Testament
4. Religious Studies 123, Early and Medieval Christianity
5. Political Science 432, Modern and Contemporary Political Theories
6. English 129, Shakespeare
7. History 020, American Civilization to 1877 *or* History 463, American Thought to 1865
8. History 422, Modernity and Its Critics *or* Philosophy 203, Nineteenth-Century Philosophy

MIDDLE ATLANTIC

317

ers on campus come mostly from the left, but not all of them. The 2003–4 Distinguished Speakers Series included Greg Louganis, Margaret Cho, Jesse Ventura, Maya Angelou, and Linda Chavez.

Penn State students hail largely from Pennsylvania—77 percent of the undergraduates, in fact. All 50 states are represented in the student body, however, as are some 130 foreign countries. Minority enrollment (graduate and undergraduate combined) stands at 15 percent. The school attracts a fairly bright student body for a state school, with the middle range of SAT scores standing at 1090–1290.

Football is king at Penn State. Coach Joe Paterno (for whom the university creamery named their Peachy Paterno ice cream) could run for any office in the state and win—at least until recently. Before the 106,000 fans at Beaver Stadium, he has won more Division I games than anyone else in NCAA history, and he and his wife have donated $4 million to the university—one of the main library buildings is even named for him. Penn State athletes have a 79 percent six-year graduation rate (averaged over four years), well above the national average for Division I athletes of 58 percent (and 56 percent for all students). The men's and women's basketball teams graduated all their players during the same time while making appearances in NCAA tournaments to boot. The 15 men's and 14 women's varsity teams are known as the Nittany Lions. The word Nittany, derived from an Indian word meaning "single mountain," is the name of a peak near campus.

Penn State's campus is a pretty safe place, according to statistics. Forty-three police officers and six security officers, along with a cadre of police interns and student officers, provide round-the-clock service. The biggest on-campus arrest categories are liquor and drug violations—610 and 149 in 2003, respectively. Other than that, the university reported nine forcible sexual assaults, 38 burglaries, four stolen cars, and three arsons. Not so bad for a school larger than many towns. Larceny is the most common non-substance-related crime.

Tuition for Pennsylvania residents is a modest $9,374, but it doubles if you're from out of state. Room and board come in at $6,230. Almost half of full-time undergraduates receive financial aid, and the average student graduates with loan debt of $18,200.

PRINCETON UNIVERSITY

PRINCETON, NEW JERSEY • WWW.PRINCETON.EDU

Late-burning scholastic light

Princeton, wrote a young F. Scott Fitzgerald in his first novel, *This Side of Paradise*, has an "alluring reputation as the pleasantest country club in America." It is a place of bright colors, he wrote, where "the quiet halls with an occasional late-burning scholastic light" held his hero Amory Blaine's imagination rapt. The young St. Regis graduate wandered the New Jersey campus drunk with the Gothic architecture and heady tradition, and sometimes drunk literally as well, always striving to make something of himself. *Daily Princetonian* chairman, perhaps, or a player on the Princeton football team.

That was 1920. Since then, everything—and nothing—has changed. This Ivy League university, consistently ranked as the top school in America by *U.S. News and World Report*, no longer welcomes just the St. Regis and Exeter sons of America's aristocracy. But the women and students of color who have swarmed Nassau's gates since Amory Blaine stepped off the train at Princeton Station show the same résumé-minded ambition. They have become, in *New York Times* columnist David Brooks's phrase, "organization kids," scheduled to the hilt. They still party hard. Wrote Fitzgerald, "Princeton was one part deadly Philistines and one part deadly grinds, and to find a person who could mention Keats without stammering, yet evidently washed his hands, was rather a treat."

And yet, for the intellectually curious, Princeton is "the finest educational institution in the galaxy," says one student. Somebody is keeping those late-burning scholastic lights aglow. Princeton is the undergraduate's Ivy. The relatively small graduate program and lack of professional schools means that big-name professors actually teach. Most humanities courses are, mercifully, nonpolitical; most professors have an affection if not a reverence for learning and have no desire to approach their disciplines as political catechisms. Couple all this with a gorgeous campus and enough activities to satisfy the amateur artist or exercise fiend, and you see why 13,695 would-be Princetonians applied for a mere 1,175 spots in the class of 2008.

VITAL STATISTICS
Religious affiliation: none
Total enrollment: 6,831
Total undergraduates: 4,801
SAT midranges: V: 680–770, M: 690–790
Applicants: 13,695
Applicants accepted: 13%
Accepted applicants who enrolled: 69%
Tuition: $31,450
Room and board: $8,763
Freshman retention rate: 98%
Graduation rate: 90% (4 yrs.), 97% (6 yrs.)
Courses with fewer than 20 students: 74%
Student-faculty ratio: 5:1
Courses taught by graduate TAs: none
Most popular majors: social sciences, engineering, English
Students living on campus: 98%
Guaranteed housing for four years? yes
Students in fraternities or sororities: none

Princeton has no true "core," but you can put together a great books curriculum by taking the Humanities 216-217-218-219 series, which is open by application and involves two seminars per term for two terms. Throw in a music history class and an art history class, and you'll be well educated indeed.

All Princeton students face a respectable set of distribution requirements in order to earn either an AB (Princeton's term for a bachelor of arts and sciences) or a bachelor of science in engineering (BSE) degree, chosen from mostly quite serious—if sometimes too specialized—courses. In addition to the classes required for one's major, AB students must take:

- One freshman writing seminar.
- Foreign language to proficiency—one to four semesters.
- One course in "Epistemology and Cognition."
- One class in "Ethical Thought and Moral Values."

Princeton has done some soul-searching of late over what role athletics should play in admissions and over the "organization kid" stereotype. Princeton's new president, Shirley Tilghman, has noted that the university should try to admit more students with "green hair." Princeton plans to expand its incoming classes by 11 percent, starting this year, in order to make room for more activists, misfits, and scholars. Financial aid has expanded in recent years to make Princeton more affordable; the proportion of students from families earning less than $50,000 a year is at its highest in history. Whether Princeton will retain its traditions while finding a place for those who don't dream of working at Goldman Sachs remains to be seen.

Academic life: I pledge my honor

Academics at Princeton are quite rigorous. Talk to a student for ten minutes and he'll bore you with how many tests he has this week, how productive he was last night, and so forth. While students pepper their schedules with "guts," and you can slack off by choosing to have a class graded "P/D/F" (pass, D, or fail), the course catalog is refreshingly free of the silly, grievance-inspired courses lurking elsewhere. Lectures are never huge, and are supplemented by "precepts"—small-group discussion sessions. Professors teach many of these sections themselves; ask which to take if you want access to the professor. Many courses past the 100 level are seminars. Princeton is a small school, and you are quite likely to get the classes you want.

One special Princeton tradition is its Honor Code. Exams are unproctored, and students must sign their tests: "I pledge my honor that I have not violated the honor code during this examination." They also sign papers with a note saying the writing represents their own work in accordance with university regulations. Students must accept the Honor Code to attend Princeton. Violations are tried by a somewhat shadowy tribunal and punishments range from suspension to expulsion.

Princeton has the resources to attract excellent professors and build stunning departments. One professor says that "the physics, mathematics, and philosophy departments are the best in the world, period." History, economics, politics, religion, classics, and the Woodrow Wilson School of Public and International Affairs (the only selective undergraduate major) are all strong. Literary types should apply for seminars in the creative writing department, where luminaries such as John McPhee, Yusef Komunyakaa, and Paul Muldoon delve into the nitty-gritty of training young writers. "Joyce Carol Oates has read more of my writing than I have of hers," says one recent alum.

Many students take Econ 101 and 102; almost all the professors for these courses are excellent, from the libertarian Elizabeth Bogan to the more left-wing (and boisterous) Uwe Reinhardt. James McPherson's Civil War classes in the history department take up where his tome *Battle Cry of Freedom* leaves off; Sean Wilentz may be a Clinton apologist, but he certainly knows how to teach American studies. Robert George's constitutional interpretation and civil liberties classes in the politics department have a reputation for tough grading, but also for being worth the C on your transcript. Students also recommend professors Peter Brown, Anthony Grafton, William Jordan, Stephen Kotkin, and Peter Lake in the history department; Robert George, Jeffrey Herbst, Stephen Macedo, Russell Nieli, Paul Sigmund, and Keith Whittington in politics; Miguel Centeno, Thomas Espenshade, Sara McLanahan, Paul Starr, Robert Wuthnow, and Viviana Zelizer in sociology; the controversial but captivating Cornel West in African American studies; Alan Blinder and Burton Malkiel in economics; Eric Gregory, Martha Himmelfarb, Leigh Schmidt, and Jeffrey Stout in religion; Oliver Arnold, John Fleming, James Richardson, and D. Vance Smith in English; Ellen Chances in Slavic languages and literature; Michael Doran in Near Eastern studies; Robert Hollander in Romance languages and literatures; Josiah Ober and Joshua Katz in classics; and Baastian van Fraassen in philosophy.

The curricula of Princeton's academic departments tend to have remained serious. For admission to the English department, students must complete one survey course on reading fiction, drama, or poetry, and one historical survey of English literature course that covers the fourteenth through eighteenth centuries, and later take classes in literature to 1800 (course offerings include multiple Shakespeare classes, one on Milton, and another on Chaucer, for instance), one class in "Approaches to Literature" (generally on literary criticism), and two classes in literature from 1800 to the present. Princeton requires economics majors to take introductory courses in microeconomics, macroeconomics, and statistics, and to pass calculus. Then they take the department's intermediate-level micro, macro, and

REQUIREMENTS (CONT'D)

- One class in historical analysis.
- Two courses in literature and the arts.
- One course in quantitative reasoning.
- Two courses in science and technology, with laboratory work.
- Two courses in social analysis.
- Senior thesis.

And, in addition to courses required in their major, BSE students need to complete:

- Four terms of mathematics.
- Two terms of physics.
- One term of chemistry.
- One term of computer science.
- A freshman writing seminar.
- Seven courses in the humanities and social sciences, including at least one class in four of these six areas: "Epistemology and Cognition," "Ethical Thought and Moral Values," foreign language, historical analysis, literature and the arts, and social analysis.
- Senior thesis.

econometrics courses (there are two levels of these, for advanced math students and those with just a calculus background). Then students must complete five other economics courses. A few offered in fall 2004 included the first-rate "American Economic History," "Public Finance," "International Trade," "Economics of the Labor Market," "Economics and Public Policy," and the genuinely worthwhile "Environmental Economics."

For a school that emphasizes undergraduate teaching in the humanities, Princeton also manages to be strong in the hard sciences, regularly attracting generous grants and major research partners. For instance, in July 2004, the U.S. Department of Energy decided to locate its international fusion energy experiment program at Princeton. The next month, the National Institutes of Health chose Princeton as the home for a new $14.8 million research center, the Center for Quantitative Biology, devoted to basic science research on the building blocks of life.

Is the Princeton classroom politicized? "Political content does influence course content, in a left/liberal direction most of the time, and I have known of left-oriented faculty marking students down for their non-left opinions," says a former freshman advisor. "But the latter cases are rare, and in general the free speech atmosphere at Princeton is much better than at other campuses I have known, like Yale."

Indeed, one of the most encouraging developments at Princeton in recent years—indeed, in the whole country—has been the establishment of the James Madison Program in American Ideals and Institutions under the directorship of Robert George, a natural law philosopher in the politics department. The Madison Program does not offer a major, but it does host lectures and conferences to which undergraduate students are invited. Students can also apply to become junior fellows of the program, which allows them to interact closely with program faculty and speakers over a meal. Students who attend James Madison Program events say that they are treated as mature, intelligent, responsible individuals and that even guest lecturers avoid "speaking down" to them. Some of the luminaries who've spoken there recently include David Novak, on the theme of religious liberty, educational researcher Abigail Thernstrom, and Daniel Libeskind, architect of the buildings that will replace the fallen World Trade Center.

The Madison Program serves to counterbalance somewhat the presence on campus of the infamous Peter Singer, who serves as the Ira W. DeCamp Professor of Bioethics at, ironically, the University Center for Human Values. Singer wrote in his book *Practical Ethics*: "killing a disabled infant is not morally equivalent to killing a person. Very often it is not wrong at all." He has since brought further embarrassment to his institution by publishing an article arguing that bestiality may be morally licit.

Like many universities, Princeton has suffered from grade inflation. A new policy, adopted in April 2004, aims to change that. "In undergraduate courses, As (A+, A, A-) shall account for less than 35 percent of the grades given in any department or program in any given year," Princeton now says. According to widely distributed grade definitions, a C+ now means "acceptable; meets basic standards for the assignment or course." Of course, no student who wins a spot at Princeton ever expects to earn less than a B. It remains to be seen whether the university can alter these expectations.

One distinctive Princeton requirement is the senior thesis. Students select a major in their sophomore year, complete an independent research-oriented junior paper (JP) or two in this field during their junior year, then undertake the major research work known as a thesis before graduating. Some people take these projects quite seriously. Many artistic students write creative senior theses—plays, novels, symphonies. Others just crank out 80 pages of something. Says one student, "If applicants aren't sure whether they'd enjoy such a project, they should consider a school where a thesis is optional."

Student life: Bickering for the fickle

Almost all Princeton students live on campus; the surrounding borough of Princeton has no affordable rentals. Freshmen and sophomores live in one of several residential colleges: Mathey (say "Matt-ee"), Rockefeller ("Rocky"), Wilson, Butler, or Forbes. A future option is the soon-to-be-constructed four-year Whitman College, financed by Ebay CEO Meg Whitman. Dorms are all coed; rooms and bathrooms are not. Each residential college has a dining hall and organizes intramural teams and activities for students.

Juniors and seniors live in dorms and dine in a peculiarly Princeton setting known as "eating clubs." These dozen mansions line Prospect Avenue or "The Street" and serve as the heart of Princeton's social scene. Every Thursday and Saturday students hit The Street in their club clothes; every Friday and Sunday morning the clubs reek of beer residue.

Each club has a character. We return to Amory Blaine: "The upper-class clubs . . . excited his curiosity: Ivy, detached and breathlessly aristocratic; Cottage, an impressive mélange of brilliant adventurers and well-dressed philanderers; Tiger Inn, broad-shouldered and athletic, vitalized by an honest elaboration of prep-school standards; Cap and Gown, anti-alcoholic, faintly religious, and politically powerful; flamboyant Colonial; literary Quadrangle; and the dozen others, varying in age and position."

The characters have evolved. Cap and Gown is athletic, not anti-alcoholic; Cottage is home to Princeton's Dixie transplants. Ivy is still detached and breathlessly aristocratic. Tiger Inn is still rowdy. About 80 percent of Princeton's students join a club during their sophomore year. Half the clubs require a "bicker"—an elaborate audition process. The other half are "sign in"; anyone who wants to join may join, space permitting. In general, bicker clubs are more selective about who they allow into their parties. Members give their friends passes; freshmen try to sneak in. If you want to join one of

MIDDLE ATLANTIC

the selective clubs, you should start meeting members in your freshman year so they'll remember you during bicker.

Choosing a club has long been a stressful process. Notes Fitzgerald: "There were fickle groups that jumped from club to club; there were friends of two or three days who announced tearfully and wildly that they must join the same club, nothing should separate them; there were snarling disclosures of long-hidden grudges as the Suddenly Prominent remembered snubs of freshman year. Unknown men were elevated into importance when they received certain coveted bids; others who were considered 'all set' found that they had made unexpected enemies, felt themselves stranded and deserted, talked wildly of leaving college."

This situation is completely unchanged.

With this long a tradition, the club system has its fans. "They broaden groups of friends outside one's department or regular social circles, provide a place to call one's own, with free snacks any time of the day," says one student. Certainly there's something stylish about it all. However, the eating club system can be a bit juvenile and cliquish, so interest in alternatives is growing. Juniors and seniors can join two co-ops or go "independent." A few dorm kitchens provide options for cooking, and Spelman—a dorm of apartments with kitchens—offers a thriving independent scene.

With 38 varsity teams competing in NCAA Division I, a huge percentage of Princeton students play sports. Princeton always fields competitive teams in the "preppy" sports such as lacrosse and field hockey. On occasion, Princeton's basketball team has relived its Bill Bradley glory days by winning the Ivy League championship, but even so the Tigers generally get knocked out in the first round of the NCAA tournament. Football is a sad story. The new, nameless Rafael Violy–designed stadium features great architecture but lousy sport. In the stadium's inaugural 1998 game, Princeton limped to a touchdown-free 6-3 win over Cornell.

No one younger than the class of 1946 expects grand football from an Ivy League school that doesn't offer athletic scholarships. On the other hand—given the competition for admission to Princeton—setting aside a few dozen for athletes who may (or may not) bring glory to their alma mater requires quite an academic trade off. A book co-written by former Princeton president William Bowen, *The Game of Life*, has set off a multiyear inquiry into the role athletics should play in admissions. The new dean of admissions, Janet Lavin Rapelye, will no doubt leave her mark here.

Even if intercollegiate athletics are a mixed bag, Princeton students love sports. About half of all students participate in intramural athletics; many more can be found on the Stairmasters in Dillon gym. Princeton's Outdoor Action program leads troops of freshmen hiking into the wilderness as part of orientation every year. Despite massive consumption of Milwaukee's Best ("Beast"), one rarely sees overweight students. One does, however, see a fair number with eating disorders, claims one of their peers.

Princeton features a newspaper, the *Daily Princetonian*, and several publications including *Tiger*, a humor magazine; the artsy, naughty *Nassau Weekly*; and the wryly conservative *Tory*. Aspiring journalists can try out for the Press Club, whose members string for local papers such as the *Trenton Times*.

Singers can join one of a fantastic number of a capella groups that blossom in Princeton's Gothic arches like weeds after rain. Those wishing a more traditional repertoire can audition for the Glee Club—or the Chapel Choir, provided they can stomach the Princeton Chapel's politically correct services. Theater and dance folks perform in Richardson Auditorium or Theater Intime and haunt the halls of 185 Nassau Street for classes and workshops. Political wonks join Whig-Clio for the debates and speeches, but in general there's not much political activism on campus. (Perhaps that's because of the lack of green-haired students.) Occasionally the College Democrats bring a speaker. The James Madison Program in American Ideals and Institutions imports more conservative folks. Every religious persuasion has its group. The university-supported Center for Jewish Life holds services and serves kosher meals. The Agape Christian Fellowship (affiliated with Campus Crusade for Christ) is there for evangelical students; the Aquinas Institute is a hub for Princeton Catholics. In general, religious students find Princeton tolerant of their needs. "Princeton is a much easier place for socially conservative Christians and Jews to get by in—indeed, even to thrive in—than any other Ivy institution with which I am familiar," says one professor. "I have had many conservative Christian students as advisees and they all seem very well adjusted to the Princeton scene, with little sense of alienation or outsider feelings." However, students who try to distance themselves from drinking or the one-night-stand hook-up scene may find their social options limited.

Princeton town-and-gown relations aren't strained—they're nonexistent. Since Princeton students socialize at the eating clubs, not many bars cater to student tastes. With a food court at the Frist Campus Center, few students venture to town restaurants except for a sandwich at Hoagie Haven or ice cream at T. Sweets. In fact, with legend saying students who pass through the FitzRandolph Gate onto Nassau Street won't graduate, it's a wonder any students at all venture toward this small town of Coach and Ann Taylor stores. The most volatile issue of town-gown relations in recent years has been an alcohol ordinance that allows Princeton borough police to enter private property if they suspect underage drinking is going on. In theory, this allows the cops to bust the eating clubs.

Some residential colleges organize bus trips into New York for Broadway shows, and the occasional student takes the NJ Transit train into Penn Station. But as one student points out, "It's hard to go to NYC for an evening, if about an hour and a half will be spent in transit each way." Theoretically, Philadelphia is also nearby—but the public transit route involves three trains. So few students go there. Most students report that their social and entertainment needs are met on campus.

Princeton has very little crime. The occasional student loses a bicycle or laptop if they're not locked up—there were 68 burglaries noted in 2003—but the only crime people still talk about is the armed robbery of the Sovereign Bank on Nassau Street in 1997. There were also 10 forcible sex offenses, two aggravated assaults, 13 stolen cars and two arsons on campus in 2003.

Tuition for the 2004–5 school year was $31,450. Room and board was $8,763. However, Princeton financial aid is the most generous in the Ivy League. Students aren't offered loans; all aid comes as grants. Princeton started this policy specifically to lessen the loan burden on young alums and to lessen the sticker shock for families who didn't think they could afford Princeton. It has worked. The proportion of Princeton students from lower- and middle-class backgrounds has risen steadily since 2001.

Princeton offers a financial aid calculator on its prospective student information Web page. A hypothetical homeowning family with two kids, a $100,000 income, and a $100,000 portfolio (excluding retirement accounts) would be expected to contribute about $15,000 a year. Princeton would cough up $25,000 worth of grants. Families earning up to about $200,000 are eligible for some aid. Given that Princeton is sitting on an $8 billion endowment, many students say it's about time the money trickled down to where it makes a difference.

RUTGERS UNIVERSITY

NEW BRUNSWICK, NEW JERSEY • WWW.RUTGERS.EDU

Tougher than the rest

Rutgers, now the State University of New Jersey, was founded as Queen's College in 1766. Like King's College (later Columbia University) in the neighboring colony, Queen's offered a cooler, drier intellectuality than the then-evangelical College of New Jersey at Princeton. Intended to train ministers for the Dutch Reformed church, Rutgers did so at a time when its faculty were the secular leaders of revolutionary New Jersey, and the school's transition to a more worldly mission came without the controversy that disturbed other institutions. Rutgers has always catered to practical folk without much pretension to forming a social or spiritual elite, and this is true even today.

While professors offer rigorous courses in fairly esoteric subjects, the university admits more than half of its applicants and makes a real effort to retain any student who does his work. Professors attempt to get to know their students personally and keep their office hours faithfully, are glad to help when asked, and are unhappy that more do not seek them out. Yet there is some disappointment that Rutgers isn't more selective, so that the quality of the student body might come up to that of the faculty; too many of New Jersey's best enroll elsewhere. President Richard McCormick, an American historian inaugurated in 2002, has spoken of making Rutgers a top-tier research institution, improving its reputation, and increasing its economic impact on the state of New Jersey—but he shows no signs of rejecting the mandate to serve a broad base. He has little choice. In spite of its population and wealth, New Jersey lacks the strong network of public four-year colleges that other states have, and this puts an enormous burden on its state university. All things considered, Rutgers does an impressive job, and may be well worth a second look.

Academic Life: I got my facts learned real good right now

Rutgers University serves around 50,000 students in three cities. The New Brunswick campus is the largest and oldest, and also the strongest and most selective in the liberal arts and sciences. Rutgers University in New Brunswick is divided into 12 colleges for undergraduates. Four of these—Douglass, Livingston, University, and Rutgers—are liberal arts colleges, each with its own academic focus and reputation. One faculty serves all four colleges, however, so students in all four colleges are welcome to choose courses from the same general catalog. Rutgers College students, for instance, will undoubtedly have Douglass or Livingston students as classmates.

Douglass is an all-women's college—the largest in the country—but only in its residential life, since students share classes with those from other colleges. Douglass students are required to take a course called "Shaping a Life" (presumably their own), which is an "introduction to the education and experience of women," and a second course from the women and gender studies department, both in addition to the general academic requirements. Livingston, founded in 1969, "is committed to offering educational programs which bring together students, faculty, and staff in a diverse and vital learning community," the college says. The goal of coursework in Livingston College is "to foster critical thinking and social responsibility by asking students to examine contemporary issues, cultural attitudes, and their own roles in society." The University College serves adult and part-time students, most of whom are commuters balancing their academic loads with family and work responsibilities.

With approximately 11,000 students, Rutgers College is the largest of the university's liberal arts colleges and the most selective. The course catalog says that "the fellows of Rutgers College have developed a distinctive educational design based on breadth and depth in traditional liberal arts disciplines." However, there is little that is distinctive in the college's requirements, and these requirements do not ensure that students achieve genuine breadth and depth in their studies.

Rutgers lists more than 4,000 courses in its catalog; most fulfill one of the gen-

VITAL STATISTICS

Religious affiliation: none
Total enrollment: 34,696
Total undergraduates: 26,813
SAT midranges: V: 540–640, M: 560–670
Applicants: 24,434
Applicants accepted: 61%
Accepted applicants who enrolled: 32%
Tuition: $6,793 (in state), $13,828 (out of state)
Room and board: $8,357
Freshman retention rate: 89%
Graduation rate: 46% (4 yrs.), 71% (6 yrs.)
Courses with fewer than 20 students: 41%
Student-faculty ratio: 14:1
Courses taught by graduate TAs: not provided
Most popular majors: social sciences, psychology, business
Students living on campus: 47%
Guaranteed housing for four years? no
Students in fraternities: 5% sororities: 5%

Rutgers has nothing like a core curriculum, or even any requirement that students take courses grounded in Western civilization. The following are the distribution require-ments faced by students in liberal arts:

- Writing skills. "Exposi-tory Writing" or its equivalent, plus an additional course with a strong writing compo-nent, chosen from a list of hundreds (including some taught in foreign languages, as well as advanced calculus, in which the writing compo-nent might not be so strong).
- Quantitative skills. One course in college-level mathematics and an additional course, which may be in mathematics or data analysis; one of these may waived if a student is placed in calculus rather than pre-calculus.
- Natural science. Two courses in biological sciences, chemistry, environmental science, geological sciences, meteorology, or physics.
- Social science. Two courses in Africana studies, American studies, anthropology, economics, geography, history, Jewish studies, political science,

eral academic requirements. Consequently, a Rutgers di-ploma means something rather different for each gradu-ate, depending on his choices. Nor is there a strong advis-ing system in place to help give students direction. "I am not too sure about advising," one student says. "I would suspect that would be more in a graduate or higher-level undergraduate setting." In fact, any undergraduate may visit an academic center if he needs help, but asking for help is not required. (The dean of the junior class says that the advising centers and the faculty members who staff them help students chart classes to fulfill requirements and meet their interests.) Once a student has declared his major, he may visit a professor in his own department for advice. Again, this is not required.

The good news is that many faculty members are ea-ger for students to understand course material, to give ad-vice on which courses to take, and to help students choose a career path or graduate school. Faculty members teach most lecture courses, and although introductory classes can be as large as 300 students, classes soon get much smaller. One political science student says, "In upper-division courses in my major, most classes are small enough that the professor will know your name." Graduate teaching as-sistants do teach weekly discussion sessions and smaller group seminars—an administrator admits that TAs teach courses "frequently." All faculty members hold office hours, and "the professors there are helpful if there is a need," says one student. Unfortunately, says an honors student, "a lot of people don't take advantage of office hours. They're al-ways happy to see you, but students rarely visit."

Rutgers has been enduring a severe budget crunch, and as a result the university recently announced a number of cuts that hit academic departments hard. Many depart-ment Web pages even include a link for people to donate money specifically to the department. Unfortunately, scarce resources have combined with increasing "diversity" man-dates to mean that more traditional scholars have a very, very tough time getting hired.

When asked to name the finest departments, faculty, and courses, students and faculty are hard pressed to nar-row their preferences. Modern philosophy is a clear strength. Rutgers offers an undergraduate medieval studies major, a commendable course of study if rounded out by a complementary minor like classics, philosophy, or English.

The English department, although characterized by one student as a "repository for [students] who don't know what else to do," boasts some good faculty and an excellent array of courses in all periods of English and American literature. Nevertheless, an English professor laments that his department has gone PC: "[Trendiness] is a national disease, but Rutgers has it worse than most places. The tragedy is that Rutgers used to be one of the top 'literary' departments in the nation." Nowadays, he says, "that's the state of things in most English departments—identity politics, junior faculty who couldn't make sense of a Donne poem to save their lives, gender blather, 'gay studies,' et cetera. It is a grim time." English majors are required to take a course in African American literature but not in Shakespeare.

While there are excellent offerings in history, many of the faculty are leftists, which affects both the offerings and the way they are taught. "As an ancient historian, I find that my department low-rates traditional disciplines such as mine," a history professor says. "For example, when our Roman historian retired, no serious effort was made to replace him. The department also pursues trendiness, with most recent hires coming in recent United States history and women's and minority history." History majors must take two courses in "global, African, Asian, Latin American, or Native American history" and can fulfill an American history requirement by taking such courses as "Ethnicity in American History" or "Women in American History."

The women's and gender studies department is particularly egregious. Courses like "Dynamics of Class, Race, and Sex," "Lesbians and Gay Men and Society," "Gender and Spirituality," and "Gender and Pop Culture" dominate its course list. Students can earn course credit for interning at the National Abortion Reproductive Rights Action League (NARAL), the National Center for the Pro-Choice Majority, or *Ms.* magazine.

Faculty and students lean "very much to the left," says one student. "And, unfortunately, it often does influence the content of the courses. Just last semester, I took a twentieth-century history course where the professor was extremely liberal and taught almost every lecture as if conservatives were the problem with society."

Ethnic studies courses are notoriously left-leaning or simply trivial. An American

REQUIREMENTS (CONT'D)

psychology, Puerto Rican and Hispanic Caribbean studies, sociology, or women's studies. One can acquire the rudiments of ancient, modern, or American history, or take something like "American Indians of New Jersey."

- Humanities. Two courses in African languages and literatures, Africana studies, American studies, art history, Chinese, classics, comparative literature, English, French, German, Greek, Hebrew, Hindi, Italian, Japanese, Jewish studies, Korean, Latin, linguistics, music, philosophy, Portuguese, Puerto Rican and Hispanic Caribbean studies, religion, Slavic languages and literatures, Spanish, or women's studies. There is a chance to learn something of real value in literature, philosophy, or even theology, or to take something dreamed up to stroke your racial pride.
- Non-Western requirement. One course from a list of hundreds, which can also, depending on the discipline, count for the science, humanities, or social science requirement.

studies course is titled "Women on the Fringe: Perceptions of Women as Social and Sex-Role Deviants in American Civilization." Students majoring in comparative literature should not expect to study the differences between the French and British Romantic periods. Instead, they are "strongly urged to pursue coursework in 'non-Western' literatures and cultures," according to the catalog. They can choose from options such as "Backgrounds of Homoerotic Literature" and "Minority Literature." As one comparative literature student describes it: "In English you focus on a lot of theory and read a lot of literature written by, as my professors have said, 'dead white guys.' And when you do read literature from other countries, you use Western standards to judge them, so you never really end up appreciating them."

Classics, political science, and archeology are all said to offer real excellence. The departments of modern languages, especially German and French, offer first-rate courses on culture and literature for majors and nonmajors on topics such as the Enlightenment. The biological sciences, especially microbiology, are world-class. Disciplines that typically have a radical slant at other colleges, such as sociology and anthropology, still retain some excellent faculty at Rutgers, including sociology professor David Popenoe, who does research on "critical perspectives on family issues" and has produced impressive demonstrations of the crucial importance of fathers. Other good professors include William C. Dowling, William Galperin, and William Walling in English; and Jack Cargill and T. J. Jackson Lears in history.

Another promising area of the university is the Rutgers College Honors Program. Although honors students are not bound to a set curriculum, they can participate in special honors-level courses, lectures, discussions, and extracurricular events. They can also elect to live in one of the honors residence halls.

Outside the Honors Program, though, student intellectual life is not especially sparkling. "My impression is that Rutgers is like any other pretty good state university," a history professor says. "Some students are genuinely interested in learning, some only care about grades and/or post-graduation jobs." There seem to be plenty of the latter kind.

Student Life: Ain't no sin to be glad you're alive

Rutgers University is not residential. No student is required to live on campus, and less than half the student body chooses to—most of them freshmen, housed together in traditional hall-style dormitories or in Clothier, a huge, eight-story high rise known as a party dorm. Every dorm has quiet hours, and most have 24-hour study lounges where students can escape the often-chaotic dorm culture. All freshman dormitories are smoke free, and each dorm has a residential advisor to enforce the rules. Although there are a few single-sex floors, men and women are often housed in rooms next to each other (there are no coed bathrooms or dorm rooms, however). The women in Douglass College live in all-women dormitories, and students can also opt to live in one of many fraternity or sorority houses. There are a number of special houses available for students interested in foreign languages, areas of the arts, or academic subjects like history, political science, philosophy, religion and spirituality, and lesbian, gay, bisexual, and transgender studies.

Amidst financial cutbacks, Rutgers seems to have little trouble in finding the resources to fund a vast array of diversity programs, coalitions, task forces, and administrative offices. The Office of Emerging Populations and Special Retention Program sponsors the Diversity Advocacy Board and something called Encounters: Orienting Students in Diverse College Communities. The Office of University Harassment Compliance and Equity oversees affirmative action at the university. The Committee to Advance Our Common Purposes is a university group whose sole purpose is to "champion our individual and collective humanity and respect for our differences." The Office of Diverse Community Affairs and Lesbian and Gay Concerns aids students in political activism, monitors alleged bias incidents, and trains residential advisors to be more open to and aware of diversity. A director in the office told us, "One of our main goals is to help these students feel comfortable on campus"; this is accomplished through the sponsorship of annual student programs like National Coming Out Day, World AIDS Week, and Queer Appreciation Week, and by providing career tips in a program called Out on the Job. The university also offers a "rainbow graduation" ceremony for graduating gay/lesbian students.

The Office of Diverse Community Affairs and Lesbian and Gay Concerns publishes *Beyond Polarities*, a gay/lesbian journal with the tagline, "Use *Beyond Polarities* with pride to construct a meaningful, queerific gay old time at Rutgers, the State University of New Jersey." The journal's name is meant to "transcend the dichotomies of man/woman and straight/gay in order to see that sexual and gender identities take form in many more shapes than we are often led to believe." These projects, of course, are funded through the university budget in many more shapes than we are often led to believe—tax dollars and student fees among them.

A recent controversy on campus centered on the tension between free expression and ethnic sensitivity. According to the *Chronicle of Higher Education,* local sandwich vendors—affectionately known as "grease trucks"—have been censured by Rutgers for the colorful names they give to sandwiches, including the Fat Dyke, the Fat Bitch, and the Fat Filipino. The school ordered the vendors to change the sandwich names or cover them with duct tape. The campus paper, the *Daily Targum,* polled students and found that 70 percent wanted the names left as they were.

SUGGESTED CORE
1. Classics 01:190:381, Greek Drama in Translation *and* Classics 01:190:391, Roman Drama in Translation
2. Classics 01:190:208, Philosophy of the Greeks
3. Religion 01:840:201, Old Testament *and* Religion 01:840:200, New Testament
4. Religion 01:840:312, Greek Christianity (Second through Eighth Centuries) *and* Religion 01:840:313, Latin Christianity (Third through Thirteenth Centuries) (*closest matches*)
5. Political Science 01:790:372, Western Tradition: Hobbes to Mill
6. English 01:350:221, Shakespeare
7. History 01:512:103, Development of the United States I
8. History 01:510:427, Intellectual History of Modern Europe

Rutgers has few formal outlets for conservative faculty or students. You'll find no conservative newspapers or student organizations—unless one counts the various religious groups. But one student says, "I am very much a conservative, and though it is a very liberal campus, I am comfortable being here. It's about making the right friends, taking the right classes, and knowing why it is you do hold the views that you do." In 2003 Rutgers' InterVarsity Christian Fellowship won a significant victory when the university conceded its right to restrict leadership positions to . . . well, Christians. The university had taken the position that this policy was inappropriate for an officially recognized student activity of a public university, but it backed down when the organization filed suit.

About 5 percent of the student body goes Greek. "Unfortunately, alcohol does play a big role for a lot of people, especially in the Greek scene," a student says. "But for many of us, we have a great social life without it." One sorority member says that "alcohol is there if you want it, but Rutgers is so large that there's not pressure to conform. There are so many different types of people, that if you don't like something you can find your own group of friends." Since almost all Rutgers students are from New Jersey, many go home on weekends. For those who stick around, the university offers other means of relaxation. The *Chronicle of Higher Education* reported on the school's "De-Stress Fest 2004," which included meditation sessions "with themes like 'Beach Escape' and 'Nature Trail' [and] combined deep-breathing techniques with the sounds and smells of the ocean or a tranquil forest." The school also distributed "relaxation kits" containing hot cocoa, herb tea, anti-stress tips, and a bottle of soap bubbles with a wand.

Rutgers boasts hundreds of intramural teams and nearly 50 NCAA Division I and III varsity sports (each campus fields its own teams). High-ranking teams in recent years have included women's lacrosse, tennis, and basketball, and men's baseball, soccer, gymnastics, crew, and track. In 1869, Rutgers and Princeton played the first intercollegiate football game; Rutgers won, 6-4.

One Rutgers senior says, "New Brunswick is no New York City, but there's plenty to do here." Comedy clubs, ethnic restaurants, shops, theaters, and other activities are a five-minute walk from campus. According to both faculty and students, the logistics of New Brunswick pose one of the primary difficulties in navigating Rutgers. The campus is sprawling, and auto congestion is acute. "Organizing the day is difficult for students," says one professor, who notes that many work to make ends meet, primarily in off-campus jobs. Areas of Rutgers University—especially Douglass College and the main academic quad of Rutgers College—are wonderfully charming with ivy-covered collegiate architecture, but other buildings look more like prison facilities.

Indeed, police have had a hard time keeping the New Brunswick campus safe. In front of academic buildings and dormitories on the College Avenue campus, the homeless and panhandlers regularly set up shop. Residents can enter dormitories only by swiping their "slash cards," and the university documents visitors; as a result, the crime rate inside dormitories, at least, is relatively low. One student who lives on campus says, "It's a good idea to *always* lock your door to your room, no matter if you know everybody in the building or not. The most common crime on campus is burglary, and students often get too comfortable with their neighbors, who might just happen to be thieves." In 2003, the university reported 11 forcible sex offenses, five robberies, four aggravated assaults, 149 burglaries, 22 stolen cars, and five arsons on the New Brunswick campus. The university maintains bike patrols, horse patrols, and van escorts. Students and faculty are advised to program the number for the University Police into their cell phones, not only to report crimes, but to request assistance for dead batteries, keys locked inside cars and rooms, and an escort from buildings to distant parking lots.

If you're a New Jersey resident, Rutgers is something of a bargain. In-state tuition for 2004–5 was $6,793. Outsiders paid $13,828. Room and board was $8,357. Admission is need-blind, but the school does not guarantee to meet every student's financial need. Some 68 percent of students receive some need-based aid.

St. John's College

ANNAPOLIS, MARYLAND, AND SANTA FE, NEW MEXICO • WWW.SJCA.EDU

Changing our minds

St. John's College marches to the beat of a different drummer. It has no intercollegiate athletic teams, academic majors, or departments. The SAT is not required for admission, and grades are not reported to students unless they ask to see them. Some newer faculty—who, in another peculiarity of the college, are called "tutors"—lack campus offices, so they work out of the coffeeshop instead. It is not uncommon for tutors and students to leave notes for one another on chalkboards next to the mailroom. A Friday night lecture on campus attracts hundreds of students and tutors and sometimes stretches past midnight. A unique spirit of common intellectual inquiry animates the college, for St. John's can justly claim to offer the best curriculum in the world: the great books of western civilization.

"St. John's is persuaded that a genuine liberal arts education requires the study of great books—texts of words, symbols, notes, pictures—because they express most originally and often most perfectly the ideas by which contemporary life is knowingly or unknowingly governed," the academic bulletin says. The books "change our minds, move our hearts, and touch our spirits."

The drumbeat in higher education is for more fluff rather than substance, for training rather than education. St. John's, however, marches on in its mission "to restore the true meaning of a liberal arts education," as the college bulletin puts it. Originally founded in 1698, the college had a respectable if unremarkable tradition until falling on hard times during the Great Depression. Bankrupt and with its accreditation in jeopardy, St. John's invited two former Rhodes scholars to take charge, each of whom was under the spell of the great books renaissance at Columbia and the University of Chicago. Thus did Stringfellow Barr and Scott Buchanan establish in 1937 the New Program. Its heart: a four-year passage through the seminal texts of the West, and no others.

Soon St. John's began to attract an odd assortment of characters: European refugees like Jacob Klein and Simon Kaplan, philanthropist Paul Mellon (who attended St. John's as an adult), visiting lecturers like Bernard Knox and Mortimer Adler. In 1964, the college opened a new campus in Santa Fe, New Mexico, in order to expand access to its program without sacrificing an intimate learning environment. The two campuses operate under one governing board but with separate presidents and faculties, and students are able to freely transfer between campuses.

Academic Life: Hardcore

All students and tutors at St. John's study the same core texts. Students spend their freshman year with Greek philosophers and writers; the sophomore year in the Roman, medieval, and Renaissance periods; junior year with the Enlightenment; and senior year with modernity. Tutors at St. John's tend to teach there for decades, and some can boast of having taught every class offered. All students begin the St. John's program as freshmen, even those who have begun or completed studies at other colleges. The advantage of this approach is that students and their classmates read the same texts together, which creates a common canon.

The heart of the academic program is a twice-weekly seminar (during all four years) in which philosophy, theology, political science, literature, history, economics, and psychology are all considered. The reading list for literature includes works by Aeschylus, Virgil, Dante, Chaucer, Shakespeare, Racine, Molière, Tolstoy, Rimbaud, Kafka, and Faulkner. The ground rules for discussion are basic. "Reason is the only recognized authority," the college explains. Some 20 students and two tutors gather to consider an assigned reading. References to earlier readings can be made, but the citation of extracurricular texts is discouraged. Classrooms at St. John's do not contain clocks. Conversation spills from seminars out into the open air. "Discussions here take place—endlessly, it seems—beneath the quadrangle's trees, in the busy coffeeshop, over meals," the *Chronicle of Higher Education* has noted. A "take your tutor to lunch" option permits students to invite tutors to dine with them. The student-faculty ratio is eight to one.

Each year, Johnnies take a mathematics tutorial in which geometry, astronomy, algebra, calculus, and relativity are covered. Greek tutorials are offered for freshmen and sophomores, French for juniors and seniors. The mathematics tutorials hinge on demonstrations, the language tutorials on translations. During the sophomore year, students also take a tutorial in musical theory and composition.

As a reflection of the importance given to dialectical inquiry, few tests are given at St. John's. "But in an important sense every day is an exam because in such small classes whether you have prepared and how well you have prepared are very evident," a student says. "With Euclid [his *Elements of geometry*], for example, in any class you might be asked to demonstrate at the board and from memory any proposition."

A third component of the curriculum comprises science laboratories. "They fit the great story," says the same student, "of how things which were separate in antiquity—mathematics and physics—were united to become mathematical physics and conquer nature itself." Laboratory classes study and in some cases replicate famous scientific experiments while seminal scientific texts are read in seminar. For example, the lab covers genetics at about the same time that students are reading Darwin in the seminar.

Finally, juniors and seniors choose from a list of 15 to 20 preceptorials offered by tutors each year. These are the only "electives" at St. John's. "The aim is to explore a book in greater detail than is possible in a seminar," says one alum. "My preceptorials on Dante's *Purgatorio* my junior year, Livy's *History of Rome*, and Machiavelli's *Discourses on Livy* were among the best classes I had at St. John's."

Other than the preceptorials, students pick and choose neither courses nor tutors. Tutors are assigned the role of Socratic midwives—drawing out conversation rather than directing it. St. John's uses this system because it discourages the elevation of individual tutors' personalities over the texts. Nevertheless, students confess to having favorites, such as Michael Andrews (currently on leave), David Bolotin, Joshua Kates, and Edward Cary Stickney in Santa Fe; Elizabeth Blettner, Mera Flaumenhaft, Anita Kronsberg, George Russell, Erik Sageng, and David Townsend in Annapolis. "The tutors I didn't like were those who talked too much and who seemed too interested in their own topics," a recent graduate says. "Overall, the tutors have a good breadth of knowledge, work hard at asking good questions to stimulate discussion, and are available for private consultation."

Each semester, students sit for an oral exam that takes the form of a conversation about recent readings and their connection to the liberal arts in general. Another form of student appraisal occurs when freshmen and sophomores attend a "don rag" session at which a student's tutors discuss his performance in the third person, with the student listening as an observer. In junior year, the don rag gives way to a student-tutor conference at which the student offers an analysis of his own work. During their first

VITAL STATISTICS
Religious affiliation: none
Total enrollment: 950
Total undergraduates: 950
SAT midranges: V: 660–730, M: 600–660
Applicants: 500
Applicants accepted: 67%
Accepted applicants who enrolled: 38%
Tuition: $30,570
Room and board: $7,610
Freshman retention rate: 83%
Graduation rate: 62% (4 yrs.), 72% (6 yrs.)
Average class size: 20
Student-faculty ratio: 8:1
Courses taught by graduate TAs: none
Most popular majors: n/a
Students living on campus: 60%
Guaranteed housing for four years? no
Students in fraternities or sororities: none

St. John's has one of the very best curricula of any school in this guide. Its solid core guarantees that every graduate emerges with the same sort of humanistic and scientific education as most of the great leaders, founders, inventors, and thinkers throughout the history of the West. In addition to selections from a fascinating array of electives, each student takes the same basic curriculum. The center of the St. John's experience is four years of year-long seminars:

- "Freshman Seminar." Termed by the college the "Greek" year, this two-semester course "begins with the *Iliad* and the *Odyssey*, continues with the dramas of Aeschylus and Sophocles, allows much time for the works of Plato, and concludes with Aristotle."
- "Sophomore Seminar." This year-long course carries students (perhaps too quickly) through the Bible, "classical Roman poetry and history," the Middle Ages, and the Reformation. "The seminar's diverse readings are thus unified by the common classical and biblical roots and by the

three years, students submit reflective essays based on the seminar readings. The essay and oral exam at the end of the sophomore year are used to determine whether a student advances to third-year studies. During the spring semester of their senior year, students are furloughed from classes for a month to write an analytical paper on a subject of their choosing. Each paper is then defended before a panel of tutors at a session open to the public.

No wonder that one student says, "When I talk to friends of mine at other schools, the difference between our educations is astounding."

Thanks in part to its non-negotiable curriculum, the campus has not become scorched earth in the culture wars. There is periodic discussion about whether the curriculum should be revised to include more works by women and minorities. A black alumnus recently wrote an article in which he declared that "St. John's is what a college ought to be, and blacks, as well as all races, should not be put off by the general homogeneity of the curriculum." He added that the great books "lengthen our attention span, teach us to cultivate humanity, help us to fully appreciate what it means to be human and to exist."

Since tutors are supposed to function as participants in classroom discussions rather than as proponents for particular ideological viewpoints, there is little opportunity for political advocacy to seep into teaching. "St. John's is probably one of the few places in this country where you have the ability to study texts on their own terms—without a professor's bias (for the most part) and a certain 'accepted' interpretation of what the books say," one student says.

Some political leftists dislike the curriculum's focus on Western civilization and scorn the approach as elitist. Yet the St. John's great books curriculum has been attacked from a few on the right as well, who argue that in the face of so many persuasive, yet conflicting, arguments, students might end up as ragpicking skeptics. One student allows that "the strength of the program is also its weakness—no secondary sources, no 'context' to help put ideas in perspective." A rhetorical question often heard on campus is, "What is a lecture, but the giving of answers to questions that have not yet been asked?" That epitomizes the great conversation at St. John's: before anything, tutors and students must begin by asking the same question.

"Religion and aesthetics are viewed as subordinate to the holy 'reason' by the majority of students," one student says. "There is quite a lot of hostility toward religiosity in general among the student body. At the same time, there are many conversions (particularly to Catholicism) that I have seen happen as people make their way to their senior year."

The Bible and several medieval and modern theologians are in the curriculum. "Tutors seem to have a basic respect for Christian beliefs, if dealt with in an intellectual rather than personal manner," a recent graduate says. She adds that students would be well advised to approach religious texts within the search for truth rather than as a "brief for certain points of theology."

With the Roman, medieval, and Renaissance periods all crammed into sophomore year, however, the program would seem to buy into the Whig view of history as the forward march of secular humanism from Socrates to the Enlightenment. One alum says that "the program is influenced by the Enlightenment and the thought of Leo Strauss—to be precise, the students spend more time reading Plato and Kant than any other authors. On the other hand, I never got the sense that tutors or the program worked on the assumption that Christianity was some sort of detour on the Road to Progress. I heard occasionally of one or two tutors (out of dozens) who were belligerent in arguing against Christianity. And there were a good number of believing Christians among the tutors. For a school that's not associated with any religion, St. John's pushes students to take Christianity seriously on an intellectual level."

After four years of great books and great conversations, what do St. John's graduates do? While we don't endorse the careerist approach to education, we know that parents and students do wonder whether young scholars who emerge from schools such as this can make a living. "Despite daily assertions to the contrary," the bulletin replies, "there is no educational device for assuring worldly success to students." A long-time tutor says, "We will not prepare you for careers, but we will give you the chance to discover a vocation." Unsurprisingly, St. John's graduates go on to do a myriad of things—and surprisingly few end up as lifers at Starbucks.

REQUIREMENTS (CONT'D)

accumulating record of responses to them," the catalog notes.

- "Junior Seminar." This year at St. John's focuses on the seventeenth and eighteenth centuries, including "the first encounter with American authors (Madison, Hamilton, Mark Twain) and a reflection upon our own way of life."

- "Senior Seminar." This year brings the student through the nineteenth and twentieth centuries nearly up to the present. Readings include *War and Peace*, *Faust*, and *The Brothers Karamazov*, and works by Hegel, Nietzsche, and Heidegger. According to the school, "In keeping with the college's mission to turn out educated citizens, the senior year also includes works central to American democracy, such as the *Federalist Papers*, the speeches of Lincoln, key Supreme Court decisions, and Tocqueville's commentary on the radical nature of the American experiment."

Students also need:

- Four years of language.
- Four years of math.
- Three years of laboratory science.
- One year of music.

One recent alumna has become a successful romance novelist. At least two others have gone on to become influential and famous Napa Valley winemakers (Larry Turley and Warren Winiarski of Turley Wine Cellars and Stag's Leap Wine Cellars, respectively). Another alum, Ronald H. Fielding, found his calling in investments. In 2003 he gave his alma mater $10 million, saying, "At St. John's, you have to deal with things that are unfamiliar and difficult and work them out. If you have to grapple with the ideas of Kant and Nietzsche, and work out the mathematics of Einstein, you gain something very valuable for the long run."

Still, St. John's is seeking to better prepare students for graduate studies and professional employment. The Annapolis campus received a $1.1 million grant a few years ago to start a summer program. In it, select students receive an internship and stipend toward a practical application of what they've learned. A survey of the activities of graduates found that 20 percent go into law or teaching and 20 percent into business careers.

Student Life: Continental divide

The Annapolis and Santa Fe campuses have different reputations. Annapolis, with its street names and buildings from colonial times, takes its character from the legislators, naval officers, and affluent professionals who live there. Students who would chafe in such a starched atmosphere might prefer the Santa Fe campus, where things are a bit more hazy. "Santa Fe is for the weed-smoking hippies to hang out in the mountains!" one Annapolis Johnny says. Some students speculate that the importance given to rationality in classrooms encourages the bacchanalian excess that sometimes prevails among students on weekends and at social occasions. One alum, however, recalls that he was able to live Gustave Flaubert's famous dictum to artists: "Be regular and orderly in your life like a bourgeois, so that you may be violent and original in your work."

Perhaps as an indispensable break from its intense academics, St. John's offers several club and intramural sports (there are no varsity teams, however). In Annapolis, a boathouse hosts a crew team; students can also sign out college-owned sailboats and dinghies. An annual croquet match against neighboring Naval Academy midshipmen attracts spectators dressed in linen to munch on cucumber sandwiches while watching the competition (the Johnnies usually prevail). Linen is hardly ever worn to play the less-civilized sport of Spartan Mad Ball, a game unique to the two campuses of St. John's, and governed by only three rules: no shoes, no sharp objects, and the game ends after three hospitalizations have occurred. A tutor reports that one recent game was notable for the presentation of two brothers at the emergency room, the teeth of the one embedded in the forehead of the other. When not engaged in active warfare, Santa Fe students go on rafting trips down the Rio Grande and ski outings in Taos, which is a couple hours away. A student search-and-rescue team also cooperates with New Mexico authorities in emergency operations. Fencing and soccer are popular at both campuses.

The Annapolis student newspaper is the *Gadfly*; in Santa Fe, it's the *Moon*. Other activities include film clubs, madrigal and theater groups, Sunday concerts, a Christian fellowship, and student government. Organized parties run the gamut from the Spring Cotillion (for which upperclassmen prepare newer students by teaching them to waltz) to the Seducers and Corrupters Party (no one would tell us what preparations for this involve). Santa Fe Johnnies fund Reality Weekend by running a casino, using

their profits to engage in ancient Greek mud-wrestling and other classical exercises at this end-of-the-year weekend of festivities. Each campus also sponsors a series of parties such as a Halloween Ball. Dances are well attended. Although St. John's strives to enforce prevailing state laws, alcohol is an indispensable social lubricant, leading one conservative student to say, "I can't say St. John's is as much of a community as I had originally hoped."

Six traditional dorms in Annapolis house students, whereas the Santa Fe campus has constructed 16 townhouse-style units for student lodging. The rooms are functional but not always spacious, and some of the Annapolis buildings show signs of aging. The mess hall, too, is spartan, but the lack of separate dining facilities for the tutors encourages conversations between students and tutors even at meal times.

Each fall some students transfer to the other campus and find that the same "Johnnie jargon" is spoken there, along with the same stock seminar questions ("What is the Greek on that?"). They fall right into step with the great books canon, the measure of a civilization, once our own, now only heard from afar.

The Annapolis campus, with its proximity to both the state capitol and public housing, has experienced some muggings in recent years; campus security has offered safety tips and police whistles. In 2003, that campus witnessed five burglaries and one arson. Santa Fe's adobe-style facilities are two miles from downtown and more isolated. In 2003, that campus witnessed one non-forcible sex offense, and seven burglaries. Both campuses offer students 24-hour computer access and have libraries with collections—and furnishings—designed to aid serious readers.

Perhaps the only way in which St. John's conforms to the norms of contemporary academe is the tuition it charges: $30,570, with room and board another $7,610. However, admissions are need-blind, and the school guarantees full aid to students who apply promptly (though aid packages may differ according to which campus one attends, an insider told us). The average student loan debt of a St. John's graduate is around $20,000.

SETON HALL UNIVERSITY

SOUTH ORANGE, NEW JERSEY • WWW.SHU.EDU

Walking to Rome

Seton Hall University is named for Elizabeth Ann Seton, the first American-born saint. This New York City aristocrat, who once hosted a ball for President George Washington, found herself ostracized and impoverished after she converted to Catholicism. When she started winning converts, the New York State legislature threatened her with legal sanctions, so Seton had to flee to more tolerant (and more Catholic) Maryland. There she founded a religious order to staff schools and missions for the poor. The university honors its namesake with its devotion to serious liberal arts education provided at a manageable tuition. Seton Hall students graduate with some exposure to the great works of Christendom through a required sequence in Western civilization. Perhaps more importantly, at a time when many Catholic schools are slouching towards Gomorrah, Seton Hall, under the leadership of Msgr. Robert T. Sheeran, is moving ever closer to Rome. For students who care about that, but who want to attend a middle-sized university rather than a tiny liberal arts college (like Thomas Aquinas, Christendom, or Thomas More, also reviewed in this guide), Seton Hall is worth a careful look.

Academic Life: Taking up a collection

Seton Hall University enrolls around 4,800 full-time undergraduates and a larger number of part-time and graduate students. Five of Seton Hall's schools and colleges offer undergraduate degrees: the College of Arts and Sciences, the Stillman School of Business, the College of Education and Human Services, the College of Nursing, and the John C. Whitehead School of Diplomacy and International Relations. For now, all undergraduates except nursing students are required to take a number of liberal arts courses, but the specific requirements depend on the college. But after several years of debate, the school has decided to adopt a common core for all schools. Its content and shape are still under discussion, but the result can only be for the good, our sources report. One requirement that will be included is a course reflecting Catholic ethics, "though it's uncertain how specific it will be," says a professor, with cautious enthusiasm. One priest on campus says that all core classes "will deal with questions central to the Catholic intellectual tradition. It looks like the first will be 'the journey of transformation,' which will take a Catholic text alongside a non-Christian one and examine our tradition in the light of others. The second will be the classic Catholic intellectual tradition—scriptures and early Middle Ages. The third will be Catholicism and postmodernity."

The core will take effect either in 2007 or 2008—and it's not clear whether it will apply retroactively to enrolled students—but the school's move toward curricular rigor means that Seton Hall is worth taking seriously. It's not just a school for blue-collar kids from New Jersey to get their business degrees from anymore.

Seton Hall students can get away with some fluffy coursework in some majors, says one student—try communications—but it's unlikely that a student would graduate without having to undertake some serious academic study. "The university has made a conscious commitment to weed out easier courses and majors and to strengthen the intellectual rigor of all programs," a business professor says. "We"re on a 'quality' kick." Seton Hall's best departments include classical studies, international relations, Catholic studies and some of the humanities. The English department, which includes poet Jeffrey Gray and fiction writer David Stephens, actually focuses (hold your breath) on *English literature*. Majors are required to take seven courses: ""Introduction to Literary Studies," "Great Books of the Western World" I and II, "American Literature" I and II, and "British Literature" I and II, in addition to seven electives from several different areas and a senior seminar. The history department is strong in American social and constitutional history and European intellectual history, and is open to considering the Catholic dimensions of these subjects—for instance, the work of the seminal historian Christopher Dawson, who has a course devoted to him here. The history major also requires breadth in the discipline, including courses in American, European, and third-world history, as well as two courses in allied fields like economics, political science, or anthropology. Communications and sociology are known to offer students a lighter load.

VITAL STATISTICS
Religious affiliation: Roman Catholic
Total enrollment: 10,800
Total undergraduates: 4,800
SAT midrange: 990–1210
Applicants: 2,355
Applicants accepted: 82%
Accepted applicants who enrolled: 26%
Tuition: $22,227
Room and board: $9,102
Freshman retention rate: 80%
Graduation rate: 39% (4 yrs.), 59% (6 yrs.)
Average class size: 25
Student-faculty ratio: 14:1
Courses taught by graduate TAs: 1%
Most popular majors: communications studies, rhetoric, criminal justice
Students living on campus: 42%
Guaranteed housing for four years? no
Students in fraternities: 13% sororities: 8%

Seton Hall's Honors Program is the crown jewel of the university's undergraduate offerings. Qualified students enjoy a rigorous curriculum, close interaction with faculty members, and intellectual camaraderie with classmates. As freshmen and sophomores, honors students take four colloquia: "Classical Civilizations" (beginning with Genesis and Plato's *Timaeus* and *Republic*); "Medieval Civilizations"; "Early Modern Cultures"; and "Contemporary Civilization" (ending with Vaclav Havel). They then take two honors seminars and complete a senior thesis. In addition to their departmental advisors, honors students can visit professors who are designated as advisors to the Honors Program, and their classes tend to be smaller than are general courses. Each year, the program offers "enrichment" field trips to art exhibits and performances in New York City and often brings scholars to lecture on campus. However, says one professor in the program, the program's quality may be challenged by the school's attempt to fit more students into the classes, raising the size of the colloquia from 30 to 45.

As Seton Hall hammers out its plan for an improved core curriculum, the school currently maintains a respectable set of requirements. All arts and sciences students must take:

- A two-course sequence in Western civilization. This requirement is met via "Art of the Western World / Music and Civilization," "Great Books of the Western World" I and II, "Western Civilization" I and II, or "Philosophy and the Classical Mind / Philosophy and the Modern Mind."
- A two-course world civilizations cluster. This is satisfied by taking classes in the study of American civilization or a third-world civilization, foreign literature in translation, or upper-level foreign language courses.

Still, the students and faculty here are impressive. The program was recently endowed by wealthy alumnus Thomas Sharkey, chairman of the school's capital campaign. "I've been with students to the Metropolitan Opera, and for some it was the first time they'd seen an opera, and they found it a transformative experience," says a professor.

Seton Hall's preprofessional majors are more intensely focused on their disciplines and don't require study in as many different areas or offer as many options. Business school students, for instance, can fulfill the behavioral sciences requirement by taking "Psychology for Business Majors," while arts and sciences students can choose from a list of 17 courses that includes "Introduction to African American Studies," "Western Political Thought," and "Introduction to Social Work." One student who switched majors during his sophomore year advises students to "get the core courses out of the way early so you can be exposed to all the disciplines before you lock yourself into a major."

Although campus literature emphasizes that Seton Hall is, above all, a Catholic university, how much that fact is emphasized in the classroom varies. Arts and sciences students completing a religious studies course requirement certainly do not have to immerse themselves in Catholic doctrine. A student in the business school could fulfill his religious studies requirement by taking "Scriptures and Computers," a religious studies course that studies "biblical software to locate passages and cross-references for thematic, literary, liturgical, and other useful purposes," according to the university bulletin.

But there is good news for serious Catholic students. Seton Hall has effectively done an end run around recalcitrant professors and other entrenched interests by creating a special Catholic studies program in which students can earn a major, minor, or certificate. The core courses for the major include "Introduction to the Catholic Vision," "Catholicism and Art," "Catholicism and Literature," "Catholic Social Teachings," "Christian Belief and Thought," and "Integrating Seminar in Catholic Studies." Students also take six electives chosen from offerings in the Catholic studies, philosophy, and religious studies departments. Students can receive credit by studying in Rome or other overseas Catholic studies programs; in 2004, patristics scholar Fr. Douglas Milewski led students on a two-week tour of Poland. In 2005, Chesterton scholar Dermot Quinn conducted students on a fortnight of Catholic Studies courses at Oxford University, which they took along with noted social theorist (and Tolkien expert) Stratford Caldecott.

Classes at Seton Hall are big if manageable—the average is 25, and the student-faculty ratio is a decent 14 to 1. But one professor notes that the university has improved these statistics by hiring many more adjunct professors, despite its stated commitment to reduce their numbers in the long run. Hardworking professors have been granted a reprieve in the form of a reduced teaching load, addressing a long-standing complaint among faculty. Around 1 percent of classes are taught by graduate teaching assistants, according to the university—a much lower proportion than in the recent past.

Seton Hall's formal advising program takes place through the Freshman Studies Program, which assigns each freshman a "professional mentor"—not a faculty member—who is supposed to help the student choose courses and a major. Each freshman is also assigned a peer advisor (an upperclassman who has done well in school) and takes a one-credit study skills course, which teaches the student how to use a computer, balance his time, and conduct research, as well as how-to-survive skills like balancing a checkbook and getting to and from New York City. Once a student has declared a major, he can seek advice from the assigned faculty advisor for the department.

In 2003, Seton Hall was named the twelfth "most connected" university by *Forbes*. Upon entering, every student is handed an IBM Thinkpad laptop; after sophomore year, students get a replacement computer. Instructors are becoming as tech savvy as their students, and many make their lectures available online. The campus is now completely wireless, so students can study, check e-mail, or read class notes anywhere—in the library, on the quad, or in their rooms.

There are many excellent professors. Some of Seton Hall's best are Joseph Marbach in political science, Deirdre Yates in communication, Richard Hughes in classics, Philip Moreman in diplomacy and international relations, Deborah Brown in Asian studies, and Msgr. Richard Liddy in religious studies. Notable history faculty include William Connell, James McCartin, and Dermot A. Quinn. The philosophy department is anchored by Robert Mayhew, David O'Connor, and Rev. John Ranieri. The dean of the College of Arts and Sciences has over the past two years conducted searches for faculty who can enhance the university's Catholic mission across a broad range of fields.

Student Life: Sisters of charity

Seton Hall students are not known to be tremendously active, politically. The campus atmosphere is correspondingly calm. One professor says, "I've heard a wide variety of views expressed by both faculty members and students; the debates are free and open and usually quite civil. In that sense, we are 'seekers after truth' rather than 'ideologues.'"

REQUIREMENTS (CONT'D)

- A course in communications.
- Two English composition courses.
- One math class.
- Two classes in the natural sciences.
- Two courses in the behavioral sciences.
- One course in ethics.
- Three courses in philosophy and religious studies (including at least one in each discipline).

All arts and sciences students must also reach the intermediate level in a foreign language, shown either through coursework or test scores.

Under the leadership of President Sheeran, Seton Hall has sought to strengthen its Catholic identity in recent years. The creation of the Center for Catholic Studies (in 1997) and the approval of an undergraduate major in Catholic studies (in 2002) are just two of the more visible results of his efforts. "Significant persons among both faculty and students are actively engaged in evangelizing this campus," a professor says. Msgr. Sheeran also invited the G. K. Chesterton Institute to relocate to campus, adding Fr. Ian Boyd and his *Chesterton Review* to the Seton Hall community. "Fr. Ian Boyd is an internationally recognized scholar with an enormously wide range of contacts," a humanities professor says. "Indeed in a real sense, he has made the institute into not only a national but an international resource."

Officially, Seton Hall supports Catholic causes, but most of the activism (particularly as regards abortion) comes from students in the seminary, not faculty or undergraduates. The campus ministry program is firm in its Catholic position on moral issues. In matters of campus life, the university has tried to remain traditional—the campus TV station doesn't show R-rated movies (when it's operational—see below), the campus radio station recently changed from heavy metal to rock, and cohabitation is not allowed in the residence halls. Still, the university administration is open to the airing of alternative views, even concerning Catholic doctrine.

Although Seton Hall has on staff several liberal faculty members—"raging communists," one student claims—political opinions, generally speaking, do not influence course content. A professor who has served on various promotion and tenure committees at the university says, "Nobody has ever asked a question about a candidate's political views or whether he/she is 'liberal' or 'conservative.' I can honestly say that we do our best to concentrate on the candidate's teaching and research capabilities. I can also honestly say that I've never heard of a faculty member being sanctioned or ostracized because of the content of his/her courses or his/her political views." But the university keeps a close watch on departments that are typically considered leftist. The course catalog explains that the women's studies program "is established in the spirit of St. Elizabeth Ann Seton, whose life of activism, spirituality, and leadership serves as an inspiration to our community." The program offers only a minor—not a major—and courses include "Women, Culture, and Society," "Feminist Theories," and courses cross-listed with other departments—for example, an African American studies course in "The Black Man and Woman," and social work classes in "Family Violence" and "The Well-Being of Women."

The main selling point of South Orange, New Jersey, is that it's close to places that are more interesting. South Orange does have a downtown area with restaurants, bars, a movie theater, and a few shops. But more importantly, there is a train station within walking distance of the Seton Hall campus that allows students to get to New York City's Penn Station in around half an hour for just $7, round trip. Students say the allows them to take advantage of the numerous internship, volunteer, and entertainment opportunities to be found in the Big Apple.

There's plenty to do on campus as well. Seton Hall's Student Activities Board posts huge calendars all over campus each week to advertise movie nights, salsa dance lessons, self-defense sessions, game nights, lectures, concerts, and open mike nights. At Pirate's Cove, a coffeeshop in the basement of the Dougherty University Center, comedians and local and student bands often perform. The student-run radio station, WSOU-FM, is usually ranked among the top three student stations in the country, but unfortunately, the television station, Pirate TV, was shut down in 2003 after a basketball player signed his autograph on a camera lens, ruining the expensive equipment. One student says that while there are activities on campus every day, students probably don't take advantage of them as much as they should. "You get so comfortable just hanging out with your friends, doing nothing, that you miss out on more enriching activities," he says. Seton Hall recognizes more than 100 student organizations, including résumé-boosting outfits like the Economics Club and the Brownson Speech and Debate Union, cultural and religious organizations, musical groups, the Setonian (the weekly student newspaper), and many others. With only around 10 percent of students participating, social fraternities and sororities are less influential at Seton Hall than they are at many schools. "It's up to you to become involved," says a student, "because nobody is going to make you be active."

The Pirates compete in NCAA Division I in the Big East conference on 12 varsity teams. Seton Hall has no football, field hockey, or lacrosse teams, mainly because there simply isn't enough space on campus for them to play and practice. The university offers fine athletic facilities for intramurals and pick-up games, as well as for personal fitness. Basketball games are held at Continental Arena at the Meadowlands, and students can catch a free shuttle service there; season tickets for students are $75.

As Seton Hall has expanded and enrollment has grown, space has become the most precious commodity on campus. Because of a lack of dorm rooms, housing is not guaranteed for students, and there is a large commuter population—just 42 percent of students live on campus. Only seniors are allowed to have cars on campus. Students who manage to secure a dorm room should have few complaints; rooms are comfortable enough, and most rooms share a bathroom with just one other room. All dormitories are coed except for one, Newman Hall—whose donor stipulated that the residence hall must be for women only—but there are several single-sex floors and wings in the coed dorms.

To prevent crime, Seton Hall's campus is enclosed within a metal fence; there is just one gate, which is staffed with a security guard night and day. To enter a dormitory, a student must swipe his identification card, and visitors must sign in. Students coming home late at night can call a campus escort service. The university recently

SUGGESTED CORE
1. Classical Studies 2301, Epics and Novels of Greece and Rome
2. Philosophy 2020, Ancient Philosophy
3. Religious Studies 1102, Introduction to the Bible
4. Religious Studies 2221, Early Christian Thought *and* Religious Studies 2222, Medieval Christian Thought
5. Political Science 1411, Western Political Thought II
6. English 2312, Shakespeare
7. History 1301, American History I
8. History 2250, Western Europe in the Nineteenth Century (*closest match*)

MIDDLE ATLANTIC

added emergency call boxes all over campus. For 2003, the last year for which statistics were available, the university reported three forcible sex offenses, two robberies, three aggravated assaults, 11 motor vehicle thefts, and 36 burglaries on campus—pretty good numbers for a school located in an area as densely populated as northern New Jersey.

Seton Hall has an active campus ministry program for Catholic students, offering mass three times daily and four times on Sundays. For students of all faiths, there are regular Bible studies, prayer meetings, retreats, and small group fellowships. The campus ministry staff will help students find local congregations regardless of their denominations. One non-Catholic student says the university's Catholic nature can easily be ignored by non-Catholics or brought to the forefront for Catholic students: "It's there if you want it, but it's never pushed on you." A promotional video for prospective students never once mentions the word "Catholic." What students can't ignore is the university's strong commitment to community service. Seton Hall's Division of Volunteer Efforts (DOVE) promotes these activities and organizes shuttle bus service to the volunteer sites.

One professor describes Seton Hall's campus as "sylvan." The beautiful Immaculate Conception Chapel and the attached President's Hall are the heart of the campus, most of which is modern in style.

In terms of cost, Seton Hall is reasonable for a private school. The tuition in 2004–5 was $22,227, and room and board was $9,102. Admissions are need-blind, although the school does not guarantee to meet every student's need. Some 90 percent of students received need-based aid last year, up from 75 percent in past years.

SWARTHMORE COLLEGE

SWARTHMORE, PENNSYLVANIA • WWW.SWARTHMORE.EDU

Quaker roots and cash

Founded during the Civil War in 1864 by Quakers as a co-educational institution, Swarthmore College has been non-sectarian since 1908. Today, some 1,500 students study on 357 acres of picturesque land in a residential suburb 30 minutes from Philadelphia. The college prides itself on famous faculty, such as pioneering gestalt psychologist Wolfgang Kohler, and graduates such as Michael Dukakis. Of course, it helps to be rich—and Swarthmore is really, really rich: the school's endowment stands at $930 million.

For a small school, that is a heck of a lot of money. On a per-student basis, Swarthmore's endowment is the ninth largest in the nation. But despite its vast wealth and sterling academic reputation, whether Swarthmore is still an elite institution depends on one's point of view. Its rankings are fantastic, and its students' average SAT scores are dazzling. Then again, as with most institutions, its curriculum ain't what it used to be. Furthermore, Swarthmore has traveled even further down the path of radical chic than most other eastern liberal arts schools—and that's a long journey, indeed. That famous communist-turned-Quaker, Whittaker Chambers, were he to attempt to speak on campus today, might well be shouted down. Worse still, he might face a sea of blank, uncomprehending faces—unsure how even to treat unfamiliar opinions.

Academic Life: A trip to Sam's Club

Swarthmore has an agenda that goes well beyond education—and extends into leftist activism. The college employs its status as a shareholder to pressure any company in which it holds even a $2,000 investment—squeezing such companies as Lockheed Martin, Dover, and Masco corporations to add the category of sexual orientation to their nondiscrimination policies, for instance.

But Swarthmore has its virtues. The students certainly work hard. "We have some genius types here, but more than that we have a lot of very hardworking people," says

VITAL STATISTICS
Religious affiliation: none
Total enrollment: 1,474
Total undergraduates: 1,474
SAT midranges: V: 680–770, M: 670–760
Applicants: 3,680
Applicants accepted: 25%
Accepted applicants who enrolled: 39%
Tuition: $28,500
Room and board: $8,914
Freshman retention rate: 95%
Graduation rate: 82% (4 yrs.), 91% (6 yrs.)
Average class size: 15
Student-faculty ratio: 8:1
Courses taught by graduate TAs: none
Most popular majors: social sciences, business, philosophy
Students living on campus: 94%
Guaranteed housing for four years? yes
Students in fraternities: 7% sororities: none

No specific courses are prescribed for Swarthmore students. The distribution and graduation requirements are:

- 32 credits total, or their equivalent.
- 20 of these credits must be outside one's major area.
- Three courses in each of Swarthmore's three divisions—humanities, natural sciences and engineering, and social sciences—in at least two different departments within each division. Out of those nine courses, three must be "writing-intensive" courses and one must be a science lab.
- A physical education requirement. All students not excused for medical reasons are required to complete a two-semester program in physical education. Credit is also given for participation in intercollegiate athletics as well as dance courses. All students must pass a survival swimming test or take up to one quarter of swimming instruction.

one student. The school is quite self-conscious about the fact that its classes are rigorous and high grades comparatively more difficult to obtain. "Anywhere else, it would have been an A," reads one popular T-shirt. Graduate schools are said to adjust for the rigor of Swarthmore's grading when evaluating applicants. One student describes the general atmosphere as "the revenge of the nerds." Another says that the best thing about Swarthmore is the quality of the intellectual environment: "You're surrounded by . . . brilliant people."

The college reports that grade inflation is not a concern. A Dartmouth college paper noted that Swarthmore has maintained 1970s standards by de-emphasizing grades. "Swatties may or may not have more work than their counterparts at Dartmouth or Amherst colleges," the article said, "but they do have lower average grades." Despite this report, one study and the testimonies of several students suggest that Swarthmore's grades are beginning to rise.

However bright and industrious they are, we doubt that Swatties are any more qualified than other students their age to design their own curricula. Yet that is what the school expects them to do. The school bulletin claims that "education is largely an individual matter." So Swarthmore's distribution requirements exert only marginal influence on students' choices. As Swarthmore psychology professor Barry Schwartz has written: "[A]t my small college . . . we offer about 120 courses to meet our version of the general-education requirement, from which students must select nine." What this means, he explains, is that "[t]he modern university has become a kind of intellectual shopping mall. Universities offer a wide array of different 'goods' and allow, even encourage, students—the 'customers'—to shop around until they find what they like. Individual customers are free to 'purchase' whatever bundles of knowledge they want, and the university provides whatever its customers demand."

Schwartz is surely right: Swarthmore's requirements may be met by choosing innumerable courses from its academic buffet. In social sciences, the seminar "Women, Family, and the State in China" would do the trick. So would "The Formation of the Islamic Near East." There are more traditional options, too, including courses on medieval and modern Europe and—why not?—the history of the good old U.S.A. In the humanities division, "Substance, Shadow, and Spirit in Chinese Literature and Culture" would meet a requirement. What about a course on English literature? "Fairy Tales and Magic Fictions," "Illicit Desires in Literature," "Subverting Verses," "Legal Fictions: Law and Literature in the United States," "Utopias," "Outsiders and Insiders in Literature and Film," and "Narrative and Confession"—all these count. But not "Shakespeare," "Dickens," or "Melville." Not "Beowulf to Milton." Not even "American Poetry." These courses are reserved for majors and the suspiciously curious. To be fair, canonical authors are also studied in many Swarthmore literature classes, which are organized thematically rather than chronologically, as if to mirror the poststructuralist rejection of literary history in favor of a kaleidoscope of splintered, politicized perspectives. Of the modern languages and English departments, one professor says, "It's a classic case of third-rate minds studying second-rate minds." The English department, says one student, seems to be to catering to the "political interests" of the student body—one more argument against such a self-service curriculum. It is not hard to see why Swarthmore's English department was singled out in a National Association of Scholars report as offering one of the worst programs among elite schools.

REQUIREMENTS (CONT'D)

■ A foreign language requirement, which may be fulfilled by completing three years of a single foreign language in high school, scoring 600 or better on a standard achievement test, taking one year in a foreign tongue, or learning English as a foreign language while remaining demonstrably proficient in another.

The college will be implementing further distribution requirements incrementally in the next few years.

The sociology and anthropology major isn't as politically charged as the English major, but it is widely acknowledged to be one of the easiest. Students do not regard mathematics as particularly well taught. Like most schools, Swarthmore has departments devoted to various races and a single sex, but these are not particularly extensive; the majority of their faculty and courses are drawn from other departments. Elective classes in the religion department include "The Body in Late Antiquity," which examines "different views of the body (human, angelic, and divine) in Late Antiquity, with special emphasis on sexuality, gender, divinity, and mystical transformation." Er, amen.

There are some very good departments at Swarthmore. Engineering, economics, political science, biology, and physics all receive high marks from faculty and students, and there are pockets of strength in psychology and philosophy. Some of the better professors include James R. Kurth and Kenneth Sharpe in political science; Barry Schwartz in psychology; Richard Eldridge, Hugh Lacey, Hans Oberdiek, and Richard Schuldenfrei in philosophy; John Boccio in physics; Rosaria Muson and William Turpin in classics; Bernard Saffran and Larry Westphal in economics; Amy Cheng Vollmer in biology; and in studio art, painter Randall Exon.

The easy accessibility of the faculty is "one of the best things about the school," says one student. When they enter, students are assigned faculty advisors, who must sign off on their course selections every semester. On choosing majors, students get faculty advisors within their departments. In general, students report, the best advice on what courses to take (and to avoid) comes from other students, not their faculty advisors.

Swarthmore belongs to the Tri-College Consortium, which also includes Bryn Mawr College and Haverford College. Students may take courses at these schools, participate in their social activities, and use their libraries. A free shuttle bus provides transportation.

In class, the political atmosphere can be "oppressive and hostile" for those who don't conform, says one student. Another says that he purposely avoids English courses because of the "tacit assumption that everyone is a liberal. . . . Professors don't really encourage debate about that." A third student says that "there's definitely some tension from some of the more radical elements on campus, who feel that it's a place for liberals." But, he says, "most Swatties are open to new, different ideas."

A professor confirms the overwhelming impression that the Swarthmore faculty and administration are "self-consciously . . . self-confidently, and self-assertedly left-liberal." The general feeling, says this professor, is that "non-leftists have something wrong with them." However, in class "one can occasionally evoke a minority of articulate conservative voices." Students report, though, that they usually feel as if they must censor themselves in the classroom; there is pressure "not to offend," and conservative students "are not terribly keen on admitting it." To its credit, Swarthmore's Office of the President maintains a special fund to bring in conservative speakers.

But the left is given pride of place at Swarthmore. On the college's Web site, one student is praised for taking a year-long college sabbatical to work on a campaign to defeat the proposed constitutional amendment defending traditional marriage. This student says, "I felt this was the most important issue facing our country."

Student Life: Organization kids

Swarthmore students are united by the nature of their ambition and habits. According to one professor, the typical Swattie is very much "the Organization Kid," a phrase coined by writer David Brooks. Swatties are ambitious achievers who have been "checking the boxes since they were kids," the professor says—young men and women who are "academic" in that they can study and discuss others' ideas smoothly and sometimes brilliantly, but not "intellectual," in that they do not tend to develop their own ideas. However, this professor continues, Swarthmore students "are even better than they were 10, 20 years ago. There really is an amazing number of insightful, proficient, innovative students. I learn from my undergraduates."

The serenity and simplicity of the 300-acre Swarthmore College campus is perhaps the chief legacy of the school's Quaker roots. The leafy, beflowered campus is dominated by its first building, Parrish Hall, which looks down on the wide, long lawn sloping down to the small Swarthmore train station and the "ville" of Swarthmore. On fine days, the lawn's white Adirondack chairs are filled with reading or resting students. Others play Frisbee or football. Nearby is a large rose garden. Carefully landscaped lawns, gardens, and stone walls punctuate the rest of the campus. An inconspicuous identifying plaque seems to accompany every tree and plant, and nearly all the buildings—including the dorms—are built of the same solid, gray stone. The uniformity, proportionality, and scale of the campus recall the peaceful convictions of its Quaker founders.

The town of Swarthmore is tiny, safe, and wealthy. The business district, such as it is, includes a pizzeria, a couple of restaurants, a small used book store, a pharmacy, and a few specialty shops. It is also dry—like Swarthmore's teetotaling founders. For students, the town of Swarthmore provides only a few basics. But with the train stopping just a couple of hundred yards from the dorms, Philadelphia's Center City and points in between are just a few minutes away. Other bars, restaurants, and stores can be found in the neighboring towns of Springfield and Media. The neighborhoods surrounding campus are lined with large, unpretentious homes and make for rewarding walks. But in their free time, most students tend to stay on campus. The college generously funds student parties—although it insists that college money not be spent on alcohol and that party hosts commit to checking IDs to restrict underage drinking.

All students are required to subscribe to the college meal plan (and the town offers few alternatives even if they weren't). In 2000, the college changed its policy to allow coed rooming, though it allows for such arrangements only for groups of three or more. In part the change was stimulated by complaints from gays on campus, who charged the school's previous housing policy with heterosexism (because single-sex housing might make life "uncomfortable" for homosexual students). The option is only available for sophomores, who get to choose their roommates; the school pairs students with others of the same sex for their freshman year, and juniors and seniors usually get to live alone.

Swarthmore's bulletin is at pains to note that although 15 percent of its "residence hall areas" are restricted for single-sex living, single-sex housing is "not guaranteed." Indeed, "students should not expect to live in single-sex housing for all four years." Visitation restrictions are voted on by students, and can include 24-hour visitation (i.e., no restrictions). Student journalists at Swarthmore recently compiled a helpful guide for Swatties intent on having sex somewhere other than in their coed rooms, offering as popular spots "a bell tower, an observatory, music-practice rooms, and a bamboo grove," and "the No. 1 locale: the student health center." The paper did discourage "shower sex," since it involved wasting water.

The political climate at Swarthmore is conventionally leftist. For instance, the school joined with Bryn Mawr, Haverford, and a few other schools in canceling games to be played in South Carolina in 2000 because of the state's confederate battle flag. Daniel Flynn, executive director of Accuracy in Academia, reported being met at a lecture he gave at Swarthmore with various kinds of abuse, including a student giving him the finger for the entire lecture. When the College Republicans proposed a Veter-

SUGGESTED CORE

1. Classics 33, Homer and Greek Tragedy
2. Philosophy 102, Ancient Philosophy
3. Religion 4, New Testament and Early Christianity
4. Religion 14H, Christian Life and Thought in the Middle Ages
5. Political Science 12, Modern Political Theory
6. English Literature 20, Shakespeare
7. History 5a, The United States to 1877
8. Philosophy 49, Marx, Nietzsche, and Freud

ans Day memorial service, leftists protested. "People here are soldier-hating, fascist liberals," says one embittered student. One conservative student says of Swarthmore students that they "want diversity in that everyone they know has a different color skin . . . not a different political ideology."

Indeed, Swarthmore may well be *too* accepting—in some ways. Swarthmore student Ivan Boothe (class of 2004) recently pled guilty to soliciting sex from a minor over the Internet and possessing and disseminating child pornography after police discovered more than 500 such images on his personal computer. He was sentenced to six to 23 months in prison and three years of probation. In the aftermath of the case, one student complained that some students chose to defend Boothe in the weekly student newspaper, the *Phoenix*, writing letters claiming that he posed no danger to the community. Another student, whose daughter was five years old at the time, responded that as a mother she considered Boothe a grave threat to the community. Later it was reported that this mother was lambasted in private forums and even criticized for not opting to have an abortion when she was a pregnant teenager. Shockingly, Swarthmore decided to readmit Boothe after he had served his jail time and to permit him to live on campus. The student paper quoted Boothe as saying "No one has said anything negative to me in person. . . . I expect when I say my name is Ivan Boothe for them to cringe, and no one does it. So either they don't know, they don't care or they're hiding it very well." Ironically, the archives of the *Phoenix* contain an article by one Ivan Boothe titled "Download Speed May Rise Slightly," which discusses the need for increased speed on the campus network—you know, in case you need to download a picture or something.

Swarthmore's alternative, conservative student newspaper, *Common Sense*, recently suspended publication for lack of editorial staff. There is also something called *Ourstory*, which, according to its editors, is "Swarthmore's biannual, all-campus diversity literary and art publication."

Student groups abound, such as Queer and Questioning Resources, Diversity Coalition, Why War?, Students for a Free Tibet, etc. A small College Republicans chapter meets on campus. And there *are* a few groups not devoted to activism, including, quite refreshingly, a knitting club known as the Knit-Wits.

The Garnet Tide compete in 22 intercollegiate sports in NCAA Division III. Intramural and club sports are said to be fairly popular, especially ultimate Frisbee. Swarthmore's decision in 2000 to drop its intercollegiate men's football and wrestling teams, and to downgrade women's badminton to club status, was not universally popular. President Alfred H. Bloom was quoted in the *Chronicle of Higher Education* as saying the elimination of the football team "makes a very big difference, because the places in our class are our most precious commodities, and we need to balance a range of interests and talents." Had Swarthmore previously been overrun with underqualified jocks? Hardly. The football team's average SAT score was nearly 1400. One professor speculates that the demise of football was driven by the school's affirmative action policies, which ate up so many admissions slots. Other Swatties suggest that losing the team was a way of ridding the school of an undesirable symbol of traditional masculinity. Many Swarthmore types "definitely do not like the traditional jock," says one student.

Crime at Swarthmore and in the adjacent neighborhoods is very low, consisting almost entirely of the occasional burglary—there were only 12 such crimes reported on campus in 2002, the last year for which statistics were available. The campus also reported one sexual assault that year as the only other significant crime. Compared to other schools, there were relatively few liquor-law violations; in fact, Swarthmore reported a decline from 13 in 2001 to only five in 2003. There were no drug violations reported. Students feel quite comfortable walking the campus and adjoining neighborhoods at night.

Swarthmore isn't cheap, but aid is generous. While tuition in 2004–5 was $28,500, and room and board $8,914, some 49 percent of undergraduates received financial aid, and the average debt of a graduate is a middling $13,533.

UNITED STATES MILITARY ACADEMY

WEST POINT, NEW YORK • WWW.USMA.EDU

The long gray line

Among educational institutions in this country, the United States Military Academy at West Point is unique. Although the institution was only founded in 1802, the site of the academy played an important part during the American Revolution. George Washington ordered Polish-born Thaddeus Kosciuszko, a hero of Saratoga, to design the fortifications for West Point in 1778. The following year, Washington transferred his headquarters there. To block any British attempt to move north, forts, batteries, and redoubts were built; a 150-ton iron chain was also stretched across the Hudson. Another hero of Saratoga, then-commander Benedict Arnold, offered to hand the strategic fort to the forces of the Crown. Had his plot not been discovered, King George might well have won his colonies back—and this book would have been published in Canada.

The French Revolution and the ensuing conflicts that engulfed Europe led such notables as Washington, Hamilton, and Adams to urge Congress to form a school for the training of Americans to lead the infant country's army. An act of Congress, signed by President Jefferson in 1802, established the United States Military Academy. Colonel Sylvanus Thayer (superintendent from 1817 to 1833) established military and academic standards, originated the Honor Code, and made engineering the basis of the curriculum. Most of the nation's first railroads, bridges, harbors, and roads were designed by West Point alums. During the War between the States, graduates such as

MIDDLE ATLANTIC

Grant, Lee, Sherman, and Jackson led armies on both sides. In the following century, West Point kept abreast of developments in both academia and warfare, producing Eisenhower, MacArthur, Bradley, Arnold, Clark, Patton, Stilwell, and Wainwright. Rapid expansion of both facilities and personnel occurred after World War II, and in recent decades minority enrollment has grown tremendously. In 1976, the first women were admitted, and cadets are now allowed to major in subjects ranging from the sciences to the humanities.

Academic Life: Military Gothic

As might be expected, the academy is rather different from civilian schools. For starters, it trains Army officers. Every cadet takes an oath "to defend the Constitution of the United States from all enemies, foreign and domestic"—that is, to be prepared to fight in this country's wars, near and far. All prospective entrants need to reflect upon this point and to remember that there can be no "conscientious objection" after the oath is administered. This was easy to forget in the peaceful days between 1989 and 2001. Things are obviously different now—as, in Kipling's words, "our far-flung battle line" holds "dominion over palm and pine."

Since its founding, the academy has summed up the "West Point experience" as development in four critical areas: intellectual, physical, military, and moral-ethical. The goal is "to educate, train, and inspire the Corps of Cadets so that each graduate is a commissioned leader of character committed to the values of duty, honor, country." These values are meant to animate "a career as an officer in the United States Army; and a lifetime of selfless service to the nation."

It's not easy to enter West Point. Admission is highly competitive, and candidates must receive a nomination from a member of Congress or from the Department of the Army. Upon graduation, cadets receive a bachelor of science degree and a commission as a second lieutenant in the U.S. Army, with a commitment of at least five years active duty. The academy graduates more than 900 new officers annually—approximately 25 percent of the new lieutenants required by the Army each year. The Corps of Cadets numbers 4,000, of whom about 15 percent are women.

Academic life at the Point is demanding. To begin with, there is a genuine core curriculum of 31 courses designed to impart a "balanced education in the arts and sciences." Combined as it is with physical education and military science, this core constitutes the military academy's "professional major." Although based upon the needs of the Army, it is further intended to establish the foundation for a field of study or an optional major. Some 75 percent of cadets do choose to complete a major in the general fields of engineering, math, or humanities and social sciences. There are currently 22 optional majors and 25 fields of study, covering virtually all the liberal arts (save classics), science, and engineering disciplines found in equivalent highly selective civilian colleges. Each of these fields of study requires a cadet to pursue nine electives in courses specified by the academic discipline. Cadets who follow this path "follow a more structured elective sequence and complete a senior thesis or design project."

Although engineering retains pride of place at West Point, the liberal arts are not neglected. The art, philosophy, and literature (APL) major, for example, offers courses from the English, foreign languages, history, law, and social sciences departments. This major is the best choice for the would-be officer who craves a true humanistic education. It features *very* solid courses. For example, the "Cultural Studies" class taught at the Point is not the politicized piffle it often amounts to elsewhere. Rather, the course considers "the thinking processes, investigative techniques, fruitful theories, and current methods of discourse relating to the study of art, philosophy, and literature, a rich nexus that contributes significantly to cultural identities." The course is team-taught and focuses on "a group of cultural artifacts like the Acropolis, the *Republic*, and the *Iliad* or, perhaps, the work of Delacroix, Nietzsche, and Goethe." This fine course is a basic requirement for the APL major. Those studying this field must then take an art history course ("Eastern Art," "Masterpieces before Giotto," "Special Topics in Art History," or "Giotto and Beyond"), and another elective ("Criticism" or "Ancient Philosophers").

This major's literature track also offers excellent courses, such as "World Literature." In many colleges such a course is a sort of random survey; at West Point it teaches students "epics and tragedies of ancient Greece and Rome, Russian novels, works of medieval Islamic literature, haiku of Japan, Continental European novels of the nineteenth century, or postmodern fiction of South America." Ethnic literature at many colleges becomes a politicized hobbyhorse, free of real academic rigor. But at West Point, the course by this name teaches texts "ranging from works like Hurston's *Their Eyes Were Watching God*, Momaday's *The Ancient Child*, and Allende's *The House of Spirits* to works by less familiar authors like Lu Xun, Naguib Mahfouz, and Kenzaburo Oe." Cadets are asked to examine works selected for their intrinsic quality and significance without reference to any political agenda.

On this major's philosophy track are courses such as "Philosophy of Mind," which "address[es] major topics in the traditional philosophy of mind and questions created by recent developments in artificial intelligence: What is mind? What is the relationship of a mind to the physical world, including the brain? What is consciousness and self-consciousness? . . . Can computers be constructed to think or behave like human beings, or to have consciousness? Readings will come from classical sources, such as Descartes, as well as contemporary literature in philosophy, cognitive science, and artificial intelligence."

VITAL STATISTICS
Religious affiliation: none
Total enrollment: 4,041
Total undergraduates: 4,041
SAT/ACT midranges: SAT V: 570–660, M: 600–690; ACT: 26–30
Applicants: 12,442
Applicants accepted: 13%
Accepted applicants who enrolled: 84%
Tuition: $0
Room and board: $0
Freshman retention rate: 86%
Graduation rate: 77% (4 yrs.), 84% (6 yrs.)
Average class size: 18
Student-faculty ratio: 8:1
Courses taught by graduate TAs: none
Most popular majors: engineering, liberal arts and sciences, general studies
Students living on campus: 100%
Guaranteed housing for four years? yes
Students in fraternities or sororities: none

MIDDLE ATLANTIC

The other side of academic life at West Point is the Military Program, which begins on a cadet's very first day. Most military training takes place during the summer. New cadets (plebes) undergo cadet basic training—or "Beast Barracks"—in the summer preceding their first academic year. Cadet field training at nearby Camp Buckner takes place during the second year. The third and fourth summers are spent "serving in active Army units around the world; attending advanced training courses such as airborne, air assault, or northern warfare; or training the first- and second-year cadets as members of the leadership cadre." Military science instruction in the classroom is conducted during the school year.

Student Life: Of poets and plebes

As might be expected, life for cadets at West Point is extremely regimented; the various uniforms worn signify the fact that one's time is carefully organized. Of course, given the intensive academic, mental, and physical training undergone, this makes sense. But the academy, anxious to produce good leaders, is not content with this. "Moral-ethical development" is important as well: the authorities aim to foster it through "formal instruction in the important values of the military profession, voluntary religious programs, interaction with staff and faculty role models, and a vigorous guest speaker program." But the biggest moral element involved is the Cadet Honor Code, summed up in the line, "A cadet will not lie, cheat, steal, or tolerate those who do." The Honor Code is supposed to govern cadet life—and it does to a great degree.

The United States Corps of Cadets, to which each cadet belongs, comprises 32 cadet companies grouped into battalions, regiments, and the corps. This structure is overseen by the Brigade Tactical Department, led by the brigade tactical officer (BTO), an active duty colonel. Other, lower-ranking officers and NCOs are assigned as tactical officers (TACs) to each of the cadet formations. They supervise each cadet's development—academic, military, physical, and moral-ethical. Acting as commanders of each unit alongside the cadet officers, the TACs act as mentors, counselors, leaders, motivators, trainers, evaluators, commanders, role models, teachers, and administrators. Thus, each one is available for counseling purposes to the cadets daily, from reveille to taps, and is involved with all cadet activities. In addition, the Center for Personal Development, a counseling and assessment center staffed by Army officers trained as professional counselors/ psychologists, provides individual and group counseling.

One consideration for women (and their parents) thinking about applying to the Point is, to be blunt, sexual. Although no one can fault the patriotism and ability of the academy's female grads, the fact remains that every few years or so there is a sex scandal at one or another of the academies. Somehow it has not dawned upon the civilian leadership of the armed forces that placing young men and women at their sexual peak in intimate proximity and under heavy pressure is a recipe for erotic activity; the fact that such things are reduced to mere pastimes in many high schools does not help. Inevitably a few commanding officers' careers are ended for such things happening on their watch. While one cannot help but think that the civilian leadership is really responsible, parents solicitous for what was once called their children's "virtue" may think twice before sending their offspring to study at the Point.

Despite the many official demands on a cadet's time, he does have plenty of options for the leisure time he gets. Golf, skiing, sailing, equestrian activities, and ice skating are all available, as are a cadet radio station, orienteering, rock climbing, and Big Brother–Big Sister. The Directorate of Cadet Activities operates the Eisenhower Hall Theatre, the Cadet Restaurant, Grant Hall, the Cadet Store, and the Cadet Bookstore, and cadets produce such publications as the *Howitzer Yearbook*, the *West Point Calendar, Bugle Notes*, and the *West Point Planner*. Some outsiders may be surprised by the existence of the *Circle in the Spiral,* the literary/art journal of the Corps of Cadets, which features poems, artwork, and stories by cadets. Since the journal's origin in 1991, it has won praise from the Columbia Scholastic Press Association and the American Scholastic Press Association.

Nor are social events lacking. There are dances almost every week, as well as annual events like Ring Weekend, Yearling Winter Weekend, and Plebe–Parent Weekend. Festivities like 100th Night Weekend, 500th Night Weekend, Dining-In, Hops, and the like help keep cadets from being all work and no play. Additionally, the Directorate of Cadet Activities sponsors 109 clubs, amongst which are competitive club teams, individual sports, hobby clubs, academic clubs, support clubs, and religious clubs. The list is dazzling, ranging from Amateur Radio, the German Language Club, and the Hunting Club, to the Korean-American Relations Seminar. The academy requires a great deal physically: each semester, every cadet participates in an intercollegiate, club, or intramural sport.

Political clubs as such do not exist, although undoubtedly most cadets would describe themselves as "conservative," whatever that might mean. But in keeping with the U.S. military's tradition of being apolitical, partisan activity as such would be frowned upon.

The physical plant is quite lovely. The distinctive nineteenth-century "military Gothic" style, found at military schools and colleges around the country, originated here. The tower of the witch's castle in the 1939 film, *The Wizard of Oz*, was actually a tower on a building here; the flying monkeys were dressed in cadet uniforms.

From the dawn of warfare, the necessity of religion to undergird the warrior's resolve has been acknowledged—at least until our own day. In 1972, federal courts ended

ACADEMIC REQUIREMENTS

Graduation from the Point (and commissioning in the U.S. Army) has rather stringent requirements. All cadets must complete a core curriculum. This includes 31 courses divided equally between the arts and sciences. All options for fulfilling these requirements are academically sound and serious. The courses required are:

- Three courses in English.
- Four courses in history (both U.S. and world).
- Two courses in "leadership."
- One course in "philosophy/ethics."
- Two foreign language classes.
- Three courses in social sciences.
- One course in law.
- Four courses in mathematics.
- Two classes in chemistry.
- One course in physical geography.
- Two classes in information technology.
- Two courses in physics.
- Three classes in engineering/design.

mandatory chapel attendance at all three service academies. Nevertheless, until and unless the civilian leadership banishes it entirely, religious life flourishes, on a voluntary basis, at West Point.

There are five chapels at West Point, each of which receives a great deal of use. Most notable architecturally, the Gothic Cadet Chapel was dedicated in 1910. The first pew features silver plates engraved with the signatures of such previous superintendents as Generals MacArthur, Taylor, and Westmoreland. This chapel features Protestant services every Sunday and hosts the Protestant Chapel Choir and the Protestant Chapel Sunday School. Its choir is famous and performs at a number of the academy's traditional ceremonies. The neoclassical Old Cadet Chapel was built in 1836. Originally located near the cadet barracks, it was removed stone by stone to its present location in 1910. Its interior contains many plaques, including one to Maj. Gen. Benedict Arnold. Located near the entrance of the cemetery, it hosts many funerals and memorials and has long been the home for Lutheran services. A third Protestant facility is the Georgian-style Post Chapel. Built in 1943, it is occupied now by a Gospel congregation.

For Catholics, there is the Norman Gothic Chapel of the Most Holy Trinity, built in 1899 and enlarged in 1959. Amongst other features, it boasts 22 stained-glass windows showing soldier-saints and memorializing Catholic alumni killed in the service of their country. Masses are held on Saturday and Sunday, with music by the Cadet Catholic Choir and the Catholic Folk Group.

Opened in 1984, the Jewish Chapel contains an extensive Judaica collection, a library, and special exhibits. Sabbath services are held every Friday evening during the academic year, augmented by the Jewish Chapel Choir.

Other faiths are active at the Point, but all are encouraged to make use of the Cadet Prayer:

> O God, our Father, thou Searcher of human hearts, help us to draw near to thee in sincerity and truth. May our religion be filled with gladness and may our worship of thee be natural. Strengthen and increase our admiration for honest dealing and clean thinking, and suffer not our hatred of hypocrisy and pretence ever to diminish. Encourage us in our endeavor to live above the common level of life. Make us to choose the harder right instead of the easier wrong, and never to be content with a half truth when the whole truth can be won. Endow us with courage that is born of loyalty to all that is noble and worthy, that scorns to compromise with vice and injustice and knows no fear when truth and right are in jeopardy. Guard us against flippancy and irreverence in the sacred things of life. Grant us new ties of friendship and new opportunities of service. Kindle our hearts in fellowship with those of a cheerful countenance, and soften our hearts with sympathy for those who sorrow and suffer. Help us to maintain the honor of the corps untarnished and unsullied and to show forth in our lives the ideals of West Point in doing our duty to thee and to our country. All of

which we ask in the name of the Great Friend and Master of all. Amen.

The artistic side of the cadet is not neglected either. The Eisenhower Hall Theatre is the East Coast's second-largest cultural arts theatre, and it presents a host of world-class performances annually. Opera, dance, symphony orchestras, staged spectaculars, country, and rock have all been performed here, and the place has been host to a wide variety of Broadway plays and important musicians, from *Les Misérables* and the Radio City Rockettes to Luciano Pavarotti, Johnny Cash, and the Twyla Tharp Dance Company.

The West Point Museum is the oldest and most diverse public collection of "militaria" in the Western Hemisphere. Starting with captured British materials brought here after the British defeat at Saratoga in 1777, the museum collections have come to include trophies from each of this nation's wars, including such rarities as Mussolini's hat. The school does not report its crime statistics; however, apart from occasional sex scandals, there seems to be little to speak of.

There is no tuition at West Point. Since all cadets are members of the Army, their education is free, and in addition they receive a salary.

SUGGESTED CORE

1. No suitable course
2. Art, Philosophy, and Literature Ep 388, Ancient Philosophy
3. No suitable course
4. No suitable course
5. Social Sciences 386, Political Thought and Ideas
6. Art, Philosophy, and Literature Ep 394, Shakespeare
7. History 103, History of the United States *or* History 153, Advanced History of the United States
8. History 363, Europe in Transformation and Revolution, 1648-1850 (*closest match*)

UNITED STATES NAVAL ACADEMY

ANNAPOLIS, MARYLAND • WWW.USNA.EDU

Anchors, aweigh!

Annapolis radiates charm. The small town on the Chesapeake is in many ways reminiscent of Williamsburg, Virginia. Tourists flock here to enjoy the colonial and Victorian
sights, and one of the most sought-after sights for tourists (alas now somewhat restricted, thanks to the events of 9/11) is the Naval Academy. The Navy had to wait more
than 40 years after the establishment of the Army's academy at West Point to get one of
its own, in 1845. Even then, it only happened because of a mutiny led by three midshipmen (the nautical equivalent of cadets) aboard the U.S.S. *Somers*.

In 1794, President George Washington was able to persuade Congress to start a
navy, specifically to combat the Barbary Pirates—unleashed when Napoleon ejected
their enemies, the Knights of Malta, from that island. However, it was the revolutionary French against whom the infant American fleet first went into battle, a year after
its first vessels were launched in 1797. But there was no regular training of naval officers for another 50 years. Then in 1842, the brig U.S.S. *Somers*, a school ship manned by
teenage naval apprentice volunteers—whose training was conducted aboard ship—set
off from the Brooklyn Navy Yard. Discipline rapidly fell to pieces and a shipboard re-
bellion erupted. A court of inquiry found that three young midshipmen had made a
"determined attempt to commit a mutiny" and sentenced them to be hanged from the
yardarm. The resulting national outcry forced Congress to act.

Three years later, Secretary of the Navy George Bancroft founded the Naval School
at Annapolis. Maryland's capital was selected to protect midshipmen from "the temptations and distractions that necessarily connect with a large and populous city." On
October 10, 1845, the seven professors were joined by a class of 50 midshipmen to
whom they taught mathematics and navigation, gunnery and steam, chemistry, English, natural philosophy, and French. As the United States grew into a world power,
their fleet became a true "blue water navy," capable of operating around the globe.
Today, the academy has expanded from its original 10 acres and 50 midshipmen to 338
acres, schooling 4,000 men and women.

Academic Life: Not all wet

Since 1933, the Naval Academy has awarded bachelor of science degrees to its graduates;
in turn, it has replaced its once fixed curriculum with the present core curriculum plus
18 major fields of study, including many elective courses. So too, training in naval technology has evolved from the days of sail to today's nuclear submarines and guided mis-
sile systems. The academy has also become a major source of new officers for the Ma-

rine Corps, which remains a part of the Navy, albeit an autonomous and extremely individualistic one. As at West
Point, jealously guarded traditions continue to provide a
sense of continuity at Annapolis year after year.

Admission is highly competitive. In addition to scholastic, physical, and leadership requirements, "to receive an
offer of appointment to the Naval Academy, an applicant
must obtain a nomination from an official source. This
normally includes a U.S. representative, two U.S. senators,
and the vice president of the United States," according to
the academy.

As its Web site says, "Every day, as the undergraduate
college of the naval service, the United States Naval Academy strives to accomplish its mission to develop midshipmen 'morally, mentally, and physically.'" Annapolis offers
each of its midshipmen a core curriculum featuring engineering, science, mathematics, humanities, and social science courses in order to "provide a broad-based education
that will qualify the midshipmen for practically any career
field in the Navy or Marine Corps." Married to this are 19
majors. Of these, four—English, history, language studies,
and political science—might be considered liberal arts. The
better students may participate in honors programs; even
postgraduate degrees may be started at Annapolis.

The English major requires two survey courses. "Western Literature I" is billed as "a balanced survey of the Western literary tradition and its backgrounds, from the ancient
Greeks through the Renaissance. Readings . . . include classical Greek and Roman epic, drama and philosophy (typi-
cally Plato and Aristotle); selections from the Old and New testaments; medieval poetry, drama, and philosophy (especially Dante and/or Chaucer); and Renaissance poetry, non-Shakespearean drama and prose." "Western Literature II" features "the Western literary tradition and its backgrounds, from the Enlightenment through Romanticism to the various reactions to Romanticism beginning in the mid-nineteenth century, most notably realism, naturalism, and modernism and its aftermath." (We believe
that very few collegiate English departments refer officially to "modernism and its aftermath," but more should.) "Shakespeare," with its study of a "representative sample
of Shakespeare's tragedies, histories, and comedies," as well as writings of the Bard's
contemporaries, is also mandatory. On this solid framework are added eight other in-
depth, specialized courses.

Even if a midshipman chooses one of the liberal arts majors, he will be awarded a
bachelor of science degree, owing to the technical content of the core curriculum. Mid-
dies pursuing any of the liberal arts majors are eligible for the Honors Program. Cho-

VITAL STATISTICS
Religious affiliation: none
Total enrollment: 4,309
Total undergraduates: 4,309
SAT midranges: V: 530–640, M: 560–670
Applicants: 4,281
Applicants accepted: 34%
Accepted applicants who enrolled: 83%
Tuition: $0
Room and board: $0
Freshman retention rate: 95%
Graduation rate: 86% (4 yrs.), 86% (6 yrs.)
Average class size: 20
Student-faculty ratio: 7:1
Courses taught by graduate TAs: none
Most popular majors: engineering, social sciences, general studies
Students living on campus: 100%
Guaranteed housing for four years? yes
Students in fraternities or sororities: none

sen for their "excellent academic and leadership performance," honors students complete a thesis or research project. They then defend it orally in front of a panel of faculty members. If successful, they graduate with honors.

An even more challenging offer is the Trident Scholar Program, which provides an opportunity for "exceptionally capable midshipmen to engage in independent study and research during their senior year. Following their selection to the program during their junior year, the first class scholars conduct independent research in an area of interest, working with a faculty . . . expert in the field. Trident Scholars carry a reduced formal courseload to give them time for in-depth research of the project and for preparation of a thesis."

Minors in Arabic, French, German, Spanish, Russian, Chinese, and Japanese are offered for those who complete four advanced courses in one of these languages.

The faculty number some 600, about evenly divided between civilian and military personnel. One of the most sought-after instructors is David Allen White, who has taught world literature at Annapolis for more than 21 years, but most faculty are said to be excellent.

Given its mission to train officers, the academy also provides professional and leadership training. Some of this is practical: Not only do four years at the Naval Academy teach the life and customs of the naval service, but as plebes, midshipmen learn to take orders and then to take on positions of responsibility themselves. They also acquire practical experience from assignments with Navy and Marine Corps units. In the classroom, such courses as "Leadership," "Ethics and Law," and "Seamanship and Navigation" round out their education in this sphere.

Added to this is what the academy calls "moral and ethical development." The school reminds students that as future officers they "will someday be responsible for the priceless lives of many men and women and multi-million-dollar equipment. From Plebe Summer through graduation, the Naval Academy's Character Development Program is a four-year integrated continuum that focuses on the attributes of integrity, honor, and mutual respect."

Student Life: Such intangibles as honor

The strongest memory that graduates of the Naval Academy take with them from Annapolis is Plebe Summer. This is the rigorous, sometimes traumatic seven-week period in which civilians are molded into midshipmen. On Induction Day, shortly after arrival, the new plebes are put into uniform and taught saluting—indeed, they will salute virtually everyone they encounter, serving officers and upperclassmen alike. The days start at dawn with an hour of exercise, finishing long after sunset. There is neither free time nor nearly enough time to do all that a plebe must do. As at the other two academies, this system is designed to separate the wheat from the chaff, retaining only those who can operate under pressure and deal with sudden changes without going to pieces—all necessary traits in an officer. At the same time, "plebing" builds a sense of identity with the academy and is the start of the sort of lifelong friendships that only hardship can bring.

At Annapolis, Plebe Summer also means an introduction to seamanship, navigation, and combat arms. By the time the school year starts, the plebe is completely familiar with the academy's and the Navy's standards—particularly regarding such intangibles as honor.

As at West Point, the school maintains a strict honor system (here called the "Honor Concept"). Annapolis's Concept states that "midshipmen are persons of integrity: They stand for that which is right. They tell the truth and ensure that the full truth is known. They do not lie. They embrace fairness in all actions. They ensure that work submitted as their own is their own, and that assistance received from any source is authorized and properly documented. They do not cheat. They respect the property of others and ensure that others are able to benefit from the use of their own property. They do not steal." Honor offenses are dealt with by brigade honor committees made up of elected upperclassmen. The school works hard to develop within the future officer a high sense of personal honor—a notion completely alien to many in the civilian world, including, often, in academia. This is why cheating scandals at Annapolis, which have occurred from time to time, are regarded far more seriously than at many civilian institutions; it is not simply wrong, it a breach of esprit de corps; it is dishonorable, and that is the worst that a midshipman can be.

ACADEMIC REQUIREMENTS

As might be expected, midshipmen are required to pass a rigorous curriculum in order to graduate and be commissioned as officers. Moreover, whereas West Point allows their cadets to forego a major and stick to the core curriculum alone, midshipmen must also take a major. The core includes the following classes:

- "Calculus" I and II.
- "Chemistry" I and II.
- "Rhetoric and Introduction to Literature" I and II.
- "Leadership and Human Behavior."
- "American Naval Heritage."
- "Fundamentals of Naval Science."

The day is quite regimented, with reveille and watches. One marches to meals and does everything in uniform. Midshipmen live in Bancroft Hall, a gigantic dorm. The 4,000-strong Brigade of Midshipmen is divided into companies. Each company has its own living area at Bancroft, called a "wardroom." Every bedroom (shared by two or more midshipmen) is wired for computers, Internet access, and phones. The companies are the focus of life at Annapolis, as each midshipman eats, sleeps, drills, and plays with the members of his own company and competes against the other companies. This in turn teaches the small-unit cohesion so integral to warfare and is the source of life-long friendships. This is also where practical leadership begins—since, as he advances year by year, the midshipman will be expected to assume leadership positions at the company, battalion, and brigade level. Although subject to careful supervision by regular naval and marine officers, it is the midshipmen who run the brigade.

The academy's athletic program is intensive, to say the least. Annapolis regards the midshipman's physical growth as of like importance to his mental and moral development; "athletic teams are an integral part of the overall education of the midshipmen." This is because "team play, cooperative effort, commitment and individual sacrifice" are integral to the role of the officer. A physical education curriculum and athletic choices are required. The academy's teams are well supported, as seen by anyone who has experienced an Army-Navy game. What's more, the football team broke a string of dismal records with a bowl appearance at the end of the 2004 season.

As attractive as the Annapolis experience sounds, in evaluating it the first thing to remember is that it is a *naval* academy. Its purpose is to train men and women to lead others in combat, whether on sea, on land, or in the air. Anyone with an ethical objection to combat should avoid taking the oath "to defend the Constitution of the United States against all enemies, foreign and domestic," lest they be guilty of perjury. Once taken, this oath becomes the cornerstone of the midshipman's, and later the officer's, personal code of honor.

While the academy has been coeducational since 1976, there are still many who question whether it is a good place for women to study. Women now account for 13 to 14 percent of entering plebes and receive the same academic and professional training as do the males. Thankfully, the academy has not tried to butcher the English language with "midshippersons." But as anyone who follows the news knows, every few years one or another of the academies undergoes a lurid sex scandal, generally involving rape, weekend orgies, or some unpleasant combination of the two. Just as routinely, the heads of some serving officers roll. While no one can contest the patriotism or the expertise of the academies' female graduates, one wishes that the civilian leadership were held accountable for such lapses instead—for having thrown people of both sexes into such intimate quarters as they currently share at the Academy. One can only suppose that they themselves were never young. Young women especially (and their parents) who are attached to a high moral code would do well to bear this in mind before applying.

Religion has always been seen as an essential moral anchor for the fighting man—and particularly for his officers. But back in 1972, the same sort of civilians who would push women into the academies became overwrought by the practice of mandatory chapel. Every cadet or midshipman had to attend the services of his religion at the chapel on Sunday (or Friday night, were he Jewish). The judiciary struck down this clear and present danger to the republic in that year, causing "right-thinking" folk everywhere (few of whom, perhaps, would send their own children into the military) to rejoice. Despite that decision, religion remains an important force at Annapolis.

Indeed, the zealous defenders of freedom have sniffed out yet another danger to civil liberties, this time in the form of prayers before meals. The proud old state military colleges, V.M.I. and The Citadel, have been forced through court action to stop this subversive practice. But at Annapolis, alone of all three academies, grace is still said before lunch. Thoughtfully, the ACLU has offered to assist any midshipmen who might want to sue the academy. So far, no one has bothered.

There's a good reason for that. Ultimately, military folk are asked to be willing to die for their country. Without a connection to something higher even than duty to country, this is simply too much to ask. But from this connection comes that essential quality in combat: courage. This is something military men from all times and most places have understood.

At Annapolis, the copper-green dome of the chapel symbolizes this realization. It serves as the focal point of the Command Religious Program, which tries to "foster spiritual growth and promote the moral development of the midshipmen within the tenets of their particular faith or beliefs." The Chaplains Office, manned by six clerics of various faiths, both conducts worship services and offers counseling. Services are held for members of the Catholic, Christian Science, Jewish, Muslim, Protestant, and Mormon faiths, while midshipmen religious organizations include the Protestant Midshipmen Club, the Catholic Midshipmen Club, Jewish Midshipmen Club, Officers' Christian Fellowship, Baptist Student Union, Fellowship of Christian Athletes, Navigators, Campus Crusade for Christ, and the Latter-Day Saints Student Organization.

The Naval Academy Chapel contains the crypt of naval hero John Paul Jones. The interior of the chapel features rose marble, ornate stone and wood features, and stained-glass memorials (some Tiffany) to past naval heroes. Hanging from the ceiling over the rear choir loft is a votive ship. Most illustrative of the spirituality of Annapolis is the Midshipman's Prayer. Here is its traditional version (a lovely interfaith one is also offered):

SUGGESTED CORE
1. and 2. Humanities Elective (HE) 217, Western Literature I
3. HE 222, The Bible and Literature
4. History (HH) 485, A History of Christianity
5. FP 340, Modern Political Thought and Ideology
6. HE 333, Shakespeare
7. HH 346/347, Revolutionary America and the Early Republic / Civil War and Reconstruction
8. No suitable course

> Almighty Father, whose way is in the sea, whose paths are in the great waters, whose command is over all and whose love never faileth; let me be aware of thy presence and obedient to thy will. Keep me true to my best self, guarding me against dishonesty in purpose and in deed, and helping me so to live that I can stand unashamed and unafraid before my shipmates, my loved ones, and thee. Protect those in whose love I live. Give me the will to do my best and to accept my share of responsibilities with a strong heart and a cheerful mind. Make me considerate of those entrusted to my leadership and faithful to the duties my country has entrusted in me. Let my uniform remind me daily of the traditions of the service of which I am a part. If I am inclined to doubt, steady my faith; if I am tempted, make me strong to resist; if I should miss the mark, give me courage to try again. Guide me with the light of truth and keep before me the life of him by whose example and help I trust to obtain the answer to my prayer, Jesus Christ our Lord. Amen.

In keeping with the American military's apolitical tradition, there are no political clubs at the academy; however, there are some 90 other extracurricular activities (ECAs—everything has an acronym here). These include musical and theatrical groups like the Catholic Choir, the Drum and Bugle Corps, and the Masqueraders; recreational groups such as Amateur Radio and the Chess Club; professional organizations like the Dolphin Club and the Semper Fidelis Society; and community service clubs, publications, and athletics. Heritage, religious, academic, and brigade support activities fill out the roster. Participation in such groups is held to be important, not only for its own sake, but also for its role in rounding out the social aspect of the midshipman's development.

Although the various programs offered by the academy take up more time than the average college student is required to give, midshipmen do get Christmas and summer vacations (leave) plus shorter periods of time off (liberty). Leave and liberty are dependent upon "assigned military responsibilities, performance in academic and military endeavors, and class seniority." Students earn more liberty and privileges each year they advance at the academy. Off-campus privileges during the school year consist of town liberty and weekend liberty. The latter allows the midshipman to leave the academy after his last military obligation on Friday afternoon and return Sunday evening.

Use of cars is restricted according to class seniority, although no midshipman may have a motorcycle within town liberty limits. Drinking is forbidden to plebes at the academy and restricted to over-21 upperclassmen. Needless to say, the use of drugs is forbidden and results in expulsion from the academy. Random urinalysis is conducted.

Almost everything a midshipman needs is available on the academy grounds: bookstore, uniform and tailor shop, cobbler shop, snack bar, barber/beauty shop, post office, and recreation rooms. There are also restaurants and an ice skating rink. Members of the Brigade eat together at King Hall and enjoy such delectables as steak, spiced shrimp, Mexican food, and home-baked pastries. Medical, psychological, and dental care is provided on site, as well as legal and financial advice. In a word, other than applying himself to his studies and other obligations, the midshipman has little to worry about. The academy does not report its crime statistics to the government, as is required of civilian schools. However, it would seem that real crime is all but negligible.

When accepted to the Naval Academy, the student joins the U.S. Navy. Not only is the education free of charge, but the midshipman earns a salary. Merit, not money, is required of entrants to the service academies.

VASSAR COLLEGE

Vassar to Yale: Drop dead

When Vassar College first opened the gates of its campus in 1865, its founders planned to offer women an education equal in quality to that available to men at Yale and Harvard. For more than 100 years, Vassar reigned as a giant of women's education. When Yale proposed a merger with Vassar in 1967, the women's college turned down the offer. Two years later, Vassar began admitting men.

Though Vassar is now coed, it still retains the self-styled "progressive spirit" that animated its founding. It claims a mission based on "toleration and respect for diversity," a "commitment to social justice, and a willingness to challenge the status quo." "Vassar's politics," says the school mission statement, "have always been the politics of inclusion." (Except, of course, for when it only included women.) It is an institution that, at least in theory, strives to exclude no one and no ideas. College admissions literature admits that "politically, our campus is more liberal-minded," but asserts that "there is a nice mix of liberals, conservatives, and everything in between!" Still, one liberal student characterizes Vassar as "very left. That definitely influences the courses, both in terms of the books read and classroom discussion."

It's easy to be tolerant of "diversity" when everyone agrees with you, of course. The consensus of sources we consulted is that if there are students and faculty at Vassar who are skeptical of "progressive" dogmas, they keep a pretty low profile.

VITAL STATISTICS
Religious affiliation: none
Total enrollment: 2,475
Total undergraduates: 2,475
SAT/ACT midranges: SAT V: 650–730, M: 630–700; ACT: 28–32
Applicants: 6,193
Applicants accepted: 29%
Accepted applicants who enrolled: 36%
Tuition: $30,895
Room and board: $7,680
Freshman retention rate: 92%
Graduation rate: 81% (4 yrs.), 91% (6 yrs.)
Average class size: 16
Student-faculty ratio: 9:1
Courses taught by graduate TAs: none
Most popular majors: English, psychology, political science
Students living on campus: 98%
Guaranteed housing for four years? yes
Students in fraternities or sororities: none

Academic Life: Our advice is, get advice

First, the good news. Classes at Vassar are small: A mere 1 percent of Vassar classes enroll more than 50 students, and most have fewer than 20. The student-faculty ratio is nine to one, and the average class size, 16. Teaching is a high priority, and, as "a majority of the faculty live on campus or nearby," according to the university, faculty form close relationships with students. "In my four years at Vassar, I have never met a teacher who has been more concerned about his research than his students," says a student. "In fact, teachers go out of their way to meet with you." A faculty member says, "There is a lot of effort to keep classes small so learning can come from discussion and joint endeavor." Teaching assistants do not teach courses. "Faculty and students work closely together," a professor says. "Inquiry and accomplishment are more valued than rote memorization and 'following rules.'"

Retiring president Frances Daly Fergusson receives mixed reviews generally, but at least one faculty member called her "outstanding." Fergusson spent 20 years leading Vassar and is said to have managed its transition to coeducation very effectively. As we go to press, her replacement has not yet been selected. According to one professor, "Tenure decisions are rigorous and scrupulously fair and very exhaustive." Despite the school's emphasis on teaching, publishing is expected. "A candidate must show evidence of more than competent teaching," one professor says. "Scholarship counts a great deal, as does service."

Vassar's strongest programs include history, philosophy, biology, and art. English is considered "excellent in spots," and the programs in the Romance languages provide fine opportunities for study abroad. The economics department offers a respectable range of courses, including introductory and advanced ones on Marxist economics along with a couple on neoclassical (free market) and game theory. Students and faculty name the following as the best teachers at the school: Nancy Bisaha, Robert K. Brigham, James Merrell, Leslie Offutt, and Michaela Pohl in history; Mark C. Amodio, Beth Darlington, H. Daniel Peck, and Everett K. Weedin in English; Nicholas Adams, Eve D'Ambra, Susan D. Kuretsky, Brian Lukacher, and Andrew M. Watsky in art history; Robert Brown in classics; Giovanna Borradori, Michael McCarthy, Mitchell Miller, and Douglas Winblad in philosophy; Peter G. Stillman in political science; Alexis Klimoff in Russian; and Deborah Dash Moore in religion. The Web site offers a student-run ranking of the faculty (for students' use only); if you do enroll, check it out.

The "Freshman Course," required of all first-year students, is a small-group seminar designed to introduce students to the "Vassar experience" and to promote "the effective expression of ideas in both written and oral work," according to admissions literature. While the courses serve as an introduction to a given discipline, they are often interdisciplinary. Nearly every department offers a freshman course; a recent catalog lists about 20, including the urban studies course "Let Them Eat Asphalt: Food, Farming, and the City," the history course "American Moments: Readings in U.S. History," and the English composition course "The Art of Reading and Writing." One student says, "The usefulness of the freshman course varies from professor to professor. I took one in the English department . . . and it was one of the most challenging courses I've ever taken at Vassar. It really taught me how to analyze my own writing in order to improve upon it without a professor's insight. [But] some students are completely unsatisfied with their freshman courses. So, just like any other course, the value really comes from whether or not the professor is good."

By the end of their sophomore year, all students must complete a course in quantitative methods. Any math, laboratory science, or computer science course will satisfy this requirement, as will select courses in anthropology, geography, and economics. Students must also demonstrate proficiency in a foreign language, but this can be done with SAT II subject test scores, by passing a proficiency exam, or by completing three semesters' coursework. And Vassar has a strong foreign language program, offering concentrations in French, German, Greek, Italian, Latin, Russian, and Spanish, as well as advanced study in Chinese, Hebrew, and Japanese. Students can also fulfill the foreign language requirement in other languages via the Self-Instructional Language Program, in which they listen to tapes, read from a textbook, and speak with native speakers.

Extracurricular academic opportunities are numerous, and interested students should comb the catalog and discuss with faculty and other students the unique internship, research, and study-abroad possibilities that are available. "There are a lot of internships from the Ford Foundation available in the summer for humanities students," one professor says. There are also research opportunities in the sciences working under faculty. Vassar participates in the Twelve College Exchange Program, so students may spend a semester or a year at schools like Amherst, Bowdoin, Dartmouth, Wheaton (the one in Massachusetts), or Williams.

On the down side, Vassar's curriculum is quite unstructured, giving students virtually free rein to overspecialize or dabble aimlessly. One student majoring in French says, "I feel that students at Vassar take a semi-wide range of courses. A humanities-minded student will branch out into other humanities departments, but they won't be found taking a couple of chemistry classes just for the fun of it." The school enjoys a reputation as one of the country's top liberal arts programs, but the college does little to ensure that students actually receive a true liberal arts education. "Skillful inquiry"—rather than the liberal arts—is "the cornerstone of the Vassar curriculum," according to the school.

In the absence of a core curriculum, finding what is most useful at Vassar could be difficult, but advising at the school is said to be strong. Entering students are assigned premajor faculty advisors. Once they declare majors, they are assigned to faculty members in their own departments. Vassar students can also seek advice from the dean of the student's class—the dean of freshmen, for instance, oversees the premajor advising program and new student orientation. The college requires that students consult with their advisors before registering for the forthcoming semester. It also offers special preprofessional advisors for students interested in medical or law school. This is important, given that 80 percent of Vassar graduates go on to a graduate program of some kind.

Vassar begins to get more serious about requirements when students start their

ACADEMIC REQUIREMENTS

Vassar's slim general education requirements are as follows. Students must:

- Take one "Freshman Course," a small-group seminar chosen from any department.
- Pass one quantitative (math or science) course by the end of the sophomore year.
- Demonstrate foreign language proficiency, either through coursework or test scores.
- Complete between 10 and 17 courses in their declared major.

work within their majors. Students majoring in history, for instance, must take 11 courses in the area, including at least one in each of four areas: European history, American history, pre-1800 history (courses such as "Renaissance Europe" or "Colonial America"), and Asian, African, Middle Eastern, or Latin American studies. They must also take an additional course in Asian, African, Middle Eastern, Latin American, or pre-1800 history. Finally, history majors complete a senior thesis. Political science majors must take 10 courses, including one in each of four major fields of study: American politics, comparative politics, political theory, and international relations. The English major was recently beefed up—while getting less specific in the types of courses required. Students who enter Vassar from this point on will need 12 English classes to complete the major, at least four of which must be at the 300 level. In their senior year, English majors must complete a 25-page paper in one of those 300-level courses. In addition, students must take "British Literature through the Eighteenth Century," two courses in literature written before 1800, and one additional course in literature written before 1900. It's possible, though unlikely, for an English major to graduate without taking a course in Shakespeare and for a history major to avoid a general survey course on the United States.

Students looking for trendy majors have plenty of choices at Vassar—the women's studies program being a good example. It offers courses like "Feminism/Environmentalism," "Gender Issues in Economics," and "Women in Film." The urban studies program takes a kitchen-sink approach. It claims to introduce "students to a temporal range and spatial variety of urban experience and phenomena" and to engage "students experientially in a facet of the urban experience." We hope that means something to students majoring in the subject, because it is entirely lost on us. A unique major at Vassar is Victorian studies, a program that combines history, literature, and sociology.

Almost half of Vassar students study abroad at some point during their four years, and the college sponsors (or cosponsors with other colleges) study in Germany, Morocco, Paris, Bologna, Sienna, Madrid, and at the British Film Academy. Vassar students are also allowed to study abroad through another college or university. The education program sponsors teaching internships at a primary school in Oxfordshire, England, and in Clifden, Ireland. Students majoring in international studies are actively encouraged to study in a foreign country.

Student Life: Shiny happy people

The Vassar campus is peaceful, and residential life is pleasant. While the school has since fallen out of first place, in 2002 *The Princeton Review* claimed that Vassar had the happiest students in the country. Located in Poughkeepsie, New York, (population 75,000), 70 miles north of New York City, Vassar's Hudson River Valley surroundings look more like a Winslow Homer painting than a modern college campus. Throughout winter, the area's average temperature hovers in the twenties, but in more temperate months, students can take advantage of Vassar's 500-acre farm, complete with hiking and jogging trails. Other favorite outdoor attractions are Sunset Lake and the Falls (a local waterfall). But don't get too close to the townies; according to the recent *Princeton Review* rankings, Vassarites don't play well with others—indeed, Vassar ranks among the top 10 schools in creating tension with the locals.

When Vassar first opened in 1865, the entire institution was housed in Main Hall, a large building with a façade designed by James Renwick. Part of Main Hall was renovated and expanded a couple of decades ago to create a mammoth College Center that houses, among other things, a snack bar, a cafe, a post office, a bookshop, a radio station, and the college pub, Matthew's Mug. Main Hall also has several administrative offices and student residences.

Four Elizabethan-style residence halls, housing about 150 students each, form a typical quad. The college has five other student residences off the main quadrangle, and approximately 20 percent of Vassar students (all upperclassmen) live in apartments or townhouses further from the center of campus. One residence hall is reserved for women only, but all other halls are coed and do not separate men and women by floor. Many bathrooms are coed, and students can share suites (though not individual rooms, theoretically) with members of the opposite sex.

Each house is self-governed, meaning that students make most of the decisions; there are no resident advisors in the buildings, so "student fellows" do most of the counseling and community programming that RAs would do at other schools. Some floors in each dormitory are set aside as "wellness corridors" or substance-free areas. Students seeking a more "holistic" living experience can apply for co-op housing, where residents cook and clean for themselves while promoting a "collaborative, healthy lifestyle," according to the college. Smoking is prohibited in residence halls unless residents decide to designate a specific smoking location. Houses also maintain quiet hours between 11 p.m. and 10 a.m. About 98 percent of Vassar students live in college-owned housing. Housing is guaranteed for all four years, but upperclassmen may have to live in double- or triple-occupancy rooms originally meant for one or two residents. The college's dining services rank among the nation's 10 most vegetarian-friendly, according to People for the Ethical Treatment of Animals, and have recently expanded their vegan options.

Vassar has no Greek system, and the absence of what Vassar calls the "Animal House" atmosphere makes the college less dependent on a drinking culture—or so claims the administration. But students do drink. One regular Vassar event was shut down by organizers a few years ago because of excessive intoxication. The "HomoHop," an annual dance open to members of all sexual proclivities, including drag queens and pornography fans, had attracted nearly 1,500 people per year. Tragically, the event was cancelled after dozens of students ended up in the emergency room with alcohol-related

SUGGESTED CORE
1. Classics 102, Reading Antiquity
2. Philosophy 101a, History of Western Philosophy I
3. Religion 225/227, The Hebrew Bible / The New Testament and Early Christianity
4. Religion 236, Christian Traditions (*closest match*)
5. Political Science 270, Modern Political Thought
6. English 240, Shakespeare *or* English 241/242, Shakespeare
7. History 275b, Revolutionary America, 1750–1830
8. Philosophy 205a, Nineteenth-Century Philosophy

MIDDLE ATLANTIC

illnesses. Raunchy Vassarites may turn for consolation to the pages of *Squirm,* the college-recognized campus porn magazine, and its sister organization, the Sex Avengers.

Students with more refined tastes have access to a vast number of cultural events; Poughkeepsie is only 90 minutes from New York City by train. Poughkeepsie itself has plenty of concert venues, dance clubs, and restaurants—the Culinary Institute of America is only minutes away, housed in a beautiful former Jesuit seminary that contains the grave of Pierre Teilhard de Chardin.

Vassar's reputation for radical, and sometimes bizarre, politics is as strong as its reputation for academic rigor. Vassar offers many explicitly politicized courses, the administration seems genuinely exhilarated at the prospects of promoting its own leftist agenda, and students are activists to the core. One student says, "I'm a senior and have only met two Republicans in four years." Conservative students exist, but they are strongly advised to keep a low profile. There are rumors that a Republican Club existed at one time, but the closest thing to it now is the newly formed Moderate, Independent, and Conservative Alliance (MICA). This club was recently approved unanimously by the Vassar Student Association and has held some forums that have been well attended and lively. It remains to be seen if it can outlive the graduation of its charismatic founder.

The Feminist Political Action Group, according to the Vassar student organization list, is for those who "agree with the terms womyn and equal power." (The group doesn't specify what sort of agreement one must have with the term 'womyn,' but presumably this doesn't refer to those who agree that it is a typo.)

Vassar is an NCAA Division III school. The Brewers compete in the Upstate Collegiate Athletic Conference against nine other small New York colleges on 23 varsity teams. Intercollegiate club sports and intramurals are plentiful and popular and include sports like billiards, bowling, water polo, and handball. There are also a number of vocal and theatrical organizations.

To judge by crime statistics, Vassar is a very safe campus. In 2003, the last year for which statistics were available, the college reported only one assault and two burglaries. All residence halls are equipped with card entry systems. The student-organized Campus Patrol monitors the campus each night and runs an escort service for students walking across campus after dark. A student-run shuttle also takes students to and from many off-campus locations. Vassar does not have a police force, but the school does employ unarmed security officers.

Tuition for the 2004–5 school year at Vassar was $30,895, plus $ 7,680 for room and board. Financial aid is readily available, but several years ago the school decided to go from 100 percent need-blind to "need-sensitive" in cases where admission is marginal. The Vassar Web site claims that more than 60 percent of students receive financial aid and that the average first-year student got more than $25,000 in 2004. Vassar awards more than $23 million in scholarships in addition to federal and state aid. But don't expect the financial aid experience to be as smooth as meeting the graduation requirements; students complain that working with the office can be frustrating.

VILLANOVA UNIVERSITY

Guiding spirit

Founded in 1842 by the Order of St. Augustine, Villanova University is named for St. Thomas of Villanova, a sixteenth-century Augustinian monk who was renowned as a "friendly and helpful" teacher. That attitude of service, and a dedication to the spirituality and teaching of St. Augustine himself, imbues the Villanova faculty. Villanova University is still run by the Augustinian order (which trained Martin Luther—a fact the group is still trying to live down). The school sits on a beautiful 254-acre campus on the historically affluent Main Line just 18 miles west of Philadelphia.

Villanova's seal proclaims "Veritas, Unitas, Caritas," or "truth, unity, and charity." All of these are still reflected, to some extent at least, in the school's intellectual and campus life. Villanova's liberal arts curricular requirements and programs remain comparatively strong; students seem to genuinely care for each other and for the poor; and Big East basketball games certainly create plenty of unity. Compared to many other of the nation's Catholic universities, Villanova seems to be on the upswing.

Academic Life: Unitas, we fall

Villanova's curriculum is better than most. While it allows a bit too much flexibility to students, it does go some way toward providing students with foundational exposure to the best of the Western, and Catholic, intellectual traditions. As one student says, Villanova "teaches students to be well-rounded people both inside and outside of the classroom." However, students still need to make wise choices to avoid politically driven courses. A professor in the social sciences says, "There is a fair amount of focus by some faculty—especially new hires in the last 10 or so years—on trendy, superficial subjects. This is especially the case in English and philosophy, with postmodernism and so-called feminism edging out other areas. However, there are also a number of faculty who refuse to succumb to superficial intellectual fashion and do their job."

VITAL STATISTICS
Religious affiliation: Roman Catholic
Total enrollment: 10,481
Total undergraduates: 6,460
SAT/ACT midranges: SAT V: 570–660, M: 590–690; ACT: 25–29
Applicants: 10,897
Applicants accepted: 47%
Accepted applicants who enrolled: 31%
Tuition: $28,200
Room and board: $9,000
Freshman retention rate: 93%
Graduation rate: 81% (4 yrs.), 86% (6 yrs.)
Average class size: 23
Student-faculty ratio: 13:1
Courses taught by graduate TAs: none
Most popular majors: biology, nursing, commerce and finance
Students living on campus: 67%
Guaranteed housing for four years? no
Students in fraternities: 6% sororities: 25%

Villanova asks of its students that they fulfill an abbreviated, loosely directed version of the traditional core curriculum—which is still more than most schools demand. Students must take:

- Two humanities seminars—one in "Ancient, Medieval, and Renaissance Thought" and one in "Modern Thought: Enlightenment to the Present." There is no common syllabus for these small-group seminars, and topics vary by instructor. Instructors are required to include texts and themes from the works of St. Augustine in both seminars.

Students in the College of Liberal Arts and Sciences face additional requirements. They must take two courses each in:

- Fine arts.
- History ("Themes in Modern World History" and one other upper-level course).
- Literature ("The Literary Experience" and one other).
- Philosophy (one of which must be "Introduction to Philosophy").
- Theology and religious studies ("Christianity: Traditions and Transitions" and another).

Students who want the best possible liberal arts education at Villanova should investigate an exciting new department called "Humanities and Augustinian Traditions" (or humanities for short). One professor calls this program "an integrated curriculum centered around the basic questions of human existence. One of the reasons for the founding of this department is the promotion of serious Catholic intellectual life at the university." According to the department's Web site, "The humanities major consists of four gateway courses, which are team-taught seminars that investigate basic questions about God, the human person, the world, and society both in relation to the wisdom of past and contemporary thinkers.... In addition to the seminars and lectures, humanities majors will take a comprehensive oral exam at the end of their first year, and will write a thesis in their senior year under the supervision of a faculty member." The aspirations of the department are lofty. It wishes to offer "a true 'liberal' education: one that seeks to liberate students' humanity by opening them to the wisdom of the past, by teaching them to think deeply, imaginatively, and critically about the problems facing our world, and by developing habits of articulate speaking and writing. A liberally educated person is someone who knows how to be fully human." Unlike many other schools that employ such rhetoric, in this program, at least, Villanova seems serious about implementing it.

Villanova enrolls almost 4,000 graduate students, but they do not teach undergraduate courses. Professors are intent on having their students learn the material. One engineering student says, "My professors do a majority of their research and such during the summer so they can focus on teaching during the school year." Another student says, "Professors are always readily available and unusually willing to help. As far as my experience at Villanova so far goes, research and publications come in a distant second to the students' needs." Professors are required to hold office hours each week, and students say they take advantage of them—and not just right before exams. Some faculty members give out their home phone numbers at the beginning of the semester and encourage students to call with questions. Thanks to the fairly good student-teacher ratio (13 to 1) class sizes tend to be manageable, averaging 23 students. One sophomore says her largest class has around 40.

Villanova's largest classrooms, typically used for introductory biology and chemistry classes, hold 100 students or so.

Every freshman is assigned a faculty advisor who is supposed to help the student select courses and give guidance on choosing a major. Once the student decides on a major, he is assigned a faculty member within the department to serve as his advisor. The advising program, students say, is strong, but some freshmen have had trouble with their premajor advisors. "An advisor who's an English professor might not know a thing about what to take if one wants to be a neurosurgeon," one student says. Another student says, "I've had friends have trouble with the random [premajor] advisors. Often they try to recruit and advise towards the major they specialize in, thinking that you are undecided rather than undeclared."

Students with excellent SAT scores and high school class ranks may be invited to participate in the university's Honors Program. To earn an honors degree, a student must take at least 12 honors-level courses, including a sophomore honors seminar, and complete a thesis senior year. Honors classes are more difficult than regular ones, and students say honors advisors are stronger and more involved in the students' academic plans. There is no special honors curriculum or separate dormitory for honors students, but students foster a sense of camaraderie by attending lectures, social events, or, occasionally, field trips to Philadelphia or New York City.

Villanova has the regular set of traditional majors, but students can also earn a concentration (eight courses) in criminal justice, peace and justice, or the ever-popular Irish studies program. Strong departments include astronomy and astrophysics (separate from the physics department) and the other pure sciences, economics, political science, and some areas of philosophy and English. English majors do not have to take a course in Shakespeare, but they can also escape without taking a course in gender and sexuality, although the subjects come up in a number of the department's course descriptions.

"Villanova has for the past six years established an ongoing, fruitful partnership with the University of Pennsylvania, funded by the National Italian American Foundation, which brings to campus a stellar line-up of tremen-

REQUIREMENTS (CONT'D)

- Foreign language at the intermediate level or above.
- Math, or one math and one computer science course.
- Natural sciences, with lab sections.

Students also must take three social sciences courses, one course in college ethics, and eight writing courses—including four designated as "writing intensive" and four as "writing enriched." The two core humanities seminars and the introductory literature course satisfy three of these.

Finally, two courses in a student's curriculum must deal with diversity, defined as having something to do with ethnic and minority experiences in the United States, women's experiences and how "gender influences experience," or the "culture, economics, politics or ecology of societies and nations other than those of Europe and the United States." Some English courses count toward the requirement. Foreign language courses do not count, but some foreign culture and literature classes do.

MIDDLE ATLANTIC

dous Italian American scholars and imaginative writers," says a professor.

The business school, the College of Commerce and Finance, is one of Villanova's best-known programs. Though the College of Engineering has a strong advising program and several excellent professors, one engineering student says, "You'd be better off going to Penn State or a similarly big school with bigger labs and more money to throw around. That's really the only program that suffers from being too little, and that's just the nature of engineering."

The best faculty members at Villanova include Eugene McCarraher and Mark Shiffman in core humanities; David M. Barrett, Lowell Gustafson, Jeanne Heffernan, Robert Maranto, Colleen Sheehan, and Thomas Smith in political science; Marc Gallicchio in history; Earl Bader, Charles Cherry, James Kirschke, Hugh Ormsby-Lennon, and Robert E. Wilkinson in English; Daniel Regan and David Schindler Jr. in philosophy; John Wojcik in chemistry; Randy Weinstein in chemical engineering; Bernard Prusak in theology; marketing professor James Mullen in commerce and finance; and Sayed Omran in Arab and Islamic studies. Under the direction of an able new director, A. Maria Toyoda, Villanova has just begun a concentration in East Asian studies.

Student Life: Ubi caritas

In the past 15 years or so, Villanova has witnessed a resurgence of Catholic identity. When Villanova introduced its new "core" curriculum 16 years ago, "reading Catholic literature and discussing it seriously became the norm on campus," says one professor. In 2003, Villanova Law School dean Mark Sargent refused to fund students wanting to intern at pro-abortion activist groups, according to the *Philadelphia Inquirer*. Sargent told the paper, "They are not going as students who happen to attend Villanova. They're going as Villanova law fellows in our name, and therefore associating us with a particular position. A line is crossed."

A popular student group is Villanovans for Life, which organizes an annual Respect Life Week, promotes pro-life causes throughout the year, and participates in the annual March for Life in Washington, D.C. Pro-abortion groups are not allowed on campus, and the student health center does not offer contraceptives or abortifacients (such as "the morning-after pill"). The BGLOV (Bisexuals, Gays, and Lesbians of Villanova) is an "unrecognized" student organization, meaning it can't receive university funding or hold official events on campus; however the group is listed on the Campus Ministry Web page. Students in the club meet regularly on university grounds and attend events together like a visit to "one of Philadelphia's favorite gay nightclubs," according to the Web page.

Appearances at Villanova can be deceiving. "On the surface [the political climate] is 100 percent liberal, students and faculty," one student says. "Beneath the surface, I'd say the student body is about 75 to 85 percent conservative." The College Republicans group "is huge and very active," says a parent. The university has two student newspapers: the *Villanovan* (on the left) and the *Villanova Times* (on the right), but the *Villanovan* garners more support from the administration and is able to publish more frequently.

Villanova maintains a Peace and Justice Center that offers courses like "Ecofeminism," "American Indian Thought and Culture," and "The Political Economy of AIDS" and sponsors student groups such as Bread for the World, the Feminist Coalition, the Coalition Against Racism, and the Environmental Group. However, there are a number of faculty members interested in the nuanced social teachings of the Catholic Church; the core humanities Web site maintains a library of work by Dorothy Day and Thomas Merton on how to integrate faith and economics.

Villanova students report few, if any, intrusions of politics into the classroom. "I think that the content of the courses can tend to make an otherwise conservative student see another point of view and maybe even change his own a little," says a sophomore, "but rarely does a student feel pressured to accept a particular ideology as gospel."

One student characterizes the typical Villanova student as "a white, Irish/Italian upper-class Abercrombie clone from a development house in the suburbs." Another student says a common nickname for the school, whose student body is around 85 percent white, is "Vanillanova." Not a nickname in which any school is likely to take comfort. Thus, Villanova's Office of Multicultural Affairs coordinates student groups like the Black Cultural Society, the Hispanic Society, and the South Asian Multicultural Organized Students Association (SAMOSA). The office also handles the Minority Vita Bank, a database of minority applicants, making hiring searches convenient for university departments. The Villanova Intermediary Persons program pairs volunteers with incoming minority freshmen to serve as friends on campus, easing their transition to Vanillanova.

If there is one part of St. Augustine's teaching that is stressed more than any other at Villanova, it is his plea for true Christian charity. "We really try to foster a sense of community on campus," says a student. The Campus Ministry office organizes volunteer opportunities like weekly trips to soup kitchens, Habitat for Humanity projects on Saturdays, prison literacy programs, charity activities through fraternities and sororities, and mission trips (in 2003 a group of students served in Nicaragua). The Pennsylvania State Special Olympics Fall Festival is the largest student-run activity of its kind in the world, and around half of the student body volunteers for the event. Most students are Catholic, but Catholics and non-Catholics agree that Christianity "is never really an in-your face type of situation," as one student says. "We don't try to downplay Christianity," says another Catholic student, "but we are accepting of all faiths. . . . My best friend here is Buddhist." Among organizations for students who remain *extra ecclesiam* are Hillel and a Muslim students group.

Many students are active in Catholic liturgical life. The Sunday masses for stu-

---

SUGGESTED CORE

1. English 2400, Western World Literature 1
2. Philosophy 2500, History of Ancient Philosophy
3. Theology and Religious Studies 2000, Fundamentals of Bible Studies
4. Theology and Religious Studies 2725, Christian Classics I
5. Philosophy 2400, Social and Political Philosophy
6. English 3250, Shakespeare
7. History 2000, Investigating U.S. History I
8. History 3351, Nineteenth-Century European Culture and Society (*closest match*)

dents (held in the morning and at 6, 8, and 10 p.m. because "there aren't too many students who want to wake up early on Sunday mornings," says one student) are entirely student run (except for the celebrant) and are "so well attended that if you get to mass after it starts there will be no seats left and you will have to stand," warns another student. There are also two masses each day during the week. The Campus Ministry office sponsors retreats, tai chi exercise groups, and other workshops, and helps students of other faiths find rides to churches or synagogues in the area. St. Thomas Monastery is home to almost 100 Augustinians, around 45 of whom are professors or administrators at the school. Said a parent about the monks, "We have met a few Augustinians. They are impressive. Their approach strikes me as gentle, compassionate, and wise."

Villanova students are not especially pious, though. One student cautions that "the average student does not take Catholic ideals completely to heart. Issues like sex before marriage, abortion, and general morality are not viewed in the same way as Catholicism would have us. In that sense the average Villanova student is not too much different from the average public university student."

Villanova's NROTC program includes about 150 midshipmen and has produced more admirals and Marine Corps generals than any other school except for the U.S. Naval Academy. The campus military center, John Barry Hall, is said to be the only federally funded building with a cross on it. Says one parent of an NROTC student, "The dedication and determination of the NROTC midshipmen is unparalleled. I met one young man who lives with and takes care of his senile grandmother (who would otherwise be alone), and takes the train to Villanova everyday." Lately, several NROTC students have chosen to minor in Arab and Islamic studies, another strong program at Villanova.

That department witnessed a tragedy in 2003, when a popular professor, Mine Ener, killed her handicapped infant daughter and herself after suffering an episode of postpartum psychosis, according to the *Chronicle of Higher Education*. The deaths shocked the campus, which was further afflicted when some pharisaical conservative commentators (including Bill O'Reilly) denounced the university for creating a memorial to Professor Ener—setting off a firestorm of controversy that led to the removal of the simple plaque.

Villanova is only a short train ride into Philadelphia (the R5 line takes you to 30th Street Station, near the University of Pennsylvania and Drexel University), but students tend to pass up Philadelphia's cultural events and nightlife to spend most of their weekends and evenings on campus. About 25 percent of women and 6 percent of men are members of Greek organizations, but since they do not have their own houses, Greek organizations are less exclusionary and more service-oriented than they are at other schools. Students will find plenty of activities on campus to occupy their free time: publications, music and theater recitals, concerts, and two-dollar movies in the student center (the midnight showing is always free).

The campus lies along Route 30 (the so-called Main Line), a couple miles down the road from Bryn Mawr and Haverford colleges. The mostly Gothic-style campus has plenty of lush green lawns and was designated a national arboretum in 1993. St. Thomas of Villanova Chapel is the dominant building on campus, but the Connelly Student Center is more frequently visited, with its dining areas, computer lounge, music listening room, art gallery, ice cream shop, movie theater, and meeting space. Outside of Connelly is a black-and-white sculpture known by students as "The Oreo," where students often advertise for events, gather for protests, or just hang out between classes. Cafes called "Holy Grounds" are conveniently located all over campus. Falvey Memorial Library offers around 800,000 volumes to the university community, and students are able to check out books from Haverford, Bryn Mawr, and the University of Pennsylvania through interlibrary loan.

The university is primarily residential. Villanova guarantees housing on campus for the first three years; most seniors live in off-campus apartments. Villanova manages 18 residence halls and 8 apartment buildings. Students can choose to live in either single-sex or coed dorms, but even the coed dorms are segregated by floor, so students never live next door to a member of the opposite sex. Villanova's luckiest juniors live in on-campus two-bedroom, one-and-a-half-bath apartments. Freshman dormitories were recently renovated; the sophomore residences need to be. Many freshmen opt for the Villanova Experience Program (VEP), learning communities in which students live together in a dorm and share a core humanities seminar. As a result of this close interaction, one student says, "usually people in learning communities get to know their hallmates a little faster." Recent VEP themes included "Leadership" and "Visions of Freedom."

Villanova is a member of the recently depleted Big East athletic conference. Basketball is huge here: Villanova Wildcats fans pack the Pavilion for each home game, but especially for those against other Philadelphia-area schools like the University of Pennsylvania and St. Joseph's University. Some students and alumni say that these athletic competitions bring more unity to the campus than does anything else.

Mostly as a result of student complaints, the university recently loosened its visitation policy to allow students to have visitors (including those of the opposite sex) until midnight on school nights and until 2 a.m. on Fridays and Saturdays. Upperclassman dorms can have these hours extended if all residents attend a session on "roommate rights and responsibilities," and thus a few dorms allow visitors (not of the opposite sex) 24 hours a day. The student handbook says, "The university . . . believes that a genuine and complete expression of love through sex requires a commitment to living and sharing of two persons in marriage. Consequently, overt sexual behavior and/or overnight visitation by a member of the opposite sex in residential facilities represent flagrant violations of the Visitation Policy and the Code of Student Conduct."

The campus is secluded enough from the outside community that it endures little crime. During the 2003 school year, Villanova reported one forcible sex offense, two arsons, and 37 burglaries. In case of emergency, students can use any of the 17 call boxes around campus to ask for help or an escort. The campus is well lit, and a card is required for entering buildings.

Villanova's tuition is at the higher end of private colleges, but it is not as astronomically expensive as the Ivies. Tuition in 2004–5 was $28,200, with room and board at $9,000. Admissions are need-blind, but the school does not guarantee to meet every student's full financial need. Almost 63 percent of all matriculating undergraduates receive some type of need-based or merit assistance.

SOUTH

AUBURN UNIVERSITY

AUBURN, ALABAMA • WWW.AUBURN.EDU

Throwback

The Methodist Church opened East Alabama Male College in 1859 but had to close it two years later with the outbreak of the Civil War. The college reopened in 1866 in financial shambles. In 1872, the Methodists transferred control to the state of Alabama, and several name changes later, the school became Auburn University.

In many ways, Auburn is a throwback to an earlier American campus: football is king, the Greeks rule the social scene, and radical political activism is next to nil among the mostly apolitical student body. But at the same time, the campus is changing: enrollment is at record levels and the university is trying to get national recognition by drawing on its roots as a public, land-grant institution. This is a difficult task for a university that occasionally suffers when the state legislature tries to address more pressing needs. Sometimes the school blunders badly—for instance, the 2004 scandal that saw trustees meddling in the choice of athletic coaches eventually led to the resignation of the school's president and a harsh punishment from Auburn's accrediting agency. The school was put on probation for a year—a penalty which was only recently rescinded after a series of administrative reforms.

Yet compared with other colleges, Auburn's atmosphere can be refreshing. When men open doors for women, it's appreciated—not deemed "sexist." "It's a conservative school," says one instructor. "It's just a very Christian, very professional atmosphere. It's dressier than a normal university campus. The girls seem more modest. It just seems cut out of the past, in the good sense." According to a student, "The campus looks great. The old buildings are well cared for and full of southern charm and beauty."

Auburn administrators also want the college to distinguish itself through a renewed emphasis on the preprofessional departments that can meet the practical needs of the state of Alabama—forestry, fisheries, information technology, and poultry science, for example. To save money, the university has chopped some programs and merged

VITAL STATISTICS

Religious affiliation: none
Total enrollment: 22,928
Total undergraduates: 18,896
SAT/ACT midranges: SAT
  V: 500–600, M: 510–610;
  ACT: 22–26
Applicants: 12,827
Applicants accepted: 84%
*Accepted applicants who
  enrolled*: 33%
Tuition: $4,610 (in state),
  $13,830 (out of state)
Room and board: $6,686
Freshman retention rate: 85%
Graduation rate: 34% (4 yrs.),
  65% (6 yrs.)
*Courses with fewer than 20
  students*: 28%
Student-faculty ratio: 16:1
*Courses taught by graduate
  TAs*: 14%
Most popular majors:
  business, engineering,
  social sciences
Students living on campus:
  16%
*Guaranteed housing for four
  years?* no
Students in fraternities: 18%
  sororities: 31%

SOUTH

383

ACADEMIC REQUIREMENTS

Unlike most schools in this guide, Auburn retains many elements of a traditional core curriculum, which it combines with respectable distribution requirements. To graduate, students must fulfill the following:

- Two freshman writing classes.
- "World Literature" I and II, writing-intensive courses that used to be called "Great Books." The first course emphasizes ancient, medieval, and Renaissance literature; the second course considers literature from the seventeenth century to the present. Syllabi can vary by instructor, and teachers are "encouraged to construct syllabi that contain a balanced representation of traditionally canonical works as well as works by women, by minority writers within Western culture, and by non-Western writers."

departments, particularly in the liberal arts, which leaves some professors questioning the university's commitment to providing a well-rounded education. Nonetheless, Auburn has a core curriculum that ensures that all students are exposed to less practical areas of inquiry than chicken reproduction or fish migration patterns.

Academic Life: Core all around

Auburn offers undergraduate degrees in more than 130 areas, including many highly specialized fields like forest engineering and "fisheries and allied aquacultures." While the university, thankfully, has retained a core curriculum that exposes each student to the liberal arts, some professors say that the emphasis on the liberal arts has decreased as the school tries to distinguish itself in other areas. If true, that would be a lamentable development.

The university is divided into nine colleges (Agriculture, Architecture, Business, Education, Engineering, Human Sciences, Liberal Arts, Science and Math, and Veterinary Medicine) and three schools (Forestry and Wildlife Sciences, Nursing, and Pharmacy), plus the graduate school. All undergraduates, regardless of major, must fulfill the requirements of Auburn's core curriculum. Unlike elsewhere, Auburn's core curriculum is not under attack, and faculty and administrators tend to agree that there is a common body of knowledge worth teaching. University literature proudly proclaims that the core curriculum not only forms the foundation for professional and career programs but also signals Auburn's "traditional commitment to the enhancement of students' personal and intellectual growth and the development of a more responsible citizenry." According to one student, the core "takes up your first two years of study, but it really ensures that all students, regardless of major, get a well-rounded education in liberal arts, math, and science."

Having a core curriculum doesn't necessarily mean students are all learning the same thing. There is no common syllabus for the core courses, and topics can vary somewhat from section to section. Individual faculty members choose what books students read and what they discuss in class, although the English department insists that instructors work "within established guidelines." In one world literature course with the theme "Literature and Exile," students read Plato's *Apology*, four books of the Old Testament, and some of Sappho's poetry; they also watch films like *The Matrix* and

Blade Runner to complement the written texts. In another such course, students read from Sophocles' *Antigone*, Shakespeare's plays, the *Aeneid*, *Sir Gawain and the Green Knight*, and *Paradise Lost*. While a few of these courses are simply titled "World Literature," many have more specific titles such as "Wildness and Craziness," "The Female Quest," and "Alienation and Belonging."

There are several truly excellent departments at Auburn, but most are outside of the traditional liberal arts areas; preprofessional programs such as veterinary medicine, agriculture, forestry, and engineering are the strongest on campus.

The shining star of Auburn's social science offerings is its Department of Economics, which is based in the university's College of Business. The department boasts solid credentials and first-rate professors with free-market orientations. The department works in conjunction with the Ludwig von Mises Institute to run reading groups and other programs and provides students with solid foundations in current economic thinking. "If you're market-oriented, you want to go to the economics department," one professor says.

The Ludwig von Mises Institute, one of the intellectual highlights at Auburn, is a nationally known educational and scholarly center. Named for the Austrian free-market economist, the institute defends capitalism, private property rights, and sound monetary policies. It publishes journals and books; maintains a popular Web site (www.mises.org); awards fellowships; runs seminars and conferences, and makes the public case for limited government. (Writers on its Web site go a little further, with some making the case that we might be better off with no government at all.) Institute president Lew Rockwell provoked debate in early 2005 by writing that elements in the conservative movement had drifted towards fascism by embracing aggressive foreign conquest and restrictions on civil liberties as part of the "war on terror." Students interested in free markets and free societies would be advised to look into the institute, which rolls out the red carpet for interested scholars.

In addition to economics, the history and philosophy departments are regarded as among the strongest at Auburn, as is the College of Engineering. Philosophy majors are directed to take three core courses (though substitutions are allowed) in the history of philosophy—"Ancient and Early Medieval Philosophy," "Late Medieval and Early Modern Philosophy," and "Recent and Contemporary Philosophy." They must then

REQUIREMENTS (CONT'D)

- One of three two-course history sequences—"World History," "Technology and Civilization," or "The Human Odyssey," which focuses on "shifts in human perception resulting from discovery and invention."
- Two four-hour science courses, including a lab and a selected sequence in biology, chemistry, geology, or physics.
- A math course.
- A philosophy course; students may choose among topics such as logic, ethics, health science ethics, or business ethics.
- One social science course in anthropology, geography, psychology, or sociology.
- Another social science course in either microeconomics, political economy, or American government.
- A fine arts course in architecture, art history, music, or theater.

SOUTH

choose seven other courses, five of which must be upper-level offerings. The history department does not provide much structure to its majors, requiring only a course in history research methods, two other survey courses, four upper-level seminars, and a thesis. But by seeking advice from professors in the department, serious students can graduate with a thorough knowledge of the discipline.

Business is a popular major, though some faculty decry its rampant preprofessionalism. For instance, interested students can attend sessions on what to wear to an interview or which utensils to use at dinner—a session that some on campus deride as "The Right Fork." Throughout the school, one professor notes a "definite pecuniary approach to education. . . . 'How much can I make?' 'Is it worth it?' These are the kinds of concerns that larger and larger proportions of students and parents openly express."

Professors to seek out at Auburn include Richard W. Ault, Roger W. Garrison, Dan Gropper, and David L. Kaserman in economics; Rafe Blaufarb in history; Henry W. Kinnucan in agricultural economics; and James R. Barth in finance.

The university's Honors College, which selects about 200 freshmen from all of the colleges and schools each year, is another of the university's outstanding programs. Students with high school grade point averages of at least 3.5 and with scores of either 29 or 1280 on the ACT or SAT, respectively, are invited into the program. During their first two years at Auburn, honors students take core courses together; the classes are small and designed to promote in-depth discussions with fellow students and faculty. Students can earn a senior honors certificate either by writing a thesis or by taking four "contract courses," which supplement regular courses with extra writing or field work. The program comes with perks—honors students live in separate residence halls, have priority at registration, and, in their final semesters at Auburn, are granted their own library carrels.

In recent years, Auburn has dedicated millions of dollars to new research initiatives in transportation, information technology, detection and food safety, biological sciences, fisheries and allied aquaculture, poultry science, and forestry and wildlife sciences. In late 2004, the university announced it had secured $15 million in state and local funding to open a 156-acre research park. The high-tech quest doesn't sit well with many liberal arts faculty. "I would like to see us produce more well-rounded kinds of students," says a professor. "A student who wants a technical education in computers or business would survive here, but they would also survive at the DeVry Institute."

The same professor laments that academics on campus often must compete with other interests, complaining that football is "valued higher than academics, by the alumni, the administration, and everybody else. . . . Auburn is generally a party school, with athletics emphasized and academics downplayed and grade inflation like you wouldn't believe." All faculty members hold weekly office hours, but students don't always take advantage of them. "Office hours tend to be underutilized though faculty are willing," a recently retired professor says. "And while the inquisitive student will find many responsive faculty and can find niches of interest, the student body, it is my impression, has other concerns—work, parties, Greek societies, athletic events."

Advising varies from college to college. Students in the College of Liberal Arts are invited to make appointments with nonfaculty advisors in the dean's office. Once a student has declared a major, he can meet with a faculty advisor within his department.

The university reports that graduate teaching assistants teach 14 percent of all undergraduate courses, but students can opt for professors by checking the class schedule. "At Auburn, the sense of the faculty and its administration has been to be very encouraging to have senior professors teach lower-division courses," the retired professor says.

As for political bias in the classroom, there seems to be little worth mentioning—quite an achievement. "There are good teachers and bad teachers," says one professor. "It's still possible to get a really good education at Auburn if you pick and choose." Another professor says that older faculty members tend to be less concerned with political agendas than their younger peers. "They're hiring new, younger faculty members, and they bring the virus with them," he says. "But it's moving in the opposite way among students. The students are less politically correct, though they might be forced to mouth the words."

Auburn does maintain a women's studies curriculum, which offers a few courses focusing on "gender roles" and "the anthropology of gender." But such courses play a lesser role in the life of the university than they do elsewhere; women's studies offers only a minor, listing almost all its courses under real departments, like English or history.

Student Life: Sweet home . . . Auburn

Auburn is the sort of place that generations of families attend in succession, where football runs deep in the blood, and where you wouldn't be caught dead wearing a T-shirt that says "Alabama." (Actually, if you did wear one, you just might be caught dead.) It was not so unusual when Auburn sent out a press release a few years ago touting a South Carolina family that was graduating its sixteenth family member from Auburn. "We have two more darling granddaughters that I'm sure will go to school here at Auburn one day," the family's matriarch said.

Football is the major focus of energy in the fall, culminating with the yearly showdown with Alabama, or perhaps a bowl game. Even in the winter and spring, more attention is paid to football recruiting than to basketball. And in this state, you're either an Auburn fan or an Alabama fan. There is no middle ground. "My family would have disowned me if I went to Alabama," says one engineering major. CBS Sportsline.com ranks Auburn's Jordan-Hare Stadium as one of the best in the nation and describes the Auburn gridiron atmosphere as "hot, humid, and totally crazy."

SUGGESTED CORE
1. Foreign Languages 3510, Greek Literature and Culture in Translation *and* Foreign Languages 3510, Roman Literature and Culture in Translation
2. Philosophy 3330, History of Philosophy: Ancient and Early Medieval
3. Religious Studies 1030, Introduction to the New Testament
4. Religious Studies 2030, History of Christianity
5. Political Science 4040, Contemporary Political Theory
6. English 4330, Early Shakespeare *or* English 4340: Later Shakespeare
7. History 2010, Survey of U.S. History to 1877
8. History 4340, European Cultural and Intellectual History *or* History 4320, Nineteenth-Century Europe, 1815–1918

SOUTH

Fraternities and sororities dominate campus social life, and there have been some well-publicized incidents of hazing. An Auburn freshman sued the local Kappa Alpha fraternity a few years ago, claiming, among other things, that he had been beaten and forced to jump into a ditch filled with garbage, water, vomit, and human waste. Although the Alabama Supreme Court ruled that the student had no grounds to sue (because he chose to endure the treatment), the university refused to recognize the local chapter. Auburn now has a clearly defined hazing policy that includes prohibitions on everything from branding to "the use of demeaning names" to "having pledges perform personal chores or errands." About a quarter of undergraduates belong to the Greek system, and many of the rest regularly attend weekend parties at Greek houses. Some fraternities, however, have banned alcohol and claim many religious, nondrinking students as members. While the Greek organizations are "relatively well behaved," says one student, "sororities and fraternities are definitely a big part of campus life."

Students who live on campus can choose from a variety of options ranging from standard dormitory rooms to furnished, air-conditioned, two-bedroom apartments. There are many single-sex residence halls for women—a whole women's quadrangle, in fact—but none for men. In coed dorms, men and women are housed in separate wings or on alternating floors, and members of the opposite sex are not allowed to spend the night.

Auburn offers hundreds of student clubs. There are around 25 religious organizations—mostly Protestant prayer groups and fellowships, but also a Jewish group and a Muslim Association. There are also groups for many different interests, including amateur radio, equestrian sports, and astronomy. The College Republicans are the biggest club on campus, with a staggering 1,500 members.

Politically, Auburn is best described as pleasant and noncontroversial. There are virtually no protests, no visible displays of angst, no significant groups of campus agitators. "There are very few leftists here," a conservative student says. "It's great but sometimes it gets a little boring. There are no real wackos to fight with." The campus atmosphere is quite traditional; students tend to be very polite and friendly, and dress is "preppy," according to another student.

Auburn has some separate programs for minority students, which some say serves to keep races segregated rather than to bring students together. Some of the programs border on the patronizing, such as the Minority Engineering Program, which provides "academic support services to entering minority engineering students," as well as remedial tutoring and mentoring for minorities, according to university literature. The university Web site offers a somewhat elaborate "Tolerance and Diversity through the Curriculum" search engine. Using the search engine, an interested student can filter courses by topics like "sexuality" or "prejudice/hate/genocide/dehumanization." The site also breaks down a number of courses into what percentage of each course deals with each topic. For example, ENGL 2210, "Great Books" II, is 11 to 25 percent "race and ethnicity," gender, "religion and spirituality," human values, and "multiculturalism and internationalism"—but only 1 to 10 percent of class time is spent on "disabilities and exceptionalities," "age and ageing," sexuality, etc. (Percentages may not add up to

100 due to rounding—or to the complete lunacy of the exercise.) Another computer program, which Auburn is actually trying to patent, is used to encourage minority recruitment without focusing exclusively on race. The software, according to the *Chronicle of Higher Education,* "groups applicants into clusters of similarly qualified students with similar backgrounds. . . . [R]ace and other criteria, such as academic performance, family income, and gender, are weighted equally."

Auburn has an active Office of Multicultural Affairs as well as a Diversity Leadership Council, which defines diversity as "the co-existence of people, processes, and functions, characterized by both differences and similarities." Black History Month in February is a big deal, with a series of lectures and concerts on themes of diversity, civil rights, and racism. The 2003 program featured as keynote speaker Maulana Karenga, the American leftist academic who invented the "African" holiday Kwanzaa. Recently, the university created an Africana studies program.

When fraternity members at Auburn attended a 2001 Halloween party in blackface, the university suspended the students and derecognized the two fraternity chapters that were involved. After a lawsuit, the university finally allowed one of the chapters to return to campus. Despite all of this a freshman says that "it is a very peaceful campus. Race is really a nonissue."

Students and professors describe the town of Auburn—known as the "Loveliest Village on the Plains"—as a university town that reflects the school's atmosphere. "It's a socially conservative town. It's very church-oriented. You see them on every block," says one professor. Some students say there's little to do in Auburn, but others claim the town is perfectly suited for study, research, dining, and relaxation. It offers many historical sites and excellent restaurants. Take, for example, the Auburn Chapel, where the first secessionist meeting in the Deep South took place in 1851. Elsewhere in town are barbecue restaurants, southern restaurants, European-style pubs, and barbers who sprinkle their conversation with talk of moonshine. Ten minutes from Auburn is Chewacla State Park, which has a quiet lake and relaxing picnic spots. It's a local favorite for swimming and hiking.

The crime rate on campus is much lower than that for the surrounding community, which in turn is much lower than national rates. The 2003 crime statistics reported 42 burglaries, one forcible sex offense, five aggravated assaults, and four stolen cars on campus—this for a school of more than 23,000 students. Some schools' football teams commit more crimes than that.

Auburn is quite reasonably priced, especially if you're from Alabama. 2003–4 in-state tuition was only $4,610, while out-of-state was $13,830. Room and board (on campus) amounted to $6,686.

CHRISTENDOM COLLEGE

FRONT ROYAL, VIRGINIA • WWW.CHRISTENDOM.EDU

To restore all things in Christ

Christendom College was founded by a group of Catholic laymen in 1977 to combat what they saw as the wholesale abandonment of the classical liberal arts tradition and religious orthodoxy in Catholic academies. As the college Web site states, "The cultural revolution which swept across the United States in the late 1960s struck a devastating blow to Catholic higher education. . . . What followed was a wholesale loss of Catholic identity in these institutions. . . . No longer could these transformed universities fulfill what had always been the primary purpose of Catholic education: to lead young minds out of narrow perspectives into the world of known truth under the guiding light of the Catholic faith." A Christendom professor says, "Even Catholic colleges seemed to be embracing the prevailing culture of utilitarianism and nihilism in their curricula. Christendom was founded . . . to be a place that is solidly Catholic and solidly grounded in the Catholic understanding of the liberal arts."

The college's purpose is to provide "a liberal arts education that would fully integrate natural and revealed truth. The purpose of a liberal arts college is to 'educate for life'—to lead the whole man to wisdom, and not just to train a worker for a job." At the heart of Christendom's understanding of truth is the Catholic faith. At Christendom "the truth of the Catholic faith is seen as central to all other truth: It unifies and illuminates the scientific and humane disciplines." A liberal arts education, according to Christendom, should not just develop intellectual abilities but "form moral character and foster spiritual growth."

The goal of Christendom College is a lofty one, nothing less than "re-Christianiz[ing] the temporal order." Christendom wants its graduates to be "energized subjects of Christ the King." The college's very name signifies this goal: "Christendom" means a Christianized social order. The college's motto is *Instaurare omnia in Christo*—"to restore all things in Christ." Christendom takes the word "omnia" ("all things") quite literally: there is no natural truth that is not seen as somehow fitting into and leading to the supernatural truth of Christ. This belief in and commitment to truth sets Christendom apart from the great run of colleges and universities today and has led the school to create a challenging and coherent program that aims to turn out well-educated and able graduates.

Academic Life: Uncommon doctors

Education at Christendom is ordered around a strong core curriculum that begins in the freshman year and continues into the junior year, culminating for most students with a semester in Rome. The core curriculum totals 84 semester hours, making up a full two-thirds of a student's coursework. In some respects, the core is just what you might expect from any liberal arts college worthy of the name: the literature and history of Western civilization, composition courses, and a foreign language form the foundation of the education.

Christendom's core goes far beyond what even many "good" liberal arts colleges require—take, for example, philosophy: Where most liberal arts colleges ask for two or three philosophy courses at best, Christendom's core requirement of six semesters of philosophy is quite impressive. The "fundamental ordering principle" of the philosophy curriculum was set by no less than St. Thomas Aquinas, the great "Common Doctor" of Catholic philosophy and theology. The purpose of this solid grounding in philosophy is to "assist the student in using reason to understand the nature of reality and to illumine further the truth of revelation."

In addition to theology and philosophy, the core at Christendom has heavy doses of history and literature. The literature program is designed to help the student to see, "through the eyes of the literary artist, both the concrete reality of human life and the ultimate reality of human destiny," according to the college. The history program, following the spirit of G. K. Chesterton's *Everlasting Man*, takes as its starting point the centrality of the Incarnation of Christ. This should not be surprising, given that Warren H. Carroll, known for the widely acclaimed series *A History of Christendom* (the civilization, not the college), was the school's founding president. According to Carroll, "for the believing Christian, the Incarnation of Christ—God becoming man—is the most important event that ever happened or could ever happen. Because it was a historical event, the Incarnation gives history transcendent importance." Four semesters of history are required in the core, and many students rate these classes as the best of their Christendom career. "The professors make history really come alive," says one student. "The method they use is sort of a 'philosophy of history,' and it makes you see how history really matters."

In reference to the curriculum, "coherence" is something of a buzzword among Christendom faculty. With an all-encompassing vision of the liberal arts driving the curriculum, the faculty and administration are at pains to create an educational experience in which each course, major, and rule for community life contributes to an integrated Catholic worldview. The core curriculum achieves that end to a large extent. "By the time students are juniors, they're all talking the same language," one professor says. "The core gives them a common set of categories and standards by which they can

VITAL STATISTICS

Religious affiliation:
  Roman Catholic
Total enrollment: 438
Total undergraduates: 371
SAT midrange: 1130–1330
Applicants: 269
Applicants accepted: 79%
*Accepted applicants who
  enrolled*: 55%
Tuition: $14,420
Room and board: $5,250
Freshman retention rate: 83%
Graduation rate: 69% (4 yrs.),
  69% (6 yrs.)
Average class size: 25
Student-faculty ratio: 13:1
*Courses taught by graduate
  TAs*: none
Most popular majors: history,
  philosophy, theology
Students living on campus:
  98%
*Guaranteed housing for four
  years?* yes
*Students in fraternities or
  sororities*: none

SOUTH

391

Christendom maintains a first-rate liberal arts core curriculum. Students must complete:

- Four semesters of a foreign language. French, Spanish, Italian, Latin, and Greek are offered. Two years of Latin are required of all students majoring in philosophy and theology; other students need four semesters of the language of their choice.
- Six semesters in philosophy. The philosophy core is arranged according to the classical Aristotelian order, comprising logic, math (Euclidean geometry), philosophy of man, metaphysics, and medieval and modern philosophy.
- Six semesters of theology. Students begin with "Fundamentals of Catholic Doctrine" in the freshman year, which is a survey of Catholic teaching, and move into the Old and New testaments in the sophomore year. In the junior year, this segment of the core culminates with courses in moral theology and Catholic apologetics.

measure and make judgments," says another faculty member. The program may fall short of coherence in a few areas, according to some faculty and students. "There is some debate here as to whether political science even belongs in the core of a liberal arts program," says a professor. And the theology department is said to be of lower quality than one would expect, if only because it has frequently been staffed with numerous adjuncts and temporary chaplains.

Only after completing the core does the student move into courses in his or her major, which must be declared at the end of the sophomore year. There are only seven majors available to the Christendom student—classical and early Christian studies, English literature, French, history, philosophy, political science and economics, and theology—though there are a host of minors, from mathematics to classical studies. The major programs are designed to integrate the knowledge the student gained in the core and to bring that knowledge to fruition. "People come to Christendom to learn the truth about reality," says Robert Rice, chairman of the English department and former vice president for academic affairs. "That's *all* of reality, which is the whole of human experience. Truth is One, and we believe that all the truths one learns in the different disciplines illuminate and complement one another. And students see this coherence and find it exhilarating." At Christendom, education is seen as having a goal, an end. One student sums up this end: "At Christendom, we're taught to know the Truth, desire the Good, and contemplate the Beautiful."

In 1997, Christendom acquired the Notre Dame Graduate School of Theology (formerly the Notre Dame Institute) in Alexandria, Virginia, about 75 miles from the undergraduate campus. There, students pursue an MA in theological studies while concentrating in systematic or moral theology or catechetics.

One might think that because of the size of Christendom (enrollment is capped at under 500 students) and the homogeneity of religious belief that there is a danger that the college is a sort of hothouse environment that indoctrinates its students, but conversations with a few students quickly clear up that impression. "The people here are very diverse; people have differing opinions on all sorts of things," one student says. "Actually, in my experience it's the secular universities which are filled with the same sort of people: doctrinaire liberals. People here have made an informed, mature commitment to the Catholic faith." Most students and graduates agree that while almost all students at Christendom are devout and practicing Catholics, there's plenty of academic diversity within the classroom—too much diversity for a few, who have complained that the school is home to views that might be called "un-American." A controversy erupted in 2001 when one student distributed handbills denouncing unnamed students and faculty as "monarchists" who allegedly sympathized with the terror attacks of September 11. This was so inflammatory, and the charges so unsupported by specifics, that the student was disciplined and later expelled. His case was widely publicized in the neoconservative press. Nevertheless, it's certainly true that some at Christendom have advocated Catholic monarchy as the best political system; several of its founding faculty members spent time in the 1970s in Spain, cultivating connections with the devout Carlist movement and working out ways to "incarnate" the faith in the institutions of society. Such ideas, however, while desperately unpopular (or unknown) in the United States, stood squarely in the mainstream of Catholic thought up until the Second Vatican Council.

Christendom does not aim to create a culture of automatic acceptance in education, but instead to introduce students to reason and to teach those students to question beliefs on all levels. Faith and reason, the two means of knowing truth in the traditional Catholic worldview, are considered the antidote to the evils besetting modernity and are at the heart of the Christendom education.

The faculty members are all dedicated to teaching, and students generally rate the quality of teaching at Christendom as excellent. Even with a student-faculty ratio of 13 to 1 (rather high for a small school), the students and professors tend to forge close relationships in and out of the classroom. They commonly lunch together on campus, and students are frequently invited to dine at the homes of professors. "With only [a small student body] and a small faculty, everyone knows each other. It's like being part of a big family," says one professor. Students will find Christendom professors to be very accessible and interested in them not only as students, but as people. "Mentoring relationships develop between faculty and students quite naturally here," one student says. "There is a high level of trust among the students for the faculty," says a professor. Another professor says,

REQUIREMENTS (CONT'D)

- Eight courses covering Western civilization, both its history and literature. This sequence leads the student more or less historically through many great books of the West, beginning with scripture and Homer's *Iliad* and *Odyssey*, moving through the Latin classics, the medieval works of Chaucer and Dante, Luther and Shakespeare, and finally recent authors such as T. S. Eliot and Pope John Paul II.

- Two classes in math and science, such as "Euclidean Geometry" and "Introduction to Scientific Thought."

- Two courses in social and political doctrine: "Introduction to Political Theory" and "The Social Teachings of the Church." The latter course is an examination of classic Catholic social doctrine concerning the state, the citizen, the common good, and wealth and poverty using scripture and the church fathers, as well as modern papal encyclicals such as Pope John Paul II's *Centesimus Annus*.

"Sometimes a student will ask to see me, and I expect he wants to talk about something in class, when what he really wants to talk about are his problems with his girlfriend." Professors who can be counted on for exceptional courses include Christopher Blum and William Fahey in classics, Trey Stanford in literature, William Marshner in theology, and Anthony Andres and John Cuddeback in philosophy. Christendom's recent hire of Christopher Shannon to teach in its history department speaks well of the college's commitment to academic excellence and scholarly rigor.

Given the Catholic liberal arts basis of the college, faculty tend to be a self-selected group firmly committed to the principles of the college. Faculty members are expected to be practicing Catholics and to assent to official Catholic teaching. To this end, faculty make a "Profession of Faith" and "Oath of Fidelity" to the church upon hiring; both must be renewed annually. Furthermore, faculty contracts state that "public rejection of, or dissent from, the teachings of the Catholic Church as interpreted by the Holy Father, or rejection of the authority of the pope as head of the Catholic Church, is grounds for the termination [of the contract]."

The moderate size of the faculty and the considerable demands of the core curriculum mean that practically all of the faculty teach courses in the core every year. This all but guarantees that students will get to know their professors early on, and quite well. "The faculty here all understand that our first and foremost responsibility is to teach," says one professor. "We have gotten better and better at 'doing' the liberal arts over the years," says Rice. "When we founded the college the core was 60 hours. Now it is 84." This commitment to a traditional approach is reflected in the choice of texts and method of teaching those texts. "We are committed to using primary texts whenever possible," Rice says. "So when we teach Euclidean geometry, we use Euclid's *Elements*. When our students read Chaucer's *Troilus and Criseyde*, they do so in the original Middle English. We use no excerpts or anthologies." This commitment means that Christendom is a remarkable ideology-free zone.

As previously mentioned, the college was founded by people who saw Catholic doctrine as well as the traditional liberal arts being abandoned by leading Catholic colleges. They saw their mission as one of restoration. "The college was founded to train lay Catholics in the liberal arts who would be loyal to the church," a professor says. This has occasionally led to an emphasis on piety over academics. Recent work done by the college in pursuit of reaccreditation, however, has brought about a new awareness of the seriousness of the academic life. "It is evident that some professors are more concerned with educating students on the faith and doctrine of the church as opposed to a traditional college education," says one student. However, this student says, "Christendom is a very Catholic school, the students are very active members of the church. . . . To not have a strong emphasis on learning about the doctrine of the church would be to ignore the reason many students attend."

The strongest departments at Christendom, are, as one might expect, philosophy and theology. The history department is also well regarded, and the program in classics is quite strong. Students and faculty both report some weaknesses in the modern languages. "The modern language courses aren't very challenging," one student says. A faculty member says, "We are trying to improve the modern languages here, and we need to." A number of students also express disappointment with their courses in political science and economics. "The poli sci courses are the weakest I had here," says one senior.

It would be easy for one to assume that students attending Christendom are seeking a vocation in religious life, and a good number of students do enter priestly or religious service. However, Christendom alumni are employed in almost every field possible, from education, marketing, medicine, and information technology to law and academia. With such a strong liberal arts background offered through the core curriculum, students and alumni express comfort in a variety of careers. Alumni tend to remain conscious of what was instilled in them by Christendom, that each one is called to help "restore all things in Christ."

Student Life: Oh, Shenandoah

Christendom students are expected to be committed Catholics, or at least sympathetic to the Catholic faith. This should come as no surprise at a college whose stated goal is "to help students through their study of the liberal arts to consecrate their intellect and will to Christ." As such, the college aims at feeding the souls as well as the minds of its students. Religious observances, such as daily mass, are an integral part of the college's life. A wide variety of Catholic devotions are popular with Christendom students, such as daily rosary or pilgrimages to various shrines. Fittingly, the college's Chapel of Christ the King dominates the campus and is likely to be the first building a visitor notices upon arriving, although just beyond the chapel, the new library of St. John the Evangelist rises above the Shenandoah River.

While the environment at Christendom is certainly ordered, it should not be thought of as controlling. Chapel functions are not mandatory, but, according to a student, "if people notice that you haven't been to mass in a while, they might ask how you're doing." There is an active social life on campus, with everything from intramural sports, limited intercollegiate athletics (men and women play soccer and basketball, and there is a men's baseball team) to numerous dances and parties throughout the year. "The social life was good and healthy and fun," says a recent graduate. Large parties and excessive drinking are rare at Christendom. More common than binges are barn dances and dinner with faculty members and their families. People at Christendom certainly do rejoice in such expressions of Catholic culture as Oktoberfest and St. Joseph's and St. Patrick's days, or the grand Medieval Fest, replete with trial-by-combat, disputed questions, morality plays, and generous feasting. With the exception of Thanksgiving the college does not observe secular holidays. One recent graduate claims that the atmosphere at Christendom fits the summation of the Christian life expressed by St. John Bosco, "Love, and then have fun."

Christendom is actively concerned about the morality and virtue of its students. "The faculty here are quite self-conscious about functioning *in loco parentis*," an administrator says. The college enforces a dress code for classes, meals, and the like. Students and faculty are expected to dress modestly and professionally at all times. Students are also expected to live on campus and must apply to the dean of student life for an exception. The dorms for men and women are separate and visits by members of the opposite sex are not permitted. The dorms themselves are relatively small (the largest hold about 50 students) and homely (in both senses of the word). There is also a high regard for the virtue of courtesy at Christendom. "Visitors are often impressed by the friendliness of the students here," says an administrator. "The atmosphere on campus is meant to establish a kind of peaceful order whereby one can more easily be disposed to practice the virtues," a college chaplain explains. Two or three chaplains serve the college each year, and there are regular visits by other priests and members of religious orders.

Christendom also fosters in its students an appreciation of culture and the arts. The college sponsors the Beato Fra Angelico Fine Arts Program to "offer students a further opportunity to experience directly the higher and more aesthetically praiseworthy fruits of Western civilization and our contemporary culture." Each year the college sponsors a regional sacred arts exhibition. There are, as well, a number of concerts and recitals on campus, and Christendom has an active choir and Gregorian chant schola (which has recently released its second CD). The college hosts a variety of speakers, both Catholic and political; past invitees include Patrick Buchanan, Rick Santorum, Robert George, and Joseph Pearce. The Student Activities Council organizes trips to concerts and other cultural events in Washington, D.C. And further afield, the college administers a Semester in Rome program wherein students spend part of their junior year studying history, art, and architecture in the Eternal City. A special course there is dedicated to the literary and historical experience of Rome—including such authors as Livy and St. Gregory the Great, and select plays of Shakespeare.

Most of the faculty and students would be considered conservative by prevailing standards, and the school was recently named as one of the top 10 conservative colleges in the country by the Young America's Foundation. But one does not find lock-step uniformity at Christendom. While radical politics don't find a home here, there is genuine disagreement about politics. "There is suspicion about Americanism and the founding among some students and faculty," one professor says. "Some here are inclined to view the whole Enlightenment project as hopelessly corrupt." There is also disagreement about the proper role and scope of government. "The classic Catholic position, as formulated by St. Thomas and others, is that good government promotes virtue among the citizens," says one professor. "But this principle is in tension with our original founding principles of limited government, and certainly contradicts the modern 'values-free' and libertine agenda of the left."

Christendom is located in Front Royal, Virginia, in the beautiful Shenandoah Valley, about 75 miles from the nation's capital. The area is truly a wonder of natural beauty, including the Shenandoah National Park, Skyline Drive (whose northern terminus is in Front Royal), and George Washington National Park. The area is renowned for hiking, wine tasting at the numerous nearby vineyards where many students work, and fox hunting. The administration has taken care to make the campus fit in with its setting, but the relative newness and small size of the college mean that one finds few imposing or architecturally striking buildings on campus. However, that does not mean the campus is not conscious of its environs. As the college's vice president for development put it at the groundbreaking ceremony for the new library, "We have to always keep in mind that whatever building we erect will probably be around long after we've gone." While Front Royal itself is a somewhat sleepy town (with the benefit of very low crime, both on and off campus), the students do a pretty good job of keeping life on campus lively. When the need for more excitement strikes, larger towns are only a few miles away, and D.C. is near enough to make a night on the town an inviting proposition. The school reported no criminal incidents of any kind on its campus in 2003.

Tuition and fees at Christendom are relatively low, in comparison to its peers in private Catholic education. Students attending the college in 2004–5 paid $19,670 for tuition, fees, and room and board, covering the entire academic year. The college offers both merit-based financial aid through scholarships and need-based financial aid in the form of work-study grants and loans. Admission is need-blind. In fall 2004, 57 percent of incoming students received some form of need-based aid. Students completing four years of academic study in 2003 left the college with an average debt of $10,050.

CLEMSON UNIVERSITY

CLEMSON, SOUTH CAROLINA • WWW.CLEMSON.EDU

For all practical purposes

The school that is now Clemson University was founded in 1889 with funds from Thomas Green Clemson, the son-in-law of American statesman and political philosopher John C. Calhoun. Although it has grown significantly since then, Clemson's mission has remained basically the same. From the beginning, Clemson students sought higher education for practical reasons. The college was built to remedy the destruction brought about by the Civil War, offering education in agriculture and the mechanical arts to South Carolina students who still had hope in the South. Becoming well versed in Shakespeare or learning the purpose of the French and Indian Wars was not exactly a priority for many of the Clemson students of yesteryear. And neither, generally speaking, is it today.

In 2002, Clemson's provost unveiled the university's academic plan—plain and simple, the institution's 10-year goal is to become one of the nation's top 20 public universities, as judged by *U.S. News and World Report*. By improving eight broad academic "emphasis areas" (for instance, general education, information and communication technology, and "family and community living"), Clemson hopes to raise its *U.S. News* ranking (which, to be clear, we think a highly dubious goal, in and of itself). But many of the university's planned improvements require money, and alas, the state of South Carolina continues to cut the university's budget each year.

Academic Life: Priority ceding

Five undergraduate colleges make up Clemson University: Agriculture, Forestry, and Life Sciences; Architecture, Arts, and Humanities; Business and Behavioral Science; Engineering and Science; and Health, Education, and Human Development. Although all students, regardless of college, have to complete several general education requirements, providing each of them with a broad and structured liberal arts education is not a priority at Clemson. In fact, in October 2003 the university voted to cut back on some of the school's already sketchy general education requirements, from 41 credit hours to 33. In part, this move was motivated by budget cuts imposed by the state of South Carolina, according to a faculty member. "Another factor was the problem many students were having in graduating within four years," he says. (The four-year rate is a pretty paltry 40 percent.) These changes further diluted the already weak core requirements at Clemson, this professor says. However, another professor claims that since "each major has its own requirements, students aren't likely to suffer as a result. It's still possible for someone to get a good education at Clemson by taking the right courses."

Clemson began as a land-grant university, and it remains strong in agriculture, engineering, and other applied arts and sciences. Clemson students are proud of their prestigious engineering program; one student estimates that "nearly half of male students here study engineering." The College of Engineering and Science is, in fact, the largest of the colleges, serving around 28 percent of the student body.

Other areas must fend for themselves. And in fact, some have. The Architecture, Arts, and Humanities College, the college that comes closest to having a liberal arts focus, is the smallest division at Clemson, enrolling just 14 percent of students. Says one professor, "One of Clemson's announced goals is to 'establish a Phi Beta Kappa chapter by the year 2010,' but that may be in jeopardy if the university continues to neglect the humanities and social sciences." On the bright side, as another professor says, "despite official neglect of the humanities by the administration, a grassroots effort on the part of faculty across the disciplines has created a distinctive 18-hour minor in the great works of Western civilization." This is clearly the place to start if one is looking for a liberal education at Clemson. To earn the minor, students must take courses from five different areas: classical civilization; post-classical literature; philosophy, religion, and social thought; the arts; and the sciences. Courses that contribute to the minor must teach "foundational texts." The program seems popular with students; professors say that the only problem is freeing up enough interested teachers from their departmental courses to teach these interdisciplinary classes. In all, the Great Works minor offers about 40 courses.

Clemson's distribution requirements are unimpressive. The humanities requirement, for instance, can be satisfied by anything from "Introduction to Women's Studies" to "African American Theatre" to "Nineteenth-Century Philosophy." For the social science requirement, solid survey courses like "The History of the United States" or "Principles of Macroeconomics" are fair game, but so are "Sociology of Mental Illness" and "Animal Welfare." One student, however, is quick to point out that while more specialized classes fulfill general education requirements, most of them have prerequisites. Therefore, "Most students are going to take the 'General History of the U.S.' or English 102," she says.

On the other hand, a professor maintains that Clemson's "bare-bones general education curriculum" allows "enough flexibility . . . that a student could avoid fundamental learning in favor of unserious courses."

Although Clemson's general education requirements provide *some* degree of

VITAL STATISTICS
Religious affiliation: none
Total enrollment: 17,110
Total undergraduates: 13,936
SAT/ACT midranges: SAT V: 540–640, M: 570–660; ACT: 24–28
Applicants: 10,620
Applicants accepted: 69%
Accepted applicants who enrolled: 42%
Tuition: $7,840 (in state), $16,404 (out of state)
Room and board: $5,292
Freshman retention rate: 88%
Graduation rate: 40% (4 yrs.), 72% (6 yrs.)
Courses with fewer than 20 students: 27%
Student-faculty ratio: 16:1
Courses taught by graduate TAs: not provided
Most popular majors: business, engineering, social sciences
Students living on campus: 47%
Guaranteed housing for four years? no
Students in fraternities: 17% sororities: 31%

ACADEMIC REQUIREMENTS

Clemson has no core curriculum and has recently pared back its distribution requirements. The new general education requirements, which are still subject to tinkering, ask the following of students:

- One course (three hours) in English Composition, and another course which fulfills the Advanced Writing requirement. These hours may be fulfilled by a single course or by a "cluster" of courses that together provide enough writing exercises equivalent to one course deemed writing-intensive. This course can overlap with major requirements.
- Three hours in oral communications. This requirement could be fulfilled either by a single course or by a group of courses. The course also may be used to fulfill other requirements.

breadth, the depth of a student's education depends on his major. An English major, for instance, is required to take courses in eight different categories (but Shakespeare isn't one of them—he is optional). Other majors are less specific with their requirements. Besides a basic course in "World Regional Geography" or "Historical Geography" and a senior seminar, the history department requires just one course in each of these areas: United States; European; and African, Asian, or Latin American history.

Faculty members say Clemson's academic strengths lie in architecture, new materials engineering, history, and chemistry. One professor says the economics department has "a well-respected 'Chicago-school' faculty, all of whom teach undergraduates as well as graduate students. Daniel Benjamin's 'Principles of Economics' class is a must for any serious student." Some of Clemson's best professors are Robert E. McCormick Jr. and T. Bruce Yandle in economics; Barton R. Palmer and Mark R. Winchell (founder of the Great Works program) in English; J. David Woodard in political science; and university president James F. Barker, who customarily teaches at least one well-loved course in architecture—most recently, a course focusing on the American small town.

As at most large state universities, the intellectual aptitudes and motivations of the students vary widely. "There are intellectually serious students in almost every class," says a professor. "The majority, however, seem excessively grade-conscious." Since many state scholarships now require a B average or better, students have become even more zealous for good grades, and faculty members say that the university has inflated grades to satisfy them. While the average SAT score for entering freshmen at Clemson has risen (to around 1210 in 2004) so have grades, due to inflation. The average GPA is just under 3.0. One faculty member says, "At Clemson, just like at Garrison Keillor's Lake Wobegon, all the women are strong, the men good-looking, and all the children above average."

Students in the Calhoun Honors College tend to be more interested in ideas than the general Clemson population and are certainly more serious academically. One student protests that this is not altogether accurate; some academically-motivated students "choose not to be a part of the Honors College," because they, like he, "merely desire to be free of [its] limitations." It doesn't seem that limiting to us. In fact, it sounds downright worthwhile. For the General Honors curriculum, students must complete at least six honors courses, most of which also satisfy the general education requirements. Members of the program are expected to complete at least one honors course each semester and maintain a GPA of 3.4 or better. Honors courses, which are more like seminars in that they encourage active student participation, are offered in many disciplines; they include everything from "Plants in Medicine" to "Greek Drama and Philosophy." Participants in the program get priority course scheduling and extended library privileges and can live, take ski trips, and attend cultural performances with other honors students. Most departments also offer a departmental honors program to their major students.

Regular classes can be as large as 300 or 400 students, and in such a course, it's unlikely that students will get much one-on-one time with the professor. However, one student reports that only one of her classes per semester had more than 200 students; "most of my classes have been small," she says.

Upon entering Clemson, each student is assigned a professional or faculty advisor, but it is the student's responsibility to seek help should he need it. "A lot of students are almost resistant to advising," a professor says. "They pick their courses and e-mail them to their advisor and try to get approval without meeting them. The quality of advising varies greatly across the university, according to the individual—some professors see it as a real vocation and spend a lot of time on it, others don't."

Graduate teaching assistants do much of the heavy lifting at the lower levels of instruction at Clemson, teaching, for instance, many of the sections in freshman composition and other introductory classes. In the sciences, students have been known to complain that their TAs, hailing from foreign lands, are brilliant but incomprehensible to native South Carolinians. According to a professor, the university has begun to hire adjunct teachers to avoid paying benefit packages to tenure-track faculty.

In the classroom, faculty members say, Clemson is much more conservative than most large state universities. "Conservative faculty members are among the most prominent at Clemson and feel completely free to speak their minds," a professor says. "For example, one moderate liberal and one strong conservative are the two most highly regarded professors in the political science department." The most provocative course in poli sci, according to the *Chronicle of Higher Education*, seems to be "Anti-Americanism: Hating the U.S. at Home and Abroad," which requires students to read essays by Noam Chomsky and rants by Osama bin Laden—not in order to accept their views, but to

REQUIREMENTS (CONT'D)

- Six hours in the social sciences. A list of about 85 approved courses has been proposed. Students are advised to choose one course that overlaps with the three-hour cross-cultural awareness requirement. About 35 courses would fulfill both.
- Six hours in arts and humanities. Students must choose one course from a list of approved literature courses—on which there are twice as many approved courses dealing with literature in translation than there are for British and American lit courses. The other course must come from a list of approved courses in areas such as philosophy, religious studies, women's studies, theater, et cetera.
- Three hours in mathematics.
- Four hours in a laboratory science, plus a course on science and technology in society.

SOUTH

analyze and critique them. With few exceptions, politicized courses are sequestered in departments like women's studies, which offers only a minor and a few courses each year. The religion department offers the basics in various faiths, in courses like "Religions of the Ancient World," "Buddhism in China," and "History of Early Christianity," with none of the classes in "religion and gender" prevalent at other schools.

Student Life: Senator Calhoun's farm

More than two-thirds of Clemson's undergraduate student body comes from the state of South Carolina, but a campus tour guide insists that Clemson is not a suitcase college. "There are always people here on campus, and there's always something going on," she says. Freshmen are required to live on campus, but around a quarter of the class leaves university housing each year for (usually) cheaper and more independent quarters. Underclassman housing consists primarily of corridor-style dormitories, while upperclassmen vie for suites and on-campus apartments. Some residence halls are reserved exclusively for men and others for women. In coed dormitories, men and women are not necessarily separated by floor or by wing.

Clemson's campus is typical of many large state universities, with a pleasant core. An outdoor theater and reflecting pool and Tillman Hall (and bell tower) are the most photographed areas of the grounds. John C. Calhoun's mansion is close to the main part of campus. Less pleasant buildings were constructed as the university's enrollment grew; some might describe them as "penitentiary style." Clemson describes its grounds as a "bull's-eye" campus: the library is at the center, surrounded by academic buildings, surrounded by residence halls, surrounded by athletic facilities, surrounded by parking (a considerable pain, say some students, but it seems a wise set-up to us).

With some exceptions, the center of a Clemson student's college life is unlikely to resemble the layout of the campus. If students' priorities had anything to do with the layout, the football stadium would be at the center, surrounded by a few on-campus bars or fraternities (after all, Clemson was ranked the number two party school by *The Princeton Review* in 2002).

Sports are very important to students and alumni. Death Valley (Clemson's football stadium) has a capacity of 80,000, and undergraduates are guaranteed free tickets for games. Area bars are packed on football weekends. On Homecoming Friday night, Clemson students participate in one of the nation's largest student-run pep rallies. Homecoming sees a large gathering of students and graduates, with Greek organizations (about 25 percent of Tigers go Greek) and other clubs constructing floats for a parade. Other popular varsity sports are volleyball and soccer. Clemson's golf team recently won the NCAA championship, the first program in college golf history to win a conference championship, a regional championship, and the national championship in the same year. Intramurals, usually organized around Greek organizations or freshman dorms, are also popular, offering in addition to the usual array of sports dodgeball, kickball, and sand volleyball. The student organization Central Spirit is dedicated to building school spirit, planning events, decorating locker rooms, painting tiger paws on people's faces, and even deciding the winner of an award given to "the person (student, faculty, or otherwise) that shows exceptional devotion towards Clemson athletics," according to Central Spirit's Web site.

And Clemson fans are nothing if not spirited. According to the *Chronicle of Higher Education*, in November 2003, Clemson fans "rushed the field to celebrate a victory over their University of South Carolina rivals, tearing down a goal post and injuring a sheriff's deputy in the process." Says a student, "The one thing that really sets Clemson apart from other schools is our school spirit. In the general population, orange is not a popular color. Here at Clemson, orange [the school shade] is a popular color throughout the week—not just on home football game days."

Racial issues are the most prevalent in campus debate. When activist Jesse Jackson came to campus in September 2003, he criticized Clemson's record on recruiting black students. As reported in the September 19, 2003, issue of the student newspaper, the *Tiger*, Jackson told his audience that Clemson needs to do more to balance the student body racially. The athletics department brings in most of its money from football games, and 75 percent of the team is black, but on the campus as a whole, black students constitute just 7 percent of Clemson's student body. (South Carolina's population is almost 30 percent black, according to the 2000 Census.)

SUGGESTED CORE
1. Great Works 301, Great Books of the Western World *or* English 403, The Classics in Translation
2. Philosophy 315, Ancient Philosophy
3. Religion 310/302, The Old Testament / The New Testament
4. Religion 307, The Christian Tradition *or* Religion 404, History of Early Christianity
5. Political Science 450, Political Theory (*closest match*)
6. English 411, Shakespeare
7. History 101, History of the United States
8. History 173, Western Civilization II

The university has lately been eager to change the racial climate on campus, and a professor complains that "an implicit policy of racial preference influences many personnel decisions." The Office of Multicultural Affairs offers more than a dozen diversity training sessions each year for faculty, staff, and students, who are taught how to "heal from the scars of internalized oppression," among other things. The office also sponsors events during various awareness months—Hispanic Heritage, Native American Heritage, Black History, and Asian/Pacific American Heritage. Black History month is really the only one of these that is particularly politicized, while the others feature mainly cultural demonstrations, like salsa dancing lessons, workshops on natural fiber dying, or an Asian food fair.

One conservative professor describes the political atmosphere on the Clemson campus in this way: "The campus mode is conservative in politics and liberal in social views. As far as I can tell, politically correct speech is not an issue. Perhaps this is because this is a southern campus, and southerners historically disagree politely."

Clemson does have a small student homosexual group, but the group speaks to a rather hostile audience: the 2003 *Princeton Review* ranked Clemson fourth among schools that do *not* accept alternative lifestyles.

SOUTH

403

Clemson students do think some issues are worth arguing about—especially when it comes to money coming out of their pockets, as with the university's steep tuition hikes. In 2003, California congressman Howard McKeon proposed legislation that would penalize colleges that increased tuition by twice the rate of inflation for more than two years in a row. If that measure had passed a couple years ago, Clemson would have lost its federal student aid programs and then some: from 2000 to 2002, the university raised tuition a whopping 62.5 percent, according to the *Chronicle*.

Clemson may not be the most cosmopolitan town, but many students enjoy the community. "Everybody's extremely friendly," a student says. "Everybody always smiles. They want to keep the small-town atmosphere. Clemson's the kind of town where you don't have to show ID to write a check." The Astro, a movie theater in "downtown" Clemson (a short walk from campus), shows movies for about three dollars. "Local businesses cater to Clemson students," a student says. "They exist because of us." One bar gives a free T-shirt to each student who visits on his or her 21st birthday. Since many Clemson students take more than four years to graduate, potentially giving them a few years of college at legal drinking age, that's probably a smart investment.

There are certainly plenty of activities to fill up students' free time. Besides homecoming, a favorite tradition is Tiger Gras, Clemson's own Fat Tuesday, with all of the usual overindulgence. Students can also take advantage of the dozens of concerts, film series, and speeches the University Programs and Activities Council organizes each year. There are open mike nights, karaoke, poetry readings, and "Coffee and Conversations" sessions each week.

Clemson's student government is active and influential on campus, students say. Although Clemson already has a few hundred student organizations, including the Calhoun Brewers Society, the Dairy Science Club, and the Dixie Skydivers, should a student want to start another one, he needs only to find 12 other interested students and a faculty sponsor.

Clemson is fairly strong in the performing arts. A Shakespeare festival is held on campus each year, and the college orchestra performs regularly. Students can often get discounted rates or free tickets for on- and off-campus events.

The university is located squarely in the Bible Belt, and Christian religious groups are among the most popular at the school. The Fellowship of Christian Athletes, Clemson Christian Fellowship, Baptist Collegiate Ministry, Campus Crusade for Christ, Reformed University Fellowship, and others hold weekly discussions and prayer groups and occasional retreats. As Clemson is a state university, religious groups do not get funding from student fees.

One great advantage of life in this small South Carolina town is that the crime rate is low, especially considering the size of the university. In 2003, there were but two forcible sex offenses, two robberies, 26 burglaries, and two stolen cars on campus—a notable decrease over the previous year.

In-state tuition for 2004–5 was $7,840, and room and board was $5,292. Out-of-state students pay double that tuition, $16,404 to be precise. Most of the financial aid that Clemson awards is need-based, but some merit scholarships are offered as well.

SOUTH

DAVIDSON COLLEGE

Full-court Presbyterian

Davidson College began as a liberal arts college for manual laborers in 1837. After the Civil War left the school destitute, Davidson rebounded to become one of the South's top colleges for men, rivaling such schools as Washington and Lee, until 1976, when Davidson first began to admit women. The college's reputation has continued to improve, and it is now one of the most selective schools in the country, producing an impressive 23 Rhodes Scholars. But the 1,700-student college has no plans to grow into a large university with graduate programs, because it recognizes that its small size has yielded its greatest virtues: close faculty-student relationships, a strong college community, and a genuine commitment to the liberal arts.

Davidson was founded by Presbyterians and is still affiliated with that denomination. The college's statement of purpose pledges to emphasize "those studies, disciplines, and activities that are mentally, spiritually, and physically liberating." The college has followed this mission through an honor code that sets the tone for student life, a liberal arts curriculum that requires students to take serious courses, a community that welcomes spirituality, and a social scene that encourages students to be physically active. As a result of the college's adherence to its mission, Davidson students are some of the most well-rounded in the nation.

Academic Life: On course

Though the Davidson course catalog calls its curriculum a "core," it would be better described as a set of distribution requirements. While we would prefer to see the genuine article—a single set of foundational courses that everyone must take—Davidson's mandated course selections are better than most, no doubt because such a high percentage of courses offered by the school are solid ones. "Davidson's broad core requirements, rather than being a burden, are a guide to making sure students have taken a diverse

VITAL STATISTICS
Religious affiliation: Presbyterian
Total enrollment: 1,712
Total undergraduates: 1,712
SAT/ACT midranges: SAT V: 630–720, M: 640–720; ACT: 27–31
Applicants: 3,927
Applicants accepted: 32%
Accepted applicants who enrolled: 39%
Tuition: $24,987
Room and board: $7,371
Freshman retention rate: 96%
Graduation rate: 88% (4 yrs.), 89% (6 yrs.)
Courses with fewer than 20 students: 70%
Student-faculty ratio: 11:1
Courses taught by graduate TAs: none
Most popular majors: social sciences, English, biology
Students living on campus: 92%
Guaranteed housing for four years? yes
Students in fraternities: 41% sororities: 0%

Davidson's excellent distribution requirements have five components:

- Core Curriculum. A 10-course set of requirements from six major disciplines that must be fulfilled before the start of the senior year. It includes literature (one course), fine arts (one course), history (one course), religion and philosophy (two courses, at least one of them in religion), natural sciences and math (three courses, at least one in math and one in a lab science), and social sciences (two courses).
- Composition. First-year students must satisfy a composition requirement through courses that offer sustained attention to writing and discussion. These courses may be selected from the English department or other departments, or the requirement may be satisfied through the completion of Davidson's first-year Humanities Program. "W" course offerings for 2004 included "Love, Death, Art," "Introduction to Shakespeare," "Religion and Food," and "Time Travel."

range of classes," a Latin American studies major says. "Despite being a numbers guy," says a math major, "I have read Plato, Milton, Flaubert, Nietzsche, and Hayek, to name a few." One faculty member says, "May a student graduate without taking a course in Milton? Yes. May a student graduate without thinking clearly and writing critically about fundamental issues in art, science, mathematics, literature, philosophy, etc.? No."

Certainly not if they enroll in the Davidson College Humanities Program. Taught by faculty from several departments who lead discussion sections of 16 students each, freshmen and sophomores in this program take a sequence of four courses focusing on the development of Western civilization, including "The Ancient World," "Late Antiquity and the Modern World," "The Renaissance to the Eighteenth Century," and "The Modern World." This program is basically a core curriculum—albeit an abbreviated one—in which students experience courses with each other in the same way they would at a school with a genuine college-wide core. Since the humanities sequence covers material from philosophy, religion, history, and literature, students participating in this program satisfy four distribution requirements. An alternative to the Western civilization core is the newer two-semester "Cultures and Civilizations" course for first-year students, which focuses primarily on "horizons beyond the West."

Although Davidson is primarily a liberal arts college, its science and undergraduate research programs are strong, and the balance it strikes between the arts and sciences is impressive. One Davidson administrator says that some of the most scientifically minded students will also minor in religion or another humanities discipline, and vice versa. The strongest departments at the school are philosophy, history, mathematics, political science, chemistry, and biology. Another highlight is the religion department, whose faculty members teach courses in, among other things, "Theological Ethics," "Introduction to the Hebrew Bible," "The Genesis Narrative," "Christian Latin Writers," and "Christianity and Nature." In other words, the common preoccupations of gender and ethnic studies are mostly absent, and religion is approached as a genuine discipline worthy of serious study.

The Davidson psychology department recently switched from offering bachelor of arts to bachelor of science degrees, giving the department a more experimental orientation. Davidson offers premed, pre-dentistry, prelaw, pre-ministerial, and teacher education programs, as well as an engineering cooperative in which students take three years at Davidson and two years in the engineering school at either Columbia University or Washington University in St. Louis.

About two-thirds of Davidson students study abroad at some point during their four years, choosing from among the school's programs in Tours, Würzburg, Cambridge, Mexico, Cyprus, Ghana, India, Zambia, Spain, and various areas associated with classical antiquity. There are universities five times Davidson's size with fewer attractive offerings. The school also offers classes in Chinese, French, German, Latin, Russian, and Spanish. A student may study another language through the college's Self-Instructional Language Program.

Within the curriculum, the most politicized departments are the interdisciplinary ones, such as ethnic studies, gender studies, international studies, and the rare Southern studies. Davidson added its "cultural diversity" requirement only a few years ago, after many peer (and more liberal) institutions had introduced theirs. However, the kooky courses one finds in other liberal arts college catalogs are missing from Davidson's; even the cultural diversity requirement can be satisfied by a number of good courses in the history or foreign language departments.

Just about every department at Davidson is reputed to be tough. One religion major says that she spends four hours a day studying: "It might be possible to get by with classes that are easier than others, but I don't know how." Another student says that every course is difficult. "I've been surprised to hear about my peers struggling more in music theory, art history, and drama classes than in their freshman science requirements like chemistry," this student says. Students recommend seeking out faculty such as Paul Miller and Randy Nelson in English; Hansford M. Epes and Burhard Henke in German; Lance K. Stell in philosophy; Karl A. Plank and H. Gregory Snyder in religion; C. Shaw Smith Jr. in art history; Maria Magdalena Maiz-Pena in Spanish; Kristi S. Multhaup in psychology; and Mark Foley in economics. "All of Davidson's professors are the best, literally," says a sophomore. "Ironically, some of the most-loved professors at Davidson are also the most challenging. I think this characterizes the academic atmosphere here well."

Davidson students and faculty agree that the school's Honor Code permeates academic and campus life. In the code, students pledge to "refrain from stealing, lying

REQUIREMENTS (CONT'D)

- **Foreign Language.** Students must reach a level of proficiency in a foreign language equivalent to a third-level course at Davidson.
- **Cultural Diversity.** Davidson believes "that all students should have the experience of studying societies or cultures that differ from those of the United States or Europe." This requirement must be fulfilled for graduation and courses may be selected from most departments—including foreign languages.
- **Physical Education.** An impressive total of four physical education courses are required. PED 101 is required of all students in their first semester; while the other three—one "lifetime" credit, one "water" credit; and one "team" credit—are fulfilled later.

SOUTH

about college business, and cheating on academic work." A supplemental Code of Responsibility aims for students to recognize that Davidson is a "college of liberal arts committed to the Christian faith" which tries to "develop the maturity of character." Any member of the Davidson community can charge a student with a violation of this code. These standards give professors the freedom to leave the room during exams and students the flexibility to take home tests and schedule their own times for finals. But beyond these benefits, students take comfort in knowing that they can trust their peers and that their professors and classmates are pledged to honesty. A student on the Honor Council says that only three or four violations occur per year, and most of those incidents are reported by the offenders themselves, not by classmates or faculty members. The library stacks at Davidson are open and students check out books from the library without electronic scanners or security beepers. Students leave laptops on their desktops when they go for a break and even leave their dorm rooms unlocked. One sophomore says that all of this demonstrates the college's underlying "atmosphere of trust."

With a student-faculty ratio of 11 to 1 and an average class size of 13, student-faculty relationships at Davidson are among the strongest anywhere. Office hours extend beyond the obligatory one or two hours a week one sees at many schools. One student reports that she and her classmates frequently pop into professors' offices to talk about class or various intellectual topics. "The time I have spent one-on-one with my professors is a highlight of my experience here," another student says. Often professors give students their home phone numbers on the first day of class, encouraging them to call with questions. One English professor says, "I don't even keep office hours anymore. I just open my door at 7:30 each morning. It's a quiet day when I don't have two or three students dropping by." The admissions director says that intellectual curiosity is the one attribute that Davidson students have in common, and that the admissions office purposely chooses students who are "ready to have intellectual relationships." All incoming students are assigned faculty advisors. Once a student has declared a major, he is assigned (or can choose) a faculty member in his major department to serve as an advisor.

Student Life: Body and soul

Above all, Davidson attracts and shapes well-rounded students: academically, socially, athletically, even morally and spiritually. Patterson Court—the organizing body of the college's six fraternities, four women's eating houses, and one coeducational eating house—lies at the center of the Davidson social scene. About 70 percent of female and 40 percent of male students belong to social/dining clubs, but students are not pressured to participate. And the clubs are not residential, so social life centers around the dormitories as much as it does around the small club headquarters. The Black Student Coalition once petitioned to organize a black fraternity on campus, but the student government wisely turned the proposition down, because they thought it would only segregate the campus racially. "The eating clubs are not sorority-ish and are not exclusive or cliquey," one member says.

Davidson has taken great pains to foster a sense of community; about 92 percent of the student body lives on campus. Before arriving, freshmen fill out an exhaustive roommate matching questionnaire and even take the Myers-Briggs Type Indicator, a personality test. Coordinators spend weeks trying to find the best fit for each student, and most roommates end up being good friends, if not also roommates as sophomores. All floors and bathrooms on campus are single sex, as are some dormitories. Most seniors live in campus apartments, which offer a pleasant transition from dorm life to the real world.

SUGGESTED CORE

For a somewhat abbreviated core, the Humanities Program (Humanities 150, 151, 250, and 251) suffices.

Beautiful Georgian-style architecture and a shaded campus fit in well with Davidson's southern location. New, modern facilities blend in with 100-year-old buildings, as the school has not abandoned its original style. The Knobloch Center contains a movie theater, post office, fitness center with climbing wall, an outdoor center, meeting rooms, student organization offices, a cafe, a bookstore, a large outdoor patio that overlooks the football stadium, and a 600-seat performance hall, home to the Royal Shakespeare Company's only North American stop. A magnificent new art/art history building, complete with two public galleries, provides private studios for art majors. And the recently renovated Dana Laboratories give students in the sciences opportunities to use state-of-the-art equipment rarely seen at schools the size of Davidson. At the center of campus, the Chambers Building is undergoing a three-year, $21 million renovation to improve classroom use and efficiency, modernize classroom instructional technology, increase the number of faculty offices, and enhance accessibility to the building.

The town of Davidson is not exactly hopping, but it is big on charm. Students who enjoy visiting needlepoint stores, antique shops, and art galleries will love the place. Admirably, instead of abandoning the downtown for suburban sprawl, town residents have striven to preserve the town; a Village Store has sold necessities on Davidson's Main Street since 1903. Four churches are within walking distance and the on-campus Davidson College Presbyterian Church offers services each week from a variety of communions, including Presbyterian, Catholic, and Episcopal—along with a nondenominational contemporary worship service. Nearby Charlotte offers bright lights and entertainment; the Blue Ridge Mountains are only two hours west; and the Carolina beaches are three or four hours to the east.

Davidson students, on the whole, are not politically active. Coursework and athletics occupy enough of their time. "While there's still a subtle conservative dominance, such things as the liberal campus publication, the *Libertas,* certainly have a presence," a student says. Membership in the College Democrats and the College Republicans is about equal, but left-leaning students are usually more vocal, especially regarding foreign wars. One student remarks, "In the two years that I have been here, I have seen the campus become somewhat more charged politically. But despite this, most debate still seems to be good-natured."

Some schools with relatively conservative credentials belie their identity at commencement by inviting speakers whose politics reflect what's popular among student activists. Not Davidson. In fact, according to *USA Today*, Davidson no longer invites famous figures for its commencement ceremonies, and hasn't since the 1960s, when "it moved ceremonies outdoors. The first year turned so hot, and the speaker droned on for so long, that the college has since limited speechifying to brief remarks by the president." Instead, the ceremony focuses "on graduates as they walk across the platform to receive diplomas and shake hands with the president." Sounds like a good plan to us.

As much as some in the administration might like to see the dominant politics of academia infuse the school's curriculum and campus life, Davidson College remains essentially southern and conservative. "However, there's definitely a balance of liberals, which I believe is increasing as the college increases its geographic draw and grows in prestige every year," says one student.

Davidson is one of the smallest NCAA Division I colleges in the country, and Wildcat athletes compete on 21 varsity teams. A fourth of the student body participates in varsity athletics, and—due in part to the physical fitness requirements—90 percent participate in intramural sports programs. All students are trained in first aid and CPR, the fitness centers are always full, and a number of students play pick-up basketball games in the evening. Davidson students are not couch potatoes.

Crime is not much of an issue at Davidson College, mostly because of its location; the most recent (2003) statistics show no violent crimes at all on campus, merely four burglaries, one stolen car, and two arsons. The college has taken steps to keep the campus safe. The grounds are well lit, campus police patrol the grounds on bikes, and residential buildings are accessible only with student ID cards. Campus social groups take turns running the Vamanos Van, a transportation service that takes students from weekend parties back to campus in an effort to curb drunk driving.

Tuition for the 2004–5 academic year was $24,987, with room and board an extra $7,371. In that year, students received more than $14 million in financial aid from college sources along with other outside sources to form aid packages. While most financial aid is need-based, Davidson sets aside over $1 million in various merit-based scholarships, which are awarded to approximately 15 percent of each entering class. Clearly dedicated to making Davidson accessible to qualified students, the college has earmarked $85 million of its five-year, $250 million campaign, "Let Learning Be Cherished," towards scholarship programs. To date, almost 80 new scholarships have been created and existing scholarships have been enriched. On a student-run blog, one anonymous student says, "If you have need, I've found Davidson to provide it. . . . The key is to ask questions—the admissions/financial aid people are some of the nicest around and will bend over backwards to help you out."

DUKE UNIVERSITY

DURHAM, NORTH CAROLINA • WWW.DUKE.EDU

The Harvard of the South?

In the 1850s, Methodist and Quaker families in rural North Carolina founded Union Institute, later known as Trinity College. This became part of the new Duke University when the James Duke family established a $40 million endowment from their tobacco business, but to this day the largest division of the university is called the Trinity College of Arts and Sciences.

The school's religious roots are evident in the school motto: *Eruditio et Religio*, "Knowledge and Religion." A metal plaque in front of the Duke Chapel even maintains that "the aims of Duke University are to assert a faith in the eternal union of knowledge and religion set forth in the teaching and character of Jesus Christ, the Son of God; to advance learning in all things of truth; to defend scholarship against all false notions and ideals; to develop a Christian love of freedom and truth; to promote a sincere spirit of tolerance; to discourage all partisan and sectarian strife; and to render the largest permanent service to the state, the nation, and the church. Unto these ends shall the efforts of this university always be administered." To readers of Tom Wolfe's *I Am Charlotte Simmons*—based in part on life today at Duke—the poignancy of these noble phrases will be apparent.

That is because the school's links to orthodox Christianity have become tenuous over the years; the Duke Chapel cut its last ties to the Methodist Church by performing homosexual wedding services in 2000. If Duke still advances any gospel, it is the Social Gospel, which it at least preaches in a more tolerant spirit than other institutions whose leftism is more secular in origin; here there seems to be a real preference for persuasion over intimidation.

Duke's ethos has been deeply marked by the 11-year presidency of Nan Keohane, a decided feminist who openly deplored the university's "Christian association" during her reign. President Richard H. Brodhead, the former dean of Yale College, where he received his education and served as professor of English, was inaugurated in 2004. He

VITAL STATISTICS
Religious affiliation: none
Total enrollment: 12,100
Total undergraduates: 6,100
SAT/ACT midranges: SAT: 1340–1530; ACT: 29–33
Applicants: 18,000
Applicants accepted: 22%
Accepted applicants who enrolled: 44%
Tuition: $32,409
Room and board: $8,830
Freshman retention rate: 99%
Graduation rate: 88% (4 yrs.), 94% (6 yrs.)
Courses with fewer than 20 students: 69%
Student-faculty ratio: 9:1
Courses taught by graduate TAs: 2%
Most popular majors: economics, public policy, psychology
Students living on campus: 86%
Guaranteed housing for four years? yes
Students in fraternities: 30% sororities: 42%

SOUTH

411

While it has no core curriculum, in the better of its two liberal arts options, Trinity College Program I, Duke requires that students take:

- Two courses in arts and literature and performance, from a list of hundreds ranging from "Shakespeare before 1600" to "Literature and Sexualities."
- Two courses in history, philosophy, or religion, from a list of hundreds including "The History of Ancient Philosophy" and "The History of Public Health in America."
- Two courses in cultural anthropology, economics, environmental sciences, linguistics, political science, psychology, public policy studies, or sociology, again from a list of hundreds including much that is solid and not a little that is silly.
- Two courses in natural sciences and mathematics, chosen from a list in which useful courses predominate.
- Two courses in quantitative studies, chosen from a list of courses all of which require some kind of mathematical analysis.

faced his first challenge in October when the Palestine Solidarity Movement held its national conference on campus. Brodhead saw to it that advocates of Israel as well as the Palestinian position were able to express themselves freely at the event. His personal leadership has done much, observers agree, to maintain Duke's reputation for civility.

Duke also has a reputation for academic excellence. *U.S. News and World Report* has ranked Duke in its top five, while the *Journal of Blacks in Higher Education* has named it as one of the best universities for black students and professors. Duke is often called "the Harvard of the South," but considering the preprofessionalism and politicization that have swept over Cambridge, Duke should consider the comparison both an honor and a warning.

Academic Life: Make your Marx

Duke has two undergraduate schools: the Pratt School of Engineering and Trinity College of Arts and Sciences. Trinity undergraduates may choose one of two programs to achieve a bachelor's degree. Program I is the more traditional and popular choice. The curriculum for Program I, revised in 2000, revolves around five interrelated sets of curricular requirements: Areas of Knowledge, Modes of Inquiry, Focused Inquiries, Competencies, and a student's major subject.

Program I undergraduates must also demonstrate competencies in foreign language, writing, and research. The language requirement can be completed by taking three courses of a language or by placing out. The writing requirement consists of the freshman University Writing Course plus two writing-intensive courses from other disciplines. Nearly every humanities or social sciences department offers a few of these writing-intensive courses. In the history department, for instance, "Europe to the Eighteenth Century," "Modern Britain," and "The Rise of Modern Science: Early Science through Newton" all qualify. The research requirement is completed by taking a research-intensive course like "The Philosophy of Religion" or "Principles of Animal Morphology."

Individual majors impose further requirements. Philosophy majors, for instance, take two survey courses, "History of Ancient Philosophy" and "History of Modern Philosophy," both of which are solid introductions to their subjects. The English major has a little more structure—nine courses distributed across five areas: writing and language; British literature; American literature; genre, criticism, and world literature; and cultural studies. English majors must also take a course on a major author—Chaucer, Milton, or Shakespeare—and two courses in British literature before 1900.

Trinity also offers Program II, which allows students to "examine and explore a topic, question, or theme as a core area of study which is not generally available as a course of study within Program I." Students in Program II are not held to the requirements of Program I, including the requirements for a major. Rather, a student submits, in consultation with an advisor, a written proposal to the appropriate academic department and to the Program II Committee, which approves or rejects the undertaking.

Students and faculty at Duke also teach special "house courses" on topics ranging from "The Grateful Dead" to "Marijuana Prohibition," "Juggling," and "Sweet Temptations: Women, Sex, and Food." House courses are offered pass/fail at half credit and students are only allowed to take two of them for credit.

Duke's department of literature used to be world famous for its enthusiastic endorsement of postmodernism, Marxism, and queer theory. Its fame has diminished, but literature students at Duke can still sample fare like "The Politics of Black Motherhood," "Why Hispanics Are Not White," and "Postmodern Lives: Labor, Sexuality, and Emotions in the Late Twentieth Century." While the English department offers a number of solid, traditional courses, the literature department focuses instead on "a unique interdisciplinary approach to the study of literature, film, and cultural forms. It enables students to engage in cross-cultural analysis" and "aims to train students to develop a sophisticated appreciation of the ways questions of race, class, gender, and sexuality arise in different historical and social contexts."

REQUIREMENTS (CONT'D)
■ Two courses in cross-cultural inquiry (identity, diversity, globalization, and power—"Advanced German Language and Culture" and "Roman History" both count, as well as the usual multicultural suspects); science, technology, and society, for which many science courses qualify; or ethical inquiry, which many humanities courses satisfy.
■ Three courses in a foreign language, or satisfactory performance on a test.
■ The freshman University Writing Course plus two writing-intensive courses from other disciplines, such as "Europe to the Eighteenth Century," "Modern Britain," and "The Rise of Modern Science," along with a great many others.
■ A research-intensive course like "The Philosophy of Religion" or "Principles of Animal Morphology," among others of less obvious value.

Political science is one of Duke's strongest departments, and if students choose the right teachers there, they will prosper. Standouts include Ruth Grant and Thomas Spragens Jr. in political theory, Peter D. Feaver in international relations, and Michael C. Munger, chair of the department and a political economist. Albert F. Eldridge and Michael Gillespie are also favorites. Most renowned by fellow academics is liberal internationalist Robert Keohane (Nan's husband); like Feaver, he is known as a tough grader.

SOUTH

Political science majors must take at least one course in each of the following areas: American government and politics; comparative government and politics; political theory; and international relations, law, and politics. They must also choose one of the areas as a concentration. According to numerous students, the excellent instruction in the political science department is tainted by the great power wielded by graduate teaching assistants, many of whom reportedly have difficulties with the English language.

Other good teachers at Duke, according to students, include James W. Applewhite, Ian Baucom, Buford Jones, Michael Valdez Moses, Thomas Pfau, Deborah Pope, Reynolds Price, Victor H. Strandberg, and Kenny J. Williams in English; Bruce Kuniholm, Alex Roland, and Peter Wood in history; Diskin Clay in classical studies; Michael Ferejohn, Martin Golding, and David Wong in philosophy; Alphonse Mutima in Swahili; Frank L. Borchardt in Germanic languages and literature; Richard E. Hodel in mathematics; and Craufurd Goodwin in economics. The influential and provocative Christian pacifist Stanley Hauerwas, who teaches in the religion department, was named "America's best theologian" by *Time* in 2001.

Duke's Department of Public Policy is an extremely politicized enclave within the university; many professors there live within a "liberal cocoon," one student complains. Classical studies is considered strong and squarely focused on sensible areas of inquiry.

In 2003 Duke's Department of Black Studies sponsored a guest appearance by "revolutionary anti-imperialist" and "political prisoner" Laura Whitehorn, who was incarcerated for 14 years for planting a bomb in the United States Capitol building. The university defended this appearance in the name of free speech.

In addition to departmental studies, Duke offers a certification program (interdisciplinary minors) in Marxism. The Marxism program's Web page says the curriculum includes "a critical appraisal of Marxist methods of analysis and their social implications, considered in the light of theoretical alternatives and changing historical circumstances. Topics covered include sexual and racial inequality, alienation, development and underdevelopment in the world system, labor processes, protest movements, and ideologies." The program is directed by Michael Hardt and Frederic Jameson. The study of Marxism was at its peak at Duke in the late 1980s and early '90s, but the collapse of the Soviet empire, coupled with the departure of some key professors, has taken a toll. "The steam has gone out of the Marxists," says one professor. "They used to have a lot of power, but now a lot of residual people like Fred Jameson are passé."

Academic advising at Duke is comprehensive, but it also places a good deal of responsibility on students. Freshmen are assigned advisors with whom they meet at least twice in the first semester. Some students say that this causes problems, since computer science professors, for instance, have little guidance to offer students who want to major in philosophy. After declaring a major (usually in the sophomore year), a student takes a faculty advisor within that major. At that point it is up to the student to take the initiative and gain all he can from the relationship. Unfortunately, most students visit advisors only once a semester, and that is only to obtain a PIN necessary for online registration.

Students do report, however, that many professors are willing to have discussions and even meals outside office hours. Some say that most faculty members are genuinely interested in teaching and helping undergraduates, but they also say that the vast majority of undergraduates show a lack of intellectual curiosity and very little interest in getting to know the faculty. One student takes the view that Duke students are "mostly there to get a ticket punched and attend some parties along the way." But one recent alumna says this anti-intellectual attitude varies from department to department, as economics and public policy majors are known for being inordinately interested in padding their résumés. Premed students are notorious grade-grubbers.

Professors teach most courses, but graduate teaching assistants sometimes teach introductory classes and often grade exams. University Writing (UWC), Duke's one required course, is usually taught by graduate students, who decide course content and class discussion. One student says UWC is a "complete waste of time" and is usually influenced by the instructors' own ideological biases. Introductory freshmen classes are often large (100 to 175 students), but by the junior and senior years, when most students are working on their majors, class sizes dwindle to a more manageable 25 or fewer.

Duke students can take advantage of the opportunities offered by other universities in the area, including the University of North Carolina at Chapel Hill, North Carolina State University in Raleigh, and North Carolina Central University in Durham. Students can take one course each semester at any of these institutions, but only if an equivalent course is not being offered at Duke during that calendar year.

Duke's William R. Perkins Library has more than 4.9 million volumes and is the eighth-largest among private universities in the United States. Duke participates in the Triangle Research Library Network, which opens the collections of the above universities to Duke students.

SUGGESTED CORE
1. Classical Studies 105, Ancient and Medieval Epic
2. Philosophy 100, History of Ancient Philosophy
3. Religion 100/102, The Old Testament / The New Testament
4. Religion 120, History of the Christian Church
5. Political Science 266, Early Modern Political Thought *or* Political Science 224, Modern Political Theory
6. English 143/144, Shakespeare before 1600 / Shakespeare after 1600
7. History 91D, Development of American Democracy to 1865
8. History 151E, European Intellectual History, 1848–1918

Student Life: Are you Charlotte Simmons?

Duke University is located in Durham, North Carolina, a town of almost 200,000 people making the transition from tobacco to technology. Lately the "Durham Renaissance" has resulted in new bars and restaurants close to Duke's East Campus. Durham still isn't a college town, but it's better now than it was a few years ago. Still, most students usually remain on campus, venturing into the surrounding areas only if they are upper-

SOUTH

415

classmen and have cars. On weekends, these students usually head to nearby Chapel Hill and its lively Franklin Street.

Duke's campus is not such a bad place to spend a lot of one's time, however, since it is undeniably one of the most beautiful universities in the country, both in its architecture and in the lovely flora that surrounds the campus. The Sarah P. Duke Gardens consist of 55 landscaped and wooded acres in the heart of campus. Duke Forest covers 7,700 acres and serves as an outdoor laboratory, a favorite picnic spot, and a jogging area.

Duke's two main campuses, the Georgian East Campus and the Gothic West Campus, are joined by a bus system. East Campus—once the all-women college—is where freshmen live. It has its own auditorium, gym, athletic fields, classrooms, art museum, and a few of the humanities departments. West Campus is the main campus and is home to most of the administration buildings and academic departments, upperclassmen dormitories and fraternities, athletic facilities, and other venues.

After the freshman year, housing is chosen by lottery; the most popular real estate is on West Campus, where all sophomores are now required to live and residents enjoy more convenient access to classes and social activities. Smoking is not allowed in any residence halls. Most dormitories are coed but divide the sexes by halls; there are no coed bathrooms. A single-sex dorm option is available for both male and female students. The university both guarantees and requires on-campus housing for the first three years, but it is expensive. As a result, half of seniors move off campus.

Two major campus events are Oktoberfest and Springfest, each of which brings bands and local vendors to the main quad. The Last Day of Classes bash brings a prominent musical artist to campus, entertaining students and giving them a chance to relax and blow off steam before finals begin.

Students say that alcohol use was "driven underground" by the administration after a student died a few years ago, having choked on his own vomit after a night of binge drinking. Fraternities and sororities at Duke must hire a university-approved bartender for all their parties and the school has been trying to provide more alternative, alcohol-free activities. Alcohol is forbidden on the freshman campus, and the policy is usually strictly enforced. When underage students drink—and they still do—they usually drink on West Campus, where drinking age laws are never enforced, and behind closed dorm-room doors. A sizable number of students smoke marijuana, the only illegal drug in wide use at the school.

Duke has a plethora of student groups of all types, and students are welcome to create another one if the university doesn't already offer it. Recently, a group of students formed a weekly debating club called the Duke Philodemic Society. The university also has a strong ROTC program. Other popular student organizations are the daily newspaper, the *Chronicle*; community service activities through the Circle K; the InterVarsity Christian Fellowship; musical groups; and various cultural organizations. Most student groups are housed in the Joseph M. and Kathleen Price Bryan Center, also home to student government offices.

A Multicultural Center recently opened—this in addition to the existing Williams

Center for Black Culture; the Women's Center; the International House; the Center for Lesbian, Gay, Bisexual and Transgender Life; and the Office of Institutional Equity. According to some students, the student body has become segregated as a result of the administration's support for "diversity," and students of different races rarely mix after freshman year, when students live next door to classmates of different religions, races, and cultures. Those students who choose to live in on-campus apartments, for instance, are usually black, while fraternities are mostly composed of upper-middle-class whites.

Although Duke has a reputation for liberalism, the student body as a whole is largely apolitical. Studying, playing sports, getting drunk, and having sex rank above political activism for most Dukies. Students on the extreme left are the most active, with liberal groups getting most of the administration's support and university funding. Rarely does a week at Duke pass without a task force report on racism, a panel on gender issues, a rally against sweatshops or the treatment of pickle factory workers, or the like. Groups like the Black Student Alliance, the Alliance of Queer Undergraduates at Duke (AQUADuke, once known as the Duke GLBT and later the Gothic Queers), and other "multicultural" groups receive significant university support.

In fact, Duke students are so apolitical that their 2002 administration building sit-in was not organized to protest anything in particular, but rather to commemorate a sit-in that took place in the good old days of '69. (Nostalgia just isn't what it used to be.) The featured speaker was a member of the administration who had been one of the original protesters. The vice president for student affairs, Larry Moneta, supported the exercise in Woodstock-era nostalgia as an opportunity for students to gain "enlightenment." "The current condition didn't come without work," he said, and "future conditions will only come with work." There were no arrests, but some students were less than appreciative. "Apparently, administrative representatives are endorsing the idea that students are entitled to take over buildings and disrupt the university as long as they feel strongly enough about some issue," one said, noting that Moneta "seems to be calling directly for students to undertake more radical actions (i.e., 'work') against his own administration." This complaint was perhaps a little naïve, as it might well have been the agenda of Moneta and the Keohane administration to use disruptive students to move the university further to the left than the majority of the faculty wanted to take it. If so, they failed.

Sports are the unifying activity at Duke. In men's basketball (and increasingly women's as well), Duke is always a strong contender for the national championship. Men's basketball players are gods on campus—gods who happen to attend class with you, even if they aren't taking notes. (See Tom Wolfe's creation, "JoJo Johanssen.") Coach Mike Krzyzewski is a living legend. The tent city that bears his name, Krzyzewskiville, is created each year before major home games, especially the one with archrival University of North Carolina. Admission works on a first-come, first-serve basis, so students get in line (in their tents) as early as a month before the game. Typically, Coach K delivers pizzas to camping students the night before the UNC game. Students also participate in intercollegiate club sports, competing against other area colleges and universities. A wide variety of intramural sports are available and these are especially popular with freshmen, who often organize teams according to their residence halls. Pick-up basketball games can always be found on both the East and West campuses.

One scandal regarding sports and sex discrimination appears to be winding down, with a victory for feminists: according to the *Chronicle of Higher Education*, a female Duke student who insisted on joining the football team in 1995 (she was a placekicker, not a linebacker) has been awarded $350,000 in legal fees, reimbursing her for the cost of suing the university after it removed her from the team. Whether this will result in a flood of female recruits to the football bench remains unclear.

Durham is prone to crime, though crime on campus decreased from 2002 to 2003. Forcible sex offenses went down from 10 to six, burglaries from 56 to 36, and referrals for drug violations from 45 to 20. East Campus and especially the Central Campus apartments are considered to be the most dangerous areas due to their proximity to the city center. But students who follow basic safety guidelines should generally feel comfortable. The university helps prevent campus crime by providing Safe Rides, a walking escort service, emergency phones, and card entry to all dormitories.

Duke is a pricey adventure, comparable to the most expensive schools in the northeast. Tuition in 2004–5 was $32,409; room and board, $8,830. However, admissions are need-blind, and all accepted students are guaranteed sufficient aid. Some 38 percent of students receive need-based aid, and the average student loan debt of 2003 graduates was $20,025.

EMORY UNIVERSITY

ATLANTA, GEORGIA • WWW.EMORY.EDU

A run for its money

Money can't buy everything, but you can't blame Emory University for trying. Drawing on a substantial endowment (in 2003, at around $4 billion, Emory's was the ninth-largest in the nation), Emory has made college life into a country club where students happen to attend classes. Look beyond the most obvious evidence of wealth—the new buildings, the technology, the lush green campus—and you'll find that Emory has spent money on less tangible items as well. Undergraduates enjoy a student-faculty ratio of just seven to one. Research opportunities and internships are available in nearly every discipline. Students can choose one of 70 majors. Money can buy a lot.

Still, about 170 years removed from its humble beginnings as a small Methodist college in Oxford, Georgia, Emory has shed much of its character and southern charm. Since its main campus moved to Atlanta in 1919, the school has seen a steady shift in priorities. The liberal arts now play second fiddle to career-driven disciplines, and classroom discussions between students and professors have become less important than research. Emory has many of the fine attributes of other top-notch schools, but between students, late-night philosophical tête-à-têtes are rare. Conversations on how to make money in investment banking are not.

Academic Life: The Emory boards

These days, the trend in academia is to let students themselves decide which courses will contribute to a broad education. Emory follows that trend: "The general education component of an Emory undergraduate education is organized to present an array of intellectual approaches and perspectives as ways of learning rather than a prescribed body of content," as the catalog puts it. Students may be paying $36,000 a year for the privilege, but at Emory, as elsewhere, they must chart their own paths. The school has no core curriculum and relatively anemic distribution man-

VITAL STATISTICS
Religious affiliation: United Methodist
Total enrollment: 11,781
Total undergraduates: 6,346
SAT/ACT midranges: SAT V: 640–720, M: 660–740; ACT: 29–33
Applicants: 10,372
Applicants accepted: 42%
Accepted applicants who enrolled: 29%
Tuition: $28,940
Room and board: $9,650
Freshman retention rate: 93%
Graduation rate: 84% (4 yrs.), 88% (6 yrs.)
Courses with fewer than 20 students: 64%
Student-faculty ratio: 7:1
Courses taught by graduate TAs: 10%
Most popular majors: social sciences, business, communications
Students living on campus: 70%
Guaranteed housing for four years? no
Students in fraternities: 28% sororities: 31%

SOUTH

419

In lieu of a core curriculum, Emory offers some loose distribution requirements. Each student must take:

- Freshman writing, either a basic composition course or a section of "Writing About Literature."
- Three courses designated as "writing-intensive."
- One course in mathematics or computer science.
- Two natural science courses (including at least one laboratory course).
- Two classes in the social sciences. Students can choose "Principles of Microeconomics," "Introduction to Gay and Lesbian Studies," "National Politics in the United States," "Introduction to General Psychology," or "Sociology of Sex and Gender," among others.
- Two courses in the humanities (one in evaluating texts and one in the arts). Choices include "Dostoevsky in English Translation," "Fictions of Human Desire," "Introduction to Classical Mythology," "History of Film since 1938," and dozens of other classes.

dates. Emory's "requirements are quite minimal and the 'fields' are very broadly defined," one professor says. "I'm sure it's quite easy to avoid courses that should be fundamental to a true liberal arts education. The laxness of the [general education requirements] may be a blessing in disguise, however, insofar as students may avoid being forced by the college to take unserious or trendy classes, which abound here as elsewhere among elite universities."

Luckily for students, Emory has pumped a good deal of its money into improving teaching at the school. Students say introductory courses (especially in biology or chemistry) can be as large as 100 students, but others are as small as four or five. Every student is required to take at least two seminars—one as a freshman and one as an upperclassman. Ninety percent of courses are taught by faculty members. However, most of the freshman English seminars are taught by graduate students—meaning that where students arguably need the guidance of professors the most, Emory doesn't provide it. However, "professors are extremely open to helping students, but also to just getting to know them outside of class," says one student. Honors theses, independent study, and research projects allow students to get to know faculty members in more formal academic relationships. Professors are required to hold weekly office hours, which students often make use of, if not for talking about ideas, then at least for improving their grades. "Emory students are generally characterized by professional ambition more than by intellectual curiosity, and there is much obsession with grades (as opposed to the work required to get them)," says a social sciences professor. Another professor says, "Most *are* obsessed with grades, but they're gifted and talented too, and are usually willing to do the necessary work to get the high grades. They have to be preoccupied by grades, in a way, because advancing to further education often depends on them. . . . Only a handful in a given year love the discussion of ideas for their own sake."

Advising begins with the Freshman Advising and Mentoring at Emory (FAME) program, which groups about 18 freshmen with a faculty advisor. Once a student declares a major, usually as a sophomore, he is assigned to a faculty advisor within that department. Advisors are usually helpful if students need them, but it is often the students' responsibility to seek them out. "Students must use their good judgment, or the guidance of a good teacher, rather than depend on Emory for guidance," says one professor.

Among Emory's strongest departments are political science, psychology, English, history, anthropology, and biology. Philosophy—particularly political philosophy—is also well respected. "Every professor in the philosophy department is great—very intelligent, and an excellent teacher," a student says. Philosophy majors are required to take an introductory logic course, two "History of Western Philosophy" courses, and a senior seminar. With a slate of excellent topics among the department's course offerings, students should have no trouble choosing electives. The English major calls for a course in poetry, two courses in English literature before 1660 and two after 1660, and two in American literature. Class offerings, for the most part, are solid, especially in British literature. Emory is one of only a few top-level schools with a dance and movement studies major, which it includes among the liberal arts and sciences. Those with an abiding interest in violence will be disappointed to learn that Emory has just discontinued its "violence studies" program.

In academic life, Emory is predictable enough that students looking for an education rather than indoctrination can pretty easily avoid problem areas—such as the interdisciplinary studies in culture and society department. One professor vividly describes it as "politicized to the tee with gay and lesbian material and postmodern crap." Some of the department's course offerings bear out the professor's choice of words: "The Politics of Identity," "Language, Space, and Embodied Experience," "North African and Arab Women Writers and the Narrative of War," and "Society, Culture, and Sexuality." One student says courses in the interdisciplinary studies department have an "abnormally easy reputation, and students take [them] with the intention of an easy A."

After a few introductory courses in women's studies and feminist thought, students majoring in women's studies can choose electives like "Language, Gender, and Power," "Multicultural History of Women in the United States," "Gender Politics," and "Lesbian, Gay, Queer Studies," which examines "lesbian/gay/queer histories and cultures, through the study of literature, film, archival sources, oral histories, and contemporary scholarship" and considers "identity, representation, gender, race, class, community development, [and] political movements," according to its course description. But the department isn't completely hopeless; Elizabeth Fox-Genovese, author of *Feminism Is Not the Story of My Life*, teaches in the department (as well as in the history department), with emphases in the areas of comparative women's history; the antebellum South; and cultural, literary, and intellectual history. Her scholarship has helped

REQUIREMENTS (CONT'D)

- One class in United States history. Choices, all of them worthy, range from "Foundations of American Society" to "History of African Americans since 1865."
- One class in "historical perspectives on Western culture." Options here include "The High Middle Ages, 1000–1350" and "The Formation of European Society: From Late Antiquity through the Early Modern Era."
- One course in "non-Western cultures or comparative and international studies." Good options here include "Ancient Mediterranean Societies" and "Introduction to Religion."
- Two courses in a foreign language.

expand the reach of her discipline beyond the narrow, bitter identity politics of sex.

Emory has almost as many graduate or professional school students as it does undergraduates. The powerful professional schools can't be ignored, says one professor, "with the massive medical school tail sometimes wagging the dog."

A two-year program for underclassmen is offered through Oxford College on Emory's original campus, 45 minutes east of Atlanta. With only 600 or so students on campus, Oxford students form stronger bonds with their classmates than they would in Emory College, but those classmates won't be quite as smart. The average SATs for incoming Oxford freshmen tend to be about 150 points below those of their Emory College counterparts.

Among the best teachers at Emory are Patrick N. Allitt, Elizabeth Fox-Genovese, and James Melton in history; Juan del Aguila, Robert C. Bartlett, Merle Black, Harvey E. Klehr, Randall W. Strahan, and Carrie R. Wickham in political science; Mark Bauerlein in English; Marshall P. Duke in psychology; Donald W. Livingston and Donald Phillip Verene in philosophy; Frank J. Lechner in sociology; and Paul H. Rubin in economics.

Student Life: The real thing

Every corner of the Emory campus smells of money. If building projects are a sign of progress, Emory must be doing very well indeed. The main and oldest part of campus is a quadrangle of pink and gray Georgia marble buildings separated by a long green lawn. On warm, sunny days (and there are plenty of those in Atlanta) students have classes here, study, play Frisbee, and talk with friends. For the number of people who study at the university, Emory has a remarkable number of buildings; the visitor cannot help but be impressed by the size of the campus. And although the school's location in urban Atlanta makes expansion rather difficult, Emory has found room in other areas. The university just completed its Clairmont campus about a mile from the main campus—students have to take a shuttle bus to reach it. But that's a small annoyance for those upperclassmen lucky enough to live there. "It looks like a country club," says one student. "We have apartments, tennis courts, cafes. My parents think I'm getting spoiled." The Cox Computer Center offers rows and rows of equipment; some workstations have two large monitors for every computer. "There's almost no reason for a student to bring a computer to campus," says one student. "There are probably two computers for every student here already."

Freshmen and sophomores are required to live on campus, and upperclassmen usually choose to live there as well. Life on campus is convenient; traffic in Atlanta is horrible, and off-campus apartments can get expensive. Except for freshmen, who live together in traditional dormitories, Emory students usually enjoy suite-style residences or on-campus apartments close to most of the academic buildings. Students select their freshman roommates online through a sort of personals service where they list their interests and expectations in a roommate. There is one all-women residence hall and several single-sex-by-floor residences, as well as several dormitories where men live next door to women.

Students have practically every dining option available to them on campus—but only one kind of soft drink. At orientation, freshmen participants are sent on a treasure hunt where they are told to find a can of Pepsi. It's a trick assignment, because it can't be done. One of the first gifts to Emory, a.k.a. "Coca-Cola University," came in 1914 from Asa Candler, the president of the Coca-Cola Company; his brother was president of the university at the time. In 1979, two brothers gave Emory more than $100 million dollars in Coca-Cola stock, and presently, a third of the endowment is invested in the company. "We watch the Coca-Cola stocks pretty closely," says a student.

Emory has no football team, and students say school spirit is rather meager in part because of that fact. Any attention paid to sports is usually directed towards the soccer and basketball teams or to intramurals, which are very popular. Emory students are required to complete four one-credit physical education courses, beginning with a "wellness and lifestyle management" course taken during the freshman year. And no country club is complete without fine fitness facilities; the George W. Woodruff Physical Education Center (known as WoodPEC to students) boasts an Olympic-sized swimming pool, basketball and racquetball courts, a climbing wall, an indoor track, weight machines, and exercise machines. When Atlanta hosted the Olympic games in 1996, Emory served as a practice facility.

The city of Atlanta is a draw for many prospective Emory students, but once they get to campus, many find that they visit the rest of the city less frequently than they had expected. The university itself has nearly everything a student could require, and the area surrounding campus, particularly Emory Village, with its restaurants and bars, has everything else. But downtown Atlanta is just a MARTA rail ride away. Students can often purchase reduced-rate tickets on campus to art exhibits and cultural performances throughout the city. Then there's the Marco C. Carlos Museum, Emory's on-campus art facility, with a fine permanent collection and interesting traveling exhibits each year.

Nearly 30 percent of students are members of fraternities or sororities, and Greek organizations provide most of the activities for weekend social life. "Greek life is strong here, but because we don't have houses, it's not as intense as it is at most other schools," says one student. Parties and drinking are prevalent on campus. "Because the majority of students are affluent, they are able to buy a lot of alcohol and throw big parties," one student says. "But most students' primary goal is academics and grades—when those are satisfied, anything else goes."

One of Emory's most active political groups is the College Republicans, which brought David Horowitz, Ben Stein, and J. C. Watts to campus recently. So ubiquitous

SUGGESTED CORE

1. Classics 101, The Hero and Anti-Hero in Classical Epic and Art
2. Philosophy 250, History of Western Philosophy I
3. Religion 150, Introduction to Sacred Texts (*closest match*)
4. Religion 230, Early and Medieval Christianity
5. Political Science 302, Modern Political Thought
6. English 311, Shakespeare
7. History 231, Foundations of American Society: Beginnings to 1877
8. History 376, European Intellectual History, 1789–1880

SOUTH

423

has been the College Republicans' presence of late that it has surprised many Emory students, including the president of the Young Democrats, who writes in a September 2003 *Wheel* editorial, "For me, all of this right-wing hoopla made me feel a little annoyed. But more than annoyed, I felt underrepresented, quiet, and probably pretty afraid. I felt thoroughly and honestly defeated. The people involved with the College Republicans have always said the conservative voice on Emory's campus is consistently overlooked, and they made it their mission to be loud last year. They were. The campus heard them."

Emory's Cannon Chapel is the site of an ecumenical worship service every Sunday morning and a Catholic mass every Sunday morning and evening. The chapel is sparse; its sign—not its architecture—identifies it as a church, and inside it looks more like a lecture hall than a place of worship. Religious student organizations abound and include Baptist Campus Ministry, Emory Christian Fellowship, Orthodox Campus Ministry, Catholic Campus Ministry, and many others. But although Emory is in the Bible Belt, it does not have the feel of a religious school. The city of Atlanta provides plenty of opportunities for students to serve in the community, including via Emory Reads (a literacy program), Habitat for Humanity, hospital volunteering, and high school tutoring.

Crime is a drawback for most other Atlanta schools, but Emory is located in the relatively safe Druid Hills neighborhood. The most common crime is burglary: 25 occurred on campus in 2003, as did five forcible sex offenses, five robberies, five aggravated assaults, 11 car thefts, and a shocking 32 arsons—a significant uptick in most categories over the year before. There are emergency phones all over campus. One female student says, "I've never felt unsafe, so I've never had to use them, but it's nice to know they're there."

Emory is upscale in its tuition as in every other way, charging $28,940, with room and board averaging $9,650. However, admissions are need-blind, and Emory promises to offer full aid to accepted students. Some 73 percent of students receive aid.

UNIVERSITY OF FLORIDA

GAINESVILLE, FLORIDA • WWW.UFL.EDU

Swamped

The University of Florida is a major public land-grant re-search university—the state's oldest and most comprehen-sive. Located in rural northern Florida, the city of Gainesville revolves around the campus and its student population.

In the 1860s, the state-funded East Florida Seminary in Ocala was consolidated with the state's land-grant Florida Agricultural College in Lake City. In 1905, the college be-came a university and was moved to Gainesville, where the first classes were held in 1906. The university became a co-educational institution in 1947. And today it is one of the five largest universities in the nation, with almost 48,000 students. Despite its overwhelming size and location in the middle of a swamp (but less than one or two hours away from various beaches), the University of Florida maintains academic excellence by being somewhat more selective in its admissions than other massive public universities. Still, the large student population, the popularity of Gator foot-ball, and a pervasive party atmosphere have a way of dis-tracting many students—and others—from the university's academic mission.

Academic Life: End around

The University of Florida has no core curriculum. Instead, it offers general education requirements. These are aimed at helping the student attain "competency in goals and meth-ods in the humanities, physical and biological sciences, mathematics, and social and behavioral sciences." It sounds like a good idea, but the general education requirements are in fact not very demanding.

If students want a traditional liberal arts education, they must pick and choose carefully, for while one can fulfill the education require-ments, including the international/diversity requirement with substantial courses rooted in the best traditions of the West, there are dozens of courses such as "Ecofeminism," "Seminar in Gay and Lesbian Literature," "Sex Roles: A Cross-Cultural

VITAL STATISTICS
Religious affiliation: none
Total enrollment: 47,993
Total undergraduates: 33,694
SAT/ACT midranges: SAT V: 570–670, M: 590–690; ACT: 25–29
Applicants: 22,458
Applicants accepted: 53%
Accepted applicants who enrolled: 57%
Tuition: $2,955 (in state), $15,827 (out of state)
Room and board: $6,040
Freshman retention rate: 94%
Graduation rate: 51% (4 yrs.), 78% (6 yrs.)
Courses with fewer than 20 students: 37%
Student-faculty ratio: 23:1
Courses taught by graduate TAs: not provided
Most popular majors: business, social sciences, engineering
Students living on campus: 22%
Guaranteed housing for four years? no
Students in fraternities: 15% sororities: 15%

Perspective," and "Women, Race, and Imperialism" that can also count as electives toward a degree, and half the classes students take in their four years are electives. Students are encouraged to use these electives as it suits their degree emphasis, but six courses at the junior and senior level have to be taken outside a student's major. An economics professor says that "students have a broad selection of courses, given the size of the university," and while a "student seeking a strong major that promotes critical thinking can blossom," so also can a "student seeking an easy way through the credentialist system . . . graduate, but that is hard to stop."

The University of Florida also must comply with the state-mandated "Gordon Rule," a requirement for which the students of the University of Florida can thank former state senator John Gordon—or, perhaps, his daughters. They graduated from a Florida university, and, according to their father, their college education did not include teaching them how to write. So in 1982 he cosponsored legislation the goal of which was to ensure that all students graduating from a public university in Florida learn how to write, demanding that current Florida students achieve competence in "communication" and "computation." To meet the communication requirement, students must receive a C or better in courses that involve substantial writing. Courses are designated as requiring zero, 2,000, 4,000, or 6,000 words. The goal (and the requirement) is to have students write at least 24,000 words before graduation.

While the policy may seem lofty, the rule's benefits only come when it is wisely applied—in other words, when the university ensures that the majority of the 24,000 words are well written and worthwhile. "The general education requirements, in my opinion, dilute the education received in this university," a business student says. "Students take the most vapid courses in the university to meet the requirements, such as 'Wildlife Issues' for a bio credit, 'Astronomy' for physical education credit, or 'Music Literature' to get 6,000 words toward the Gordon Rule."

Sometimes students fall into these "vapid" courses not because they want to bypass more serious options, but because the courses they want are not available—the downside of attending such a large public institution. One student says that since "there are few electives offered per semester . . . students have to settle for a class they didn't want to get into in order to graduate." This student bemoans the lack of faculty in some departments. Indeed, there are 23 students for every UF faculty member, not a good ratio even for such a large school. "The extremely low tuition means that a number of courses are large lectures, but junior- and senior-level courses are kept relatively small," a professor says.

Despite UF's size, a psychology major says, "professors are very accessible as far as I have seen. Most professors post office hours and all are required to have office hours at some point during the week." Although the university attracts a number of good students (the university Web site says 77 percent of those admitted were in the top 10 percent of their high school classes, but doesn't give the percentage for those who actually enrolled), students "often do not take advantage of office hours," a professor says. The problem is worst in the large lecture classes, however. One student in the Honors College says that all of her professors have been very friendly. However, she says that "the larger classes are less 'personal' and therefore there is less contact with the instructor."

Graduate teaching assistants often assist with large lecture classes. A psychology major says, "The role of the TA depends on the professor. In some classes the TA is there to answer all questions by the students, grade exams and quizzes, and hold review sessions." Another student says that the role of TAs varies depending on the subject matter. About 20 percent of her classes have been taught by TAs and sometimes the "system seemed to work very well." Yet a student in the business department says "many students complain about how bad some TAs are with dissemination of information, heavy accents, and lack of communication." Nearly all upper-division courses are taught by professors.

University leadership is aware of the complaints by many students regarding the lack of quality educators during certain phases of their education. At the start of 2004, the university saw the installation of a new president, James Bernard Machen, who seems committed to reforming the school. Along with flamboyant gestures such as a Harley-Davidson ride through the campus to promote voter registration, Machen has worked to increase funding for teaching—instituting a $150 million dollar, multiyear fundraising campaign to be used for graduate studies, faculty research, salaries and benefits. The fundraising campaign is part of the larger goal to make the University of Florida a top-10 school through the improvement of faculty, raising academic standards, and—lest anyone forget—enshrining "diversity" at the university as a top priority. Well, as Meat Loaf once sang, two out of three ain't bad.

Advising is the responsibility of each college, and therefore the quality varies from college to college. The Academic Advising Center serves the whole university. It consists of professional advisors, not faculty, who help students choose majors and satisfy course requirements. In some departments and colleges, students must meet with an advisor before they can register for courses for the following semester, while other departments and colleges have a faculty advisor on staff, available for students who voluntarily seek his or her assistance.

The Honors Program "seeks to provide the richness of a small-college experience with the vast resources of a major research university,"

ACADEMIC REQUIREMENTS

With no core curriculum in place, UF imposes certain loose general education requirements:

- Composition (three credits).
- Mathematical sciences (six credits). Three credits must be from approved mathematics courses; the other three may be approved courses outside of the mathematics department, such as computer science.
- Humanities (nine credits).
- Social and behavioral sciences (nine credits).
- Physical and biological sciences (nine credits).
- International/diversity focus (six credits). These six credits are not in addition to the 36 general education credits listed above but instead are to be used to satisfy some of those requirements. This requirement is not as politicized as one might guess. For example, a student who wanted to fulfill a humanities requirement and a social and behavioral sciences requirement could also fulfill the international/ diversity focus requirement by registering for a language course or enrolling in a class such as "The Bible as Literature."

SOUTH

427

according to the university. The program offers smaller classes, special honors sections of large courses, exclusive dorms, program-dedicated advisors, and a unique social and academic community for elite students during their first two years on campus. That said, some of the special courses offered in this program strike us as more quirky than "core"—for instance "The Tao of Star Trek," "An Introduction to Theories and Methods in Hiphop Cultural Studies," and "History of Rock and Roll." In other words, even UF honors students should not expect a great books education along with that fantastic tan. However, the Honors Program does offer an alternative to massive classes and impersonal sections led by teaching assistants.

In the classroom, professors seem to allow students to express a variety of opinions without fear. And while the faculty, unsurprisingly, leans leftward, a number of conservative professors can also be found. More importantly, an atmosphere of freedom seems to prevail. One such faculty member says, "I have been here for over 30 years and am not aware of anyone's being turned away or hounded after being hired for political views. Occasionally a student protests the professor's foisting his or her opinions in class."

Some of the best academic programs at Florida include business, nursing, journalism, psychology, education, engineering, agriculture, and microbiology. Solid professors include Stephen McKnight in history; Sanford V. Berg and David A. Denslow in economics; Thomas Auxter in philosophy; Richard Conley, David M. Hedge, and William A. Kelso in political science; Mary E. Collins in soil and water sciences; Bonnie Moradi and Carolyn Tucker in psychology; William Marsiglio and Hernan Vera in sociology; and Gordon E. Greenwood and Rodman B. Webb in educational psychology.

The intellectual curiosity of the student body flickers, with some bright spots. A faculty member says, "I see the spectrum: village idiots to intensely motivated students." A student says, "Most talk is of football and parties and how drunk one got the night before. But then of course, there are groups and clubs on campus that provide intellectual stimulation." He adds, "This university is what you make of it. You can get a high-quality education if you choose to, by taking hard, challenging courses and professors that stimulate your interest. However, I have seen that most students do not do this and basically slide into graduation and a degree."

Student Life: In the sun

Gainesville is a college town. The mild winters and hot summers allow for outdoor activities year-round, and there are beaches within an hour's drive (though popular destinations such as Daytona Beach, Orlando, Tampa, Jacksonville, and St. Augustine are all within two hours' drive). Ninety percent of students are Florida residents. And when there's no football game or other activity to keep them around campus, students tend to go home on the weekends.

However, football is the life of the party at UF. On Saturdays in the fall, the Gators attract about 85,000 fans into Ben Hill Griffin Stadium, otherwise known as "The Swamp." UF has a very physically active student body, so it should come as no shock that this large, southern university prides itself on being consistently ranked among the top five NCAA programs in the nation in overall athletics for both men's and women's sports. In recent years, the revived men's basketball program has become a focal point of school spirit as well. Parties tend to revolve around Gator football and basketball games. "Football games basically shut down the campus on Saturdays, and parties are ubiquitous," a student says.

Gator Growl, an annual pep rally held before the homecoming game, brings to campus nationally recognized comedians and musicians. A full weekend of parties takes off from there. One student recalls visiting UF "during Gator Growl and instantly knew I wanted to come here. The school you see with your parents is not always the school you see on the weekend." Fortunately, UF is big enough to accommodate students who do not want to concentrate all their extracurricular time on football-watching or drinking. "Whatever you like doing, you will find," a student says. "If you dig the Greeks, we have them; if you like clubs, we have enough to make your head spin; if you like museums and performing arts, we have them; if you like clubbing, we have it—although the quality and variety is debatable; if you like movies, we have those too." Every Friday, the Student Government Association sponsors Gator Night at the Reitz Student Union as an alternative for students looking for fun away from the party scene. Usually, there is a midnight movie followed by free breakfast.

While most freshmen live on campus, only about 22 percent of the entire student body does. With the exception of Mallory Hall, which is just for women, all other on-campus residences are coed. However, male and female students are not allowed to share a dorm room and do not share bathrooms. (Actually, Florida law prohibits male and female students from cohabitation in on-campus apartments unless they are married.) With minimal space available on campus, the university does not guarantee housing for all four years. But Gainesville itself provides comfortable quarters and a welcoming ambience for students, as the city revolves around student life. Students at UF tend to pay a good bit of attention to their physical appearance, and the Florida sunshine lets them flaunt it. One more modest female student says, "I feel a little uncomfortable walking through campus while all of the girls are dressed in practically nothing."

Political activism on campus is surprisingly balanced. Students are not activists, but both conservative and liberal perspectives are regularly aired on a range of topics. Students typically voice their discontent not in the classroom, but rather in the mainstream student newspaper, the *Florida Alligator*, or through gatherings in Turlington Plaza to plug for this or that cause, movement, or idea.

The most hotly contested topic of local interest during the last few years con-

SUGGESTED CORE

1. Classics 2100, The Glory that Was Greece
2. Philosophy 3100, Ancient Greek Philosophy
3. Religion 2210/2240: Hebrew Scriptures / New Testament
4. Religion 3500, History of Christianity
5. Political Science 4053, Great Political Thinkers: Machiavelli to Marx
6. English 4333, Shakespeare
7. History 2010, United States History to 1877
8. Philosophy 4644, Continental Philosophy

cerned Gov. Jeb Bush's push to end race-based admissions throughout the state of Florida. In 1999, Bush signed an executive order "eliminating race and ethnicity as factors in college and university admissions" starting in 2001. In 2002, the UF administration responded by announcing it would accept the top 5 percent of each high school graduating class in the state—in the hope that this would "diversify" the campus. In the first year of this plan's implementation, the university accepted about 300 students who otherwise would not have qualified; that same year, UF denied admission to about half of its 26,000 applicants—a case of inequity which seems to recreate the worst abuses alleged to result from quotas. The same year saw a 43 percent increase in minority enrollment, much to the enthusiasm of those who believed the state was not doing enough to atone for past discrimination.

Only 15 percent of students join a fraternity or sorority, but there are more than 450 student clubs and organizations, as well as some 60 intramural sports in which to participate, all of which help make this giant university seem a little cozier. In addition, there is a remarkably vivid religious presence on campus. Besides the usual Turlington Plaza preachers, thousands of students, and even some faculty, join religious groups—embracing Christian, Hindu, Muslim, Jewish, and other faiths.

Crime on and off campus is increasing, nearly doubling from 2002 to 2003, something that surprises many of those that considered Gainesville a relatively isolated town. The year of 2003 saw 55 on-campus burglaries, 12 forcible sex offenses, two aggravated assaults, one robbery, and one arson in the residence halls. The university provides a free pick-up service for any students who feel uncomfortable walking on campus, as well as emergency stations around campus. One female student says that usually "an officer will be there within 30 seconds." For the most part, students feel safe, but they are also cautious about dangers like date rape drugs and walking alone at night.

The University of Florida is generally considered affordable, and for those students seeking aid, plenty of options are available. The tuition for in-state students in 2004–5 was $2,955, and $15,827 for those out of state; room and board were $6,040. Says one student, "The good thing about UF is that for many Florida residents with good test scores, [a state merit] scholarship pays full tuition and cost of books. I know many friends who are at UF specifically for this reason." Freshmen enter UF with an average need-based loan of $2,971 and total gift aid averaging $4,799.

FURMAN UNIVERSITY

Un-conventional

Though Furman University is now religiously independent, its Baptist heritage defines the school. Furman was founded in 1826 by the South Carolina Baptist Convention and named for the prominent preacher, organizer, and southern secessionist Richard Furman. When Furman University broke formal ties with the Baptist convention 166 years later, some alumni and professors feared that this move marked the beginning of the school's secularization—sending it down the worldly path to prestige already trod by Duke, Vanderbilt, and Emory, all of which started out as similarly faith-based institutions. Indeed, over the past two decades, Furman has risen steadily in reputation; once an excellent regional university, Furman is now one of the top liberal arts schools in the nation. Happily, it still maintains many of the things that have made it stand out, such as a strong religious tradition, close faculty-student interaction, and a true liberal arts curriculum. Students hail from more than 46 states and 31 foreign countries (in 2004), but the college draws a third of its students from the state of South Carolina and around 75 percent from the Southeast. Perhaps that is one reason Furman has retained a unique atmosphere and fairly traditional orientation. In fact, if the reports of students and professors there can be trusted, Furman is one of the friendliest schools included in this guide.

Academic Life: Doing serious well

Leaders at Furman have long sought to establish the university as a serious liberal arts institution and have crafted a solid curriculum worthy of the school's good name. "Furman does 'serious' well," a professor says. "Fully 50 percent of the requirements for graduation are required courses and all of those are solid academically. Furman is committed to the traditional liberal arts." Although some students occasionally complain that the school's general education requirements involve too many classes, most students seem to realize the benefits. "You're going to be able to stick your toes in a lot of

VITAL STATISTICS
Religious affiliation: none
Total enrollment: 3,359
Total undergraduates: 2,807
SAT/ACT midranges: SAT V: 580–690, M: 590–680; ACT: 25–30
Applicants: 3,849
Applicants accepted: 58%
Accepted applicants who enrolled: 33%
Tuition: $25,888
Room and board: $6,912
Freshman retention rate: 92%
Graduation rate: 77% (4 yrs.), 84% (6 yrs.)
Courses with fewer than 20 students: 55%
Student-faculty ratio: 12:1
Courses taught by graduate TAs: none
Most popular majors: social sciences, business, visual arts
Students living on campus: 90%
Guaranteed housing for four years? yes
Students in fraternities: 35% sororities: 40%

Although there is no core curriculum, Furman's general education requirements are relatively strong. Only a handful of courses satisfy each of these requirements, so although "Race and Ethnic Relations" is offered in the sociology department, it cannot contribute to a student's general education social science requirement. Only good, broad introductory classes in economics, education, political science, psychology, sociology, and anthropology—fulfill the following requirements:

- A basic English composition course, where "the thematic emphasis in each section varies," but "all sections focus on expository and argumentative writing, with particular attention to analytical strategies, grammatical correctness, and organizational methods."
- A three-course humanities sequence: "The Roots of Western Civilization," "The Search for New Authorities," and "Revolution, Progress, and Anxiety."

different areas and see what you like and what you don't," says one student.

While Furman administrators may hope to increase its national visibility, they seem to realize that big grants and research projects are less important than undergraduate teaching. Furman is a university—and not a college—only because of its two small graduate programs: a master of science degree in the department of chemistry, and a master of arts degree through the department of education. Classes are taught entirely by faculty members, including the English composition courses, which other universities pass off to harried graduate students. The student-faculty ratio is 12 to 1. Introductory classes usually have approximately 25 to 30 students, while upper-level courses in the major often include only 10 students per class. The largest classes, according to students, are the humanities sequence courses, with around 100 students. However, these courses also meet in smaller sections during the week—again, with a professor, not a teaching assistant. Business and political science classes, two popular areas at Furman, may be larger than those in other departments. "The professors at Furman are excellent," says a junior psychology major. "They are very approachable. I really enjoy my classes." Strong professor-student interaction encourages undergrads to be genuinely interested in coursework rather than just in making the grade. "Furman students are curious and motivated," says one professor.

Furman students have plenty of opportunity for extra help, should they need it. The Center for Learning and Collaboration, a writing lab and technology help center, is frequented by students. On-campus tutoring is free. Furman's James B. Duke Library, named for one of Duke University's founders, was recently renovated to allow for a capacity of 800,000 volumes and to provide wireless Internet access throughout the building. An interlibrary loan with area libraries can get books to Furman in a couple of days, and a Furman identification card permits students to use the library at any college in South Carolina.

Along with a classroom approach to the liberal arts and sciences, Furman also promotes something that it calls "engaged learning," encouraging students to participate in internships in the Greenville area to supplement their classroom experiences. Students can often receive course credit for the internships. According to the *Chronicle of Higher Education*, Furman offers two courses, "Medical Sociology" and "Medical Ethics," which combine internships at local hospitals with intensive study of the philosophical and social implications of medical practice. Students attend lectures, view films, discuss books—and work in any of 11 clinics at hospitals, including neurosurgery and neonatal intensive care. Meeting patients and working with them gives students insights into medical practice "in a way that I can't express to them," says one professor. Preprofessional courses in business administration, accounting, and music performance are also encouraged. On top of what's offered at the Career Services Center, Furman students find their job prospects strengthened by a strong alumni network.

The strongest departments at Furman are chemistry, psychology, and political science, while faculty members say physics, theater, and sociology are among the weaker areas. Students say some of the best teachers at the school are T. Lloyd Benson and David S. Spear in history; Stanley J. H. Crowe in English; David H. Bost and Alvin L. Prince in modern languages and literatures; Jonathan Grieser in religion; Paul R. Rasmussen in psychology; and Silas N. Pearman III in health and exercise science.

Furman uses what it calls a "modified trimester calendar"; students take three courses in the fall, two courses (five days a week) in the winter, and three courses in the spring. "The winter 'crunch time' is difficult, but the calendar makes classwork very manageable. You only have a few classes on your plate at any time," says a junior accounting major.

Student Life: Everyone's home

Furman left the South Carolina Baptist Convention in 1992, leading some on campus to worry about the school's religious identity. "Furman is on the slippery slope to secularism," warns one professor. "We are still very traditional, but the administration is not committed to maintaining a Christian identity." Although there is no religion requirement in the curriculum, and while Furman is nondenominational, it is not quite secular. The Charles E. Daniel Memorial Chapel, with its cross-topped steeple, looks like a small town's First Baptist Church, and it is one of the most promi-

REQUIREMENTS (CONT'D)

Instead of this humanities sequence, students may take one introductory history course, one introductory religion course, and one literature course (in English or a foreign language). Of course, we recommend the humanities sequence.

- One additional humanities course in the classics, English, history, a foreign language, philosophy, religion, or theatre arts.
- One to three courses in mathematics (depending on the student's precollege achievement).
- Two courses in the natural sciences.
- Two in the social sciences.
- One in the fine arts.
- One in health and exercise science.
- At least one course in the university's Asian-African program, which offers about 40 from which to choose. Among them are "Religions of the World," "Chinese Philosophy," and "History of the Modern Middle East," so students are likely to find solid fare here, too.

Students must also demonstrate intermediate proficiency in a foreign language, either through coursework or test scores.

SOUTH

433

nent buildings on campus. It holds a university worship service each Sunday morning and a Catholic mass each Sunday evening, although one student reports that there is an underlying tension between Catholics and Protestants on campus. The dining hall displays the words "Unto thee, O God, do we give thanks" and "Give us this day our daily bread." The Baptist Collegiate Ministry is still the largest student group on campus, hosting a "Tuesday Night Together" Bible study each week and mission trips, retreats, and concerts throughout the year. One Catholic student says religious activities are there if you want them, but "you're certainly not going to feel persecuted if you don't." A student-led Religious Council oversees the university's various ministry groups, of which there are several; in addition to the Baptist Student Union, Young Life, a new Orthodox Christian Fellowship, and the (Catholic) Newman Apostolate are also active. To find out what students are doing with their time, visit the selection of Web logs maintained by the University on its home page, at www.engagefurman.com/diary.

Furman students fill life outside of the classroom with countless activities—from parties to academic clubs to community service work. But students say they spend most of their free time socializing with friends in their rooms. Furman is a residential campus, and with the recent completion of several new halls, the university now requires that students live on campus for all four years of college. Freshmen and sophomores usually dwell in traditional corridor-style halls or suites, while upperclassmen can use the school's on-campus apartments as a transition into life after graduation. "There's really no reason that you'd even want to live off campus—there are so many different choices in housing," says a senior. Before Furman's split with the Baptists, men lived on one side of campus and women lived on the other, but today most dormitories are coed by floor—men live on one floor, women on the next. Furman is still traditional enough that students are permitted in the rooms of members of the opposite sex only during visitation hours—10 a.m. to 2 a.m. daily—and must be escorted by a resident. Freshmen arrive on campus a week before classes start and compete on teams with dorm mates, building camaraderie and school spirit. A highlight of the week is a meet-and-greet party with the university president. Students are matched up, almost randomly, with dates for the event.

Since Furman moved to its present campus in 1957, no building is more than 50 years old. Most of the buildings are of red brick, but while none are jarringly ugly, the beauty of the campus comes from nature, not architecture. The grounds are well-shaded with a great variety of arboreta—walkways are lined with magnolia, pine, and oak trees. The main focus of the campus is a 30-acre man-made lake, which dozens of ducks and geese call home. Running trails and picnic tables surround the lake and the dining hall shows off excellent views of the water. On one small peninsula stands the Bell Tower, a replica of a tower that once stood on Furman's earlier downtown campus. A college tradition calls for every student to be tossed into the lake on his birthday.

The Paladins compete in NCAA Division I athletics and are members of the Southern Conference along with Wofford, Davidson, Appalachian State University, the Citadel, and the University of North Carolina–Greensboro. Furman school spirit seems to be strong: The football team, although only Division I-AA, draws up to 15,000 fans for each home game, a heck of a turnout, considering that the student body totals about 3,300. Soccer games are also well attended; the women's team holds the record for the longest winning streak in the Southern Conference. There are also club sports (including an equestrian team) and intramurals, the latter usually organized around freshman dormitories or fraternities.

Greek organizations claim around a third of the student body, but the university has tried to keep fraternities and sororities from becoming too exclusive. Furman has a "delayed rush" system which begins in January, so freshmen get to know their hallmates before they go Greek. Fraternity and sorority houses are off campus and almost entirely nonresidential. They are used mainly for meetings and social events.

Furman is officially a dry school, but the administration does make special concessions for charity events on the outskirts of campus. Drinking does play some role in campus life, usually behind closed dorm-room doors or at off-campus bars. Students operate a sort of designated-driver shuttle service to downtown Greenville that runs from 8 p.m. to 2 a.m. on Thursday, Friday, and Saturday nights.

Cultural events at Furman are not only plentiful, but required. Students must attend at least 36 Cultural Life Program (CLP) events during their four years on campus. One student estimates that the university offers around 200 each year, meaning that a student need only attend about 5 percent of them. But many students go more frequently. A single week in March 2005 listed the following activities: a brown-bag lunch in the chapel, a symposium on the separation of church and state, two films, a festival of ten-minute plays by students, a talk by the widow of a hero of Sept. 11, 2001, a talk on stem-cell research, an a cappella concert, and a seminar on church music. Most students say the CLP requirement not only encourages students to attend cultural events, but also pushes the university to offer them.

Furman students may be interested in politics—the political science department is one of the university's many strong areas—but Furman is by no means an activist campus. The most active political groups on campus are the College Republicans and the College Democrats, who hold a debate at the end of each year. "It gets pretty heated," says one student.

The most salient political issue on campus of late has concerned the perceived homogeneity of the Furman student body, which has a reputation of being overwhelmingly white, upper middle class, and politically and religiously conservative. In fact, 10

SUGGESTED CORE

1. Classics 32/33, Greek Literature in Translation / Roman Literature in Translation
2. Philosophy 31, Historical Foundations of Philosophy I
3. Religion 11, Introduction to Biblical Study
4. Religion 40, Church History (*Or, for an abbreviated version of courses 1, 2, 3, and 4, take Humanities 11, The Roots of Western Civilization*)
5. Political Science 61, Modern Political Thought
6. English 61, Shakespeare
7. History 40, The United States to 1820 *and* History 41, The United States 1820–1890
8. Humanities 13, Revolution, Progress, and Anxiety

percent of Furman students are minorities, and the university—almost to the point of obsession—is pushing hard to increase that number via special, minority-only programs. "Furman's really doing a lot of things to bring a lot more 'diversity,'" says one student. There's a black student weekend for potential recruits, a minority recruiting specialist in the admissions office, a minority freshman orientation program, and plenty of minority-only events on campus. The Office of Multicultural Affairs runs three diversity training programs: "Building Community through Unity," "The Inclusive Leader," and "Walk a Mile in My Shoes." There is also a Student League for Black Culture (SLBC), which holds regular meetings and sponsors a speaker each Martin Luther King Day. Some students and faculty fear that all of this focus on race will lead to excessive politicization on campus.

Socially, Furman students are more traditional than their counterparts at other top schools. A September 2003 *Paladin* article reported on a study that compared the dating habits of students at Furman and Clemson University, which is about 30 miles away. The study found that 64 percent of Furman students thought that sex outside of marriage is wrong, compared to only 38 percent of Clemson students. The survey also reported that 40 percent of Furman students had had sex, versus 69 percent at Clemson.

Furman is secluded enough from the city of Greenville that crime from the city rarely filters through the campus gates. In 2003, the university reported just four aggravated assaults, one forcible sex offense, one arson, three stolen cars, and 17 burglaries. The most common arrest: alcohol violations, of which there were 112. But a September 2003 *Paladin* editorial charged that the university has done little to ensure campus safety: there is no campus-wide emergency call system, many areas of campus are poorly lit, and most gates to the campus are open even at night. Furman Public Safety does operate a nighttime safety escort service and offer self-defense courses for women.

Furman is not particularly expensive. Tuition in 2004–5 was $25,888, room and board $6,912. Moreover, the school's financial aid is fairly generous—admissions are need-blind, and some 67 percent of students receive some need-based aid. The average recent graduate owes $19,170 in student loans.

GEORGE MASON UNIVERSITY

FAIRFAX, VIRGINIA • WWW.GMU.EDU

Technopolis

Named after a lesser-known patriot—a champion of the Bill of Rights, and Virginia's delegate to the Constitutional Convention—George Mason University was founded just 47 years ago as a branch of the University of Virginia, becoming independent in 1972. The school calls itself the "Innovative University for the Information Society." In keeping with President Alan Merten's focus on "technology across the curriculum," this public university has indeed thrived in the science and technical fields, especially in serving its graduate students, who constitute nearly 40 percent of the student body. George Mason plans to finish a $40 million laboratory by 2006 to study countermeasures to bioterrorism, reports the *Washington Post.*

The school has also amassed an impressive faculty, including some leading economists. But GMU is still trying to get undergraduate education right. With only 53 percent of entering students graduating within six years, Mason's graduation rate is low. One student says, "It has taken me five years to finish college because I could not get the classes I needed." And it could get worse, at schools across Virginia. A recent article in the *Chronicle of Higher Education* claims there is a "capacity crunch" at GMU and all Virginia state schools. Although more students with stronger academic records are applying to George Mason, state funds are not keeping pace. But strong students who find a place at Mason will find sufficient resources to support them. "Students with the determination to focus on the material have the opportunity to receive a world-class education from professors with richly varied experiences and backgrounds," says one student.

Academic Life: Home rule

Some of the best academic decisions made by George Mason in recent years have come, believe it or not, from a committee. First under the leadership of former rector Edwin

VITAL STATISTICS	
Religious affiliation: none	
Total enrollment: 28,874	
Total undergraduates: 17,408	
SAT/ACT midranges: SAT V: 490–600, M: 500–600; ACT: 20–25	
Applicants: 10,103	
Applicants accepted: 69%	
Accepted applicants who enrolled: 33%	
Tuition: $3,942 (in state), $14,310 (out of state)	
Room and board: $6,240	
Freshman retention rate: 81%	
Graduation rate: 27% (4 yrs.), 53% (6 yrs.)	
Courses with fewer than 20 students: 32%	
Student-faculty ratio: 15:1	
Courses taught by graduate TAs: 18%	
Most popular majors: business, social sciences, engineering	
Students living on campus: 24%	
Guaranteed housing for four years? yes	
Students in fraternities: 5% sororities: 5%	

SOUTH

437

George Mason offers a very abbreviated core curriculum and boasts some of the better general education requirements of any large school in this guide. Students must take:

- Two courses in basic writing skills. In addition, at least one course in a students' major must be writing-intensive.
- One course in oral communications. Either "Oral Presentations," or "Interpersonal and Group Interaction."
- One course in information technology.
- A course in quantitative reasoning.

  Students must also fulfill distribution requirements by taking eight courses in various disciplines, including:

- One course in literature from about twenty mostly solid choices such as "Classical Mythology," "Greek and Roman Epic," or "Major Writers."
- One course in the arts. "Drawing" I or "Beginning Ballet" would count, as would "High Renaissance Art in Italy: 1480–1570."
- Two courses in the natural sciences, including a lab.
- U.S. History.

Meese II, attorney general in the Reagan administration, and now under Rector Sydney O. Dewberry, the surprisingly powerful and traditionally conservative GMU Board of Visitors has been instrumental in positive curricular reforms that have considerably improved the prospects for liberal education at George Mason. GMU has an impressive economics department, enough solid courses for students to obtain a sound liberal arts education, and some state-of-the-art facilities. Furthermore, all this is available at a relative bargain, despite recent increases in tuition.

Under the board's direction, specific courses on "U.S. and Western institutions, traditions, and economies" have been added to the curriculum, despite a resolution from the Faculty Senate that condemned the board for "micromanaging" and imposing what the senate called an "academically inferior" plan. This is not the first time the board has locked horns with and prevailed over the faculty group, which one professor describes as "retreating and retreating and retreating" in recent years. Relations with the board improved when Meese visited the Senate in February 2003 and the faculty was given a nonvoting seat on the board's Faculty and Academic Standards Committee—though not on the Board of Visitors.

Despite (or perhaps because of) limited faculty input, GMU has a stronger curriculum than most schools. One student says, "The general education program at George Mason is superb. It ensures that dedicated students will be exposed to a wide variety of disciplines, producing well-rounded, informed individuals with global perspective and proficiency in subjects outside the specialized fields."

Once students declare their majors, they face stronger departmental requirements. English majors, for instance, must take a survey course on writing and literature and at least one course in each of the following areas: literature before 1800, literature before 1915, non-canonical or minority literature (e.g., "Folklore of the Americas" or "Tabloid Culture"), and another upper-level elective. English majors must also take four or more courses in a genre such as contemporary world literature, poetry, or medieval and Renaissance literature. Unfortunately, it is nevertheless possible for English majors to avoid Shakespeare and British literature altogether.

History majors must take two courses in United States

history; two in European history; two in global, Latin American, African, Asian, or Middle Eastern history; and a course titled "Introduction to the Historical Method." As in English, students can avoid important areas of the discipline if they really want to.

Students who want more structure may opt for one of the university's alternative educational paths. One of these tracks, Mason Topics, directs freshmen through the general education requirements according to a particular theme. On-campus students live together on "living/learning" floors in the residence halls. They attend films and lectures together and form study groups. A recent year's topics included "The Classical Presence," "The Global Village," "The Information Society," and "The American Experience." Another path, the New Century College, was once a college of its own and today offers an interdisciplinary approach along with the flaky "experiential" and "integrative" flavor of "learning communities"—the same weak pedagogy that led to its censure by the Board of Visitors and absorption by the College of Arts and Sciences in 1999. One former New Century student says, "I encourage all students, especially conservatives, to avoid New Century College. It remains politicized and out of touch with reality."

Elite students may fulfill their general education requirements through the Honors Program, which offers smaller classes and greater access to top faculty. Offered by invitation only, admission is based on a student's entire academic record, including high school GPA, standardized test scores, and leadership qualities. Students are given access to the best resources and faculty on campus, as well as their own lounge and computer lab, priority registration, and their own floor in university residences. Through an integrated curriculum of interdisciplinary courses, honors students "learn to probe the foundations of knowledge, develop new skills in addressing complex issues, and think independently, imaginatively, and ethically." Some recent honors courses have included "A Liberal Arts Approach to Calculus," "An Introduction to Chaos Theory and Nonlinear Dynamics," and "Technology in the Contemporary United States."

The faculty is especially important at GMU. One student claims, "Mason is effective at recruiting top talent, as evidenced by the experts representing us in fields such as

REQUIREMENTS (CONT'D)

- "History of Western Civilization." Students in this course use the same books and are expected to watch a video lecture (featuring a GMU professor) each week. Professors also share a set of guidelines for teaching the course.

- Any one of dozens of courses to fulfill the one-course "global understandings" requirement. Choices from a variety of disciplines include courses such as "Modern Japan" and "Global Perspectives on Spirituality and Healing."

- One course in the social and behavioral sciences.

- A synthesis course in which students are supposed to "engage in the connection of meaning and the synthesis of knowledge" and "demonstrate advanced skills in oral and written presentation." The synthesis requirement is fulfilled by taking one upper-division course from just about any discipline. Current approved courses include titles such as "Free Speech and Ethics," "Comparative Study of Religion," "Reason, Science and Faith in the Modern Age," or a "capstone" course from a major.

SOUTH

439

economics, neuroscience, conflict resolution, and politics. They are attracted to Mason's spirit of creativity, exploration, and independence." But some of the 55 majors offered by George Mason attract better scholars than others. The English department, for instance, has garnered criticism for, in the words of one student, "replacing courses that examine individual genius with those that examine culture (e.g., African American literature), all in a sad egalitarian effort to avoid having students even discriminate good works of literature from bad works." English course descriptions and a faculty that includes a number of experts in gender studies, minority literature, and pop culture support this assessment. But despite student comments that "educators in that department are mainly socialists or Marxists," the department has left room for some interesting courses in writing and rhetoric as well as a few solid literature courses. Recommended faculty here include Michael Kelley.

Other top teachers at Mason include Robert Ehrlich in physics; Ivanka Atanassova and John Orens in history; Joseph Becelia, Dennis Pluchinsky, and Hugh Sockett in government and international politics; Charlie Jones and Steven Weinberger in linguistics; Brita Caminiti and James Levine in foreign languages; and Robert L. Sachs and Daniele C. Struppa in mathematics. Struppa is also dean of the College of Arts and Sciences.

Most of George Mason's politicized departments can be found in the social and behavioral sciences area, from which students must take one course; it includes sociology, psychology, anthropology, and women's studies.

A notable exception in this group is Mason's free-market-oriented economics department. Mason's economics department was recently ranked number one out of some 69 such departments in the region, according to *Applied Economics Letters*. This came as no surprise considering the number of big guns on staff. In August 2001, highly regarded economist Donald Boudreaux left the Foundation for Economic Education to succeed Walter E. Williams as chair of the GMU economics department, which is famous for its quality faculty as well as for its focus on the Austrian, Chicago, and public-choice schools of economics. Williams has described GMU's economics department as "probably the nation's, if not the world's, only completely free market department." The department faculty, according to another professor, "deliberately ignores political correctness, and the conventional economic wisdom, and purveys the revealed economic truth in its undergraduate instruction, irrespective of current relativist predilections." One student calls the faculty, "amazingly brilliant . . . with a passion for economics." The resulting curriculum is described by one student as "diverse and challenging, but also fun." Recent additions to the faculty include George Mason's second Nobel Prize–winning economist, Vernon Smith, who along with colleague Bart Wilson offers a new undergraduate course titled, "Contemporary Society in Multiple Perspectives," which explores classical economics and game theory with a problem-solving lab. Besides Boudreaux, James Buchanan (now emeritus), Smith, and Williams, other excellent professors in the department include James T. Bennett, Peter J. Boettke, Bryan D. Caplan, Tyler Cowen, Larry Iannacconi, Dan Klein, David Levy, Russell Roberts, Charles K. Rowley, Thomas Rustici, Alexander Tabarrok, Gordon Tullock, and Richard E. Wagner.

Students report that in the classroom—at least outside of the politicized departments—professors strive for balanced teaching and an open atmosphere of genuine tolerance. Another student says, "Many professors are explicit about their biases, but present both sides of the issue. They are usually open-minded about students who disagree with them, provided they support their arguments with evidence. . . . Mason is pretty tolerant towards all political and religious viewpoints, particularly in comparison with other universities."

Upon arrival, students are appointed professional advisors, moving on to faculty members upon choosing their majors. "Professors tend to be very accessible and warm," says one student. Another students says, "Students have access to advisors, but some do not take advantage of it. However, it is more difficult to meet with the more experienced advisors." But while professors are willing, students' wills are weak. One professor says, "I have office hours every week and fewer than ten students come to see me during the semester." Most of this is due to a general lack of intellectual curiosity among students. Many students describe George Mason as a "commuter school" that does little to encourage contact with a faculty advisor until late in a student's career.

With numerous outlets for libertarian interests, including various institutes, think tanks, the economics department, and the mostly conservative Board of Visitors, one professor reports that the student body as a whole is conservative. A student concurs: "I have noticed more vocal conservative students and a comparatively open environment towards all political viewpoints." GMU houses the Institute for Humane Studies, which promotes the study of liberty in the conviction that a greater understanding of human affairs and freedom will foster peace, prosperity, and social harmony. IHS offers scholarships, grants, internships, and seminars to students at GMU and across the country.

Some of the most visible groups are apolitical groups directed at students from specific countries like the "Indian Students Association," and almost every conceivable religion is represented on campus. However, Mason also retains some of the typical collegiate political atmosphere. In addition to the University's Diversity Advisory Board—a "melting pot of ethnicity," as described by the chairman of this board—the school spends money on an Office of Diversity Programs and Services, a Multicultural Research and Resource Center, a Black Peer Counseling Program, and a Women's Studies Research and Resource Center—all of which engage in the same hodgepodge of counseling, workshops, sensitivity training, and lectures devoted to feminism, racism, sexism, classism, homophobia, and the like.

SUGGESTED CORE

1. Classics 340, Greek and Roman Epic
2. Philosophy 301, History of Western Philosophy: Ancient
3. Religion 251/252, Biblical Studies: The Old Testament / The New Testament
4. Religion 371, History of Western Christian Thought I
5. Government 324, Modern Western Political Theory
6. English 335/336, Shakespeare
7. History 121, Formation of the American Republic
8. Philosophy 335, Nineteenth-Century Philosophy

SOUTH

Student Life: Spontaneous generation

George Mason's nondescript modernist architecture can best be described as "spontaneous." A mere 32 years have passed since the university declared its independence from the University of Virginia and built its own facilities. The diverse student population of 17,000 undergraduates is shaped by a commuter-school culture that lacks deep roots and leaves much student activity similarly spontaneous. In short, the traditional college experience is hard to find here. "This is the most apathetic campus I have ever been on," complains one student, "Being a commuter school and not having a football team kills any attempt at building school spirit." Surrounded by a ring of trees that makes George Mason look like a park to outsiders, the school is located in the middle of a wealthy Washington, D.C., suburb, only a short distance from the capital and its attractions—perhaps too short a distance. And often too close to home; as one instructor put it, "Students come to school, attend class, and leave. There is no sense of community." A student concurs, "I think independent, self-motivated students who are technologically savvy and enjoy writing and making interdisciplinary connections will thrive here." This commuter culture, however, may be changing. According to a recent article in the *Chronicle,* out-of-staters account for the fastest-growing segment of the freshman class and "construction zones have become a common sight in the past few years as the university has added new classrooms and dormitories."

Student life organizes itself around a network of more than 200 organizations. "Students must get involved with organizations if they want to get to know people at Mason," says one student. The list includes ethnic interest groups from the Nepalese to the Bolivian and everything in between. Other groups focusing on politics, religion, science, and technology leave students with many options but also reflect the fragmented nature of the campus community. Students seem to recognize this. A recent poll found that nearly 40 percent of students were "dissatisfied/very dissatisfied" with their "sense of belonging at Mason." "The administration tries hard to make Mason a more welcoming place," reports one student, "but it is difficult because of Mason's best asset—diversity. There are so many different ethnic groups here, which is great because I have learned a lot about other cultures, but generally everyone keeps to his group."

Only 24 percent of the undergraduate population lives on campus; those who do have a suitable number of options, including single-sex and coed halls. There are no coed dorm rooms or coed bathrooms in university housing. The 15 fraternities and 11 sororities do not have university housing, but some maintain off-campus residences. The university guarantees housing for students who remain on campus, but once a student chooses to live elsewhere, he may not get a spot if he wants to return. On-campus residence halls are newer and contain many amenities but are commensurately expensive, and the university faces an acute housing shortage. Ambitious plans to build more halls are intended to more or less double the on-campus population by 2007. George Mason has a few themed residence areas like healthy living, substance-free, and women's studies floors, as well as sections for those enrolled in the several "paths through general education," like the Honors Program and Mason Topics. This "living/learning program" lets students studying together live as a group on floors like "The Global Village."

Facilities on the 677-acre campus are impressive. In 2002, the library celebrated its millionth volume. It offers resources enough for most students. More ambitious undergraduates and graduate students make use of the extensive interlibrary system, which involves many D.C.-area institutions. There are excellent online databases and a popular "Ask a Librarian" feature, which gets students immediate help with resources through online discussion. Part of the library is housed in the George W. Johnson Center, a gargantuan 320,000-square-foot complex with computer labs, student services, class space, and a four-story open atrium where students can gather between classes and take advantage of a food court, banks, the campus bookstore, and various other services. The nearby Center for the Arts includes a 2,000-seat concert hall, two smaller theaters, dance studios, and assorted music and fine arts studios. Innovation Hall, a 104,000-square-foot "tele-education" facility, was completed in 2003.

The university has several athletic fields, and the Patriot Center seats 10,000 for indoor sports (and rock concerts), an impressive number given that only 330 athletes compete in the university's 22 men's and women's NCAA Division I sports programs. Varsity teams include baseball, basketball, cross country, golf, lacrosse, rowing, soccer, softball, swimming and diving, tennis, indoor and outdoor track and field, volleyball, and wrestling. Many intramural sports are also available.

Mason is the scene of a disproportionate number of crimes. In 2003, the school reported 16 forcible sex offenses, one robbery, five aggravated assaults, 19 burglaries, 20 car thefts and three arsons on campus. These security problems have led to an on-campus escort service, "lots of police," according to a student, and a university stalking policy implemented in 1999 that was the first in the nation. Despite the statistics, one professor says, "Everyone here feels quite safe."

Tuition in 2004–5 was $3,942 for Virginia residents and $14,310 for out-of-staters. Room and board averaged $6,240 per year. Admissions are need-blind, but the school does not guarantee to match each applicant's need. Some 48 percent of students received aid packages, averaging $7,600. The average student loan debt of a 2004 graduate was $14,500.

UNIVERSITY OF GEORGIA

ATHENS, GEORGIA • WWW.UGA.EDU

Eat a peach

Only recently have people begun to take the University of Georgia seriously. For most of the time since its founding in 1785, it has been regarded as little more than a training ground for agriculture students. Students at the state rival, Georgia Tech, represent UGA as a school full of rednecks, jocks, and giggly sorority girls. Fifteen years ago or so, that crude characterization wasn't all that far from the truth, but UGA is now on the rise, drawing better students and more prestigious faculty.

The quality of the student body has improved largely as a result of the state of Georgia's HOPE Scholarship program, through which in-state students can receive full tuition scholarships. The program has allowed UGA to become more selective because it has induced many of the state's top students to stay in state. And HOPE students must maintain a B average in order to keep their scholarships.

The curriculum has quite a bit going for it, too. UGA's distribution requirements are comparatively strong and the Honors Program is highly regarded. Throw in a low-key political atmosphere, a fantastic college town, and a strong sense of school spirit, and UGA is clearly an excellent choice for students interested in state-school options in the South.

The student body is 86 percent white, and this troubles many. As the *Washington Post* reports, only about 6 percent of the students are black, while the state of Georgia is more than 25 percent black. Many in-state black students choose Georgia's historically black colleges over the University of Georgia, and for whatever reason, blacks and whites in Georgia remain much more segregated (at least when it comes to higher education) than they are in other states. Following a lawsuit, UGA was recently forced to abandon its system of awarding extra points in its admissions process to members of racial minorities. The university is therefore looking for some way to offer an advantage to minority students on the "edge" of admission, and has added a couple of admissions counselors specifically committed to recruiting minority students.

The University of Georgia is a major state school in a conservative state. Since 88 percent of its undergraduates come from Georgia, it is not surprising that they push the school to the political right. On the other hand, as UGA's academic star has risen, the school has attracted more national scholars and faculty members and fewer regional ones, which has resulted in a gradual shift leftward among the professoriate. Even so, most students and faculty characterize the school as traditional and conservative. As one professor says, "Conservatives are much more comfortable voicing their opinions here than at most other large state universities."

Academic Life: Keep HOPE alive

Georgia's curriculum, which the university calls a "core," consists of a set of distribution requirements that collectively provide students as broad an education as one could hope for at a large school. While students at the University of Georgia have flexibility in choosing their courses, it's impossible for them to get away with taking courses in just one or two disciplines, and most of the courses that fulfill the College of Arts and Sciences' requirements are introductory-level ones in fundamental areas, like "Introduction to Economics," "Introduction to Western Literature," and "Introduction to Political Theory." Furthermore, one-third of the courses UGA students take are general education courses. One junior says the university course requirements are helpful: "A lot of students don't have any idea what they want to major in, or even what topics are out there. The curriculum really gives students the chance to explore."

The Georgia state government has mandated that all students fulfill a United States and Georgia history requirement, either by passing an exam given during orientation or by taking an approved course in U.S. history. Students also must satisfy a United States Constitution requirement and a Georgia Constitution requirement, either by passing a test, completing "American Government," or taking a combination of other courses in the political science and history departments. Students in Arts and Sciences must also fulfill a cultural diversity requirement by taking one course in African American, Native American, Hispanic American, or Asian American studies. Almost every course that fulfills these requirements seems politicized, but courses like "Topics in Romance Languages" and "American Indian History to 1840" are less so.

UGA students also must fulfill an "environmental literacy" course requirement. According to a science professor, courses in this area are typically solid. "Ecology here is science rather than politics," the professor says. "Same with agriculture; if you want to talk about the world hunger problem, you go and find agriculture experts who can tell you exactly what's going on."

The state of Georgia offers an extraordinary reward for above-average students—a sum of money equal to full tuition and fees plus $150 for books. This HOPE (Helping Outstanding Pupils Educationally) Scholarship program is funded by the Georgia Lottery and is available to any in-state student who achieves a B average in core academic areas while in high school. The scholarship is renewable for college students who main-

VITAL STATISTICS

Religious affiliation: none
Total enrollment: 33,405
Total undergraduates: 25,019
SAT/ACT midranges: SAT V: 560–660, M: 570–660; ACT: 24–28
Applicants: 13,267
Applicants accepted: 62%
Accepted applicants who enrolled: 53%
Tuition: $3,368 (in state), $14,684 (out of state)
Room and board: $5,756
Freshman retention rate: 93%
Graduation rate: 41% (4 yrs.), 74% (6 yrs.)
Courses with fewer than 20 students: 35%
Student-faculty ratio: 18:1
Courses taught by graduate TAs: not provided
Most popular majors: business, social sciences, education
Students living on campus: 27%
Guaranteed housing for four years? no
Students in fraternities: 15% sororities: 18%

UGA maintains quite a strong set of general education requirements. The school divides its curriculum into five parts: "essential skills," institutional electives, and distribution requirements in the humanities and fine arts, natural sciences and mathematics, and the social sciences. Students must take the following:

- "English Composition" I and II.
- One math course.
- One humanities course. Choices range from "Greek Culture" to "Introduction to Interpersonal Communication."
- A humanities course from a department other than one's major, or a fine arts course.
- A four–credit hour laboratory science course.
- A three–credit hour laboratory course, or a second four-hour course. Three-hour choices include "Physical Science" and "The Ecological Basis of Environmental Issues."
- Another course in science, mathematics, or technology. Choices range from "Mathematics of Decision Making" to "Introduction to Personal Computing."
- "American Government" or several alternative courses, though students may test out of these.

SOUTH

tain a 3.0 grade point average. As the state's flagship public university, the University of Georgia has felt the consequences of the HOPE program more deeply than any other school. A study conducted by two University of Georgia economists and funded by the National Science Foundation reported that, since the institution of the HOPE scholarship in 1993, UGA admissions have become more selective and the academic profile of UGA students has correspondingly improved. One HOPE recipient says the scholarship has kept him and a lot of other students academically focused. "My parents wouldn't be too happy if I lost a full scholarship," he says. The university reports that the incoming class of 2006 had higher SAT scores and GPAs than any other class in UGA's history, and some alumni remark that they could never have gotten into the school had they applied now.

One professor who has taught at the university for several years attests to the changes wrought by the HOPE program: "University of Georgia students are dramatically better than they were 15 years ago. Large numbers of gifted students who would previously have fled to private universities in the Northeast are now flocking to the University of Georgia." In fact, the study mentioned above found that 76 percent of Georgia students with SATs of 1500 or higher (out of a possible 1600) have stayed in state since HOPE started.

Perhaps as a result of the influx of these higher-caliber students, the school's Honors Program has blossomed to become a program that *U.S. News and World Report* has called "an Ivy League experience at less than half the price." (Or less, if you get it on a HOPE scholarship.) One professor refers to it as "our crown jewel." The strength of this program, naturally, lies in the rigor of its courses. Most of the honors courses fulfill distribution requirements—that is, for most introductory-level courses, there is a corresponding honors course. The catalog description for one honors course ("English Literature from 1700 to the Present") promises that students will read Pope, Swift, Johnson, Blake, Wordsworth, Coleridge, Keats, Tennyson, Arnold, Browning, one or two nineteenth-century novelists, Yeats, Woolf, and Joyce. "United States Survey to 1865," also open only to honors students, emphasizes primary sources from America's founding through the Civil War.

By taking on more work, honors students also can receive credit for most upper-level courses. Juniors and seniors in the program are welcome to enroll in graduate-level courses. Classes in the Honors Program tend to be smaller and more difficult, and the professors in the program are some of the best at the university. UGA has a few honors dormitories, but are they not exclusively reserved for honors students, and besides some special lectures and advisors, there is little to the program outside the classroom.

The administration would like to see the school ranked in the same tier as the so-called "public Ivies." Before this happens, Georgia must raise the bar in certain areas. For one thing, 26 percent of freshmen do not graduate in six years, and only 41 percent graduate in four years. As one professor in the sciences says, this is not because the courses are terribly demanding. Some faculty cite the lack of intellectual curiosity among students. "Making the grade is the chief objective of a strong portion of our undergraduates," says one professor. And there is considerable variance in the difficulty of the school's majors. "Education is the most obvious" example of an easy department, says one professor. "If one can get by the university-wide requirements, A's and B's are a sure thing in the College of Education for the rest of one's four years. On the other hand, majors like math, chemistry, physics, and computer science are brutally tough."

Although UGA has become a rather large research university that enrolls some 25,000 undergraduates, most students say their professors are focused on teaching. One says, "I've never run into a situation where my professor has put his own research over his teaching responsibilities." Undergraduate instructors are required to post office hours and some have an open-door policy. "For the most part, professors are very accessible to students and friendly, too," the student says. "That's what I found so surprising at such a large university: my professors know my name and are happy to talk to students." UGA uses graduate teaching assistants in the same way as most big universities: professors teach large lecture courses twice a week and TAs lead smaller discussion groups once a week. Upon entering UGA, each student is assigned a professional, nonfaculty advisor who helps the student choose a major. Once the student

REQUIREMENTS (CONT'D)

- "American History to 1865" or "American History since 1865," though again, students may test out.
- Four courses from at least two social science departments. Choices range from "Applied Microeconomic Principles" to "Multicultural Perspectives on Women in the United States."
- One course demonstrating environmental literacy, like "Soil and Water Resource Conservation" or "Fungi: Friends and Foes."
- One semester of physical education.
- Four or five credits of electives approved by one's advisor.

Each department also requires a level of oral communication and basic computer skills appropriate for the major.

In addition, the College of Arts and Sciences maintains a few requirements of its own, including competency in a foreign language (to the third-semester level), the successful completion of one literature course, one biological and one physical sciences course, one history course, and two courses in social sciences other than history.

SOUTH

has selected a major, he is assigned a faculty advisor within his major department.

Faculty members most often mentioned as dedicated to undergraduate teaching include Jonathan Evans and James Kibler Jr. in English; Noel Fallows in romance languages (Spanish); James C. Cobb, John C. Inscoe, and Kirk Willis in history; Thomas M. Lessl in speech communications; David Hally in anthropology; Ronald Blount in psychology; Allen C. Amason in management; Keith S. Delaplane in entomology; John Pickering in ecology; Daniel E. L. Promislow in genetics; and Dwight R. Lee and David B. Mustard in economics. Hamilton Jordan, White House chief of staff under President Jimmy Carter, will serve this year as a guest lecturer; students interested in government should make a point of catching his talks.

Agricultural programs and the sciences are particularly strong, in part because they receive more state and federal funding. Eleven percent of undergraduate degrees are awarded in business management, but after business, degrees are more evenly distributed among disciplines.

Student Life: Positively Athenian

One couldn't ask for a better college town than Athens, Georgia. For many students, Athens is the deciding factor in choosing to come to UGA. The town has everything: plenty of bars and restaurants, a movie theater, shops, and a renowned music scene: Athens is the birthplace of such bands as REM, the B-52s, and Widespread Panic. Some of the popular locales for catching good local bands are the historic Georgia Theatre, Wild Wing Cafe, and 40 Watt. The on-campus Performing Arts Center and downtown Classic Center both host world-class performers such as the Atlanta Symphony Orchestra. Students can easily get cheap tickets to these events.

UGA has the largest College Republicans chapter in the country, and the CRs also are the largest student group. One leader of the club says that the group is the most politically active on campus and that its members are highly mobilized, bringing conservative speakers and political candidates to campus several times a year. Politically, the town of Athens is to the University of Georgia what Chapel Hill is to the University of North Carolina and Austin is to the University of Texas: its leftism hardly makes it representative of the state as a whole.

UGA lies in the heart of the Bible Belt and consequently has a number of Christian student groups whose members tend to be traditionally minded. Faculty members in the Christian Faculty Forum say they feel free to express their beliefs, hold meetings, and bring in speakers. Lately, this group and several of the Christian student groups have heard the protests of detractors who say religious groups at a public university violate the separation of church and state. So far, though, the Christian groups remain strong, and, as one professor says, "help balance the landscape a bit." Many of the groups that receive the most support from the administration are more liberal, including the Lambda Alliance, a homosexual group. The *Red and Black*, the university newspaper, is well known for its liberalism. In the university as a whole, says one professor, "there are all perspectives, but overall, people are level-headed. Tolerance of diverse views is prevalent, but as in most circumstances where 35,000 people assemble, exceptions could be found if one looked for them." Students living on campus may participate in Diversity Awareness Week at Georgia—or DAWG Days—which is sponsored by the Residence Hall Association. According to the housing Web page, "Topics covered include race and ethnicity, religion, sexual orientation, body image and size-ism, and students with disabilities, to name a few." President Michael Adams has told the *Red and Black* that he is squarely behind these efforts.

Georgia students are patriotic, to the point of controversy. When a group of UGA students recently sought approval to build a memorial for university alumni (all alumni) who had fought and died in war (all wars), the proposal was defeated because, as a University Council representative explained, "A war memorial by its nature is going to exclude someone on this campus: females, non-Anglo males, African Americans, homosexuals, and international students. For the memorial to be more inclusive, service to other nations and in organizations like the Peace Corps should be honored." If this sort of logic continues to flourish at UGA, the school is well on its way to becoming a public Ivy after all.

Despite the fact that a large percentage of the student body hails from Georgia, the university does not typically clear out on the weekends. "It depends on if there's a home football game," a student from an Atlanta suburb says. "If there is, nobody leaves town." But Athens and the area have so many attractions that "not as many go home as you'd think" even on other weekends. The bright lights of Atlanta are within an hour-and-a-half drive and students head there together at least a few times a year. For outdoorsy students, the Appalachian Mountains are about two hours northeast.

Talk to any Georgia student and within a couple of minutes your conversation is bound to shift to football. Most students' social lives in autumn revolve around home games. The Georgia-Florida game is the most coveted ticket of the year. Football is the center of campus life—indeed, the stadium is located at the heart of the campus. Other varsity sports also have been gaining popularity lately (although the men's basketball program recently was wracked by a scandal). Intramural sports are popular and plentiful.

Around one-third of the student body lives on campus, and the university guarantees housing only for freshmen. Many more students would prefer to live on campus but are denied the opportunity because of a housing crunch, which may soon be eased somewhat when the university completes various remodeling projects. Those who live on campus reside in huge freshman dormitories, suites in East Campus Village, or in

SUGGESTED CORE

1. Classics 1020, Classical Mythology *or* Classics 4220, Classical Epic Poetry (*not offered on a regular basis*)
2. Classics 3000, Classics of Ancient Western Philosophy
3. Religion 4080, New Testament Literature
4. Religion 4001/4080, Old Testament: Hebrew Bible Literature / New Testament Literature
5. Political Science 4020, Political Philosophy: Hobbes to Nietzsche
6. English 4320, Shakespeare I
7. History 2111, American History to 1865
8. History 4373, Nineteenth-Century European Intellectual History

other on-campus facilities. The university offers one men-only dormitory and several women-only residences, including Brumby Hall, a 950-student dorm that has limited visitation hours. UGA does not have any coed dorm rooms or coed bathrooms. The university's "learning communities" are another housing option. In Rutherford Hall, students in the College of Arts and Sciences live down the hall from faculty members and attend special academic programs. Another residence hall maintains special tutoring, advisors, study areas, and classrooms for the students who live there. Students studying French or Spanish can immerse themselves in these languages by living in similar special residences.

The food on campus is less than stellar—by popular demand. The school has attempted to offer upscale, health-oriented items in its cafeterias, but Georgians aren't fooled by fancy fare. According to the *Chronicle of Higher Education,* "students don't want fancy stuff—they want Chef Boyardee. At lunch *and* dinner. They also want cereal to be available all day. And they want chicken strips. Lots of chicken strips. . . . And pizza." Popular variations on the latter include "chipotle chicken pizza, chicken fajita pizza, and even 'McCheeseburger' pizza." Sounds like more UGA students need to try studying abroad—for instance, in that *other* Athens across the sea.

Rentals in Athens (Georgia), including nearby houses, downtown lofts, and scattered apartment buildings, are rather pricey. Almost one-fifth of the student body goes Greek, and Greek organizations play a significant role in campus social life for both members and independents. Weekend parties at the houses are popular and generally are open to all students.

The campus crime rate is not that high, but the city of Athens has some dangerous areas. On campus, students coming home late at night can take advantage of the escort van service. The school offers an extensive and effective bus system for students. There are emergency phones all over campus. Almost all dormitories have a hand geometry reader that ensures that only people who belong in the dormitories can enter, and community desks in the dorms are staffed 24 hours a day. In 2003, the last year for which there are statistics, the campus had 18 burglaries, eight motor vehicle thefts, six robberies, and one case of arson.

For students from Georgia, this school is an amazing value, with 2004–5 in-state tuition only $3,368. It's even pretty reasonable for non-Georgians; out-of-state tuition was $14,684. A typical room and board plan costs just under $6,000 per year. Admissions are need-blind, and 27 percent of students receive aid. However, the school does not guarantee to cover the full need of every student admitted. The average student loan debt of a recent graduate is $18,900, the school reports.

GEORGIA INSTITUTE OF TECHNOLOGY

ATLANTA, GEORGIA • WWW.GATECH.EDU

Eyes on the prize

Some say a better name for the Georgia Institute of Technology would be the "North Avenue Trade School." At Georgia Tech, most students enter knowing which career they want to pursue; a degree is just the means of attaining it. As students and faculty emphasize, college life here is not about exploring the major disciplines or gaining a broad base of knowledge—that is what high school was for. The liberal arts sit on the university's back burner, and most engineering students just enroll in them to satisfy curriculum requirements. Students here are so indifferent to the liberal arts for their own sake that even humanities course descriptions are saturated with the words "science" and "technology." But academic life at Tech is rigorous and intense. "One thing I believe about Tech is that they really want you to *earn* your degree," an engineering student says. "My degree from Georgia Tech will be something of immense pride and satisfaction. I will know that I earned it on my own merits and not anyone else's."

Located in the heart of Atlanta, Georgia Tech provides students with the advantage of living in the South's unofficial capital, which provides a fantastic number of educational, professional, cultural, and recreational opportunities. A few Tech students even find time to enjoy them.

Academic Life: It does compute

Academic life, as one computer science major puts it, is exceptionally tough, "but it will be well worth the hundreds of all-nighters and stress levels of '11' once I get my degree and am looked at by future employers as one 'who knows what the heck I am doing' because I graduated from such a highly ranked school." The chance to land a good job, not love of learning, seems to be the primary motivation for most Georgia Tech students. "Purely intellectual curiosity is

VITAL STATISTICS
Religious affiliation: none
Total enrollment: 16,841
Total undergraduates: 11,546
SAT/ACT midranges: SAT V: 600–690, M: 640–740; ACT: 25–32
Applicants: 8,561
Applicants accepted: 70%
Accepted applicants who enrolled: 43%
Tuition: $3,638 (in state), $17,980 (out of state)
Room and board: $6,526
Freshman retention rate: 92%
Graduation rate: 26% (4 yrs.), 72% (6 yrs.)
Courses with fewer than 20 students: 38%
Student-faculty ratio: 14:1
Courses taught by graduate TAs: not provided
Most popular majors: engineering, business, computer science
Students living on campus: 53%
Guaranteed housing for four years? no
Students in fraternities: 21% sororities: 24%

always rare, but [here], it's rarer than usual because the nature of the institute selects and rewards extreme task focus," one professor says. "Grades are most students' concern, especially in a course not part of their major."

Georgia Tech students must go through quite an ordeal before they can embark on their careers. Most engineering students require five years to graduate, and sixth- and seventh-year seniors are not uncommon. The course requirements for the engineering program are so rigorous that they discourage students from taking a wide variety of courses before settling on their majors. And a few years ago, Georgia Tech increased the required percentage of hours in the engineering major. As one professor says, "While the training might be better, it's arguable whether people are as well or better educated."

"Georgia Tech is not like the typical college people see in the movies; most students show up here knowing what they want to do, and do only that," says a student. "Since engineering is the university's main focus, most people do not take a wide variety of classes." It's hard enough just fulfilling the minimum. Another engineering student says, "You can't come to Tech and think it will be like high school, where a minimal amount of studying will get you an A. Do that your first semester at Tech and you will flunk out."

Georgia Tech began as and remains a technical institution, but it does require courses other than those in engineering and the sciences. Upon entering Georgia Tech, students choose from among the university's six colleges: College of Engineering, College of Computing Sciences, College of Sciences, College of Architecture, the Ivan Allen College of Liberal Arts, and the DuPree College of Management. Georgia Tech is most renowned for its engineering program, and these and related courses are by far the most difficult. Georgia Tech's nationally recognized engineering facilities include the Manufacturing Research Center, where both undergraduate and graduate students "examine manufacturing processes, applications, and technical solutions," according to its Web page. Undergraduates participate in cutting-edge research that directly supports Tech's academic programs in engineering. In 2005, eight of the 11 programs offered in engineering were ranked among the country's top 10 by *U.S. News and World Report.*

Not all engineering students can compete at this level. "Most engineering majors who do poorly tend to switch to easier coursework that can be found in [the] management, industrial engineering, and English majors," says one student. The engineering disciplines, with the exception of industrial engineering, require high-level math and physics skills that professors expect students to master quickly and to use in classes.

The College of Computing is also highly regarded. It conducts interdisciplinary research and participates in instructional programs within other academic units on campus. Students gain hands-on experience while developing logical and analytical skills in their computer courses. Computer science majors are required to take 21 semester hours of free electives, but many use this flexibility to take courses within their major department rather than to broaden their knowledge in other areas. Nearly every computer science and engineering program in the country emphasizes group learning and cooperation, but at Georgia Tech the computer science department has been known for forbidding this practice—a prohibition that has led to controversy in the past. A couple of years ago the *Chronicle of Higher Education* reported that, of 187 students investigated, more than 130 were penalized for "cheating" on a computer programming assignment. A parent of one of the students in question says his son was "accused of 'discussing' his computer science homework" (which was worth less than 2 percent of the grade) "and charged under a vague no-collaboration rule with cheating." More recently, the school has made efforts to defuse this issue, even going so far as to redesign the main introductory computer course for majors so as to permit collaboration on homework—and to shift almost the entire focus of grading onto tests and other in-class work.

The College of Sciences offers undergraduate and graduate degrees in mathematics and the natural sciences in a high-tech environment. The campus includes a new Biotechnology Complex.

The Ivan Allen College of Liberal Arts, which dates only to 1990, does not contain Georgia Tech's most highly touted academic programs; only 703 undergraduates (out of more than 11,000) are enrolled, garnering less than 5 percent of freshmen admitted in each of the last four years. But the university recognizes that it must develop its liberal arts programs in order to become a full-service university. "Georgia Tech is no longer a regional engineering school, it is a national and international technological university, which means it has to have strong humanities and social sciences," the dean of the Ivan Allen College said recently. Even within the liberal arts college, students cannot avoid mathematics and the sciences. For instance, instead of a philosophy department, Georgia Tech has a "philosophy, science, and technology" department, replete with courses like "Environmental Ethics," "Introduction to Cognitive Science," "Science, Technology, and Human Values," and "Ethics and Technical Professions." The only ancient philosophy course concludes with "the early development of science in the fourteenth and fifteenth centuries." And instead of "history," Tech has a "history, technology, and society" major. It features such courses as "Engineering in History," "The Scientific Revolution," "Technology and Science in the Industrial Age," and "Technology and Society." The English department has just four courses (four!), all in basic composition. And two of those are considered remedial and not offered for college credit.

ACADEMIC REQUIREMENTS

Georgia Tech has no liberal arts core, but it does require a solid base of technical classes and a few humanities courses as well. Students must take:

- Two English composition courses.
- A calculus class.
- A computer science course.
- Two introductory-level humanities courses. Choices range from "History of Art" to "Literary and Cultural Postmodernism."
- Four science/math/technology courses, including a second calculus course for all students who are not liberal arts majors.
- Four social science courses, one of which must satisfy the statewide United States/Georgia history and constitution requirements—usually fulfilled by "The United States to 1877," "The United States since 1877," or another survey course. Other choices include "Ancient Greece" and "Science, Technology, and Gender."

Ivan Allen College's School of Literature, Communication, and Culture offers bachelor of science degrees in science, technology, and culture (STAC) and computational media, with postgraduate degrees in information design, digital media, and human-computer interaction. These programs seem to assume that the future of communications (if not the traditional humanities *per se*) is to be primarily electronic. This school has very few actual literature courses; the emphasis, again, is on science and technology.

Tech's College of Architecture, one of the oldest and most highly respected schools of its kind in the country, offers majors in architecture, building construction, and industrial design; the school is a national leader in city and regional planning. The college's curriculum challenges students to create innovative projects in modern lab facilities, especially through the IMAGINE (Interactive Media Architecture Group IN Education) lab, a highly advanced computer modeling system for what might be called investigations in theoretical architecture. On a less theoretical, even more whimsical plane, a Tech College of Architecture grad student recently won a medal in a national industrial design competition with a sleek, modern, and apparently highly ergonomic . . . cat box.

Many students believe the quality of Tech's faculty is its most valuable asset. Fifty-five faculty have received Presidential, National Science Foundation (NSF) Young Investigator, or NSF Career awards. Professors teach most courses; only a few are conducted by graduate teaching assistants. More often, Tech uses TAs in the same way most state universities (and several Ivies) use them: for teaching laboratory sections, holding office hours, grading papers, and leading weekly discussion sections.

One student says, "Professors are excellent at what they do, extremely intelligent, and know the subject. They have won high-dollar contracts for the school from huge companies, have tenure at the school, and do major research for which they get recognition." Not surprisingly, then, many professors are interested in their research above all else. One student says that while faculty members are ready to help if asked, "normally the chain of command is notes, books, Internet, TAs, newsgroups, professors. Professors are generally seen as a last resort. Their line of reasoning is that in the work force, you can't just go to the boss and say, 'How do you do this?' because they will think that you don't know what you're doing."

Freshmen are assigned advisors and are required to visit them, but upperclassmen can use their advisors to whatever degree needed. "In my experience, they offer suggestions and help you figure out classes," one student says. "However, they are very willing to let you plan your academic career."

Students name as some of the best professors at the university George F. Riley in electrical and computer engineering, George L. Cain Jr. and Marcus C. Spruill in mathematics, William Leahy in the College of Computing, Ahmet Erbil in physics, and Charles A. Eckert in chemical engineering. Among active and visible younger faculty are marine biologist-biochemist Julia Kubanek, aerospace engineer and NASA contact Robert Braun, and nanotechnology guru Z. L. Wang.

SOUTH

Student Life: No time for rambling

Coursework at Georgia Tech is tough. Students spend vast amounts of time in the library, in laboratories, and in front of their computers. With less than a third of the student population graduating in four years, some students can't afford to "waste time" with extracurricular activities or social events. But one student says, "We aren't called 'Ramblin' Reck' for nothing. We work hard and study lots, then play hard . . . in that order." That may be, but it also isn't for nothing that *The Princeton Review* recently ranked Tech second in the country for "least happy students."

Atlanta and Georgia Tech have grown and prospered together for more than a century. Alas, Atlanta city planners built Interstate 75/85 between Georgia Tech and its Midtown neighborhood, dividing the two both physically and psychologically. The separation eventually led to a steady decay of the Fifth Street area, creating problems for the Midtown community and for Georgia Tech.

But changes are occurring for the better. Atlanta universities, including Emory, the Atlanta University Center, and Georgia State, have had their neighborhoods transformed, revitalized, and made safer. Georgia Tech's surrounding area also is on the upswing. Pioneer investors are shaping a more vibrant place to work, live, learn, and play. The Technology Square Project is expected to bring a special character to the Midtown renaissance by anchoring its technology core and creating an artery between the Tech campus and Midtown by way of the Fifth Street Bridge. The still-developing project welcomes pedestrians with the open-front School of Management building and retail outlets, including a new school bookstore, a first for Midtown.

Downtown Atlanta has plenty of attractions for Georgia Tech students anxious to get off campus and away from the books. The High Museum of Art is one of the best museums in the South. Underground Atlanta is a subterranean marketplace with shops, bars, and cafes. The Varsity, a legendary quick-paced hot dog and burger joint, serves students and locals alike; it was started by Frank Gordy, a Tech dropout, in 1928. Sports fans can enjoy Atlanta Falcons football at the Georgia Dome and Atlanta Hawks basketball at Philips Arena. The Atlanta Thrashers ice hockey team began play in 1999 (and stopped, at least for a while, with the 2004 NHL strike). Atlanta Braves games at Turner Field are popular spring and summertime events.

Georgia Tech athletics are popular among students, area alumni, and Atlantans, who often claim a partial ownership of the university—or at least of Tech sports. The Yellow Jackets compete in the Atlantic Coast Conference (ACC), home to such power-

SUGGESTED CORE

1. Literature, Communication, and Culture 2202, Ancient and Medieval Literature and Culture
2. Philosophy, Science, and Technology 3102, Ancient Philosophy
3. No suitable course
4. History, Technology, and Society 2032, Ancient Rome—From Greatness to Ruins (*closest match*)
5. Philosophy, Science, and Technology 2050, Philosophy and Political Theory (*closest match*)
6. Literature, Communication, and Culture 3228, Shakespeare
7. History 2111, The United States to 1877
8. Literature, Communication, and Culture 2112, Evolution and the Industrial Age (*closest match*)

SOUTH

455

houses as Duke, Florida State, Maryland, and North Carolina. Tech struggles from time to time, but overall its sports programs are strong. In the past decade, Tech has won a national championship in football, sent its basketball team to the Final Four, and won ACC titles in golf, baseball, and women's volleyball. All games are free for students. And despite the workload, Tech consistently ranks among the top 25 schools in the nation in graduating its student-athletes (although it helps that Tech athletes are disproportionately more likely to major in management than in engineering). The university also offers intramural sports, including sand volleyball, flag football, ultimate Frisbee, and wiffleball.

Besides sports, Georgia Tech offers plenty of extracurricular activities. Student clubs include those devoted to recreation, leisure, publications, and artistic and cultural productions, as well as honor societies, volunteer groups, and organizations for political, religious, cultural, and diversity purposes. Not surprisingly, Georgia Tech also has a number of academic and professional groups, like the Earthquake Engineering Research Institute, the Institute of Electrical and Electronics Engineering, and the *Journal of Student Research and Technology*.

Tech is hardly a political hotspot: no sit-ins, no political rallies, and few professors pushing political agendas. After all, Tech's main strength lies in its science and engineering fields, and it's hard to make such courses partisan. While some courses in the Ivan Allen College, particularly in the social sciences, are politicized, and one professor in Ivan Allen says, "I've seen some politically correct junk thrown at students, where they are forced to read ridiculous books to satisfy the curriculum of the course— to satisfy the political leaning of the professor," the same professor goes on to say, "It's not super conservative here at Tech, and it's not as liberal as many colleges and universities have become either. Most students here are ready to learn 'science-y' stuff more than [they are] politics, music, arts, and literature."

A recent graduate echoes this professor's description of campus political life: "Since most of my coursework was engineering, I feel that I saw very little political influence. Not even politicians can change the multiplication table. I think conservatives and liberals both feel comfortable there. Students are very concerned for themselves and, as such, care little about someone else's political agenda. They're engineers, they want the grades, the degree, the job, the money. . . . That's what matters there."

Fifty-three percent of Georgia Tech undergraduates choose to live on campus; the rest live in the surrounding area. "To tell you the truth, campus housing is pretty scarce and many students, after their required freshman year, choose to live off campus or in Greek life housing," one student says. First-year students have the option of participating in Freshman Experience (FE), which offers a set of traditional dormitories on the east side of campus. Most of the dorms are single sex and all dorms have an official escort policy for members of the opposite sex. All FE dorms are supposed to be alcohol-free, and all have upperclassmen as resident advisors on each hall, a required meal plan, and 24-hour low-noise rules. Undergraduates who are not a part of FE have limited options for housing. Traditional-style halls typically are single sex with two-person rooms. Some suite-style buildings are available, as well as four apartment com-

SOUTH

plexes originally built for the 1996 Olympics. Apartments are usually the most coveted living options on campus; since housing is decided by lottery and by class, seniors usually snag these prime spots.

Student safety is of great concern at Georgia Tech. The university has a police force of 48 sworn officers and a budget of $2.8 million. The latest crime statistics, from 2003, report two forcible sex offenses, two robberies, one aggravated assault, 40 burglaries, and 70 stolen cars on campus—rather a lot, but not so surprising given Tech's urban location. The university has increased night-time lighting on campus during the last several years and now uses campus-wide e-mail alerts to identify suspicious activities. The campus police also track repeat offenders and have instituted a K-9 unit with police dogs. Campus safety programs feature extensive crime awareness workshops at freshmen orientation.

As a state-assisted school, Georgia Tech is considerably less expensive than other universities with comparable reputations. In 2004–5, tuition for Georgia residents was only $3,638, while outsiders paid a more standard (though still relatively low) $17,980. The housing and meal plan cost $6,526. Almost three-quarters of the student body comes from Georgia; all in-state students maintaining a B average are eligible for the state's Helping Outstanding Pupils Educationally (HOPE) scholarship and the free tuition that comes with it. *Money* magazine consistently ranks Tech as one of the nation's best academic values.

HAMPDEN-SYDNEY COLLEGE

FARMVILLE, VIRGINIA • WWW.HSC.EDU

The alpha male

Hampden-Sydney College in Farmville, Virginia, is a small school that provides an excellent liberal arts education to its approximately 1,100 students. And all of those students are men. Hampden-Sydney is one of only three remaining all-male institutions of higher education in America. What is more, its curriculum was never neutered. *Insight* magazine has named Hampden-Sydney as one of the 15 finest institutions that "still teach the fullness of the Western academic traditions."

Hampden-Sydney was founded during the American Revolution and is named for John Hampden, who earned the title "father of the people" for leading resistance to Charles I's government. Algernon Sydney, the college's other namesake, was a republican philosopher and an inspiration to both John Locke and America's founding fathers. Patrick Henry, revolutionary and anti-federalist hero, helped found the college and sent six of his sons to the school. He aimed to help Virginia create "useful knowledge amongst its citizens" by supporting the college. James Madison, father of the American Constitution, also helped to shape the college during its formative years. Steeped in the history of English and American political thought and classical liberalism, Hampden-Sydney has not abandoned its roots, and for this reason alone it is a unique and noteworthy institution.

Academic Life: You can't male it in

Hampden-Sydney provides a challenging curriculum that encourages breadth and depth, and although the school does not have a true core, its distribution requirements are structured and thorough. The nucleus of the Hampden-Sydney curriculum is its Western culture requirement: three specific courses focusing on the West's classical beginnings and its development through the present. The courses cover three eras of history: "beginning" to A.D. 900, 900 through 1800, and 1800 to the present. They are taught by professors across departments and share a focus on five common events (such as the rise of Athens and democracy or the Industrial Revolution) and five common readings (from sources such as *The Wealth of Nations* or *The Origin of Species*). According to the catalog, "These materials often become the subjects of college-wide colloquia, making students and professors companions in their search for understanding." The courses include broad sketches of politics, art, religion, philosophy, and the intellectual history of Western society, and combine history with the reading of great books. "A professor may discuss the possibility that eternal truths or human nature exist, as well as taking the typical historicist approach so prevalent in the humanities and social sciences in most colleges," says one professor. Another professor who teaches one of these courses says, "In my Western Culture 101 class, students read the Bible, Homer's *Iliad*, Sophocles' *Oedipus Rex* and *Antigone*, Aristophanes' *The Clouds*, Plato's *Apology*, Aristotle's *Politics* (Book One), Plutarch's lives of Alcibiades and Caesar, and St. Augustine's *Confessions*. Today we had a nice discussion about Caesar's ambition." Another faculty member says, "The core courses are serious, though, as anywhere, there are perceived differences in difficulty, depending on the instructor. To some degree, the differences are mitigated by the assessment procedure, which establishes common standards and goals." After taking the three courses in Western civilization, students then need two American studies courses, chosen from a short list of courses in the history, English, political science, and religion departments.

Hampden-Sydney's curriculum and faculty members encourage intellectual curiosity. "This semester we had nearly 50 students take a course on Plato and Aristotle," a professor says. "We had to open a new section of the course to accommodate the demand. So many students seem to be searching for something more than just careers."

Just as rigorous as these general requirements are the demands of major departments. English majors take two survey courses, one in English literature and one in American literature. Each student also studies comparative literature, the literature of a period of his choice, the literature of a specific author, and Shakespeare. Finally, each English major must complete a senior thesis. The English department does offer courses on ethnic literature, postcolonialism, and the cinema, but not nearly as many as at most schools. Unfortunately, English requirements for nonmajors are not as demanding. Students may select from a broad list of courses that includes both "The History of English Literature" and "Multi-Ethnic American Literature." One English faculty member says, "Our department used to be more traditional than it is now. The trend is definitely in the direction of requiring less literature written before the twentieth century." In the history department, majors need three courses in American history, one in European history, and two outside of these areas, plus a colloquium. The U.S. history requirement can be satisfied by classes like "American Intellectual History," not the bizarre courses you find at many other liberal arts schools.

Professors and students say that English, modern languages, and history are more politicized than most other departments. Still, says one professor, "there is less nuttiness here than at most places. In our English courses, for example, texts are read and

VITAL STATISTICS
Religious affiliation: Presbyterian
Total enrollment: 1,082
Total undergraduates: 1,082
SAT/ACT midranges: SAT V: 520–620, M: 520–630; ACT: 21–28
Applicants: 1,207
Applicants accepted: 69%
Accepted applicants who enrolled: 38%
Tuition: $21,878
Room and board: $7,370
Freshman retention rate: 81%
Graduation rate: 61% (4 yrs.), 65% (6 yrs.)
Courses with fewer than 20 students: 69%
Student-faculty ratio: 10:1
Courses taught by graduate TAs: none
Most popular majors: social sciences, psychology, philosophy
Students living on campus: 95%
Guaranteed housing for four years? yes
Students in fraternities: 34%

SOUTH

459

ACADEMIC REQUIREMENTS

Hampden-Sydney has a genuine core curriculum, which students are encouraged to complete during their first two years. Requirements are as follows:

- Rhetoric 101 and 102 and one course from classical studies, English literature, or classical and modern language literature. Students must also reach the intermediate level in a foreign language.
- Two introductory courses chosen from biology, chemistry, astronomy, or physics (including at least one with a lab component).
- One mathematics course and one additional math or science course outside the student's major.
- An introductory social science class in economics, political science, psychology, or sociology.

taught, not the latest literary theories." The English department offers four or five courses of suspicious relevance to the discipline. In "Postcolonial Literature," for instance, students examine, "the idea of nationality, the construction of history, categories of race and class, the complexities of cultural inheritance, and problems of narrative transmission." But courses such as this are not the norm. Judging from the course catalog, at least, the history department offers nothing but serious classes. "At Hampden-Sydney, there are no trendy departments," says another professor. "Everyone takes books and ideas very seriously. There are individual faculty members who present the 'latest' ideas, but generally in a sober and thought-provoking way." One student says, "The faculty is liberal, but I know several conservative professors. While [most] are liberal in their personal beliefs, I have never had a professor try to push his/her beliefs on me or politicize the class."

For the most part, politics, faculty or student, is not a salient feature of the Hampden-Sydney landscape. Students do not protest or stage sit-ins, and only rarely do they organize for political causes. The college's new Intercultural Affairs Office tries to promote tolerance on campus by "creating an environment that is sensitive to the diversity of a multicultural community" and by offering "academic, administrative, and social support" to minority students. But by and large, modern academia's obsession with the clichés of diversity has bypassed Hampden-Sydney.

Outside of the classroom, the college political atmosphere is just as sedate. One of the few liberal groups is the Student Environmental Action Coalition, part of a national "network of progressive organizations and individuals whose aim is to uproot environmental injustices through action and education." The school also hosts the Republican Society, dedicated to the study of American politics and "the philosophies of the Republican Party." Its president says that while the group is by far the most politically active group on campus, with 100 members, they "are not the 'in-your-face' type." He says, "I think liberals and conservatives feel comfortable on campus." Students have also organized the Society for the Preservation of Southern Heritage, dedicated to "the Constitution of the United States, a strong family unit, religious faith, courage, honor, and integrity."

Except for a few explicitly political speakers, most guest lecturers are academics who speak about their specialties. The college recently hosted a three-day conference on the "war on terrorism" that featured presentations by Gen. Doug Brown, Commander of the U.S. Special Operation Center, and reporter Seymour Hersh, among others. This conference was organized by the Wilson Center for Leadership in the Public Service, an umbrella organization for leadership, public affairs, and public service programs.

One of the strongest departments on campus is political science, which is also a popular major. At Hampden-Sydney, the political science department emphasizes the evaluation of contemporary political problems in light of the writings of the great Western and American political thinkers. Classics, though only three professors strong, is considered one of the college's best teaching departments, as is the school's largest, economics, in which 30 percent of Hampden-Sydney students major. The science departments are also good; faculty single out chemistry as strongest.

The faculty has a reputation for sensible research in traditional areas, with only a couple of professors recently undertaking scholarship in areas like popular culture, film, and women's studies. But even in the popular culture realm, ideas are taken seriously. One Hampden-Sydney professor is editing a book titled *Political Philosophy Comes to Rick's: Casablanca and American Civic Culture*. The rhetoric faculty is predominantly female, and some of their research interests are limited to women; the same holds for the foreign language department. The second course in the rhetoric sequence can be "theme-based"—a type of class that at many schools is a forum for the discussion of the professor's pet ideology. But a professor in another department asserts that these rhetoric courses at Hampden-Sydney are "not politicized." The themes are intended "to excite the students," he says. Another senior faculty member says, "It would be hard to find a professor trying to indoctrinate in the classroom here."

Hampden-Sydney assigns each incoming student a faculty advisor and a peer advisor. In addition, to help new students adjust to college Hampden-Sydney requires that its students take an advising seminar, which is taught by the faculty advisor and aided by the peer advisor. Once a student selects his major, he is assigned a faculty advisor within his department. Students must visit their advisors each semester before registering for courses.

Since Hampden-Sydney does not have graduate students, faculty teach all courses. The college has a good student-faculty ratio of 10 to 1, and 69 percent of Hampden-Sydney's classes are limited to fewer than 20 students. No classes enroll more than 50. "Our professors are in their offices most of the time when they aren't teaching, so it's not a problem finding them," a political science major says. "Most of my professors

REQUIREMENTS (CONT'D)

- Western Culture 101, 102, and 103.
- Two courses in American studies, U.S. history, English, political science, or religion.
- International studies, which consists either in studying abroad or taking one course in international history or culture; "History of East Asia," "The Transformation of Post-Communist Societies," and the religion course "Islam" all satisfy this requirement.
- One course from a short list of classes in religion or philosophy.
- One or two courses—depending on the class—in fine arts, chosen from a list that includes "Introduction to Music Literature," "History of Western Art," and "Introduction to the Visual Arts," among others.

SOUTH

give out their home telephone numbers on the first day of class, and I have called them at home many times. I think that is one of the unique and best aspects about Hampden-Sydney." Some of the best teachers at the college include William Jones, David Marion, and James Pontuso in political science; Anthony Carilli, Saranna R. Thornton, and Kenneth Townsend in economics; James Arieti in classics; William Shear and Alexander Werth in biology; Lawrence Martin in English; Victor Cabas Jr. and Susan Robbins in rhetoric; and Ralph Hattox and James Simms Jr. in history.

Hampden-Sydney students value the small classes and personal attention they receive at the school. As one student recalls, professors "won't let you hide in the back" of a small class and fall asleep. Most classes are structured as a combination of lecture and participation. Life at Hampden-Sydney is tough academically. The school's four-year graduation rate of only 61 percent demonstrates that some students are obviously unprepared for the curriculum they encounter.

Student Life: Living (mostly) white males

Of course, the most distinctive thing about Hampden-Sydney is that there aren't any women in class. "Being all-male is nice during the week because you do not have to deal with dating or being distracted by a good-looking young woman," a student says. "You also have the chance to form a unique brotherhood with your fellow students." Another student who went to a coed high school says, "I get a better education in the all-male classroom. Class discussions are vastly improved because more students are willing to talk and share their opinions." Hampden-Sydney men aren't completely deprived of female company. School parties attract women to campus each weekend, and many fraternities host dances and mixers with nearby sororities. A number of women's colleges that maintain a close social relationship with HSC are within driving distance. In fact, a popular bumper sticker reads, "I pay tuition to Sweet Briar, but my daughter goes to Hampden-Sydney." Longwood University, a coed school known primarily for teacher education, is only a few miles away and also helps enliven the social scene. On weekends, students sometimes visit the University of Virginia, Virginia Tech, the University of North Carolina, and North Carolina State, all within a comfortable drive. One student says, "There is normally something to do, but some weekends are slow, and Farmville is not a town with a night life."

Hampden-Sydney's rural, isolated setting helps bind the campus community together. Ninety-five percent of students live on campus, which is the locus of most social activity. The school provides a free house for visiting women. Because of the school's Honor Code (see below), visitors are allowed to come and go as their hosts wish. The few students who choose to live off campus can opt for a college-owned cottage or (with permission) test their luck on the housing market. One of Hampden-Sydney's dormitories offers a substance-free floor.

The college is home to America's second-oldest collegiate debating society. Since 1789, the Union-Philanthropic Literary Society has served as an extracurricular intellectual forum for students. Its most notable members have included William Henry

Harrison, Patrick Henry's son Edward, and honorary members Robert E. Lee and Henry Wadsworth Longfellow. The group's broad interests have always reinforced the school's liberal arts tradition. Its discussions also provide one of the few outlets for political controversy on campus. "Some faculty members grumbled when the boys debated whether feminism was killing free speech, but no one tried to stop the debate," says one professor. "We are pretty old-fashioned down here. We say mostly what we like and we are pretty civil about the whole thing."

Student social life is heavily influenced by the Greek system, which includes 11 social fraternities, one professional fraternity for chemistry and related majors, and 15 honor fraternities. Roughly one-third of Hampden-Sydney men join these groups. But one nonmember says, "There is not a sharp division between Greeks and non-Greeks as on some campuses." Aside from college-sponsored speeches and lectures, most social, musical, and cultural events revolve around the Greek houses; these events are usually open to the entire campus. Each spring, students participate in Greek Week, a campus-wide festival.

The Hampden-Sydney Tigers compete in eight varsity sports in the NCAA Division III Old Dominion Athletic Conference—and Title IX obviously isn't a problem. Students have organized seven more intercollegiate club teams, including swimming, rugby, and wrestling. The school also has a strong intramurals program in which 80 percent of the student body participates. Hampden-Sydney's biggest social event is the annual football game against the school's archrival, Randolph-Macon College. Tailgating before football games is a perennially popular activity.

There is a certain demographic homogeneity at Hampden-Sydney. Ninety-two percent of students are white, and 60 percent come from Virginia. "The typical HSC student is a white male who wears polo shirts and khaki shorts," says one student, "but the school is comfortable for those who don't fit the profile."

The college offers a number of Christian groups for interested students, and one member says the school is a "good place to grow in your faith because of growing campus ministry groups like the Baptist Student Union, InterVarsity, Chi Alpha Fellowship, and the Fellowship of Christian Athletes." But, he says, "The strong party culture provides a testing ground for a person's beliefs." The ministries and religion professors, as well as local churches, provide spiritual support. Most students are Protestant, but a Jewish and a Catholic student group exist.

Farmville, Virginia, is a small town known for its furniture stores and agriculture. Prospective students should expect to encounter the typical symbols of rural southern life, from fields of tobacco to the equally pervasive (and possibly more harmful) Wal-

SUGGESTED CORE
1. Classical Studies 203, Greek Literature in Translation
2. Political Science 310, Classical Political Philosophy
3. Religion 102, Introduction to Biblical Studies
4. Religion 221, History of Christian Thought I
5. Political Science 413, Early Modern Political Philosophy
6. English 333/334, Shakespeare
7. History 111, The United States to 1877
8. Philosophy 304, Nineteenth-Century Philosophy

SOUTH

463

Mart SuperCenter. The campus blends in well with the rural setting. Shady, tree-lined paths connect the red-brick buildings, which look like old Virginia courthouses.

Hampden-Sydney's academic and social excellence is founded on one of its oldest traditions, the Honor Code. Because one of the main goals of life, the school believes, is to live a "moral existence," the Honor Code assumes that all students will "behave as gentlemen" and will not lie, cheat, or steal. The system is administered by a court of student leaders, and service on the court is considered an honor. One alumnus, Steven Colbert of Comedy Central's *The Daily Show*, reports that he still takes the Honor Code so seriously that decades after he left Farmville he can recite its text from memory. At Convocation, a ceremony at which new students sign the Honor Code for the first time, Hampden-Sydney men wear coats and ties, a sign of the dignity the ceremony commands. Faculty members affirm that the honor system works. Exams are not proctored, and, one professor says, "in my personal experience of 40 years, never need to be." In keeping with its mission to cultivate "good men" as well as "good citizens," Hampden-Sydney also has a long-standing tradition of student volunteerism. Through the student-run "Good Men, Good Citizens" group, students participate in a wide variety of community services.

Students and administrators say the Honor Code and the college's rural location are largely responsible for keeping the campus as safe as it is. In 2003, the last year for which statistics were available, the school saw a total of 30 burglaries and one forcible sexual assault. Violent crime is extraordinarily rare.

For the 2003–4 school year, Hampden-Sydney put more than $7 million of its own funds into financial aid awards to 80 percent of students. Tuition and room and board for 2004–5 totaled a bit over $29,000 per year. Some 52 percent of students receive need-based financial aid.

LOUISIANA STATE UNIVERSITY

BATON ROUGE, LOUISIANA • WWW.LSU.EDU

Every man a kingfish

Louisiana State University traces its roots to two powerful, controversial men. The school was founded just before the Civil War, by Gen. William T. Sherman, and received its first influx of serious money from Gov. Huey Long. The Kingfish relocated the school to its current location on a 2,000-acre campus adjacent to the Mississippi, where he sought to build a first-class university with prominent faculty and winning athletic teams. Now, as in the Kingfish's own day, that grand aspiration remains only partially fulfilled, providing a lesson about the effects of chronic underfunding and a populist tradition that sometimes overwhelms academic excellence.

LSU enjoyed its greatest renown during the middle decades of the twentieth century, when the university earned the nickname "Parnassus on the Mississippi." The school was a leading outpost of the Southern literary revival, hosting Robert Penn Warren, Cleanth Brooks, and the journal they edited, the *Southern Review*. In political philosophy, too, LSU had a stream of distinguished professors, including Eric Voegelin, Willmoore Kendall, and Charles Hyneman. Among the notable persons who spent time in graduate study at LSU during this era were Hubert Humphrey, Richard Weaver, and Robert Lowell. Walker Percy once taught there, and several retired faculty members can still be found who knew him personally. A revived and altered *Southern Review* continues to flourish, as do several excellent academic departments. Nevertheless, the intellectual environment at LSU no longer seems so dazzling.

The university accepts nearly 78 percent of applicants and has a high average class size of 21 students. It has found gold and growth in research, which brings upwards of $8 million to the university each year. The finer faculty members, of which LSU has dozens, must accommodate a wide range of students—from the intellectual elite of the state, produced by excellent parochial and magnet schools, to standard-issue slackers. Still, there are more good courses and faculty at LSU than at many state universities,

VITAL STATISTICS

Religious affiliation: none
Total enrollment: 32,241
Total undergraduates: 26,387
SAT/ACT midranges: SAT
  V: 520–630, M: 530–640;
  ACT: 22–27
Applicants: 11,077
Applicants accepted: 78%
*Accepted applicants who
  enrolled*: 66%
Tuition: $2,855 (in state),
  $9,655 (out of state)
Room and board: $5,882
Freshman retention rate: 85%
Graduation rate: 25% (4 yrs.),
  58% (6 yrs.)
*Courses with fewer than 20
  students*: 31%
Student-faculty ratio: 22:1
*Courses taught by graduate
  TAs*: 14%
Most popular majors:
  business, education,
  social sciences
Students living on campus:
  23%
*Guaranteed housing for four
  years?* no
Students in fraternities: 10%
  sororities: 17%

SOUTH

465

LSU imposes modest distributional mandates on students, who must take:

- Two courses in English composition.
- Two courses in analytical reasoning (math or logic).
- One course in the arts.
- Three courses in humanities. These may include foreign languages, communications classes, or classical studies, such as "Introduction to Philosophy" or "Modern Europe."
- Three courses in the natural sciences.
- Two courses in the social sciences, such as "Human Geography: Americas and Europe," "Introduction to Psychology," or "American Government."

and focused students can still find excellent teachers, distinctive academic resources, and hearty fellowship in an atmosphere friendly to patriotism and faith on one of the most beautiful campuses in America. But they had better like heat and humidity.

Academic Life: Loss of honors

Louisiana State University wants you to know that it is a research university on the rise. In fact, the first goal in LSU's mission states that "the vision of Louisiana State University is to be a leading research-extensive university." Former chancellor Mark Emmert (who left LSU in 2004) wrote in his welcome letter: "With more than 85 research centers, institutes, labs, and programs, LSU is at the forefront of producing cutting-edge science and technology." Many of the university's initiatives seem directed at keeping the school's status as a "research-I" institution and fending off the challenge of the University of Louisiana in Lafayette—a one-time regional university that is now attempting to contest LSU's longtime status as the state's flagship school. With all that research going on, it's easy to forget that there are roughly 26,000 undergraduates hanging about the place, some of them even aspiring towards a liberal education. It remains to be seen if the new chancellor, former NASA director Sean O'Keefe, will show more interest in undergraduate liberal education than in the numbers-driven search for national prominence.

Aware that it has long underfunded LSU—particularly during the 1990s—the state of Louisiana has backed the school's ambitious "Flagship Agenda," a plan which aims, among other things, to "increase undergraduate admission standards and recruit and retain top students." To this end, the school has received money to "add 150 faculty members, increase graduate assistants by 50 percent, double the number of postdoctorate positions, and increase annual library collections and access to scholarly material by 50 percent." Already, a number of departments, including English, have received funding for more tenure-track professors, reducing their reliance on adjunct faculty. There have been some transitional problems in implementing this shift to tenure-track teaching. Many nontenured instructors in the mathematics and English department were let go at once, resulting "in huge sections of the introductory classes in each subject," reports one student. "I cannot imagine how anyone could effectively teach an English composition class to 100-plus people," he says.

Unfortunately, none of this new tax money has found its way to the single best resource for a true liberal arts education on campus: LSU's Honors College. This program, for which a separate application is required, promises "the benefits of a small liberal arts environment within a large research university." Honors students can choose to live together in the Laville Honors House, which is the site of weekly teas with Honors College faculty members. Students complete a traditional major in one of the regular academic colleges, which means that participation in the Honors College can coincide with studies in fields outside the humanities. Up to 10 years ago, one could get as good a grounding in the liberal arts in the LSU Honors College as that available at most Ivy League schools, according to graduates.

However, the Honors College is not what it used to be. One melancholy professor says that "the LSU administration has not treated the Honors College honorably," noting that in the past, "the Honors College was staffed largely by graduate faculty members, and the core courses were taught at a consistently high level. Since then, LSU has used the Honors College to recruit students, but failed to fund it. As a result, while the level of student intelligence and interest is high, the core courses are largely staffed by adjunct professors. The level of instruction is about average for freshman courses generally at LSU, and that is very uneven."

Unfortunately, a freshman may qualify for the Honors College and not be admitted, because admissions have been restricted to 600 students—regardless of how many freshmen meet the criteria. Even students who are admitted to the program may be turned away from one of the freshman core courses, since honors only has the money to accommodate 250 to 300 students, according to a source on campus. This casual neglect of the best place for liberal education at the school suggests a profound distortion of priorities. As one professor says: "Undergraduate education is quite low on the administration's agenda for the university: There is no prestige or money in teaching young people." It is telling that the university can find money to hire 150 new faculty members to teach specialized courses on their latest research in various departments, while refusing to fund classes in ancient literature, medieval studies, and the Renaissance. Indeed, some of those foundational classes are beginning to be replaced in the Honors offerings by narrow, politicized courses. Not promising.

The University College Center for Freshman Year is responsible for students' initial academic advising; once he declares a major, a student transfers to an advisor in that department. While in the University College, students begin completing the university-wide general education requirements. One student cautions that the school's survey

REQUIREMENTS (CONT'D)

Students face a second set of requirements once they enter one of LSU's 10 colleges, which include Agriculture, Art and Design, Arts and Sciences, Basic Sciences, Business, Engineering, Education, and Music and Dramatic Arts. For example, a student entering the College of Arts and Sciences and majoring in a humanities area must take:

- Freshman English.
- Two courses in literature.
- One humanities class outside English or foreign languages.
- Courses up to the fourth semester in a foreign language (or show equivalent test scores).
- A year-long course in the biological or physical sciences (with lab), plus an additional science class.
- One math course.
- One additional course in analytical reasoning.
- Two courses in history.
- Three courses in the social sciences.

courses can result "in a disappointingly shallow education," and for that reason, serious scholars should seek out more challenging classes—for instance, by taking the honors sections when they are offered. "LSU is a large state university, so of course there are a thousand ways to graduate while avoiding the most serious matters of study," says one professor. "But there are also some very fine faculty in a number of fields, and the student who wants to look will find them quickly enough."

Given its financial constraints, LSU offers an impressive number of strong academic programs. In the humanities, English, political science, history, philosophy and religious studies, music, and theater are notable for their quality instruction. The English department's requirements for majors are suspect, though; majors are required to take classes like "Critical Strategies," "Modern Criticism," and an ethnic or women's literature course. Happily, students must also choose at least one course on Milton, Chaucer, or Shakespeare. Trendy courses tend to be taught by assertive and often intolerant academics who hail from major universities outside the South—and who aren't thrilled about living in Louisiana, often cracking jokes at the expense of local politics and mores. Such professors often make a point of trying to "enlighten" their more conservative charges, and they have been known to detect evidence of "retrograde" views (for instance, traditional Christianity) in student papers and to grade them accordingly. One student who cited Thomas Aquinas in a final paper in a required class received a zero (not an F, a *zero*) for the assignment—which would have led to her expulsion from the graduate program. (Her paper was subsequently accepted at a national conference.) When her justified grade appeal was routinely denied, she was forced to threaten the university with a lawsuit before the English department finally backed down. This happened 10 years ago, but the offending professor is still on the faculty, so beware.

The safest bet, says one graduate, is to "ask other students about a professor's politics and fairness before taking his class, particularly in the English or French departments. Or go visit the professor before you register, and talk with him. Air your views openly, and see how he reacts. If you catch the slightest hint of hostility, look for another section or course."

The LSU geography department is one of the finest in the country. The economics department is free market–oriented, although professors use econometric rather than theoretical approaches to the subject. The political science department is strong in political theory, thanks to the heritage of the great theoretician Eric Voegelin, a former professor. Students interested in learning the history of ideas should seek out the faculty associated with the Eric Voegelin Institute and enroll in their courses—which are among the best theory classes offered anywhere in the United States.

On the other hand, the mass communications school, while growing in size and reputation, is "soft academically," in the words of one student. Students have been known to describe classes in such subjects as journalism as "the easiest they have ever taken." Students in the business school are not known for their intellectuality. "Business majors may hardly ever if at all walk into the library," says a student. Another calls these business students "ethically challenged."

Of course, at such a big school one is bound to find intellectual gems. Among the many fine professors on campus are John R. Baker, Charles Bigger (emeritus), Edward Henderson, Gregory Schufreider, Mary Sirridge, and John Whittaker in philosophy and religious studies; James and Edith Babin, James Bennett, Anne Coldiron, Kevin Cope, Brian Costelo, Bainard and Christine Cowan, Rebecca Crump, William Demastes, Michael Hegarty, John Lowe, David Madden, John R. May, Robert McMahon, Elsie Michie, Susannah Monta, Lisi Oliver, Malcolm Richardson, James Wilcox, and Michelle Zerba in English; Gaines M. Foster, James D. Hardy Jr., Paul F. Paskoff, Karl Roider, and Victor L. Stater in history; and Cecil L. Eubanks, Mark Gasiorowski, Wayne Parent, Ellis Sandoz, and James Stoner in political science.

Official statistics indicate that almost 8 percent of all classes have more than 100 students. The student-faculty ratio is rather depressing, at about 22 to 1. Even with these numbers, one student seems surprised that in most of her honors courses, "the instructor has known the name of every student in the class." Professors are said to be accessible. "The teachers are willing to personally help you and take time out for you," a student says.

Graduate student teaching assistants teach some course sections, particularly in areas such as English, math, and the basic sciences. Except for the Honors College, the advising system at LSU is weak. The otherwise excellent history department, for instance, has one undergraduate faculty advisor to handle the academic needs of all LSU history majors. One student says the advising program "operate[s] like a factory, and an inefficient one at that." The school is said to be revising its long-inadequate freshman composition courses and developing a plan for writing across the curriculum—two worthy initiatives, given the inadequate high school English education that most LSU students have received.

Student Life: We'll have good fun on the bayou

LSU sits on more than 2,000 acres in Baton Rouge, population 230,000. The school has begun spending money on restoring its lovely, long-decaying campus. LSU's stately Italian Renaissance–style buildings (modeled on those at Stanford, which Huey Long visited and decided to copy) and classic art deco theater are now undergoing a thorough rehabilitation. The school is opening a new art museum in once-desolate downtown Baton Rouge, featuring "14 galleries totaling 13,000 square feet of state-of-the-art exhibition space with soaring 16-foot ceilings and beautiful lighting," according to the uni-

SUGGESTED CORE
1. Classical Studies 3020, Classical Epic in Translation
2. Philosophy 2033, History of Ancient and Medieval Philosophy
3. Religious Studies 1004/ 1005, Old Testament / New Testament
4. Religious Studies 4928, Augustine, Anselm, and Aquinas
5. Political Science 4082, History of Political Theory from Machiavelli to Nietzsche
6. English 2148, Shakespeare
7. History 2055, The United States to 1865
8. History 4113, Modern European Intellectual History since 1850

SOUTH

versity, to house LSU's impressive collection of fine and decorative arts. The English department building, Allen Hall, is graced by lovely WPA murals.

The campus is bordered on the west by the Mississippi River, and two mounds made by Native Americans more than 5,000 years ago stand at the northwest corner of the campus. Live oak trees and colonnaded passageways dot the campus. For nightlife, students head to blues and jazz clubs for live music and "meat market" bars for dancing. Tigerland, a group of apartments and bars near campus, is a popular place to go on weekends, as are The Varsity, where bands play; Louie's, a greasy spoon close to campus; and The Chimes restaurant.

Students also hang out at the LSU Union, which includes a bookstore, theater, games area, and food stands; or at the Parade Grounds, a grassy area where students play intramurals, lie in the sun, study, and play Frisbee. Baton Rouge's downtown has begun to see a renaissance of arts and small businesses. The city is also host to the Jimmy Swaggart Bible College—which frequently dispatches young evangelists to preach on the LSU campus against immorality and immodest dress—and St. Agnes Church, a parish served by nuns of Mother Teresa's order, which offers a weekly Latin mass. (Students dissatisfied with the watery doctrine preached at the campus Catholic chapel take refuge at such neighboring parishes.) The Baton Rouge Zoo is large and well worth visiting—as is the art deco Louisiana State Capitol.

Student life at LSU is vibrant—if not particularly healthful. Drinking makes up a significant part of social life on campus, as students throng local bars in defiance of the under-21 drinking laws—which Louisiana adopted only under enormous pressure from the federal government. Nearby New Orleans still features drive-through daiquiri shops, and Cajuns to the school's south and west tend to take "one for the road" quite literally, flouting bans on open containers. If you prefer eating to drinking, Baton Rouge is a wonderful town to learn the intricacies of Cajun and classic Southern cooking; it also hosts a surprising variety of ethnic restaurants.

Among LSU's numerous student organizations are agricultural and equestrian clubs, the usual Greek houses, religious clubs, and ethnic groups. Some of the more unusual include the Wargaming and Roleplaying Society, the Hip-Hop Coalition, and the Poker Strategy Club. A service group called Ambassadors and student government are comparatively popular among students. There are also many Christian groups.

The Greek system has a strong presence at LSU. Although only 10 percent of men join fraternities and 17 percent of women join sororities, one student says, "Their influence is way bigger than those numbers represent. Greek students have a big profile on campus. They're the ones holding office in student government." In 2003, nine disciplinary actions were taken against fraternities and sororities for violations ranging from alcohol to assault to hazing. "Fraternities keep doing stupid things and getting into trouble here," says a student. "We've had a couple kicked off campus." Indeed, several years ago two fraternities were removed from campus until 2005 and another was put on probation until 2006.

Tiger football games are what really lie at the center of LSU students' social lives. LSU won a share of the 2003 national championship, bestirring its historically fervent football fans. As one student says, "There is nothing better than to go to an LSU football game and sit in the student section. Everyone around you is so pumped." Tailgating is extraordinarily popular, as alumni and others fill vast parking lots with pickup trucks containing propane stoves to heat gumbo and barbecue. The city of Baton Rouge clogs with traffic and pretty much closes down on game days as Louisianans converge from all over the state to throng the massive, Stalinist-modern Tiger Stadium. If you don't like football, leave town—well in advance.

The LSU athletic program is one of the best in the nation, with strong gymnastics, swimming, baseball, and men's and women's track teams. The women's and men's basketball teams also have many fans. Students take part in a number of intramural sports, including ultimate Frisbee, wallyball (think volleyball played on a racquetball court), and flag football. At the LSU Union, students can enroll in art instruction or courses in wine tasting and Cajun dancing. Too few students take advantage of such worthy opportunities, however.

If the orientations of LSU's student organizations may be used as a guide to the political temperature of the campus, it may be indicative that just 10 of the more than 300 clubs have political purposes. (By contrast, there are 25 religious clubs.) "There's no overemphasis on politics here," says a student. "It's not a topic you really hear about." You're much more likely to hear people talking about, say, hunting and fishing. LSU's College Republicans is consistently one of the largest such chapters in the country, at more than 1,000 members, while the College Democrats boast only 200.

"Louisiana is a culturally conservative state and it shows in the student body. There are no hippies, no love-fests on the Parade Grounds," says one student. A professor says, "Generally speaking, I would describe LSU students as conservative and religious but grounded in common sense and decency rather than fanaticism." The most prominent churches on campus are the Catholic and the Baptist chapels.

No students are required to live on campus, though many choose to live either in the dorms or in residential colleges—which range from the quaint and traditional (with ceiling fans) to the huge and hideous (which are at least air conditioned). Happily, students no longer live under the bleachers of Tiger Stadium—as they did well into the '90s. (Huey Long couldn't get legislators to fund a stadium, so he built dorms in a stadium shape and planted grass in the middle. No, we're not making this up.)

Some residence halls are single sex, while others separate the sexes by floor. Women's dorms maintain a curfew for the opposite sex, though enforcement depends upon one's residential advisor. Students may opt to live in one of several living-learning communities. The Information Technology Residential College is designed to provide students training in just that. Herget Residential College was created "to foster a sense of community and to create an environment that encourages and facilitates academic effort and achievement." Students take some classes together and meet regularly with residential college mentors. The Vision Louisiana program is for students who "want to affect the future of Louisiana." A four-year program during which students must live in the residence hall at least two years, Vision Louisiana endeavors to apply material covered in courses towards solving problems facing the state.

Perhaps LSU students' penchant for heavy drinking is why liquor-law and drug violations are up to 10 times as frequent as at universities of similar size. LSU's assault and burglary statistics are also high. Because the school adjoins one of the poorest neighborhoods in Baton Rouge, crime is a persistent problem on campus; 2003 crime statistics include two rapes, one robbery, 85 burglaries, 11 assaults, and 22 stolen cars on campus. Compare this with Georgia State's report of only 13 burglaries and three assaults for the same year (and note that Georgia State is in downtown Atlanta). The LSU Police Department provides awareness and safety training to students, but there are only 16 emergency call boxes located on campus.

Like most state schools, LSU is quite a bargain for residents of the state—who, thanks to Huey Long's populist "homestead exemption," pay very low local taxes, one reason the school is underfunded. It's also pretty cheap for out-of-staters. In 2004–5, the school charged $2,855 to in-state students and $9,655 to those from out of state. Room and board was a modest $5,882. LSU's admission process is need-blind, and the school provides aid to about 43 percent of students. The average student loan debt upon graduation is $15,997.

UNIVERSITY OF MISSISSIPPI

OXFORD, MISSISSIPPI • WWW.OLEMISS.EDU

A fable

Ole Miss has all the advantages of student life at a relatively small, southern, traditional state school. Rebel fans support their teams—especially football—vigorously, and throw grand parties before, during, and after football season. Campus life is peppered with traditions like the school cheer and lingo like "the Grove" and "the Square." And if university-town Oxford ever feels too small, Memphis is less than an hour's drive away. Yes, student life at Ole Miss is enticing.

But be watchful, or academic life may pass you by. It is possible to get a top-notch education at Ole Miss—but it's by no means necessary. Remarks a professor dryly, "Students can indeed graduate with a narrow knowledge base, particularly by majoring in 'soft' disciplines, which rarely demand more than rote memorization." Fortunately, good professors are also attracted to the school's picturesque location and traditional sensibilities; consequently, there are a good many quality courses at Ole Miss. If students remember to take them.

Academic Life: Light in August— and other months

"There is an incredible opportunity to get a fulfilling education," says a recent graduate. "At Ole Miss I gained leadership experience, confidence, and exposure to many great programs and organizations." Therein lies the rub. Exposure to programs is one thing, but the real question is, "Do Ole Miss students get exposure to great ideas and thinkers?"

Not necessarily. While the University of Mississippi's curricula and distribution requirements differ substantially across its academic sub-units, its "core" requirements are inconsequential. You might not even know you were in the center of the real-life version of William Faulkner's fictional Yoknapatawpha County if you relied solely on the distribution requirements. The number of courses that fulfill the distribution requirements varies wildly from one discipline to another. For instance, the six-hour requirement for social science may be met by any course at all in anthropology, economics, political science, sociology, or psychology— or Journalism 101. And so it goes: any course in the history department fulfills the six-hour history requirement; any course offered by the art history department meets the three-hour fine arts requirement; and to make the three hours in the humanities, students may take any course in classical civilization, African American studies, philosophy, religion, or, if these don't suit, pick from a list of 10 approved courses from other departments.

VITAL STATISTICS
Religious affiliation: none
Total enrollment: 14,497
Total undergraduates: 11,820
SAT/ACT midranges: SAT: 980–1240; ACT: 20–26
Applicants: 6,999
Applicants accepted: 80%
Accepted applicants who enrolled: 42%
Tuition: $4,110 (in state), $9,264 (out of state)
Room and board: $5,610
Freshman retention rate: 81%
Graduation rate: 34% (4 yrs.), 54% (6 yrs.)
Courses with fewer than 20 students: 40%
Student-faculty ratio: 21:1
Courses taught by graduate TAs: not provided
Most popular majors: business, education, social sciences
Students living on campus: 28%
Guaranteed housing for four years? no
Students in fraternities: 25% sororities: 35%

The natural science requirement seems, by comparison, positively rigorous. Students must take a full year of coursework in any one area: astronomy, physics, biology, chemistry, or geology, and another course from a second department (the only exception being that students who take astronomy courses to fulfill the first requirement may not take physics to fulfill the second, and vice versa). Two of these courses must have a laboratory component.

The University of Mississippi offers 86 baccalaureate degrees through the seven undergraduate colleges on its Oxford campus. Surprisingly, only a minor in religion is offered, although one can get a degree in just about everything else, including criminal justice and exercise science. Should these options not satisfy, the College of Liberal Arts offers an interdisciplinary bachelor's degree that allows a student to combine any three minors.

One unique and prestigious degree offered is a bachelor of arts in southern studies. Ole Miss is the home of the Center for the Study of Southern Culture, which has been, for nearly 30 years, the premier place to study the writings of Mr. Faulkner (long-

SOUTH

time resident of Oxford, who wrote so much about the place that he said, "I discovered that my own little postage stamp of native soil was worth writing about and that I would never live long enough to exhaust it") and the works of other southern luminaries. Thanks to a grant from John Grisham (another one-time resident of Oxford), each year the English department hosts a visiting southern writer. Courses offered through the center vary by semester but include such gems as "Southern Literature and the Oral Tradition," "An Economic History of the South since the Civil War," "The Fiction of Faulkner's Yoknapatawpha County," and seminars on various major southern authors. Oxford's Square Books boasts signed editions of Faulkner and other major writers and serves as a hangout for literary types on campus. Faulkner's old home, Rowan Oak, stands in town and is certainly worth a visit.

The rigor of major requirements does, of course, vary. The Department of English (strong particularly in nineteenth- and twentieth-century American literature, southern literature, and creative writing) requires of its students six hours of 300-level seminars, a course in Shakespeare, and seven upper-level electives. The history department demands 33 hours that "show a reasonable balance between United States and non-United States history courses." All history majors must take a two-course sequence on the history of Europe, two senior seminars, and at least two upper-level courses on the history of non-Western nations.

Thankfully, Ole Miss generally offers solid courses. The English department offered, in 2004–5, classes on Shakespeare, Chaucer, major authors of Britain, surveys of southern and of Greek literature—and only a couple of suspect courses like "Gay and Lesbian Literature and Theory."

The same is true for the history department, which offered "The Roman Republic," "European History: Late Middle Ages and the Renaissance," and "African American History since 1865." But, to help out majors searching for that "reasonable balance" between U.S. history and non-U.S. courses, the courses offered in the latter category seem a bit flightier ("Race and Ethnicity in Latin America," for example). Nonetheless, there are a good many quality courses that cover history outside of the United States.

The pickings in the philosophy and religion department are slim. Philosophy courses cover only the very basics: "Introduction to Philosophy," "Logic," "Aesthetics," and, for some reason, "Buddhism."

Academic advising is mandatory, but—as with the distribution requirements—its quality varies by school. Students in the College of Liberal Arts are assigned faculty advisors, but those in the School of Business Administration and School of Accountancy are guided by an academic advising center. The university's Web site makes it clear that, whatever the method or college, "students have the primary responsibility for planning their individual programs and meeting graduation requirements." Says a student, "The process usually involves a lot of waiting, but that can be avoided if students take advantage of early advising, appointments, etc." A student in the College of Liberal Arts says, "I think the system works very well. . . . Having the same advisor for the entirety of one's undergraduate career is helpful."

Professors at Ole Miss are readily available to students. "In general, the faculty are eager to help when called upon," says a student. "Because Ole Miss is rather small, undergraduates here are much more likely than they are at other public universities to receive instruction from full-time members of the faculty rather than graduate students," says a professor. Nevertheless, Ole Miss *does* make use of teaching assistants, who teach lower-level courses, particularly those that students take to fulfill distribution requirements—but that is due, in part, to the budget crisis facing the school. State support has dwindled to one-fourth of the university's funding, and tuition payments represent the university's largest source of recurring income. As a natural consequence, the number of students admitted has increased while the pace of hiring new faculty has not kept up. The student-faculty ratio is a rather dismal 21 to 1. "More has to be done with less," says a professor, "and graduate programs are under threat."

Students from the University's Honors College and the Croft Institute for International Studies are, according to one professor, "the cream of the crop." The composite profile of a Sally McDonnell Barksdale Honors College student is an SAT score of 1310 (ACT 30) and a high school GPA of 3.85. Not bad. Honors college students are required to take at least 29 hours of honors credit and must keep a 3.5 grade point average. They take freshman and sophomore seminars, complete a research project undertaken with a faculty mentor, and write a senior thesis. The remaining credit hours come from specially designated honors courses in regular departments. These courses offer smaller enrollment and more discussion. Honors students must also attend two performances, conferences, exhibits, or guest lectures each semester and volunteer 10 hours per semester in community service. The honors college Web site claims, "[We] offer an education similar to that at prestigious private liberal arts schools . . . but at a far lower cost." And that may well be true: the course selection at Mississippi is better than at some elite, diversity-addled Yankee colleges. The 30 honors classes offered in Spring 2005 included solid choices like "Greek Literature in Translation," "Art Appreciation: Western," and "Principles of Macroeconomics."

The Croft Institute for International Studies admits just 45 students each year, who must complete the institute's curriculum in addition to that of the College of

ACADEMIC REQUIREMENTS

The University of Mississippi is like most state schools in that it imposes only weak, unhelpful distribution requirements. On the other hand, given the school's traditional orientation, many of the courses that satisfy these requirements are good. All undergraduates must take:

- Six hours of English composition.
- Three hours of mathematics.
- Six hours of laboratory science.
- Fifteen hours in the humanities, social/ behavioral sciences, and fine arts, with at least three hours from each category.
- A one-hour course called "The University in Principle and Practice."

  Bachelor of arts students must also take:
- Six hours in a foreign language at the intermediate level or above.
- Three more hours in mathematics.
- Three to five more hours in natural science.
- Six hours in history.
- Three more hours in the social sciences.

Liberal Arts. Students take four core courses introducing them to international studies, East Asia, Europe, and Latin America. Subsequently, students take another four courses each in two concentrations: thematic (such as "global economics and business") and geographic. Students have a chance to examine their chosen area firsthand, as all international studies students are required to study abroad.

Although the university administration has engaged in "top-down decision-making," according to a professor (for example, a couple of years ago administrators decided to transfer the economics department from the business school to the College of Liberal Arts against the unanimous vote of the economics faculty), at present there is no overt pressure to conform to any particular political point of view. "But there certainly are places where leftist and statist ideologies find their ways into the curriculum, particularly in the English, history, and sociology departments," the professor says. However, students do not complain—to us, anyway—of professors' political views unduly affecting course content. "The typical UM faculty member's interest tends to focus on cutting-edge research," a professor says. Another professor says, "More and more faculty are showing interest in interdisciplinary topics such as bioinformatics (biology plus computers) or conservation biology."

Some schools and departments are known to be more exacting than others. The School of Pharmacy and the EH Patterson School of Accounting are rigorous, and the economics, English, and physics departments of the College of Liberal Arts are particularly strong. However, one professor says, "the marketing and management majors, two examples with which I am most familiar, are widely perceived as easy insofar as they emphasize 'practical' knowledge over 'theory.' These majors prepare students for entry-level jobs in the banking, insurance, and real estate industries, but fail utterly to equip them with the intellectual tools necessary for a lifetime of learning."

Highly recommended professors at Ole Miss include Benjamin F. Fisher IV, Donald M. Kartiganer, Colby H. Kullman, and Joseph R. Urgo in English; William F. Chappell, John R. Conlon, and William F. Shughart II in economics; Robert B. Westmoreland in philosophy and religion; Alice H. Cooper and John W. Winkle in political science; David S. Hargrove in psychology; and Dale L. Flesher, Tonya Kay Flesher, and Morris H. Stocks in the School of Accountancy.

Student Life: The unvanquished

Oxford, Mississippi, is a charming community of 13,000 located just 70 miles south of Memphis, Tennessee. It is also a university town—Ole Miss being Lafayette County's biggest employer—and subsequently boasts an abundance of restaurants, bars, and boutiques in the historic downtown area (known as the Square) surrounding the Lafayette County Courthouse. (Faulkner wrote about the courthouse, too, in *Requiem for a Nun*, and it is quoted on a plaque next to the courthouse: "But above all, the courthouse: the center, the focus, the hub; sitting looming in the center of the county's circumference like a single cloud in its ring of horizon, laying its vast shadow to the uttermost rim of horizon; musing, brooding, symbolic and ponderable, tall as cloud, solid as rock, dominating all: protector of the weak, judiciate and curb of the passions and lusts, repository and guardian of the aspirations and hopes. . . .") A student says, "By far, the most popular place to hang out in Oxford is the Square, which truly feels like a movie set. There are upwards of 30 bars and restaurants around the town square area, so many students opt to spend time there at night." So many students spend time there, in fact, that another student reports, "Lines to get in to the most popular bars can begin around 7 p.m. on Thursday nights." Hopes and aspirations, indeed!

Yes, Ole Miss is something of a party school. One student calls bar-hopping an "art" in Oxford. He says, "Since the bars close at 1 a.m., 'late nights' are very common. These involve going to someone's house after the bar and continuing the party." About one-third of students at Ole Miss go Greek, and many students follow family lineages to the university in the hopes of affiliating themselves with the same fraternity or sorority. Says a non-Greek, "Each sorority or fraternity is steeped in its own tradition. Still, interaction between non-Greek and Greek students is great." Says a professor, "Sorority and fraternity activities dominate the social calendar throughout the year, but football is the number one priority in the fall."

SUGGESTED CORE
1. Classical 307, Greek Literature in English Translation
2. Philosophy 301, History of Philosophy I
3. Religion 310, The Old Testament and Early Judaism *and* Religion 312, The New Testament and Early Christianity
4. Religion 373, Ancient Christianity *and* Religion 375, History of Medieval Christianity
5. Philosophy 331, Political Philosophy (*closest match*)
6. English 385, Shakespeare
7. History 105, History of the United States to 1877
8. History 341, The Darwinian Revolution (*closest match*)

Ah, football season, when "bars are always packed with football celebrations," according to a student. "Football is the lifeblood of Ole Miss," says a student. "There are more traditions associated with Ole Miss football than I can write in one day." The biggest and best of these traditions is, of course tailgating in "the Grove," which one student describes as "an elaborate experience." The Grove is a 10-acre wooded area in the middle of campus where tens of thousands of students, alumni, and fans gather with tents and large spreads of food. These tailgates have become famous, even making the pages of *Sports Illustrated*. A student says, "Game-day attire is very strict: Children either have cheerleading outfits or Ole Miss jerseys on, girls have heels and dresses . . . and the guys have suits and ties. If you don't follow these fashion rules, then you're obviously with the visiting team." Another student describes it as "cocktail party meets hardcore tailgating."

Other sports are not nearly as beloved as football. However, of its 18 men's and women's sports teams, Ole Miss has a strong tennis team and women's soccer team. The University of Mississippi also offers an active intramural program, serving more than 6,500 participants each year. There are the usual suspects here, along with whiffleball, walleyball, and special events like bingo and Texas hold 'em tournaments.

Because student life is so enticing, "Ole Miss seems to have a large percentage of fifth-year seniors. Many students choose to spread classes out for a lighter courseload each semester," says a student. And a recent graduate says, "Ole Miss has a lot of great

SOUTH

477

qualities and traditions, but I must say that very few of the students that chose the university did so based on academics." Professors' analyses bear this out. One sums up his students' attitudes this way: "To generalize, the majority of the students at Ole Miss view classes as something to get through in order to graduate. Most do not come to office hours, except toward the end of the semester when it usually is too late. Opportunities to exploit class time as a forum for exploring ideas are few and far between, since the typical student does not want to stand out from the crowd by asking questions and would never risk challenging an instructor's opinion." Still, he adds, "While about half of the students in the undergraduate classes I teach—targeted primarily toward business and engineering majors—are not strongly motivated to excel academically, about 10 to 15 percent of my students are very good, equal to the best I have taught anywhere." Another professor considers his students "often interested in learning" but "lacking in all of the skills they need in order to learn. High schools are not doing a very good job of teaching studying skills and time management."

In fact, enough freshmen have trouble making the transition to college, getting caught up in Ole Miss's traditions and morning-afters, that the university's administration has implemented a program called Freshmen Absence-Based Intervention (FABI). Designed to "circumvent student absences and potential student failure," according to its Web site, FABI calls upon professors who teach lower-level courses to report to a secure Web site the names of freshmen with "excessive absences." The burden of the intervention falls upon the student's residence hall advisor and academic advisor.

In describing her peers, one student uses three words: "Conservative. Conservative. Conservative." Another student says, "Ole Miss is an extremely conservative southern school, and most of the students value that." This is perhaps explained by the student profile: two-thirds of Ole Miss students hail from Mississippi, many of them from small towns, and, according to a professor, "many of our students come from families with incomes far above the statewide average; significant numbers have been born into wealth." Professors, of course, tend to be more liberal.

While the student body tends toward the right, the student newspaper, the *Daily Mississippian*, has been traditionally dominated by liberal students, according to a professor: "Lip service is paid to 'diversity' and the homosexual agenda is in full flower on the paper's editorial page." One professor considers UM's atmosphere to "very much allow for free speech," and students and professors report that both sides of the political spectrum feel comfortable in making their voices heard.

The College Republicans are large and active. The student government is popular on campus, as is the student programming board, which brings in musicians, comedians, and hosts the annual beauty pageant—something that would have already been halted at other schools. Otherwise, "few of the professional or special-interest organizations seem to be popular or prestigious," says a student. Most of the nearly 200 student organizations fall along religious, professional, or Greek lines. The more unique ones include the Anime Club, which watches, yes, Japanese cartoons; the Financier's Club; and the Feral University Rebel Rescuers, whose mission is "to humanely control and maintain the homeless cat population on the University of Mississippi campus."

For a school that had to be desegregated at gunpoint by federal marshals some 40 years ago, Ole Miss is now quite comfortably multiracial—if still rather segregated, by student choice. Some 13 percent of the student population is black. As one professor told the *Daily Mississipian*, "It's a problem that all campuses face and a problem that all aspects of society face. . . . I haven't noticed it being much different there than here. In fact, I'd say there are more mixed groups here than elsewhere." Despite the occasional controversy over the display of the Confederate battle flag—once a staple at football games—the school has avoided much of the interracial animus (and resulting heavy-handed "diversity" initiatives) that afflicts other schools north and south.

Students who do not reside in one of the 28 fraternity and sorority houses can live in university housing. Some 28 percent of students live on campus, and freshmen are required to do so. There are set visitation hours, but during the first week of classes in the fall residents may vote to extend the hours. Some residence halls are reserved by sex. The university is embarking on a multimillion-dollar project to renovate most of the residence halls, adding amenities like kitchen facilities, study floors, music practice rooms, and courtyards.

The school is pretty safe; in 2003, it reported two forcible sex offenses, nine burglaries, and two stolen cars on campus.

Whether you're from Mississippi or not, this school is quite inexpensive, with 2004–5 tuition a mere $4,110 for in-state students and $9,264 for nonresidents. Room and board cost $5,610. Admissions are need-blind, and while the school cannot afford to guarantee full financial aid to all, 85 percent of students get some of kind of aid. The average debt of a recent graduate is (a surprisingly high) $18,500.

Morehouse College

Expecting respect

Founded in 1867 to educate freed slaves, Morehouse College began as the Augusta Institute in the basement of Springfield Baptist Church. The college moved to Atlanta 12 years later, eventually changing its name to commemorate a Baptist leader in that city. Morehouse remains the only historically black, all-male college in the country. With the all-female Spelman College, Clark-Atlanta University, Morris Brown College, the Interdenominational Theological Center, and the Morehouse School of Medicine, it is a member of the Atlanta University Center, the "largest private educational consortium with a predominately black enrollment in the world." Students in any one of these schools can enroll in courses at any of the others, thereby taking advantage of resources their own schools may not offer.

Few if any cities boast as rich a history of black leadership in industry, government, and education as does Atlanta, and Morehouse College plays a pivotal role in maintaining this tradition. As renowned former Morehouse president Benjamin E. Mays told the graduating class of 1961, "There is an air of expectancy at Morehouse College. It is expected that the student who enters here will do well. It is also expected that once a man bears the insignia of a Morehouse graduate he will do exceptionally well. We expect nothing less."

The spirit of Mays's charge continues to this day. "The House," as the college is reverentially called, is as profoundly steeped in tradition as any American academic institution, including the military academies. During the annual Freshman Week prior to each fall term, new freshmen are led to Sales Chapel, where upperclassmen impart the legends of such alumni luminaries as Martin Luther King. Throughout the week, upperclassman may at any time subject freshman to impromptu drills in the hallways, testing their knowledge of the school's history and lore. The week ends with a celebratory trip to a nearby amusement park that the school rents for the purpose, and with "Spirit Night," a torch-lit rally where students are regaled with inspirational speeches about the meaning and tradition of becoming a "Morehouse man."

Morehouse's Leadership Center was established almost 10 years ago to prepare students for ethical leadership and to instill in them "character, civility, and a sense of community." The "Morehouse man" works towards all of these ideals. While most college students roll out of bed to attend class in jeans—at best—students at Morehouse frequently don coats and ties (obligatory for new students during Freshman Week). And while most colleges try to put students and professors on an equal footing, at Morehouse the deference of students to their professors (not to mention upperclassmen) is tangible. A professor from another university says, "I don't think I've seen so pronounced a sense of respect and decorum in any school such as what I witnessed during my days at Morehouse College."

Academic Life: . . . Period

Today, Morehouse is led by President Walter E. Massey, a noted physicist and a graduate of the class of 1958. Under his direction, the future looks good for Morehouse. Upon taking the helm, Massey said his main goal would be to renew "Morehouse's commitment to a culture of excellence." And indeed, under Massey's guidance Morehouse has reasserted its grand tradition while meeting the demands of the twenty-first century—academically, socially, and politically. Two projects Massey has instituted are the Leadership Center, which sponsors a lecture series, and the Institutional Values Project, which, according to its mission statement, organizes discussions and surveys about how to make Morehouse "one of the best liberal arts colleges in the nation . . . period. And the college of choice for African American males." In academics, Massey has emphasized the real-life application of pure science to the business world, as well as interdisciplinary approaches.

Morehouse's alumni roster includes some of the most distinguished men in twentieth-century America, including Martin Luther King Jr., NAACP chairman Julian Bond, filmmaker Spike Lee, actor Samuel L. Jackson, Olympic gold medalist Edwin Moses, and Atlanta mayor Maynard Jackson—all, in one way or another, archetypal "Morehouse men." Among all-black colleges and universities, Morehouse consistently ranks at or near the top, and the school is considered by many to be one of the finest colleges in the South . . . period. While test scores for entering freshmen are nothing special, numbers do not tell the story. As one parent says, "I was more concerned with what I thought Morehouse could do to enrich my son—both as a man and as an intellect—than what its numbers could do for my ego." Her point is well taken, for while many liberal arts colleges have loosened academic requirements, Morehouse continues to impose on its students a rather structured set of courses. The college wants not only to give students a broad exposure to the liberal arts, it also wants to create a shared base of knowledge that its students can build on in subsequent courses and later in life.

To satisfy the requirements of the college-wide curriculum, students take a variety of courses in both the sciences and the humanities. "There is no leeway allowed in completing the courses," a professor says. "Students are encouraged to finish the core

VITAL STATISTICS

Religious affiliation: Baptist
Total enrollment: 3,000
Total undergraduates: 3,000
SAT/ACT midranges: SAT V: 470–580, M: 470–590; ACT: 18–25
Applicants: 2,785
Applicants accepted: 66%
Accepted applicants who enrolled: 41%
Tuition: $13,732
Room and board: $8,748
Freshman retention rate: 84%
Graduation rate: 32% (4 yrs.), 65% (6 yrs.)
Courses with fewer than 20 students: 62%
Student-faculty ratio: 17:1
Courses taught by graduate TAs: none
Most popular majors: business, engineering, biology
Students living on campus: 40%
Guaranteed housing for four years? no
Students in fraternities: 3%

SOUTH

481

Morehouse maintains a reasonably impressive core curriculum, one that is supplemented by some worthy distribution requirements. All students must take:

- "Freshman Assembly," "Sophomore Assembly," and "Junior Assembly"— which entail attendance at a minimum of six Crown Forum events each year, for a total of 18 events.
- "Freshman Orientation," which the college Web site describes as "a two-semester orientation to academic and social life at Morehouse."
- "English Composition" I and II, though students with high placement scores are exempt from one of these courses.
- "World Literature" I.
- "World History" I and II.
- "College Algebra" and "Finite Mathematics" or "Precalculus."
- Beginning and intermediate courses in a foreign language.
- "Introduction to Religion."

before the junior year, so they are eligible for Phi Beta Kappa." Morehouse puts a premium on maintaining a certain sequence of courses; each major has a (strongly) suggested four-year plan worked out in advance and made available through the course catalog, and the academic advisement process reinforces this approach. There is no question of a student falling through the cracks at Morehouse.

Of course, this emphasis on structure and uniformity comes at a certain cost; courses intended for all students must to some degree be gauged to those at the lowest level of academic preparation. For instance, the English department offers an introductory writing course, basically designed to get students up to speed. It is required of all students. One student describes it as "a bit of a cakewalk" and "not what I would call a college-level course." Likewise, all Morehouse freshmen take "World History," a two-course sequence in which students learn about the American, African American, and European experience. A faculty member who has taught the courses complains that the sequence is little more than a "pastiche of Western civilization and African civilization" that was "poorly thought out. . . . What it turned out to be was a course where one would go in and teach his or her expertise." The reading list for the class includes *An African-American Odyssey*, a world atlas, and *World History: Topic Approaches*, a textbook written by none other than the Morehouse College history department. A department staffer explains that "some professors got together and published their own interpretations of history."

To satisfy the science and mathematics requirements, all students take a two-course sequence in mathematics selected in accordance with their field of study. Students not majoring in science must also take a course in physical science and one in biological science, while science majors take in-depth introductory science courses. While some say the science requirements are weak and give non-science majors an easy way out, and one professor bemoans the "dilution of science in the interest of expediency," another faculty member says that the system provides "useful and applicable general scientific principles without overwhelming the student with minutiae."

And some requirements are clearly commendable. Unlike most colleges, Morehouse still requires intermediate-level proficiency in at least one foreign language. Six languages are offered. Foreign languages are grouped administratively into one department, offering majors in Spanish and French and instruction in German, Japanese, Russian, and Swahili.

To satisfy the humanities requirement, students choose four courses from a list of only 11 that includes "Introduction to Philosophy," "African American Music: Composers and Performers," and "History of Jazz." The social sciences list, from which students must choose two courses, includes courses like "Principles of Economics" and "Criminology." A "World Literature" course is taken during the sophomore year that, according to the course bulletin, introduces students to "works from oral traditions and writings, including Biblical literature, poetry, drama, fiction, and essays. Works are selected to expose students to cultural contexts of Africa, Asia, Europe, and North and South America."

Most assessments of Morehouse suggest that the college's academic reputation rests primarily on a few select departments, especially engineering, business administration, and biology—some of the most popular fields of study at the school. Biology majors are usually on a premedicine track, and many of the top Morehouse premed students go on to enroll in the college's own medical school.

The excellent business administration department is enhanced by its contacts with entrepreneurs in the city of Atlanta. The department's curriculum is traditional in format, requiring students to pick a major area of concentration in accounting, finance management, or marketing, among others. The department also encourages its students to minor in economics. A former student in the department describes the coursework as "extremely rigorous, but certainly worthwhile." Top professors in the business administration department include Keith Hollingsworth and Robert Ledman in management and Alan Aycock in finance.

In the humanities, the religion department receives good reviews, not surprising given Morehouse's close ties to the Baptist church. Religion majors must take seven specific courses, including introductions to the Old and New testaments, world religions, "Ethics and Religion," "Philosophy of Religion," and "Introduction to Theology," in addition to electives in the department. Lawrence E. Carter and Aaron L. Parker are recommended professors in the religion department.

The history department is also considered among the school's best, although students disagree about the quality of the pedagogy. To declare a major in history is quite a commitment, as students have to take 14 specific courses and six electives. The core includes two-semester courses in "World History: Topical Approaches," "History of the United States," "History of African Americans," and "History of Africa," as well

REQUIREMENTS (CONT'D)

- "Introduction to Philosophy" or "Introduction to Philosophical Ethics."
- One of six music courses.
- "Survey of Visual Arts" or "Introduction to African American Art."
- Two social science courses. Choices include "Principle of Economics and National Government," "Introduction to Urban Studies," and "Psychology of the African American Experience."
- Two physical education courses, like golf, swimming, badminton, basketball, tennis, "fitness for the nontraditional student," or "individualized fitness for the nontraditional student," the last two by permission only.
- Business 322, Computer Science 101, or a higher level computer science course. Students may test out.

SOUTH

483

as single-semester courses in "Ancient History," "History of Modern Europe," "Latin American/Caribbean Studies," "Revolution and Modernization," "Great Men and Women of America," and "Public Speaking," an English course. Students recommend Alton Hornsby Jr. and Daniel Klenbort in history.

Morehouse's small community allows students to have closer relationships with faculty members than they might at other schools. Professors often give out home telephone numbers and encourage students to come to them for advice. "I was never made to feel rushed whenever I went to professors with questions," says one student. "And I almost always felt like they cared, whether I was talking about my work in their classes or someone else's." Upon entering Morehouse, each student is assigned a faculty advisor; once he selects a major, he is assigned a faculty advisor within that department. A sizable and attentive tutoring network is also available to help students stay on track. "If there is one thing to be said about Morehouse," says a former student, "it's that I never felt like I was simply on my own when it came to any academic difficulties I might have had. I always felt comfortable asking for help. I felt like they wanted me to succeed." Since Morehouse does not have graduate students, there are no teaching assistants on campus. While only 80 percent of instructors have PhDs or other terminal degrees, those who do not are concentrated in part-time instructor and lecturer positions and in lower-level courses.

Morehouse is a school for men, but since the college allows cross-registration with other historically black colleges in the area, most classrooms are mixed gender. This doesn't necessarily sit well with all Morehouse men. "While I was generally interested in what my female peers had to say," says a former student, "I didn't always want to be politically sensitive, and when women were present, I sometimes felt I had to be." Another sore spot is Morehouse's African American studies program, which was, somewhat surprisingly, only recently initiated. Some students say that this department is particularly politicized, though many courses at Morehouse are taught from an Afrocentric perspective (e.g., "Race and the Law," "Theories of Afrocentricity," "Intercultural Communication"). Even liberal students say that attempts to give an African American twist to some courses often feel forced, and some conservative students say that such attempts border on dishonesty. Of the required sophomore world history course, one conservative says that the course is nothing more than "tawdry multicultural claptrap"; a professor replies, "I teach my courses from an African-centered perspective—period." On the bright side, one former campus radical complains that although Morehouse professors tried to situate their subject matter more within the context of the black experience, the pedagogy was still mired in "Eurocentric" assumptions.

One unique Morehouse institution is known as Crown Forum, which takes place in the Martin Luther King Chapel and occurs at least once a month. Crown Forum owes its name to a phrase penned by one of the school's most distinguished alumni, Howard Thurman, who wrote: "A crown is placed over our heads, that for the rest of our lives we are trying to grow tall enough to wear." Crown Forum consists of lectures on ethics, culture, leadership, or current events. "A lot of schools tout their traditions to suck you in but don't do much else to reinforce them once you arrive," a student says. "Crown Forum means you don't forget the traditions." Students are formally inducted into Crown Forum in their freshman year and are expected to attend a minimum of six Crown Forum events in each of their freshman, sophomore, and junior years.

Student Life: School Daze

Morehouse boasts a vibrant life outside the classroom, with a number of student organizations, opportunities for co-recreation with neighboring schools (particularly with Spelman), athletic activities, and even something of a Greek culture (though its status has recently become rather precarious—see below).

Morehouse fields teams in football, basketball, track and field, tennis, cross country, and golf at the varsity level and competes as an NCAA Division II school in the Southern Intercollegiate Athletic Conference. In 2003, Morehouse was forced to disband its soccer team because of NCAA violations, according to the *Chronicle of Higher Education*. It appears that the NCAA edict—the harshest assessed since the "death penalty" inflicted on Southern Methodist University football in the 1980s—was reflective not of corruption, but of inexperience and judgment errors. Soccer has since returned to intramural status, and the college also has intramural competitions in football, basketball, volleyball, and occasionally other sports.

Most Morehouse students are grounded in their religious faith, and thus the college has a variety of religious groups, including the Fellowship of Christian Athletes and the Morehouse Gospel Theatre Ensemble. There is a growing affinity for Islam among students, and the school has two organizations devoted to Muslim concerns. These groups are responsible for some of the more vociferous political activity on campus, according to one source.

On the whole, there isn't much political controversy on campus. "Morehouse has some pretty radical students and professors and some pretty conservative ones," says one student, "but I think that because we're all black and all guys, there's just less focus on politics. . . . There's not much opportunity to play 'us' versus 'them.' We're all pretty much on the same page." But another student, for the very same reason, expresses concern that Morehouse "reinforces the patriarchal hegemony so often associated with and manifested by black men." Out of this concern have sprung organizations and demonstrations aimed at promoting "gender sensitivity"—particularly in the wake of a nationally publicized 2002 incident in which a student, since expelled, reacted violently to what he interpreted as a homosexual advance on the part of another student.

In terms of electoral politics, most students identify with the Democratic Party, although there is also a significant Republican presence on campus. Both parties have

SUGGESTED CORE
1. No suitable course
2. Philosophy 310, Ancient and Medieval Philosophy
3. Religion 210/211, Introduction to the Old Testament / Introduction to the New Testament
4. Religion 400, Introduction to Theology (*closest match*)
5. Political Science 462, Modern Political Theory
6. English 377, Shakespeare
7. History 215, History of the United States to 1876
8. Philosophy 312, Nineteenth-Century Philosophy

SOUTH

485

student organizations, though the College Republicans have only recently become especially active. Students say that both groups demonstrate a good deal of respect toward one another. Discussions between them tend to "actually be discussions, very civil," reports one student.

Apart from sharing classes with female students, Morehouse men have plenty of organized opportunities to consort with women from neighboring schools. Morehouse men are even assigned a "Spelman sister," a relationship that they usually maintain throughout their Morehouse careers. And the city of Atlanta is not exactly bereft of females.

Morehouse once had a thriving Greek system, but fraternities have been under fire lately. Indeed, the most controversial area of student life concerns the fraternities. There is a strong fraternity tradition at black colleges, most famously illustrated in Morehouse alum Spike Lee's film *School Daze*—but it is the *School Daze* image of the fraternity that Morehouse would like to get away from. More than 10 years ago, Alpha Phi Alpha lost its charter after a hazing incident that resulted in the death of a student. Five years ago, two fraternities lost their charters due to hazing. Fraternities have since fallen out of favor, but there is some speculation that they are about to make a resurgence, mainly because "brotherhood" is so much a part of the Morehouse experience.

There are two student-run publications on campus: the *Torch*, which is the school yearbook, and the *Maroon Tiger*, the student newspaper.

Around 40 percent of Morehouse students live on campus. The college does not guarantee housing for all four years, but the housing director says there is sufficient space for students who request it. Freshmen are required to live on campus unless they receive special permission. They reside in separate dormitories from upperclassmen. Students can choose from among residence halls with various themes, including environmental awareness, leadership, "well-roundedness," and "men mentoring men." All students living on campus must agree to a substance-free policy, meaning no smoking, alcohol, or drugs are allowed on campus. The housing office says the school has a "zero-tolerance" policy towards violations.

Although Morehouse lies in the heart of Atlanta, statistics show that the crime rate is stunningly low—the only crimes reported on campus in 2003 were two robberies, one burglary, two arsons, and five car thefts. Campus police patrol the grounds and will escort students at any time to or from the library, the Atlanta University Center complex, MARTA public transportation stops, and various other locations in the vicinity.

The expense of attending Morehouse has been a growing concern for students; a number of students we interviewed spoke of having dropped out at various times in order to raise money to attend the school, even though Morehouse has generous funding available, giving aid to a whopping 89 percent of its students and practing need-blind admission. The cost for tuition, room, and board was roughly $22,000 for the 2004–5 year, cheaper than many comparable liberal arts colleges, but nonetheless impossibly expensive for many students and families. On the other hand, the difficulties students have in attending seem only to increase the loyalty that Morehouse men feel toward their college.

NEW COLLEGE OF FLORIDA

SARASOTA, FLORIDA • WWW.NCF.EDU

A study in choice

The New College of Florida has spent the past few years working to reinvent itself as a major independent player not only in the state of Florida, but also on the national level as a unique option in liberal arts education. What makes New College distinctive is that it provides a challenging and demanding liberal arts education—without giving grades. The college lets students choose their own educational paths, but it also demands that they understand, explain, and defend their choices if they hope to earn a diploma. All in all, an interesting departure from the (mostly atrophied or corrupted) traditions of American higher education.

New College is in fact new. It started as a private institution in the 1960s and later became a satellite campus of the University of Southern Florida. In 2001, the Florida legislature established the college as the public independent honors college for the state. This granted the college both the freedom to control its own budget and independence in making tenure decisions—but it also brought the school under closer scrutiny by lawmakers. Now shorn of the anonymity it enjoyed as a mere department of the University of South Florida, the school has gained national notice.

The college maintains that it is the school of choice for students who can manage the freedom and responsibility of building their own education. There are four principles to the college's educational philosophy:

1. In the final analysis, students are responsible for their own education.

2. The best education demands a joint search for truth by exciting teachers and able students.

3. Students' progress should be based on demonstrated competence and real mastery rather than on the accumulation of credits and grades.

VITAL STATISTICS
Religious affiliation: none
Total enrollment: 692
Total undergraduates: 692
SAT/ACT midranges: SAT V: 630–720, M: 590–670; ACT: 26–30
Applicants: 716
Applicants accepted: 53%
Accepted applicants who enrolled: 49%
Tuition: $3,452 (in state), $18,460 (out of state)
Room and board: $6,006
Freshman retention rate: 80%
Graduation rate: 50% (4 yrs.), 65% (6 yrs.)
Courses with fewer than 20 students: 64%
Student-faculty ratio: 11:1
Courses taught by graduate TAs: none
Most popular majors: n/a
Students living on campus: 68%
Guaranteed housing for four years? no
Students in fraternities or sororities: none

SOUTH

487

There is no core require-
ment at New College. To
graduate, students must
fulfill a series of
intellectual "contracts"
approved and evaluated
by faculty members and
also complete some
independent study
projects, a senior thesis,
and an oral exam. The
four requirements are as
follows:

- Successful completion of
  seven student contracts.
- Satisfactory completion of
  three independent study
  projects, each representing four full weeks of
  academic study that occur
  in January over the winter
  break. Faculty members
  remain in residence
  during this time to assist
  students in research.
  Projects are then submitted for evaluation.

4. Students should have opportunities to explore, in depth, the areas that interest them.

We can't say we agree with all the implications of this creed
(particularly of points 1 and 4), but New College seems to
apply it responsibly and imaginatively, to worthy effect.

New College is one of the smallest public schools of
its kind, at almost 700 students; some say the school needs
to grow to 800 or 1,000 to increase its viability and reputation. However, the current students aren't eager to see any
changes, glad as they are with the school's guaranteed small
classes, low student-teacher ratio, and lack of teaching assistants. As the school garners acclaim in print and respect
from graduate and professional schools that accept its
alumni, New College will continue to cement a reputation
as a solid place for self-directed students who wish to specialize early. If that's what you're looking for. . . .

Academic Life: The discipline of independence

Most colleges nowadays let students pick the vast majority
of their courses, with little guidance from the curriculum
other than lax distribution requirements. New College goes
further—allowing students to set their own goals in each
class as well, and judging them by how well they've achieved
them. This isn't as New Age as it sounds. Students are required to work closely with faculty mentors in choosing their
academic paths and with the teacher of each class in setting
their individualized goals. This flows from the college's core values of independent learning and individual responsibility. This nontraditional approach to education doesn't
seem to have lowered the standards of the college; the institution boasts a strong freshman class each year and is consistently ranked highly among colleges. The academic
mentors (here called "sponsors") who help students draw up their curricula are known
for urging students to take classes that are challenging and difficult.

New College has a strong appreciation for the liberal arts, and it is structured
according to the philosophy that nothing can be learned if one is a "passive spectator"
in academic activities. Instructors constantly push for engagement and persistence on
the part of their students, and it is the students who decide what requirements will
define their educational careers. At the beginning of each semester, students write academic contracts that are planned paths of study. Instead of grades, a student's progress
is measured in terms of goals, activities, and the student's personal criteria for success.
Goals range from becoming a more active participant in the classroom to working on
projects that will increase the student's chances of acceptance into graduate school.

Goals can be short or long term, and students are encouraged to discuss in the contract how their activities during the term relate to their goals.

While the college offers a large amount of freedom in the academic program, students work closely with the advice of faculty members to build an academic career that explores and defines what the student determines a liberal arts education to be. These faculty members, who serve as the student advisors, also review student contracts at the end of a term. Faculty advisors are responsible for identifying problems in teacher evaluations or student patterns. If a student is demonstrating a lack of participation in particular classes, the sponsor will work with the student to write a contract for the next semester that addresses this issue. At the same time, patterns in positive behavior are looked for to shape future work. This type of relationship with the student's sponsor is all part of the aim of New College to set students on a path toward continued learning once out of college by exercising the independence and personal responsibility learned in college. You could certainly—and in many places, will—acquire less useful skills from an education.

At freshman orientation, students are introduced to faculty advisors, who guide the students through the writing of their first academic contracts. "A sponsor is much more than what students find in the traditional role of a faculty advisor at most major universities," the college states. "At New College, the sponsor is not an individual the student seeks out twice a year to sign off on paper work. At New College, the sponsor is one of the lead actors in the shaping of the student's future."

New College's entire philosophy of education revolves around the student-designed contract. Teacher evaluations and the certification of the contract by the academic advisor determine if a student satisfactorily completes the semester. Students need seven contract certifications to graduate. Graduation is not based on grades; students will receive a "satisfactory" if they have completed the terms of the contract, or an "unsatisfactory" if they have not.

The nontraditional academic structure does not mean that New College is academically lax. According to the fact book put out by the state of Florida on New College, its main academic focus in admissions is the student's secondary education and admissions essay. Class rank is considered; however, standardized test scores and recommendations are more important. Some 84 percent of entering freshman have SAT scores above 1200 or ACT scores of 27 or higher, with average GPAs of 3.6. Refreshingly, the college does not make admissions decisions based on race or ethnic background.

REQUIREMENTS (CONT'D)

- Defense of a senior thesis. Each student presents his or her research to a committee composed of three faculty members, one of them the sponsor of the project. The bulk of the final year is spent completing this project.
- The oral exam. Finally, a student has a baccalaureate exam, or "bacc." During the oral exam, the three faculty members that constitute the thesis committee give an oral exam to the student covering the student's thesis topic and entire academic career at New College. The exam is open to the college community and after it is assessed and the final contract is complete, the faculty votes on the student's eligibility for graduation.

SOUTH

While Advanced Placement courses are becoming more and more common in high schools, first-year students at New College start as true freshmen; the college does not accept AP credits. Student have mixed views about this, regretting the loss of expected credits but noting the benefits of doing more challenging work. "At other schools I would have 12 completed hours before I started," says one. "In the end, I still chose New College and having the AP experience had many benefits. I was prepared for my college work and the first year was not as difficult a transition in terms of the classroom environment."

The school offers 30 majors in the fields of arts and sciences in addition to individually arranged special topic and multidisciplinary majors. New College provides a number of worthy options in the liberal arts and lists foundational courses in each department, such as "The Canon of British Literature," "The Philosophy of Science," "Renaissance and Reformation Europe," "The Sociology of Sustainable Communities," and "Modern Philosophy." Missing are many of the trendy, politicized courses offered at other universities. New College does not appear to be compelled to offer "diversity" and gender-based classes; students interested in that kind of thing can find it in an independent tutorial.

The student-faculty ratio is 11 to 1. The school employs 66 full-time faculty, almost all of whom hold PhDs or other terminal degrees. As there is no graduate program at New College, no classes are taught by graduate teaching assistants. The average class size is 17 students, with 64 percent having fewer than 20. The faculty is known for creating class subsections that serve as discussion groups and project teams, and for holding problem and practice sessions to supplement class material. These sessions are arranged between the instructor and students and are not tracked by the registrar's office. With no teaching assistants and the flexibility in schedules, one student boast that he gets "to learn what I want to learn, with brilliant professors."

Some of the best teachers at New College include Magdalena E. Carrasco in art history; Aron Edidin and April Flakne in philosophy; Arthur McA. Miller and John F. McDiarmid in British and American literature; John D. Moore and David Rohrbacher in classics; and Kim Anderson in visual arts.

Student Life: Branch office

Students describe New College's social life as a laid-back environment where students and teachers pride themselves on genuine openmindedness and cosmopolitan tolerance. This extends from classroom debates—where a wide range of opinions are welcome—to an open acceptance of student "lifestyle choices." Students at New College do not fit the stereotypes often bandied about regarding Florida college students. Greek life, weekend parties, and beach-based hedonism don't really thrive here. Instead, New College students seem to be mellow, intellectually curious nonjoiners.

Most students we consulted said that the population of the college is predominantly liberal and fairly activist, as is true at most campuses. However, they insist that students and faculty alike are respectful of dissent. There is a constant stream of debate on campus, which takes place among bright, mutually respectful students. "It isn't all 'bleeding-heart liberals' here," says one student. "My roommate and I are libertarians and you can find a few Republicans. There are actually more of them at New College than people think—they are just more likely to be overshadowed by the College Democrats or some loud liberals."

New College is perhaps a little too tolerant towards the drug culture. Students agree that substance abuse is fairly common: "Yes, drug use is visible, but it is not terribly more prevalent than what one would expect to find at another school. New College is small enough that you know who is doing what and where it is," says one student. Students do not feel peer pressure to do drugs—but at the same time, if one is curious, they are easy to find. One student says, "I would not say that there are many people who do drugs recklessly; everyone knows the consequences and keeps an eye on one another."

Students looking for life outside the classroom or the bong party have many options available, including some 55 student organizations, including the usual Republican, Democrat, and Green party organizations, Amnesty International, Student Farmworker Alliance, CIPHER (a libertarian group opposed to the "war on drugs"), and PRIDE, which provides the usual run of gay rights programs. Athletic organizations include ultimate Frisbee and scuba. One of the more interesting and popular organizations is Nice RAK (Random Acts of Kindness), a philanthropic organization that looks for unique forms of community service—such as taking out the trash for the housekeepers and giving away free bus passes. Art films are a popular staple of student entertainment on campus. The school also brings a wide variety of speakers to campus; in one week in April 2005, New College hosted sex educators speaking about female gratification and conservative former congressman Bob Barr—not at the same event, mercifully. Religious organizations on campus include InterVarsity Christian Fellowship, the Multifaith Council (which sponsors "nondenominational Bible studies"), the Muslim Students Association, and the Jewish Alliance.

New College's campus reflects the fact that it was formerly a branch of the University of South Florida. The grounds are small and not really designed to give the feel of an independent college. "On my first visit to New College," says one student, "I was slightly surprised by the feel of the campus. I only knew of it having a strong academic reputation so I was expecting the campus to feel older. Instead, the first time I was on campus it felt like a small, spread-out community college." New College, since gaining independence, has been doing much to change this perception. Recent building projects and campaigns are meant to create more of a traditional campus environment. Still,

SUGGESTED CORE
1. Classics 80477, Greek Civilization
2. Philosophy 80504, Classical Philosophy
3. Religion 20534, Jewish Scriptures *and* Rel 20059, Christian Scriptures
4. History 80518, Medieval Europe (*closest match*)
5. Political Science 80531, Introduction to Classical Political Thought (*closest match*)
6. English 20042, Shakespeare: Plays and Poetry
7. History 80512, Topics in American History to 1877
8. Philosophy 20528, Modern Philosophy (*closest match*)

SOUTH

491

students complain that the campus does not have the atmosphere one expects from a four-year institution. "New College continues to feel like a branch of something else," says one.

However, New College students agree that small is beautiful; most of them list the school's size as one of their reasons for enrolling and staying. "My high school had 3,000 [students], and my first college had 35,000," one says. "I think the size of New College is perfect. I love recognizing everyone and constantly feeling like I am surrounded by my friends."

The school provides housing to incoming students and almost all make use of it—as do 68 percent of students generally. The college offers coeducational dorms and apartments, but no special housing for married students. Rules do exist in housing facilities and dorms, but those rules are fairly slack and rarely enforced. Students maintain good relationships with resident advisors (RAs) and the social philosophy often associated with New College continues into the RA relationship. "You talk to your friends at other colleges about how you smoked with your RA and how you had to come up with a costume for queer ball that involved liquid latex and bondage tape," says one student, with evident fondness.

Many would consider Sarasota an ideal place to be young and carefree. The campus is conveniently close to the beautiful Florida beaches, and a moderately warm and sunny climate is found throughout most of the year. However, students at New College complain that the areas surrounding campus are less than exciting. "The actual campus of New College is accessible to the actual city of Sarasota by car, but Sarasota is not the bustling metropolis that it claims to be," one says.

The campus is safe, if not exactly drug-free. Students see campus security and police more as a support network than a curb to their freedom. Students told us that campus police are of the opinion that the drugs and drinking found on campus cannot be stopped—so instead, officers make themselves available to those who might need help. The feeling of community at New College is one of the leading reasons that criminal activity—outside of recreational drug use—is very rare. For the latest year that data was available, 2003, the college recorded only two burglaries and two stolen cars.

The 2004–5 tuition and fees total for residents was $3,452; non-residents paid $18,460. Room and board averaged $6,006. New College was dubbed a top value in public higher education by *The Princeton Review* in 2005. The school offers both need-based financial aid and general aid and gifts, but does not provide need-based financial aid for nonresidents. There are three criteria for non-need-based awards: academics, leadership, and state/district residency. Of the students who received need-based aid, 79 percent of their need was met. One-third of students graduating in 2003 had taken out loans, for an average debt of $9,612.

UNIVERSITY OF NORTH CAROLINA

CHAPEL HILL, NORTH CAROLINA • WWW.UNC.EDU

The first shall be . . .

"First," proclaims the University of North Carolina's litera-ture. "First among public universities. First in innovative academic programs." Indeed, in 1795, the University of North Carolina at Chapel Hill was the first public state uni-versity in the fledgling United States. As for those "innova-tive academic programs," there is no doubt that UNC is of-ten on the cutting edge. Whether this is a good thing is de-batable.

Innovative programs aside, UNC has its virtues. Faced with the facilities of a large and prestigious research uni-versity, the charm of Chapel Hill's college-town atmosphere, a multitude of student organizations, a strong faculty, hun-dreds of courses, and a decent set of distribution require-ments, a student at the University of North Carolina can certainly graduate with a sturdy foundation in the liberal arts and have a good time along the way. He can also waste much of his time. As at most state schools, students have to take care to choose wisely if they are truly to get their money's worth—even if they're only paying in-state tuition.

Academic Life: Going to Carolina

UNC has a highly regarded Honors Program that offers sepa-rate, smaller sections of existing courses and select semi-nars on other topics. Each year, some 200 applicants to Chapel Hill are selected for this program, which carries with it enhanced financial aid. Others can apply to transfer into the school during their freshman year. Students praise the program, part of the Johnson Center for Undergraduate Excellence, for its rigor in liberal arts. One student says, "Honors advisors have done very well. I've heard good re-views." but adds, "They aren't pushing people hard enough for an honors program." Moreover, since the Honors Program relies for most of its classes on existing under-graduate selections from the College of Arts and Sciences, some of which are trivial or politicized, it's hardly an intellectual utopia. For instance, Honors offers seminars such

VITAL STATISTICS

Religious affiliation: none
Total enrollment: 26,878
Total undergraduates: 16,525
SAT/ACT midranges: SAT
    V: 590–690, M: 600–700;
    ACT: 25–30
Applicants: 18,850
Applicants accepted: 35%
*Accepted applicants who
    enrolled*: 53%
Tuition: $3,205 (in state),
    $16,603 (out of state)
Room and board: $6,245
Freshman retention rate: 95%
Graduation rate: 67% (4 yrs.),
    81% (6 yrs.)
*Courses with fewer than 20
    students*: 54%
Student-faculty ratio: 14:1
*Courses taught by graduate
    TAs*: not provided
Most popular majors:
    social sciences, commu-
    nications, business
Students living on campus:
    43%
*Guaranteed housing for four
    years?* no
Students in fraternities: 11%
    sororities: 19%

SOUTH

493

The Basic Skills General Education requirement at Chapel Hill requires all students to take:

- Two courses in English composition.
- At least three courses in a foreign language.
- Two courses in mathematics.

On top of these, students must complete distribution guidelines divided into five areas (called "Perspectives"), taking:

- Two "aesthetic" courses (one in literature, one in fine arts). Choices range from "High Renaissance Art" to "Sexuality and Visual Culture" and "The Fifties."
- Two courses in natural sciences (at least one with a laboratory component).
- Two courses in history, either Western, non-Western, or comparative.
- Two courses in social sciences. Choices range from "Economic Statistics" to "Defining Blackness."
- One course in philosophical perspectives. Choices include "Social Ethics/Political Thought" and "Feminism."

as "Writing with an Accent: Latino Literature and Culture" and the Marxist-inflected "Comedy and Class." Still, received wisdom does stand a chance of meeting challenge from young minds exposed to readings from Machiavelli, Hamilton, Descartes, and Franklin, all found in the honors seminar "The Elements of Politics," or from students who have taken "Verdi's Operas and Italian Romanticism" or "The Romans," with readings from Petronius to Virgil.

Although it insists on nothing like a core curriculum, UNC's distribution requirements do a better job than most at attempting to require some breadth of knowledge of its students. According to a student, it works: "You cannot graduate with a very limited area of knowledge—it's impossible." Unfortunately, the wide latitude students are given in choosing courses means that someone could easily blunder through four years and not encounter truly foundational texts and thinkers.

Students report strong relationships with faculty members, who generally maintain open-door policies. Upon entry to the university, students receive advice from professional advisors or faculty members in the Academic Advising Center. Once students have declared majors, they are assigned to "advising teams." A philosophy student, for instance, would be assigned to "Team 95" along with those studying art, classics, music, drama, linguistics, religious studies, English, and American studies. Just a half-dozen advisors are assigned to all the students majoring in these areas. However, students are also assigned faculty advisors within their majors. One student says that "academic advising here is exceptional. Every student has at least one advisor . . . and each is focused on making the best out of each student's experience." Other students are more skeptical. "Advising is available but it doesn't come knocking on your door in the freshmen dorm; you're competing with other students. You only have so much time with the professor—you're in the waiting room with about 10 other students."

Recommended departments at UNC include business and biology. The Kenan-Flagler School of Business has an excellent nationwide reputation (except in the eyes of a "sexual orientation issues" consulting firm that, according to the *Chronicle of Higher Education,* gave the school a failing grade when it comes to "tolerance"). In 2004, The Center for Entrepreneurship received a $3.5 million grant that it plans to use on internships with local companies. The English department is noted for its attention to teaching, its traditional curriculum, and its freshman composition program. The classics department and the school of journalism and mass communication also are among the best in the nation. The art history department's strength is in teaching, but it is also boosted by the university's impressive art collection.

Students name the following faculty members as among the best teachers at the university: Jean S. DeSaix, William M. Kier, and Patricia J. Pukkila in biology; James W. Jorgenson in chemistry; George W. Houston, Sara Mack, and Kenneth J. Reckford in classics; novelist Doris Betts (emerita) and Michael McFee in creative writing; Barbara Day in education; Michael Salemi in economics; Christopher M. Armitage, Reid Barbour, Larry Goldberg, Philip Gura, Trudier Harris-Lopez, Fred Hobson, Joy S. Kasson, Ted Leinbaugh, George Lensing Jr., James Seay, Thomas Stumpf, and Weldon Thornton in English; William L. Barney, Judith M. Bennett, E. Willis Brooks, Peter A. Coclanis, W. Miles Fletcher, Jacquelyn D. Hall, John F. Kasson, Roger W. Lotchin, and Jay M. Smith in history; Robert Lauterborn in journalism; Sue E. Goodman in mathematics; James Ketch and Thomas A. Warburton in music; Laurie E. McNeil and Lawrence G. Rowan in physics and astronomy; Michael Lienesch, Kevin McGuire and Thomas Oatley in political science; Peter Iver Kaufman and Ruel W. Tyson Jr. in religious studies; and Anthony Oberschall and John Shelton Reed (both emeritus) in sociology.

Somewhat surprisingly at a university of North Carolina's size, students seem to be comfortable with course enrollment numbers. Outside of introductory courses, there are said to be few huge classes, except for a few in the drama and government departments. Large classes are broken up into recitation sessions, which are led by graduate student teaching assistants. "Most of the introductory-level classes are taught by TAs, but once you move into the more major-specific courses, you usually get professors," says a student. Philosophy and history courses fill up quickly, as do core classes.

The extent to which politics affects classroom policies and discussion varies by professor, of course. One professor says, "In the classes I teach . . . I have a good mix of conservative and liberal students, and the conservative viewpoint is well represented in

REQUIREMENTS (CONT'D)

The College of Arts and Sciences, the largest academic unit at UNC, requires its students to take four more courses from among the five Perspectives groups.

In addition to these requirements, students must complete two physical education courses and a course that fulfills a cultural diversity mandate, which can overlap with one of the other required courses. Close to 300 courses are on the cultural diversity list.

UNC requires that juniors and seniors pursuing the bachelor of arts degree fulfill even more general education requirements. Students must pass upper-level courses in four of the five perspective areas, and these courses cannot be in their major field of study. In their majors, students face breadth requirements. A political science major, for instance, must take an economics course. Since the 1940s, all students had been required to pass a swimming test, but this beautifully archaic requirement was tossed aside in fall 2005.

SOUTH

495

student comments during discussions. My impression is that it is easy for conservative students to feel comfortable here among their peers, though they may feel uncomfortable with some of the faculty's prejudices in certain courses." But one student says, "If I have one complaint about UNC it's that it is very, very liberal. The faculty is horribly one-sided, which leads the students to also be one-sided. Political biases absolutely influence the course content. Conservatives generally feel intimidated in class to speak out when they disagree with a professor."

No small wonder. According to the *Chronicle of Higher Education*, in the spring of 2004, a student expressed his disapproval of homosexuality as part of a class discussion. His English professor sent an e-mail to her class chastising the student, labeling him a "white, heterosexist, Christian male" and "a perfect example of privilege." Under pressure from a Republican congressman, who encouraged the Office of Civil Rights and the U.S. Department of Education to investigate possible free speech violations, the university chastised the professor and sent an observer to the professor's classes for the rest of the semester.

Less admirably, in the past two years Chapel Hill has tried to deny recognition to one Christian organization because they wouldn't admit—well, non-Christians, and tried to deny another Christian group the right to Christian leadership. This policy has spawned lawsuits, one of which is ongoing.

Chapel Hill can be surprisingly "tolerant," however. In spring 2004, a faculty member allowed a three-day *Playboy* photo shoot featuring nude female undergraduates at his home. According to a fellow faculty member, as of September 2004 there had been little administrative disapproval of the professor's widely publicized shenanigans. One weary student says, "If this were a different university, I would be appalled, but here, I'm not surprised."

The student body at UNC is not as liberal as the faculty. According to one professor, "There are many conservative or conservative-leaning groups. Pro-life organizations, College Republicans, Campus Crusade, and InterVarsity Christian Fellowship groups have memberships numbering in the high hundreds." But many active groups on campus do lean leftward politically. UNC students' activist interests are expressed in organizations like the Carolina National Organization for the Reform of Marijuana Laws, Carolina Otaku Role-Playing Society for Evil, and the Carolina Lesbian/Gay/Bisexual/Transgendered Film Society.

Student Life: In the Pit

The city of Chapel Hill is often hailed as a great college town with a vibrant culture, cheap eats, and hopping nightlife. The February 2003 issue of *Rolling Stone* ranked Chapel Hill fourth among college towns for live music. Students go to Franklin Street in the evenings. "It's a madhouse," says a student. The madhouse is particularly evident on Halloween, when thousands of people pour onto Franklin Street for a giant costume party. With Durham and Raleigh (home to Duke and North Carolina State, respectively) nearby and both the mountains and the beach within a three-hour drive, as well as Coker Arboretum right on campus, UNC students never suffer from a shortage of things to do. When on campus, students hang out at The Pit, a sunken cement and brick area in the center of campus where one sees and hears all sorts of people, from pot-smoking hippies to a boisterous preacher warning of the apocalypse. The area is flanked by a dining hall, the campus bookstore, a library, and a make-shift student center. Spray-painted signs advertise upcoming events and publicize student groups.

The university boasts about 400 clubs, teams, and student organizations, including the Carolina Paintball Club, the Carolina Shag Club (named for a popular southern dance), and the Carolina Surfing Club. "There is always something going on," a student says. "They have everything from games to cookouts to movie nights on the campus lawn to make-your-own gingerbread house at Christmas." Another student reports, "There are almost always frat parties . . . and the bar scene is very popular." About 15 percent of students go Greek. "Greek life is very popular but surprisingly academic. Most fraternities and sororities are highly involved in community service and professional organizations. They are also more sophisticated than at many other schools I've seen," a student says. A faculty member says, "Greek students at UNC have a consistently higher GPA on average than non-Greek students."

SUGGESTED CORE
1. Classics 30, The Heroic Journey
2. Philosophy 56, Ancient Philosophy
3. Religious Studies 21/22, Introduction to the Hebrew Bible / Introduction to the New Testament
4. Religious Studies 63, Medieval Philosophy
5. Political Science 64, Modern Political Thought
6. English 58, Shakespeare
7. History 21, American History to 1865
8. History 126, Modern European Intellectual History

Houses of worship on campus seem to be at best satisfactory and at worst substandard. One student says, "They aren't bad. . . . There are some churches that cater to undergrad students. They're definitely adequate." Another student found more to praise in the student-run religious clubs than the chapels themselves: "I attended the Newman Catholic center every Sunday last year as a freshman; there were a lot of student-run programs there; I was happy to see that. As I got more involved I realized that it was very liberal. One priest said that abortion within the first three weeks was okay. I now go to the church off campus. Generally, Campus Crusade and InterVarsity have two very strong chapters here; I go to a Bible study with them and retreats. They are very strong without the university's help."

Collegiate sports—led by basketball, of course—are very important to life at UNC, at least when the teams are doing well. At more than $28 million for eight years, North Carolina's contract with Nike is the largest of its kind. Students are heavily involved in sports, either by supporting the school's teams or by participating on club teams and in intramurals. There are 40 club teams, ranging from Australian rules football to roller hockey. Women's sports has a mixed tradition at Chapel Hill. On the bright side, three women went to the 2004 Summer Olympics in Athens. On the other hand, in April 2004 the university settled a sexual harassment lawsuit to the tune of $70,000 in favor of a female soccer player who claimed she was sexually harassed by her coach. As part of

SOUTH

the settlement, the coach in question must participate in eight years of sensitivity training.

The university is in the middle of a billion-dollar construction program that includes an addition to the School of Nursing and a $60 million mixed-use complex called Rams Head Center. It will accommodate 700 cars in its three-level garage as well as a recreation center and a dining facility.

Campus housing is extremely limited. "South Campus is the 'ghetto' while North Campus is much more desirable," says a student. But that may change with four new residence halls on South Campus, built at a cost of $47 million in housing revenue bonds. There is no distinction between upperclassmen and freshman housing, so all undergrads apply for the same slots. UNC does not guarantee housing, but most students who want housing can get it—at least in some form. New apartment-style housing is currently under construction for students with children. As of fall 2005, a new undergraduate apartment community will be available in Odum Village.

Only a little more than 40 percent of students live on campus, but those who live off campus tend to live nearby in fraternity or sorority houses or in apartments. There are a variety of theme housing options, including language houses, Unitas (a program that attempts to minimize stereotypes and prejudices by assigning roommates based upon their racial, ethnic, religious, and other differences), the Academic Enhancement Program, and Women's Perspectives. There are also substance-free areas of dorms available. North Carolina is southern enough that it still offers both all-men and all-women dormitories, although coed halls are also available. Visitation policies vary from hall to hall; some allow visitors (with roommate consent) until 1 a.m., while others allow visitors throughout the night. Says a student, "RAs are relaxed about housing policies and generally do not keep a strict watch on students." According to the current housing policy, a guest's stay is limited to no more than 72 consecutive hours. Guests of the opposite sex may not use the suite/floor bathroom, using instead a public restroom available in the building. And a guest may stay or sleep only in his or her host's room.

Incoming freshmen are required to attend orientation. Apart from the typical administrative activities, freshmen are paired with upperclassmen mentors and may attend mini-classes about diversity and sexual education. The summer reading is also discussed at length, but "it's a waste of time," says one student. Some complain that the choice of readings tends to be politicized. "I would suggest having two shorter books that give two sides of an issue," says a fair-minded undergrad.

One UNC tradition is the Honor Code, a policy that is taken very seriously by students. All students pledge to adhere to the code, which prohibits lying, cheating, and stealing. "Cheating is the most common offense but is by no means taken lightly," says one student. The code, however, doesn't mention public nudity: A less serious UNC tradition consists of streaking through the library at midnight on the first day of exams. One witness says, "It's quite a, um, show." Burglary and motor theft were the most prevalent types of crime during the 2003 calendar year, according to the *Daily Tarheel*. Crime on campus decreased overall that year; in 2003 there were five cases of robbery, four cases of aggravated assault and 28 cases of burglary. Liquor-law violations led to 13 arrests, and 31 drug-related arrests were made on campus. In 2004, an 18-year-old woman was raped in Morrison Residence Hall. One male student says, "I feel completely safe walking around campus, but most of the women walk in groups and carry pepper spray." The university offers the SAFE Escort service and a shuttle, called Point-2-Point, for getting across campus at night. However, the Department of Public Safety was forced to cut its budget by $2 million dollars for the 2002–3 school year. With such financial constraints, it does not seem probable that safety efforts will be expanded further.

UNC requires all incoming freshmen to own laptops (in order to facilitate a multimedia learning experience, says the university). This added expense comes on top of likely tuition increases; the Board of Governors is considering a proposal to raise tuition $300 a year for three consecutive years. In 2004–5, tuition was $3,205 for in-state and $16,303 for out-of-state students, plus room and board at $6,245. Admission to UNC–Chapel Hill is not need-blind. Obviously, students who are residents of North Carolina are treated to a lower price tag, but the bill can still run high either way. The usual options are available to students trying to pay for their education, including some decent scholarship opportunities. The university's Carolina Covenant enables eligible students from historically low-income families to attend and graduate debt-free if they work on campus 10 to 12 hours weekly. In 2004, over half of the student body received some form of financial aid. If a student applies and is eligible, UNC will meet 65 percent of his costs. The rest is up to students and their parents.

OGLETHORPE UNIVERSITY

ATLANTA, GEORGIA • WWW.OGLETHORPE.EDU

Third time the charm

Oglethorpe University is the successor to an institution of the same name chartered in 1835 to provide southern Presbyterians an alternative to Princeton. Named after Georgia state founder James Edward Oglethorpe, it actually began in Midway, a small town near Milledgeville (then the state capital), in 1838. In keeping with its primary mission, the university's curriculum consisted primarily of Greek, Latin, classical literature, theology, and natural sciences. Oglethorpe's most distinguished son from this period was poet Sidney Lanier, a member of the class of 1860. As with many of his classmates, he marched away to the War between the States. He survived, but the conflict ruined the school; the Oglethorpe adage is that the institution "died at Gettysburg." That may be an exaggeration, but as its official history says, "its students were soldiers, its endowment was lost in Confederate bonds, and its buildings were used for barracks and hospitals." An attempt to revive the place in the new capital of Atlanta in 1870 likewise withered, in just two years' time.

Nevertheless, Oglethorpe's memory lingered, and it was rechartered in 1913. Two years later, the cornerstone to the new campus was laid at its present spot on Peachtree Road in north Atlanta, in the presence of members of the classes of 1860 and 1861. The new president was Dr. Thornwell Jacobs, grandson of a one-time Oglethorpe professor. Jacobs presided over the new school for almost 30 years, intending it to be a "living memorial" to James Oglethorpe. As part of this notion, Gothic revival architecture inspired by the honorary alma mater of Oglethorpe, Corpus Christi College, Oxford, was employed in the new buildings, while the Oglethorpe crest of three boars' heads and the motto *Nescit Cedere* ("He does not know how to give up") became the university coat of arms. During his 1732 voyage to Georgia, Oglethorpe had been inspired by the tenacity of the stormy petrel, a hardy seabird. This became the school's mascot.

Although the new institution was quick to claim lineage with the old, restoration did not include links with the Presbyterian Church. So nonsectarian was the revived university that there was and is no chaplaincy—though there are a few vestigial remnants of the religious past.

Liberal arts did remain the school's focus, although business and education courses joined the curriculum. In its first three decades, Oglethorpe received major contributions from several individuals, most notably William Randolph Hearst. The "Chief" gave Oglethorpe a large tract of land; in response, Oglethorpe campus's body of water, 30-acre Silver Lake, was renamed Lake Phoebe after the publisher's mother.

For about a decade, Oglethorpe University was involved in major college athletics; its football teams defeated both Georgia Tech and the University of Georgia, and it produced baseball hall-of-famer Luke Appling. But this effort was dropped when Dr. Jacobs became convinced that it detracted from academic pursuits. Oglethorpe University began the then unheard-of practice of awarding honorary doctorates—to a decidedly mixed band of public figures, including Woodrow Wilson, Walter Lippman, Franklin Roosevelt, Bernard Baruch, Amelia Earhart, and David Sarnoff. But the most famous of Dr. Jacobs's efforts was the "Crypt of Civilization," an enormous hoard of twentieth-century artifacts sealed in the foundation of Phoebe Hearst Hall in 1940; it may not be opened until the year 8113. We wish the university good luck with that.

Adding to the academic emphasis were the efforts of Philip Weltner, who became president in 1944. He installed an educational paradigm he dubbed the "Oglethorpe Idea," which boasted that it would serve to "make a life and to make a living." The Oglethorpe core required about one-half of every student's academic program to include courses in "Citizenship" and "Human Understanding." Oglethorpe also encouraged close personal relationships between faculty and students, all to the purpose of crafting, in Dr. Weltner's words, "a small college superlatively good." The late 1960s saw a vast expansion of the school's physical plant. More importantly, the school escaped that era and the next decade with its commitment to liberal education largely intact. That alone should inspire students to explore this corner of the South which seems to have risen again.

VITAL STATISTICS
Religious affiliation: none
Total enrollment: 1,049
Total undergraduates: 900
SAT midranges: V: 550–660, M: 490–620
Applicants: 761
Applicants accepted: 66%
Accepted applicants who enrolled: 35%
Tuition: $21,900
Room and board: $7,100
Freshman retention rate: 87%
Graduation rate: 58% (4 yrs.), 60% (6 yrs.)
Average class size: 12
Student-faculty ratio: 12:1
Courses taught by graduate TAs: none
Most popular majors: business, psychology, communications
Students living on campus: 54%
Guaranteed housing for four years? no
Students in fraternities: 33% sororities: 25%

Academic Life: Just admit it

Oglethorpe prides itself on providing, in its own words, "a superior education in the liberal arts and sciences and selected professional disciplines in a coeducational, largely residential, small-college environment within a dynamic urban setting. Oglethorpe's academically rigorous programs emphasize intellectual curiosity, individual attention and encouragement, close collaboration among faculty and students, and active learning in relevant field experiences."

According to the university, an education here will instill the abilities to "read critically—to evaluate arguments and the evidence, and to draw appropriate conclusions . . . to convey ideas in writing and in speech—accurately, grammatically, and persuasively," to reason "logically and think . . . analytically and objectively about important matters" and to become capable of "the most thoughtful reflections on right and wrong and an allegiance to principles of right conduct, as reflected by Oglethorpe's Honor Code."

SOUTH

501

Oglethorpe does a better job than most colleges at providing students a disciplined humanistic curriculum in order to guarantee that they receive a liberal education. The school's mandatory core consists of the following classes:

- "Narratives of the Self" I and II. According to the catalog, students consider "a variety of fictional and philosophical constructions of the self, the relationships of memory to personal identity, and the disjunction or harmony between public and private selves. The authors considered in the courses may include Homer, Socrates, St. Augustine, Montaigne, Shakespeare, Descartes, Cervantes, Lao Tsu, Nietzsche, and Toni Morrison."

- "Human Nature and the Social Order" I and II. Here Oglethorpe students focus "on the relationship between individuals and communities, examining the extent to which the 'good life' can be pursued within the confines of any

Tall orders, indeed, but Oglethorpe's rigorous curriculum certainly does encourage students in their pursuit of such lofty goals. Alas, its admissions standards seem to militate against them. Oglethorpe recommends—perhaps wistfully—that those wishing to enter Oglethorpe should take in high school four years of English, three years of math (to include Algebra I, Algebra II, and geometry), and at least three years of science—among other worthy prerequisites. But this kind of prep is not required—which is a boon to many of the students who do indeed gain admittance.

According to one student, "Standards for academics and extracurricular activities desperately need to be raised. Admissions standards are so low that extracurricular activities, SAT scores, and academic skills are fairly irrelevant. For example, most students don't even have to write an admissions essay to be accepted into Oglethorpe. OU administrators are so concerned about increasing admissions that they'll simply take what they can get." Another says: "For a school that paints itself as a 'selective liberal arts university,' its admissions standards are intolerably low. Its newly instituted affirmative action program has also worsened this problem. Oglethorpe is recklessly striving towards the goal of increasing admissions, both minority and nonminority, at the expense of gaining a quality student body." One female student rather angrily underlined this problem, saying, "Admissions just instituted a massive affirmative action program, resulting in vastly lowered standards for minorities. I'm just shocked at the degree to which Oglethorpe will misrepresent itself and mangle its already low standards in order to gain students."

At Oglethorpe, faculty advisors are assigned through a distinctive, integrated program. Essentially, an entering freshman chooses one among a long list of courses designed to introduce him to college work and then uses that class's teacher as his advisor until he chooses a major. The classes change each semester; those offered in fall 2005 included "Hands-On Biology," "Music, Television, Films and their Impact on Culture and Society," "¡Sí, Amigo!: Getting To Know the Spanish-Speaking World," "Mr. Wizard: Physics Toys and Demos," and "The Siege of Atlanta." Upperclassmen also serve as teaching assistants or "mentors" to freshmen—earning credit for an education class. Later, students choose advisors in their major fields. As one student wrote on the school's Web site, "At Oglethorpe, you will have an advisor in your field of study who will assist you each semester with registration for classes. More importantly, though, you will also develop a relationship with your advisor over four years, and he or she will become a source of support and motivation, and a connection to internships and career options. My advisor . . . goes out of her way to schedule meeting times with me and ensure that I am taking all of the courses I need. She contacts other professors and administrators with any questions or concerns I may have. She worked with me through my internship at Hands on Atlanta and has sat down with me on many occasions to work through a difficult paper or assignment. Most importantly, she really knows me—my academic interests and career goals and also my hometown, my hobbies, and my personality."

Oglethorpe offers 22 majors in its bachelor of arts program. There are 10 other courses of study, two of which are Latin and Greek. In addition to having solid courses on history and literature, the American studies major offers "African American Politics." English weighs in with two women's studies courses and "African American Literary Traditions." But by and large, the course options are exceptionally solid—even in sociology. One instructor says, "Normally sociology is just a cesspool, but at this university, the traditional family is affirmed and proven. The class on 'The Family' [is] where all the nonsense about the alternative family is rebutted." Recommended sociology faculty include Brad Lowell Stone and Alan Woolfolk. Other professors list politics, history, sociology, biology, and English as the strongest departments on campus. Accounting also has a good reputation for placing its graduates with national firms. The weakest: physics, chemistry, psychology, and education.

Politicized faculty do exist at Oglethorpe. One professor calls his colleagues mostly "moderates to conservatives." However, he says, "Some of my colleagues behave very badly and I think politicize their classrooms and make diatribes. . . . The difference is that here, it's a small campus and word gets around. Once the student knows the lay of the land . . . he can navigate to avoid those courses." One student says it's not so easy: "Students will generally run into problems when trying to avoid certain professors, though. The available courses are so scarce that students are often forced to select the few courses offered in their area of major, no matter who the professor is." But things are not nearly as bad as they

REQUIREMENTS (CONT'D)

social order. These courses investigate issues such as the nature of human excellence and virtue, the character of justice, the origins and sources of social order, and the status and legitimacy of political power. . . . Authors such as Aristotle, Locke, Smith, Tocqueville, Marx, and Weber are read."

- "Historical Perspectives on the Social Order" I and II. In their junior year, students follow "the rise and fall of civilizations from antiquity through the Renaissance" and "the problems of modernity, such as the rise of the modern state, nationalism, revolution, and globalization."

- Either "Science and Human Nature: Biological Sciences" or "Science and Human Nature: Physical Sciences."

- Either "Music and Culture" or "Art and Culture," each of which seems to focus on traditional, Western forms and their development over time.

- "Great Ideas of Modern Mathematics."

- At least one semester of a foreign language at the second-semester elementary level or higher.

SOUTH

503

might be. Says an instructor: "There is a solid cadre of decent, dedicated teachers here, folks . . . who do not go in for postmodernist cant, do not coddle students, and do take the books and subjects they teach seriously. There are also the standardless flatterers." And certain professors (we don't like to mention names) who conduct frequent, off-topic tirades against President Bush in classes ostensibly about philosophy. One politics professor, a student reports, frequently makes shocking factual errors—like "confusing *Scott v. Sanford* with *Plessy v. Ferguson* for an entire class period or insisting that President Bush can run for a third term in 2008 because he 'wasn't elected' in 2000." The same teacher "can also be a bit hostile to conservative ideas when she's grading."

Politics professors Joe Knippenberg and Brad Smith have been pointed out as especially good. As one faculty member puts it, "OU is not a 'conservative' institution in the manner of Hillsdale, although we have a larger percentage of conservative faculty members than all but a few schools in the country. . . . We neither hire nor promote people based upon their political views—just teaching, scholarship, and service. We are a 'traditional' liberal arts college. So, for example, at OU every sophomore takes a year-long core course titled 'Human Nature and the Social Order' in which the students read Aristotle, Augustine, Aquinas, Hobbes, Locke, Smith, Tocqueville, Weber—all original texts. I would put the course up against any required course in the country."

Thanks to such dedicated teachers and a good core curriculum, and despite slipping admissions standards, it seems that a student is likely to gain a remarkably traditional liberal arts education at Oglethorpe—even if he majors in business. And that's no mean achievement for a school in 2006.

Student Life: Not what it seems

Oglethorpe's Web site notes that "the student body, while primarily from the South, has become increasingly cosmopolitan; in a typical semester, Oglethorpe draws students from about 30 states and 30 foreign countries." Perhaps as a result, the school shows few signs of being particularly rooted in its region. This can lead to some unhappy surprises among students who chose Oglethorpe in search of a distinctly conservative environment—rather than for its admirably traditional curriculum (which is far more important, in our view).

One student said that "in pre-admissions Q & A panels, I was told that this was a very conservative and political campus. In actuality, the campus is extremely apolitical and apathetic, but most students who are interested in politics are overwhelmingly liberal. We have a grand total of five [College] Republicans. . . . There are certainly some positive aspects in the arena of academics, but overall there's a vast disparity between what Oglethorpe actually is and what Oglethorpe says it is."

Another student says: "OU is not a happy place for conservatives. For the most part, it's a political ghost town. The overall sense of apathy on campus is very frustrating." This student says that College Republicans, for example, "have trouble getting students interested, while gay rights groups, environmental groups, and the liberal Black Student Caucus don't seem to be having as much difficulty."

Oglethorpe has its nuts-and-bolts challenges beyond mere ideology. One of these is student residences. Although commuter students are permitted to live in their family homes, freshmen and (since 2005) sophomores are required to live on campus. The school maintains that on-campus living is an integral part of an OU education: "At Oglethorpe

University, we strive to create a living and learning community for students that is supportive and challenging at the same time. We think living on campus is about the people in the community and you're going to love our people." Alcohol and tobacco are not forbidden, but the administration makes much of a program called the "Substance-Free Living (SFL) Community." Clustered on a floor in Dempsey Hall, SFL students make a commitment to their roommates and hallmates that they and their guests will refrain from the use of tobacco, alcohol, and illegal drugs while on the floor and will not return to their rooms in a state of intoxication.

Smoking is forbidden in New Residence Hall and Traer Hall. The three dorms of the Upper Quad permit smoking in the rooms "on the first and second floors of the Upper Quad as long as students have permission from roommates and suitemates." On Greek Row stand two sororities and four fraternities, which attract around 30 percent of students as members.

Since the school is located in Atlanta, there are limitless possibilities for amusement and cultural enrichment and a number of other major schools within easy reach. Campus groups include the University Singers, Amnesty International, Black Student Caucus, College Democrats, ECOS (Environmentally Concerned Oglethorpe Students), Executive Round Table, Feminist Majority Leadership Alliance, Film Club, International Club, International Issues Discussion Forum, OUTlet: Students Against Homophobia, Phi Delta Epsilon (a premedical society), and the aforementioned plucky little band of College Republicans.

The school has no official chaplains—which is not a great handicap in a major city with plenty of churches and synagogues from which to choose. There are three religious societies at OU—Atlanta YAD: Jewish Student Union; Fellowship of Christian Athletes; and the Oglethorpe Christian Fellowship. The latter group employs a full-time minister and holds gatherings for those students who wish to worship together in the conservative Protestant manner. Every Wednesday night at eight they meet in the Emerson Student Center for prayer, singing, and Bible study. In keeping with the university's (long-buried) Presbyterian roots, the Oglethorpe Christian Fellowship is a member of the Reformed University Fellowship, a ministry of the Presbyterian Church in America. Catholic students go to mass off campus. One suburban parish that traditionally minded students might enjoy is St. Francis de Sales in suburban Mableton, which offers the old, chanted Latin liturgy (with diocesan permission).

Although it sits in a major city with its share of urban blight, Oglethorpe's campus is amazingly harmonious; in 2003, the school reported only two burglaries and a single stolen car. The last time someone was robbed on campus appears to have been in 2001.

SOUTH

As private universities go, Oglethorpe is quite reasonably priced, with 2004–5 tuition at $21,900 and room and board at $7,100. The school works hard to garner financial aid for students. In 2005, the Financial Aid Office awarded more than $7 million in scholarships and grants. Remnants of the university's denominational past are the Oglethorpe Christian Scholarships, "awarded to freshmen and transfer student who are residents of Georgia and who demonstrate active participation in their churches," as well as the usual academic qualities.

RHODES COLLEGE

MEMPHIS, TENNESSEE • WWW.RHODES.EDU

Graceland

Rhodes College is one of the hidden treasures of American higher education. The college is blessed with a community built on trust and honesty, professors who enjoy teaching outside of their narrow specialties, students who appreciate the college's strong core curriculum and the broad education in the liberal arts and sciences that it yields, and strikingly beautiful collegiate Gothic architecture. The school also boasts a $198 million endowment—"more than it knows what to do with," says one professor. But it seems to be spending wisely.

The school has gone through more name changes than most in its history. Founded in 1848 in Clarksville as the Masonic University of Tennessee, it was later renamed Stewart College. In 1925, the school moved to Memphis and took the name Southwestern Presbyterian College. By 1945, the school was ready for a new moniker, Southwestern at Memphis (although it remained Presbyterian). Finally, in 1984 the school was rechristened Rhodes College after a former president.

Rhodes boasts an excellent curriculum and dedicated faculty and its graduates do very well. The admissions department says that 95 percent of Rhodes graduates who apply to business, divinity, and law schools are accepted. Rhodes students may not have the highest test scores, but they are typically serious about their education. "As in any school there exists a minority of students who would rather get by with as little work as possible," says one student. "But even the slackers will learn from their friends, if nothing else." And yet, for whatever reason, the college's national reputation is strong among professional educators but not the public at large. Rhodes is happy to describe itself as "one of America's premier liberal arts colleges"—and it certainly is. Indeed, the literature for prospective students is perhaps too modest—not a complaint we would make about most schools.

Academic Life: Two roads converge

Rhodes students choose between two core curricula, both of which reflect the school's essentially Christian vision of education: "The Search for Values in the Light of Western History and Religion" and "Life: Then and Now." Each program is four courses long, with students taking one core course each semester during their first two years. Students who choose the first program—known around campus as "Search"—receive a broader introduction to the liberal arts and Western tradition. During the first year, they read the history and literature of the Hebrews, Greeks, and Romans, with an emphasis on the early Christians. They also study the Bible within the context of Greco-Roman history, culture, and thought. Second-year students use the knowledge garnered during the previous year to study how the ancients shaped the development of Western civilization. By reading the works of various major philosophers, religious figures, and political theorists of the last thousand years, students come to their own conclusions about the Western tradition through the guidance of their professors. One student who chose "Search" says, "The Search program and the Life program involve the study of how the Bible was written, with a strong focus on cultural context. Many have found this a challenge to their beliefs; others have found it encouraging." An upperclassman who participated in "Search" says, "In my upper-level classes, I've found that it helps to have the same foundation as my classmates have had. Professors don't have to explain everything all over again."

"Life," the second path, is focused primarily on theology and Biblical studies. The first semester introduces students to the study of the Bible, its central themes, and its historical and cultural context. During the second semester, students are introduced to the major themes of Christian thought through the study of works by various religious thinkers. Students also discuss contemporary theological issues in light of the work of the great theologians of the past. Having completed this introduction to the Christian tradition, sophomores choose two final courses, including one biblical studies course (for example, "Prophets," "Gospel of John," or "The Letter to the Romans") and another Bible-related course in theology, religious history, or philosophy (for instance, "Responses to Moral Confusion" or "Philosophical Theology").

VITAL STATISTICS
Religious affiliation: Presbyterian
Total enrollment: 1,553
Total undergraduates: 1,541
SAT/ACT midranges: SAT V: 590–700, M: 600–690; ACT: 26–30
Applicants: 2,345
Applicants accepted: 69%
Accepted applicants who enrolled: 27%
Tuition: $27,874
Room and board: $6,904
Freshman retention rate: 87%
Graduation rate: 71% (4 yrs.), 73% (6 yrs.)
Courses with fewer than 20 students: 69%
Student-faculty ratio: 11:1
Courses taught by graduate TAs: none
Most popular majors: social sciences, biology, English
Students living on campus: 75%
Guaranteed housing for four years? no
Students in fraternities: 51% sororities: 58%

SOUTH

Rhodes's curricular sequences are solid and sturdy. Students must complete:

- English 151, "Critical Reading, Thinking, and Writing."
- Three semesters in a foreign language (or test out).
- Either "The Search for Values in the Light of Western History and Religion" I & II, or "Introduction to the Biblical Tradition" and "Introduction to the Theological Traditions," or one course in biblical studies and one in Bible-related studies (theology, philosophy, comparative religion).
- One course in literature or film, ranging from "Shakespeare's Major Plays" to "Fantasy, Science Fiction, and Horror Film."
- One course in history or philosophy, ranging from "Medieval Philosophy" to "Seminar in Contemporary Feminist Theory."

The curriculum is both rigorous and coherent, insiders agree. "The Rhodes approach to a broad liberal arts education is as good as you are going to see," a professor says. "The college is committed to it, and so are most of the faculty." This person continues, "How well it works in practice varies widely from student to student. For those who want it, they can get it here. For those who are determined to remain narrow, they can succeed as well."

Most students complete the distribution requirements during the same period that they take the four-course core program—during their first two years at Rhodes. After this grounding in the fundamentals, they begin to pursue a major, choosing from among 24 traditional disciplines; the college does not offer many newfangled ones. The college also offers seven interdisciplinary majors, most of which combine this or that discipline with international studies. In consultation with faculty members and their academic advisors, students can also create a major by concentrating in two or three academic departments. Each entering freshman is assigned an academic advisor who helps him select courses and a major. Once he has declared a major, he is assigned a different faculty advisor within his major department.

Frequent, close faculty-student interaction is one of Rhodes's primary selling points. Class sizes are small (averaging around 15 students per class) and the student-faculty ratio is a healthy 11 to 1. But the main reason for the strong relationships between students and faculty is that the administration has never pressured professors to publish. As a result, faculty members focus the vast majority of their attention on teaching. There are no virtually no graduate students at Rhodes, except for a few people working on M.S. degrees in accounting—and hence, no teaching assistants. This means that students and professors build direct relationships. "The professors at Rhodes place teaching as their highest priority," a religious studies major says. "That is a huge advantage of a small school like Rhodes. Professors know who you are and are interested in your academic success, even if you are not majoring in their departments." One professor says that "there is no more pressure to publish" at the expense of good teaching now than there was in the past: "I'm very confident that our primary mission is teaching." Students name the following as particularly good teachers: Joseph Favazza, Luther Ivory, Steven McKenzie, and Bernadette McNary-Zak in religious studies; Marshall McMahon in economics; Kathleen Anne Doyle and Amanda L. Irwin in Spanish; and Patrick Shade in philosophy.

Particularly outstanding departments at Rhodes are biology, English, and political science. Some say that the measure of a good liberal arts college is the extent of its foreign language curriculum. If that is true, Rhodes is in good shape. Rhodes has majors in French, German, Greek and Roman studies (including language studies in ancient Greek and Latin), Russian, and Spanish, as well as a minor in Chinese and course offerings to the intermediate level in Hebrew and Italian.

To judge from the course catalog, one would think that the religious studies department's orientation was rather traditional, with an emphasis on biblical studies and Christian theology. Students choosing to major in religious studies must take "Introduction to the Biblical Tradition," "History of Christian Thought," courses on both the Old and the New testaments, and a course in the religions of Asia, among others. But one Christian student who has taken several courses in the religious studies department says she found the department to be rather unorthodox: "Two or three faculty members claim to be Christian. The rest do not profess any beliefs." Others have said that the department is out of sync with the rest of the Rhodes community. The chair of the department, who makes most of the hiring and tenure decisions, specializes in liberation theology and ecology. The good news, however, is that the religious studies department is the exception, not the rule, and most students and faculty at Rhodes respect and support the faith tradition with which the school is associated.

For the most academically gifted students, the Honors Program provides an opportunity to engage in a more intense academic experience. During senior year, the honors student works with a faculty member by taking one to three honors tutorial courses, culminating in a "project of a scholarly and creative nature." The "directed inquiry" option allows students to work closely with faculty members in independent study courses. One of college president William Troutt's initiatives has been to better integrate Rhodes College into the Memphis community, and one way this has been accomplished is through internships. While gaining practical experience with area companies like FedEx, International Paper, and Merrill Lynch, students can earn course credit in various departments.

Rhodes's academic opportunities are not limited to its Memphis campus. About 30 percent of Rhodes students study abroad. Through joint programs with the University of the South at Sewanee, Rhodes students can study in several European locations.

REQUIREMENTS (CONT'D)

- One other humanities course. The choices include "Athenian Society and the Dramatic Festivals of Dionysus" and "Nomads of Inner Asia."
- Three courses, including one laboratory course, from at least two of these areas: biology, mathematics/computer science, chemistry, physics/astronomy, and geology.
- Three courses from at least two of these areas: anthropology/sociology, political science and international studies, economics, and psychology. The choices include "Constitutional Law and Politics" and "Victims of Progress."
- Two courses from any two of these areas: art, music, and theatre—or three one-hour applied music credits. The choices include "Music in the Baroque Period," "Art and Spirituality in the Middle Ages," and "Children's Literature, From Page to Stage."

SOUTH

Students can also transfer credit from approved study-abroad programs at various American and international universities. Rhodes conducts two shorter foreign study programs in Honduras, where participants study coral reef ecology and participate in service learning. Exchange programs within the United States are also available. For instance, students interested in engineering can earn a dual degree by taking three intensive years of coursework at Rhodes and two years of engineering courses at Washington University in St. Louis. Many creative opportunities are available for the ambitious student who seeks them, and the college is eager to expand these even further.

Rhodes is an enticing option for the student who wants a superior liberal arts education free of the tiresome political biases one finds at many other schools. Students say the student body is moderate to conservative, while most faculty members tend to be liberal but not radical. "The Rhodes community is more conservative than anything else," a student says. "It rarely influences course content in any noticeable way." Another student says that she took a course on the American presidency during an election year. Her professor invited the class over to watch the election returns, but refused to reveal for whom he had voted. "He tried so hard not to influence us politically," the student says. The academic disciplines themselves are straightforward. A major in English is a major in English—not in ethnic, gender, or any other form of resentment studies. Even women's studies, an interdisciplinary minor, balances its courses on feminism and gender studies with reasonable fare such as "History of Southern Women" and "Women in U.S. History." And Rhodes is one of the few liberal arts colleges to not offer even a single course in gay/lesbian literature or the like.

Members of the Rhodes community are quick to comment on the importance of the college's Honor Code in academic and student life. Many professors give unproctored or take-home exams, trusting that the work that students submit will be their own. "Nearly all of my tests last year were unproctored," a student says. "I can honestly say that in all of those exams I know of no instances of that trust being abused. Cheating is not an option at Rhodes."

Recent years have seen Rhodes College moderate its relationship with the Presbyterian Church (U.S.A.). The college bulletin still notes that the school is affiliated with the church and that this relationship is "more than assent to a set of vague values or sentimental emotions." But one professor says that "the symbolic and rhetorical trappings of church relatedness have been gradually disappearing." Indeed, religious studies is one of the more politicized departments on campus. But religion remains important to the majority of students; Christian study groups and social organizations are very popular. Because there is no college church, religiously committed students worship in local congregations or in small campus groups and have no need to conform their faith to academic fashion.

The school's library of 267,000 volumes has long been insufficient, but a recent $40 million donation led to the construction of the new Barrett Library.

Rhodes still remains virtually undiscovered, and the statistics are somewhat paradoxical. It has a 69 percent acceptance rate, and only 27 percent of those accepted actually enroll. Many of the highly talented applicant pool are drawn away to institutions less committed to traditional values and located in more swinging settings; those who choose to attend are self-selected and consequently tend to be the sort of people a serious student would want to spend four years with.

Student Life: Rhodes's scholars

The student body is predominantly white, Anglo-Saxon, and Protestant, and this is a concern to administrators who are educating students to make their lives in a multiracial and multicultural society, and who feel a desire to reach out to the conservative Christian black population of the South. For them, multiculturalism is not a code word for hatred of America and Western civilization. "The admissions department is trying as hard as it can to attract minorities, but, as it is, many racial minorities feel overwhelmed by a 'sea of white,'" one student says. The Office of Multicultural Affairs was meant to be temporary when it was established in 1990, but it now employs a full-time director who sets up workshops, orientation programs, and mentoring programs matching minority freshmen with minority upperclassmen. The director says that the mandatory freshman orientation features a day dedicated to multiculturalism. The office also advises several cultural groups, including All Students Interested in Asia, Black Student Association, Diversity Group, Hispanic Organization for Languages and Activities (HOLA), The Ministry (a religious group), and Rhodes Indian Cultural Exchange (RICE).

SUGGESTED CORE
1. Greek and Roman Studies 211, Myth and Community in Ancient Greece and Rome
2. Philosophy 201, Ancient Philosophy
3. Religious Studies 101, Introduction to Biblical Literature
4. Religious Studies 214, Early Christian Literature
5. Political Science 314, Modern Political Philosophy
6. English 230, Shakespeare's Major Plays
7. History 231, North America in the Colonial and Revolutionary Eras
8. History 326, Modern European Intellectual History

Rhodes might be having trouble recruiting students, but a visit to the college's gorgeous Oxford-like campus is enough to dispel any speculation that the campus itself is to blame. Thankfully, Rhodes has been inflexible when it comes to architecture. Every building on campus is of gray-orange stone, with slate roofs and stained glass windows in the Gothic style. With 100 acres and only 1,553 students, Rhodes has plenty of room for expansion—and plenty of room for studying outdoors, playing ultimate Frisbee, and other activities. Generous donations have allowed for facilities uncommon at schools of Rhodes's size. The Bryan Campus Life Center is an activities hub that includes a large dining hall, a performance gymnasium, another three-court gym, a fitness center, an outdoor swimming pool, reception halls, and plenty of lounge and social areas for students and faculty.

Some 75 percent of students live on campus in one of the school's many living options. As dorm rooms go, Rhodes's are very comfortable; some even have private bathrooms and wood-burning fireplaces—and nothing makes a campus smell nicer in winter time. The dormitories are located on the outer edges of the campus, with the academic buildings and other campus facilities in the center. The college recently built a set of townhouses, called East Village, each of which includes a living room, kitchen, bedrooms, and bathrooms; all told they house 200 students. Freshmen usually live together in their own dorms. The college requires its students to live on campus for their first two years. Students are separated in dorms by sex, but the college does not have a strict visitation policy. A little more than half of Rhodes students are members of fraternities or sororities. The groups have their own houses with meeting and social spaces, but since the Greek system is not residential, the groups don't dominate the campus scene. One recent alumna says that the fraternities and sororities "are not all that exclusive" and that independent students feel comfortable attending Greek parties.

Students spend most of their free time on campus, but occasionally they remember that they are in Memphis, Tennessee, a city that offers an attractive smorgasbord of restaurants, bars, shops, blues clubs, and other forms of entertainment. The center of all the hullabaloo, Beale Street, is a short drive from campus. Elvis's Graceland is nearby as well.

Although Rhodes has no church building on campus, many students are religiously committed and regularly attend services in the area. Two small rooms in dormitories serve as on-campus chapels. One of the most active campus organizations is Rhodes Christian Fellowship, which is affiliated with the evangelical InterVarsity Christian Fellowship; the group meets every Wednesday night for prayer and a speaker. Other religious groups include Westminister Fellowship, Catholic Student Association, Fellowship of Christian Athletes, Interfaith Circle, and the Jewish Student Union. One member of the Rhodes Christian Fellowship says, "As a Christian, my faith has grown tremendously since I arrived at Rhodes. The student body here has been very encouraging, and it is not unpopular for students to show interest in religious functions. I would say that Rhodes passively encourages spirituality by making resources readily available, but by no means does it force beliefs upon anyone."

The campus as a whole is not usually politically active. Even the conservative bent of the student body is subtle. One student says, "It's usually a matter of when discussing politics, more veer right than left, and afterwards, both parties go to the cafeteria to eat together." Says another, "Those who try to make politics a more public issue have trouble getting others to rally around them."

Community service is probably the most popular extracurricular activity; fully 80 percent of students volunteer for one cause or another. The Kinney Program, founded more than 40 years ago, organizes opportunities on campus and in the Memphis area and recruits students to participate. Rhodes students independently run a downtown soup kitchen, lead a Habitat for Humanity group, and volunteer countless hours as tutors in public schools, at Memphis's renowned St. Jude Children's Research Hospital, and dozens of other places. Students active in community service can apply for a scholarship, take courses to supplement their hands-on learning, and earn academic credit for service internships. A student affairs coordinator, also an alumna, says that this spirit of volunteerism is the one thing she is most proud of about Rhodes: "I bet you wouldn't find a more service-committed student body anywhere."

The $23 million Bryan Center, dedicated in 1997, has encouraged students to become more active in athletics. Around a quarter of the student body participates on at least one of the 19 varsity sports teams. Club and intramural sports options abound. The Rhodes Lynxes compete in the Southern Collegiate Athletic Conference; Sewanee is their main rival.

Rhodes has one of the safest campuses in this guide. Statistics for 2003 show 12 burglaries and two arsons, but no violent crime. A stone wall surrounding the campus helps keep stragglers out, and campus policemen on bicycles cover the grounds. The college offers a student escort service around the clock as well as plenty of crime prevention workshops.

A Rhodes education is offered at the going rate; the school charged a tuition of $27,874 in 2004–5 and an additional $6,904 for room and board. Some 55 percent of students receive some need-based aid. Admissions are need-blind, although the school does not promise to supply all needed aid.

SEWANEE,
THE UNIVERSITY OF THE SOUTH

SEWANEE, TENNESSEE • WWW.SEWANEE.EDU

This one can be shared

The University of the South, commonly referred to as Sewanee, maintains a reputation as a unique institution. Geographically isolated yet not too remote, the Domain (as the campus is called) is adorned with beautiful buildings and thousands of acres of forest and fields. In 1941, poet William Alexander Percy wrote of Sewanee, his alma mater: "It's a long way away, even from Chattanooga, in the middle of woods, on top of a bastion of mountains crenulated with blue coves. It is so beautiful that people who have been there always, one way or another, come back. For such as can detect apple green in an evening sky, it is Arcadia—not the one that never used to be, but the one that many people always live in; only this one can be shared."

Sewanee is also unique in the way in which a living tradition of manners and academic seriousness pervades the school; that, besides beauty, is another reason why talented teachers and students have been attracted to Sewanee for many years. Estab-

SOUTH

513

lished by the southern dioceses of the Episcopal Church just before the Civil War and grandly named the University of the South, the school saw decades of hard times both during the war (when Union troops blew up the cornerstone of the chapel) and afterwards, when it closed for a time. It reconvened in 1868 with nine students and four professors. Oxford and Cambridge universities sent books to help stock the struggling school's library, and with time and dedication Sewanee became a seat of learning and maturation for generations of southern men. It became coed in 1969 and abolished mandatory Saturday classes in the 1980s.

Sewanee has thus far maintained an atmosphere of high respect for the life of the mind. Its students are intellectually curious, its faculty inviting and eager to teach. Students usually dress up for class, and honor students wear black gowns designating their mark of distinction. The school is a warm, friendly community. If it can avoid shedding its traditions to placate the insatiable forces of political correctness, Sewanee will remain, in the best sense, a university of the South.

Academic Life: Southbound

Sewanee's mission, according to the college bulletin, is "to develop the whole person through a liberal arts education of high quality. . . . The college's aims include training in personal initiative, in social consciousness, in aesthetic perception, in intellectual curiosity and integrity, and in methods of scientific inquiry." A student who thirsts for knowledge and is ready to learn is naturally easier to teach, so that's the kind of student Sewanee tries to recruit. "The approach to education here is intellectual, not mechanical," says a professor in the sciences. "Some students think about the practical so little that they're scrambling for jobs the last semester they're here." Not that Sewanee alums have too much trouble in that department; 97 percent are either employed or in graduate school within a year of graduating.

Sewanee has historically imposed a fairly traditional set of distribution requirements on its students. This is under review; according to one professor, the school is in the process of hiring a new dean whose role will entail revamping the curriculum to "look like everyone else's." We hope this initiative fails completely, because, as it stands, Sewanee establishes a solid educational foundation and stresses the importance of good writing skills. (The school requires all students—even those majoring in the sciences—to take at least two courses designated as "writing-intensive." The university's Writing Center, staffed with students skilled in the craft, is open every day.) Professors say that the college is in the process of reinventing itself in order to score better on those empty-headed rankings that some students use to choose a school. That's another innovation we hope will crash and burn.

For now, a student can satisfy Sewanee's "core curriculum" by choosing the interdisciplinary humanities path—four team-taught courses on the Western cultural tradition. Beginning with "Tradition and Criticism in Western Culture—the Ancient World," and continuing with courses in the medieval, the early modern, and the "Modern World—Romantic to Postmodern," the plan allows students to fulfill four distribution requirements while reading great books—Plato's dialogues, the *Odyssey*, the *Aeneid*, St. Augustine's *Confessions*, the *Canterbury Tales*, *Paradise Lost*, and many others—and by exploring the art, history, politics, and music of each period as well.

Sewanee recently instituted the First-Year Program based on research that indicated students spoke more highly of their academic experience when it started with small, intense classes. The program offers 15 or so seminar-style courses on topics like "Ethical Issues in Student Life," "Our Place in the Universe: An Introduction to the Science of Astronomy," and a course team-taught by a German professor and a music professor on "The Struggle between Good and Evil: Fairy Tales in Literature and Music." Frequent field trips and shared dorm space encourage discussion outside of the classroom.

Students do feel a sense of connection with the faculty. In part, these relationships build through students' assisting with faculty research or taking independent study classes, but one professor says the close connection is a result of the small community: "We see students outside the classroom all the time. Interaction with students is not only common, it's expected." Another professor says that Sewanee has "enough serious students who are grateful for the leisure to study to make teaching here rewarding." In the National Survey of Student Engagement, Sewanee receives high marks each year, in particular for student-faculty interaction. Freshmen are assigned faculty advisors by dormitory, so small groups of hallmates normally share both faculty advisors and an upperclassman proctor. After the first year, students are welcome to choose a faculty advisor and to change advisors at any time. Students say their advisors are knowledgeable and willing to offer support and guidance. The student-faculty ratio is 10 to 1, and the average class size for freshmen is 19 students, with just 13 students in the typical upper-level course.

Despite its small size (about 1,350 undergraduates plus a tiny seminary program that qualifies it as a university), Sewanee has educational opportunities across the curriculum, even in its smallest departments. The philosophy department has just four faculty members, yet it offers a major and a minor. The English department—the most popular major on campus—has been home over the years to many literary figures of national note, including Monroe Spears, Andrew Lytle, Allen Tate, and Caroline Gordon. The library stores an extensive collection of original Faulkner papers and students may take a course that allows then to study them. Home of the nation's oldest and most prestigious literary quarterly—the *Sewanee Review*, edited by George Core—the department is traditional in focus; for example, majors are still required to take two

VITAL STATISTICS
Religious affiliation: Episcopalian
Total enrollment: 1,377
Total undergraduates: 1,359
SAT/ACT midranges: SAT V: 580–660, M: 570–660; ACT: 25–30
Applicants: 2,070
Applicants accepted: 64%
Accepted applicants who enrolled: 30%
Tuition: $32,700 (includes room and board)
Freshman retention rate: 88%
Graduation rate: 74% (4 yrs.), 78% (6 yrs.)
Average class size: 15
Student-faculty ratio: 10:1
Courses taught by graduate TAs: none
Most popular majors: English, history, economics
Students living on campus: 92%
Guaranteed housing for four years? yes
Students in fraternities: 70% sororities: 68%

SOUTH

515

courses in Shakespeare and two others in English literature before 1750.

In history, another excellent department, majors are required to declare a focus on the history of the United States, Europe, Great Britain, or Africa/Asia/Latin America, and then to take at least five courses in this concentration and four outside it.

The environmental studies program, which offers a concentration but not a major, is also said to be excellent; the university's immense land holdings are an asset to the program. The department is interdisciplinary; faculty members are on staff in other university departments like anthropology, biology, forestry, and geology.

In 2000 the school was ranked by some guides as a top-25 liberal arts college. By 2003 it had fallen to 33, so the school took the serious step of hiring a Chicago image consultant to help it play catch-up with its peers. Sewanee was anxious to shake a certain party-school image that it had acquired and to overcome the perception that it was geographically isolated (which is essentially true). Sewanee also hoped to increase applications so it could drop its acceptance rate and appear more selective. One faculty member says that although Sewanee's acceptance rate is quite high—two out of three students who apply get in—the school makes no concessions to those who are unprepared. That comes as a shock to some students, and about 12 percent of freshmen don't come back as sophomores. One freshman says, "Amongst my friends there is a general feeling of being overworked. Sewanee prides itself on preventing grade inflation."

The Chicago-based consulting firm recommended bringing in Mary Maples Dunn, the president of Smith College, to inspect the curriculum. Dunn's immediate response was exasperation: there were no human sexuality courses and the words gay and lesbian appeared nowhere on campus. This has been corrected, so to speak. The school now offers a women's studies minor. And other majors are changing for the worse, too. "New faculty members are often allowed to teach courses that they create, and the coherence of many majors in the humanities has been lost or severely damaged," a professor says. "There is no sense among the younger faculty of what a major should consist of, and the older members of the faculty seem willing to let the young have their way. Sewanee is experiencing 10 years late what other liberal arts colleges have experienced." One professor accused the consulting firm of "mindless reductionism" and suggested that the school is being stripped of its traditions. It's not the first time Yankees blew something up at Sewanee.

The extent to which the code words "multiculturalism" and "diversity" are used to cloak aggressive ideological agendas is a subject of some disagreement. One professor notes that these terms "are seldom heard and affect the curriculum in minor ways if at all. Most efforts to import cultural diversity actually originate with the students involved in a handful of extracurricular groups." But another faculty member disagrees, insisting that "the ideas behind the words are having an impact."

Yet both of these professors say that the curriculum has—at least till now—escaped largely unscathed. "Our liberal arts curriculum is still strongly oriented toward the cultural legacy of Europe and toward canonical texts in most disciplines," another professor insists. "This is a campus where the most popular major is English and where the two most popular classes in that major are [in] Shakespeare and Chaucer."

Students in all majors are required to reach the fourth-semester level in a foreign language. (Sewanee offers majors in French, Spanish, German, Greek, Latin, and Russian as well as study in Italian, Chinese, and Japanese.) The university offers opportunities for study abroad through its own programs or through partnerships with other colleges and universities. Students enrolled in the European studies program choose one of two study options—"Ancient Greece and Rome: The Foundations of Western Civilization" or "Western Europe in the Middle Ages and the Renaissance"—and spend four weeks at Sewanee before heading overseas to York, Durham, and Oxford, followed by five weeks on the Continent.

Students recommend the following instructors: William Brown Patterson, Charles Perry, Woody Register, and Susan Ridyard in history; James Peters in philosophy; Gayle McKeen in political science; and Robert Benson, Thomas Carlson, Wyatt Prunty, and Dale Richardson in English.

The faculty are said to be more liberal than the students are, but not across the board. While most faculty members are genuinely fair-minded, one instructor is known to penalize a grade if a student refuses to use gender-neutral language. "I'm not sure that any Sewanee department is 'politicized' in that it is dominated by an intolerant leftist agenda," says a faculty member. But so much is in transition now at the school that it's hard to say where the school will stand when many of the senior faculty members—who tend to be more conservative than the new hires—retire. One faculty member says, "A great deal could change very quickly after that, and I might be giving very different answers. . . . But for now Sewanee is a good and valuable place."

The most public debate so far concerning Sewanee surrounds the school's name. The official name of the school is University of the South, but everyone refers to it as Sewanee. Because it was interested in attracting more minorities (the school was 92 percent white in 2004) and the word "South" purportedly provoked negative images, the board considered changing the name of the school to "Sewanee" officially. Ultimately the administration decided against the change, though it now more liberally uses "Sewanee" in its marketing materials.

ACADEMIC REQUIREMENTS

In lieu of a genuine core curriculum, the University of the South imposes a respectable set of distribution requirements. Students must take:

- One course in English composition.
- Foreign language courses through the intermediate level.
- One course in mathematics.
- Two courses in natural sciences (at least one with a lab). Options include "Cognitive Psychology" and "Comparative Sexual Behavior" (which thankfully does *not* include a lab).
- An introductory course in history.
- One course in social sciences. "World Politics" or "Global Gender Issues" would do.
- One course in philosophy or religion, such as "Ancient Philosophy from Homer to Augustine" or "Feminist and Womanist Religious Ethics."
- One course in art, art history, theater, or music, ranging from "Greek and Roman Art" to "The Films of Alfred Hitchcock."
- Two courses designated as writing-intensive.
- Two courses in physical education.

SOUTH

517

Student Life: Owners of their Domain

The campus at Sewanee is about as pleasant a place as you can find—unless you're a hopeless city slicker. Perched on a flat-topped mountain in the Cumberland Plateau of southern Tennessee, Sewanee is a good distance from any urban center: Chattanooga is 55 miles to the east, and Nashville is 92 miles in the other direction. The 10,000 acres known as the University Domain includes the town of Sewanee, the college campus, and plenty of space best described as the great outdoors. Town-gown relations are nearly perfect—mainly because the university manages the town. Students volunteer at the fire department, serve on emergency medical service teams, tutor children at nearby Sewanee Elementary School, and visit the elderly at the Sewanee Senior Citizens' Center.

The school provides so many extracurricular options that four years isn't enough to sample them all. "The *joie de vivre* [is now] remarkably similar to what I remember" a generation ago, says one alumnus. "So many events are scheduled not only during the weekends but during the week that we are not likely to become a suitcase college," a professor says. In fact, another professor says, the Residential Life office faces problems each Christmas and spring break in getting students out of their dorms. "And many of [the students] do anything they can think of to remain on campus during the summer," says this professor. In their free time—besides studying—students spend time with special-interest clubs like the university orchestra, community service organizations, or sports teams. An on-campus movie theater provides convenient entertainment every night except Thursday. Greek life is very popular, with some 70 percent of students counting themselves as members. "There is a strong frat scene, and little else," says one student. "However, there is very little pressure on those who do not want to drink. Many people participate in the social scene and do not drink."

For outdoor enthusiasts, the Domain is heaven. The Sewanee Outing Program, which organizes group activities and loans climbing, hiking, camping, and caving equipment, points out that the 8,000 acres of undeveloped land include "50 climbing sites, 13 lakes, 27 caves, 65 miles of trails . . . and countless streams and waterfalls." That's not bad for a small state, let alone a small university. In addition to the Outing Program, the school offers a Canoe Club and a Climbing Club. Indeed, the beauty of the university's grounds and architecture are a key element of the school's personality. Wide, expansive lawns are ringed with huge trees and numerous flowers, with most buildings of native sandstone. These include a new dining hall, which looks as if it had been constructed a century ago, when the Collegiate Gothic style enjoyed wide popularity. Anyone considering Sewanee should visit the campus; he'll never want to come home.

The Sewanee Performing Arts Series sponsors six major theater, music, or dance performances each year, and theater arts majors can elect to spend a semester of their junior year in New York City at the Michael Howard Studio. Sewanee also hosts several academic events every year, including the Sewanee Writers' Conference (founded with money from the estate of Tennessee Williams) and the Medieval Colloquium, both of which draw nationally known scholars and writers to campus. Those with vocal talent may join the University Choir, which sings for the services in All Saints' Chapel.

More than 90 percent of students live on campus, and Sewanee has plenty of housing options. The university offers more single-sex dormitories than it does coed living spaces. Most dorms are arranged in suites with a common bathroom for every one or two students, making the wait for a shower a short one. Some of the residence halls saw service in the campus's days as a hospital, inn, and military academy. Emery Hall, once a morgue, is now a small women's dormitory. Not surprisingly, ghost stories abound. Fraternity and sorority housing is considered to be on-campus housing.

"Sewanee's students are, for the most part, rich kids from traditional, conservative, southern families," says a faculty member. "That's just the nature of the place." Since Sewanee administrators would like to see that change, the admissions department holds a special weekend each year for prospective minority students. If they enroll, they are offered a special freshman orientation retreat. But Sewanee's student body remains less than 10 percent black, and though this is sometimes decried in the student newspaper, the *Sewanee Purple*, the university has changed only slightly over the past couple decades. "We're known as a conservative school with a mostly white student body," says a faculty member. "As much as Sewanee tries to change that, it's hard for people to get over a long-time stereotype."

SUGGESTED CORE
1. Classics 351, Greek Literature in Translation *and* Classics 353, Latin Literature in Translation
2. Philosophy 203, Ancient Philosophy from Homer to Augustine
3. Religion 141, Introduction to the Bible
4. Religion 301, Christianity 100–1300
5. Political Science 302, Recent Political Theory
6. English 357 and 358, Shakespeare I and II
7. History 201, History of the United States
8. Philosophy 319, Nineteenth-Century Philosophy

Generally, students are "moderately right leaning," says a student. "There tends to be a strong majority of students who favor conservative social positions. . . . However, there is a large minority of center-left students as well." Many of the student political groups are issue-based, like the Gay-Straight Alliance, Free Tibet, Sewanee Peace Coalition, and Students for Life, rather than party-oriented. "There is probably a majority in support of leftist environmental policies, but at the same time there is a general majority in favor of keeping marriage between heterosexuals, an aggressive foreign policy, limiting abortion, and preserving the influence of religious institutions," one student says. Both conservative and liberal students generally feel comfortable voicing their views.

One of the more famous alumni is Rev. Vicky Gene Robinson (named for his parents, Charles Victor and Imogene—he prefers "Gene"), the first openly gay Episcopalian bishop. Robinson maintains good relations with the school. One of the five members of the selection committee who nominated Robinson was Rev. Joe Goodwin Burnett, who at the time was a professor of pastoral theology at the Sewanee School of Theology.

The University of the South welcomes religious activities and groups, and although the school is officially Episcopalian, other denominations are supported. Baptist Christian Ministries and the Sewanee Catholic Community are active student groups. Still, as a parent of a prospective student says, "You can cut the Episcopalianism at Sewanee with a knife." The university bulletin reports that about a third of Sewanee students say they are Episcopalian. Sewanee's campus has three chapels—St. Luke's Chapel, the Chapel of the Apostles, and All Saint's Chapel. There are two traditional eucharistic services every week and an "informal folk mass" called "Growing in Grace." The school also supports Bible studies, the Canterbury Group (for Episcopalian students), a Centering Prayer group, and other activities. Sewanee even refers to its academic year with terms from the church calendar—the year is divided into the Advent and Easter semesters, not fall and spring.

Crime is remarkably low (in fact, not a single assault has taken place in years). The only crimes in 2003 were 26 burglaries (double from the previous year) and one stolen car. One security brief attributed the general increase of burglary on campus to the increase in gadget-sized technology.

Tuition, room, and board at Sewanee totaled $32,700 in 2004–5. About 60 percent of the students receive some sort of financial aid, admissions are need-blind, and the school uses its endowment of $240 million to provide 100 percent of each student's demonstrated need.

SPELMAN COLLEGE

Living up to a legacy

What is now Spelman College began in 1881 in the basement of Atlanta's Friendship Baptist Church. The students, most of them former slaves, were there to learn to read and write; the Bible was their main text. John D. Rockefeller and his wife visited the school in 1884 and soon gave enough money to provide for Spelman's immediate future. Today the student body comprises more than 2,100 students (all women) from 41 states and 15 foreign countries.

For its first 100 years, the college struggled to make a name for itself. But under the leadership of Johnetta Cole from 1987 to 1997, Spelman became known as one of the country's better private, independent, liberal arts colleges, leading some to call it the black Radcliffe. Cole successfully conducted a $113 million capital campaign, garnering $20 million from Camille and Bill Cosby and $1 million from Oprah Winfrey. In 2005, *U.S. News and World Report* added Spelman to its list of the Top 75 Best Liberal Arts Colleges. From what we've learned, Spelman earned its spot.

Not surprisingly, for a school with Spelman's heritage and whose student body is 97 percent black, Spelman emphasizes African American literature and culture in its curriculum. But it explores these subjects with a sense of historical and cultural seriousness—unlike too many race and gender-oriented programs of study. By and large, Spelman students are proud of their school and are quick to say that even though their school is different from other top colleges, it can certainly compete with them. "It is very empowering attending Spelman," a senior says. "Knowing that you are part of a legacy of excellence makes you strive to live up to that legacy and everything that people expect when they hear that you are a student at Spelman College."

Notable alumnae include Pulitzer Prize–winning novelist Alice Walker; Marian Wright Edelman, founder of the Children's Defense Fund; and actress Keshia Knight Pulliam, formerly of *The Cosby Show*.

VITAL STATISTICS

Religious affiliation: none
Total enrollment: 2,186
Total undergraduates: 2,186
SAT/ACT midranges: SAT V: 490–580, M: 490–560; ACT: 20–24
Applicants: 4,345
Applicants accepted: 47%
Accepted applicants who enrolled: 33%
Tuition: $15,305
Room and board: $8,040
Freshman retention rate: 91%
Graduation rate: 63% (4 yrs.), 76% (6 yrs.)
Average class size: 17
Student-faculty ratio: 11:1
Courses taught by graduate TAs: none
Most popular majors: social sciences, psychology, English
Students living on campus: 62%
Guaranteed housing for four years? no
Students in sororities: 5%

SOUTH

Academic Life: The content of its character

Spelman calls its general education curriculum a core, but in reality only two specific courses are required:

- "The African Diaspora and the World" (two semesters).
- "First Year Composition," which requires a grade of C or better.

Students also take one course each in:

- Humanities. Choices include "World Literature: Ancient to 1600" and "World Literature: 1600 to the Present," or any course from the philosophy and religion department.
- Fine arts. Options range from "Studies of Women in Theatre and Drama" to "Women in Dance: Sexism, Sexuality, and Subversion."
- Social sciences. Courses offered range from "Survey of European History" II and "Introduction to Economics" to "Cross-Cultural Perspectives on Gender."

Spelman College offers 26 majors, most of them straightforward and traditional. There are no peace and justice or ethnic studies departments. Nor is there a formal African American studies major—although a student could create her own curriculum for this and other majors through an interdisciplinary "independent major" option. The Ethel Waddell Githii Honors Program is constituted similarly to other colleges' honors programs for high-achieving students, but has significantly more structured requirements, including special honors-level core courses in English composition, mathematics, and philosophy. A sampling of honors electives includes "Biomedical Ethics," the alarming "Mao-Zedong's Thought in Africa," and "Women in Japanese Society." Honors students are required to write and defend a substantial senior thesis.

In most cases, requirements for the majors offer some of the structure that the general education requirements lack. For instance, the English department requires 11 courses of its majors: "Introduction to Literary Studies," "Advanced Exposition," "Seminal Writers in the African American Tradition," a course in U.S. literature, "Shakespeare," a course in British literature, and two courses in gender studies, international literature, and critical theory. English majors fulfill requirements in chronological periods, as well: one course in literature before 1800, one between 1800 and 1900, and one after 1900.

The history major is not quite as structured, although students are more likely to graduate with real breadth in the discipline than their colleagues at some more prestigious schools. History majors must take a course called "Historical Methods," which the department calls "an introduction to researching and writing" and which addresses "the skills needed to successfully complete the major." Another required course is "Making of the Modern World," in which the texts include *The Atlantic Slave Trade*, *The French Revolution and Human Rights*, *Auschwitz: True Tales From a Grotesque Land*, and a world history reader. Besides these specific courses, history majors must take five electives, three courses in their region of concentration, and one from among five other geographic areas. Eleven total courses are required.

The best departments at Spelman are economics, biology, and philosophy and religion—which offer solid course selections in the foundational areas of the disciplines. One student praises the foreign language department, even though the range of tongues taught is limited; Spelman offers majors in Spanish and French, as well as instruction in Japanese and Latin.

Comparative women's studies is the most politicized of Spelman's departments; the program promises (warns?) that majors will "analyze the ways in which gender, race, ethnicity, class, and sexuality construct the social, cultural, and biological experience of both men and women in all societies," "analyze images of women in literary texts, the media, and the arts" and "recognize the masculine bias in the history of knowledge." One course called "The Black Female Body in American Culture," according to the catalog, "addresses the relationship between constructed corporeal representation of black women and American culture. . . . The black female body is analyzed in terms of the body itself as a text and as a site of political struggle." Care to write a 30-page paper on Janet Jackson's "wardrobe malfunction"? This may be the department for you.

Whatever your interests, if you're studying at Spelman you'll find plenty of help from supportive faculty members. "One of the great things about Spelman is that the professors are genuinely interested in their students' success. Most are very easy to get in contact with in their offices, via e-mail, etc.," an economics major says. "There is no excuse for a student to not be able to talk to her professor if she is having a problem." Another student says, "I usually find myself in a professor's office at least once daily. Most students feel comfortable approaching professors about class work and other academic advice. I . . . have developed personal relationships with my professors and have maintained them throughout the four years." Teaching assistants do not teach, but they do help with laboratory portions of science classes.

Spelman students receive strong academic advice and support throughout their years at the college. Each is assigned an advisor upon arrival (usually a faculty member), who helps her select courses and choose a major. Once the student has declared a major, she can choose a faculty advisor within her major department. Students must visit their advisors before registering each semester. Spelman is intensely committed to student counseling and preparation—and, if necessary, remediation, usually provided through the college's academic support centers. At the College Writing Center, students can get advice on assignments from peers and faculty. Each month, the center holds writing workshops and lectures. The Learning Resources Center helps students make the transition from high school to college with workshops on study habits, noncredit courses, and peer tutoring. Students say the Office of Career Planning and Development is exceptionally helpful, and most seniors spend a number of hours there during their final year.

REQUIREMENTS (CONT'D)

- Natural sciences.
- Computer literacy.
  Student also must complete:
- 16 credits in a foreign language, or through the intermediate level.
- Two courses in health and physical education—for instance, a dance class.
- Two courses in mathematics, at a level determined by placement tests.
- "First-Year Seminar," which consists of attendance at convocations and public events.
- "Sophomore Assembly," also requiring attendance at important events.
- One course in international or women's studies. Thankfully, this can be fulfilled by taking a course in any number of departments, including the foreign language departments.

SOUTH

523

Students name as the best professors Marilyn A. Davis and Jeanne T. Meadows in political science; Cynthia Neal Spence in sociology; Bernice J. deGannes Scott and Jack Stone in economics; James Hale in computer science; Stephen Knadler in English; Teresa Edwards and P. Nagambal Shah in mathematics; and Roy Martinez, chair of the philosophy and religion department.

Spelman is part of the Atlanta University Center Consortium, an association of historically black institutions of higher education. Its partners include Morehouse College, the Interdenominational Theological Center, Morehouse School of Medicine, Clark Atlanta University, and Morris Brown College. Spelman students can take courses at other members of the consortium, with whom they share the Robert W. Woodruff Library. Spelman also encourages students to participate in the Domestic Exchange Program, in which women study for a semester or year at places such as Bates, Bryn Mawr, or New York University. One student who spent a semester at Stanford University says the exchange program gave her "the mainstream, large-university experience." The dual-degree engineering major allows students to take three years at Spelman and two years in an engineering program at another school (such as Columbia or Dartmouth), after which the student earns both a liberal arts and an engineering degree. Spelman does not sponsor any study-abroad programs of its own but does allow students to participate in other schools' programs in Europe, Ghana, the Dominican Republic, the West Indies, and elsewhere.

In general, what ideological activism is present at Spelman is sponsored by the administration and the faculty, not students. In November 2003, Spelman hosted the SisterSong Women of Color Reproductive Health and Sexual Rights National Conference. Faculty members may be overwhelmingly liberal, but one student says that "classes aren't really influenced by [bias] except for maybe in the political science department." But if the department is biased, this is not reflected in the catalog. Courses like "Racism and the Law" are kept to a minimum, and political science majors are required to enroll in "Ancient and Classical Political Theory," "American Constitutional Law," and "National Government in the United States." Would that more political science departments were so politic.

In March 2003, Spelman hired its ninth president, Beverly Daniel Tatum. Tatum, who served as acting president at Mount Holyoke College prior to coming to Spelman, is touted as a "scholar, teacher, author, administrator, and race relations expert." She is the author of *Why Are All the Black Kids Sitting Together in the Cafeteria? and Other Conversations about Race.* Tatum inherits an endowment of $215 million—highest of any of the schools in the Atlanta University Center Consortium.

Student Life: On general decorum

If pressed, students and faculty ("mostly Democrats," says one student) characterize Spelman as left-leaning. Conservative-minded Spelman scholars might find a home with the Students in Free Enterprise group and numerous religious organizations. Other political groups include Amnesty International; Afrekete, a group for "gay, gender free, bisexual, lesbian, transgender, and gay friendly individuals"; and the Feminist Majority Leadership Alliance. This last group performed a genuine service in 2004 when it called vivid, public attention to the antifemale, violent, and pornographic nature of the lyrics sung by many hip-hop artists—causing a major rap artist to cut ties with Spelman.

Although Spelman College is officially not affiliated with any religion, many students are religiously committed and continue to practice their faith while at school. There are 15 religious organizations on campus, including Campus Crusade for Christ, Catholic Newman Organization, Movements of Praise Dance Team, New Life Inspirational Gospel Choir, and Christian Leaders of Tomorrow, as well as the Baha'i Club and An-Nissa, a Muslim religious group. Campus Ministries offers a number of activities for students, including religious services, prayer sessions, counseling, and lectures and seminars. The Sisters Chapel (the eponymous sisters are John D. Rockefeller Jr.'s mother and aunt) holds religious services and the weekly convocation. At one time, the convocation was a religious service, but it "is now more information-based . . . with a musical interlude," says one student. Occasionally, freshmen and sophomores are required to attend.

In 2004 Spelman College launched the Sisters Center for WISDOM (Women in Spiritual Discernment of Ministry). This project, funded by the Lilly Endowment, seeks "to develop and empower the total person [and to] re-establish and strengthen our ability to integrate faith commitments and contextual experiences into curricular and cocurricular activities."

Many students say they chose Spelman College because it is a comfortable place to study. "Though it is pretty competitive, students are also supportive of one another and want the best for all of their friends," a student says. Another student suggests that Spelman is only for those who are truly "intellectually driven." Political activism comes well behind coursework and extracurricular activities in most students' minds.

Socially, Spelman is much more conservative than many of the schools in this guide. A student guidebook called the *Spelman Woman* lists a number of commendable traditions that students are expected to follow. On general decorum, the guide notes, "Although the campus is small and has a very comfortable, homey feeling, it is still an academic community where business is conducted. Therefore, some behaviors are less than acceptable. The following list notes a few unacceptable public practices: the use of profanity, combing hair in public places, wearing hair rollers to class and in administrative offices." On smoking: "Though most Spelman students are legally old enough to smoke, the college does not encourage the practice as the health risks associated

SUGGESTED CORE
1. English 331, The Epic and Its Origins
2. Philosophy 230, History of Western Philosophy: Ancient and Medieval
3. Religion 311, Old Testament Literature and History *or* Religion 312, A Survey of Christianity
4. Religion 303, The History of Religious Thought
5. Political Science 417, Political Thought from Machiavelli to the Present
6. English 310, Shakespeare
7. History 211, 212, Survey of American History
8. Philosophy 231, History of Western Philosophy: Modern (*closest match*)

with smoking run counter to the college's ultimate goal." The guide discourages all manner of vulgarity. For instance: "Campus activities such as date auctions, slumber parties, and pajama jams often reflect negative images of the women who plan those events and Spelman College." Spelman women tend to dress more formally than students on other campuses—even in an all-female environment, dresses, makeup, and carefully arranged hair are the norm, a testament not so much to femininity as to Spelman women's desire to appear polished and professional at all times. The guide even offers a primer in business etiquette.

The fact that Spelman is an all-women school doesn't really hit students until they return to their dorms at night. One student says, "We are an all-female institution, but we still interact a great deal with males"—particularly the men from Morehouse College. "They attend our classes; we can attend theirs; we socialize on the different campuses, so it's not like you are around women all the time," she says. Only a very small percentage of Spelman students participate in social sororities, but many students attend fraternity socials at Morehouse College. Most student social life occurs on either the Spelman or the Morehouse campus, but the bright lights of Atlanta occasionally pull students away from their studies. Restaurants, sporting events, night clubs, and other cultural attractions are plentiful. Spelman is an NCAA Division II school and offers varsity teams for basketball, cross country, golf, soccer, tennis, track and field, and volleyball. There is also a cheerleading team and a few extramural athletic programs in which students compete against area schools like Piedmont and Maryville.

The college boasts a historic campus of 32 acres that dates back to 1883 and is located only five minutes west of downtown Atlanta. More than 60 percent of students live on campus in one of Spelman's 10 residence halls. In 2004 the renovation of Packard Hall won an Atlanta Urban Design Commission Award of Excellence. Most rooms are double occupancy, but there are a limited number of singles, triples, quads, and even five-person rooms. The visitation policy is quite strict: Male visitors must sign in and out of the dormitories with the dorm hostess at the designated check-in area, be escorted at all times, and are only allowed in the buildings from 6 to 11:30 each evening. Men are never permitted to spend the night in the residence halls.

Community service is popular among students, and the city of Atlanta certainly has plenty of need for it. Almost half the student body participates in some form of volunteer activity. The West End neighborhood, where Spelman is located, has some of the highest poverty, incarceration, and AIDS infection rates in the country—although the college itself is sufficiently policed, beautifully manicured, and the site of very little crime. One student says Spelman is "a small campus and has security located at both gate entrances. This provides a sense of security for students who live on campus." In 2003, the last year for which statistics were available, the college reported 19 burglaries on campus and no other crimes.

As private colleges go, Spelman is affordable; 2004–5 tuition was $15,305, room and board $8,040. Some 90 percent of students receive some form of financial aid—20 percent of them merit-based scholarships. The average student graduates with a debt of $16,500—not bad, for the formative experience she has enjoyed.

TULANE UNIVERSITY

NEW ORLEANS, LOUISIANA • WWW.TULANE.EDU

Green wave

Throughout its 171 years, Tulane University has gone through several reorganizations. In 1834, it began as the Medical College of Louisiana, later merging with the new University of Louisiana. In 1884, a wealthy businessman, Paul Tulane, donated more than a million dollars—enough for the school to become private and change its name to honor its benefactor. Tulane University moved to the green, wide boulevards of uptown New Orleans and built much of the gracious campus that stands today on St. Charles Avenue—along one of the last remaining city streetcar lines. The university has grown to almost 11,000 students, some 70 percent of them undergraduates.

Money helped in 1884, and money is needed again. Tulane is still picking up the pieces from the disastrous, almost 20-year tenure of its former president, Eamon Kelley, who resigned in 1998. Under Tulane's current president, Scott Cowen, private donations have risen dramatically; two cofounders of Yahoo, who are Tulane alumni, recently gave $30 million—apiece. Upon his arrival, Cowen announced that he intended to raise $700 million to "bolster the school's standing among elite research institutions." Tulane has already collected $470 million and expects to reach its goal by 2008. The school intends to spend the money on nuts-and-bolts items, like expanding and renovating the library, overhauling the baseball stadium, and boosting its endowment.

Tulane is a beautiful school with a long tradition, not to mention some renowned scholars and programs in the humanities and sciences. However, Tulane's rather casual approach to the curriculum means that a student who wants a genuine education must arrive at Tulane with that purpose firmly in mind. He will also need a fair degree of self-discipline to avoid drowning in the pleasures of America's most delightfully dissipated city.

VITAL STATISTICS
Religious affiliation: none
Total enrollment: 10,754
Total undergraduates: 7,829
SAT midrange: 1240–1420
Applicants: 14,000
Applicants accepted: 55%
Accepted applicants who enrolled: 21%
Tuition: $31,210
Room and board: $7,925
Freshman retention rate: 86%
Graduation rate: 62% (4 yrs.), 73% (6 yrs.)
Average class size: 22
Student-faculty ratio: 10:1
Courses taught by graduate TAs: none
Most popular majors: business, social sciences, engineering
Students living on campus: 42%
Guaranteed housing for four years? no
Students in fraternities: 12% sororities: 15%

SOUTH

527

Tulane has no core curriculum and rather loose distribution requirements. Students in its liberal arts colleges must prove competency in three major areas:

- Writing. Students complete (or test out of) English 101, a composition class, then take either a four-credit writing-intensive course in any one of many departments, or add a writing practicum to a seminar from a long list of approved courses. In 2005, these included many worthy-sounding classes: "Colloquium in Ancient History," "Colloquium and Field Work in Ancient and Medieval Mediterranean Civilizations," "Seminar in Modern British History," "Psychopharmacology Lab," and "Darwin and Darwinism," along with some likely clunkers: "Women in Africa" and "Advanced Feminist Theories."
- Foreign languages. Students take (or test out of) a course at the intermediate level.
- Formal thought. Students take (or test out of) a course in math or symbolic logic.

Academic Life: Safety first

Six undergraduate colleges make up Tulane University: the School of Architecture, the School of Business, the School of Engineering, the two liberal arts colleges—Newcomb College for women and Tulane College for men—and the University College, which largely caters to part-time and night students. Despite the separate colleges for men and women, Tulane University is entirely coed; Newcomb and Tulane colleges share a common curriculum, faculty, and residential space. Students enrolled in the liberal arts colleges will find that the only distinction is in what is printed on their diplomas.

Most Tulane students are "relatively motivated," says a professor. "I suppose that a really clever but lazy student could manage to hawk out the easy courses in [the curriculum], and then go on to major in soft fields like communications or sociology," one professor says. "Most of them don't, however. As an advisor, I am often impressed at how many of my students have backgrounds in calculus, for instance. Or in hard languages like German, Russian, or Latin."

One thing affecting student motivation is the fact that Tulane has acquired the reputation as a "safety" school. One student, who chose Tulane for its virtues, bemoaned her classmates' attitude: "Most of the students here are here because they didn't get into their first choices, which is disappointing. (Most people applied to Ivy Leagues, or schools like UVA and Duke.) I wish more people wanted to be here because it is such a fun and interesting school."

One of Tulane's best departments is philosophy, which has done a remarkably good job of hiring and promoting faculty devoted both to their research and their students. The spectrum of scholarship represented in the department is broad, with faculty specializing in ancient philosophy, metaphysics, continental philosophy, epistemology, ethics, logic, and other areas. Philosophy majors are required to take a two-course sequence in the history of philosophy, a course in logic, one in ethics, and two upper-level courses on special topics like Aristotle, empiricism, the philosophy of the mind, or metaphysics. Besides the standard philosophy major, the department also offers two other tracks, "law, morality, and society" and "language, mind, and knowledge."

The political science department is also comparatively strong, with several excellent faculty members. One professor says the department is "considered one of the best teaching departments in the university," despite its members' impressive publishing and research records. A student majoring in political science says, "The professors in that department are great." The history department, on the other hand, lists a paucity of fundamental courses, some say because it lacks funding for professors to teach them.

Some of Tulane's best teachers, students and faculty say, are John Patton in communications; Ronna C. Burger, Gerald Gaus, John D. Glenn Jr., and Eric Mack in philosophy; W. David Clinton, Thomas Langston, Paul H. Lewis, Gary A. Remer, Andrea Talentino, and Martyn Thompson in political science; George L. Bernstein, James Boyden, Kenneth W. Harl, Colin M. MacLachlan, and Samuel C. Ramer in history; Michael P. Kuczynski in English; James McGuire in physics; William L. Alworth (emeritus) in chemistry; Harvey and Victoria Bricker in anthropology; Prospero Mesa in Spanish; and John Edwards in economics. The Murphy Institute of Political Economy offers an undergraduate degree, and the economics department tends to be libertarian. Judith Schafer stands out as a dedicated teacher in the Murphy Institute.

For some time, students have feared that they might lose their favorite teachers because Tulane could not afford to offer them competitive salaries; this is no doubt an issue that President Cowen will address with his newfound cash. One way he has raised that money is by encouraging faculty to publish widely and to secure grants. Some faculty members have complained that this gets in the way of teaching undergraduates. One student says, "As at any institution, there are a number of faculty members who are interested only in their research." Faculty say salaries at Tulane are lower than at comparable institutions, and many of the school's distinguished faculty members have left Tulane to assume endowed chairs or head departments elsewhere. Others stay, it is said, because they simply love living in New Orleans. Who can blame them?

If technology research is your interest, Tulane will accommodate you; the school has partnered up with the federal government on major initiatives to fight bioterrorism. According to the *Chronicle of Higher Education*, the school is a partner "in two federally financed biodefense research consortiums" and operates "one highly secure Biosafety Level 3 laboratory and is building three more. The university's scientists are developing

REQUIREMENTS (CONT'D)

Tulane also requires a course in the "foundations of Western culture," which can be fulfilled with solid courses—or by taking "Dance History: Primitive through Nineteenth Century." A second course is required in "non-Western and Latin American cultures"; among the classes that qualify are "Egypt under the Pharaohs," "Women, Development, and Communication in the English-Speaking Caribbean," and "Race, Ethnicity, and Nationalism," along with about 100 other options.

Students must also take:

- Three courses in humanities and the fine arts (at least one from each).
- Three courses in the social sciences (from at least two different departments).
- Three courses in mathematics and the sciences (from at least two disciplines). One must have a laboratory component.

vaccines against anthrax, plague, and other diseases."

Tulane's student-faculty ratio is an impressive 10 to 1, and most professors are said to be eager to help students. An international relations major says, "While they are all involved in research, professors literally drop everything during office hours or a scheduled appointment to make sure you understand." A freshman says "professors are so accessible, I find that I can get a better caliber of education in a couple hours of one-on-one sessions than I do in the classroom, particularly in my weaker subjects."

The advising program, students say, is not so good, at least for underclassmen. Freshmen are assigned to professional advisors in the deans' offices of their respective colleges and are required to have "advising sessions" before registering for classes. "These advising sessions . . . are a joke," one student says. "They treat the students like cattle, pushing them in and out." Another student says, "It's kind of a joke for freshmen. However, once you declare a major, you get assigned a real advisor, who knows your name, can write letters of recommendation for you, and is generally interested in seeing improvement." Another student found that freshman advisors were hard to track down; she switched to another, and still another, before she finally had a productive meeting and was able to register for her classes—late. "It was a hassle more than anything," she says.

Tulane tried to leap onto the national PC bandwagon some 15 years ago when administrators campaigned for race-based faculty hiring, mandatory "sensitivity training," and more "diversity" in the classroom. Faculty members fought back, quashing the ideas by taking them to alumni. "After losing that battle, the administration contented itself with small, piecemeal initiatives, like supporting black studies and women's studies, benefits for gay partners, and the like—issues that didn't rouse the alumni community enough for them to be stopped," says one professor. Like most schools, Tulane employs a largely liberal faculty, with a few conservative and libertarian faculty in (almost) every department. "It is common to see articles, pictures, and cartoons on professors' doors ridiculing President Bush," a political economy major says. "Those faculty who are conservative tend to fly below the radar."

Students say faculty sometimes plug their views in class, but one can avoid politicized classes by shunning departments like women's studies, sociology, and Latin American studies that focus to distraction on race, class, and gender. "One of the sociology professors I had openly condemned capitalism, while in a history class concerning modern France, all we read were selections from French Marxists," one student says. "In a Spanish reading class . . . the reading selections were made up of articles advocating gun control and the mass redistribution of wealth and condemning the family unit as being antifemale." Another student says political biases often influence the content of courses, but he also says that "if you are vocal about opposition to received liberal views, the faculty generally let you speak your mind and will engage in debate with you in and out of class."

A new program requires freshmen to read a book the summer before entering Tulane. The latest selection was *The Color of Water: A Black Man's Tribute to His White Mother*, by James MacBride. Lectures and discussions on the book are then held throughout the first semester—at least, in theory. According to a freshman, "Discussions, however, weren't really enforced, and if you weren't in freshman English . . . it wasn't even brought up."

Student Life: Fat Tuesday— and Wednesday, Thursday, etc.

For prospective students, Tulane's biggest selling point is (and probably has always been) the eclectic city of New Orleans, which really does look and feel Caribbean. Around three-quarters of the Tulane student body comes from more than 500 miles away; a quarter of the school comes from the Northeast. The uptown campus (the medical school is in a grubby part of downtown) is pleasant and situated in a "desirable neighborhood," as the real estate lingo has it. Just across St. Charles Avenue, which borders the campus, is the Frederick Law Olmstead–designed Audubon Park, which includes a public golf course, jogging and walking trails, and lagoons. Across Magazine Street at the opposite end of the park is Audubon Zoo, one of the nation's finest. Right down the block is the Jesuit Loyola University, which houses a more working-class, unpretentious sort of student.

SUGGESTED CORE
1. Classical Studies 122, The Greek Mind
2. Philosophy 201, History of Ancient Philosophy
3. Classical Studies 314/ 322, Hebrew Bible / New Testament
4. Classical Studies 220, Ancient Christianity
5. Political Science 478, Modern Political Theory
6. English 446 and 447, Shakespeare I and II
7. History 141, The United States from Colonization to 1865
8. Philosophy 310, Nineteenth-Century European Philosophy

The Mississippi River flows by the zoo on the other side of a huge levee that keeps New Orleaners from drowning—since the entire city sits below sea level. The St. Charles Avenue streetcar runs up and down that street, providing an easy and enjoyable way for Tulane students to visit the French Quarter. In New Orleans, says one student, "There is always something going on, such as concerts. There is too much to do here for only four years." Another student says there's nothing like sitting under the live oaks, listening to the streetcars go by, and enjoying the weather—that is, when it's not too hot and muggy to emerge from the air conditioning.

Tulane is a notorious party school whose students somehow find time to do a little homework and study for some tests. Students say alcohol plays a tremendous role in most students' social lives. "Being in New Orleans, how could you avoid it?" says one. The university has tried to steer students away from drinking by banning alcohol on campus for underage students. A junior says that the prevalence of drinking has decreased some, but mostly, it has moved off campus, where alcohol is easy to obtain. Other students insist that drinking doesn't get in the way of classwork. "It's not unusual that some of the best students and most active participants in campus life are some of the hardest partiers on the weekend," one student says. "But they get an impressive amount accomplished in the meantime." Another says, "We are certainly a school full of serious academics, but a lot of those academics are as good at drinking as they are in the classroom." Try that argument with your parents, and see how far it gets you.

SOUTH

Students say they spend their free time participating in extracurricular activities with religious organizations, community service associations, and other groups like Mock Trial and the Tulane Literary Society. There are historic churches and synagogues all around the city—including the downtown church universally called "Jesuit," where novelist Walker Percy walked in one day and asked for instruction in the Catholic faith, and the parish from which *A Confederacy of Dunces*' Ignatius Reilly was banned for demanding a requiem for his dog. (The author, John Kennedy Toole, was a Tulane grad.) The French Quarter, on the other hand, has its Wiccans.

With several exceptions, the Tulane student body is not known for its political fervor. Politics are considerably less exciting than simply living in New Orleans. The College Republicans is the most active and outspoken of the student political groups, sponsoring local politicians and national names—like Phyllis Schlafly, recently—and a Conservative Awareness Week each year. On the left, Tulane ACLU, Free the Planet (an environmental organization), Students Organized Against Racism (a pro-affirmative action group), and MOSAIC (a gay rights organization) are all active. (A gay activist group in New Orleans seems slightly redundant; it's one of the most actively gay cities in America.) The College Democrats have become more organized in recent years; you'll see them chalking sidewalks with anti-Bush slogans, and sometimes (one student tells us) ripping down the posters of the rival Socialist Workers Party,

The university's weekly student newspaper, the *Tulane Hullabaloo*, appeals to campus conservatives to voice their views. "The *Hullabaloo* staff has a great sense of journalistic integrity," says a conservative student. "Most are liberal, but I think that the views section does a fantastic job of incorporating all viewpoints, so I commend them on that."

Even as the *Hullabaloo* seeks political variety on its opinion pages, the Tulane administration has long been on a quest for ethnic "diversity." Students who want to help with freshman orientation must first attend "diversity training" sessions, "which basically say how horrible white people are," says a student. The Office of Multicultural Affairs sponsors a Multicultural Preview Conference each year for new minority students and a Diversity Convocation each fall. Through the Multicultural Council, the university supports a dozen ethnic-based student organizations—among them, the African American Congress of Tulane, Latin and American Student Association, and the Tulane Chinese Student Association. At commencement, Tulane's "multi-ethnic graduating students" can attend a special graduation celebration reception. Two years after its creation in 2001, the President's Special Task Force on Diversity found that minorities were underrepresented in top positions at the university and that "there is an uneven distribution of females and minorities across the academic ranks," particularly at the level of professor. It also reported that minorities thought Tulane was less friendly in its campus climate than white students did. The task force recommended that Tulane actively recruit minorities and females to administrative and tenure-track faculty positions, but thus far no major, concrete initiatives towards this end have been announced.

Sports are less important than drinking games, but they still have a place on campus. The Green Wave fields 16 varsity teams, and club and intramural competitions are also popular. After bitter complaints from students, alumni, and local fans, Tulane rejected a budget-driven proposal that would have either eliminated the football team (which has enjoyed considerable success in recent years) or downgraded it from NCAA Division I to Division III. President Cowen has been engaged in another football dispute over the past few years, fighting to gain Tulane a better shot at entering lucrative bowl games.

All residence halls are coed (separated by floor) except for two women-only dorms. Housing is guaranteed only for incoming freshmen. Housing options include on-campus apartments, suites (four single rooms that share a common bathroom), and traditional dorm rooms. The all-women Josephine-Louise Hall is a bastion of southern propriety, requiring visitors to register at the front desk from 8 p.m. to 8 a.m. and male visitors to be escorted at all times.

Unfortunately, although in recent years major crimes have declined slightly, New Orleans is also one of the most violent cities in the nation. Students should not avoid Tulane for fear of crime, but they should be extremely careful once they arrive and remember that in New Orleans, dangerous neighborhoods sit right next to safer ones. On-campus offenses for 2003 rose slightly over 2002 and included three forcible sex offenses, three robberies, three aggravated assaults, 38 burglaries, 11 stolen cars, and two arsons. Students can call for an escort at any time, day or night, and blue light emergency phones are available all over campus.

Tulane charges Ivy League–level tuition—$31,210 in 2004–5, and $7,925 for room and board. It does practice a need-blind admission policy, fortunately, and has a variety of need- and merit-based scholarships available. Aid is provided to approximately 41 percent of students.

VANDERBILT UNIVERSITY

NASHVILLE, TENNESSEE • WWW.VANDERBILT.EDU

Name dropping

On one reckoning the modern conservative intellectual movement began in 1933 when a young Socialist Party activist arrived at Vanderbilt from the University of Kentucky and found the Agrarians there were not the poltroons he expected, but men and women of intellect, erudition, feeling, and character. It was years before Richard Weaver finally abandoned his own "progressive" ideology, but Vanderbilt provided the decisive demonstration of a viable alternative. For many students, it still does. Although endowed by New York rail tycoon Cornelius Vanderbilt and reaching an international constituency—only 20 percent of its students come from Tennessee—Vanderbilt has, until recently at least, cherished its southern roots. There was even some controversy when the name of Confederate Memorial Dormitory was sanitized to Memorial Dormitory, though it never became a major issue.

Students and faculty agree that Vanderbilt has a fairly conservative student body. The administration wants high national rankings, and so recent years have seen Vanderbilt attempt to conform more closely to the political expectations of the academic establishment. In the classroom, this has meant more courses with obvious political agendas; on the rest of the campus, it has meant increased funding for diversity programming, liberal speakers, and politically correct campus groups.

Even so, Vanderbilt attracts fewer radical faculty members and more outright conservative faculty members than do most top-tier schools. One philosophy major says that, in the classroom, Vanderbilt has achieved enviable political balance. "The faculty leans to the left, but it has not been my experience that other views are unwelcome. In fact, I have had two philosophy courses taught by fairly libertarian professors and a number of economics courses. The level of bias varies by department, but it is not all that bad here."

The student body may be conservative, but liberals tend to be more outspoken, writes a student in the *Vanderbilt Hustler*: "Vanderbilt has a reputation of having a very conservative student body, but the conservatives have been a fairly silent majority in comparison to their more vocal and activist counterparts." One conservative student says, "The biggest group on campus is the College Republicans, but the most in-your-face groups are the gay group (LAMBDA) and the Vanderbilt Feminists." While no overtly political group can receive university funding, according to one writer for the *Vanderbilt Torch*, a conservative opinion publication, only conservative groups are neglected. He complains that "liberal groups such as the Black Cultural Center, LAMBDA, and VandyFems [Vanderbilt Feminists] . . . receive tens of thousands of dollars."

Academic Life: The house that Vanderbilt

Students in Vanderbilt's College of Liberal Arts and Sciences must fulfill a set of broad distribution requirements, or what Vanderbilt calls the College Program in Liberal Education (CPLE). An admissions officer explains that the Vanderbilt curriculum aims to teach students "life skills"—that is, competency in four areas: quantitative, analytical, problem solving, and communication. Vanderbilt recognizes the value of a broad liberal arts education, noting that companies recruit students with these four skills, not simply proficiency in one academic discipline. "Majors don't decide what you do," the admissions officer says. Through the distribution requirements, liberal arts students gradually master these skills, but other requirements in writing, mathematics, and foreign languages emphasize these skills further.

For the writing requirement, students take English 100W, a basic freshman writing course that can be skipped with sufficient scores on the writing portion of the SAT. Students also take one or two additional writing-intensive courses, depending again on test scores, and qualifying classes are offered in virtually every humanities department. Good scores on the SAT II mathematics test can satisfy the mathematics requirement, in lieu of a course in calculus or statistics. The basic foreign language requirement calls for proficiency to the elementary level, but students can satisfy the international component of the distribution requirements by continuing to the intermediate level or by studying abroad.

Unfortunately, few students appreciate the value of a broad liberal arts education, and some of the courses designed to meet the requirements are not well taught; a recent reform has addressed these issues with some degree of success. A history major says that some students view CPLE requirements as a chore, a hurdle to jump before reaching the real goal—one's major. But according to one student who values the CPLE requirements, "If you graduate from Vanderbilt with a degree from Arts and Sciences (perhaps excluding women's studies) you will have a great deal of knowledge and be prepared to enter the workforce."

Most of the courses that satisfy the CPLE requirements are serious, fair, and straightforward. However, the curriculum allows for so much flexibility that the traditional components of a genuine core curriculum—American history, ancient philosophy, European intellectual history, and the like—can easily be avoided. For example, the women's studies course "Women's Experience in America" and the music department's "American Music" satisfy the American component of the history requirement. These

VITAL STATISTICS

Religious affiliation: none
Total enrollment: 11,294
Total undergraduates: 6,272
SAT/ACT midranges: SAT
    V: 620–710, M: 650–730;
    ACT: 28–32
Applicants: 11,170
Applicants accepted: 38%
*Accepted applicants who
    enrolled*: 37%
Tuition: $29,240
Room and board: $9,736
Freshman retention rate: 95%
Graduation rate: 80% (4 yrs.),
    86% (6 yrs.)
*Courses with fewer than 20
    students*: 67%
Student-faculty ratio: 9:1
*Courses taught by graduate
    TAs*: 5%
Most popular majors: social
    sciences, engineering,
    psychology
Students living on campus:
    83%
*Guaranteed housing for four
    years?* yes
Students in fraternities: 34%
    sororities: 50%

SOUTH

535

In lieu of a core curriculum, Vanderbilt imposes certain distribution and other requirements. Students in the College of Arts and Sciences must take the following:

- English 100 and two other courses with a writing component chosen from a list including "Introduction to Philosophy" and beginning courses in foreign languages.
- A basic course in mathematics.
- One year of a foreign language.
- A higher-level math course or a third semester of foreign language; students are strongly urged to take both.
- Two courses in American history and culture, chosen from a list including "History of the United States" and "Gender, Sexuality, and Race in Early American Culture, 1600–1865."
- One semester of study abroad; an intermediate-level foreign language course plus either one advanced course or one course taught in English on the culture of that language area; or two survey courses in early, classical, medieval, European, East Asian, Latin American, or African civilization.

may provide genuine insight into important aspects of American culture, but surely they do not impart a thorough grasp of American history as it is traditionally understood. One economics major says, "My courseload is quite rigorous by choice, but you could create an easy schedule for yourself with a little research."

Students wishing to enroll in a truly broad liberal arts curriculum would do well to take Humanities 140 and 141, a two-course sequence titled "Great Books of the Western Tradition." Another good choice is Humanities 150 and 151, listed as "Humanities," a two-course program with this description: "Analysis and discussion of a selected number of the great works of literature, philosophy, and the arts, representative of the main periods and intellectual movements in Western civilization. The works are studied primarily in relation to the permanent humanistic values of our culture."

One of Vanderbilt's best departments is philosophy, which emphasizes American thought, continental philosophy, and the history of the discipline. Philosophy majors at Vanderbilt are required to take a course in logic, one in ethics, and one course in two of the following three areas: ancient philosophy, medieval philosophy, and modern philosophy. The department is seen as very balanced, with few politicized courses. John Lachs, a distinguished scholar of American philosophy, teaches an interdisciplinary course in liberty together with a historian and an economist, covering the history of the idea of liberty, the significance of choice in economic life, and the consequences of denying choice, as in the late Soviet Union.

In contrast, students view the political science department as having a few good scholars but still suffering from the lingering effects of a war between proponents of a heavily statistical approach and those who favor qualitative and theoretical methods. In 2003, the department was placed in "receivership status" until a new chair and three faculty could be appointed. The situation is under control again, though there are some vacancies, and it may be some time before Vanderbilt becomes a happy environment for prospective political science majors.

Vanderbilt's women's studies department, which began offering majors in January 2002, offers—to understate things—nontraditional courses. The course description for "Pornography and Prostitution in History" promises to teach students about "commercialization of the sex trade, Renaissance to the present." Topics include "political scandal, capitalism, globalization, [and the] effects of technological change, from the printing press to the Internet." Readings come from "anthropology, psychology, and feminist theory." Women's Studies 270, "Lesbian Studies: Identity, Desire, and Representation," probably would not have been in the course catalog a decade ago. The department offers course credit for internships at organizations "focused on women, feminism, or gender," such as the National Abortion and Reproductive Rights Action League and the National Women's Health Network. We hope some enterprising women apply for credited internships at groups such as Feminists for Life, to test the department's evenhandedness.

The Margaret Cuninggim Women's Center, a university-funded organization with its own campus building, holds meetings for the Vanderbilt Feminists and presents lectures and conferences such as "Gender and Sexuality," sponsored by the Warren Center for the Humanities. This particular discussion featured two lectures: "Homoerotic Flows: Sexuality Studies in Transnational Perspective" and "The Incredible Shrinking Public: The Sexual Politics of Neoliberalism." Other events have been more mainstream.

Vanderbilt's religious studies department offers a wide array of traditional-sounding courses such as "Themes in the New Testament," "Pauline Interpretation of Christianity," and "Introduction to Southern Religion and Culture," alongside a few that would make some of Vanderbilt's founders wince.

Vanderbilt's best professors include John Lachs in philosophy; Michael Bess and Joel F. Harrington in history; Camilla P. Benbow in psychology; Roy Gottfried, Mark Jarman, and John Plummer in English; Robert W. Pitz and Greg Walker in mechanical engineering; Lori T. Troxel in civil and environmental engineering; Douglas Hardin in mathematics; Stephen Buckles and John Vrooman in economics; David Weintraub in physics and astronomy; Robert Innes in human and organizational development; and Michael Rose in musicology.

Vanderbilt, fortunately, still places a good deal of emphasis on the academic relationship between professors and students. Students are almost guaranteed to know at least one of their professors, as they are required to take one seminar during their first year at Vanderbilt. These freshman seminars are limited to about 15 students, and most are taught by senior faculty members, giving students an experience that is rare at schools of Vanderbilt's size. One student says, "I think freshman seminars are some of the best classes Vandy has to offer, and I really enjoyed mine."

REQUIREMENTS (CONT'D)

- Three courses in the humanities from at least two disciplines chosen from a list including Classics 115, "The Good Life," and Theater 15W, "Treasure or Trash."
- Two laboratory or three lecture courses in basic astronomy, biology, chemistry, geology, or physics.
- One course in science and society, chosen from a list including "Goethe and the Natural World" and "The Racial Imagination," both in the German department.
- Two social science courses chosen from a list including introductions to anthropology, economics, political science, psychology, and sociology, as well as society and medicine.

SOUTH

537

Vanderbilt has also been able to keep classes small. The student-faculty ratio at Vanderbilt is nine to one, with an average undergraduate class size of 19 students. Professors, not graduate teaching assistants, teach 95 percent of undergraduate courses. Graduate students usually lead the weekly discussion sections attached to large lecture courses and grade most tests and papers. "In my experience, the professors are quite approachable," one student says. "I've eaten dinner at the homes of some professors. They give advice if you ask for it, and nine times out of 10, the professors are quite understanding and helpful to students."

The formal advising program is weak. Each entering freshman is assigned a faculty advisor, who is supposed to help him choose courses and, eventually, a major. Once the student has declared a major, he is assigned to a faculty member within that field. Unfortunately, many students still do not meet with their advisors as often as they should, though they are now required to do so before they can register.

As for the courses themselves, a junior says, "the courseload here is not so rigorous that students can't find time for extracurriculars and socializing, but succeeding here does take work. The administration pressures departments to avoid the grade inflation that occurs at other schools." That pressure has yielded varied success. One engineering student says that "liberal arts majors don't have anywhere near the workload carried by engineers or premed students," which fact is, of course, a common perception, one that may not take the differing nature of the disciplines into account.

Distinctively among major universities, Vanderbilt claims to have retained the conviction that higher education is first of all character formation, the education of the whole person. The school has announced a new initiative to make ethics and character development the integrating theme of the curriculum. (Indeed, in the Mandarin translation the school has chosen for advertising in China, Vanderbilt calls itself "the academic center of virtue," according to the *Chronicle of Higher Education*.) In the wrong hands, this could, of course, degenerate into another attempt at universal ideological indoctrination, but given the strength of intelligent traditionalism on campus, there is good hope that at Vanderbilt it will take a more benign form. As for how it is implemented, time will tell.

Student Life: A night at the Opry

Realizing that a large part of college education occurs outside the classroom, Vanderbilt encourages students to live on campus and guarantees students housing for four years—in fact, the school requires all students to live on campus until their senior year. Students live in any of 30 residence halls, which include singles, doubles, efficiency apartments, one- or two-bedroom apartments, suites for six, and lodges that hold 10 students. A tour guide claims that in recent years there hasn't been enough interest among students in single-sex dorms for the university to create any, but many of the dormitories have single-sex floors. There are no coed dorm rooms or bathrooms at the school.

Vanderbilt offers a series of special-interest houses incorporated into the traditional residence hall system. For example, one house is devoted to residents interested in philosophy, while another might be for students who wish to speak a particular foreign language. In addition, groups of 10 or more students who want to establish their own special-interest house are generally allowed to do so; the most frequent focus of such self-made groups is some sort of community service project.

Dorm life at Vanderbilt is comfortable, as most students enjoy such amenities as music practice rooms, laundry facilities, study rooms, common social areas, and convenience stores called Varsity Markets, which stay open until 1 or 2 a.m. Freshmen live apart from upperclassmen. Vanderbilt has ambitious plans to transform student life through the creation of residential colleges that integrate the living and learning environments. Students entering now may not have the benefit of these, but they may feel the unsettling effect of impending change. On the other hand, they may soon have an opportunity to participate in off-campus service learning opportunities as an "alternative spring break."

> ### SUGGESTED CORE
>
> *For a somewhat abbreviated core, the following Humanities series is recommended:*
> Humanities 140/141: Great Books of the Western Tradition
> Humanities 150/151: Greek, Medieval, and Renaissance Periods / and Modern Period, Seventeenth Century to Present

The campus itself is composed of many different styles of architecture, some of which are quite stately in themselves but do not blend well into a whole. Except for one large lush green lawn, the main campus is quite compact, and one student claims that for arts and sciences students the longest walk from a dorm to a classroom is about five minutes. And that walk will be under trees: the campus was granted arboretum status in 1988.

Many students say that campus life revolves around the Greek system, which about 40 percent of undergraduates join. A recent article in *Seventeen* portrays Vanderbilt as having a student body composed of rich kids obsessed with materialism. In the article, one student says, "At Vanderbilt University, it's easy to feel like you just landed at a country club." The editor, a Vanderbilt alumna, writes, "When I think of Vanderbilt, the sorority aspect of things really sums it up."

Lately, as the university has tried to bring in a more diverse student body, some on the left wing of the faculty have attacked the Greek system as a bastion of elitism. One senior says that the typical Vanderbilt student is "wealthy, conservative, attractive, well-dressed, drives a BMW, and is Greek." There is a certain amount of truth in this characterization. Vandy men wear jackets and ties to football games, and most students are reasonably well turned out for classes. The same student complains that "Vanderbilt is a very hierarchically based institution, and people who are not comfortable displaying their wealth and size-two figures should go someplace else."

On the other hand, the Bishop Joseph Johnson Black Cultural Center, named in 1984 for the first black student admitted to Vanderbilt (in 1953), pledges to serve as the "'home away from home' for African-descended students." The center sponsors programs for black students, including a "Knowledge at Noon" social hour, a lecture series featuring black scholars, a tutoring/mentoring project, Black History Month events, and several black student organizations. The Black Graduates' Recognition Ceremony, held the day before the university commencement, "is designed to honor all black graduating students with specially woven Kente stoles from Ghana." Similar attempts are made to help Asian and other atypical students to feel at home. Perhaps more might be done to accommodate "majority" students from less affluent backgrounds.

Nashville is an entertainment paradise, at least for country music fans. With the Grand Ole Opry and music performances every evening, as well as a number of other attractions, one would think that many Vanderbilt students would find it hard to stay on campus. But one student says that with their many academic and extracurricular responsibilities, including school-sponsored events like comedy shows and music night at the Pub (an on-campus bar and restaurant), most students venture into the city only about twice a month, and some students not at all. Once outside of Nashville, students must drive a ways to really get anywhere. Memphis is three hours to the west and the Great Smoky Mountains are four hours to the east.

As a member of the Southeastern Conference, the Commodores compete—if that's the word—against such football powerhouses as Florida, Auburn, and Georgia. The *Chronicle of Higher Education* cited Vanderbilt for its "student-fan apathy. . . . Attendance at Vanderbilt Stadium is so anemic that after a 2003 Vandy victory over Kentucky, it took fans a pathetic 10 minutes to tear down the goalposts." And Kentucky went 4-8 that year.

The school maintains membership in the conference even while retaining strict educational requirements for its players. The basketball team is more competitive. Intercollegiate club sports and intramural sports are also popular with students. In 2003, Vanderbilt's chancellor announced his plans to "help integrate the university's sports program more fully into campus life," according to a *Chronicle of Higher Education* article, by eliminating the athletics department and creating a new Office of Student Athletics, Recreation, and Wellness. Soon after the announcement, the athletic director resigned.

Crime is not the major problem at Vanderbilt that it is at most urban schools, but safety is certainly a concern. The most recent statistics, from 2003, reflect an increase in several areas of criminal activity on campus. The school reported 26 forcible sex offenses, 16 automobile thefts, 10 robberies, three arsons, 18 aggravated assaults, and 89 burglaries. The campus is not completely sealed off from the city, and it is believed that most of these offenses were committed by townies. Campus police offer several programs to curb campus crime. A walking escort service offers security for students crossing campus at night, and a nighttime van service stops at the library, dormitories, and other major buildings. Dormitories can be accessed only with student ID cards.

Vanderbilt is expensive, with 2004–5 tuition at $29,240, and room and board charges of $9,736. However, admissions are need-blind, and the school guarantees to meet the full financial need of all who enroll—offering need-based grants to 35 percent of students. The average student loan debt of recent grads is $20,364.

UNIVERSITY OF VIRGINIA

CHARLOTTESVILLE, VIRGINIA • WWW.VIRGINIA.EDU

So long as reason is left free

Thomas Jefferson memorialized his three most prized accomplishments in his self-composed epitaph, which reads: "Here was buried Thomas Jefferson: Author of the Declaration of American Independence, Of the Statute of Virginia for religious toleration & Father of the University of Virginia." Jefferson founded U.Va. in 1816 and designed the grounds himself, including the library building, which Jefferson called the Rotunda, a red-brick, white-columned building whose crowning dome was inspired by Rome's Pantheon.

 Kiplinger's magazine recently ranked Charlottesville as the "Best College Town" in the country, while *U.S. News and World Report* ranks U.Va. second among public universities. In fact, the school consistently rates among the top universities in the nation no matter who is doing the rankings. Thanks in part to a $1.6 billion endowment, U.Va.'s architecture and campus grounds are some of the most beautiful in the country. Moreover, many top-notch professors here concern themselves with the "enduring questions," while their bright students can be counted on to take academics (or at least their grades) very seriously. Although its required curriculum is underwhelming, the University of Virginia has so many pockets of excellence that it is well worth considering.

Academic Life: Whereas God hath created the mind free

The intellectual quest for truth that Thomas Jefferson envisioned would characterize the school he created is best represented today at his university by the Echols Scholars program. Students in this honors program comprise 8.5 percent of incoming freshmen in the College of Arts and Sciences; those applicants who demonstrate academic excellence, intellectual leadership, and evidence of the ability to grapple with complex topics are invited to join the program. Echols Scholars live together, register early for classes,

VITAL STATISTICS
Religious affiliation: none
Total enrollment: 23,341
Total undergraduates: 14,129
SAT/ACT midranges: SAT V: 600–710, M: 630–720; ACT: 26–31
Applicants: 14,627
Applicants accepted: 39%
Accepted applicants who enrolled: 54%
Tuition: $5,131 (in state), $21,172 (out of state)
Room and board: $5,960
Freshman retention rate: 96%
Graduation rate: 83% (4 yrs.), 92% (6 yrs.)
Courses with fewer than 20 students: 49%
Student-faculty ratio: 15:1
Courses taught by graduate TAs: 15%
Most popular majors: social sciences, engineering, business
Students living on campus: 46%
Guaranteed housing for four years? no
Students in fraternities: 30% sororities: 30%

and are exempt from distribution requirements. Echols Scholars are usually high-achieving, career-oriented students, and their natural affinity for learning coupled with regular advising usually prevents them from misusing this complete curricular freedom. (Speaking of abuses, in 2005 a dean of the Echols program was removed from the program and ordered to cease his "inappropriate contacts" with female students—which apparently included invitations to drinks, leg-patting, and unwanted hugs, according to the *Chronicle of Higher Education.*)

Another choice for ambitious students is the Bachelor of Arts with Honors program. U.Va., unlike other universities, does not award honors to graduating students based upon grade point average. Rather, students must apply to pursue a course of independent study for their third and fourth years of college, during which time they study under departmental tutors. Candidates are evaluated by visiting examiners from other colleges and universities and may receive degrees with "honors," "high honors," or "highest honors" as the only grades for two years of work, or else they may be recommended for an ordinary BA—or no degree. Students who wish to be considered for a degree with distinction must apply to the distinguished major program of their departments. A senior thesis and some graduate courses are usually required, and most departments do not accept everyone who applies.

As for the rest of U.Va.'s students, there is no core curriculum, and the university's distribution requirements are so vague a student would have to work hard *not* to fulfill them by graduation. Even the 12 credits (three or four classes) of natural sciences and mathematics are difficult not to fulfill, given that the departments under that rubric range from astronomy to economics to environmental sciences. "I see our 'core curriculum' as little different from those elsewhere," a professor says, "Students can construct a program that is as easy or hard as they wish."

More curricular structure is provided by the major requirements in each specialty. The top-ranked English department, for example, requires its students to take two pre-1800 courses, a senior-level majors' seminar, and a three-course sequence on the history of literature in English. An English professor says, "We're full of postcolonial theory, currently very fashionable, but we're also very strong in traditional areas such as Shakespeare and medieval literature." Another professor notes that "while the department is quite strong, it offers comparatively very little in the way of theory compared to Michigan or Duke." We don't think that's anything to feel badly about.

The religious studies department has recently added more structure to its major requirements. Students must take three courses in a single religious tradition, two courses in another religious tradition, one course in a third tradition, and a senior-level majors' seminar. With 29 full-time members and six joint members, the department is the largest of its kind among public universities in the United States. It offers an undergraduate major in religious studies, an undergraduate minor, and a full program of graduate studies. The department's undergraduate program has been highly rated for years, and it deserves its reputation.

In addition to the English and religious studies departments, other highly regarded disciplines at U.Va. include history, economics, and political and social thought

(PST). The School of Commerce is also solid. Professors that come highly recommended by students include John M. Owen and Larry J. Sabato in politics; James Davison Hunter and W. Bradford Wilcox in sociology; Kenneth G. Elzinga in economics; James F. Childress, Charles Marsh, Charles T. Mathewes, Vanessa Ochs, Donald Polaski, Augustine Thompson, Heather Anne Warren, Robert Louis Wilken, and William M. Wilson in religious studies; Gordon Braden and Paul Cantor in English; Edward L. Ayers, Michael F. Holt, and Jon Lendon in history; James Ceaser in government and foreign affairs; David Herman in Slavic languages and literatures; and Louis Nelson in the School of Architecture. On the other hand, the mathematics department "has proven to be so poor," according to one student, "that students will take calculus from the engineering school."

The U.Va. advising program is rather meager, which is all the more unfortunate given the great freedom students have. "Many advisors are not aware of the curriculum or what to advise," says a student. Each student is appointed an academic advisor before he arrives on campus, whom he can replace after he chooses a major. All advisors are teaching faculty. Students were once required to see their advisors twice per year to get the codes necessary to register for courses, but now, unfortunately, they can receive their codes by e-mail. Officially, students must still see their advisors first in order to have the code sent, but "last semester, I saw an e-mail from my advisor. I opened it assuming he had suggested a time to meet, and he'd actually just sent me my code," says a student.

Given the paltry distribution requirements and its lack of commitment to student advising, it is a good thing U.Va. offers so many good courses. There are, to be sure, a number of trendy or unserious options, but as of yet they have not displaced more traditional classes. Each semester nearly every department offers at least a few worthy courses—often quite a few.

U.Va. students do tend to be serious. Going to office hours and attending review sessions are de rigueur, although often these efforts are put forth in the pursuit of grades rather than out of intellectual curiosity. Students at Virginia worry that a 15-hour courseload makes them look like underachievers and they haggle with professors over B-

ACADEMIC REQUIREMENTS

U.Va. imposes only some loose requirements of study. Students must take:

- A six-credit first-year writing course (some students are exempt).
- A three-credit writing-intensive course in any subject.
- Four semesters of a foreign language. Students who already know another language may test out.
- Six credits of social science. Many courses count, ranging from "The Politics of Western Europe" to "Witchcraft."
- Six credits of humanities. Choices range from "Chaucer" to "Queer Theories and Queer Practices."
- Three credits of history. Choices run from "The Roman Republic" to "The History of U.Va. in the Twentieth Century."
- Three credits with a "non-Western perspective." Options here include the normal suspects, plus the more unusual "Augustine of Hippo" and the "History of Urban America."
- Twelve credits of natural science and mathematics. Choices here range from "Life beyond the Earth" to "Statistics."

Note that one class may fulfill several requirements simultaneously.

SOUTH

pluses. Grade inflation is, consequently, a problem. Rarely does a student receive a C or lower, especially in the liberal arts. One professor says, "The weakness of U.Va. is the student sense of entitlement: 'I deserve an A for showing up—just like in high school.'"

Students are highly career-oriented as well, a characteristic that several of them find irritating. "Everyone's pretty keyed up here about grades. It's a pretty intensely 'success-centered' environment," says one. Another says, "There is a high percentage of 'go-getters' who are often arrogant." One professor says that U.Va. students are "more careerist" than those he taught at two other esteemed public universities, and another faculty member considers the "careerist orientation of many of [U.Va.'s] students" the university's primary weakness. He says, "Most students do not seem to be interested in the material for its own sake. They seem to view U.Va. as a fun and interesting spring-board to better and bigger things." However, another professor reports that many of his students "have a strong liberal arts ethos and so choose courses purely out of intel-lectual excitement."

Introductory courses are large. One instructor of a popular survey course in physics reserves four classrooms—he teaches in one and pipes his image over video to the other three. Large courses are taught by professors, but the smaller discussion sections are usually taught by graduate teaching assistants. Once students reach the sophomore and junior level, class sizes shrink dramatically, typically to 20 or 30 students. Even in large courses, professors are friendly and accessible, particularly to students who ex-hibit an eagerness to learn. University Seminars (USEMs) are offered to first-year stu-dents as a way to connect students with faculty. These once-weekly courses are kept to about 20 students and are taught by esteemed professors. Unfortunately, they can be highly specialized and politically biased, since they are often used to introduce stu-dents to the professor's current research. Nevertheless, it is still to a student's advan-tage to scan the listings for a solid course.

"U.Va. is a liberal institution but it is located in a conservative state," one profes-sor says. "It also has a tradition of civility. The broader political climate and the tradi-tion of civility mean that the institution is fairly tolerant toward conservatives on the faculty and in the student body. I think U.Va. is one of the better universities for con-servatives." Most professors, unsurprisingly, tend to be liberal, and one student reports that political biases "certainly do" affect course content. Students recommend a close reading of course syllabi and using the two-week trial period each semester to drop a class if necessary.

A recent push for more "diversity" has affected U.Va.'s curriculum. One professor considers the university's "liberal curricular drift" to be a significant concern. Students are already required to take one non-Western perspectives course that "deal[s] substan-tively with a culture other than the Western cultural heritage, including minority sub-cultures in the West." The departments of anthropology and studies in women and gender are reported to be highly politicized.

"In all of my experience, professors at the university have been incredibly acces-sible to their students," one student says. "If anything, it is the students' own lack of initiative that might hinder the interaction." Another student says, "Professors won't find you, but because so few students actually come to see them for anything not related to grades, they tend to be very appreciative when one does." At least one professor invites his students to Thanksgiving dinner. Others give students opportunities to help with research.

Student Life: The impious presumption

U.Va. is nestled amid the eastern foothills of Virginia's Blue Ridge Mountains in the city of Charlottesville (population 40,000). The University of Virginia's prime location—within minutes of the mountains, three hours from the beach, and two hours from Washington, D.C.—means that students (especially those with cars) haven't any excuse to be bored. Despite its small size, Charlottesville offers a surprising number of cultural events. The Virginia Film Festival and the Virginia Festival of the Book are both held there, and big-name performers often make a tour stop at the Performing Arts Center. The Downtown Mall is a brick pedestrian walkway lined with shops, restaurants, bookstores, and coffee houses. Closer to the university is The Corner, a similar shopping and eating district. The university sponsors an event just about every night of the school year, and students and townspeople alike attend the lectures and concerts. There are also, of course, numerous Civil War and other historical sites (including Jefferson's wonderful home, Monticello) nearby.

U.Va. offers hundreds of student organizations. From Disciples of Bob Barker to the Sullen Art Society of Creative Writers, from the Cigar Society at U.Va. to its Swing [Dancing] Club, the career-driven Cavaliers show a playful side. Popular organizations include Madison House, a center for various service projects; UGuides, students who give tours of U.Va.; singing groups; the First-Year Players, a theater troupe; student government; Honor Council; and various Christian groups, especially the Reformed University Fellowship. A group opposed to political correctness, the Individual Rights Coalition, is also active. The school boasts a number of "secret societies," most of which are philanthropic organizations. (If any are misanthropic, they aren't telling.) The school's official newspaper is the *Cavalier Daily* and is known by students as the *C.D.* The student-run publications are organized within the Consortium of University Publications (COUP). This group is financially and editorially independent of the school and includes members such as *Critical Mass* (a self-described leftist magazine) and *Virginia Advocate* (a monthly conservative journal). "Despite the relatively large size of the school, the many student organizations provide a great means for finding a smaller community within the larger university," says a student.

The Queer Student Union is one of several highly active gay groups on campus.

SUGGESTED CORE
1. Religion 121/122, Old Testament: Hebrew Scriptures / Early Christianity and the New Testament
2. Religion 205, History of Christianity I
3. Religious Studies 369, John and the Book of Revelation
4. Religious Studies 236, Elements of Christian Thought
5. Political Science 302, Modern Political Theory
6. English 250, Studies in Shakespeare
7. History 201, American History to 1865
8. History 380, Origins of Contemporary Thought

SOUTH

545

The law school boasts a Lambda Law Alliance; gay fiscal conservatives gather as Log Cabin Republicans; and queer alumni run a group called the Serpentine Society. The school's first gay fraternity has also recently opened (Delta Lambda Phi). The Minority Rights Coalition is a consortium of various minority groups that police the campus activities and engage in activism.

The Honor Council is a student-run manifestation of the Honor Code, established in 1840. If a student is convicted of lying, cheating, or stealing, the only possible penalty is expulsion from the university. Some students have even had their degrees revoked after graduation, as was the case in a notorious scandal in 2002, where 158 charges came to the council from a single professor after software he designed caught numerous acts of plagiarism and paper-sharing. Most students take the code seriously, and exams are often unproctored. The Honor Code has come under some fire recently for adhering too much to the letter rather than the spirit of the law: rape, for example, does not fall under the single-sanction guidelines, so that a convicted plagiarist is expelled automatically, while a convicted rapist is not.

First-years (Jefferson himself eschewed terminology like "freshman" or "senior" because he believed that no one was ever done learning) are required to live on campus in dorms. The dorms are generally grouped into "old" and "new," the former being closer to central campus (in U.Va.-speak, the campus is the "grounds"), but the latter offering more amenities. Housing in the first-year dorms is segregated by gender only by floor or by suite. Upperclassmen residential assistants (RAs) run freshman orientation, which is mostly a recounting of university regulations but does include a sensitivity training program. Students may also apply to live in one of three residential colleges: Hereford, Brown, or International Residential College (IRC). Hereford is the largest and houses about 500 students, most of which live in single rooms. These students take charge of the budget and have opportunities to bring in speakers or sponsor events. The 200 residents of Brown College—who have a reputation for quirkiness—live closest to the central grounds, but have to share their rooms. While it is possible to see a Marxist rooming with a free-market business school student here, one might also be treated to a great books seminar put on by a resident faculty member. The newest residential college, IRC, is organized along the lines of a parliamentary government with elected officials. All the colleges are modeled on the residential experience at the Ivies or in England. They offer community meals and have faculty members living among the students.

Upperclassmen can move off campus, but many choose to enter a residential college or one of the language houses. Some fourth-years apply to live on the Lawn in classic and ornate single rooms in the original part of campus, where students and professors used to live and study side-by-side. This historic part of the university was declared a World Heritage site by UNESCO in 1987.

At U.Va. there has been a great emphasis on "diversity," essentially focused on race relations. A new Diversity Center has been opened in the Student Union and a new director of diversity is being added to the staff. While the administration seems concerned about race relations on campus, the students do not. While many admit that self-segregation is a problem, they recently voted down a plan that would have altered the housing system. The lower, older part of campus is 90 percent white and is the location for most of the Greek activity. The upper campus is much more diverse, and since foreign students tend to gravitate to that location, it is a self-perpetuating quality. According to U.Va.'s Voices of Diversity Web page, "the university's deans are now being evaluated, in part, on their ability to increase diversity," and one professor reports that the administration requires faculty to go through "sensitivity training." U.Va.'s newest application for admission requires applicants to answer one of five questions, two of which are: "What kind of diversity will you bring to U.Va.?" and "Discrimination exists. Reflect briefly on a moment when discrimination affected you or someone around you."

More controversially, the university has proposed requiring a diversity training course for first-year students. Students who organized against this initiative found their meeting disrupted by U.Va.'s student council president, who walked into the meeting and wrote "www.davidduke.com" on the chalkboard below the organization's Web address. Classy.

Sports are considered a big part of the college experience and U.Va. students rally behind their Cavaliers, especially in men's basketball, football (students dress up for games), and men's soccer. The university recently enlarged the football stadium and has begun building a $128 million basketball arena, a project that has elicited disapproval from some teaching faculty who would prefer that the university divert fundraising efforts from the project to academics. "Our academic buildings are falling down around our ears," says one professor.

Even with so much else to do, a primary occupation of U.Va. students is drinking. Students call themselves Wahoos, after the fish that supposedly can drink twice its weight. Only one-third of the student body goes Greek, but parties on Rubgy Road are the center of attention on weekend (and some weekday) nights. In some cases the Wahoos' devotion to drinking can go too far. A dangerous "tradition" (it started in the mid-'90s) that the school takes very seriously is the "fourth-year fifth," in which fourth-year students (mostly Greek men) drink a fifth of alcohol—each—before the final football game. Each year the university president issues a strongly worded letter, Alcohol Awareness Week is scheduled around the game, and students are asked to sign a pledge stating they won't engage in the dangerous stunt. The 2004 letter from the president reminded students of the 1997 death of Leslie Ann Baltz, a student who fell down a flight of stairs after drinking a fifth. The president also mentioned that 11 ounces of liquor is considered lethal for a 120-pound person (15.5 ounces would do in a 150-pound male, and a fifth equals 26.5 ounces).

Students who don't drink report that there are plenty of other activities to keep them entertained—movies at the student center and Frisbee golf, for example—but finding interesting nonacademic alternatives to Rugby Road does take some imagination.

Charlottesville, a relatively small town, is generally safe. However, the community has been shaken by a series of sexual assaults since 1997. The university does offer a free student escort service—recently revamped to discourage drunken students who regularly used the system as a free designated driver. There are 170 blue-light emergency telephones spaced throughout the grounds, and cellular telephones programmed with 911 are available for student loan at the libraries. In 2003, the school reported 23 forcible sexual assaults, two robberies, four aggravated assaults, eight burglaries, and five stolen cars on campus.

In-state tuition in 2004–5 was only $5,131; for out-of-state students it was $21,172, with room and board another $5,960. Financial aid is generous. Admissions are need-blind, and the school commits to covering the needs of any student who enrolls. About 45 percent of undergrads get some form of aid. The average in-state student leaves the school with $12,000 in debt while the average out-of-state student leaves with $16,000. However, the school has decided to emulate those Ivies that make attendance free for working-class students, promising "that no one will leave U.Va. owing more than a quarter of the four-year cost of attendance for in-state students."

WAKE FOREST UNIVERSITY

WINSTON-SALEM, NORTH CAROLINA • WWW.WFU.EDU

Sleepers, wake!

The Student Center at Wake Forest University features a large painting of Christ cleansing the temple. Traditional Christians might wonder how the university will fare at the second coming. Founded by Southern Baptists in 1834, Wake Forest was fairly recently an explicitly Christian institution. Lately, however, the school has gone chasing after a national reputation—and like many other religious universities, it has found it useful to repudiate the religious convictions of its founders. As one student says, "Wake Forest's current connections to its Southern Baptist heritage are little more than lip service."

Wake Forest seems to regard its religious past as an embarrassment. Down the road at Duke University, a school founded by Methodists, national rankings rose as it gradually junked its denominational heritage. So Wake Forest has followed suit. While the North Carolina Baptist Convention deems homosexual behavior sinful, Wake Forest pays employee benefits to same-sex partners of faculty and staff, and Wait Chapel now allows same-sex commitment ceremonies to be performed there. Baptists deplore drinking, but Wake Forest sells alcohol on campus and its students abuse booze with notorious enthusiasm. The student newspaper, by no means a conservative organ, complained in 2003 that the university offends Christian students by secularizing such public observances of religious origin as the lighting of the "Advent tree."

The residue of its past still clings to the Wake Forest curriculum and culture, however. And that is a good thing. Despite the recent addition of a cultural diversity requirement, Wake's general education curriculum is still better than most. The university maintains a number of outstanding academic departments, and it draws a good number of intelligent and morally serious, if not terribly intellectual, students. Perhaps divine grace, in its gratuitousness, has kept Wake Forest from falling as fast and as far as it might have deserved.

Many had hoped that the new president, Nathan O. Hatch, a graduate of Wheaton College who had spent his professional life at Notre Dame and serves on the National Advisory Board of the Salvation Army, would reassert the school's religious identity. However, Hatch wrote recently in the *Chronicle of Higher Education* in praise of the secularization of Catholic universities that took place in the 1960s. If that is an indication of the direction in which he intends to lead Wake Forest, it won't be a Southern Baptist school again anytime soon.

Academic Life: Waking the dead

Wake Forest's catalog informs students that they "have considerable flexibility in planning their courses of study." But they must use this flexibility to navigate a fairly serious set of distribution requirements in the following five divisions: history, religion, and philosophy (three courses); literature (two courses); fine arts (one course); social and behavioral sciences (three courses); and natural sciences, mathematics, and computer science (three courses). Typically, the courses that can be used to satisfy these requirements are introductory. One professor laments that "students take the most popular courses and often repeat what they took in high school." The university makes further stipulations. Students must take at least one introductory class in each of the following seven categories: the history, religion, *and* philosophy departments, the natural *and* pure sciences, and the social *and* behavioral sciences. Thus, the curriculum does a decent job of guaranteeing that students will graduate with a good deal of educational breadth and at least a few foundational courses under their belts.

However, the rigor of some of these courses is open to question. One student says that there are many fluff classes available, especially in the communications, sociology, and political science departments. "A liberal arts student can truly graduate knowing very little beyond a limited scope," he says. "For example, the basic American and Brit-

VITAL STATISTICS

Religious affiliation: Baptist
Total enrollment: 5,483
Total undergraduates: 4,104
SAT midranges: V: 610–700, M: 630–710
Applicants: 6,289
Applicants accepted: 47%
Accepted applicants who enrolled: 38%
Tuition: $30,210
Room and board: $8,500
Freshman retention rate: 96%
Graduation rate: 75% (4 yrs.), 86% (6 yrs.)
Average class size: 19
Student-faculty ratio: 10:1
Courses taught by graduate TAs: none
Most popular majors: social sciences, business, communications
Students living on campus: 78%
Guaranteed housing for four years? no
Students in fraternities: 33% sororities: 53%

SOUTH

549

Wake Forest's require-
ments fall short of a
traditional core curricu-
lum, but they come
closer than most other
schools' requirements.
Students must take:

- A first-year seminar.
  According to the school's
  Web site, these small
  classes "are designed to
  help students begin to
  develop analytical, critical
  thinking, and verbal
  expression skills early in
  their college careers."
- English 111: "The Writing
  Seminar." (Students may
  be exempted under certain
  circumstances.)
- One foreign language
  course beyond the
  intermediate level,
  depending on high school
  preparation.
- Health and Exercise
  Science 100 and 101.
- "Basic Problems of
  Philosophy."
- "Introduction to Reli-
  gion," "Introduction to
  the Bible," or "Introduction to the Christian
  Tradition."
- "Western Civilization to
  1700" or the more diffuse
  "World Civilizations to
  1500."
- "Europe and the World in
  the Modern Era" or
  "World Civilizations since
  1500."
- Literature—one course
  each from two of these
  three groups: "Introduc-

ish literature courses are becoming less substantive in my
opinion. A quick glance at their reading lists would reveal
that these classes are not filled with the great authors but
rather works of radical chic with perhaps a play of
Shakespeare or some Hawthorne thrown in." Indeed, when
the curriculum committee revised the distribution requirements a few years ago, faculty members tried to get the
philosophy department to put more "variety" in its curricular offerings for underclassmen. Luckily, this initiative failed,
and introductory philosophy students still get exposure to
the classic texts of the great philosophers. One student says
that he thinks introductory philosophy is "the crown jewel
of the undergraduate curriculum, one that almost all students find challenging yet rewarding."

While the school offers a broad spectrum of majors,
most of the trendy interdisciplinary areas like women's studies, ethnic studies, and urban studies are only offered as
minors and therefore do not have the power or popularity
that they do at other universities. The business school program is reputedly very challenging, as are the hard sciences
(chemistry, biology, and physics). One student says that "the
liberal arts are increasingly becoming subject to political
correctness and are drifting from traditional texts and subjects."

Outside of the business school and the hard sciences,
Wake's better departments include economics, mathematics, and the foreign language programs, including German,
Russian, Spanish, and French. "Philosophy remains a bastion of good, solid academic tradition," a professor says.
"They're unwilling to go along with faddish multiculturalism." A classical languages major says that his department is "one of the few liberal arts departments at Wake
Forest that still avoids being politicized." Wake offers a
unique minor in early Christian studies, in which students
take courses on the New Testament, the age of Augustus,
and the Greco-Roman world and select relevant courses in
the art, history, religion, and philosophy departments.

Wake Forest's course catalog is fairly tame politically.
But the political science department tends to promote the
politics of the left. Students report that three years ago a
political science professor showed a video by the People for
the American Way in his class, claiming that it offered a
fair depiction of American conservatism. And there are in-

formal connections between the department and the International Socialists club (not an official university organization). The religion department includes courses like "Feminist and Contemporary Interpretations of the New Testament" and is said to take a dim view of traditional Christianity, Baptist or otherwise. "That department is highly politicized and heavily influenced by liberal theologies," a student says. "For instance, a student I know who wishes to become an Episcopal priest has majored in Greek and avoids most religion classes because of their content." A student reports that in his sociology class on deviant behavior, the correct answer on an examination identified religious objections to homosexuality as bigotry. Another student says that his art professor compared early Christians to the Taliban.

Many of the courses that satisfy the cultural diversity requirement are predictably politicized, such as "Feminist Political Thought" and "Postcolonial Literature," which one student says is taught by a "young English instructor who also uses the campus to host meetings of the local International Socialists group." The student says, "To borrow from the joke of the old Soviet workers, 'They pretend to teach us, and we pretend to learn.'" Students minoring in the humanities must take "Innovation and Inclusivity," a course that examines "(1) paradigms such as psychoanalysis, Marxism, feminism, and liberation theology, (2) debates about political correctness and multiculturalism, and (3) strategies used by minority and non-Western voices," according to the course description.

Wake Forest does put a good deal of emphasis on international studies (though they are only offered as minors), including Asian studies, East Asian studies, German studies, international studies, Latin American studies, Russian, and East European studies. Certificates are offered in Italian studies and Spanish studies. The school owns residential study centers in London, Venice, and Vienna and runs its own study-abroad programs in these cities as well as in Benin, Cuba, Ecuador, Mexico, France, Spain, China, Japan, Russia, and elsewhere. There is a residential language center for students who wish to speak Russian or German on a regular basis. More than 50 percent of Wake Forest students study abroad during their college years.

The school's Honors Program allows Wake's most

REQUIREMENTS (CONT'D)

tion to British Literature" or "Studies in British Literature"; "Introduction to American Literature" or "Studies in American Literature"; and world literature, chosen from 42 courses.

- One course in fine or performing arts.
- One course each from three of these groups: "Introduction to Economics"; "Introductory Psychology"; "Introduction to Communication and Rhetoric"; anthropology, political science, and sociology.
- Three science courses from two departments. The best choices for nonmajors are "Biology and the Human Condition," "Everyday Chemistry," and "Introductory Physics." The last two also meet the quantitative reasoning requirement.
- One course designated as a quantitative reasoning course. This requirement should be met by at least one course taken for the science requirement.
- One course designated as a cultural diversity course. Curiously enough, "European Drama" and "The Old South" qualify here, alongside any number of courses that study the developing world and minority groups.

SOUTH

551

academically talented upperclassmen to take small-group seminars together. Those who take at least four honors seminars can graduate with distinction. In the English department, the honors courses are mostly specialty courses in topics like Chaucer, Milton, Victorian poetry, or the literature of the South. Topics for honors seminars in other disciplines vary by semester. Students who feel too restricted by the university's course requirements can apply to the Open Curriculum program, offered for students with "high motivation and strong academic preparation," according to its Web page.

One of the initiatives put in place by former president Thomas Hearn Jr. was a campus-wide emphasis on technology. Every freshman receives an IBM ThinkPad and color printer, the cost of which is absorbed into tuition and fees. The university upgrades the computers after two years, and students can keep them after they graduate. Wake also has computer labs and printer clusters all over campus. These technological trimmings have earned the school a distinction as one of the nation's "most wired" campuses, according to *Yahoo! Internet Life* magazine. But at least one professor labels these efforts a grand marketing ploy that only serves to distract students—and their tuition-paying parents—from focusing on the quality of the liberal arts education the school offers.

The close relationships between faculty and students often touted by the Wake Forest administration appear to be genuine. The student-faculty ratio is an impressive 10 to 1. Admissions literature says that the school "maintains its high academic standards by assuring that undergraduate classes, lectures, and seminars are taught by faculty members, not teaching assistants." (Teaching assistants only teach the lab sections of science and language courses.) Wake Forest faculty members do generally value teaching over research. Students say their professors are accessible and almost always welcome students even outside their scheduled office hours. Freshmen are assigned faculty members as advisors, but these advisors primarily serve only to make sure that students are satisfying the necessary distribution requirements.

Some of the best professors at Wake include Charles M. Lewis in philosophy; Robert Utley in humanities; William Moss and Eric Wilson in English; Roberta Morosini and M. Stanley Whitley in Romance languages; J. Daniel Hammond, John C. Moorhouse, and Robert M. Whaples in economics; John V. Baxley, Richard D. Carmichael, Elmer K. Hayashi, and James J. Kuzmanovich in mathematics; Kevin Bowen, Stewart Carter, Brian Gorelick, and Dan Locklair in music; Helga Welsh in political science; James P. Barefield in history; Mark R. Leary in psychology; and James T. Powell in classical languages.

Wake Forest is one of the dwindling number of colleges that still has an honor code. Entering freshmen attend an honor assembly in which a professor delivers a sermon on being honest and forthright. Students then sign a book. By doing so they agree to the code and demonstrate that they know the consequences for violating it—possible expulsion.

One recent campus controversy is worth reporting. Late in 2004 professor of English Jim Hans deplored the availability of grants from the Kaufman Foundation for relating entrepreneurship to the liberal arts; he was answered by nine of his colleagues. There are several noteworthy points about this exchange. The discussion was carried on with a civility depressingly rare in such confrontations. And the forum for it was provided by the *Old Gold and Black*, the student newspaper. All of which makes Wake Forest a comparatively civilized place these days.

Student Life: If a beer falls in the forest . . .

In spite of the headlong secularization of Wake Forest, one of the most popular groups on campus is the Baptist Student Union, a social and spiritual group that sponsors summer missions, prayer groups, local ministries, intramural sports teams, and other social events. Musically inclined students can choose from a large number of groups, most of them Christian in nature. The InterVarsity Christian Fellowship hosts prayer and discussion groups on campus, and the Wake Forest Baptist Church holds services in Wait Chapel every Sunday morning. The Wake Forest Catholic Community has daily mass and three masses on Sunday in Davis Chapel, and there is also an Orthodox Christian Fellowship.

Wake Forest's Office of Multicultural Affairs, a university-funded department, sponsors many activities for ethnic minority students, including new minority student orientation, the Martin Luther King Jr. Celebration, Black History Month, Asian Awareness Week, Multicultural Summits, and minority tutoring and scholarships. The office also advises the Black Student Alliance, one of the more active political groups on campus. A guide for multicultural students says that 10 years ago, nearly half of Wake Forest's black student body was there on athletic scholarships. Since then, the university has tried to dramatically increase its number of minority students and faculty. So far, however, minority enrollment has only risen slightly, from 12.2 percent in 1998 to 13.2 percent in 2003, according to Wake Forest's annual *Fact Book*. A January 2003 article in the *Old Gold and Black* puts minority enrollment at about 10 percent in the late 1980s.

One of the most influential political groups on campus is the Gay-Straight Student Alliance, which passes out rainbow stickers to faculty members and encourages them (with great success) to display them on their office doors. The feminist groups on campus also sponsor many events. Aside from these groups and the presence of a few "international socialists," however, the Wake Forest student body is notable for its lack of interest in political activism. One student suspects that a poll would show most students on the center-right.

Wake Forest is situated in the old tobacco town of Winston-Salem, North Carolina, a city of around 175,000 people. The school is only a short drive from downtown but is separated from the city by a wooded area. Almost all of the campus buildings are of red brick, and a tree-lined quad with the chapel on one end and the main adminis-

SUGGESTED CORE
1. Classics 255, Classical Epic: *Iliad, Odyssey, Aeneid*
2. Philosophy 232, Ancient and Medieval Philosophy
3. Religion 102, Introduction to the Bible
4. Religion 372, History of Christian Thought
5. Political Science 115R, Modern Political Thought
6. English 224, Exploring Shakespeare
7. History 251, The United States before 1865
8. Philosophy 352, Hegel, Kierkegaard, Nietzsche (*closest match*)

SOUTH

tration building on the other marks the center of the campus. Magnolia Court, containing dozens of varieties of the trademark tree of the South, is especially beautiful in the spring. Reynolda Gardens, originally owned by tobacco giant R. J. Reynolds, comprises 125 acres of woodlands, fields, and nature trails, in addition to four acres devoted to a formal garden and a greenhouse.

Living off campus is the exception, not the rule. While all of the residential halls are within close walking distance of the campus's center, the coveted rooms are on the Quad, central to Wake's academic and social life. Most of the dormitories have men and women divided by floor; the university did away with its all-women residence hall a few years ago. Theme houses allow students to live with friends with shared interests in the languages or the arts. There are no coed dorm rooms or shower areas on campus, although some theme houses do have coed bathrooms. Substance-free (no smoking or alcohol) dormitories for freshmen and upperclassmen offer an escape from substance-laden peers.

And substance use, particularly of alcohol, *is* heavy at Wake Forest. In the last decade or so, the community has seen fraternities and their parties become much more widespread. Students say that every weekend is a party weekend. Binge drinking is a genuine problem, with students frequently sent to the emergency room for detoxification. A university-run poll of Wake Forest students revealed that almost 60 percent of upperclassmen and 40 percent of freshmen were binge drinkers (in other words, they had consumed five or more alcoholic drinks in one sitting in the past two weeks). In 2002, some fraternity members were arrested for animal cruelty and abandonment after police found a drunk, dehydrated pig missing its tail. The pig was apparently a prop at a Sigma Phi Epsilon weekend party. (In 2002, the university did see a 34 percent drop in the number of disciplinary actions due to liquor-law violations on campus, but this may simply reflect less enforcement.)

Of the campus culture at large, one student says, "The typical Wake Forest student is usually upper middle class and often from a southern state. Someone like myself—lower class and the first person in the family to go to college—is less common but by no means ostracized."

Winston-Salem, though not exactly a cultural metropolis, has its attractions. The Winston-Salem Warthogs are a minor league baseball team affiliated with the Chicago White Sox. Excellent medical facilities and high-tech companies employ many of the city's residents. The real advantage of living in Winston-Salem, though, is its proximity to other cities. Students sometimes visit nearby Greensboro for concerts and sporting events, and the Research Triangle of Durham (home of Duke University), Chapel Hill (University of North Carolina), and Raleigh (North Carolina State University) is only an hour or two to the east. For outdoor enthusiasts, Asheville and the Blue Ridge Mountains are two hours to the west.

Wake Forest offers plenty of things to do on campus in the evenings and on weekends, often attracting lecturers and cultural performances to its halls. One student says, "At least once at Wake, one should attend a performance of the Lilting Banshees, a satirical student comedy group." Wake Forest athletics are probably dearer to students than anything else. The Demon Deacons compete on 16 intercollegiate teams in the Atlantic Coast Conference. The men's basketball team is usually a contender. Students also have plenty of nonvarsity options, including 23 intercollegiate club teams. Intramural teams include basketball, bowling, inline hockey, tennis, and many others.

Students and statistics agree that Wake Forest is a fairly safe campus. One student says that "the real danger exists when going into Winston-Salem," which has some sketchy areas. The university police maintain a strong presence on campus, and a free bus service offers rides around campus at night. The university does report a good number of burglaries each year—44 in 2003, down from 50 the previous year and 97 the year before that—but the incidence of other crimes is very low. In 2003 there were only four assaults, four forcible sex offenses, one robbery, and one motor vehicle theft.

Wake Forest is fairly expensive, with a 2004–5 tuition of $30,210 and estimated room and board costs of $8,500. However, admission is need-blind, and all students who enroll are guaranteed sufficient financial aid; some 68 percent get some need-based assistance.

WASHINGTON AND LEE UNIVERSITY

LEXINGTON, VIRGINIA • WWW.WLU.EDU

A stately state

Washington and Lee University was founded in 1749 as Augusta Academy. The school's name was changed after George Washington saved the school from going under in 1796. The name of General Robert E. Lee—who taught there after the war—was added after his death in 1870. Since its beginnings, W&L has been one of the South's—indeed the nation's—preeminent liberal arts institutions. It has produced four Supreme Court justices, 27 senators, 31 governors, and 65 congressmen. The white columns and brick buildings, the coat of arms over the dining hall door, the honor code, and a traditionalist student body all attest to the school's aristocratic roots and intellectual seriousness.

However, W&L's identity may be changing in ominous ways. The current administration, stung by low rankings in national college guides, has hired a public relations firm to help it manage its image and rise higher in such (we think arbitrary and futile) lists of schools. A document produced by the firm—the so-called Cleghorn Report—has spurred high-level controversy on campus, as many prominent alumni and some faculty worry that the school is on the road to losing its special character. We hope that's not the case, but there is ample reason for concern.

SOUTH

For instance, the report refers to Washington and Lee's alleged reputation as a southern school, heretofore a source of pride among alumni, as a "black mark" for the institution, even though (a) the school *is* located in the South, after all, and there is not much to be done about that, and (b) at least one analysis indicates that the school has as much nationwide representation among its students as do schools like Williams and Carleton. There is also concern that the report presages a movement to increase enrollment as a way of diluting W&L's particularity. As one long-time professor has written, "many of us worry that . . . the university runs a risk of losing those characteristics that have made this a great place to learn how to conduct our lives." As things stand now, Washington and Lee is a national treasure, and it would be a shame to lose it.

Academic Life: Grade deflation

Like so much else at this school, Washington and Lee's curriculum can fairly be characterized as traditional. Truly bizarre classes are hard to come by, and the school does not generally offer today's trendy majors like media studies or ethnicity studies. There are departmental honors programs at W&L, but competition is stiff. The philosophy department requires that each honors student have an overall GPA of at least 3.3 and that he write and defend an honors thesis during his senior year. University Honors, W&L's general honors program, requires that participants take one reading course and three honors-level seminars; past topics have included "The Great Depression," "Pilgrimage in Religious Traditions," and "Evolution of Consciousness." Each University Honors student must also complete a thesis during the senior year.

Although W&L does not have a true core curriculum, the distribution requirements take up more than one-third of the credits required for graduation. One student says that with the "many general education requirements spanning many fields, students at W&L get a very broad education outside their majors." However, what guarantees students a broad liberal arts education is the solid course offerings.

Major requirements impose further curricular discipline, as most departments mandate breadth of knowledge in the student's field of study. The English department requires majors to take at least three courses in each of three areas: earlier British literature, later British literature, and American literature.

Academic advisors are on hand to help students chart their academic courses, and by all accounts advising at W&L is fantastic. The student-faculty ratio is a healthy 11 to 1. Each freshman faculty advisor is supposed to have no more than six advisees and usually hosts a dinner for them at the beginning of the year. Freshmen are assigned advisors from the School of Liberal Arts and are encouraged to change advisors once they settle on a major. Professors—even department heads—do not seem to begrudge their advising responsibilities. Advisors are said to be very accessible and generally meet with their advisees at least three to four times a year. "My advisors have been very helpful in guiding me in my course planning and making sure I stay on track," a student says. "The advisors are definitely interested in helping students and finding internship opportunities." Another student says, "A lot of people get jobs through professors, who take a real interest in them." Many also find work through a "massive network of alumni," he says.

A student interested in independent study or lab experience should have no trouble finding a mentor. At W&L, many students benefit from regular interaction with their professors—who, students say, are genuinely interested in teaching, not just research. Faculty members are very approachable and keep extensive office hours, of which many students take advantage. "The student-professor relationships found at W&L are one of the most wonderful things about the school," says a student. "All my professors know my first name, we speak when we see each other, I go over to dinner at their houses, have their home phone numbers—I could go on." Another student says, "I've spent over three hours in professors' offices this week and it's Wednesday." A professor says, "Since W&L has an open-door policy, students often stop by to talk about ideas. Class discussions frequently spill outside the classroom into office hours." One professor reports that "many faculty serve on committees that involve students as active and equal participants."

"Professors teach all classes," one student says. "And when I mean teach, I mean teach. They don't just get up in front of a class and dictate for an hour." On the rare occasions that teaching assistants grade papers or exams, professors look them over as well. With the exception of a few introductory courses in math and English, most classes—96 percent of them—have fewer than 30 students. Students report few problems getting into the classes they want.

VITAL STATISTICS
Religious affiliation: none
Total enrollment: 2,166
Total undergraduates: 1,760
SAT/ACT midranges: SAT V: 660–730, M: 660–720; ACT: 28–31
Applicants: 3,649
Applicants accepted: 30%
Accepted applicants who enrolled: 43%
Tuition: $27,960
Room and board: $7,225
Freshman retention rate: 94%
Graduation rate: 87% (4 yrs.), 90% (6 yrs.)
Average class size: 16
Student-faculty ratio: 11:1
Courses taught by graduate TAs: none
Most popular majors: history, politics, economics
Students living on campus: 61%
Guaranteed housing for four years? no
Students in fraternities: 79% sororities: 74%

As part of the effort to transform the school, teaching excellence now has less importance in tenure decisions and research is now weighted more heavily, a development tht worries some alumni and high-profile supporters of the school, who regard its emphasis on teaching as one of its most distinctive strengths. Their fears have only been confirmed by a recent decision not to extend tenure to a popular and highly rated teacher because of a lack of publications.

There are, of course, still many excellent professors on campus. Students particularly recommend Jim Casey in economics; William Connelly, Lucas Morel, Mark Rush, Robert Strong, and Eduardo Velasquez in the politics department; Ted Delany, J. D. Futch, and Taylor Sanders in history; Robert Johnson in math; Art Goldsmith and David Harbor in geology; Ellen Mayock in Spanish; Eric Uffelman in chemistry; Julie Woodzicka in psychology; Marc Conner, Genelle Gertz-Robinson, and Suzanne Keen in English; and George R. Bent in art. The English department is particularly strong. W&L's Journalism School (actually a department within the College of Arts and Sciences) is well regarded by those on campus as well as by those who hire reporters.

SOUTH

W&L is not yet plagued by the serious grade inflation that has afflicted many other universities. "This is actually problematic," says one student, "because our grades are much lower than many Ivy League schools where grade inflation is rampant, but their academic curriculum is no more difficult than W&L's." Students, at least, maintain that there are no easy A's to be had. W&L's Honor System, widely respected, means that professors place a good deal of trust in the honesty of students, who are allowed to schedule their own final exams and often have closed-book take-home exams.

Many students find W&L's atmosphere intoxicating. Says one, "Washington and Lee is all about the little things that can't be measured by *U.S. News and World Report*. Teachers who really care. A campus that's beautiful. Friendly people with character and integrity. A killer social life. If studies took into account all the little things that really make schools what they are, Washington and Lee would be number one." Perhaps so. But while W&L still stacks up favorably against just about any other school one could name, an increasing emphasis on the shibboleths of diversity threatens to overwhelm what makes the school unique. The introduction of a black studies and a women's studies program, the politically correct tone of campus publications, a squeamish administration, and a trend towards hiring what one alumnus calls "radicals" as teachers could mean that W&L is changing inexorably—in the same way that many once-distinctive religious and regional schools have already done. Places like Vanderbilt—the last home of W&L president Thomas Burish, who blundered recently by admitting to a gathering of students that he wished to remake W&L into the "Williams of the South." They didn't cheer.

Student Life: Lee, reclining

Washington and Lee's student body has, over the years, earned a reputation for conservatism. That may be changing. One student says, "The average student is still a Republican, but great scholarship offerings, more international students, and a diversification of programs have definitely shifted the students to the middle." The W&L professoriate is more politically liberal than the student body, but students say that professors' personal ideologies rarely dictate course content or classroom discussions, so students of various persuasions feel comfortable. Says one liberal student, "One of my economics professors, who's clearly left-leaning, had us reading Milton Friedman the other day." Says another student, "It's a conservative's heaven, but liberals still feel comfortable." And a faculty member says, "The best antidote to political correctness is a faculty committed to learning, by which I mean a faculty who still want to learn and not just teach. This sense of wonder preserves fairness. I am happy to say that I have colleagues with just this disposition."

W&L students are generally conservative, and right-leaning student groups are the most active and vocal, though one student was quick to protest *The Princeton Review*'s 2004 ranking of W&L as the school "most nostalgic for [Ronald] Reagan." There is a small gay and lesbian group, but that is about the only active organization that could be called radical. "Students are able to express any views they may have," one says.

The small town in which Washington and Lee is situated has helped to create an atmosphere in which students study hard and then let out stress over a glass of beer—or six. Although fraternity and sorority members participate in community service activities and other events, their houses are also centers of student inebriation. "Partying is a major social activity at W&L," one student says. "With its small-town location, the entire social scene revolves around Greek life activities and parties." Another says, "We are social animals. We consume more alcohol than the average college student." Greek parties are open to the whole campus, and W&L has a deferred rush system, which is supposed to allow for more intermingling among students before they select a house. One student says, "Prospective students should know that if they are not at all interested in the Greek system when they come here, they are in for a very long four years." But another says that she enjoyed "a strong college experience" even though she did not join a sorority. "The opportunities on campus are numerous," she says, and she has been "completely happy without the totally defined social structure offered by the Greek system."

Lately, the administration has been attacking this deeply rooted system, since it perceives the predominantly white fraternities and sororities as obstacles to multicultural integration. Saying that the Greek system not only causes racial problems but is also an insurance liability, university officials have effectively forced drinking off campus. But W&L students are not so easily sobered; the administration's aggressive policy has had the unintentional consequence of raising the number of DUI violations. Another professor argues that the attack on the Greek system is in the service of learning, not multiculturalism. He adds that "hazing is another worrying reality at W&L. There was an egregious case last year that resulted in the suspension of a fraternity for a full year."

W&L students do not exaggerate their partying capabilities. According to university publications, a whopping 47 percent regularly engage in binge drinking (six or more drinks in one evening). A professor reports that in the last decade the university has had half a dozen alcohol-related deaths—alarming for a school of this size.

One source says that the administration is trying to remake W&L, purging its specifically southern character through the implementation

ACADEMIC REQUIREMENTS

In the coming year W&L plans to revamp its general education mandates. The current distribution requirements are:

- One course in English composition (students can test out).
- One intermediate course in a foreign language or equivalent test scores.
- Two courses in literature. All options are excellent, ranging from "Medieval and Renaissance Studies" to Chinese, Greek, and Roman literature in translation.
- Four courses from at least two of the areas of fine arts, history, philosophy, and religion. Qualifying courses include "Ancient and Classical Art," "History of American Business," and "Basic (Theatrical) Scenic Design."
- Three courses in science and mathematics, including four credits of lab. One course must be in math or computer science.
- Three courses in the social sciences. All options are introductory surveys of major disciplines—not trendy electives.
- Five courses in physical education, plus a swimming test.

SOUTH

559

of a full-blown diversity program modeled on those in place at northeastern, liberal schools. "At times it seems that some students are favored for scholarships or opportunities because of their race," one student says.

Washington and Lee students may be drinkers, but they're not slackers. Classrooms are competitive. One student says, "The workload can be daunting." Another says, "Most people here intend to succeed and take classes seriously." Still another reports that "Intellectual discussions can occur anywhere at any time . . . in places you wouldn't expect, such as locker rooms." Most students are involved in more than one club or organization, of which there are over 200—including two student newspapers, one radio station, and a cable television station. W&L is an NCAA Division III school—which means its athletic program cannot offer scholarships, but that doesn't mean sports are insignificant; W&L fields some 21 varsity teams as well as club programs in men's and women's fencing, rugby, lacrosse, water polo, and squash.

Fittingly, "the honor code established by Gen. Robert E. Lee remains a strong force in the W&L community. It is taken very, very seriously and is extremely effective," according to a student. The school calls this code its "moral cornerstone." Incoming students pledge to abide by this code, which is run by their peers. Offenses against honor include lying, cheating, stealing, and other breaches of trust. For students found guilty, there is only one punishment—expulsion. The Honor System is a manifestation of General Lee's "one rule" at the university: that every student be a gentleman. The Speaking Tradition, for instance, dictates that when people pass each other, they say "hello," even if they are strangers. (One student reports that the tradition has deteriorated into somewhat of a "nod and grunt" tradition, but that nevertheless it continues to promote friendliness.) General Lee and his family are buried below the centrally located Lee Chapel. Traveller, Lee's horse, is buried outside the chapel. A marble statue of Lee reclining sits, oddly, where an altar might normally be. (Thankfully, the building is used more for meetings, concerts and speakers than for religious services.) In short, Lee's presence is still palpable at the university. One student considers him "the physical embodiment of what all W&L students aim to be: honorable, of integrity and character." The Lee Chapel is the site of most public events; one professor recalls, with a certain irony, that when filmmaker Spike Lee came to speak on campus, he stood in front of the tomb of General Lee, flanked left and right by Confederate battle flags. "He knew what he was getting into," the teacher says.

Students are required to live on campus for their first two years, beyond which the university does not guarantee housing. About two-thirds of the student body lives on campus. All residence halls are coed, but men and women are separated by floor and there are no coed bathrooms or dorm rooms. On-campus housing includes fraternity and sorority houses, where many students live as sophomores. Other than these, the university offers a few interesting housing communities. The Chavis House, a manifestation of W&L's diversity program, is, as the university announces in tortured diversity-speak, a "physical space on campus where African American (and other American ethnic/racial minorities) cultures and traditions are not only tolerated but actively appreciated." It is named for John Chavis, a "free black who completed his studies" in

1799, when the university was known as Liberty Hall. (W&L's *second* black student, sad to say, didn't arrive until 1966.) The International House has similar aims. The Outing Club House is used for presentations and speakers and as a launching pad for most of the group's trips. It also features an indoor climbing wall, a bike workshop, a library, and gear for all types of outdoor activities. There is also a substance-free housing option. Resident advisors live in freshman housing. Freshman orientation is mandatory; the primary topics of discussion include respect for the Honor System, general tolerance, and sexual assault awareness and prevention.

W&L's rich history is reflected in a number of its traditions. The Fancy Dress—or as some students call it "Fancy Stress"—is a 95-year-old annual event and a favorite among students. In a different tradition, members of the secret Cadaver Society sneak out at night to leave their symbol on banners and sidewalks. Other student groups include the W&L Swing Dance Club and the Liberty Hall Volunteers, who participate in Civil War reenactments, portraying the unit formed of students from Washington College in 1862. In the spring, students take field trips to the Maury River to float, tan, and socialize. During each presidential year, most W&L students participate in a mock convention. Whether it is a Republican or Democratic convention varies; students represent the party out of power. Through grassroots research in all 50 states, students predict the candidate the party will nominate—with uncanny accuracy, erring only once in the last 55 years. In January 2004, W&L students bucked the perception that Howard Dean was headed for the Democratic nomination and accurately predicted the selection of John Kerry.

W&L lies in the heart of the Appalachian town of Lexington, Virginia (population 7,100), also home to the Virginia Military Institute. Students say there is not much to do, but beautiful parks and mountain hikes are just minutes away. The small downtown offers a coffeeshop and a couple of bars. The rural setting provides a sense of security. The 2003 crime statistics reported nothing apart from three burglaries. Liquor-law violations dropped from 52 in 2002 to only 22 in the following year.

Nobody said this kind of school comes cheap. Tuition for 2004–5 was $27,960, and the least expensive room and board arrangement cost $5,975. Only about 35 percent of the student body applies for financial aid each year, and 22 percent of students get it. The average student loan debt of a recent graduate is $15,634.

SUGGESTED CORE

1. Classics 203, Greek Literature from Homer to the Early Hellenistic Period *and* Classics 204, Augustan Era
2. Philosophy 141, Ancient Philosophy
3. Religion 101/102, The Hebrew Bible: Old Testament / Introduction to the New Testament
4. Religion 250, Early Christian Thought: Orthodoxy and Heresy
5. Politics 266, Modern Political Philosophy
6. English 210, Shakespeare
7. History 107, History of the United States to 1876
8. History 326, European Intellectual History, 1880 to Present (*closest match*)

SOUTH

561

COLLEGE OF WILLIAM AND MARY

WILLIAMSBURG, VIRGINIA • WWW.WM.EDU

Nobility stoops to conquer

The College of William and Mary is the second-oldest college in the United States, so naturally, the school has some of the oldest and most remarkable traditions in the country. Chartered by self-styled British monarchs William III and Mary II in 1693, the school—like the rest of the United States—severed its ties with England in 1776. William and Mary founded the first Phi Beta Kappa chapter and America's first honor code system. Thomas Jefferson, James Monroe, and John Marshall are among its alumni. The college has scores of reasons to be proud of its past—and unlike many other colleges, it is.

Known in the media as one of the "public Ivies," William and Mary believes it has an obligation to provide a quality education to Virginians. The admissions department, therefore, reserves a majority of its slots for state residents, even though more out-of-state than in-state students apply. And no wonder. The college's focus on undergraduate teaching, its strong sense of community, and its historic, seductively beautiful campus make it an attractive option for serious students all over the world.

A major administrative change is in the works at William and Mary. President Timothy J. Sullivan has retired after 12 years of service and has been replaced by Gene R. Nichol, former dean of the law school at the University of North Carolina at Chapel Hill. In an interview with the *Virginian Pilot*, Nichol promised to place increased "diversity" at the mostly white southern school "center stage in the college's agenda." Yikes. A vocal critic of the Bush administration, Nichol claimed that he would keep his personal politics separate from his leadership of the school. Fine, but what about the dreary, conventional politics of academia? William and Mary bears close watching in the years to come.

Academic Life: It worked for Thomas Jefferson

William and Mary revised its curriculum several years ago so that students would graduate with a broader understanding of the liberal arts. Indeed, W&M is one of the few public universities whose administration still seems to have retained a genuine liberal arts orientation and is moving closer to that ideal rather than further from it.

"We believe it's important to not become too narrowly focused as an undergraduate," an admissions director and W&M alumnus says. "Our students learn how to approach problems from different points of view." Hence, the curriculum is designed so that equal thirds of a student's courses come from the general education requirements, electives, and a student's concentration. One recent alumnus says that students "must learn something of both the humanities and the sciences—although various paperwork games can be played to avoid a few things. However, the education requirements are established so that not too much can be worked around."

W&M's academic departments generally provide solid, rigorous courses for the requirements, with a result that falls just short of a traditional core curriculum. A government and economics major says, "There are about two or three 'less serious' classes that I know of, but I think even that is only relatively speaking." Another student gripes, "There's no such thing as a free 'A' around here."

A student concentrating in English at William and Mary must take at least one course on Chaucer, Shakespeare, or Milton; one on English literature before 1800; one on English lit after 1800; an American literature course; and a fifth course in the study of a genre, like "English Novel to 1832" or "Epic and Romance."

W&M is well known for its American history program. Reliably good courses include "Early American History," "Antebellum America," and "History of American Foreign Policy." However, students note that the history department can be politicized; courses like "Consumption, Goods, and American Society" and "Colonialism and Resistance in the Americas" bear this out.

According to faculty and students, the college's strongest departments are biology, classical studies, economics, anthropology, the School of Business, geology, physics, and religion. Government has some excellent professors, but it has become increasingly politicized in recent years. An undergrad says, "Some conservative students were afraid to jeopardize their GPAs by speaking out in class." A government major says, "In the grand scheme of things, William and Mary's not too liberal, but it's definitely more liberal than conservative."

Additional departments where students say that professors' political leanings influence learning include sociology, religion, and economics. However, one student who has taken a broad range of courses says, "In some humanities, there is a definite left-wing slant, but the professors who demonstrate that prefer for a student to analyze and challenge rather than to parrot. It is most valuable to be a thinker rather than a follower." Other students have made the following statements: "I've never felt indoctrinated"; "The majority of faculty welcome different opinions and will encourage intellectual debate"; and "[T]eachers will confess that they've given money to the Democratic campaign, but they'll criticize [Democrats] as much as they criticize Bush."

College literature, as it is apt to do, boasts of the school's commitment to teach-

VITAL STATISTICS

Religious affiliation: none
Total enrollment: 6,920
Total undergraduates: 5,582
SAT/ACT midranges: SAT V: 620–730, M: 630–710; ACT: 27–31
Applicants: 10,161
Applicants accepted: 35%
Accepted applicants who enrolled: 40%
Tuition: $7,095 (in state), $21,795 (out of state)
Room and board: $6,020
Freshman retention rate: 90%
Graduation rate: 71% (4 yrs.), 91% (6 yrs.)
Courses with fewer than 20 students: 41%
Student-faculty ratio: 11:1
Courses taught by graduate TAs: none
Most popular majors: social sciences, business, psychology
Students living on campus: 75%
Guaranteed housing for four years? no
Students in fraternities: 33% sororities: 34%

SOUTH

563

While it's not a tradi-
tional core, the curricu-
lum at William and
Mary imposes substan-
tial general education
requirements that can
be met by mostly solid
introductory surveys.
Students take:

- One course in mathemat-
  ics and quantitative
  reasoning, such as
  "Principles and Methods
  of Statistics."
- Writing 101, another basic
  writing course, or a
  writing-intensive freshman seminar within the
  department of the
  student's concentration.
- Two courses in the natural
  sciences (one physical
  sciences class and a
  biological sciences class,
  plus a supplemental lab),
  such as "Great Ideas in
  Physics" or "Insects and
  Society."
- Two courses in the social
  sciences. Choices range
  from "Principles of
  Microeconomics" to
  "Sport Psychology."
- Three courses in world
  cultures and history. At
  least one must be in
  Western civilization, such
  as "American History,"
  "History of Europe," or
  "Introduction to the
  History of Christianity."
  Another must cover
  material outside Europe,
  such as "Gender in Non-
  Western Cultures," or

ing, and students agree. "Professors are accessible and friendly, I haven't had anyone who wasn't willing to help," says one student. A second student says, "They are great mentors and advisors." The student-faculty ratio is 11 to 1, very good for a public university. An administrator says, "When you walk into a classroom, that person in the front is a professor. What a novel idea!" Students say that professors teach all their courses, while graduate teaching assistants lead weekly discussion sections for only the largest lecture courses.

The college has put into place programs that allow students to get to know their professors—the freshman seminar, for example. As freshmen, students are assigned premajor faculty advisors for the transition from high school to college. "My freshman advisor has been very helpful, but you need to be proactive about what your requirements are as a freshman and use your advisor as a supplement to that," one student says. Later on, students get faculty advisors from within their major departments; at that point, a student says, "We're able to get whatever we need from the process."

For all its emphasis on teaching, William and Mary does place pressure on faculty to publish, to the point that a recurring campus controversy centers on this or that favorite teacher being denied tenure. One student claims in the student publication *Flat Hat* that a sociology professor's contract was not renewed because of "insufficient research potential," while another student says that an "incoming professor has a prestigious publishing record, but [since] he cannot teach he should not have been hired." As one editorial in the *Flat Hat* notes, "the 'save the professor' letter has become a bit of a cliché."

Faculty members also wish they got paid more: a 2003 faculty survey by the college found that a whopping 69 percent of faculty have considered leaving the institution, mostly in search of bigger paychecks. Although 80 percent of faculty who replied to the survey said they were at least moderately satisfied with their jobs, then-president Sullivan at the time called the survey results "sobering news." Students actually voted for a "Save-A-Professor" program, which uses $5 from each student's activity fee to create a fund to pay three professors a special $10,000 bonus annually for a three-year term. The award is designed to encourage the "best and favorite professors" to stay at the college.

Some of the best professors mentioned by students include Thomas Finn (emeritus) and Hans Tiefel in religion; Phil Kearns in computer science; George Greenia in modern languages and medieval and Renaissance studies; Clayton Clemens, George Grayson, and Emile Lester in government; Sarah Stafford in economics; Hans C. von Baeyer and Robert E. Welsh in physics; James Axtell and Dale Hoak in history; John Conlee and Kim Wheatley in English; Gerald H. Johnson (emeritus) in geology; and Lawrence L. Wiseman (emeritus) in biology.

A student-run writing center helps struggling writers perfect their essays. In the sciences, students study and work on projects together; you'd have to search hard to find the cutthroat premed students that are the norm at some larger research universities.

Student Life: Playing real good for free

The 1,200-acre William and Mary campus is located at the end of Duke of Gloucester Street, just off the grounds of Colonial Williamsburg. Ignore the thousands of tourists, and the town is a scene from eighteenth-century America, complete with rustic taverns, fife and drum parades, the governor's residence (from when Williamsburg was the capital of Virginia), apothecary shops, and "interpreters" in historic garb. Some W&M students work in the town's shops and museums, and all students can visit the attractions for free. (However, if a student wants to leave Williamsburg he'll face major highway construction: Virginia plans to repave 60 miles of Interstate 64, Williamsburg's main lifeline, over the next several years.) Students complain of strained town-gown relations over things like limits on the number of people allowed to live in a rental unit, sound ordinances, and resistance to building off-campus apartments. Another thorny and unresolved issue has been students' ineligibility to vote in Williamsburg.

The main part of the William and Mary campus—the part where tour guides naturally spend the bulk of the tour—is an extension of the colonial style of the surrounding town. The Wren Building is the nation's oldest academic building to have remained in continuous use; in it, Thomas Jefferson, James Monroe, and John Tyler all studied, dined,

REQUIREMENTS (CONT'D)

cross-cultural courses, such as "The Crusades."

- One course in literature or the history of the arts. Choices here are much too broad; you could fulfill this requirement with anything from "Jesus and the Gospels" to "Introduction to Black Studies."

- Two credits in creative or performing arts. According to the college's Web site, many of the courses satisfying this requirement are two- or three-credit courses. To use one-credit courses, a student must take both courses in the same creative or performing art. Options here range from "Intermediate Jazz" to "Synchronized Swimming" I.

- One course in "philosophical, religious, and social thought." Options include "Modern Religious Thought: The Enlightenment to the Present," "Philosophy of Kinesiology," and "Death."

A student must also reach the fourth-semester level of proficiency in a foreign language and demonstrate an understanding of computers by taking an appropriate course within his or her major or by taking a computing proficiency exam upon matriculation.

SOUTH

565

and attended class. The centuries-old trees and brick buildings bring a charm to what the admissions department calls its "ancient campus." William and Mary has obviously expanded since its colonial beginnings, and beyond the main part of the campus the architecture is less pleasing.

"The school is growing too quickly in size," a student says. "Lots of construction is eating up the open space that's left on campus." In October 2004, the college began clearing space for four new tennis courts next to the Commons Dining Hall, which will also be renovated. The new tennis courts will replace those next to Adair Gym in order to make way for the construction of a 500-space parking deck. In April 2004, construction crews broke ground on the building that will eventually hold W&M's new nuclear magnetic resonance spectrometer, which will be one of the most powerful in the world. The college is also building a new dorm over what used to be students' favorite soccer fields.

Roughly three-quarters of the student body lives on campus. William and Mary only guarantees housing for freshman and seniors, but seniors often choose to live off campus anyway. Students who want campus housing tend to get it. Freshmen live together in all-first-year dorms. Most campus dormitories are coed by wing or floor, but students can live in single-sex dorms if they so choose. One benefit of the school's Honor Code is that at the beginning of the year, students and their RAs make their own decisions about campus living spaces, voting on quiet hours, visitation rules, etc. The dormitories are generally nothing to write home about; however the coveted lodges, cottage-style houses in a central campus location that house seven people each, are always the first to be chosen in the housing lottery. The off-campus Ludwell apartments are growing in popularity, housing mostly juniors and seniors. Special-interest housing includes an international house and substance-free housing. Students eager to improve their language skills can opt to live in French, German, Russian, Italian, Japanese, or Chinese theme houses, home to both fluent and nonfluent speakers.

Fraternities at William and Mary are mostly residential. About a third of students participate, but students say Greek life has an even stronger presence on campus than this statistic indicates. Weekend frat parties are popular and open to the entire student body. Greek organizations host fundraisers for charity, says one student, "that often take the form of laid-back Saturday afternoon sports tournaments." In 2004, a pledge was hospitalized with a sky-high blood alcohol level and injuries sustained during pledge week. The responsible irresponsible fraternity had its charter suspended. After an alleged rape at a fraternity party in 2003, the college cracked down on alcohol at Greek parties. Now it's a matter of policy that a fraternity must report to the administration whether it intends to have a "wet" or "dry" party; if the party is "wet," the revelers can expect a heavy police presence. An astonished student tells us that former president Sullivan himself once joined police outside a fraternity party.

The Office of Multicultural Affairs oversees most of the "cultural diversity" activities on campus, which have included the Celebration of Cultures, African Culture Night, Korean Harvest Festival, and the Hispanic Heritage Month Banquet. In general, the most active political groups on campus are on the left, including the Amnesty International chapter, Student Environmental Action Coalition, and the LAMBDA alliance, which holds a Gay, Lesbian, Bisexual, and Transgendered Awareness Week. (Some more conservative Virginians are known to call the school "William and Larry" because of its supposed reputation for being friendly to homosexuals.) W&M students have started a chapter of the ACLU to accompany existing branches of Planned Parenthood and the NAACP. Student publications include the *Standard*, the *Remnant*, the *Flat Hat*, and the *Progressive*. Conservative groups are in a distinct minority. These include the Students for Life, a nascent club called Students for Academic Freedom, and the College Republicans, who are generally "quiet," says one student. Not so the libertarian group Sons of Liberty. In fall 2003, the college condemned and shut down a satirical bake sale put on by the group that protested race-based affirmative action by selling brownies at University Center—$1 if the buyer was black or Hispanic, $2 for whites and Asians. After a threat of litigation, the school allowed them to conduct the next bake sale without hindrance.

W&M athletes, the Tribe, have some of the highest graduation rates in NCAA Division I sports. Aside from the 23 varsity sports programs, W&M also has plenty of club and intramural teams; nearly 90 percent of the student body participates in sports. However athletic participation does not always equal a fan base: "Turnout for sporting events is very low," says one student. Although there was a bump in attendance at football games in 2004 because "they've been winning," there's usually only a full house at homecoming. "If you're looking for a big sports school, this is not the place," says a freshman.

Religious activities are fairly popular on campus, with interdenominational groups remaining the largest. There are 33 religious clubs ranging from Quaker to Catholic, Hindu to Hillel. A student says, "Within walking distance there's a Jewish temple, six or seven different Protestant denominations, a Catholic church. If you're Baptist, Lutheran, or Episcopalian, there's a house of worship you can walk to in three minutes." Another says, "There is a really vibrant religious community within Williamsburg and William and Mary, especially if you are Christian; Catholicism is the largest represented religion here, they are very active and do a lot in the college community."

Since most students live on campus, much of social life is centered there. The University Center Activities Board (UCAB) organizes each week in the spring and fall an event called Fridays at Five, where bands play outside at a pavilion for free. Other UCAB events include student talent shows, on-campus movie screenings, comedians, and speakers. Popular hangouts include The Daily Grind (an on-campus coffeehouse open until 3 a.m.), the Cornerstone Grill, and Deli's. At the Yule Log Ceremony, held

SUGGESTED CORE
1. Classical Studies 410, The Voyage of the Hero in Greek and Roman Literature *or* Classical Studies 411, Sacred Violence in Greek and Roman Tragedy
2. Philosophy 331, Greek Philosophy
3. Religion 204, Christian Origins
4. Religion 331, The World of Early Christianity
5. Government 304, Survey of Political Philosophy II
6. English 205, An Introduction to Shakespeare
7. History 121, American History I
8. History 392, Intellectual History of Modern Europe II

SOUTH

567

just before winter exams, the college president reads "The Night Before Christmas" and students enjoy apple cider and Christmas cookies. The Last Day of Classes Bash is an all-day event held in the Sunken Gardens.

William and Mary is a school that loves tradition, including a number of quirky legends. One of the best-known revolves around the Crim Dell bridge: if a couple kisses there, they are destined to marry—unless one throws the other off. A bawdier tradition centering around the Crim Dell bridge is the W&M "triathlon," which includes a jump into the Crim Dell, streaking the Sunken Garden, and jumping the wall to the old governor's mansion in Colonial Williamsburg. And there's something of a Frisbee cult at William and Mary. One student says "there are people who enjoy some pretty weird things. You'll be up at three in the morning and see kids throwing Frisbees at lamp posts."

According to one student, the typical William and Mary undergrad is "nerdy, dedicated to his studies but able to relax well." Students report that because of their workload, they must be driven to have a social life. As one student puts it, "I know plenty of people who stay in all weekend and get their work done." Another student says, "People here are serious about their futures. . . . We're focused and we have direction."

William and Mary boasts a low crime rate, mostly because of its setting, but also because of the Honor Code and the prevailing atmosphere of trust. "I don't walk by myself at night at three in the morning on the weekend, but . . . I've never felt unsafe," a female student says. One particular bathroom on campus attracts homosexual cruising year-round—enough to win it mention on a national gay Web site. In 2003 the college reported one forcible sex offense on campus, four burglaries, and one robbery. On-campus arrests included 13 liquor-law violations and six drug abuse violations. The campus police provide a nighttime escort service and a van that shuttles students to area bars and parties. There are emergency phones all over campus.

For a school of this caliber, William and Mary is an excellent value—for Virginians, who in 2004–5 paid only $7,095 tuition; out-of-state students paid $21,795; room and board were $6,020. The school practices need-blind admissions, however. About 50 percent of students receive some type of aid—half that many get it based on need. The college covers most Virginia residents' need. For nonresidents, the college uses a combination of need and merit to determine how much help it can provide. According to the school, a financially strapped (though not necessarily average) 2004 graduate of W&M borrows about $15,000 to $20,000 to pay for his undergraduate years.

WOFFORD COLLEGE

SPARTANBURG, SOUTH CAROLINA • WWW.WOFFORD.EDU

So very normal

The wave of radical change that swept over American academia in the 1960s transformed most colleges in this guide, both in their curricula and in their social attitudes, to the point where older alumni often hardly recognize anything about their alma maters, apart from the buildings and (sometimes) the mascots. Even religious schools were confronted by fundamental challenges to their mission and identity—a test too many of them flunked. So it's refreshing, if only for the sake of genuine diversity, to come across a college that didn't turn into a pumpkin one midnight in 1968. Perhaps because it's located in a state mostly ignored by the nation's intellectual elite, Wofford College seems to have escaped the rage for uniformity that overwhelmed most colleges in the United States. Instead, it has maintained, to an astonishing degree, continuity with its own best traditions and those of its region. And it has done so without becoming a narrow, ideologically driven place that anyone could legitimately call "fundamentalist"; instead, the conservatism that prevails at Wofford arises organically from the beliefs of its student body and a significant number of the faculty and administration. Even those who do not share them have chosen to respect them, instead of trying to rip them up root and branch.

"Most of the people running Wofford are creatures of the [college] culture," says one professor, "and they know better than to try to change the students in outrageous ways." That doesn't mean that undergrads aren't challenged to defend and criticize their own views. But it does mean that the school doesn't treat its students' religious beliefs and social views as symptoms to be treated through curricular chemotherapy. This fact alone makes Wofford special—the fact that it's so very *normal*. "It's as close as you can get anywhere to an old-fashioned southern college experience," a teacher says. He means that in the best sense: Wofford was one of the first private colleges in its region to accept black applicants, voluntarily, and its student body has a healthy racial variety.

If you're a socially conservative student (especially if you're a southerner at heart),

VITAL STATISTICS	
Religious affiliation: United Methodist	
Total enrollment: 1,133	
Total undergraduates: 1,133	
SAT midrange: 1160–1350	
Applicants: 1,317	
Applicants accepted: 66%	
Accepted applicants who enrolled: 30%	
Tuition: $28,740 (includes room and board)	
Freshman retention rate: 93%	
Graduation rate: 79%	
Average class size: 17	
Student-faculty ratio: 12:1	
Courses taught by graduate TAs: none	
Most popular majors: social sciences, business, biology	
Students living on campus: 87%	
Guaranteed housing for four years? yes	
Students in fraternities: 50% sororities: 60%	

Without a true core curriculum, Wofford still tries to guarantee breadth of studies with decent distribution requirements. Students must take:

- "Freshman Humanities."
- "Freshman English" and one sophomore level course such as "Introduction to the Study of Literature" or "Survey of American Literature."
- "Western Civilization" (either before or after 1815).
- An introduction to philosophy or a sophomore-level philosophy course such as "Bio-Medical Ethics."
- A course in religion. Available offerings range from "Religions of the World" to "Søren Kierkegaard."
- Another sophomore- or higher-level philosophy or religion course; the other Western civilization course; or a course from the "Peoples and Cultures" list, such as "Ethnic American Literature" or "African Philosophy."

and if you're looking for a school that offers some strong liberal arts courses, a solidly free-market economics education, and a close-knit community of good-natured students and committed teachers, Wofford is a wonderful place to spend four years. It isn't a high-powered academy that submerges all students in the "great books" or the Gospel, and because the school unfortunately does not have a rigorous core curriculum, it's possible to get through the school without having attained a deep understanding of Western culture. But the school offers *many* serious courses in the important works of our civilization; and in those small classes taught by accessible, interested professors, you'll find fellow students who aren't cynical, jaded, or bigoted against the material they're learning. "I find that students are hungry for the classics," says one faculty member. "I've taught them recently, and students said they'd wished they read these earlier. They were blown away." Such enthusiasm can be contagious—and books read in that spirit will resonate quite differently in the mind, and form the character more profoundly, than the same works considered suspiciously as relics of an oppressive, alien past.

Wofford's low profile on the national scene may be its greatest asset, some supporters say. Students report that it keeps Wofford administrators from conforming too closely to the trends and politics of other universities. "The best part about Wofford is that they're just not interested in all of the foolishness you find at other schools," says one alumnus. "Students just won't have it." Wofford's donors likely wouldn't have it either. A major benefactor of the school and the region is textile king Roger Milliken, a conservative philanthropist and sometime backer of Patrick J. Buchanan. President Benjamin Dunlap is reputed to be mildly liberal, but students and faculty say he knows better than to push ahead with a radical agenda. Students, on the whole, are southern conservatives with traditional views. As such, they are not usually gripped with political fervor.

The college acknowledges and reflects its Methodist roots, and although there is no required chapel attendance or Bible course required in the curriculum, Wofford tries to "create a campus atmosphere congenial to the development of Christian character," as the college catalog says. The fall convocation each year begins with a prayer, and along with a diploma, each graduating senior receives a Bible signed by all of Wofford's faculty members. "It's one of the school's greatest traditions," says a student.

Academic Life: Small is beautiful

Wofford's catalog says the "curriculum emphasizes the traditional but calls also for the experimental, always in accord with the liberal arts focus of the college." The word "experimental" at most other schools would imply an emphasis on postcolonial literature in the English department and a major in the study of sexualities (we speak specifically of that erstwhile Methodist university one state to the north, Duke), but at Wofford the word means merely a few more projector screens in the classrooms and wireless Internet in the library.

Wofford College's core curriculum, if that's the word, is limited to Humanities 101, taken by all freshmen. The seminar-style course concerns "humanistic inquiry, with special attention given to value questions and issues," according to the course description. It is taught by a foreign language, philosophy, English, history, or other humanities professor who designs the course himself. In 2003, one of the sections was titled "Love and Death in Western Literature"; students in this class read *Antony and Cleopatra*, Flannery O'Connor's *A Good Man Is Hard to Find and Other Stories*, and George Bernard Shaw's *Heartbreak House*, among other texts. Another section, "Authority, Obedience, and Commitment," studied several of Plato's dialogues, Shaw's *Saint Joan*, and *The Autobiography of Martin Luther King, Jr.*, among other works. While such a free-form course must be fun for professors to invent, and might turn out to be quite worthwhile indeed, it could also end up as an idiosyncratic exercise. There seems to be too much luck of the draw here. Students should inquire in advance about what's taught in particular sections, and choose accordingly.

Comparatively thorough distribution requirements make up about a third of the courses needed for graduation. In a bigger school, this would be depressingly inadequate, but the very poverty of Wofford's course offerings means that the faculty have little opportunity to offer worthless fluff, and few of the faculty would be so inclined anyway. As with the freshman humanities course, finding out about the topic prior to signing up is a good idea for the first of the English requirements, the writing-intensive "Seminar in Literature and Composition." According to the course catalog, this class "focuses on a literary figure, genre, nationality, or period." Well that narrows things down, doesn't it? Topics covered recently "range from 'F. Scott Fitzgerald and the Jazz Age' to 'American Ethnic Fiction' to 'D. H. Lawrence.'" In other words, call ahead and pick the right section. The second English requirement is a little clearer: students must pick one of two surveys of English literature—up to 1800, or from 1800 to the present.

Other requirements include the potentially admirable course titled "History of Modern Western Civilization," either from the Renaissance to 1815, or from 1815 to

REQUIREMENTS (CONT'D)

- A two-year introductory foreign language sequence, or one advanced course.
- A two-course sequence in biology, chemistry, geology, physics, or psychology; or an introduction to science with one semester in a life science and one in a physical science; or an intensive physics course.
- A course in art, music, or theater, such as "Survey of the History of Western Art" or "African Art."
- A course in mathematics.
- Freshman physical education.

SOUTH

the present. However, one faculty member complains about this requirement: "Notice where it starts—in the early modern period. Students can finish their education without knowing anything about the classical period or the Middle Ages. That's a real problem. The general education requirement leaves a lot of wiggle room. A student can get through without having read many major works, if he's motivated to avoid them."

On the positive side, the majority of Wofford's courses avoid the narrowness and trend-sniffing characteristics of other schools' catalogs. In the English department, for instance, one will find courses in early-to-modern British literature, two Shakespeare courses, surveys in American fiction and poetry, a course in southern literature (students in this class read the Agrarians, Faulkner, Welty, Warren, O'Connor, and Dickey), and good classes in poetry, drama, and literary criticism. The history major requires three courses in American history; a course in early European history; one in modern European history; a course in the "modern Middle East, modern East Asia, modern imperialism, colonial Latin America, or modern America"; two senior-level reading courses in history; and another senior-level course taught by a prominent historian serving at Wofford as a visiting professor—a rotating position that attracts some eminent scholars, such as William Leuchtenburg and Robert Remini. Religion course offerings are solid, ranging from broad but worthy classes such as "Christian Ethics" and "Religions of Asia" to deeper, more specific subjects like "The Johannine Literature" and "History of Christian Theology: The Ecclesial/Political Relationship." The classes in the fine arts department are mostly historical, with a few studio workshops offered for creative students. All the offerings meeting the science requirements are serious classes; even the psychology courses require lab work and experiments.

Wofford's history department contains a number of competent and dedicated faculty, but with its newer hires some fear it is drifting toward the sort of hyperspecialization characteristic of the profession. English has its strengths—including, again, several highly regarded professors—but one faculty member says that it suffers from "the most noticeable grade inflation on campus."

One Wofford professor cracks that philosophy students "are not required to master arguments or even the history of philosophy, but are encouraged to be creative and do philosophy themselves," noting that the department is also held to be among the more politically liberal at Wofford. But the listed requirements for the major seem solid enough: one course in "Metaphysics and Epistemology," a three-course history-of-philosophy sequence ranging from antiquity to the nineteenth century, a "course in logic and/or reasoning," and a course in ethical theory, followed by a senior project.

Wofford offers 24 majors, seven minors, and interdisciplinary programs in computational science, gender studies, information management, Latin American and Caribbean studies, and the very rare nineteenth-century studies. There is a creative writing concentration within the English major, and in a delightful tradition, each year Wofford publishes and distributes 2,000 copies of the best novel written by a student—thereby launching a new southern writer on the scene. Authors who have read on campus include Doris Betts, Lee Smith, George Garrett, and Bill Bryson.

The most popular majors are biology, business, economics, and government. Along with the language departments, these are also known as the most influential departments at the school, and in diametrically opposed senses, the "strongest." One professor explains: "The economics and government departments are uniformly conservative, and the government department in particular takes a philosophical, even classical approach to the study of politics. In these departments the questions and concerns animating traditional liberal education still thrive." The faculty in the biology and language departments, on the other hand, are "evangelical" neo-Darwinians and "crusaders for the biotech enterprise," including such practices as stem-cell research and cloning. One teacher calls them "rabid in their disdain for religious and philosophical critiques of modern scientific hegemony" and says that they are prone to "attract many of Wofford's better students away from liberal arts." How effective they are at convincing South Carolinians of the validity of scientism is another question; one biology professor took a secret poll of senior biology majors and found to his despair that more than half rejected Darwinian evolution. Whatever one thinks of this, it certainly provides evidence of the strength of Wofford students' native conservatism.

All four professors in the economics department can be described as "thoughtful Hayekians," which means that they are reasonable advocates of the market. The government department, already mentioned as being fairly conservative, has faculty who emphasize historical and theoretical perspectives on political science rather than number-crunching statistical approaches.

There is a gender studies program at Wofford, but it is not a major, and it seems pretty tame. Courses that satisfy the program requirements include "Women in Renaissance Art," "Topics in Modern Intellectual History," and "History of American Women"—in other words, classes that are probably worth taking. The intercultural studies program consists of practical courses intended to help business students communicate when in other countries. It requires advanced study in a foreign language and at least one semester of international study. African American studies consists of one course in "African American History," which appears to be a rather serious class, as well as a few courses in race and ethnic relations in sociology. What's more, no matter what the politics of the professor, it's unheard-of for conservative students to be graded down for expressing their views.

Wofford's smallness means that its course catalog is not the usual Shoney's buffet of esoteric options. But in some areas, choices can be disappointingly few. In the languages, for example, majors are available only in French, German, and Spanish (with

SUGGESTED CORE
1. English 336 European Masterpieces: Antiquity to the Renaissance (*closest match*)
2. Philosophy 351, Western Philosophy in Antiquity and the Middle Ages
3. Religion 201, The Old Testament / Religion 202, The New Testament
4. Religion 203, The Christian Faith
5. Government 392, Modern Political Thought
6. English 305, Shakespeare (Early Plays) *and* English 306, Shakespeare (Later Plays)
7. History 201, History of the United States, 1607–1865
8. History 380, Europe in the Age of Anxieties, 1850–1914 *or* Philosophy 353, Nineteenth-Century European Philosophy

SOUTH

573

some courses offered in ancient Greek and in Chinese). What's more, "the language departments are evangelical in their crusade for multiculturalism," according to a faculty member. While in some ways small academic departments can be a drawback, they can also be an asset. "You know all your professors here, and they know you," says a student. Wofford's size also helps to keep it focused on its role in the formation of undergraduate minds and hearts. Another student says, "This is not a research institution, so the reason professors choose Wofford is because they love to teach and help students. This is apparent the first minute you walk on our campus." Students have the option of taking some classes at nearby Converse College, which means more choices for those who don't find their interests represented at Wofford.

Classes are compact—the largest classroom holds just 60 students. Professors hold office hours weekly, but their doors are almost always open. One student says, "My friends at other institutions can't believe I know professors as I do, and that I actually feel comfortable going by their offices or homes, or stopping them on the sidewalk to ask them questions." Every student is assigned a faculty advisor who helps him choose courses and, when necessary, a major. Freshmen and sophomores are required to meet with their faculty advisors before registering for classes. Once a student declares a major, he is directed to the care of the department chair or another faculty member within the major department. One student says she found her advisor to be a "great resource for class recommendations, encouragement, and advice on post-college options." A peer tutoring program pairs upperclassmen with students who request the extra help.

Some of the best professors at Wofford include Robert C. Jeffrey and Frank M. Machovec in government; John McArthur, Timothy Terrell, and Richard Wallace in economics; John Cobb and George Martin in English; Ellen Goldey in biology; and Charles Bass in chemistry.

A one-month winter interim session allows students to undertake "projects" that, while they wouldn't necessarily make for good semester-long courses, are interesting nonetheless. Four projects are required for graduation. In 2004, offerings included "Chemistry in Popular Media," "Jazz History," and "Washington: Soldier to Statesman." There are also preprofessional internships, volunteer work, independent study, and travel interims (including trips to Australia and New Zealand, London and Ireland, Chile, or Hawaii). Or try the scuba project, which includes three weeks on campus earning diving certification and one week diving off the Dutch island of Bonaire. Students can also design their own projects. A few years ago, two Wofford men traveled throughout South Carolina researching "hole-in-the-wall" diners. One student says, "My interims have been some of my most unique learning experiences during my college career."

Wofford's Sandor Teszler Library houses 250,000 volumes, but students can also avail themselves of the holdings of Converse College and the University of South Carolina-Spartanburg through interlibrary loan.

Student Life: Tradition a'plenty

President Dunlap says Wofford's greatest and most obvious attributes are the friendliness and authenticity of its students. "The stuff that all the other colleges claim to have, Wofford really has," he says. Students agree. One sophomore says, "There really is a Wofford family. You know everyone." The students are mostly courtly, polite, and well-rounded—southern ladies and gentlemen—according to one professor. He says that they have mostly "modest ambitions. They want to go to professional schools, teach school, get married, and raise families," he said. "They don't overvalue either academics or athletics, but balance the two. However, they'll do hard work when asked, and they really appreciate the opportunity to learn."

For most Wofford students, social life *is* Greek life. More than half the students are members of a fraternity or sorority, and each chapter has its own house. "On an average weekend night, we have 600 to 700 people down here," says one student. Local bands and theme parties are frequent and popular. Greek organizations, students say, foster a close-knit atmosphere that brings many alumni back to campus every year for homecoming or to participate in other traditions. Mostly because of fraternities and sororities, Wofford is said to be rather cliquish—fraternity rush begins during the second week of school, with sorority rush starting a week later. But at least "there is a clique for everyone, and they're not segregated," says one student. "You have your core friends, and then everybody else you're friendly with." In 2003, about 66 percent of Wofford students came from the state of South Carolina, and 19 percent hailed from North Carolina, Georgia, or Florida. "We definitely have the 'good ol' boy' label here, but Wofford is actually a very diverse campus," a student says. "You meet people of all different backgrounds." That depends on your frame of reference, of course. During 2002–3, for instance, Wofford enrolled just two international students. They probably just haven't heard of Wofford over in Bangalore.

Besides the Greek system, the Wofford community begins to form in the freshman dormitories. Some 87 percent of students live on campus; in fact, students are required to live on campus unless they live with their parents or other relatives, but exceptions can be made. Most residence halls are coed, but Wofford is still traditional enough that it offers one all-female dorm (with access limited to residents only) as well as one all-male dorm. The meal plan is fairly standard, requiring freshmen to take (or at least pay for) 12 meals on campus per week; for the other meals, students use "Terrier Bucks," a more flexible way of spending as much or as little as the student wishes.

Wofford enrolls only 1,100 or so students, but the school competes at the NCAA Division I level as a member of the Southern Conference, along with Davidson College, Furman, and Western Carolina University, among others. Moreover, it has the tenth-best graduation rate in the nation for student-athletes in its division. And though small, Wofford has some of the best athletic facilities in the region, thanks to an athletic building donated by Carolina Panthers owner and Wofford alumnus Jerry Richardson. In return for the gift, the Panthers use Wofford as their summer training center each year—not a bad deal for Wofford. The college also opened a new baseball stadium in 2004. About 40 percent of Wofford students play on one of the school's 17 varsity teams. Intramurals are also popular and are usually organized by fraternity. As every Wofford student is quick to say, the college is deeply rooted in tradition. For Saturday afternoon football games, for instance, men wear ties, women wear dresses, and alumni and local residents flock to the stadium.

The lovely campus was designated an arboretum in 2002 in recognition of its thousands of trees of hundreds of different species. The college has built several stunning facilities in recent years, including the $15 million Milliken Science Center and the Franklin Olin Building, which houses high-tech computer and language labs. The college's first building was Old Main, which was restored in 2001 and is home to several academic departments and Leonard Auditorium. Spartanburg is an attractive southern town "out of the 1950s, where you can get anywhere in 15 minutes," a professor says.

Wofford College is, for most students, within an easy drive from home—and many visit their parents on weekends. But the college is not a suitcase school. "Typically there is always something going on during the weekend, from a band party at one of the fraternity houses to a play production by Wofford's theater department to a sporting event," a student says. He adds that students complain "about times when they do need to go home, because they are afraid they will miss something at Wofford." Besides attending parties (a major component of life outside the classroom), Wofford students occasionally find time for other activities. However, Spartanburg has no college town to speak of, and students spend most of their time on campus or in the off-campus houses nearby. Every Wofford student must hit the Beacon, Spartanburg's legendary hamburger joint, at least a few times. Order your sandwich "a' plenty"—covered in onion rings and fries, dripping in grease—along with the customary sweet tea.

Lately the college has pumped up its arts and concerts calendar, encouraging intellectual and cultural interests for students and Spartanburg-area residents. The World Film Series, featuring independent foreign movies, is free for students. Musical performances are said to be well attended by students. Many Wofford students are active in community service work through the college's Twin Towers Project, Habitat for Humanity, mentorships, and soup kitchens.

Wofford's Office of Multicultural Affairs, formed in 2000 and administered by the dean of students' office, is comparatively uninfluential. A brochure for the office, "Developing Leaders for a Multicultural World," says its mission is to "act as an educational supplement by preparing members of the campus community for living in an increasingly multicultural world via three major components: multicultural programming, diversity education, and leadership development." Programs include a Human Diversity Week held each fall and events to celebrate Black History Month each February.

The school hosts just a few political organizations, including College Democrats, Amnesty International, College Republicans, and the South Carolina Student Legislature. The nonpartisan Public Policy Committee hosts politicians and political leaders on campus each year, such as Congressman Mark Sanford (when he was running—successfully—for governor of South Carolina in 2002), then-incumbent governor Jim

Hodges, and Michael J. Copps, a Wofford alumnus and member of the Federal Communications Commission. Various Christian denominations are represented on campus, with a Newman Club for Catholics; Baptist, Presbyterian and Episcopalian student groups; and a Gospel-oriented ministry called "Souljah's for Christ."

On the Wofford campus itself, crime is very infrequent, with just one aggravated assault and 14 burglaries reported in 2002, and none of these in 2003—when, however, five cars were stolen. Students should be careful when leaving the confines of the grounds, because the areas directly bordering the campus are "sketchy," as one student says. Another student, a fraternity member, says, "Wofford is a pretty 'wet' campus, and public safety often looks the other way when they see underage drinking. You have to be pretty stupid to get an alcohol violation." As there were no liquor-law arrests made on campus between 2001 and 2003, he seems to be telling the truth.

As private universities go, Wofford is a bargain, with a price tag of $28,740 for tuition, room, and board. Admission is need-blind; however, the school cannot afford to guarantee full financial aid to all students. Still, some 54 percent do receive some need-based aid, and the average student loan debt of recent grads is only $12,281.

Midwest

CALVIN COLLEGE

GRAND RAPIDS, MICHIGAN • WWW.CALVIN.EDU

The institutes of the Christian religion

The Christian Reformed Church has a long and notable educational tradition of cultivating a certain kind of purposeful intellect, one informed by broad worldly learning and committed to Jesus Christ—that is, both liberal and obedient. Calvin College has advanced this tradition since 1876, when it was founded to "engage in vigorous liberal arts education that promotes lifelong Christian service." The college "pledges fidelity to Jesus Christ, offering our hearts and our lives to do God's work in God's world. . . . We offer education that is shaped by Christian faith, thought, and practice. We study and address a world made good by God, distorted by sin, redeemed by Christ, and awaiting the fullness of God's reign."

Historically, Calvin's students and faculty have been drawn mainly from the Dutch Reformed population that founded the college. But the dominance of the Dutch has waned as the college has sought a broader range of students and faculty. The rationale behind this effort, Calvin administrators claim, is scriptural: "A commitment of the community is to seek, nurture, and celebrate cultural and ethnic diversity, in obedience to the biblical vision of the kingdom of God formed 'from every tribe and language and people and nation.'"

The issue of diversity raises a question for Calvin College that has faced college administrators, faculty, and students across America since the early 1980s, when Jesse Jackson called for the end of the Western civilization requirement at Stanford University: Can a college promote diversity for its own sake while maintaining a commitment to, and a belief in, excellence? A new curriculum introduced in 2001 gave indications that Calvin is trying to have it both ways. Whether Calvin's struggle to maintain its historical commitments while keeping "up to date" will make it a better school remains to be seen.

VITAL STATISTICS

Religious affiliation: Christian Reformed Church
Total enrollment: 4,180
Total undergraduates: 4,127
SAT/ACT midranges: SAT V: 540–670, M: 540–670; ACT: 23–29
Applicants: 1,721
Applicants accepted: 98%
Accepted applicants who enrolled: 53%
Tuition: $17,770
Room and board: $6,185
Freshman retention rate: 86%
Graduation rate: 57% (4 yrs.), 76% (6 yrs.)
Courses with fewer than 20 students: 37%
Student-faculty ratio: 12:1
Courses taught by graduate TAs: none
Most popular majors: business, social sciences, education
Students living on campus: 56%
Guaranteed housing for four years? no
Students in fraternities or sororities: none

MIDWEST

Students at Calvin do not face a traditional core curriculum, but rather a set of serious, respectable distribution and other requirements, chosen from a uniformly solid selection of courses. They are as follows:

- Two "gateway and prelude" orientation classes taken during the first year.
- Seven "core competency" requirements in such areas as rhetoric, health and fitness, and foreign languages, and 13 "core studies" requirements—including a minimum of one course each in history, philosophy, literature, mathematics, the arts, persons in community, societal structures in North America, global and historical studies, the physical world, and the living world. At least two courses in biblical or theological foundations are also required.

Academic Life: Harmony of the law

The overriding principle at Calvin, says one professor, is "coherence" between the Christian identity and educational activity of the college. This is reflected, according to several observers, in the president's style in running the college. President Gaylen J. Byker is noted for calling programs to account for their fidelity to the principles of the college. "He has held people's feet to the fire," says one professor. According to another, the president "tries to rein in the pressures and influences that are not consistent with the identity of the college. He has promoted a greater sense of the need for Calvin to be more self-conscious and deliberate about its identity."

Calvin's adoption of what it calls a "core curriculum" in 2001 was the most significant curricular reform at the school in decades. Needless to say, strengthening a core curriculum runs counter to the trend at virtually all other colleges surveyed in this guide. If only it truly *were* a core curriculum—now that would be stop-the-presses sort of stuff. For while the new curriculum is a step in the right direction, the result is still a set of distribution requirements that offers too much wiggle room and not enough of a common intellectual foundation to be called a true core. Students may choose from a variety of courses to fulfill a particular curricular category or test out of a requirement altogether. Any one of fifty classes meet the "global and historical studies" requirement, for example. Furthermore, certain professional-degree programs (ranging from fine arts to nursing, recreation, and social work) have a "modified core curriculum"—modified, that is, to suit the major. Athletes are exempt from the "one-hour skill-enhancement" requirement, high school courses can get a student out of foreign language and science requirements, and a C in college preparatory mathematics is good enough to excuse a student from the core math requirement. In sum, the "core" seems to be a compromise between the need for curricular structure and the market demand for student choice.

However, as compromises go, it's a pretty good one. The document that describes the rationale and content of the core curriculum is impressive. It identifies a set of skills and a body of knowledge that the school believes all liberal arts graduates should have—something many schools are loathe to state for the record—and structures courses designed to provide those skills and knowledge. The catalog states: "The courses in the core are designed to impart a basic knowledge of God, the world, and ourselves; to develop the basic skills in oral, written and visual communications, cultural discernment, and physical activity; and to cultivate such dispositions as patience, diligence, honesty, charity, and hope that make for a life well-lived."

Embedded in Calvin's mission and in the college's view of the core curriculum is an eagerness to engage the world of affairs, including the practical and secular world of professions. "We're not fundamentalists," says one professor. "There is no problem here engaging the world and tackling the toughest intellectual or scientific issues of the day." Another says, "We reject the anti-intellectualism and defensiveness which characterizes too much of the Evangelical community." And one professor who has taught at other institutions says, "This place is very open to discussion of ideas; there is true intellectual freedom. I couldn't do the kind of scholarship I'm doing anywhere else."

Calvin's Christian commitment is apparent even in courses that appear at first to have little connection to religious issues. According to a professor, Calvin insists that students do three things throughout their education: "Think about biblical assumptions concerning human beings and how they apply to the issue being studied; think about the Christian vision, seeing scripture as a whole; and ask: What can we expect from human beings? What institutional frameworks make sense for them?" In taking this approach, this professor says it becomes readily apparent that "some things, some ideological movements, don't fit" the Christian worldview.

The core curriculum, to its credit, strives for integration between different disciplines and attempts to sequence courses in such a way that they build upon each other. The program's evident goal is to develop within each student a coherent body of knowledge, which the student can "put to work" with the skills he will have learned: this is the essence of Calvin College's idea of a liberal arts education. Those seeking a liberal arts education as "an end in itself," therefore, may be disappointed by Calvin's pragmatic emphasis. Calvin is not interested in becoming a great books school; however; the new curriculum holds out the possibility that students (at least those who are required to fully participate in the core) will share a unified experience of reading from a common body of canonical texts. Despite its traditional orientation, the school is open to legitimate new areas of learning; Calvin is the only Christian college in the United States to offer four continuous years of language studies in Chinese and Japanese, or to offer an Asian studies major.

While navigating their way through the core curriculum at Calvin, students will

REQUIREMENTS (CONT'D)

- A one-course requirement in the area of "cross-cultural engagement." The guidelines for these courses state that in them students will "learn how to distinguish between enduring principles of human morality and their situation-specific adaptations; to witness other cultural embodiments of faith, and thus to reflect on the substance and definition of one's own faith by comparison." This is very unlike other schools' "diversity" requirements, which typically exist for the purpose of promoting cultural relativism.

- A "core capstone" course during the final year. This is typically a small seminar with a major research project undertaken in the student's major field of study; its purpose is to integrate rigorous scholarship with a Christian worldview.

MIDWEST

want to make time for contact with the stronger departments at Calvin—including English, philosophy, classics, chemistry, religion, and physics—as well as some of the college's outstanding professors. These include W. Dale Brown, Edward Ericson Jr. (emeritus), Susan Felch, and James Vanden Bosch in English; Kelly James Clark in philosophy; Kenneth D. Bratt in classical studies and the Honors Program; Ronald L. Blankespoor in chemistry; John R. Schneider in religion; and Calvin Stapert in music.

In order to be hired at Calvin, faculty must not only belong to the Christian Reformed church or another church in fellowship with it, but must also sign a confessional statement pledging their adherence to the three principle documents of the Reformed faith: the Heidelberg Confession, the Belgian Confession of 1561, and the Cannons of Dordt. (They are permitted to make minor reservations regarding these articles, but they must agree to them in substance and principle.) In addition, it is mandatory for faculty members to send their children to Christian Reformed schools; in order to send their children to other schools (public, Catholic, or home school, for example) they must receive a special exemption from the college provost. This last requirement draws the most resistance, but so far attempts to change it have failed. These requirements preserve Calvin from many of the relativist and deconstructionist fads that have swept through other church-related institutions, rendering them religious in name only.

While Calvin does officially call for "gender-inclusive" language in academic writing, there have been no attempts to introduce more radical speech codes or "sensitivity training." Radical ideology remains far in the background at Calvin. "There are some professors whom everyone knows are liberal, but they don't try to use their classes to advance their agenda," says a student.

However, it would be fair to say that outspoken conservatives are made to feel unwelcome in some departments. Conservatives, says one faculty member, "feel some pressure to prove they're not right-wing crazies." Even so, according to a professor, "conservatives are not hard to find here." There is a Conservative Study Group at Calvin that serves as a forum for ideas and a source of support for interested faculty.

Calvin professors share a deep and abiding commitment to excellence in undergraduate teaching. Faculty are expected to make teaching their top priority, and the quality of a professor's teaching weighs heavily in the college's decision to grant tenure. But this commitment to teaching has not impeded the quality or quantity of scholarship produced by Calvin's faculty. One faculty member says that he is "tremendously impressed" by the scholarship of the Calvin faculty, whom, he believes, "would be considered an asset to any great college or university."

The overall intellectual atmosphere at Calvin is described as vigorous. Communicating the Christian vision does not restrict the educational content at Calvin to apologetics. Calvin's denominational affiliation and confessional commitment do not stifle debate, but rather provide the community with important things to talk about, in the belief that objective truth can be sought and found. Professors encourage the examination of and debate over first principles, and students and faculty agree that there is a lively exchange of ideas in and outside of the classroom. There are several lecture series on campus each year that bring in noted writers, artists, and intellectuals of various stripes.

Calvin classes are all taught by faculty, and the student advising system is thorough. Arriving freshmen are expected to meet with faculty advisors during summer orientation, when they choose their first-semester classes. Then in October the school suspends classes for two "advising days," during which all students meet again with advisors. Those who have chosen majors huddle with mentors appointed by their departments, while others are put with advisors who specialize in helping undecided students.

Student Life: Such children ought we to be

Calvin College is unreservedly and unapologetically Christian and Reformed, and its policies and priorities as well as the campus climate and culture must be understood through this lens. To those unfamiliar with the Christian Reformed faith in general and Calvin College in particular, many of the restrictions and policies may seem severe. When one stands back, however, and considers the destruction wrought on university and college campuses over the course of the past 50 years by college faculty and administrators lacking any first principles from which to approach their work, Calvin's faculty regulations seem not only reasonable but laudable.

Indeed, the college has fostered an environment open to prudent reforms but not mere change for its own sake. The climate at Calvin is one in which students feel as though they are a part of something beyond themselves, something that is manifest in the school's historical role in propagating their faith and nurturing their intellects. As such, Calvin has escaped, though it is not by any means impervious to, the political conflagrations that have engulfed most college campuses. In other words, the political climate at Calvin is not determined by fads and forces external to the university; it grows organically out of the questions that arise when shared beliefs and convictions are brought to bear on issues and ideas within the academic setting.

Calvin students are serious, according to professors: "There aren't many programs where you can be a slacker and get through," says one. Given Calvin's whopping 98 percent acceptance rate, this is rather surprising. But according to Calvin's director of admissions, this approach is deliberate. "We believe in extending the opportunity to receive a good education to as many students as possible. Once the student is here, it's up to him or her to live up to the opportunity and meet the standards of the college."

By all accounts, those standards are high. "The proof of our rigorous expectations is in the lack of grade inflation here," says one professor. "Each year, only two or three students graduate with a 4.0 average." Indeed, some graduate and professional

SUGGESTED CORE
1. Classics 211, Classical Literature
2. Philosophy 251, History of Philosophy I
3. Religion 121, Biblical Literature and Theology
4. Religion 243, History of Christian Theology I
5. Political Science 306, History of Modern Political Thought
6. English 346, Shakespeare
7. History 252, The American Republic, 1763–1877
8. Philosophy 335, Nineteenth-Century Philosophy

schools are known to add points to the GPA of Calvin graduates to make them comparable to other schools with less exacting standards.

This commitment to providing educational opportunity is also reflected in the amount and variety of sources of scholarships for Calvin students. There are 50 pages of academic scholarships listed in the college catalog, some of which are open to all students, and some restricted to students in certain disciplines. There are numerous means of support available at Calvin for diligent students.

All this results in close relationships between students and faulty. "It is the rare student who feels remote or distant from the faculty," a professor says. Many students echo this opinion. "I've had dinner at a professor's home on a number of occasions," one student says. "The professors are very approachable," says another. "Here at Calvin," says a professor, "you have the opportunity for really wonderful mentoring relationships to develop between students and faculty." This, it would seem, is further evidence of the salutary effect of Calvin's historical commitment and its present-day charge to educate in accordance with the tenets of Reformed Christianity. That is, by taking its charge as a Christian college seriously, Calvin's students, faculty, and administration enjoy the considerable cultural benefits that an authentically Christian community accrues over time.

The religious identity of the student body is overwhelmingly Christian, but Christian Reformed pupils make up only 50 percent of the student body—a surprisingly small figure given the historical identity and close denominational affiliation of the college. By all accounts, students of non-Reformed backgrounds are made to feel welcome. "We are almost all agreed on the central beliefs of the Christian faith," says one such student, "so we get along pretty well."

Of course, very few colleges have been unaffected by the multiculturalist winds that have blown through universities and every other institution in the public square during the past several decades. At Calvin, however, multiculturalism is mild and muted compared to that which dominates many secular campuses. "Calvin College is multipigmented, not multicultural," says one professor. He says that there is growing awareness that there is a Christian culture at Calvin that needs to be appreciated and fostered for its own sake. "The Christian Reformed culture is interesting in its own right," he says. Another professor notes that a "certain amount of 'white guilt'" has motivated the college to expend a great deal of energy recruiting minority faculty and students. But even students recruited from non–Christian Reformed backgrounds are mostly Christian and therefore sympathetic to the values of the college.

All freshmen and sophomores (except those who are 21 or older) are required to live on campus or at home with their parents. For most underclassmen, this means living in one of the school's residence halls, which house men and women on separate wings. Juniors and seniors typically opt to live in college-owned housing on the other side of the highway. Even students in these apartments must adhere to a policy that forbids visitors after midnight (1 a.m. on weekends). Restrictions are even tighter in the residence halls, where students are not allowed to have members of the opposite sex in their rooms unless the door is open.

Even so, Calvin's code of student conduct is fairly relaxed, considering the Calvinist affiliation of the college. Students are not required to sign any pledge regarding behavior. "Responsible freedom," is the code at Calvin: students are expected to refrain from drinking, smoking, sexual immorality, and the use of obscene language on campus. Judicial bodies made up of students and faculty enforce the code of conduct. The college takes seriously its role in forming the conscience of its students. Interestingly, in recent years a growing number of students have voiced a desire to see the college make even stricter demands.

While the students at Calvin are serious, that seriousness doesn't prevent them from finding diversions. The Student Life Division at Calvin offers, in its own words, "a wide array of programs and services that are consistent with, and complement, the educational opportunities that abound at Calvin." Music is important on campus: the school has five different choral ensembles, an excellent orchestra, and a contemporary Christian ensemble. There are numerous intramural sports, as well as a variety of intercollegiate athletic teams. Arts organizations include a Writer's Guild and a theater group. There is a campus newspaper, *Chimes,* and a literary journal, *Dialogue.* Students participate in a number of political groups, including the College Republicans, College Democrats, even the Calvin Students for Christian Feminism.

Calvin residents aren't so politically predictable as one might think—given the school's theological conservatism. According to online columnist William Norman Gress, about a third of the faculty, and 100 students, issued protests about the Iraq war—which they considered unjust—when President Bush came to speak at the 2005 commencement. This won two professors who led the protest the epithet of "bad Christians" from superhawk radio commentator Sean Hannity.

The city of Grand Rapids offers just enough attractions to be appealing to those from smaller towns and disappointing to those from larger ones. The area of Grand Rapids surrounding Calvin is extraordinarily safe; crime at the school, including the areas bordering campus, is nearly nonexistent.

Calvin has been designated by *The Fiske Guide to Colleges* as one of "America's best value colleges." Costs are below the national average for other four-year private colleges—2004-5 tuition was $17,700 and room and board, $6,185. Calvin offers both need-based and merit-based aid. The average financial aid award in 2004 was $13,200; 61 percent of students receive some aid.

CARLETON COLLEGE

NORTHFIELD, MINNESOTA • WWW.CARLETON.EDU

Educating Carl

Carleton College, a small, private liberal arts college in Northfield, Minnesota, likes to think of itself as an undiscovered gem waiting to be unearthed by a savvy prospector. However, since *U.S. News and World Report* labeled Carleton fifth among "Best Liberal Arts Colleges" in 2005, the school isn't much of a secret. With no graduate school, the college's focus is trained squarely on undergraduate learning; unfortunately, its curricular requirements don't set it apart from hundreds of other schools.

Founded by a group of Congregational churches in the 1800s, Carleton has been coed from the beginning—the first graduating class of 1874 had one man and one woman—and that tradition of Upper Midwestern progressivism is still alive. Says one student, "Carleton is the sort of place where you could walk by your floor lounge at any time and hear a friendly argument or discussion of any political or social issue between students." Carleton is also known for being intimate, if not isolated: Northfield is 45 minutes from Minneapolis, and the winters are long and hard. Perhaps for that reason the school presents itself as a place where nonconformist personalities serve to warm those winters. President Robert Oden, inaugurated in 2002, likes to go fly fishing in such vacation spots as western Iceland. The admissions Web page contains profiles of the school's zaniest students, such as two classmates who started the Carleton Stone Skipping Society, of all things, as a way to reconnect with the soothing childhood experience of tossing pebbles in water. "Many people think of the typical Carl [as Carleton students are known] as being pretty 'granola,' but we're not all vegans walking around in our bare feet when there's no snow on the ground," says one dissident "Carl." Not all, anyway.

At Carleton, students will find an intense intellectual atmosphere and especially good training in the hard sciences. That, plus plenty of Minnesota friendliness, helps take students' minds off the weather.

Academic Life: Rule of threes

Carleton operates on the trimester system. During each 10-week term, students take three courses at a time. The system has its benefits: with only three classes, students can focus more intensely on the topics at hand. But with such short terms, exams are always just around the corner, and some students complain about the calendar's hurried pace. The trimester system does serve a practical purpose—the first trimester ends right before Thanksgiving, and the second doesn't start until after New Year's Day, freeing students—at least those from out of state—from suffering six weeks of frigid Minnesota winter. (It also allows industrious students to earn a little spending money by working seasonal retail jobs all December.) Those who don't take to the cold report that the middle trimester (January to March) requires unusual feats of endurance. Some say they just hibernate in the library until spring.

Among colleges its size, Carleton is also unique for having world-class programs in the natural sciences. The college is usually one of the top liberal arts colleges for sending students on to receive PhDs in the sciences. Its natural science departments' focus on individual lab work even gives Carleton a leg up on most large universities. And the chemistry department is so strong that it propels many students to choose careers in chemistry even when they hadn't been planning on it.

Carleton's distribution requirements are nothing to boast about, however. Carls must complete 10 courses, and students are given relatively free rein to choose, creating either an education based on the classics, a trendy modern one, or some mix of the two. "Students have a choice of courses within these requirements, and I have no doubt that some students leave here with something less than a full exposure to the liberal arts by selecting courses that are a bit lightweight," a faculty member says. "But in general, most students get a solid exposure to the liberal arts, and maintaining the freedom they have to choose courses is important enough that I am willing to let the occasional student slip by with a less than ideal liberal arts experience."

Carleton does impose a Recognition and Affirmation of Difference (RAD) requirement, which is fulfilled by choosing one of a number of RAD–approved courses. Such courses are "centrally concerned with issues and/or theories of gender, sexual orientation, class, race, culture, religion, or ethnicity as these may be found anywhere in the world" and require "reflection on the challenges and benefits of dialogue across differences." Many of these courses are of dubious value, such as "Gender, Sexuality, and Schooling." But other classes sound more worthy, such as "The History of Imperial China." "Basically, you just have to take a humanities class on something other than white Western civilization and you're okay," one student says.

Students view life at Carleton as intellectually intense and its courses as designed to be challenging. "I have never and don't think I will ever encounter as rigorous an academic environment as at Carleton," says one recent graduate. Says a current student, "Instead of grade inflation, grade deflation is almost the norm here." Another recent graduate agrees: "Grade inflation is minimal compared to what I've seen at other schools."

VITAL STATISTICS
Religious affiliation: none
Total enrollment: 1,764
Total undergraduates: 1,764
SAT midrange: 1300–1480
Applicants: 4,700
Applicants accepted: 29%
Accepted applicants who enrolled: 35%
Tuition: $30,501
Room and board: $5,650
Freshman retention rate: 97%
Graduation rate: 87% (4 yrs.), 90% (6 yrs.)
Average class size: 18
Student-faculty ratio: 9:1
Courses taught by graduate TAs: none
Most popular majors: biology, English, economics
Students living on campus: 89%
Guaranteed housing for four years? yes
Students in fraternities or sororities: none

Once a student declares a major, his study gets more structured. English majors are required to take two introductory British literature courses (which cover Chaucer to the Victorians), an introduction to American literature, and literary theory; they can then choose one course in each of four major areas of English.

The best departments at Carleton are the hard sciences and political science. One politics professor says, "In my own field . . . there are more courses whose readings are classic texts than there are at most leading universities." Al Montero of the political science department is "liked by everyone," says a student, and "although his poli-sci intro class is one of the most difficult intros, it is one of the most popular." Mark Krusemeyer in the math *and* music departments; Alison Kettering in art history; Laurence Cooper, Robert Packer, Steven Schier, and Kimberly Smith in political science; and Nathan Grawe and Michael Hemesath in economics are named as some of the college's best teachers. Harry Williams, a history professor, receives high marks from students for outside-the-box courses on everything from early African American journalists to black conservatism.

Classes at Carleton are small. The median class size is 18, and 35 percent of classes have 13 students or fewer. Only extremely popular or introductory classes are ever full. A large class at Carleton consists of 40 students, and no class ever enrolls more than 80. Professors teach all discussion sections and lab sections—Carleton has no graduate school, and therefore no teaching assistants. And while at some schools students never even meet their professors, at Carleton it is not uncommon for students to eat dinner at their houses and play on intramural teams with them. "Faculty were always very open and encouraging; they wanted to see you outside of class," says one recent grad. "The professors are *extremely* approachable," says another. At Carleton, office hours are used for professor-student discussion and for extra help with course material—not for "grade-grubbing."

Formal advising is one of the school's weak points. "Until you choose a major sophomore spring, you have some randomly assigned advisor," one student says. "Mine wasn't too helpful, so I just ended up talking to older students and professors and just figuring it out for myself. The departmental advisors are of course much more helpful." Each entering freshman is assigned a faculty advisor and a "student registration facilitator" to help students choose classes, but students decide how much to rely on them for advice. Since faculty are usually friendly and accessible, students don't have trouble finding wise counsel.

Around 70 percent of students go on to graduate education, most for PhDs instead of MBAs. Since most students are not headed immediately toward Wall Street or the business sector, the competitive preprofessionalism rampant at other colleges is less prevalent at Carleton. "Unlike [the situation] at many other schools, the average Carl competes with herself or himself and not other students," says one student. A faculty member says, "The intellectual curiosity of students at Carleton is one of the institution's greatest strengths. I regularly talk to students outside of class or they send me articles about topics not directly related to class material." Another professor says, "Carleton students seem comparatively unconcerned with grades."

Approximately 65 percent of students study abroad at some point. Many choose Carleton's own international programs, which allow students to take trimesters in Spain, England, China, Mexico, Australia, France, Russia, or Ireland—or join study-abroad programs sponsored by other schools.

Student Life: On the ascetic education of man

Carleton's political environment is sometimes as extreme as its weather. A campus publication once jokingly referred to Carls as "Northern Commies." Conservatives or even moderates are clearly outnumbered—"overwhelmed" says one Carleton student. A professor says, "I have heard stories of how some conservative students hide their politics to avoid losing friends." However, since intellectual debate is one of the few activities available during certain months in Northfield, students find the college more tolerant than many others. "Most of the students and professors are liberal, but there isn't the preachiness that you find at other colleges. Even in liberal classes, I've found that the professors won't stomp on your opinions for being conservative, and the students are able to look past ideological differences," a student says. The Carleton Conservative Union publishes an alternative paper, the *Observer*. The same group has sponsored a "conservative coming-out" cookout on behalf of the worldview that once dared not speak its name. "The college is generally a politically liberal place, but it also values liberalism in the classical sense," a faculty member says. "In recent years there has been a growing public conservative presence."

While the administration can tolerate a lack of conservatives, a lack of racial diversity is quite another thing. In the eyes of the administration, the 19 percent of students who are Asian, Hispanic, Native American, or African American is not enough. "As far as ethnic makeup, it is not as diverse as the college would like," one student says; the administration has apparently had a rough time convincing minority students to attend school in the snowdrifts of Minnesota. The school recently hired a new director of multicultural affairs "to support the academic and social development of students of color." Carleton students already support each others' development; as many students and faculty report, Carleton students tend to get along admirably. "For the most part, people listen to each other's opinions and

---

ACADEMIC REQUIREMENTS

Carleton's distribution requirements are as follows:

- Two courses in arts and literature, which can be satisfied by "Shakespeare I," "Amazons, Valkyries, Naiads, and Dykes," and other courses.
- Two classes in the humanities, like "Introduction to Western Philosophy" or "Environmental Justice."
- Three courses in the social sciences, such as "Breakfast with the *Times*," which uses the *New York Times* as a starting point for teaching economics, or "Principles of Psychology."
- Three courses in mathematics and natural sciences.
- A freshman writing course, culminating in a writing portfolio for faculty review.
- Four terms of physical education. Options range from aikido to modern dance.
- An upper-level class in a foreign language or sufficient scores on standardized tests.

experiences and are accepting of each other," reports a student. "I know people who grew up on poor Minnesota farms and got their books for free as well as those who had a new car every year."

Housing at Carleton invites a certain stoicism. "Some of the housing is quite old, but that only serves to give it character," one student says. "I liked the majority of my accommodations through four years." Almost 90 percent of the student body dwells on campus, and students must apply for an exception to live off campus. There are a variety of "shared interest living areas," such as the Women's Awareness House and the African American Awareness group. Greek houses are banned at Carleton. A housing crunch a few years ago inspired Carleton to build new townhouses, which have become some of the choicer picks for students. (Sophomores generally get the worst housing, since freshmen are coddled and upperclassmen are rewarded for seniority.) One student says, "There is a wide range of quality when it comes to on-campus housing. There are nice dorms and then there are glorified closets." Students with high picks in the housing lottery get the nice dorms or apartments.

The college has no single-sex dorms but does have a few floors designated for men or women only. Carleton is one of the few schools in the country that offers coed bathrooms and dorm rooms, although students do not room with members of the opposite sex unless they request it. The college also has several substance-free housing options, in which students pledge that they will not drink, smoke, or use drugs (while in the building, at least). Choosing the right housing at Carleton is important, since students will see a lot of their rooms from the inside. "Living in the dorm that first year is an experience every freshman should have," a student says. "A majority of friendships are forged during the first few weeks of school when students are staying up late in common areas talking and experiencing life away from home for the first time. As the year passes and it gets colder more of the day is spent indoors." As Carleton's own promotional material admits, a Minnesota winter takes some adjustment for students from almost any other part of the country.

But Carleton students do enjoy the outdoors, especially in the fall and spring. Intramural sports are popular, particularly ultimate Frisbee. "Everyone, I mean everyone, plays Frisbee," says one student. Carleton's intercollegiate ultimate Frisbee teams are excellent and have a large following. Few of Carleton's other intercollegiate teams, which compete in the NCAA Division III, can say the same. Carls go to football games more to see the "Gender Neutral Cheerboys" (Carleton's politically correct and oh-so-tongue-in-cheek pep squad) and the marching band, the "Honking Knights," than to watch the games. For students looking for big-time basketball or football programs, Carleton is obviously the wrong school.

Most popular Carleton activities are of the participatory sort. Students put together their own plays, music groups, and dance groups, to which even novices are generally invited. Other student groups tend to center around the ethnic (the Coalition of Hmong Students, for instance) or the bizarre (e.g., the Reformed Druid society). Students looking for staple activities, though—such as writing for the college newspaper—will have to accept that the small and laid-back nature of the school works against reaching professional quality. The *Carletonian*, for instance, does not even have an updated Web site.

Students report that Carleton is not as cliquish as some other small colleges. One student says, "It's not like going to high school all over again—unless you want it to be, and then you and your 10 friends can have popularity contests while everyone else ignores you."

The school's isolation does limit students' social options. Drinking is often the preferred activity at dorm parties, and students who are of age visit the Northfield bars—all two of them. Nearby St. Olaf College's students ("Oles") come to Carleton on weekends, since St. Olaf's is dry. As for the illegal stuff, "pot is not hidden," as one recent graduate attests. "The school does not enforce strict regulations on drugs and alcohol," says another Carl.

For those yearning for the big city, a shuttle bus takes students the 45 minutes to Minneapolis–St. Paul on weekends. There students can take advantage of Twin Cities attractions, bars, theaters, restaurants, and assorted professional sports teams. For the most part, though, students stay on campus, and prospective students should anticipate a small community where students see familiar faces everywhere. With only 500 students or so in each class, one may grow a little tired of the dating options by senior year.

Freshman orientation is uneventful and "a little long," according to one student, but good for meeting people. Usually, students read a common book during the summer prior to their enrollment and discuss it in small groups once on campus. Most students report that the pre-freshman trips to rugged locales (such as the Boundary Waters) are especially helpful for group bonding and for promoting the individual competence Carleton likes to think it instills.

And of course there are some unique Carleton traditions. The college Web site names some of the main ones, from blowing bubbles at faculty members during opening convocation to playing broomball and going "traying" (using a dining hall tray as a sled) on the snowy hills. The Primal Scream allows students a lung-venting session during exams. Then there's "Schiller," an old bust of the German poet that a select few students get to keep during their time at Carleton. Schiller tends to show up at important events. Every time Schiller appears, all the students cheer—and some of them try to steal it.

Otherwise, there is little crime on campus. In 2003, the school reported three forcible sex offenses, eight burglaries, two arsons, and one stolen car. Slipping drunkenly on the ice seems to be the greatest danger.

Student costs for the 2005 academic year were $36,151, including tuition, room and board, and fees. Aid is available for those who demonstrate a need, but students must present evidence of attempts to get funding from outside sources in order to get

SUGGESTED CORE
1. Classics 112, The Epic in Classical Antiquity
2. . Philosophy 270, Ancient Philosophy
3. Religion 221, Jesus, Paul, and Christian Origins
4. Religion 121, Introduction to Christianity
5. Political Science 251, Modern Political Philosophy
6. English 130, Shakespeare
7. History 120, History of American Society to 1865
8. Philosophy 274, Continental Philosophy

university funding. About half the students who apply for need-based aid receive it. To attract top students, Carleton offers small scholarships to National Merit Scholars, enrolling as many of them as some much larger schools. Carleton also allows families to lock-in current tuition prices years in advance through prepayment. The average recent graduate owes $15,698 in student loans.

UNIVERSITY OF CHICAGO

CHICAGO, ILLINOIS • WWW.UCHICAGO.EDU

Old school

The University of Chicago, one of America's foremost universities, belongs in a class of its own. Other schools also boast students of the highest caliber and a professoriate to match, but the University of Chicago has developed a culture of academic sobriety and commitment to traditional liberal learning that sets it apart from its peers in the Ivy League and elsewhere. Long after most of America's other outstanding institutions of higher education surrendered their rigorous core curriculum requirements, Chicago continues to require its undergraduates to obtain a broad liberal education grounded in the great works of Western civilization, through one of several "core" sequences chosen from a mostly excellent list.

However, the past decade has seen an ongoing struggle within the university over the interdisciplinary core curriculum, and there are signs that the university may not be holding the line against pedagogical and ideological pressures. Tempers have cooled in recent years, and student activism and alumni concern about the core seem to have died down. One student says, "The university has gotten smarter about how to effect the changes they want. When [former president] Hugo Sonnenschein proposed major changes to the core as a whole, it caused near riots. Now [that] the changes are made piecemeal . . . it's much harder to get people worried and up-in-arms about little changes here and there."

It seems that the administration has other concerns too. A professor says, "If I had to characterize the flavor/goals of the current administration, it would certainly be complementary themes: bringing the university back to its Chicago roots—that is, a concern for and interest in the surrounding areas, being a good neighborhood, and reconnecting with the city and its leadership; and diversity—attracting more faculty and students of color/ethnic backgrounds." But despite this emphasis on the D-word, a freshman entering the University of Chicago can obtain something very like the old Common Core experience. There can be no doubt that a Chicago education is a very special product when viewed in the context of the academic marketplace, a product that is becoming increasingly rare and may well be irreplaceable. Attending the University of Chicago would still be an excellent choice for almost any prospective student. We hope that in 10 years we can still say the same.

Academic Life: Subtraction by division

In addition to its reputation for academic excellence, the University of Chicago is well known for offering an especially rigorous and serious scholarly environment at the undergraduate level—almost monastic, some might say—due in part to the proportionately large number of graduate and professional students. Recent growth in the undergraduate population, however, has somewhat lessened this feeling. For most students at the University of Chicago, academics come first, second, and third. The pressure can be intense, but for many prospective students the hyper-intellectuality of the school, along with the Common Core, is one of the university's top selling points. Grade inflation, though minimal, is not unknown at Chicago, nor are frivolous courses, and it is indeed possible for a student to skate through to graduation without taking the most demanding classes. But he would be very much the exception.

> **VITAL STATISTICS**
>
> *Religious affiliation*: none
> *Total enrollment*: 13,400
> *Total undergraduates*: 4,400
> *SAT midrange*: 1290–1430
> *Applicants*: 5,361
> *Applicants accepted*: 62%
> *Accepted applicants who enrolled*: 30%
> *Tuition*: $28,689
> *Room and board*: $8,450
> *Freshman retention rate*: 98%
> *Graduation rate*: 83% (4 yrs.), 90% (6 yrs.)
> *Average class size*: 25
> *Student-faculty ratio*: 4:1
> *Courses taught by graduate TAs*: none
> *Most popular majors*: economics, biology, English
> *Students living on campus*: 66%
> *Guaranteed housing for four years?* yes
> *Students in fraternities*: 12% sororities: 5%

Chicago's Common Core was designed in the 1930s by, among others, Robert Maynard Hutchins, the school's president from 1929 to 1951, and the eminent American sociologist David Riesman. Its purpose was, and still is, to ensure that students matriculating at Chicago are liberally educated regardless of their major. But more than that, the Common Core allowed for the education of students in the manner the university has long been famous for: rigorous, thorough, and critical. It made possible the intellectual environment that separated Chicago from other schools. Whether one went on to concentrate in physics or philosophy or neurology, the Common Core—which even today occupies most of an undergraduate's first two years on campus—ensured a quality of thought other places could only wish for.

Although the Common Core is for many a great attraction to the university, some fear that it is gradually morphing into a set of distribution requirements. The fate of the Western civilization sequence is representative: this three-quarter sequence of the Common Core has been largely replaced by the two-quarter course "European Civilization." (For now, one course in Western civilization is still offered—instead of the former

Chicago is one of the only well-known schools in America whose core curriculum is worthy of the name. The core requirements at Chicago allow some options— almost all of them good. In addition to a major and some electives, students must complete six quarters (total) in three critical areas (students choose to emphasize one of the three):

- Humanities. There are seven humanities sequences from which to choose, not all of them offered in any given quarter. They range from "Greek Thought and Literature" and the highly regarded "Human Being and Citizen" to more modern fare such as "Media Aesthetics: Images, Sound, Text."

- Civilizations studies. Sequences include such area studies as "History of European Civilization," "Judaic Civilization," and "America in Western Civilization." Students may also complete the civilization studies sequence requirement by participating on one of nine study-abroad programs.

10; there are 13 or 14 sections of European civilization.) Defenders of this change say that the new courses allow for the study of classic texts in greater depth, are more focused on the Enlightenment and expansion of Europe, and retain the discussion-based format and historical breadth of the former sequence. But critics fear that this change represents a step away from Chicago's tradition of requiring broad-based humane learning. As Stephen Balch, president of the National Association of Scholars, wrote in the *Chronicle of Higher Education,* "Whatever its strengths, the new sequence is not the same as 'Western Civilization,' because students opting for it will no longer encounter the big picture, from classical antiquity through modernity, so ably provided by the traditional program." One professor counters that students seem to prefer the new arrangement: "After years of declining enrollments, there is now a chronic staffing shortfall because of the increased student demand." In 2004, Chicago introduced a course that meets the civilization requirement without actually introducing students to a major world civilization. Instead, the two-quarter sequence named "Colonizations," according to the university, "approaches the concept of 'civilization' from an emphasis on cross-cultural/societal connections . . . exploring the dynamics of conquest, slavery, colonialism, and their reciprocal relationships with concepts such as resistance, freedom, and independence." Not promising. We certainly can't think *this* a good development.

Another required sequence is in humanities, where the student must select from a disparate array of options— some much better then others. The most academically serious students scoff at the humanities sequence in "Reading Cultures: Collection, Travel, Exchange." According to one professor, this is really a social sciences course that is "in the hands of the multicultural folks." On the other hand, "Human Being and Citizen" remains highly respected. In this sequence, students read the very best works of the Western tradition, beginning with Homer and continuing into the twentieth century. Unfortunately, one professor says that it is increasingly difficult to find teachers for the course who really believe in its implicit philosophy. "It is a great books course, and the humanities faculty would get rid of it if they could, because we read primary sources in this course rather than the secondary sources they're pushing." Other excellent humanities sequences include "Philosophical Perspectives on the Humanities" and "Greek Thought and Literature."

Academic advisors, who typically work with the same students throughout their undergraduate careers, work for the dean of students. While some undergraduates have reported finding the academic advisors helpful, the more common view seems to be that they are either useless or counterproductive. The burden of finding the best classes to take rests upon the shoulders of the student himself. Fortunately, by all accounts professors, and their graduate teaching assistants are readily available to provide assistance with academic questions. In addition to keeping regular office hours, students report that faculty often give out home phone numbers and will arrange to meet with students at whatever time is convenient for them. This accessibility is facilitated by small class sizes; even the core humanities classes are capped in the mid-twenties. Senior faculty teach some large freshmen courses; others are taught by postdoctoral appointees who have yet to obtain a tenure-track position or by graduate students. According to one student, "Some of the best teaching in the college is done by graduate students, particularly those in the Committee on Social Thought, who routinely win the graduate teaching awards."

The University of Chicago is famous for its faculty: more than 70 Nobel Prize winners have been affiliated with the institution in one capacity or another. But the Nobel laureates form only a small portion of Chicago's outstanding faculty, many of whose best professors still teach undergraduate classes. These include Constantin Fasolt, Hanna Gray, and Katy Weintraub of the history department; Paul J. Sally Jr. in mathematics; James Redfield in classical languages and literatures; Charles Lipson, John Mearsheimer, and Nathan Tarcov in political science; Nobel-winner Gary Becker and James Heckman in economics; the philosophy department's Jonathan Lear and Robert Pippin; Leon Kass (currently on leave of absence) and Mark Lilla of the Committee on Social Thought; Amy Kass (also on leave) and Herman Sinaiko in humanities; Ralph Lerner of the social sciences division and the Committee on Social Thought; Bertram Cohler, also of the social sciences division; Michael Fishbane in Jewish studies; Isaac Abella in physics; Jean Bethke Elshtain, Jean-Luc Marion, and David Tracy in religion; Wendy Olmsted, chair of the Fundamentals Program; and a great many more.

Subjects that students may choose for their concentrations are grouped into five "Collegiate Divisions": Biological Sciences, Humanities, New Collegiate, Physical Sci-

REQUIREMENTS (CONT'D)

- **The arts.** Classes here include "Introduction to Art," "Drama: Embodiment and Transformation," and introductions to Western and world music.

  Students also take:

- Six quarters of natural sciences or mathematics, including two quarters of biological sciences, two of physical sciences, and one of math.

- Three quarters of social sciences. Sequences include "Power, Identity, and Resistance," "Self, Culture, and Society," "Democracy and Social Science," "Mind," and "Classics of Social and Political Thought."

- Three quarters of physical education.

- Three or four quarters of a foreign language, although students may demonstrate proficiency through placement testing.

ences, and Social Sciences. We particularly recommend that students who want an intensive liberal arts curriculum (beyond the core) look at one concentration: the New Collegiate's "Fundamentals: Issues and Texts." Students in fundamentals, or "fundies," choose six classic texts to study in detail in light of one overarching question. For example, the question "What is justice?" might be pursued through selected works of Plato, Aristotle, Cicero, Dante, Rousseau, and Marx. Students concentrating in fundamentals write a research paper in their junior year and in their senior year must take a comprehensive exam on all six of the texts they have chosen.

Two other excellent interdisciplinary programs exist outside the New Collegiate Division: the highly eclectic but sophisticated Interdisciplinary Studies in the Humanities (which includes a theater-centered option that includes creative writing and stage production seminars), and "History, Philosophy, and Social Studies of Science and Medicine." The Committee on Social Thought is world famous for the quality of its faculty and students, and for good reason. In the postwar years it served as the home of many refugees from European totalitarianism, and it still carries on the tradition of inquiry associated with famous scholars and writers like Hannah Arendt, Saul Bellow, and Allan Bloom.

Among the social science sequence options, "Classics of Social and Political Thought" and "Self, Culture, and Society" are the best choices. They come closest to "exemplifying the 'old core,'" in the words of one faculty member. For those with an interest in performance, composition, or musicology, "Music in Western Civilization" offers another excellent option.

According to one professor, "The teaching of foreign languages seems to have been much enhanced by the recent multiplication of overseas programs. . . . They are serious academic programs, not fun-and-games abroad."

Not all sciences at Chicago are created equal, so students should be particularly choosey when fulfilling the largest core requirement—the six quarters of natural sciences. "The physical scientists take teaching very seriously" says a faculty member. "They're extra good citizens, have some excellent courses, and don't have any trouble with staffing." Biology, however, is not as reliable, according to another professor. "They regard teaching as a burden. But they still have some very good courses, and they can attract some humanists who come there and find that they like what they see." Thanks to the Common Core, there is a good chance that even students who choose a concentration from the hard sciences will receive a very good liberal education at Chicago. On the flipside, because much of the first two years are dedicated to the Common Core, the University of Chicago may not the ideal institution at which to be a premed student. The university is not, by and large, oriented towards preprofessional training—which, say its defenders, is one of its great strengths. But premed students are able to tend to their prerequisite work in science by counting some of those courses as part of their Common Core. Says one professor, "The college is making special efforts to guide and counsel premed students both in their training and in their preparations for applying to and being interviewed by medical schools."

The political climate at the University of Chicago is more diverse than that at many institutions, and perhaps for that reason more subdued. Arguably, Chicago is among the least politicized campuses in the country. In part that is thanks to the premium placed on the life of the mind at Chicago, which is encouraged by the university's tradition of fostering critical inquiry and discussion. Many specific schools of political thought find representatives on campus, from Lionel Trilling-style liberals to Straussian neoconservatives to more radical types attracted to postmodern thought. At universities across the country, one in 20 students majors in economics. At the University of Chicago, it's one in five. "That by itself," says one professor, "probably gives the place more political balance." The university has, by and large, managed to maintain a civil level of discourse among these various factions—though some at Chicago complain that the various intellectual cliques do not mix it up nearly enough and are too apt to remain within their own circles.

Some departments are more politicized than others. The departments of English, Near Eastern languages and civilizations, and sociology get relatively poor grades in this regard. One professor says that the English department in particular is "full of methodologists and ideologues." Another teacher says that "English is politically correct in a big way. . . . They no longer believe in great texts, but only cultural studies." Students wishing to study literature seriously often take refuge in the fundamentals program highlighted above. One member of the economics department says it is less political than in the past and characterizes the faculty as "heterogeneous, . . . devoted to a wider range of theoretical and empirical issues, including game theory, auction theory, long-term economic growth, etc." Conservative professors can be found in a number of other departments, too, from political science to the Committee on Social Thought. The distribution of such professors throughout the school suggests that political considerations play less of a role in deciding who gets tenure at Chicago than elsewhere. Students report that younger professors and graduate students seem more ideological and less inclined to question their own beliefs than are senior faculty.

Student Life: Talking philosophy

Social life at Chicago is not so different from elsewhere, but it is more subdued and definitely more intellectual. Students do throw parties, and while alcohol does not play a major role at university events, it does in the private revels of many of the students.

"ScavHunt" is a yearly celebration of insanity featuring a list of items to be scavenged—ranging from the bizarre to the sickening. Last year's list of more than 280 items included a bicycle built for 12, a team member's umbilical cord, and an Easy-Bake oven with a Special Edition Sylvia Plath inaction figure. But Chicago undergraduates also attend open lectures in their spare time and talk philosophy in coffeeshops. Whatever the university itself may lack in planned social activities, the city of Chicago amply provides. Students may avail themselves of all that the city has to offer, from the many world-class museums to shopping on the Magnificent Mile, famous blues joints such as Kingston Mines, and beer-soaked Cubs games in the bleachers at Wrigley Field. There are several excellent independent and used bookstores on or near campus.

The architecture of most of the university's academic buildings matches the serious purpose of the college itself, the graceful Gothic buildings impressing upon student and visitor alike the institution's grounding in scholarly traditions dating back to the High Middle Ages. (The university, of course, is not that old. It was founded in 1890 by John D. Rockefeller.) Recently the university has taken to erecting more modern buildings, including a $125 million graduate school of business opened in 2004 and designed by renowned architect Rafael Vinoly; the Gerald Ratner Athletic Center; and the Max Palevsky Residential Commons. A 430,000-square-foot Interdivisional Research Building is scheduled to open in 2005. With Starbuck's, high-end condos, and new landscaping, the university's campus and (once-blighted) Hyde Park neighborhood has probably never looked so posh.

The op-ed pages of the main student newspaper, the *Maroon*, are generally open to contributors from different points of the political compass, although the paper's own editorial line tends to be liberal. Thoughtful conservatives have an outstanding publication of their own, however, in the *Chicago Criterion*, a monthly political magazine. Right-leaning intellectuals should check out the Edmund Burke Society, based at the university's law school, for Oxford-style debates on philosophical topics. Both College Republicans and College Democrats are active on campus. More controversial than national politics are issues pertaining to Chicago's own identity; especially in the battles over the curriculum, students have played an active role—and usually on the side of retaining the Common Core.

Recreational activities on campus can hardly compete with the lures of Chicago, one of America's great cities, but there are many university-sponsored activities, including 19 men's and women's varsity sports teams, 43 intramural clubs, and more than 300 student organizations, including a large number of religious groups. First-year students are required to live in on-campus housing; all 11 dormitories on campus are coed, although single-sex floors are available. Residential students may eat at any of three dining commons or two à la carte locations. The 11 undergraduate residence halls are divided into 38 "houses," which were created to break up the living system into more human-scale, community-oriented units. Resident masters are senior faculty or staff members who live in the larger residence halls. Smaller halls share a resident master or participate in a larger hall's programming. Resident masters organize a program of social and cultural events that may include guest lectures, dinners, residence hall special events, and trips for opera, theater, and sporting events—usually for very low prices. Several halls are a bit of a hike (or a short bus ride) from campus. Broadview, for example, which houses about 200 students, is "a pleasant 15-minute walk from the main quadrangles," according to university literature. Stony Island is a 20-minute walk, but at least it offers apartments for upperclassmen. Hitchcock and Snell halls, among others, are located on campus.

The campus itself and its immediate environs are fairly safe and patrolled frequently by university police (the largest private police force in the city), who can be summoned from any of 300 emergency phones placed strategically around campus. In 2003, the school reported two sexual assaults, two robberies, 41 burglaries, and five stolen cars on campus. Students who are alert have little to fear.

Chicago is expensive but worth it, with 2004–5 tuition at $ 28,689 and room and board at $8,450. Admissions are need-blind, and Chicago guarantees to meet the need of any student it accepts. Some 70 percent of students receive need-based aid. The average student loan debt of a 2002 graduate (the most recent figure available) was $16,124.

FRANCISCAN UNIVERSITY
OF STEUBENVILLE

STEUBENVILLE, OHIO • WWW.FRANCISCAN.EDU

New evangelization

The Franciscan University of Steubenville is virtually unique among Catholic schools. First of all, it stands out, along with a handful of others, by proclaiming an orthodox Catholic commitment to the unity of faith and human knowledge, or *fides et ratio*. As evidence of this commitment, it actually obeys the pope—for instance, when the late Pope John Paul II ordered that Catholic colleges and universities require theologians who teach to possess a *mandatum*, or certificate of doctrinal orthodoxy, from the local bishop. Fewer than one in 10 schools complied. Steubenville was one of the faithful few.

While many of America's most prominent Catholic universities were succumbing to the pressures of secularization and modern disbelief—remaining Catholic in name only—Steubenville was intensifying its mission to be a "Catholic and a Franciscan institution, [and] to promote the moral, spiritual, and religious values of its students."

MIDWEST

601

At the same time, its history over the last 30 years, especially as regards the Catholic charismatic movement, has led to something new—a Catholic/evangelical cross-pollination more reminiscent in style, if not in substance, of such Protestant institutions as Biola or Covenant than of the neo-Scholastic cloisters of the pre–Vatican II Catholic university.

Founded in 1946 by the Franciscan Friars of the Third Order Regular, by the early 1970s Steubenville had become a regional commuter college, undistinguished in its commitment to the Catholic faith or Catholic teaching; its campus life was distressed by moral infirmity, including drug and alcohol abuse. An alumnus describes the school at that time as "a community college with an interesting history." But with the appointment as president of Fr. Michael Scanlan in 1974, things changed. At a time when many colleges were reeling from a decade of student protest, Steubenville, under Fr. Scanlan's magnetic leadership, began to cultivate its present reputation as a locus of charismatic piety and orthodox Catholic education.

Father Scanlan moved Steubenville in another direction not by looking to the educational experts of the day, but by mining the depths of his own Catholic faith and tradition and harnessing the energy of the budding Catholic charismatic renewal. Steubenville University turned toward Catholic tradition as other Catholic schools were turning away; Steubenville became, nearly overnight, a Mecca (or, better, a Lourdes) for conservative Catholics across the nation. It became known for its theological study, charismatic enthusiasm, and evangelical outreach. The "unity of all truth" once described by Cardinal John Henry Newman is, according to the university's mission statement, the beginning and end of an undergraduate education at Steubenville.

Through broadcasts on the Catholic cable network, EWTN, as well as massive student retreats held each summer and the university's growing academic press, this small Catholic school in a town that students call "the armpit of Ohio" now has an international reputation as a center of Catholic education and activism.

Academic Life: The whole truth?

Despite the university's much-talked-about emphasis on the "unity of knowledge," Steubenville has not adopted a genuine core curriculum. Steubenville abandoned its rigorous core program in the 1960s, during its Dark Age; perhaps its unique identity as an institution with Catholic vision and evangelical verve has delayed the maturing of a unified program from disparate origins and goals. In any case, while there has been debate among faculty and administrators as to whether to reinstate a true core, today none exists. Steubenville continues to limp along with the lax, borderline anarchic requirements inherited from the 1960s.

Steubenville's general education requirements are extremely loose—yet no less baffling because of that. Courses offered in the same academic department can and will apply to different core concentrations. Thus, English composition courses are considered communications; English literature courses apply to the humanities requirement. For some reason, American history counts as social science, but European history is considered humanities. One department, anthropology, offers courses applicable to the communications, humanities, natural science, and social science core concentrations. One wonders how anthropology of religion (or, more likely, Christian anthropology) missed being included in the theology requirement.

The two staples of functional literacy, the courses every community college tries to push first—English composition and basic college-level mathematics—are in the same core group (communications) as are a sufficient variety of other options that make them both fairly convenient to avoid, if one wishes. As one professor says, "Students can graduate with only one course" in English literature, which could leave one reading anything from Shakespeare or Milton to Andre Dubus, Larry Woiwode, and Ron Hansen. All worthy authors, but not equally . . . foundational. Either way, a student attending Steubenville, unless he is enrolled in the university's Honors Program, will have to chart his own path, putting together his own "core" liberal arts program before advancing to his major courses. The good news is that it is possible to do that at Steubenville, though it does require planning and thoughtfulness as well as an intellectual maturity that is rare among college freshmen.

Steubenville offers most of the majors that one finds at today's "multiversity"—from philosophy and literature to marketing and sociology—minus, thankfully, areas like feminist, gay/lesbian, or cultural studies. Majors require a minimum of eight upper-level courses. The school also offers an unusual minor in human life studies (essentially pro-life advocacy) and courses in history, literature, political science, and sociology that track church teachings closely.

Students round out their undergraduate programs with electives, which the savvy undergraduate student will use to take the liberal arts courses not required by the university—for example, the history course, "Colonial America," or various courses in the English department. The bachelor of arts degree also requires two courses of a foreign language, but the bachelor of science degree does not.

The Honors Program provides the structure the general curriculum lacks—but only for the university's top students, who must maintain at least a 3.0 GPA to remain in the program. Students can apply for the program after being admitted to the university if they meet certain academic criteria; Steubenville recommends a B-plus high school GPA and an SAT of at least 1100 (according to the old scoring system), which does not exactly amount to academia's highest fence. However, since the program would benefit virtually any Catholic student, that is probably not a bad thing. And while the entrance

VITAL STATISTICS

Religious affiliation:
  Roman Catholic
Total enrollment: 2,374
Total undergraduates: 1,913
SAT/ACT midranges: SAT:
  1040–1270; ACT: 21–27
Applicants: 846
Applicants accepted: 84%
*Accepted applicants who
  enrolled*: 53%
Tuition: $16,070
Room and board: $5,350
Freshman retention rate: 84%
Graduation rate: 80% (4 yrs.),
  88% (6 yrs.)
Average class size: 22
Student-faculty ratio: 15:1
*Courses taught by graduate
  TAs*: none
Most popular majors:
  theology, education,
  business
Students living on campus:
  64%
*Guaranteed housing for four
  years?* no
*Students in fraternities or
  sororities*: not reported

While most of the courses at Steubenville are good to excellent, the arrangement of its requirements is less Roman than Byzantine (and we don't mean "iconic"). For some reason, mathematics and drama are considered part of one core group—along with foreign languages, computer courses, and English composition. Courses in the same department frequently apply to different core groups. As a result, one could emerge from Steubenville with a sound liberal education—or as a semi-schooled pious dilettante. The choice is the student's. And it shouldn't be.

Students must complete:

- Five courses in communications. Courses that qualify include English composition, foreign languages, speech, drama, mathematics (including statistics), computer science, and some music courses. One may choose anything here from "Elementary Applied Algebra" to "Critical TV Viewing."

criteria may not be exactly stunning, the program itself is very good. Students take a chronological sequence of courses covering the great works of Western civilization. The classes consist of small-group seminars, encouraging students to actively participate in their education rather than having information spoon-fed to them. Honors seminars include the following: "Early and Classical Thought," "Later Classical Thought," "The Early Fathers," "Medieval Thought," "The Renaissance," "The Enlightenment," "The Nineteenth Century," and "The Twentieth Century." In almost all the courses, students read primary texts; in "Later Classical Thought," for instance, students read Plato, Aristophanes, Aristotle, Plautus, Terence, Virgil, Plutarch, Cicero, Seneca, Lucretius, and Tacitus. The course on the twentieth century features works by C. S. Lewis, T. S. Eliot, and G. K. Chesterton.

The selection of authors and periods covered in the Honors Program is impressive, and students complete almost all of their general education requirements via the program; indeed, the school might be well-advised to institute its strictures as a universal requirement. Steubenville students who are not enrolled in the Honors Program can use it as a model when selecting their own classes. Although some complain about the lack of academic rigor across the board at Steubenville, the school does provide several opportunities for good students to challenge themselves. Some academic programs allow students to take graduate-level courses during their senior year.

The theology department at Steubenville has long been highly regarded, attracting a number of well-known professors and an enthusiastic and sizable number of majors. Students who major in theology have nearly every semester planned for them. As freshmen, they take "Foundations of Catholicism" and "Christian Moral Principles." Other required courses are "Principles of Biblical Study" (a two-semester course), "Theology of the Church," "Theology of Christ," and "Sacraments," in addition to several departmental electives. One student says that Professor Scott Hahn has made the theology department one of the most recognized departments at the university. Other excellent professors there include Patricia Donohue-White and Regis Martin.

Elsewhere in the university, the level of academic rigor varies by department, according to a recent alumnus. This student majored in philosophy and theology and found his philosophy courses much more rigorous than his theology classes, with some exceptions. Indeed, the philosophy program is considered to be particularly strong, though some see it as "rather disjointed." John Crosby, Patrick Lee, and John White are considered notable scholars and fine teachers in this department. Other good teachers at Steubenville include James Gaston, Kimberly Georgedes, and Fr. Conrad Harkins in history; Douglas B. Lowry in economics; Benjamin Alexander and Justyna Braun in English; and Stephen Krason in political science. The classics, political science, and history departments are also among the university's top programs.

The biology program has fallen some since its beginnings, but laboratories and equipment in the recently built Saints Cosmas and Damian Science Hall have helped deflect criticism that the school is only concerned with the liberal arts. The university recently added a more rigorous bachelor of science degree (the biology department had previously only offered a BA). The nursing program also is good.

Each year about 100 students attend classes at Franciscan's campus in Gaming, Austria. What makes this program especially attractive is that the cost of tuition, room, and board in Austria is the same as at the Steubenville campus. This trip exposes idealistic young Americans to one of the oldest and grandest sites of Catholic civilization. One student says the program "was a highlight of my undergraduate experience."

One of the greatest benefits of attending Steubenville, students say, is the quality of faculty-student interaction. Professors, not graduate students, teach all classes. Unfortunately, however, the university does not require students to build these relationships with their professors through advising, and the formal advising program is "a rather loose one," says one student. "Students are given a formal advisor only to sign their class schedules each semester and to ensure that they will graduate on time. Beyond that, advising is left relatively open." Another student says that while one of his advisors had him map out his course choices several years in advance, he had another advisor who "barely took the time to read my course schedule." The good news is that most faculty members are more than willing to assist students who put forth the effort to seek them out. "Most of the professors who teach here do so because of the university's mission

REQUIREMENTS (CONT'D)

- Five courses in humanities chosen from departments such as art, European history, literature, philosophy, or theology. One course is required from these three areas: history, literature, and philosophy. Choices here include "Dante's Divine Comedy," two Shakespeare courses, and "Contemporary Christian Fiction."
- Two courses in natural sciences. These come from biology, physics, chemistry, and physical anthropology. One specially worthy course here is "Human Embryology."
- Two social science courses, selected from American history, political science, economics, psychology, and sociology. Options range from "History of the United States" to "Catholic Political Thought."
- Two theology courses, chosen from courses like "The Trinity," "The Sacraments," "The Catechumenate and RCIA," and "Youth Ministry I."

and their . . . desire to mentor students with the same religious and ideological convictions," a philosophy student says. "Mentoring students is therefore one of the things they like most about their jobs."

Some observers inside and outside the university claim that academic rigor at Steubenville has been compromised by the university's commitment to charismatic Catholicism. "Students go there primarily because of its evangelical zeal and missionary spirit, and only secondarily because of its intellectual reputation," says a recent alumnus. "The result is that the university, I think, tries to accommodate these students while providing for more rigorous academic opportunities for those so inclined." While Steubenville may want to increase the level of academic rigor, says the student, "the university seems conscious of the fact that it cannot make such changes too quickly without sending students into shock."

Some students and faculty have even complained that in certain cases students' enthusiasm for Catholic causes—pro-life work, missionary service, and evangelism—hinders their academic performance. "Some of the students are much more concerned about being active in missions than they are in attending academic conferences, meeting various secular and national leaders," a student says. That the politics and academics at Steubenville reflect a Catholic and evangelical zeal should come as no surprise, as this is written into the very mission of the university; religious fervor is precisely the reason many students choose Steubenville. The mission statement reads, in part, "Through academic life and co-curricular programs, the university promotes the ongoing and deepening of life in the Lord Jesus Christ and in the church." Since that pretty much describes the founding mission of Salamanca, the Sorbonne, Oxford, and Cambridge, it's nice to know that at least a few schools in Christendom are still interested in doing the same.

Student Life: Road to glory

Steubenville students tend to have a considerable and well-justified fondness for their school. Although the university may fall short in providing a coherent core curriculum that binds students together intellectually, students usually do form strong spiritual bonds through their common faith. "The spiritual growth that one gets is by far the best thing here at Steubenville," a student says. "There are some who don't grow, but the atmosphere encourages holiness and sound morals, which can only be helpful to academics and in putting future life choices in perspective." The university provides dozens of opportunities for students to grow in their Catholic faith. One student says, "These are simply too numerous to go into [in] any detail." The university has three daily masses, daily confession, many other daily liturgical activities, and larger liturgical (and generally charismatic) events on the weekends. A centralized volunteer office called Works of Mercy helps students connect with a number of service groups, including prison ministry, homeless ministry, and pro-life outreach.

With a few exceptions, unmarried students are required to live on campus for the first three years of college, a policy that is "rooted in the university's commitment to build a sense of Christian community on campus," according to the housing Web page. Still, only 64 percent of the student body lives on campus. All dormitories are single sex and mixed by class. Each residence hall has a small chapel for prayer and monthly mass. Since 1974, the school has fostered a "household system," by which (in principle) any group of three or more students (of the same sex) could draw up a constitution of daily and spiritual life, as a stimulus for living in Christian community. Over 20 such groups exist on campus today, and the system appears to be thriving, although some students and, especially, alumni (who tend to retain an intense interest in life at the alma mater) have expressed concern about increasing intervention in household organization and administration by the campus Office of Student Life.

Steubenville sits in an isolated setting on a high plateau overlooking the Ohio River—think Rust Belt, or think *The Deer Hunter,* which was filmed nearby. But this does not mean that students have trouble filling up their free time. "College life in Steubenville is fun, so long as you go to Pittsburgh—45 minutes away," one student says. "Many students go camping here, too. There are ways to have a blast. And there are plenty of enthusiastic people to have fun with." Another writes, "Some students go to other people's houses off campus, some stay on campus, which I think can't hurt. . . . The campus is quite nice, and there are lots of things to do." In fact, some students (particularly those who plan to study for the priesthood) find campus social life pervasive—even overwhelming, as the close-knit community and shared values of the students foster easier communication and tighter bonds than would likely be found in the alcohol-tempered alienation of, say, a large state school. "People are so enthusiastic about being together—you could be doing something every night, if you let yourself," one student says.

As one might expect, many of the school's extracurricular clubs and activities reflect the Catholic and charismatic nature of the university. Even the name of the campus coffeeshop is a religious pun: "Heavenly Grounds." A student-run, all-male singing group dedicated to the Catholic Church's new evangelization is popular and holds competitive auditions each year. The Baconian Society, the university's highest honor society, (named after the thirteenth-century syncretistic philosopher Roger Bacon) meets regularly. Students interested in business and economics may become members of the Free Enterprise Club, in which students compete against other Ohio colleges in developing programs that foster a better understanding of the workings of the market economy. The largest organization on campus, Human Life Concerns, discusses and supports issues that affect the sanctity of human life.

SUGGESTED CORE
1. English 209, World Epics
2. Philosophy 311, Ancient Greek Philosophy
3. Theology 102, Introduction to Scripture
4. Theology 302, Early Christian Life and Thought *and* Philosophy 312, Medieval Philosophy
5. Political Science 292, Political Philosophy II
6. English 324, Shakespeare's Histories and Comedies *or* English 325, Shakespeare: The Tragedies and Tragi-Comedies
7. History 345, America: From Independence to Civil War 1776–1860
8. Philosophy 316, Kant and Later Modern Philosophy

MIDWEST

607

Parents need not worry that their child's faith will be undermined at Franciscan by speakers, plays, or other events. For example, in 2002 the university hosted, among many other programs, the Catholic Writers Conference, a Priestly and Religious Vocations Awareness Fair for students, and the Catholic Women's Conference, which featured Patti Mansfield, a leader in the Catholic charismatic revival movement. In 2005, as the Jesuit Fordham University was mounting *The Vagina Monologues,* Steubenville hosted *You're a Good Man, Charlie Brown.*

The greatest advantage of attending Steubenville, one student says, "is its conservative environment." Upon further reflection, though, the student adds, "This is also a potential problem because when kids graduate from here, when they are challenged by other philosophies and ideas, I don't know if they will be able to respond adequately to attacks."

Steubenville takes a keen interest in the value of health and sportsmanship, but unlike many similarly sized schools, it has not deluded itself or its alumni into thinking that it needs to cram a 60,000-seat pleasure dome with boisterous fans each weekend in order to be considered a legitimate center of higher education. Quite the opposite: Steubenville has no varsity teams at all. Instead, students compete against area colleges and universities on club teams in rugby, baseball, volleyball, basketball, cross country, and soccer. There are also plenty of intramural sports, like ultimate Frisbee, flag football, volleyball, and basketball.

Crime is infrequent in rural Steubenville, though it has increased recently. In 2003, there were two aggravated assaults and 19 burglaries. The university offers safety workshops and provides a safety escort service to and from various campus locations after dark.

Among private universities, Steubenville is not especially expensive, with 2004–5 tuition set at $16,070, and room and board at $5,350.

GRINNELL COLLEGE

GRINNELL, IOWA • WWW.GRINNELL.EDU

Question authority

Founded in the little town of Grinnell on the prairies of Iowa in 1846, Grinnell College (originally Iowa College) is named for Josiah Bushnell Grinnell, an abolitionist minister. The college was founded, in its words, to educate students "for the different professions and for the honorable discharge of the duties of life." It began as an institution that was self-consciously progressive (in the positive sense). Grinnell was, in fact, the first college west of the Mississippi to grant a bachelor's degree to (and one of the first to admit) both black students and women; in antebellum days the town of Grinnell served as a stop on the Underground Railroad. Grinnell went on to play a sizable role in the Social Gospel movement, which elevated political action over the preaching of doctrine.

The college's tradition of political engagement has continued with a strong emphasis on community service. More than 350 students participate in 20 volunteer programs. It can certainly be said that with regard to its self-conscious, if not self-righteous, radicalism, Grinnell has displayed admirable consistency over the years. Today it has a reputation as a place where granola-crunchers and hardcore lefties of all varieties feel particularly comfortable. (Think "Swarthmore West.") And Grinnell takes the old bumper-sticker slogan, "Question Authority," quite seriously: Priding itself on a system of open curriculum and self-governance, Grinnell refuses to use its authority to require its students to take more than a single specific course.

For students with the motivation and intellectual preparation to give structure to their own educational careers, or at least to seek out worthy advice, there is an excellent liberal arts education to be had at Grinnell. But as it says on those mail-order toys: "You get to put it together." The faculty is strong, the students bright, the community close, the location bucolic—and the $1.2 *billion* endowment is the largest per student in the country. If a student can live with Grinnell's politics, he could do much worse than this little college on the prairie.

VITAL STATISTICS

Religious affiliation: none
Total enrollment: 1,556
Total undergraduates: 1,556
SAT/ACT midranges: SAT V: 640–760, M: 650–730; ACT: 28–32
Applicants: 2,970
Applicants accepted: 51%
Accepted applicants who enrolled: 29%
Tuition: $25,820
Room and board: $6,870
Freshman retention rate: 93%
Graduation rate: 81% (4 yrs.), 88% (6 yrs.)
Courses with fewer than 20 students: 63%
Student-faculty ratio: 9:1
Courses taught by graduate TAs: none
Most popular majors: social sciences, biology, English
Students living on campus: 88%
Guaranteed housing for four years? yes
Students in fraternities or sororities: none

Academic Life: Recommend it, and they will come

Whatever curricular course they choose, Grinnell students are expected to study hard. "There are a few less serious classes, but not many," a science major says. "The most common such courses are in science for non-science majors (such as physics for poets). For some people these classes are actually challenging, but there are a fair number of students who take them because they want a class that will not be so time-consuming." Another student says that "the courseload here is extremely rigorous and requires excellent time-management skills; I personally have close to five hours of homework each night, which is about the average here."

The only course the college requires by name of all students is a first-year tutorial. It is then left to the curricula in the various majors to impose a little structure on students' education; however, some majors have serious requirements and others allow inordinate flexibility. English majors, for instance, must take eight courses in all, but only one is a set course (in English literature through the eighteenth century). After that, English majors must choose either the second introductory semester or a course in "Postcolonial Literatures." English students also take one course in American literature and must show proficiency in a foreign language—something that ought to be one of the general education requirements, if Grinnell had any. What students read and study in these courses varies according to each professor's fancy. However, one syllabus for "Traditions of Literature II," a course that covers the Romantics to modernism, reveals that students study traditional fare: Wordsworth, Yeats, Byron, and Dickens, with no heretofore oppressed voices or secondary sources.

In the Grinnell history major, students must complete eight upper-division courses within the department. The department recommends but does not require that students choose courses in the areas of United States, European, and non-Western history, as well as one course in preindustrial history. So a history major could (though he probably wouldn't) graduate without ever reading the Constitution. The department also recommends (sensing a theme here?) that students reach proficiency in a foreign language and in quantitative analysis, both of which it deems "essential for serious study of history." Again, course content depends on the faculty member. A basic course in American history includes the following readings: *The Narrative of Frederick Douglass*; *Tituba, Reluctant Witch of Salem*; and *For Cause and Comrades: Why Men Fought in the Civil War*. And while students don't read primary sources such as the *Federalist Papers* or the works of John Locke, a book on the founders' attitudes towards slavery, *Jefferson's Pillow: A Black Patriot Confronts the Myths of the Founding Fathers*, is required reading.

By now the Grinnell strategy should be clear: recommend but don't require—even if the course is considered essential. The vast majority of students will follow the recommendations anyway, but no one will resent them as they would the imposition of requirements. Or so goes the theory. This allows the school to defuse administration-student tensions, to avoid being cast in the role of an "authority," and to allow students, many of them teenagers, to maintain a feeling of complete independence. It is not a strategy wholly without merit. But it leaves plenty of room for error.

Students say that they are encouraged by their advisors not to be too narrow in their selections and to take courses from various academic disciplines. "It is rarely a problem that anyone graduates from Grinnell without meeting these recommendations," a senior political science major says. Another student says, "Academic advising here is excellent, as advisors give very sound advice to students on what courses to take and also help in the career preparation of students." Still, students retain great latitude in their study options. "Students here have a great deal of freedom in choosing their courses," one student says. "So it is possible to be anywhere on the spectrum from extremely focused to as broad as possible." A professor says, "Transcript analysis has shown that about 85 percent of Grinnell graduates have a balanced liberal arts program. Thus, the question arises for the faculty; do we want to legislate requirements in order to 'catch' the other 15 percent? So far, the answer has been 'no.'"

At Grinnell, 63 percent of all classes contain fewer than 20 students, and only 1 percent of courses enroll more than 50 students. One-quarter of all classes have fewer than 10 students, and the student-faculty ratio is 9 to 1. And because Grinnell is exclusively an undergraduate institution, there are no graduate teaching assistants. Thus, Grinnell provides students with small classes and close interaction between faculty and students. In fact, according to one administrator, there is almost a master/apprentice relationship between professors and students, especially in the junior and senior year, when it is not uncommon for students to publish papers and attend conferences with their teachers. "Professors are very accessible," a senior says. "All of them have regular office hours, and if a student is unable to make them, almost all professors are willing to set up some other appointment." Another student says, "If one needs to meet a professor, it's usually done the same day. The professors here know everyone in their classes by name, usually by the second day of class." For most faculty members, teaching is a clear priority over research or publishing. One student says that most teachers conduct research during the summers so that during the academic year they can focus on . . . teaching.

ACADEMIC REQUIREMENTS

Grinnell makes many recommendations to students, but few demands. Only one, actually:

- First-year tutorial. The heart of Grinnell's liberal arts program, and the only course that is required of all students, this seminar is limited to 12 students per section. A four-credit course taken in the first semester, the tutorial is not a core course, since students can choose from a wide-ranging list of topics such as "Yeats and Joyce," "Baseball," and "The Myth of the Middle Class." The course is meant to introduce students to what Grinnell expects of them by way of reading, writing, and speaking at the college level. The tutorial usually culminates with a research project. The professor with whom a student takes the tutorial also serves as his advisor until the student declares a major, when he gets a new faculty advisor from his major department. Beside the tutorial, the only requirements students face are those set by their majors. Otherwise, they must simply complete a total of 124 hours of coursework.

At all levels of the curriculum, Grinnell College students receive an education rooted in active experience. For example, students in archaeology participate in "knap-ins," where they "flint knap" (shape stones into arrowheads and other prehistoric tools). Students studying classical Greek might spend a year in Athens visiting museums, libraries, national monuments, and archaeological digs. In fact, nearly 60 percent of Grinnellians study off campus, usually abroad, for a semester. Study of international issues receives great emphasis at Grinnell, with strong interdisciplinary concentrations and a new Center for International Studies.

Students name the following professors as some of the best on campus: Michael Cavanagh in English; Charles Duke in physics; Brad Bateman in economics; Bruce Voyles in biology; George Drake and Sarah Purcell in history; Robert Grey, Ira Strauber, and Barbara Trish in political science; and David Campbell in environmental studies. The best departments—biology, history, and English—are also among the most popular. The most politicized areas of study are Grinnell's 12 interdisciplinary concentrations, including Africana studies, gender and women's studies, and global development studies.

More religious or conservative students will sometimes feel uncomfortable in the Grinnell classroom. For example, the history department's "Collapse of the Eurocentric World Order" course uses Leninist theory to examine the history of the twentieth century. But the good news is that professors generally try to keep their politics outside of the classroom. One conservative student says that, although both students and faculty are "pretty far left," most of his professors "have been very good about teaching material from a wide range of viewpoints, many of which they disagreed with." He says, "The professors I've had also have always made it clear when they are talking about something they personally believe" as opposed to established facts. Another student says, "Professors have told me personally they enjoy classes where conservatives are present, as it makes for a better discussion. I have never heard of any professors discriminating against students on the basis of their political beliefs." On the other hand, many conservatives may find it easier to keep their opinions to themselves on this very liberal campus.

Student Life: No, it's Iowa

Grinnell is particularly keen on racial and cultural diversity. Around 13 percent of the student population is a member of some minority, but Grinnell has recently been taking significant steps to increase minority faculty presence as well. The college is a member of the Consortium for a Strong Minority Presence, whose main goal is to help minority scholars land faculty positions at top-notch liberal arts schools. The Office of Multicultural Affairs lists nine student organizations for self-described minorities, including the Coalition of Anti-Racist Whites (CARW) and Queer People of Color (QPOC). The real minorities on campus, though, are the conservatives. The president of the College Republicans says, "We have nearly 20 people on our mailing list, which is kind of amazing given the very liberal leanings at this school." However, according to its Web site, the Grinnell College Republicans (whose mission is to "ensure the conservative voice is heard amidst the sea of liberal propaganda") recently became affiliated with the National College Republicans and "has been growing rapidly ever since." Another student says that at Grinnell, "liberals feel very comfortable. Conservatives probably feel very out of place. Sometimes liberalism here feels a little like anticon-servatism rather than its own set of beliefs."

Technically, all Grinnell students are required to live on campus, but each year about 15 percent of the student body receives special permission to live elsewhere. Most of the college's dormitories house fewer than 100 students, and students can choose to live on either coed or single-sex floors; no dorms are entirely single sex. Some residence halls have coed bathrooms, but a housing official says that hallmates vote at the beginning of the year on whether to have coed bathrooms—and if even one student objects, bathrooms remain single sex. Grinnell does not offer coed dorm rooms. Nonsmoking dorms are available, and since the fall of 2004, the college also has been offering a substance-free residence hall. Most halls are locked at 10 p.m. and do not reopen until 6 a.m., but students can always enter by way of electronic access cards. To ease overcrowding and improve older facilities, the college recently opened four new residence halls. Grinnell has no Greek system.

The college Web site lists more than 160 student organizations, from the Beard and Mustache Society, to Habitat for Humanity, to Grinnellians for the Advancement of Sexual Pleasure, which, prompted by the Feminist Action Coalition's widely successful masturbation workshop, recently hosted a seminar on sex toys. There are also a number of other student movements dealing with racism, economic disparity, and cultural diversity. The Stonewall Resource Center (SRC) is a "confidential and safe space to serve the campus's gay, lesbian, bisexual, and transgender community and allies." In fact, Grinnell's whole campus is a "safe space" for these students, whose groups (along with other student organizations) receive considerable support from the college. On its Web page, SRC links to five pertinent student groups at Grinnell: Stonewall Coalition (an umbrella group), Grinnellians Escalating AIDS Response (GEAR), a Coming Out Group (a support group for students "questioning their sexual identity"), Queer People of Color, and Bilnc (a student group for bisexual students).

The first intercollegiate football and baseball games west of the Mississippi were played in Grinnell, and the home teams won. Today, the Grinnell Pioneers and its NCAA Division III athletic program field 20 varsity teams in the Midwest Athletic Conference. The college also has a well-developed intramural program and club sports for intercollegiate competition, the most popular of which are football, rugby, and ultimate Frisbee. The college has demolished its old gym and is constructing a new one, with the first phase due to be completed in early 2005. In fact, there has been a recent

SUGGESTED CORE
1.–3. Humanities 101-I, The Ancient Greek World *and* Humanities 102-II, Roman and Early Christian Culture
4. Religious Studies 213, The Christian Tradition (*closest match*)
5. Philosophy 264, Political Theory II
6. English 121, Introduction to Shakespeare
7. History 111, American History I
8. Philosophy 234, Nineteenth-Century Continental Philosophy

flurry of building projects on campus. In addition to the new physical education facilities and dorms, Grinnell has also opened a new admissions building and a science center. A campus center with a restaurant, office space, post office, craft workshops, and dining hall is in the works as well. Perhaps as a physical monument to the college's commitment to diversity, Grinnell's oval-shaped campus is punctuated by varied architectural styles. Goodnow Hall, the college's turn-of-the-century library, is Romanesque; today, the refurbished building houses the school's anthropology department. Steiner Hall, a Greek Revival building, houses classrooms and faculty offices. Just north of Steiner Hall lies the structure that "defines the very character of Grinnell College as a liberal arts institution"—the neo-Gothic Herrick Chapel, which reflects the school's missionary roots. The college now uses it for both religious services and secular events. The campus also includes prominent Tudor, modern, and Victorian buildings.

As a small college in a small town, Grinnell is closely integrated into its local community. The college lies in the center of town between Park Street and East Street. A railroad runs right through campus. Students gather regularly at the town gazebo, located adjacent to campus, to engage in the protest *du jour*. The college would like to strengthen its ties to the town even further. It hosts "Town and Gown" events several times each year to encourage students and employees to interact more with the Grinnell townsfolk. Students pay an activities fee along with tuition, that funds campus events such as Disco, the Titular Head Festival (a film festival), the Mary B. James (a cross-dressing party), Waltz (a campus-wide formal), and performances by artists such as the Russian National Ballet and the Prague Chamber Orchestra.

Grinnell is a pretty safe place—like most of Iowa. In 2003, the school reported two forcible sex offenses, 14 burglaries, one stolen car and five arsons on campus. Between 2001 and 2003, the school reported only one liquor-law arrest, but this is surely just a matter of lax enforcement. Drug use among students is frequent and unhidden. Over the same three-year period, 27 referrals were made to campus disciplinary bodies regarding drug use. In 1998, the college created the safety and security department, but it relies on the local police force for serious cases.

Tuition and fees for 2004–5 were $25,820, with an additional $6,870 for room and board. Grants and scholarships form the bulk of Grinnell's financial aid, which is awarded primarily on the basis of need and is not considered in admissions decisions. In 2002–3, Grinnell allotted approximately $20 million to scholarships, grants, and other aid. Over $15 million of that was gift aid.

HILLSDALE COLLEGE

HILLSDALE, MICHIGAN • WWW.HILLSDALE.EDU

On its own

As its motto proclaims, Hillsdale College has been "educating for liberty" since 1844. The college was established by Free Will Baptists but has always been officially nonsectarian. Hillsdale was the first American college founded on the principle of nondiscrimination against blacks and women. The college has a tradition of standing strong against the prejudices of its age and of articulating an integrated vision of what it means to be liberally educated. During World War I, the college successfully resisted an order from the federal government to racially segregate its Army ROTC unit. In 1975, when the government sought to impose racial quotas in admissions and hiring and to collect statistics on the racial composition of student bodies, the administration remained true to its independent tradition and went to court. After the Supreme Court decided in 1985 that any college enrolling even one student who accepted federal financial aid was susceptible to federal micromanagement, Hillsdale responded by refusing all federal funding. Since then, the college has successfully raised money to provide private financial aid for its students, including need- and merit-based scholarships, and in the last two decades, Hillsdale has transformed itself from a party school into a genuine liberal arts college with a national following.

According to its mission statement, "The college considers itself a trustee of modern man's intellectual and spiritual inheritance from the Judeo-Christian faith and Greco-Roman culture, a heritage finding its clearest expression in the American experiment of self-government under law." The school is thus conservative in the sense that it seeks to transmit the Western heritage to its students, and that it does so through a rigorous liberal arts curriculum. But Hillsdale is also a politically conservative school, as its programs, institutes, publications, and the make-up of its student body attest. If that's not your cup of tea, please turn the page—there are *plenty* of other schools from which you can choose.

VITAL STATISTICS
Religious affiliation: none
Total enrollment: 1,230
Total undergraduates: 1,230
SAT midrange: 1150–1380
Applicants: 907
Applicants accepted: 77%
Accepted applicants who enrolled: 43%
Tuition: $16,800
Room and board: $6,700
Freshman retention rate: 85%
Graduation rate: 61% (4 yrs.), 69% (6 yrs.)
Average class size: 21
Student-faculty ratio: 11:1
Courses taught by graduate TAs: none
Most popular majors: business, social sciences, biology
Students living on campus: 86%
Guaranteed housing for four years? yes
Students in fraternities: 35% *sororities*: 45%

Academic Life: The long view

Hillsdale presents its students with an impressive core curriculum, along with other requirements:

- Two semesters of "Rhetoric and the Great Books." Students study literature from the ancient world (Plato, Aristotle, the Bible) up through the twentieth century, along the way reading authors such as Shakespeare, Cervantes, Voltaire, Rousseau, Goethe, Dostoevsky, Kafka, T. S. Eliot, Camus, and Samuel Beckett. Except for a basic writing handbook, students read primary sources.
- A course in the physical sciences.
- A course in the biological sciences.
- "Western Heritage to 1600."
- A course on American history.
- A class on the U. S. Constitution.

Hillsdale's commitment to the Western heritage and to a rigorous liberal arts education is most fully expressed in its core curriculum. In fact, Hillsdale's curriculum is so demanding that some faculty are concerned about the attrition rate of students who arrive ill-prepared. A major effort has been made to improve retention. Still, about 15 percent of freshmen do not return for their second year, and nearly 30 percent of those who begin college at Hillsdale do not graduate in six years. The students who stay, however, report that they enjoy the core curriculum; after all, it's what attracted most of them, and its compelling contents are taught by dedicated faculty. One student says the core curriculum instills "a deeper passion for a greater understanding of knowledge, truth, virtue, and character." This passion is recognized and valued even in the "real world"—98 percent of Hillsdale graduates gain employment or admittance to graduate school within six months of receiving their degrees.

The college's commitment to its educational vision is less strong in the natural sciences, insiders report, noting a tension between advanced technical studies and integrated liberal education. In our view, the principal shortcoming of Hillsdale's core curriculum is that it does not require more training in philosophy and theology. But civic religion is not neglected; recently, the college added a course on the U.S. Constitution to its core, making it one of only five colleges in the country to require study of our founding document—and three of those are military service academies.

Hillsdale offers 25 majors in the humanities and natural sciences, six interdisciplinary majors, and eight preprofessional programs. Students generally focus on majors in their junior and senior years, after they have completed the requirements of the core curriculum. The chemistry, biology, English, history, classics, and political science programs are particularly strong, and professional and preprofessional programs like business, prelaw, and premed are popular—perhaps too popular, according to some faculty. Even at this liberal arts school, some students are more interested in their future careers than they are in learning for learning's sake. But one student notes that "business majors take the same core as any other major, and thus come out able to think, speak, and write in a more coherent fashion than most business majors from other schools."

Majors in political economy and American studies are also strong—a rare thing at an American college. Christian studies, an interdisciplinary program, is exceptionally fair and balanced. The department's Web page says the program's "uniqueness lies in its stress on a thorough and appreciative knowledge of the biblical and theological elements woven into the culture and imagination of Western civilization and in its attempt to interpret man and society from the perspective of the Judeo-Christian tradition." Students majoring in the discipline begin with three core courses in the Bible and theology, then go on to take pertinent courses in various departments, such as a history of the Reformation and classes in "Christianity and Politics," "Humanistic and Christian Psychology," and "The Philosophy of Religion."

The classics department has recently witnessed a renaissance: surging enrollment in Latin classes (more than 20 percent of a recent freshman class enrolled in Latin 101) required the hiring of a third full-time faculty member in that department. The music program is also burgeoning, spawning many musical groups on campus.

For those who aspire to study abroad, Hillsdale offers programs at the Universität des Saarlandes in Germany; Oxford University; St. Andrews in Scotland; and summer schools in Würzburg, Tours, Seville, and Regent's College in London. Hillsdale also sponsors a program through which students can take internships in politics or journalism for credit in Washington, D.C.

Students also choose one elective each in philosophy/religion (either "Introduction to Philosophy" or "Introduction to Western Religion"); literature/classical studies (three options here—"Greek Civilization," "Roman Civilization," or "Greek Mythology"); the fine arts, including history of art (ancient or recent), music, and theater; and the social sciences.
- A foreign language (for those pursuing BA degrees).
- Two courses in "physical activities."
- Two seminars chosen from offerings of the Center for Constructive Alternatives.

Hillsdale reports a less-than-selective 77 percent acceptance rate. It's worth noting, as one alumnus told us, that "because of the kind of place Hillsdale is, many students who might be rejected simply do not apply." The recently reinvigorated Honors Program provides an elite experience for students willing to undertake a challenge. Honors students must take seminars in their sophomore and junior years and complete a thesis during their senior year to present before the college community. Honors students enjoy discussions with speakers brought in by the Center for Constructive Alternatives (see below), special sessions with faculty members to discuss course readings, and cultural excursions to nearby urban centers. They are also encouraged to undertake community service projects. About 30 students are accepted into the Honors Program each year, mostly as freshmen.

One student says, "The faculty members are wonderful, with rare exceptions, both inside and outside of the classroom. They are professional but accessible and very helpful with students beyond their formal duties in class." Another student says, "I've had class in professors' houses, been to parties and dinners with my professors many times, and have always found them to be available to talk with on any subject whether or not it is officially office hours, even if I've only had one class with them in the last four years." Yet another student reports that "when the professor steps into the classroom he is not some 'god of the subject,' but instead, a friend." Each student is assigned a faculty advisor, and students say the system is useful for those who actually seek advice. One student says it "has been very helpful to me on the times when I've needed to use it, but I usually plan out my courses by myself and only go to my advisor to get his signature." The student-faculty ratio is 11 to 1. Since Hillsdale has no graduate program, no courses are taught by graduate teaching assistants. Adjunct teachers do help out, but for the most part, courses are taught by full-time faculty.

Some eminent faculty members long associated with Hillsdale have retired over the last couple of years. They have been replaced by new professors with solid credentials. Indeed, observers have noted that the general quality of instruction has steadily improved in recent years. Hillsdale, of course, naturally attracts scholars who share its regard for the liberal arts and its conservative outlook, especially its academic conservatism. Among the best teachers at Hillsdale are Robert R. Miller Jr. and Francis Steiner in biology; Lee Ann Fisher Baron and Christopher A. VanOrman in chemistry; Joseph Garnjobst and David Jones in classics; Gary Wolfram in economics; Andrew Cuneo, Michael Jordan, John Reist, Stephen Smith, John Somerville Jr., and David Whalen in English; Brad Birzer, Tom Conner, Burt Folsom, Sir Martin Gilbert, Victor Davis Hanson, Mark Kalthoff, and John Willson in history; Thomas J. Burke, James W. Stephens, and Donald J. Westblade (the new head of the Honors Program) in philosophy and religion; Kenneth G. Hayes in physics; Mickey Craig, Robert Eden, and Will Morrisey in political science; Don Ernst and Fritz Tsao in psychology; Peter Blum in sociology; and Michael Bauman, the director of the Christian studies program.

The Center for Constructive Alternatives does an admirable job of enlivening intellectual life at Hillsdale. The program is famous for bringing to campus big-name speakers, from politicians like Ronald Reagan and Margaret Thatcher to public intellectuals like Walter Williams and Lynne Cheney. Although the CCA is most notable for bringing conservative speakers to campus, it has sponsored others, such as George McGovern and Stanley Fish, as well. Students must attend at least two CCA lectures as part of the core curriculum requirements. Through the Shavano Institute for National Leadership, the CCA seminars and lectures have spread Hillsdale's reputation throughout the country. Hillsdale publishes the texts of the speeches in its monthly journal, *Imprimis*, which is distributed to more than one million people. Hillsdale also runs the Hoogland Center for Teacher Excellence, directed by David J. Bobb, which instructs teachers "in the best of the liberal arts tradition for the advancement of liberty," according to its Web page. Through the Hoogland Center, teachers can attend seminars such as "The Cold War" and "Will Free Markets Protect the Planet?"

One student complains that in the history, political science, and economics departments, "political biases definitely shape the courses. . . . Liberal theories are usually brought up by teachers in those departments only to be attacked." This student says, "This is definitely not a comfortable campus for liberals, as the college's overall philosophy is explicitly conservative. However, there are sections of the student body that are liberal or at least open and receptive to liberal ideas." Indeed, students and faculty describe Hillsdale as a place where various sociopolitical views are tolerated. The difference is that conservative ideas are not attacked as a matter of course.

In its official literature, Hillsdale repudiates "the dehumanizing, discriminatory trend of so-called 'social justice' and 'multicultural diversity' which judges individuals not as individuals, but as members of a group and which pits one group against other competing groups in divisive power struggles." In short, there is absolutely no PC nonsense at Hillsdale, either inside or outside of the classroom.

Hillsdale sees its political mission as nonpartisan. But there are certain political consequences of an education in the liberal arts, as put forth in the faculty's statement on academic freedom, drafted originally by Russell Kirk. It stands in marked contrast to the notion of academic freedom prevalent at most institutions today. In part it reads: "[A]cademic freedom in particular requires attachment to a body of truth, made known through the order and integration of knowledge. Of such truths the college is the conservator and renewer, and the primary function of the college is to transmit, through these truths, some measure of wisdom and virtue."

SUGGESTED CORE
1.–3. Classical Studies 301, Greek Civilization *and* English 101, Freshman Rhetoric and Great Books
4. Religion 213, History of Christian Thought I
5. Political Science 314, Modern Political Philosophy
6. English 471/472, Shakespeare
7. History 105, The American Heritage
8. Philosophy 217, Nineteenth-Century Philosophy

The political atmosphere at Hillsdale is overwhelmingly conservative. Long-time president George Roche III successfully promoted Hillsdale's national reputation for conservatism as a way to raise money after the school decided to refuse all federal aid, although at the time some thought that this focus on fundraising detracted from the college's educational mission. By the end of Roche's tenure, many students and faculty found the political atmosphere at the school stifling, not because of its conservatism, but because of Roche's domination of all aspects of the school's life. Roche left Hillsdale under a cloud of personal scandal in 1999, raising questions in the minds of many about the future of the school—which had for so long virtually been identified with him.

The college was most discreet, not to say secretive, about the reasons for his departure. Whatever his failings, however, Roche had managed to build an institution strong enough to survive him. According to one student, "It didn't change things on a day-to-day basis, in terms of academics and student life. Things went on pretty much as usual."

Hillsdale's board of trustees hired Larry Arnn, who had been president of the Claremont Institute in California for 15 years, to serve as the college's president. Arnn, who was inaugurated in 2001, holds a doctorate in political science, and, although he had been out of academia for some time, he has proven to be a quick learner who rapidly acquired the skills needed for his new position, according to a faculty member. Whereas some faulted his predecessor for focusing too much on fundraising, Arnn has emphasized the importance of Hillsdale's commitment to liberal education and has expressed his determination to make Hillsdale the finest liberal arts college in the country. He has also stressed the role that liberal education must play in the renewal of American political life. While Roche maintained tight control over all aspects of the college and had little use for those who did not see things his way, Arnn has fostered an environment that one faculty member characterizes as "totally open." Arnn also made a point to reach out to students after his inauguration. "He is focused on education, very accessible, and very supportive of student life," says a student. "He has done a good job of getting to know students and even dines in the cafeteria several times a week."

Not everyone is pleased with the choice of Arnn. A student libertarian group that (cheekily) calls itself Hillsdale Liberals (classical liberals, that is) posted on its Web site a column by prominent historian Thomas DiLorenzo, who dubbed Arnn a "Straussian neocon"—that is, a supporter of the welfare state and an interventionist in foreign policy. He cited a former professor who suggested that Hillsdale students are now being encouraged to support Bush administration policy rather than to apply strict standards of classical liberal restraint. Of course, to many (such as the school's teaching fellow, and Bush speech consultant, Victor Davis Hanson) that would be a good thing. In any case, it's refreshing to report on a school where *these* are the kind of debates that take place on campus.

Student Life: Only the location is far out

Hillsdale's 200-acre campus is attractive but modest. Although not lacking in the essentials, Hillsdale could stand to improve some of its facilities, such as the natural science labs, and some of the older buildings need renovation. In response to these needs, President Arnn has produced a long-term expansion plan. New buildings for the administration and faculty and a music hall were recently completed, and work will soon be finished on yet another set of classroom and office buildings. The campus computer network was also recently upgraded.

Some 45 percent of women and 35 percent of men participate in the Greek system at Hillsdale, making it an important center of social life. There are three fraternities and three sororities, each with its own residence on campus. The administration has expressed concern about excessive drinking in the Greek system, but the situation does not seem to be any worse at Hillsdale than at other schools, and if anything it is probably better. One student surmises that there are more fines assessed at Hillsdale than at other schools, but that students accept these disciplinary measures as part of the Hillsdale vision. Among the student body, there are both studious intellectuals and ardent partiers, but most students lie between these two extremes.

One self-described "political moderate/liberal" student says that Hillsdale faces the same problem that some other liberal arts colleges face: a lack of intellectual diversity among students. The difference here, of course, is that students lean right rather than left. This student says, "The vast majority of students are tolerant of liberals as people, but there is a very small minority that has absolutely no respect for and resents liberal viewpoints." It says much about the political atmosphere at Hillsdale that while there is a thriving College Republicans club, the College Democrats "tend to disappear every three years or so when [the founders] graduate," as one student says.

The school's official student newspaper, the *Collegian*, boasts that it is Michigan's oldest college newspaper. Over its 125-year publishing history, however, the paper has been tinkered with repeatedly by the administration. When the head of the journalism program, Tracy Lee Simmons, came to campus, he "said his one concern . . . was interference from the administration. Simmons didn't think he could teach students to be professional journalists and allow them to be censored," according to a *Collegian* article. "I was determined the *Collegian* would not be a public relations arm of the college," he said. And today, students say, it isn't. The *Collegian* is now an independent newspaper, and administrators don't see the newspaper until they pick it up at a campus distribution point just like everyone else.

Hillsdale College is tucked away in rural south-central Michigan in the center of the town of Hillsdale (population 8,000), an hour and a half west of Detroit and three hours east of Chicago. The isolation means that students get more reading done and form a strong community on campus—which is the center of Hillsdale social life, offering plenty of activities during the week and on weekends. Students and faculty members alike comment on how vibrant the intellectual life of students is, with active extracurricular reading groups in all fields, a literary magazine, and a theological debating society. Indeed, one faculty member says, "The real divide on campus is not between liberals and conservatives, or Greeks and non-Greeks, but between Catholics and Protestants." There is also a small but vocal Orthodox community.

The divide in the Hillsdale region, however, is between the college and nearby towns. Both the neighboring burg of Jonesville and Hillsdale are depressed industrial towns, and there is some tension between the working-class "townies" and middle-class members of the college community.

Athletics are popular at the college; almost half of the student body participates in varsity athletics. However, four sports were cut recently due to financial difficulties. Hillsdale competes at the NCAA Division II level in a variety of men's and women's sports and offers a number of intramural and club sports. The athletic facilities are relatively new. Faculty members say students sometimes have trouble balancing their studies with sports. Nevertheless, sports do not overwhelm the college environment.

Hillsdale students are required to live on campus in one of the 10 dorms or six Greek houses, although exceptions are made for married students and those who enter at an older age. Hillsdale is conservative socially, too. All residences are single sex. The visitation hours, although recently relaxed somewhat through the efforts of the student government, are rigorously enforced, according to one residential advisor. Male and female students are allowed to visit each other in dorm rooms until 1 a.m. on weekends, until 7 p.m. on Sundays, and until 10 p.m. on Tuesdays and Wednesdays.

Some female students recently requested that more lighting be installed on campus so that they could feel safer walking home at night. But the crime rate at Hillsdale is low; indeed, Hillsdale is one of the safest schools in this guide. During the 2003–4 academic year, the only crimes on campus were five burglaries.

Hillsdale is cheaper than many colleges in this guide, with 2004–5 tuition at $16,800, and room and board at $6,700. Admissions are need-blind, although the school cannot guarantee to meet the full financial need of applicants. Some 65 percent of students do receive need-based aid, and the student loan debt of an average recent graduate is $15,700.

UNIVERSITY OF ILLINOIS AT URBANA-CHAMPAIGN

URBANA-CHAMPAIGN, ILLINOIS • WWW.UIUC.EDU

Popping the cork

"U of I gives you just as good an education as you could get anywhere else," says one University of Illinois (UIUC) student with pride. Located in Urbana-Champaign, about 125 miles south of Chicago, UIUC has a reputation as one of the country's top public universities, attracting to its campus a bevy of bright students and highly regarded faculty and maintaining more than a few excellent academic departments.

"This is a research university," says one professor. "We are not a teaching college. People don't come here to get small classes and individual attention. They come for the sports, for the first-rate facilities, and to make contact with some of the best thinkers in their field." Whether many Illini actually take—or get—the opportunity to interact with the "best thinkers in their field" is an open question. In any case, UIUC would be performing a higher service if it required its students to confront a few more of the "best thinkers" not currently on the faculty—Thucydides, Augustine, Dante, Tocqueville, chaps like that.

Academic Life: Optional history in the land of Lincoln

Illiniois has no core curriculum, though its meager set of distribution requirements has become more structured over the past decade. Ten years ago, students were only required to take two English composition courses, so it could hardly have become *less* structured. In addition to the two-semester English composition and three-semester foreign language requirements, students must now take a total of 10 other courses distributed among broad liberal arts and science categories.

Freshmen may choose to begin their college experience by enrolling in the First-Year Discovery Program, which offers very small classes (up to 20 students) in a variety of disciplines, letting new students get to know faculty members. This is not always possible in the required behemoth "intro" courses—so opting for this program seems like a wise move for anyone entering UIUC.

It's easy to get lost in the system at this university, which offers plenty of good courses—and at least as many paths of least resistance. The curriculum is unstructured and the catalog lists an enormous range of disciplines—almost 150 of them. "Students are pretty much adrift to take whatever they want; there's no real cohesion or body of knowledge they are building," one professor says.

A College of Liberal Arts and Sciences (LAS) professor complains that even in more traditional disciplines, faculty members' interests tend to focus on new, trendy areas of research rather than on more traditional topics, so that it is not uncommon for students to be fooled by course titles. A course in the Old Testament, for instance, may turn out to consist of feminist complaints about Yahweh and patriarchy. (The business school is more cautious; one professor says that the school's courses "cover the fundamentals with an eye to the contemporary.") Of course, at a school as big as Illinois, it is statistically almost inevitable that a number of serious, well-taught courses will still be offered. Illinois is particularly well known for the quality of its programs in engineering, the sciences, journalism, and business. The College of Agriculture is one of the oldest in the nation, and its programs are widely respected. Other departments with strong programs include economics, labor and industrial relations, geography, and history.

The classics department has a distinguished history, several world-class scholars, and five majors to choose from: classical archeology, classical civilization, classics, Greek, and Latin. The religious studies program is also surprisingly good for a state university. Religious studies majors are required to take eight courses: "Comparative Perspectives," "Hebrew Bible in English," "New Testament in English," "Philosophy of Religion," a course in Asian religions, one in Western religions, and a two-course sequence on Western civilization from the history or comparative literature departments. ("Western Civilization from Antiquity to 1660" and "Western Civilization from 1660 to the Present" qualify.)

With its unstructured curricular landscape dotted by various academic land mines (as well as gold mines), it is unfortunate that the university's advising program is ane-

VITAL STATISTICS
Religious affiliation: none
Total enrollment: 40,687
Total undergraduates: 29,632
SAT/ACT midranges: SAT V: 560–670, M: 620–730; ACT: 25–31
Applicants: 21,986
Applicants accepted: 68%
Accepted applicants who enrolled: 48%
Tuition: $6,460 (in state), $19,380 (out of state)
Room and board: $6,848
Freshman retention rate: 90%
Graduation rate: 58% (4 yrs.), 80% (6 yrs.)
Courses with fewer than 20 students: 33%
Student-faculty ratio: 14:1
Courses taught by graduate TAs: 26%
Most popular majors: business, engineering, social sciences
Students living on campus: 39%
Guaranteed housing for four years? no
Students in fraternities: 19% sororities: 22%

The rather loose general education mandates at UIUC require the following courses:

- One or two courses (depending on each class's demands) in composition. These seem to be straight-forward rhetoric/college writing classes.
- One topic-driven class in advanced composition. Options range from "Writing in the Disciplines" to "Humane Education with Companion Animals."
- One course in "Cultural Studies: Non-Western/U.S. Minority Culture(s)." Choices include "Masterpieces of East Asian Literature" and "Introduction to African American Film."
- One course in "Cultural Studies: Western/Comparative Culture(s)." Options extend from "Religion and Society in the West" to "Brazilian Women's Literature."
- Students must complete a third-semester course in a language other than their own.

mic. "Teaching professionals," faculty hired by the university to teach introductory courses, serve as departmental advisors. One political science major says that the system is "in dire need of review." The university provides a kind of virtual online "advisor" in the form of an informative Web page, upon which many students rely instead of consulting a teacher. One student reports that he has "not yet felt the need for advising"—a statement that illustrates just why students need advising. Students are expected to discuss an academic strategy with a (human) advisor and to hand in a "major plan of study" by the start of their junior year.

The Honors Program is available to students who maintain a 3.25 GPA. Students in the program can take special honors courses, but they are not granted separate housing facilities. Honors students often enjoy smaller classes and can even register for courses before the rest of the university. If a particular course is not offered as an honors course, a student can sometimes complete extra coursework on his own and receive honors credit for doing so. The bad news, however, is that a number of the honors seminars deal with the trendiest areas of academia. The English department, for instance, offers honors seminars such as "Middle-Class Women and the Marriage Plot" and "Langston Hughes and Claude McKay: Race and American Poetry," along with seminars on Shakespeare and autobiography.

Illinois has a student-faculty ratio of about 14 to 1. A full 26 percent of classes are taught by graduate students rather than by professors. This is far above the norm, even at state universities. "Many departments have a problem finding faculty to teach basic courses due to the lack of professors carrying a full-time load for whatever reason," a professor says. "The courses that suffer are introductory-level ones." A student says, "My big lecture courses were taught by professors, but a majority of my classes and all of my accompanying discussion sections were taught by TAs."

Students express a certain ambivalence about UIUC professors overall. When they are good, they are said to be very, very good. This category includes Kevin Waspi in finance; Thomas Rudolph in political science; Keith Hitchins in history; Robert McKim and Rajeshwari Pandharipande in religious studies; and James Dengate in classics. But not all teachers live up to the title. One student says, "Illinois has some professors that are very accessible and some you will never be able to get any help from. In my opinion, professors often depend way too much on

TAs. A lot of times it is the TA who has office hours that you go to." Another student says, "All professors hold office hours and check their e-mail frequently, but there are a select few who advise you to talk with your TA before seeking advice from them." When in doubt, look up the school's annual "Incomplete List of Teachers Ranked as Excellent by Their Students." Just remember that some teachers may have earned popularity by easy grading.

Like Harvard and many other Ivy League schools, Illinois suffers from pervasive grade inflation. "It's notorious," says a professor. "One introductory-level teacher was known for giving half the class As and the other half A-pluses. It's a pact. Students don't harass the professor and the professor gives them easy grades." Of course, not all professors are willing to compromise, and lazy students sometimes get burned.

And some professors are unhappy with their charges. "I have students who fall asleep or read the newspaper in my class," says one teacher. "A lot of them just don't show up." Another professor says of his students, "Most seem to be interested in graduating and instrumental learning that can aid their careers." A colleague says, "Some students do get very involved, but I would say those are the exception, not the rule." A student says, "If you're smart, that's cool. But a lot of people just try to get by. They don't want to put in the effort."

Professors and students agree that the LAS faculty has a heavy leftward tilt. One professor describes it as "highly politically correct." A student agrees: "The College of [Liberal] Arts and Sciences is exactly what it says: liberal—way left." One professor we spoke to cautions conservative students to think twice about the school if they were planning on an English major.

Nor do politics stop at the classroom door. At UIUC, one student says, political bias "usually comes through in the way that course material is presented." Another student recalls that an anthropology professor "spent 10 minutes ripping on George Bush and then began the lesson on an entirely unrelated topic." A few students report blatantly ideological attempts to punish students who disagree with instructors. "I wrote a paper for my Rhetoric 105 class [a freshman writing course] in which I argued against gay marriage," a student says. "The teaching assistant gave me a D on the paper because 'you can't argue for that sort of position without appealing to hate and religious bigotry.' I had to go to the department chair to get the grade raised to a C, and that's all I could do."

REQUIREMENTS (CONT'D)

- Two classes in humanities or the arts. Options range from "Shakespeare on Film" to "The Archaeology of Illinois."
- Two natural sciences or technology courses. Choices include "General Chemistry" and "Introduction to Fibers and Textiles."
- Two courses in social/behavioral sciences. Students may study anything from "Microeconomic Principles" to "Women's Lives."
- One course in the "Quantitative Reasoning I" group. Choices are limited to a course in economics or math or a philosophy course in symbolic logic.
- One course in the "Quantitative Reasoning II" group. Students may choose anything from an introductory physics course to "Measure and Evaluation in Kinesiology."

Support services at UIUC have been politicized, thanks to a previous administration mired in the pseudo-intellectual bog of diversity discourse. "'Diversity' was the favorite word of our [former] chancellor [Nancy Canton]," says one student. "[Canton] proclaimed diversity to be the most important element of a philosophical education," says a professor. "You'd think it would be education." One of Canton's legacies, created in 2002 by the Chancellor's Committee on Diversity, is the Center for Democracy in a Multiracial Society, a research-oriented project that is "organized around a commitment to the practice of democracy and equality within a changing multiracial society." Canton left in spring 2004 for Syracuse University and was replaced by Richard Herman, a mathematician, who seems at first blush to be less ideological than his predecessor.

Courses that fulfill the cultural studies general education requirement include "Sex and Gender in Classical Antiquity" and "Minority Images in U.S. Film." Academic departments at Illinois are being pressured to "diversify" their course offerings and hire preferred minority candidates. When a British history professor retired recently, he was replaced by a professor who specializes in the history of an indigenous group on a Pacific island. The classics department reportedly had to argue doggedly to persuade the dean to hire someone who specializes in Roman history. The political science department was ordered to hire an expert in Asian American politics, practically a nonexistent field. Because of the administration's multiculturalist obsession, "more serious areas get neglected," says a professor. Looking for the most politicized departments at UIUC? Try English, education, history, and women's studies.

Student Life: Beer and Champaign

The University of Illinois at Urbana-Champaign sits on 1,454 acres in the heart of the state. Located within three hours of Chicago, Indianapolis, and St. Louis, and situated in a city with a population of 100,000 residents, the university has an unmistakably midwestern feel. The oldest part of the campus, the picturesque Quad, recalls a park. It is surrounded by imposing buildings that house most of the LAS departments. The neighborhood known as Campustown is dotted with shops, coffeehouses, bookstores, restaurants, and bars. The Krannert Center for the Performing Arts mounts theatrical and operatic productions every year, as well as numerous chamber and orchestral performances.

Of the more than 40,000 students, however, few take advantage of cultural attractions in the area. When they are in town at night, they're usually drinking. There are bars "within 50 paces of the Quad" says one student. Says another, "When you get here, your first priority is to get a fake ID." To get into the bars one must be only 19 years of age, even though the official drinking age is 21. The university is usually ranked as one of the top 20 party schools in the nation, "but it's not for lack of other things to do," says a student.

No indeed; the university has almost 900 registered student organizations, among them the Nintendo 64 Club, the Illini Bowling Club, the Illini Aviation Club, Knittingillni (a knitting club), the Swing Society, and the Brain-Ring Club (whose members promote traditional Russian intellectual games).

The Student Government Association is large and active, though it tends to throw its weight behind left-wing causes. Church organizations are particularly popular on campus. "There is a very large religious presence here at Illinois," says a campus minister. "There is a substantial Catholic presence at the Newman Foundation, but also a wide variety of Protestant organizations, such as Campus Crusade for Christ and InterVarsity Christian Fellowship."

As befits a Big Ten school, after drinking campus life centers primarily on athletics, especially men's basketball and football. The emphasis on sports helps to explain the endless, tedious controversy over the university's mascot, Chief Illiniwek, who emerges during halftime at football games.

It seems that the use of the Chief offends a few American Indian groups and many more leftist academics. After more than 800 faculty members signed a petition against the Chief, a larger group of students and faculty formed to support it. The chancellor became so fed up with the debate that he sent an e-mail to the entire university community prohibiting anyone from discussing the mascot controversy with a crucial constituency—prospective student-athletes. A group of faculty members vehemently objected to this free-speech ban, the ACLU filed a suit against the university, and the chancellor backed down.

One professor insisted that prospective student-athletes "should be aware that they're participating in the denigration of a race of people." The Save the Chief group insists that the mascot is a symbol honoring the school's tradition and its historical roots—noting that each year, the student selected to be the Chief spends time in South Dakota on a reservation learning dances and talking with community members. The debate over the Chief drags on: according to the *Chronicle of Higher Education*, in March 2005 the Illinois Native American Bar Association filed a lawsuit against the university, claiming that the Chief's appearance at games violates the state's Civil Rights Act of 2003.

And from our "I-can't-believe-it's-come-to-this" file, UIUC's pre–St. Patrick's Day bar fest was recently the occasion of controversy when the alcohol-related activities surrounding the festival were denounced by one professor as being anti-Irish, anti-Catholic, and racist besides. The university administration refused to act on his complaint—probably at the insistence of Irish-American students.

The Illini Pride organization is a fan club that holds barbeques and other events to support the teams. The homecoming celebration has been taking place since 1910. It consists of a one-week festival complete with parade, pep rallies, and lots of drinking.

The Greek system is enormously popular on campus. Roughly a fifth of students

SUGGESTED CORE

1. Classics 221,
   The Heroic Tradition
2. Philosophy 203,
   Ancient Philosophy
3. Religious Studies 101,
   The Bible as Literature
4. Religious Studies 108,
   Religion and Society in
   the West I (*closest match*)
5. Political Science 372,
   Modern Political Theory
6. English 218, Introduction to Shakespeare
7. History 170,
   U.S. History to 1877
8. History 360, Enlightenment to Existentialism *or* History 361, European Thought and Society since 1789

belong to a chapter, making the UIUC system one of the largest in the country. Illinois also boasts a strong intramurals program, offering about 20 sports, including badminton, basketball, flag football, miniature golf, and ultimate Frisbee.

Outside the classroom, students report a good deal of tolerance for different viewpoints. Says one student, "I have had no problem being an open conservative on campus." In addition to many liberal student organizations, including the left-leaning *Daily Illini* student newspaper, the campus does have a few conservative organizations. The conservative student newspaper, the *Orange and Blue Observer* appears to have published its last issue in February 2003. The Campus Republicans are not as active as in the past.

Freshmen are required to live in university residence halls, in a fraternity or sorority house, or in one of the five privately owned certified residence halls. More than three-quarters of entering students choose to live in a university residence hall, of which there are several kinds, including one in which students agree not to have visitors of the opposite sex in their rooms, a substance-free hall, and men-only and women-only dorms. There are no coed dorm rooms or coed bathrooms at the university.

UIUC also offers theme housing to students. These residences are markedly less politicized than similar houses at other schools. Some are "living/learning communities," each focusing on a different theme, including "Global Crossroads," "Leadership Experience through Academic Development and Service," "Unit One" (a group that offers art workshops, credit courses, and field trips), "Women in Math, Science, and Engineering," and "Weston Exploration," which offers workshops like "Career Development: Theory and Practice," "Principles of Effective Speaking," and "The College Experience." The program also holds a number of discussion sections in the Weston Residence Hall, encouraging students to discuss academic subjects with hallmates inside and outside the classroom.

The crime statistics on campus are disturbing. In 2003, the last year for which statistics were available, the university reported 36 aggravated assaults, 12 forcible sex offenses, five robberies, 19 aggravated assaults, 67 burglaries, two stolen cars, and one arson on campus. It is tempting to blame this on the school's urban location and large size—until one looks at, say, New York University, which is just as big, and is located, ahem, *in New York City*. NYU has about one-third the crime. Students can use the university's SafeRides escort service for protection and emergency phones are located all over campus.

Tuition at Illinois is affordable—an average of $6,460 in 2004–5—for in-state students. Out-of-state undergrads paid an average of $19,380. Add to that about $7,000 in room and board. The school made it to *Kiplinger's* "Best Value: State Schools" list, and it's notable that financial aid is not as widely used here as at other schools—perhaps because it's relatively cheap. Only about 30 percent of students receive aid. Admission is need-blind, but this is not saying much. The financial aid office functions mostly as the administrative arm of government aid programs. Tuition does fluctuate according to one's choice of academic division, but students have the option of "locking in" the tuition rate at which they entered.

INDIANA UNIVERSITY – BLOOMINGTON

BLOOMINGTON, INDIANA • WWW.IUB.EDU

Love and basketball

Indiana University is in many ways typical of large state research universities. It has many, many programs (some of them highly ranked), attracts plenty of capable students, sits in an attractive college town, and suffers from a serious case of ideology. Here as elsewhere, administrators and many faculty have carried the concern for "diversity" to almost mind-bending extremes. Still, as at many state universities, one can get a real liberal arts education at Indiana, but it takes some careful choosing.

What sets IU apart from many of its state-school peers is its students' love affair with basketball. Fathoming the depths of IU students' passion for hoops illuminates much about university culture—just compare the way their faces brighten at the mention of a top-rated basketball recruiting class with their relatively lackluster enthusiasm for *academic* classes. Coursework is rarely the primary reason students go to IU, recently ranked by one publication as the top party school in the nation—regardless of whether or not, in a given year, the Hoosiers beat Purdue.

"The best part of IU is that there's always something going on," says one student. And another points out that, if nothing else, "the campus is beautiful." When things get a bit crazy, an evening stroll through the arboretum, past Dunn Meadow, beside the Union, across the Jordan River, and through the woods along Indiana Avenue is of great restorative value. So is a basketball game.

Academic Life: Ministry of truth

Indiana University has the liberal arts rhetoric down. "Our experience demonstrates that the liberal arts help develop the rigor of mind needed for advanced study in any field and for the pursuit of a richer life through the enlargement of mind and spirit," the university says. Among the 11

VITAL STATISTICS	
Religious affiliation: none	
Total enrollment: 37,821	
Total undergraduates: 29,549	
SAT/ACT midranges: SAT V: 490–600, M: 500–620; ACT: 22–27	
Applicants: 21,132	
Applicants accepted: 83%	
Accepted applicants who enrolled: 36%	
Tuition: $5,756 (in state), $16,791 (out of state)	
Room and board: $5,872	
Freshman retention rate: 88%	
Graduation rate: 41% (4 yrs.), 71% (6 yrs.)	
Courses with fewer than 20 students: 40%	
Student-faculty ratio: 18:1	
Courses taught by graduate TAs: not provided	
Most popular majors: business, education, communication	
Students living on campus: 42%	
Guaranteed housing for four years? no	
Students in fraternities: 16% sororities: 18%	

Indiana University maintains no core curriculum but rather imposes certain broad mandates with regard to course selection. To obtain a bachelor of arts degree in the College of Arts and Sciences, students must complete the following:

- "Fundamental Skills" Requirements. Students must take three credits each in English composition and intensive writing, as well as a four-course sequence in a foreign language. They must also "demonstrate mastery of a fundamental skill in mathematics, which is defined as a level of proficiency equivalent to three years of high school math." Students may test out of all of these requirements save that of intensive writing.
- Distribution Requirements. Students choose four classes in each of three distribution areas: arts and humanities, social and historical studies, and natural and mathematical sciences. The most restrictive area still offers more than 250 choices.

major goals of IU's liberal arts curriculum are "appreciation of literature and the arts" and "critical and creative thinking." Even so, embedded in IU's traditional-sounding liberal arts philosophy are goals surely motivated by more contemporary concerns. The administration aims to teach students "intellectual flexibility and breadth of mind" so that they can "[be] sensitive to others' views and feelings." Students must learn to "practice scientific methods" because they will enable them to "distinguish conclusions that rest on unverified assertion from those developed through the application of scientific reasoning." And students "study . . . the international community" in order to "cultivate an informed sensitivity to global and environmental issues."

Moving from rhetoric back to reality, however, the university's requirements for a BA degree are so unstructured as to be nearly irrelevant. Furthermore, only a portion of the approved courses would have a place in a true liberal arts core curriculum.

For students who seek an academic challenge and a rigorous introduction to the Western tradition, IU offers its Honors College, with its own set of courses spanning many departments and disciplines. One honors course, called "Ideas and Experience," centers on the theme "Literature as Quest" and includes readings from the *Epic of Gilgamesh,* Xenophon's *Anabasis, The Divine Comedy*, the journals of Christopher Columbus, and *Pilgrim's Progress.* Another, "Rhetoric and Democratic Public Culture in Ancient Greece," introduces students to rhetoric through Plato, Aristotle, Thucydides, and Demosthenes. Other promising honors courses include "Russian through Pushkin," "Spiritual Autobiography," "Beethoven and His Era," and "Human Nature." By piling up five or six of these courses, a student could gain a fairly comprehensive foundation in the humanities.

IU is a research university, and it has a vast number of departments and programs to prove it; students can graduate with a degree in anything from telecommunications to folklore. If the dozens of liberal arts majors aren't enough, there are always the interdepartmental majors that combine areas like computer science and philosophy.

One of the worst aspects of the school is the obsession of IU's administrators with "diversity"—a nebulous ideal that they seem intent on cramming into every nook and cranny of the curriculum. They state as much in their own documents. "Curricular infusion" is one of three approaches IU uses to prepare "students for a more diverse world," the other two sides of the "diversity triangle" being "faculty enhancement" and "student enhancement." The model is described in a report made at the behest of the vice president for student development and diversity. The 2001 report (updated in 2003) says, "Together, operating synergistically, the results can be the enhancement of student learning about the many dimensions of diversity." The whole report is a brilliant example of skewed educational priorities expressed in clunky, ideological jargon.

Someone must be able to understand it, though, because the plan is going swimmingly thus far. Spring 2004 courses included "Representation of the Body" (which considers "why sex-differentiated body rituals have become so salient in recent times. The course concentrates on the creation and institutionalization of sexual difference through representations of the body"). A quick scan down the fall 2004 course listing found the 300-level history seminar "Issues in United States History" taught with the following focuses in mind: "People in Motion, Cultures in Contact," "History of Latinos in U.S. Education," "America's Wars and Armed Forces," and "Latino Immigrants in U.S. Society." Two English courses that sound as though they ought to be safe—"Literary Masterworks" and "Twentieth-Century American Fiction"—are actually quite discouraging. The "masterworks" class includes no American and British fiction; in the class on America, the course materials ask: "While reading a wide range of texts written throughout the century, can we identity patterns and shifts in American literary representations of regionalism, race, and ethnicity?"

Students have noticed the emphasis. One says the diversity policy is "almost fanatically enforced." Another says, "In classes that I've been in, we've dealt with a lot of racial and feminist topics." Says another, "Politics definitely intrude upon the classroom." Yet another student claims that "a lot of the professors are really liberal, and to be successful in those classes, you almost need to tell them not your real opinion but what they want to hear." Professors and students alike warn particularly of liberal bias in the political science department.

Faculty are also feeling the pressure to get on board with the university's "xenomania." A diversity assessment committee recently recommended rewarding faculty who comply with diversity efforts and starting a Diversity Resource Center where

REQUIREMENTS (CONT'D)

- A "Topics Seminar" Requirement. Students must take one of the "topics" courses, which are freshmen seminars taught by tenured professors, usually about subjects of current interest to the individual instructors. Consequently, these courses can be highly specialized or present a political bias. Spring 2005 topics courses included one whose "fundamental question" was "What role does the mass media play in crime control?" and another called "Latinos and Other Immigrants."

- A "Culture Studies" Requirement. Students must take six credits that meet the criteria for culture studies. Two lists are provided for this endeavor, one with almost 400 approved courses, and another with a scant 75. Students may take two courses under the non-Western perspectives rubric or one course from that category in addition to a course focusing on modern Western Europe.

consultants would train professors on how to introduce themes of diversity into their courses. Other recommendations include, of course, increased recruitment of minority students and faculty, including a "grow our own" program that would "identify undergraduates with doctoral potential," and developing "more campus-wide dialogue and discussion on diversity issues in both formal and informal settings." Not only do faculty feel pressure from the administration; one student warns that whenever a professor makes a comment that diverges from campus orthodoxy "a student is ready to report it."

Still, the administration does have its lucid moments. When, in 2002, IU's Black Student Union demanded the removal from a university building of a mural by Thomas Hart Benton depicting Ku Klux Klansmen burning a cross, the chancellor refused. She called the piece of art a remembrance of Indiana's "shameful past." Of course, the chancellor also promised to institute a program discussing issues raised by the mural, to divert some financial resources to art that reflects the diversity of IU, to increase diversity initiatives, and to annually assess the university's progress toward diversity goals. (It should be noted that Benton was no partisan of the Klan, but a patriotic liberal and a supporter of the New Deal.)

In 2003, the administration again stood up for free speech. A business professor wrote on his Web log that he opposed hiring male homosexual teachers because, among other characterizations, they are "generally promiscuous." Some angry students and faculty demanded the removal of the statements, which were posted in university Web space. But IU's lawyers found that no policies had been breached, according to the *Chronicle of Higher Education*.

Indiana University's president, Adam Herbert, came on board in 2003. In his speeches, President Herbert has made clear his commitment to liberal arts education—as well as to diversity. He even quotes John Henry Newman's *The Idea of the University* . . . in the service of diversity, that is. In his remarks at IU Bloomington's 2003 9/11 Diversity Reception (that's a mouthful), Herbert agreed with Newman that a university is a place where truth is found "by the collision of mind with mind, knowledge with knowledge." From this Herbert leapt to the conclusion, "That is why the idea of university and diversity go hand in hand."

Nonetheless, the administration's attempts to indoctrinate can be thwarted by a savvy student; and a core body of knowledge *can* be acquired at IU. The sheer number of courses that the university offers means that a student has the resources for a remarkable education at hand, but he'll have to fashion it with care.

IU's music school is top ranked, as is its business school. It also has a formidable language program that offers instruction in more than 40 languages, including Estonian, Zulu, Lakota, and Twi. The biological sciences at IU seem likely to experience a renaissance, thanks to generous gifts from the Lilly Endowment. According to the *Chronicle of Higher Education*, Lilly gave IU $26 million in 2004 to help it attract "top scholars and researchers," and another $53 million in 2005 for life sciences research.

Indiana University has gone the way of the virtual university in some respects. Students are only required to see their academic advisors—who may or may not be faculty members—during their freshman year. Afterward, while students are "encouraged" to see their advisors, the online computerized student advising system "monitors" students' progress toward meeting degree requirements. IU's literature actually emphasizes students' responsibility (in boldface) for "planning their own programs and for meeting the following degree requirements for graduation." In other words, don't bother us. Not surprisingly, students aren't impressed by this hands-off system. One student says, "It's much better to talk to a former student than to your advisor. . . . A lot of times [the advisors] don't know what's going on." In addition, GradPact, the university's plan to ensure students have the opportunity to graduate in four years, has been cancelled because of the costs associated with coding and maintaining the necessary software. Nonetheless, students often find professors within their majors to be both accessible and willing to give informal advice.

While professors may be accessible, few students bother to access them; most undergrads stay away from office hours unless they are having trouble understanding something. In a survey of senior students, 16 percent of respondents said they "never discussed ideas from readings for classes with a faculty member outside of class," and 48 percent said they had only "sometimes" done so.

Students report that freshman survey courses often include 100 to 250 students. Professors teach most classes, with the exceptions of some introductory foreign language and English composition courses, but graduate assistant instructors lead the smaller discussion sections and give the grades. "What I've found to be the biggest difficulty are the foreign instructors here. It can be really hard to understand their accents, and the lectures can be really dry," says a student. "It's almost better to learn it from a textbook rather than waste your time." Another student recommends teachers who are "somewhat older" rather than the "younger teachers," noticing that, in his experience, professors with tenure care more about teaching and less about their research.

One student tells of a professor who was "more concerned about her statistics than how students did in her class. She made her grade distribution a perfect bell curve, and to make it that way, she gave people participation points according to what she needed them to be rather than what they deserved." The professor was likely concerned about grade inflation, a persistent problem at IU and one administrators are trying to tame. Nevertheless, in the first semester of the 2003–4 academic year, more than two-thirds of the departments in the College of Arts and Sciences awarded students an average GPA of better than 3.0.

SUGGESTED CORE

1. Classical Studies C311, Classical Epics
2. Philosophy P201, Ancient Greek Philosophy
3. Religious Studies R210, Introduction to the Old Testament / Hebrew Bible *and* Religion 220, Introduction to the New Testament (*closest matches*)
4. Religious Studies R330, Christianity 400–1500
5. Political Science Y382, History of Political Theory II
6. English L220, Introduction to Shakespeare
7. History H105, American History I
8. History B300, West European Intellectual History (*closest match*)

Student Life: Hoop it up

Indiana University is nestled among the rolling hills and pastoral landscape of southern Indiana in the town of Bloomington (population 70,000), which many consider to be the "perfect" college town. Bloomington is a friendly town with a nice mix of human types. So, for example, while People for the Ethical Treatment of Animals named IU as one of the 10 most "vegetarian-friendly" colleges in 2002, there are plenty of meat-and-potatoes folk around, too.

Three lakes, two wineries, and a renovated downtown with brewpubs, shops, and cafes provide entertainment in Bloomington. The bars lining Kirkwood Avenue are hotspots for students. There is a festival nearly every month in the town, including ones dedicated to the arts, beer, and chocolate. Bloomington also offers many cultural events, as does IU's first-rate music school; as a result, "there are concerts all the time," says a student. Students also go camping, boating, fishing, and bicycling at nearby parks.

IU students have hundreds of student organizations at their disposal. Two of the most popular are the Student Athletic Board (some 1,000 members strong), which is charged with increasing attendance at athletic events, promoting school spirit, and coordinating homecoming; and the Indiana University Student Foundation, which is in charge of the Little 500 bicycle race—the largest intramural bike race in the country, famously memorialized in the movie *Breaking Away*. The College Republicans chapter is also quite large at IU: their mass meetings regularly draw several hundred students.

Given the administration's insistent diversity rhetoric, it is no surprise that radical groups have power at IU. OUT, the gay, lesbian, bisexual, and transgender student group, wields particular influence. It sponsors the Miss Gay IU drag pageant, teaches workshops like "Male Sensual Pleasure," and administers the SafeZone sticker program. There are more than 50 programs and services listed on IU's diversity resources Web page, and a number of like-minded student-run organizations such as Multicultural Outreach Recruitment Educators and ONE IU, which "seeks to foster racial understanding via interaction and communication across racial lines."

In a more traditional vein, "drinking is a pretty popular activity here," says one student. "Students drink throughout the week, and at least as many people outside of the Greek system drink as those inside it." University officials reportedly are "cracking down" on fraternity parties, according to a student. "When I was a freshman, there would be real old-school frat parties with bands. The whole atmosphere of Greek life is changing as far as parties go." Says another student, "Alcohol enforcement in Bloomington is ridiculous. . . . I have known many 21-year-olds who have gotten arrested walking home from the bars; it's an atmosphere that almost promotes drunk driving. Many student organizations have worked and are working hard to change the school's current alcohol policy, which many feel is unrealistic and outdated."

The reported crackdown may be in response to *The Princeton Review*'s ranking of IU as the top party school in the nation in 2002, a distinction that university officials emphatically reject. However, IU ranked first in the number of drug arrests in 2002 among all four-year U.S. universities, and second in alcohol arrests. In part, these rankings reflect IU's increased enforcement efforts, but if the campus social scene were "not fueled by alcohol" and incensed by pot, there would of course be fewer offenders to arrest.

Says one student, "A lot of people [at IU] are really smart, but they're the same ones partying on the weekend. I've also been surprised by how poorly some people I know write." Students are, according to another of their peers, "more concerned with their social life than with academics," but they'll "do what they have to do to get their degrees." Another student sighs that her fellow students "are going to find the easiest way they can to get to graduation." Coursework is said to be manageable, depending on the student's program of study. "What most students find most rigorous are the attendance policies. It takes some time to figure out how to get good grades without going to class," says a recent graduate.

Some students protest this characterization: "In fact, academics are probably the main reason people come to IU, especially when it is packaged in this great atmosphere," says one. Another says, "I won't lie to you, we do party here, but to say that students are not concerned with getting a good education is absurd. I find the atmosphere of the school to be very academically focused, and have not met one person who has done the bare minimum to graduate." Apparently, IU is large enough to accommodate all ranges of intellectual curiosity.

Then there is that matter of basketball. After the legendary/infamous Bobby Knight was ousted in 2000, Coach Mike Davis led the men's basketball team to the NCAA national championship game in 2002. The team has struggled some since— though, to students' delight, it still wipes the floor with Purdue every year. Basketball exercises a uniting force at IU; there are more requests for student tickets than can be accommodated. After each big win, "we flood through Sample Gates and onto Kirkwood Avenue to party," says a student. Another student says, "Kirkwood was unreal after the Final Four game when we knew we were going to the national championship. It was like Mardi Gras." The men's soccer program has also been historically good, winning its sixth Division I national championship in 2003.

Students play sports too. The intramural program is one of the biggest in the country, offering 27 sports—everything from billiards to euchre to indoor soccer. "Intramural sports are huge here," says a student. "There's every sport imaginable offered." More than 450 teams are registered in the intramural basketball leagues alone. The student recreational sport center is extolled by students for its pool, weight room, basketball courts, and track.

IU has four "neighborhoods" of residence halls grouped together. Different residence halls feature such varied amenities as a music practice room, a game room, an exercise room, a convenience store, a library, and a McDonald's. One residence hall offers a co-op program in which students receive a reduction on rent (up to 40 percent) in exchange for cleaning and doing such chores as taking out the trash and cleaning the bathrooms. IU offers no single-sex residence halls but does provide single-sex floors for those who would like them—in fact, most floors are single sex, as are all dorm rooms and most bathrooms. Students who do not specifically request limited visitation hours (ending at midnight weekdays and 2 a.m. weekends) are automatically assigned to residence halls with unrestricted visitation hours. "Most upperclassmen live off campus," says a student, "but parking is horrible. There are times when you've got 15 minutes between classes and a 20-minute walk."

IU is relatively safe, given its size. The school reported six forcible sex offenses, one robbery, five aggravated assaults, 49 burglaries, and one stolen car on campus in 2003.

Indiana is not a pricey school, especially if you're a local. In 2004–5, in-state tuition was only $5,756, while out-of-state tuition totaled $16,791. Room and board came in at an average of $5,872. Admissions are need-blind, but the school does not make guarantees about levels of financial aid. Approximately 40 percent of students receive some assistance.

UNIVERSITY OF IOWA

IOWA CITY, IOWA • WWW.UIOWA.EDU

Good workshop, but no tools

A University of Iowa geographer once described the school as "centrally located," which was apparently shorthand for "the middle of nowhere." Iowa City is almost four hours from the nearest major city. But famous folks have *been* there. Flannery O'Connor studied here, for a time, at the famous Writers' Workshop founded by Paul Engel. So did John Irving, Jorie Graham, Andre Dubus, Wallace Stegner, Kurt Vonnegut, and a number of famous others.

But it's debatable at best whether this stellar program has any impact on the quality of the typical undergraduate's education. For like virtually all state schools, Iowa maintains only an unimaginative, pedestrian curriculum; students will not necessarily encounter the great authors and texts of the West—the Bible, Thomas Aquinas, William Faulkner—that helped form the mind of Flannery O'Connor. Nor need they encounter Flannery O'Connor. Some university representatives might name underfunding of the liberal arts as the biggest problem facing UI today, but its unfocused curriculum is much more troubling.

Academic Life: In hock

UI's Code for Student Life proclaims, "As members of the academic community, students are encouraged to develop a capacity for critical judgment and to engage in a sustained and independent search for truth." By "independent," the code really means "unsupervised." The approved courses that fulfill Iowa's general requirements *could* provide a student with something like a core body of knowledge, but only if that student knows where to look.

Persistent budget cuts, it is claimed, have kept the University of Iowa from attaining its goal of 700 professors in the College of Liberal Arts and Sciences. Although student enrollment figures in the college hit a 10-year high in 2003, the number of tenure-track faculty decreased by 7 percent over the same period, as departing professors were either replaced with less expensive visiting professors or not at all. The dean of Liberal Arts and Sciences called the budget cuts "devastating" to her plans to hire more faculty; she predicted larger class sizes and fewer courses. Budget cuts are also driving off teachers. A recent survey indicates that 81 percent of faculty who quit in fiscal year 2003 left the university for better pay. The university ranked 39th in average faculty salaries in fiscal year 2004 among 60 universities studied, and ninth out of 11 schools in its peer group. Time will tell whether legislative initiatives or the current university-wide billion-dollar fundrais-ing effort will restore undergraduate faculty to desirable levels.

One academic bright spot at UI is the Honors Program. Entering students with strong records are invited to join, and other students whose GPAs meet or exceed 3.2 may join later. Each semester, honors seminars are offered for juniors and seniors, and most departments offer independent studies. Students may also opt to research a senior project with the guidance of a faculty member and thereby earn a degree with honors. Honors seminars in 2004 included "Philosophy of Religion," "Work and Family Issues," and "Mystery Fiction and the Ancient World."

Iowa does not require students to take a cultural diversity course, but students may take one to fulfill a general education requirement. Course offerings include "Education, Race, and Ethnicity," "Literature and Sexualities," and that foundational course, "Human Relations for the Classroom Teacher." The university also offers more than 90 study-abroad programs as part of a strategic commitment to "internationalizing the undergraduate, graduate, and professional curricula."

The English department has recently improved the requirements for its majors,

VITAL STATISTICS

Religious affiliation: none
Total enrollment: 28,442
Total undergraduates: 20,135
SAT/ACT midranges: SAT
  V: 530–660, M: 540–670;
  ACT: 22–27
Applicants: 13,874
Applicants accepted: 83%
*Accepted applicants who
  enrolled*: 35%
Tuition: $4,702 (in state),
  $15,354 (out of state)
Room and board: $6,350
Freshman retention rate: 83%
Graduation rate: 36% (4 yrs.),
  66% (6 yrs.)
*Courses with fewer than 20
  students*: 49%
Student-faculty ratio: 14:1
*Courses taught by graduate
  TAs*: not provided
Most popular majors:
  business, social sciences,
  communications
Students living on campus:
  28%
*Guaranteed housing for four
  years?* no
Students in fraternities: 8%
  sororities: 12%

Students in the College of Liberal Arts, which enrolls the bulk of undergraduates, must fulfill the following requirements—many of them in their first semester or year:

- Three to eight semester hours of rhetoric, depending on their ACT verbal scores. This amounts to the English composition/ writing requirement.
- One course in historical perspectives. Among the courses fulfilling this requirement are "Western Civilization," "Introduction to Islam," and "Philosophy and the Just Society."
- One course in humanities. Courses include "Major Texts of World Literature," "Contemporary Brazilian Narrative," "Classical Mythology," and "Literature and Sexualities," to cite just a few out of many, many choices.
- One course in quantitative or formal reasoning. No course in mathematics is required, though math through algebra is required for admission to the university. Students can also opt for a course in computer science.

who must take at least one course from the following six areas: literary theory and interdisciplinary studies, medieval and early modern literature and culture, modern British literature and culture, American literature and culture, transnational literature and postcolonial studies, and nonfiction and creative writing. Students are also required to take at least two courses from three historical periods, including early literature through the seventeenth century, eighteenth- and/or nineteenth-century literature, and twentieth- and/or twenty-first-century literature. The history department's distribution requirements include two classes each in American, European, and non-Western history, along with one course studying a period before 1700.

Students at UI must meet with an advisor before registering for classes, but they report that the quality of advising varies wildly. Although one lucky student reports, "I have spent hours talking to advisors about school and just life in general, and they have always been a great resource," many agree with another student's claim: "My first advisor was a joke." Students are assigned advisors (not teaching faculty but "advising professionals") at freshman orientation. Students switch to teaching faculty advisors upon choosing a major. Says a student, "Some departments are better than others at advising. In big majors, people have to find their own way through." Unfortunately, students don't always take advantage of the opportunities available to them. As one professor says of his advisees, "I usually have a couple of students who will come in on a regular basis, but most don't bother."

The university's sheer size means that students can always find solid classes among the masses. The strongest programs at Iowa are traditionally found among the fine arts. The Writers' Workshop is still highly regarded. The studio arts and theater programs are also strong. The university was the first to accept creative work in theater, writing, music, and art on an equal basis with academic research. The English, history, sociology, and political science departments earn high rankings but are uneven. Recommended professors include Evan Fales and Thomas Williams in philosophy; Ralph Keen and David E. Klemm in religious studies; and Brooks Landon, Garrett Stewart, and Jonathan Wilcox in the English department. The communications program is one of the best in the country.

While professors feel the push to produce innovative research, and some classes are massive, students report they have a good rapport with faculty. At such a behemoth university, students have to make the effort to search out professors, but once they do, they will "find them very accessible," says a student. "I have never had professors who weren't very excited to have students come to their office hours." Students' middling intellectualism is confirmed by a student who says, "Classes here are manageable. They don't prevent you from having a social life." There are classes taught entirely by teaching assistants, notably the required freshman rhetoric courses. Sometimes students develop better relationships with TAs than with professors. "TAs are more accessible and know people's names," one student says. A professor says, "I don't want to be harsh, but the UI doesn't care all that much about teaching. It has awards and programs, of course, but the bottom line is that this is considered a 'research institution,' which means that if you are a great researcher and a crappy teacher, you will still get raises and promotions." The student-faculty ratio is 14 to 1.

Students say that classroom indoctrination or intolerance is rare at Iowa, which is good news. Sadly, the course catalog contains plenty of examples of politicized, overspecialized, and ephemeral courses. One need look no further than the first-year seminars, which are designed to allow freshmen to work closely with faculty members. These courses are capped at 15 students—good. But professors often design them around their current research—not so good. Seminars offered in the spring of 2005 included "Being Young in Africa," "Exploring Mt. Everest," "The Social Roots of Academic Ability," and "Listening to the World," where students could "reflect on the role of sound in our lives." As to majors, among the vast crowd listed in the catalog you will find both women's studies and (we're not kidding) a BS in leisure studies.

Under Iowa's Four-Year Graduation Plan, students can sign a contract with the university guaranteeing that graduation will not be delayed by closed classes and limited course offerings. Many UI students opt to take courses at nearby Kirkwood Community College, the largest community college in Iowa, where tuition is cheaper and class size is smaller. "A symbiotic relationship has been forged between the two institutions through dual enrollment and a growing number of transfer students," says one professor.

REQUIREMENTS (CONT'D)

- One course in the social sciences, chosen from a list that includes "Media and Society," "Introduction to Human Geography," and "Health for Living."
- Two courses in the natural sciences, including one with a lab. Choices include botany, earth history, astronomy, physics, and chemistry.
- Two additional courses chosen from two of these areas: cultural diversity, fine arts, foreign civilization and culture, historical perspectives, humanities, physical education, and social sciences.
- One section of "Interpretation of Literature." All students (except English majors) must take this course. As one of only two university-wide required courses, the course description is sufficiently ambiguous to accommodate the number of sections—82 in one recent semester—offered by so many different instructors.
- Fourth-semester competency in a foreign language (any of 15 languages, from American Sign Language to Zulu).

Student Life: Not heaven—Iowa

Approximately 64 percent of students hail from Iowa and 21 percent from adjoining states—primarily Illinois—and the political leanings of the student body reflect the centrist populism of this region of the country. On the right, there is a We Support Bush club *plus* a Students for George W. Bush club; in the center, there is the Democracy Matters organization (whose goal is "to educate . . . about the corrupting power that special-interest campaign contributions have on America's political system"); and on the left there are the Iowa International Socialist Organization and the Campaign Against War, one of whose primary goals is protecting "civil liberties in our current climate of neo-McCarthyism." One student calls Iowa's open atmosphere its best asset. And another student says, "I am a conservative and I enjoy this campus; it is a challenge and a wonderful platform for discussions."

The priorities of Iowa's administration are evidenced by the following anecdote. When faced with a $7 million budget cut in 2003, President David Skorton said, "The university will protect student financial aid, the library acquisitions budget, and our equal opportunity and diversity efforts." This at a university with undeniably under-staffed liberal arts departments. Skorton's welcome letter to students makes clear the university administration's main concerns: research and diversity. "At Iowa, we've nurtured innovation and creativity across and between disciplines for decades, and we've been committed to making our educational programs accessible to people from diverse walks of life and cultural backgrounds since our inception. And we keep our eye on the future, responding to the new challenges of a global, interdependent, multicultural, and technologically advanced society." As for religious diversity, well, a pamphlet describing Danforth Chapel, a reconstruction of a pioneer chapel whose plans were worked on by Grant Wood among others, reassures readers that the wood and tooled-copper cross that sits atop the altar "can be removed."

The general attitude of Iowa students toward Iowa City, according to a student, is: "When people get here, they can't wait to get out of here. When they leave, they can't wait to get back." While Iowa City may not be the "Athens of the Midwest," as the charming overstatement has it, it does have a certain appeal and a surprising amount of cultural activities.

Iowa City is a community of 63,000 located on the east side of the state on the Iowa River. The downtown area, within walking distance of the university, features a bricked pedestrian walkway lined with shops, restaurants, and coffeeshops. Throughout the summer and in early fall, Iowa City hosts a free Friday night concert series, and the Jazz Festival in early July draws a large crowd. A few times per year, the city holds a Gallery Walk with receptions at 15 downtown sites. "There's strong community support of the arts program," says a music major at UI. The Devonian Fossil Gorge is Iowa City's star attraction. It was revealed when a 1993 flood washed away tons of soil and trees to reveal a 375-million-year-old ocean floor. The Amana Colonies—seven villages founded by German immigrants in 1844—are only 25 miles away and offer old-world charm and shops.

The campus covers 1,900 acres, and its buildings are constructed in Greek-revival and modern styles. Iowa City affords plenty of recreational areas, including a skate park, a walkway by the Iowa River, and a state park a few miles away where students can swim, sun, fish, rent canoes, hike, and bike. Students also go to "the res," a reservoir with a bird sanctuary and abundant deer.

UI has more than 370 student organizations; the biggest ones are Students Today Alumni Tomorrow Ambassadors, Student Government—and RiverFest, the student organization that mounts Iowa's four-day April celebration, drawing 20,000 people for live music, an art fair, and biking and running races. Students often hang out at The Summit, Atlas World Grill, Java House, and Tobacco Bowl. "There is a wide range of activities, from dancing in a bar, to listening to a classical band or choir at Hancher [Auditorium]," a student says. "Whatever you want to do, whether it's playing sports or watching them, playing an instrument or listening to them, dancing or watching them, Iowa has it in spades."

Around 90 percent of freshmen live in the 10 residence halls, even though students are not required to live on campus. UI offers a number of "learning communities" designed to "provide a supportive and engaging environment where students are challenged intellectually and have the unique advantage of bonding with other students who have similar academic goals." Students are selected on a first-come, first-served basis. There are learning communities for health sciences, women in science and engineering, honors, international crossroads, leadership in business and entrepreneurship, performing arts, transfer students, and refreshingly, men in engineering. There is also a "quiet house" option. All halls are officially substance-free; that ban includes the use of tobacco products in residence halls. All residence halls are coed, with men and women separated by floor or wing.

Around 10 percent of students join fraternities or sororities, but Greeks hold a disproportionate number of leadership positions on campus. The main occupations of Iowa students? "We go to football games and we go to bars," a student says. As is to be expected at a Big Ten school, sports are important. The front of the newsletter for St. Paul Lutheran Chapel and University Center announces "Take Note! On Saturday, Iowa plays Wisconsin in football" before going on to church news. "Sports are advertised a lot, especially guys' football and basketball," says a student. UI offers 12 varsity teams for women and ten for men. The school mascot is Herky the Hawk; Herky is short for Hercules, of course. Iowa has a ban on scheduling games with teams with Native American mascots (excepting Illinois, apparently), deeming the use of such mascots "demeaning and offensive."

SUGGESTED CORE

1. Classics 20E:030, Greek Civilization
2. Philosophy 026:111, Ancient Philosophy
3. Religious Studies 032:001, Judeo-Christian Tradition (*closest match*)
4. History 16E:111/112, Medieval Intellectual History 300–1150 / 1150–1500
5. Political Science 030:132, Modern Political Theory
6. English 008:147, Shakespeare
7. History 16A:061, American History 1492–1877
8. History 016:003, Western Civilization III (*closest match*)

MIDWEST

"The worst part of UI is its bar scene," says a student. His lament is justified. Official statistics show disciplinary action amounting to an average of nearly 500 liquor-law cases per year and an average of 120 drug-related *arrests* per year over the last three years for which statistics were available (2001–3). In 2003, Iowa reported 145 on-campus drug arrests and its liquor violations are anywhere from two to 10 times as many as those reported at state universities of similar size. "Partying is pretty big here," a student says. "Underage drinking is always in the news," says another. "One reason the statistics are so spectacular is that the university and city cooperate to crack down on—and report publicly—alcohol-related activity," says one professor. But a student reports that "student government actually hands out cups, kind of encouraging underage drinking." Students report that freshman regularly get served at bars and that "bar crawls are pretty prevalent." In fact, the drinking scene is so popular that university administrators are considering a university detoxification center where students arrested for public drunkenness would be housed until the following day. Proponents point to a telling statistic: 17 percent of graduates leave the university with a criminal record because of public intoxication.

The university's other safety statistics are about the same as those reported at similar universities. A female student reports, "I feel very safe here." The UI Department of Public Safety offers self-defense training and recently implemented a special department dedicated to the investigation and prevention of sex crimes—eight sexual assaults were reported in 2003). In the same year, the school reported 53 burglaries, two robberies, three aggravated assaults, and four stolen cars. There are emergency phones located throughout campus, and there is a student-run safety escort service.

As a state school, Iowa is a pretty good deal for residents: in-state tuition in 2004–5 was only $4,702 ($15,354 for nonresidents), while room and board was $6,350. Admissions are need-blind, and the school undertakes to cover student need with a combination of grants, work-study, and loans. Some 42 percent of undergrads who apply for it receive need-based aid. The average student loan debt of those recent graduates who borrowed was $17,044.

UNIVERSITY OF KANSAS

LAWRENCE, KANSAS • WWW.KU.EDU

No place like home

The University of Kansas, located on a high ridge in a state known for its flat fields, sticks out from its surroundings in more ways than one. Founded in 1864 as Kansas's main state university, KU has risen steadily in reputation to become, first, one of the top public universities in the Midwest, and now one of the more highly regarded public schools in the nation.

    The university is currently fighting its way out of a financial crunch brought on by drastic state budget cuts. KU has managed to avoid eliminating staff positions and closing academic programs only by raising tuition significantly and by adding special fees to popular programs. But even so—and while it certainly has some of the usual political and curricular deficiencies associated with large state universities—KU offers one of the best state-school educations now available. For one thing, it is a rarity in that it maintains a humanities and Western civilization department and comparatively strong liberal arts requirements. But given the mammoth size of the school and its impersonal approach to teaching, it's not for everyone. "A student who is at high risk for getting lost in a large, bureaucratically inclined institution should stay away from this place," says a professor. But self-directed students who know what they want to study can probably find it here.

Academic Life: Lost civilizations

Of the 11 undergraduate schools at the University of Kansas, four admit freshmen—the College of Liberal Arts and Sciences (CLAS), the School of Architecture and Urban Design, the School of Engineering, and the School of Fine Arts. The remaining seven schools require that a student first enroll in the College of Liberal Arts and Sciences, and that is where nearly half of KU undergraduates end up choosing majors.

    All students attending KU—or thinking of attending KU—should take a long, hard look at the humanities department. Much of what is valuable in this department

VITAL STATISTICS
Religious affiliation: none
Total enrollment: 28,905
Total undergraduates: 21,343
ACT midrange: 21–27
Applicants: 10,442
Applicants accepted: 69%
Accepted applicants who enrolled: 59%
Tuition: $4,163 (in state), $12,117 (out of state)
Room and board: $5,216
Freshman retention rate: 83%
Graduation rate: 26% (4 yrs.), 57% (6 yrs.)
Average class size: 23
Student-faculty ratio: 20:1
Courses taught by graduate TAs: 20%
Most popular majors: business, communications, visual and performing arts
Students living on campus: 23%
Guaranteed housing for four years? no
Students in fraternities: 14% sororities: 17%

The University of Kansas has no core curriculum, but it does maintain a decent set of distribution requirements for students in its College of Liberal Arts and Sciences—including a few common courses which hold out the promise for some unity in a KU education. Students must take:

- Any three introductory English courses, two covering composition and one in literature.
- One course in oral communication or logical argument.
- Two introductory classes in math (or one in math and one in biology).
- Two specific courses in humanities and Western civilization. These cover many of the classic works of the West, from the ancient world through the Middle Ages to the dawn of modernity.
- One class dealing with a non-Western culture. Approximately 150 courses qualify here, and fortunately only a few of them seem to be exercises in guilty hand-wringing; students can fulfill this requirement with good courses like "Imperial China" or "Introduction to Ancient Near Eastern and Greek History."

can be traced to the influence of the late, great liberal educator John Senior—author of, among other works, *The Death of Christian Culture*. Working at what must have seemed the darkest moment in American academic history—in 1970, as campuses erupted into violence and curricula were being disemboweled at hundreds of famous colleges—Senior and a few of his colleagues conceived and launched a program at KU called "Integrated Humanities." Starting with a reading list that matched any great books program in the country—and requiring the study of Latin—this program became far more than a 24-credit sequence in Western culture. Senior and his colleagues organized stargazing expeditions, arts fairs, and formal waltz balls. Many of the program's students discovered or rediscovered religious faith as a result of immersing themselves in the common literature of what used to be called "Christendom." And herein lay the program's downfall, according to Robert Carlson, author of *Truth on Trial: Liberal Education Be Hanged*, the definitive history of the program. "Integrated Humanities" had been under attack since its inception by academics and activists who detested its "ethnocentric" and seemingly reactionary focus on Western civilization. The program's critics seized upon the religious affiliations of its founder, accusing him of proselytizing his students. These and other charges, through relentless repetition in the media, eventually stuck—and by 1979, integrated humanities had effectively been dismantled by the KU administration. According to those who saw it happen, the school broke up the program by making its courses ineligible to meet the school's core requirements—a devious strategy that proved effective. Still, the remaining elements of a core curriculum and the significant number of worthy courses still offered at KU by serious scholars exist largely because of Senior's noble, doomed experiment the very existence of which today goes unnoticed on campus. It is little more than a rumor, like the tale of a lost civilization that, once you do a little digging, turns out to have been our own.

KU students can still earn a major or a minor in the humanities, and within the field may choose to specialize either in literature or Western civilization. As the course catalog puts it, one may choose "areas such as philosophy, religion, history, theatre, literature, women's studies, and the arts. Your major might combine courses to focus on such interdisciplinary topics as peace, humor, or hunger. Popular courses such as the 'Masterpieces of World Literature' series, the 'Biography of a City' series, and 'Science, Technology, and Society' are offered, along with many others."

The university Honors Program is another option that serious students should consider. Although the program has no separate, fixed curriculum, honors students can take courses that are more challenging—and always smaller, at 20 to 25 students. Freshman honors students also take a one-credit seminar that introduces them to the program and to general study habits; the instructor of the course becomes the student's advisor. Most honors students live together in special housing, "an enriching environment conducive to learning," according to the program's Web page.

Sadly, honors classes and upper-level courses within their majors are about the only places students will have the opportunity to develop relationships with faculty. Introductory courses enroll as many as 500 students. Graduate students teach roughly 20 percent of courses.

Freshmen are assigned professional advisors in the Freshman-Sophomore Advising Center, where they get some help in choosing a major and in picking courses that fulfill the general education requirements. Once a student has declared a major, he can visit with a faculty advisor within that department, but he shouldn't expect to receive much personal attention there. "Unfortunately, many teachers are not available outside of class," a journalism major says. "Sometimes the size of the school can hinder a student from getting the type of advice and help he needs. KU is not a personal place, and you do not get much individual attention here." Students in some of the smaller departments have better experiences. "Many [professors] are widely published, but I have never had a professor who wasn't willing to bend over backwards to meet with any students by appointment," says a student in such a department. "Whenever I walk into a professor's office hours without appointment, he's never been too busy to help." Says one professor to prospective students, "Be aggressive in getting to know faculty. If you want to hide and be anonymous, KU is a place to do it, but if you want to get individual attention, you can make that happen, too. Shop around for courses and faculty. Let faculty challenge you. Whether you would call yourself liberal, conservative, indifferent, insane, or whatever, don't shy away from the seri-

REQUIREMENTS (CONT'D)

Students earning a BA also face nine "principal course distribution" classes and a language requirement:

- Three courses in humanities—one in history, one in literature and the arts, and one in philosophy and religion.
- Three from natural sciences and mathematics.
- Three from social sciences. Students take one course in culture and society, one in individual behavior, and one in public affairs. There are more than a dozen choices in each category, ranging from "Principles of Human Geography" to "Women's Studies: An Interdisciplinary Introduction."
- Foreign language courses through the fourth semester. KU offers instruction in 28 languages, including Cherokee, Croatian, Haitian, Wolof, Yiddish, and the more common western European tongues. The university uses placement exams to identify the appropriate courses for those students who already have some foreign language skills; proficiency exams are available for those who wish to test out of the requirement.

ous business of thinking, an activity that can be handsomely enhanced through the offerings of many KU faculty, even some with whom you may vehemently disagree."

As the quality of instructors varies, so does the quality of students. "My students run the gamut from intellectually curious to not so much," a music professor says. "Many come by to talk about ideas, but some seem to be only interested in filling requirements and making good grades."

Some of the best departments, professors say, are those in the humanities, as well as music, aerospace engineering, and the preprofessional areas. Students say some of KU's best professors are Allan Cigler, Sharon O'Brien, Thomas Heilke, and Burdett Loomis in political science; Anthony Genova in philosophy; Albert W. Burgstahler in chemistry; David M. Katzman and William Tuttle in American studies; Douglas A. Houston in business; Stephen Ilardi in psychology; Leslie Tuttle in humanities; Douglas Atkins, Steven Faulkner, and Dennis Quinn in English; and Jonathan H. Earle and Phillip S. Paludan in history. According to a professor, "Public administration is a top-ranked department in the narrow niche field of urban affairs, and it has just started up an undergraduate major. The majority of political scientists in this country would tell you that PA is an intellectually weak field, a stepsister subfield of political science, and certainly of little note for liberal arts interests at the undergraduate level. The fact that the administration is investing in this department in a College of Liberal Arts and Sciences may be a bad sign."

KU's greatest weakness, says one professor, is a lack of financial resources. "When I came to KU 30 years ago, the state of Kansas was supplying well over two-thirds of the budget. Now it is down to less than one-third. Private contributions and research grants have made up some of the difference, but the situation is not good, and it is getting worse." In 2002, the university slashed 159 staff positions and several programs because of an $18.8 million state budget cut. The university was also unable to offer regular salary raises, according to a university press report. Some of the missing money has been replaced by increased tuition and fees. "These are being used for faculty lines, program development, maybe even capital projects in some schools. Buildings are going up, the [business] school is hiring 14 new faculty lines and developing five majors, et cetera," says one veteran teacher.

During the Vietnam War era, the University of Kansas was known as the Berkeley of the Midwest. In 1971, activists burned down the Kansas Student Union, threw a Molotov cocktail through the Navy ROTC's office window, and harassed ROTC students. Some of that spirit still remains at the university. "The state of Kansas is very conservative overall," says one student, "However, Lawrence is very liberal—much like Bloomington, Indiana, or Austin, Texas." One right-leaning professor warns, conversely, that "a significant aspect of Kansas conservatism is a populist anti-intellectualism." When such populists look at a school like KU, they resent its elitism more than its actual politics, and look for chances "not to improve the curriculum, but to reduce humanities and similar offerings in favor of more business-school and other brick-laying options," he says.

Students differ about the degree to which political bias affects classroom instruction. A journalism and political science major says, "Even the political science courses I have taken remain unbiased." Another student says, "I never felt uncomfortable because my views differed from the professor's." Still, other students report that many courses—especially those in the social sciences—are politicized. And one particular student complains to us of professors who ridicule the ideas of conservative students and applaud those who share the professor's views.

Student Life: "Mount" as a relative term

The state of Kansas might call to mind cornfields and tornadoes spinning over huge expanses of flat land, but the city of Lawrence is in one of the few hilly parts of the state, and the campus itself is on top of Mt. Oread, making the starting time of that 8 a.m. math class only half the battle. And while many large state schools can boast of precious little in the way of architectural splendor, KU's limestone campus is truly one of the Midwest's most beautiful. The university's master plan, completed in 2001, dropped $155 million on capital construction and landscaping. Newly constructed buildings include a lavish Student Recreation Fitness Center. This 98,000-square-foot facility "features a 1/7-mile suspended track, a 42-foot climbing wall, 15,000 square feet of cardiovascular and resistance training equipment, free weights, aerobics and martial arts studios, and indoor and outdoor basketball and volleyball courts," boasts the school. KU has also completed a $10.3 million expansion and renovation of its music building, Murphy Hall—which now has "new rehearsal halls, faculty offices and a computer laboratory, plus an expanded music and dance library." The newly completed Hall Center for the Humanities features "a 120-seat conference room, a seminar room, a serving kitchen, and offices for Hall Center staff and research fellows." The school is still working on an 80,000-square-foot, high-tech engineering complex.

Only a fifth of students, mostly freshmen, live on campus. All dormitories are coed, except for two all-women residence halls, but men are always housed in a separate wing from women and nobody lives next door to a member of the opposite sex. KU has a strictly enforced housing policy that requires a male student to be escorted by a female student when visiting the female wing of a hall (and vice versa). In the two women's residence halls, men must be out by 11 p.m. on weeknights but can stay overnight throughout the weekend. KU offers several options for students who wish to live with other students of similar interests. There are also quiet floors for upperclassmen and scholarship halls, where students share all cooking and housekeeping responsibilities.

Around 15 percent of KU undergraduates are members of a fraternity or sorority, and most members live in the organizations' houses. Fraternities and sororities con-

SUGGESTED CORE

1. Classics 230, Greek Literature and Civilization
2. Philosophy 288, Ancient Philosophy
3. Religious Studies 124, Understanding the Bible
4. Religious Studies 315, History and Literature of Early Christianity
5. Political Science 301, Introduction to Political Theory (*closest match*)
6. English 332, Shakespeare
7. History 128, History of the United States through the Civil War
8. Philosophy 560, Nineteenth-Century Philosophy

tribute to KU's reputation as a party school, and drinking plays an enormous role in campus social life. "There is very much a culture of alcohol here, and it can seem at times like the only thing to do here is get drunk," says one student. "But Lawrence has culture other than alcohol." Another student says, "Students at KU can drink as much or as little as they wish. The alcohol is available and accessible to all ages. . . . However, it is not the focus of the university's activities." Lawrence itself provides plenty of options for weekend and nighttime entertainment—live music, shops, bars, and restaurants. Students rate it highly as a college town.

One of the best attributes of large state universities is that there's usually another student who shares your interests—and at KU there's no better way to find such students than by joining one of the almost 500 student clubs. The 75 or so academic organizations are mostly preprofessional societies like the Pre-Dental Club, the Public Interest Law Society, and the Athletic Training Students' Association, but there are also intellectually oriented ones like the Philosophy Club, which sponsors an essay contest each year and occasional lectures by professors in the discipline. Religious clubs, especially evangelical Christian ones, are also quite popular at KU, and no student should have trouble finding a group that shares his faith: discussion groups, Bible studies, and prayer sessions abound. Some local churches shuttle students to Sunday services. KU is one of the few state schools with a chapel on campus. Danforth Chapel is nondenominational; its Web page says that it is a place for "individual meditation and prayer" as well as weddings, memorial services, and student activities. "A variety of conservative and not-so conservative Christian student communities thrive here," says one professor. "The St. Lawrence Catholic Center has a (deservedly, in my opinion) wonderful reputation for intellectual integrity and engagement, as do a few evangelical churches with strong youth and student programs."

On campus, left-wing students are the most outspoken and active. "I would say that liberal elements are much more comfortable on campus, and conservatives just don't speak out enough," says a student. "Groups like Queers and Allies and a student animal rights organization are some of the most outspoken at KU." Another conservative student says, "It seems as if some organization is always protesting against some cause or another. So much so, that I begin to become immune to what these groups are saying." But there are always exceptions to the rule. The school's most recent Rhodes scholar, Robert Chamberlain, class of 2002, "was an outspoken conservative, and he deferred his admission to Oxford to do a tour of duty in Iraq, a move that was clearly noted in university publications," according to one professor. "Precisely because I *am* a conservative, I made common cause with many of my much more liberal colleagues in opposing the invasion of Iraq," this professor says. Clearly, there is room for dissent, complex thinking, and bipartisanship at KU—which is a very good thing.

The College Republicans are said to be very active on campus, as are the College Democrats, but both groups usually stick to party politics rather than ideological issues, often bringing state politicians to speak on campus. Political clubs can obtain financial support through the Center for Campus Life (using student fees), but a representative from the office says most of the funding goes to general expenses like office supplies and fliers for the political club. "Controversial funding for speakers or pro-tests, for instance, would have a much harder time finding financial support," he says.

One of the few interests that nearly every Jayhawk student shares is sports, and basketball above any other. How could they not, at this school where James Naismith, inventor of the game, worked for nearly 20 years? Kansas has been a perennial con-tender for the NCAA men's basketball championship for decades, but the team has not won the crown since 1988. Besides varsity athletics, KU offers 25 intercollegiate club teams and many intramural ones, usually organized around residence halls and Greek houses.

Crime is relatively infrequent for a school of KU's size. The most common cam-pus crime is burglary, and students who lock their doors and watch their laptops rarely become victims. The SafeRide service escorts students from one end of campus to the other between 11 p.m. and 3 a.m. In 2003, the school reported six forcible sex offenses, four aggravated assaults, 86 burglaries, and five stolen cars on campus.

Even though it has risen steadily and unpredictably in recent years, tuition at KU is still low, especially if you come from Kansas. In 2004–5, in-state students paid $4,163, while out-of-staters had to pony up $12,117. Room and board cost $5,216. In response to vigorous student complaints about unpredictable prices, the school has introduced a four-year guaranteed tuition rate plan. Starting in the fall of 2007, incoming students will pay the same base tuition rate for their first four years of college, thus avoiding any annual increases.

KENYON COLLEGE

GAMBIER, OHIO • WWW.KENYON.EDU

For whom the bell tolls

Every quarter hour, bells clang loudly from Kenyon College's Church of the Holy Spirit, resonating throughout Gambier, the quaint clapboarded town in north-central Ohio that has been home to the college since 1828, when the four-year-old school moved here from Worthington, Ohio. "There's nothing better in Gambier than walking around the town on a warm Friday afternoon listening to the bells' melody," says one recent graduate.

In 2002, the Board of Campus Ministries announced that the bell would henceforth be rung for every execution in the United States as well. Giving new meaning to old traditions is emblematic of life at Kenyon College. The school's hallowed Peirce Hall features stained-glass depictions of some of Western civilization's greatest heroes, but some fear that the meaning of their work and lives has slowly been transformed through the prism of fashionable, politically correct interpretive categories. At Kenyon, old achievements have mingled with new promises to reshape the vision of Bishop Philander Chase, who founded Kenyon as an Episcopal seminary for men.

President Robert Oden, a staunch civil libertarian, left for Carleton College in 2002, and Kenyon named Georgia Nugent as its new president in February 2003. Under Oden there was a sense that ideological diversity and the open exchange of ideas were valued, and President Nugent is following in his tradition. In her inauguration speech she expressed admirable sentiments, saying, "I urge us to look forward, not in a way that breaks with the past, but that reconnects us with it." One professor says that if Nugent "is 50 percent of what Oden [was], we'll be lucky.

Bishop Chase's legacy still informs many traditions at Kenyon, including its college songs and dances and its Collegiate Gothic buildings. And college officials and students remain devoted to the Hill, as the Kenyon campus is commonly known—and some of them even stand by its oldest and finest qualities.

Academic Life: Senior exercises

Kenyon College has no core curriculum, such as used to characterize liberal arts colleges. Instead it offers a set of "curricular guidelines." Students must take at least two courses in each of four academic divisions: social sciences, natural sciences, fine arts, and the humanities. Kenyon students also must meet a (rather weak) foreign language requirement that can be fulfilled by a unit of introductory-level courses or through sufficient test scores. And, to accommodate graduate schools' demands for students with skills in quantitative analysis, Kenyon students now have to take one half-unit of quantitative reasoning, usually in the mathematics, psychology, or economics departments.

After completing most of their distribution requirements, Kenyon students declare a major, choosing from a list of 18 departments that offer 38 majors between them. Most of the majors that Kenyon offers are in traditional disciplines, but students can add concentrations or minors from interdisciplinary departments like African American studies or women's and gender studies. A few students each year create their own interdisciplinary curricula and pursue "synoptic" majors.

One interdisciplinary department popular among first-year students is the Integrated Program of Humane Studies (IPHS), which introduces students to the classic texts of Western civilization in seminar-style tutorials. Over the course of a year, students study the Hebrew Bible, Plato, Virgil, Shakespeare, Aristotle, Nietzsche, Mann, Virginia Woolf, Kafka, Foucault, and others. After the first year, around a dozen students choose to concentrate in IPHS, taking courses such as "Dante and Machiavelli" and "Modernism and Its Critics." Though the IPHS curriculum offers incoming students a solid year of worthwhile reading and writing, it is an underdeveloped major.

Political science remains a favorite department among students and is highly respected among Kenyon faculty for the quality of its instruction and its commitment to exploring fundamental issues. The department provides an impressive year-long freshman seminar, "Quest for Justice," an introductory class for majors—popular among nonmajors too—that includes readings from the Bible, Thucydides, Tocqueville, Rousseau, and the American founders. Political science majors are also required to take a course called "Liberal Democracy in America" and must choose another American politics course in addition to three courses in comparative politics and international relations. Students also take one upper-level seminar.

Kenyon's English department first gained widespread recognition with the arrival of the Southern Agrarian poet, literary critic, and *Kenyon Review* founder John Crowe Ransom in 1937. Poet Robert Lowell transferred from Harvard to Kenyon to study under Ransom. Poet James Wright and novelists E. L. Doctorow and William Gass further helped establish Kenyon's English department as among the best in the country. The department has slipped since those glory days—although, granted, that was a hard act to follow. Although it still offers such solid courses as "Advanced Fiction Writing Workshop," "The Epic," and "Chaucer," the department has gone the way of

VITAL STATISTICS

Religious affiliation: none
Total enrollment: 1,634
Total undergraduates: 1,634
SAT/ACT midranges: SAT V: 620–730, M: 610–690; ACT: 26–31
Applicants: 3,808
Applicants accepted: 38%
Accepted applicants who enrolled: 32%
Tuition: $32,980
Room and board: $5,570
Freshman retention rate: 96%
Graduation rate: 81% (4 yrs.), 84% (6 yrs.)
Courses with fewer than 20 students: 70%
Student-faculty ratio: 10:1
Courses taught by graduate TAs: none
Most popular majors: social sciences, English, visual and performing arts
Students living on campus: 98%
Guaranteed housing for four years? yes
Students in fraternities: 27% sororities: 10%

English departments almost everywhere in placing undue emphasis on postcolonialist and postmodernist approaches to literature, giving students choices like "Queer Shakespeare." Several students and professors now say that the department is overrated.

One aspect of Kenyon's academic life that is not overrated is the senior exercise, which consists of a departmental project or comprehensive exam. Every student completes his Kenyon years with this ordeal, placing all Kenyon seniors in the same stressful boat. In the social sciences and in the humanities, a student can satisfy the requirement by writing a chapter-length paper on a broad topic determined by his advisor. In other departments, such as economics and political science, majors take a comprehensive test.

Little about Kenyon is career-oriented. One professor says, "Students are our main 'business' in that we take them, their intellectual growth, and our teaching and learning seriously—intensely so." Consequently, professors expect students to be enthusiastic about their educations and to want to learn for the sake of learning. Professors nurture students' intellects with constant book recommendations, additional reading assignments, and vigorous teaching. "We don't get caught up in rankings, future financial earnings, or prestige in general," says one student. "We immerse ourselves in learning." According to college literature, nearly 70 percent of Kenyon graduates enter graduate school within five years.

Upon entering the college, incoming students are paired with faculty advisors and upper-class counselors (UCC) of the same potential major, both of whom help ease the transition from high school to college. "Without my advisor and UCC, choosing courses would have been a little overwhelming," says a recent alumnus. Though classes like the creative writing seminar with writer-in-residence P. Frederick Kluge and the "North by South" history seminar with William Scott and Peter Rutkoff are perennially full, students can petition professors to be admitted. The college boasts a student-faculty ratio of 10 to 1 and an average class size of 18. Most courses meet conference-style around large tables, which encourages discussion.

Unfortunately, a few years ago the college lifted its commendable "Ten-Mile Rule," which had mandated that professors live within a ten-mile radius of the college. Now some professors commute from Columbus and other satellite towns across north-central Ohio, which veteran professors and administrators say limits student interaction with professors. One professor says, "I now see that [lifting the rule] has eroded the quality and integrity of the residential college we once were."

Nonetheless, most professors enjoy their relationships with students; according to a recent survey, 93 percent of first-year students have dined at a professor's house. At Kenyon, a professor and student might run into one another at the college bookstore and talk about a difficult concept or chat about graduation or summer plans. Even absent the Ten-Mile Rule, most professors are still highly accessible, and most doggedly encourage students to visit them during office hours. One student says, "If you're not going to office hours, you're missing out on a wealth of knowledge." Students often crowd the hallways outside professors' offices during finals week.

Kenyon faculty members are never entirely apolitical, whether in tenure or hiring decisions or in promoting their own beliefs on campus. Two professors mention their distaste for what one calls the "unspoken agreements among many or most people that ensure the hiring of people who are politically acceptable." Another professor says that a "darker side to faculty relations in certain areas" is unavoidable. "A few of us are maintaining rational discourse as best we can." It is clear from these comments that there are professors with conservative sentiments at Kenyon, and that, though they feel beleaguered, they also feel free to complain privately to their students about it. Students say they rarely encounter overt indoctrination inside the classroom, but sometimes suspect political agendas in the curricula of a few especially politically active professors. Regardless of their beliefs, though, students usually feel comfortable enough to express varying viewpoints. According to one student, "Politics stop at the classroom door."

In 2002, the college dedicated two buildings for the natural sciences and mathematics to form a new science quadrangle. In addition to the completion of Kenyon's impressive music facility, Storer Hall, a few years before that, the new buildings represent a renaissance for the long-ignored mathematics, music, and natural sciences departments. A master plan foresees the construction of a new fine arts center and additional student housing, plus the renovation of existing buildings. A new fitness, recreation, and athletic center is scheduled to open this year.

The list of excellent professors at Kenyon is long. It includes Fred E. Baumann, John M. Elliott, Kirk E. Emmert, Pamela K. Jensen, Joseph L. Klesner, David M. Rowe, Devin Stauffer, and Stephen E. Van Holde in political science; Jennifer Clarvoe, Adele Davidson, William F. Klein, P. F. Kluge, Perry Lentz, Sergei Lobanov-Rostovsky, and David Lynn in English; David E. Harrington, James P. Keeler, and Richard L. Trethewey in economics; K. Read Baldwin and Provost Gregory P. Spaid in art; E. Raymond Heithaus, Haruhiko Itagaki, and Joan L. Slonczewski in biology; Robert E. Bennett in classics; Wendy MacLeod and Harlene Marley in drama; Reed Browning, Michael Evans, and Roy Wortman in history; Bradley Hartlaub and Judy Holdener in mathematics; Natalia Olshanskaya and Carlos Piano in modern languages and literatures; Benjamin R. Locke in music; Juan E. De Pascuale and Joel F. Richeimer in philosophy; John Idoine and Paula C. Turner in physics; Allan Fenigstein and Michael Levine in psychology; and Royal Rhodes in religious studies.

ACADEMIC REQUIREMENTS

Kenyon's distribution guidelines call for students to take 18 courses outside their major, including:

- Two courses in the fine arts. Examples include "Music Theory" and "Screenwriting."
- Two classes in humanities. "Sanskrit" and "Afro-Caribbean Spirituality" both qualify, among others.
- Two courses in natural science. Courses include the traditional hard sciences, as well as mathematics and psychology.
- Two courses in the social sciences. Courses range from "History of the Early Middle Ages" to "Socialism at the Movies."
- One introductory foreign language class (unless students test out of this requirement).
- One course demonstrating quantitative reasoning. Most science, mathematics, and economics courses count.

Student Life: Quiet in the land—usually

"There's obviously a lot to love about going to a school on a hill in the middle of Amish country, and there's obviously a lot to hate," says a recent alumnus. This love-hate emotion is one to which most Kenyon students admit. The college's 1,000-acre campus in Gambier, Ohio, home to just 1,400 year-round residents, is about 45 minutes northeast of Columbus and 90 minutes from Cleveland. The village has seemingly undergone little change since its founding, adding only a bank, two small inns, a nationally renowned bookstore, two coffeeshops, a college bar, and a post office. Not bad for a small town—but here's the catch: only two village buildings are *not* owned or operated by the college. The Village Market, one of the private enterprises, still allows residents to purchase groceries on credit slips, greets customers by their first names, and is a welcome sanctuary from urban anonymity. The director of admissions describes Kenyon's atmosphere as one of "incredible community."

Suburban sprawl is beginning to encroach on the area around Gambier, however. Knox County's population grew nearly 15 percent between 1990 and 2000, and Kenyon officials are justifiably worried that new developments popping up around Gambier will damage the college's rural image and threaten its splendid isolation.

Middle Path, a mile-long gravel walk, runs the length of the campus and is the thoroughfare connecting the college's main academic buildings. The path is anchored at the north end by Bexley Hall and at the south by Old Kenyon, a historic dormitory. Former president Oden once remarked that the path is symbolic of lifetime learning—a straight path with numerous disciplines stemming from it.

Kenyon is strictly residential, mandating that all 1,600 or so students live in college housing and purchase the college board plan. A handful of seniors live off campus, but few exercise this option, since most enjoy the college apartments and dormitories; besides, the housing market is tight in Gambier and Mount Vernon, a neighboring town of 15,000. Single-sex or coed floors, suites, apartments, smoking or nonsmoking dorms, and substance-free housing are all available. All residence hall bathrooms are single sex, as are dorm rooms. Students can also apply for special-interest housing if, for instance, they want to live with the Black Student Alliance or an unrecognized sorority.

Though students report that they spend most of their time studying, the college offers more than 120 student organizations, ranging from the Stairwells to Students for Creative Anachronism. The *Kenyon Collegian*, the college's official weekly newspaper, is a hastily written source for campus news and weekly commentary. ALSO, the Allied Sexual Orientations club, has considerable influence on campus and frequently marches against injustice, perceived or otherwise, and sponsors speakers. The *Kenyon Observer*, a 13-year-old conservative monthly, has witnessed a recent renaissance and has graduated gifted writers who have worked at *Commentary*, *National Review*, the *Weekly Standard*, and *Public Interest*.

In any given year, the college has only around 50 politically vocal students, who express their views in various campus media outlets like the conservative *Observer*, the mainstream *Collegian*, or the radical *Voice*. The Crozier Women's Center and the Snowden

Multicultural Center both pursue liberal agendas. The women's center annually sponsors Take Back the Night, a march against violence against women that students say usually turns into an anti-male event, and has hosted the controversial *Vagina Monologues*. Activists United is an umbrella organization that sponsors lectures against sweatshops, the death penalty, international free trade, and related issues. Campus conservatives have hosted lectures by Andrew Sullivan, Bay Buchanan, Alan Keyes, and Ward Connerly in the past few years, typically through the fledgling College Republicans organization. A recent attempt to bring John Derbyshire of *National Review* to campus met with difficulties. According to the *Collegian*, a balking professor and a scheduling conflict conspired to postpone Derbyshire's seemingly inoffensive lecture, titled "Prime Obsession: Bernhard Riemann and the Greatest Unsolved Problem in Mathematics." Examples of genuine intolerance at Kenyon are few.

Kenyon students are regularly rated among the happiest in the nation. Outside of class, academic departments and a Student Lectureships Committee regularly host lectures; student bands perform; and would-be poets recite at coffeehouses. But Gambier is still a quiet college town. For those who find it too quiet, the college offers a free shuttle to Mount Vernon and a cheap Saturday shuttle to Columbus. One student says, "The biggest fear one could face in Gambier is boredom." Students generally work hard, but several professors remark that students' interest in writing well and reading more is quickly slipping. "Students do not read as much as they used to," one faculty member sighs.

According to college officials and recent campus antidrinking campaigns, drinking is far too prominent on campus. The administration imposed drinking-game restrictions in the fall of 2003, resulting in a heated debate between college officials and the student body as represented by the student council. The college also employs several security officers to help enforce liquor laws both old and new and to secure the safety of students.

Although only one bar in Gambier serves alcoholic beverages until the legal closing hour (2 a.m.), the college's 12 fraternities and sororities do their part in hosting the student parties and dances that form the backbone of Kenyon's social life. The college hosts an annual winter ball—the Philander's Phling, named in honor of the college's founder—which attracts scantily dressed drunken students every year in a rather ironic tribute to a bishop. The college also hosts an annual raucous weekend in May called Summer Send Off, usually featuring musical performances, barbecues, and recreational activities.

SUGGESTED CORE

1. Classics 111, Greek Literature in English, Epic and Lyric
2. Philosophy 200, Ancient Philosophy
3. Religious Studies 310/225, Hebrew Scriptures: The Old Testament / The New Testament
4. Religious Studies 320, Medieval Christianity (*closest match*)
5. Political Science 221, History of Political Philosophy: The Modern Quest for Justice
6. English 220, Shakespeare
7. History 101, United States History, 1492–1865
8. Sociology 112, Social Dreamers: Marx, Nietzsche, and Freud

MIDWEST

Kenyon is a member of the NCAA Division III North Coast Athletic Conference along with Oberlin, Ohio Wesleyan, Case Western Reserve, and archrival Denison University. Though the college offers 22 intercollegiate teams and several club and intramural teams, the school has a thin reputation for athletic prowess. Kenyon's swimming program is an exception; the men's team has maintained the longest national championship streak in NCAA history—an incredible 24 years. The women's swimming team has won 19 straight conference titles. Other notable intercollegiate teams include women's tennis, men's soccer, and men's lacrosse. The new $60-million Center for Fitness, Recreation, and Athletics is scheduled to open in fall 2005.

Students can call for walking or driving escorts when out late at night, and blue-light emergency phones are available all over campus. In 2003, Kenyon reported one forcible sex offense and no other crimes—meaning that the campus is generally very safe.

Kenyon is very expensive, with tuition in 2004–5 at $32,980 and room and board averaging $5,570. Admission is not need-blind, but students who do get in are guaranteed financial aid to meet their full need.

MACALESTER COLLEGE

SAINT PAUL, MINNESOTA • WWW.MACALESTER.EDU

Global positioning

When Presbyterian Liberal Arts College opened in Saint Paul, Minnesota, in 1885, its leaders probably didn't plan to found a cosmopolitan institution. But the school, now known as Macalester College, has remade itself as a center of globalist education. Half of the student body studies abroad at some point, the school's International Center gives an award to the most internationally minded senior, and the flags of all United Nations member states wave as graduates march across the stage at commencement.

It was immediately following World War II that the college first began this push for global identity, offering special programs for foreign students and a number of study-abroad programs. Around this time, Macalester began to attach itself to the Scottish heritage of one of its earliest benefactors, a businessman and philanthropist from Philadelphia named Charles Macalester. In 1948, the Scottish Clan of MacAlister adopted the school as a member, and since then Macalester has take up everything Scottish— from the student pipe band to the school's athletic teams' name, the Scots. The college formerly held an annual Scottish Faire, which was one of the most popular events on campus. Unfortunately, Macalester's generous endowment has been outrun by the management's spending and the beloved event has been discontinued for financial reasons.

Macalester has the same excellent credentials as many other top-notch liberal arts colleges: strong student-faculty relationships, a commitment to scholarship, and a close college community. But while its internationalist flavor is unique and certainly represents a strength for students interested in foreign studies, Macalester's administration, faculty, and many of its students are obsessively committed to that multiculturalism which political philosopher Paul Gottfried has called a "secular theocracy"—to the detriment of the school's academic mission.

Academic Life: Around (the rest of) the world

Macalester outlines a general curriculum for its students but leaves the rest unstructured; students can potentially graduate with huge gaps in their education. For instance, some have complained that the history department does not offer a course that covers the founding of the United States and its early history (unless you count classes such as "Gender and Sexuality in Colonial and Nineteenth-Century North America").

Students are offered plenty of unorthodox options at Macalester College. The urban studies program contains an interdisciplinary major that combines courses in anthropology, economics, history, sociology, political science, and geography—all seemingly centered on racial tension in America. Since its participants receive little depth in any given area, even administrators warn, "All students will not be equally proficient in all skills." International studies is a popular major that augments Macalester's focus on globalism; students in this major learn humanities and social sciences in conjunction with a foreign language and a semester abroad. The women's studies department allows majors to choose 12 courses from a list chock-full of courses like "Lesbian, Gay, Bisexual, and Transgender Studies: Sexual Margins, Colonial Legacies." The American studies program, according to one student, "has nothing to do with white people." While it is tempting to dismiss such courses as shallow, one conservative student who has perforce attended some warns against such dismissal. "They do come from a thought-out worldview, and you do have to think to contradict them properly."

Two-thirds of all classes at Macalester contain fewer than 20 students and only 2 percent of classes enroll more than 50 students. With a student-faculty ratio of 11 to 1,

VITAL STATISTICS
Religious affiliation: Presbyterian
Total enrollment: 1,900
Total undergraduates: 1,900
SAT/ACT midranges: SAT V: 640–740, M: 620–710; ACT: 28–32
Applicants: 4,405
Applicants accepted: 39%
Accepted applicants who enrolled: 28%
Tuition: $26,638
Room and board: $7,350
Freshman retention rate: 93%
Graduation rate: 74% (4 yrs.), 81% (6 yrs.)
Courses with fewer than 20 students: 68%
Student-faculty ratio: 11:1
Courses taught by graduate TAs: none
Most popular majors: social sciences, psychology, foreign languages
Students living on campus: 68%
Guaranteed housing for four years? no
Students in fraternities or sororities: none

Macalester offers students close relationships with professors. Teaching assistants do not teach courses. But while Macalester has traditionally made teaching its highest priority, in recent years the administration has placed increased emphasis on research. Whether this shift in focus will diminish the quality of teaching or student-faculty relationships is yet to be seen. "Professors are definitely accessible to students," one student says. "I, for one, often feel intimidated by professors and don't ask for very much help, but I think as I chose my major, I became more relaxed with the professors in my department and more willing to get advice."

Each student must complete a special freshman course during his first semester on campus. These small classes focus primarily on writing instruction. Past offerings have included the religion course "Introduction to the Bible," the French class "Tolerance and Intolerance," and the English course "American Voices: The American Novel." Instructors for these courses usually serve as advisors for new students. After a student declares his major during his fourth semester, he is assigned a faculty advisor within his department—though he is welcome to switch advisors at will. Students are required to consult with their faculty advisors before registering for new courses each semester. With such an unstructured general education curriculum, students had better seek out guidance.

Beyond the freshman writing course, Macalester has no further writing requirements. Furthermore, Macalester is so focused on international issues that it has apparently forgotten to require any specific knowledge of the Western tradition. Students can graduate without ever having taken courses in Western civilization or American history; they can fulfill their humanities and social science course requirements with classes entirely outside of the Western tradition. Even the domestic diversity requirement manages to avoid mainstream U.S. history, focusing instead on the cultures of diverse populations within the United States with courses like "Ethnographic Interviewing" and "Sports in the Afro-American Community." One professor says, "Macalester's curriculum is still too unstructured. Curricular sprawl is the rule."

Many, many academic courses complement Macalester's focus on the curious, the queer, and the foreign. A history course, "Racial Formation, Culture, and U.S. History," discusses "the construction of racial identities" and "the linking of material privileges and power to racial locations." The history department also features "The Politics of Food in Latin America," an offering that blames food shortages and malnutrition in Latin America on U.S. foreign policy. Then there is "Gender and Sociopolitical Activism in Twentieth-Century Feminist Utopias," which relies on an evaluation of utopias, dystopias, and "ecotopias" to provide students "with a genealogy to . . . construct visions of sociopolitical change." The program also "offers an opportunity to link with a local minority/women's organization." "The Politics of Sexual Minority Communities" in the political science department asks students to question the sexual origins of American communities; to explore homosexuality as a social, physiological, and religious construct; and to study how American politics and law embody these constructs. "Global Governance" investigates the emergence of "global civil society" and "the implications of these changes for democracy, social justice, etc." Large swathes of

Macalaster's curriculum seem designed to promote multiculturalist ideology.

It should be noted that Macalester also offers many fine, traditional academic courses, even as it actively encourages students to study politically charged and narrow topics. One conservative professor says that though the campus is strongly liberal, people feel comfortable voicing their views, and politics does not enter into hiring and tenure decisions. "We are conscientious about that," the professor says.

Future professions do not seem to concern Macalester students or faculty unduly; although most biology majors are premed, economics, for instance, is generally taught more with an eye to theory rather than application. There is no business degree. Nevertheless, according to the professor, "Hierarchically structured curricula that do not lead to a lucrative profession and are not 'trendy' (e.g., physics, math—except for computer science—foreign languages and literatures) have a hard time at Macalester." Another says that only "a small minority of students are authentically curious."

The best departments at Macalester are economics, art, the sciences, and the foreign languages. The classics department is also solid, and its majors concentrate on important areas within the discipline. Students report that the following professors are among the best at Macalester: Mary Hark in art, J. Andrew Overman in classics, Karen Warren in philosophy, Vasant A. Sukhatme and Sarah E. West in economics, David Dressoud in math, Sarah N. Dart in linguistics, and Sung Kyu Kim in physics.

One worthy option for seniors is the Honors Program, which requires an above-average GPA, imposes additional work, and culminates in the writing of a senior thesis.

Student Life: So long to the faire

Macalester has taken a number of aggressive steps to promote interest in non-Western cultures. A few years ago, the college created its Council for Multicultural Affairs, which is staffed by students, faculty, and administrators and is supposed to advise the president on multicultural issues. The college is recruiting a dean of race and ethnicity, while apparently planning to retain its existing dean of

ACADEMIC REQUIREMENTS

Macalester's rather easygoing distribution requirements run as follows. Each student must complete:

- One "First-Year" course, during the freshman year. These special sections of ordinary courses in various departments contain no more than 16 students and are writing-intensive.
- Two courses in the social sciences. Options here range from "Foundations of U.S. Politics" to "Feminist and Queer Theories and Methodologies."
- Two courses in the natural sciences.
- Two courses in mathematics.
- Three courses in the humanities and fine arts (including at least one course in the humanities and one in the fine arts). Humanities options include "Ancient World I: Greece" and "Postcolonial Theory." Art choices range from "Renaissance Art" to "Art of the Last Ten Years."
- One course in "international diversity" and one in "domestic diversity." Courses to fulfill these requirements can be found in over a dozen departments.
- A fourth-semester course in a foreign language or the equivalent.

multicultural studies and dean of multicultural life. The latter runs his own department, which is meant to contribute to a "spirit of diversity." Part of this department is the Lealtad-Suzuki Center, the college's multicultural center, which offers a first-year program called "Pluralism and Unity" and sponsors Safe Zone, an organization committed to "creating a safe environment and community for all people regardless of sexual orientation, race, ethnicity, national origin, gender, religion, age, or ability." The Train the Trainer program helps students, faculty, and staff teach others in the Macalester community about diversity issues. And the monthly Soup and Substance lunch series is a discussion for students and faculty; past topics have included "Ain't I a Woman? Listening to the Voices of Women Students at Mac" and "Why Are the Black Kids Sitting Together in the Cafeteria?"

They might better have asked, "Why are all the black kids sitting at *one table* in the cafeteria?" Macalester's obsession with matters of race has not paid off when it comes to attracting students of color. According to the college, only 3 percent of students fall into that prized category. The number of preferred minorities in matriculating classes has been falling recently, and the class of 2005 contained the fewest nonwhites at Macalester in 13 years—even though the acceptance rate for those minorities has been rising.

Many students share the ideological predilections of the Macalester administration. According to the *Chronicle of Higher Education*, graduating international students are encouraged to carry a flag of their home country to the commencement ceremony. When a Jordanian student wanted to carry a Palestinian flag, the college prohibited her from doing so, since Palestine is not an official United Nations member state. After considerable protest, however, she was allowed to wave a flag from her seat during the ceremony. One student who transferred from Macalester to another midwestern college claims that "Macalester is a breeding ground for radicals."

Nevertheless, a College Republicans group called MacGOP has recently been organized. Apparently, at least some of their members are pleased with their choice of college. One says, "I'm really glad that I chose Macalester. It has given me the opportunity to grow and deepen my beliefs, to be challenged both in the classroom and in the dorms, and the chance to be involved in ways I couldn't have at other schools."

Larger groups include Queer Union, the Student Organization for Animal Rights (SOAR), Afrika!, and Feminists in Action. "I don't think that conservatives are very comfortable on campus," an art major says. "The political leaning of Macalester is definitely, without any doubt at all, left. Recently in the Minnesota elections when the Republican Party won many of the positions, it seemed as though the campus was in mourning, or that it was the end of the world or something." The college newspaper, the *Macalester Weekly*, overflows with opinion pieces alternately excoriating President Bush, American imperialism, and multinational corporations.

In 2002, *The Princeton Review* ranked Macalester first on a list of colleges where "students ignore God on a regular basis." (Macalester is officially a Presbyterian school, so this ranking must have had John Knox spinning in his grave.) Then–college president Michael McPherson anticipated that this ranking would hurt Macalester's image, and he tried to set things right for the next year by encouraging religious students to fill out *The Princeton Review*'s online survey. McPherson sent an e-mail to an admissions officer saying, "I'll bet this is driven by some question on their Web survey about how often you pray. If that's right it would be easy enough to get 10 students or something to log in and say they pray a lot or something. This is going to be a pain with religious alumni." When the complete e-mail chain was forwarded to 100 or so students, McPherson apologized and called his comments "flip and insensitive," according to a *Macalester Weekly* article. "Macalester is very big on respecting people of other faiths, but I think that Christianity, specifically, isn't often thought of in this light," a Christian student says. "Christianity is often an easy target for mockery. And so, being a Christian at Mac is both difficult and exciting."

Weyerhaeuser Chapel gets a lot of use as a site for speeches, conferences, performances, and weddings. In the basement is the chaplain's office (and the campus mosque). Downstairs hosts dinners, prayer services, receptions, small-group speakers, and the like. The chaplain is a Presbyterian minister, Rev. Lucy Forster-Smith. Her associate chaplain, a recent Macalester graduate, according to the school Web site, "is intensely involved in the national movement for the full inclusion of gay, lesbian, bisexual and transgendered persons within religious communities." Catholic students may resort to Fr. Jim Radde, S.J., "a conflict management consultant, mediator and restorative justice practitioner," who reports that he "enjoys international folk dancing and is venturing into watercolor." Rabbi Shoshana Dworsky looks after the spiritual needs of (presumably Reform) Jewish students. Religious clubs on campus include the Council for Religious Understanding, Fellowship of Christian Athletes, Mac Catholics, Mac Jewish Organization, Mac Protestants (a liberal group), Mac Unitarians, the Muslim Student Association, Macalester Association of Alternative Spiritualities (Wiccan), and the Macalester Christian Fellowship (a more evangelical group).

Most Macalester students live on campus in college-owned housing. In fact, freshmen and sophomores are required to live on campus. Each year, about 70 percent of students live on the grounds, where they can choose to live on single-sex floors; all dormitories are coed, but bathrooms are not. There are also substance-free dorms for those who select them.

Some students who would prefer to live on campus are denied the privilege each year because of housing shortages, although the completion of a new residence facility may relieve this situation. The two-year housing requirement puts a heavy load on the residential system and limits the spaces available to juniors and seniors. Macalester

SUGGESTED CORE

1. Classics 194, Amazons and Aristotle: The Art and Literature of Ancient Greece
2. Classics 230/Philosophy 230, Ancient Medieval Philosophies
3. Religious Studies 119, Introduction to the Bible
4. Religious Studies 121, Early Christianity, Heresy, Orthodoxy, and Gospels
5. Political Science 160, Foundations of Political Theory
6. English 140, Shakespeare
7. History 190, American Civilization (*closest match*)
8. Humanities 158, Nineteenth-Century European Culture

claims that increased demand among upperclassmen for on-campus housing is a result of improved amenities like the new student center. The administration has long-term plans to expand dorm space, but with funds tight there are no hard dates for completion. Off-campus housing can be difficult to secure as well, since Macalester's campus lies near two other small colleges in a prime real estate area, and housing is commensurately expensive. But often, juniors and seniors have no other choice.

Athletics have long been popular at Macalester, with many students participating in one way or another. The school fields 21 varsity teams, and the Scots compete in the Minnesota Intercollegiate Athletic Conference (MIAC), a league of small colleges in the area. The football team plays a different schedule, shunning the MIAC to play as an independent in the NCAA Division III. Some years ago the school president suggested eliminating football altogether because of lackluster results and a thin roster, but popular pressure to keep the team prevailed. Thus were the Scots able to go 1-8 in 2003. And again in 2004. In addition to varsity athletics, Macalester offers many club and intramural sports.

Outside the classroom, students enjoy the social life that Macalester and the area surrounding the campus offer. One student says, "There are lots of events going on all the time—interesting lectures, dances, soccer games, plays. I think people tend to hang around or near campus all the time even though downtown isn't too far away, simply because they are pretty busy with weekend homework." Still, with both the College of Saint Catherine and the University of Saint Thomas nearby, the college's urban setting is lively. The original nineteenth-century college was housed in Old Main, a squat prairie-looking castle. Another notable structure, Carnegie Hall, was built in 1910 during Andrew Carnegie's Johnny Appleseed phase; today it houses the social science department. The campus brushes up against Grand Avenue, a business district that caters to trendy urbanites.

Macalester has a fairly safe campus, given its urban location. In 2003, the school reported two forcible sex offenses, four burglaries, two stolen cars, and one arson. The campus is patrolled by security officers, and with the student escorts program students can call for a walking buddy at night for up to one mile off campus. Emergency phones are located throughout the campus.

With 2004–5 tuition at $26,638 and room and board at $7,350, Macalester is a moderately pricey place. And the school is considering putting an end to need-blind admissions, which it had practiced for decades, citing financial shortfalls. The school does offer some merit-based scholarships and need-based financial aid that takes into account how many kids a family has in college.

MIAMI UNIVERSITY

OXFORD, OHIO • WWW.MUOHIO.EDU

In plain sight

At the center of Miami University's campus lies a bronze medallion imprinted with the university seal. Along with an open book representing the accumulation of knowledge, a globe symbolizing the present-day world, and a telescope looking into the future, the seal proclaims the motto *Prodesse Quam Conspici*— "To accomplish rather than to be conspicuous." This is an apt slogan for Miami, a public school whose steady academic ascent seems to have gone almost unnoticed. Sadly, however, the humanities at Miami are in no better shape than at most liberal arts universities throughout the land. If this university aspires to greatness, it will have to tighten up its curriculum requirements so that students cannot avoid confronting enduring thinkers and fundamental texts.

Academic Life: According to plan

Miami University literature claims that the campus's Georgian architecture is "the perfect setting for the classic liberal arts foundation that all students receive at Miami." Certainly, the architecture is better than the curriculum: Miami students do not have to complete a true core and are free to fulfill many of their distribution requirements with less-than-worthy courses. A student is allowed to pick between, for example, "Introduction to Shakespeare" and "Literature and Sexuality." And so on. In the social science category, students are offered both "American Political System" and "African Americans in Sport." The choices—too many choices—are theirs. Miami's liberal arts plan does at least make sure that students are exposed to different areas—but

VITAL STATISTICS
Religious affiliation: none
Total enrollment: 17,151
Total undergraduates: 15,059
SAT/ACT midranges: SAT V: 560–640, M: 580–660; ACT: 25–29
Applicants: 14,977
Applicants accepted: 71%
Accepted applicants who enrolled: 33%
Tuition: $18,256
Room and board: $7,010
Freshman retention rate: 91%
Graduation rate: 72% (4 yrs.), 79% (6 yrs.)
Courses with fewer than 20 students: 37%
Student-faculty ratio: 17:1
Courses taught by graduate TAs: 11%
Most popular majors: business, education, social sciences
Students living on campus: 45%
Guaranteed housing for four years? no
Students in fraternities: 22% sororities: 27%

students can, as one says, "skate through the distribution requirements rather easily." And while each department at Miami offers solid courses, they're mostly served up alongside politicized or overspecialized fare. For instance, in the fall 2004 semester, the history department offered "Survey of American History," a solidly informative course—as well as "Homosexual and Lesbian Experience." To top off the Miami academic experi-

According to the "Miami Plan," all students face the following distribution requirements. The first set of mandates, called "Foundation" courses, address five specified areas. Students take:

- Two courses in English composition.
- Four courses in fine arts, humanities, and the social sciences.
- Three courses in the natural sciences.
- One course in mathematics, formal reasoning, or technology.
- One course in United States cultures and one in world cultures.

Specific qualifying courses are earmarked in each category.

The second set of requirements, called "Focus" courses, involve nine hours of a "thematic sequence" outside a student's major.

The other general education requirements are as follows:

- One seminar course during freshman year.
- A "Senior Capstone Experience" course. This is purportedly "the culmination of the undergraduate learning experience." The academic seriousness of such courses varies.

ence, the history department offered in the same semester the following senior capstones: "U.S. Youth Culture," "Holocaust," "International Relations," "Judaism and Early Christianity," "Churchill," "Islamic and Middle Eastern History," and "American Presidency."

Another academic weakness is the main freshman writing course, English 111. A professor says, "The university achieves small class sizes and individual attention through the employment of numerous graduate students and adjunct faculty who are poorly trained and barely coordinated. In practice, too many of these classes are exercises in indoctrination; 'good writing' is writing what the instructor wants to hear." He complains of "low standards: bad diction or grammar go unnoticed—or at least unpunished."

Majors at Miami run the gamut from the traditional liberal arts to exercise science, family studies, and women's studies. The stringency of major requirements varies by department. The English department, for instance, has a long list of rules attempting to ensure that its majors obtain breadth of knowledge; nonetheless, the quality of course offerings fluctuates, and majors can graduate without ever having taken Shakespeare, though they must take at least one course in "ethnic, minority, or women's literature." The religious studies department, on the other hand, only has general guidelines for the 24-credit-hour program and but a single required course, "Methods for the Study of Religion."

Miami University's School of Interdisciplinary Studies, known more commonly as the Western College Program, offers students a bachelor of philosophy degree in interdisciplinary studies, environmental science, or environmental studies. The program "has an education style of a small college within a major university. It offers faculty in residence, discussion classes, opportunities for research . . . and participation in a wide range of student activities," according to Western's Web site. The 250 Western students face additional requirements—specified courses designed for the program such as "Creativity and Culture" and "Social Systems." Each student constructs a "statement of educational objectives" in conjunction with a faculty advisor in order to tailor the student's remaining curriculum to his career objectives or academic interests. Western provides the student with no more than a shot at a true humanities education, though some may find the smaller community comfortable. And one Miami student calls Western Campus "a liberal world of its own."

Outside of the liberal arts, Miami has been building up its engineering program. Says a professor, "Miami will never be an engineering school like MIT, Caltech, etc., but this enhancement is a good thing for the university because it helps to counterbalance the facile and trendy leftishness of so many faculty in other parts of the university." The engineering faculty reportedly adheres to high intellectual standards and strong work habits and encourages students to take courses beyond engineering and math.

It is the Richard T. Farmer School of Business that is most popular and "has a lot of pull on campus," says one student. The business school is nationally renowned, in particular, for its accounting, economics, and entrepreneurship programs. According to a professor in the school, "the business program encourages academic experiences with a marketplace focus. In particular, the 'Laws, Hall & Associates' (advertising) and 'Interactive Media Studies' (Web development) programs involve teams competing to satisfy corporate clients." Business school students agree that the coursework is rigorous. And ever since the university recently admitted to a grade inflation problem (in spring 2001, the average GPA at Miami was 3.17), the business programs have become even more difficult. "They have been cracking down and making courses harder," an economics student says. "Grade inflation is not university-wide, though they fail to see this. The problem lies with individual departments." Thomas Hall and Norman Miller of the economics department (which often ranks in the top five in the nation for undergraduate studies) are noted as excellent teachers, as are David Rosenthal and Jan Taylor in the business school and Ryan Barilleaux and Augustus Jones in political science.

The student-faculty ratio at Miami is an underwhelming 17 to 1; students say that introductory and required classes such as English composition or science lab sections often employ graduate students as instructors. About 70 percent of first-year courses have enrollments of fewer than 30 students. Students report having no trouble registering for the classes they want.

Most students say Miami University professors are

REQUIREMENTS (CONT'D)

Students in the College of Arts and Science face further requirements:

- **Foreign language.** Students must demonstrate at least a fourth-semester proficiency in a foreign language.
- **Humanities.** Students must complete a total of nine semester hours from at least two of the following areas: history, literature, philosophy, and religion.
- **Social science.** Students must complete a total of nine hours from at least two of the following categories: anthropology, economics, geography, political science, psychology, and sociology.
- **Natural science.** Students must take 10 hours in the natural sciences, including at least three hours in physical science, three hours in biological science, and one laboratory course.
- **Formal reasoning.** Students must choose one course from a list of 10 approved courses in formal reasoning, a category that includes mathematics, statistics, logic, and linguistics. Some courses fulfill both Miami Plan and College of Arts and Science requirements.

dedicated to teaching and accessible to students, but at least one undergrad has had trouble. "Some professors are mainly there to perform research, and teaching is second. I have run into this a number of times. I would estimate 20 percent of teachers are more concerned with research. Maybe I have just had some bad luck." Another student chose Miami University based upon the faculty's dedication to teaching and is not disappointed by her choice. "Students are the number one priority here," she says. Professors are required to hold office hours, and many Miami students take advantage of this time to ask for advice on courses, career advice, résumé help, or just to talk. Before declaring majors, students visit advising centers, where professional advisors help them select majors, courses, or both. Once a student has declared a major, he is usually assigned a faculty advisor in his department, although some students report having nonfaculty advisors.

Perhaps because of the popularity of its business school, most Miami University students tend to be more or less conservative. The faculty is predominantly liberal. How much their opinions filter into class instruction depends on the professor and department. Faculty in the business school tend to be more conservative, or at least careful to be as objective as possible, while some faculty in the liberal arts departments "heavily influence the content of the course through selective teaching and misrepresented facts," says one student.

The administration, too, seems to have an agenda, at least in terms of serving that jealous god, "diversity." The president's long-term goals for the university include "increasing diversity of the faculty, staff, and student body." According to the school's Web site, minority enrollment has indeed increased 26 percent in the last six years. The school's attempts at outreach have included programs that help prospective students who might not have had as many educational opportunities as others—programs such as the Building Bridges to Science program, which awards stipends to selected minority students in order to allow them to engage in laboratory research.

Other initiatives are more questionable. Miami has hired a "multicultural librarian" to "assist students, faculty, and library staff in addressing a range of diversity issues," according to the university Web site. Saying that it wants its students to receive a more "rounded" education, the university has added course offerings to reflect its diversity-driven agenda. The most obvious example is the black world studies program, which offers majors and minors comprising courses that are "concerned with historical and contemporary production of black experience(s)."

There are also multicultural training sessions for faculty and staff—basically indoctrination attempts. In these classes, everyone from support staff—employees of the police department and housing, dining, and guest services—to graduate study directors and department chairs learns how to "creat[e] a supportive atmosphere for students of color." The university has created a Center for Black Culture and Learning and a Center for World Cultures and Learning to assist in its multicultural and diversity initiatives. Furthermore, in conjunction with a pansexual student group, the school supported an "Awareness Week" in the spring of 2003.

Student Life: The beaches are at the other Miami

Oxford, Ohio, is home to 8,500 year-round residents, but when school is in session, the population almost triples. The town boasts a surprising number of restaurants and businesses on its main, brick-paved street. Oxford residents enjoy international foods at a large grocery store (Jungle Jim's), ski slopes in nearby Indiana, and a renowned outdoor theater troupe. With Cincinnati and Dayton each about 40 miles away and Indianapolis 100 miles to the west, Miami University students live in a relaxed rural atmosphere that is also within easy distance of larger cities.

Students have formed more than 300 organizations. Approximately 10 percent of them are religious; Campus Crusade for Christ has one of its largest chapters here, with more than 900 student members. Many other clubs are either career related (about 20 percent) or sports oriented. The HawkHeads, the student fan club, is popular, as are the Miami Swing Syndicate and the Miami Dropout Club, an organization dedicated to skydiving. The few politically active liberal student groups at Miami, like Miami Students and Staff against Sweatshops, tend to concentrate on specific issues.

Religious students at Miami won an important battle in September 2001 when the university settled a lawsuit with 11 former and current students over the allocation of student fees to various student organizations. The students sued Miami for denying religious organizations access to the same university funding granted to political groups. Under the terms of the settlement, Miami devised a new system to allocate funding based on groups' activities and events: the money is now allocated for specific activities and events rather than to organizations in general.

Miami students are very interested in sports, if not as participants, then as spectators. Miami has eight men's varsity sports, 10 women's sports (including synchronized skating), and more than 40 club sports. Intramurals are dominated by the wildly popular broomball, a game rather like hockey but whose participants wear sneakers and slide across the ice with a mallet and puck. Almost 200 broomball teams sign up each season.

Most Miami students are involved in more than one extracurricular activity; some are in as many as five or six. Students aren't hesitant to characterize the typical undergraduate. "The 'typical' Miami student is changing, but still leans toward being a white, upper-middle-class, J. Crew–wearing student that was extremely involved in high school extracurricular activities," says one. Another student says that the typical Miami student is "active, an overachiever, studious with a fun side, upper-middle class, and con-

SUGGESTED CORE
1. Classics 211, Greek and Roman Epic
2. Philosophy 301, Ancient Philosophy
3. Religion 211, Introduction to the Religion of Ancient Israel (*closest match*)
4. Comparative Religion 232, The Development of Christianity, 100 to 451 (*closest match*)
5. Political Science 303, Modern Political Philosophy
6. English 134, Introduction to Shakespeare
7. History 111, Survey of American History I
8. Philosophy 402, Nineteenth-Century Philosophy

MIDWEST

fident about his/her future." About one-fourth of Miami students are members of fraternities or sororities, and Ohio high school counselors report that prospective students consider Miami a "Greek university."

Both conservatives and liberals feel comfortable on campus, in large part because the university is hardly a hotbed of political activity. In fact, in March 2004, Spectrum, the university's "gay, lesbian, bisexual, trans, queer straight alliance" teamed up with Miami's College Republicans to cosponsor a lecture given by the homosexual executive director of the Log Cabin Republicans. In true civility, both sides reportedly appreciated the talk, "Opening the Dialogue: Gay and Republican," while "not completely support[ing] everything [the speaker] said," according to the *Miami Student*. Another speaker who appeared recently, in 2005, was Ward Churchill, the infamous University of Colorado at Boulder professor of ethnic studies who compared the victims of September 11, 2001 to Adolf Eichmann. Miami students raised little fuss—in contrast to other campuses, where Churchill's proposed appearances sparked firestorms.

Says one student, "Overall, the student body as a whole is rather apathetic when it comes to politics." One issue did rouse the university in 2003, when a conservative columnist for the *Miami Student* was fired. The editorialist had criticized two professors in the French department for showing explicit films in their courses. The ensuing controversy, however, focused not on pornography in the classroom but on the student's journalistic practices: He had not seen the film himself (*Ridicule*; it was merely R-rated, and far from titillating) before he wrote his column. He was given the option by the student editor in chief either to apologize or be fired. He chose the latter.

A second issue that awakened befogged political sentiments at Miami was a 13-day strike that began in September 2003 by the labor union of Miami's facilities employees. The union and the university had butted heads regarding raises and wages. According to the *Miami Student*, several hundred students came to events and to picket lines to support the union workers, and about 100 faculty attended in full academic regalia.

Freshmen are required to live in university housing, and each hall has a theme and plans social events around it. All halls are smoke free. Coed halls are single sex by floor; official visiting hours are from noon to midnight on weekdays and unregulated on weekends. Living-learning communities allow students to live with classmates with similar academic interests. Most upperclassmen move off campus, and some go off-off-campus: so many Miami students spend a semester in a study-abroad program that Miami ranks tenth in the nation for the number of students it sends abroad. The university maintains its own campus in Luxembourg.

As focused as Miami students are on academics, it's no surprise that two of their traditions center on exam success. Students who step on the bronze medallion in the campus center are sure to fail their next tests, says the legend. This ominous warning is counterbalanced by the sundial found a few hundred yards away. For good luck on their next exams, students rub the head of one of its bronze turtles.

The school's location helps keep crime at bay; during 2003, the school reported six forcible sex offenses, 36 burglaries, one stolen car and four arsons.

Currently, around 70 percent of Miami's students come from the state of Ohio, but that proportion may decrease soon. In 2004, the university implemented a tuition hike that charges out-of-state tuition rates to in-state students, calling it a "progressive" move that "embraces the best practices of private-sector universities while fully meeting Miami's responsibilities as a state-assisted public university of Ohio." Tuition in 2004–5 was $18,256 per year; room and board charges were $7,010. All Ohio residents automatically receive a sizeable Ohio Resident Scholarship as well as an Ohio Leader Scholarship. The former is a fixed amount, but the latter varies according to need, merit, or even intended major. The minimum sum of these two scholarships for Ohio residents is $10,000. "The fact that Miami is partly supported by the state of Ohio is good news—it costs less than comparable private universities—and bad news—it conforms itself to various educational fads, as public universities usually do," says a professor. Nearly 75 percent of Miami students receive financial assistance.

University of Michigan

Ann Arbor, Michigan • www.umich.edu

That's affirmative

The University of Michigan prides itself as the "leader and the best," or at least Michigan's 107,000 football fans would like to think so on autumn Saturday mornings as they file into Michigan Stadium to watch the Wolverines (usually) pummel an opponent. But Michigan leads in more than just Big Ten football. Whether it is Michigan's focus on research or its unwavering devotion to racial diversity, Michigan has arguably become the standard bearer for America's public research universities. The direction in which it's leading them is, of course, another question.

Michigan has made headlines with its seven-year battle in defense of affirmative action, which finally ended in 2003 with the U.S. Supreme Court's decision to allow the university to use racial preferences in admissions. Although faculty and students still discuss affirmative action on campus, the debate now centers more on the effects of the decision—for instance, on minority applicants and enrollment. Students say the Supreme Court's decision has been overshadowed by other political issues, including a proposal to add a gender and sexuality requirement for liberal arts students. The university is a popcorn popper of outrageous ideas, and conservatives face quite a struggle in countering them.

Michigan has so many remarkable features that it's a shame many of them are overshadowed by political correctness. The university is huge, boasting 39,000-plus students, 7.6 million library books, 315 buildings, and 17,000 trees representing more than 150 species. Then there is the massive budget (nearly $1.2 billion in fiscal year 2004, larger than that of four *states*), which allows Michigan to attract some of the nation's best scholars and most talented students. Unfortunately, it is up to the student to find the university's strengths, along with professors who can teach and friends who enjoy learning.

Academic Life: Michigan, my Michigan

There is no question that the University of Michigan employs some of the nation's finest scholars, including several Nobel Prize winners. Of course, the extent to which these celebrity instructors are accessible to undergraduates varies. The University of Michigan is a research institution, and as one student says, teaching "always comes second, after getting published." This student charges that although professors dutifully hold office hours and teach the obligatory lecture courses, "in reality, they largely couldn't care less about the classes they're teaching." Another student says that the quality of instruction is uneven: "They know what they are talking about, but do not know how to present it to a class." Students also warn of difficulties getting into upper-level courses, which often fill up quickly. "You practically have to beg, borrow, and steal to get into any 400-level classes," says one student. Lectures are generally given in the German style: professors read them and students take notes, sometimes in one of the world's largest lecture courses, Chemistry 1800.

The University of Michigan can seem overwhelmingly large to many students, and the formal advising program does little to make it seem more manageable. Advising for students in the College of Literature, Science, and the Arts (LSA) is divided into two parts: general advising and concentration advising. If a student needs help choosing a major or has questions on how to satisfy the general education requirements, he is invited to make an appointment with a professional or peer advisor in the LSA Advising Center. Once a student declares a major, he can visit a concentration advisor within his department. In the history department, for instance, 10 professors hold office hours once a week specifically to advise students who have questions about the major. Students do not have specific faculty advisors assigned to them, and many students never establish academic relationships with faculty members. Students report that most of the informal academic advising they receive comes from teaching assistants, whom they typically get to know from the discussion sections of larger lecture courses. During the weekly discussion sections, TAs gloss over course readings and delve more deeply into areas in which students have questions.

Students name the following faculty members as the best undergraduate teachers: Gary Solon in economics; Ejner Jensen, John Knott, and Ralph G. Williams in English; H. D. Cameron, Ludwig Koenen, David O. Ross, and Charles Witke in classical studies; Astrid Beck and Scott Spector in Germanic languages and literatures; John

Fine, Diane Owen Hughes, David Lewis, Rudolf Mrázek, and William G. Rosenberg in history; Ronald Inglehart and Greg Markus in political science; and Christopher Peterson in psychology. Almost every department has its bright spots, but the most respected departments nationally are history, political science, classical studies, anthropology, chemistry, physics, engineering (all areas), Judaic studies, Chinese language and literature, the Medieval and Renaissance Collegium, psychology, economics, business administration, mathematics, Near Eastern studies, neuroscience, and art history. This extensive list alone should give the reader a sense of the broad basis of Michigan's academic reputation.

Michigan's philosophy department is strong. Majors are required to take courses in logic, the history of philosophy, value philosophy, mind and reality, and an advanced small-group seminar. Unfortunately, a course in ancient philosophy is not required. The classical studies department offers concentrations in classical archeology, classical civilization, ancient Greek, and Latin. Excellent courses include "The Ancient Greek World," "Greek Drama," and "Plato's Dialogues."

Michigan's art department features one innovative course especially worth looking into: "Food: From Farming to Feasts," which teaches students about the entire process of growing food, from farm to market, according to the *Chronicle of Higher Education*. Students dig potatoes and carrots, harvest fruit, make preserves, sell produce at a farmer's market, and serve their food at a homeless shelter. Yes, we said art class: assignments include creating artworks based on one's experience on the farm, and creating ceramic serving platters to donate to the shelter. While such a course shouldn't replace a survey of Renaissance painting, it does sound intriguing—particularly for students who might have grown up assuming that steak spontaneously generates in little shrink-wrapped packages.

Michigan's Honors Program is one of the most respected in the country. In years past, the program selected students based solely on academic merit, but recently, after receiving pressure from a number of minority student groups, Steven Darwall, the program's director, announced that he hoped to increase the program's "diversity" by altering the admissions criteria. However they are admitted, honors students face a special curriculum that can also satisfy the university's general education requirements. First-year students are required to take a humanities course on the ancient Greeks and another honors humanities course during the second semester. In addition to these, honors students must take two honors courses each semester. The honors literature

VITAL STATISTICS

Religious affiliation: none
Total enrollment: 39,533
Total undergraduates: 24,828
SAT/ACT midranges: SAT V: 580–680, M: 630–720; ACT: 26–30
Applicants: 21,293
Applicants accepted: 62%
Accepted applicants who enrolled: 45%
Tuition: $8,014 (in state), $25,840 (out of state)
Room and board: $7,030
Freshman retention rate: 96%
Graduation rate: 67% (4 yrs.), 87% (6 yrs.)
Courses with fewer than 20 students: 46%
Student-faculty ratio: 15:1
Courses taught by graduate TAs: not reported
Most popular majors: social sciences, engineering, psychology
Students living on campus: 37%
Guaranteed housing for four years? no
Students in fraternities: 16% sororities: 15%

Michigan imposes no core curriculum, but liberal arts students in the College of Literature, Science, and the Arts (one of 11 undergraduate colleges) must take the following courses:

- Two courses in the natural sciences.
- Two classes in the social sciences, such as "Principles of Economics" I and "Introduction to Political Theory"—or "The Politics and Culture of the Sixties" and "Language and Discrimination: Language as Social Statement."
- Two courses in the humanities, such as a survey of Western civilization or ancient philosophy—or classes like "How To Be Gay: Male Homosexuality and Initiation" and "The Dynamics of the Black Diaspora."

offerings include "Introduction to Poetry," "Great Books of Japan," and "Faust." Some students in the program (80 percent of freshmen and 30 percent of sophomores) choose to live in special honors housing, allowing them to "extend their intellectual lives beyond the classroom and live with like-minded peers," according to the program's Web page.

Michigan's Great Books Program, led by H. D. Cameron of the classical studies department, is particularly praiseworthy. The program does not consist of a core of courses but instead allows students to sign up for courses on an à la carte basis (regrettably, only four courses are offered each year). Most classes are reserved for honors students, but exceptions are made for other interested undergrads. A two-semester sequence on the great books exposes students to canonical works from ancient Greece through the Renaissance. The history course, "Debates of the Founding Fathers," is about the "making of the American Constitution, both as an intellectual and as a political event." In "Great Books of Modern Literature," students read *Don Quixote*, *Faust*, *Crime and Punishment*, *Madame Bovary*, and *Huckleberry Finn*.

The Residential College (RC) is a 900-student liberal arts unit within LSA in which students are rather secluded from the rest of the university. RC students are "alternative" types, says one student, who describes them as "typically more freewheeling, bombastic, [and] significantly more liberal as a group than most other students." RC students have their own dormitories, academic space, smaller classes (around 15 per class), and special advising, but students can also take courses outside the RC. RC students can choose concentrations in arts and ideas in the humanities, creative writing and literature, drama, or social science, or they can create their own major. According to the program's Web page, RC concentrations are more "inquiry-driven and interdisciplinary in approach, drawing on a range of perspectives and resources to develop an integrated, broad-based program of study." Arts and ideas, probably the best of these concentrations, lets students choose from among courses like "Classical Sources of Modern Culture: The Heritage of Greece" and "Shakespeare and Rome: The Figure of Rome, Shakespeare, and Sixteenth-Century Painting."

Political life on campus unfortunately seeps into the classroom. As one student says: "It is often difficult to be the only person in a class to take a conservative stance on an issue and have to defend it against 30 of your classmates. It is even more difficult to write a paper and get a good grade when you disagree with what the professor said. Sometimes you have to sell out on your political beliefs for a good grade." Social sci-

MIDWEST

ence classes tend to be more biased than others, but one conservative student says, "This bias is tolerable [because] it is almost always dispensed in regard to the material covered in a course. For example, a sociology professor could advocate universal health care coverage when studying gaps between the rich and the poor, but won't give an anti–Iraq war lecture or praise John Kerry or Michael Moore."

However, Michigan will not allow students to escape without some exposure to campus correctness. The school imposes a one-course race and ethnicity (R&E) requirement, which, says one student, is "basically a course on why the white man is evil." According to the *University Record*, an R&E course must incorporate: "(a) The meaning of race, ethnicity, and racism, (b) racial and ethnic intolerance and resulting inequality as it occurs in the United States or elsewhere, and (c) comparisons of discrimination based on race, ethnicity, religion, social class, or gender." Students select from a list that includes "Introduction to Women's Studies," "Rhetorical Activism and U.S. Civil Rights Movements," "Literature and Social Change," "Introduction to the Study of Latinas in the United States," "Introduction to Arab Culture and Language," and "Environmental Justice: Domestic and International."

As if the R&E requirement weren't bad enough, the university also allows creative expression courses to satisfy distribution requirements. A recent *Michigan Review* article complains that such measures have meant that a "strong classical education has been tossed aside and replaced with a cheaper, dumbed-down, cute and fuzzy, touchy-feely version that churns out moronic alumni who are unable to argue effectively, write profoundly, or think critically."

If, for some reason, you enrolled in the women's studies course "Introduction to Lesbian, Gay, Bisexual, and Transgender Studies," which discusses such issues as "identity development, simultaneous oppressions, internalized and externalized homophobia, coping with heterocentricity, sexism, and racism, and early and contemporary history/herstory of same-gender attraction and transgender experience"—well, you probably knew what you were getting into. The same goes for "Women's Reproductive Health" and "Material Girls: Race, Gender, and Sex," both of which are also offered through the women's studies department.

However, students who enroll in either the Great Books or the Honors program can count on receiving a serious, intellectually challenging education—which is more than many other state schools can offer.

REQUIREMENTS (CONT'D)

- One more course in each of the above areas or in math or creative expression.
- Two courses in English composition.
- One course in quantitative reasoning. This can be satisfied by an introductory course in calculus or "Games, Gambling, and Coincidences," among others.
- One course in race and ethnicity. The mostly lamentable choices include "Race and Ethnicity in Contemporary American Television" and the more interesting "Origins of Nazism."

  Students must also demonstrate proficiency in a foreign language at the fourth-term level, either through coursework or tests. With almost 40 languages to choose from, including Swedish and Sanskrit, students should have no trouble finding one of interest.

Student Life: Numbers games

With a total enrollment of almost 40,000, the University of Michigan is practically a city unto itself, but students can make it seem a lot smaller by taking advantage of certain campus residential options. Less than half the undergraduate population, mostly freshmen, lives on campus. The university guarantees housing for the first year only. Michigan's dormitories include high-rise apartment buildings, old-fashioned houses, and large halls housing more than 1,300 students. Most of the dormitories are coed, separating sexes by floor, but the university does have three all-female dormitories for women who request them. The Martha Cook Building, a quieter residence with sit-down dinners several times a week, is an all-women dormitory that maintains limited visitation hours for men—but living there costs more. The university does not have coed bathrooms or coed dorm rooms.

For those who choose to live off campus, the housing department provides information and advice on finding apartments, but rent is generally high and housing should be arranged more than six months in advance (unless you enjoy walking a mile to class). Most students choose to live in the "student ghetto" south of campus, but many other options exist.

Although only 16 percent of students join fraternities or sororities, some students say the Greek system dominates campus life, at least on the weekends. Especially during their first semester, students often attend house and fraternity parties, usually held in the organizations' off-campus houses. One student says that "beer cans litter Frat Row" and that on the weekends "drunk, skimpily clad individuals can often be seen walking the streets."

If students' social lives center on something other than the fraternities and beer, then that thing is the school's athletics program. Football games at "the Big House" (Michigan Stadium, college football's largest stadium, with a seating capacity of 107,501) are incredibly popular. Students can buy season tickets for $142, including tickets for games with Michigan's three greatest football rivals—Michigan State, Ohio State, and Notre Dame (when they play in Ann Arbor). The atmosphere at men's basketball games is considerably more subdued; Michigan's Crisler Arena is often said to be the quietest in the Big Ten Conference. (Participation in men's basketball can be lucrative, however; Michigan was banned from postseason participation in 2004 because it was discovered that four former players had been paid a total of $600,000 by boosters.) Hockey fans, on the other hand, are known for their out-of-control antics and lewd cheers. The university offers students an extensive intramurals program—more than 40 sports, from broomball to table tennis—and fields 34 teams for intercollegiate club sports competition, including water polo, rifle sports, and ninjitsu.

Ann Arbor, one of the nation's great college towns, is just a short walk from the dorms. Both on and off campus, Michigan students have a vast number of musical and cultural performances from which to choose, as well as theatre, film, and comedy acts. Students enjoy canoeing on the Huron River or jogging in Nichols Arboretum, playing Frisbee in the Diag (the central part of campus named for its diagonal sidewalks), or studying outdoors. As one student says, Michigan is "a very relaxed place to go to school."

Michigan's sheer size can make some students feel like just a number, but, as one student says, "the best thing to do is check out a bunch of organizations and groups at the beginning of the year and try to get involved in anything. It is difficult to make friends in class, so if you can become active in a group, you can have a core set of friends and expand from there." Surely one of UM's 700 clubs will be of interest.

One student writes that the housing department makes it nearly impossible for openly conservative students to become resident advisors. For one thing, the application requires a one-page essay answering the question, "What is your definition of diversity?" There is, of course, just one right answer. RAs-in-training play a game, called "Cross-the-Line," in which students are singled out by declaring their political and moral beliefs—whether they believe in affirmative action, for instance, or whether they consider themselves allies of "lesbian, gays, bisexuals, and transsexual individuals." During the following week, all new RAs must wear the rainbow triangle symbol around campus and then write a paper on how they felt while doing so. ("Like a hypocrite" is probably not the right answer.)

The *Michigan Daily*, the official student newspaper, strives mightily to maintain impeccable left-liberal credentials. Some of the more active groups on campus include Defending Affirmative Action and Integration By Any Means Necessary, Anti-War Action!, and Students Organizing for Labor Equality, an anti-sweatshop group. The latter organization was recently successful in persuading the university administration to drop its lucrative contract with Nike because the company engaged in unfair labor practices. Students for Choice sponsors a few big-name speakers each year. The University of Michigan chapter of the ACLU focuses on trying to keep enforcement of marijuana-possession laws to a minimum. With so many active liberal student groups, conservatives on campus are clearly outnumbered. Their newspaper, the *Michigan Review,* publishes biweekly. There are active College Republicans and Students for Life groups on campus.

Crime at the University of Michigan, although it has decreased slightly over the past decade, is still a cause of some concern. In 2003, the last year for which statistics were available, 22 forcible sex offenses and 10 assaults were reported on campus. Some 67 burglaries, seven arson cases, and 16 car thefts were also reported. But one junior says, "I feel very safe on campus. In a college community, it is pretty easy to spot people who do not belong." Emergency phones are placed throughout campus, and policemen patrol the campus and surrounding streets on bikes.

SUGGESTED CORE

1.–3. Great Books 191 *and* Great Books 202
4. History 308, The Christian Tradition in the West from the New Testament to the Early Reformation
5. Political Science 302, Development of Political Thought: Modern
6. English 267, Introduction to Shakespeare
7. History 160, The United States to 1860
8. History 416, Nineteenth-Century German and European Thought

---

For students from Michigan, this school is undeniably a bargain—a place with an Ivy reputation for only $8,014 (in 2004–5). Out of state students paid $25,840. Room and board was $7,030. Admissions are not need-blind, nor does the school guarantee to meet students' full need. Only 40 percent of students receive need-based aid, and the average student graduates with around $19,400 in loan debt.

MICHIGAN STATE UNIVERSITY

EAST LANSING, MICHIGAN • WWW.MSU.EDU

For granted

Beginning with the very land on which it stands, Michigan State University is an unpretentious place. To visitors used to campuses with landscaped gardens and perfectly manicured lawns, MSU's campus, filled with giant trees, seems like a walk in the untamed woods. MSU is, in fact, unabashed about its agricultural orientation; its brochure, "Things to See and Do at MSU!" lists among the university's attractions a botanical garden, butterfly and bug houses, and a 4-H children's garden. MSU's agricultural program is as old as the school itself. Founded in 1855 as Michigan Agricultural College, the university has at its center Beaumont Tower, which marks the site of the "first building in the United States erected for the teaching of scientific agriculture," according to the university. "Here began the first college of its kind in America, and the model for land-grant colleges established under the Morrill Act of 1862."

Having taken the prototypical, utilitarian approach adopted by most land-grant schools toward education, MSU has precious little to be pretentious about. It is sprawling, unfocused, and in many ways undemanding. It has a well-deserved reputation as a party school. Intercollegiate athletics are a high priority. But, as at virtually any land-grant school, for the student who doesn't mind doing his research before enrolling and is good at sniffing out good courses and professors, there are a few pockets of excellence at MSU.

Academic Life: The untamed woods for the trees

Beyond its rather sparse general education mandates, MSU makes moderate demands of its students. The College of Arts and Letters requires students to reach proficiency in a foreign language to the second year. Students in this college must choose two "cognates," areas of concentration outside their majors. Some departments require a specific cognate, and each cognate must be a "cohesive body of knowledge." Completion of a cognate involves taking about four courses. Economics majors, for instance, might take a cognate that includes four of the following five courses: "Survey of Accounting Concepts," "Introduction to Finance," "Introduction to Business Law," "Management Skills and Processes," and "Introduction to Marketing."

Members of MSU's Honors College are not bound by the same academic requirements as other students. They may substitute courses to fulfill degree and major requirements, choosing classes the student thinks "would contribute in a meaningful way to the student's overall program," according to the school's Web page. Honors students also "may choose from literally hundreds of course offerings to fulfill their general education requirements." Honors students take one writing course, two courses in arts and humanities, two in the natural sciences, and two courses in the social sciences. Before selecting courses, honors students must have the approval of a staff advisor or professor for their schedules. Special honors sections are available in many departments. They usually are smaller, more interactive, and move at a quicker pace.

For all students, Michigan State assigns faculty advisors within their major departments and encourages students to make at least one or two visits per year. But in most majors, students visit a "specialist-advisor," a staffer trained to advise students on careers, courses, and professors within the major. Thus, students may never have one-on-one interaction with faculty members. In short, if students don't seek out their assigned faculty advisors, those advisors certainly won't come looking for them. The result, as one student puts it, is that at MSU "advising isn't so great. It didn't do a lot for me. I would have rather not taken some classes they recommended. I'd give them a 4 out of 10."

One outstanding department on campus is the James Madison College, a residential college dedicated to "liberal education in the study of public affairs for undergraduates," which one professor calls, "a truly excellent institution with a program as good as any in the country." Another professor calls it one of the university's greatest intellectual strengths, and people outside of MSU praise it as well. Madison students live in Case Hall in a small-college learning environment where, one students says, "if a Madison student does not establish a good relationship with a professor by the end of the first semester, it is his own fault." Classes are conducted in an informal seminar

VITAL STATISTICS	
Religious affiliation: none	
Total enrollment: 44,836	
Total undergraduates: 35,408	
SAT midranges: V: 490–620, M: 515–650	
ACT median: 22	
Applicants: 21,834	
Applicants accepted: 79%	
Accepted applicants who enrolled: 44%	
Tuition: $6,188 (in state), $17,033 (out of state)	
Room and board: $5,458	
Freshman retention rate: 90%	
Graduation rate: 36% (4 yrs.), 71% (6 yrs.)	
Courses with fewer than 20 students: 21%	
Student-faculty ratio: 18:1	
Courses taught by graduate TAs: not provided	
Most popular majors: business, communications, social sciences	
Students living on campus: 42%	
Guaranteed housing for four years? no	
Students in fraternities or sororities: not reported	

MSU has no core curriculum, but a student does have to fulfill three sets of requirements: the university's, his college's, and his major's. All students, regardless of major, need 30 credits from writing courses and "Integrated Studies" (a fancy name for distribution requirements). The required courses are:

- Two "Writing, Rhetoric, and American Culture" courses. To start with, all university students complete a composition course, designed not only to strengthen writing skills but also to "broaden students' understanding of the American experience." Topics students may choose include "American Radical Thought," "Women in America," and, believe it or not, "Men in America." Students must also complete a writing course within their degree program.
  n Two "Integrated Social Sciences" courses in the social, behavioral, and economic sciences.

style, and the college regularly offers academic programs, speakers, and social events. Madison is, in other words, virtually a self-contained enclave within the larger university. It also boasts many of the brightest students at MSU; 30 percent of the 2003 Phi Beta Kappa class consisted of Madisonians, and Madison alumni have been Rhodes, Truman, Marshall, and Fulbright scholars. "The James Madison College offers some of the best faculty and classes in the university, making it one of the best public colleges in the country," one student says.

During their first year, Madison students take two year-long courses: "Identity and Community: An Approach to Writing" and "Introduction to the Study of Public Affairs." Madison students are also required to take a course in microeconomics and one in macroeconomics, attain second-year competency in a foreign language, and participate in a "field experience" (such as an internship). In addition, students must take around 17 of their courses within Madison College, choosing from classes like "Classical Republicanism," "Military Issues After 9/11," and "African American Politics." If you attend MSU, we highly recommend applying to this college.

The Lyman Briggs School of Science is similar to Madison College; it offers a residential, smaller-scale learning environment dedicated to the study of the natural sciences. The school houses academic courses, student residences, computer laboratories, classrooms, offices, a dining hall, and a convenience store all under one roof. The 1,500 Briggs students may choose from six main concentrations within the school and 26 coordinate majors from the College of Natural Science, ranging from astrophysics to zoology.

The best departments at MSU outside of Madison College and the Briggs School are agriculture (particularly the veterinary and animal science programs), business and the hard sciences (physics, chemistry, mathematics), music, and biology. The foreign language programs at MSU are quite good, and the engineering departments are particularly strong. One professor claims that they are given much more support than the humanities departments. In fact, another professor says, "I would not come to MSU to major in English, philosophy, or indeed any of the 'pure' humanities." Outstanding faculty at Michigan State include Constance Hunt, Louis Hunt, and M. Richard Zinman at James Madison College; James Seaton in English;

William Allen and Jerry Weinberger in political science; and Daniel R. Ilgen in psychology.

Graduate student teaching assistants are used extensively at Michigan State. Indeed, the university depends on them so heavily that it must cater to their union's demands. One student estimates that 70 percent of his introductory classes were taught by TAs. Students usually encounter professors only after moving into higher-level courses, and even in those classes, teaching assistants are often on hand to grade papers and the like. One student says that, especially in the sciences, "TAs without enough proficiency in English are a real problem . . . to the point that a huge chunk of MSU students now take math at the neighboring community college." The university is relying more on "teaching specialists," who may or (often) may not have a PhD, to teach large introductory courses.

Once students finally do make contact with professors, they find the experience worthwhile. "Professors are extremely accessible to students and in almost all cases I have found them to actually go out of their way to be accessible to students," says a student. Professors hold regular office hours, though one student reports that very few students take advantage of them. "When they do, it's usually when they really need help or after they've performed poorly on a test or paper," the student says.

Like most faculties in the nation, Michigan State's is left of center, but it is not as politically active as the administration. Professors try to leave personal political ideology out of the classroom, and students say that they largely succeed in remaining neutral while stimulating conversation and debate. There are exceptions. One student says, "Some professors here have no qualms whatsoever about using class as a forum for political beliefs." According to one professor, political and intellectual diversity is nearly nil, especially in the social sciences and humanities. The English department, for example, thinks that it is "part of our land-grant mission to make the traditions of world literature in English available to, speak for, and include those who have been typically left out—most notably, women and minorities." One English professor says the department is becoming less traditional, deemphasizing literature in favor of cultural studies. "The English department is leading the way down the multicultural diversity path," this pro-

REQUIREMENTS (CONT'D)

Students must also complete:

- A sequence of two classes—one 200-level course and one 300-level course. Choices include "Social Differentiation and Equality," "Power, Authority, and Exchange," and "Time, Space, and Change in Human Society."
- Two "Integrated Arts and Humanities" courses. Students must complete one course numbered below IAH 211 and one other IAH course numbered 211 or higher. Course titles include "United States and the World," "Europe and the World," "Music and Culture," and "Literature, Culture, and Identity."
- Two natural science courses and a laboratory. Each student must complete three credits in biological sciences, three in physical sciences, and a two-credit laboratory experience taken concurrently. The university offers dozens of courses to fulfill these science requirements, such as "History of Life," "World of Chemistry," and "Navigating the Universe."
- At least one math course for those students who do not test out of it.

fessor says. According to another professor, the freshman writing department has taken on a decidedly more technical inclination, adding new courses in such areas as "digital writing," while fewer freshman writing courses are taught by tenured faculty than in the past. The department offers many "innovative" courses such as "Chillers & Thrillers: Pop Lit," "Studies in Ethnic Film," "Literature for Young Adults," and "Language Use in the African American Community." English majors have to take at least one course in ethnic literature, non-Western literature, or women and literature, in addition to the three other course requirements: "Introduction to the Study of English"; a course in English-language literature either pre-1660 or 1660–1789; and another course in literature, either 1789–1900, since 1900, or in modern media and culture. English majors are not required to take a course in Shakespeare. History majors have to take at least one African, Asian, or Latin American course in addition to courses in American and European history.

The College of Social Sciences houses many of the most politicized departments on campus, including the African Studies Center, the Center for Latin American and Caribbean Studies, and the Women's Studies Program. Although there is no African or African American studies major, students can focus on these subjects through the American studies program. In 2003–4, the provost proposed the dissolution of the College of Arts and Letters and the merger of some of its parts with Social Sciences, with the leftovers becoming part of Communication Arts and Sciences. This caused considerable turmoil among humanities faculty, some of whom saw the proposal as exemplifying the decline of the liberal arts on campus.

Student Life: Economies of scale

MSU's campus takes up most of the town of East Lansing, Michigan, whose population of 50,000 increases significantly when the 35,000-plus undergraduates return to campus each fall. Naturally, the town caters to students, who often visit local shops, entertainment venues, restaurants, and of course, bars. Different areas of the city are easily accessible, and bus tickets are cheap.

MSU operates the largest residence hall system in the country. Freshmen and sophomores are required to live on campus, but after the first two years most students move off campus. There are several special housing options for particular academic interests and racial/ethnic groups, and the university also has alcohol- and smoke-free housing options. All dormitories are coed, with men and women usually separated by floor. The food at MSU is generally good, say students.

Some students choose to spend at least one semester away from campus; during the 2002–3 school year, the university offered nearly 200 study-abroad programs, in more than 60 countries, "on all continents," according to the school (though we looked in vain for the Antarctica program). MSU brags that it sends more students abroad than any other research institution (2,460 during 2003–4). More than 3,000 MSU students take part in service-learning experiences in more than 400 community service organizations in conjunction with seventy MSU classes each year.

Hundreds of student organizations at MSU cater to nearly every whim, whether one's interest is juggling, cuisine (Les Gourmets puts on a seven-course, black-tie dinner each year), making documentary films, or simply being (try the Art of Healing and Breathing Club). Members of the Apple Club promote the use of Macintosh computers, and the Society for Creative Anachronism "recreates the Middle Ages as they should have been." There are no fewer than 20 agriculturally oriented clubs on campus, including the Michigan State Sustainable Agriculture Network, and there are as many religious clubs. Although the university does have an active College Republicans group and a new Russell Kirk Society—named for the historian of ideas who once taught at MSU—a conservative newspaper, the *Spartan*, recently folded.

MSU is a Big Ten school with strong basketball, football, and hockey programs, and sports serve to unite the far-flung student body. MSU claims to have the largest intramural sports program in the nation; interested students can participate in activities from skydiving to rollerblading. Varsity athletes compete on 23 teams, and Spartan football games are graced by a state-of-the-art mechanical engineering student–built chariot, pulled by two Andalusian horses imported from Spain, thanks in part to a $50,000 foundation grant.

Campus structures are built to the scale of a large state university. MSU is home to a world-class atom-smasher, the National Superconducting Cyclotron. The MSU libraries house more than four million volumes, plus an additional quarter-million rare books in a special collection. The Wharton Center for Performing Arts contains two theaters: the Great Hall and Festival Stage, which can hold 2,500, and a smaller theater with 600 seats. MSU is also home to the Kresge Art Museum, which contains more than 5,000 works of art as well as classrooms and art studios. The Alumni Memorial Chapel is suitably inclusive—except of God, who is represented in this "sacred space" only by one stained glass window containing eight small circles that are supposed to stand for different religions. The rest of the windows reframe religious concepts in secular terms, including groaners like the "Stations of the University" and the "Cardinal University Virtues." Other windows celebrate values like brotherhood, patriotism, inspiration, creativity, and school activities.

Diversity is a mantra at MSU. Glossy brochures boast that Michigan State really is racially diverse: some 20 percent of the student body are members of U.S. racial or ethnic minority groups and another 3 percent hail from other nations. The university's obsession with multiculturalism pervades campus, where one professor calls it "the new religion." The Multicultural Center in the student union hopes to "advance diver-

SUGGESTED CORE
1. Classics 350, Greek and Roman Literature in Translation
2. Philosophy 210, Ancient Greek Philosophy
3. Religious Studies 150, Introduction to Biblical Literature
4. Religious Studies 320, Christianity (*closest match*)
5. Political Science 372, Modern Political Philosophy
6. English 421, Shakespeare or English 221 Honors, Introduction to Shakespeare
7. History 202, U.S. History to 1876
8. History 338, European Intellectual History: Modernism and Post-Modernism

sity within community" through poetry slams, cultural film series, and other aware-ness programs. MSU's stated policy of nondiscrimination includes one of the longest lists of protected categories in the land, including height, weight, veteran status, and political persuasion. The university's Office of Affirmative Action, Compliance, and Monitoring publishes a pamphlet called "Bias-Free Communication: Guidelines for Communicating in a Diverse Community," which is, essentially, a speech code. (Fortu-nately, the guidelines are only recommendations and not requirements.) Among the recommendations: "Use gender-neutral words/phrases in your language, e.g. journal-ist, fire fighter, chairperson. Avoid the use of 'man' or 'woman' in job titles," and "when discussing families, be inclusive of families that are headed by same-gender partners or lesbian, bisexual, gay, or transgendered single parents and recognize the presence of LBGT youth in families."

As for the student body, "The liberal students are the noisiest," says one student. Another student says, "Liberal students definitely have much more of a voice on cam-pus. The student governments are overrun by them. . . . The conservative movement on campus is struggling." In characterizing students' academic interests, one jaded stu-dent says, "Mixology 101 and Fornication 219 are the most popular classes." Another student says the typical MSU student is "ambitious, open-minded, loves to have a good time, and is a party animal." Fraternities and sororities are strong at Michigan State, and if a student isn't one of those who participate in Greek organizations, he has likely attended one of the Greeks' many parties. MSU is consistently ranked in or near the top 10 in lists of party schools, and numbers bear out this reputation. In 2003, the school reported 655 liquor-law and 141 drug arrests, along with 14 forcible sex offenses, 11 robberies, 16 aggravated assaults, 116 burglaries, 26 stolen cars, and three arsons on campus. According to one professor, much of the crime is committed by nonstudents who come to campus to party with their friends. Students say they are rarely worried about becoming the victims of serious violent crimes (though perhaps they should be). Having their laptops stolen or being busted at parties are matters of greater concern.

For the 2003–4 academic year, in-state tuition was $6,188 for in-state students and $17,033 for out-of-staters. Room and board was another $5,458. Admissions are need-blind, though the school does not promise to meet a student's full aid need. Some 61 percent of students receive gift aid, and the average debt per student for seniors in 2003 was $21,037.

UNIVERSITY OF MINNESOTA – TWIN CITIES

MINNEAPOLIS AND ST. PAUL, MINNESOTA • WWW.UMN.EDU

Fraternal twins

The state of Minnesota has always had an independent streak at least as wide as the Mississippi, which has its headwaters there. The state skews in different directions politically—it elected the nation's only Reform Party governor, the wrestler Jesse Ventura—and it's perhaps best known outside the region for Lake Wobegone, the fictional yet evocatively real hometown of (University of Minnesota grad) Garrison Keillor. The University of Minnesota–Twin Cities is likewise hard to categorize. Well-regarded in national rankings of large public research institutions, the university is a mixture of disparate elements, offering practically everything—some of it excellent. The university was founded as a prep school in 1851, before there even was a state of Minnesota. It closed during the Civil War, but reopened in 1867 as a land-grant school. By the middle of the twentieth century it had established itself as one of the leading public universities in the nation. The state university system has opened branches in Duluth, Morris, and Crookston during the past 60 years, but this essay focuses only on the nearly 50,000-student Twin Cities campuses—one in Minneapolis, one in St. Paul.

Academic Life: Feeling Minnesota

Students can study just about anything at the University of Minnesota: there are more than 150 majors available in the school's 20 colleges, including everything from aerospace engineering to interior design to mortuary science to urban forestry. What you can't find at the university is a core curriculum. Minnesota has what it calls the Diversified Core Requirements, a set of distribution requirements that all undergraduates must complete. With few requirements and a broad course selection, they do not guarantee a student a foundational liberal arts education.

VITAL STATISTICS
Religious affiliation: none
Total enrollment: 49,474
Total undergraduates: 32,474
SAT/ACT midranges: SAT V: 540–660, M: 560–680; ACT: 22–28
Applicants: 17,158
Applicants accepted: 76%
Accepted applicants who enrolled: 40%
Tuition: $5,962 (in state), $17,592 (out of state)
Room and board: $6,302
Freshman retention rate: 86%
Graduation rate: 24% (4 yrs.), 56% (6 yrs.)
Courses with fewer than 20 students: 50%
Student-faculty ratio: 15:1
Courses taught by graduate TAs: not provided
Most popular majors: social sciences, business, engineering
Students living on campus: 22%
Guaranteed housing for four years? no
Students in fraternities or sororities: not reported

MIDWEST

Minnesota's "Diversified Core Requirements" include:

- Two courses in the physical and biological sciences, including one with lab or field experience.
- One course in "mathematical thinking," such as "Introduction to Logic," "College Algebra and Probability," or "Statistics."
- One or two first-year writing courses (depending on which college the student is enrolled in) and four writing-intensive courses overall, including two upper-level classes and one in the student's major.
- Five courses in social science and humanities, including at least six credits in social science fields, six credits in the arts and humanities (including one course in literature and one course in other humanities), and three credits that fall under the category of "historical perspectives."

Literally thousands of course combinations satisfy the liberal education requirements, and if that doesn't work, students can add to the list with a simple application process. For one of their required science courses, for instance, students can take either "Chemical Principles I" or the less fundamental "Geology and Cinema." (Earthquake movies?) The range widens in the history and social sciences area. For Minnesota's purposes, "The Black Family," "American Indian Women: Ethnographic and Ethnohistorical Perspectives," "Anthropology of Death," "Principles of Microeconomics," "Intimate Relationships," "Medieval Islam," and "Gay Men and Homophobia in American Culture" are the functional equivalent of classes on ancient Greece, Rome, and Byzantium. For arts and humanities, just about any literature is as good as another: Persian poetry, Chinese literature, Greek mythology, the Bible, even courses like "Introduction to Shakespeare" or "Great Books." The shame is not that the university offers such a wide variety of courses, but that it refuses to differentiate between the icing and the cake.

Most of the university's seven colleges offer honors programs, and these are usually an improvement over the general curriculum. The one in the College of Liberal Arts, for example, offers special honors courses taught by "selected teachers," smaller sections, discussion groups, and seminars, as well as "special faculty advisors," according to the catalog. The honors programs are recommended by those on campus as a good way to wring the most out of what could otherwise be a meager general education. "Any student who can get in, should," says one professor. "Class sizes are small, and the instructors mainly excellent."

The quality of advising for non-honors students varies from college to college; generally, certain professors, upperclassmen, grad students, and professional advisors share advising duties, and many do a good job. As at most big schools, the advising becomes more valuable the more effort the student makes to keep in contact with his advisor. Even within the College of Liberal Arts, how much students interact with advisors depends on the department. A freshman interested in economics, for instance, can make appointments with college-wide advisors; once he declares a major, he can meet with a peer undergraduate advisor in the economics department or the faculty member who is the department's designated advisor. But with more than 350 students majoring in economics each year, it is undoubtedly hard for students to have extensive one-on-one interaction with the departmental advisor.

Students have ample opportunity to perform research at Minnesota. One way to get involved is through the Undergraduate Research Opportunities Program, which gives more than 450 students each year stipends to assist faculty members with research or perform their own research under faculty supervision. In 2004, the university's sponsored research topped $520 million dollars.

Students at large state universities should expect some large classes; Minnesota is no exception. The university reports that 188 of the 3,349 classes it offered (about 6 percent) in a recent semester had more than 100 students. However, about 20 percent of all classes enrolled fewer than 10 students. Teaching assistants handle the discussion sections in larger classes; faculty members maintain that their TAs are well prepared to teach by the pedagogical courses offered them by each department. One student comments that in some classes professors "rush in, give the lecture, and rush off to finish their work, leaving a T.A. to fend off questions and teach the rest in discussion classes." Students also sometimes have trouble getting the courses they want, professors say, because of the high demand. "It's a rarity if undergrads get out of here in four years. And often it is just a matter of the courses they need not being available," one student says. In the Big Ten conference, Minnesota ranks ninth out of 11 schools in graduation rate; barely more than half (56 percent) of incoming freshmen graduate in six years, according to the university. Fewer than a third graduate in four years.

Besides facts such as these, one can scarcely generalize about a school so large and varied as Minnesota. "Colleges are much more autonomous here than at most other schools—the social, political and intellectual atmosphere differs pretty widely across the various colleges," says one professor. Another professor refers to the local and student papers to keep abreast of what's happening on campus—even in his own department. There are, to be sure, politicized disciplines at this school. Cultural studies and comparative literature (one program with several tracks) was formed from a ménage of disbanded humanities departments a number of years ago. The course list includes a hodgepodge of literature (loosely defined), pop culture, and multiculturalism. The department also offers a major in cinema and media culture that includes classes like "Oppositional Cinemas," which looks at "the ways diverse national cinemas engage the international hegemony of Hollywood cinema." But there are also very good teachers in the program, including several who have won the university's top teaching awards, and the program is growing.

The English department's literature program is beset with plenty of politicized

REQUIREMENTS (CONT'D)

The College of Liberal Arts, home to the most undergrads, also requires proficiency in a second language equivalent to four semesters of college courses.

Finally, a student must earn three credits in each of the following four "designated themes of liberal education":
- "Environment."
- "Cultural Diversity."
- "International Perspectives."
- "Citizenship and Public Ethics."

The courses that meet these criteria can and usually do overlap with the "core" courses; in fact, some of the distribution requirement courses even count for two themes.

MIDWEST

offerings ("Gay, Lesbian, Bisexual, and Transgender Literature," "Introduction to Black Women Writers in the United States," and "World Englishes," for example) but also provides ample opportunity for more solid offerings, such as "Historical Survey of British Literature" and "Introduction to Shakespeare." "It used to be great, the best," says one professor. There are still good professors, but the department is torn between traditional scholars and cutting-edge theorists; when a professor from the traditional group (who also happened to be a political liberal) won a university teaching award, half the department walked out of the announcement in protest.

Among the best programs at Minnesota are history, economics, philosophy, psychology, political science, chemical engineering, materials science, biochemistry, microbiology, the foreign language departments, and the Academic Health Center, which includes the health sciences. Try these recommended professors: Thomas J. Bouchard Jr., William Grove, and Matthew McGue in psychology; Thomas Clayton and Peter Firchow in English; Bernard Bachrach, David Kieft, and James D. Tracy in history; John Archer, Robin Brown, Richard Leppert, and Harvey Sarles in cultural studies and comparative literature; Marvin Marshak and Oriol T. Valls in physics; Anatoly Liberman in German; and Ian Maitland in the Carlson School of Management. John Dolan in philosophy is now professor emeritus but still active; interested students should pay him a visit. One professor says, "It is easy for a determined student to find out who has won awards for excellence in teaching, which courses actually teach something, which professors really care about their students." Former president Mark Yudof put money into undergraduate teaching, starting a teaching awards program that carries a $15,000 bonus and a salary increase of several thousand dollars for distinguished professors.

Yudof, who resigned in 2002 to become the chancellor of the University of Texas system, also left as his legacy a strong commitment to the promotion of campus "diversity"—ethnic, not intellectual. Indeed as one student says, "There is a huge emphasis on making everyone feel comfortable here. However, that does not seem to include conservatives." In the 2003 admissions process, prospective Minnesota students were "subject to individual review of their personal circumstances," according to a *FrontPage Magazine* article. The university calls it "holistic assessment," and says admissions "will be based on an overall assessment of each applicant's academic record and individual circumstances. . . . Diversity of all kinds, from race to geography, is also taken into account." What this means is that admission is no longer guaranteed for students who meet minimum qualifications for test scores and grades, as it had been in the past. Evidence of overcoming some sort of adversity (anything race-related will probably do nicely) will now be a big plus when it comes to the admissions committee. The article quoted then–executive vice president Robert Bruininks as saying: "The policy is not an attempt to control admission, but rather an attempt to create a more diverse university community." But, as the article concludes, however the university chooses to characterize it, "The upshot is that hardworking, smart, and well-balanced Minnesota kids are going to have a harder time getting admitted to UMinn unless they can develop some hardships to tout." Bruininks, for his part, was inaugurated in November 2002 as the new president of the university, with widespread faculty support.

Student Life: Where all the children are above average

SUGGESTED CORE

Humanities 1001, 1002, 1003, 1004, 1005, and 1006 (Humanities in the West I, II, III, IV, V, and VI) suffice.

Minnesota students can live in campus dorms, residential colleges, special-interest houses, or private off-campus housing. The university guarantees housing for first-year students, and about 70 percent of freshmen select the campus dorms, which are located in either Twin City. Recently, dorms filled up and some students were housed in nearby hotels. Two dorms (Territorial and Frontier halls), both on the Minneapolis side and both coed, are freshmen-only. Opened in the fall of 2002, Riverbend Commons includes suites and some apartments, as well as a number of language houses. Some residential halls offer discussion seminars for freshmen on a variety of academic topics. All dormitories are coed, although men and women are separated by floor or wing, depending on the configuration of the building. There are no coed bathrooms or dorm rooms.

Students living on campus can choose from three visitation policies: unlimited visitation, a limited policy (in which members of the opposite sex are only allowed on the floor during certain hours), and a full visitation restriction (in which members of the opposite sex are not allowed on the floor at all). It is encouraging to note that despite the university's pursuit of multiculturalist credentials, very few of the 20 or so special-interest houses on campus are dedicated to a particular race or politics. Most are academic, honors, arts, language, or career-oriented; exceptions are the Women's Studies Cluster, Environment House, and the Global Studies House.

Minnesota undergrads come primarily from Minnesota (74 percent), Wisconsin, and the Dakotas, states that have a reciprocity agreement with the state of Minnesota for in-state tuition rates.

If the extensive list of more than 400 student groups is any indication, the homogeneity in students' backgrounds is no indication of homogeneous interests. The AB Kilombo Capoeira club, for example, is "dedicated to teaching authentic *capoeira* [a form of martial arts], traditionally of Bahia, Brasil." There is the Mafia Club, Queer Men, Queer Women, Stonecutters (here on Earth "to split the rocks of ignorance that obscure the light of knowledge and truth"), the Theatre of the Relatively Talentless, University Pagan Society, the Vedic Cultural Society, and the Zoological, Exotic, Avian and Wildlife Medicine Club. Among others, that is. The university also has groups promoting the culture of Afghans, Africans, American Indians, Asian Americans, Greeks, Hmong, and Liberians, again, among others.

Political organizations are mostly on the left side of the ledger, though there is a pro-life group and one called Students for Family Values, which says it stands for "social conservatism and the preservation of the family." Other recognized groups include Students Against War/Students For Global Justice, Minnesota Public Interest Research Group, Student Organization for Animal Rights, and Atheists and Humanists. There are also chapters of the conservative law students' Federalist Society and a large and active College Republicans chapter—which brought the largest representation of any university to a recent College Republicans national convention. "In the '90s, the campus was wracked by the culture wars," a professor says. "But by 2000, the fever had subsided. The mood is more equivocal on campus." And tipsy: campus police referred 886 cases for liquor-law violations in 2003.

Faculty may well be more partisan than the students. The Senate Social Concerns Committee recently submitted a resolution calling on the board of regents to "enter into no further bond underwriting agreements with Lehman Brothers, Inc., until Lehman Brothers ends it financial backing of the private prison industry." The committee has also submitted a resolution opposing university involvement in the Mount Graham telescope project in Arizona because the land is considered sacred by Indian tribes and ecologically delicate by environmentalists.

According to its own masthead, the campus paper, the *Minnesota Daily*, is "the world's largest student-produced and managed newspaper." A well-written, award-winning newspaper with a liberal editorial page that also publishes opposing views, it got in hot water with some readers recently for including a pro-life advertising insert, but it held its ground in saying that the insert was handled according to the paper's advertising policy. But for the most part, as one faculty member says, "The campus paper is way over on the left and it is very influential." In 2004, a group of students started the *Minnesota Patriot* newspaper as a conservative biweekly alternative to the *Daily*. The *Daily* receives $5.73 in student fees from each full-time student. The *Patriot* receives nothing.

Other groups are underwritten by student service fees. A panel of students decides how these fees are to be allocated and the process is clearly biased. In 2004–5, each student will pay more than $4 to liberal groups such as the Queer Student Association. The conservative group, Students for Family Values, receives 19 cents. All student groups are required to sign an Equal Opportunities Statement that requires them to allow anyone to be a member, vote, and hold office, even if they do not uphold the group's beliefs. Maranatha Christian Fellowship achieved a small victory recently when it sued the university, claiming the agreement infringed on their religious freedom. The university settled out of court and now religious groups must sign a modified agreement which states that, "religious student organizations may require their voting membership and officers to adhere to the organization's statement of faith and its rules of conduct."

There are—at the moment at least—11 men's varsity teams and 11 women's teams. The university has tried to cut a few more: men's gymnastics and both golf teams were slated for whacking in an effort to help the athletic department budget. But private contributions are allowing these programs to continue for a few more years, at least. There are also dozens of club and intramural sports and good facilities for nearly all of them.

The campus is fairly safe for an urban area, and university police are good about patrolling by bike and car. Considering the size of the campus and the number of students, very few burglaries and assaults have been reported in recent years, especially in residence halls. However, for the campus as a whole, burglaries shot up from 33 in 2001 to 84 in 2003. There were also 16 forcible sex offenses, five robberies, three aggravated assaults, 11 stolen cars, and 24 arsons. Each residence hall has a security monitor on duty from 9 p.m. to 7 a.m. nightly.

Tuition for a normal-to-heavy courseload at the university in 2004–5 was $5,962 for Minnesota residents, $17,592 for nonresidents. Housing ranged from $3,730 to $4,432; an unlimited meal plan cost $2,906. Admissions are need-blind, and the school arranges, with loans, to cover all financial need; 44 percent of undergraduates receive some financial aid. Average student loan debt for recent graduates is $13,668.

NORTHWESTERN UNIVERSITY

EVANSTON, ILLINOIS • WWW.NWU.EDU

Think about your direction

A little more than 150 years ago, Northwestern University was founded to serve students in the Northwest Territory—an area that became the states of Ohio, Indiana, Illinois, Michigan, Wisconsin, and Minnesota. Northwestern comprises not only the Weinberg College of Arts and Sciences, our main concern here, but the School of Communication (formerly Speech), the School of Education and Social Policy, the McCormick School of Engineering and Applied Science, the School of Continuing Studies, the Medill School of Journalism, and the School of Music, as well as the Graduate School, the School of Law, the Feinberg School of Medicine, and the Kellogg School of Management. Medill is regarded as one of the top journalism programs in the country, and its alumni are consistently listed among the winners of the Pulitzer Prize.

Northwestern has always stood a little outside the contemporary mainstream. In the sedate 1950s, for example, British orientalist Alan Watts was the Episcopalian chaplain; he moved on to become the guru of the original Beatniks. Today, Northwestern is a national university in the heart of the nation, attracting some of the brightest students and faculty from not only the Midwest but from the entire country. The administration would like to gain even more prestige nationally and internationally, and admission has become much more selective over the past few years. The school also is trying to boost its profile as a research university, and faculty members are being pushed to publish more, while at the same time still attending to their teaching duties. Some may feel the temptation to cast envious glances at the nearby, world-class University of Chicago, but Northwestern has its own virtues, including a real suburban charm.

MIDWEST

Academic Life: Good directions

Weinberg College of Arts and Sciences enrolls nearly half of Northwestern's 8,000 undergraduates; the School of Engineering and School of Communication enroll another quarter, with journalism, music, and education making up the rest. Weinberg has a set of distribution requirements similar to those found at other midsized private universities—no better, and no worse.

Although the list of courses approved for distribution requirements is short, it does include some that appeal to grudge-driven identity politics rather than the traditional topics of higher education. The only upside of this is that students who desire traditional content do not sit in classes populated by those who would resent the imposition. Northwestern students typically have the foresight to choose courses from a variety of disciplines. One professor says few students graduate from NU without taking a broad range of classes.

Northwestern is one of only a few universities using the quarter system (three quarters plus a summer session), which means students face grueling exam periods no fewer than six times a year, counting midterms and finals. "I always feel like I'm studying for some final or another," one student says. "But if you're willing to not wait to the last minute for every little thing, it's manageable." Time management is one key to success here; the other is course selection. For each quarter, the courseload should be balanced between demanding and less demanding workloads, and integrated so that work done for one course contributes to the others as well. Of course, that's good advice anywhere.

Freshmen at most universities start their college careers by taking large introductory courses. The Northwestern curriculum encourages another path, requiring all undergraduate students to take two seminars during their first year. This arrangement allows students to discuss academic ideas in intimate class settings; freshman seminars include no more than 15 students. But freshmen should choose their seminars wisely, as academic rigor varies by course and instructor. Recent offerings have included the English course "Shakespeare and the Culture of Violence," the history course "Commonplace Cruelty: Forced Migration and the Making of Early America," and "Philosophy of Art." The "Race, Gender, and City Life" sociology seminar has this course description: "While men might hail from Mars and women from Venus, they both often live in cities. What happens when these worlds meet? Do men and women experience the city differently? How does gender influence the city? What impact does an urban space have on gender? In addition to exploring these issues, we will also explore the intersections of sexuality, race, and class during this course." Students should be especially careful in choosing freshman seminars because their seminar instructors are also their premajor advisors and the evaluators of their writing proficiency.

The best students in the College of Arts and Sciences have the opportunity to participate in the College Scholars Program, which intends to "nurture creative scholarly and artistic talent at the undergraduate level," according to its coordinators. Although there are no formal requirements, scholars in this program typically take advantage of grants for research in the arts and sciences. In addition to working on independent projects, students attend regular lunches with their peers in the program, participate in small workshops with visiting academics, and together visit cultural venues in the Chicago area.

One humanities professor says there is palpable pressure to "publish or perish," and that faculty members are supposed to spend 45 percent of their time on research, 45 percent on teaching, and 10 percent on administrative projects. Professors in the sciences, where the pressure to publish is perhaps greatest, tend to have lighter teaching loads than their colleagues in the humanities. Northwestern president Henry S. Bienen recently told the student newspaper that scientists at NU must win more grants or risk the consequences. "If you're not using our space well and productively and being competitive for research, don't think you have dibs on that space forever," he said. Despite the new emphasis on research productivity, though, one freshman says his "professors seem generally interested in students. I haven't had one yet that wasn't concerned with my academic soul."

The admissions department boasts that NU faculty members teach approximately 98 percent of courses. In larger lecture courses, professors typically teach twice a week, with students breaking up into smaller discussion groups, taught by graduate teaching assistants, once a week. Northwestern professors generally are accessible to their students, and one faculty member says that more than a few students take the opportunity to go to office hours and get academic advice from their professors. Still, relationships with faculty are not as close as one would find at a smaller liberal arts institution. One music major says she doesn't think many of her classmates go to office hours, although they should: "In a huge lecture, going to office hours can make your face in the crowd stand out. Some NUers recognize this, but I don't think most do." Students are assigned faculty advisors within their major departments but also are welcome to visit professional advisors at the Academic Advising Center if they have questions about various disciplines or are unsure of which major to select. Students are required to meet with their advisors before registering for classes, but most see this as a mere formality and say that genuine advising rarely occurs in these meetings.

The best departments at Northwestern are English, psychology, economics, and history. Students name the following as particularly strong professors: T. H. Breen and Edward Muir in history; Mary Kinzie in English; Sarah E. Fraser, Sandra L. Hindman (emerita), and Lyle Massey in art history; Kenneth Seeskin in philosophy; Martin Mueller

VITAL STATISTICS
Religious affiliation: none
Total enrollment: 16,266
Total undergraduates: 8,001
SAT midrange: 1310–1480
Applicants: 14,137
Applicants accepted: 33%
Accepted applicants who enrolled: 41%
Tuition: $29,940
Room and board: $9,393
Freshman retention rate: 97%
Graduation rate: 84% (4 yrs.), 93% (6 yrs.)
Courses with fewer than 20 students: 73%
Student-faculty ratio: 7:1
Courses taught by graduate TAs: 2%
Most popular majors: social sciences, history, communications
Students living on campus: 65%
Guaranteed housing for four years? no
Students in fraternities: 30% sororities: 39%

Students in North-western's liberal arts college do not face a core curriculum but, instead, a series of distribution requirements and other mandates. First, students need to take two courses—from a fairly selective list of classes published at the beginning of each year—in each of six areas:

- Natural sciences. Choices have included "Genetics and Evolution" and "Sound Patterns in Human Language."
- Formal studies. Options have included "Finite Mathematics" and "Harmony."
- Social and behavioral sciences. Choices have included "Introduction to Microeconomics" and "Gender, Power, and Culture in America."
- Historical studies. Options have run from "Classical Greece" to "Roots of Feminism."

and Robert Wallace in classics; and Andrew Baruch Wachtel, who also serves as dean of the Graduate School, in Slavic language and literature. With more than four million volumes in Northwestern's combined libraries, the university's book collection ranks tenth among America's private universities.

In the past, NU officials have adamantly denied the existence of grade inflation. A couple years ago, a *Daily Northwestern* reporter checked the numbers after NU provost Lawrence Dumas told a *Chicago Tribune* reporter that grade inflation didn't exist at Northwestern. Lo and behold, the reporter found that As and A-minuses made up 46 percent of all grades that semester. Dumas was so embarrassed that he investigated the problem, but he found little support among faculty and students for curbing the tide. Students complained that graduate schools and employers compare grades and that deflated Northwestern grades would hurt their chances of being selected. And faculty members are so conscious of teacher and course evaluations that they fear upsetting students by assigning low grades—lest they endanger their chances at tenure. The same story is told at hundreds of other schools.

Although there are only a handful of reported incidents of plagiarism at NU each year, a recent outbreak prompted faculty members to look more closely at their students' work and its sources. In an introductory philosophy course, 12 students were found to have copied text they found on the Internet into their final papers. Incoming freshmen now are asked to sign a statement declaring that they understand the university's position on academic honesty. What may be more to the point, the Writing Program is making an effort to educate new students in the skill of paraphrase and the conventions of citation, which many high schools do not teach effectively. After all, it is more tempting to download a paper when you don't have a clue how to write one.

Students and faculty describe Northwestern as a school that is generally conservative. The administration seems slower to cave in to student pressures than what might be expected—which isn't to say administrators don't eventually cave in. Some years ago, Asian students staged a dramatic hunger protest aimed at forcing the administration to establish an Asian American studies department. In 2000, after five years of candlelight vigils and letters to the university president, administrators finally granted them the program, offering a minor and two full-time faculty members.

As a general rule, the engineering school and science departments are fairly conservative, while the social sciences and humanities departments are more liberal. An exception to the latter is economics, which houses several noteworthy free-market economists. The comparative literary studies, gender studies, and race and ethnicity studies programs are predictably bad. The Weinberg College of Arts and Sciences encompasses six politically correct studies departments: Asian American studies, Latin American and Caribbean studies, Jewish studies, gender studies, African American studies, and Hispanic studies (formerly called the Spanish and Portuguese department).

The primary reason these departments are dubious is that, like the Balkan states, they keep splintering into narrower and narrower entities ("ghettoes," as some put it) with diminishing intellectual returns. A professor in the social sciences calls the profusion of politically correct departments a waste of university resources and says that if the departments are really necessary, Northwestern should follow the example of Stanford in lumping them together in one department: ethnic and identity studies. As it stands, there is continual pressure for new ethnic studies departments. The Asian American studies department is basically a Chinese studies department, and the South Asian and Indian students find this unfair. The professor asks, "What next? A South Asian American studies department?"

For the most part political pressures at Northwestern are not overwhelming. One social sciences professor who has sat on committees to hire new faculty members says politics "has not undermined things viciously" when it comes to hiring. But in his own department, he has seen cases in which committee members have eliminated candidates whose views were not politically acceptable. In one case, he says, a distinguished candidate was passed over simply because he was black and conservative. A few years ago, the Hispanic caucus in the law school refused to support the hiring of a black libertarian law professor because they already had four blacks, and hiring another one would "send some sort of message"—to whom or about what, we have no idea. At the same time, the law school hired former Weather Underground leader Bernadine Dohrn, who has never been admitted to the bar because of her criminal record, as head of its Child and Family Justice Center. At least she never planted any bombs at Northwestern.

Students say their professors are much more left-leaning than they are, and both students and faculty agree that the student body is mostly nonideological. One professor says his students are "mostly interested in studying and graduating, and you find few activists on the left or the right." A liberal student says some of her professors are "very, very leftist, some middle of the road." The student body has liberals and conservatives, she says, and "there's a place for both, but I really don't take the conservatives seriously." One social sciences professor says his students do not get as inflamed over classroom political issues as they did 10 or 15 years ago, For example, he has noticed that students now use "he" as the indefinite pronoun instead of the more politically correct "he/she" or simply "she." "They've relaxed a great deal," he says.

Student Life: North by Northwestern

Students at Northwestern have many of the social habits that students at other first-rate schools have. In other words, as one journalism major puts it, NU is "definitely not a party school," although students do attend parties at friends' off-campus apartments occasionally. Students, especially economics and political science majors, are said to be heavily career-oriented. More than a third of undergraduates are members of fraternities or sororities, but even these organizations are not especially focused on partying. In fact, of the 18 recognized fraternities, only three allow alcohol. The Greek system at NU is consequently low key. Many students attend quarterly semi-formals sponsored by student organizations. Ethnic organizations like the black student group For Members Only are not particularly active throughout the year, but they do sponsor social events periodically.

Northwestern does have the usual cadre of politically active students. On the right, the weekly *Northwestern Chronicle* offers news and commentary from a conservative point of view. The *Daily Northwestern* is more liberal. The College Republicans have a strong following and sponsor conservative speakers a few times each year. Recent lecturers at Northwestern have included James Carville, Paul Begala, Pat Buchanan, Star Parker, Jerry Springer, and Phyllis Schlafly. Cornel West gave a lecture on Martin Luther King Day in 2003, and the Muslim group has long been slated to host Noam Chomsky, although he hadn't come to campus as of this writing. The Bisexual, Gay, and Lesbian Association (BGALA) is an "A-status" group, meaning it receives school funding to operate and to sponsor events. One BGALA member says that the group gets decent press coverage and respect on campus.

While NU admissions literature touts the proximity of Chicago as a selling point, NU students rarely leave the upper-class suburb of Evanston to head downtown. One would think that Chicago's nightlife, at least, would draw more students, but students spend most of their time on campus or at nearby apartments. Students in Northwestern's School of Music perform frequently on campus, including at well-attended senior recitals, and the school sometimes hosts musicians from Chicago's jazz venues. The university also sponsors festivals like the annual Dillo Day, during which students drink tremendous amounts of alcohol and listen to big-name bands.

The Northwestern Wildcats, members of the Big Ten Conference, field varsity sports in baseball, basketball, golf, soccer, swimming, tennis, football, wrestling, cross country, fencing, field hockey, lacrosse, softball, volleyball, and cheerleading/dance.

Northwestern isn't known for its success in most of these sports, and beyond a small core of devoted followers, the stands only swell when things are going well. As one student says, "When the team is good, football is relatively huge with sold-out crowds. When the team isn't any good, attendance drops off significantly." The latter is historically more common. The NU student body rarely keeps up with other campus sports; says one student, "If you ask a random Northwestern student, 'How's the such-and-such team doing?' he wouldn't have any idea." But Northwestern isn't completely uninterested in athletics. Some NU students play on intramural and club teams as a break from classroom pressures. NU's modern recreation centers allow students to participate in swimming, racquetball, aerobics, and other sports. The Sailing Center maintains a fleet of sailboats and provides instruction and programs on Lake Michigan.

The university only guarantees housing to incoming freshmen, but a student housing official says his department has never denied housing to any student who has a sincere desire to live on campus. "We have a delicate balance between housing availability and demand. Students who live off campus choose to live there," says the official. About two-thirds of Northwestern undergraduates live on campus. Residents choose from a wide variety of living arrangements, from small houses to huge dormitories. Students also have the option of single-sex or coed residences and can take their meals at any of the dining halls, which are located in the residences.

Northwestern has managed to keep campus crime down during the past few years, but vigilance is still necessary. Says one student, "At night, most girls I know don't walk alone." At least on campus, violent crime is low. In 2003, the last year for which statistics were available, Northwestern posted just four forcible sex offenses and six robberies. There were 50 burglaries.

Northwestern stands with other well-known schools in charging a hefty tuition: $29,940, and an additional $9,393 for room and board. Admissions are need-blind, however, and the school guarantees to meet the full financial need of students. Some 50 percent of students receive need-based aid.

SUGGESTED CORE

1. Classics 240, The Literary Achievement of Greece and Rome
2. Philosophy 210-1, History of Philosophy
3. Religion 210/211, Introduction to the Hebrew Bible / New Testament Origins
4. Religion 361-1, Foundations of Christian Thought I
5. Political Science 201-2, History of Political Thought II
6. English 234, Introduction to Shakespeare
7. History 210-1, History of the United States
8. History 350-3, Intellectual History of Europe: Nineteenth Century

UNIVERSITY OF NOTRE DAME

SOUTH BEND, INDIANA • WWW.ND.EDU

Land o' Lapsed

The University of Notre Dame has long been the most visible Roman Catholic university in the United States, thanks in large part to its high-profile football program. But the university also came to prominence for making an excellent education accessible to the Catholic middle class. Although for years the university has had an excellent law school and many professional and graduate divisions, its primary strength throughout most of its existence has been the high caliber of its undergraduate curriculum.

In decades past, students could rest assured of both the authentic Catholic identity of the school and the personalized attention of the excellent teaching faculty. All this was undermined in 1967, when Catholic college and university officials gathered at Notre Dame's retreat in Land O' Lakes and decided that the Catholic identity of their schools was a liability in an increasingly secular age. As the Land O' Lakes statement put it: "To perform its teaching and research functions effectively, the Catholic university must have a true autonomy and academic freedom in the face of authority of whatever kind, lay or clerical, external to the academic community itself." This reflects a post-Protestant reading of academic freedom, and its consequences on Catholic colleges have been profound—breaking down their intellectual immune systems, rendering once-faithful institutions helpless to resist whatever political pathogens sweep through the rest of academia. As a result, too few Catholic colleges in the United States are, well, Catholic.

Certainly Notre Dame has not escaped infection. But a healthy core of resistant students and faculty has remained, leaving some vitality within its curriculum, and some observers optimistic about a resurgence of faithful scholarship on campus. We watch and wait.

Notre Dame's recently retired president, Fr. Edward Malloy, was a long-time advocate of the separation of church and school and a frequent critic of Vatican policy. He lambasted *Ex Corde Ecclesiae*, the church's official statement on the centrality of the faith to Catholic higher education. That document ordered the theological faculty of Catholic universities to submit to their local bishops a statement of their fidelity to key tenets of Catholic doctrine, a document called the "mandatum." This Vatican initiative has been ignored at many Catholic universities; Father Malloy was a leader in this campaign of disobedience. (Here's an easy test for parents wondering about the Catholic commitment of a given school: call the theology department chairman and mention the word "mandatum." If the person on the other end of the line responds with enthusiasm, this is a school you can trust. If he gags on his latte, find somewhere else to spend your money.)

Father Malloy's replacement, Fr. John Jenkins, is a specialist in medieval history and St. Thomas Aquinas, but it is not yet clear what direction he intends to take the school. Several students and faculty members devoted to preserving the Catholic identity of the school are cautiously optimistic. (If his steadfastness in the face of criticism over the 2004 firing of the football coach is any indication, their optimism is well placed.) According to a student, "Father Jenkins doesn't seem to be a slave to what the Ivies are thinking or doing. I can't say the same about Father Malloy."

There is a sizable contingency at Notre Dame that would like to mute the school's Catholicism and soften its liberal arts focus. This movement has certainly achieved some success over the last few decades. But there is nevertheless a strong, nearly intractable grassroots Catholicism at Notre Dame that flourishes thanks in large part to the surprisingly strong Catholic identification of the student body. There is also evidence that a good number of faculty and administrators at Notre Dame still wish to resist the secularization of the university. One journalist who covers Catholic universities is hopeful about Notre Dame: "Well over half of the theology faculty have asked for and received their mandatums. It sounds as if most of the resistance has been coming from the old-guard, tenured faculty above the age of 45." This good news confirms our judgment that even if the outcome of Notre Dame's identity crisis remains unresolved, it is still possible to obtain a challenging Catholic liberal arts education under the shadow of the Golden Dome and Touchdown Jesus. As one professor says, "A serious student with a solid Catholic background will be able to obtain a great education at Notre Dame."

For all the struggles over the school's religious identity, however, it may be the push for "white-collar vocational" education that poses the biggest danger to Notre Dame in the long run. "The careerist drive is a great threat," one longtime professor says, calling the craving for prestige "the engine of secularization. We hire faculty who we see as qualified not because they add to the catholicity of the school but because they help in our quest for momentary greatness."

Academic Life: Under the golden dome

Freshmen at Notre Dame enroll in the "First Year of Studies" before they choose a major and go their separate academic ways. Students' feelings about these university seminars are mixed. With small class sizes, getting into a first- or even second-choice seminar is

VITAL STATISTICS

Religious affiliation:
  Roman Catholic
Total enrollment: 11,415
Total undergraduates: 8,311
SAT/ACT midranges: SAT:
  1300–1450; ACT: 30–33
Applicants: 9,745
Applicants accepted: 30%
*Accepted applicants who
  enrolled*: 59%
Tuition: $31,100
Room and board: $6,930
Freshman retention rate: 98%
Graduation rate: 95%
Average class size: 20
Student-faculty ratio: 13:1
*Courses taught by graduate
  TAs*: 7%
Most popular majors:
  business, engineering,
  premed
Students living on campus:
  76%
*Guaranteed housing for four
  years?* no
*Students in fraternities or
  sororities*: none

sometimes difficult. The composition courses are particularly demanding as they require each student to submit a final writing portfolio at the conclusion of the class.

The First Year curriculum is not a true core curriculum, as students may fulfill requirements with a number of courses. First-year seminars are offered in 12 disciplines in the College of Arts and Letters, with more than 50 different university seminar sections. Different mathematics courses are recommended by the university depending on students' future plans, but it is worth noting that most Arts and Letters majors do not require a calculus sequence.

Overall, the quality of the first year at Notre Dame is largely dependent on the academic curiosity of the student. While freshmen can fulfill their requirements with a range of courses, many of these courses are excellent introductions to the fields of literature, philosophy, theology, and history. One professor notes: "It's possible to do a pretty good job in general by picking and choosing your courses, but the offerings are quite uneven." Certainly, it is possible to find some very good professors.

Says one, "Notre Dame still hires a core of substantial scholars; because of its tradition and the high quality of the applicant pool in all areas you can find solid people." Students can find out for themselves at the school's Web-based professor reviews. While these can be an excellent resource for a newcomer, they are anonymous comments from students and should therefore be taken with a grain of salt; easy graders probably score high.

While many entering students think they've already made up their minds on their majors, many First Year of Studies students find themselves indebted to the program for introducing them to fields previously unknown to them. "Rather than rushing into a decision based on my general interests, I had time to allow both the new disciplines I was never exposed to in high school and the changes I was undergoing both as a student and as a person to affect my choice," one student says. "My current major is a perfect fit, and I can honestly say that I never would have considered it without the freedom of the First Year of Studies."

First-year students are assigned professional advisors (some with teaching experience, some without) who are supposed to help students make the transition from high school to college by choosing appropriate courses and, eventually, academic majors. With 14 full-time advisors to serve a freshman class of 2,000, it is unlikely that any student establishes a lasting relationship with his advisor. The extent of advising in the major depends on the discipline; some departments match faculty advisors with a small group of students, while others have one faculty member serve as the undergraduate advisor for the entire department.

After completing the First Year of Studies requirements, students enroll in one of four colleges (Arts and Letters, Business Administration, Engineering, or Science), according to their majors.

The College of Arts and Letters is the oldest and largest division of the university, and it is the home of Notre Dame's justly renowned Program of Liberal Studies (PLS). Known around campus as the "great books" major, PLS offers a three-year sequence of seminars and tutorials conducted in the Socratic method. Starting with the *Iliad* and ending with Ralph Ellison's *The Invisible Man,* the program's reading list is impressive and should attract any Notre Dame student serious about a liberal arts education. The program's excellent faculty includes Frederick Crosson (emeritus), Mary Katherine Tillman (a John Henry Newman scholar), Phillip Reid Sloan (director of the undergraduate program in science, technology, and values), and Walter J. Nicgorski (editor of the *Review of Politics* and a professor in the political science department).

Outside the PLS program, students are free to flourish or founder, but there are several patches of excellence, even genius. The philosophy and political science departments are particularly strong. Highly respected nationwide, the philosophy faculty includes Alfred Freddoso, Alasdair MacIntyre, Ralph McInerny, Alven Nieman, David O'Connor, Alvin Plantinga, and David Solomon (who heads the Center for Ethics and Culture). Philosophy majors must complete a two-course sequence in the history of philosophy, a course in formal logic, two upper-level courses in contemporary philosophy, and three upper-division electives.

Recommended political science faculty include Mary M. Keys, Daniel Philpott, and Michael P. and Catherine H. Zuckert. This major requires students to take introductory courses in American government, international relations, comparative government, and political theory; four advanced courses; and two writing seminars.

The classics department, under Chairman Keith Bradley, has made substantial efforts to improve its academic program by attracting faculty such as the internationally renowned Cicero scholar, Sabine MacCormack, and by holding several weekend conferences and lectures throughout the year. Other outstanding faculty members at Notre Dame include Seamus Deane, James P. Dougherty, John E. Matthias, and Thomas Werge in English; Jay Dolan, George Marsden, John McGreevy, Thomas F. X. Noble, and James Turner in history; and Charles K. Wilber (emeritus) in economics.

Students and alumni have long griped about the theology department, home to well-known professional dissidents from doctrine. As one professor says of theology at Notre Dame, "It's awful. The [former] president always rushe[d] to their aid and [said] things that are completely incompatible with the teachings of the Holy Father." Pro-

ACADEMIC REQUIREMENTS

Freshmen must enroll in the First Year of Studies (FYS) and take:
- One semester of a university seminar in any of 12 disciplines.
- One semester of "First Year Composition."
- Two semesters of mathematics.
- Two semesters of a natural science.
- Two semesters of physical education or ROTC
- One additional elective.
- Three additional courses (program requirements or electives).

After freshman year, in addition to the requirements of their majors, students must complete:
- A course in history.
- A course in social science.
- Two courses each in philosophy and theology, including "Foundations of Theology" and "Introduction to Philosophy," both of which are offered in a number of different sections with widely varying reading lists.
- One course in fine arts or literature. Students have many different options in fulfilling these, some sounder than others.
- All Arts and Letters students are required to reach intermediate proficiency in a foreign language.

fessors warn that faithful Catholics are much less likely to be hired by the theology department or given leadership positions than religiously uncommitted specialists or rebels. However, there is some indication that even this department is beginning to get better. As one student says, "About theology, I would say that it is definitely improving. Many of the students in the department are faithful to the church's teachings, and the department seems to be taking this into consideration in courses offered and by cross-listing courses from the philosophy faculty. In particular, the writings of John Paul II have become of major interest to students, and the faculty is beginning to use them as a focal point in courses. Ralph McInerny's directed readings course on papal encyclicals and Adrian Reimers's course on the 'Theology of the Body' have both developed from a couple of students coming in for weekly discussions to full-sized classes." Noteworthy professors in theology include Michael J. Baxter, Fr. Brian E. Daley, and David Fagerberg.

A number of institutes, think tanks, and study centers further enhance intellectual life at Notre Dame. Students should check out the programs, lectures, conferences, and seminars offered by the Cushwa Center for the Study of American Catholicism, the Erasmus Institute, the Center for Ethics and Culture, the solid and scholarly Maritain Center, and the Medieval Institute. Each fall, the Center for Ethics and Culture holds an annual conference that is highly regarded by students.

Notre Dame is home to the Kroc Institute for International Peace Studies, which was made possible by a $50 million bequest from Joan Kroc, widow of the founder of McDonald's. The institute's director, R. Scott Appleby, is an oft-quoted and left-leaning ideologue. Most recently, the institute made headlines because an incoming member of the faculty was denied a visa by the Department of Homeland Security because of his associations with Islamist groups. The institute has called repeatedly for tinkering with the very structure of the Catholic church—supposedly to prevent future sex scandals.

A notable academic change at Notre Dame in the recent past has been the division of the economics department. In fall 2003, the department split into the Department of Economics and Econometrics—which places special emphasis on quantitative study—and the Department of Economics and Policy Study, which makes more room for quantitative and theoretical approaches and concerns.

Student Life: Touchdown Jesus

For serious Catholics, student life at Notre Dame has much to commend it. On the most raw, blustery, and steel-gray of South Bend winter days, young men and women can be found at the Grotto, a replica of the shrine of Our Lady of Lourdes. Masses are held several times daily in the extraordinary basilica, and they are well attended. Most dorms have their own chapels with daily mass. As a former student says, "They're a well-scrubbed student body. Most are from professional families and most are headed for the professions. There's not a lot of countercultural stuff there."

Students and alumni firmly assert that they are happy with the differences between Notre Dame and the Ivies, but as the school moves closer to the secular model of elite eastern schools, an array of ideologies has rushed in to fill the void left by the retreat of the church's influence on campus life. Annually, amid protests from campus groups such as the Knights of Columbus, there is a campus production of *The Vagina Monologues*, a toxic play that celebrates lesbian statutory rape.

The campus, like most others, has taken on the burden of diversity training. Incoming freshmen are required to attend a lecture concerning homosexuality and the need to be "inclusive." Students who prefer to sit this one out are fined $25. This is the only fine of this type on campus, but it's money well spent. The school's assistant vice president for student affairs has helped form the Standing Committee for Gay and Lesbian Student Needs. This group, while not officially recognized by the school as a student organization, gets in by the back door as a recognized "standing committee." One of its leaders also runs the school's residence assistant training program. A "gay week" is held in October and during a recent observance the school constructed a wooden door frame, through which students were invited to "come out." The school also sponsors a day on which some students and faculty wear T-shirts that say "Gay is OK with me." Other students protest this activism by dressing more formally than usual.

Unlike many Catholic schools, however, there remains at Notre Dame a substantial constituency for the church's teachings. For instance, several years ago the student government presented the board of trustees with a report that argued that the university wasn't doing enough to ensure the institution's Catholic identity. Students wanted Notre Dame to highlight its "intense Catholic character" in admissions. The students were worried by the decline in the percentage of Catholic professors. They also wanted the mandatory theology course to include "a serious study of Catholic dogma and doctrine." There is a new conservative student newspaper, the *Irish Rover*, which has called for Notre Dame to remain true to its liberal arts roots and the Catholic faith.

There are no coed dorms, and a priest or a nun lives in every dorm. These rules, which would appear draconian on most college campuses, have long been a part of life at Notre Dame (at least since women were first admitted in 1972). Former president Fr. Theodore Hesburgh, who governed the university for some 20 years, is said to have remarked that Notre Dame would have coed dorms only over his dead body. While

SUGGESTED CORE

1. Classics 455, Classical Epic
2. Philosophy 301, Ancient and Medieval Philosophy
3. Theology 100/180/200, Foundations of Theology: Biblical / Historical
4. History 392, History of Christianity to 1500
5. Political Science 243, Political Theory
6. English 340, Shakespeare in Performance
7. History 115, Growth of the American Nation
8. Philosophy 221, Philosophy of Human Nature (*closest match*)

Notre Dame's Program of Liberal Studies would provide an excellent core, for students willing to major in the program. Those who do should take the following:

- Program of Liberal Studies 180, Literature University Seminar I and II
- Program of Liberal Studies 281-282, Great Books Seminar I and II
- Program of Liberal Studies 381-382, Great Books Seminar III and IV
- Program of Liberal Studies 481-482, Great Books Seminar V and VI

some students agitate for a general loosening of social policies at the school, others indicate that the enforcement of these regulations is not always particularly tight. Hard liquor is officially prohibited in the dorms, for example, but students say that lots of drinking occurs. Violations of visiting hours are punished harshly. Other rules are also closely followed: freshmen are not allowed to have cars on campus, and hazing is prohibited.

There is an active pro-life movement on campus. A few years ago, the movement's leader pressured a reluctant administration into speaking up publicly in opposition to abortion. As a former student says, "They just sort of went to the administration and said, 'Why aren't you more openly pro-life?' That got them moving on the issue." Other student groups include ROTC, several chorales (including a liturgical choir), Habitat for Humanity, an undergraduate investment club, Humor Artists (a comedy troupe), and a nationally ranked parliamentary debate team.

The city of South Bend and its bordering neighbor, Mishawaka, do not have much to offer in the way of excitement. Indeed, it is remarkable just how little either city caters to the Notre Dame student. Nowhere is there a strip of bars, pizza joints, restaurants, coffeehouses, and shops targeting students—certainly nothing like what one usually finds at other major midwestern universities. As a result, students tend to stay on campus; however, the addition of a modern theater should help make that a bit more enjoyable. The Michael Browning Family Cinema at the DeBartolo Center for Performing Arts is the new 200-seat, state-of-the-art THX home of ND Cinema.

The campus itself is lovely, especially during the fall, and despite the uninspired architecture of many of the newer buildings. The golden dome of the Main Building glimmers on the north end of campus, right next to the Basilica of the Sacred Heart and the Norte Dame Grotto. Beyond the basilica and grotto lie two small lakes. On the other side of campus are two crucially important buildings: the massive Hesburgh Library and Notre Dame Stadium. These edifices are visually connected by the presence of "Touchdown Jesus," a 14-story-high mosaic on the south wall of the library that looks down on the recently renovated and expanded stadium. The stadium, of course, is the home of Notre Dame football. Athletics—as well as many other social activities—revolve around the sport, which the school started playing back in 1887. The school gets precious national exposure thanks to an exclusive contract with NBC to carry all of its home games. Other sports have also been quite successful, including baseball, women's soccer, and, recently, men's and women's basketball. In all, there are 13 men's teams and 13 women's teams.

Campus crime is infrequent. In 2003, the school reported just one forcible sex offense, one aggravated assault, four stolen cars, one arson, and 49 burglaries; alcohol-related arrests have fallen.

Notre Dame may have started out as a school catering to blue-collar immigrant kids, but it isn't cheap today. Tuition in 2004–5 was $31,100, with room and board at $6,930. Admissions are need-blind, and the school pledges to meet accepted students' full need. Some 49 percent of the 2004–5 student body qualified for need-based assistance. The average amount of that assistance was just over $21,000, $16,000 of which came from the school in the form of a grant or scholarship. The school makes it a priority not to burden the student population with loans. Less than 50 percent of recent grads had outstanding loans, and those that did had an average debt of between $15,000 and $20,000, the school reports.

OBERLIN COLLEGE

OBERLIN, OHIO • WWW.OBERLIN.EDU

Boundless, desolate fields

In 1833, Alsatian pastor John Fredrick Oberlin sent two Yankee ministers west to found a college "where they could train teachers in and other Christian leaders for the boundless and most desolate fields of the West." Oberlin College was the result. Since its founding, Oberlin has been one of the most progressive liberal arts colleges in the country. In 1841, the college awarded AB degrees to three female students—the first in the nation. Two years after the college's founding, its leaders pledged that Oberlin would be a place where "youths are received as members, irrespective of color." By 1900, one-third of all African American college graduates in the United States had graduated from Oberlin. And in 1865, the college founded its world-renowned music conservatory.

Oberlin has grown considerably in reputation and influence from its small midwestern roots and in the process has left its original Christian mission far behind. The college now demonstrates its progressivism with a curriculum soaked in ethnic, class, and gender obsessions. Liberation theology has replaced traditional Christian doctrine, and "Introduction to Religion" courses now include subtitles like "Women and the Western Traditions," "Feminist Religious Thought in a Multicultural Perspective," and "African Religions and Their Thought Systems." Oberlin challenges its graduates to use their educations to "make a difference in the world around them," and so Oberlin students are known for their social activism, intellectual firepower—four Oberlin students earned Fullbright awards in the 2004–5 academic year—and dedication to putting their education to social use. As a *New York Times* article put it, "While Yale was worrying about God, and Harvard was worrying about the classics, Oberlin was concerned with the world beyond." To what extent Oberlin's world beyond bears any resemblance to the actual world is open to question. However, while in the tight-knit world of Oberlin, students can at least establish strong relationships with professors and classmates, who happen to be some of the nation's finest.

Academic Life: Music to hear

Oberlin has two main residential colleges: Arts and Sciences and the Conservatory of Music. Around 2,250 students choose Arts and Sciences. Oberlin College has no core curriculum, nor even a decent set of distribution requirements. With such a minimalist curriculum, students can—and sometimes do—avoid all serious courses and devote themselves instead to studies in women's and ethnic issues.

Arts and Sciences offers 45 majors. Some of these provide little more structure than the basic college requirements. Others, though still fairly weak, have improved somewhat over the years. According to a study conducted by the National Association of Scholars, in 1964 Oberlin's English department had no required courses; today, English majors must take two courses in English literature before 1700, one in literature between 1700 and 1900, and one in literature from 1900 to the present. Courses in poetry, narrative fiction, and drama are also recommended. Unfortunately, English majors have the option of selecting "concentration majors," which allow them to dump some of the traditional English courses for trendier ones. For instance, students can concentrate on African American studies, modern culture and media, or women's and gender studies, among others. History majors can also avoid foundational courses. In fact, they are only required to take two courses in each of two sections: the first section includes European and United States history, and the second includes African, Asian, Caribbean, Russian, and early Jewish history. Oberlin students do not have to complete a thesis or pass comprehensive departmental exams prior to graduation.

Unfortunately for students, a good deal of Oberlin's political activity occurs within the classroom. One professor says segments of the Oberlin faculty are "ideological and aggressive." An article from the Web-based *FrontPage Magazine* sums things up this way: "At Oberlin, it's difficult to tell where activism ends and education begins." Conservative columnist Michelle Malkin, an alumna of Oberlin, recalls, "For the most part, it was an incredibly politically correct culture." A professor says, "The whole public atmosphere is pretty much confined to the left. In the rhetoric that is constantly used at this place, in questions of sexual orientation and racial divides, there is a real balkanization that has taken place in recent years."

The college imposes a daunting three-course cultural diversity requirement that can be fulfilled through dozens of politicized courses; however, students may also choose to complete the requirement by taking courses in foreign languages or world history. In other words, "cultural diversity" doesn't necessarily mean ethnic/gender/class propaganda.

Many members of Oberlin's faculty, however, while liberal, are not knee-jerk radicals. In an essay titled, "What's Conservative About Conservation," David Orr, an environmental studies professor, asks how conservatives—supposedly hostile to cultural dynamism, cherishing the social bond between the living, the dead, and the yet-to-be-born, and guided by prudence—can be "hostile to the cause of conservation." In other words, instead of cheaply attacking conservatives' approach to the environment with leftist platitudes, Orr actually attempts to draw out inherent contradictions within conservative political rhetoric.

Founded in 1865, Oberlin's Conservatory of Music is the college's finest academic offering. Enrolling about 600 students, the conservatory offers bachelor of music degrees in music theory, music history, music education, performance, composition, jazz studies, and other areas. Degree requirements are similar to those of Arts and Sciences, and the core curriculum is identical (i.e., there is none). Including individual major guidelines, students have to complete at least 124 credit hours (around 35 to 40 courses), half of which must be earned at Oberlin. The conservatory does offer master's degrees, but they are limited to Oberlin undergraduates who wish to gain additional knowledge in a specific area. Oberlin also offers a five-year double-degree program for students who wish to pursue degrees from both Arts and Sciences and the conservatory.

The natural sciences are also very strong at Oberlin. One professor says, "I think natural science at Oberlin is a little-known jewel—it has a crucial function in maintaining [Oberlin's] academic caliber and does attract some of the best students." In fact, three Oberlin graduates have won Nobel prizes, all in the sciences. To support the prodigious number of students who go on to pursue PhDs in engineering and the natural sciences—among four-year institutions, Oberlin is ranked first in this department—the college recently completed construction of a new science facility to replace 40-year-old Kettering Hall. The Oberlin Science Center includes two large lecture halls, a science library, and classrooms that integrate laboratories into a traditional classroom setting.

Other strong departments at the college include classics, philosophy, politics, and mathematics. Excellent professors include Jeffrey Witmer in mathematics; David Benzing, Yolanda Cruz, and Roger Laushman in biology; and Martin Ackermann in physics.

Oberlin's academic calendar is a typical two-semester schedule, but there is also a winter term in January that "enables students to discover the value of self-education . . . that a structured curriculum during the academic year cannot accommodate," according to the college viewbook. (Where can we find this "structured curriculum"?) During this interim term, students can elect to study abroad, perform community service, or focus on their majors through interactive projects. Students are required to earn credit for projects conducted during these four weeks. In 2004, students spent this time participating in a performance anxiety workshop and touring with a string quartet. Other examples of past winter term projects include shadowing a doctor, working at a battered woman's shelter and studying Peruvian folk dances. One student analyzed her

VITAL STATISTICS

Religious affiliation: none
Total enrollment: 2,827
Total undergraduates: 2,807
SAT/ACT midranges: SAT V: 640–730, M: 610–710; ACT: 26–31
Applicants: 5,824
Applicants accepted: 39%
Accepted applicants who enrolled: 32%
Tuition: $30,975
Room and board: $7,643
Freshman retention rate: 93%
Graduation rate: 64% (4 yrs.), 79% (6 yrs.)
Courses with fewer than 20 students: 68%
Student-faculty ratio: 10:1
Courses taught by graduate TAs: none
Most popular majors: biology, English, history
Students living on campus: 73%
Guaranteed housing for four years? yes
Students in fraternities or sororities: none

Oberlin has no core curriculum and fairly weak distribution requirements. On top of their major requirements, students cannot count more than 84 hours within a single division (Arts and Humanities, Social and Behavioral Sciences, or Natural Sciences and Mathematics) toward graduation. Therefore, at least 28 hours must be taken outside the division with the highest number of credits. Students must also earn nine credit hours in each of three divisions:

- Humanities. Just about everything will count, from "Shakespeare and Film" to "Boundaries of Yellow: Navigating Terrains in Contemporary Asian American Literature."

extensive childhood diaries and wrote an analytical paper on what she had learned. The same student, during another winter term, obtained half of her credit by working at the local historical society and the other half by putting together a schedule of physical exercise.

One of the benefits of this small college is that students have the opportunity to forge lasting relationships with professors. Upon entering, each Oberlin student is assigned an academic advisor to help choose courses, majors, and future careers. With such an unstructured curriculum, students could benefit from some guidance in planning an educational program; unfortunately, Oberlin does not require that students meet with their advisors for extended amounts of time, and some students end up forging their own curricular paths with little faculty input. The college offers several colloquia each year for first- and second-year students, with enrollments limited to just 15 students. "Many of those courses are excellent due to the small class size and their interesting subject focus," a student says. But some of the colloquia offerings are of marginal importance: One first-year course is titled "Race and Ethnicity in American Politics." And another in the history department is called "National Schizophrenia in Japan and Sub-Saharan Africa 1945–Present: Tradition, Modernity and the Modern Artist." However, students can also choose the second-semester French language course (taught in French), "Le Voyage dans la Literature Francais," which includes a study of *Tristan et Iseult,* as well as texts from Rabelais and Voltaire.

Students unsatisfied with typical course offerings can participate in the college's popular Experimental College (EXCO), which offers student-run courses on subjects ranging from "The Passion of the Christ," an exploration of the film and the Gospels from a Christian perspective, to the downright dangerous "Introduction to Knife Throwing Performance." In 2004 alone, students organized more than 70 courses. These courses count in small bits toward the hours needed for graduation, and while they don't replace regular classes, students do use EXCO offerings "to pad our schedules a little bit," one says. Oberlin maintains study centers in England and Spain, and has affiliations with other colleges' programs throughout the rest of the world.

Student Life: Masterpieces for rent

Oberlin, Ohio, population 8,600, is 35 miles southwest of Cleveland. Given the lack of cultural options in its surroundings, the college works hard to create entertainment options on campus. Admissions literature points out that 1,000 activities are offered on campus in a given year, including 400 concerts, 200 film screenings, two operas, and 60 theater and dance productions. "Nearly every day, a respected scholar, community leader, or artist is lecturing somewhere on the Oberlin campus," the school points out. The town of Oberlin offers a few perks of its own, including good bookstores (the Co-op and Mind Fair Books) and coffeeshops like the Java Zone and Main Street Mercantile Store and Tea Room (known as the Merc). The Apollo movie theater is in an art deco building in the downtown area and features current films at low prices.

The music conservatory boasts incredible facilities: 150 practice studios, around 170 Steinway grand pianos, 40 music studios, a music library, and electronic and computer musical instruments that are rare in most undergraduate institutions. Additionally, the conservatory supports the Oberlin College Artist Recital Series, which for 110 years has offered performances by professors, students, and visiting artists like the Cleveland Orchestra, Opera Atelier, and the Juilliard String Quartet. Says one student, "Because of the conservatory, there are a lot of musical performances, most of which are fun and showcase excellent talent."

Besides campus performances, cooperative activities, studying, and heading into Cleveland, students "otherwise go to the Feve (the only bar) or to the Oberlin Inn for pitchers night," says one student. Last year, one of the most popular and controversial events was Safer Sex Night, an all-college dance originally intended to educate students about the dangers and consequences of sex. According to the *Oberlin Review*, at the 2003 Safer Sex Night, education videos were broadcast on monitors throughout the buildings and students arrived scantily clad—some in nothing more than a bumper sticker. At the same time, faculty members performed demonstrations on how to safely use condoms, birth control, and other contraceptive devices. The newspaper reported, "Students dealt with the heat in a variety of clothing, from full suits to nothing more than a well-placed cowboy hat." Another popular annual event is the Drag Ball, recently dubbed the "Mardi Gras of the Midwest" by *Rolling Stone*. The ball annually attracts about 1,500 students, faculty, and administrators, including school president Nancy Dye.

Oberlin's brand of political radicalism is aimed primarily at the liberation of desire, or "expanding boundaries." As *FrontPage Magazine* has said, "Oberlin embodies a far-left paradise of agitation, Marxist activism, and sexual licentiousness." The Oberlin Chapter of the National Organization for the Reform of the Marijuana Laws is perhaps

REQUIREMENTS (CONT'D)

- **Social Sciences.** Options here range from "Political Change in America" to "Gender, Nature, and Culture."
- **Natural Sciences.** The choices are many, including "Meteorite Impacts in Space and Time" and "The Brain: An Introduction to Neuroscience."

Students must also take at least three winter-term credits and show proficiency in writing and quantitative skills by completing courses or passing tests. They must also meet the school's cultural diversity requirement, which consists of three courses—more than any other school in this guide imposes.

the archetypal student political group. Students eager to "make a difference in the world" seem to thrive here and organize around groups such as the Peace Activists League and the Oberlin Action Against Prisons. That, coupled with campus visits from sex-toy entrepreneurs, porn stars, and self-avowed butch-lesbian socialist Carmen Vasquez, seems to bear out the assertion that Oberlin really is a far-left paradise. No small wonder then that the college does not have a College Republicans chapter or any other organized group associated with the conventional right, aside from the Oberlin Pro-Life Union of Students.

A campus columnist suspects that conservatives do exist but are "too scared to organize." Malkin's experience at Oberlin bears this out. She recounted in a column that when she criticized Oberlin's affirmative action program, she encountered a "vicious response." Malkin wrote: "It's an extremely liberal campus. Even if you tread very lightly on political sacred cows, there [is] a huge negative response."

Officially, Oberlin says it enjoys political dialogue, but campus debates have the feel of those that used to occur between the acolytes of Trotsky and Stalin rather than debates between fundamentally opposed worldviews. If mentioned at all, academically unfashionable views tend to be met with scorn rather than genuine intellectual consideration. "Even the campus newspaper recently acknowledged that digging up a Republican among the student body is nearly impossible to do—they found only two—and conservative, or even moderate, voices are virtually nonexistent," reports *FrontPage Magazine*.

Oberlin has no fraternities or sororities, instead offering cooperatives. The several on- and off-campus cooperatives house more than 500 students and offer dining services. Each cooperative is based on a particular theme and identity, ranging from the Kosher House to the Third World Cooperative. Co-op members divide tasks such as cooking and cleaning and take their attachment to the co-op seriously.

Other housing options at Oberlin include traditional dormitories and theme houses. The college no longer has single-sex dormitories, but it does section off various areas of dorms to be all-women or all-men. There are a few coed bathrooms on campus, but a housing representative explains that these are restricted to coed floors on which there is only one bathroom. At the beginning of each school year, students vote on whether to make the bathroom coed, and the decision must be unanimous. Oberlin offers a good deal of flexibility in its meal plans, from an all-inclusive plan to a monastic seven-meals-a-week option. Students can choose from among six dining halls at Oberlin, all of which follow strict health guidelines to meet the expectations of this mostly health-conscious community.

Health concern seems not to extend to the use of liquor and other drugs. Liquor-law violations are common. Students say that many Oberlin students are drug users and heavy drinkers. An *Oberlin Review* article reported that students, speaking anonymously, found drug use to be widely popular. One student says it is "really, really easy" to obtain drugs at Oberlin.

Oberlin students are a unique lot, as one sophomore reports: "Oberlin fits a particular type of person. It's a little off the mainstream in its culture. If a prospective student was looking for an alternative experience or was himself/herself a little off the mainstream, then Oberlin is a good fit." Extracurricular clubs cover a wide range of interests, including the Oberlin Chess Club, student radio (WOBC), and a Zionists club.

Conservative religious students (and to some extent, Christians of any political leaning) will feel out of place at Oberlin. A letter to the editor printed in a November 2004 edition of the *Oberlin Review* sounds a voice in the wilderness: "Spring 2002 saw a series of attacks on Christianity that the administration and faculty did nothing to prevent or apologize for. . . . The artistic and academic condemnation and disrespect of Jesus and his followers reached a feverish peak. An art show called 'The Rape of Mary,' a religion professor personally attacking Christian students, threatening the Protestant chaplain's position. . . . For the past three years, Oberlin . . . has vented its frustration at the government on people of faith."

So maybe it's telling that on the Oberlin Web site for student organizations, faith-based clubs are listed under the same category as identity organizations such as La Alianza Latina and Lesbian, Gay, Bisexual, and Transgendered Union. Still, there is a pro-life club on campus, a Christian fellowship, a Hillel, and a Muslim students association, as well as a "Queers and Allies of Faith" group. Local houses of worship include a Lutheran church, several evangelical and Pentecostal denominations, a Friends meeting, a Unitarian Universalist fellowship, and a Catholic church. Jewish religious services are either held at the Hillel center or at Talcott Dining Hall.

Clubs are governed by the Student Senate, whose budget committee controls how much money student organizations receive from the annual fee levied against each student. Campus publications include the *Oberlin Review*, the weekly student newspaper; the *Grape*, a magazine focused on world affairs and opinion; *Scope*, a student publication dedicated to artistic endeavor; *Oberlin on Oberlin*, "an online publication chronicling student life and student concerns"; and *Enchiridion*, Oberlin's literary magazine.

The Allen Memorial Art Museum is a leading college museum and is especially strong in its collection of seventeenth-century Dutch paintings, Japanese prints, Chinese paintings, and contemporary art. Founded in 1917, the museum is a significant cultural asset. Art history and other humanities courses frequently take advantage of the museum's resources for classroom presentations. Allen Museum also maintains a 400-piece rental collection that allows students, faculty, staff, and Oberlin residents to rent signed prints by Warhol, Picasso, and Toulouse-Lautrec, as well as paintings and sculptures by other artists. The rental days occur twice a year; those renting in Septem-

SUGGESTED CORE
1. Classics 101, Homer's *Iliad* and the Myths of Tragedy *and* Classics 102, Homer's *Odyssey* and the Myths of Comedy
2. Philosophy 215, Ancient Philosophy
3. Religion 205, The Hebrew Bible *and* Religion 208, The New Testament
4. Religion 217, Christian Thought and Action: Early and Medieval
5. Politics 232, European Political Theory: Hobbes to Marx
6. English 208, Shakespeare and Film (*closest match*)
7. History 103, American History to 1877
8. Politics 234, European Political Theory: After Marx

ber return the works in December, while February rentals are returned in May. Students get first dibs on the collection, and some even camp out for the best choice.

Although John Heisman, the coaching legend whose name now adorns college football's most prestigious award, began his coaching career at Oberlin, the college hasn't seen the likes of him lately. But that may be changing, as one professor says that "athletics are more of a priority with the college than they have been in the past." Oberlin recently hired Vin Lananna as athletic director; he was a U.S. track and field coach at the Olympics in Athens, and prior to that, coached several Stanford teams to national titles. Lananna was also allowed to hire a number of additional coaches and assistant athletic directors. So if in five years or so Oberlin's teams are not more competitive, it won't be from lack of aggressive financial commitment. Oberlin is a member of the North Coast Athletic Conference, an NCAA Division III group, and offers 22 varsity sports. Students can also participate in club sports (including karate, the marching band, and ice hockey) and intramurals (including basketball, table tennis, soccer, and softball).

Crime at Oberlin is typical of a smaller college in a rural town. Statistics in 2003 showed 37 burglaries and three forcible sex offenses. Walking safety escorts are available, student shuttles run from 9 p.m. to 2 a.m., and an emergency telephone service is in place to help students in need.

With tuition at $30,975, and room and board at $7,643, Oberlin makes for an expensive trip to left field. Nor does the school practice need-blind admissions. However, students admitted will find their full financial need met. During the 2002–3 academic year, more than 56 percent of the student body received financial aid from the college.

OHIO STATE UNIVERSITY

COLUMBUS, OHIO • WWW.OSU.EDU

The "big" in Big Ten

Ohio State is big; it sits on a 1,644-acre campus, one of the world's largest, and enrolls the nation's second-largest student body, behind only the University of Texas at Austin. The school traces its history to 1870, when it began as the Ohio Agricultural and Mechanical College. Its curriculum was the subject of much debate: whether 'twere better to stick to the agricultural and mechanical arts, or to offer a more traditional curriculum including the humanities. The latter view won the day, as the university decided that it would offer just about every subject under the sun—even the liberal arts.

Still, among the OSU liberal arts faculty, it is a common view that students looking for a serious humanities education would be better served elsewhere. Only "focused, savvy undergraduates" interested in going on for a graduate or professional degree, according to one professor, should choose Ohio State. Another professor nominates Miami University and Ohio University as better Ohio public schools for the liberal arts, and Michigan and Wisconsin as better Big Ten choices. Another professor takes exception to this. "A discerning and determined student can gain a good liberal arts education here," she says. "The problem is that he or she shouldn't have to struggle against the system to do it."

Academic Life: 50,000 of your closest friends

OSU's general education requirements give the student plenty of wiggle room. Thus, although a student may have to arrange his schedule so as to incorporate a few mandates, he will surely be able to find a course to his liking—not exactly the goal of a liberal arts curriculum.

One worthwhile initiative, which students considering OSU should certainly investigate, is the Honors Program. Honors students typically come from the top 10 per-

VITAL STATISTICS

Religious affiliation: none
Total enrollment: 50,995
Total undergraduates: 37,509
SAT/ACT midranges: SAT V: 520–630, M: 550–660; ACT: 23–28
Applicants: 16,954
Applicants accepted: 76%
Accepted applicants who enrolled: 47%
Tuition: $7,479 (in state), $18,066 (out of state)
Room and board: $6,909
Freshman retention rate: 88%
Graduation rate: 31% (4 yrs.), 62% (6 yrs.)
Courses with fewer than 20 students: 43%
Student-faculty ratio: 14:1
Courses taught by graduate TAs: not provided
Most popular majors: social sciences, business, engineering
Students living on campus: 25%
Guaranteed housing for four years? no
Students in fraternities: 6% sororities: 7%

Ohio State's general education requirements vary, but in Arts and Sciences, students face the following mandates:

- At least two courses in "writing and related skills," including an introductory composition course. The other class may be selected from a long list, including "The U.S. Experience as Reflected in Literature," "African American Voices in U.S. Literature," and "U.S. Folk Experience."
- Two "mathematics and logical analysis" courses. Students may test out of these or take approved courses in computer science, linguistics, or philosophy.
- One course in "data analysis." Applicable fields of study range from social work to astronomy.
- Four courses in the natural sciences, including one two-course sequence, at least one course in the biological sciences, one course in the physical sciences, and one lab.
- Three courses in the social sciences from a list of about 60 approved courses of varying quality. One example is "Language across Cultures," the aim of which is to "shed light on cross-cultural similarities and differences."

cent of their classes and have average SAT scores above 1300. They are eligible for merit scholarships and may live in one of four special residence halls. They may also choose from among more than 240 honors classes, which in fall 2004 included a mix of basics like "Honors Chemistry" and a few heavy-handed ideological courses (e.g. "Cross-Cultural Perspectives"), as well as interesting and challenging topics like "The Faust Theme" and "Art of the Ancient World." These courses are taught by elite faculty and enjoy smaller enrollment. The Scholars Program is a similar initiative, whose 300 participating students live in housing specific to their academic interests, take advanced classes, and enjoy personalized advising and mentoring opportunities. Scholars travel each year to a "world-class city," go on retreats, and engage in community service. One professor goes so far as to say that both of these programs compare "favorably with a decent middle-of-the-road Ivy League education."

Outside these programs, the picture is less impressive. After fulfilling the school's (rather lax) general education requirements, students go on to complete a major. Students of history, for instance, must take but two required courses: an introduction to the historical method, and a senior seminar designed to hone their research skills to approximate those of professional scholars. History students must take a minimum of 50 hours in their major, including at least 20 credit hours in one geographical region and 15 from two or more other regions; at least 10 credit hours in courses studying history before 1750; and the same number in history after that date. (Classes at OSU are taught on the quarter system, and most classes are worth five credit hours.) These are respectable requirements, and many of the departmental course offerings are excellent, but there are also the usual clunkers, like "History of Modern Sexualities." You'll notice that American history is *not* one of the requirements for the major.

Ohio State's Academic Plan, revised in 2003, reflects the institution's priorities well. The plan maintains that OSU is committed to building "a world-class faculty" and developing "academic programs that define Ohio State as the nation's leading public land-grant university." It also claims that OSU is committed to upgrading "the quality of the teaching and learning environment" and "enhanc[ing] and better serv[ing] the student body." To do all this, the

MIDWEST

university intends to build new libraries, add classroom space, and focus on the use of new technologies. In addition, OSU plans to "better serve the student body" by making admission more "selective." But this is window-dressing stuff. Improving the school's rankings, physical plant, and technological infrastructure will do little to enhance its substantive educational offerings. In fact, because the budgeting system was changed to a "responsibility-based system," one professor reports trouble getting approval to teach small classes—since each department is rewarded based on the raw numbers of students it processes. "Seems contradictory to me—promoting larger classes while saying that undergrad education will improve," the professor says.

Ohio State administrators may not care if OSU becomes a national model for teaching undergraduates, but as they state in their Diversity Action Plan, they do want it to be "a national model for diversity." Towards this end, OSU vigorously pursues various affirmative action policies. Among other costly plans, OSU's historic Hagerty Hall reopened in January 2005 after six years of renovation; it now houses the technologically advanced World Media and Culture Center, as well as various foreign language departments. Propaganda coming out of the highest echelons of bureaucracy include "The President and Provost's Diversity Lecture and Cultural Arts Series: Excellence through Diversity," which amounts to lectures on topics such as "Strategic Priorities, Strategic Funding," "How the Media Teach about Diversity," "Diversity and the American University Professoriate: National Imperative or Political Correctness?" and "Nine Ways of Looking at a Poor Woman."

Reports about classroom politicization are mixed. According to one political science professor, OSU has "a very open political climate. Liberal and conservative voices are heard. The campus community is very tolerant." The same professor says that professors in her department "pride themselves on being neutral and playing 'devil's advocate' when one political opinion is expressed." A conservative student agrees. "I have had left-leaning, moderate, and conservative professors. I can say that I have never felt uncomfortable in a class, though. As a conservative, I have always been given a chance to voice my opinion, and even encouraged to do so, even when the professor is obviously liberal." Despite these claims, one faculty member maintains that

REQUIREMENTS (CONT'D)

- Five courses in the arts and humanities, including a two-course sequence in history, one literature course, and one visual/performing arts course. Students may choose among two-semester survey sequences such as "Western Civilization from Antiquity to the Seventeenth Century" and "From the Seventeenth Century to Modern Times," or they may skip the West entirely and study world history or the history of Africa only. To meet the visual/performing arts requirement, they may choose among many, many alternatives, including music, medieval and Renaissance painting, and landscape architecture.

- Three courses that will satisfy the "Diversity Experiences" requirement. One course must cover "social diversity in the United States" and two courses must concentrate on "international issues," including one with a non-Western focus.

- One course from a list titled "Issues in the Contemporary World."

  Students must also show proficiency in a foreign language or complete coursework through the fourth-semester level.

MIDWEST

"some topics are relatively taboo." This professor says that at least one "activist Christian" was denied tenure for political reasons. One student gives this example of one-sided intellectual dialogue: "The faculty offered a seminar last school year to discuss in a forum the current situation of the war in Iraq. . . . Not one of the faculty members on the panel supported the war in Iraq, defended current U.S. policy, or even offered to play devil's advocate. . . . OSU has a long way to go in terms of academic freedom," he says.

The most politicized departments are said to be the usual suspects (African American, African, and women's studies), but also include psychology and English. Says a professor regarding the English department, "Too often I hear from students that they've been ridiculed or even downgraded on their work for their beliefs (whether political or religious), or that they've simply kept their mouths shut or parroted what they knew was the party line in order to get decent grades. . . . It's fairly widespread, and seems to be worst in classes taught by TAs. Many of our students refer to the 'American Experience' second writing course as 'Indoctrination 101.'" The professor adds that "there are many dedicated teachers in the English department, and as long as students stay away from taboo subjects or don't air their religious views, they find the department surprisingly warm . . . for such a large one."

Currently, OSU is best known for its Fisher College of Business and College of Engineering. The school offers more than 170 degree programs, covering everything from jazz studies to turfgrass science. While none of the departments "specialize in undergraduate education," as one professor reports, nearly all have some excellent teachers. Undergrads should try Janet Box-Steffensmeier in political science; Eric Fisher, Howard Marvel, and Gene Mumy in economics; Rick Livingston in comparative studies; Edward Crenshaw in sociology; In Jae Myung in psychology; Phoebe S. Spinrad in English; and Harding Ganz in history.

Because OSU is such a large campus, it is very important for students to "get connected," says a professor. "It is a big place. To not get lost, one needs to connect with professors about related [research] interests." Smart students will generally stand out at OSU. They may also be a bit bored. Since OSU accepts more than 75 percent of its applicants, classes must "be structured for a heterogeneous clientele," as one professor gently phrases it. On the plus side, ambitious students will find it easy to stand out. Says a professor, "Those who want to distinguish themselves from the horde at OSU can do so quite easily because most of their undergrad colleagues aren't coming to see their professors and are happy with a C." Once a student identifies the professor with whom he would like to study and "makes a reasoned pitch, works hard, and shows his talent," he will, according to the same professor, receive a "remarkable undergrad education working with some of the top scholars in his field."

Students in the College of the Arts and Sciences are appointed two advisors—one of whom may (or may not) be a faculty member. Despite this "dual-advising system," OSU stresses students' responsibility to navigate the academic labyrinth. In the university's own words to its students, "You are responsible for knowing the requirements of the curriculum you are pursuing, . . . scheduling an appointment with your assigned academic advisor(s) regularly, . . . [and] getting updated . . . major information." With six-year graduation rates hovering around 60 percent during the past three years, and the four-year rate at a measly 31 percent, this system doesn't seem particularly effective.

OSU's freshman retention rate of 88 percent, while not spectacular, is certainly better than its graduation rate statistics. Part of the reason may be the considerable time and energy spent on new arrivals at OSU. The university offers a series of orientation events as part of the First-Year Experience Program (FYE), in which students, during their first quarter on campus, are invited to "attend special lectures, seminars, and gatherings" intended to address issues they will face in adjusting to college life. Upperclassmen meet with freshmen to discuss the new academic demands and social challenges; seminars by faculty members introduce research methods and principles; and eminent writers arrive with fanfare and read from their bestselling books, after which students are invited to discuss and debate the contents. The themes for 2004–5 events blended the practical and appropriate with a helping of the ideological. Seventeen- and eighteen-year-old students could certainly gain from the insights of their elders on such topics as "Academic Engagement and Exploration," "Financial Awareness," "Leadership," "Drug and Alcohol Use," "Physical Health and Wellness," and "Anxiety and Mental Health." We're a little more dubious about what they'll gain from seminars titled "Celebrating Diversity" and "Safe Sex." There are also FYE course offerings, ranging from solid fare to the ideological or strangely specialized. The 2004–5 FYE courses included "Culture and Observation: Designing for Diversity" and "Where Are All the Extraterrestrials?"

Professors at OSU can be surprisingly approachable. One student in a class of 100 says that "the professor went to great lengths to make himself accessible. He ran two separate homework problem help sessions (in addition to one run by the TA), and he [didn't] end them until all questions [were] answered. . . . I have been impressed by the effort he expends in order to serve his students." Students should seek out professors like this—especially since many of their lower-level courses will be taught by graduate students.

One way to avoid OSU's massive lecture classes is to take survey courses at one of the school's regional campuses. According to a student at the Columbus campus, "Many freshman students (myself included) feel that their first year of study is wasteful. . . . If one can avoid coming to the main campus and save money in the process by attending a regional campus closer to home, it would be well worth it." A student at the Newark campus says that "it is much better to take history classes [here] because the class size is much smaller. Thus, more attention [is] given to individual students." Well-regarded

SUGGESTED CORE
1. Classics 101, Masterpieces of Greek Literature in Translation *and* Classics 102, Masterpieces of Latin Literature in Translation
2. Philosophy 301, History of Ancient Philosophy
3. English 280, The English Bible
4. History 507, History of Medieval Christianity
5. Political Science 210, Modern Political Ideologies (*closest match*)
6. English 220, Introduction to Shakespeare
7. History 151, American Civilization to 1877
8. History 513.01, The Age of Modernity in the Nineteenth Century

professors at the Newark campus include David Paul and Rachel Paul in political science, as well as Mitch Lerner in history.

Student Life: It's a riot

Ohio State's campus is located in Columbus, the state's capital. It is the largest city in Ohio and, believe it or not, the fifteenth-largest in the nation. Naturally, there is plenty to do in the city on any weekend and most weeknights. Hockey fans can catch the NHL's Blue Jackets—when they're not on strike—while soccer supporters can get a dose of the city's MLS team, the Columbus Crew. The prosperous city hosts a substantial arts scene, including museums, a symphony, and a ballet. The city is student-friendly: for example, students can use their university ID cards to ride the local buses for free.

Yet in the fall, OSU students tend to be consumed with football. In 2002, the Buckeyes went undefeated and won the national championship. Even when the team has suffered a defeat or two, Ohio Stadium, otherwise known as "The Horseshoe," is usually packed to its 101,568-seat capacity (during a 2002 game against archrival Michigan, 105,539 fans somehow squeezed in).

Students gather to party before, during, and after OSU sporting events, especially football games. Unfortunately, win or lose, students and locals sometimes lose control of their emotions, and "parties" become "riots." Following that big 2002 game against Michigan, 60 people were arrested, 100 fires set, and nine cars torched—all this despite a record police presence. Two years earlier, after a home loss to Michigan, one student was stabbed, three police officers injured, 11 students arrested, and 129 fires started. Police had to use tear gas and wooden bullets to bring the rioters under control.

These riots usually begin at big parties in off-campus residences where hosts retain little control over who attends. Ironically, these mammoth house parties are the direct result of, in one student's opinion, the university's acting in its own self-interest. Over the last few years OSU, in collaboration with the city government, has used the power of eminent domain to drive out several bars on High Street, ostensibly in the name of revitalization. As a result, the campus drinking scene has moved to less centralized and less watched areas. The closing of close-to-campus bars, says one student, has severely dampened campus nightlife and increased concerns about drunk driving.

Students at Ohio State can take advantage of the 550 clubs the university offers, none of which officially entail rioting. This number includes at least three dozen honor societies and nearly 40 religious organizations. "Most students at Ohio State are involved in at least one club or activity," a student says. "There is nearly a club for every ethnic group and language." The College Republicans chapter has a sizable membership. The College Democrats are not as popular, although according to one student, that is only "because there are several smaller liberal clubs on campus representing specific liberal interests." The mainstream student paper, the *Lantern*, is an "unapologetic mouthpiece for the extreme left wing," says one student. The *OSU Sentinel* represents conservative views.

In campus politicization as in academics, OSU is no Wisconsin or Michigan—and in this case that's a good thing. Political fervor is simply absent at Ohio State. As one student says, "Ohio State is generally a conservative campus; students more so than professors. However, since conservatism is the norm, rarely do conservative groups gain a lot of attention."

Nonetheless, one student considers the influence of the gay and lesbian community at OSU to be pervasive. He points to the FYE seminar called "Guess the Straight Person," as well as to the placards frequently displayed on university busses. The buses carry messages from the Gay, Lesbian, Bisexual, and Transgender Student Services office advertising ways students can work to stop "homophobia." Among the recommendations: "Do not assume everyone is male or female."

Beyond the gridiron, intramural sports are quite popular. The large campus has many areas for running, cycling, and enjoying nature in the warmer months, and the new Recreational and Physical Activity Center opened in June 2005. On fine days, "the Oval," a grassy area in the heart of the campus, offers a place for students to study, socialize, and get a breath of fresh air.

The vast majority of students—91 percent—are from Ohio. Only about a quarter live on campus, and relatively few (5 percent) join sororities or fraternities. There are three female-only residence halls, none exclusively for males. The coed dorms house women and men in a variety of ways, sometimes on different floors, sometimes on the same floor but in different wings, and sometimes on the same floor and same wing. All the bathrooms are single-sex and all dorms are smoke-free. Housing options include the Living-Learning Program, which pairs students with other students who share similar "interests, lifestyle, or commitment to an academic program." Some of these 40 programs include the Afrikan American program, Substance Free program, First-Year Business Focus Community, and Women in Engineering program.

The occasional riot is not the only crime about which students at OSU ought to be concerned. The part of Columbus surrounding campus is notable for its high crime rate. In 2003, the school reported nine sexual assaults, nine robberies, two aggravated assaults, 165 burglaries, 14 stolen cars, and three arsons on campus—and that was a significant improvement over 2002 statistics. One new professor says, "I used to live within walking distance of the campus of the University of Texas at Austin. . . . I planned to live within walking distance here, but it truly is not safe." The campus police department offers both vehicle and walking escorts to students who want them.

Ohio State is quite a bargain for students from the state. While regional campuses are cheaper, even the main campus in Columbus charged only $7,479 in tuition for local students (compared with $18,066 for those from out of state) in 2004–5. Room and board was $5,328 in Columbus. Ohio State practices need-blind admissions and provides aid to some 58 percent of students. The average loan burden of recent graduates is $15,963.

PURDUE UNIVERSITY

WEST LAFAYETTE, INDIANA • WWW.PURDUE.EDU

It takes a tough team to play for a tender school

If you attend Purdue, the thing you're going to hear most often from outsiders—apart from lame chicken jokes—is the question "What is a boilermaker?" According to tradition, this nickname for Purdue students originated in 1889. In a year when the football team was struggling, discouraged coaches hired several husky men from the Monon Railroad to play football. After enrolling in one course, the men started playing and won one game after another. An angry newspaper in a rival college town wrote uncomplimentary stories calling the team "sluggers," "cornfield sailors," and "boilermakers." The last name struck the fancy of Purdue students and has been a nickname ever since.

Purdue is a public land-grant university, founded in 1869 to educate the sons of Indiana. The school currently enrolls 30,747 undergraduates—about two-thirds from the Hoosier state. Most people think of Purdue as the home of Big Ten sports and big-time engineering. But Purdue is about more than jocks and joists. The school offers degree programs in 12 academic colleges and schools with approximately 200 majors. The university does boast one of the top engineering departments in the country, as well as a very successful MBA program.

Purdue faculty and graduates have pioneered aviation and space travel, earning it the nickname "Cradle of Astronauts." Indeed, some 22 Purdue alumni have been chosen for space flight—including Neil Armstrong, the first man to walk on the moon, and Eugene Cernan, the last man to do so. Purdue and Massachusetts Institute of Technology have furnished more astronauts than any other nonmilitary institution, and Purdue alumni have served on more than 40 percent of all manned U.S. space flights.

Academic Life: The battle of arts and sciences

Purdue is best known to those outside the state of Indiana as a haven for engineers—since one in 50 engineers in the United States is Purdue-trained. Purdue has granted the most engineering degrees of any American school to women, and its School of Technology produces more graduates in engineering technology than any other public institution in the country. Nevertheless, the School of Liberal arts is the biggest college at the university. Other popular programs of study include management, pharmacy, hospitality and tourism management, agriculture, and communications.

Purdue is a heavily preprofessional school with no core curriculum. However, students in all colleges of the university are required to fulfill a set of distribution requirements; the school makes some effort to supplement a technical education with at least a smattering of humanities and social and behavioral science courses. Most of the colleges require 18 hours (or six classes) spread across various departments—not an imposing or impressive mandate. You can find strong liberal arts courses at Purdue, but many technologically oriented (and other) students fill the hours outside their majors with "fluff" classes. A student in the engineering program explains, "I understand the concept of needing to know more about 'the world around me' besides math and my electrical engineering program—however, when students have the option of 'Society, Culture and Rock and Roll' or 'Introduction to the Ancient World' for the history requirement, many of us are going to take the class that sounds more fun."

Purdue describes itself as an institution focused on research, and it is certainly able to make good on that claim. A program introduced by the provost's office called "Study in a Second Discipline" is the university's latest attempt to broaden the research areas of faculty members within the different colleges. The program allows for tenured faculty members to study outside of their current disciplines for either a semester or a year, focusing on a subject that can supplement their current teaching. One mathematics professor is applying the modeling used in the courses he currently teaches to the field of immunology, while another who teaches in the discipline of nutrition and food sciences is studying toxicology. While still in its infant stages, this cross-disciplinary program has been lauded as a means of keeping professors from becoming stale and giving them an opportunity to expand their areas of study.

Similarly, the College of Science offers an Interdisciplinary Science major that encourages students not only to give themselves a firm scientific background but also to branch out into a cross-disciplinary area from any of the other colleges. Obviously there is potential for abuse—among the suggested areas are women's studies and African-American studies—but one can also imagine a student exploring more traditional fields that would positively inform his predominantly preprofessional training.

Students describe most professors at Purdue as dedicated and knowledgeable—which they'd better be, given how many pupils they must teach. Purdue's student-faculty ratio is only 15 to 1. But teachers make an effort to be accessible, students report: "All professors have office hours and are pretty easy to get in touch with. However, it's always helpful to introduce yourself to your professors since you're one of the thousands of students they have." While English composition classes are usually limited to about 25 students, and a foreign language class will average about 30, chemistry classes might consist of a lecture section of 250 to 300 students and a laboratory of 25. Math

VITAL STATISTICS

Religious affiliation: none
Total enrollment: 38,653
Total undergraduates: 30,747
SAT/ACT midranges: SAT V: 500–610, M: 530–650; ACT: 22–28
Applicants: 24,003
Applicants accepted: 80%
Accepted applicants who enrolled: 35%
Tuition: $5,962 (in state), $18,570 (out of state)
Room and board: $7,020
Freshman retention rate: 86%
Graduation rate: 31% (4 yrs.), 66% (6 yrs.)
Courses with fewer than 20 students: 36%
Student-faculty ratio: 15:1
Courses taught by graduate TAs: not provided
Most popular majors: engineering, business, education
Students living on campus: 30%
Guaranteed housing for four years? no
Students in fraternities: 18% sororities: 17%

Purdue's School of Liberal Arts (one of many colleges there) imposes the following required coursework, drawn from a specific list of courses:

- Six to seven hours of English composition and communication, including a two-semester sequence in English composition and a one-semester course in oral communication.
- Three to twelve hours demonstrating a proficiency in a foreign language. Many students satisfy part of this requirement with high school language classes.
- Twelve hours of mathematics (such as statistics and algebra) and natural sciences (including a lab), with two courses in each field.
- Three hours of Western heritage and civilization. Students have the option of studying the Bible, the ancient world, or Latin literature.

classes usually combine a lecture of 200 to 250 students with a "recitation" (weekly seminar with a teaching assistant) of 30 or so. Class size does shrink as students move further along in their majors.

A few of the colleges, including the College of Liberal Arts (CLA) and the College of Science, offer honors programs for exceptional students. The CLA Honors Program supplements the courses meeting distribution requirements with such gems as "Survey of Greek Literature in Translation" and "West European Democracy," courses that are not quite overwhelmed by the predictable offerings examining gender roles and multiculturalism. CLA honors students also benefit from smaller class sizes, early registration, and a greater opportunity to interact with professors and visiting scholars. Generally, to take honors classes, a student must have a GPA of over 3.0.

Advising and registration at Purdue is in the midst of change. Currently, Purdue is the only university in the Big Ten system that does not permit online registration. Each college or school has a staff of academic advisors that students are required to meet with at least once each term to register for classes. Starting in 2008, students will be able to register online, replacing a 30-year-old administrative computing system that many students viewed as cumbersome and antiquated. The new system will allow students to register themselves for classes, check their financial aid status, and also observe how dropping a class will affect their tuition.

The university administration is in the midst of hiring 300 new faculty members in order to reduce reliance on graduate teaching assistants in the beginning levels of undergraduate work. Faculty teach only 74 percent of undergraduate classes; the rest are led by one of the 2,000 TAs and research assistants on campus.

A popular program with both students and faculty alike is the tradition of the "Old Master." For the past 50-plus years, the university has invited back 10 distinguished alumni for three days to interact with students and teachers in the dining halls, dormitories, and classrooms. Recent masters have included the first female director of the National Science Foundation, various space travelers, and the director of the American Red Cross.

The online student writing lab receives high marks from students—attracting not only undergraduates and graduates, but Web users from around the world. The service received almost 2.4 million hits from more than 125 countries in 2003. However, many students complain about the library facilities and the lack of documents and periodicals. Purdue has 15 libraries but ranks poorly compared to its peers in current periodicals per student.

Student Life: Hugs for sale

More conservative than most universities, especially compared to its sister schools in the Big Ten, Purdue hosts students who are not overtly politicized or overly excitable. A little more than two-thirds of Purdue students are drawn from Indiana, and more than nine-tenths of the student body is white. (However, Purdue does enroll more international students than any other public university in the country.) Students from outside the state and from larger metropolitan areas are at times a bit shocked to find that "Purdue is traditional Midwest, Christian and conservative," as one student says.

Almost 60 percent of the student body is male—a ratio that rises when you visit the local watering holes. "If I was standing in a bar at Purdue and I threw a quarter, the odds of it hitting a guy instead of a girl are about four to one," a student comments. The student body is known as professional and courteous, "everyone is generally really nice here," says another student. "I like to think that we are a rather personable university." The university actually devotes a portion of its campus to encouraging small courtesies. On the "Hello Walk," for instance, which cuts through the front mall, students are expected to greet each person they pass with a smile or a hello. In the past year, two Purdue students set up a table once a week in the union giving compliments to every person who walked by—and hugs upon request. Only in the Midwest.

Weekends in fall are dominated by football, while many school rituals revolve around athletics. Saturdays start at 7 a.m. with "Breakfast Club," which entails going to bars in costumes before heading to the stadium for tailgating. Another major event is Grand Prix, "our annual go-cart race," a student explains (think of it as the counterpart to the Little 500 at Purdue's fellow state school and archrival, Indiana University). Organizations on campus build cars for a speed competition, which anchors a week of revelry every spring. Students say social life at Purdue is usually active and offers a wide variety of choices; however, weeknights are much calmer than

REQUIREMENTS (CONT'D)

- Three hours of United States tradition. This requirement focuses on the country's cultural legacy and role in the world. General American history and literature courses dominate the offerings.
- Six hours in non–United States cultures, such as one course in the history or politics of Asian and Islamic cultures and another on global, political, and economic systems.
- Three hours in the arts, such as art history, dance, music, theatre, fiction, and poetry.
- Six hours in "racial and ethnic diversity," including one class on racial and ethnic minorities in the United States and one course on "gender issues." This monster may be fed by most courses crosslisted with women's studies in a variety of liberal arts disciplines.
- Six hours split between a social ethics course (one may choose anything from a general macroeconomics course to biomedical ethics or law and philosophy) and a psychology course.

weekends. "With so many students in difficult engineering programs, there is no time to take off to go to the bar," claims one undergrad.

For those who take the time to hoist a glass, the Greek system at Purdue is popular, encompassing almost 20 percent of students. This gives Purdue the third largest Greek system in the United States. But non-Hellenists need not be intimidated, a student insists: "I have many friends who are not Greek; 80 percent of the student body doesn't join a house. The Greek environment is so diverse, many people in houses intermingle with independents." Many fraternities or sororities fail to conform to the typical "frat" house stereotypes, and some are even alcohol-free.

Other social options are plentiful at Purdue. Intramural sports dominate the calendar during the fall and spring. With over 600 student organizations on campus, few find themselves lacking for something to do outside of class. Political and religious groups exist for almost every belief system under the stars. There's a strong Christian community on campus, students report, and a nondenominational chapel. But it is much more common for students to attend one of the churches in the area.

As at many large schools, freshman are not required to live on campus—however, about 85 percent of them choose to do so. The residence hall system holds nearly 11,000 undergraduates students and also houses some married and graduate students. Students have the option of coed living; four of the 11 undergraduate residence halls are coed by wing. Men and women do not share the same floors.

Students who choose not to live in dorms can be found in one of the Greek houses or in one of the many apartment buildings that surround campus. Another housing option is cooperative living. Members of cooperative houses take turns with cooking and cleaning—making this a cheaper option than sorority and fraternity houses. Students rush one of the seven women's or five men's houses—whose typical population ranges from 14 to 60 members.

Purdue's is a relatively safe campus. Crime statistics from 2003 show no increase in criminal incidents over previous years. The most common offenses are underage alcohol violations, with theft and burglary being the next most common; there were 28 burglaries during the year on campus. Six sex offenses and six motor vehicle thefts were also reported.

Purdue is reasonably priced, as these things go. For the 2004–5 academic year, tuition was $5,962 for Indiana residents and $18,570 for nonresidents. Room and board was $7,020. The university provides both need- and merit-based financial aid. About 48 percent of students take out loans, with an average debt upon graduation of $16,641.

ST. OLAF COLLEGE

NORTHFIELD, MINNESOTA • WWW.STOLAF.EDU

Ye shall have a song

Founded by Norwegian Lutheran immigrants in 1874, St. Olaf College of Northfield, Minnesota, still thinks of itself as "a college of the church." The school's mission is to provide "an education committed to the liberal arts, rooted in the Christian gospel, and incorporating a global perspective." St. Olaf attempts to adhere to this mission by providing its students with solid liberal arts options, a biblical studies course requirement, a large international studies and study-abroad program, and (optional) daily chapel.

The church with which St. Olaf is affiliated, and from which it receives considerable funding, is the Evangelical Lutheran Church in America. In fact, St. Olaf is the Lutheran college that provides the most seminarians to that church. Interestingly though, this "college of the church" offers a major in religion, but not theology, and religion majors are not required to take any Lutheran theology. The ELCA is an old mainline denomination whose leadership in the last few decades has tended to drift with the times, most controversially and prominently on matters of sexuality. The college seems to be right there with the church leaders. A religion professor's recent article in the *Minneapolis Star Tribune* compares people who oppose gay marriage based on biblical interpretation to those who used scripture to support slavery. In 2003, the college helped sponsor the Knutson Conference on Sexuality, Spirituality, and the Church, the goal of which was to "discuss ways in which the church could become an inclusive and welcoming institution for gay, lesbian, bisexual, and transgender . . . people," according to the *Manitou Messenger,* St. Olaf's weekly student newspaper. One student complains of the "politicization of chapel at St. Olaf" and says that liberal Lutherans seem to be the most keen on St. Olaf chapel services. More traditional students often attend the Baptist church in Northfield instead.

On the bright side, St. Olaf continues to value the great works of Western civilization, to promote spiritual growth through various religious organizations and ac-

VITAL STATISTICS

Religious affiliation:
  Lutheran
Total enrollment: 3,046
Total undergraduates: 2,976
SAT/ACT midranges: SAT
  V: 600–710, M: 590–700;
  ACT: 25–30
Applicants: 3,144
Applicants accepted: 64%
*Accepted applicants who
  enrolled*: 38%
Tuition: $30,950
Room and board: $5,800
Freshman retention rate: 93%
Graduation rate: 79% (4 yrs.),
  84% (6 yrs.)
*Courses with fewer than 20
  students*: 44%
Student-faculty ratio: 13:1
*Courses taught by graduate
  TAs*: none
Most popular majors:
  social sciences, visual
  and performing arts,
  English
Students living on campus:
  96%
*Guaranteed housing for four
  years?* yes
*Students in fraternities or
  sororities*: none

St. Olaf has a fairly structured set of requirements. All students must fulfill a series of general education courses divided among three types. The first, foundation studies, focuses on the development of basic verbal, mathematical, and physical skills. The requirements include:

- One "First-Year Writing" and four "Writing in Context" classes.
- Foreign language classes; students must reach the intermediate level in a foreign language, either by taking courses or by testing out.
- One class in oral communication.
- One course in mathematical reasoning.
- Two different quarter-credit courses in physical activities or dance, or one half-credit course in physical education.

Core studies introduce "the different fields of knowledge and diverse ways of knowing that are at the heart of the liberal arts." Students are required to take two courses each from the following areas:

- History of Western culture. Choices include "Ancient Warfare," "American Consumer

tivities, and to teach an appreciation of the arts through its excellent music programs. Especially if they take, as they should, one or more of the optional "Conversations" sequences in the humanities, students who choose St. Olaf should get a first-rate education.

Academic Life: That cerebral Minnesota climate

While St. Olaf doesn't prescribe a set core curriculum, it maintains a respectable set of requirements. Dozens of courses fulfill each of these requirements, but the curriculum is structured enough that it "indeed does demand the fundamentals of a top-quality education, including forced, yet meaningful study of the humanities, sciences, and foreign languages," according to a professor. The single best way to complete most of these requirements is through St. Olaf's five-course Great Conversations curriculum. Here students encounter and grapple with the Western tradition by reading the great books. "Connors" share a dorm for their first year, eat meals and go to events together—obtaining many of the benefits of a traditional core curriculum. These are interdisciplinary courses in which students and faculty explore the history, ideas, and artistic and literary achievements of the era in question. Courses for Great Conversations include "The Tradition Beginning: The Greeks and the Hebrews," "The Tradition Continuing: Romans and the Christians," "The Tradition Redefined: The Medieval Synthesis," "The Tradition Renewed: New Forces of Secularization," and "The Tradition in Crisis: Dissenters and Defenders." This last course takes students through the nineteenth century, including the thought of Darwin, Marx, Freud, Dostoyevsky, Nietzsche, Wollstonecraft, and the artistry of Beethoven, Ibsen, and Picasso.

St. Olaf provides instruction in French, German, Spanish, Chinese, Greek, Latin, Japanese, Norwegian, and Russian. The Nordic studies concentration is a tribute to the college's historical roots. Students develop competence in the Norwegian language and take five courses across the curriculum—a history course in "Modern Scandinavia," a religion course in "Lutheran Heritage," and a philosophy course in "Kierkegaard and Existentialism" all contribute to the concentration.

International study, including study abroad, is highly encouraged at St. Olaf. In 2003, St. Olaf ranked first in the United States in the number of students and the percentage of the student body (80 percent) who studied abroad. The college sponsors or cosponsors programs in 45 countries and on every inhabited continent; in Africa alone, there are seven programs. Another option is the study/service programs that the college runs in several countries. Last year, students took classes and worked in Indonesia, Korea, Russia, and South India.

St. Olaf's small student body (about 3,000 students) and its relatively cerebral climate allow students to develop close academic relationships with their instructors. Faculty members interact with students outside the classroom frequently and show genuine concern for them. Students say most of their classmates are interested in academic topics even outside of class; residence hall debates are common.

Every student is assigned a faculty advisor upon entry to the school, and the student can change advisors later on if he chooses to do so. One student says, "I have had an excellent academic advisor over the past three years, and I think the majority of students would echo this." The Academic Support Center is staffed with peer advisors trained to help their fellow students with essays and courses they have already taken.

Students say the best professors at St. Olaf are Edmund Santurri in religion; Theodore Johnson and David Van Wylen in biology; Beth Abdella in chemistry; David Wee in English; and Daniel Hofrenning in political science. Students speak highly of the entire philosophy department, but especially of Edward Langerak and Charles Taliaferro, and they also praise the sciences. St. Olaf educates many future health care professionals, including doctors, nurses, and others. The renowned music department is one of St. Olaf's most obvious academic strengths; the department lists 70 faculty and staff members (some part-time) and offers five different degrees catering to those who would teach, compose, or perform.

Politics don't dominate St. Olaf, but they are present. One professor maintains that "within every department at St. Olaf, you have your conservatives and liberals and your indifference." One student says that "it is a challenge at times attending an institution that only seems to want to promote left-wing ideas. . . .

REQUIREMENTS (CONT'D)

Culture," and a dance course titled "The Rise of Ballet."

- Multicultural studies. Options range from "Race and Class in American Culture" to "Immigration Ethnic Studies."
- Natural sciences (biology, chemistry, or physics), including one course with a lab.
- Studies in human behavior and society, from two different departments.
- Artistic and literary studies. One could study the literature of the Romantic period or "Children's and Young Adult Literature."
- Biblical and Theological Studies. All students take "Bible in Culture and Community," and one other course in Christian theology, such as "The Bible, Slavery, and Civil Rights," or "The Bible and the Problem of Suffering."

Students also take one "integrative ethics" course based on Christian theology, in which questions of justice, morality, rights, and responsibilities are the focus. These courses are offered in various disciplines to juniors and seniors, often in their majors.

At first, I was fearful of speaking up or making political comments in class, but once I did I realized that there were many students in concurrence with me and that the professor (at times) appreciated having an opposing view in class."

In February 2004, St. Olaf hosted the Nobel Peace Prize Forum, which many professors encouraged their students to attend. Jimmy Carter was the keynote speaker, and the event featured some 50 related peace seminars and workshops, such as "Being Peace" (a dance workshop) and "Peace and Change through Public Art," which claimed to promote nonviolence by rendering apologies to Native Peoples. According to Katherine Kersten of the Center of the American Experiment, "The forum presented views from the far left of the political spectrum, excluded dissenting perspectives, and then issued repeated 'calls to action' to students." Conservative students proposed adding their own speaker to offer a dissenting view, but they were turned down. They complained unsuccessfully to the administration, then formed a committee called St. Olaf Students for Intellectual Diversity. They appealed directly to the college regents, documenting St. Olaf's policies on academic freedom and the liberal bias they felt pervaded the campus. The regents listened with sympathy and concern, and many expressed strong support. However, some organizers have experienced a backlash of criticism from administration and faculty. President Christopher Thomforde accused a student leader of launching a "campaign against the college," and according to Kersten a few professors have singled out conservative students for criticism in class.

Student Life: Um! Ya! Ya!

St. Olaf is not racially diverse (the student body is only 1 percent black), but it desperately wants to be. As the college Web site readily admits: "We don't claim to be the most diverse college in the nation, but we're working on it." To make up for it, so to speak, they promise to "make sure that every student encounters some strange ideas and even some strange people." The college supports an office of Community Life and Diversity that regularly sponsors affirmative action workshops and multicultural lectures; the dean of Community Life and Diversity reports directly to the president of the college. Students can even major in American racial and multicultural studies (ARMS), taking an introductory course in the discipline plus at least seven other courses from various departments. "Dance in America," "Food, Work, and Culture," a social work course called "Erasing the Border," "History of Jazz," and "Slavery in the Americas" all contribute to the ARMS major.

Nearly every St. Olaf student (96 percent) lives on campus. In fact, most students are required to live at the college for four years. Cars are allowed by permit only and the college encourages students to stay on campus to learn and live together. Living options are plentiful, from smaller houses to a 12-story, 300-person residence hall, and from single rooms to quads. All dorms are coed, but men and women are separated by floor. Several houses along St. Olaf Avenue and Lincoln Avenue have been converted into dorm rooms for upperclassmen. These "honor houses" are organized into various themes. Residents agree to speak mostly the chosen foreign language in the language houses, for example, and students can propose service projects for other theme houses. In an interesting development that highlights the school's respect for environmental stewardship, St. Olaf applied for and got a $1.5 million grant from Xcel Energy to fund the construction of a wind turbine on campus. When finished, it will generate one-third of the college's electricity.

SUGGESTED CORE

For a slightly abbreviated core, the St. Olaf Great Conversations sequence suffices.

According to one student, St. Olaf is a very social campus, despite the fact that it is officially dry. Students are fairly well rounded in their social lives, attending cultural events, lectures, sporting events, and other activities with their classmates. The campus "nightclub," the Lion's Pause, draws students by serving up pizza, shakes, and "pop" (as soda is called in the Midwest) and by bringing in local bands and some nationally known artists.

Students have plenty of clubs to choose from—academic organizations like Quiz Bowl, the Chess Club, and the Economic Society or other special-interest groups like the Ballroom Dance Club, the Fly Fishing Club, or various student media organizations. St. Olaf's College Republicans has more than 400 members and is the largest chapter in the state. Musical opportunities, even outside the academic setting of the music department, are numerous. Even the college fight song is musically unique: it is said to be the only one in the country written as a waltz, the chorus consisting entirely of repetitions of this stunning text: "Um! Ya! Ya!" (The verse is considerably more clever; it includes this line: "We fight fast and furious, our team is injurious.") The college's music ensembles—band, orchestra, Norseman Band, philharmonic, jazz ensemble, and Collegium Musicum (which performs music of the medieval, Renaissance, and Baroque styles)—give students opportunities to hone or showcase their talent. No discussion of St. Olaf would be complete without mentioning the St. Olaf Christmas Festival, a musical worship service shared with the public that has become a regional holiday institution. The college sold more than 270,000 copies of its first CD, *Great Hymns of Faith*.

St. Olaf may be a "college of the church," but one student says it seems that way only for those who participate in religious activities. "You can be as involved in the church as you want to be, but it depends on the student," she says. "If you didn't attend the events, I don't think you would consider St. Olaf as a college of the church." Daily chapel "gives students a break . . . to reflect upon their day, life, and its meaning," says another student. "I have found the daily chapel speakers to be quite interesting." Religious groups are plentiful and include student organizations like Inter-Religious Dialog, Christian Activities Network, Fellowship of Christian Athletes, Catholic Students Association, BASIC (Brothers and Sisters in Christ) Bible Study, InterVarsity Christian Fellowship, Student Christian Outreach, Care Ministry, and Student Congregation (a group that organizes many of the spiritual activities on campus).

Sports, varsity and otherwise, are popular at St. Olaf. Of the college's 27 NCAA Division III varsity teams, football and soccer draw the most spectators, but the Oles are especially proud of their Alpine and Nordic ski teams. The college reports that 80 percent of the student body competes in intramurals, with teams usually organized around residence halls.

And St. Olaf is not as remote as one might think, though a Minnesota winter or two will sure make it feel that way. Minneapolis and St. Paul, the Twin Cities, are only 35 miles to the north. Set in the rolling farmland of southeastern Minnesota, Northfield's motto is "Cows, Colleges, and Contentment." A fourth C—crime—is thankfully not prevalent. In 2003, the college reported five forcible sex offenses, 15 burglaries, and three motor vehicle thefts. An article in the student newspaper reports that burglaries have been on the rise lately; most often, these involve laptops stolen from unlocked dorm rooms. The newspaper reports that no actual break-ins have occurred. To prevent violent crime, students can make use of the Safe Ride service, which will escort them across campus at any time before 1 a.m.; at other times, Public Safety will transport students back to their residence halls.

St. Olaf's tuition in 2004–5 was $30,950, with $5,800 charged for room and board. Approximately 60 percent of first-year students receive need-based financial aid—72 percent from scholarship and grant assistance, 11 percent from loan assistance, and 11 percent from student employment. The college says that 83 percent of all new students who applied for need-based aid received assistance and that the average award was $17,000 for the 2002–3 school year. St. Olaf's admission decisions are need-blind.

WABASH COLLEGE

CRAWFORDSVILLE, INDIANA • WWW.WABASH.EDU

The men of Wabash

Of the more than 3,000 colleges and universities in the United States, only three have an all-male student body. Wabash College in Crawfordsville, Indiana, is one. And despite some subterranean grumbling, it seems determined to keep its distinctive character. A Wabash professor observes that the school seems to mirror "what liberal arts colleges must have looked like 40 or 50 years ago." Students strike up solid relationships with their professors (and fraternity brothers) and delight in such traditions as thrive in small colleges with strong identities. It's not a monastery, though. The professors aren't exclusively male, and there is much socializing with the fairer sex at other colleges, albeit only on weekends.

Alas, Wabash is feeling the pressure to conform, though not without serious resistance. Some faculty, and many students, warn that Wabash administrators and newer professors seem inclined to abandon Wabash's particularity in the hopes of falling in with the academic zeitgeist. Such a transition is unlikely to happen soon, since the college naturally attracts students who value its unique atmosphere. In fact, many of them consider Wabash an academic arcadia.

Academic Life: Love it or leave it

Part of the reason Wabash students get the "broad base of understanding" about which its catalog boasts is that there are only a limited number of trendy, ideologically motivated courses. Students hoping to graduate without serious study should look elsewhere. "The college leans toward a great books ethos without actually claiming it," says one professor. "There are some of the typical courses you will find elsewhere, on film, masculinity, race, and feminism, for example, but the college is actually fairly conservative in its attitude toward topical classes geared toward contemporary concerns."

Strong faculty-student relationships also help Wabash stand out. Professors of varying political and social persuasions seem to uphold the college's dedication to en-

VITAL STATISTICS
Religious affiliation: none
Total enrollment: 850
Total undergraduates: 850
SAT midranges: V: 530–650, M: 550–660
Applicants: not reported
Applicants accepted: 49%
Accepted applicants who enrolled: 37%
Tuition: $22,275
Room and board: $7,053
Freshman retention rate: 82%
Graduation rate: 63% (4 yrs.), 68% (6 yrs.)
Average class size: 13
Student-faculty ratio: 10:1
Courses taught by graduate TAs: none
Most popular majors: English, history, political science
Students living on campus: 99%
Guaranteed housing for four years? yes
Students in fraternities: 62%

MIDWEST

729

Wabash's catalog and Web site note that the college curriculum "allows maximum flexibility while providing the broad base of understanding that is the core of the liberal arts concept." Two classes are required of every Wabash student:

- The freshman tutorial. In the 2004–5 school year, the college offered 20 freshman tutorial courses in such diversified areas as "Homer's *Iliad*," Turgenev's "Fathers and Sons," "Ethnomathematics: A Humanistic Perspective of Mathematics," and "The Future of Life: Conservation and Preservation of the Environment."

- The sophomore "Cultures and Traditions" two-course sequence. These courses emphasize what the college considers "important texts and cultural contexts"; the course Web page elaborates that "during the fall semester, for example, you will read from great texts long hallowed in the Western tradition, Homer's *Odyssey* and Plato's *Republic* for instance; you will think about the problem of war through texts that cross time and cultures; and

couraging genuine intellectual curiosity and a sincere grappling with the great ideas. One professor observes that, since the college is in Indiana, this "personal contact and engagement with professors" is offered as a substitute for "oceans, mountains, or even girls." Teaching, not research or publishing, seems to be the chief preoccupation of Wabash professors, as exemplified by their open-door policy. "I have never gone by an 'office hours' schedule with my professors," one student says. Even with professors with whom he had little regular contact, "I have never had difficulty reaching them. Most professors include their home numbers on the syllabus." The advising program also has a good reputation: each student is paired with a faculty advisor who helps the student select classes, a major, and sometimes even a postgraduation career, students report.

Wabash is small—there are fewer than 900 students—and maintains a student-faculty ratio of 10 to 1. Even large lecture classes normally demand a research paper and/or essays rather than relying on multiple-choice tests. "Writing is of prime importance," one professor says. "This is true across the board." A recent graduate says, "What particularly impressed me about Wabash is the premium it places on writing. In most classes, students regularly are assigned 10- to 15-page reports; tests are in essay format, almost never multiple choice." Professors have the time and show the willingness to grade these more complex, demanding assignments. Every Wabash student must, in order to graduate, pass a comprehensive examination in his major—usually six hours of written exams and one hour of oral exams. All this makes it virtually impossible for a student to graduate without truly engaging his major discipline and even his minor ones. Interestingly, some professors do not proctor their exams, trusting students to uphold a standard of honesty set out in Wabash's extraordinary honor code, which it calls the "Gentleman's Rule."

Students and faculty say that being a single-sex school strengthens Wabash's intellectual focus. A professor says classroom discussions are open and honest because students can "say what they think, without worrying about trying to impress girls" or "adjusting their remarks to placate feminist or other current orthodoxies." But the Wabash faculty is not immune to recent intellectual trends, especially in social science courses, which one student complains "place a premium on personal feelings, resulting in classes . . . with students acting as panelists, professors as hosts." Another says that though "critical thinking is rewarded to a certain degree . . . it always helps to regurgitate at least a few of the professor's perspectives." Overall, however, the intellectual atmosphere is serious and demanding. One student says that "professors expect you to come to class prepared, and most of them can tell pretty quickly whether you are."

Wabash's strongest departments are in the humanities, especially the classics department. The religion department, says one professor, "is explicitly oriented toward theology and Christian history, which is rare these days for religion departments." Perhaps as a result, religion is one of the college's most popular departments—though this may be threatened by the impending tenure of a "Bible scholar" that, in the view of a professor from another department, "has shown himself to students as openly hostile to . . . faith." Requirements for this major include two courses in the history of Christianity; two courses chosen from a selection that includes "The Hebrew Bible," "Christian Thought," and "American Religion"; two courses in a non-Christian religion; and a senior seminar, in addition to electives. The premed program, including the biology and chemistry departments, is also reportedly rigorous, yielding a high acceptance rate at medical schools. The arts have been disparaged as among Wabash's weaker offerings, but a number of professors dispute this.

Students say the following professors are among Wabash's best: David Kubiak in classics; Dan Rogers in modern languages; David Blix, William Placher, and Stephen Webb in religion; and Edward B. McLean (emeritus) in political science.

Students desiring a break from masculine rigors in Indiana can join the roughly one-quarter of juniors who take advantage of generous off-campus programs and internships. While encouraging established ones—for example, study abroad in Scotland is supposed to occur in Aberdeen—Wabash is notably open to approving foreign study elsewhere. "If a student has an idea for an interesting project of any sort, the funding for it will likely be found somewhere," a professor says. The college's Center of Inquiry in the Liberal Arts, meanwhile, sponsors lectures and conferences on teaching and the liberal arts, and at the

REQUIREMENTS (CONT'D)

you will explore some of the great texts of classical Greece and classical China in their cultural and historical contexts." The Hebrew scriptures are also studied, and although one professor points to the absence of any required course in Western civilization, a look at the Greeks and the Israelites at least covers two of its chief pillars. Neither is there an American history requirement, though many students do take some courses in that area.

Wabash's distribution requirements are as follows:

- Three courses in literature and the fine arts.
- Two courses in history, philosophy, or religion.
- Three courses in behavioral science. Almost any course in the economics, political science, or psychology departments counts.
- Three courses in natural science or mathematics.
- One additional course in math, natural science, or behavioral science.

Students must also demonstrate proficiency in English composition and in a foreign language, and they must pass the senior oral and written comprehensive exams.

center's weekly brown-bag lunch sessions attendees can study the educational philosophies of such varied figures as Kierkegaard and Leo Strauss.

One professor figures that probably 90 percent of the faculty is guided by left-liberal presuppositions, but he also thinks that they are in part restrained from imposing them by a student body that seems disinclined to take such suppositions seriously. Another adds that professors "are careful, for the most part, not to try to proselytize," not least because they are "committed to good pedagogy, which tempers their prejudices." A student reports that "Wabash has a strong, conservative holdout in a few of its departments." Indeed, Wabash students' independent streak is well known, and students aren't slow to protest when they think a professor prefers political indoctrination to teaching. Still, since taking the conservative position at faculty meetings can be a risk to one's popularity, this give-and-take may be in danger, professors say. "The body of Wabash certainly enjoys robust health," one says. "But I do worry about the future state of its soul."

Student Life: Gentlemen rule

Astoundingly, Wabash College imposes but one rule on its students: "A Wabash man will conduct himself, at all times, both on and off campus, as a gentleman and a responsible citizen." Thanks to this "Gentleman's Rule," a professor reports, "the level of self-government is extraordinary. The honor code is in place here and for the most part the students rise to the occasion." Another says: "Does it work? Mostly, I think." In 2002, the rule was applied when the fiery student paper, the *Wabash Commentary* (called by some the "scourge of the faculty and administration") described a professor's wife as "fat and ugly." The student senate deemed this conduct ungentlemanly and pulled the paper's funding. "If you do something seriously wrong and have to go speak to the dean," a student says, "he will ask you one question: Is that gentlemanlike? If you say no, then you're incriminated." How long can such a rule last in the current academic atmosphere? So far, at Wabash, gentlemen still rule.

This aspiration has survived and has perhaps been enhanced by the Malcolm X Institute for Black Studies. Founded in 1970, in 2003 it was moved to a new $2 million building that, according to the school's Web site, captures "the symbolism and spatial arrangement found in a traditional African village." (This would be an African village that also has rooms for lectures, classes, and offices.) The institute tutors black students at the college and in the town of Crawfordsville; but so far Wabash is too small, with too few black students, to have an all-black fraternity house. Americans of African descent have accordingly integrated all-white fraternities (or not joined any) while using the Malcolm X Institute as a social outlet.

Wabash does not use a race-based points system in its admissions decisions, but race is a factor. One of the elements of the college's strategic plan is to expand "admissions efforts to attract a student body that reflects the rich ethnic, religious, cultural, and economic diversity of our nation." Wabash provides multicultural scholarships—good for $12,500 per year—to "students of color who have contributed to their communities and who demonstrate high academic achievement." The admissions department holds a Multicultural Recruitment Weekend each year to attract black students. Some years ago, a campus gay group was formed, called 'shOUT, for "Wabash OUT"; it fought for and won club recognition, including funding for meetings, lectures, and, an "alternative party" where attendees, many from area colleges, dressed in traditionally female garb. The school was one of the first in the region to mount the gay Marxist play *Angels in America*.

Wabash admissions officers arguably have to struggle a bit harder than those at other liberal arts colleges. Central Indiana is not exactly a magnet for students, and an all-male college doesn't attract the timid. The promotional literature is appropriately lofty; instead of advertising that the college has lavishly appointed computer labs or a five-star dining hall, the viewbook promotes "brotherhood," "honor," and the pleasures and duties of manhood. One professor says that there is a real sense of camaraderie at the school, and the all-male environment necessarily shapes the entire mood of student life, both academically and socially. Among most on campus there is a genuine respect and even reverence for the way things were done 50 or even 100 years ago. "At Wabash, tradition is king, and the thought of going coed is never vocalized," a student says.

SUGGESTED CORE
1. Classics 102, Greek Drama (*closest match*)
2. Philosophy 140, Philosophy of the Classical Period
3. Religion 141/162, Hebrew Bible / History and Literature of the New Testament
4. Religion 171, History of Christianity to the Reformation
5. Political Science 335, History of Political Thought: Hobbes to the Twentieth Century
6. English 216, Introduction to Shakespeare
7. History 141, America to 1877
8. History 131, Nineteenth-Century Europe (*closest match*)

While most all-male and all-female schools have other universities nearby for interaction with the opposite sex, the closest female college students to Crawfordsville are an hour away, at DePauw, Butler, Purdue, and the University of Illinois; Indiana University is a little further. Women visit on weekends, for parties or football games, but more often Wabash students pile into a car and head out to meet or visit them. "Many students have girlfriends at nearby schools," says one student, and weekends are accordingly much loved. Under the title "Women who love men love Wabash," a recruitment book quotes a student: "Why does my girlfriend always love coming to Wabash on weekends? Because Wabash men know how to treat women. She refers to the guys on her own campus as 'boys.' And that tells me all I need to know about why she and her friends are here, dating Wabash men." It stops short of saying, "Go to Wabash, the chicks will love it," because of course gentlemen don't speak that way. Nonetheless, a business reply card sent by the school asks prospective students to check one of two boxes: "boy" or "man." Students will admit, of course, that plenty of Wabash students fail the test and continue to be "boys" long after they graduate; but as extolling manhood is in the present hour such a rarified pursuit, this aspiration encourages at Wabash a certain nobility unlikely to be found on other campuses.

The well-attested Wabash camaraderie is developed chiefly through the college's strong fraternity system, to which not quite two-thirds of students belong. "Fraternity life here, as opposed to most other places, is integral to the school and supported by the administration," a professor says. Non-Greeks usually find other grups to join, such as a newspaper or varsity athletic team. Chapel sing is a favorite Wabash tradition, in which fraternity members (and, recently, independents) compete to see who can sing the school song the loudest. A few weeks later, students gather to sing the alma mater together until their voices are hoarse.

As members of the NCAA Division III, Wabash offers no athletic scholarships, and sports practices are kept to a maximum of two hours daily. Nonetheless, the small-college atmosphere gives many students the chance to compete as varsity athletes. The annual Monon Bell football game between Wabash and DePauw is the oldest continuous small-college football rivalry west of Pennsylvania. On the eve of the game, freshmen keep watch all night for intruding DePauw students and their inevitable pranks. Intramural sports—which include wrestling, swimming, weightlifting, basketball, football, and soccer, among many others—are also quite popular.

Some may consider Crawfordsville, Indiana, a serviceable place to raise a family, but the typical college student is liable to find its evening entertainments wanting. In their free time, students accordingly attend parties—"at least one party every weekend," a student says—and while drinking can get enthusiastic, there's little alcohol consumed during the week. The college also pays for some entertainment expenses, including tickets to Indianapolis Colts football games.

As one might expect, crime is rare. The 24-hour emergency phones, lighted pathways and sidewalks, foot and vehicle patrols, as well as late night transport/escort service may hint at overkill, but it's hard to argue with success. In 2003, the college reported just five burglaries and one stolen car on campus. "Thefts do occur every once in a while, mostly money," a recent graduate says. "But if anything big is stolen, nobody suspects another Wabash student."

In 2004–5, tuition at Wabash was $22,275 and room and board $7,053. The Wabash student body hails from a wide variety of economic backgrounds. "It is not possible for any professor, unless he purposely tries to find out, to know the socioeconomic status of a student," a professor says. Another says that "is because, given the all-male classroom, students do not dress for success; they dress down," so "there is little preppiness and the millionaires look just like full scholarship kids." Some 70 percent of Wabash students receive need-based scholarships; another 13 percent are there on merit scholarships.

WASHINGTON UNIVERSITY

ST. LOUIS, MISSOURI • WWW.WUSTL.EDU

Truth and consequences

Washington University began as Eliot Seminary for young men in 1853. It was originally named after William Greenleaf Eliot, first chairman of its board of trustees—and T. S. Eliot's grandfather. At William Eliot's request, the name was changed within a few years to honor someone rather grander. Since then, Washington University in St. Louis has distinguished itself as among the top universities in the country, one that is able to attract some of the nation's best students—and most renowned faculty.

University literature claims that "teaching, or the transmission of knowledge, is central to [Washington University's] mission, as is research, or the creation of new knowledge." There seems to be a good deal of sincerity in Washington's dual emphasis on both teaching and research. Increased funding for famous professors and their research projects—including several eight- and nine-figure grants—has attracted more students to the university; applications have more than doubled. Some students, especially in engineering and the sciences, may find that the school's rising reputation has come at the price of reduced opportunities to interact meaningfully with professors. Nonetheless, Washington University has much to offer the hardworking, savvy student, including a sterling reputation, respectable alternatives to the general education curriculum, and a fairly nonpoliticized educational environment.

VITAL STATISTICS

Religious affiliation: none
Total enrollment: 13,380
Total undergraduates: 7,433
SAT midrange: 1350–1520
Applicants: 19,822
Applicants accepted: 22%
Accepted applicants who enrolled: 33%
Tuition: $31,100
Room and board: $10,064
Freshman retention rate: 99%
Graduation rate: 88% (4 yrs.), 89% (6 yrs.)
Average class size: 18
Student-faculty ratio: 7:1
Courses taught by graduate TAs: not provided
Most popular majors: finance, psychology, engineering
Students living on campus: 75%
Guaranteed housing for four years? no
Students in fraternities: 25% sororities: 25%

Academic Life: Gateway arch

Washington University, like most schools today, offers relatively weak distribution requirements. Students do not have to take any introductory-level courses in areas like English, U.S. history, or philosophy. "The curriculum is very flexible and has fewer requirements than other universities," a history major says. "Students who wish to avoid graduating with a broad liberal arts education will be able to at Wash U."—as will many students who simply do not know what a broad liberal arts education ought to entail. Although students are not required to take a foreign language course or to demonstrate proficiency in a language other than English, they *are* required to fulfill cultural diversity and social differentiation requirements. Apparently, an understanding of "cultural diversity" is more important than understanding . . . people from other countries when they're speaking. A professor says these requirements "are not as restrictive and PC as the comparable requirements in the school's old curriculum. There is a much broader range of courses that students now can apply to these requirements, not just courses from women's studies and African-American studies, as was typical in the past."

As one professor says, "There is much gold here, but many undergraduates choose to overlook it." One place to find it is the first-year program "Text and Tradition," which introduces students to some of the more important texts of Western civilization. It is Washington University's best stand-in for a core curriculum. Students enrolled in this program take five courses, including "Classical Literature," which makes the case for a liberal education and in which students study the Old and New testaments, Homer, Aeschylus, Sophocles, Thucydides, Virgil, Dante, Chaucer, and Shakespeare. Another course, "Early Western History," traces the path of Western history from the rise of Athenian democracy to the Renaissance. Later, students choose three seminars from among "The Emergence of the Modern Mind," "The Rise of the European State," "Puzzles and Resolutions," and "The Great Economic Thinkers." Completion of the Text and Tradition courses and seminars nets a student a minor in humanities, and students who have completed it give the program high marks.

Another noteworthy freshman option is FOCUS, a year-long seminar program that explores one major topic from the perspective of a variety of disciplines. Eight FOCUS groups were offered in one recent year, including "The Search for Values," "Cuba: From Colonialism to Communism," and "Walled Worlds: Life in Medieval Italy." The university is working hard to increase the number of freshman seminar courses. "We want to encourage students to think more deeply about issues and to get into discussion with the faculty and with their peers," says one professor. A new option, based on the Text and Tradition program, is the Interdisciplinary Project in the Humanities (IPH), "a rigorous interdisciplinary program for students seeking honors" that aims to provide a clearly defined, integrated humanities education. It also includes a language requirement. Designed as a major, IPH "combines an introductory core—a concentrated study of texts central to the European and American philosophical, religious, and literary traditions—with an area of concentration" based on a student's interests.

After several years of work, Washington's College of Arts and Sciences has now approved a new curriculum, effective for the class of 2005. One member of the committee says, "Part of what we were able to do was eliminate the old system in which every 'victim group' had begun to demand that a course be required for its purposes. In the old curricular system, the number of course requirements and the definition of which courses fulfilled those requirements had become cumbersome and indefensible." The heart of the new curriculum is a set of "cluster courses" in four distribution areas: natural sciences and mathematics, social sciences, textual and historical studies, and language and the arts. The point is to develop the student's understanding of the subject beyond what he can learn in just one course.

In the new curriculum, *every* course is eligible to satisfy a requirement in one (or more) of the clusters, many of which are interdisciplinary. "The idea of clusters," says the professor who served on the curriculum committee, "is not just to get more depth in a particular field, but rather to develop a broader context in which to understand the content and viewpoints of a particular field." One example of the more than 250 clusters is "Greek Language and Philosophy," in which students take two beginning courses in ancient Greek and one in ancient philosophy. A cluster on "The Universe" includes "Stars, Galaxies, and Cosmology" and a choice between "Solar System Astronomy" and "The Solar System." The list of cluster courses includes many laudable and interesting topics—and time-wasters such as "Gender, Sexuality, and Culture: Education and Identity," which includes "Gender and Education," "Topics in Women's Studies—Women, Feminism, and Popular Culture," "Lesbian, Gay, and Bisexual Identity Development," and "Construction and Experience of Black Adolescence."

As at all research universities, there exists at Washington a tension between teaching and research. Commitment to teaching certainly varies from professor to professor—although professors, not grad students, do teach most courses. A student says, "Most departments make it a priority to allow professors time to teach. . . . I doubt you'll find it better anywhere else, unless you go to a school where professors do nothing but teach." One professor says, "It is difficult to generalize about the teaching versus research issue. Most of the (science and non-science) faculty I know take their teaching very seriously and put a great deal of time into it. On the other hand, there is very strong pressure to get research grants."

Indeed, Washington University has a first-class seat on the federal gravy train. The school ranks sixth among private research universities (and thirteenth among all universities) in the amount of federal research grant money it hauls in. Some departments are expected to keep the money coming. The result: While one student says that in the humanities "professors are extremely accessible to students," science professors remain much more aloof. A graduate student says that "industrialization" is a major problem at Washington University, as "the hard sciences have more prestige here than the liberal arts, and I'm quite sure more

---

ACADEMIC REQUIREMENTS

The new Washington University curriculum, which takes effect in fall 2005, requires of students:

- One course in English composition in the freshman year.
- One class in quantitative analysis (i.e., formal mathematics, statistics, etc.).
- One class that fosters "an understanding of cultural diversity."
- Yet another class "substantially focused on such forms of social differentiation as race, class, gender, and ethnicity."
- One approved upper-level writing-intensive course.
- A "capstone experience" in the senior year, such as joining a faculty member in a research project or completing a special project in one's chosen major.

Students must also complete three classes in each of four distribution areas:

- Natural sciences and mathematics.
- Social sciences.
- Textual and historical studies.
- Language and the arts.

In each of these areas students must take at least two courses that form part of a "cluster" of related classes.

money, too." He says that "older faculty teach far more than they publish, while newer faculty have considerable workloads in both teaching and publishing."

The university does assign advisors to freshmen, but they seldom become close to the students. One student says, "Students are best served by seeking out for themselves professors whom they would like to advise them," since advisor assignments are usually "random and sometimes wholly inappropriate." Premajor advisors are not necessarily faculty members, but after declaring a major, a student is assigned a faculty advisor within his discipline.

Professors most often mentioned as particularly strong teachers include Eric Brown in philosophy; Gerald N. Izenberg and Mark Gregory Pegg in history; Ryan K. Balot and George M. Pepe in classics; and Richard M. Kurtz in psychology—his abnormal psych course is "legendary," says one student.

Of course, those students interested in the hard sciences and engineering can use the university's emphasis on research to their own advantage. Opportunities abound for student research. The school's world-renowned medical center attracts many premedical students. One student claims that most entering freshmen intend to be doctors, but after realizing how intense the program is, only a fraction of them actually graduate premed. The premed program and the other sciences are the "university's crown jewel," says another student. Another well-respected program is philosophy-neuroscience-psychology, an interdisciplinary program that studies the mind and brain.

Overall, the faculty in the history department are excellent, and one graduate student in the classics says that his department "keeps a lower profile but is second to no department in commitment to teaching." With Nobel laureate Douglass North (who actually teaches freshmen), the economics department is also strong, as are the School of Fine Arts and the School of Architecture. The School of Engineering and Applied Science attracts some of the nation's very best faculty and students. One engineering major says, "Professors [in engineering] tend to be *very* accessible." Many students say the business school is less rigorous than the rest of the university, although it has improved in recent years.

Some departments are weaker than others. For instance, a sample semester for the religious studies department shows only a handful of courses offered: "Miracles, Marvels, and Magic," "Christianity in the Modern World," "Classical Chinese Philosophy," "Scriptures and Scripturalism," and introductory courses in Islam, Judaism, Sufism, and East Asian religions. Washington University is obviously no longer Eliot Seminary. The major in religious studies emphasizes cross-cultural perspectives on religion (as in the course, "Sorcerers and Shamans: Carlos Castaneda and Don Juan"). The philosophy department offers no medieval philosophy courses and only recently added "Ancient Philosophy" to its yearly rotation. The department is heavy on the philosophy of mind and science and has two faculty members who specialize in feminist philosophy. One student says that the political science department isn't theoretical enough, focusing on "electoral minutiae, never political philosophy."

As at many research universities, professors say that Washington University students tend to be more career motivated than intellectually oriented. The fact that such a large percentage of freshmen intend to become doctors and that the business school is so popular suggests that most students enter Washington University having already chosen a profession. One economics student says that the university tries to put on a "Harvard of the Midwest" air with its academic intensity, but he says, "I get the impression that the student body is generally more concerned with making the grade and/or landing a job than they are with engaging in the intellectual life." But one faculty member says that there are very few students who are completely uninterested in the course material. "I'd rather have students who are engaged for the wrong reasons (grades) than students who are unengaged entirely," he says. "Very few Wash U. students are just showing up." A humanities student says, "It's a large enough university that you will find people of all types. In my experience, however, most people are quite intelligent and a number are downright brilliant."

Washington University faculty are not notable for their politicization. Even in the humanities, it is quite possible to avoid political rhetoric and posturing. One student says that he has only experienced political bias in two courses at WU—such as a Spanish course that drew almost all of its passages from feminist texts. "To learn the past tense we would have to recite sentences like, 'Juana told Paco that the company did not employ enough women as managers,'" the student says. Another student suggests that "most professors encourage discussion and it is possible to present conservative opinions in assignments without being marked down."

SUGGESTED CORE
1. English 241C, Masterpieces of Literature I
2. Philosophy 347c, Ancient Philosophy
3. Religious Studies 106/307F, Bible: Values, Ideologies and Politics / Historical and Theological Introduction to the New Testament
4. Religious Studies 101F, Introduction to Christianity
5. Political Science 301b, Development of Western Political Thought
6. English 195C, Shakespeare
7. History 209c, America to the Civil War
8. History 442, European Intellectual History: 1789–1890

Student Life: Good friends but nowhere to go

About three-quarters of the undergraduate population—including all freshmen—lives on campus in one of the 10 residential colleges in an area known as South Forty. Each of these residential colleges includes one to three buildings and gives students the feel of a smaller university community. The university only guarantees housing for freshmen, most of whom live in all-freshmen dormitories. The majority of the residential halls are coed, but students can request to live on all-men or all-women floors. There are no coed bathrooms or dorm rooms. The residential life office offers an apartment referral service for students who choose to live off campus, and the university also owns some apartments near campus that are closer to classroom buildings than the dormitories. Some students with similar interests elect to live in small-group housing; past years have seen groups formed for students interested in "Islamic lifestyles," health, theater, journalism, and community service.

The typical Washington University student is too focused on grades and a career to sign up for the latest rally or protest. In general, the campus trends to the left. Several editorials—written by conservatives and liberals alike—in *Student Life*, the main student newspaper, characterize campus liberals as being "knee-jerk," unorganized, and unable to defend their political positions. One self-described "proud liberal Democrat" writes, "Liberalism dominates the political culture at Washington University," and names several political groups—College Democrats, Progressive Action Coalition, and Students for Choice—that outshine their conservative counterparts. However, this student and many other liberal students claim to crave more intellectual and political diversity among their peers and instructors. A graduate student says that no speaker has been shouted down by protesters in the six years he has been on campus.

The most politically active liberal groups on campus tend to be issue-based, including various environmental groups, Students Taking On Multicultural Pursuits (STOMP), Southpaw (a progressive action group), and Green Action. Washington University also has an active and well-organized Conservative Leadership Association, which sponsors three major speakers on campus each year, holds weekly meetings, and hosts a reading group on classic texts. One member says proudly, "We *are* the right-wing conspiracy." CLA also publishes the *Washington Witness*, a biweekly conservative newspaper that offers news and opinion from a conservative-libertarian point of view. One conservative student says CLA's activities "encourage open-minded debate and have shifted WU's paradigm to the right over the last six years or so." The College Republicans, College Libertarians, and Students for Life are also active.

Fraternities and sororities attract one-quarter of the student body. Students say that Greek life dominates the weekend social lives of students, especially freshmen. "For the first two years, if you don't like frat parties, or frat-like dorm parties, then you probably have good friends but nowhere to go with them," says one student. However, all parties are open to the entire campus. Washington University students deny that they attend a party school. One professor says, "The university has become much more conscious of the drinking problems in recent years." Recent survey results indicated that Washington students drink less alcohol than they claim to. The university tries to publicize these statistics and to let students know "it's okay not to drink." With hundreds of campus organizations, students should have no problem occupying their free time in perfect sobriety. There are several active Christian groups, including the Baptist Student Union, Campus Crusade for Christ, and InterVarsity Christian Fellowship, several Jewish groups, and clubs for members of many other religious faiths.

Washington University's hilltop campus is located in a quaint upper-class suburb of St. Louis only minutes from the city. Forest Park—which includes 1,300 acres of forests, lakes, and hills, plus the St. Louis Zoo, St. Louis Art Museum, and Missouri History Museum—is just across the way. Most of the university architecture is neo-Gothic, down to the last arch and gargoyle. Several buildings were designed by the famed architects Walter Cope and John Stewardson. Graham Chapel, one of the oldest buildings on campus, is also one of the most frequently photographed. Although there is little university interaction with the surrounding neighborhoods, many students volunteer in the city, building houses, feeding the poor, teaching English to immigrants, or interacting with attention-starved children. The city of St. Louis offers a number of cultural activities. Sports fans can catch a Cardinals, Rams, or Blues game, and the St. Louis Symphony Orchestra is very popular.

The Washington University Bears compete on NCAA Division III teams in every major sport. The women's basketball team, the university's main source of athletic pride, won four consecutive national championships from 1998 to 2001. Plenty of intramural sports are also available.

Safety is a concern for most Washington University students, especially those living off campus. The university police department provides free security escorts at any time of night (or day), more than 100 emergency phones, and frequent crime prevention workshops. Campus crime statistics, however, list few incidents; 2003 saw two forcible sex offenses, 18 burglaries, four stolen cars, two robberies, and one arson on campus.

Undergraduate tuition in 2004–5 was $31,100. Room and board added another $10,064 to the price tag. Admissions are not need blind, but about 60 percent of undergraduates receive financial aid, based on either merit or need. The average student loan debt of a 2004 graduate was high, at about $30,000.

WHEATON COLLEGE

WHEATON, ILLINOIS • WWW.WHEATON.EDU

For Christ and his kingdom

Wheaton College was established in 1860 by evangelical Christians, and although (or perhaps because) it is officially nondenominational, it is the most respected conservative Protestant institution of higher education in the United States. Unlike most Christian institutions of higher education, both Catholic and Protestant, Wheaton has retained a strong commitment to both liberal arts education and Christian orthodoxy, resisting those trends in theology and education that swept the nation around the turn of the century and in the first decades after World War II. In an age of moral and intellectual relativism, Wheaton stands out for its conviction that truth exists, that it can be known, that it is binding on all men and women, and that knowing it "will set you free." (John 8: 32) In all its endeavors, Wheaton seeks to integrate faith and the intellectual life; even its top-notch faculty members must make a profession of faith. Although Wheaton believes that liberal education is a good thing unto itself, ultimately, as its

MIDWEST

motto states, the college undertakes all things "for Christ and his kingdom." And Wheaton's curriculum, though subject to legitimate criticism, is much stronger than one has a right to expect these days. In sum, Wheaton College offers a robustly Christian liberal education for serious evangelical students.

Academic Life: That I might learn thy statutes

Wheaton's brand of liberal education is firmly oriented toward serving the Christian church in thought and action. First of all, only students who demonstrate familiarity with the Bible and firmness of faith will gain admission—the application requires a pastor's recommendation and an autobiographical essay that speaks to the student's religious background and beliefs. And enough such students apply that Wheaton can afford to be selective. In 2004, 2,133 candidates applied for only 576 seats in the freshman class, and over half ranked in the top 10 percent of their graduating classes. This is one reason the college has been able to maintain high moral and intellectual standards over the years. The drawback, says one student, is that those with "un-Wheatonian" views are often not admitted, and that makes the college rather homogeneous. The president, Duane Litfin, while remaining committed to Wheaton's religious mission, has recently tried to shift more emphasis to Wheaton's commitment to liberal education. President Litfin's vision for Christian education is expressed in his book *Conceiving the Christian College*, which deals with the challenge of offering a faith-based education in the twenty-first century.

Although Wheaton's general education requirements do not constitute a core, they come pretty close. Choices are limited, and students end up graduating with an understanding of the fundamentals of Western culture and history. And for the most part, students and faculty see these courses as essential to a Wheaton education, not as just prerequisites for the major. As one student says, the general requirements are "the strength of the liberal education offered at Wheaton. . . . Generally, among students and faculty there is a good attitude toward the core courses." Most students support the program. If there is resistance, it amounts to complaints that the curriculum is "incoherent" and "arbitrary."

In theory, faculty members are required to integrate their Christian faith into their lessons, but in practice, according to one student, that integration is not always so thorough. "Often professors resent the specific 'integration' protocol, leading them to do a single 'integration' class or present material completely unrelated to the subject matter," this student says. Nevertheless, the integration of faith and learning, as measured by the Faculty Personnel Committee and administration, is tied to promotion, tenure or reappointment, and post-tenure review.

Each student is assigned a faculty member to serve as his academic advisor and to help him navigate through the curricular requirements. "We cannot register for classes without meeting with our advisors," one student says. "I talked with my advisor many times because I respect his opinion and experiences." The student-faculty ratio is 13 to 1, and the average class size is 23. Courses are almost evenly divided between lectures and small-group seminars, and only about 3 percent of courses have more than 50 students. Teaching assistants "are just that, teaching assistants," says a student; they do not teach courses.

One student says professors are "extremely accessible," often meeting with students outside of class, whether in formal office hours or over lunch, either at the dining hall (where Wheaton buys lunch for teachers who eat with a student) or at professors' homes. "I have a real sense that the professors at Wheaton are here for me, and I would feel comfortable talking to any of them one-on-one about classes and even about life," another student says. Faculty members and students alike report that there is a great deal of intellectual and spiritual interaction between teachers and students. "Faculty members are people who students aim to emulate," says a student. "They are mature Christians who are also at the top of their fields. They are at Wheaton because they want to teach and make a positive impact on students' lives."

Given the school's commitment to traditional Christian education, it shouldn't be surprising that Wheaton is popular among home-schooled students. The admissions department reports that 10 percent of the class of 2007 was homeschooled at some point, and it creates special recruitment materials geared to them.

Wheaton offers a wide array of 40 majors in the humanities, fine arts, and natural sciences. The college is especially strong in music, literature, economics, history, political science, philosophy, and biblical and theological studies. The sciences—particularly math, biology, chemistry, and environmental studies—are also strong, along with education and sociology.

In almost every department, students will graduate with a solid understanding of the discipline. Philosophy majors, for instance, are required to take an introductory course called "Issues and Worldviews," a logic class, and two semesters in the history of philosophy, from early Greece to the present. English majors must take 36 hours in the discipline, including "Classical and Early British Literature" and "British Literature, Seventeenth Century to Twentieth Century," plus another course in British literature before 1800, one focusing on British literature after 1800, a course on an important literary figure, one special topics course, and one advanced writing course. The Conservatory of Music is nationally renowned and gives regular performances that enliven the cultural scene at Wheaton. And there are a few unique majors, like Christian formation/ministry and liberal arts engineering, as well as certificate programs in third-world

VITAL STATISTICS

Religious affiliation: Nondenominational Christian

Total enrollment: 2,897

Total undergraduates: 2,439

SAT/ACT midranges: SAT V: 620–720, M: 600–710; ACT: 26–31

Applicants: 2,133

Applicants accepted: 49%

Accepted applicants who enrolled: 57%

Tuition: $21,100

Room and board: $6,660

Freshman retention rate: 96%

Graduation rate: 76% (4 yrs.), 85% (6 yrs.)

Courses with fewer than 20 students: 50%

Student-faculty ratio: 13:1

Courses taught by graduate TAs: none

Most popular majors: social sciences, philosophy, business

Students living on campus: 87%

Guaranteed housing for four years? yes

Students in fraternities or sororities: none

Wheaton's curriculum is centered on 42 to 46 hours of coursework in four learning "clusters":

- Studies in Faith and Reason. This block ensures that students will graduate with some understanding of the Old and New testaments. It also includes a theology course, "Christian Thought," and philosophy components. Students may choose from "Issues and Worldviews in Philosophy," "Contemporary Moral Problems," or other courses with permission.
- Studies in Society. Students take one of three history courses: "World Civilization," "World Civilization to 1600," or "Problems in World Civilization." They choose two social science courses out of 15, including, "Biculturalism," "Political Philosophy," and "Introduction to Sociology."

issues, urban studies and even gender studies (this might be the only school in America where such a program might not be so pernicious). Wheaton also has a small graduate school, offering doctorates in psychology and biblical and theological studies as well as master's degrees in other disciplines.

Wheaton is blessed with a number of outstanding teachers. Among the best—and this is most certainly not an exhaustive list—are Alan R. Jacobs, Roger Warren Lundin, and Leland Ryken in English; Mark A. Noll and Kathryn T. Long in history; Sandra Fullerton Joireman and Ashley Woodiwiss in political science; W. Jay Wood in philosophy; Joel Sheesley and E. John Walford in art; Jeffrey K. Greenberg and Stephen O. Moshier in geology; Gary M. Burge, Mark A. Husbands, and Daniel J. Treier in biblical and theological studies; Kenneth Chase and Mark Lewis in communications; Peter J. Hill in economics; and Lisa McMinn in sociology.

Students who wish to prepare for future careers can participate in Wheaton's preprofessional programs in health or prelaw. There is an Army ROTC unit on campus and an accelerated MA program in theology. Students who wish to study abroad can do so in England, France, Spain, Germany, Mexico, the Holy Land (in some years), Latin America, Russia, Argentina, and East Asia.

The library boasts extensive holdings. The Wade Center, a quasi-independent research library, holds the most complete collection of C. S. Lewis's materials outside of England and impressive collections of the works and personal libraries of the Oxford "Inklings" J. R. R. Tolkien, Owen Barfield, Charles Williams, and Dorothy Sayers— along with those of kindred spirits like G. K. Chesterton and George MacDonald. Wheaton also holds the complete papers of Madeleine L'Engle, Malcolm Muggeridge, Fredrick Buechner, and other prominent Christian writers. The Billy Graham Center, named for Wheaton's most famous alumnus, houses archives relating to mission activity and organizes programs related to global evangelization. The Center for Applied Christian Ethics brings in scholars to address contemporary issues. Wheaton also houses the Institute for the Study of American Evangelicals, which sponsors conferences, publishes a quarterly newsletter, and conducts research projects.

Since Wheaton students, faculty, and administrators share so many religious and intellectual convictions, the college has fewer fiery debates than one would find at other liberal arts colleges. The campus is certainly not politicized in any conventional way. "The political climate here is, of course, famously, overwhelmingly, stereotypically conservative," a faculty member says. "Any political controversies here are so trivial as to be not worth mentioning." However, that may be changing. One professor says, "Students and faculty alike note that in recent years (and specifically in response to the Iraq War) a more vigorous political conversation representing diverse perspectives has begun." At Wheaton, there is much more focus on evangelical than on political activity. Students started a College Republicans club a few years ago, which is large and active in local political campaigns during election years. There is also a College Democrats club. The student body is generally more conservative than the faculty, where the views of evangelicals who are theologically orthodox but politically liberal are well represented. Proponents of radical liberationist or identity politics are not highly visible, and in the classroom, political biases rarely influence course content. One student says, "Professors do not push their own agendas as much as [they] present all sides of an issue and [allow] students to take what they will." Overall, Wheaton is a safe place for students of all political persuasions. Most agree that academic freedom is alive and well here. "Wheaton students are open to listening to new ideas and thinking critically about problems," says one student. "I do not think there is much opposition or prejudice."

Student Life: You can dance if you want to

Every aspect of Wheaton College is shaped by its evangelical Christian character, including life outside the classroom. Wheaton administrators know that if they were seen as moving in a liberal or modernist direction, donors and alumni would be riled. That is one reason, according to a faculty member, that it took so long for the Wheaton Statement of Responsibilities to be revamped. But in February 2003, the board of trustees did away with the statement, replacing its list of obligations and "dos and don'ts" with a "Community Covenant," which is more positively stated and explains its restrictions within the context of Christian goals and ideals.

For many years, upon entering Wheaton, students were expected to sign the Statement of Responsibilities, which required, among other things, that they refrain from using tobacco and alcohol and gambling during the academic year. Faculty had to sign the statement, too, and the prospect of forgoing wine at dinner for the next 30 years kept some excellent Christian but non-teetotaling candidates away. As critics of the statement often pointed out, under the terms of the statement, Wheaton heroes like

---

REQUIREMENTS (CONT'D)

- **Studies in Nature.** At least one laboratory course is required, along with half a semester of biology or geology and half a semester of astronomy, chemistry, or physics.
- **Literature and the Arts.** Students pick one text-based course (such as "Classics of Western Literature") and one fine arts class (such as "Introduction to Music").

  Other requirements are:
- **Freshman Block.** Half a semester of "Theology of Culture," half a semester of kinesiology (wellness).
- A senior "capstone" course in the student's major.
- **Competency,** either through coursework or test scores, in biblical content, a foreign language, mathematics, speech, and writing.

C. S. Lewis and G. K. Chesterton could never have taught at the school, inveterate pub-goers and pipe-smokers that they were. (At the Wade Center, there is even a large portrait of Dorothy Sayers with a cigarette.)

For students, the primary practical consequence of the new Community Covenant is that it essentially lifted a 143-year-old absolute ban on social dancing. The first dance, held in the fall of 2003, drew more than 1,000 people. The prohibition against social dancing (except square dancing or folk dancing) had created resentment among students, and in a statement, President Litfin explained: "Wheaton's community covenant must evolve constantly to meet the ever-changing needs of the campus. In other words, is it properly calibrated for the needs of the people of Wheaton College in the twenty-first century?" The school now places the burden of prudential judgment on students when considering whether to dance. The restrictions on alcohol and tobacco and gambling still apply (to students), however. But students are not typically resentful of these policies. Instead of being a hindrance to social life, these restrictions actually make Wheaton a more comfortable place for students, since the majority understand and agree with them. According to the *Chronicle of Higher Education*, Wheaton ranks second only to Brigham Young University in campus sobriety.

Wheaton undergraduates are expected to attend chapel services three days a week and are encouraged to attend church somewhere off campus on Sundays. Most are also involved in some kind of active mission work during school, assisted in their efforts by the Office of Christian Outreach.

Expectations for a wholesome lifestyle come as no surprise to students arriving on campus. The Wheaton philosophy is made clear enough on the college's application form, which asks students to complete an essay (described by one student as "intimidating") about their faith and relationship with Christ. All in all, students find that not only is there "spiritual freedom" at Wheaton, but that their spiritual growth is encouraged and fostered. One student says that it is hard to describe the typical student. "We come from all different backgrounds and family histories. There are, however, things that most Wheaton students have in common. Wheaton students share a commitment to Jesus Christ that influences everything we do." Another student adds that the typical student is active in sports and in music performance.

The leafy suburb of Wheaton, Illinois, is only 25 miles from Chicago. The park-like campus is pleasant. There is a range of architectural styles represented on campus, but with a few exceptions nothing seems entirely out of place. Most buildings are constructed of red brick and designed in a vaguely Georgian style. There is ample evidence of planning for future growth. The new $22 million multi-use Todd M. Beamer Student Center (named for one of the Flight 93 passengers who struggled with hijackers and died on 9/11) has opened, providing a vital and much needed space for campus social interaction. On campus, the Conservatory of Music puts on a wide variety of performances. Wheaton has plenty of other activities to occupy students' free time, including movies, lectures, and social events.

In spite of its theological conservatism, Wheaton is concerned with issues like multiculturalism, albeit with a Christian veneer. The administration and faculty engage in much hand-wringing about the fact that Wheaton is 87 percent white, but some say little can be done to change the school's demographics; comparatively few nonwhite students apply. Currently, each academic department must review the degree to which it has incorporated "diversity" in its curriculum. But so far, at least, there is no policy demanding that professors incorporate this strange god into the classroom. One faculty member says, "After examining the course topics, most departments have concluded that they have included a variety of viewpoints. Nobody wants to make multiculturalism the main focus of the discipline." There is an Office of Multicultural Development (OMD) that tries to ensure that Wheaton's minority students feel comfortable and affirmed. The OMD's Web page places a great deal of stress on the fact that its vision and labors are founded on a "distinctly Christian worldview." The OMD offers a mere handful of benign student diversity organizations such as Koinonia, an Asian American fellowship; "Unidad Cristiana," a Latino fellowship; and the Wheaton College Gospel Choir, a multi-ethnic choir. "Multicultural (or interracial relations) and gender issues are seen within the context of a Christian community," one student says. "Instead of accentuating differences, students are encouraged to be content with the gender and racial group in which God has placed them, all the while pursuing unity in the body of Christ." This gives reason to hope that the OMD's activities are innocuous.

SUGGESTED CORE
1. English 101, Classics of Western Literature
2. Philosophy 311, History of Philosophy: Ancient Greece through the Renaissance
3. Bible/Theology 211/213, Old Testament / New Testament
4. Bible and Theology 316, Christian Thought
5. Political Science 347, Renaissance and Modern Political Thought
6. English 334, Shakespeare
7. History 351, American Civilization to 1865
8. History 349, Origins of Contemporary Europe (1870–1950) (*closest match*)

Wheaton says that it wants students living on campus in order to promote an intimate Christian community, and most students seem to embrace that concept wholeheartedly. Although the residence halls are single sex, the school owns apartment buildings (more than 100 apartment units) that are coed. Wheaton also owns 20 houses to accommodate graduate families or groups of six to 10 undergraduate students. Dormitories have limited visitation hours (for underclassmen, three hours on weeknights, and even then students must leave the door wide open) that are actually enforced. Apartments and houses, open only to upperclassmen, allow members of the opposite sex to visit until 2 a.m., but, as the director of residence life explains, residents are on the honor system. Presently, the campus lacks dorm space to accommodate every undergraduate, so each year approximately 250 students are allowed to live off campus.

Wheaton's athletic teams participate in the NCAA Division III, meaning that the school does not offer athletic scholarships for its 17 varsity teams. In addition, club and intramural sports are very popular. Team victories (and wedding engagements) are often celebrated with the ringing of the Tower Bell of Blanchard Hall.

Tuition for 2004–5 was $21,100, while room and board was $6,660. About 50 percent of undergraduate students receive some form of financial aid or scholarship.

UNIVERSITY OF WISCONSIN – MADISON

MADISON, WISCONSIN • WWW.WISC.EDU

The state of the *Onion*

Founded in 1848, the gargantuan University of Wisconsin–Madison is known as one of the best public universities in the country. Students at the school have available to them a number of excellent academic departments, and outside the classroom there are more than 600 academic and social clubs, learning-centered dormitories, and two daily student newspapers. The university's setting in the state capital also gives students the opportunity to participate in state politics. Of course, they can also participate in a protest or two. Professors and students take ideas seriously at UW–Madison—especially their *own* ideas.

The UW–Madison faculty acknowledged its commitment to academic freedom in 1894 when it told its board of regents: "Whatever may be the limitations which trammel inquiry elsewhere, we believe that the great state university of Wisconsin should ever encourage that continual and fearless sifting and winnowing by which alone the truth can be found." These words, later emblazoned on Bascom Hall, the seat of the university administration, were taken to heart by two undergraduates in 1988 when they launched the *Onion,* a must-read satirical weekly paper with a print circulation of over 369,000 and two million Web hits weekly. And there is in truth a great degree of freedom at UW–Madison; in fact, when it comes to choosing classes, a bit too much.

The state views the university as a great cash and research magnet. In late 2004 "Gov. Jim Doyle of Wisconsin announced a $750-million biotechnology, health-sciences and stem-cell research plan, including $375-million for a research institute to be housed on the University of Wisconsin's Madison campus. Stem cells were first isolated there in 1998 by the pathologist James A. Thomson," reported the *Chronicle of Higher Education.* So any students interested in playing at Dr. Frankenstein by cloning embryonic human beings and breaking them down into spare parts . . . step right this way. The *Chronicle* helpfully notes that such research is much less controversial in academic science circles than are experiments on primates—which offend animal rights activists. One more argument for forcing science majors (among others) to study philosophy . . .

Academic Life: Area man lacks direction

You won't be surprised to find out that UW–Madison doesn't have a strong core curriculum, but rather hopes to encourage students to widen their knowledge through distribution (or "breadth") requirements. But it might startle you how to find out just how lame those distribution requirements are. "The breadth requirements are very weak and have been that way ever since 1970," one professor says. "We have a 'cafeteria approach' and because of that, education is narrow." But even these weak requirements, which can be fulfilled by hundreds of choices, are seen as a burden by some Madison students, who look at the policy as an obstacle that stands between them and the real business of learning (i.e., their major).

Certainly the most genuinely onerous requirement for UW–Madison students is the ethnic studies requirement. Classes that satisfy this requirement are usually politicized, such as "Black Feminisms" and "Gender, Race, Ethnicity, Class in Comparative Perspective"—which promises to study "the problem of 'difference' and the designation of groups as 'deviant' [with a] focus . . . on the connections between gender, race, ethnicity, class, and their incorporation into the values and ideas of Western civilization." Students say that the ethnic studies requirement is often viewed by professors as an opportunity to foist a multiculturalist ethos upon impressionable freshmen. To escape the politics, one might study something exotic—and genuinely interesting—such as "Introduction to Yoruba Life and Culture."

One program that takes the business of learning seriously is the Integrated Liberal Studies (ILS) certificate program. The program was founded in 1948 with the intention of creating an interdisciplinary program that resembled a classical liberal arts curriculum. Courses are offered in Western history, philosophy, politics, art, literature, and the history of science—and most are excellent, such as "Western Culture: Political, Economic, and Social Thought," "Genres of Western Religious Writing," and "History of Western Culture." The first semester of "History of Western Culture" focuses on early Western civilization until the fall of Constantinople in 1453. Along with history texts like *The Rise of the West* by William McNeill and *The Early Church* by Henry Chadwick, students in the course also read primary texts like the *Aeneid*, the *Odyssey*, the *Iliad*, and Dante's *Inferno*.

The ILS program is affiliated with the Bradley Learning Community, which allows 250 serious students to live together. Bradley offers students reserved spots in high-demand courses, seminars and noncredit courses, and greater access to the university's top professors. During the first semester, almost all Bradley students participate in the Bradley Roundtable, a seminar that aims to ease the transition from high school to college. Each Monday night, the entire Bradley community has dinner

---

VITAL STATISTICS

Religious affiliation: none
Total enrollment: 41,169
Total undergraduates: 29,766
SAT/ACT midranges: SAT V: 560–670, M: 600–700; ACT: 26–30
Applicants: 20,495
Applicants accepted: 66%
Accepted applicants who enrolled: 42%
Tuition: $6,220 (in state), $21,060 (out of state)
Room and board: $6,500
Freshman retention rate: 93%
Graduation rate: 42% (4 yrs.), 79% (6 yrs.)
Courses with fewer than 20 students: 42%
Student-faculty ratio: 13:1
Courses taught by graduate TAs: 25%
Most popular majors: biology, engineering, business
Students living on campus: 24%
Guaranteed housing for four years? no
Students in fraternities: 9% sororities: 8%

All students at the University of Wisconsin must complete a series of general education requirements:

- Two courses in communications (mostly written). Students can test out of one of these with AP or placement test scores.
- Two courses in quantitative reasoning—but again, students can place out of one of these with sufficient test scores.
- Five courses in "breadth requirements." These include two natural science courses (or only one, if it includes a laboratory component); two humanities/literature/arts courses, ranging from "Western Culture: Science, Technology, Philosophy" to "Relief Printmaking"; and one social studies course, such as "England to 1688" or "Gender and Work in Rural America."
- One course in "ethnic studies" that is supposed to "facilitate understanding of what it means to live in a society that displays hostility to an individual based on

together and hears a lecture by a university faculty member, after which students break up into small groups for discussion.

UW's College of Letters and Sciences (L&S) is the largest division in the university, comprising 39 departments and five professional schools. Students earning bachelor of arts degrees in this college must fulfill some additional requirements; hundreds of courses can fulfill them.

The most solid L&S programs, according to several professors there, include sociology, political science, economics, Slavic, and German. History offers an impressive range of courses, but majors in the department do not necessarily graduate with a solid grasp of major historical eras. For instance, history majors face a United States history course requirement, but they can fulfill it by taking specialty courses like "The American Jewish Experience: From Shtetl to Suburb," "Women and Gender in the United States to 1870," or "History of Wisconsin." The university's weakest departments are those that confuse activism with scholarship; these include both the women's studies and the global culture programs.

Students rate highly the following professors: William Cronon, Robert Frykenberg (emeritus), Stanley Payne, and John Sharpless in history; Donald A. Downs in political science; Lester Hunt in philosophy; David Becker and Patricia Fennell in art; James L. Baughman in journalism; and Harold Scheub in African languages and literature.

The university's top students are invited to participate in honors programs offered by the various schools and colleges at Madison. These programs give students an opportunity to obtain more meaningful interaction with professors, but that's about all. Honors students listen to the same lectures as their non-honors classmates but attend additional discussion sections. There is no separate curriculum. At such a large state school with such a wide range of talents, a strong honors program would seem essential. "I don't think the administration has gotten behind [the idea of a separate honors college] as much as they should because they have other agendas," one professor says. Honors students have the option of living in Chadbourne Residence Hall (a huge 650-student dorm), but students are not necessarily housed together. A housing official says, "Our philosophy is that we don't want honors students to be so secluded that they miss the whole university experience." Honors students in L&S may also participate in "First-

Year Interest Groups (FIGS)" or "Biology Interest Groups (BIGS)," clusters of three classes that about 20 first-year honors students take together in small learning communities. Students register for the same three courses or sections under a coordinated theme such as "Multi-Racial Americas," "Transforming Earth: Place-Making," or "Causality and Free Will."

There is no doubt that Wisconsin can be intimidating for new students. The school's 185 departments list more than 8,700 courses every year, 136 undergraduate majors, and instruction in at least 40 foreign languages. Obviously, students need direction, but Wisconsin's formal advising program does not offer much. Incoming freshmen are assigned faculty or professional advisors. After choosing a major, each is assigned an advisor (usually a faculty member, but sometimes a graduate student or staff member) within that major. Students told us that their advisors were not so much interested in helping them plan their education as making sure they graduated on time. A humanities professor says that a first-rate education is possible at UW–Madison, but students "have to know how to get that education before they get here, because they won't get any help from the advisors when they come to Madison. All undergraduates who have talked to me about career programs say advisors were usually useless or not helpful."

While the average class size is 29, at a school as large as Madison many introductory courses are the size of a high school graduating class. Large lectures are usually supplemented by discussion sessions that include up to 30 students and are led by graduate teaching assistants. Unfortunately, most students at UW–Madison do not get a chance to participate in small seminars with professors until they are juniors or seniors—if ever.

While the quality of UW students has improved as the university has become more selective over the past decade or so, one professor in the liberal arts says that many students still arrive unprepared. The fault, he says, lies with the inadequacy of high schools. This professor says he teaches a course that often touches upon the writings of Plato and Karl Marx—two authors most of his students have never read before. "This is just basic literacy, but my students don't have any reference," he says. "We've created a college environment that de-emphasizes academics for socialization and being good citizens; very little here is related to disciplined learning." "If

REQUIREMENTS (CONT'D)

stereotypes of fundamental and frequently unalterable characteristics of race, religion, sex, or national origin." Options here range from "Africa: An Introductory Survey" to "Introduction to Lesbian, Gay, Bisexual, and Transgender Studies."

Liberal arts students in the College of Letters and Sciences face the following additional requirements:

- Courses in a foreign language to the intermediate level.
- Three units of mathematics (college-level high school courses can substitute).
- Four additional courses, including two courses in any kind of literature. For the purposes of this requirement, courses like "Introduction to Ethnic and Multicultural Literature," "Literature and Popular Culture," "Shakespeare," and "Introduction to British and American Literature before 1914" are deemed equivalent.
- Four courses in the social sciences.
- Four courses in the natural sciences.

you have a choice, this isn't a good place to be an undergraduate," one liberal arts professor says. "It is easy to get lost. It is hard to find peer groups to share academic interests." All professors interviewed for this essay lamented the fact that grade inflation is a serious problem at Wisconsin. "What is needed is an institution-wide policy so one does not penalize one's own students by grading them tougher than others do," one professor says. "There should also be some sort of national policy, as we do not want to penalize UW students in relation to those at other schools."

Student Life: I enjoy drinking beer

Madison has been known for its student activism ever since the campus saw massive antiwar protests in the 1960s. While radical liberal student groups are still active at UW and often dominate campus debate, the vast majority of students are uninterested in politics. Protests, however, are common. They usually originate on Library Mall at the center of campus and, depending on how large they are, head east down State Street to the State Capitol or up Bascom Hill to the home of the university administration. One of the larger recent protests was against the war with Iraq. It drew as many as 5,000 students at its peak, according to the *Chronicle of Higher Education*.

Free speech is an ongoing issue of concern on campus, but in this regard things are looking better than ever: the university recently did away with both its student and faculty speech codes. Not that unpopular speech is always welcomed. One professor says that the university still tries to restrict free speech rights with "climate" and "professional conduct codes." In addition, the university intends to create a new diversity czar by appointing an associate chancellor to monitor "diversity" and "campus climate." "The administration is very consumed by the desire to attain diversity based on defining people in terms of their race or ethnicity rather than the independence and quality of their minds," says one professor. "But I see more of a problem here in terms of free speech and related problems, not in terms of academic excellence. Unfortunately, the drive for diversity defined in terms of racial characteristics has strangely led to calls for sensitivity and censorship rather than calls for equal respect of students' capacities to deal with challenging ideas." One recent graduate says: "UW–Madison is a place for someone grounded in his belief system. Make no mistake, someone will question who you are, what you believe, and why you believe what you believe."

The most active groups on the left are the Wisconsin Public Interest Research Group, UW Greens, and MEChA (a Chicano racialist movement). On the right, the College Republicans are active, and one alumnus says the *Badger Herald* has become more libertarian lately. One conservative student told us he is happy for the opportunity to confront different worldviews. "This is a very political campus and you have the opportunity to become politically involved," the student says.

"Getting involved" goes well beyond politics. The sheer size of the university means that there is an organization for just about any interest a student might have. Students can join just about anything: Ballroom Dance Association, Campus Girl Scouts, the Molecular and Environmental Toxicology Student Association, or one of the student newspapers. Students can attend lectures by visiting professors or activists, join fraternities, sororities, or other social organizations—or just go back to their rooms after class to play videogames. The temptation for many new students, however, is to become overcommitted and spend an inordinate amount of time on extracurricular activities.

UW has a reputation for being a school with plenty of partying, and hence excessive drinking. The administration believes that there is a campus-wide drinking problem and is working to alleviate the problem. Recently, local bars agreed to eliminate drink specials on Friday and Saturday nights, which led two students to file a complaint alleging a violation of antitrust laws. According to the *Chronicle of Higher Education*, "The bars' owners say they agreed to the ban at the urging of the university's chancellor."

Activities for students who do not drink or attend house parties are bountiful, according to a student. "There is a wide variety of activities available for students during the week and on the weekends as an alternative to partying," she says. "The Memorial Union and Union South offer everything from free movies to live bands, dance lessons, game nights, well-known speakers, fun mini-courses, open mic night, and so much more. There are also 600 clubs and organizations on campus for students to get involved with."

The historic Memorial Union sits on the edge of Lake Mendota and serves as the main meeting place for students. It even has a hotel for visitors and the famous Rathskeller, a large hall containing fireplaces, large wooden tables, a cafeteria, and a small bar. The union also has a terrace on the lake where students can study, listen to concerts, or simply relax while soaking in the sun (at the right time of year) and the beautiful vista. The Memorial Union is also home to the UW Hoofers. The Hoofers comprise several different outdoor programs that allow students, for a nominal fee, to head out of Madison and explore Wisconsin or other parts of the country. Students can go sailing, backpacking, scuba diving, hang gliding, rock climbing, or simply attend one of the Hoofers' many socials.

The University of Wisconsin is pleasantly situated in a vibrant location that combines a fine urban area with two large glacial lakes, Mendota and Monona. Although some students complain about the long, harsh winters, most find the inclement weather offset by the myriad social opportunities. State Street is the main off-campus student gathering place. While the street usually fills up with bar-hopping revelers on the weekends, it also has dozens of coffeeshops, restaurants, and bookstores. On weekends, students and Madisonians often spend the day window-shopping or enjoying one of the many outdoor cafes. A multimillion-dollar arts center was recently built on State Street, close to the university and the capitol building.

SUGGESTED CORE

1. Classics 555, The Literature of Ancient Greece
2. Philosophy 430, History of Ancient Philosophy
3. Religious Studies 348/ 349, Literary Aspects of the English Bible: Old Testament / New Testament
4. Religious Studies 318, Medieval Social and Intellectual History, 1200–1450
5. Political Science 502, Development of Modern Political Thought
6. English 162, Shakespeare
7. History 101, American History to the Civil War Era
8. History 513, European Cultural History, 1815– 1870 (*closest match*)

As a member of the Big Ten, the university fields several high-profile athletic programs. Fans from the university and around the state are extremely loyal to the Badger football team (whose football stadium, the fourth-oldest in the nation, is now undergoing renovations). Basketball games have lately been very well attended, too. Hockey games have always been popular. Students also have plenty of club sports to choose from, and intramurals are popular especially among freshmen and sophomores, many of whom organize basketball (or ultimate Frisbee, sand volleyball, floor hockey, or other sports) teams from their dorm halls.

Only around a quarter of undergraduates live on campus, although most students stay there for their freshman year. The undergraduate residence halls are divided into smaller "houses" of 50 to 80 residents. Dorms are as diverse as the students who inhabit them. Some dorms, especially those abutting campus on University Avenue, are well known as party halls. Quieter spots include Chadbourne Residential College and the Lakeside Dorms on Lake Mendota. The school's all-women dorm, Elizabeth Waters, is located on a hill overlooking the lake and is especially popular for students in the Women in Science and Engineering program. There is also a Multicultural Learning Community. The university has no coed dorm rooms or bathrooms, and even in the dormitories, men and women are separated by floor or wing. Many students, however, choose to leave the dorms at the first possible opportunity. One current student has little good to say about UW residential life. "I despised the dorms," she says. "Rooms were too small, food was terrible, it was too loud, and I felt like I was in jail. I got out ASAP."

For its size, UW is rather safe. In 2003, the school reported 13 forcible sex offenses on campus, six robberies, two aggravated assaults, 32 burglaries, and six arsons. In 2002, the school won the dubious honor of the highest number of liquor offenses in the United States, according to the *Chronicle of Higher Education*—some 837. The university provides SAFEwalk and SAFEride escort services for students who need to cross campus at night.

UW–Madison tuition for 2004–5 was $6,220 for residents and $21,060 for those from out of state. Room and board was $6,500. In 2002–3 the university granted need-based financial aid to 51 percent of students.

WEST

- University of Washington
- Gonzaga University
- Reed College
- Whitman College

WASHINGTON

MONTANA

OREGON

IDAHO

WYOMING

NEVADA

- University of California at Davis
- University of California at Berkeley
- Stanford University
- Brigham Young University
- University of Colorado

UTAH

COLORADO

- Colorado College
- U.S. Air Force Academy

CALIFORNIA

- University of California at Santa Barbara
- Thomas Aquinas College

ARIZONA

- St. John's College

OKLAHOMA

LOS ANGELES AREA —
California Institute of Technology
Claremont Colleges
Pepperdine University
University of California at Los Angeles
University of Southern California

- University of California at San Diego

NEW MEXICO

- University of Arizona

- University of Dallas
- Southern Methodist University

TEXAS

- Baylor University
- Texas A&M University
- University of Texas

- Rice University

UNIVERSITY OF ARIZONA

TUCSON, ARIZONA • WWW.ARIZONA.EDU

Know when to fold 'em

The University of Arizona was founded in 1885 in what was still the Wild West. The project almost didn't get off the ground, since the state provided funding for the school's building, but not for the land on which it would be built; that had to be donated by citizens of the town. Only when two gamblers and a saloonkeeper donated 40 acres did the university find a home. The school opened in 1891, and has grown by hundreds of acres and thousands of students. Today, the University of Arizona has almost 37,000 students and offers more than 150 majors—and it is expected to grow rapidly in future decades.

Nevertheless, because tuition hikes have been banned by state legislators, university administrators have been identifying programs to cut in order to save dollars and focus the direction of the institution. "There are not enough unrestricted dollars to give all [the programs] the resources they need to attain excellence," university president Peter Likins has written. Numerous programs in the university have already been cut or are facing elimination. The humanities program and the bachelor of liberal arts degree, the School of Planning, and the School of Health Professionals are among a few programs that were eliminated in 2004. "As part of budget issues in recent years I believe our administration has trimmed [programs and departments] to a bare minimum," a professor says.

In the spirit of improvement, the administration at Arizona has acknowledged that its admission standards, which now let in 83 percent of applicants, are hurting its reputation and must be changed in order to "focus" the university. Admissions standards will be boosted for the freshman class of 2006, as the university will only grant automatic admission to the top 25 percent of all high school seniors in the state, not the top half. The transition from being a university with wide-open arms to a more competitive one should alter the intellectual landscape at Arizona, but it is far from clear how the humanities and liberal arts will fare in the future.

VITAL STATISTICS

Religious affiliation: none
Total enrollment: 36,932
Total undergraduates: 28,368
SAT/ACT midranges: SAT V: 500–610, M: 500–620; ACT: 21–26
Applicants: 23,725
Applicants accepted: 83%
Accepted applicants who enrolled: 29%
Tuition: $3,508 (in state), $12,278 (out of state)
Room and board: $6,810
Freshman retention rate: 79%
Graduation rate: 31% (4 yrs.), 57% (6 yrs.)
Courses with fewer than 20 students: 31%
Student-faculty ratio: 19:1
Courses taught by graduate TAs: not provided
Most popular majors: business, communications, social sciences
Students living on campus: 21%
Guaranteed housing for four years? no
Students in fraternities: 7% sororities: 11%

WEST

Academic Life: Raising Arizona

In 1997, the University of Arizona beefed up its general education requirements, expanding the numbers and variety of courses a student must take, regardless of major. However, the requirements are still too easy to satisfy with courses of uneven quality, which means that a fair number of students will waste their time in overspecialized or politicized classes. New students should carefully read course descriptions, ask upperclassmen for advice, and seek out some of the better professors (listed below). Still, the revised curriculum is an improvement of which many professors speak well. The liberal arts and science education received by undergraduates at Arizona, one professor says, is "very broad, thanks to our revised education program."

Additional help for students comes from professors, who are eager to work with students if the students will but seek them out. "It is easy for students to avoid faculty and advisors or get lost," a professor says. "But those students who avail themselves of the opportunities to meet with advisors and faculty are never neglected." An English professor says that there are "very strong opportunities for students to interact with faculty." "I have an open-door policy and try to have daily interaction with students in my classes and other students in our major," says another professor.

In an award-winning student outreach endeavor, Arizona has what is called the Faculty Fellows Program. Over thirty professors and administrators have currently volunteered to be "faculty aces" and to dedicate time each week to interacting with students outside the classroom. The goal, a professor says, is "to be more proactive in achieving faculty accessibility." The university helps the aces by picking up the tabs for their informal "office hours" with students, which have included brown-bag lunches out of doors, concerts, movies, and hikes.

Teaching assistants are a part of the learning environment at Arizona, though to what degree depends on the department. "There may be teaching assistants helping me, but I'm in charge and the class is mine," a business professor says. "In my college, we will use TAs in certain classes after they have proven effective in work with a faculty member, and as part of their PhD learning experience." Other departments do not use TAs as instructors, but as at most large schools, the introductory composition courses required of all students are frequently taught by TAs.

Students and professors typically speak of the intellectual climate as dependent on the individual's desire to find it, and in some respects create it. Openness is valued, they say. One graduate student describes the intellectual environment as pretty tolerant, "more so than at other state universities where I have taught. . . . I have not witnessed any egregious acts of censorship or political correctness."

Departments that shine at Arizona are almost invariably in the sciences and the business school: optics, astronomy, analytical chemistry, geology, and management information systems. In animal sciences, the equine and race track industry programs are strong, as are the veterinary science and microbiology programs. Agriculture education and classics also get high marks.

Teachers of note include Jon Solomon, David Soren, and Cynthia White in classics; Christopher Carroll, Roger Dahood, Lawrence Evers, Robert Houston, Gregory Jackson, and Charles Scruggs in English; Richard Eaton and Roger Nichols in history; and John Z. Drabicki and Price V. Fishback in economics.

Many departments host distinguished-speaker series to augment the educational experience, and the provost offers a faculty-community lecture series in which faculty present their ideas to students and the public. One lecture series especially pertinent to this guide was the Vital Signs series held in the 2003–4 academic year by the College of Humanities. The series focused on the role of humanities in the corporate university. "It's hard to get students excited when they're just here to get a degree in order to get a job," English professor Maribel Alvarez told the student newspaper, the *Daily Wildcat*. "Intellectual production is not valued enough." Clearly not—why else would the school have seen its humanities program as expendable?

Student Life: Stay on the sunny side

Just as students in the North would rather not have to deal with winter, Arizonans would just as soon skip summer, when Tucson bakes and, as a student says, "life comes to a halt." Fortunately, summer sessions are optional. During the rest of the year the climate is very pleasant. "Southern Arizona is a resort mecca," one professor says. "It's hard to find a more desirable location for a major university." Another says, "If students like sunshine and blue skies, our campus is the right place to be. Very few rainy and gray days seem to make all of us take a brighter view of life."

Tucson, about an hour north of the border with Mexico, has about 500,000 residents, so it's got big-city attributes like a symphony, ballet, opera, and theater that smaller college towns lack—though they may not be of the caliber expected by some. "Tucson is quite remote," one student says, "so if you are used to the activities associated with the city, you may be disappointed here. It is also a long way to the nearest body of water." The collision of Old West, American Indian, and Mexican cultures makes for a colorful medley of mariachi music, powwows, rodeos, and festivals. With the picturesque Sonoran Desert providing the backdrop, outdoor activities such as hiking and cycling are a common diversion.

ACADEMIC REQUIREMENTS

Arizona has no core curriculum, but rather some loose general education requirements. Students must take the following:

- Two freshman composition courses and one writing-intensive class.
- One math or logic course.
- Two or four semesters of a foreign language. BA students take four courses; other students take two. (Students may test out.)
- Two courses in "traditions and cultures." Choices include "History of Western Civilization" and "Love in World Religions."
- Two courses concerning "individuals and societies." Options have included courses like "Gender in Contemporary Society" and "Lesbian and Gay Studies."
- Three natural science courses. The scientific content here varies greatly: surveys of physical geography and weather fit the bill; so does "Food, Nutrition, and You."
- One arts course.
- One humanities class.
- One gender, race, class, ethnicity, or non-Western-area studies course. Options include "Survey of Mexican Folk Music" and (for some reason) "Rock and American Popular Music."

WEST

One of the most appealing sights around Tucson is the nearby San Xavier mission, acclaimed and admired by many as the finest example of mission architecture in the United States. Students can easily make the trip to San Xavier, a fully functioning Catholic church served by Franciscan friars. Since 1888, the mission has operated not only as a church, but also as a school to serve the Tohono O'odham people, a nation with a population of more than 24,000 people living on more than 2.7 million acres of land, some of that only miles from the University of Arizona.

The campus itself is also beautiful, with palm trees spread amongst southwestern-style redbrick buildings and more modern structures. On-campus living is guaranteed only for freshmen; however, the university recently completed the construction of three new dormitories, and with no plans to remove any of the older buildings, it is not too difficult for upperclassmen to find housing. There are a variety of single-sex, coed, and special-interest dorms, including dorms for honors students, and on-campus apartments. The coed dorms maintain separate bathrooms for men and women. The residence halls have no dining areas, which detracts a bit from the campus living experience, but they do have kitchens (community or private), and there are 30 or 40 fast-food, bistro, and cafeteria-style eateries spread across campus where students can use the money they deposit on a meal card.

The Greek system is vibrant but not dominant; Arizona is not as much of a party school as some other big state universities. In fact, one fraternity officer ran for student government president for 2004–5 on a platform of making UA into, well, the party school he'd expected. "I don't understand why people stress so much and get bent out of shape over bad grades," he told the *Wildcat*.

A good percentage of Arizona's student body is made up of out-of-state students, so there is opportunity to interact with a critical mass of students from different states and nations, as well as a reasonable chance for qualified students from outside Arizona to gain admission to the school's more outstanding programs.

Arizona starts out freshmen with a mandatory, two-day summer orientation session. The schedule in 2004 was overwhelmingly practical, with little room for indoctrination. The first day consisted of placement exams, meetings, introductions to campus career resources and other programs, and a block party. On the second day, students picked up their ID cards, attended a session called "Just the Facts," listened to the dean of students, and went through advising (students come out of orientation registered for their first semester), with optional activities scheduled for afterwards. Parents and guests are encouraged to attend, and there are special sessions, such as one on paying for college, just for them.

There are over 500 student groups at Arizona. In addition to the political and fraternal organizations, there are ethnic and religious groups, a literary magazine, and support centers of all kinds. The Arizona Academic Hammock Society promotes "fellowship, education, and peace through hammocking at the University of Arizona," and the Gentle-Men's Club "promote[s] and provide[s] resources for social etiquette and gentlemen-like conduct," according to their official Web listings. The campus has a dozen or so political groups, including Republicans, Democrats, Libertarians, the Arizona Israel Alliance, and the Alliance for Peace and Justice in the Middle East. There seems to be far more interest in pursing hobbies and individual interests than social justice. The campus activism environment rarely rages. Events that have drawn crowds in recent years include a meeting with regents about tuition increases to finance what many students view as never-ending construction and to help offset state budget cuts. Many students also view the administration as being overly focused on pleasing alumni.

Through the Spring Fling, a student-run carnival that is billed as the largest of its kind in the nation, student clubs can make money by running game and food booths. There was controversy a few years ago when the event was moved from campus—where it had been held for decades—to a larger park several miles away. The scent of that controversy still hovers over the carnival, but organizers haven't returned the festivities to campus.

Given the school's location in a medium-sized city and the size of its student body, crime is not a major issue at the University of Arizona. However the school is not completely safe. Three murders of faculty members by a disgruntled student in 2002 still haunt the campus; however, criminal offenses seem to be diminishing. The university reported seven forcible sex offenses, three aggravated assaults, 21 burglaries, two car thefts, and one arson during 2003. By way of unusual distinction, Arizona employs a rehabilitated prof with a violent adolescent past. According to the *Chronicle of Higher Education*, Robert B. Bechtel (now a professor of environmental psychology at the university) shot and killed one of his fellow undergraduates at Swarthmore College, but was found not guilty by reason of insanity. Prof. Bechtel "has said he was a victim of bullying in college . . . [and] recently testified to Arizona legislators about his violent past in order to support antibullying initiatives in Arizona schools," the periodical reported. Swarthmore College denies that Bechtel was persecuted and points to his later-diagnosed mental illness as a more likely explanation of his behavior.

Students from Arizona will find their home school a real bargain; 2004–5 tuition for them was $3,508. Out-of-state students paid $12,278. Room and board was $6,810. Admission to the university is decided without reference to a student's financial need. Thiry-nine percent of undergrads receive need-based aid, and the average student loan debt upon graduation is $16,012.

SUGGESTED CORE
1. Classics 250a, Classical Literature in Translation
2. Philosophy 260, Ancient Philosophy
3. Religion 220A/220B, Literature of the Bible, Old Testament / New Testament
4. Religion 300, Christian Literature and Thought *or* Philosophy 261, Medieval Philosophy
5. Philosophy 262, Early Modern Philosophy
6. English 231, Shakespeare's Major Plays
7. History 442, History of American Society and Thought: Pre–Civil War
8. History 412b, European Intellectual History, 1870–Present *or* Philosophy 263, From Hegel to Nietzsche: Nineteenth-Century Philosophy

BAYLOR UNIVERSITY

No separation

"For Church, for State," reads the motto of Baylor University, a school founded 150 years ago by Baptist missionaries. As the world's largest Baptist university, Baylor has worked to uphold its unique mission. Scores of America's most prestigious colleges and universities were founded on similar principles but have over the years become all but completely secularized. At Baylor, the missionary spirit of its founders has not been forgotten. While many schools have eliminated or dumbed down their academic standards, Baylor's have remained comparatively strong. And the Baptist tradition continues to permeate its academic programs and the social life of its students. As one professor told us, "If you want to be an insider at Baylor, you can't just be from Texas—you have to be a Texas Baptist."

Baylor University is now in the midst of some turmoil, which one might characterize as a battle between such insiders and those who wish to broaden the school's vision and raise its profile. The controversy centers on the implementation of "Baylor 2012," a 10-year plan begun in 2002 and championed by an energetic university president, Robert B. Sloan Jr. Under the plan, Baylor pledged to seek "a new level of excellence" and national prominence. Now, such rhetoric would normally make us suspicious; at most schools with a historic religious or regional identity, fine phrases like these are invoked by administrators who wish to water down or liquidate that identity, and remake the school in the image of . . . well, the secular, northeastern graduate schools where they got their own PhDs. (In such cases, we'd have to agree with the proverbial old Southern lady who declared "I'm against all change—even for the better.")

But something quite different was happening at Baylor. As then-president Sloan wrote in 2002, Baylor "aspires to what few institutions, if any, have ever achieved. Within the course of a decade, Baylor intends to enter the top tier of American universities while reaffirming and deepening its distinctive Christian mission." This two-pronged goal struck many as a grand and noble objective: Baylor was to become "the Protestant Notre Dame." As part of this plan, Sloan hired more foreigners and non-Texans than had ever been seen at Baylor, and even a few Roman Catholics. This did not sit so well with the school's board of regents—and the speed and vigor with which Sloan implemented the plan alienated even some of its supporters. In 2005, Sloan's opponents managed what one professor called "a classic political coup d'etat." Sloan was forced out as president in spring 2005, stepping down to the position of chancellor, a job that focuses on fundraising, recruitment, and the general advancement of the university (including Baylor's bid for the George W. Bush presidential library). On June 1, 2005—

his first day on the job—interim president William Underwood, a Baylor law professor and practicing lawyer, replaced Provost David Jeffrey, a Sloan appointee and champion of Baylor 2012. Jeffrey has returned to his former position as Distinguished Professor of Literature and Humanities. As of press time, the search for a permanent president was underway

The plan remains, at least on paper. Baylor will still attempt, for instance, "to develop a world-class faculty." As part of his plan, Sloan had already recruited 33 new faculty members dispersed among nearly every department in the College of Arts and Sciences, in addition to 36 faculty members in the other schools. The numbers alone indicate that the plan is an enormous undertaking, but the quality of the faculty members is also very high. Recent hires at Baylor include Thomas Aquinas scholar and former Boston College professor Thomas Hibbs as the new dean of the Honors College, physicist Bennie Ward, classicist Julia Dyson, and Beethoven scholar Robin Wallace, just to name a few of the more impressive additions. One professor said of the recent coup, "This won't make it a less valuable intellectual environment for students. Unless all the faculty who were brought in were to leave—which I don't expect—teaching here will remain impressive. These people are terrific folks, and I think they're going to forge an intellectual community here."

Besides hiring a higher profile and more religiously varied faculty and placing greater emphasis on research (which means adding doctoral programs), Sloan's plan included making the school a "truly residential campus" by erecting more and better academic facilities (which also requires building a large and controversial debt) and boosting athletics even more—despite the highly publicized murder of a men's basketball player in 2003 and its ugly aftermath (about which more below). In addition, the Board of Regents recently established the aforementioned Honors College for the university's top students.

So, despite Sloan's ouster, and largely because of his accomplishments, Baylor's combination of religious commitment and academic rigor makes it a unique and robust institution. Its attempt to strengthen that combination while becoming a major research university is "an audacious undertaking in the face of historic trends in church and society," in the words of the *Christian Century*. Let us hope that it succeeds without tearing itself apart.

VITAL STATISTICS

Religious affiliation: Baptist
Total enrollment: 13,799
Total undergraduates: 11,580
SAT/ACT midranges: SAT V: 530–640, M: 550–650; ACT: 22–27
Applicants: 10,917
Applicants accepted: 73%
Accepted applicants who enrolled: 35%
Tuition: $19,880
Room and board: $5,712
Freshman retention rate: 82%
Graduation rate: 43% (4 yrs.), 72% (6 yrs.)
Courses with fewer than 20 students: 35%
Student-faculty ratio: 16:1
Courses taught by graduate TAs: not provided
Most popular majors: business, education, communications
Students living on campus: 34%
Guaranteed housing for four years? no
Students in fraternities: 13% sororities: 17%

Academic Life: The examined life

ACADEMIC REQUIREMENTS

Students in the College of Arts and Sciences at Baylor face a structured list of required courses and areas of study. All students must take:

- Four courses in English. This requirement includes a two-semester introduction to "Thinking, Writing, and Research"; a course in British literature (introducing students to the works of Chaucer, Shakespeare, Milton, the Romantics, and the Victorians); and a course in either American or world literature.
- Two courses in religion. This requirement is usually satisfied with one course in the Old Testament and one course in the New Testament.
- Two semesters of history, including one course in either world history or American history and one course titled "American Constitutional Government."

Change involving faculty often leads to controversy, and big change leads to big controversy—as former president Sloan can attest. "The conflicts," reported the *Christian Century*, "are . . . numerous. The Baylor community is clashing over the school's newly articulated religious identity; over ratcheted-up demands on faculty for research and publication; over financial decisions endorsing higher tuition fees, expensive new PhD programs, new buildings and more debt; and over how these new policies have been arrived at and implemented."

In the past, Baylor placed its greatest emphasis on undergraduate teaching, but with the Baylor 2012 plan, the school's focus shifted more toward research. For one thing, faculty members now will be required to publish a certain amount each year, and, as one student says, "there will be consequences to putting pressure on faculty members," including, perhaps, less frequent interaction with undergraduates in and out of the classroom (although one professor points out that this effect may be balanced by another: smaller class sizes). As things stand now, most students say that professors are usually very accessible and willing to help students—as long as students put forth the first effort. "It has been my experience that Baylor professors on the whole are genuinely concerned with the personal and academic well-being of their students, regardless of the student's interest in their fields of study," a political science major says. Professors teach almost all courses, although students say graduate teaching assistants sometimes run labs or weekly discussion sections, especially in larger introductory courses.

The most basic reason for resistance to Baylor 2012, besides the often clumsy and sometimes secretive way in which the plan has been presented and put into effect, is a dispute over the nature of the university's religious identity. The *Christian Century* suggests that many faculty are uncomfortable with the C. S. Lewis–style "mere Christianity" brand of orthodoxy that was promoted by the Sloan administration. The newly hired faculty are all serious and practicing Christians—the *Century* reported (prior to the June 1 changes) that the "provost interviews all finalists for faculty positions" and that "about a quarter of the interview [is devoted to] the candidate's religious life. If the candidate does not satisfy the department's or the provost's criteria, he or she is rejected"—but this does not satisfy some of the old-line Texas Baptists. They distrust ecclesial or credal Christianity, and their fideism leads them to look askance at bringing the faith to bear on what they see as the realm of secular scholarship. Thus, at the heart of the controversy at Baylor is which sort of Christianity should predominate at the institution. As the *Century* puts it, "traditional Baptists disagree with Sloan's contention that Christianity has intellectual content." But to the recent administration and newer faculty members, "faith is more than atmospheric." According to one graduate student, Sloan did manage the feat of creating an institution that "has become a home to outstanding Christian thinkers of diverse disciplines and faith traditions." Not everyone can find a home here, however. Leading "intelligent design" theorist and critic of mechanistic evolution William Dembski has left Baylor—where he once ran a center for the study of intelligent design, according to the *Chronicle of Higher Education*. "My work is too controversial for [Baylor]," he told the magazine. Sloan's administration had supported Dembski—but other faculty froze (and ultimately forced) him out, the *Chronicle* reports.

Of the schools in this guide, Baylor has one of the most solid curricula, though it isn't quite a traditional core. Indeed, as the school's Web site justifiably boasts, "according to a study on general education requirements conducted in April by the American Council of Trustees and Alumni, Baylor is the only school that meets [ACTA's] highest criteria." Baylor's general education requirements dictate more than half of a student's coursework; for instance the English study required of all students in Arts and Sciences is more structured than the requirements for English *majors* at many other schools. With such a foundation, students are well-prepared to pursue further work in their chosen majors. Nonetheless, as admirable as they are, the general education requirements leave more wiggle room than they should. As one junior says, it is "relatively easy" to satisfy the requirements: "Courses are as easy or as difficult as you want them to be, and you can choose courses to fit how much you want to be challenged. I have friends taking advanced Latin and the classics for their general ed courses, but I also know plenty of people who consistently enroll in blow-off courses just to get by." Only half of the credit hours must be completed on the Baylor campus, and one student says that because of this "it is possible to transfer a significant amount of credit hours before matriculation. Once here, students are able to enroll in less demanding courses in order to boost their GPAs. For instance, I took 'Packard Physics'

REQUIREMENTS (CONT'D)

- Three social science courses to be selected from anthropology, economics, geography, political science, philosophy, psychology, or sociology.
- Two semesters of chapel. Students and faculty gather on Mondays and Wednesdays in the chapel. Attendance is recorded and students receive a pass or fail grade at the end of the semester.
- Two semesters of physical education.

  BA students must also complete three courses in the fine arts, each of which must be chosen from a different area in the field. They must also demonstrate proficiency in a foreign language.

  BS students are required to take one additional course in mathematics as well as three science courses. At least one of these must be in chemistry or physics and one in biology or geology, and one must include additional laboratory work.

(physics for BA students) and 'Shake and Bake' (in the geology department, on earthquakes and other natural disasters)."

About 200 freshmen can participate in an alternative program, the Baylor Interdisciplinary Core, which satisfies general studies requirements while providing a more coherent and integrated education. Students in the program take courses in three areas: "World Cultures," "The Natural World," and "The Social World," usually focusing on primary texts. Freshmen begin with a set of three courses: "Examined Life I: Human Development and College Life," "The World of Rhetoric I: Writing and Speaking," and "World Cultures I: Roots of Culture," a survey course in early cultures, Western and non-Western. The course syllabus for "World Cultures" shows the following texts as required: the Bible, the *Analects* of Confucius, Euripides' *Ten Plays*, Homer's *Odyssey*, *The Ramayana*, several Platonic dialogues, and Virgil's *Aeneid*. Sophomores in the program take two to three courses per semester. Juniors take one course in "Biblical Heritage and Contemporary Ethical Issues." In the senior course, "Differing Visions and Realities," students supplement biblical readings with contemporary books, articles, and films.

The major fields of study impose further curricular rigor and seriousness. English majors, for instance, must take four intermediate courses in British and American literature (and there are only five such courses from which to choose), plus advanced courses in early British literature and late British literature and one advanced course in American literature. All seniors in the English department are required to pass a comprehensive examination. English majors have few options when it comes to electives within their major, and those options they do have are generally restricted to courses that—in a radical departure from national standards—actually have something to do with literature. History majors take fundamental introductions to world history and the history of the United States, selecting four of the following five courses: "World History through the Fourteenth Century," "World History from 1400 to 1750," "Modern World Civilizations since 1750," "History of the United States to 1877," and "History of the United States since 1877." Students then choose two additional American history courses and two European history courses, plus one general history elective.

In choosing majors, Baylor students have fewer choices than colleges with less focused missions, but the payoff is that the disciplines at Baylor are generally solid all around. Students speak highly of the academic programs in philosophy, business (especially the school's entrepreneurship program), nursing, law, the sciences, theology, and music. The premed program and engineering school are highly regarded nationally. While the African studies program is not as politicized as those at some schools, the Latin American studies program appears to suffer from Sandinista envy.

Baylor offers structure in choosing courses but places less emphasis on academic advising. Students receive advisors based on their majors and the number of credit hours they have completed. Although efficient, this system may prevent students from getting to know any one particular advisor well. Advisors, according to the Academic Advisement Web page, "help students fulfill their academic goals and potential. In addition to selecting classes, professional advisors assist students with reviewing degree audits, finding a major, developing academic plans, and clarifying personal goals." Faculty also serve as advisors in many cases.

The recently boosted list of fine professors at Baylor includes: Thomas Hibbs in the Honors College; Richard G. Durán in French; J. Randall O'Brien in religion; David Corey, Mary Nichols, and Richard B. Riley in political science; Julie Sweet in history; D. Thomas Hanks Jr. and Ralph Wood in English; Robert Miner in philosophy; Alden Smith in classics; Robyn Driskell in sociology; Sara Stone in journalism; Francis Beckwith in the Institute of Church-State Studies; and John A. Dunbar in geology. Joseph McKinney is widely considered to be one of the nation's foremost experts on international trade.

Student Life: Shall we dance?

Deep in the heart of Texas, Baylor lies in Waco, a medium-sized city on the banks of the Brazos River. An hour and a half from both Dallas and Austin, Waco appears to be a hospitable setting for a college campus; however, most students admit to often escaping on weekends to one of the two larger cities. Many of the attractions offered in Waco, such as museums and concerts, are actually products of Baylor, whose presence helps make Waco something of a thriving city.

Student life at Baylor is very much what one expects from a Christian university, and a Baptist one at that. Baylor is an ideal place for a Christian student to earn an education without attending a small, fundamentalist college or university. That being said, many students note that there is an expectation that one is at least Christian, if not Baptist, and those who are not of the same persuasion feel some discomfort. Baylor and most of its students offer no apology for such an environment and actually welcome their reputation as an openly Christian university of higher education.

In 2004, Baylor began requiring all incoming freshmen to live on campus. To make this possible, the university completed a $33 million residence facility. Students living on campus must abide by the university's strict visitation policies, which include restrictions on when (and, implicitly and explicitly, how) visitors of the opposite sex may be entertained. In dormitories, visitation hours extend from 1 to 6 p.m. Sunday through Thursday, and 1 to 10 p.m. on Friday and Saturday. A recent alumnus says that students do obey the visitation policies. "I've heard a few stories about those who do not, but I think it's rare. If students want to be together they are going to find other places—most know someone with an apartment or house," the alum says. Students

SUGGESTED CORE
1. Classics 3302, Greek Civilization *and* Classics 3301, Roman Civilization
2. Philosophy 3310, History of Philosophy: Classical Philosophy
3. Religion 1310, The Christian Scriptures *or* Religion 1311, New Testament Survey
4. Religion 1350, The Christian Heritage *or* Religion 3330, Introduction to Church History
5. Political Science 4373, Western Political Thought: Modern
6. English 432, Shakespeare: Selected Plays
7. History 2365, History of the United States to 1877
8. History 4339, Cultural and Intellectual History of Modern Europe

WEST

living in university-owned apartment buildings have more liberal visitation hours, 10 a.m. to 2 a.m. Under no conditions may students have overnight guests of the opposite sex. Men and women live in separate residence halls, except for a few living areas for married students. Because Baylor is located in a fairly large metropolitan area, finding housing off campus is not difficult.

Students may find some of these regulations overly intrusive, but Baylor is emphatic that it "operates within the Christian-oriented aims and ideals of Baptists." To fulfill its mission, Baylor expects that "each Baylor student will conduct himself or herself in accordance with Christian principles as commonly perceived by Texas Baptists"; in other words, students arrive on campus knowing that Baylor is serious about being a Christian community. One student says that there are non-Baptists and even some non-Christians on campus and that they "are welcome to a certain degree . . . but it's more difficult for them to fit in."

Baylor prohibits alcohol in all residences and smoking in all university buildings, but, as one student says, "alcohol is present on campus just as it is on any campus." Many students drink in their dorm rooms or at private parties. To cut back on drinking, Baylor has implemented a policy that requires school officials to inform parents when their children violate alcohol laws or policies. The administration insists that the new policy is not punitive: "If a student has an alcohol problem, we want to help them with that. We don't want to have students suspended. We're not out to get them." A student says, "Baylor police don't go looking for alcohol violations, but they would punish a drunk student who showed up on their doorstep." The Department of Public Safety patrols the campus constantly. This university police force also monitors 20 emergency call boxes placed throughout the campus.

Because of its strong religious tradition, those outside of the university community sometimes perceive Baylor as oppressively conservative. But while Baylor students may be more conservative than those found at other universities, the campus is actually very apolitical. As with most colleges and universities, Baylor is home to College Democrats and College Republicans, but the groups are small for a school of almost 14,000 students. Most students spend their time outside of class and studying in more popular, nonpolitical organizations. About half of Baylor students participate in the university's popular intramurals program on teams organized by residence halls or other groups. Baylor's chapter of Habitat for Humanity is extremely popular, as is the Baptist Student Union.

The campus is home to a strong Greek community. Baylor's system includes 14 fraternities and 9 sororities. The school will only allow students who maintain a 2.5 grade point average to attend Greek activities; Baylor sororities themselves require a 2.75 GPA to join. Rush is open only to second-semester freshman and upperclassmen.

Prior to 1996, the school had interpreted its Baptist religious commitments as dictating that students should not dance. But today Baylor allows dances on campus as long as they are sponsored by an official university department and open to all Baylor students; Greek organizations, therefore, cannot host private dances on campus. One of Baylor's most popular traditions is a university-wide holiday known as Diadeloso. In

1934, the university decided to give students a break from hectic spring classes, and ever since students and faculty have enjoyed the tradition. The festival includes parties, dinners, sporting events, and concerts. At a recent Diadeloso celebration, students were entertained by visiting snake handlers. Baylor also enjoys "Dr. Pepper Hour," when students gather for fellowship, music, games, and a "frosted Dr. Pepper." This began in 1953, when the student activities coordinator wanted to give students an opportunity to take a break from studies and socialize together each week. The tradition stuck.

Other university traditions center around Baylor athletics. The Baylor Line, organized by freshmen, helps welcome the football team to the field by waving flags. The student body also names "yell leaders" who lead fans in organized cheers. And at every homecoming, fans remember the "Immortal Ten," basketball players who died in a 1927 train wreck. There is no doubt that the green-and-gold-clad Baylor Bears athletic teams are a huge part of student life. Competing in the powerful Big 12 Conference, Baylor has struggled of late in some of the more popular sports, especially football, but the school excels in less costly sports like golf and men's and women's track and field.

A more recent tragedy occurred in July 2003, when Patrick J. Dennehy, a Baylor men's basketball player, was found dead; his former teammate and roommate Carlton E. Dotson is now in prison after having been charged with Dennehy's murder. This death shined a harsh light on the school's sports program, leading both the athletics director and the head basketball coach to resign. Officials were later found to have committed a series of abuses, including improperly finagling free tuition for two players, misleading university investigators, failing to report positive results of drug tests, and providing players with free meals, rides, clothes, and other goodies, according to the *Chronicle of Higher Education*. Former president Sloan imposed sanctions against the program, banning the basketball team from postseason tournaments, cutting its budget, and restricting its recruitment activities. Apart from this incident, Baylor's crime statistics reflect a remarkably safe environment. In 2003, the only crimes on campus were 33 burglaries and two arsons.

Tuition at Baylor for the 2004–5 academic year was $19,880, and room and board was $5,712. The university does offer an installment plan to help with the cost of tuition, and approximately 75 percent of students receive some form of financial aid. The average amount borrowed per student is a considerable $37,976.

BRIGHAM YOUNG UNIVERSITY

PROVO, UTAH • WWW.BYU.EDU

Not without the Spirit of God

Brigham Young University is, no doubt, a distinctive university. Founded in 1875 as a small, pioneer academy, the school is named for one of the best-known presidents of the Church of Jesus Christ of Latter-day Saints (LDS), whose members are usually known as Mormons. BYU's first president, Karl Maeser, directed that instructors "ought not to teach even the alphabet or the multiplication tables without the Spirit of God." His vision continues today, but few universities elicit stronger feelings than does BYU. Many see the school as a comfortable community, especially for LDS members, while a few find it stifling. But BYU is unafraid of criticism and unapologetic about what it is: a devoutly religious presence in a secular world, dedicated to a sacred purpose. Faculty members do deliberate over whether BYU should be primarily a ministry of the church or strive toward offering a first-class education within an LDS setting. But this continuing, low-key debate has not prevented the school from requiring a rather traditional and rigorous curriculum of its students.

The university's unbending honor code governing most aspects of student life (from academic integrity to standards for attire), its academic requirements in religion, and its control of academic affairs are peculiar nowadays. "BYU is not the place for everyone," says a faculty member. But those who share the institution's vision should find themselves happily at home.

Academic Life: We're on a mission from God

Academics—as everything else at BYU—are traditional but inclusive of the teachings of the LDS church. Consider BYU's curriculum. All students must complete a two-course sequence on the Book of Mormon, one of the church's revered and holy texts. The university also requires one course dealing with the New Testament and another on the Book of Doctrine and Covenants, a collection of modern revelations to early church leaders. These requirements are not meant to be inclusive of other religions or beliefs, nor are they exploratory courses in theology. Rather, they border on the catechetical. Students who are not members of the LDS Church are strongly encouraged to first take the "Introduction to Mormonism" class before completing the rest of the religion requirements.

Students are faced with a challenging general education curriculum. BYU's major requirements are about as stiff as the general education requirements—which is to say, there is some flexibility, but not much. An English professor says that a decade ago, majors could "pick and choose so much that students could avoid Shakespeare if they wanted to." But since then, the faculty has instituted a core in the department. English majors must complete two specific courses in the fundamentals of language and literature as well as a three-course sequence on British and American literary history. Unlike English programs at most schools, BYU also requires a course in Shakespeare. Students go on to complete at least one course from two of the following three areas: early British, later British, and American literature. The department also has students take a course in "Language, Rhetoric, and Theory" and another in "Diverse Traditions and Methods." Finally, majors complete nine elective course hours and a senior seminar involving detailed research and writing. Constituting a total of 42 credit hours, the English major at BYU is challenging and comprehensive, ensuring that students are exposed to the fundamentals of the English language and the Anglo-American literary tradition. And the English department isn't even known as being particularly demanding.

The philosophy program is. Students take five courses under the rubric "sources and methods," two "historical periods" courses, one "values and conduct" course, two "following knowledge and reality courses," and 12 additional credit hours. Totaling 42 credit hours, the requirements for BYU philosophy majors are, again, much more structured than those at most universities, where students sometimes have complete flexibility in choosing their curricula. Comparative literature prescribes nine courses, requires the completion of an individualized reading list, a thorough knowledge of two language traditions relevant to the program of study (including an upper-level language course), and 12 hours of electives. Chemistry requires at least 25 specific courses, for a total of 74.5 prescribed hours (20 of which overlap with the general education requirements).

Brigham Young's two-tiered advising system is intended to guide students through these academic requirements. Undeclared students can visit the undergraduate Advisement Center, where full-time, nonfaculty advisors or trained graduate students help students with academic problems. Students who have declared majors meet with advisors within their departments. If a student wishes to speak with a particular advisor, he is free to wait, but generally, students are part of a pool and don't have their own personal guides. With this system, students may have a hard time establishing personal relationships with professors, but the help is usually there if students need it.

VITAL STATISTICS
Religious affiliation: Church of Jesus Christ of Latter-Day Saints
Total enrollment: 34,609
Total undergraduates: 30,847
SAT/ACT midranges: SAT V: 550–660, M: 570–670; ACT: 25–29
Applicants: 7,329
Applicants accepted: 76%
Accepted applicants who enrolled: 59%
Tuition: $3,280 (LDS members), $4,920 (nonmembers)
Room and board: $5,790
Freshman retention rate: 95%
Graduation rate: 27% (4 yrs.), 70% (6 yrs.)
Courses with fewer than 20 students: 39%
Student-faculty ratio: 20:1
Courses taught by graduate TAs: none
Most popular majors: business, social sciences, education
Students living on campus: 20%
Guaranteed housing for four years? no
Students in fraternities or sororities: none

Students at BYU face something rather close to the traditional core curriculum. Each must take:

- Two courses in the Book of Mormon.
- One first-year writing course and one advanced writing and oral communication course.
- One quantitative reasoning course (students may test out). Students choose from 100- and 200-level math, formal logic, and statistics courses.
- One course or more from a list of approved advanced math and foreign language courses to meet the "Languages of Learning" requirement. Math choices include mathematical modeling, calculus, and higher-level logic and statistics courses. The foreign language departments offer over 50 qualifying courses, ranging from the usual language courses to "Second-Year Serbo-Croatian" and "Old Icelandic Language and Literature."
- Two courses in world civilization, one before and one after 1500.
- One course in the New Testament.

Just what does it mean that the university and LDS Church exercise academic control at BYU? Probably not what you think. "The vast array of courses use exactly the same textbooks that are used in other strong undergraduate institutions," says a professor. "The curriculum reflects the religious teaching of the church wherever it is relevant. . . . Both faculty and students in the secular courses feel free to bring LDS teachings and values into the discussion of literature, politics, or whatever—and that's why they feel more free here than they would elsewhere, where they would be discouraged from doing that." Says a student, "In math class you learn math, in science you learn science. However teachers are free to use the gospel of Jesus Christ as they are teaching, such as beginning the class with prayer." This does not mean that open dissent from the teachings of the LDS church is allowed. "Does a person have a right to voice one's beliefs? Certainly. Would he or she be allowed to openly espouse those beliefs and continue as a faculty member or student on the BYU campus? Almost certainly not," says a BYU professor. One faculty member explains that professors can discuss, for instance, abortion politics in class, but cannot openly advocate legal abortion. In the same way, he says, "Professors can't argue that the Book of Mormon is a bunch of foolishness. One of the main purposes of this university is to provide a comfortable place for Mormons to study." In 2002, the administration proposed a ban on all R-rated material in BYU classrooms, which prompted university-wide debate and in the end was rejected in favor of a set of principles according to which each teacher was expected to act responsibly in choosing suitable materials.

The percentage of non-Mormon faculty members is about the same as the percentage of students who are not Mormons: about 2 percent. The university requires that its faculty members, if Mormon, be LDS members in good standing, which means tithing, attending church regularly, being chaste, and a number of other things. Non–LDS members must still follow the school's honor code—no alcohol, premarital/extramarital sex, etc. "BYU is really far beyond what you'd expect of most religiously affiliated schools," one professor says.

BYU is an enormous university, enrolling nearly 31,000 full-time undergraduates. Around half the courses enroll between 20 and 50 students. The student-faculty ratio is 20 to 1, which means that students cannot expect to get the individualized attention characteristic of smaller liberal arts colleges. While the school says that none of its courses are taught entirely by graduate teaching assistants, one student reports that "in large general education classes, TAs have most of the personal interaction with students." One student points out that honors students enjoy the benefits of small classes all the time, even for general education classes.

Nonetheless, another student says, "at the largest private religious university in the country, you would be surprised to discover that most professors are at least somewhat regularly available to help their students." In one student's experience, "My professors are very anxious and willing to help. I have talked to four different professors about performing undergraduate research, and each was excited about the idea and ready to help me get started, in many cases even providing some funding." Another student says, "Most professors have office hours. There are a lot of resources available to students in many aspects—professors, advising, even free counseling, but many students don't realize it and therefore don't take advantage of them."

One faculty member says BYU has an "unusually strong commitment to teaching," and it is generally agreed that publishing comes after pedagogy in faculty members' minds. Students and professors name the following faculty members as some of the best at the university: Stephen E. Robinson in ancient scripture; J. Scott Miller and Dilworth Parkinson in Asian and Near Eastern languages; John F. Hall in classics; Larry H. Peer in comparative literature; Larry Shumway in humanities; Terrance F. Olson in marriage, family, and human development; James K. Lyon in Germanic and Slavic languages; Paul E. Kerry in history; James Cannon in mathematics; Ralph Hancock in political science; and Erin D. Bigler and Hal Miller in psychology.

Not surprisingly, the politics at BYU are conservative, if anything. Courses promoting any leftist theory are simply absent from the BYU curriculum. Says a professor, "The university's avowed stance is to stick to the fundamentals rather than to turn to a curriculum tricked out to serve either left- or right-wing interests." The English department's course offerings do include feminist and postmodern approaches to literature. A faculty member says, "I would say that the faculty teaching these courses definitely promote such approaches."

REQUIREMENTS (CONT'D)

- One course on the Mormon Book of Doctrine and Covenants.
- The wellness course "Fitness and Lifestyle Management," or a combination of alternative physical education courses.
- One course in American heritage, or the more in-depth combination of one American government course and one early American history course .
- A "Global and Cultural Awareness" course. These courses about foreign cultures help students when they go off on missions.
- An arts course. Choices include "Introduction to Dance," "History of Jazz," and "Northern Mesoamerican Art."
- A "letters" course. Options here include "The Italian Renaissance," "Literature of the Latter-day Saints," and "History and Philosophy of Science."
- One biological science course.
- One physical science course.
- One social science course.
- Three to four religion electives.

Although BYU is not a major research institution and spends relatively little on research (the annual average between 1996 and 2000 being just under $15 million), the university has been successful, ranking first (among 118 institutions analyzed) in the number of inventions reported relative to research spending, according to the *Chronicle of Higher Education*. BYU promotes small-scale research projects as a way to connect instructors and students, many of which culminate in marketable products. A student confirms this, saying, "There is a new focus on undergraduate research at the university. As a result, students have great opportunities to conduct research, publish scholarly papers, and secure funding." The School of Technology and Engineering owns five supercomputers, one of which has been ranked in the top 200 in the world. Any student who finds a faculty advisor can access the computer for research.

Student Life: Why ask Y?

Brigham Young University's campus is stunning. The snow-capped Wasatch Mountains tower over the school and town, and the skiing, camping, hunting, hiking, and rock climbing in the surrounding backcountry are among the best in the country. "The outdoor opportunities are what really set BYU apart as far as location goes," says a student. "Rock Canyon is only minutes from campus, Utah Lake is just across town, and world-class ski resorts are within an hour's drive. Moreover, Salt Lake City is only 45 minutes away for those who are more interested in shopping and nice restaurants." But Provo (population 111,000) can hold its own: its residents are closely tied to the university, and the communities share cultural, entertainment, and recreational resources.

"Cultural events are a big part of student life," says a student. "BYU has many talented performing groups, including choirs, . . . big ballroom dance programs, and the like." In fact, two-thirds of BYU's student performance groups tour internationally. The Utah Symphony Orchestra frequently performs on campus, and Provo is only 20 minutes from Park City, new home of the world-famous Sundance Film Festival.

Nothing is more important to BYU's mission of building a community of faith than the social and moral life of its students. Not surprisingly, then, the university has taken a great interest in student life and has plenty of guidelines and regulations in place to support students in their faith.

The honor code requires all students—even the several hundred who are of other faiths—to live by the standards of the Church of Jesus Christ of Latter-day Saints. The honor code requires students to avoid "sexual misconduct," which is defined as "premarital sex, cross-dressing, and homosexual conduct." And BYU is serious about the consequences: any of the above is grounds for suspension or expulsion. For instance, a female cast member from MTV's "The Real World" was expelled from the university for rooming with male members of the show during filming.

The BYU honor code even governs students' personal grooming habits: Men must wear their hair short and above the ears, and neither men nor women may dye their hair odd colors. Men must keep their sideburns short and are not permitted to wear a beard. Recently, the honor code was changed to prohibit women from wearing more than one earring in each ear. The dress code regulates the length of shirtsleeves, shorts, and skirts. Men's clothing is "inappropriate when it is sleeveless, revealing, or form fitting," according to the grooming standards. Women's clothing is inappropriate when it is one of those three or when it is "strapless, backless [or] has slits above the knee." Until 1998, BYU's campus theater edited versions of popular Hollywood films in order to "to avoid violent, sexual, or vulgar scenes," says a student. When film studios objected, the school stopped editing the films—in fact, it closed the theater altogether. While these policies appear excessive to some, BYU sees the regulations as part of its commitment to creating a distinctive moral atmosphere. Not surprisingly, BYU's embrace of the old *in loco parentis* role prompts a few complaints from students, especially when it comes to the school's visitation and curfew rules.

Housing at BYU, like academics and politics, is built around the ideal of a "Gospel-centered community." It pretty much goes without saying that BYU does not have any coed dorms, bathrooms, or halls. Visitors of the opposite sex are restricted to visiting hours, which usually end around midnight. Even students who live off campus are required to obey university regulations regarding visitors of the opposite sex. Although some students find the visitation rules too restrictive, the church and the university insist that they promote an environment conducive to academic success, not to mention chastity, and most BYU students agree.

Although BYU does not require any of its students to live on campus, university culture has developed so that most freshmen choose to do so and most upperclassmen do not. A staggering 80 percent of students live off campus. "This is, in part," says a student, "because nearly all of the young men leave on a two-year mission for the church after their freshman year, and when they come back they are ready for a change and live off campus." It is also due to the fact that off-campus housing costs about half of what it costs to live on campus. Students who live off campus have to live in university-approved housing, and approval is based on whether the housing in question allows the student to adhere to the standards of the honor code. So, for example, studio apartments (where the bedroom and living space are combined) do not pass muster, nor do housing facilities that allow unmarried men and women to live together. Under the system, the owners of the housing complexes become coregulators, informing their tenants of the codes of conduct, warning or evicting tenants in cases of minor or major infractions, and reporting misdeeds to the university.

As anyone familiar with the teachings of the LDS church will not be surprised to learn, alcohol consumption is banned by the school's honor code. So are tea and coffee. Consequently, the only Greek-letter organizations on campus are academic in nature.

SUGGESTED CORE
1. Classical Civilization 110, Introduction to Greek and Roman Literature
2. Philosophy 320R, Studies in Ancient Philosophy
3. Ancient Scripture 211/ 212, The New Testament *and* Ancient Scripture 301/302, The Old Testament
4. Philosophy 330R, Studies in Medieval Philosophy
5. Political Science 202, Western Political Heritage 2
6. English 232, Shakespeare
7. History 220, The United States through 1877
8. History 306, Nineteenth-Century Europe

WEST

Even with all this, a student says, "It is my experience that most of the students do not complain about the honor code—rather, they enjoy the freedom that it brings and the atmosphere that it creates. . . . Because everyone is following the honor code there is an incredible amount of trust among BYU students, even if they have never met before. . . . A student is given two to five days to take a test in the testing center. There is nothing to stop a student from telling his classmates what was on the test other than his word of honor, and BYU students are honorable." This student allows that "a few don't like some of the rules, but they abide by them anyway. After all, they chose to come to BYU."

Student government at BYU isn't like that at most other universities. "The university changed the way student government was administered since some students were just running for office and then resigning early in their terms so that they could list their election on their résumés," says a professor. Consequently, student government, or rather, the student service association (BYUSA) is now oriented toward service and extracurricular activities. Says one club president, "There is freedom to do things, but you must work to make it fit within university policies."

There are hundreds of clubs available to students, but many students find social fulfillment instead in their respective "wards." BYU students are organized geographically into units of about 150 students each. Wards include non-LDS students in their activities as well as students from other nearby colleges, should other students live nearby. The wards are almost exclusively staffed by students themselves, and almost every student has an assignment connected to his ward, such as teaching Sunday school or organizing social activities. "The ward unit meets for church every Sunday, for a 'Family Home Evening' every Monday night, as well as for weekly or monthly activities," says a student. Groups of wards combine to form a "stake," and there are more activities organized by the stake.

For many BYU students, college is largely a place to meet future spouses, and wards are ripe for such endeavors—married and single students are placed in different wards. "BYU is a good place for LDS kids who come from places where there aren't many Mormons to meet other LDS kids—most of them hoping to find one to marry," a student says. The university even publishes marriage statistics on its Web site: upon graduation, more than half of BYU students are already married. The importance of family to both BYU and the LDS church are evident in campus events; indeed, while the honor code lists the dos and don'ts, campus life actively enforces the broader values the institution seeks to instill. Each year, the school holds a "Family Expo" designed to promote LDS church family values; the theme for 2003 was "Teach Me All That I Must Do To Live with Him Someday." The Center for Women's Services and the Student Honor Association recently cosponsored a "modest fashion show." Students modeled everything from casual wear to wedding dresses. "A big part of student life is the weekly devotional every Tuesday at 11 a.m.," says a student. "It gives students a chance to get a spiritual message from professors or leaders of the church.

BYU's 21 varsity sports provide ample opportunities for spectators. The Cougars compete in the NCAA Division I in the Mountain West Conference. The university's intramurals program includes about 30 activities each year, ranging from flag football to inner-tube water polo. "Intramurals are a big deal," a student says.

Most students are genuinely happy at BYU, believing the university serves its purpose well. Says one student, "Everyone here is willing to help you, whether it is watching your stuff for a second when you leave the room or helping you study a subject you don't understand. There is an incredible spirit of cooperation amongst the students and not competition." One student, currently serving his two-year mission requirement, reflects this widespread attitude: "I love BYU. Yes, its policies are very parental, but they also tend to reflect the generally accepted standards of church members worldwide, and that is the community BYU has been created to serve. The atmosphere at BYU is wonderful, happy, and very free to me."

Crime at Brigham Young is rarely a problem. In 2003, the campus saw just one sexual assaults, eight burglaries, and five stolen cars—a drop from previous years. However, Provo is reputed to have a growing drug problem and gang presence. Thus, even though the town and campus are quite safe, the university takes steps to protect students. BYU operates a full-service police department to patrol the campus and not long ago piloted a Safewalk program, which provides escorts for students throughout the night.

Brigham Young is one of the most affordable schools in this guide—including state universities. In 2004–5, members of the LDS church—whose tithes underwrite the school—paid only $3,280 in tuition, while nonmembers paid (a still modest) $4,920. Room and board, regardless of what church one belongs to, was but $5,790. The admission process is need-blind, but the school does not attempt to meet the full need of admitted students. Approximately one-third of undergraduates receive financial aid, and the average loan burden of graduates is $11,500.

UNIVERSITY OF CALIFORNIA AT BERKELEY

BERKELEY, CALIFORNIA • WWW.BERKELEY.EDU

What it is ain't exactly clear

One year after the September 11 terrorist attacks, the University of California at Berkeley held a day of remembrance sponsored by the chancellor's office. After discussing the course of events, organizers decided that the event would exclude singing of the "Star Spangled Banner" and "God Bless America" because the songs were too patriotic, too divisive, too political. Additionally, it was decided that instead of distributing red, white, and blue ribbons, white ribbons would be given to attending students so that politics wouldn't "disrupt mourning and grieving." The American flag was to be excluded, since, according to the Graduate Assembly, it has "become a symbol of U.S. aggression toward other countries and seems hostile." When Berkeley College Republicans took to the open microphone during the ceremony to speak of patriotism, they were shouted down by the crowd.

Welcome to the University of California at Berkeley, where student activism is as celebrated as are the university's top academic programs. From Mario Salva's Free Speech Movement in 1964, to the 1969 People's Park clash, to a short-lived post–September 11 patriotic renaissance on Sproul Plaza (the campus's legendary nerve center of student activism), Cal-Berkeley has become synonymous with political tumult.

But activism aside, Berkeley has earned a formidable academic reputation since its 1868 founding. Set at the base of the Oakland foothills in the East Bay bohemian town of Berkeley, this sprawling campus is home to 33,000 students, one-third of whom are engaged in graduate work. Students seeking warm professors, small classes, and a traditional liberal arts education may find Berkeley intimidating and politically stifling. Those who disagree with the university's politics must be brave, academically focused, and willing to confront bureaucratic obstacles and political proselytizing. This, of course, is no small task.

Academic Life: We shall overcome (lax requirements)

As at many universities founded before the 1920s, Berkeley's first students enrolled in a strong core curriculum of Latin, Greek, natural history, mathematics, English, and history. Of course, things are different today—radically different. The now-gargantuan state university (comprising 14 colleges) no longer requires its students to take even a semblance of that traditional liberal arts curriculum. While the school imposes certain breadth requirements, they are malleable to the point of absurdity. "It's pretty easy to make your own schedule and avoid classes you don't want to take," one student says.

In the College of Letters and Science (L&S), students are required to take courses in certain areas. (L&S enrolls three-quarters of the school's undergraduate population and half of all PhD candidates. It offers 60 majors in 37 departments and employs nearly 800 faculty members, or about half of all faculty at Berkeley.) For instance, to complete the entire arts and literature requirement, students can take courses like "Third World Cinema" or "Literature and Sexual Identity," opting out of more traditional courses on American or British literature. Hundreds of courses fulfill the requirements in other areas. One professor maintains that "our students still graduate with a fine education," and no doubt many of them do. Yet with such broad requirements and the large selection of requirement-fulfilling classes, the university does next to nothing to ensure it.

A writing-intensive course is required of all Berkeley students, but these are frequently laden with predictable political agendas. Students can fulfill the requirement with courses from departments like African American studies, Asian American studies, and women's studies.

One professor says the economics, political science, history, and—contrary to stereotype—sociology departments are *not* terribly politicized: "In fact, they are among the best in the nation." The economics department promotes a variety of viewpoints with the goal of finding the greatest efficiencies in a mixed economic system.

Several departments recently altered their course requirements to be more lenient. For instance, history majors now must take 12 classes, including four lower-division courses that are surveys of American history, European history, any other world region's history, and an elective. History majors must also take a premodern history class (any one will do), four upper-level courses, and two seminars—one that focuses on research and one in comparative history. The department offers solid courses among the pap, fluff, and vitriol—courses like "European Civilization since the Renaissance," "New York and Philadelphia," "E Pluribus Unum—Nation Building in the Early American Republic," and "Early Greece: Bronze Age to the End of the Archaic Period." The history department requires that upper-level classes be part of a field or concentration to be defined by historical time period, geographical region, or a "theme," with topics such as gender history, colonialism and imperialism, urban history, and race and ethnicity. Given the full range of possible classes and requirements, history majors could still manage to take all of their upper-level history classes on gender or race. Additionally, the department allows stu-

VITAL STATISTICS

Religious affiliation: none
Total enrollment: 32,814
Total undergraduates: 22,880
SAT midranges: V: 580–710, M: 620–740
Applicants: 36,580
Applicants accepted: 25%
Accepted applicants who enrolled: 41%
Tuition: $5,406 (in state), $23,226 (out of state)
Room and board: $12,554
Freshman retention rate: 97%
Graduation rate: 53% (4 yrs.), 87% (6 yrs.)
Courses with fewer than 20 students: 58%
Student-faculty ratio: 16:1
Courses taught by graduate TAs: not provided
Most popular majors: social sciences, engineering, biology
Students living on campus: 35%
Guaranteed housing for four years? no
Students in fraternities: 10% sororities: 10%

The University of California at Berkeley imposes certain curricular requirements, which seem deceptively strict. In fact, given the vast number of courses that would fulfill most of them, they would be hard not to meet merely by accident. All undergraduates must:

- Demonstrate writing and reading proficiency. This can easily be satisfied by sufficient standardized test scores or high school courses.
- Show some knowledge of American history and institutions. Many students fulfill this requirement in high school; others complete an introductory course during their first year.
- Complete a requirement called "Berkeley Campus American Cultures," which is meant to "provide students with the intellectual tools to understand better their own identity and the cultural identity of others in their own terms," according to the university catalog. Students choose from courses like "Lives of Struggle: Minorities in a Majority Culture" and "History of the United States: Colonial Settlement to the Civil War."

dents to combine these fields and encourages them to derive their own plans of study. With dreary predictability, Berkeley has cut Western civilization courses and a senior thesis from its degree requirements in history.

The English department is no more traditional. "[It] has the reputation of being dominated by professors who deconstruct classic texts in order to read into them their own political agendas," says one professor. The department offers several concentrations, including sexual identities/gender studies; folklore, popular culture, and cultural theory; and Anglophone and multicultural studies. Happily, it also requires courses in "Literature in English: Through Milton," "Late Seventeenth through Mid-Nineteenth Century," and "Mid-Nineteenth Century through the Twentieth Century," in addition to a course in Shakespeare—a requirement absent from most schools' English lists these days.

Students say that among the best professors here are John McWhorter in linguistics; A. James Gregor and Nelson W. Polsby in political science; Ann Swidler in sociology; Richard M. Abrams, Thomas A. Brady, Gerald D. Feldman, and David Hollinger in history; Ronald S. Stroud in classics; David J. Vogel in business; and John R. Searle in philosophy.

Students register for classes online, but "one cannot get all the classes one wants without going on a waiting list," says a junior business major. It's not unusual for students to stay five years just to complete their graduation requirements, loose as these may be. Classes are large but are mostly taught by professors. Weekly discussion sections, on the other hand, are led by graduate students, a typical arrangement at large universities. According to students, professors are available for meetings outside class and regularly make themselves accessible during office hours. The university does not assign teachers to advise students before they have declared their majors. Berkeley instead has the Office of Undergraduate Advising, staffed by professional advisors rather than faculty members. Once a student has declared a major, he can visit an advisor within his major, but even here, the student does not have a specific faculty member who is responsible for him or to whom he is accountable. In the English department, for instance, students can schedule appointments with major advisors, and drop-in sessions are available each day.

Faculty members say grade inflation is not as bad at Berkeley as it is at other schools, but statistics contradict them. Stuart Rojstaczer, a professor at Duke University, recently examined the national grade inflation trend, and found that on average, GPAs have increased 0.144 points per decade; Berkeley's increased 0.15 points in the past decade. Grades may look better than they actually are, but students compare their own grades to those of their classmates. Berkeley is incredibly competitive, and it is no coincidence that it was a Berkeley professor who developed one of the first Web sites aimed at detecting plagiarism. According to an ABCNews.com article, when one Berkeley neurobiology professor submitted papers for 320 students to the site a few years ago, 45 of the students were found to have plagiarized at least some material.

Political bias in the classroom is widespread, and it tends to fall in one direction—care to guess which one? In 2004, the National Association of Scholars found that there were nearly 10 Democratic faculty members for every Republican faculty member. In 2003, an English graduate student, Snehal Shingavi, advised "conservative thinkers . . . to seek other sections" of his themed writing course titled "The Politics and Poetics of Palestinian Resistance." Some students and several national news outlets blasted Shingavi for his exclusionary policies, contempt for intellectual diversity, and brazen political agenda. (Though one might admire him for his candor—better to warn off students than punish them with poor grades.) "The unstated rule on the campus is that one is free to speak and to be as extreme as one wishes, but only so long as one speaks from the left," says a political science major.

The women's studies department includes the usual dismal offerings; the names alone should warn away the wary from "Gender Mathematics and Science," "Sex, Gender, and the Bible," "Russian, French, and American Novels of Adultery," and "Sex, Reproduction, and the Law." One student says the department is "abominable."

And here's one fact worth a thousand anecdotes: Berkeley's African American studies department offers more courses than the economics department.

In the name of education, Berkeley also offers what students call "de-Cal" courses, short for "Democratic Education at Cal." The courses, which focus on culture, race,

REQUIREMENTS (CONT'D)

Students in the liberal arts college must take one course in each of seven areas:

- Arts and literature. "Shakespeare" would count; so would "Reflections of Gender, Culture, and Ethnicity in American Dance."
- Biological science.
- Historical studies. Choices include "European Civilization from the Renaissance to the Present" and "Cruising the Caribbean, 1492–1970."
- International studies.
- Philosophy and values. Choices here include "Man, God, and Society in Western Literature" and "Existentialism in Literature and Film."
- Physical science.
- Social and behavioral sciences. Choices range very widely, from "Introduction to Archaeology" to "Introduction to Chicano Culture."

Liberal arts students are also required to:

- Show second-semester proficiency in a foreign language.
- Take or test out of a course in quantitative reasoning (mathematics, statistics, or computer science).
- Complete two writing-intensive courses.

gender, and sexuality, encourage students to initiate classes in "academic interests out-side the boundaries of established disciplines." Students plan the course syllabi and schedules, but they work with faculty members to arrange the courses. An official in the de-Cal program says, "We don't like to use the words 'instructor' or 'teacher.' We call them 'facilitators,' because the students lead the discussions. [Facilitators] don't really instruct or teach." Students participating in the courses can receive from one to three units of credit for each course (a normal course counts for four units). Recent de-Cal classes have included "Beverly Hills, 90210: The Philosophy behind the ZIP Code," which discussed how the popular TV show's themes (rape, sexuality, drinking, popu-larity, eating disorders, etc.) influenced the self-images of its adolescent audience; "Breasts: Their Natural History," which first examined the breast biologically and later culturally and symbolically; "The Erotic as Power"; an array of classes that discussed the political, social, and cultural importance of "The Matrix," "The Simpsons," "The West Wing," and "Will and Grace"; and "Copwatch," in which students were taught to recognize the common "abuses" of police work and went on shifts to observe and docu-ment police misconduct. There are cities in California where such a course might con-tribute to good citizenship—but Berkeley probably isn't one of them.

Student Life: Admit that the waters around you have grown

In March 2002, the *Daily Cal* reported the closure of the Normandy Massage Parlor, a Berkeley joint that had been raided by police because it was a front for a prostitution ring. It was the second Berkeley prostitution ring shut down that year. A February 2003 *California Patriot* article revealed that a Web site sponsored by the UC–Berkeley Queer Alliance and hosted on the university network was being used to organize anonymous sex in campus bathrooms. The article said that police were aware of this sort of thing, but had so far not been able to stop it. The city of Berkeley, which the university catalog used to call the "Athens of the Twentieth Century," has plenty of drug paraphernalia stores, tie-dyed T-shirts, vagrants and runaways, communist bookstores, and, well, gen-erally looks as unkempt as the hippies who once thought it paradise. One student living in what is nicknamed "Berserkeley" says, "I like the fact that the weird people are the predominant people, so being normal is weird." Telegraph Avenue is Weirdness Central.

Still, Berkeley is a functioning college town with its share of pleasant restaurants, good bookstores, and interesting shops. In their free time, students especially enjoy sampling the local music shops and bookstores. Amoeba Music, one of the area's larg-est music stores, sells both new and used CDs. Moe's Books was recently voted by stu-dents as the best area bookstore and for 40 years has served the area with over 100,000 volumes. There are also popular smoke shops, used clothing stores, and body piercing parlors in town. The reliable Bay Area Rapid Transit (BART) train system runs through-out the Bay Area, as does an extensive but less punctual bus system.

Since Berkeley offers relatively low in-state tuition and reserves spots for Califor-nia residents, a large proportion of students—89 percent—come from California. Thus, Berkeley has a more parochial student body than do some other prestigious public universities, such as the University of Michigan or the University of Virginia. However, UC–Berkeley is not primarily a residential campus, as only 8,000 students, most of whom are first years, live in the university dorms. As at most large urban universities, students usually move off campus into theme houses, Greek houses, or privately owned residences after their freshman year. Housing is offered on a space-available basis, and late applicants are usually forced to live in non-university-owned residences. Most residences are coed, but the university does have one all-women dorm and one all-men dorm. In many coed dormitories, men and women are separated by floor. Berkeley does have coed bathrooms in most dormitories; students should certainly be aware of this before signing housing contracts. Theme houses are university-owned facilities in which students with common interests live together. For instance, a student can choose to live in the African American house; the gay, lesbian, bisexual, and transgender house; or the "women in engineering and science" house. Most students purchase dining debit cards, deducting the cost of meals in university dining halls with each swipe. The campus has five dining halls in addition to five restaurants.

Since classes are rarely scheduled on Fridays, weekends at UC–Berkeley traditionally begin on Thursday evenings. Besides the dozens of bars and clubs in Berkeley, the school is also home to more than 40 Greek organizations, to which about 10 percent of undergraduates belong. According to several students, Greek life is robust and the organizations are very active throughout the school year. This seems likely to change in the wake of a 2005 decision to ban "alcohol consumption at all events held by campus fraternities and sororities," according to the *Chronicle of Higher Education*. The school's dean of students explained the ban by pointing to an "alarming increase in problems with alcohol abuse, hazing, fights, and badly managed parties." We wonder how strictly the school will crack down on other intoxicating substances.

The school's proximity to San Francisco (15 minutes by BART) and the area's wide selection of restaurants and cultural attractions offer a welcome distraction from intense studying. But if trips to San Francisco or crowds at local bars don't sound appealing, students can participate in the activities of the many student groups on campus. UC–Berkeley has nearly 700 student groups, including sketch comedy troupes, traditional Korean drumming squads, film leagues, dozens of bizarre activist groups, and more common political organizations like the College Democrats and the College Republicans. Many of the activist groups are leftist and go beyond the traditional Green Party and Democrat college organizations. Berkeley's student organizations include the International Socialist Organization, Left Turn, Berkeley Stop the War Coalition,

SUGGESTED CORE
1. Classics 34, Epic Poetry: Homer and Virgil
2. Classics C36, Greek Philosophy and Ancient Philosophy
3. Religious Studies 119, The English Bible as Literature
4. Religious Studies 120A and B, Origins of Christianity
5. Political Science 112B, History of Political Theory
6. English 17, Shakespeare
7. History 7A, Introduction to History of the United States
8. History 163A and B, Modern European Intellectual History (*closest match*)

WEST

Berkeley Democratic Socialists of America, Students for Justice in Palestine, Berkeley ACLU, Progressive Labor Party, the Assyrian Student Alliance, the Somali Student Association, and the Berkeley Anarchist Discussion Group. All student groups must register with the Associated Students of the University of California (ASUC), a powerful body composed of student senators who help determine campus policy on student groups. ASUC also allots more than $1 million annually in student fees to various groups. The university hosts several hundred lectures, art shows, and other student and professional performances each year.

The *California Patriot*, a monthly conservative magazine, has garnered national attention for its assessments of Berkeley's hard left. In February 2002, radical ethnic separatists stole a print run of 4,000 copies. The group responsible, MEChA, is a student movement that teaches the superiority of the Mexican race, holds anti-Semitic views, and promotes the return of California, Arizona, and New Mexico to Mexico. For a while, invigorated College Republicans formed alliances with moderate Democrats to isolate the hard left, and they staged opposition rallies in Sproul Plaza. Things have since returned to normal. According to members of the Berkeley GOP, relations with the university Democrats became a bit frostier by the time of the 2004 elections. "They're much more cautious" in cooperating with the campus right, says one student.

The student-run paper, the *Daily Californian*, covers news well, but compared to other university dailies lacks substance. Other publications available on campus include the radical *MIM Notes*, the official publication of the Maoist International Movement, and the International Socialist Organization's national paper, the *Socialist Worker*.

Surprisingly, amidst the plethora of leftist organizations, Berkeley maintains a thriving and successful ROTC program, and the CIA and Department of Defense recruit from Berkeley during campus career fairs.

Berkeley fields 25 varsity athletic teams in the Pac-10 Conference. The Golden Bears maintain a heated rivalry with Stanford. The school also has a number of intramural offerings and excellent facilities to accommodate them.

Berkeley is consistently among the top five universities in arrests for alcohol, drugs, and weapons. Crime statistics for 2003 show 30 motor vehicle thefts, 10 robberies, nine assaults, 11 forcible sex offenses, more than 110 arrests for drug law violations, and 80 burglaries—all on campus. The university is so intermingled with the city of Berkeley that it is hard to separate the two or to insulate students from urban pathologies (or the city from pathological students). The university has tried to curb crime with self-defense workshops, night escort services and shuttles, and round-the-clock patrols.

Berkeley is a good deal for students from California, with 2004–5 tuition at only $5,406. Adventurous souls from other states paid $23,226. Room and board was a very high $12,554. Admission to the school is *not* need-blind, but two-thirds of students receive some form of financial aid. The average student loan debt of recent graduates is $16,354.

UNIVERSITY OF CALIFORNIA AT DAVIS

DAVIS, CALIFORNIA • WWW.UCDAVIS.EDU

Green thumb

Originally conceived as a school of agriculture, the University of California at Davis was added to the state higher education system in 1905. During World War II, the Davis campus closed, trading plowshares for swords as young GIs trained on campus. Only after the war did Davis add a liberal arts program, and not until 1960 did the number of non-agriculture students match the number of agriculture students. With the relative decline in the number of students seeking agricultural training, the challenge for UC–Davis has been to find its niche as a modern public university in a state full of excellent public universities.

Liberal arts students now outnumber agriculture students almost two to one at UC–Davis, although the school still maintains strong programs in areas like agronomy, pomology (the study of fruit cultivation), avian science, and fermentation. And the school has moved far beyond the old stereotype of a "cow college." According to the *Chronicle of Higher Education*, the school "takes an interdisciplinary approach to agriculture by incorporating social science, economics, and land-planning policy into its environmental science major." The *Chronicle* notes that the school's wine program "has a worldwide reputation among winemakers."

One result of the influx of liberal arts students and faculty has been the development of a more politically charged campus. Students have at times made issues like abortion and the crisis in the Middle East into matters of intense local concern. Still, some say UC–Davis is the most relaxed of the schools in the University of California system. The town of Davis is surrounded by farmland. Most students ride their bikes to class and to extracurricular events. Some students even bypass the dining halls to grow their own food in university-owned cooperatives. And while UC–Davis wants to be known as more than an ag school, its roots in the local soil make UC–Davis refreshingly distinctive.

VITAL STATISTICS

Religious affiliation: none
Total enrollment: 30,230
Total undergraduates: 23,472
SAT/ACT midranges: SAT V: 510–630, M: 570–670; ACT: 21–27
Applicants: 32,506
Applicants accepted: 60%
Accepted applicants who enrolled: 25%
Tuition: $6,936 (in state), $23,892 (out of state)
Room and board: $10,234
Freshman retention rate: 93%
Graduation rate: 51% (4 yrs.), 81% (6 yrs.)
Courses with fewer than 20 students: 31%
Student-faculty ratio: 19:1
Courses taught by graduate TAs: not provided
Most popular majors: social sciences, agriculture, engineering
Students living on campus: 20%
Guaranteed housing for four years? no
Students in fraternities: 8% sororities: 9%

WEST

Academic Life: Germination

Like many schools with an agricultural heritage, UC–Davis imposes rather scant distribution requirements. All students must take:

- A basic writing proficiency course known as English 57 (or show college-level writing proficiency through SAT II, AP, or other writing test scores).
- Three courses in "arts and humanities." Choices include "The History of Western Civilization" and "Chinese Painting." (Arts and humanities majors are exempt.)
- Three courses in "science and engineering." (Science and engineering majors are exempt.)
- Three courses in the social sciences. (Social science majors are exempt.)
- A course in "social-cultural diversity." Choices include "Black Images in Popular Culture," "Sports in American Society," and "Theory and History of Sexualities."
- Three "writing experience" classes, which may come from almost any academic department.

UC–Davis has three undergraduate colleges: the College of Letters and Science, the College of Engineering, and the oldest of the three, the College of Agricultural and Environmental Sciences. Requirements differ by school. Strangely, a student is exempted from general education courses in the area in which his major falls; for instance, a history major does not have to take any other courses in arts and humanities beyond the required courses for his major. The result of these loose guidelines is that outside their majors, students have virtually free rein in choosing courses—which sounds to us less like liberty than license. Among the school's scant requirements are writing-intensive courses, which do not necessarily teach writing or English skills explicitly. One professor calls the writing requirement "weak," saying that "in many instances, writing is required but not carefully examined for its quality."

Each major provides a little more structure than do the distribution requirements. History majors, for example, must complete a total of 15 courses designed to introduce them to the histories of a broad sampling of geographic areas. The introductory courses include two courses in each of the following areas: Western civilization, Asian civilization, United States and Latin America, and Africa. English majors must complete introductory work in writing, reading, drama, fiction, and poetry before advancing to more challenging coursework. Each English major must also complete a required class in literary criticism, choose one of three courses on Shakespeare, and take courses in medieval, Renaissance, British, and American literature. These fine requirements should give English majors a solid foundation in their chosen area of specialization. UC–Davis also gives structure to the political science major through carefully selected requirements. After completing introductory work in American politics, comparative politics, international relations, and political theory, as well as an introductory course in statistics, political science majors then choose eight electives at the advanced level.

For most majors, UC–Davis requires at least 15 courses; most other universities ask students to take only about 10. On the other hand, UC–Davis's courses are shorter—and may provide less depth—because the school runs on a 10-week quarter system. The difficulty of courses at Davis varies widely. One student says, "Students can get away with taking easy courses, but most people are smart enough to know it's a bad idea to do this." Another student says that most classes are rigorous, "but students can take a full load and still have time for social activities."

The best programs are in economics, biology, psychology, and English; the agricultural programs also remain strong. A computer science major says his department "isn't that stellar, and I've learned the most through a job I've had." Ethnic studies departments are filled with faculty members who are usually more activists than scholars. Students say that some of the best teachers at the school are Winder McConnell in German, Jay Mechling in American studies, Victor Caston in philosophy, Peter Lindert in economics, and Larry Peterman in political science.

Upon arriving at the university, students are encouraged to visit the Advising Services office for information on fulfilling the general education requirements; there they will meet with professional advisors or peer advisors (undergraduates). Once a student has declared a major, he can meet with a faculty member in his department. One peer advisor says that in her major, psychology, there is just one faculty member responsible for all the department's majors. So although a student will meet with a faculty advisor, it is unlikely that the two will foster any real relationship. Students say that advisors in the sciences tend to be more knowledgeable and helpful than those in the liberal arts. An engineering student says, "So far, the advising program has been fine for me, but I have heard some horror stories."

UC–Davis is a large state school, and although the admissions department claims that the university is able to keep class sizes small, the typical class enrolls between 20 and 60 students, certainly more than at most liberal arts institutions. Professors teach most courses, but basic composition and introductory foreign language courses, as well as laboratory classes, are often led by graduate teaching assistants. Although some students are able to develop serious academic relationships with their professors, most students are more interested in life outside the classroom. "I find few students with any deep intellectual curiosity," says one English professor. "The majority want the diploma as [a] job-hunting credential." Indeed, as much as the university would like to change its focus from an agricultural/vocational school to a more academically diverse one, it has had trouble attracting students who care about learning and take every opportunity to gain knowledge from their instructors.

REQUIREMENTS (CONT'D)

- One course in American history and institutions. This can be fulfilled by passing one of the approved courses in history, political science, economics, Native American studies, African American and African studies, or Asian American studies. It can also be satisfied through high school American history coursework, or AP testing.

  Students in the College of Letters and Science must also fulfill a "breadth requirement" by taking three upper-division courses in a department outside their major departments; three upper- or lower-division courses in art, music, or dramatic art; or a minor in any university program. Some degrees also require students to show proficiency—either through coursework or tests—in a foreign language.

One exception is the Integrated Studies Program, a residential honors program for the university's top 70 freshmen. The program Web page says that courses are taught by "10 faculty members committed to undergraduate teaching who are disciplinary specialists with a particular interest in how their field is related to other disciplines and to contemporary issues." Honors students take three special honors courses and two seminars. Honors courses offered last year included "Playing Shakespeare," "Americans Debate Their Rights," and "The Constitution."

One conservative student says, "Fortunately, most professors are professional and try to keep their classes neutral. I have taken three political science courses [and] many general elective studies and in all cases I found I was unable to discern their political leanings." However, some professors join in the campus political debate by providing politicized courses. To mention just a few among a wide variety, the history course "Crime and Punishment in Early Modern Europe," according to the catalog, "examines the impact of gender, sexual orientation, ethnicity, and class in processes of criminalization." The women's studies course "Colonialism, Nationalism, and Women" explores the relationship between feminist theory and postcolonialism. If your feminist theory is a little rusty, you can take any numbers of courses as a primer, including "Introduction to Feminist Theory," "Feminism and the Politics of Family Change," "Contemporary Masculinities," or several courses dealing with feminism in film. "Feminist Approaches to Inquiry" seeks to redefine "traditional disciplinary practices [and] current issues and methodologies" according to feminist beliefs. May we suggest a wine course instead?

Student Life: Down on the farm

When college students fantasize about attending school in sunny California, the town of Davis is not generally the place they have in mind. Still, Davis, located 15 miles west of Sacramento in the fertile Sacramento Valley, is a friendly and welcoming place. With a population of just 56,000, Davis is dominated by its large student population, making it one of the few real college towns in the UC system. The central campus is adjacent to downtown Davis, which caters to students but has a folksy, artsy, environmentally friendly character of its own, with a community theater and plenty of art galleries and shops. Davis's campus, the largest in the California system, includes more than 5,200 acres. Peppering the grassy fields of the campus are a number of eclectic academic and residential buildings, many of which hint at the mission style common at California's universities.

About 90 percent of incoming freshmen choose to live in university-owned housing, although it is not required. Most freshmen live in double-occupancy rooms, but the university also offers some singles and four-person suites. UC–Davis housing includes both coed and single-sex floors and one women-only residence hall. All dorm rooms, however, are single sex, as are all bathrooms. Freshmen are guaranteed housing, but after the first year, housing availability is limited enough that the university cannot guarantee it for every student—in fact, only a fifth of the total student body does live on campus. Of these, approximately 30 students live in a community called (after one of Tolkien's hobbit holes) "Baggins End," in which residents have three acres of garden space to plant and maintain. As the housing Web page says, "the living environment . . . emphasizes community, cooperation, and responsibility." There are also a few other cooperatives available for students who choose to live in them.

The African Diaspora house "focuses upon the academic and cultural enrichment of UC–Davis students interested in the social, political, and cultural concerns of the African diaspora"; it is managed by a private company rather than the UC–Davis residential office. Students say housing costs are more reasonable than in some other college towns, especially those in California, but still more expensive than nearby Sacramento or Woodland. Students living off campus can commute to campus by the Unitrans bus system (which is free) or by bike—an impressively popular mode of transportation. The university reports that there are more than 40,000 bikes in Davis, and the city has made bicycle commuting safe through various citywide measures.

> ### SUGGESTED CORE
>
> 1. Classics 140, Homer and the Ancient Epic
> 2. Philosophy 21, History of Philosophy: Ancient
> 3. Religious Studies 21, Hebrew Scriptures *and* Religious Studies 40, New Testament
> 4. History 130A, Christianity and Culture in Europe, 50–1450
> 5. Political Science 118B, History of Political Theory
> 6. English 118, Shakespeare
> 7. History 17A, History of the United States
> 8. History 147A, European Intellectual History, 1800–1870

Further housing options are provided by fraternity and sorority houses. With 22 sororities and 30 fraternities, Davis provides students plenty of Greek options, although fewer than 10 percent of students join.

More than 96 percent of UC–Davis students come from California, but an admissions officer says that the university does not reserve a certain percentage for in-state residents. Many are first-generation college students who work part-time to subsidize their tuitions. Some say there is no typical UC–Davis student, and what one student calls "unsophisticated" another student calls "normal." And that is a word not often heard at UC–Davis's sister schools in Berkeley or Los Angeles.

The UC–Davis Aggies are currently in the second year of a four-year transition period from NCAA Division II to Division I. UC–Davis will join the Big West athletic conference in most sports once it completes the transition. With 25 varsity sports teams, from football to women's water polo, the Davis athletic program offers opportunities for various tastes and talents. The university also maintains several club sports, such as cycling, fencing, and ice hockey, and its extensive intramurals program caters to 14,000 students every year. The university's athletic facilities include an equestrian center.

The Davis campus is active politically, despite its agricultural focus. Recently, when a group of students organized a public protest against abortion by passing out literature and displaying images of aborted fetuses, many UC–Davis students claimed to be personally offended, according to the student newspaper, the *California Aggie*. Angry students, who said they felt assaulted by the images, asked the administration to reconsider its free speech policy. A feminist student associated with the Women's Center

WEST

proclaimed, "We're having the university take another look at the policy especially because their information was so misleading and full of inaccuracies." She added that the protest would have been welcome if the antiabortion group had used "accurate" information. More recently, the antiabortion group, Human Life Alliance, ran a paid advertisement in the school newspaper. Outraged, the student senate passed a resolution demanding that the newspaper accept only more "accurate" advertisements. Some members of the senate earnestly argued that the paper hand over its advertising fee to a group like Planned Parenthood or, weirdly, "an agency that works toward ending racism and anti-Semitism," according to the *Aggie*. A member of the conservative activist group Young Americans for Freedom says, "The leftists control the student government and abuse their power when they see fit to do so, but the dedicated conservatives on campus do fight back and hold their own. The campus is definitely a political battlefield."

The ideological battles extend well beyond the abortion debate. The Davis campus has been the target of a number of hate crimes, including an arson attack on a synagogue and a violent assault on several Asian students. Tension between the Jewish and Palestinian communities has been particularly high in the past several years. The university's Cross-Cultural Center has been the locus of much controversy. Various political and ethnic groups elect "interns" to represent their interests at the multicultural center. When Palestinian representatives set up screensavers with pictures of Israel's flag aflame, Jewish representatives became incensed and demanded that their opponents remove T-shirts reading "Free Palestine." Not exactly the kind of improved ethnic relations the university had in mind when it created the Cross-Cultural Center, we're guessing. Given the bubbling political tensions present on campus, it is not surprising that students have organized many politically oriented groups, including pro-Palestinian and pro-Israel groups, pro-life and pro-choice groups, the College Democrats and the College Republicans, the conservative Young Americans for Freedom and the liberal Third World Forum. One student says that the most active liberal groups are Students for Justice in Palestine, the International Socialist Organization, and two university-funded organizations: the aforementioned Cross-Cultural Center and the Lesbian, Gay, Bisexual, Transgender Resource Center.

Among Davis's long-standing traditions is Picnic Day, a springtime festival dating to 1909 that includes food, concerts, competitions, and crafts. Diversity Days, a "celebration of campus differences," is, as one might guess, of more recent vintage. Last year's festival included a forum on the war on Iraq, a lecture titled "The Struggle for Peace and Justice in Guatemala," and a number of musical performances.

To prevent campus crime, the university has instituted a number of safety services. First, all students who live on campus are required to take a seminar on personal safety. The Campus Violence Protection Program also holds safety and self-defense courses for students. The school provides an escort service for students out late at night and has placed emergency call boxes all around campus. Not all students feel safe, however, and some have raised concerns about inadequate campus lighting. "I don't feel safe walking at night on campus," one female student says. The most common crimes on and around the Davis campus are burglaries and thefts. In 2003 there were 64 burglaries on campus (after 81 the previous year), 13 motor vehicle thefts, and 19 forcible sexual offenses.

Admission to UC–Davis is need-blind, and roughly half of the undergraduate student body receives need-based financial aid.

UNIVERSITY OF CALIFORNIA AT LOS ANGELES

LOS ANGELES, CALIFORNIA • WWW.UCLA.EDU

The multi cult

Most students who choose to attend the University of California at Los Angeles know what they're getting into before they move to the city. So it's not too surprising that students accentuate the positives—sunny beaches, Hollywood glamour, and in-state tuition—and try to ignore the negatives, which include huge classes and very little interaction with professors. Some students find the atmosphere so pleasing that they even linger at the school for a few extra years.

Another way in which the southern California milieu is reflected at UCLA is through the school's vaunted "diversity"; UCLA's literature boasts that it is the "most multicultural" university in the country. There is a large nonwhite population, but that in and of itself is not enough to make UCLA a "multicultural" environment, at least in the eyes of ideologues. Rather, it is the school's proliferation of ethnic studies programs, courses obsessed with race, and segregated graduation ceremonies that give it top multicultural honors. One needn't subscribe to melting-pot ideology—the mirror image of difference-obsessed multiculturalism—to wish that UCLA took more seriously its opportunity to unite the ethnically divided southern California community by offering a common curriculum and integrated campus life.

Academic Life: San Andreas faults

Upon application, UCLA students choose to pursue a degree in one of the university's five undergraduate programs: the College of Letters and Science, the School of Engineering and Applied Science, the School of Arts and Architecture, the School of Nursing, and the School of Theater, Film, and Television. With almost 23,000 students (graduate and undergraduate), Letters and Science is by far the largest academic entity at UCLA and indeed is the largest letters and science school in the University of California system. UCLA is on a quarter calendar, so students graduate having taken more courses than the typical college student. It is not always clear whether this is a good thing, as we shall see.

As at most state schools, the quality of a UCLA education depends heavily on the motivation and choices of the student. "There are definitely certain classes here at UCLA known for being easy," says one student, "but the number of challenging classes far outweigh[s] them." One engineering major says that the courseload is rigorous, particularly in the sciences, but for other majors "it really depends on what the student is after. Students can choose four difficult classes a quarter or get by with one or two and some fluff courses."

Some 13 percent of the student body does not graduate within six years. In-state tuition is only $6,485 a year, though it is expected to go up because of the California budget deficit. In a recent letter to students, UCLA president Robert Dynes warned students and parents that fees would rise faster than financial aid, requiring greater family contributions. Still, the school's relatively low price—along with the fringe benefits of living in L.A.—evidently prompts some students to take their sweet time in finishing up. To counter this trend, the administration has recently been trying to implement a "minimum progress per quarter" requirement. The idea is unpopular with students, especially with those who work part time.

Some of the better teachers at UCLA include Steven A. Hardinger in organic chemistry; James Q. Wilson (emeritus) and Victor Wolfenstein in political science; Sebastian Edwards in economics; Michael J. Allen, Edward I. Condren, and Debora K. Shuger in English; Martie Haselton in psychology; and Ruth Bloch, Patrick Geary, Carlo Ginzburg, and Richard Rouse in history. Special marks have also been given by students to Marc Trachtenberg (political science). "He is incredible—very rational, very balanced, very accessible, infectiously excited about his subject, and a true academic," says one. "He is one of the founders of the Historical Society, an organization set up to counter the postmodern orthodoxy of the American Historical Association."

The biology, chemistry, and economics departments are among the university's strongest. The philosophy department is one of the best in the nation; according to its Web page, "The undergraduate program in philosophy is not directed at career objectives. . . . Philosophy is taught to undergraduates primarily as a contribution to their liberal education." Philosophy majors take 13 courses in the department, including three basic courses in Greek philosophy, medieval and early modern philosophy, and modern philosophy, plus seven others divided among the history of philosophy, logic and semantics, ethics and value theory, and metaphysics and epistemology. Students say Sean Kelsey and Gavin Lawrence in the department are particularly good.

As Hollywood is only a short distance away, it comes as no surprise that UCLA's department of film, television, and digital media is the best in the country. It is also one of the most competitive; each year 1,400 applicants vie for the 60 spots reserved for undergraduates. Once admitted into the junior/senior year program, students can take courses like "History of Documentary Film," "Writing for Animation," "Producing and Directing Remote Multicamera Production," "Cinematography," "World Media Systems," and "Film Editing."

UCLA offers 114 majors in its five undergraduate schools, and many students choose to double-major or earn minors. For students interested in research as undergraduates, UCLA is an excellent choice. The Student Research Program offers about 1,500 slots per year in a range of projects; in addition to the experience, it "is a good way to create close, long-lasting relationships with a couple professors," a student says. The Undergraduate Research Center also supports student research in the humanities and social sciences every year.

Some of the larger lecture classes at UCLA enroll more than 300 students. "In a class such as that, the one way to form a real relationship is to go to the professor's office hours and to make yourself known by participating and asking questions," a student says. "It is not impossible to make an impression on a professor in a class of that size; it just requires some effort." Typically, professors teach larger courses and have graduate teaching assistants lead weekly discussion sections. In the smaller departments like philosophy and some of the languages, students are more likely to know their instructors well. The university's advising program varies from department to department. The College of Letters and Science offers a peer counseling program with "undergraduates trained to provide counseling and respond to student questions and concerns." Once a student has declared a major, he can visit a faculty or staff advisor in that department. The classics department, for instance, has one faculty member and one staff member to answer the questions of all the students majoring in the subject. There are also extra advising resources for athletes, honors students, and students who represent the first generation in their families to attend college.

With smaller class sizes and distinguished faculty members, one would think that the university's Honors Collegium would give advanced students the opportunity to do exactly what its mission says: "to learn, think critically and creatively, and communicate effectively." But most of the seminars offered as part of the program focus on nonfoundational topics. Courses with titles like "Perils of Living in Space: Introduction to Space Weather," "Roots of Patriarchy: Ancient Goddesses and Heroines," and "Midwives, Mothers, and Medicine: Perspectives on the History of Childbirth Stress and Coping" do not inspire confidence. The college's General Education Cluster Pro-

VITAL STATISTICS
Religious affiliation: none
Total enrollment: 24,946
Total undergraduates: 24,946
SAT/ACT midranges: SAT: 1180–1410; ACT: 24–30
Applicants: 43,199
Applicants accepted: 23%
Accepted applicants who enrolled: 37%
Tuition: $6,485 (in state), $17,304 (out of state)
Room and board: $11,928
Freshman retention rate: 97%
Graduation rate: 57% (4 yrs.), 87% (6 yrs.)
Courses with fewer than 20 students: 49%
Student-faculty ratio: 18:1
Courses taught by graduate TAs: not provided
Most popular majors: economics, psychology, biology
Students living on campus: 35%
Guaranteed housing for four years? no
Students in fraternities: 14% sororities: 11%

ACADEMIC REQUIREMENTS

Like all institutions in the University of California system, UCLA requires its students to complete only two university-wide requirements (as opposed to the four required until very recently):

- "Subject A" (two quarter courses of writing proficiency) or English as a second language. Many students place out by earning an appropriate score in English on standardized tests.
- An American history and institutions course. This requirement can be satisfied by either foundational courses or "American Popular Literature," "History of the Chicano Peoples," or "African American Literature since the 1960s."

Students in the College of Letters and Science face a few more requirements. They must do the following:

- Show proficiency in quantitative reasoning by taking a basic statistics, math, or computer science course.
- Take or test out of three quarters in a foreign language.

gram allows entering freshmen to participate in interdisciplinary study in small-group seminars, thereby fulfilling one-third of their general education requirements. While the program gives freshmen the chance to get to know their professors and fellow students well (students stay with the same peers all year), the price of participation is a willingness to endure the program's dreary, heavy-handed ideological agenda. For example, in one cluster, "Interracial Dynamics in American Culture, Society, and Literature," students study the "construction of race and its position in [twenty-first-]century American society." The college viewbook spotlights a student taking the cluster "Sports and Racism," which he says was the best choice in his academic career. One can only wonder what the worst choice was.

UCLA has more ethnic studies departments than even the most ardent multiculturalist could reasonably hope for: African American studies, American Indian studies, Asian American studies, Chicana/o studies, European studies, Islamic studies, Latina/o American Studies, Near Eastern studies, women's studies, East Asian studies, Indo-European studies, and lesbian, gay, and transgender studies. Many of these departments are politicized, simply mediocre, or both. The women's studies department offers such intellectual gems as "Maya Women and Contemporary Social Change," "Women Healers, Ritual, and Transformation," and "The Media and Aggression against Women." Many women's studies courses are cross-listed with the lesbian, gay, and transgender studies department, including "Sexuality and the City: Queer Los Angeles," "Chicana Lesbian Literature," and "Gay and Lesbian Perspectives in Pop Music." In the ethnomusicology department, students earn credit for "Music of Bebop" and "The Cultural History of Rap."

Even more traditional departments have been infiltrated. A classics professor proudly proclaims in the course catalog that "issues of politics, religion, race, ethnicity, gender, and sexuality provide an overall framework of analysis in almost all my courses." Fortunately, UCLA does not as yet have a cultural diversity requirement, although some activists have been pushing for it for years. One volunteer for the group Women 4 Change laments, "I have heard that a student can graduate without taking any ethnic studies or sensitivity training courses." We trust that this shocking situation will soon be remedied.

Student Life: Off to see the wizard

UCLA's viewbook boasts that the school is "a university of diversity." If diversity means simply the presence of many different races and ethnicities, UCLA is indeed an incredibly diverse school, with Asian and white students at 33 and 38 percent, respectively, Hispanic students at 15 percent, and black students at 4 percent. However, the *Chronicle of Higher Education* reports that the current minority population is only about 80 percent of what it was before 1998, when the University of California system abolished racial preferences in admissions. UCLA is making every effort to attract more minority students, says a student, by implementing programs to help students from disadvantaged socioeconomic backgrounds succeed academically (for instance, by offering free tutoring).

Predictably, though, races and ethnicities at UCLA tend to segregate themselves. It is a telling fact that UCLA sponsors segregated graduation ceremonies. "Lavender Graduation" is a commencement ceremony for gay, lesbian, bisexual, and transgender students. Most notably, "La Raza Graduation" is sponsored by Movimiento Estudiantil Chicano de Aztlán (MEChA), a Mexican liberation group with the motto, "For the race, everything. Against the race, nothing." In its "Plan Espiritual de Aztlán" MEChA has declared: "In the spirit of a new people that is conscious not only of its proud historical heritage but also of the brutal 'gringo' invasion of our territories, we, the Chicano inhabitants and civilizers of the northern land of Aztlán from whence came our forefathers, reclaiming the land of their birth and consecrating the determination of our people of the sun, declare that the call of our blood is our power, our responsibility, and our inevitable destiny." In essence, this means detaching the formerly Mexican southwestern United States, and reuniting it with a "revolutionized" Mexico.

Other race-specific ceremonies are held for blacks, Filipinos, Pacific Islanders, and American Indians. The university helps fund all of these. One student finds that many black and Latino students do self-segregate, but says, "It seems to me this is more a function of cultural segregation. Inner-city students, who are predominately black or Latino, do not mix much with students from suburban areas, who are generally white or Asian."

REQUIREMENTS (CONT'D)

- Take three courses in "foundations of the arts and humanities," including one from each of the following three categories: literary and cultural analysis, philosophical and linguistic analysis, and visual and performance arts analysis and practice. There are hundreds of courses to choose from, including foundational studies in various disciplines and much narrower classes.
- Take three courses in "foundations of society and culture"—one in historical analysis, another in social analysis, and a third from either subgroup.
- Take four courses in the "foundations of scientific inquiry," including two from life sciences and two from physical sciences, with a laboratory credit accompanying at least one course from each subgroup.

Depending on his major, the UCLA student can exempt himself from two general education courses. For example, an English major is exempt from one general humanities course and the literature course requirement.

Campus activism usually centers on the issues of race and ethnicity. The American Indian Student Association (AISA), a small but militant group, stages an anti–Columbus Day celebration each year. Many AISA members refuse to enter the anthropology building because it houses Indian bones (there are European and African bones there, too). When the School of Education invited First Lady Laura Bush to campus to give the commencement address, students raised a ruckus. Although Mrs. Bush is a former teacher and librarian who is active in education issues, the campus daily reported that students found her credentials "shallow" and thought that she was invited only because of her politics. In the end, Mrs. Bush declined, but not before days of UCLA student protests. And when the *Daily Bruin* ran an Independent Women's Foundation ad listing the "Top 10 Most Common Feminist Myths," UCLA feminists demanded that the *Bruin* run an apology and admit its error, reports columnist John Leo. One student said, "I think it was a violent ad, a very hostile ad. It breeds a very bad attitude toward women."

UCLA, in short, can often seem like a haven for hellraisers, with protests each week, chalked messages such as "Free Palestine" and "Living Wage Now" all over campus, and leftist student groups holding meetings nearly every night. But the fact is that a relatively small group of students stages these events. One of the most popular political organizations is Student Empowerment!, a coalition of leftist and minority student groups that really does use the exclamation mark in its name. Recently, some students have been fighting to have nonstudent workers unionized and their wages increased. Conservative students have outlets with the Bruin College Republicans, who, when it isn't an election year, spend most of their time putting pressure on the *Daily Bruin* to balance its coverage.

Residential life at UCLA is mainly for freshmen. About 90 percent of all first-years choose to live on campus, but only about 35 percent of the total undergraduate population does. The university guarantees housing for only two years, but it does provide apartment and house-share listings and a roommate matching service, and maintains five off-campus apartment buildings so students won't be left out in the cold—or rather, the Los Angeles sunshine. By 2007, the school expects to be able to guarantee four years of housing to those who want it. If a student does live on campus, he will find himself in one of four high-rise dormitories in one of two buildings with residential suites (two bedrooms, no kitchen), or better yet, in one of two village-type apartment complexes. All on-campus dormitories are coed, but some have floors that are separated by sex. Bathrooms are all single sex.

Besides housing, UCLA has all the amenities of a small town. The school has its own police department and power plant, 12 restaurants, three coffeehouses, movie theaters and other entertainment halls, medical services, and plenty of athletic facilities. But students aren't exactly trapped on campus. The typical UCLA student is active in all kinds of areas. One student says that many of her friends do volunteer work and community service in Los Angeles on the weekends. At night, students enjoy clubs, restaurants, and shopping. Third Street Promenade, a popular attraction accessible by bus and car, has movie theaters, restaurants, and shops and is close to the Pacific Ocean and Santa Monica Pier. Westwood itself, where UCLA is located, offers attractions and nightlife closer to home.

On campus, dorms sponsor events such as ice cream socials and other get-togethers but are mostly geared toward freshmen. Fraternities and sororities, while off campus, are growing in popularity. Fraternity Row, in Westwood, swarms with parties, especially on Thursday nights. Besides the Greek system (to which more than 10 percent of students belong), other popular student organizations include community service groups, activist and political groups such as CALPirg, groups devoted to voter registration and inner-city tutoring, and various campus media outlets. UCLA helps fund several ethnically oriented magazines, including *Al-Talib* (a Muslim paper), *Ha'Am* (Jewish), *La Gente de Aztlan* (Chicano, Latino, and Native American), *Nommo* (African), *Pacific Ties* (Asian), and *Ten Percent* (gay, lesbian, transsexual, and transgender).

UCLA attracts all sorts of speakers, lecturers, and performers; recent guests have included Bill Gates, Whoopie Goldberg, and Tom Hanks, as well as a host of political speakers, including a few conservative ones. UCLA has excellent music and theater departments, and student-run productions are usually of very high quality (and cheap, too).

Maintaining muscle tone is as important to most UCLA students as a healthy tan. Athletics at UCLA are consequently very popular. In addition to 22 varsity teams (and a whopping 88 combined NCAA national titles, best in the land), UCLA offers many opportunities for club and intramural sports. The intramurals Web page claims it coordinates the sports activities of more than 2,200 teams each year. It has been three decades since the Wizard of Westwood, John Wooden, held the reins of UCLA's men's basketball team. Wooden won 10 titles while at UCLA. Since he retired, the team has managed to win only one—not good enough for the Bruins' fans. They now place their hopes in a new coach, Ben Howland, who was hired before the 2003–4 season and has raised expectations for the team.

Religious life at UCLA runs the gamut; the chaplaincy offers clerics of every major faith—although few of these clergy appear to hew to the traditional morals of their respective faiths. The University Catholic Chapel offers such attractions as "Cornerstone, the LGBT [Lesbian, Gay, Bisexual Transgendered] group." The Wesley Foundation proclaims on its Web site "We do not believe that homosexuality is sinful. . . . Lesbian, gay and bisexual persons, no less than heterosexual persons, have the capacity for experiencing sex that is truly sacramental. Far from being sinful, such sex is truly holy and good." And so on, through most denominations. Traditionally religious students at UCLA would do well to find a conservative congregation off campus.

SUGGESTED CORE
1. Classics 40W, Reading Greek Lit: Writing-Intensive *or* Classics 41W, Reading Roman Lit: Writing-Intensive
2. Philosophy M103A, Ancient Greek and Roman Philosophy
3. Study of Religion 130, Readings in the New Testament
4. Study of Religion 119M, The Christian Church, 100 to 1517
5. Political Science 111B or 111C, History of Political Thought
6. English 90, Shakespeare
7. History 13A and 13B, History of the U.S. and Its Colonial Origins
8. History 222E, Cultural and Intellectual History of Modern Europe, Nineteenth Century

Crime on campus isn't much of a concern. One graduate student says that he feels safe on campus, but he's a big guy. "Were I a 110-pound female student, I wouldn't walk around campus at 3 a.m. as I commonly do now," he says. Another student notes that streets on and around campus are well-lit, and that campus security officers (in this case, specially trained students) are available from dusk to 1 a.m. to escort fellow students who feel uncomfortable. There is also a campus van service that runs until midnight during the academic year. Another student says that "most of the criminal activity doesn't [happen] on the campus, but on the outskirts." In 2003, the last year for which statistics were available, the school reported 12 forcible sex offenses, five robberies, 176 burglaries, 43 stolen cars, and six aggravated assaults on campus.

In 2004–5, in-state tuition at UCLA was $6,485, compared to $17,304 for students from out of state. Room and board was an additional $11,928. Unlike Berkeley, admission to UCLA is need-blind, and 54 percent of undergrads get some form of need-based financial aid. The average Bruin graduates with a student loan debt of $12,775.

University of California at San Diego

San Diego, California • www.ucsd.edu

The science of it

The University of California at San Diego, one of the newer campuses in the massive University of California system, has undeservedly stayed in the shadows of its better-known sister schools in Los Angeles and Berkeley. Unlike them, UCSD is not known either for athletic prowess or ideological fervor. Instead, it has gone quietly about its business of building excellent programs, particularly in the sciences. The school boasts a major supercomputer, advanced research facilities, and cutting-edge faculty, eight of whom are Nobel laureates. Unfortunately, UCSD has not lavished the same affection on its liberal arts classrooms as it has on its laboratories, and there are a few departments at the school that should just plain be avoided. But science-minded students would be hard put to find a better place than lovely San Diego, with its balmy climate, coastal location, and bustling downtown, to spend their college years.

Academic Life: Six colleges in search of a plot

UCSD is divided into six colleges: Revelle, John Muir, Eleanor Roosevelt, Thurgood Marshall, Earl Warren, and Sixth College. Admission to UCSD is accompanied by an assignment to one of the colleges (applicants rank the colleges in order of their preference for the particular "educational philosophy" of each). In some respects, the colleges are quite independent: each has its own provost and advising staff, residence halls, dining halls, and educational philosophy—as manifested in the subjects emphasized by the college's unique general education requirements and core sequence. Yet the differences between them are not all that substantial. General education requirements are consistent enough between colleges to ensure that a student in any college will at least be exposed to a healthy range of academic disciplines, though none of the colleges has a curriculum that approaches a true core. Moreover, all of the majors at UCSD are open to all students regardless of which college they are assigned to.

The one requirement common to all UCSD students is this: They have to work—hard. "This is not a place to go and party," says one student, who adds that the university has "a totally different atmosphere. Our school has a semi-professional feel to it, with a lot of people who have taken on a responsibility in their lives and act like it." In addition, UCSD, like other California universities, schedules its academic year in quarters rather than semesters, making classes "information packaging sessions," in the words of one student.

The educational philosophy and academic specialties of each college can be surmised from its namesake. Revelle College is named after Roger Revelle, an eminent scientist perhaps best known for his work on the issue of global warming (a research subject on which UCSD still leads) and the founder of UCSD. Of all the colleges at UCSD, Revelle has perhaps the most traditional and rigorous general education program—although Eleanor Roosevelt College does require of freshmen a serious sequence in the cultural history of the West. In contrast, John Muir College—home to the departments of critical gender studies, contemporary issues, and, of course, environmental studies—vies with Marshall and Warren for offering perhaps the most lax general requirements.

The other colleges offer special courses and distribution requirements consistent with their educational philosophies or missions. Warren College, for example, requires

---

VITAL STATISTICS

Religious affiliation: none
Total enrollment: 24,663
Total undergraduates: 20,339
SAT/ACT midranges: SAT: 1130–1360; ACT: 23–29
Applicants: 41,330
Applicants accepted: 42%
Accepted applicants who enrolled: 22%
Tuition: $4,566 (in state), $15,870 (out of state)
Room and board: $12,750
Freshman retention rate: 94%
Graduation rate: 50% (4 yrs.), 78% (6 yrs.)
Courses with fewer than 20 students: 47%
Student-faculty ratio: 19:1
Courses taught by graduate TAs: not provided
Most popular majors: social sciences, psychology, economics
Students living on campus: 33%
Guaranteed housing for four years? no
Students in fraternities: 10% *sororities*: 10%

Aside from the general requirements for all University of California students—a writing class and a course in "American History and Institutions"—the distribution mandates are different at each of the six colleges making up UCSD. They are, in brief, as follows:

Revelle College

- A five-course sequence in an interdisciplinary humanities program with intensive writing instruction.
- One course in the fine arts.
- Three lower-division social science courses, two of which are in the same social science and the other in American cultures.
- Three quarters of calculus.
- Five courses in the natural sciences (four quarters total of physics or chemistry and one quarter of biology).
- Fourth-quarter proficiency in a foreign language.
- Either a minor or a three-course "area of focus" that is different from the type of major a student is taking.

all students to take "Ethics and Society" and offers minors in law and society and health care–social issues. Marshall College requires its students to take a three-course sequence in "Dimensions of Culture: Diversity, Justice, and Imagination." According to the course catalog, the "Diversity" course focuses on "socioeconomic diversity in examining class, ethnicity, race, gender, and sexuality as significant markers of difference among persons." In stark contrast—yes, we're kidding—the "Justice" class looks at "racial justice, political representation, economic justice, gender, and justice . . . and rights of cultural minorities." And in case some essential politically correct topic somehow got missed in all that, the college also requires students to take courses in both third-world studies and ethnic studies. "They basically teach you that everything that you have been taught is a lie," says one student of the ethnic studies department. "I've had a real problem with that."

Sixth College, which opened in 2002 and isn't named after anyone yet, emphasizes the intersection of culture, art, and technology, and requires each student to take a three-course interdisciplinary sequence in that area. It promises to be the most elaborately equipped of the colleges, featuring its own "chief technology officer" (a position more commonly found in the corporate headquarters of Silicon Valley), and a "digital playroom" that offers students high-end equipment on which to collaborate on high-tech projects. Hewlett-Packard donates pocket PCs for every student and residence advisor, so no one will ever find himself unplugged from the matrix.

In all colleges, the general education requirements are quite broad and open to many alternative means of fulfillment. Except at Roosevelt, students at UCSD do not need to take many demanding courses in the area of Western civilization, and the areas they are required to study lack the cohesiveness that is the mark of a true liberal education. This doesn't please those who want students to have a traditional education. "If I had to make a criticism of the system here," says one professor, "I would say that the students are not getting enough attention as far as general education is concerned. . . . You can ask [students] basic questions about history or the world and they're just ignorant. All my courses turn out to be general education courses, because I can't assume [students have learned] anything."

These weaknesses aside, UCSD does have a number of excellent programs, engineering and the natural sciences chief among them. "We really have an astounding department of biology," a professor says. "And we have pretty good departments in physics, chemistry, and computer science." These departments are bound to continue to be strengths under the leadership of new chancellor Mary Anne Fox, a well-known chemist.

In contrast, only some of the departments in the humanities measure up to this standard. "The humanities departments are variable," the professor says. "There are some very good people here and there in history and philosophy. On the other hand, we can't always keep them." Perhaps most worthy of note are the political science department, well known for its emphasis on Latin American politics, and the theater department, described by one person as "really quite outstanding." Other generally worthy departments include economics, psychology, and sociology.

There are several departments at UCSD that don't cut it. One professor notes that "we're very weak in things like classics. We have [only] one or two people who can teach Greek and Latin subjects with any authority." This professor calls the literature department "a mess," but notes that this is not a problem found only at UCSD. The ethnic studies department, steeped as it is in left-wing ideology, should be avoided. "It's a very politicized organization," says a faculty member. One student who took an ethnic studies course said that when an unknown party criticized his professor in a letter to the powers that be, "she basically showed how this letter victimized everyone in the room and how it was oppressive."

But even the ethnic studies department produces good instructors, and George Lipsitz in that department is one of many fine professors at UCSD. Others include Arthur J. Droge in literature and Steve Erie, Peter Irons, Gary Jacobson, Samuel Kernell, and Stanford Lakoff (emeritus) in political science. Professors are also generally easy to get in touch with.

Students should expect large class sizes. "The general education classes were usually in auditoriums with about 200 to 300 students per class, or frequently 150 to 250," says one student. "As for lower-division classes for majors, there are 80 to 120 and for upper-division courses there are 40 to 80." Another student says that "my classes have ranged from 50 to 200 [people]."

UCSD is "definitely research oriented, not teaching oriented," one professor says, although "there have been and are excellent teachers." Teaching assistants conduct a

REQUIREMENTS (CONT'D)

Roosevelt College

- An admirable-sounding six-quarter core sequence, "Making of the Modern World," which moves from pre-history to the present, focusing on the West.
- Two courses in fine arts, one of which must include non-Western content.
- Basic conversational and reading proficiency in a modern foreign language, or advanced reading proficiency in a classical language.
- Two courses in math, computer programming, or formal logic.
- Two natural science courses.
- One upper-level writing-intensive course.
- Three courses focusing on one geographical region.

Muir College

- One additional writing course.
- One (three-course) social science sequence.
- One mathematical or natural science sequence.
- Two sequences selected from two of the following areas: fine arts, humanities, or foreign languages.

REQUIREMENTS (CONT'D)

Thurgood Marshall

- Three writing-intensive "Dimensions of Culture" courses: "Diversity," "Justice," and "Imagination."
- Two humanities courses, one of them focused on "diversity."
- One fine arts course.
- One course each in biology, chemistry, and physics.
- Two courses in math and logic.
- Four courses outside the area of one's major.

Earl Warren

- One additional writing course.
- "Ethics and Society."
- Two classes in calculus, symbolic logic, computer programming, and/or statistics.
- Two six-course "programs" in different departments and in a department different from one's major.

significant proportion of classes, especially at the introductory level. "A lot of people, I think, don't like that," says a student, who points out that language difficulties with TAs who are not native speakers of English can be very frustrating. "I'm trying to learn advanced calculus and I have a TA who just came here four years ago," he says. "It has happened more than once."

However, students do have many research opportunities available to them, especially in the sciences. One of the most highly regarded programs is the Undergraduate Research Conference, in which outstanding undergraduate students have the opportunity to present research papers to faculty. Students can also graduate with honors in a department by completing an honors thesis. "Every year the faculty are very enthusiastic about the theses," a professor says. "There's no question that represents a lot of work." The Scripps Undergraduate Research Fellowship, which focuses on marine and earth sciences, takes place during the summer at the Scripps Institute of Oceanography. It provides a generous stipend plus housing and travel expenses. A number of scholarships are out there for promising undergraduates, and there are dozens of research centers on campus where cutting-edge research is routine. For instance, in 2005, 21 undergraduates conducted a study with Mexican immigrants to trace how effective U.S. policies are at border control, according to the *Chronicle of Higher Education*. The same newspaper has reported that UCSD is one of the only schools in the U.S. to employ the most advanced Internet protocol, Internet Protocol 6, which San Diego engineers use "to control a giant electron microscope in Osaka, Japan, and see live, ultrasharp images produced by the device."

Despite some flaws, UCSD can be a fine school for serious students who are willing to put in the time and effort to make their education a success. "Be as diligent as possible going through your coursework in order to get out of this place in four years or less," says one student, "because the primary purpose of a UCSD student is to step to the next level." Another student agrees: "It's truly a quality education. . . . At worst, it's a step behind Berkeley and UCLA."

Student Life: The institute of oceanography

Like most academic institutions, UCSD is a solidly liberal place, but there is also a good amount of openness on campus. A professors says he feels "far from being unfree." This professor says it is not like it was "in the seventies, when you could really get in trouble for not being 'one of them.'" This is not to say that the forces of political correctness are absent from UCSD. But proponents of serious ideology have usually been defeated (sometimes in court) or simply deemed irrelevant and embarrassing. People of every race and culture at UCSD have too much serious work to do.

The most recent exception to this norm occurred when the university initiated disciplinary action against the *Koala*, a satirical student publication, for allegedly disrupting an open meeting of MEChA, a radical Chicano nationalist group that advocates, among other things, the seizure of several southwestern American states by Mexico. Two reporters from the *Koala* and a photographer attended the meeting and later published a parody of the organization. FIRE, the Foundation for Individual Rights in Education, took up the *Koala*'s case, sending a letter to remind Vice Chancellor for Student Affairs Joseph Watson that in 1995 he had "issued an unequivocal defense of the right to free expression." The issue then, ironically, dealt with MEChA's right to publish racist and hateful speech against a Latino INS officer who died in the line of duty, calling him a "traitor . . . to his race" and declaring that "all the *migra* pigs should be killed." UCSD has since dropped all charges against the *Koala*.

Despite a few defeats, however, the Left still maintains a strong hold on certain areas of UCSD life. Groundworks, an alternative bookstore where many students must purchase their books is, according to one student, "extremely . . . radical." He says, only partially tongue in cheek, that "you know your teacher is a Communist if he asks you to pick up your books there."

The other pseudo-Marxist institution on campus is the Ché Cafe, which one student describes as "a little cafe that models itself after Marxist and Communist rhetoric and ideology. Everyone who works there is equal; there's no head." Recently, the cafe fought off a university order that it drop links to a Latin American terrorist organization—the FARC guerrilla army of Colombia—from its Web site.

Luann Wright, whose son graduated recently from UCSD, was sufficiently concerned by the political content of his writing class that she created a Web site (www.noindoctrination.org) for students at schools across the country to post confidential assessments of the political bias they've faced in the classroom. (The site also allows professors to post responses to their critics.) Wright said of her son's class, "All the essays they had to read were race-related, and I thought that was a little odd for a writing course." The Web site has endured a storm of criticism from professors who fear that anonymous criticisms will damage their careers. But Wright is more worried

REQUIREMENTS (CONT'D)

Sixth College
- A three-course, partly writing-intensive sequence called "Culture, Art, and Technology."
- A computing course.
- Two courses in social sciences.
- Two courses in humanities.
- Two courses in natural sciences.
- One course in math/logic.
- One course in statistical methods.
- One course in ethnic or gender studies.
- One course in ethics.
- Two courses in music, theatre, dance, or visual arts.
- One upper-division project with a two-unit course in "practicum communication."

WEST

803

"about what goes on in the classroom." She told the *Chronicle of Higher Education,* "I feel we're doing our students a grave disservice when we have this sort of education where students take a writing course that is really more of a social programming course."

For most UCSD students, life goes on with politics in the distant background. "The vast majority of the students are apathetic," says one student. "I would say we have a number of Republican and conservative students, but Democrats still outnumber them 65 to 35." And, it should be noted that religious groups have a powerful voice on campus. "Any time when religion is involved," says this student, "that's a hot issue. We have a number of Christian conservative students with very strong convictions. They're a force."

UCSD has the inherent advantage of being in San Diego, a beautiful, vibrant city on the Pacific coast that has plenty of things to do and see year round—a fact that may not be immediately obvious to those who consider the city merely a glorified naval base. San Diego has so many attractions and diversions that while on-campus life "is pretty boring," as one student puts it, UCSD students can easily find sources of entertainment. First and foremost, the beach is less than 10 minutes by foot. One block away from campus, there is a shopping center with nearly everything else, and there are three major malls within a few miles of campus. There are dozens of other things worth seeing, as well.

UCSD, as one student puts it, "is very anti-Greek. They don't welcome Greeks and they don't have any policies that make being a Greek easy." There are more than a dozen Greek organizations at UCSD, though many of them are "multicultural." And, because of UCSD's policy on alcohol—"no tolerance," as one student describes it—there aren't any "real parties in the dorms. But, of course, there's always Tijuana." The Mexican border town is only about 30 minutes away, and thus students are able to indulge in plenty of vices: Tijuana has an unsavory reputation and is known mostly for its corruption and violence. Students who drive across the border should exercise common sense and caution, and be sure to comply with all Mexican laws and regulations—especially those regarding automobile insurance—to avoid any unnecessary trouble and incarceration. (If you have an accident in Mexico and lack Mexican auto insurance you can end up in prison.)

Life on campus thankfully does not come close to imitating Tijuana, but neither is it completely dead. There are a number of student clubs and organizations to get involved with, from religious groups such as the InterVarsity Christian Fellowship to political groups such as the College Republicans, along with publications like the *Guardian*, the campus newspaper, and the *California Review*, a recently reestablished conservative alternative. Also notable is the Sun God Festival, an annual concert where fun is had by all.

There is an active Office of Religious Affairs at UCSD. Under its aegis operate the Newman Center Catholic Community at UCSD, Hillel, the Foundation for Jewish Campus Life, the University Lutheran Community, the Wesley Foundation, the Unitarian Universalist Campus Ministry, and the Canterbury Episcopal Community. The general atmosphere of its programs is indicated by its Web site's proclamation that "promoting racial, religious, ethnic, and cultural tolerance and appreciation of diversity on campus is a major goal of the O.R.A."

There are no major sporting events at UCSD of the type that one sees at UCLA or USC (the football team is relegated to club status). But there are a number of varsity-level squads at UCSD, including men's and women's teams in basketball, crew, cross country, soccer, volleyball and water polo. The Tritons jumped from NCAA Division III to Division II in 2000.

Housing on campus is generally clustered around each college, and there are a variety of options for students who live on campus. The residence halls offer both single and double rooms, along with some suites for eight to 10 students, and there are on-campus apartments as well (mostly for returning students). The university guarantees housing to students for two years, but space is exceedingly limited, and students who want to live on campus should be aware that some rooms house up to three students. Rooms and suites are, according to the college's Web site, "gender specific, and most buildings are coed." Students who smoke should be mindful of California's strict anti-smoking laws, which UCSD vigorously enforces.

Crime is something of a concern on campus. While violent crimes and sexual crimes are infrequent, there have been problems with theft, especially involving automobiles. "Auto theft and auto break-ins have been a big issue," a student says. "A lot of cars have been broken into or stolen." In 2003, the school reported one nonforcible and seven forcible sex offenses, 62 burglaries, 52 stolen cars, and two arsons on campus.

USCD calls itself "the affordable choice compared to private universities," and indeed it is. In 2004–5, in-state tuition was only $4,566; out-of-staters paid $15,870. Room and board ran $12,750. Approximately half of UCSD's students receive some form of financial aid, 96 percent of it need-based.

UNIVERSITY OF CALIFORNIA AT SANTA BARBARA

SANTA BARBARA, CALIFORNIA • WWW.UCSB.EDU

The normal school

What is today the University of California at Santa Barbara was founded in 1909 as the Santa Barbara State Normal School of Manual Arts and Home Economics. It later became a teachers' college before finally joining the University of California system in 1944. UCSB is now a member of the Association of American Universities, one of only 63 universities in the United States or Canada to hold that distinction, and a reflection of the well-deserved recognition—in 2003, UCSB was one of *Newsweek*'s "Twelve Hottest American Colleges"—it is getting on the national stage. Three Nobel Prizes in three years will do that, as will three Fulbright awards to three different faculty members in just one year, all accompanied by eight national research centers. It also helps that students and teachers don't waste much of their time on radical politics.

Most of the nearly 18,000 or so undergraduates at UCSB are attracted to the school's science-centered programs and the chance to participate in top-flight research, but Santa Barbara also has some good liberal arts departments. Although the university has no core curriculum, there are many substantial courses available that can help students gain a solid liberal arts foundation if they choose wisely. If you need another reason to go to UCSB, consider this: the campus itself is on—*on*, not near—the beach. The climate is so temperate that the university includes a weather report on its home page.

On a more troubling note, according to vocal critics who have set up their own Web site (www.thedarksideofucsb.com), the university has been lax about disciplining students who flout laws against drug use, drinking, and vandalism. A recent promise by the school that it would crack down has only partly mollified those who accuse the administration of leaving students' safety and peace of mind to chance.

Academic Life: Science more than letters

The University of California at Santa Barbara is divided into five colleges, three of which offer undergraduate degrees: the College of Engineering, the College of Creative Studies, and the College of Letters and Science, which offers the bulk of the liberal arts programs and has by far the most students (about 17,000). Letters and Science offers 80 majors and interdisciplinary programs, as well as 30 minors. Its departments are organized into three divisions: Humanities and Fine Arts; Mathematical, Life, and Physical Sciences; and Social Sciences.

UCSB is known as a research institution, and its strengths accordingly lie in the sciences. Several departments are among the best in the nation, especially physics. Two of the physics department faculty have won Nobel Prizes (albeit in chemistry)—Walter Kohn (in 1998) and Alan Heeger (in 2000). Research is not limited to the faculty: more than 20 percent of undergraduates (including freshmen) participate in some form of research, and there are abundant opportunities—not just in the hard sciences, but in the humanities and social sciences as well—for those who seek them. According to the annual report from the UCSB Office of Research, "A recent *Science Watch* study of U.S. universities in 21 fields placed UCSB among the top 10 highest-impact institutions based on the citation rate of faculty research papers." Perhaps not incidentally, Chancellor Henry T. Yang is an aerospace engineer.

The humanities departments have award winners of their own. The classics department is good, especially professors Apostolos Athanassakis, Borimir Jordan, Robert Morstein-Marx, Robert Renehan, and Jo-Ann Shelton. Other good professors in the humanities include Harold Drake in history; Christine Thomas in religious studies; and C. Anthony Anderson, Anthony Brueckner, and Matthew Hanser in philosophy. The film studies department is considered by some to be the best in the country, and alumnus Michael Douglas recently donated $1 million toward a new media and television center. The department of religious studies at UCSB "is one of the major centers in North America for the study of religions"; its Web site boasts that the department once employed Paul Tillich.

There are only a few politicized distractions in the curriculum; it seems scientists just aren't as likely to put up with them. "Strange and bizarre courses are very few since UCSB mainly focuses on the hard sciences," says a student. But the very few distractions, when they do occur, are glaringly distinct. The black and Chicano studies departments get most of their business by helping students fulfill a particular general education requirement.

For a student who knows what he or she would like to study and what courses to take to get there, the College of Creative Studies is an interesting alternative. With fewer than 300 students, "the creative studies major is for talented students who are committed to advanced and independent work in one of the disciplines represented in the college," according to the catalog. These disciplines—"emphases," rather than majors—include art, biology, chemistry, computer science, literature, math, music composition, and physics. A student must complete a separate application for this college and

VITAL STATISTICS

Religious affiliation: none
Total enrollment: 21,026
Total undergraduates: 18,121
ACT midrange: 21–28
Applicants: 36,963
Applicants accepted: 53%
Accepted applicants who enrolled: 20%
Tuition: $7,062 (in state), $24,018 (out of state)
Room and board: $11,500
Freshman retention rate: 91%
Graduation rate: 49% (4 yrs.), 75% (6 yrs.)
Courses with fewer than 20 students: 47%
Student-faculty ratio: 17:1
Courses taught by graduate TAs: not reported
Most popular majors: biology, social sciences, business
Students living on campus: 29%
Guaranteed housing for four years? no
Students in fraternities: 8% *sororities*: 10%

There is no core curriculum at UCSB, but rather a patchwork of requirements designed to create what the university calls "the common intellectual experience of all UCSB students." Given the sheer array of choices—good and bad—that students face in fulfilling these requirements, it is unlikely that any two students end up with a "common intellectual experience." All students at UCSB have two basic requirements:

- An English composition requirement aimed mainly at ensuring that students can speak English. Students can test out of this.
- A course in "American History and Institutions." Many students test out.

Students in the College of Letters and Science also have these requirements:

- Two additional writing courses. These can include small freshman seminars on topics like "An Engineer's View of the Cell," and "Genetic Modification of Food Crops."
- A foreign language requirement met by taking three semesters of a language or by testing out.

first be accepted by UCSB in general before gaining admission to the creative studies major. The student is responsible for the general university degree requirements (writing, American institutions, and foreign language) and must also take eight creative studies courses outside his or her area of emphasis.

There is also an undergraduate Honors College, which consists of six honors credit units per year and earns a student a diploma with distinction as long as he maintains a B average. Some of the courses are graduate level, while some undergraduate courses may count for honors credit if students attend honors discussion groups in lieu of the regular discussion groups. Incoming freshmen are automatically considered for admission to the honors program, and typically about 10 percent will be invited to join based on high school GPA and SAT I/II scores. Current students and transfer students who take a minimum of 12 units per semester and maintain at least a 3.5 GPA are also eligible for admission. Honors students have access to the graduate student library, an honors study center, priority registration, special academic awards, field trips or research lectures, and a mentorship program that pairs current honors students with new ones.

Outside of the honors program, students say the best advice comes from faculty advisors in their majors. Although there is a general education advising office on the campus, most students prefer to simply consult their faculty advisors as soon as they pick their majors. "They can sometimes be helpful," one student says about the advising office, "but they don't always know the whole story. The professors have a better grasp of the requirements of their own departments and are more willing to work with you about your research."

Once in class, students can generally expect to find professors (in the upper-level courses) or lecturers (in the lower-level ones) doing their own teaching. Graduate teaching assistants handle some discussion sections and the grading in larger, lower-level courses. Class sizes for some general education courses can range from 200 to 800. Seventeen percent of classes have 50 or more students. The official student-faculty ratio is 17 to 1.

Despite the large classes, students are impressed with the faculty. They report that their professors are outstanding teachers and mentors who have proven track records. "My professors have been the most important part of my education here and have encouraged me, guided me, taught me, and trained me," says one student. Another student calls her professors "amazing and helpful."

What professors won't do is inflate students' grades—at least, not as much as at other schools. The scientific nature of the university works against grade inflation, and a student says that for the most part, what you earn is what you get. Besides instructors, students have plenty of other academic resources available to them. The Donald C. Davidson Library is a major research facility with 2.6 million books and bound journals, according to the university Web site. The UCSB Arts Library is in a separate building and features more than 60,000 sound recordings.

Student Life: On the beach

UC–Santa Barbara and UC–Berkeley share the "UC" in their names, but little else in terms of campus activism, multicultural obsession, and the like. Look on the UCSB Web site at the most recent memos from Chancellor Yang to the campus: they have nothing to do with student protests, politically correct initiatives, or Pavlovian diversity training. Rather, they are about hiring administrators, improving technology, and expanding the new marine science building.

But if the UC university presidents agree on any topic, it is most likely budget woes. Coming hard on the heels of a previous budget cut, a second cut totaling $373 million for the 2004–5 school year presented some serious challenges to UCSB, as well as all other California universities. It reduced fall 2004 freshman enrollment by 10 percent, increased tuition by 10 percent, cut spending on faculty by 5 percent, drastically reduced the amount of available financial aid, and tightened the budget strings around virtually every department of the university, from outreach and research to administration. Chancellor Yang assured students that although research and instruction budgets were being cut, undergraduates would be suffering the least compared to other areas of the university.

UCSB students do not regard their campus as politically oriented. "We find that we tend not to get into political arguments with the gen-

REQUIREMENTS (CONT'D)

- At least six courses that each entail "one to three papers totaling at least 1,800 words."
- One class in "quantitative relationships"—a few dozen from the science, math, and technology area will do the trick.
- One course that pertains to a "non-Western culture."
- A class that focuses on "ethnicity," either on a U.S. minority or on "the experiences of oppressed and excluded racial minorities" in the U.S.

BA students in the College of Letters and Science must also take the following:

- Three courses from science, mathematics, and technology.
- Three social science classes. (BS students only need two.)
- Three courses in "civilization and thought," with at least two coming from a three-course sequence in a certain area (like philosophy or art history) and the other course dealing with the non-Western world. (BS students take two.)
- Two classes in arts. (BS students need one.)
- Two courses in literature. (BS students need just one.)

eral population, but rather find an intense debate among those involved in Associated Students [student government] or the campus administration," one says. "Our research comes first." The editorial pages of the student newspaper are mostly without the incendiary comments found at other schools, although the paper does engage in political issues by endorsing or opposing propositions from the state and commenting regularly on local Isla Vista news and events.

Associated Students (AS) distributes funding to campus organizations, which range from the conventional to the absurd; 470 groups are registered with the Office of Student Life. The Mark Twain Anti-Imperialist Forum receives school funding, as does the Unicycle Club, the Zen Sitting Group, Mellow Moods, and Students Stopping Rape. Student government provides a number of other services, including a campus radio station, a magazine, a faculty and staff newspaper, a number of service committees, and a bike shop where students can borrow tools. The College Republicans claim some 300 members. The university has a handful of decidedly niche organizations, like the Academy of Film Geeks, and multiple ethnic and multicultural clubs. But more clubs fall under the heading of "recreation" than any other category. The place is, after all, on the beach.

Greek life is required to be rather sober. Since 2002, "all Greek-lettered organizations are required to have alcohol-free social events," according to the university. "Alcohol-free social events are defined as the following: any social event consisting of more than 30 chapter members and/or individuals shall be deemed a social event. Alcohol may not be present at any social event that is initiated, sponsored or organized on property owned, rented, or otherwise used as chapter facilities. Social events where alcohol is served must be held at a facility that is provided by a licensed and insured third-party vendor." Moreover, "hazing is absolutely forbidden."

There is a standard campus speech code that essentially bars slander and libel. For the most part, students can express their views without fear of reprisal, so long as they make sense while they're doing it. According to one student, Santa Barbara students do not fear punishment or ostracism for unpopular beliefs, but since UCSB is "predominantly a hard science school, there is a communal belief that everything has to test for validity, no matter who says it."

A "test for validity" seems to apply, in the main, to faculty hiring decisions, as well. If there is a bias, it's one toward where the professor did his or her graduate work. For example, it's probably a good sign that a number of professors in the religious studies department earned degrees at the University of Chicago; several philosophy professors come from UCLA, and classical studies tends to hire from Berkeley and Harvard.

As mentioned previously, UCSB isn't just near the beach, it's basically *on* the beach. The signature shot of the college shows university buildings arrayed above the Pacific Ocean, with the campus extending out above the sea on a spectacular point of land that also encompasses a lovely lagoon. Four beaches are actually part of campus. The view to the east is of the Santa Ynez Mountains. The setting would be a stunning site no matter what was built there, but the university has completed the West Coast feel with a collection of "California modern" buildings with terracotta roof tiles set among lush greenery. "I find the buildings here express a certain exuberance and positive outlook that California had before the Vietnam War," a student says. A section of the catalog titled "Inspiration Points" exaggerates only slightly in its introduction: "Palm-framed vistas of the blue Pacific and the golden Santa Ynez Mountains. The scent of eucalyptus mixed with the saltwater breeze. Breathtaking natural beauty combined with enormous intellectual vitality. This is [UCSB], and there is no other campus quite like it, anywhere."

Unfortunately, you may not be able to live there. Only freshmen are guaranteed housing on campus. They live in standard dorm rooms and suites—although some have excellent views. "Each hall is in close proximity to a dining facility and within walking distance to classes and the ocean," the university notes. All dorm floors are coed, and while the university offers special-interest floors and floors dedicated to specific ethnic groups, not many students opt for these. There are no coed bathrooms or coed dorm rooms. Students of age can drink in the dorms, but cannot do so in public or with more than five people in the room at a time. A code of conduct for the dorms, including restrictions on overnight guests from off campus (a two-night limit, with such visits banned over Halloween, Mardi Gras, and finals week), is said to be strictly enforced.

SUGGESTED CORE
1. Classics 36, Ancient Epic
2. Philosophy 20A, History of Philosophy
3. Religious Studies 115A/116A, Literature and Religion of the Hebrew Bible: Old Testament / The New Testament and Early Christianity
4. Religious Studies 127A and B, Christian Thought and Cultures of the Ancient World and Middle Ages
5. Political Science 188, Modern Political Theory
6. English 15, Introduction to Shakespeare
7. History 162, America in the Early Republic
8. History 123A, Europe in the Nineteenth Century (*closest match*)

Upperclassmen may live off campus in university-owned apartments or can rent from private owners in the community of Isla Vista, at most a five-minute walk to campus. About 75 percent of students live in private housing. Rental prices are steep, with an average of $2,500 per month for a three-bedroom place, and many of these expensive apartments are complete dives, according to several stories in the *Daily Nexus*. Seven miles of bike paths lie in and around campus. These are used by an estimated 14,000 cyclists each day.

UCSB students, 91 percent of whom are from California, come mostly from upper-middle-class families. The largest minority group on campus is Hispanic Americans, who make up 18 percent of the student body. Some 17 percent are Asian Americans, and 3 percent of students are African Americans.

Students like the range of options available to them in their free time, be it surfing (the surfing team has won six recent national championships while maintaining a collective 3.0 GPA), golfing, or patronizing the attractions near State Street in downtown Santa Barbara. The city also has a zoo, parks, a symphony, and other cultural attractions. More than 80 percent of students participate in intramural or club sports. The school's athletic teams (the Gauchos) are quite active. The Thunderdome, the arena

WEST

811

for the basketball teams, seats 6,000 spectators and is considered one of the least desirable NCAA Division I courts (for visitors). There are 10 men's sports and nine for women, plus club sports ranging from equestrian polo to surfing and alpine racing; intramural teams include tennis and squash.

The university calls its Arts and Lectures series "an essential component of education," according to the university Web site, and it hosts about 125 cultural events each year. These include performances, films, and lectures. The 2004 schedule included films (*To Be and To Have, Bus 174*), lectures (Lester Brown, Bruce Feiler), special events ("An Afternoon with Al Franken"), readings (Anne Lamott), and performances (Stephen Petronio Dance Company).

Freshman orientation is not mandatory for UCSB students, but about 90 percent attend. The program consists mainly of a chance to take proficiency exams, register for classes, and get acquainted with university and dorm life.

There are a very large number of more or less orthodox religious groups on campus, ranging from evangelical organizations like ACTS 1:8 (Spirit-Filled Christians on Campus), Christians in the Scientific Community, Hillel, a Holocaust Remembrance Week group (a Hillel affiliate), the Islamic Peace Fellowship, a Catholic student group, the Orthodox Christian Fellowship, Sun Lotus (Nichiren Buddhists at UCSB), and the University Christian Fellowship.

Isla Vista is a congested area; with about 25,000 people living in 1.5 square miles, it is said to have the highest population density in California. Ten years ago the area was more or less a continual party, with, according to a student, kegs of beer "rolled up on skateboards" being a common occurrence. It still tends toward excess, and it is less safe than the campus itself, but police departments are becoming more involved in the community and it's not the free-for-all it once was. Despite this, there have been recent tragedies. In 2001, a UCSB freshman who had been drinking and using drugs drove his car through a stop sign at about 60 miles per hour, killing four people (two of them fellow students) and injuring another. (The freshman was found by a jury to be legally insane; he was sentenced to a mental hospital.) In 2004, a student at Santa Barbara City College was killed by a young Isla Vista resident in a fight. The *Daily Nexus* contains a weekly police report, which recounts fairly regular instances of arrest for intoxication, inhalation, or aggression.

Despite the complaints which have been leveled against the school, in comparison with other large universities, the incidence of on-campus crime at UCSB is rather low, with petty theft the most common offense. In 2003, the school reported one nonforcible and nine forcible sex offenses, four robberies, one aggravated assault, 58 burglaries, four stolen cars, and three arsons. In all but one category, those numbers are up from recent years—a negative trend that critics are pressing the school to reverse.

UCSB is a pretty good deal for local students, who in 2004–5 paid only $7,062 in tuition. Out-of-staters paid $24,018. Room and board totaled $11,500. Admission is need-blind, and 45 percent of students receive some form of need-based assistance.

CALIFORNIA INSTITUTE OF TECHNOLOGY

PASADENA, CALIFORNIA • WWW.CALTECH.EDU

Math camp

The California Institute of Technology calls itself the "world's best playground for math, science, and engineering." It's also one of the world's best universities for combining learning, research, and accomplishment. Since the liberal arts are not its focus, where Caltech imposes a solid core curriculum is in mathematics and the sciences—though the school requires a respectable number of liberal arts classes as well. The recognition Caltech gets—and it has had plenty, topping the *U.S. News* rankings in recent years—is richly deserved. In 2003, *Kiplinger's Personal Finance* ranked Caltech first among more than 1,300 schools "for its quality and low price after students receive financial aid." The institution wastes little time, in or out of the classroom, on political ideology, which is seen as incompatible with scientific objectivity—an objectivity that benefits Caltech's approach to the humanities as well.

The arts didn't always take a distant back seat to the sciences on the Pasadena campus. Caltech was founded in 1891 as Throop University, where 31 students studied arts and crafts. Then in 1907 George Hale, an astronomer and director of the Mount Wilson Observatory, joined the board; by 1921 he, along with chemist Arthur Noyes and physicist Robert Millikan, had changed the school to the California Institute of Technology. NASA's Jet Propulsion Lab is now run by Caltech, along with many other top-flight research projects, and 29 Nobel Prizes have been awarded so far to faculty and alumni. Students have plenty of opportunities to participate in research projects with their professors.

Caltech is not an ivory-tower laboratory where students are a mere pretext; instead, they are seen as the future of the university—and a critical part of its present, especially in the collaborative, labor-intensive, and highly remunerative world of laboratory science. Caltech president David Baltimore, perhaps the only American college president ever to boast a Nobel Prize in

VITAL STATISTICS
Religious affiliation: none
Total enrollment: 2,171
Total undergraduates: 896
SAT midranges: V: 700–770, M: 750–800
Applicants: 2,761
Applicants accepted: 20%
Accepted applicants who enrolled: 37%
Tuition: $27,309
Room and board: $8,814
Freshman retention rate: 98%
Graduation rate: 77% (4 yrs.), 88% (6 yrs.)
Courses with fewer than 20 students: 63%
Student-faculty ratio: 3:1
Courses taught by graduate TAs: not provided
Most popular majors: engineering, physical sciences, biological sciences
Students living on campus: 90%
Guaranteed housing for four years? yes
Students in fraternities or sororities: none

Caltech demands of students that they master the core subjects and disciplines of the scientific method. Students must take the following:

- Five terms of mathematics: calculus, ordinary differential equations, and infinite series; linear algebra; vectors and analytic geometry; calculus of several variables; and probability.
- Five terms of physics: classical mechanics, electromagnetism, waves, quantum mechanics, and statistical physics.
- Two terms of chemistry: lecture courses in general and quantitative chemistry.
- One term of biology: a topical course introducing a variety of tools and concepts of modern biology.
- One freshman "menu" course: a term of astronomy, geology, environmental engineering and science, energy science, or number theory.

medicine, has been called upon to balance competing interests in an institution profoundly dependent on cooperation. So far, he seems to be succeeding.

Academic Life: The liberal sciences

Caltech has recently received a literal embarrassment of riches—a whopping $600 million gift over 10 years (the largest private donation ever given to an institution of higher learning) from alumnus Gordon Moore (cofounder of Intel) and his wife Betty. This fistful of dollars, a third of which has already come to the school, has sparked some dispute on campus. Moore designated his largess to encourage "collaborative work among disciplines" and to help Caltech compete with wealthy universities that possess 10 (Yale) or even 20 (Harvard) times Caltech's $1.15 billion endowment—hardly a pittance in ordinary terms, but not enough to enable bidding wars. And while the unassuming billionaire has been accommodating about seeking mutually agreeable uses for his gift, his goal in targeting Caltech as the recipient of a uniquely huge donation is that "by putting all your money in one place, you get more bang for your buck." And, at Caltech, most of the bang and most of the bucks come from the faculty. So that's where the university is spending much of Moore's money.

In a journal called the *Scientist*, Caltech vice provost David Goodstein explains Caltech's unique finances. Many, if not most, universities, rely on student tuition as the cash cow that keeps the land flowing with milk and honey, as it were; Goodstein points out that at the University of Southern California, students offset 60 percent of that school's expenses through undergraduate tuition. At Caltech, tuition accounts for only 3 to 4 percent of the university's net costs. On the other hand, Goodstein notes, professors *average* $600,000 to $700,000 a year in grant money. The hard scientists bring millions to the campus, pumping in the lifeblood of the university.

If you're considering Caltech, you should meditate for a moment upon its name; this is not a university or a college—so don't expect a broad liberal arts education here. However, if your interests are in hard sciences or technology, expect to find a school that insists upon providing a thorough, balanced grounding in scientific disciplines. Rather than encouraging early specialization, Caltech demands that its students work through what we can only call a science core curriculum. As one student says, "It would

WEST

not be far wrong to consider the program a 'liberal sciences education.'" The school states on its Web site that "[t]he breadth and depth of the Caltech core curriculum are virtually unequaled in American higher education." These aspirations are admirable, and the school seems to live up to them.

The university explains its science-heavy curriculum in this way: "The boundaries between scientific disciplines get blurrier by the week, and the most creative scientists are the ones who have a good grasp of developments in all the major scientific fields—not just their own. The need for intellectual range and flexibility can only increase in the future. The way we see it, the Caltech core curriculum has redefined the term 'liberal arts education' for the twenty-first century." The result? A student in engineering says: "I know enough math and physics to totally switch into those areas."

These requirements are in addition to those of a student's major (called an "option" at Caltech, probably because it's one of the rare things they get to choose). Of the 24 options that lead to a BS degree, several are divided further into "areas of study" or "concentrations." Those who opt for engineering and applied science may concentrate in mechanical engineering, for example. Students choosing this discipline face a "core" set of courses there, too, including a required seminar, one of three applied math courses, 12 specific mechanical engineering courses, and two semesters of labs, one of which is required by name. Mechanical engineering optioners get to pick a grand total of two electives in the field.

The university is arranged into six divisions; it says it has no departments within those divisions, treating each as an interdisciplinary group of scholars, nicely amplifying and exemplifying the message of the core curriculum. Five of the divisions are scientific (biology, chemistry and chemical engineering, engineering and applied science, geological and planetary science, and physics, mathematics, and astronomy).

The sixth division is humanities and social science. While few go to Caltech to major in the traditional liberal arts—one recent alumnus says, "People who go to tech to study anything outside the sciences are doing themselves a disservice"—those who do choose this division can expect an education uncluttered by specialization and political correctness. Students have six options to choose from: business economics and management, economics, history, history and philosophy of science, social science, and

REQUIREMENTS (CONT'D)

- Two terms of introductory lab courses: freshman chem lab, plus one other lab chosen from offerings in applied physics, biology, chemistry, engineering, or physics.
- Two terms of science writing: students research, write, and revise a 3,000-word paper on a science or engineering topic, which is then published in an online journal established for that purpose. Students work with faculty mentors on the contents of the papers and receive editorial guidance from science writing instructors.
- 12 terms of humanities and social sciences: two terms that emphasize writing; two terms of introductory social sciences; two terms of advanced humanities; and two terms of advanced social sciences. The remaining four courses are electives.
- Three terms of physical education.

literature. In literature, for example, the course list hits the most foundational—and often neglected or politicized—authors and texts: some representative course titles include "Drama from the Middle Ages to Moliére," "Chaucer," "Shakespeare," "Milton," "Twentieth-Century British Fiction," "Twain and His Contemporaries," and "Austen, the Brontës, and Woolf." Still, students who choose Caltech for the humanities are probably missing out on the university's best opportunities.

The real strength of Caltech lies, unsurprisingly, in technology—particularly in research. Besides managing NASA's world-famous Jet Propulsion Lab, the school runs the NASA Infrared Processing and Analysis Center on campus. The Beckman Institute conducts research in chemistry and biology. Just launched in 2003 is the SIRTF Science Center, which supports NASA's infrared Spitzer Space Telescope. The university also hosts a Laboratory for Molecular Sciences and the Materials and Process Simulation Center. Caltech owns and operates the Palomar Observatory in San Diego County and sponsors (with NASA and the University of California) the W. M. Keck Observatory in Hawaii.

Students use these facilities as part of their coursework, in the production of their senior theses, or in the course of their campus jobs. (Research assistants earned as much as $5,000 in recent years.) "So many profs need help," says one student, that "each student has the opportunity to develop cutting-edge research during his undergraduate career." Summer Undergraduate Research Fellowships (SURF) fund about 75 research proposals each year. SURF projects are conducted by each student for some 10 weeks, working with a professor or grad student. Each student then writes an article and presents his findings at the university's SURF Seminar Day in the fall.

Even apart from collaborating with them on research, students have no trouble getting attention from their instructors. Professors teach most classes, with teaching assistants leading additional discussion sessions. The ratio of undergrads to faculty is an astounding three to one (undergraduates, at just 41 percent of the student body, are in the minority at Caltech). The faculty is as distinguished a lot as you're likely to find anywhere, with four Nobel winners on the staff. Students especially like the teaching styles of Niles Pierce in mathematics, Steven Frautschi in physics, Axel Scherer in electrical engineering, and Christopher Brennen, Fred E. C. Culick, Melany Hunt, and Richard Murray in mechanical engineering. Students get further help from their faculty advisors, professors assigned to them when they choose an option. The Career Development Center provides useful class and work advice. And the Ombuds Office explains and interprets university policies, provides a place for student or faculty complaints or concerns, and handles other problems that don't get taken care of elsewhere. However, a student says that "most students don't take advantage of these services, because they listen to the upperclassmen instead."

With such a faculty, it is no surprise that virtually every program at Caltech is excellent. One faculty member says it is impossible to single out the best departments: "We have so many Nobelists, National Medal winners, and so on in all the departments." This isn't gross immodesty, just a statement of fact. It is fair to say, however, that physics, engineering, chemistry, astronomy, and biology are very strong in every respect. Departments in the humanities and social sciences are not bad, but do not equal the quality of the engineering and hard science departments.

Academic pursuits are governed by the university's Honor System, which consists of one sentence: "No member of the Caltech community shall take unfair advantage of any other member of the Caltech community." Most exams are take-home and none are proctored, and collaboration is encouraged on most homework assignments. Students routinely get keys to research facilities and can use them day or night. Discussions of the Honor System form part of freshman orientation. The rest of orientation consists of "Frosh Camp," wherein the entire incoming class camps with some faculty and administrators in the San Jacinto Mountains for three days. This practice is a refreshing alternative to the diversity indoctrination and cultural sensitivity seminars that go on at many schools' orientations.

Caltech recently joined forces with the independent Center for Excellence in Education, and in 2004 began hosting Research Science Institute summer programs for exceptional high school students, inviting 35 of them to campus each summer for classroom training and research. If those students go on to attend Caltech, at least they will know in advance how hard they will have to work. Grades at Caltech are not inflated—if anything, they're deflated. "I think the average GPA is 3.2, and the students work *really* hard for that," says a senior. "For instance, most classes have one homework set a week, and that set could last 10 hours or more. The *least* time I've spent on a homework set would have to be four to five hours, but usually I'm working a lot longer." Rumor has it that some grad schools automatically add up to 0.7 points to the GPAs of Caltech students when considering them for admission. And if grad schools aren't doing that, they should be.

SUGGESTED CORE
1. Humanities 3a, The Classical and Medieval World (*closest match*)
2. No suitable course
3. No suitable course
4. History 111, The Medieval Church (*closest match*)
5. Social Sciences 202, Political Theory
6. Literature 114, Shakespeare
7. History 2, American History
8. Humanities 3c, European Civilization and Modern Europe

Student Life: The sorcerers' apprentices

Caltech is only 40 miles from Disneyland but the school is less the Magic Kingdom than a very intense math camp. Caltech is never going to be a party school. Nor, given the economic realities, will it ever be mistaken for a country club. Since Caltech runs mostly on the overhead expense deductions from faculty grant money, the incentive for improving student accommodations is limited. A Caltech education is a challenging apprenticeship in the modern sorcery of the technological elite—and apprentices have never had it easy.

Caltech is not a political campus. Despite this, Caltech students are not disengaged, by any stretch of the imagination, and are far from passively subservient in their "apprenticeships." In recent years, students have repeatedly been galvanized to action

WEST

817

on matters directly pertaining to their perception of their own needs and those of the university. For perhaps the first time in the university's history, sizable and largely successful student protests have arisen at Caltech, and it appears that the target of these protests, the university administration, is responding.

For instance, back in December 2002, "more than 200 undergraduates, about a quarter of the undergraduate population, gathered . . . for a protest during finals week," according to the *Pasadena Star-News*. The causes were several: cutbacks due to budget shortfalls, an increase in the health insurance deductible, a ban on freshman parking on campus, and the famous amount of work expected from students. As one protester wrote, "It is difficult to keep believing Caltech cares when the institute receives unprecedented generosity as our health insurance is slashed and when we see new buildings being built all around us." Wrote another student: "The administration seems determined to get rid of the few things that make Caltech unique and tolerable."

After the rally, according to the *Star-News*, the administration did roll back many of the budget cuts and reverse a few changes. "Everything we complained about was either fixed or better explained to us," says a student interviewed for this guide. Since then, President Baltimore has rolled out ambitious proposals, dedicating part of the Moore donation to a revitalization of student housing and improvements addressing the daily physical conditions of student life.

There have been other, smaller issues about which students have recently made their voices heard, such as an attempt on the part of the administration to "reform" the traditional and popular house system on campus and plans for a massive modern sculpture on Beckman Lawn, a green space on campus where students relax and throw Frisbees. The sculpture, "Vectors," by nationally known artist Richard Serra, was to be a metal wall diagonally bisecting the entire lawn, putting an end to Frisbee and marring, at least in some students' minds, an otherwise attractive yard. Students were angered that they were not consulted or informed about the project; opponents of the sculpture protested by using the time-honored Caltech tradition of pranking, assembling on the lawn a satirical "Vectors" from scrap metal, with the sculpture's $1.3 million price tag prominently displayed. The Beckman Wall was left unbuilt.

As one can see, free speech is not normally a problem on the Caltech campus, in class or out of it. "As a rule, I'd say all the professors make themselves available to their students, as well as being open to new viewpoints," one says. "Given, of course, that the viewpoints are backed up with some sort of thought."

Multiculturalism and quotas apparently play little role in hiring decisions and a very small one in admissions—the Caltech faculty is only 13 percent female, and minorities make up only about 12 percent. In 2002, it was reported that Caltech had the lowest percentage of black students in its freshman class of any top-flight school in the country—a total of three students. (Ten others who were accepted declined to enroll.) This failure to be sufficiently "progressive" has not gone unnoticed. A 2001 university report concluded, "In essence, to achieve its full potential, Caltech needs to hire more women faculty, be more proactive in nurturing its junior faculty, and make itself friendlier to the working family."

Caltech is only 11 miles of Pasadena Freeway away from Los Angeles, so students have plenty of choices for out-of-class activities—if they can find time for them. The university Web site insists that it's a myth that "all Caltech students do is study; there's no time for a social life." There may indeed be some time for nonacademic activities, but not much. Students who took advantage of all the things Los Angeles has to offer would soon find themselves flunking out of Caltech.

In living the studious life, though, Caltech students find a supportive community. As one student says, "Teachers are absolutely more collaborative than competitive. . . . Caltech is a challenge, but we want everyone to make it through. Support is completely mutual." The core curriculum puts every student in the same boat, and the residential system, which is governed by the Campus Life Office, promotes a comfortable atmosphere. Students are required to live on campus for their first two years, usually in one of eight coed houses. Caltech does not provide any on-campus single-sex residence halls, but according to a housing assistant the office makes an off-campus residence available for women each year. Some on-campus community houses do have coed bathrooms, and a housing official says there are a few coed dorm rooms on campus as well. Each on-campus residence houses 65 to 100 students of all different classes. House members dine together and often play intramural sports as a team; in addition, study groups often form from the houses. Freshmen try out the residential houses during what is called "Rotation," which follows freshman orientation. They submit their preferences, and a student committee makes the final assignments. Very rarely does someone get assigned to a house below his second choice. Rooms are designed in the typical college dorm style; the weather, however, is uniquely Californian.

Campus housing is guaranteed for four years, and some students remain in the same house for their entire careers. Others can enter a lottery for off-campus, university-owned housing, which is basically next door to campus.

The university admissions office tries to persuade prospective students that if they enroll they will not be surrounded by nerds running around with slide rules and taped eyewear, and they are right: there is no typical Caltech student. "We have a lot of pranksters, clubbers, partiers, videogamers, and the occasional athlete," a student says. The student government group, Associated Students of the California Institute of Technology, publishes *little t* (the title comes from the proper way to write Caltech—"Cal Tech" is wrong), a guide for campus living. There are dozens of student groups, most of them nonpolitical and many of them science-related, covering all types of interests, including performing arts, religion, and recreation.

The admissions office Web page is less successful in debunking the myth that "you have to be a genius to get in here." The bottom line is that while "genius" might not be required, really good grades are. Just 20 percent of applicants are accepted, and while the school says there is no SAT cutoff score for consideration, the *middle* 50 percent of admitted students in 2004–5 had Verbal scores ranging from 700 to 770 and Math scores ranging from 750 to 800. The Web page also reports that "most admitted students . . . rank in the top 5 percent of their high school classes." (And by the way, as one might expect, the university has a smoking fast Web site with great design.)

Some Caltech students even play sports at the NCAA Division III level. Caltech has 10 varsity teams for men and eight for women, and while we'd hate to jump to any stereotypical conclusions, the men's soccer team *was* 1-19-1 in 2003. Men's basketball lost every game it played in 2003-4, sometimes failing to top 20 points. Lest you think we're being hard on the men, women's basketball also lost every game it played that year, once when scoring but six points in 40 minutes of "action." Women's volleyball was 6-24. The men's football team, on the other hand, has remained undefeated since 1993—when the program was eliminated, leaving behind indelible memories of home games drawing hundreds to the 90,000-seat Rose Bowl and such cheers as "Secant, tangent, hyperbolic sine, three point one four one five nine!" and "What makes the world go round? *Angular momentum*!"

The grandest tradition at Caltech, and one at which the place excels, is Ditch Day, a fixture since 1921. On this day, seniors leave campus and undergraduates attempt to trash their rooms—filling them with sand, gluing furniture to the ceiling, even disassembling cars or cement mixers and reassembling them in the rooms. Seniors don't just let this happen, of course. They turn their rooms into high-tech fortresses to withstand the siege. Some rely on sheer muscle, like a bunch of cinderblocks, or "complex, imaginative puzzles carefully planned out months or even years in advance," according to the university. "The original objective has undergone a subtle shift, from keeping underclassmen out of rooms to challenging them to get in." Underclassmen have told us that, in their desperation to decipher an essential clue, they actually find themselves remembering material from a long-repressed course." The Web page says it best: "It's a peculiarly [Caltech] kind of fun."

Apart from this officially sanctioned vandalism, Caltech's Pasadena campus is remarkably safe. The only crimes on campus in 2003 were 79 burglaries and three stolen cars.

Caltech is fairly pricey—though cheaper than some comparable Ivies—with 2004-5 tuition at $27,309 and room and board at $8,814. The school practices need-blind admissions and guarantees to meet the full financial need of students who enroll.

CLAREMONT COLLEGES

CLAREMONT MCKENNA • HARVEY MUDD
PITZER • POMONA • SCRIPPS

CLAREMONT, CALIFORNIA • WWW.CLAREMONT.EDU

Sailing the five Cs

The Claremont Colleges are a consortium of five under-graduate colleges and two graduate universities located within the same square mile in Claremont, California. The first of these, Pomona College, was founded in 1887. In the late 1920s, Pomona president James Blaisdell decided to create a group of residential colleges based on the Oxford system. Scripps College was founded in 1926, followed by Claremont McKenna (CMC) in 1946, Harvey Mudd in 1955, and Pitzer College in 1963. The Claremont Graduate University was founded in 1925 and the Keck Graduate Institute of Applied Life Sciences began in 1997.

Almost 5,500 undergraduates attend the Claremont colleges, each of which is distinct. CMC is widely considered to be one of the top schools in the nation for students interested in the study of government, management, and public policy and has developed a strong commitment to genuine study of the liberal arts. These are also a high priority at Pomona College—spiced with unfortunate doses of academic trendiness. Pomona is particularly prominent in the social sciences and the humanities. Scripps College is an all-women college with a solid music program whose curriculum emphasizes, alas, women's studies and multiculturalism. Harvey Mudd is an excellent science and engineering school that promotes hands-on research, both on campus and through internships. Pitzer focuses on the social and behavioral sciences and is generally recognized as the most "progressive"—and weakest—of the five. It also imposes the fewest core or distribution requirements; students are asked to design, "in cooperation with their advisors, an individualized program of study which responds to the students' own intellec-

CMC VITAL STATISTICS

Religious affiliation: none
Total enrollment: 1,124
Total undergraduates: 1,124
SAT/ACT midranges: SAT V: 630–720, M: 640–720; ACT: 28–33
Applicants: 3,528
Applicants accepted: 22%
Accepted applicants who enrolled: 37%
Tuition: $29,210
Room and board: $9,780
Freshman retention rate: 97%
Graduation rate: 80% (4 yrs.), 87% (6 yrs.)
Average class size: 17
Student-faculty ratio: 8:1
Courses taught by graduate TAs: none
Most popular majors: social sciences, psychology, biology
Students living on campus: 96%
Guaranteed housing for four years? yes
Students in fraternities or sororities: none

WEST

821

General education requirements—taken in addition to the demands of any major—differ among the five Claremont Colleges. They are broken out separately below.

Claremont McKenna
- Two courses in science, at least one with a full lab.
- One math class, either "Calculus" or "Discrete Mathematics."
- An intermediate class or the equivalent in a foreign language.
- Two courses, "Literary Analysis and Composition" and "Questions of Civilization."
- Courses selected from two of the following fields, which may not include a student's major: foreign literature, advanced literature, philosophy, and religious studies.
- Courses in social sciences outside a student's major, chosen from three of these fields: economics, government, history, and psychology.
- Three semesters of physical education or two seasons of a sport.
- Senior thesis.

tual needs and interests." To which we can only say: If students were ready to do that, why would they need a school?

While each of the colleges is separate, each draws upon the vast array of resources that the group offers. The colleges share 12 campus buildings, athletic facilities and teams, a student newspaper, and plenty of social activities. Perhaps the best perk, though, is that Claremont students can enroll in almost any course at any of the other colleges. So a student can benefit from the strengths of the four other colleges, making the weaknesses at his own more bearable. Generally speaking, the Claremont colleges boast dedicated and accessible faculty members, first-class facilities, excellent academic programs, small classes, and an intimate intellectual and social community. The colleges' peaceful campuses are just an hour's drive from the bustle of Los Angeles.

Academic Life: Five-finger exercise

Although the curriculum varies from Claremont college to Claremont college, most are quite strong, and each school emphasizes the importance of a well-rounded education. Pomona campus literature explains, "The heart of a Pomona education lies in training the mind broadly and deeply, in developing the kind of intellectual resilience that equips our students for life-long learning." Even the science-heavy Harvey Mudd says it "seeks to educate engineers, scientists, and mathematicians well versed in all of these areas and in the humanities and social sciences."

It is generally accepted that Pomona, CMC, and Harvey Mudd are the toughest of the Claremont colleges, followed closely by Scripps. Pitzer is the least selective of the schools. For the most part, students arriving at any of the colleges need to be prepared to work. But CMC's intellectually rigorous education draws enthusiastic reviews rather than groans and moans from its students, 97 percent of whom return to the school following their freshman year. "It's a really solid education," says one student. "It's very focused and very leadership oriented. In terms of education quality, it's very good. I compare notes with friends back east at Ivy League schools and wouldn't trade my education at all. I think I'm very well served."

With few exceptions, CMC requires each student to complete a senior thesis under the direction of a faculty reader. This is, according to the catalog, "a major research paper or creative project of substantial length." This requirement, rare in today's higher education landscape, usually strikes CMC students as a privilege, not a burden. "I think it's wonderful because it really gives you the opportunity to take what you've learned over the past four years [and use it], and you have a reader whom you work with very closely," a student says. Complaints about the thesis are generally the wailing and gnashing of teeth "from people at the eleventh hour," according to one student.

There is little departmental sprawl at the Claremont colleges. Each college has its academic strong suits and relies on the other Claremont colleges to make up for its deficiencies. CMC, for instance, contains only 11 academic departments; one is a science program shared with several other Claremont schools, and another is military science. Claremont's government and economics departments are top notch, and its international relations program is also highly regarded. "The government department is arguably the best in the country for providing a sound liberal arts education with a major in government," says one professor. Says another: "The economics and government faculties are outstanding. . . . Many of them have had high-level Washington experience [as] presidential appointees, cabinet secretary appointees, and extensive involvement in politics at the national and state levels." "The government department has a wide variety of approaches to the study of politics: political philosophy, political history, constitutional history and constitutional law, institutional history and analysis," a professor says. "This is not a department dominated by rational choice modeling or . . . minutiae."

Unfortunately, not all of CMC's departments live up to the exemplary standards of these programs. Students report that the history department is the most politicized. "The focus is more on modern history," says one. "The program isn't what it could be." In fact, the combined history course offerings at all Claremont colleges are lacking. One recent alum complained of "no sense of continuity or permanence. . . . There are no ancient history courses." Instead, classes include such marginal topics as "Visual Culture in California." No courses were offered in ancient or premodern European history in the spring 2004 term. Although one student says that the CMC literature department has "your typical left-wing literature professors," a 2003 gradu-

REQUIREMENTS (CONT'D)

Pomona College
- The interdisciplinary freshman seminar "Critical Inquiry."
- Two writing-intensive courses.
- One speaking-intensive course.
- One physical education activity.
- An intermediate-level foreign language or its approved equivalent.

Students must also take courses to fulfill each of the following 10 goal-based categories (with no more than three courses from the same discipline): read literature critically; use and understand the scientific method; use and understand formal reasoning; understand and analyze data; analyze creative art critically; perform or produce creative art; explore and understand human behavior; explore and understand a historical culture; compare and contrast contemporary cultures; think critically about values and rationality.

To graduate, a Pomona student must also complete the "senior exercise," "a self-designed capstone experience."

Harvey Mudd College
- Four semesters of mathematics.
- Three semesters of physics and associated labs.
- Two semesters of chemistry and associated labs.
- Two semesters of humanities and social sciences.
- One course each in biology, computer science, and engineering.
- Two courses in different disciplines in each of the following areas: arts and literatures, humanities, and social sciences.
- The "integrative experience," a course or project that "integrates science or technology with contemporary society." Courses include "Global Warming," "Introduction to the Anthropology of Science and Technology," and "Science and Religion in the Western Tradition." Student-initiated projects must include a substantial paper and an oral presentation.

ate who still visits friends on campus says that there is "only one typically left-wing lit teacher there." He also maintains that both the psychology and literature departments are "excellent," especially recommending Psych 90, which he describes as "grounded in reality."

At Pomona, the English department is particularly strong. Scripps has excellent art, art history, and music departments. Pitzer's sociology department is highly regarded, but incredibly politicized (to the left).

Among the best faculty at CMC are Joseph M. Bessette, Mark Blitz, Alan Heslop, Paul Kapur, Charles R. Kesler, Chae-Jin (C. J.) Lee, James H. Nichols, John J. Pitney Jr., and Ralph A. Rossum in government; William O. Brown, Eric Helland, Manfred Keil, Marc Massoud, and W. Craig Stubblebine in economics and accounting; and Robert Faggen, John Farrell, and Nicholas Warner in literature. At Pomona, the best professors include Paul Hurley in philosophy and Martha Andresen in English. At Pitzer, look for Barry Sanders in intellectual history, Albert Wachtel in English, and Newton Copp in biology. At Scripps, John Geerken in history and Michael Deane Lamkin in music are excellent. At Harvey Mudd, try Michael E. Orrison in mathematics and Stephen C. Adolph in biology.

Most classes—in all five schools—are small and inviting, allowing students to interact freely with their professors. While there are occasionally some very large courses—primarily in classes that everyone needs to graduate—"the average class is probably 12 to 15 students," a CMC student says. "Some introductory general education requirement classes are where you'll have 30 students, but a class bigger than 20 is an exception." Faculty-student closeness is impressive. "I can basically drop by their office anytime," says one student. "I've had dinner with a number of their families, in fact. It's very easy to get in touch with them, and they really care about the instruction of the students. . . . We're at a teaching college." Another student says, "It's great—you can talk to your professors and meet them at office hours without any lines. After you've taken one class with them, they know you. They have a rapport with you." A Pitzer student says, "Professors are very accessible. They are here for one purpose—to share their wealth of knowledge with the students. Some even give their home phone numbers." This closeness is "not merely a 'feel good' asset—it has practical benefits for students," says a professor. Take the all-important letters of recommendation when it comes time to find a job or graduate school. "We can discuss the students in detail, rather than writing vague generalities," the professor says.

Teaching assistants rarely teach. "The use of TAs is minimal, and they are only used when there is an extraordinary demand for a certain class," one student says. "In these cases, [the college] may add a section taught by a TA from the Claremont Graduate University in addition to the already scheduled sections."

In addition to solid courses, students will find at the Claremont colleges a multitude of research opportunities. Perhaps most notable are the Henry Salvatori Center for the Study of Individual Freedom and the Rose Institute of State and Local Government. The Salvatori Center, "within its general study of freedom . . . focuses particularly on the American Constitution—its founding principles and subsequent construction—and on questions of political philosophy and applied ethics." The Rose Institute allows students to get involved with the political process, working on "election simulations, election analysis, redistricting research, fiscal analyses, studies of California demography, and polling." Harvey Mudd offers its students plentiful opportunities to gain research experience as summer interns working alongside faculty members. The school's Corporate Partnership Program allows students to apply for scholarships from corporations like the Boeing Company, Dow Chemical Company Foundation, Motorola, and General Motors. Through the school's Clinic Program, corporations commission students to work on research projects throughout the school year and present them at the end of the year.

Also important are the diverse off-campus study opportunities that the Claremont colleges offer their students. As a group, the Claremont colleges have a very high participation rate in study-abroad programs. According to campus literature, 40 percent of CMC students spend at least a semester studying abroad during their time in school; about half the students from Pomona, Pitzer, and Scripps study abroad. Harvey Mudd's participation is much lower (about 15 percent). Students can participate in a semester program in Washington, D.C., or in foreign-study programs in countries around the globe—from Kenya to Vietnam to Ecuador to Great Britain, or closer to home in Canada and Mexico. Pitzer College reports that most students who study abroad go outside western Europe and the English-speaking world. Some of its most popular programs are in Botswana, China, and Nepal.

REQUIREMENTS (CONT'D)

Scripps College
Scripps begins its requirements with the following three-semester series of "core" courses in interdisciplinary humanities:
- Core I, a course with 200 first-year women and 13 professors in which students study "some of the major debates and concepts that have shaped [modern] intellectual life."
- Core II, an interdisciplinary, team-taught seminar chosen from dozens of courses.
- Core III, a seminar that culminates in a "significant self-designed project under the supervision of a single faculty member."
- One freshman writing course.
- A class in math or logic.
- Three courses in a single language to the intermediate level.
- One course each in fine arts, letters, natural sciences, social sciences, women's studies, and "interculturalism."

Pitzer College
A first-year, writing-intensive seminar.

- Three courses in "Interdisciplinary and Intercultural Exploration." With advisor approval, students each choose three courses that address topics of special interest to them, from "at least two disciplines and more than one cultural perspective."
- One course in "social responsibility and the ethical implications of knowledge and action." This course might involve "either community service, community-based fieldwork, or an internship," or consist of an "independent study with an experiential component."
- Two courses demonstrating "breadth of knowledge" in both humanities and the fine arts and in behavioral sciences.
- Two courses in the social and behavioral sciences.
- One course in the natural sciences.
- One course in mathematics/formal reasoning.

Student Life: The bar monkey

While the Claremont colleges share many resources, each has its own feel and typical student. One CMC student helpfully provides the following stereotypes: "Pomona: pretentious liberal intellectuals." (An alumnus adds that they tend to be "filled with guilt over their parents' success.") The student continues: "Pitzer: hippies and meatheads. Scripps: lesbians/bisexuals; artsy types. CMC: more conservative, beer-drinking, ambitious students. Mudd: math and science nerds; study a great deal, and often have quirky habits such as unicycle riding."

Approximately half the student body (in each college) comes from the state of California, however, and students from the different schools interact frequently. One student says, "There is definitely a feeling of individuality with respect to each school, but since so much is shared—classes, sports, facilities, etc.—there is also a feeling of overall commonality among the five Claremont colleges."

Claremont McKenna is "one of the most politically balanced schools in the country, with a good variety of views and with healthy representation among both liberals and conservatives," says one faculty member. The fact that it is balanced makes it appear overwhelmingly conservative to liberals. A survey conducted by the *Claremont Independent*, a conservative student publication, found that around a third of CMC students identified themselves as conservatives. "We have to be one of the most evenly split colleges in the country," says one student. A professor says 35 percent of faculty members are registered Republicans—"a huge percentage compared with most other institutions in Claremont and beyond." CMC's political environment is healthy and open, and regardless of a student's political leanings, he will find his views taken seriously and thoughtfully. "We're a very politically conscious campus," says one student, "but dissenting from orthodoxy is not a problem." Another student says: "Whatever side you come from, you always have allies in the classroom."

Pomona College likes to think of itself as the most intellectual of the Claremont colleges; its students, while mostly liberal, are said to be mostly nonideological. For the most part, Scripps College follows the trend of other small liberal arts schools for women. Many of its course offerings are presented from a feminist perspective, and Scripps students may find it hard to avoid such classes. While the goal of these politicized courses—at least for some Scripps administrators—may be to indoctrinate students with left-liberal views, their tactics don't always work. The *Claremont Independent* quotes one rare Scripps conservative: "Being at Scripps made me more conservative. I had to defend myself, and it made me see the flaws of liberal arguments more. Scripps forced me to delineate my beliefs." Pitzer College seems to be less balanced. One student calls Pitzer "hopelessly liberal." Owing to its engineering and "hard" science bent, students say Harvey Mudd is the least political, as students there are likely to spend more time working on class projects and internships than they are attending protests and political rallies.

Perhaps the best way for students to hone their critical thinking skills is through the Marian Miner Cook Athenaeum, the site of lunch and dinner meetings four times a week featuring lectures by prominent speakers, along with less-frequent concerts and performances. The Athenaeum is open to students at any of the Claremont colleges—students just use their meal ticket there instead of at the dining halls. "The speakers provide our students with a range of perspectives and interests that most students elsewhere don't confront," says a professor.

Students and faculty, in fact, can't say enough good things about the Athenaeum. Not only does it offer a decent meal, but it also allows students to visit with their professors *and* hear a number of incredible speakers. "Recommend everyone go to the Athenaeum," one student tells us. One professor explains the program this way: "It is a very good adjunct to our education: many prominent and interesting speakers, presented in pleasant surroundings . . . with opportunities usually to talk with the speaker afterwards." Traditionalists will approve of the dress code. "It's a formal setting," says one student, "a coat-and-tie type of thing."

A look at the list of speakers shows an impressive array on both the right and the left. "The speakers have been a little more loopy [in recent years] but there's always a balance," one person on campus says. Recently the Athenaeum has hosted Tony Kushner (playwright and author of *Angels in America: A Gay Fantasia on National Themes*), former attorney general Janet Reno, David Brooks (*New York Times* columnist), Alan Charles Kors (the director of the Foundation for Individual Rights in Education), and the Los Angeles Chamber Orchestra Soloists.

Students at all of the Claremont schools are a politically active bunch, according to some students. They have been visible in protests against the war in Iraq. A February 2003 teach-in featured a number of different perspectives from a dozen or so professors, according to the five-college student newspaper, the *Claremont Collage*—but all of

CMC SUGGESTED CORE
1. Classics 60, Greek Civilization Through Its Literature
2. Philosophy 112, History of Philosophy: Ancient
3. Religious Studies 20po, The Biblical Heritage
4. Religious Studies 122po, The New Testament and History of Early Christianity (*closest match*)
5. Government 80, Introduction to Political Philosophy (*closest match*)
6. Literature 64, Shakespeare
7. History 80, Forging a New Nation, America to 1865
8. Philosophy 115, History of Philosophy: The Nineteenth-Century Philosophies of Revolution and Evolution

WEST

the perspectives were antiwar. And in March 2003, around 300 students and faculty participated in an antiwar strike and march through the five colleges, according to the *Collage*. A *Chronicle of Higher Education* article says that the Pomona College Conservative Union countered a fall 2002 "Fast for Peace" event with a "Barbeque for a Free Iraq," tempting antiwar protesters, who had been fasting for 56 hours, with juicy hamburgers.

Another protest that draws a crowd of activists is the annual Take Back the Night march against domestic violence. Unfortunately, such worthy issues are often accompanied by antimale and profeminist ideology. The 2003 event, for instance, included excerpts from the lurid feminist play *The Vagina Monologues*. "Most of these [protests] are things that come from up on Pitzer," says one CMC student. Another CMC student says, "Claremont McKenna's mode of activism is [to] drive down and work on a campaign—not just as a volunteer but help with the campaign, work within the system. The world has plenty of sweaty activists."

Religious life at the Claremont Colleges is overseen by a joint Office of the Chaplains, based at McAlister Center, which maintains a Volunteer Service Center. Events and activities include: Volunteer Study Break (recruiting evenings), canned food drives, the Oxfam Hunger Awareness Program, Community Service Awareness Week, Habitat for Humanity builds, tree plantings, and alternative spring break trips. Denominational activities are held—an easy task given that the full-time chaplaincy staff includes a Catholic priest, a Protestant minister, and a rabbi.

In 1999, CMC hired as chief executive Pamela Gann, a former dean of Duke University's Law School who has kept an exceptionally low public profile. She's known as a good fundraiser—while at Duke, the *Chronicle of Higher Education* reports, she helped scare up $17 million for the law school's first capital campaign. While at McKenna, Gann has supported affirmative action in admissions and hiring decisions. The *Claremont Independent* reports that under her tenure CMC secured a $700,000 grant for new faculty positions for minorities and diversity programming in the curriculum. Claremont McKenna, according to the article, plans to increase acceptance rates for minority applicants 2 percent by next year, with the ultimate goal of building a 37 percent nonwhite student body. Gann has also been active in trying to "diversify" the CMC curriculum. One professor says Gann is "pushing for 'diversity' courses and emphasizing novelty of various kinds, which will probably come first in the humanities and in psychology." On the other hand, Pomona College seems to have made an excellent choice in its new president: David Oxtoby, who previously served as dean of physical sciences at the University of Chicago. A college press release says Oxtoby "deeply understands, and eloquently articulates, the essential role for liberal arts in this new century." Oxtoby has also emphasized the importance of ideological diversity and free speech on campus.

The town of Claremont is charitably described as sedate and not inaccurately as boring, at least for college students. "There aren't your normal college-town things in Claremont," says one student. However, just because Claremont isn't Ann Arbor doesn't mean that there is nothing to do—just that it takes slightly more effort to find activities. All five undergraduate colleges are located within a square mile, but they are all in California, of course, so although the architecture on the individual campuses does vary some, you're bound to find plenty of palm trees, lush green lawns, and sunshine. The Claremont colleges share a number of facilities. Bridges Auditorium is the site of many of concerts, lectures, and performances, which are usually open to all Claremont students. The four libraries—Honnold/Mudd for the humanities and social sciences; Denison Library (at Scripps) for the humanities, fine arts, and women's studies; and two science and engineering libraries at Harvey Mudd—also make resources available for all Claremont students. These include two million volumes and 6,000 periodicals. The $17 million Keck Joint Science Center opened in 1992. Scripps has an excellent music program and facilities, including three performance centers. Other shared resources are the dining facilities—students are welcome to take meals at any of the Claremont cafes or dining halls.

The Village, Claremont's town center, contains a number of shops, restaurants, and bookstores, but this represents the sum total of entertainment within walking distance of campus. Given this situation, a car is most certainly helpful. Los Angeles is about 40 miles to the west, although getting there can take upwards of two-and-a-half hours if traffic is heavy. CMC's Web site prominently lists the many things to do and see in Los Angeles. That list even mentions Los Angeles's horse-racing venues, some of which are seedier than others. Closer to home are the suburban cities of Pomona and Ontario, which are both only a few miles away and offer shopping and other entertainment options. Students who want to visit the beach head for Los Angeles or Orange County.

Despite the sleepy environs, life on the Claremont campuses doesn't lack activities. "Everyone has fun to some degree because there's so much going on," a student says. There are dozens of student groups and plentiful athletic opportunities, and the close-knit atmosphere makes it easy to find and make friends.

Students can join clubs that are either exclusive to one campus or available to students from all five. These clubs range from the far left to the respectable right. As one student says, "We take advantage of what goes on at other campuses, because in a sense we're all one campus." Student groups include Civitas, a well-supported community service group; the Pro-Life Society; and InterVarsity Christian Fellowship, the largest student group on campus. There are chapters of both the College Republicans and College Democrats, a pep band, a fencing club, and the aforementioned *Collage*. Students of the five colleges also share membership in other organizations, including a debate union; Hillel; a Lesbian, Gay and Bisexual Students' Union; the traveling, competing Claremont Colleges Ballroom Dance Company; the Asian Pacific Islander Awareness Committee; and several academic student groups and honor societies.

The Claremont colleges boast an impressive athletics program. Claremont McKenna, Harvey Mudd, and Scripps make up CMS athletics (Claremont, Mudd, Scripps). Students from these three colleges compete on varsity teams together. The men are known as the Stags, the women as the Athenas. Their archrivals are the Pomona-Pitzer Sagehens. Both groups offer 18 varsity sports as well as a number of intramural teams, which are normally organized by dorm. A few club sports—rugby, lacrosse, Frisbee, and volleyball—offer intercollegiate competition for those who do not have the time or ability for varsity sports.

Except for three fraternities at Pomona, there is no Greek system on the campuses, nor is there any push for one. This means that students are left to their own devices when it comes to partying, something Claremont students reportedly do a good deal of—although the campus has become dryer of late. "People drink, but not nearly as much as when I was a freshman," a student says. "The climate has changed, and people don't drink nearly as much—the keggers *used* to start on about Wednesday." However, another student says that "student life tends to revolve around alcohol consumption."

Some students are concerned about the campus's seemingly lax attitude toward demon rum. "I almost decided not to come," says one student regarding her reaction to the college's wet reputation. "The drinking policy is really a downfall, and it is, I think, a serious problem." Even so, another, nondrinking student reported that he "felt no pressure to drink." CMC does appear to have a relatively tough policy regulating alcohol consumption—the school expressly forbids underage students from touching the stuff, and where alcohol is permitted, it is strictly controlled; moreover, the college boasts a "substance-free dorm." A few years ago, science students at Harvey Mudd put their technical minds to use and created something called a Bar Monkey, basically an automated bartender seemingly from a frat movie fantasy. Students type in the drink they want and the Bar Monkey serves it up. When administrators found out about it, the creators were charged with selling alcohol illegally, but the Bar Monkey is now allowed on campus as long as it is not used in a public place. The basic idea seems to be that it is better to have a wet campus with controlled conditions than to have students wandering off and getting into trouble in bars.

Scripps, in common with many women's colleges here and abroad, has a number of interesting social traditions that reflect the atmosphere of gentility in which such institutions first arose. Among these are the Wednesday Afternoon Teas, the Medieval Dinner near Christmas time, the May Fete, the Rose Garden and the Graffiti Wall, and the four-times-yearly Candlelight Dinners.

Housing on campus is abundant and adequate. Most Claremont students live on campus—close to 95 percent of CMC, Mudd, Scripps, and Pomona students, and about 70 percent of Pitzer students. At CMC, all dorms are coed, but floors, suites, or apartments are separated by sex. Residence halls, only about two to three minutes away from each other at most, are mixed by class—freshmen often live next door to seniors. And there are no freshman-only floors at CMC. This leads to camaraderie both within residence halls and between them. "Dorm life is a blast," says one student. "It feels kind of like a family." There is also a central dining facility where students take their meals— "very good for college fare," says one student—and there are enforced quiet hours in dormitory housing.

All dorms at Pomona are also coed, but rooms are single sex. Pomona freshmen are divided into sponsor groups—10 to 15 freshmen along with two sophomore "sponsors." This arrangement is supposed to help build a close-knit community for fresh-men, but for some students, it may be a little *too* close-knit. Depending on the sponsor group, students may find themselves sharing a bathroom with a member of the oppo-site sex. "Remind me not to send my daughter here," says a housing worker.

At the all-women's Scripps College, students are also free to apply to live in one of the other Claremont colleges' buildings. Scripps residence halls are mixed by class. Each residence hall has a "multicultural educator," whose job is pretty much described by her title.

Harvey Mudd residence halls are all coed, but female students can petition to live on an all-female wing or can live in all-female suites. All rooms are single sex. Some bathrooms are coed; however, the director of residence life claims that he asks on a housing questionnaire whether the student is comfortable sharing a bathroom with the opposite sex, and no student has a coed bathroom against his will. Harvey Mudd dormitories consist of four traditional style halls known as the "Quad" and "Outer" dorms, which are mostly suites and apartments. Academic classes are mixed through-out the residence halls. And finally, Pitzer College residences offer only coed dorms, but one has an all-women floor. The housing department was noncommittal on whether or not they offer coed dorm rooms. Coed bathrooms are allowed in some theme halls.

Crime is a moderate concern on campus. "I don't think people worry at all," says one student. "We're in a sleepy little town." Students say that they don't feel unsafe, but they also say the largest problem is theft, so students should use common sense in safeguarding their belongings. The 2003 campus crime statistics from the five colleges counted some 82 burglaries, one aggravated assault, three robberies, eight forcible sexual offenses, and nine stolen cars. Those are pretty good statistics for a combined student body of almost 7,100.

Claremont McKenna College charged tuition of $29,210 in 2004–5; room, board, and required fees came to $9,780. However, admission is need-blind, and all admitted students are awarded 100 percent of their needed financial aid. More than half (56 percent) of undergrads receive financial aid.

COLORADO COLLEGE

Around the block

Founded in 1874 by General William Jackson Palmer, builder of the Denver and Rio Grande Railroad and the same visionary who laid out plans for the town of Colorado Springs, Colorado College is one of the few western colleges with a genealogical connection to traditional New England scholarship. Indeed, the college claims to remain dedicated to the "traditional principles of a liberal arts and sciences education as envisioned by its founders more than 125 years ago." A small school of about 2,000 students, Colorado College boasts a disproportionately large endowment of more than $350 million, the second largest of any school in Colorado. As the only liberal arts college in the Rocky Mountains, Colorado College identifies itself with the adventurous spirit of its forefathers and of the region itself. President Richard F. Celeste sums up the school's ethos in the phrase "Rock and Block," emphasizing Colorado College's most distinctive features: its stunning geographic backdrop at the foothills of Pike's Peak, and a unique academic schedule, the "block system," that emphasizes smaller classes, more writing, more discussion, and in-depth study of one subject at a time.

Academic Life: Downfield blocking

An impressive student-faculty ratio of 10 to 1, exceptionally small classes taught exclusively by professors, excellent test scores, and 12 Rhodes scholars (four in the past 10 years) justify Colorado College's claim to be the only "top-tier college in the Rocky Mountain region." But it is the celebrated block system that sets this small liberal arts college apart from most American schools. Along with Cornell College in Iowa, and a few other schools, Colorado College is distinctive for this system, which divides the academic year into eight 25-day segments. Students take one course at a time and professors teach only one. The plan allows for great flexibility; each class sets its own meeting times. A Shakespeare class may read a play one day and act out a few scenes the next, or an archeology class may meet at a dig site in southeastern Colorado. A four-day break separates each segment from the next, and many students take advantage of college-sponsored recreational activities such as biking in Aspen, white-water rafting on the Colorado River, or climbing a volcano in Mexico. The plan is, according to the school, the "hallmark of Colorado College's academic program," and it naturally affects all aspects of campus life. One student says the block system "suits most who come here very well. It is often the main pull for many students. Those it doesn't work for generally leave—thus the higher than normal freshmen attrition rate. One negative aspect is that it creates a constant sense of urgency that hangs over many of the students; while they aren't juggling four classes, they are required to take in and process huge quantities of information in a very short period of time." A professor says that "it works very well for our particular students, both in the short term (they make quick progress in their studies) and over time (they are well prepared for professions, professional training, and life.) It doesn't of itself integrate whole subject matters."

With more than 40 majors and as many minors available (including a distinctive program in Southwest studies) as well as the opportunity to design their own programs, students have a remarkable number of choices. The structure of the college-wide curriculum seems somewhat weak, but some of the requirements for majors are more structured. Even the self-designed majors must have faculty advisors who give oversight, and the major must have "depth," with courses at the junior and senior levels that build on lower-level courses. English majors, for instance, take courses in the literature of the Middle Ages and the Renaissance, Shakespeare, the period from 1660 to the English Romantics, the nineteenth century, and the twentieth century, plus a course in prose fiction. On the other hand, English students must take an "alternative literature course" in minority, non-Western, or women's literature.

In the hope of offering "students a breadth of learning among the divisions of the college," according to the school's Web site, the school requires that half of the required 32 units be outside a student's major. Students are allowed to double major in two different departments or in a traditional department and interdisciplinary program, provided there are no more than three courses in common between the majors. A student can pursue a "thematic minor" of five units from two departments outside the major. There are dozens of these minors to choose from—a student may even design his own—but each is interdisciplinary in approach. Those suggested by the school include "The Ancient World," "Journalism," "Environmental Studies," and "Non-Violence: Theory and Practice." Or, instead of a thematic minor, students may choose a departmental minor, such as foreign language, which is modeled on the departmental majors and is often a "more traditional disciplinary program," according to a professor.

The process by which students choose courses is also distinctive. Since all classes at Colorado College are limited to 25 students (32 for team-taught blocks), competition for seats is sometimes especially high—lots of people want to take "Ecology of Belize," for example, not least because it is taught in Belize. This has led to an auction each spring for spots in the following year's courses. Students get 10 "points" per block,

VITAL STATISTICS

Religious affiliation: none
Total enrollment: 2,044
Total undergraduates: 2,011
SAT/ACT midranges: SAT V: 600–690, M: 610–690; ACT: 25–30
Applicants: 4,172
Applicants accepted: 44%
Accepted applicants who enrolled: 32%
Tuition: $30,048
Room and board: $7,620
Freshman retention rate: 91%
Graduation rate: 77% (4 yrs.), 84% (6 yrs.)
Courses with fewer than 20 students: 67%
Student-faculty ratio: 10:1
Courses taught by graduate TAs: none
Most popular majors: economics, biology, English
Students living on campus: 73%
Guaranteed housing for four years? yes
Students in fraternities: 11% sororities: 16%

with which they bid on coveted spots in popular classes. If their bid is not quite high enough to get them in, they are placed on a waiting list and promptly notified of any last-minute openings. The system is competitive but, with a bit of tactical finesse, four years is usually ample time for a student to get into the courses he craves.

Students are aided in forming their curricular strategies by faculty advisors assigned even before they reach campus. Students are encouraged to visit their advisors at least three times per semester through their second year, when they choose other advisors from within their majors.

Student mentors chosen from among upperclassmen help freshmen in the First-Year Experience program. This program comprises the first two blocks a freshman takes and consists of courses that emphasize writing and research skills, introduce students to the college's library and academic facilities, and work to strengthen oral presentation abilities. These blocks also introduce freshmen to the interactive, small-seminar style that characterizes classes throughout the college. Classes are often unified by a particular theme that can be explored in depth during the three and a half weeks. The most recent course catalog lists a curious variety of courses from which students may choose, ranging from the solid ("The Renaissance and the Reformation: Crisis and Dissent") to the possibly too-specific or too-broad ("Air," "Kafka in Translation"), to the discouraging ("Exploring Gender").

All in all, despite a few weak and politicized areas such as women's studies and the social sciences division, the resources for an excellent traditional liberal arts education abound at Colorado College. But for its success, the school relies primarily upon the quality and self-motivation of the serious students it attracts and the guidance of individual devoted professors. According to one professor, students continue to show a strong interest in canonical Western subjects and authors, such as Shakespeare—while also dabbling in multicultural studies. Some of the best professors at the college include Marc Snyder in biology, Fred Tinsley in mathematics, Sam Williams in religion, John H. Riker in philosophy, Susan A. Ashley in history, Eve Noirot Grace in political science, Eric Popkin in sociology, and the entire neuroscience department.

Neuroscience and psychology have achieved high visibility in recent years, strengthened by the new Tutt Science Center, which also houses mathematics, environmental science, psychology, and geochemistry. The building, designed by internationally renowned architects Moore, Rubel, and Yudell, is a model of environmental sustainability. Monitors throughout allow students to measure a variety of parameters (the ambient carbon dioxide level, for example) so they can learn about and participate in using the building in more efficient ways. Across the campus, traditional buildings are undergoing restoration and "green" renovation.

Colorado College's previous president, Kathryn Mohrman, strongly supported the school's international program. More than 15 percent of CC's student body studies abroad in a typical year in one of eight international study programs run by the college in Europe, Mexico, and Japan. Colorado College is ranked fourth among bachelor's institutions in the number of students studying abroad, according to the *Chronicle of Higher Education*.

Student Life: Blocked in?

Colorado College likes to think of itself as "situated in a metropolitan area." That area would be Colorado Springs, which has a metro population of nearly half a million and is only an hour from Denver. But the proximity of the 14,110-foot Pikes Peak, the Garden of the Gods (the nation's most spectacular city park), hundreds of miles of hiking and biking trails, and the recent sighting of a moose grazing near the construction site of a new residence hall point to the wilder nature of the school's environs.

Freshman Outdoor Orientation Trips (FOOT) introduce newcomers to the region and its opportunities for backpacking, hiking, biking, camping, mountain climbing, and windsurfing. Such outings are not only encouraged by the college's location and prevailing culture but also by the very structure of the block plan, which provides four-day breaks between each class. And even during a block, with no simultaneous classes demanding attention, professors sometimes take students on extended field trips, taking advantage of the college's mountainous Baca Campus and several woodland cabins.

Such excursions are welcomed by Colorado College students, 73 percent of whom live on campus. In fact, all unmarried students except seniors, locals living with their parents, and some military students are required to live in campus housing. Housing accommodations include five residence halls, 12 small houses, and the on-campus West Ridge Apartments—which are, according to one student, "the most luxurious student housing I've ever seen." These facilities offer a suitable variety of arrangements, including both coed and single-sex options, theme houses organized around a central topic (such as social activism, music, or philosophy), six language immersion houses, a multicultural house, and units for those in search of quiet study or substance-free accommodations. There are no coed bathrooms or dorm rooms in the residence halls.

President Celeste's former position as director of the Peace Corps makes him well-suited to preside over Colorado College, which is ranked 11th among small colleges and universities for producing active Peace Corps volunteers. The school's service orientation is not only evident among the volunteering graduates, described as "ambitious to make a difference in the world," but also among the remarkable 75 percent of the student body active in community service projects through 35 student-run community service organizations.

ACADEMIC REQUIREMENTS

Under the newly revised general education requirements, students must fulfill a "Critical Perspectives" requirement consisting of:

- Two blocks of "The West Through Time," emphasizing the contributions of Western culture.
- Three blocks of "Diverse Cultures and Critiques."
- Two blocks of "Scientific Inquiry," one of which must contain a significant lab or field component in which data from the natural world is collected and interpreted.
- A relatively weak foreign language requirement that may be fulfilled by completing a pair of introductory-level classes, by taking a test, or by having studied a language for four years in high school. The whole requirement can be dropped if "the student presents acceptable evidence of a learning disability making language study impossible."

Not all clubs are wholly devoted to service. Many interests are served by nearly three dozen student organizations, from the Aikido Club and Chess Club to the various gay rights clubs (including Empowered Queers United for Absolute Liberation, or EQUAL, and the Queer Straight Alliance), the Feminist Collective, and even the Young Republicans. "It is a liberal campus," one student says. "Conservatives can expect to regularly have their viewpoints challenged." Conversely, one professor says that "neither conventionally conservative nor liberal students have been particularly prominent, though both exist here." Three fraternities and three sororities attract about 13 percent of the student body. Students govern themselves through the Colorado College Campus Association and the Student Honors Council, which since 1949 has administered an honor code that allows exams without proctors and holds hearings when there are allegations of plagiarism or cheating. There is a strong chapel program, and an associated chaplain was recently added to the already vigorous activity of the campus ministry program.

With the immediacy of the outdoor environment as well as Colorado's generally high state of athletic fitness compared to the nation as a whole, it's not surprising that 78 percent of students participate in the college's intramural program, and around a quarter of students have energy enough for the school's varsity sports programs—which have spawned 15 Olympic athletes, including five gold medalists. (Not coincidentally, the U.S. Olympic Committee has a major training site in Colorado Springs.) Of the varsity teams, only women's soccer and the famed men's hockey team play in the NCAA Division I. Other sports—10 women's varsity teams and eight men's teams—compete at the NCAA Division III level.

Crime is not a big concern; however a dramatic on-campus murder (of a campus radio announcer, not a student) in the spring of 2002 remains unsolved. In 2003, the college reported four forcible sex offenses, two aggravated assaults, seven burglaries, and one car theft. Residence halls are accessible only with an identification card. The college has a 24-hour security patrol that runs a number of crime prevention workshops and an escort service for students walking around campus late at night.

Tuition, room, and board for the 2004–5 school year totaled $37,668. Some 57 percent of students receive need-based aid (including grants, loans, and student employment). Merit-based scholarships are available to students majoring in the natural sciences.

UNIVERSITY OF COLORADO AT BOULDER

BOULDER, COLORADO • WWW.COLORADO.EDU

The Boulder doesn't fall far from the mountains

The University of Colorado at Boulder was founded in 1874 as the state's flagship institution. With a grant of forty-five acres and $15,000, the school began with a single building, Old Main (which still stands), and a daunting mission—to educate the citizens of a state that was still very much part of the wild West. At the school's opening in 1877, students and faculty sang the university anthem, "We Hail Thee! Great Fountain of Learning and Light." Some 127 years later, that "fountain of learning and light" comprises nine academic colleges and serves nearly 32,000 students on a stunning, six-hundred-acre campus in the heart of the Rocky Mountains.

The campus is spectacular and the faculty generally outstanding. Even the curriculum is remarkably good for a state school. The student body, on the other hand, is subject to fits of mob violence and seemingly bent on alcoholic self-annihilation, and attempts by the administration since 1997 to deal with the pandemic of substance abuse have provoked student rioting. Nevertheless, the university is large and diverse enough that a student with a strong sense of self-discipline can find support in a vital religious community. A student who wishes to pursue a traditional liberal education here will find the means to do so, but little encouragement.

Academic Life: Skills and content

What the University of Colorado calls a core curriculum is merely a set of requirements in "skills acquisition" and "content areas." The student who values a traditional education and somehow finds herself at Boulder can find solid courses to satisfy each requirement. One who wishes to avoid this will be able to do so very easily, except for math and science.

VITAL STATISTICS

Religious affiliation: none
Total enrollment: 31,943
Total undergraduates: 26,182
SAT/ACT midranges: SAT V: 530–630, M: 550–650; ACT: 23–28
Applicants: 19,360
Applicants accepted: 85%
Accepted applicants who enrolled: 31%
Tuition: $3,480 (in state), $20,592 (out of state)
Room and board: $7,564
Freshman retention rate: 84%
Graduation rate: 36% (4 yrs.), 66% (6 yrs.)
Courses with fewer than 20 students: 45%
Student-faculty ratio: 18:1
Courses taught by graduate TAs: 16%
Most popular majors: social sciences, business, communications
Students living on campus: 22%
Guaranteed housing for four years? no
Students in fraternities: 8% sororities: 11%

CU–Boulder has no core curriculum but does maintain extensive and respectable distribution requirements. Each student must complete the following:

- A foreign language requirement, met by passing one course or testing out. Sign language counts.
- A quantitative reasoning and mathematical skills requirement, met by passing a course or a test. One course that counts is "Telecommunications I."
- A lower-division writing course. Choices range from "Writing in Arts and Sciences" to "Conversations on the American West." Students may test out.
- An upper-division writing course. Choices range from "Critical Thinking and Writing in Philosophy" to "Multicultural Perspectives and Academic Discourse."
- An upper-division course in critical thinking. Well over 100 courses count, ranging from "Introduction to Abstract Mathematics" to "The Japanese American Internment."
- A history course. Choices range from "Economic History of Europe" to "Sub-Saharan Africa to 1800."

The "skills" are knowledge of a foreign language, writing, quantitative reasoning, and critical thinking. Only the critical thinking requirement and half the writing requirement require coursework. The foreign language requirement can be satisfied by taking three foreign language courses in high school, a third-semester college-level class, or by examination. Sufficient quantitative reasoning and math skills can be demonstrated by passing one to two math courses or a proficiency test. The lower-level written communication requirement can be satisfied by ACT, AP, or SAT scores.

The upper-level "writing" courses are offered by various departments. Examples include "Multicultural Perspectives and Academic Discourse," "Scientific Writing in Kinesiology," and "Critical Thinking and Writing in Philosophy." The course in "critical thinking" is intended to help students "learn how to construct, defend, and criticize arguments; identify and assess tacit assumptions; and gather and evaluate evidence." Courses that count include "Japanese-American Internment," "The Sixties: Critical Black Views," and "Policy Implications of Climate Controversies." On the other hand, "Seminar in Classical Antiquity," "Intellectual Roots of Italian Renaissance Art," and the "History and Philosophy of Physics" also fulfill the critical thinking requirement.

In addition to the skills requirement, students must take one course in each of the following content areas: historical context, cultural and gender diversity, United States context, contemporary societies, and ideals and values. Two courses must be taken in literature and the arts, and four courses, including a laboratory course, in the natural sciences.

Several of the seven content-area requirements can be satisfied by completing politicized courses in gender and ethnicity; indeed, the number of such courses can seem overwhelming. The cultural and gender diversity requirement, for instance, can be fulfilled by choosing classes like "Economics of Inequality and Discrimination," "Understanding Privilege and Oppression in Contemporary Society," "Introduction to Lesbian, Gay, Bisexual, and Transgender Studies," and "The Social Construction of Sexuality." The United States context list includes a number of trivial courses, and the literature and the arts area lists courses like "Feminist Theory/Women's Art" and "History and Philosophy of Dance." The contemporary societies requirement can be satisfied by courses like "Contemporary Black Protest Movements," "Gender, Race, and Class in Contemporary U.S. Society," and "Disabilities in Contemporary American Society." But even the diversity requirement can be satisfied by a course in traditional Asian civilization, and economics courses count for contemporary society.

Around half of Colorado's classes contain fewer than 20 students, and 85 percent enroll fewer than 50. As usual, introductory-level courses for underclassmen are the largest. The university claims that students won't have trouble getting into required courses and will not be prevented from graduating because of limited course availability. To back up this claim, CU has implemented a "Graduation Guarantee" under which students entering with a minimum amount of academic preparation are guaranteed to get into all the courses they need within four years. If the college cannot meet that promise, additional courses are free.

The Honors Program at CU–Boulder is one of the strongest in the country, and since a central honors council decides whether a student should graduate with honors, the distinction actually means something. A student in the program can choose honors-level courses in any department and can graduate with honors by taking at least four such courses and writing a thesis as a senior. The honors department also offers a number of interdisciplinary courses, including "The Figure of Socrates," "Science and Mysticism," "Election 2000," and "Mind, Brain, and Ways of Knowing." An honors dorm is available for one hundred freshmen participants, but living there is optional.

Several departments at CU–Boulder stand out. The sciences are generally very good. The aeronautical engineering program is well respected, and NASA recruits many CU students. The physics department is singled out by students and faculty alike as especially strong. In 2003, two faculty members won the Nobel Prize in physics. Some humanities faculty, however, are unhappy with the disproportionate emphasis they believe the university puts on the sciences. "The scientists support the school with federal grants, so basically, anything they want, they get," says one professor. Another professor says, "This school is basically supported

REQUIREMENTS (CONT'D)

- A course in cultural and gender diversity. The more than 100 choices range from "Introduction to Traditional East Asian Civilizations" to "Multicultural Leadership."
- A course in American society and culture. There are over fifty options here, including "Colorado: History, Ecology and Environment."
- A lower-division course in literature and the arts. Choices range from "The Figure of Socrates" to "Fairy Tales of Russia."
- An upper-division course in literature and the arts. Options include "Goethe's Faust" and "Feminist Theory and Women's Art."
- A two-semester science sequence.
- Two additional science courses.
- A one credit science laboratory.
- A course in contemporary societies. The more than 50 choices range from "Principles of Microeconomics" to "That's Amore: Introduction to Italian Culture."
- A course in ideals and values. Choices range from "Introduction to Philosophy" to "The Future of Spaceship Earth."

WEST

by the grants that the sciences bring in." Humanities receive much less outside support, and thus get less from the university itself, according to professors. Given the political slant of some of them, that may be just as well.

The University of Colorado made headlines in 2005 when Professor Ward Churchill was forced to resign the chair of the ethnic studies department after Bill O'Reilly exposed his nationwide audience to Churchill's published remark that the victims of the World Trade Center attacks were comparable to Nazis like Adolf Eichmann, who was kidnapped, tried, and executed by Israel. This remarkable statement was based on Churchill's assumption that the Central Intelligence Agency had an office in the Twin Towers, which they in fact did not, not to mention his callous disregard for the lives of the thousands who were in no way part of the U.S. command and control structure. When the governor of Colorado called for Churchill's removal, a group of students supporting him successfully disrupted an open meeting of the Board of Regents convened to discuss the incident. By March, the university's president, Elizabeth Hoffman, had herself resigned, but not Churchill. At press time the university was still attempting to buy out Churchill's contract him and get him the heck out of Dodge. Meanwhile, the Tribal Clerk of the United Keetoowah Band Cherokee in Tahlequah, Oklahoma, has denied that Churchill is a member of the tribe, a membership he has often claimed. He had even been expelled as an impostor in 1993 from the radical American Indian Movement. It was on the basis of Churchill's claim to be not only an Indian, but a national spokesman for the Indians, that the University had evidently waived the customary requirement of a doctorate in his hiring.

Outside the sciences the academic quality of departments varies. "There are a lot of people very committed to mainstream teaching in English and American history," says one professor. Political science is considered a radical department by several faculty. Two of the most popular departments, psychology and environmental studies, are not recommended by more traditionally oriented faculty. One conservative student says the most politically radical departments are sociology and art, although, he says, the art department is "very tolerant of differing views." Another professor says that sociology, which was once heavily Marxist, is "starting to get better" as retiring professors are replaced by better scholars. For undergraduate teaching, the foreign languages, especially French, Spanish, and Italian, are quite strong.

English is described as "weak and chaotic" by one professor, though this person adds that "if you're intelligent and resourceful you can make your way through—just ask around to find good professors." One English department professor says glumly, "If we believed in truth in advertising, we would change the department's name to cultural studies." The requirements of the English department bear out this professor's lament. Majors must take a course in "Literary Analysis and Literary Theory," three courses in English and British literature, and one in American literature. But they also must take a course in advanced theory, genre studies, or popular culture, and one in multicultural or gender studies. The history department is more traditional. It requires a two-course survey of American history, two introductory courses in Western civilization, and one course focusing on a non-Western nation or region.

Students who need help in choosing courses may consult with their faculty advisors, but Colorado insists that "the relationship between you and your advisor is one of shared responsibility." Some students remark that there is "a lot of bureaucracy," and to get used to doing things yourself if they need to be done. Not much help should be expected from the administration. Students unsure of their majors are shuffled into the Open Option program and assigned an advisor from a pool. Once a student chooses a major, he is assigned to an advisor from his department. Professors also advise students unofficially, of course. "All of the professors I have had are interested in helping the students and make time to help students who want to succeed," an economics major says.

Some of the best professors at the university include E. Christian Kopff in the Honors Program; David Gross and Patricia Limerick in history; Paul W. Kroll in East Asian languages and civilizations; Jay Kaplan in economics; and Thomas R. Cech in chemistry. In 2004, Nobel Laureate Carl Weiman was named national Teacher of the Year by the Carnegie Foundation for the Advancement of Teaching and the Council for Advancement and Support of Education. Weiman, who moved his Nobel Prize press conference up 15 minutes so as not to be late for his freshman class in physics for non-scientists, donated the prize money to the university fund for the improvement of science teaching. For the sake of teachers like this you can put up with a lot of nonsense (like that surrounding Ward Churchill).

Since 1948, the university has organized a Conference on World Affairs, a symposium that comprises a wide variety of thinkers and celebrities. In 2004, program speakers included feminist Susan Faludi, Peter Copeland, the editor and general manager of Scripps Howard News Service, and essayist Richard Rodriguez.

When asked to characterize CU's students, one professor says, "They have a very strong commitment to looking good and skiing." A student acknowledges, "The workload could be heavier. But students are not so tied down by their schoolwork that they can't afford to party midweek or cut class on a Tuesday to ski." But there are also ample opportunities for talented and motivated students to participate in the intellectual life of CU–Boulder. "The best students are well taken care of," a professor says. "If you're an average student, you're on your own." Alas, there are many average students. According to university figures, 24 percent of CU students ranked in the top 10 percent of their high school classes, and 57 percent ranked in the top quarter.

SUGGESTED CORE

1. Classics 4110, Greek and Roman Epic *or* English 2602, Introduction to Western European Literature
2. Philosophy 1010, Introduction to Western Philosophy: Ancient
3. English 3312, The Bible as Literature
4. Religious Studies 3000, Christian Traditions (*closest match*)
5. Political Science 2004, Survey of Western Political Thought (*closest match*)
6. English 3000, Shakespeare for Non-majors
7. History 1015, History of the United States to 1865
8. History 4414-3, European Intellectual History 1750–1870

Student Life: Dude, where's my couch?

From any campus dorm room, students at CU-Boulder may have a view of the Rockies, the campus pond, or a mountain meadow. But only 22 percent of students live on campus. Most CU students flee university housing after their first year. Housing options on campus range from small houses to high rises. All dormitories are coed, but in some cases, men and women are separated by floor. Coed bathrooms and dorm rooms are only available for married students, who are normally housed in university-owned apartments. Many dormitories offer a Residential Academic Program, which allows students to take small courses with faculty members within the residential setting. Some of these classes focus on science or engineering, others on multicultural education.

The campus setting in the heart of the Rocky Mountains attracts an environmentally conscious student population; its reputation as a school for potheads attracts, well, potheads. The result is the presence of a significant population of politically radical students—or at least a significant population of students *posing* as radicals. One undergrad says the school has been called the "liberal lighthouse of the West." Another calls it the "Berkeley of Colorado," saying, "Boulder is known for its new age thinking and care-free approach to life. There is a sizable population of hippies, and Greenpeace activists are everywhere."

Sounds like a riot—literally. Protests are a common occurrence. During the build-up to the war on Iraq, the university unplugged the microphones being used by student protesters, saying that the protest was interfering with classes being held in adjacent buildings. When the students attempted to force the university to turn the microphones back on, police were summoned. The students began to fight the police, who responded with mace and tear gas. Those responsible for the protest were arrested and suspended from school. One was charged with a felony.

Although only about a tenth of CU–Boulder students are members of a sorority or fraternity, it was voted the number one party school in the nation by *The Princeton Review* for several years. When it dropped to ninth place in 2004, a student told the *Denver Post*, "Well, we're going to make it to No. 1 again. That's all I have to say." The administration has attempted to get tough on drinking, and a 1997 crackdown led to serious riots. Six resident advisors were fired in 2002 after they admitted to drinking on campus, in violation of the uiversity's zero-tolerance policy. One student reports that "nearly every student of age" can be found in the bars on any given night, and no doubt a certain number of the underaged. In fall 2004 a male freshman died of acute alcohol poisoning in a fraternity initiation.

The city of Boulder is described as "pretty lax" about marijuana. Farrand Field is home to a "smoke-fest" every year on April 20, and a student reports, "The cops don't care; they simply park their cars at the side of the field and watch." Thousands of students participate.

CU–Boulder has a full calendar of campus speakers—"about three or four speakers every night," according to one student. Despite the fact that Focus on the Family, the influential conservative Christian organization, is located less than ninety miles away (in Colorado Springs), liberal speakers at CU outnumber conservatives by a wide margin.

Students in the Art & Revolution group "challenge the corporate state's mind control machine and mainstream advertising by creatively resisting its influence on the community." The Support Native Resistance group works to free the Dineh nation from "Peabody Coal, the United States, and other oppressors." The World Federalist Association intends to achieve peace through international law. Other politically oriented student groups include Justice in Northern Ireland, Young Democratic Socialists, the Green Party, Hemp Initiative, and Amnesty International. To counter these leftist student groups, conservative students started a Students for a Better America group, but the university made life difficult for it by denying funding for "Freedom Week," intended to raise awareness of conservatism. CU also has chapters of the College Republicans and the Campus Libertarians. One student advises, "You must be tolerant and open-minded when you come to CU. You will be immersed in a liberal society, probably more liberal than you grew up in."

"If you don't ski, bike, hike, climb, etc.," says a student, "you don't belong here." The university offers dozens of intramural sports, from basketball to broomball, but students looking for more stringent competition can try out for an intercollegiate club or varsity team. The Colorado Buffalos compete in the Big 12 conference with collegiate powerhouses like Texas and Oklahoma in 17 varsity sports. Represented by their mascot, a buffalo named Ralphie, Colorado has excelled in football. Unfortunately, it has also excelled in sleazy recruiting practices.

In 2004 a grand jury investigated reports that visiting football recruits were taken to sex parties and generously plied with drugs and alcohol. The judge refused to release their report to the public, but a recruiting assistant was indicted after admitting using the university telephone to call an escort service. He claimed that he hired the ladies exclusively for his own use, but they testified to the contrary. Auditors found no evidence that university funds had been used to pay for their services. Heretofore suppressed rape charges also surfaced, and reports that the university threatened a woman who attempted to report rape by a sports star. A columnist for the *Denver Post* scoffed at university president Betsy Hoffman's assertion that this scandal would not be allowed to "taint" the "reputation" of the school: "CU didn't have much of a reputation before—other than as a professional party school... and a school that produced dozens of football players who got into trouble with the law (one became a murderer) and a school where fraternity members burned sofas in the street and as a school down the street from where Mork and Mindy lived." Harsh, but close enough to the truth to hurt. The president didn't help matters by stating in a deposition that "c**t" applied to a woman is not necessarily abusive, but may also be a term of endearment. Football recruits are now supervised by coaches or parents, forbidden to to go to bars, clubs, and parties, and subject to an 11 o'clock curfew. It is hoped that some will nevertheless choose to play for the Buffs.

Boulder (population 100,000), the bohemian capital of the West, boasts that it is home to more than 128 "new religions." At the same time, says one Christian student, "CU is an excellent place for students to grow in their faith. There are a multitude of Christian groups, service groups, Christian service groups, and other such activities.

WEST

Come to CU ready to be challenged in your faith, and do not come to CU expecting to be able to be open with your faith without attracting some flak." The city's cosmopolitan atmosphere is highly appealing to many students. Each year Boulder hosts the Colorado Shakespeare Festival and numerous music festivals. Other celebrations are of less general interest. In spring 2002, three campus women's groups sponsored Women's Sex Night, also known as "Sexpressions." During the event, students celebrated their sexuality with interpretive dance, musical performances, and poetry.

The school's largely wooded campus has won worldwide acclaim for both its natural and architectural beauty. The university has made a conscious effort to maintain continuity. Most buildings exhibit a Western style known as Tuscan Vernacular, which uses local stone and distinctive red tile roofs. Students walking from dorms to their classes may cross a number of creeks and streams, but it is generally a safe bet that the water will stay underfoot: Boulder averages more than three hundred sunny days per year. Students who find the campus beautiful will not be disappointed when they venture in to town—*Sports Illustrated* recently ranked Boulder the fifth-best college town in America. And with the Rockies surrounding the entire campus, students looking for outdoor activities of any kind should have no trouble finding them. Hiking, mountain biking, and skiing are extremely popular. "It's about a five-minute walk to the mountains," a student says, exaggerating only slightly. "That's probably why a lot of people come here." (About half the student body hails from outside Colorado; that group represents each of the other states plus 80 foreign countries.) Some of the top ski resorts in North America are within a two-hour drive, including Vail and Aspen, and if the urge strikes, there are abundant opportunities for whitewater rafting, snowboarding, backpacking, horseback riding, and climbing—in fact, students who are short on time can even climb some of the buildings on campus, such as the Engineering Center. There are numerous outdoor-oriented student organizations, including cycling, flying, and soaring clubs. The university is also home to the Fiske Planetarium, the CU Heritage Center, the CU Museum of Natural History, and the CU Art Galleries.

The university community is not often struck by individual violent crime. In 2003, the last year for which statistics were available, the university reported nine aggravated assaults, three robberies, and 22 forcible sex offenses on campus. To protect student safety, the university keeps dormitories locked, and the campus has plenty of emergency call boxes and round-the-clock police surveillance. A safety escort service not only helps students get around campus but also escorts students throughout the city of Boulder. All dormitory visitors must present a student ID card or be escorted by a resident.

Boulder is rather a bargain for Colorado residents; in 2004–5 they paid only $3,480 in tuition; nonresidents paid a hefty $20,592. Room and board was $7,564. Admissions are need-blind, although the school doesn't promise everyone full financial aid. Some 55 percent of students do receive such a package, and 44 percent get some need-based aid. The average student loan debt of a 2002 graduate was $16,000.

UNIVERSITY OF DALLAS

IRVING, TEXAS • WWW.UDALLAS.EDU

The Lazarus effect

A small but growing number of regional colleges across America are gaining prestige and acceptance among prospective students and academics alike by claiming to offer their students a true liberal arts education in a traditional religious environment. The University of Dallas is one such school. Known for its exceptional focus on an authentic and rigorous core curriculum, dedicated faulty, and serious student body, it remains to be seen whether this Catholic school can stay faithful to its strong religious and liberal arts tradition even as it pursues an aggressive capital campaign and aims to raise its national reputation. Right now, at least, among regional liberal arts colleges one would be hard pressed to find a school offering a stronger core. As one UD professor puts it: "I think it may be the best education available." In addition, the university's Web site notes that in 1988 UD became "the youngest university in America to receive a Phi Beta Kappa chapter, a prestigious membership granted on the basis of academic excellence."

Founded by the Sisters of St. Mary of Namur in 1956, the university "seeks to educate students of seriousness, intelligence, and spirit . . . so they may develop the intellectual and moral virtues which will prepare them for life and work in a changing and problematic world, achieve a mature understanding of their faith, and become men and women who act responsibly for their own good and for the good of their family, community, country, and church." Over the years, Dallas has maintained and even improved on its commitment to such values, and it has done so without much money at its disposal. But that is a particular problem the university has struggled with in recent years; as one administrator puts it, "2003 was yet another year of financial despair at UD." Several years ago, President Msgr. Milam Joseph was hired with a mandate to improve the university's financial health. He tripled the school's marketing and public relations staff and launched a campaign to raise $104 million. The funds were earmarked for new student life facilities, a rectory for Dominican priests, academic scholarships, new

VITAL STATISTICS

Religious affiliation: Roman Catholic
Total enrollment: 3,047
Total undergraduates: 1,087
SAT/ACT midranges: SAT V: 560–670, M: 550–660; ACT: 23–28
Applicants:
Applicants accepted: 87%
Accepted applicants who enrolled: 34%
Tuition: $19,604
Room and board: $7,026
Freshman retention rate: 86%
Graduation rate: 70% (4 yrs.), 74% (6 yrs.)
Average class size: 20
Student-faculty ratio: 12:1
Courses taught by graduate TAs: none
Most popular majors: biology, business, English
Students living on campus: 61%
Guaranteed housing for four years? no
Students in fraternities or sororities: none

WEST

845

The University of Dallas has one of the most serious and valuable core curricula in the country. All students must complete the following:

- Four courses in philosophy. Three are required for all students: "Philosophy and the Ethical Life," "Philosophy of Man," and "Philosophy of Being." Students also choose one elective.
- Four courses in English, composing the "Literary Tradition" sequence. The first course is a focused and intensive study of classic epic poetry, the second studies the Christian epic poem, the third is on dramatic tragedy and comedy, and the fourth is on the modern novel.
- Three electives in math.
- Three electives in the fine arts.
- Two electives in the sciences, one biological and one physical.

faculty positions, and the university endowment. While such improvements were desperately needed, Joseph's efforts raised suspicion among some students and faculty who believed that the university's commitment to bring in large donors and raise its national profile would come at the expense of the school's liberal arts mission. Msgr. Joseph retired in 2003, but the board of trustees remains, and they are, as one student says, "Monsignor's board. Very bottom-line oriented."

In the summer of 2004, Francis M. Lazarus became the university's seventh president. As the former provost of the University of San Diego, Lazarus has the financial savvy to shepherd Dallas into the black. So far, he has managed to increase enrollment and to cut the school's debt by cutting expenditures. Both his fiscal skills and his academic background will be needed—the former to pay the bills, the latter to maintain the university's traditional educational focus. It's a nearly impossible line to walk, but the University of Dallas needs if it is both to survive and to prevail.

Academic Life: The way

What sets UD apart from many of its peer institutions is the way in which its core curriculum actually does set students on a path to the moral and intellectual virtues. The core at UD is "designed to foster the student's pursuit of wisdom through formation in intellectual and moral excellence, to foster a mature understanding of the Catholic faith, and to encourage a responsible concern for shaping contemporary society." UD was the very first university to receive accreditation from the American Academy for Liberal Education, a group committed to recognizing schools that have solid core curricula. That group's endorsement is quickly becoming the gold standard for those looking for a true liberal arts curriculum.

All students at Dallas must take the two-year core, for as the university eloquently explains: "Reflection reveals to us that this tradition [of great books and ideas] is a conversation among the greatest minds, discussing the issues of greatest concern to all of mankind. To assess this tradition, to accept, to modify, to reject any part of it, to think and to live in freedom with it or from it, we must all join this conversation at the highest possible level with every resource at our command. A true core curriculum enables us to do that. It teaches us to listen attentively to the most powerful and articulate voices from the past, to reflect long and deeply on what they say, to engage in animated argument with each other about what they mean, and then, after sifting and weighing and testing, to make up our own minds." To which we can only say, "Amen."

There is very little leeway within the core—either in terms of texts studied or in course selection—which is part of the reason that the core at Dallas is an authentic liberal arts program. It gives undergraduates a common bedrock of texts, authors, and ideas from which to approach their majors—and their lives. In addition to traditional majors, students may complete a preprofessional or dual-degree program (e.g., predentistry or a joint BA/MBA program). Additional concentrations (e.g., journalism or medieval and Renaissance studies) may also be pursued.

It is not only the university that maintains the importance of the core; the students at Dallas are its biggest supporters. "My friends who went to more prestigious universities didn't have to study nearly as much as I did," says one recent graduate. "You had to study at UD. And you had to *read* original sources, not a textbook." It is little wonder that English and politics are two of the most popular majors (the others being biology and business leadership). Both students and faculty consider English, politics, theology, and philosophy to be strong departments. The medical school acceptance rate for Dallas graduates is 90 percent, indicating both that the science departments are excellent and that spending two years on core classes does nothing to prohibit students from pursuing a plan of study outside the liberal arts. The administration at the University of Dallas takes seriously its mission as a Catholic liberal arts university and has built a core curriculum that reflects that seriousness of purpose. Consequently they have attracted and nurtured a faculty and student body that embodies the mission of the university.

REQUIREMENTS (CONT'D)

- Four set civilization courses, two in Western and two in American civilization.
- One set course in politics, with special attention to the Declaration of Independence, the *Federalist Papers*, and *Democracy in America*.
- One set course in economics. This course has a free-market emphasis but is presented with attention to Catholic social teaching.
- Two set theology courses: an introductory course in biblical scholarship, and "Western Theological Tradition."
- One to four foreign language courses (through the intermediate level). Choices include ancient Greek, French, German, Italian, Latin, and Spanish Credit is given for high Advanced Placement scores.

Dallas students may augment their introduction to the liberal arts by participating in the Rome program at Due Santi, the university's campus located about 10 miles from the heart of the Eternal City. The program is designed to deepen students' knowledge of the subjects, authors, and ideas presented in the core curriculum. About 85 percent of Dallas students participate in the program. "The semester in Rome is certainly formative," one professor says. "The students become more sophisticated, cosmopolitan, and appreciative of history, other cultures, and the universality of the faith."

In addition to the bachelor of arts degrees offered through the Constantin College of the Liberal Arts, the university also offers a BA in business leadership through the College of Business. Established in 2002, the College of Business houses both the

WEST

undergraduate program and the Graduate School of Management. Undergraduate students majoring in business leadership are also required to take the university core requirements. Additionally, business majors take a slate of courses in business leadership—in ethics, social justice, and environmental or biotechnical science—as well as traditional business offerings in marketing, accounting, finance, and business law.

In recent years, many at the University of Dallas worried about the future of the university core and the mission of the university in general. As previously mentioned, the administration of former president Joseph, according to some students and faculty, was not fully committed to the school's liberal arts mission. Many perceived Joseph as being too quick to employ professional fundraisers rather than academics. "Msgr. Joseph and others want to make it a much larger school, more versatile—with more computers and majors—and drag it away from the liberal arts," an alumnus complained at the time.

The installation of President Lazarus, however, reaffirmed UD's strong commitment to not only the Catholic virtues that built the university, but also its dedication to its traditional liberal arts focus and curriculum. President Lazarus has ushered in financial debt reduction not by catering to donors or sacrificing traditional courses, but instead by cutting costs. One of Lazarus's first acts was returning a large sum of money borrowed for renovations, as the administration was not able to justify extending the current debt without plans of repayment. This approach, while controversial—many faculty took some issue with the lack of salary increases and higher health insurance premiums—has helped rebuild some of the school's depleted endowment. Meanwhile, the concerns felt previously by faculty and students that in some way the liberal arts focus of the university would be lost have largely been laid to rest.

Teaching at Dallas is strong, as both graduates and professors from peer institutions attest. Some of the best undergraduate teachers include John Alvis, David Davies, Fr. Robert Maguire, and Gerard Wegemer in English; Richard Dougherty and Thomas G. West in politics; Angelo G. Giuliano and Margaret Turek in theology; William A. Frank and Fr. James Lehrberger in philosophy; Thomas W. Jodziewicz in history; Hazel Cazorla and Alexandra Wilhemlsen in Spanish; William Doyle in economics; Richard Olenick in physics; and Frank Doe in biology. Professors in general play an important role in the life of the university, taking an active role in university social events and extracurricular programs. Students uniformly give them high praise: "The professors really live what they teach," says one student. "They write what they think, and they behave the way they preach."

Though Dallas faculty receive high marks from their students for teaching, they are also actively involved in their respective disciplines, publishing and attending professional meetings. "UD faculty are the best in the country," one student says. UD expects junior faculty to publish in order to be awarded tenure, but even tenured faculty continue to publish. "There's peer pressure to keep going," says one professor. "Everyone wants to pull his weight." There is no evidence, however, that publishing demands detract from professors' work in the classroom. To the contrary, professors appear to be dedicated to the school's liberal arts mission and to recognize its value within a broader humane context; they are happy to be in a place where open support for the traditional canon of the West is not viewed with suspicion.

Class sizes, while they have grown over the years, remain moderate (the average classroom contains 20 students). Although there are some graduate students on campus, none of them are primary teachers of undergraduate courses. Upon enrolling in the university, each entering freshman is assigned a faculty advisor who helps to guide the student through the ins and outs of the core curriculum—not that there are many choices to make. After the first year, a student may select a new advisor from among the faculty in his major department or the university at large.

Student Life: Not there to entertain

The University of Dallas has earned a reputation of greater fidelity to Catholic orthodoxy than the vast majority of Catholic schools—and this one fact alone attracts the interest of many students and parents. As Catholic as Dallas is—about 70 percent of its undergraduates identify themselves as such—students and faculty report that non-Catholics generally feel comfortable at the school. There is little proselytizing by individuals, and none by the university itself. (Protestant worship services are available on campus.) Says one professor about non-Catholics, "Those I have spoken with have expressed some surprise that no one ever approached them about becoming Catholic."

The fundamental agreement between Dallas students on core religious matters is an important contribution to the school's community atmosphere. "You are surrounded by kids who will enforce the school's ideas that there is truth, it can be known by man, and it is unchanging," a student says. And as another student puts it, "For being such a small school, everyone really finds his niche. There are always people who have common ground with you, and it's easy to find them." One professor says that the students are "hard working, respectful, and bright. I certainly do not see our students as closed-minded or set in their ways and thinking. They are, I think, truly open and unafraid. Many of them are devout Catholics and that does provide a standard for their judgments. They are open to anything compatible with authentic Catholicism."

The presence of the university has contributed to the development of a substantial Catholic community in the area. Students can and often do attend mass at the beautiful Cistercian monastery nearby or the Dominican priory on campus. Mass is said at the university's modernist Chapel of the Incarnation twice daily; many students attend, but there is little pressure, if any, for them to do so. It is possible to "get through UD and not learn anything about your faith," says one student. "[But] if you want to practice and grow in your faith there is opportunity to do so and you would never be ridiculed for it."

It should be mentioned that the University of Dallas takes a refreshing and productive view of the university's role in "entertaining" students. As the university hand-

WEST

book makes plain, the university attracts bright, imaginative, and forceful students, and the living quarters, recreational facilities, and social activities all conspire to create a proper environment for their moral and intellectual development: "The satisfaction of students is not here the aim of educational endeavor." The campus, in other words, is a place of learning, not a pleasure dome. According to the *UD General Bulletin*, students are "expected to form among themselves a community of persons sharing in a common goal, and to work out activities, academic or social, that relate harmoniously to the enterprise of learning."

UD students do manage to have fun. Indeed, undergraduates are notable for their lack of puritanical joylessness. Parties in the private apartments adjoining the campus are common, and the annual Groundhog Day party finds students in the woods with a keg or three. Charity Week brings many students together for more constructive festivities. And for students with wheels, the Dallas–Fort Worth metroplex offers abundant cultural opportunities and activities.

Students do not generally attend UD for its sports programs. Still, all of campus was in awe when the long-suffering UD basketball team made the NCAA Division III tournament for the first time in school history in 2004. Not too long ago, there was talk of starting a football team (after all, the place *is* in Texas) but this idea aroused controversy (and costs a lot of money) and was subsequently shelved. Some intramural sports are offered, including football, soccer, basketball, volleyball, and softball, and they are popular. Rugby is a club sport with a good-sized student following. The school has nearly completed a $2 million expansion of its fitness center.

Dedicated to the cult of student choice, many schools are proud of the plethora of clubs and activities they make available to students (clubs and activities that are typically funded by ever-increasing student fees). Dallas seems to have achieved a balance between offering some clubs, such as the University Democrats and the Crusaders for Life, without creating an overwhelming activist environment. As one might expect, religious groups are among the most active and students find many options for service both in the church and the surrounding community.

That surrounding community is located in the city of Irving, which has precious little to recommend it, least of all natural beauty. Many students complain that the university is not placed in a student-friendly neighborhood; there are no stores, coffeehouses, restaurants, or bars within easy walking distance. "I never really saw Dallas because I didn't have a car," says a recent graduate. "If you don't have a car, you're lucky to make it to the grocery store." The university's Dallas Year program tries to overcome this limitation by organizing outings for freshmen to the opera, museum, concerts, and sporting events (although Texas Stadium, home of the Dallas Cowboys, is within walking distance). The convenience of the Dallas–Fort Worth airport is an advantage, but along with its pile-of-bricks architectural style, the university's location is clearly its greatest weakness.

Single-sex dormitories are available. Coed dorms do not include coed floors or bathrooms. Visitation hours for members of the opposite sex are quite restricted, and students entertaining members of the opposite sex must keep the door "bolted"—that is, extend the deadbolt so that the door cannot close. About 61 percent of students live on campus; students are required to do so until they are 21 unless they are married, are veterans, or are living with their parents. Many students find off-campus housing across the street from campus; other apartments are relatively easy to find in nearby neighborhoods. Students perceive the campus and its environs to be safe. The only crimes on campus in 2003 (the most recent year reported) were three car thefts and one burglary. Crime can be a problem in south Irving, but this ethnically varied area is also more interesting than the standard suburban soullessness of north Irving, where UD is located.

Undergraduate tuition in 2004–5 at UD was $19,604, while room and board was $7,026. As with most universities, financial aid is offered in the form of loans, grants, scholarships and work-study programs. Students seeking need-based aid must first complete the Free Application for Federal Student Aid and then apply for loans and grants or the work-study program through the university. Merit-based scholarships are available. The average aid gift for new students is $11,320; about 63 percent of the undergraduate population receives need-based financial aid.

GONZAGA UNIVERSITY

SPOKANE, WASHINGTON • WWW.GONZAGA.EDU

Capitalized "Catholic"

St. Aloysius Gonzaga died in the sixteenth century while caring for young people who suffered from the bubonic plague. The patron saint of youth never could have known that a Jesuit university would bear his name 300 years later, half a world away. About half the student body at Gonzaga University is Catholic, and a very small number of faculty members are priests of the Society of Jesus. The university's president, Fr. Robert Spitzer, cares deeply about Gonzaga's Catholic identity and has kept the university on a more traditional path than almost any other Jesuit university in the land. In its literature, the university claims that its "students develop their total selves, and love who they become." One student agrees: "My experience with Gonzaga has been one of immense value." A professor says, "I love this university. I attended it as a student. I teach here and two of my children attended it. I believe that the educational experience is very good. Students are challenged in their classes, taught to think critically . . . and are truly committed to the Catholic ideal of service."

Academic Life: Almost there

The most crucial part of the Gonzaga undergraduate experience is what the university calls its core curriculum, in which students take a series of courses from philosophy, history, mathematics, literature, and religion. All students, no matter their major, are required to take these distribution requirements, which are vastly superior to what most schools (even most Catholic ones) have to offer. But they're not quite a core. "In general, there is an overall lack of clear coherence in the university core and the requirements of the college," a professor says. "There was once a coherent vision that governed the university's educational kingdom, but what is left is a loose association of various territorial fiefdoms." A student says, "The core offers courses in Western civilization (and several of the better history professors take these classes very seriously), English requirements, and several classes in religious studies. But the best I can say for the religious studies classes is that they give one an idea of how and what theological liberals think." A professor says, "The large core is surely a great resource. I'm not convinced that the core is utilized to its full potential, however. There is not as much coordination among departments as there might be . . . or even within individual departments." But as another student says, "Gonzaga has enough of a core curriculum and enough good professors teaching core classes to guarantee that liberal arts students are exposed to quite a lot, and most of them do seem to broaden their knowledge considerably."

Gonzaga also offers an impressive Honors Program, which through colloquia and seminar sections provides a solid core curriculum for students who qualify. The program is kept small and is quite competitive. Its students have access to Hopkins House, their own special (nonresidential) house with kitchen, Internet, and other facilities. There is some concern that the program is being politicized. For example, one component was described as follows: "The freshman colloquium introduces students to issues of class, race, gender, and sexual orientation." But one honors student says, "Overall, the program is structured to foster thinkers who can shape society wisely, not indoctrinate students to some political agenda. As a conservative student, I have not felt uncomfortable in the program at all."

Gonzaga has allowed some traditional majors to decline. The classical languages department, for instance, has only two faculty members: One is an instructor and one is a retired Jesuit priest. "Classics [was] about to die here and [was] only saved by the dedication of several professors, most of whom have 'regular jobs' in other departments," a classical languages major says. A professor says, "The state of the classics is a disgrace." The university offers more than twice as many courses in women's studies as it does in Latin and Greek. The philosophy department, however, is alive and well. "A large portion of the philosophy department [faculty] is quite traditionalist, and the chances of a student ending up in a good, interesting, and challenging philosophy class at least once are very high," a student says. Since all students must take four courses in philosophy, this is important. As one philosophy professor says of his department, the largest in the Pacific Northwest: "We have a strong and diverse course offering with some excellent instructors devoted to teaching the tradition." Other good departments at Gonzaga include the natural sciences, music ("small, but good"), and the business school. Students can earn a concentration in Catholic studies, which "holds great promise," according to one professor. Some students hope it will become an independent major. "The good news," says one professor, "is that an increasing number of students arriving on campus are serious about their studies and about a liberal education; it is my impression that we have many more students than in the past who are taking responsibility for their education."

The most politicized academic departments at Gonzaga are women's studies, international studies, and religion. The biology department has also been criticized for its politics by both students and faculty. Although one religion professor prefers the term "centrist" to characterize his department, other faculty members speak of its "dominant political liberalism" as a weakness. Courses like "Gender and Politics" and "Lan-

VITAL STATISTICS

Religious affiliation:
  Roman Catholic
Total enrollment: 6,169
Total undergraduates: 4,118
SAT/ACT midranges: SAT
  V: 540–640, M: 550–650;
  ACT: 24–29
Applicants: 4,310
Applicants accepted: 74%
*Accepted applicants who
  enrolled*: 32%
Tuition: $21,730
Room and board: $6,430
Freshman retention rate: 92%
Graduation rate: 63% (4 yrs.),
  79% (6 yrs.)
Average class size: 23
Student-faculty ratio: 11:1
*Courses taught by graduate
  TAs*: none
Most popular majors:
  business, biology,
  psychology,
Students living on campus:
  56%
*Guaranteed housing for four
  years?* no
*Students in fraternities or
  sororities*: none

Five schools at Gonzaga serve undergraduates—the College of Arts and Sciences, the School of Education, the School of Business Administration, the School of Engineering, and the School of Professional Studies. All students are required to complete the core requirements of the university and of the individual school or college.

Gonzaga's university-wide distribution requirements are as follows:

- Thought and Expression. This is a set of three courses designed to be taken simultaneously in one of the semesters of an undergraduate's first year. It includes "English Composition," "Critical Thinking," and "Speech Communication."
- Philosophy. Three courses in philosophy are taken in sequence: "Philosophy of Human Nature," "Ethics," and one upper-level elective chosen from among courses such as "Ancient-Medieval Philosophy," "St. Thomas Aquinas," "Marxism," and "Postmodern Thought."

guage and Cultural Identity" are typical of those offered in women's studies. In Gonzaga's English department there's good news and bad: Yes, there's a Shakespeare requirement. But the only course offered during a recent semester that fulfilled it was also cross-listed in women's studies. One English major calls this "an unfair requirement for those that wish to take a course that had previously been focused on education rather than indoctrination." Approximately one-quarter of undergraduates enroll in either the business or engineering schools. The Engineering School facilities have been recently improved, though they are inadequate for major research.

Students say professors are accessible and usually personable. About half of all undergraduate courses enroll 20 to 50 students; only a handful of lecture courses enroll more. One undergraduate says, "I've never met [a professor] who didn't seem to think of himself as a teacher first—even the ones who do publish a lot. Professors do advise students, and TAs are virtually unknown." Another student says, "The majority of professors are very interested in the students. I have only heard of a few that are more concerned with getting published." A professor who has taught at Gonzaga for more than 30 years maintains that he and his colleagues are "very accessible."

Gonzaga is hiring more adjunct professors and there are more fixed-term appointments than in the past. The size of the university's entering freshman classes has rapidly expanded, rising by 125 in just three years. "In the past," says one faculty member, "we took pride in telling parents that even full professors teach their share of lower division, freshman-level courses every semester. But three years of good enrollments (two of which were exceedingly strong) have taxed our abilities."

Advising duties make up one of the four pillars of promotion at Gonzaga. All students are assigned a faculty advisor and must meet with that advisor at the beginning and middle of each term. But how strong this relationship becomes depends largely on the student. Many students visit their advisors only to have them sign off on the courses they wish to take. But most do take advantage of their faculty resources. "Developing relationships seems to be a crucial element in Gonzaga's education," says a student.

Students think that the best professors are Harry C. Hazel in communication arts; John Beck in economics; Teresa Derickson, Tod Marshall, Michael Pringle, and Mary Sagal in English; Stephen E. Balzarini, Robert Carriker, Kevin Chambers, Eric Cunningham, and Andrew Goldman in history; Brian Clayton and Douglas Kries in philosophy; Michael Connolly and Blaine Garvin in political science; and Edward Schaefer and Gary Uhlenkott in music.

One of Gonzaga's jewels is the campus it owns and operates in Florence, Italy. The Florence program, established in 1963, allows students to spend part of their undergraduate years in one of the world's great cities.

While other Jesuit universities (this means you, Georgetown) have kept their Catholic identity at arm's length, Gonzaga's administrators revel in it. "Under the leadership of Fr. Robert Spitzer," says one professor, "the trustees and administration are committed to maintaining and increasing" the school's Catholicity. In the university alumni magazine, in which most university presidents would spout uncontroversial clichés, Spitzer writes regularly on themes such as the pursuit of virtue, ethics, the social teaching of the church, the relationship of rights and the common good, the relationship between faith and reason, and the practical aspects of prayer. "In the past two years," says the above professor, "the university has seen a great rise in student-initiated Catholic activism, making Gonzaga an increasingly friendly place for those who wish to learn about their Catholic heritage."

Students and professors acknowledge that Gonzaga's students tend to lean rightward. One student says, "The student body is moderate to slightly conservative, while the faculty is liberal in the majority," but "both liberals and conservatives feel comfortable on campus. Both the left and right have active political groups." Students say faculty biases do sometimes influence course content. "Though many professors will push their ideology on their students," one student says, "there are very few, if any, cases of a professor's political views affecting his grading." A fellow student says, "Though the faculty is weighted heavily toward the left, it is possible to get around that." The College Republicans are an active presence on campus, but the university also has Young Democrats and a newer Campus Libertarians group. Other active student groups include the Gonzaga University Right to Life organization and a group called

REQUIREMENTS (CONT'D)

- Religious Studies. Three courses in religious studies are taken in sequence: one in scriptural studies, one in Christian doctrine, and one in applied theology.
- Mathematics. One course in mathematics is required at the introductory level or above.
- One course in English literature—either "Literary Genres" or (for honors students) "Honors Literature I."

All students in the College of Arts and Sciences face an extended core curriculum that also includes:

- Two courses in history.
- One course in the fine arts.
- A laboratory science course.
- One course in either math or science.
- A course in British or American literature
- Two courses in social sciences.
- One course in either foreign language or culture.
- One course in social justice. Social justice courses cover "issues related to experiences of difference (like race, class, gender, ethnicity, or sexual orientation)," according to the catalog.

Helping Educate Regarding Orientation (HERO), the gay rights group.

Gonzaga does have some of the politicized, bureaucratic flimflam that is characteristic of the contemporary university. The university has, for instance, a director of multicultural education; an associate vice president for diversity; Unity House, a center that "conducts cultural and justice related events"; and an Academic Cultural Excellence Program that awards scholarships to select students. Religious studies is known for its leftist inclinations, offering courses like "Christian Doctrine from a Feminist Perspective." After approval by university administrators, a grant from AmeriCorps funded the opening of a Gay Lesbian Bi-Sexual Transgender Resource Center in 2004. In its first months of operation, the center has been "a rallying point for gay activism," says one student. Another student says, "Homosexual issues have been pretty overt the past couple of years, with a week every year dubbed 'National Coming-Out Week,' barbecue and all."

Student Life: Cinderella no more

Gonzaga will never be famous for its architectural distinction. The university has 87 buildings spread over 108 acres, including an art museum, a gymnasium, a science facility (new in 2003), a fitness center (also new in 2003), and a student center that houses memorabilia from the career of Bing Crosby, Gonzaga's most famous alumnus. The McCarthey Athletic Center, which seats 6,000 for basketball games, opened in fall 2004. The administration building, constructed in 1898, was once the entire college. Today, it houses the College of Arts and Sciences, administration offices, and many classrooms. Major university masses and academic convocations are held at St. Aloysius Church, while most other services are held in the newly renovated university chapel.

Only about half the student body lives on campus, and most of those who do are underclassmen. The university requires freshmen and sophomores who do not stay with their families to live at Gonzaga, where most freshmen live in double rooms in dormitories. Some upperclassmen find housing in university-administered apartment buildings. Gonzaga has both single-sex and coed dormitories; in the coed halls, men and women are separated by floor or by suite. All students who live in residence halls are required to be on a meal plan. Students also have the option of academic theme houses, where students live in groups united by a common activity or interest.

Gonzaga offers a wide variety of extracurricular opportunities. Students can choose from a variety of one-credit "activities" courses per semester, which many say are a great opportunity to meet new people and build relationships with fellow students. "Beginning Bowling," "Alpine Skiing," and "Intermediate Social Dance" are among the choices. Students can help operate the campus television and radio station; contribute to *Spires*, the campus journal of scholarship and opinion; write for the *Gonzaga Bulletin*, the weekly student paper; or have their original creative work published in *Reflection*.

As the university has strengthened its ties to the church, many students have strengthened their own ties to their faith. "There is a regular (and rather large) group of students who attends daily mass, and a much larger number of students on Sunday," a student says. Students participate in service groups like the Knights of Columbus and Catholic Daughters of America, prayer groups, retreats, and liturgical services through the university's strong University Ministry office. One professor singles out the Newman-Stein Fellowship, a Catholic social and intellectual group, as "an impressive atmosphere for students to live out their faith." Another professor agrees that, "Newman-Stein has made significant contributions to campus culture." The school also hosts Protestant and ecumenical groups, as well as a Protestant chaplain.

Gonzaga is large enough (at around 4,000 undergraduates) that it is hard to characterize the typical student. "While every student is unique, there are certain characteristics that we find are common among young men and women who want a solid Catholic education," a student says. "Many students here are committed to the pursuit of knowledge and the truth in their lives." In demographic terms, most Gonzaga students are Catholic, white, and middle class, and about half come from out of state. Students and faculty say that most students are happy while on campus, and some like the school enough to encourage their siblings to attend. But Gonzaga loyalty doesn't always translate into dollars for the school; only 28 percent of graduates donate to their alma mater.

No true Gonzaga Bulldog will let you forget the university's excellent athletics program. The university fields 14 teams in the NCAA Division I. The past few years have seen dramatic success for the men's basketball program, which has gone to the NCAA tournament every year since 1999. Women's basketball is on the upswing as well. For a while, Gonzaga was the nation's favorite underdog every March, but the team can no longer sneak up on anyone. The school dominates the West Coast Conference in men's basketball and women's crew.

Most students feel safe on Gonzaga's urban campus, even though the city of Spokane has a higher crime rate than its population and location would seem to warrant. In 2003, there were two aggravated assaults, one forcible sex offense, 17 burglaries, 12 stolen cars, and one arson on campus. After more than 400 liquor-law violations in 2003, there is increasing concern over alcohol's role on campus.

More than 95 percent of students receive financial aid. "Financial aid from Gonzaga is very good—many students I know, including myself, came here because the school offered a better financial package than the other places to which we applied," says one student. Tuition, fees, room, and board cost about $28,000 in 2004–5. For students who graduated in 2000, the average debt was $21,357. Admission is need-blind.

SUGGESTED CORE

1. English 485, The Epic
2. Philosophy 401, History of Ancient Philosophy
3. Religious Studies 105, Old and New Testament
4. Religious Studies 205, The History and Teachings of Christianity
5. Political Science 331, Modern Political Thought
6. English 205, Studies in Shakespeare
7. History 273, History of the United States I
8. Philosophy 411, History of Modern Philosophy II *or* Philosophy 412, Modern-Contemporary Philosophy (for non-majors) (*closest matches*)

PEPPERDINE UNIVERSITY

MALIBU, CALIFORNIA • WWW.PEPPERDINE.EDU

Useful things

"An educated man without religion," wrote George Pepperdine in 1937 on the occasion of the dedication of the university that today bears his name, "is like a ship without a rudder or a powerful automobile without a steering gear." With this in mind, the founder of Western Auto Supply and lifelong member of the Churches of Christ endowed his school with the intention of building an institution to prepare young men and women for a "life of usefulness in this competitive world" and to help them "build a foundation of Christian character and faith which will survive the storms of life." According to one student, "In all his comments about the school, Mr. Pepperdine appears to be the posterboy for the Protestant work ethic. But the school has a laid-back, Bohemian edge as well. [Being at] Pepperdine is something like this: the beautiful daughter of an 1880 Kansas farmer marries one of the Beach Boys—and you ended up at the wedding."

Today it may be said of Pepperdine University that, with a few notable exceptions, it remains exceptionally true to the aspirations of its founder. Pepperdine's brand of higher education is essentially aimed at cultivating a practically oriented—rather than intellectual—graduate who embraces Christian values, is conservative in disposition, and is poised for a life of leadership and purpose. While Pepperdine has not been impervious to the dubious ideological reforms that have swept through the academy over the past few decades, its strong Christian identity makes it attractive to students interested in pursuing their studies at a school with a relatively sound liberal arts curriculum, a religious orientation, and a warm, friendly atmosphere.

Then too, it doesn't hurt that Pepperdine has one of the most beautiful campuses of any institution of higher education in the nation. Located about a half-hour away from the hectic environs of Los Angeles (and a light-year away from that city's moral milieu), the college's campus in Malibu overlooks the beach. And while the physical setting of a college may not seem all that important, one should not underestimate the value of natural beauty (God's second great book, after the Bible, according to Augustine) in cultivating a sense of the good life, or what George Pepperdine called "beautiful Christian living." On the other hand, a grad student says that "the downside is that this half-hour buffer zone from LALA land also makes the Malibu campus feel insular. Besides the ocean and beautiful beaches, there is not much activity in the vicinity. Malibu is a hideout for stars and is prone to quietude and privacy."

Pepperdine does not have the same approach to the liberal arts that one might find at, say, the University of Dallas, Thomas Aquinas College, or even Hillsdale. The general education requirements cannot be considered a core curriculum, one in which all undergraduates are required to take the same foundational courses. Still, Pepperdine's interdisciplinary curriculum is much better than most, and a student can construct with little difficulty a solidly traditional liberal arts education, especially through the school's Great Books Colloquium. Students will find support from a serious and accomplished faculty, and they will encounter small classes, ample opportunities for close instruction, and an atmosphere in which teaching, rather than research, is still considered the primary task of the professor. In this case, the claim of an institution's promotional literature is true: Pepperdine's most distinctive feature "is its commitment to academic excellence in the context of Christian values."

Academic Life: Service ace

Pepperdine University consists of five institutions—Seaver College, the undergraduate institution; the School of Law; the Graziadio School of Business and Management; the Graduate School of Education and Psychology; and the School of Public Policy, which opened in 1997. Seaver College offers a variety of majors that, for the most part, reflect the school's abiding interest in cultivating "productive" graduates. Majors are divided among seven divisions. The Business Administration Division offers majors in accounting, business administration, and international business studies. The Communications Division offers, among others, majors in journalism, advertising, and public relations. These two divisions, predictably, are the most popular among students, defining Seaver College as a de facto "service" school rather than a liberal arts school, one that emphasizes the skills needed to survive in the workaday world rather than the intellectual facilities needed to understand it.

Indeed, Pepperdine is well known for its programs in business administration and sports medicine, and it offers a sound economics program as well. Students may also pursue a BA through the Center for International Studies and Language, with concentrations offered in Asian studies, economic studies, European studies, political studies, and Latin American studies. The other, less popular, divisions at Seaver are Humanities and Teacher Education, Natural Science, Religion, Fine Arts, and Social Science.

The general education requirements, according to one professor, "are heavy," but they do "provide the students with a balanced liberal arts education." This is especially noteworthy for students who major in business or communications-related fields, who at some other institutions typically are exempted from whatever "core curriculum" may exist.

VITAL STATISTICS

Religious affiliation:
 Churches of Christ
Total enrollment: 7,919
Total undergraduates: 3,201
SAT/ACT midranges: SAT
 V: 550–650, M: 560–660;
 ACT: 24–29
Applicants: 6,024
Applicants accepted: 29%
*Accepted applicants who
 enrolled*: 41%
Tuition: $28,630
Room and board: $8,640
Freshman retention rate: 89%
Graduation rate: 63% (4 yrs.),
 80% (6 yrs.)
*Courses with fewer than 20
 students*: 63%
Student-faculty ratio: 12:1
*Courses taught by graduate
 TAs*: none
Most popular majors:
 business, communications, psychology
Students living on campus:
 62%
*Guaranteed housing for four
 years?* no
Students in fraternities: 24%
 sororities: 29%

While Pepperdine's undergraduate unit, Seaver College, does not quite impose a traditional core curriculum, its General Education Program is leaps and bounds superior to most other schools' distribution requirements in terms of the courses that are required and the material that is covered. Students must take the following:

- A two-course sequence in English composition and literature during freshman year.
- A freshman seminar "designed to build community among a small group of freshmen" and "provide academic and personal advice," according to the catalog.
- A three-course religion sequence.
- A three-course sequence on Western heritage.

Students wanting a more rigorous education in the humanities and liberal arts should consider Pepperdine's Great Books Colloquium, a two-year, four-course sequence modeled after the celebrated St. John's College program. The only prerequisites are eligibility for English 101 (which any native speaker of English will be able to meet) and "a willingness to commit oneself to the time and effort required by the courses." According to the catalog, "Students should be advised that the reading load is much heavier than that for the freshman composition course and that the writing assignments are comparable. However, past students have testified that the greater challenge has given them precisely what they desired from a university education: an opportunity to read fine works, rigorous training in writing and discussion, a forum for sharing ideas, and a close-knit group in which to grow intellectually."

Since its inception nearly 15 years ago, the Great Books Colloquium has been a great success, attracting 15 to 20 percent of the incoming freshman class each year. Its popularity is due, in part, to the fact that completing the sequence is equivalent to completing five of the required general education classes. Additionally, the colloquium is broad enough in its scope and light enough in its required commitment to attract and reward students who are not pursuing a liberal arts–related major or who wish to spend a year abroad with one of Pepperdine's international study programs. Finally, the attractiveness of the program can also be traced to the intellectual demand that it places on students: where much is expected, much will be delivered. Good students seek out a challenge, and also other good students. In the Great Books Colloquium, they find both.

Great Books courses are not identical across sections in their reading lists, and this makes them something less than they could be, at least in terms of promoting a common base of knowledge. Nevertheless, the colloquium is one of the highlights of a Pepperdine education—and the colloquium faculty especially love the program: "I think that, in addition to the international programs, this is one of the jewels in the Pepperdine crown," says one. Another professor says that the program is "where I have found the best students I've had."

Pepperdine's small undergraduate population (there are just 3,200 students in Seaver College) makes getting to know professors fairly easy. "If you are a motivated student and you find professors with whom you hit it off," a professor says, "you can do a lot of one-on-one." "I was able to go to [my professor's] office and shoot the breeze about politics for hours," a student says of one of her teachers. "The faculty members are extremely accessible. I really feel spoiled; the personal attention available to every student is staggering. All of my teachers know my first name, and I maintain personal relationships with many of my teachers."

One reason that Pepperdine receives such laudatory remarks about its faculty is the school's insistence that faculty are primarily teachers, not researchers. Graduate students do not teach classes, professors do. While research is valued, two out of the four standards used to determine tenure and promotion have to do with teaching. "Here at Pepperdine, teaching is the priority," a faculty member says. "There's an increasing emphasis on research, but the teaching part is more important than ever."

Indeed, there are a number of truly outstanding professors at Pepperdine, though many, including James Q. Wilson and Ted McAllister in the School of Public Policy, generally do not teach undergraduate courses. Some of the best undergraduate faculty at Pepperdine include Ronald W. Batchelder in economics; Michael G. Ditmore in English; Darrel Colson and Michael Gose in Great Books; Don Thompson in mathematics; Stephen V. Monsma and J. Christopher Soper in political science; and Ronald C. Highfield in religion. Kenneth Starr, the former independent counsel of Whitewater/Lewinsky fame, was recently named dean of the Pepperdine School of Law, a job he temporarily delayed taking in order to pursue his investigation of President Clinton.

Only a few courses—primarily ones in religion and the humanities—are taught in large lecture halls. Most courses at Pepperdine are quite small; some 63 percent enroll fewer than 20 students. The student-faculty ratio is 12 to 1.

Students can participate in one of Pepperdine's many study-abroad programs. Seaver College offers year-round residential programs in Germany, England, Italy, and Argentina, along with summer programs in 17 countries around the world. More than 50 percent of Pepperdine students choose to study in foreign lands, and the *Chronicle of Higher Education* has listed it among the universities that send the most students abroad. What is more, foreign students constitute 6 percent of the Pepperdine student body and represent more than 52 nations. Students attending Pepperdine get a truly international and intercultural experience not even approached by most universities' ideological commitment to "non-Western perspectives."

Student Life: Watch the waves

George Pepperdine had a clear and precise notion of what the political atmosphere at his school would be like. "All instruction," he wrote, "is to be under conservative, funda-

REQUIREMENTS (CONT'D)

- Three semesters (or the equivalent) of a foreign language.
- One course in behavioral science (psychology or sociology).
- Two courses in American heritage.
- One course in non-Western heritage. Most of these courses are in Asian studies, and seem less ideologically charged than non-Western courses at other schools.
- One basic laboratory science course, such as "Principles of Biology."
- An elementary course in mathematics.
- A course in rhetoric and public speaking.

mental Christian supervision with stress upon the importance of strict Christian living." The mandate was clear in 1937, but today Mr. Pepperdine would not always be pleased with the political climate of the school that bears his name.

"The popular perception is that Pepperdine is a conservative place," one faculty member says." But, he adds, "that's pretty much the [perception of the] donors." One prominent alumnus says he has "heard the horror stories for years" from conservative students who say that "despite its conservative reputation, a host of conservative donors, and lavish alumni and Law School [events] featuring prominent conservative speakers, the fact of the matter is that conservative professors are nonexistent at Pepperdine when it comes to the courses that really affect a student's view on politics and government." Moreover, according to one participant, "in the MBA program the teachers and students seem very much at odds with the administration, and roll their eyes when they have to mention adjustments in curriculum or behavior to fit a 'Christian lifestyle.'"

Certain departments—notably political science and sociology—are known by those who notice such things to lean left. One student says that in a sociology class, most of what the professor presented in class was "strictly liberal"; students, for example, had to watch the film *Roger and Me,* which was then used as the basis for an assignment on social class in America. Another exercise in this course included playing Monopoly, during which there "were different standards for different classes of people, the moral being that as the rich get richer, the poor get poorer." Such exercises may be more indicative of certain disciplines, especially sociology, than they are of the general tenor of Pepperdine's political climate; it is difficult to say. Certainly, however, Pepperdine has not been immune from the ideological drift of the humanities and social sciences: buyers beware.

Pepperdine's convocation requirement, under which students must attend 14 lectures or concerts per term, features events that "are usually religious, sometimes political, and always liberal in nature," according to a student. "If there are conservative speakers, they never talk about politics, only religion." A case in point: Linda Chavez spoke about religious issues, whereas Elaine Brown, a former high-ranking member of the Black Panthers, spoke entirely about politics—although she did quote the Bible a few times.

These matters aside, Pepperdine remains a comparatively traditional campus. "Pepperdine is a noncontroversial, nonconfrontational kind of campus. It is politically boring," a student says. "The general attitude outside of religious hot topics is almost complete apathy." An alumnus says that "there aren't many organized liberal groups on campus" and that "many students are from wealthy Republican families who sent their kids there to protect them from the ravages of popular culture. . . . Their view tends to reflect a hybrid between popular culture and the Republican views of their parents." In recent years, some students have worked to start a conservative campus newspaper and to bring conservative speakers to campus with outside funding—but lacking much organizational structure, these efforts have flagged.

Pepperdine, as one faculty member says, has no "town-gown relationship." For one thing, there's not much of a town; students have to drive most anywhere they want to go off campus. But Pepperdine offers many activities to keep students occupied—perhaps more than it should. "Sometimes there are too many social distractions, along with the beach, which keep students from studying," says one professor. This, after all, is an age when colleges and universities feel compelled to provide students with every form of distraction—from world-class exercise facilities and theaters to dorm room Ethernet links (for downloading music), massage therapists, and lavish dining facilities that would have made Julia Child blush. Case in point: at Pepperdine, there is a 24-hour recreational facility, the Howard A. White Center, where students can play table tennis or billiards or watch a big-screen television. According to one student, "the exercise facilities are the thing most lacking on campus. The gym is much smaller and simpler than the gyms at most schools of this size, although celebrities and NBA stars can be seen playing basketball from time to time."

SUGGESTED CORE
1., 4., 5., and 8. Great Books I, II, III, and IV
2. Philosophy 300, Ancient Philosophy
3. Religion 101/102, Old Testament / New Testament
6. English 420, Major Writers: Shakespeare
7. History 520, Colonial and Revolutionary America

The off-campus distractions are considerable. Los Angeles is but 30 minutes away (when there is no traffic—ha!) and is easily accessed via the Pacific Coast Highway. Of course, it provides all of the attractions and vices of a world-class city. Santa Barbara is two hours away. Santa Monica offers the Third Street Promenade, whose stores, shops, and restaurants are popular with students. In Malibu, there are many "destination" restaurants and stores frequented by college students.

Housing at Pepperdine is limited, but freshmen and sophomores under 21 who aren't living with their parents are required to live on campus. The university believes that "students profit more from living on campus than from living off campus," according to the catalog. Life on campus is comfortable, but there are a few strict rules—no alcohol, no firearms, no candles, no pets, and no one from the opposite sex in your living area from 11 p.m. to 11 a.m.

Freshmen live in eight-resident suites, each with a double bathroom, a living area, and four double bedrooms. The suites are clustered six to a hall surrounding a main lobby with a fireplace, television, and laundry room. Out of the twenty-three residence halls on campus, all but one are designed along these lines. The remaining residence hall is a tower complex reserved for 275 sophomores and upperclassmen; it has two wings for men, four for women. The tower has double rooms, and each pair of doubles shares a bathroom.

The school has recently added the Drescher Apartments, which are situated on a hill overlooking the main campus adjacent to the new graduate business and public policy schools. This new structure houses a mixture of graduate students and upperclassmen who are in good academic standing, four students in each four-bedroom apartment, and affords the campus's most spectacular views.

Pepperdine has a number of competitive athletic programs. The Waves are well known in water polo, tennis, and volleyball circles; there are seven varsity sports for men, seven for women. For lesser athletes, there are also a variety of club and intramural sports. And of course, spectatorship is popular. "The homecoming basketball game is huge—everyone from the school goes, packing the Firestone Fieldhouse, and the camaraderie is amazing," a student says. A homecoming *basketball* game is necessitated by the fact that the Waves do not play football.

But it is Pepperdine's religious commitment that draws many students, and Pepperdine expects its students to pursue religious interests. Even so, as one student says, "the relative conservatism of the student body is not evident in the way the girls dress. I have never seen such short skirts in my life." Still, the college strongly encourages students to join a church, and it offers Seaver-wide worship assemblies, devotionals, small-group Bible studies, and an on-campus ministry. A student notes that the first three questions a student asks a peer at Pepperdine are, "What is your name?" "What is your major?" and "What church do you attend?" To answer the latter query: 80 percent of the students at Pepperdine say they come from a Christian religious background, with Roman Catholic the most prevalent (17.6 percent) and the Churches of Christ close behind (16.9 percent). The university is careful to mention in its student catalog that services are held every Sunday and Wednesday at the Malibu Church of Christ, but also points out that there are other congregations nearby that welcome students. One professor says that there is a "healthy mix between the devout and the not-so-devout" among Pepperdine students.

Pepperdine is one of the most crime-free campuses in the nation. Serious crime is unknown; burglaries have been decreasing, and liquor and drug violations are substantially less frequent than at comparable institutions. In 2003, the only crimes reported on campus were 40 burglaries and one stolen car. There's also a healthy attitude toward community service on campus, represented by Pepperdine's Step Forward Day. Students help pick up trash in Malibu, clean up local schools, and pack lunches for the homeless. "It is truly a thrill to see so many students involved," says one student.

It's not cheap to study in Malibu. Pepperdine's 2004–5 tuition was $28,630, and room and board cost $8,640. Approximately 75 percent of Pepperdine students receive some form of financial assistance each year. Typically, all financial assistance packages contain some loan awards.

REED COLLEGE

PORTLAND, OREGON • WWW.REED.EDU

The fourth R

With a relatively demanding curriculum and a number of rigorous courses, Reed College is neither for the academically lazy nor the intellectually timid. At its heart lies a core freshman course in Western civilization, which along with a senior thesis, bookends an intensely challenging journey into higher learning.

This tiny school in Portland, Oregon, was founded in 1908 by a bequest from pioneer Simeon Reed and his wife Amanda. The first classes were held in 1911, and since then the school has grown into a student body of 1,300 undergraduates, plus about two dozen master's candidates. Notable "Reedies" run the gamut from Apple founder Steve Jobs (he attended briefly) to the comedian Barry Hansen, better known as the D.J. "Dr. Demento" (he graduated). Reed has become increasingly selective over the years, admitting only about half its applicants. Despite its emphasis on traditional learning, in many ways the school is unorthodox and even eccentric. For years, Reed has refused to supply *U.S. News and World Report* with information for the magazine's annual college rankings, something most schools are eager to supply. But during its recent search for a new president—a process that is extremely secretive at most schools—Reed posted the résumés of its three finalists online.

As it wraps up a vast renovation and reconstruction effort, Reed is ready to greet students with a slew of new academic and residential facilities. The college has spruced up old dorms, expanded the library, and erected new buildings, including an auditorium, during this multiyear project. Overall, the school has increased the square footage of its buildings by almost 30 percent—made possible by a $112 million capital campaign begun in 1995.

VITAL STATISTICS

Religious affiliation: none
Total enrollment: 1,341
Total undergraduates: 1,312
SAT/ACT midranges: SAT V: 660–750, M: 610–710; ACT: 28–31
Applicants: 2,485
Applicants accepted: 47%
Accepted applicants who enrolled: 29%
Tuition: $30,670
Room and board: $8,070
Freshman retention rate: 85%
Graduation rate: 49% (4 yrs.), 70% (6 yrs.)
Courses with fewer than 20 students: 80%
Student-faculty ratio: 10:1
Courses taught by graduate TAs: none
Most popular majors: social sciences, English, history
Students living on campus: 57%
Guaranteed housing for four years? no
Students in fraternities or sororities: none

Academic Life: Reeding, writing, and arithmetic

Reed freshmen are greeted with a week-long orientation program featuring field trips, a

WEST

865

job fair, and an introduction to the academic departments. Then the work begins. The one core class, Humanities 110, began in 1943 as a way to combine the history and literature of ancient Greece and Rome. It now incorporates elements of philosophy, art history, and political science as it leads students from Homer to Aristotle in the first semester and from Augustus to St. Augustine in the second. A professor sums up the school's traditional attitude toward the importance of this academic foundation: "We study the Greeks because they invented history and philosophy in the West."

Humanities 110 is team taught, and students are divided into sections with no more than 16 in each group. In addition to the weekly three-hour seminars, the entire freshman class of Reedies meets three times a week for one-hour lectures, which are just as important for the teachers as for the students. The professors are eager to impress their peers and rarely fail to deliver an illuminating and lively performance. "We look at this class as one *we* can really learn in," says a professor. "And just because a lecturer said something about a work doesn't mean the students take it as gospel."

During their first year, students each write at least four major papers per semester, and their performance is evaluated regularly throughout the year. As sophomores, most students choose to continue their liberal arts education with a survey class on medieval Europe, modern Europe, or classical Chinese civilization. As the school catalog asserts, "The humanities curriculum places primary emphasis not upon information, important as that may be, but upon the development of disciplined thinking and writing through the interpretation of works of art, literature, or other means by which people have expressed themselves and ordered their lives, individually and socially." Reed's philosophy of learning for learning's sake runs the risk of devolving into self-referential theorizing about theories. In recent years, instructors have accentuated this tendency by combining Reed's traditional emphasis on primary materials with the esoteric analyses characteristic of modern scholarship. But one professor says that instructors balance the two approaches well.

By current standards Reed has managed to preserve scholarly rigor. The departments of economics and history, frequent victims of politicization at other schools, include few classes that could be considered academically suspect. Economics majors are required to take a broad survey course called "Introduction to Economic Analysis," as well as "Microeconomic Theory," "Macroeconomic Theory," and a choice of either "Survey of Econometric Methods" or "Theory and Practice of Econometrics" (the latter focuses more on statistics than the former). The history department requires students to take a basic humanities course (like "Early Modern Europe") and six other history courses, including at least one in each of three areas: Europe, the United States, and regions or nations outside Europe, the United States, and Canada. Students must also take at least one course on history before 1800 and one on history after 1800, but these can overlap with the geographical requirements.

The focus of the psychology department is straightforward, emphasizing scientific research. An unusually intense Chinese department emphasizes the history and literature of China through the ages in a format largely devoid of multiculturalist ideology. Even the dance department concentrates on traditional Western forms of expression. The music department, which attracts many accomplished musicians to the school, provides an array of instruction and performance opportunities and waives many related costs for majors in their junior and senior years.

Even the English department is solid in its courses on Shakespeare and other important authors and eras. However, it also features some less substantial classes, such as "Ethnopoetics," which investigates "poetic strategies through a discussion of spirituals, nommo, dialect, blues, jazz, collage, narrative cycles, and oral style."

The most politicized department at Reed is probably anthropology, which offers separate classes on the anthropologies of dreams, colonialism, and eating. Another class, "Sex and Gender," explores "the biological attributes by which a person is deemed 'male' or 'female.'" Who knew it was such a thorny question?

In all, the school offers 34 majors, of which 12 are considered interdisciplinary, including mathematics-economics and chemistry-physics. A quarter of Reed students major in its strong science programs, particularly biology and physics. History, English, and psychology are the most popular liberal arts majors. Across the board, traditional disciplines dominate; very few Reedies graduate with a major that includes the word "studies" in its title. Then again, even the American studies interdisciplinary program is quite rigorous, requiring students to fulfill all the requirements of a traditional major in addition to classes specific to the concentration.

Most students who graduate from Reed eventually go on to pursue further learning; across all fields, the percentage of Reed students who become doctoral candidates is the third-highest in the nation. Not surprisingly, about a third of Reed students eventually go into education as a profession, which is about as many Reedies as enter law and business combined. Within two years after graduation, 65 percent of Reedies have found their way to still-higher education.

Reed emphasizes "self-assessment" as a means of evaluating academic achievement. As the college literature puts it, "the college does not wish to divide students by labels of achievement." Nevertheless, most professors do give grades in addition to providing extensive commentary on student work. Compared to

ACADEMIC REQUIREMENTS

Reed does not have a traditional core, but it does require all freshmen to take one admirable two-semester course on Western civilization . Otherwise, students must take at least two units in the same discipline in each of the following areas:

- Literature, philosophy, religion, and the arts. Options range from "Studies in Fiction: Desire, Sexuality, and Twentieth-Century British Fiction" to "Ancient Philosophy."
- History, social sciences, and psychology. Choices include everything from "European Diplomatic History: 1848–1914" to "Sport and Society."
- The natural sciences.
- Mathematics, logic, foreign language, or linguistics.

Students must also complete these requirements:

- Three semesters of physical education, an obligation that can be fulfilled by activities like snowboarding, bowling, badminton, or belly dancing.
- A junior qualifying examination.
- A senior thesis and oral examination.

other schools, Reed has experienced very little grade inflation. It also invites parents to become part of the learning process—encouraging them to take part in their children's reading and to discuss the choice of texts with professors, according to the *Chronicle of Higher Education*. That's just plain refreshing.

Incoming freshmen are assigned faculty advisors within their expected fields of study. Students are assigned faculty advisors within their major departments once they have finalized their program selection, usually during the sophomore year. All students must pass a junior qualifying exam—the "junior qual"—in their majors before being promoted to senior status. History majors complete "a critical essay dealing with a given issue or problem within a particular historical field and period." For English majors, the exam has three parts "involving questions about a piece of fiction, a critical or theoretical essay, and a poem or poems (all of which are generally handed out to be read before taking the exam)," according to the department Web page.

At Reed, to paraphrase the bumper sticker, every degree is considered an honors degree. A senior thesis is required of all students, typically running from 60 to 120 pages. The completed works are archived by the school at its designated "thesis tower," and the thesis title of each student is listed in the program at graduation. "Most talk about it being the high point of their education at Reed," a professor says. "And it makes a PhD dissertation seem less daunting." The project culminates with a two-hour oral exam held before a group of professors from both inside and outside the field of the subject matter. The annual thesis parade, in which students file from the steps of the library to the registrar's office with champagne corks flying and their monographs in hand, is among Reedies' most beloved traditions. "It looks like a World Series victory," says a professor.

Technology at Reed is state of the art, and the course material for most classes can be accessed online. Many of the school's classrooms boast Internet connections and high-tech projection screens. The library's Instructional Media Center has a language laboratory, music listening room, and an array of electronic devices for student use. Reed offers a tantalizing array of foreign studies programs in a dozen countries and invites students to submit their own proposals for consideration as well. After winter break, students return to campus for a freewheeling 10 days before regular classes begin; during this time, called "Paideia," they can take fanciful not-for-credit courses. Not long ago, the college offered a short course on how to build catapults.

Students say the intellectual relationships between faculty members and students are exceptionally close. The student senate even allocates money so that students can take faculty and staff members to lunch. Students say the best teachers at Reed include Peter Steinberger in political science, Lisa M. Steinman in English, Walter G. Englert in classics, Robert H. Kaplan in biology, and David Griffiths in physics. Classics professor Nigel Nicholson won the 2004 Oregon Professor of the Year award from the Council for Advancement and Support of Education and the Carnegie Foundation for the Advancement of Teaching.

Ethics at Reed are guided by the school's all-encompassing Honor Principle, which holds the entire community responsible for "maintaining standards of honesty and mutual trust in their academic and social lives. . . . The honor principle also demands the respectful concern of each person for the other, and exercise of conscionable judgment in all actions toward individuals and their property." Exams are not proctored, and students are free to take their tests with them—to the dorms, the library, or a local coffeeshop—on the presumption that they will not cheat. Upholding the tradition is considered a badge of honor among students. In addition, the student senate appoints a "J-board" each year of nine students who hear and resolve disputes.

Politics are present but not dominant on campus. "It is easier to be a liberal at Reed than a conservative," says one professor. As for the instructors, "most faculty don't talk politics with each other," the professor says. Other professors admit, however, that both the faculty and the student body lean decidedly toward the left. But, in general, political disputes are intellectualized at Reed, with students pouring their partisan energies into papers rather than rhetoric. This fundamental bias toward the books is illustrated by a favorite Reedie chant at sports competitions: "Hegel, Kant, Marx, Spinoza! Come on Reed, hit 'em in the nozza!"

Student Life: No time to Reed-lax

No doubt about it, Reed is a stressful place. About 15 percent of the incoming freshman class does not return, and over a quarter of the student body does not graduate in six years. "We do sometimes worry that we're asking students to do too much," says a professor. "It's demanding from the day the students get here."

Primed to help is Student Services, a multipurpose entity that provides students with everything from academic support to mental health treatment. In addition to one-on-one tutoring (students can get at least one hour a week, and often a second, free of charge), the school offers a math center and writing assistance. But the demands pay off. According to the *Chronicle of Higher Education*, Reed ranks among the top baccalaureate schools in the nation in producing Fulbright scholars.

Student organizations, of which there are more than 60, include the Organic Grower's Union, Beer Nation, and the apocalyptic club Chunk 666. A queer alliance and feminist union are also present on campus, and their members are among the more politically active students.

Reed College's address is on Woodstock Boulevard, a name that aptly describes the student body's overall leanings. But Reed students are usually too busy to engage in direct political action, seeing themselves as too high-minded for crass partisanship; hence, there is neither an active Republican nor Democratic club on campus. Instead

WEST

students tend to gravitate together on the basis of issues in groups such as Amnesty International; organizations focused on ecological issues are especially popular.

Practically all students live on campus during their freshman year, while many move off campus after that. University housing, limited in comparison to most small liberal arts colleges, is awarded by lottery. Upperclassman advisors and recent graduates (not necessarily from Reed) reside in the dorms to offer support and guidance. An unusual phenomenon at the school is the migration back to the dormitories by many seniors eager for dining plans and on-campus amenities while they focus on their theses. Dormitory life has improved in recent years with the construction of three new residence halls. Reed also offers language houses and theme houses that vary from one year to the next. There are no fraternities or sororities. All dorms are coed, though there are some all-female floors. On the other floors, men and women often share bathrooms.

Reed does not participate in NCAA competition, but there are intercollegiate club sports in men's and women's rugby, coed soccer, men's basketball, coed squash, and ultimate Frisbee. The most unusual student hobby at Reed involves working at its nuclear reactor. This facility is unique in that it is not associated with a graduate school or a nuclear engineering department—and is run almost entirely by undergraduates who have obtained a license to do so. It is often used for research projects. Other popular hangouts include the thoroughly equipped sports center and the campus theater, which welcomes participation from students in all majors. Also frequented is the Douglas F. Cooley Memorial Art Gallery, where studio art students can exhibit their work.

Reed is situated on what was once known as Crystal Springs Farm. The scenic 100 acres feature topography ranging from a wooded canyon to wetlands. Populated by swallows, shrews, salamanders, and a variety of fish, the canyon and its fauna have served as the objects of study for a number of senior thesis projects. There is even a section of the school Web site devoted to trees on campus, and the Canyon Clean-Up Day is another tradition cherished among Reedies.

The nucleus of off-campus student activity is the Gray Fund, which sponsors a seemingly endless array of free field trips throughout the year, from skiing to whitewater rafting. When an event is oversubscribed, students and faculty are chosen by lottery to attend the event, but practically everybody ends up going on one excursion or another. The school has a ski lodge on Mt. Hood, which it encourages students to reserve; it also loans out skiing and camping equipment free of charge. Reed even helps subsidize tickets for many events in Portland. But despite the many extracurricular activities available, the books have first priority. Students can easily spend weeks without going off campus, buried in texts in their rooms or in the library. "Reed is not for everyone," says a professor. "It's a college for bright, motivated students who really want to work hard but also want the rewards of working hard. Anything you ask them to do, they rise to the occasion and do it really well."

There have been reports of pervasive drug and alcohol use on campus, as well as some controversy regarding the school's relatively lax policy towards substance abuse. (The school's anti-tobacco policies are, however, strictly enforced.) The annual spring

Renaissance festival, known as Renn Fayre, is considered the high point in the campus calendar for illegal indulgences (most of which were unknown in the West during the relevant historical period; perhaps the students should stick to mead).

Aside from a smattering of break-ins, the Reed campus is virtually crime free; in 2003, three burglaries and seven motor vehicle thefts were reported. There were no campus liquor-law arrests in 2003, though 20 liquor violations and nine drug violations were referred for college disciplinary action. The school operates a bus service until 2 a.m. The area of Portland surrounding the school is also relatively safe.

The cost of attendance at Reed in 2004–5 was $30,670 for tuition and $8,070 for on-campus room and board. Reed does not offer institutional aid based solely on merit and not all students with need are offered institutional assistance. Rather, continuing students are given priority in the funding decisions, so some first-year and transfer students may not receive aid until their second year. According to the college Web site, "Reed meets the full demonstrated institutional need of all students who have attended Reed at least two semesters." Admission is need-blind, but "the financial aid process is merit driven and admitted students who have the strongest admission applications are most likely to receive institutional financial aid."

RICE UNIVERSITY

HOUSTON, TEXAS • WWW.RICE.EDU

Against the grain

William Marsh Rice, a wealthy New Englander, made his fortune in Houston before deciding to found an institute for higher education. Rice traveled around the world studying universities in order to draw upon the best of them for his school. He was particularly taken with Princeton and Oxford and therefore used them as models in the founding of the Rice Institute in 1912, which later became Rice University. Though William Rice wasn't alive to see the school launched—he had been murdered a dozen years earlier by scoundrels who tried to alter his will and steal his fortune—the college indeed opened. It became a small institution of the highest quality where students lived in residential colleges and faculty-student relations were warm and intense.

Although it is now much bigger, those attributes still characterize the university. Teaching is still emphasized: with Rice's student-faculty ratio of just five to one, no student need fall between the cracks. Socially, Rice University is very comfortable: its residential college system offers students the close-knit community atmosphere of a smaller school along with the resources of a larger one. And the lively if sprawling city of Houston lies all around.

Then there is Rice's comparative affordability—the university consistently ranks as one of *Money* magazine's "best college buys." Add all this to an excellent academic reputation and a stellar student body, and it is easy to see why Rice has become nationally known as a Texas alternative to the Ivy League.

Academic Life: No way of knowing

In 2004, David W. Leebron, former dean of the Columbia University School of Law, became president of Rice, where he also teaches political science. Rumor has it that one reason his predecessor, Malcolm Gillis, resigned was the defeat of his highly structured, postmodern curriculum, "Five Ways of Knowing." Unfortunately, there is now on the table a proposal from the new administration that would remove curriculum decisions from faculty control. "I expect a reemergence of something like Five Ways of Knowing," a professor says. Another Rice veteran says, "For as long as I've been here, the Rice Board of Trustees, which poses as conservative, has consistently supported the election of presidents who are no friends of Western civilization. Nobody seems to know why."

In its course bulletin, Rice University says its academic philosophy "is to offer students . . . both a grounding in the broad fields of general knowledge and the chance to concentrate on very specific academic and research interests. By completing the required distribution courses, all students gain an understanding of the literature, arts, and philosophy essential to any civilization, a broad historical introduction to thought about human society, and a basic familiarity with the scientific principles underlying physics, chemistry, and mathematics."

If only. Alas, Rice's distribution requirements are pretty mediocre, mandating just four courses in each of three areas. Group I is designed to "develop students' critical and aesthetic understanding of texts and the arts; . . . lead students to the analytical examination of ideas and values; . . . introduce students to the variety of approaches and methods with which different disciplines approach intellectual problems; and . . . engage students with works of culture that have intellectual importance." Catchy. To achieve all this, a student must choose from a list of more than 200 courses in the departments of art, art history, English, philosophy, medieval studies, classics, theater, women's studies, foreign languages, and many others. So no Rice student is guaranteed to gain an understanding of "the literature, arts and philosophy essential to any civilization," because he can fulfill these requirements by taking a women's studies course such as "Introduction to Lesbian, Gay, Bisexual, and Transgender Studies" rather than, say, "British Writers." And so on.

Group II focuses on "human society," serving as a catch-all for the social sciences, and Group III covers "analytical thinking and quantitative analysis," including math and the hard sciences.

One professor says, "Our distribution requirements are really very flexible now. Some of us fought pretty hard to make it happen." Rice's curriculum used to be more structured, according to one professor, who called it "a terrible ideological straitjacket. . . . Some of us in the sciences led the fight for a largely laissez-faire plan, similar to that at Brown. We were successful. . . . At this time, anybody has the right to take courses in queer theory, postmodern interpretations of everything, etc. But nobody is required to take them." Another professor says, "I have a vision of a curriculum that could be better. It is possible to miss some courses that I think are fundamental." Still, "when our graduates write back from graduate school, they tell us it is easier—and professors at those universities, usually regarded as the top tier, commend us for the preparation of our students."

The degree to which departments promote traditional areas of study and free discussion varies somewhat. The sciences, engineering, and social sciences, according to one professor, appear to "have nonideological faculties and tolerate believers of all stripes quite readily." The same professor says that "the humanities departments are definitely getting a lot more politicized." For example, the history department lost its two medievalists in 2000 and has no plans to replace them. Another professor called the atmosphere in the department "stiflingly present-minded." The "Study of Women and Gender" department has strong support from the university administration, so much so that the administration is willing to pay people to take its classes. "They have received funding to offer graduate students who take three gender studies classes $3,000 per year in addition to their normal stipend," a professor says. "This is unprecedented. For graduate students, this is actually quite a bit of money. It has also influenced the admission of graduate students within individual humanities departments."

Opinions vary slightly on what effect campus politics have on student expression. One professor says, "I think students are rather free to express their views on anything." Another says, "One can speak freely here, and there is, as far as I know, no case of classroom intimidation of beliefs, as one hears about elsewhere." However, one student says, "We may have a fairly decent number of conservatives at Rice, but it's hard to know. Many of us are afraid to voice our opinions in class or in papers for fear of being shot down by the almost monolithically liberal faculty."

Traditionally, students at Rice had ample opportunities to develop relationships with their professors, who were said to be very accessible during office hours and outside of class. One student said her physics professor used to eat lunch once a week in

VITAL STATISTICS
Religious affiliation: none
Total enrollment: 4,959
Total undergraduates: 2,822
SAT median: 1410
Applicants: 7,501
Applicants accepted: 24%
Accepted applicants who enrolled: 39%
Tuition: $18,850
Room and board: $8,018
Freshman retention rate: 95%
Graduation rate: 89% (6 yrs.)
Average class size: 11
Student-faculty ratio: 5:1
Courses taught by graduate TAs: 3%
Most popular majors: engineering, social sciences, natural sciences
Students living on campus: 76%
Guaranteed housing for four years? no
Students in fraternities or sororities: none

WEST

873

Rice has no core curriculum and very weak distribution requirements. On top of the mandates for each major, Rice requires students to take four courses each from three extremely broad subject areas:

- Arts, values, and culture. Any of some 200 courses in the departments of art, art history, English, philosophy, medieval studies, theater, women's studies, and foreign languages qualify.
- Human society. These courses come from departments such as anthropology, economics, history, psychology, and sociology.
- Analytical thinking and quantitative analysis. Appropriate departments for these courses include math, computer science, physics, chemistry, and biology.

the student dining hall so students would come by and talk to him—in addition to his regular office hours. But as "old guard" professors retire, many of those who are replacing them exhibit a different ethos, insiders say. One faculty member says, "One problem with the younger faculty is that they have little patience, if any, for the claims of undergraduates and generally do not join residential colleges and have lunch there. This will become a large issue as most of the best teachers and scholars are on the verge of retirement." Science professors tend to be more involved in research than humanities professors are, but one student says that they at least "try to involve undergraduates" in their work. "There are many opportunities for engineering/science students to work in a professor's lab, which is a wonderful chance to learn skills and get to know professors better."

Some of the best teachers at Rice, students say, are J. Dennis Huston in English; Richard J. Stoll in political science; Baruch Brody, Tristram Engelhardt, and George Sher in philosophy; John S. Hutchinson, James Tour, and Kenton Whitmire in chemistry; Don Johnson in electrical engineering; Raquel Gaytan in languages; James Thompson in statistics; Ewa Thompson in Slavic studies; and Steve Klineberg in sociology.

Teaching assistants, who at Rice are undergraduates, help with review sessions; graduate students, sometimes called instructors, teach some introductory courses. The formal advising program "is a bit subpar, especially the general advising before declaring a major," says one student. Upon entering college, every student is assigned a faculty advisor based on his area of interest. Once he declares his major, he is assigned to the designated advisor for his major. Because there are usually just one or two official advisors assigned to a department, it's hard for students to get much time with them. "The advisor in your major department usually understands the issues of that department quite well, but typically just rubber stamps whatever you've already decided to take," a student says. "Some people create de facto advisor relationships with professors who are not technically their advisors and get them to sign their registration forms. The rules are really sort of loose."

Rice has traditionally been strongest in the sciences and engineering, and many students are in premed, a program that can be intense. One premed student says, "At Rice, most people are very serious about their work, but I've never felt threatened by any competitiveness among my peers. There's no competition in a cutthroat way, and many students study together, helping each other learn the material." Rice premed students typically have some of the highest MCAT scores in the country.

The School of Architecture is also highly regarded. Students in the program must complete additional distribution requirements, foundation courses in architecture, and a "preprofessional sequence" in their junior and senior years. The Shepherd School of Music is excellent in music theory, history, and performance.

Rice's strict honor code is vigilantly enforced by students. Cheating on an exam, besides resulting in an automatic F, could lead to expulsion. For falsifying some data on a lab report, a two-semester suspension is not unusual. However, according to one staff member, "In the last year, there was a large cheating scandal. A group of athletes took a take-home test together. According to the rules, this was a pretty clear-cut case of expulsion but the former president, Malcolm Gillis, stepped in and reduced the penalties. There was a big outcry on campus."

Student Life: Houston, we don't have a problem

Rice's residential college setup, modeled after the Oxford system, organizes nearly every aspect of social life at the school; some students choose Rice precisely for this reason. The nine colleges are proportionally filled with men and women, different races and ethnicities, partiers and bookworms, jocks and artists, business majors and philosophers. As a result of this mixing, Rice students self-segregate much less than at other schools—there are no ethnic awareness halls, for instance, nor political-issue or gender-issue dormitories. Students are integrated ethnically, politically, and culturally—whether they like it or not. As a result, the residential colleges lack distinctive character. Paradoxically, Rice students defend their colleges fiercely. "Everyone thinks his college is the best," says one student. "It's really like a big family," another student says. "You know everybody in your college." The college communities are first formed during freshman orientation, when students meet their fellow classmates and advisors, participate in strange contests, and learn why their own colleges are superior. "It felt like summer camp," says a student.

Unfortunately, Rice University's residential colleges don't have enough room for its 2,800 undergraduates, and a significant number have to live off campus, missing the benefits of the college system. Rice has built another college (Martel) but has no plans to add others in the near future.

Although students are free to mingle with members of other colleges—residential college dining halls are open to all students, for instance, and all classes and extracurricular activities include students from other colleges—a student's closest friends usu-

WEST

ally come from his own college. "It's so random how they assign you to the colleges, but it really determines who you're friends with and what you do for the next four years," a student says. Residential halls vary some from college to college. All dormitories are coed, but each college offers a few single-sex floors, and all bathrooms and shower areas are single sex. Students in the newer colleges enjoy suite-style living (three or four singles with a common room and bathroom), while the older ones offer more pleasing architecture. A faculty master lives in a house next door to the residence halls of each college and serves as a live-in advisor.

Rice colleges have their own traditions. Baker, for instance, has something called the "Baker 13," which involves students running through campus wearing nothing but shaving cream; this occurs on the 13th and 31st of each month (or 26th if the month does not have a 31st). Weiss College goes "pumpkin caroling" every Halloween, Lovett College throws a casino night each February, and Brown College's residents are bound to be dunked in the Fairy Fountain on their birthdays. Rice students say there is never a lack of events on campus to occupy what free time they have. "We work incredibly hard, but students know how to leave work behind and have a good time," says one student. Student groups range from the Aegean Club and the Rice African Students Association to the Wine Society and the Zen Club, which meets for "regular sitting meditation."

Roughly half of Rice's student body hails from Texas, so, not surprisingly, students tend to be more conservative than their instructors. But only a handful of students are active politically. "Rice is tolerant to a fault," says one professor. "Students go about their business. There is little burning intellectual fervor, but also no radical protests, strikes, or disruptions." Political views are voiced in columns or letters to the student newspaper, the *Rice Thresher*, rather than in demonstrations. "The student body is largely apathetic," an undergrad says.

Drinking is more popular than politics. The university's biggest and most beloved tradition (since 1957) is the annual Beer-Bike contest. Preceded by a week of activities—picnics, a baseball game, a big dinner, beer debates (professors drink at a pub, then debate topics with students)—students then get down to business with chugging and biking races (usually, but not always, separate contests). Even as many universities are cracking down on alcohol use and abuse, no one dares to attack Beer-Bike. Everyone participates in the festivities, even the college president. "Rice is a wet campus with a relatively relaxed alcohol policy, so plenty of students drink," a student says. "There is a lot of drinking on campus, but there are also a lot of things to do for those who don't drink. I've never felt any pressure to drink," says another.

Cultural shows, dances, operas, and other musical performances (both student recitals and professional ones), political lectures, and the residential colleges' themed parties are favorite attractions. Rice Village, with its restaurants and shopping, is a 15-minute walk from campus. Hermann Park, which features a public golf course and the Houston Zoo, is literally across the street. The Museum District, home to the Houston Museum of Fine Arts—the nation's sixth largest—is also within walking distance. Five miles away stands Houston's revitalized downtown, replete with theaters, concert halls, and the city's best nightlife. The city's new light rail service is now in operation, with Rice University one of the main stops. Minute Maid Park (formerly Enron Field), home of the Houston Astros, is located east of downtown.

Churches of almost every denomination stand near campus, and many are accessible by foot. InterVarsity Christian Fellowship and Campus Crusade for Christ are the largest and most active religious groups on campus. In fact, in an opinion piece in the *Rice Thresher,* an atheist complained, "As a non-Judeo-Christian at Rice, I appear to be in the minority." A public controversy at Rice arose when head football coach Ken Hatfield related his conservative Christian views on homosexuality to the *Chronicle of Higher Education,* saying that though he might not kick a homosexual athlete off his team, he would think hard about it. When his comments drew fire from some in the Rice community, Hatfield apologized and pledged to follow the university's nondiscrimination policy. Other worldviews at Rice are represented by Hillel, the Muslim Students' Association, Secular Students of Rice, and Hindus at Rice.

Football is king in the state of Texas, but Rice has a hard time competing with the likes of the University of Texas and Texas A&M, each only a couple hours away. Maybe team members are too busy studying; Rice athletes have the highest student-athlete graduation rate in Division I. Students naturally show more enthusiasm for teams that are playing well. Rice students typically express more interest in intramural sports than they do in varsity athletics and can also choose from 26 intercollegiate club sports.

Rice is a reasonably safe place. It reported two forcible sex offenses, six assaults, three burglaries, and two stolen cars on campus in 2003. However, bike thefts are common. Rice's campus is self-contained and pedestrian-friendly. "I've never felt at risk," says one student, "but you have to remember you're in Houston."

Rice University is significantly cheaper than many other schools of comparable quality, with tuition only $18,850, and room and board $8,018. Admission is need-blind, and the school promises to meet every student's full need. Some 79 percent of students receive financial aid, and the average student loan debt of a 2003 graduate was $12,900.

SUGGESTED CORE
1. Classics 107, Greek Civilization and Its Legacy (*closest match*)
2. Philosophy 201, History of Philosophy I
3. Religious Studies 122, The Bible and Its Interpreters
4. History 202/203, Introduction to Medieval Civilization I: Early to Middle Ages / II: High to Middle Ages
5. Philosophy 307, Social and Political Philosophy
6. English 321, Shakespeare
7. History 117, The United States, 1776–1877
8. History 370, European Intellectual History from Bacon to Hegel

University of Southern California

Los Angeles, California • www.usc.edu

Believing its own press

In 2005, the University of Southern California celebrated its 125th anniversary, and on the occasion administrators spoke loftily about how far the university has come since its humble inception in 1880, when Los Angeles was a provincial backwater of some 10,000 inhabitants. As one professor said, "USC . . . is moving from being a loose constellation of professional schools to being a real university." Perhaps, but as one student tells us, "The university has no common vision and no interdepartmental communication. USC is atomized, as is each department."

One indicator that a university's "footprint" is growing is when massive gifts start to come in from accomplished alumni who want to put their names on things. In 2004, USC received $52 million from Andrew J. Viterbi, a USC graduate and cofounder of the cell-phone giant Qualcomm for whom USC has named the Viterbi School of Engineering. This gift was just part of a massively successful fundraising campaign by the university, which raised $2.85 billion in only nine years—nearly three times its original goal, according to the *Chronicle of Higher Education*. Half that money has gone into the school's endowment, meaning that it will probably never hurt for money again. As for that other paltry $1.425 billion, the university has already mapped out plans to spend some of it on "a new student center, a life sciences building, a fine arts center, and a sports arena," as well as a faculty hiring binge, which is expected to attract 100 "world-class" professors in the fields of biology, "urban studies and globalization, and language and culture," reports the *Chronicle*.

USC has a number of truly world-class professional programs already, and it more than adequately prepares its students in these programs to compete in the outside world. Classes are usually small and inviting, and in pockets there is a sense of close-knit community. But, as with all schools, certain parts of USC are stronger than others. In other words, caveat emptor.

Academic Life: Ready for my closeup

Many of USC's strong professional programs are known throughout the world, especially the School of Cinema-Television—which regularly produces top-flight screenwriters, editors, and directors—and the Marshall School of Business. At USC the high achiever will find that the sky is the limit. However, the basement is also an option. As one student says, "You can just slide through one of the easier schools . . . and get no education." Of the school's pallid distribution requirements, another student says, "I don't know anyone who didn't just consider them a thing that you have to do." In fact, he says, the prevailing attitude toward the requirements is "just get an A and get it over with." Even if students aren't serious about these courses, it seems that USC is; one professor notes that the school has grown stricter about which courses fulfill these mandates. What is more, some of them with offbeat titles are in fact good classes, poorly named—it's a marketing thing. "In many departments and among many faculty, there is an effort to avoid looking traditional or canonical," the professor says. "The titles look like conference titles."

However, there is a better way to go through USC—one which offers students a genuinely demanding, enriching education. The Honors Core, or "thematic option," is offered by the College of Letters, Arts, and Sciences as an alternative way to complete the general requirements. Some consider the honors program the school's crown jewel. "I doubt that there is any Ivy League school that has as tough an academic challenge," says one honors student. According to USC, the honors curriculum "is arranged around four core courses which focus on the history of Western civilization through the close reading of primary literature and philosophical texts." It is heavy on reading and writing, and it focuses on all the right things—according to the catalog, it includes "major texts within the Western tradition; biblical and classical through contemporary sources," looking at "critical problems in the development of scientific thought" as well as an "analysis of historical change, social and political theory." Unfortunately, the program only admits 200 to 250 students each year, and the average enrollee has a high school GPA of 4.15 (weighted average) and a 1440 SAT score—which means that this program is slightly harder to get into than Harvard.

Another worthy initiative at USC is its Renaissance Scholars award, which is given to select students who combine study in two widely divergent fields—physics and theology, or computer science and poetry, for instance. Students whose majors and minors come from such disparate disciplines, and who graduate with a 3.5 average or better, are eligible for the special designation (akin to an honors diploma). These scholars also compete for a $10,000 scholarship to the graduate school of one's choice. In essence, the program is a noble attempt to encourage science-minded students to develop a mastery of one of the liberal arts—and to spur campus poets and filmmakers to gain expertise in one of the hard sciences.

VITAL STATISTICS

Religious affiliation: none
Total enrollment: 29,264
Total undergraduates: 16,271
SAT/ACT midranges: SAT: 1260–1440; ACT: 27–31
Applicants: 29,278
Applicants accepted: 27%
Accepted applicants who enrolled: 34%
Tuition: $25,358
Room and board: $8,852
Freshman retention rate: 96%
Graduation rate: 61% (4 yrs.), 82% (6 yrs.)
Average class size: 26
Student-faculty ratio: 10:1
Courses taught by graduate TAs: none
Most popular majors: business, social sciences, visual arts
Students living on campus: 36%
Guaranteed housing for four years? no
Students in fraternities: 18% *sororities*: 21%

USC has no core curriculum and rather anemic distribution requirements. However, these can be met through the admirable Honors option described in this essay. Besides a two-course introductory writing sequence and one upper-level writing course, all students must take one course from each of the following six broad categories:

- Western European and American culture. Options here are excellent, including "Origins of Western Literature and Culture" and "Philosophical Foundations of Modern Western Culture."

In addition to the school's distribution requirements, students face a mandatory diversity requirement—one course selected from a list of many that won't help students who are dedicated to learning about other cultures gain useful knowledge about them. To choose just one example, it seems unlikely that students will use the theories and practices presented in Comparative Literature 445, "Eurocentrism," for much of anything—unless they become corporate diversity enforcement officers.

While USC is more conservative than most other western schools when it comes to the political orientation of its students, there is no denying that both students and faculty with traditional views have experienced problems when it comes to expressing themselves in the classroom. "The politicization of speech in the classroom is clearly confined to certain humanities departments—English, comparative literature, and somewhat in political science and history," says a professor. Some students would add the religion department to that list. "Although most professors are willing to listen, there are issues which will invite ridicule," a student says. "If a student wishes to discuss religion, and he does not agree with the professor, that student will be made to look like a fool." Another student says, "I think you can see a humanistic, liberal secularism to everything on campus."

As one professor notes, "things are uneven" at USC, and "a lot can depend on what faculty you get, and what departments and what courses." A student says, "USC, in a lot of ways, is really school-by-school." Another student reports, "Unfortunately there is no continuity in teaching ability. Many professors are primarily researchers who are obligated to teach a course every semester, often quite begrudgingly. Very, very few professors at USC will equip students to be citizens, to be financially wise, to be discerning, or to be good. This simply does not happen. There is no consensus about what constitutes knowledge or what constitutes a noble life."

Among the outstanding faculty at USC are Gene Bickers in physics and astronomy; Peggy Kamuf in the French and Italian department; Leo Braudy in English; Paul Knoll in history; Sharon Lloyd in philosophy; John Bowlt in Slavic languages and literature; John Furia Jr. and Don Hall in the School of Cinema-Television; Howard Gillman in political science; Ed Cray and Jack H. Ryan in the School of Journalism of the Annenberg School for Communications; and Juliet Musso, Gary Painter, and Richard Sundeen in the School of Policy, Planning, and Development. One student says, "The best professor on the USC campus is Dallas Willard in the philosophy department. He has been at USC for over 30 years and is an excellent resource for guidance about what professors and courses to take. Additionally, he is the best human being I have ever met and goes out of his way to care for his students in every dimension."

USC also offers opportunities for undergraduates to get involved in research, not just in the sciences but in the social sciences as well. "The president and the provost have continually pushed faculty—and I think they're serious about it—and the faculty have begun to respond" to this call to include undergraduates in research, a professor says. Among other programs, thematic option students can participate in an annual undergraduate research conference. The topics of research papers at the 2004 conference, "Rank-o-philia," reflect well on the intellectual curiosity and creativity of the thematic option students. Topics ranged from "How the Ranking of Foreigners Affected Their Lives" to "Rank in Schools: A Tale of Two Countries." There are also opportunities for undergraduates in the Summer Undergraduate Research Internship Program at the Southern California Earthquake Center. And USC boasts a program called the Academic Culture Initiative (ACI). "This allows undergraduates to get more out of the classrooms," one student says. "In ACI, there are programs such as the Research Clearinghouse, which is a database that matches undergraduates with faculty that are doing research." Student work presented at the ACI 2005 Undergraduate Symposium for Scholarly and Creative Work ranged from the original composition "Passacaglia: For Piano and Cello" to the paper "Reversible DNA Binding of Photo-responsive Surfactants." Another ACI program is the Student Speakers Bureau, in which students develop and fine tune their speaking skills, sometimes before alumni groups. The ACI also does academic weekend retreats and book salons and encourages faculty to take their students to lunch. "Basically, this program is meant to deepen academic life on campus," the student says.

USC's music program is excellent. There is a fine program in linguistics, and the department of Slavic languages and literature is also well regarded. USC's School of Cinema-Television deserves special mention for being one of the best, if not the best, in the world. As one student says, "I'm 21. Give me $40 million and I could make a feature film better than the one I saw last week in the theatre. I realize how well prepared I am." At the very least, the program teaches self-confidence. And where else could you find something called the "Hugh M. Hefner Chair for the Study of American Film?"

Class sizes at USC are generally small; it is typical for there to be fewer than 30 students in upper-division courses. Students are concerned about the teaching quality. "Some professors I've had have made me question the tenure program," a student says.

REQUIREMENTS (CONT'D)
■ **Alternative cultural traditions.** Choices here include "Chinese Literature and Culture" and "Race and Sexual Politics in Southeast Asia."
■ **Principles of scientific inquiry.** Mostly solid introductory courses.
■ **Applications of science and technology.** Here, too, the list of choices is good.
■ **Literature, philosophy, and art.** Students have the option of taking one of two survey courses on general themes relating to the liberal arts.
■ **Contemporary social issues.** Choices here range from the sublime ("Religion and the State: Changing Boundaries") to the meticulous ("Understanding Race and Sex Historically").

WEST

881

"At a university like USC, tenure is mostly based on research and not teaching. Sometimes, unfortunately, it shows." Another student says, "It is vital that you not rely on your academic advisor when choosing courses or professors," since he or she is likely to steer advisees "towards the most popular or most professionally decorated teachers" regardless of teaching ability or course content. "I suggest looking at the course catalog, getting an idea of the interesting courses, and then going to the Web sites of the professors who are teaching them. From the lists of books they've published and the descriptions of their specialties, one will get a sense for their potential biases. Then I would write an e-mail to the teacher to ask questions about the nature of the course. If possible meet with the teacher beforehand, or sit in on the first class to really get a feel for its direction. This may sound paranoid, but believe me, it is not only worthwhile, it is necessary if one is to avoid a disaster," he says.

But there is no dearth of excellent professors at USC, and while some courses are larger—especially the lower-level intros—many professors are quite reachable. "They're accessible," says a student. "You can send an e-mail to a professor and get an answer within an hour." Professors are expected to keep at least four office hours per week. "The administration tells us to be there for our students," a professor says.

Student Life: Have your people call my people

Student life at USC is a motley assortment of activities, undertaken smack-dab in the heart of Los Angeles, with all its diversions. "It's L.A., you know," a student says. "There are unlimited options." Another student says that those attending USC can try "anything and everything." "There isn't too much of a night life around USC," says another student. "So students with cars flee campus for Westwood, Hollywood, Santa Monica, Pasadena, Huntington Beach" and other Los Angeles suburbs known for their bright lights and swanky bars. Most of these destinations are a short car trip away, and they offer everything that a college student could want—restaurants, shopping, bars, and, of course, the warm, sandy beaches of the Pacific Ocean. The university also sponsors movies and dorm events. However, "the campus itself is pretty uninviting for general hanging out," a student says. "There isn't a central student union that has air hockey and hot chocolate, so most hanging out goes on in the dorms. . . . It's easy to feel trapped at USC. The campus is essentially a two-square block island dropped into a horrible area of downtown Los Angeles. A car spells freedom, but this is often not a possibility for many students."

USC sits near the center of U.S. popular culture—Hollywood—so students can expect to be exposed both on and off campus to the whole panoply of postmodern weirdness. On campus, there are plenty of student groups catering to nearly every interest. Students recommend Troy Camp and Spirits in Action, two of USC's prominent philanthropic organizations. There are numerous ethnic clubs and various preprofessional societies, as well as an extremely active contingent of religious groups. According to one student, because of the dynamic Christian religious groups on campus, "a lot of Christians on other campuses look to us and say 'that's what we want on our campus.'" "USC is a little more conservative than UCLA or the University of Washington or [the University of California at] Berkeley," says one student. Another notes that the new Unruh Political Student Association "is meant to foster political discussions and events through this student-based group sponsored by the Unruh Institute of Politics. So far, they have encouraged events from both sides politically." Of course, there are probably more than two sides to every question—but still, this sounds to us like a good sign.

Athletics play a big role in campus life. USC's principal rival—hated crosstown foe UCLA—is always a welcome target for Trojan partisans. "Even if you are not a major sports fan, it's hard to avoid being pulled into Trojan pride and whipping out your victory sign when USC beats UCLA or Notre Dame," a student says. The school also boasts plenty of club and intramural sports.

USC has a well-entrenched Greek system, with 48 recognized Greek organizations on campus, including an ecumenical Christian fraternity, Alpha Gamma Omega, and a Jewish house, Alpha Epsilon Pi. Greek life is pretty much confined to Fraternity Row along 28th Street just north of campus. "The Row is generally open only to people in the Greek system," says a student. "They only very infrequently have open parties to which everyone is invited." Another student calls it "a world unto itself," but he also notes that it does carry weight around the college: "The Greek system is huge at USC."

Housing at USC is "primarily coeducational," according to the school's Web site, although men and women are assigned to different wings or floors of certain buildings and they have their own bathrooms. Seven residence halls are primarily for freshmen, who make up the vast majority of the dorm population, although many of USC's school-run apartments are also set aside for first-year students. While the university says on its Web site that 10 to 15 percent of the spaces in university housing are set aside for returning students, students say rooms are sometimes hard to come by. "There are some nice dorms on campus, and none of them are infested or particularly dirty," a student says. "But USC does have a housing problem now, which has caused some four-person apartments to now hold five people. Also, it is almost impossible not to share a room if you stay in USC housing, and many students move out of USC housing after their freshman year."

Dorm life gets mixed reviews from most students. "The dorms here are not nice, and are basically boxes in a building," says one student. Even the housing options intended for students who prefer quieter quarters get tepid marks from some. "I lived in the honors dorms my freshman year, which made me understand why, when the recruiters were wining and dining the scholarship recipients, they only mentioned the camaraderie and not the accommodations," a student says.

SUGGESTED CORE
1. Classics 150, The Greeks and the West
2. Philosophy 100, The Western Philosophical Tradition: Classical Beginnings
3. Religion 311, The Bible in Western Literature
4. Religion 480, History of Christianity
5. Political Science 371, European Political Thought II
6. English 430, Shakespeare
7. History 351, The American Revolution
8. History 312, The Age of the French Revolution and Napoleon

The Deans' Halls are open to students who are the recipients of various university scholarships and those participating in honors programs. Other special-interest housing includes three residential colleges that house faculty members as well, and special-interest floors for students interested in business, cinema, substance-free living, or limited visitation. There are floors devoted to programs or groups such as Women in Science and Engineering. On-campus houses for Jewish and Muslim students feature kosher and halal kitchens, respectively. There are also special floors for black and Latino students in Fluor Tower. "Diversity" at USC seems to involve less the mixing of cultures than their self-segregation, says one student: "Unfortunately the Koreans all hang out with other Koreans and the African Americans all hang out with other African Americans. There is no USC community—there are tiny communities that often fail to interact."

The food is generally good, and it is available at numerous restaurants on campus and at one central dining facility. Freshmen in the dorms should expect to be forced onto the college's meal plan.

Students can't complete their USC experience without brushing up against traditions. They include kicking the light poles on the way to the Coliseum for a football game, the rivalry with UCLA, the annual Skull and Dagger prank, homecoming, the famous fight song, and taping up Tommy Trojan—the school's mascot—to save him from pranks at the hands of interloping UCLA students. "USC is nothing," says a student, "if it's not tradition-rich."

The school boasts excellent study facilities; Leavey Library, which holds the most often-used books, is open all day, every day. However, "Doheny is the largest and most gorgeous library on campus," says a student, who points out that the library has "stained glass windows, 10 floors of book stacks, and the quiet and solemnity of a convent."

Students disagree on the impact of crime on campus, though many point nervously to the dangerous neighborhood, known for homelessness and gang activity, surrounding the school. In 2003, the school reported 12 forcible sex offenses, 13 robberies, one aggravated assault, 20 stolen cars, and 91 burglaries on campus—not a terrible record for an urban school, but not indicative of idyllic peacefulness, either. The north side of campus, where most students live, is generally safer. Avoid the south and west sides of campus, especially at night. "I feel very safe on campus, even at night, because we have a good Department of Public Safety here," a female student says. However, another considers "the entire USC area . . . incredibly dangerous" and recommends that "all Metro buses are to be avoided." The school operates a fleet of "Campus Cruisers" that ferry students around in safety for up to two miles surrounding campus.

One thing many students have in common is money—a lot of it. One undergrad who relies heavily on financial aid jokes that "one in four USC females has had a nose job." The school is expensive, no question about it, with 2004–5 tuition at $25,358, and room and board at $8,852. However, admissions are need-blind, and the school commits to meet the full need of any student who enrolls. One needy student says that USC "has one of the best financial aid programs in the country." About 60 percent of students get need-based aid, and the average USC graduate owes $18,000 in student loans.

SOUTHERN METHODIST UNIVERSITY

DALLAS, TEXAS • WWW.SMU.EDU

Oh Lord, won't you buy me

Southern Methodist University is known simultaneously as one of the leading schools in the Southwest and as the finishing school for the children of the Texas business elite—there are probably more Mercedes-Benzes with Jesus fish parked here than anywhere in the world. But the school has steadily been developing its serious side, attracting serious scholars not only in areas in which the school is traditionally competitive (such as business and fine arts), but also in political science, history, psychology, and engineering. Whether the average freshman will fully appreciate and take advantage of the educational opportunities here is another question.

A massive fundraising campaign that ended in 2002 resulted in 80 new endowments for academic programs, 171 new student scholarships and awards, 16 new academic positions, and 14 new or renovated facilities. The university's literature claims that as a result it has been greatly strengthened in key academic areas, including science and technology. There's more to Southern Methodist University than meets the eye, and one doesn't need to be a future first lady (Laura Bush is one of SMU's prominent alumni) to prosper here. With a little investigation and effort, one can even design for oneself a college education of substance.

Academic Life: That education business

Southern Methodist University is one of the more prestigious places to pursue a business or related degree in the region. SMU is a principal training ground for Dallas's professionals, and its Cox School of Business offers the most popular majors—business and finance. One special opportunity for select business undergraduates is the BBA Leadership Institute, a seminar program taught by outside business leaders and professionals. Part of the Cox School, the program offers classes and seminars that address real-life business situations.

VITAL STATISTICS

Religious affiliation:
   United Methodist
Total enrollment: 10,901
Total undergraduates: 6,208
SAT/ACT midranges: SAT
   V: 540–640, M: 560–660;
   ACT: 24–28
Applicants: 6,434
Applicants accepted: 65%
*Accepted applicants who
   enrolled*: 31%
Tuition: $25,358
Room and board: $8,852
Freshman retention rate: 88%
Graduation rate: 53% (4 yrs.),
   71% (6 yrs.)
*Courses with fewer than 20
   students*: 51%
Student-faculty ratio: 12:1
*Courses taught by graduate
   TAs*: not provided
Most popular majors:
   business, social sciences,
   communications
Students living on campus:
   40%
*Guaranteed housing for four
   years?* no
Students in fraternities: 29%
   sororities: 35%

Southern Methodist does not have a traditional core curriculum, but it does maintain a respectable set of distribution requirements. Unfortunately, most of the seemingly substantive mandates can be met by taking bizarre or politicized classes. All students must take the following:

- Two English composition classes.
- One mathematics course.
- One class in information technology.
- Two laboratory courses, at least one of which must be selected from biology, chemistry, geology, or physics.

Students also take one course each from five of the following six categories:

- Arts. Choices range from "History of Cinema Comedy" to "Women and Music: 'Like a Virgin': From Hildegard to Madonna."
- Literature.
- Religious/philosophical thought.

Beyond that, the university has a solid academic reputation in the humanities that has actually been improving lately. English, political science, history, and psychology are well-regarded among the liberal arts at SMU, and its theater and arts programs are nationally recognized. The university seems genuinely to wish to fulfill the mandate of its Master Plan of 1963, which stated that "professional studies must rise from the solid foundation of a basic liberal education."

SMU promises to provide small classes, and in fact prides itself on this; a bare majority of courses have 20 students or fewer. The University Honors Program is even better, allowing about 600 students to take intimate seminars on topics not offered broadly, with enrollment in each course capped at 20 students. Teaching assistants rarely serve as primary instructors.

When freshman enter the university through Dedman College, they are oriented through the General Education Curriculum, in which the liberal arts are divided into such groupings as "cultural formations" ("interdisciplinary humanities and social sciences options, emphasizing writing") and "perspectives" (arts, literature, religious and philosophical thought, history, politics and economics, and behavioral sciences). Students majoring in the humanities, mathematics, the natural sciences, and the social or behavioral sciences remain in Dedman College. Others apply to the School of Engineering, the Cox School of Business, or the Meadows School of the Arts.

Given the preprofessional slant of most students who enroll at SMU, a freshman looking for a liberal education will need to choose carefully in order to find a college education imparting substantive and foundational literacy in Western literature, history, and thought. There are hidden treasures available to budding humanists who seek them out. One graduate student says that his "sense is that, if so inclined, an undergraduate could successfully carve out a substantive 'classics' curriculum at SMU."

Good courses include "Currents in Classical Civilization," which is billed as an interdisciplinary cultural study of the epoch and includes some exposure to primary readings; "Myth and Thought in the Ancient World," an exploration of the conceptual and philosophical underpinnings of ancient understandings of reality in Western and non-Western cultures; and "Thinking in the Ancient World," which boasts a more global orientation. A greater emphasis on philosophical discourse as distinct from cultural overview might be found in "History of Western Philosophy—Ancient." Other worthy choices for the intellectually curious include "Introduction to the Hebrew Bible" and "Christ as Cultural Hero," described as "[a]n exploration of the impact of Jesus on the history of Western culture, not only in religion and philosophy, but also in the fine arts, literature, and politics." Devout Christians should of course be prepared for discussion of revisionist theories and possibly irreverent material. One should probably steer clear of "The Social-Scientific Study of Religion" and "Ways of Being Religious." An indispensable foray into the Middle Ages could be had through "Philosophical and Religious Thought in the Medieval West," or, for a more romantic and colorful twist, "The World of King Arthur." "Medieval Thought" appears to be more of a survey, but it does have an interesting focus on the interaction between Christendom and the high culture of medieval Islam. Moving forward to the most vital period in understanding English-speaking culture at the period of its decisive emergence from the medieval worldview, "The World of Shakespeare" should be seriously considered. Coming toward the present, students should look at "History of Western Philosophy—Modern," "Social and Intellectual History of Modern Europe," and "Out of Many: History of the United States to 1877."

Given the school's practical bent, one might be surprised to learn that medieval studies has some very enthusiastic and learned practitioners at SMU. Professors Bonnie Wheeler and Stephen Shepherd are described as "excellent medievalists." Dr. Wheeler is "a passionate teacher of Chaucer," according to a student, and is said to actively attract students to medieval studies.

A student describes the university's English department as "professionally distinguished" and has high praise for some of its professors. There is an annual literary festival on campus, and the university also publishes *Southwest Review*, one of the four oldest continuously published literary quarterlies in the nation. Two literature professors specializing in poetry, Willard Spiegelman and Thomas Arp, are especially well respected (Spiegelman as a highly articulate and excellent guide to the understanding and appreciation of poetry, Arp as the author of a widely used poetry textbook).

In the history department, recommended professors include Jeremy Adams and Edward Countryman. One student who did not go out of his way to tailor his core

REQUIREMENTS (CONT'D)

- History/art history. Because these two disparate categories are thrown together, students can avoid studying anything more venerable than the "History of Photography." The dozens of other choices include "Mortals, Myths, and Monuments of Ancient Greece" and "Out of Many: History of the United States to 1877."
- Politics and economics.
- Behavioral sciences. Students also must take:
- Two Cultural Formations classes. Options include solid courses, as well as "Wives, Lovers, Mothers, Queens: Expressions of the Feminine Divine in the World Religions," "Cultures and Constructions of Gender, Sexuality, and the Family in South Asian Religions," and "Lesbian and Gay Literature and Film: Minority Discourse and Social Power."
- One course that reflects "human diversity." Choices here include "Female Trouble: Stories of Women" and "Surrealism and the State: An Introduction to Eastern European Literature."

curriculum felt in retrospect that the classical, Enlightenment, and modern eras got adequate attention while the Middle Ages and the Renaissance were somewhat neglected in the more popular survey history courses. But judicious choices in fulfilling one's requirements (not to mention electives) can very much counteract this tendency.

SMU offers some exceptional opportunities for political science majors. The university is home to a relatively new but prestigious political studies institute, the John Goodwin Tower Center for Political Studies (named for the former senator), which focuses on international relations and comparative politics. The center was established to support teaching and research programs in international studies and national security policy. One could hardly think of a more relevant area of concentration in these tense and ideologically inflamed times, when diplomacy not only appears to be something of an endangered art, but also seems to have fallen into a perhaps undeserved level of disrepute. The center's Web site emphasizes that it is "a unique institution in American higher education because . . . [its] focus is clearly upon the enhancement of undergraduate education within the larger research interests of a university." The center offers a limited number of research fellowships to undergraduate students. The recipients develop research projects under faculty supervision for publication or presentation to professional organizations or faculty committees. Fellows receive stipends of up to $500 per semester for a maximum of four consecutive semesters. The Tower Center has also worked with distinguished polling organizations such as Zogby in conducting research into the views of the American public on foreign nations and international politics.

The university's Meadows School of the Arts is also highly esteemed. Its facilities include the Bob Hope and Greer Garson theaters, funded by those performers. The Meadows School has earned a prominent place nationally among American art schools and offers diverse programs in the visual arts (art and art history), performing arts (dance, music, and theater), and communications (advertising, cinema-television, corporate communications and public affairs, and journalism), as well as an excellent program in arts administration.

Student Life: Greek envy

SMU is located in Highland Park, an affluent section of Dallas with many dining, cultural, and nightlife attractions and conveniences. Some consider the school a haven for rich kids more concerned with their choices of fraternities or sororities than with their academics, kids who drop references in casual conversation to which of their parents or which of their friends' parents are senior corporate executives. In fact, the stereotypical SMU student is an affluent Texan or southern preppy. While the campus is overwhelmingly white, there has been an increase in Hispanic students in recent years. At the same time, many students emphasize that the climate is basically upbeat, open, and friendly, with little snobbery publicly evident. The university administration has been engaged in a push for "diversity" in recent years. Given the context of SMU's tradition of rather homogeneous social elitism, one might imagine that the "diversification" efforts are not necessarily as obnoxious as they usually are in other campus settings, where they might be more gratuitous and ideologically driven.

The campus is built in a stately Georgian style. Various new facilities have been built in recent years, such as an art museum and football stadium, and the library has been expanded. Renovations and expansions of both the fitness and recreation center and the business education center are ongoing. The 14 residence halls are all coed and have high-quality accommodations.

Students who need a break from the upper-class environs of Highland Park can study during the summer at SMU's campus in beautiful Taos, New Mexico. Located in a former Civil War fort, SMU–Taos is "contained within the Carson National Forest and surrounded by the Sangre de Cristo Mountains"; it stands "at an elevation of almost 7,500 feet," according to the *SMU Daily Campus* (the online version of the student newspaper). One student told the paper, "I loved SMU-in-Taos because it is the perfect place to get class credit while also having tons of fun and doing everything outside." Classes are held from May through August in subjects such as "anthropology, art, communications, cultural formations, English, history, religion, wellness," and several of the sciences.

Entering freshmen at SMU are required to take courses comprising a "wellness program," an attempted primer on methods for maintaining personal well-being and balance in undergraduate life. Most call the classes "easy"; the word "fluff" also comes up. SMU enumerates "seven areas of personal wellness": social, physical, emotional, occupational, intellectual, environmental, and spiritual. There's something of an emphasis on an "I'm OK, you're OK" self-consoling approach to life issues in the program. One student says, "I think that the part about making good life choices is great, but the part that basically says that 'no one is ever wrong' really bothers me. There has to be some standard. Nevertheless, 'wellness' is my favorite class because it is a big stress reliever and it encourages closeness among students."

The existence of and early emphasis on the wellness program is emblematic of a university administration that is known (and looked upon with gratitude) as being highly solicitous of the personal needs of individual students. The administration is said to very actively seek the views of students on matters affecting campus life and to be quite willing to spend money to address frequently voiced concerns. Professors are considered easily accessible and often show an unusual degree of willingness to give one-on-one attention to freshmen. The university also provides what it calls an "academic safety net" for its students in the form of the Learning Enhancement Center,

SUGGESTED CORE
1. Engl 4362, Heroic Visions: The Epic Poetry of Homer and Vergil
2. Phil 3351, History of Western Philosophy (Ancient)
3. Reli 3319/3326, Introduction to the Hebrew Bible / Introduction to the New Testament
4. Reli 3349, Early Christianity *or* Hist 2321, Philosophical and Religious Thought in the Medieval West
5. PLSC 3361, Modern Political Thought
6. Engl 1320, The World of Shakespeare
7. Hist 2311, Out of Many: U.S. History to 1877
8. Phil 3370, Nineteenth-Century Philosophy

where students can take seminars on time and stress management, receive writing tutorials, or enroll in an elective that builds study skills.

Around a third of each class pledges fraternities or join sororities; many upperclassmen live in Greek houses. Although students involved in Greek life frequently go out of their way to insist that the social atmosphere at SMU is open, friendly, and nonexclusive, there's no denying the heavy social dominance of the fraternities. It's to the point where recent graduates have reported that some young women actually choose to transfer to other schools when they don't make the sororities of their choice.

Social life revolves around the weekly fraternity parties. It's said that the weekend begins on Thursday night, to the degree that Friday sees much class-skipping. Friday night is devoted to relentless revelry, Saturday to recovery, and Sunday to cleaning up and gearing up for the week ahead. Campus parties continue to draw seniors and juniors who have moved off campus.

Special-interest club social activities are common during the week; theater and political groups are popular. Social and student government "leadership development" activities, such as the Leadership Consultant Council (LCC), Program Council, Student Foundation, and Student Senate, are also unusually prestigious at SMU. The Texas House of Representatives passed a resolution in 2003 that "recognized [LCC] as one of the best student leadership development organizations in the nation." The university is not a bad place to be if one has interest in a political career or in becoming, say, an up-and-coming corporate attorney—especially if you're a Republican.

The SMU student body leans toward being moderately conservative. Many note that the professors are generally more liberal than either the "decidedly Republican" student body or the larger community, although the faculty is said to be less left-leaning than comparable universities. Liberal students at SMU further describe Dallas itself as "a very conservative city" and note that this fact has its influence. One fairly neutral student states flatly that the campus "is located in an extremely conservative community and surrounded by a conservative urban area. Occasionally I've observed some liberal groups who have placed fliers around campus. The school newspaper seems to be more to the left."

One active student says that political activity "on campus is enjoyable because groups are allowed to flourish. Almost every Young Conservatives of Texas event brings liberals to the table to argue over the national/international issues of the day." A debate between the College Republicans and the SMU Democrats was well attended in fall 2004, and a large crowd turned out for President George W. Bush's appearance at SMU the day before the election.

The student newspaper, the *Daily Campus,* in fact has a fairly healthy reputation for vigorous debate between contributors of various viewpoints. One recent exchange was between a proponent of the "intelligent design" critique of Darwinian evolution, championed by biologist Dr. Michael Behe, and SMU's own Dr. John Wise. This exchange was notable for the newspaper's willingness to give Behe's views a serious hearing in the first place.

At the same time, SMU students tend to look askance at anything overzealous or radical in tone or content as being extremist and distasteful. While not notably liberal by any means, the campus is not as overtly conservative as Texas A&M; most students feel that there is not a highly pronounced ideological flavor to the campus. The overall milieu is nevertheless not terribly hospitable to those who identify strongly with the hard left. Conservative students, conversely, would probably feel slightly more at home than usual—especially if they are studying business or prelaw.

Some students have nevertheless noticed elements of political correctness they find irksome. The Office of New Student Programs requires its student leaders to take part in a diversity exercise that one student says "demeans every white, rich, male who happens to be fortunate enough to be born with a mom *and* a dad in the home." Privileged treatment of "designated victim" groups can occur. One freshman reports that recently the school axed the debate team for not having enough members while at the same time leaving intact the homosexual organization, which had fewer members.

A student observes that there seem to be "a large number of students involved in on-campus Christian ministries." Campus Crusade for Christ alone draws roughly 100 students to its weekly meetings. Although it was founded by what is now the United Methodist Church and its Perkins School of Theology still serves as a United Methodist seminary, SMU is nonsectarian and welcomes students of all faiths. In fact, while 28 percent of students are Methodist, 20 percent are Roman Catholic, with the remainder mostly from other Protestant denominations. Perhaps responsive in part to a slightly more overt Christian presence than is evident at some other schools, the university offers a course titled "Bioethics from a Christian Perspective" which can be taken to fulfill core requirements. "SMU has a strong group of ethicists, including Robin Lovin at the Perkins School of Theology," says one student.

SMU is not known as a draw for feminists, although some are present and they host relatively noncontroversial events such as the "antiviolence against women" march called "Take Back the Night."

Highland Park has also historically been a dry neighborhood; there aren't any bars within six blocks of campus, promoting a more sedate immediate community environment. There is ample police presence, and female students say they feel quite safe. In 2003, the school reported three forcible sex offenses, one robbery, one aggravated assault, 18 burglaries, four stolen cars, and two arsons.

With 2004–5 tuition and fees at $25,358, and room and board at $8,852, the cost of attending SMU is in the middle range of private schools. Admission is need-blind, and more than 70 percent of undergraduates receive some form of financial aid from the school. The average SMU undergrad exits school owing $16,906 in student loans.

STANFORD UNIVERSITY

PALO ALTO, CALIFORNIA • WWW.STANFORD.EDU

Make yourself useful

By all accounts Leland Stanford, founder of Stanford University, was a remarkable man. Trained as a lawyer, Stanford was also a successful businessman and politician. A practical man, Stanford helped build the western portion of the first transcontinental railroad. As a politician, he was instrumental in establishing the California Republican Party, served as California's governor, and was elected to the United States Senate in 1855. For all of his practical successes, however, Stanford also attached great importance to the study of general literature and to the liberal arts. "I think I have noticed," Stanford once said, "that technically educated boys do not make the most successful businessmen." Cultured citizens, Stanford argued, were also useful citizens.

Leland Stanford's insight appears to have been lost on those who now look after his patrimony. Stanford University's reputation as a leader in both the sciences and the liberal arts diminished when it abandoned its Western civilization requirement in 1987 after a storm of student protest led by Jesse Jackson, who led the infamous chant, "Hey hey, ho ho, Western civ has got to go." These events placed Stanford at the center of a two-decade-long nationwide movement that has virtually removed the systematic study of Western civilization from college campuses across the country.

Today, instead of Western civilization, Stanford requires courses in world cultures, American cultures, or gender studies. Perhaps as a result, Stanford students have turned away from the liberal arts towards technical fields such as computer science and engineering. The growth of the high-tech sector and the transformation of Stanford's Silicon Valley home in Palo Alto from sleepy farmland to the center of the new economy has further solidified the university's position and reputation as a leader in the technical, rather than the liberal, arts.

John Hennessy, an engineer, software pioneer, and Silicon Valley insider, became Stanford's president in 2000. There has been little to contradict fears voiced upon his appointment that the liberal arts would continue to decline under Hennessy's leadership. One professor now calls the school "Stanford Tech." A recent decision by the Stanford University Press to reduce the number of humanities volumes it publishes can be viewed as a further indication of the university's de facto decision to abandon the liberal arts and instead go "high tech." One professor we contacted disagrees that Stanford has abandoned the liberal arts, however: "In fact, of four broad areas of concentration (humanities, social sciences, engineering, and natural sciences), engineering is the smallest. Overall we are fairly well balanced across these four areas, a claim that no other top institution can make," he says. The Stanford philosophy department was rated number six in the United States in 2004 by *The Princeton Review*'s Philosophical

Gourmet Report. And one of the uses to which Stanford is putting its technical prowess will benefit humanistic scholars around the world: The school is working with Google, the New York Public Library, Oxford University, and the University of Michigan to make scholarly collections available free online, according to the *Chronicle of Higher Education*.

In any case, there is little question that Stanford continues to attract the "best and the brightest," both in terms of faculty and students: Stanford graduates constitute nearly half of the United States Supreme Court (Justices Breyer, Kennedy, O'Connor, and Chief Justice Rehnquist); 18 Stanford graduates, including Sally Ride, have served as astronauts; and in 2003, Stanford was behind only Harvard and the University of Texas at Austin in the number of incoming National Merit Scholars. However, Stanford students are no longer required to gain a solid grounding in the literature and history of Western civilization. Students who want a broad, humane education at Stanford must piece it together at a school that is hostile to traditional education—but excels in the technical fields. In other words, Stanford specializes in solving the question of "how" to achieve a goal. It has perhaps forgotten the fine art of asking "why?"

Academic Life: The decline of Western civ

"Stanford provides the means," the school's catalog states, "for its undergraduates to acquire a liberal arts education." True enough. Students who are mature and savvy will figure out how to take advantage of Stanford's remaining courses in the liberal arts. As one conservative student journalist wrote, "Stanford definitely has its share of politicized courses with their multicultural dogma. But the courses which form a foundation in Western civilization, although not mandatory, are readily available for the taking."

The best option for Stanford students interested in spending their four years of expensive education in broadening their minds is the Program in Structured Liberal Education (SLE), a sequence of three courses that stands as one of the last traces of Stanford's once-strong Western civilization requirement. SLE is a "year-long, residential, rigorous writing and literature course that intensely covers the canon of Western civilization along with some material on Hinduism and Buddhism (also reflective of actual civilizations)," says a past participant. According to the program Web page, SLE emphasizes primary texts that help students answer questions like "What is knowledge? What is the relationship between reason and passion? How does the concept of

VITAL STATISTICS
Religious affiliation: none
Total enrollment: 18,836
Total undergraduates: 6,555
SAT/ACT midranges: SAT V: 680–770, M: 690–780; ACT: 29–34
Applicants: 19,172
Applicants accepted: 13%
Accepted applicants who enrolled: 66%
Tuition: $29,847
Room and board: $9,503
Freshman retention rate: 98%
Graduation rate: 77% (4 yrs.), 93% (6 yrs.)
Courses with fewer than 20 students: 69%
Student-faculty ratio: 7:1
Courses taught by graduate TAs: 17%
Most popular majors: social sciences, engineering, biology
Students living on campus: 91%
Guaranteed housing for four years? yes
Students in fraternities or sororities: 13%

justice change over time? Is coherent meaning possible in the modern era? Can one live a spiritual life in the contemporary world?" SLE freshmen live together in three houses, allowing them to learn and discuss ideas outside the classroom.

Students say professors at Stanford are accessible to undergraduates, despite the pressure to publish that many faculty members sense. "I've yet to have a professor, of any rank or stature, not return an e-mail," one student says. "In terms of access to professors, you really can't beat Stanford." A science major says, "It obviously depends on the courses . . . but I've generally found that professors are very welcoming and helpful when approached." Graduate teaching assistants rarely teach courses, but they do often lead discussion or laboratory sections for larger lecture classes. One student says of the faculty, "They're generally competent; a few are outstanding; [most are] reasonably available." Each freshman is assigned to an academic advisor, who is a faculty member, a staff member, or graduate student, and also to a peer, upperclassman academic advisor. Once the student declares a major, he is assigned (or chooses) a faculty advisor within his major department. One student says, "Every student has a faculty advisor, but quality varies dramatically, and the good ones are in high demand."

The Diversity Myth, a book by two former editors of the conservative campus paper the *Stanford Review*, provides a detailed account of Stanford's liberal curricular bias and political atmosphere. In it, students report that the most left-leaning courses can be avoided simply by reading the course titles. "So long as you avoid the one or two nutcases, you're in fine shape," one student says. "One of my favorite professors here is a committed Marxist, and arguing with him is a pastime of mine. I've never felt any pressure to submit to his views or felt as though he'd grade me more harshly if I disagreed with him." Another student says, "I did take a class on medical ethics where the professor was generally unbiased except on the issue of abortion, where she spent an inordinate amount of time trying to shoot down every opposing idea."

Stanford's humanities departments are diluted with politically correct programs, such as the Center for Comparative Studies in Race and Ethnicity, African and Afro-American studies, and feminist studies. In the feminist studies program, which has been around for more than 20 years, "the courses offered . . . use feminist perspectives to expand and reevaluate the assumptions at work in traditional disciplines in the study of individuals, cultures, social institutions, policy, and other areas of scholarly inquiry," according to the department. Students enroll in courses that question the "male supremacist social system," such as "Girls on Film," "Feminist Perspectives on Science," and "Lesbian, Gay, and Bisexual Studies." Feminist studies has, as one student puts it, "a huge" presence on campus, sponsoring lectures, activist workshops, and essay contests.

"Many of the political science classes are liberal and PC, but if you look you can find some classes that are taught by conservative professors," a student says. Another says, "Stanford has high-quality courses and instruction, but obviously it's up to the students to make sure they get the education that they want." The editor of the *Stanford Review* has written of the school, "The professors in the schools of Humanities and Sciences, Engineering, Earth Sciences, Business, Law, Medicine, and Education are consistently superb. I mention both undergraduate and graduate programs to highlight the important synergy between the two. For example, one of my best advisors freshman year was a graduate student in the Business School who was pursing a PhD in economics. My major advisor, a health economics professor, has an MD and PhD in economics from Stanford. Even if you do not think you will have many encounters with some of the graduate schools, it is important to realize that there are positive externalities from having successful schools and departments in all fields. The benefits overflow in subtle but important ways."

A number of Stanford faculty members are tabbed by students as outstanding teachers, including John B. Taylor in economics; Judith L. Goldstein in political science and public policy; Philip Zimbardo (emeritus) in psychology; David Kennedy and Norman Naimark in history (history boasts three Pulitzer Prize winners: Kennedy, Carl Degler (emeritus), and Jack Rakove); William H. Durham in anthropological sciences; John C. Bravman in materials engineering; Kathleen M. Eisenhardt in management; Brad D. Osgood in electrical engineering; Douglas D. Osheroff in physics; George Springer in aeronautics; Eric Roberts in computer science; Michael Bratman in philosophy; Roger Noll in economics; former Reagan administration member Martin Anderson at the Hoover Institution; and Robert McGinn at the Center for Work, Technology, and Organization.

Several of Stanford's academic programs, especially political science and economics, are bolstered by the university's affiliation with the Hoover Institution, a privately endowed think tank located on campus. Three current Hoover affiliates are Nobel laureates: economists Gary S. Becker, Milton Friedman, and Douglass North. Political science, especially, is reputed to have excellent undergraduate teaching, with several professors having filled key administrative positions in Washington, D.C. Secretary of State Condoleeza Rice is currently on leave from the political science department.

Political science majors must declare a concentration in international relations, American politics, political theory, or comparative politics and take at least four courses in that area. For breadth, majors must take two courses in another area and one more course in a third area. Economics majors face a more struc-

ACADEMIC REQUIREMENTS

Stanford has no core curriculum. Instead, the university requires that students complete the General Education Requirement (GER), one year of foreign language study, and the university-wide writing examination. Students must complete the following:

- A year-long introductory humanities sequence. The first quarter deals with some classic primary texts of the West. Other sections (students can choose among many) are said to be often blatantly politicized.
- Three courses in natural science, applied science and technology, and mathematics. More than 100 courses fulfill this requirement.
- Three courses in humanities and social science. Hundreds of courses qualify—of widely varying quality and content. Some good options include "The Rise and Fall of Europe" and "History of Greece."
- Two courses selected from 125 choices in world cultures, American cultures, or gender studies. These classes are said to "offer little more than leftist politics," according to a student.

tured curriculum, including six core courses: "Principles of Economics," "Introduction to Statistical Methods," "Basic Price Theory," "Intermediate Microeconomics," "Intermediate Macroeconomics," and "Econometrics." In addition to these introductory courses, economics majors must also choose four courses from a short list, pass a "Writing in the Major" course, and take four other electives.

But the strength of Stanford now resides in its science and engineering programs, which attract the overwhelming majority of incoming freshmen and, if one includes the medical school, house the majority of the university's tenured faculty. Over the years, Stanford has been able to attract a core group of premier physicists, including several who have been awarded the Nobel Prize (Steven Chu, Robert Laughlin, Douglas Osheroff, Burton Richter, and Richard E. Taylor). They develop and conduct research at the Stanford Linear Accelerator Center, a world-renowned center for physics.

Over the years students and faculty in both the humanities and sciences have complained that grade inflation is a problem at Stanford. "Grade inflation does seem to exist in many classes," a student says. "A popular saying at Stanford is something like, 'You must work hard to get an A but you must do absolutely nothing to earn a C.'" Nevertheless, Stanford remains eminently competitive, especially with regard to undergraduate admissions. To address what some thought was an overly competitive undergraduate application process, Stanford, like Yale University, recently decided to eliminate its early decision option for incoming freshmen.

Student Life: Silicon (Valley) implants

"There is a definite liberal slant among the students and faculty at Stanford," says one undergraduate. This opinion is widely held, as the *Stanford Review* attests: "As at most universities and California institutions, the ideology is predominantly left-of-center. The rallies in White Plaza, the petitions that sweep through the dorms, the proposals for boycotts, and the ubiquitous propaganda all assert liberal values."

The politicization of Stanford's campus is everywhere apparent. On any given day, members of the student body might demonstrate against racism, human rights abuses in foreign countries, sexism, homophobia, general intolerance, or logging. The annual "grape debate" asks students to vote, dorm by dorm, on whether grapes will be served in their dining hall. The Grape Education Committee provides students with information on the ins and outs of grape production prior to the vote. The whole event appears to have evolved from student sympathies for the United Farm Workers Organizing Committee, a group that protests the sale of grapes by nonunion farm workers.

Perhaps as signified by the creation of the Islamic studies program, Stanford is becoming increasingly multicultural when it comes to religion, and some students consider this to be a turning away from the school's original mission. In February 2003, the Queer-Straight Social and Political Alliance, with the blessing of the Office of Religious Life, held a "Stanford Freedom to Marry Day" on a campus plaza. The senior associate dean for religious life, Rabbi Patricia Karlin-Neumann, presided over four same-sex wedding ceremonies in Memorial Church—a picturesque Christian chapel built by Mrs. Stanford as a tribute to her late husband.

While there appear to be any number of outlets for liberal-minded students, faculty, and administrators at Stanford, there are also places where conservatives might find solace. One, of course, is the Hoover Institution, which frequently sponsors lectures, has an active internship program, and is a resource for reasoned scholarship on issues of considerable public interest. Even though the university appears to regret its relationship with Hoover, interested students would do well to become acquainted with its programs.

Stanford is located in the midst of the soul-crushing monotony of suburban Silicon Valley. Even with downtown San Francisco only 45 minutes away, students find little reason to leave campus, for both in architectural splendor (the buildings are inspired by the California Mission style, with red-tiled roofs and sandstone walls) and in student amenities (the one-of-a-kind Stanford Linear Accelerator Center, the seven million volumes of the library system, the newly renovated residence halls) the campus seems to have it all. The university, fully self-sufficient, even has its own shopping center, with stores such as Macy's and Nordstrom's.

Students, many of whom are self-described intellectuals, are keen on student organizations, and Stanford appears to offer a student club or society for every interest. Hundreds of clubs, ranging from the academic to the preprofessional to the athletic to the multicultural, are available. Clubs include the Jewish Graduate Student Organization, the Bocce Ball Club, Women and Youth Supporting Each Other, and the ReJOYce in Jesus Campus Fellowship.

Conservative students should certainly check out the *Stanford Review*, an alternative to the school's official newspaper. Recently, according to the *Review*, the paper has come under assault due to several controversial articles, and the university is trying to prevent its door-to-door distribution in the dorms. One conservative student waxes effusive over the extracurricular opportunities at Stanford. As he wrote in the *Stanford Review*: "Education is not confined to the classroom. The proverbial late-night discussions and absorbing dinner table conversations with your friends are certainly part of what I mean. I also consider the cornucopia of cool programs sponsored by various student organizations to be part of the educational experience. For example, a little over a week ago I attended talks by James Lilly, former U.S. ambassador to China, sponsored by the Forum for American-Chinese Exchange at Stanford; Abbas Milani, an Iran scholar, sponsored by the Persian Student Association; L. Paul Bremer, [former] head of the Coalition Provisional Authority in Iraq, sponsored by the ASSU Speakers Bureau and Stanford in Government; and [Lt. Col.] Daniel Yoo of the U.S. Marine Corps, who served in Afghanistan and is currently a National Security Fellow at the Hoover

SUGGESTED CORE
1. Classics 18, Greek Mythology
2. Philosophy 100, Greek Philosophy
3. Religious Studies 15, The Hebrew Bible *and* Religious Studies 25, Introduction to New Testament Literature
4. Religious Studies 24: Introduction to Christianity (*closest match*)
5. Political Science 130B, History of Political Thought II: The Origins of Modern Democracy
6. English 163, Shakespeare
7. History 165A, Colonial and Revolutionary America
8. History 136A, European Thought and Culture in the Nineteenth Century

Institution. The last event was one of a weekly series called 'Pizza and Politics,' which the *Stanford Review* sponsors in conjunction with the Hoover Institution. I have been participating in these lunches since I was a freshman, and I have been amazingly fortunate to have shared meals with the likes of Milton Friedman and Thomas Sowell."

Most students live on campus all four years, as Bay Area housing prices are exorbitant. Housing is guaranteed for four years. In general, students enjoy living on campus; as one student says, "Stanford's on-campus housing is wonderful." There are many different styles of living, from apartments to house-style units, dorms, and co-ops. Dormitories are all coed with some single-sex floors, but fraternities and sororities, of course, provide single-sex living options. Although there are no coed dorm rooms, some bathrooms are coed. Many of the dorms and houses are theme oriented, including Muwekma-Tah-Ruk for American Indian students, Okada for Asian American students, Ujamaa for African American students, and Casa Zapata for Latino students. Some have unofficial designations, such as the "gay" or "lesbian" house. The *Stanford Review* has voiced criticism of the ethnic dorms, citing those who say "that the dorms encourage the formation of . . . 'separatist enclaves.' . . . [S]ince many minorities live in ethnic theme dorms, there are simply fewer minorities to contribute to cross-cultural exchange on the rest of campus, especially in nonethnic theme dorms."

Undergraduate students are not the only ones living on campus—58 percent of graduate students and 30 percent of faculty also reside on "the Farm," the nickname for Stanford's scenic 8,200-acre spread.

Stanford's considerable cultural resources have recently come together in the Cantor Center for the Visual Arts, which opened in 1999. The center includes the historic museum building, a Rodin sculpture garden, and a new wing with a bookstore and space for special exhibitions. The 27 galleries in the Cantor Center exhibit a diverse standing collection, including everything from Miro to O'Keeffe to Renaissance paintings and African masks.

Cardinal athletics are an important part of student life at Stanford. Since 1980, the Cardinal (not Cardinals, plural; the name refers to the school color) have won almost 70 NCAA team championships, more than any other school in the nation over that span. In all, the university boasts 95 national championships. Tiger Woods, Mike Mussina, and John Elway are three former Cardinal athletes who have gone on to superstardom. The *Chronicle of Higher Education* cites Stanford as a national role model for Title IX compliance, a much-criticized federal law that requires universities to provide for women the same level of athletic support as they do for men. The university also has a number of intramural and club sports, plus several noncredit recreation programs in activities such as Afro-Caribbean dance, rock climbing, and golf.

Palo Alto offers students plenty of distractions, especially restaurants and shops, but it "just isn't a college town, and there isn't much there for Stanford students," says one student. Another student says Palo Alto is a pleasant enough town, but that it "is somewhat pricey. A better bet is Castro Street in Mountain View [five miles from campus]. . . . The area is more middle class and less yuppie, the food is cheaper, and there aren't as many crazies around."

Most students say they feel safe on campus—despite a recent explosion in sex crimes, which leapt from five incidents in 2002 to 38 in 2003. Also in 2003, the school reported 142 burglaries, 35 stolen cars, one robbery, one aggravated assault, and two arsons. Directly off campus, students say Palo Alto attracts many homeless people, who, one student says, "may threaten to kill you." Students returning home late at night can call for an escort if they don't feel safe.

Stanford offers a world-renowned education and charges a commensurate tuition: in 2004–5, students paid $29,847, and $9,503 for room and board. However, admissions are need-blind, and the school is committed to providing all enrolled students with adequate aid.

University of Texas at Austin

Austin, Texas • www.utexas.edu

The university as Wal-Mart

Barry Schwartz, a professor of psychology at Swarthmore College, laments the "intellectual shopping mall" the modern university has become in an article aptly titled "The Tyranny of Choice" in the *Chronicle of Higher Education*. Universities, Schwartz argues, treat students like consumers. They offer an array of products—i.e., classes and majors—from which the student-consumers may choose, and so respond to some degree to changes in consumer taste and sentiment.

If the typical university is a mall, then, as one student says, the University of Texas at Austin "is the Wal-Mart of higher education"—a one-stop shop where all political ideologies, oddball hobbies, and career interests are nurtured or, in some cases, pandered to. UT has more than 40 active student-run political groups, and it awards bachelor's degrees in more than 120 subjects. In keeping with its home state's belief that "more is more," UT is the largest single-campus university in the United States. That fact does not frighten off the throngs of freshman applicants, who have only grown in number since UT passed the 50,000-student mark.

Academic Life: Attention, shoppers!

At a place where the student body has long since overflowed the 40 acres originally allotted for the university, vast amounts of freedom and choice demand a high degree of

WEST

899

individual responsibility or qualified assistance. Yet academically, most UT students go it alone. "What we can't do at a place like UT is maintain any serious quality control," a professor says. "That someone has 'earned' a BA at a large state university means nothing." What universities like UT do instead, the professor says, is "magnify the dangers that are inherent in the modern elective system—they offer a smorgasbord of dislocated and quirky courses on a far larger scale. They also offer the raw materials for classic liberal education, if you know how to find them and put them together."

The flip side of an abundance of choice is that there's a niche for everyone, a situation most students praise. Rapidly locating and scurrying into that niche is critical at such a massive school. While UT students are not unfriendly, the vast majority of faces will be unfamiliar as you're hoofing it across the sprawling campus from class to class. "I feel about as much camaraderie with my fellow students at UT as I do with someone off the street who wears the same brand of shoes I do," a student says.

At many colleges it is easy to be a science or engineering major and never encounter the great works of the West; at UT, that is also possible for liberal arts majors. "Play your cards right in UT's liberal arts college and watch yourself learn nothing toward a classical education," a student says. "All in all, you can get a liberal arts degree from UT and really have no education at all."

Though UT's general distribution requirements fall far short of a core curriculum, the university offers several programs that enhance the majors or serve as challenging interdepartmental options for advanced students. Plan II Honors, a major in itself, is a core-like sequence designed for students who show high proficiency in both language and mathematics. Plan II students are very, very bright: the average combined SAT score of the entering Plan II class of 2003 was 1450, and 84 percent were in the top 5 percent of their graduating classes.

Plan II seeks to foster a tight community through common coursework and small class sizes. Freshmen begin with a year-long English literature course and a semester of logic. That is followed by "Problems of Knowledge and Valuation," a two-semester philosophy session, in the sophomore year. Freshman and juniors take seminars whose quality and relevance vary. Fall 2004 freshman selections included, for example, "Business of Music Performance" and "Emerging Selves." Most Plan II seminars and sequences are heavy on writing and rewriting, and in their fourth year, students write (and probably rewrite) a thesis of 7,500 to 15,000 words. (Outside Plan II, only honors-track students write theses.) Virtually anything can be a "thesis," including artwork (accompanied by a paper), performances, and scientific studies. "Morale in Plan II is high, and rightly so, both for students and teachers," says a professor. "However, it does not have its own faculty and depends on the departments. Individual faculty members are usually eager to teach and offer courses in the program, but the departments are not always happy to see their best faculty drawn off to teach a course that has a maximum enrollment of 15." Like Plan II students, but to a lesser degree, students who enroll in the College of Liberal Arts' Freshman Honors Program benefit from smaller class sizes and honors sections of introductory courses during their first two years. In addition, these students receive helpful advice concerning their academic schedules and broader career goals. Liberal arts students with 60 hours of completed coursework and a UT GPA of at least 3.5 may apply to the Liberal Arts Honors Program (Upper Division), which provides special seminar-type classes and an honors diploma.

Other schools and departments offer special programs. The McCombs School of Business has the Business Foundations Program, directed toward students who are completing a nonbusiness major but desire more courses applicable to the real world. The College of Natural Sciences offers the Dean's Scholars Program, which facilitates undergraduate research projects and interaction between students and faculty. Computer science's Turing Scholars Program does the same for young programmers.

As might be expected of a school its size, the academic advising at UT is mediocre except in very small majors and special freshman programs. The average student is best off educating himself in detail on degree requirements and interests and acquainting himself with the inch-thick book of course offerings, and only then meeting with an advisor to double-check. "You get as much out of the advising process as you put in," one student says. "Advisors are just happy if you have your act together ahead of time so they can lift your bar and move down the list. However, advisors are generally knowledgeable, and when prompted, can be quite helpful in helping you determine what courses and instructors best fit your needs. But they don't waste time providing this support if you don't ask for it." A professor says that advising is better in some of the smaller departments, like classics and philosophy.

Some assistance may come from faculty and graduate student teaching assistants, who hold regular office hours. Students commend faculty for generally being willing to reach out to anyone willing to show up. "I've never met a professor who wasn't more than happy to receive students for inquiries, and they seem to pride themselves on being very available to students who want to complement the class setting with one-on-one tutelage," a student says. A professor says, "There is an overall atmosphere and opportunity that should not be short-changed. I think the brighter students who already have some sense of their own interests and direction really have a good time here and get a good education."

Another professor says that "UT's students are significantly better than those at the average flagship state university—not quite up to the level of students at Berkeley or Michigan, but close." Because UT is so large, it is difficult to characterize the intellectual character of students at large. One professor says "students are less curious

VITAL STATISTICS
Religious affiliation: none
Total enrollment: 50,377
Total undergraduates: 37,377
SAT/ACT midranges: SAT V: 540–660, M: 570–680; ACT: 23–28
Applicants: 23,008
Applicants accepted: 51%
Accepted applicants who enrolled: 57%
Tuition: $4,260 (in state), $12,960 (out of state)
Room and board: $6,184
Freshman retention rate: 93%
Graduation rate: 39% (4 yrs.), 74% (6 yrs.)
Courses with fewer than 20 students: 34%
Student-faculty ratio: 18:1
Courses taught by graduate TAs: not provided
Most popular majors: social sciences, business, engineering
Students living on campus: 18%
Guaranteed housing for four years? no
Students in fraternities: 9% sororities*: 12%

The University of Texas has no core curriculum but does impose certain distribution requirements—which are certainly too easy to meet. All students must take the following:

- One rhetoric and composition course and two courses that have a "substantial writing component." These courses can be used to fulfill other requirements as well. The quality and content of these courses vary greatly according to section.
- A course called "Masterworks of Literature." Be sure to check the syllabus before you choose a section; teachers' ideas of what a "masterwork" is differ all too widely. If you see words like "race," "class," or "gender," keep looking.
- Enough courses to attain (or tests to demonstrate) fourth-semester proficiency in a foreign language.

than in the past," but another says that students "in the past year or two, have begun showing more interest in academic studies than I've ever seen here." In this, as in everything else at UT, both curious and apathetic students can find a niche, and one's view of the enterprise will depend on one's vantage point.

UT relies heavily on graduate students to teach everything from massive lecture courses to small seminars. "Too much of the burden of teaching still rests with graduate students," says a professor. "Unfortunately, financial support for graduate students has not kept pace with support in a given field available elsewhere, and this means that UT is not competitive with universities of similar or higher rank. The quality of graduate students inevitably suffers."

UT can boast of many professors known for their excellent teaching and advising. Among them are J. Budziszewski, Roderick Hart, David Prindle, Alan Sager, and Jeffrey Tulis in government; George Forgie, John Leffler, Brian Levack, William Louis, and Guy Miller in history; David Hamermesh and Dale Stahl in economics; Norval Glenn in sociology; John Ruszkiewicz in rhetoric and composition; Randy Diehl, Phillip Gough, Joseph Horn, Robert Josephs, Peter MacNeilage, James Pennebaker, and Del Thiessen (emeritus) in psychology; Karl Galinsky in classics; Jean-Pierre Cauvin in French; William Guy and Michael Starbird in mathematics; James Garrison, Ernest Kaulbach, and Martin Kevorkian in English; Daniel Bonevac, Robert Kane, and Robert Koons in philosophy; and Marvin Olasky in journalism.

Majors in the business school, including the professional program in accounting and the Business Honors Program, are considered some of the best in the country. Many other UT departments rank highly; philosophy is excellent, as are psychology, classics, and linguistics. In the natural sciences, physics, math, and chemistry are all solid, as is the computer science department.

Budding journalists at UT have access to a unique resource—the original notes made by reporters Woodward and Bernstein, during their investigation of Watergate. The Harry Ransom Humanities Research Center holds these notes and will soon receive additional materials that had been withheld to protect the (now-exposed) identity of "Deep Throat," Woodstein's principal source, according to the *Chronicle of Higher Education*. Those interested in another presidency should visit the Lyndon Johnson Presidential Library, also in town.

Religious studies is not a road to salvation, UT insiders report. "Students should be cautioned that most religious studies courses are hostile to religion," says a professor, "though a growing number of courses that treat religion with respect, unaffiliated with that program, are springing up."

Majors to which the least-prepared students gravitate are education and English. These are also two of UT's most politicized departments. The latter, for example, offered in Fall 2004, "Poets and Punks: British Culture after 1945" in which students studied the new relationship between the "radical bohemian avant-garde" and literature, the end of which was putting "Graham Greene . . . in the service of Sex Pistols—to the considerable illumination of both." The professor's stated aim is to "inject volatility into conventional notions of the hierarchy of high and mass culture." Another English course during the same semester instructed students to "collect and edit slang items."

Perhaps the most prominent political issue on the UT campus is race and its use in admissions. After a recent Supreme Court decision permitted it to reinstate the use of race in admissions, the university announced its intention to do so for the entering class of 2005–6. Given that state law since 1997 has required UT to automatically admit all high school graduates in the top 10 percent of their classes who wish to enroll—a policy that has put an extraordinary strain on the resources of the nation's largest university—how the policies' combination will play out is a source of concern. Texas legislators, concerned about the "dumbing-down" of the school, are revisiting the "10 percent" law, with an eye to making more room for SAT scores and other qualifications in admissions decisions, reports the *Chronicle of Higher Education*.

Even before race reentered the admissions picture, the UT administration had assembled a Task Force on Racial Respect and Fairness. The panel, which submitted its report for public comment in January 2004, was itself noteworthy for its lack of intellectual diversity; entire colleges, such as that of natural sciences, evidently had no representation on the panel. Among many other suggestions, the task force proposed that (1) incoming freshman be required to sign an "affidavit" with their admission acceptance adhering to a university-crafted definition of "fairness and respect"; (2) the school appoint a vice president for diversity and equity; (3) all future public relations initiatives demonstrate a multicultural and inclusive program; (4) the school rate student groups with regard to how much they "respect and promote diversity"; and (5) awards be given to faculty who include multicultural learning in the classroom.

REQUIREMENTS (CONT'D)

- Two courses in American government, one including "Texas content." Some sections that fulfill the government requirement come with tags that identify the angle the course may take, such as the apparently straightforward "Congressional Elections" and the possibly partisan "Poverty and Politics."
- Two courses in American history.
- Two courses each in two of the following areas: anthropology, economics, geography, linguistics, psychology, and sociology.
- Three courses in mathematics and the sciences. At least one of the courses must be in math.
- Two courses in "general culture," one of which must be in architecture, fine arts, classics, or non-logic (not necessarily illogical) philosophy.

WEST

903

President Larry R. Faulkner responded by emphasizing UT's commitment to race-based admissions, by instituting a cross-cultural requirement for incoming freshman (not to be a "single, specific course, but rather a subject-area elective chosen by each student from a list of eligible courses"), by approving a vice provost for diversity position, and by allotting $500,000 per year for diversity programming. "The diversity worries are serious," says one UT professor. "Not only could that money be used for several other big hires; in my experience, diversity programs usually heighten racial tensions. I have sensed very little racial tension on campus, but a small, committed group of activists seems to have the ear of the administration." Another professor is concerned about the task force's recommendation that faculty search committees and applicant pools always be racially diverse: "It could be the downfall of departments that so far have resisted politicization. In practice, I could imagine this involving faculty from radical departments like African American or Mexican American studies being placed on search committees for hiring faculty in philosophy, government, classics, etc."

Student Life: Keeping it weird

Though they may agree on little else, nearly all of UT's approximately 51,000 students confess to one thing: Austin may be the perfect college city. It's a place where weird people are known to congregate, and where normal people are known to have gone and become weird. There's even an active community group called "Keep Austin Weird"—it seems that many longtime locals haven't exactly been delighted to see their bohemian city steered towards normalcy by Silicon Valley types and assorted other yuppies associated with Austin's burgeoning technology industry. But Austin is not Dallas or Houston, at least not yet. Formalities are rare: in Austin, "dressing up" still just means wearing your Ropers instead of your Birkenstocks. The town is renowned for unpretentious intellectuality in a region full of down-home pleasures such as the annual Wiener Dog Races in the nearby town of Buda, which attracts fanatical dachshunds and their owners from around the country.

Just as the city of Austin's politics are unrepresentative of the state of Texas as a whole, so is its remarkable natural beauty, as it is adjacent to the Texas Hill Country. To cool off after a rigorous run or ride on one of the city's many hike-and-bike trails, students can paddle a canoe down Barton Creek or take a chilly dip in spring-fed Barton Springs Pool, both of which are situated within Zilker Park, a downtown beauty that spans 351 acres. As the state capital, Austin provides many opportunities for students to release their political energies; the capitol building is within walking distance of campus. On campus, fraternities and sororities are present and lively, though unable to exact control over the campus social scene, given UT's sheer size and rebellious tendencies. Hundreds of student organizations fit almost every need or interest (but all that's necessary to start another group is three interested students). The Longhorn Hellraisers, to name just one nonpolitical organization, paint their faces burnt orange and white, take off their shirts (it's men only: women can join the Hellraiser Honeys), and scream at basketball and football games.

Language clubs, film series, and discussion groups abound. The Geneva Society promotes theological discussion, and the student newspaper, the *Daily Texan*, rivals many midsized city newspapers in its professionalism. Alternative publications come and go, but the humor magazine *Texas Travesty* is always good for a laugh, and the *Austin Review* and *Contumacy* are conservative outlets focused on local and campus politics, respectively. UT has many religiously oriented student organizations. Christian students wishing to remain so should generally avoid the churches adjoining campus, sources tell us. Catholic students, for instance, should skip the Catholic Student Center, perhaps in favor of more traditional liturgies at a local parish like Sacred Heart.

Football is king in Texas, and in an age of mushy sentimentality it is refreshing to see the healthy, hearty hatred that persists between the Longhorns and the Texas A&M Aggies. In recent years, the Horns have generally gotten the better of their rivals. Perhaps the most successful intercollegiate sport at UT in recent years has been the men's swimming program, though the men's and women's basketball teams are usually among the nation's best as well. Intramural sports are quite popular, though some of the playing fields are unfortunately situated a couple miles north of campus.

SUGGESTED CORE
1. Classical Civilization 301, Introduction to the Ancient World: Greece
2. Philosophy 329, History of Ancient Philosophy
3. Religious Studies 318, The Rise of Christianity (*closest match*)
4. History 309, Western Civilization in Medieval Times
5. Government 347, Introduction to Political Theory (*closest match*)
6. English 321, Shakespeare: Selected Plays
7. History 315, United States, 1492–1865
8. History 332, European Intellectual History, from the Enlightenment to Nietzsche

Residence hall living is not the norm at UT. The university's 11 residence halls have a combined capacity of just over 6,800, even with the mammoth Jester Hall, which holds just shy of 3,000 residents. The vast majority of students live off campus, many in private dormitories adjoining the campus. For those who do live on campus, single-sex dormitories are available for both men and women. There are no coed dorm rooms or bathrooms.

Freshman orientation on campus is available but not required. Much of the programming is suspect, so incoming students may want to give it a pass. One sophomore recalls attending an orientation program on diversity. "We were told to accept everything and be open-minded to all. Those who did not would be considered intolerant, racist, and close-minded," she says.

Similarly, one UT senior claims that "diversity of skin color, diversity of national origin, etc., are valued, but diversity of thought, in general, is not." Another student says, "Any outspoken conservative thought is generally regarded as unenlightened, racist, and narrow-minded. Intelligence is gauged by how few convictions a student holds, how often they 'experience' other cultures, and how quickly they denounce traditional moral values." One professor says, "Lots of students drop my course when I tell them I am conservative and Republican. . . . I have over the years been called a Nazi, UT's Rush

WEST

Limbaugh, and so on, although my evaluations are very good, especially considering I am always near the top on questions like excessive workload and time spent on my class versus others. . . . Students have told me about being penalized [in other courses] for their conservative writings or about having to write what the professor wants, not what they really think."

Despite a climate sympathetic to left-wing ideology, students report the university administration to be generally fair in allowing "all voices to be heard," according to one student. An affirmative action bake sale hosted by the Young Conservatives of Texas provoked no statement of regret or rebuke from the administration—which set it apart from other Texas schools. However, a campus pro-life group had to overcome bureaucratic barriers, including being prohibited from using the Tower Mall, being forced to follow policies only inconsistently applied to other groups, and being subjected to occasional faculty abuse. Once, when a woman who had had an abortion tried to talk about her experience, she was shouted down by a radical professor with a bullhorn. The professor, who violated a university policy against unapproved amplification devices, suffered no consequences, but the university police got a reprimand for confiscating the bullhorn.

Famous nationwide for its offbeat and often radical, if not large, protests, the West Mall steps beneath UT's famed clock tower are as active as ever. On the West Mall and in other university-designated "free-speech zones," students are allowed to hold sound-amplified events between 11:30 a.m. and 1:30 p.m. The Young Conservatives of Texas have been tastefully rowdy in recent years, and socialists and Greens are always protesting something. The Campus and Community Involvement Office, though notorious for its bureaucracy, is the institutional backbone behind the 40-plus political groups on campus. These include everything from Students for a Fair and Safe Shuttle, whose mission is to "support UT shuttle workers," to Raising Awareness about People Trafficking (RAPT). In 2003, the school reported eight forcible sex offenses, two robberies, four aggravated assaults, 64 burglaries, nine stolen cars, and two arsons. Students report feeling reasonably safe on and around campus, and given the size of the school the incidence of serious crime on campus does not appear to be high. There are, however, occasional incidents on Guadalupe Street (the "Drag"), which borders the campus's west side and tends to collect runaways, vagrants, and the weirdest of the weird. (Ever seen the cult movie *Slacker*? It's set at UT and provides a pretty accurate picture of this side of campus life—and generally makes the school look quite appealing.)

UT is especially attractive to Texas residents, with a 2004–5 tuition of $4,260; out-of-state students paid $12,960; room and board cost $6,184. The school practices need-blind admissions, and while it can't meet all student aid needs, it claims to meet "the need of most students, and particularly those with higher needs," according to the school's financial aid office. Around 38 percent of students get need-based aid, and the average student loan debt of a recent graduating class was $17,000.

TEXAS A&M UNIVERSITY

COLLEGE STATION, TEXAS • WWW.TAMU.EDU

Marching orders

Texas A&M University at College Station has undergone rapid changes during the last 40 years, none greater than in 1963, when the school converted itself from an all-male military academy to a full-fledged coeducational university. But Texas A&M, which every year hosts a traditional candlelight "Aggie muster" ceremony, has retained much from its military-school past. The university still sponsors the Corps of Cadets, which, with 2,000 members, is the largest uniformed body of students outside the three U.S. service academies. And it is still in agriculture and mechanics that the university excels. However, A&M is actively attempting to improve its liberal arts programs.

Academic Life: Cloned sheep may safely graze

As do the other state universities in Texas, A&M requires students to complete something called a "core curriculum." This amounts to a rather paltry set of distribution requirements. "The Core Curriculum provides breadth. . . . When you have the opportunity to select among various courses, select those that will give you the opportunity to explore a possible major, or make selections that enhance your degree goals," the university Web site lamely advises.

The agricultural and engineering programs at Texas A&M are among the finest on campus. Roughly 20 percent of the undergraduate population majors in some type of engineering. Virtually every engineering program offered, from aerospace to petroleum, ranks among the top 20 in the nation, and several are among the top five.

The university's offerings in the College of Agriculture and Life Sciences are certainly extensive. A student interested in this area can even major in somewhat obscure fields like agricultural journalism, dairy science, or wildlife and fisheries sciences. The College of Veterinary Medicine is widely considered to be one of the most advanced in America.

VITAL STATISTICS
Religious affiliation: none
Total enrollment: 44,435
Total undergraduates: 35,732
SAT/ACT midranges: SAT V: 520–640, M: 550–660; ACT: 23–28
Applicants: 17,324
Applicants accepted: 72%
Accepted applicants who enrolled: 57%
Tuition: $5,955 (in state), $13,695 (out of state)
Room and board: $6,887
Freshman retention rate: 90%
Graduation rate: 32% (4 yrs.), 76% (6 yrs.)
Courses with fewer than 20 students: 19%
Student-faculty ratio: 20:1
Courses taught by graduate TAs: 27%
Most popular majors: business, engineering, agriculture
Students living on campus: 25%
Guaranteed housing for four years? no
Students in fraternities: 3% sororities: 6%

The self-described "core curriculum" (which isn't) at Texas A&M requires the following:

- Two courses in communication, including "Composition and Rhetoric," plus another from a list of 10 approved courses in English, communication, or agricultural journalism.
- Two classes in mathematics. Almost all mathematics courses—and three philosophy courses—count.
- Two or three courses in the natural sciences, including a lab. This can be fulfilled through introductory courses in biology, botany, chemistry geology, physics, zoology, anthropology, horticulture, entomology, or renewable natural resources.
- One course in the humanities, either history, philosophy, literature, the arts, culture, or language. Hundreds of courses are eligible—including some from women's studies and Hispanic studies.
- One class in visual and performing arts. More than 80 courses qualify, such as "Beginning Modern Dance," "Beethoven's Life and Music," and "Dance and Modern Cultures." The two philosophy courses

In 2000, the college was the birthplace of the first animal specifically cloned for disease resistance. (For the record, we're not at all convinced that this is cause for rejoicing.) After testing hundreds of cattle, Bull 86 was found to be naturally disease-resistant to brucellosis, and resistant to tuberculosis and salmonellosis under laboratory conditions. Cells from Bull 86 were used to produce a genetic clone, Bull 86^2. Since then, Texas A&M researchers have also cloned goats, pigs, and cats, making the university the "first academic institution in the world to have cloned four different species," according to the university. Happily, the Texas legislature seems likely to ban human cloning, setting at least some limit to the mad science practiced at College Station.

The Lowry Mays College and Graduate School of Business receives high marks, with its programs in accounting, management, and marketing ranked among the top 25 in the nation in popular surveys. The College of Architecture, with more than 1,500 students, is one of the largest in the United States.

And by the way: Texas A&M also has a College of Liberal Arts, albeit one with only 12 departments, 25 majors, and 7,300 students (or about 16 percent of the 44,000 on campus).

Students majoring in a liberal arts discipline must take a few extra courses required by the College of Liberal Arts, including two "literature in English" courses, one additional humanities course, one additional social and behavior sciences course, two literature courses, and two intermediate-level foreign language courses. An "international cultures" course is also required. While this requirement can be met by a few questionable courses like "Intercultural Communication" and "Force and Violence in the Political Process," courses like "French Literature in Translation," "Eastern Europe since 1453," and "Western European Government and Politics" qualify as well.

Of course, the extent of major requirements varies by department. English majors on the literature track must take at least 12 upper-level courses, including: "Survey of English Literature to 1800," a specialty writing course, two British literature courses (including a study of pre-1800 works), two American literature courses, a course in Shakespeare, and a senior seminar. In addition, English majors must take "Introduction to Linguistics" and a course in English history. History majors, on the other hand, can expect to take two courses either on world civilization or world history as well as a seminar on the history of the United States. Students interested in studying the classics must major in something else; classics is only available as one of the college's several minors, as are religious studies, women's studies (only recently added), comparative cultures, and five others. The American politics component of the department of political science ranks among the top 20 in the country, and the economics department consistently appears in rankings of the top 40 programs.

Even though Texas A&M raised tuition rates by 18 percent for the 2004–5 school year, and although 60 percent of the revenue was to go toward new faculty hires, the journalism department was recently shut down (despite student protests) because the university "could not afford to hire the extra professors needed to sustain the program," according to the *Student Press Law Center*. Now, Texas A&M offers only an "interdisciplinary" journalism minor.

In "Vision 2020," the university's long-range planning document put forth in 1997, the university states its intention to add courses and departments in the liberal arts. According to university literature, already, "during the past ten years, the College of Liberal Arts has moved from the periphery to the center of Texas A&M University"—although the engineering departments would probably dispute that. The lack of a strong liberal arts college has hurt A&M's standing in the academic community, but students—many of whom see little point in a liberal arts or fine arts degree—have not complained too much.

The university's former president, Ray Bowen, left the helm in 2002 to take a faculty position in mechanical engineering. He was replaced by Robert M. Gates, who served as director of the Central Intelligence Agency in the early '90s. Bowen's departure and Gates's arrival were welcomed by many at the university. Bowen had made several moves that some alumni thought were aimed at conforming A&M to the progressivism often characteristic of elite public universities, such as Bowen's Vision 2020 report, a set of 12 recommendations designed to make Texas A&M one of the top 10 public universities in the nation by 2020. One of the goals posited by the plan was to "diversify and globalize the A&M community."

REQUIREMENTS (CONT'D)

are "Philosophy of Art" and "Philosophy of Visual Media."

- One class in social and behavioral sciences addressing anthropology, economics, political science, geography, psychology, sociology or communication.
- Four classes in U.S. history and political science. Thanks to the Texas legislature, there is a four-course citizenship requirement, including the required political science courses, "American National Government" and "State and Local Government," as well as a choice of two American history courses, usually satisfied by a survey called "History of the United States," but which can also be fulfilled by one course on Texas history and another on U.S. history.
- Two classes in international and cultural diversity. Better choices among the 200 possibilities include "The History of England" and "World Literature"—but only if a student thinks he can live without "Sociology of Gender" or "Pacific Rim Business Behavior."
- Two courses in kinesiology (physical education).

To achieve this result, Bowen adopted a "plan that will require students to take six hours of international or cultural diversity classes." Conservatives contend that the plan was implemented merely to pacify critics who say that A&M students suffer from their allegedly culturally deficient surroundings. One conservative student says that the multiculturalism requirement is "just one step in a larger plan to sacrifice the values that make A&M special" for greater academic reputation and prestige. The student follows this assertion with the worst accusation one can make against an A&M president: "He wants to make us just like the University of Texas."

President Gates has followed in Bowen's footsteps in ways many students and alumni find disturbing. As one student says, he "seems to be pushing the same Vision 2020 that Bowen did." Despite state budget cuts, Gates has established a new vice president and associate provost for institutional diversity who will implement "a campus-wide program to support diversity," including compulsory diversity training for members of the Student Government Association and the campus daily, the *Battalion*.

However, a writer for the *Texaminer* says that "Gates deserves credit for not joining the stampede of Texas colleges . . . that are restoring racial preferences in admissions following the U.S. Supreme Court's decisions in the University of Michigan cases." In a statement on the university's Web site, Gates says that "students at Texas A&M should be admitted as individuals, on personal merit—and on no other basis." Still, Gates emphasizes that Texas A&M will redouble its efforts to recruit and enroll minority students.

One professor describes the average faculty member as "at least moderately conservative" and the average student as "pretty conservative." He adds, "Some, maybe even many, midlevel administrators are hostile to the views of the [typical] A&M student and consequently seek to transform the largely Christian, conservative student body into something more 'representative.' Consistent with this, faculty now undergo a mandatory diversity class in which orthodox Christian and conservative beliefs are treated essentially as the root of bigotry, and, by implication, as inconsistent with the diversity thrust at A&M." Women's studies, while a notoriously politicized department, is small, offering only a minor for undergraduates, and lists only a dozen or so courses each semester; naturally it doesn't have the influence that it does at some schools.

Texas A&M is a huge university, so it is not surprising that fewer than half of all classes enroll fewer than 30 students. Graduate teaching assistants teach 27 percent of the undergraduate courses offered at the university and often lead weekly discussion or laboratory sections as well. One student says, "Professors as a whole are accessible to students [during] office hours." The advising program is "not well advertised, so students need to be aware of the services on their own," this student says. Underclassmen who have not yet decided on a major can speak with professional advisors in the General Studies Program, the "keynotes" of which are, according to the program, "exploration and flexibility." More often, students visit their major advisors (either faculty members or professional advisors), who help their students choose courses, fulfill degree requirements, and prepare for graduation and careers. A&M has a number of capable professors. These include Robin Smith in philosophy, David Vaught in history,

D. Bruce Dickson in anthropology, and R. Douglas Slack in wildlife and fisheries sciences.

As at most large public universities, academic rigor varies from department to department, and intellectual curiosity varies from student to student. Nearly a quarter of Texas A&M student-athletes major in agricultural fields, compared to just 3 percent of all A&M undergraduates. As the associate athletics director for academic affairs told the *Chronicle of Higher Education*, many of these athletes study cattle and crops "because agriculture has been supportive, friendly, and willing to accommodate the needs of students who have grades below 2.25." You see, in Texas, this fact is nothing to hide.

The A&M honors program is a bit tougher. Honors students, who must maintain a 3.5 GPA, remain enrolled in their respective schools and departments. They are not, therefore, "lock[ed] into a four-year program separate from the regular curriculum," the university Web site boasts, but instead pick and choose from the 300-plus honors-level courses offered throughout the university. An honors student can also enroll in one of the honors study sequences: the Engineering Scholars Program, the Business Honors Program, or the College of Liberal Arts Honors Plan. The liberal arts plan begins with a freshman honors seminar (past seminar offerings have included "Toleration in Theory and Practice" and "Rites of Passage across Cultures and within American Subcultures") followed by two sophomore courses, "Foundations of the Liberal Arts: Humanities" and "Foundations of the Liberal Arts: Social Sciences."

The "foundations" courses, however, are not quite as foundational as one would hope. A recent year's sophomore courses focused on "Twentieth-Century Revolutionary Movements" and offered reading lists that included Antonio Gramsci's *Prison Notebooks* and *Petals of Blood* by Ngugi wa Thiong'o—marginal (if interesting) texts. In recent years, the junior seminar has offered "U.S. Movie Censorship, 1900–1998" and "Bodies and Buildings." Other university-wide honors program courses range from "Child Development for Educators" and "Political Systems of Latin America" to "History of the United States" and "The Marriage Institution."

SUGGESTED CORE
1. Classics 352, Greek and Roman Drama *or* Classics 361, Greek Literature in Translation
2. Philosophy 410, Classical Philosophy
3. Religion 211/214, Hebrew Scriptures / New Testament
4. Religious Studies 220, History of Christianity: Origins to the Reformation
5. Political Science 350, Modern Political Thought
6. English 212, Shakespeare
7. History 105, History of the United States
8. Philosophy 414, Nineteenth-Century Philosophy

Student Life: Shout it out

To many Aggies, College Station is the center of the world. Most Aggie alumni make at least one pilgrimage a year to visit campus to watch their beloved football team at Kyle Field. In fact, CBS Sportsline.com declared: "There are simply no other fans who get into their team more than Aggies."

WEST

Texas A&M is a member of the Big 12 athletic conference, and as such, sports—especially football—are a high priority. In addition to the 18 varsity teams, students have 30 club sports and dozens of intramural teams—including a Playstation 2 tournament—from which to choose.

Instead of cheerleaders, the Aggies have "yell leaders." If the Aggies win, students throw the yell leaders into a campus fountain (a.k.a., the Fish Pond). And if A&M loses, students and alumni stay in the stands to practice school yells for the next game. Midnight yell practices, held the night before every home game, often attract as many as 30,000 people. Another remnant of Texas A&M's past is the tradition of kissing one's date after each touchdown, extra point, or field goal.

Most students at Texas A&M prefer to tailgate and drink beer before (and after, and between) football games, listen to country music, and just make it through their engineering classes. The dearth of coffeehouses in College Station is Anheuser-Busch's gain, as the city is full of terrific honky-tonks, dance halls, and restaurants. Favorites include the Dixie Chicken, which proudly proclaims "more beer sold per square foot than anywhere in the world." The owners of the Dixie Chicken have done so well they have a virtual monopoly on nightlife in College Station; they also own the Chicken Oil Company, Dry Bean Saloon, Shadow Canyon Dance Hall and Saloon, and Alfred T. Hornback's. One local is quick to point out that while there are only a few coffeehouses, there is a vibrant music scene, including popular open-mike nights at bars frequented by local singer-songwriters and their fans. "This may not be Austin," he says, "but it is in fact an important center for Texas-style country music." Another Aggie favorite is Wings 'N More, which serves up some of the nation's best wings in varying degrees of hotness.

Certainly there are plenty of conservatives in College Station. "As a university, Texas A&M has made no apologies for the conservative leanings of its student body. God, country, family, and A&M are still ideals worth dying for in the eyes of the average student" wrote a student recently in the *Texaminer*, a campus conservative magazine. The outspoken student newspaper, the *Battalion*, is said to alienate both left- and right-wing students alike.

While there are many opportunities for political involvement at Texas A&M, student life more characteristically revolves around organizations that enhance the "Aggie spirit." Thousands of students each year were proud to consider the building of a massive bonfire as their primary extracurricular activity—until a tragic accident in 1999 crushed 12 students under the pile of wood and buried the tradition. The construction of a bonfire memorial, including a "Tradition Plaza," "History Walk," and "Spirit Ring," was dedicated in 2004. Some persistent students and alumni have resorted to an off-campus bonfire, which drew several thousand people last year.

Many students also join the Corps of Cadets because of its prestige on campus. Because almost all of Texas A&M's many traditions have their genesis in the school's military past, the corps serves a vital role at football games. For example, to be a member of the Fightin' Aggie Band, one must first be a member of the Corps of Cadets, as the band wears military uniforms and marches military style.

Only about 5 percent of Texas A&M students are involved in Greek life. Instead, Texas A&M boasts the largest student-union program in the nation, with more than 800 university-recognized clubs and organizations. If you can't find one that interests you, you aren't looking: the groups cover all corners, from Aggieland Mariachi to the Philosophy Club to a group dedicated to water polo. The list of student organizations includes 76 religious groups, most of them Christian, including Aggie Promise Keepers, Resurrection Week, and Christian Business Leaders. One student says, "I'd have to say that a lot of A&M students turn to religion-based recreation, such as Bible study, praise and worship groups, and other religious social activities."

The food in the residence halls at Texas A&M leaves much to be desired, according to some students. Aggies are not required to live in residence halls; in fact, there are fewer than 8,000 on-campus housing spaces available for non-Corps students. Twenty-one residence halls (amazingly) are single sex. The coed dorms split men and women by floor. There are no coed bathrooms or bedrooms in the residence halls.

Like most other large universities, students at Texas A&M are occasionally victims of petty thefts in the residence halls. Remarkably, though, there were only 29 such occurrences reported on campus in 2003. Campus police are most active in citing rowdy and underage drinkers, arresting 161 students on campus in 2003; additionally, disciplinary action was taken on a total of 347 liquor-law violations. Compare these numbers to schools of comparable size, such as the University of Texas or Indiana University. Campus police at UT arrested about half as many students for liquor violations but took disciplinary action against a comparable number of students in 2002, the last year for which statistics are available. Indiana University, on the other hand, arrested three times as many students for liquor violations and disciplined over twice as many students as Texas A&M did in 2003. One student says, "Alcohol is a major part of local culture, but so is Christian temperance." A free student CARPOOL service drives home an astonishing average of 100 tipsy students per weekend night.

Texas A&M's 2004–5 tuition was $5,955; out-of-state students paid a moderate $13,695. Room and board cost $6,887. The admission process is need-blind, and about 40 percent of undergraduates at Texas A&M who apply for it receive some need-based financial aid. According to the school's Web site, A&M students received a total of more than $329 million through scholarships, grants, loans, waivers, work-study, and on-campus student employment in the 2003–4 school year. The average loan burden of recent graduates is $15,450.

THOMAS AQUINAS COLLEGE

SANTA PAULA, CALIFORNIA • WWW.THOMASAQUINAS.EDU

For a chosen few

Thomas Aquinas College was founded in 1971 specifically to address the substantial secularization of many Catholic institutions of higher learning. The problems at Catholic schools, according to the founding document of TAC, had become so acute that such schools displayed "a growing inability to define themselves in such a way as to justify their continued existence as Catholic institutions." The document, "A Proposal for the Fulfillment of Catholic Liberal Education," states:

> The view that liberal education begins in wonder and aims at wisdom—that is, a knowledge of an order which human reason does not create but can discover and understand—has by and large been replaced by the notion that such an education aims at a kind of cultural enrichment, so that the primary focus of study becomes the works and inventions of man rather than the larger order of which he is a part.

Thomas Aquinas's founders put their solution to this problem into effect with an initial class of 33 students eager for an educational experience modeled after the great books movement but enriched by the notion that faith is not antithetical to reason. That effort continues, indeed flourishes, such that the college expects to reach its planned capacity of 350 students in 2005.

Thomas Aquinas College differs from its secular great books predecessor, St. John's College, by defining itself as "dedicated to Catholic liberal education." Colleges with great books programs—whose classes examine the works of Homer, Euclid, Plato, Aristotle, Virgil, the Bible, Aquinas, Shakespeare, Newton, Milton, Tolstoy, Twain, Eliot, and Einstein—give students the most thorough grounding in the literature and thought of Western civilization.

They are also not for everyone. Most students prefer more conventional programs. The students who flourish at great books schools have an intense, persistent desire to read Homer, et. al. They embrace (or cheerily endure) the quirks of their college environments, and are unfazed by the prospect of explaining their undergraduate studies to condescendingly curious human resource professionals at future job interviews.

One of our editors is a proud alumnus of a great books program. But he recalls that the most miserable students he knew at school were those who were there because *someone else* thought studying the great books was a good idea. Students who plan to enroll at a great books school should be strongly attracted to the works on the program. They should also visit the school, overnight if possible. As one TAC student says, "It *is* very important to visit first, long enough to go to a few classes and see what it's like."

WEST

Academic Life: With the program

"The Program" at Thomas Aquinas College, a curriculum that consists entirely of the study of great and enduring texts and thinkers, creates a learning environment that binds its students together in a way that not even the school's secluded location could. There are no majors or specializations. Each graduate of Thomas Aquinas receives a bachelor of arts degree in liberal arts, but rest assured that this is no "general studies" diploma. The 146 required credit hours include 28 in mathematics, 24 in philosophy, 12 in foreign language, 24 in theology, 28 in scientific laboratory, four in music, 24 in various seminars, and two dedicated to a senior thesis.

All the classes at Thomas Aquinas are a year long and are taught in the Socratic method, wherein a tutor serves as a facilitator for classroom discussion about a reading. This engagement takes place around a table, day after day, as students are guided, never lectured. The college considers its permanent faculty to be the authors of the great books themselves—that is, Shakespeare, Dante, Milton, Galileo, and others you may have heard of.

Students are not trained as historians—note the lack of history courses—or as literary scholars, but rather as educated readers. Ideas and their connection to truth are the focuses of this great books approach. "I think [the tutor method] is the best method of teaching for undergraduate study," one student says. "We don't have to listen to dry lectures where someone's opinions are forced on us. Instead, comprehending the text is what drives the class." The tutor method "allows students to figure things out on their own, and so understand them thoroughly," another student says. "The tutor method doesn't work as well when the subject matter is very specific, and the students are too ignorant about the matter to discuss it intelligently, as sometimes happens in lab, math, and language." A member of the administration sums up TAC's strength: "Habituating students to give and to listen to reasons for what is said."

Unlike colleges where you can major in the subject you're best at, everyone at TAC studies the same demanding and varied curriculum, with resulting disparities in ability in the classroom. One student says, "There's sometimes a huge gap in understanding among the students in the math and laboratory classes, and though the tutors try to make sure everyone is on the same page, it's sometimes a struggle to keep up with those who really have an aptitude for the material."

On top of the heavy reading load, students write, though relatively little due to the school's goal of fostering exceptionally thoughtful, rigorous writing. "I write less as a student at Thomas Aquinas College than I did as a high school student," says a student who attended an evangelical Christian high school. "We are asked a question (e.g.,

VITAL STATISTICS

Religious affiliation:
  Roman Catholic
Total enrollment: 331
Total undergraduates: 331
SAT median: 1296
Applicants: 184
Applicants accepted: 82%
*Accepted applicants who
  enrolled*: 60%
Tuition: $17,700
Room and board: $5,500
Freshman retention rate: 84%
Graduation rate: 61% (4 yrs.),
  64% (6 yrs.)
Average class size: 15
Student-faculty ratio: 10:1
*Courses taught by graduate
  TAs*: none
Most popular majors: n/a
Students living on campus:
  99%
*Guaranteed housing for four
  years?* yes
*Students in fraternities or
  sororities*: none

Thomas Aquinas offers perhaps the strongest core curriculum of any school in this guide. The general outline of every student's course work is as follows:

Freshman Year
- Seminar: Major Greek authors.
- Language: Latin, English composition.
- Mathematics: Euclid.
- Laboratory: Classical, medieval, early modern scientific treatises.
- Philosophy: From Plato to Aquinas.
- Theology: The Bible.

Sophomore Year
- Seminar: From Virgil through Spenser.
- Language: Latin.
- Mathematics: From Plato through Copernicus and Kepler.
- Laboratory: From Aristotle to atomic theory.
- Philosophy: Pre-Socratics and Aristotle.
- Theology: Augustine through Aquinas.

Why does Euclid prove alternate proportionality of ratios twice?) and we have to answer it from the text. More of the thoughts in my college papers are originally my own than is typical for college writing assignments, I think."

Freshmen write five short papers, one each in math, language, theology, philosophy, and literature. Sophomores write four longer papers, and juniors write two 1,500-word papers in theology and philosophy. Seniors flesh out a thesis on a question from the curriculum of their choosing.

Secondary sources for papers are discouraged or even forbidden. The campus library provides little in the way of second-hand opinions to affirm or discourage students' own. Rather than these types of commentaries, the library houses alternate translations of the curricular works plus other books by studied authors. The St. Bernardine of Siena Library also includes impressive items of interest to the public: pages from Bibles dating from A.D. 1123, Hittite seals dating from circa 1200 B.C., and one of 47 known illuminated reproductions of the Gutenberg Bible.

Some of the books on the program stand in stark contrast to the college's vision of the world. The school explains its book choices: "Some are regarded as masterworks, while others serve as sources of opinions that either lead students to the truth, or make the truth more evident by opposition to it." Thus, Engels, Freud, and Marx appear alongside Augustine and Dante. The college accepts no transfer students. Those who wish to switch to Thomas Aquinas from another college must start over as freshmen, but such a leap is surprisingly common. One student says that he transferred to Thomas Aquinas after attending a Catholic university on the East Coast. "I saw that I learned a lot more in my seminar class in which we were reading the great books than in my other classes combined," he says. "There are a lot of students like me here, who have spent a year or more elsewhere and have come to TAC looking for something a little different. My roommate, for example, graduated last year with a degree in mechanical engineering and is now halfway through his freshman year, and he loves it."

One student explains her decision to leave an Ivy League university after three semesters to enroll at Thomas Aquinas like this: "It would be extraordinarily easy to graduate [somewhere else] without a decent, even halfway respectable knowledge of math and the sciences, for example, unless one majored in one of those fields. . . . [At my old school] intellectual discussions were not engaged in with much seriousness, and the students attached an excessive degree of importance to the opinions of their professors rather than taking the time and energy required to form their own thoughts on the subject."

In the small seminars, labs, and classrooms—which never exceed 20 students and average far fewer—students analyze texts and conduct experiments in search of the truth. But the Catholic college makes no secret of what it hopes students will find in their learning. "A college dedicated to Catholic liberal education is responsible first and foremost for helping its students perfect their intellects under the light of the truths revealed by God through the Catholic Church," the school says. Catholic faculty members take an oath of fidelity and make a profession of faith at the beginning of their terms as required by *Ex Corde Ecclesia*, but non-Catholic faculty (so long as they do not teach theology) and students are welcome.

Students describe the workload as heavy but rewarding and their peers as hard working. Grades are given, but intellectual progress is emphasized more. The school uses a form of evaluation called the "don rag," a twice-yearly ordeal in which a student faces all his tutors and essentially listens to them talk about him. Many students say language, math, and lab are among the most difficult classes to pass.

With such small class sizes and no lectures, individual personalities and their combinations in each class have a significant effect. "The best classes are those where many people are passionate about whatever it is we're reading," says one student, who adds, "if there are four or five 'big talkers' in a section . . . it can be difficult for quieter students to participate."

Faculty are very accessible and continue classroom discussion over meals, as students and tutors dine in the same area. Tutors also open their homes to students for dinner-and-seminar get-togethers and on holidays. Underclassmen enjoy the added benefit of their elders' having taken the same course sequence, a situation they describe as liberating. "Relationships on campus are so much stronger because everyone has taken the same academic route," one student says. "Students' conversations are deep and serious because there is an intellectual bond from our common experiences."

"TAC students typically form strong, lifelong friendships," says one graduate. "The small student body, the relative isolation, and the commitment to an idiosyncratic philosophy of education all foster strong bonds of friendship. The rigors of Latin and the mathematical classes, especially first-year Euclid, constitute a kind of hazing initiation. Also, the TAC alumni form a mutual support network. It's a lot like the 'old school boy' network in England."

Teachers at TAC are not really expected to publish, and some never do. That's good for faculty-student relationships, but some say that because they don't submit

REQUIREMENTS (CONT'D)

Junior Year
- Seminar: From Cervantes through Kant to Thomas Jefferson.
- Music: From Plato to Mozart.
- Mathematics: From Archimedes to Newton.
- Laboratory: From Descartes to Newton.
- Philosophy: From Aristotle to Aquinas.

Senior Year
- Seminar: From Tolstoy through Marx, up to documents of Vatican II.
- Mathematics: From Pascal to Lobachevski.
- Laboratory: From Newton to Einstein.
- Philosophy: Aristotle and Aquinas.
- Theology: Aquinas.

WEST

917

their work to outside critique by colleagues in the field, a few of the tutors at TAC are occasionally prone to dogmatism—an attitude which transmits itself to some of the students. One distinguished Catholic professor at a graduate school says of TAC students he has taught, "They are so utterly convinced that they are right, and that they know everything important already, that it's impossible to teach them anything. I had one who insisted he knew more about Aquinas than I do—and he doesn't. He simply refused to do the readings I assigned him. Instead, he dropped out. I think such dogmatism is a result of the kind of education they get there." One alumnus recalls TAC's president, Thomas Dillon, saying that the point of the curriculum is to study St. Thomas Aquinas and to give the students what they need to study Aquinas. Students begin with the Bible in the first year and end with Aquinas's *Summa Theologiae* in the junior and senior years.

Another graduate complains, "What makes things difficult is that the core faculty at TAC . . . believe they have a monopoly on philosophical truth. Basically, Plato and Augustine said some good things, but the only sound thinkers are Aristotle and Thomas Aquinas. A Catholic must be a Thomist, and an Aristotelian one, at that. All schools or traditions of Thomism are corrupt and depart from Thomas's true principles, except for the Laval School which now exists at TAC. People have zero interest in other academics or philosophers, even Catholic ones. This chauvinism is hard for students with a cosmopolitan inclination." Others, however, characterize this complaint as exaggerated.

Thomas Aquinas College constructs the education it offers on strong assumptions about the limits of reason in knowing all things. While nonreligious great books colleges such as St. John's encourage free inquiry and do not take stands as institutions on particular issues, Thomas Aquinas follows Catholic doctrine. High school students who think they might be interested can get a taste of Thomas Aquinas's style in the two-week Summer Great Books Program for High School Students, which began in 1997. Selected readings in this program, which costs $800, include Sophocles' *Antigone* and Kierkegaard's *Fear and Trembling*.

Student Life: The rules

Thomas Aquinas College is a genuine community—in the same sense as, say, a small Swiss village. One student recalls how the college responded when a fellow student was seriously injured in a car accident. "For the entire time that he was in danger of death, the entire school—students, tutors, staff—would get down on their knees during the lunch hour in the cafeteria." The student recovered and resumed his studies. The torrential California rains of January 2005 cut off access to the school. Many students had returned from Christmas vacation, but the staff and faculty weren't able to drive to campus. So the students built sandbag dams to protect buildings from flooding, yanked sodden carpets out of the dorms, and took over cooking duties in the dining hall.

As a real community, Thomas Aquinas College has real standards. And it expects its students to abide by them. Recently, the college expelled a number of students who admitted using drugs and drinking (they were under age) off campus (on-campus drug and alcohol use, as well as dorm visits from members of the opposite sex, are also punished by expulsion). And most of the students supported the administration's action. After this incident, Dean Michael McLean met with each class at TAC, and the discussion was helpful, according to both sides. The college has a strong interest in fostering a moral environment for its students. One student says that the college acted correctly, noting that the college "risks losing the respect of its students if it does not hold to the rules it sets out."

> **SUGGESTED CORE**
>
> **The college's required curriculum suffices.**

A recent incident involving the board of governors of Thomas Aquinas College is demonstrative of the mores to which the school adheres. Former board member Andrew Puzder is president and chief executive of CKE Restaurants, a group that includes a restaurant chain that had recently featured *Playboy* founder Hugh Hefner in its commercials. TAC president Thomas Dillon made no secret of his disdain for the advertisements and arranged for Puzder's removal from the board.

In January 2004, Thomas Aquinas boasted of its pupils in a news release titled "Persevering Students Help Close Abortion Clinic." Twice a week for six years, 10 to 15 students had gone to a clinic in nearby Ventura to pray and counsel in front of it. When that clinic closed, the release noted, the students redirected their energies toward the Planned Parenthood clinic in the same town. "I am very proud of our students," a college chaplain said. "Most of our campus ministries—and our pro-life group is no exception—are spontaneous in character."

As a Catholic school that takes its faith seriously, Thomas Aquinas College is a great place for students who share its faith. Other students might best look elsewhere. TAC has firm rules about social life—dormitories are segregated by sex, and visits by members of the opposite sex are strictly forbidden. Students must abide by a curfew—11 p.m. on weeknights and 1 a.m. on weekends—unless they have made prior arrangements with a prefect.

At Thomas Aquinas, the virtue of modesty is taken seriously: men wear slacks and collared shirts, women wear dresses and skirts. Good manners are the only kind. "People in the world often lament that 'chivalry is dead,'" one female student says. "That is not the case at Thomas Aquinas College. Men almost always open doors for women and treat them as ladies. With most couples I know the guy walks the girl to her dorm at night." Public displays of affection are forbidden. A female student says, "I feel like the role of the wife as simultaneous homemaker and homeschool teacher is greatly idealized, whereas the proper role of the father is construed as mostly that of the provider and head." Another female student says that while many women graduates of the college do pursue traditional roles as wives and mothers, the administration has always encouraged her to pursue her plans for postgraduate study.

Involvement in the tight-knit Thomas Aquinas community is a full-time job, and the college administration intends for it to be that way. To help foster the intellectual society it works so tirelessly to create, the college requires unmarried students to live

WEST

on campus unless they live with their families or are granted special permission by the dean to live elsewhere. Such permission is very rarely given. The hope is that over dinner, on the volleyball court, and in the common rooms of dormitories, the lingering, eternal questions from the formal learning setting will be further reflected upon and discussed.

With the completion of a sixth dormitory, dedicated in October 2004, on-campus housing construction is now complete. Dorm rooms are designed for two, and after the freshman year students are welcome to pick their own roommates. Administration-appointed prefects, like residential advisors, enforce rules and look after the dorms. Current students advise prospective students that there are no Internet, phone, or cable connections in rooms, although computers and cell phones are allowed. Punishment for watching a movie in one's room is kitchen work.

To balance the intense academic load, a student offers some suggestions: "get off campus at least once a week," and "exercise as often as you can. . . . Go to mass daily. Sit with different people at meals. Learn to dance." Dancing (swing and ballroom) is one of a number of extracurricular activities that students themselves organize. Two seniors are appointed each year to plan off-campus ski trips and hikes as well as on-campus dances and barbecues. There's also an annual St. Patrick's Day bash.

The college has recently hired a part-time athletics director. Students compete on intramural teams or in Ventura County leagues, but not in intercollegiate sports. Hikes in the Los Padres National Forest are frequent, and more serious hikers may join the Bushwackers, a campus group dedicated to maintaining forest trails. The campus theater troupe, the St. Genesius Players, specializes in Shakespeare, and there is a *schola*, an all-male ensemble that performs Gregorian chant at mass. A sizeable barrel-vaulted chapel, designed by neotraditionalist architect Duncan Stroik of the University of Notre Dame, will be built on the campus soon.

Unsurprisingly, many extracurriculars at TAC have an academic flair. Each year on St. Thomas Day, students and faculty face off in Trivial and Quadrivial Pursuit competition—a much-anticipated "stump the student" game. Literary-minded students and tutors contribute essays, caricatures, poetry, and humor to the student-published magazine, *Demiurgus*, a self-described "medium for free thought and ideas," and more formal essays and reviews to the official campus publication, the *Aquinas Review*. Informal language groups for French, German, Greek, Hebrew, and Latin meet over meals.

Students are typically enthusiastic about religious life. Mass is offered—but never required—thrice daily except on Saturday, when it is held twice. Other liturgical ceremonies, including the rosary and compline, are well attended. Confessions are heard before and after every mass. Eucharistic adoration is scheduled for several hours each day. Non-Catholics are more than welcome at the school, with the standard restrictions on receiving communion and other activities reserved for Catholics only. "Truth is, after all, universal," is the school's position. As one student says of the religious environment, "Everything you could possibly need to become a saint is available right here." One student warns, however, that "TAC is a very, very strongly Catholic campus. Non-Catholics face tremendous social pressure to convert. If you persevere and hold

WEST

on to a non-Catholic religion in your four years there, you're going to catch some grief."

The dating scene at Thomas Aquinas is highly unusual. Whereas most college students see dating during these years as a kind of buffet—try a little of everything— dating at Thomas Aquinas is viewed as a serious step toward marriage, though men and women do have friendships outside of romantic relationships. Most relationships are exclusive, and, again, the school's small size makes dating around difficult and awkward. "Living here is like living in a tiny southern town," a student says. Another says, "The official self-presentation makes TAC look passionless, perhaps puritanical. In fact, TAC is something of an American Catholic 'Love Boat.' A large percentage of TAC alumni end up marrying other TAC alumni. Dates, romances, and many Jeeves-and-Wooster-like love situations dominate much of campus life. Many TAC students go there for the purpose of finding a mate. Couples go on 'rosary walks' and other outings. Dorms are single-sex, but there are oodles of flirting opportunities. . . . The park-like section of TAC, just below the main campus, provides edenic privacy for couples."

For those who heed the earlier advice about getting off campus, Thomas Aquinas benefits from its location in Southern California. Museums such as the Huntington Library, the Santa Barbara Museum of Art, and the Reagan Library are within driving distance, and those lonesome for city hustle and bustle make the 70-mile drive to Los Angeles. The Pacific Ocean is 20 minutes away, and the harbors at Ventura and Santa Barbara offer whale watching tours, deep-sea fishing, and outings to the nearby Channel Islands for diving, snorkeling, and sightseeing.

In terms of cost, Thomas Aquinas is quite affordable for a private college. Tuition in 2004–5 was $17,700, room and board $5,500. The school does not say whether admissions are need-blind, but it does promise to provide full aid for all who attend. Approximately 73 percent of students receive some form of financial aid—and 59 percent receive gift aid that does not have to repaid. A majority also work campus jobs.

UNITED STATES AIR FORCE ACADEMY

COLORADO SPRINGS, COLORADO • WWW.USAFA.EDU

Into the wild blue yonder

Of the three armed services, the Air Force is by far the youngest. This, of course, is simply because prior to the invention of the airplane, the skies were clear of all human traffic. But shortly after the Wright Brothers made their famous flight at Kitty Hawk, the usefulness of their invention for military purposes became obvious. The War Department created, in 1907, the Aeronautical Division as part of the Army's Signal Corps to study "ballooning, air machines, and all kindred subjects." Two years later, the Army bought its first warplane from the Wright Brothers. It was not, however, until this country entered World War I that American military aviation really took off. American pilots and planes proved their mettle over France, and on May 24, 1918, the United States Army Air Service was born.

Although the initial reaction of the government to peace was to cut the funding of the Air Service, men like Brig. Gen. William "Billy" Mitchell, the man in charge of it, continued to beat the drums for an expanded military presence in the air. Although Mitchell himself was court-martialed in 1925 for insubordination (he had openly and publicly attacked the Army leadership), the following year many of his ideas about the role of the Air Service were vindicated when the service was augmented and dubbed the United States Army Air Corps. In 1941, a few months before Pearl Harbor, the service became the "United States Army Air Forces." World War II saw tremendous growth in the service's size and advancements in technology, culminating in the jet engine and the atomic bomb.

Prior to that war, West Point had produced the Air Force's officers. But the Cold War made training of a larger number of Air Force officers essential. Having grown from 305,827 personnel in 1947 to nearly one million by 1954, the Air Force required about 1,200 new junior officers a year, and they needed more technological training than was available at the Point. In 1954, President Eisenhower signed the Air Force Academy Act. The architecture of the place was "Space Age"; as Secretary of the Air Force Harold E. Talbott declared at the time: "We want the academy to be a living embodiment of the modernity of flying and to represent in its architectural concepts the national character of the academy. . . . We want our structures to be as efficient and as flexible in their design as the most modern projected aircraft." So it is: the architecture of the place does have a "futuristic" tone to it, even 50 years later.

Academic Life: Active duty

Its stunning location at Colorado Springs sets the Air Force Academy apart. The academy is state-of-the-art in every way—just what one would expect in a school so given over, by necessity, to the mathematical and the technical. There are laboratories, observatories, and a library containing more than 700,000 books.

In keeping with the service's Army origins, academy students are called "cadets." As at the other two academies, cadets are organized into a self-run corps, the 4,000-strong Air Wing. Although the curriculum is heavy on science and math, it is possible to gain a solid liberal arts education here. But Colorado Springs' educational program is not solely about scholastics. As much time and thought are put into developing both the cadet's personal character and his leadership abilities. This is no ordinary college.

That too is something that the prospective Colorado Springs applicant must consider. If he graduates, he will receive an appointment and serve as a commissioned officer in the Air Force for at least eight years after graduation, with at least five of those on active duty (and the balance in the reserves). At the end of the day, the military is about warfare; lives are at stake and it is not a videogame. Upon entrance to the academy, each cadet swears on his honor to "defend the Constitution of the United States against all enemies, foreign and domestic." Despite the many advantages an academy education offers, if parents, the applicant, or both have conscientious objections to combat, Colorado Springs is not the place to go.

Criteria for acceptance are rigorous. As the academy's own Web site says, "A well-rounded program of academic, leadership, and athletic preparation is important. You must also carefully consider whether you possess the characteristics of dedication to duty, desire to serve others, ability to accept discipline, morality, and the enjoyment of challenge." A nomination to the academy is essential. This must come from either of your senators, your congressman, or the vice president. If you're interested in this or any of the service academies, you should write to one of these worthies as soon as possible.

The Center for Character Development (CDC) is a prominent feature of academy life. On the one hand, it features the Honor division, which guides a cadet committee in administering the Honor Code ("a cadet will neither lie, cheat, nor steal, nor tolerate anyone who does"), a traditional feature of life at all three academies. Those found guilty of violations will generally be expelled. But the CDC also harbors the Human

VITAL STATISTICS

Religious affiliation: none
Total enrollment: 4,157
Total undergraduates: 4,157
SAT midranges: V: 590–670, M: 620–710
Applicants: 12,430
Applicants accepted: 15%
Accepted applicants who enrolled: 67%
Tuition: $0
Room and board: $0
Freshman retention rate: 88%
Graduation rate: 73% (4 yrs.), 75% (6 yrs.)
Average class size: 23
Student-faculty ratio: 8:1
Courses taught by graduate TAs: none
Most popular majors: engineering, business, social sciences
Students living on campus: 100%
Guaranteed housing for four years? yes
Students in fraternities or sororities: none

The Air Force Academy presents a challenging academic environment, offering no easy ways out. The school imposes a highly technical core curriculum. All students take the following instruction.

Fourth-Class Cadets

- Basic Cadet Training (BCT).
- Basic Physical Training.
- "Applications of Chemistry."
- "Introduction to Computer Science."
- "Language and Expression."
- "Military Theory and Air and Space Power."
- "Modern World History."
- Calculus I and II.
- General Physics I.
- "Fourth-Year Experience."
- Physical education.

Third-Class Cadets

- Combat Survival Training.
- "Soar for All" or "Basic Parachuting."
- "Global Engagement."
- "Fundamentals of Aeronautics."
- "Fundamentals of Mechanics."
- "Introductory Biology" (with lab).
- "Principles of Microeconomics."
- "Masterpieces of Literature."
- "Introduction to Military History."

Relations Division, which tries to develop officers who "believe individual differences of race, color, national origin, religion, and sex are to be valued; act in ways that support and encourage others to develop to their fullest potential; do not demean or debase others; accept individual differences and understand how they contribute to high productivity and mission accomplishment."

As mentioned, there is a highly technical core curriculum. As might be expected, given that these are literally life-and-death topics for Air Force officers, the scientific courses are taught painstakingly and well. Most classes the cadet attends in his first two years are required core courses. But in the last two, he can focus on electives leading to his major, of which there are 32. Of these, English, foreign area studies, history, humanities, legal studies, political science, and social studies fall under the liberal arts banner.

The Humanities Division says that its mission is to "teach future Air Force leaders an appreciation for the culture they've promised to defend and the ability to speak, listen, write, and read effectively." For example, "Classical Masterpieces" is billed as "a study of influential genres of the classical tradition, including epic, drama, and history. Authors have included Homer, Sophocles, Aristophanes, Thucydides, Vergil, Tacitus, and Dante. Key concepts to be studied include the role of the hero, the nature of political institutions, and the relationship between man and the divine—in short, the foundations in Greek, Roman, and medieval European culture." There are standard survey courses in both British and American literature, but there are also a number of classes dealing with the application of English to technology, such as "Communication in the Information Age."

The humanities major is perhaps the most well-rounded liberal arts degree one can obtain at Colorado Springs. As the catalog says, "The major includes courses from each department in the humanities (English and fine arts, foreign languages, history, and philosophy). A wide variety of elective options allow students the flexibility to tailor the major to individual interests. In addition, the divisional options make the major ideal for students who wish to minor in either foreign languages or philosophy."

There are, of course, a great many strictly military courses, as well as airmanship and aviation, designed to prepare the cadet for his career in the Air Force. In addition, all manner of military training is conducted during the summers.

Student Life: Honor among doolies

Arrival at the Air Force Academy means exchanging civilian gear for a uniform, having one's hair cut, taking the oath, and in general beginning the transition into military life. This is the beginning of Basic Cadet Training (BCT). Instead of calling new cadets "plebes," as at West Point and Annapolis, the fresh arrivals at Colorado Springs are called "doolies" (derived from the Greek *duolos*—slave). While a doolie's life is not as bad as the name makes it out to be, it is far from easy. BCT is extremely challenging and meant to separate the wheat from the chaff. Often it results in lifelong friendships.

The first half of BCT occurs in the Cadet Area, and in it doolies are instructed in military customs and courtesies, the Honor Code, Air Force heritage, marching, and room inspection. The second portion of BCT takes place in Jack's Valley, a wooded area on the academy grounds. This training is particularly physical; among other things the cadet will learn small-unit tactics and firearms. BCT ends with the Acceptance Parade, which marks the doolie's entrance into the Cadet Wing and the commencement of the school year.

Colorado Springs' Cadet Wing is a formation that mirrors unit organization in the Air Force. Drawn from the first-class (senior year) cadets, the Cadet Wing commander oversees four cadet group commanders, who in turn look over the commanders and their staffs of 36 squadrons, each comprising about 110 cadets. Supervising these cadet officers are air officers commanding (AOC), who are located in each squadron and group. Life at the academy, from meals at Mitchell Hall to intramural athletics and living arrangements within the dorms, is lived entirely within the framework of the squadrons.

Each year at the academy brings the cadets specific challenges. The fourth-class cadet will end his first year "with an initial foundation of Air Force history, heritage, honor, discipline, drill, and followership skills." The military strategic studies (MSS) course featured is "Introduc-

REQUIREMENTS (CONT'D)

- "Introduction to Management."
- "Probability and Statistics."
- General Physics II.
- "Politics and American Government."
- "Geopolitics."
- "Introduction to Behavioral Sciences and Leadership."
- "Air Base Design and Performance."
- Glider or parachuting instruction.
- Physical education.

Second-Class Cadets
- Military training options.
- Operations Air Force field trip.
- "Introduction to Astronautics."
- "Electrical Signals and Systems."
- "Energy Systems."
- "Law for Commanders."
- "Ethics."
- Academic elective courses.
- "Foundations of Aerospace Power."
- Physical education.

First-Class Cadets
- Summer training.
- Military training options.
- "Engineering Systems Design."
- "Advanced Composition and Speech."
- Academic elective courses.
- "Foundations of Aerospace Power."
- Physical education.

tion to Military Theory and Air and Space Power." The third-class year involves learning survival, land navigation, and water survival skills that are tested during an intensive, three-week trek through the Rockies. Here the cadet must find his way, build his shelters, and forage for food. Airmanship is taught, and third-class cadet military training focuses on turning followers into leaders. The third summer involves practical training in Air Force military skills, as second-class cadet military training prepares the cadet to be a primary trainer of third- and fourth-class cadets. "Foundations of Aerospace Power" is the MSS class taken. First-class cadets take over command positions in the Cadet Wing. The MSS class is "Introduction to Joint and Multinational Operations."

While this is a challenging schedule, to be sure, a throughgoing athletic program supplements it. *Sports Illustrated* has named the academy the "most athletic school in the country." Every cadet takes two physical education courses each semester; it is mandatory for him to participate in either intercollegiate or intramural sports as well. There are more than 40 athletic teams available. But athletics at Colorado Springs are not intended purely for physical fitness, important as that is. Team sports are regarded as a vital part of cadets' education, instilling in them "a sense of initiative, self-confidence, and the knowledge that they are part of something greater than themselves." Intercollegiate sports are also big, and most of the teams are members of the NCAA Division I Mountain West Conference.

To allow for all the required academic, military, and athletic training, daily life is carefully regimented. There are four 50-minute periods each morning and three each afternoon, although cadets may have additional academic instruction after classes or during other unscheduled times. Cadets march to breakfast and lunch, and (save for those involved in intercollegiate sports) play on intramural teams two afternoons a week after classes. On the other three afternoons there are squadron activities or free time. Evenings after dinner are spent studying in one's room or at the library, as are those Saturday mornings not given over to parades and inspections. Saturday afternoons and Sundays are generally free. The fall and spring semesters last 17 weeks each; the summer term lasts 10.

During BCT, the doolie may not have visitors or phone calls. During the body of the fourth-class year, phone calls and visitors are permissible on Saturday afternoons and evenings and on Sunday mornings and afternoons. Third-class cadets are given limited chances to leave the campus and visit the local area. Such privileges increase each year, although "unsatisfactory performance in military training, academic studies, or athletics restricts . . . free time, while above-average work increases" it. Only the top two classes may own and operate cars at the academy. There are generally three weeks of summer leave (except BCT summer), approximately two weeks of Christmas leave, and a week during the spring.

Despite all of this, there are plenty of activities for social and other leisure events. Although doolies do not socialize with upper-class cadets, the latter have no distinctions among themselves socially. Arnold Hall, the academy's student union complex, features formal and informal social events, as well as pizza or other snacks, dancing, television, games, movies, and live performances by popular entertainers. A military reception and ball are featured once a year, thus giving the cadet the chance to wear the formal uniform and hone the social skills he will need as an active duty officer.

Weekend skiing is popular among cadets, and ski equipment may be checked out from Cadet Recreation Supply in Vandenberg Hall. Just west of the cadet are the Cadet Recreation Lodge and the Lawrence Paul Pavilion, which are used for squadron parties and picnics. Nearby Farish Memorial Recreational Area offers picnic areas and hiking.

In addition to the aforementioned sports, the school hosts competitive teams ranging from parachuting to debating. Pride of place among recreational clubs goes to the Cadet Ski Club, but Amateur Radio, the dramatic club called the Blue Bards, equestrian and hunting clubs, and rodeo are just a few of the many others. In keeping with the apolitical traditions of the American military, there are no political clubs at the academy, although many if not most cadets would likely describe themselves as conservative. Civic involvement is encouraged through volunteer community service. There are also mission support clubs, such as various choirs and drill teams, and professional organizations.

In 1972, the courts ruled that chapel attendance could no longer be mandatory for cadets. Nevertheless, the nondenominational chapel remains the architectural crown of the campus. It has been described as being "at once old and new, physical and spiritual, solid and soaring, of the earth and of outer space." Equipped with 17 stunning spires, the chapel has several levels, each serving one of three faiths (Protestant, Catholic, and Jewish). Mormon cadets attend a church of their own in Colorado Springs.

Currently, several Protestant chaplains at the academy are weathering a storm of media criticism for encouraging their flocks to evangelize their fellow cadets. After a lawsuit was filed by a secularist advocacy group, representatives of the Yale Divinity School—hardly an evangelical hotbed—conducted an investigation. Among other incidents, it reported that an academy official told cadets that those who are not "born again will burn in the fires of hell," according to the *Chronicle of Higher Education*. Whether one believes this or not, it is hardly a morale booster. The academy has responded to critics by beginning "a training program called Respecting the Spiritual Values of all People, or RSVP, which consists of 50-minute small-group sessions led by academy chaplains, lawyers, and commanders. Each cadet, as well as each faculty and staff member, is required to participate in RSVP training," reports the *Chronicle*. The training is run by the new Climate and Culture Office, and by the end of May 2005 each of the 9,000 people on campus was expected to have attended the first program. The official investigation of the harassment issue and its aftermath are still unfolding, and new RSVP sessions are in the works.

SUGGESTED CORE

1. English 360, Classical Masterpieces
2. and 8. Philosophy 390, The Great Philosophers
3. No suitable course
4. History 325, History of Christianity (*closest match*)
5. Political Science 301, Political Theory
6. English 353, Shakespeare
7. History 351, The Foundations of Modern America

For those who do not wish to argue over religion, there is always sex. In 1976, women were admitted to all three academies. Now while there is no doubt of the patriotism or prowess of the Air Force Academy's alumnae, there is a basic biological fact that the civilian leadership has chosen consistently to ignore: the tendency of people of opposite sexes kept in close quarters to . . . well, fraternize. Or worse, even here where the behavioral expectations are so high. This human proclivity manifests itself every few years in the form of a sex scandal at one or another of the academies—most recently, at Colorado Springs. Again, according to the *Chronicle*, "Successive commanders at the Air Force Academy failed over the course of a decade to acknowledge the seriousness of sexual assault and harassment at the Colorado Springs campus, and the service only recently imposed measures to change a climate that tolerated abuse of female cadets, the Pentagon inspector general has found. The inspector general's findings . . . said sexual assaults against women were reported almost 150 times over 10 years but that little action was taken until the accusations became public in 2003." Other crimes, while not reported by this or other service academies, do not appear to be an issue on campus.

As members of the U.S. Air Force, no tuition is required from cadets. In fact, they receive a salary while attending. Money or the lack thereof is not a consideration for applicants.

UNIVERSITY OF WASHINGTON

SEATTLE, WASHINGTON • WWW.WASHINGTON.EDU

We'll always have Seattle

The University of Washington has all the deficiencies of many large state research universities. The teaching is uneven. The advising program for approximately 28,000 undergraduates is atrocious. The liberal arts curriculum is dreadful. Housing is a problem. Students and faculty are outspokenly political and politicized, and not just when participating in protests on Red Square, a central campus location where radicalism flourishes. (And yes, it actually is named Red Square.)

But the oldest public university on the West Coast has one thing that other large state research universities don't: Seattle. It's a city that inspires love among its residents, wistful nostalgia among its exiles, and, more often than not, astonishment among its visitors. Along with the usual advantages of state schools—including, in Washington's case, affordable in-state tuition and a national reputation—the Seattle advantage helps to make up for what UW so sorely lacks. But that is, without question, a lot to make up for.

Academic Life: Mass market

The behemoth known as the University of Washington includes 17 schools and colleges, 12 of which offer degrees for undergraduates. This essay will focus on the College of Arts and Sciences, the academic home to some 40 departments and two-thirds of the undergraduate student body.

UW students are offered plenty of "flexibility." The course catalog is a heavy volume listing upwards of 5,500 courses, 140 majors, and 90 minors. The reasonable freshman should seek advice from a faculty member on how to make the most of his time at the university. However, some students graduate from UW without ever having received advice from their professors regarding courses, majors, or their careers after college. One honors student says, "I rarely go to office hours except to turn in papers, and this seems to be the average." The college viewbook even

VITAL STATISTICS

Religious affiliation: none
Total enrollment: 39,199
Total undergraduates: 27,732
SAT/ACT midranges:SAT V: 520–640, M: 550–670; ACT: 23–28
Applicants: 15,950
Applicants accepted: 68%
Accepted applicants who enrolled: 45%
Tuition: $4,458 (in state), $15,661 (out of state)
Room and board: $7,968
Freshman retention rate: 92%
Graduation rate: 42% (4 yrs.), 69% (6 yrs.)
Courses with fewer than 20 students: 37%
Student-faculty ratio: 11:1
Courses taught by graduate TAs: not provided
Most popular majors: economics, business, engineering
Students living on campus: 17%
Guaranteed housing for four years? no
Students in fraternities: 12% sororities: 11%

WEST

quotes a student as saying, "My freshman year, I was in 'Intro to Mass Communication' along with 500 other people. I talked to my professor *once* in office hours. To this day he still remembers my name. So few students take advantage!" A senior says, "Office hours are extremely underutilized. Whenever I go to office hours, I'll hardly ever be interrupted."

Even so, another student reports, "UW does have an unbelievably wide variety of courses, but they do have the faculty to cover them. There are very few other institutions in which an undergrad could take a course in Uighur language or mathematical biology and still have a superbly qualified instructor who encourages practical application of the course. Far from offering irrelevant courses, the University of Washington is one of the few places [where] one can attend courses that are diverse at the same time as being capably instructed and applied. . . . Many of the arts and language departments here have stellar faculty and first-rate programs."

The university offers one-size-fits-all advising on selecting courses and majors. Students who have not declared majors can visit the Undergraduate Advising Center, where they make 30-minute appointments with professional advisors, not faculty members. Once students have declared a major, they are assigned departmental advisors, who, according to a specialist in the advising center, are full-time professional advisors or graduate students "fully trained in advising."

The many huge classes at the introductory level are taught by professors, graduate teaching assistants, or both. In a typical intro-level course, the professor teaches the class two days a week, and students break up into smaller discussion groups led by TAs once a week. "TAs normally grade most papers and exams and generally have a lot more contact with students than the professors do," says one student. As students begin to specialize in their majors, class sizes grow smaller and students have more opportunities to create relationships with faculty members.

Informal "freshman seminars" of 10 to 15 students provide another opportunity to interact more closely with UW faculty. The offerings, though, are not always appealing. The pickings for fall 2005 included "Gay, Lesbian, Bisexual, and Transgender Images in Film"; "How Chemistry, Biology, and Physics are Used to Make New Products We All Use"; "What Is Philosophy?"; "Recovery of Function from Central Nervous System Trauma"; and "Queer 101: Exploring Gay, Lesbian, Bisexual, and Transgender Issues."

An alternative to the standard Arts and Sciences curriculum is the University Honors Program, a four-year track in which students usually take one designated honors course per quarter. In lieu of the areas of knowledge requirements, honors students enroll in a three-quarter sequence on "Western Civilization," "World Civilization," and "Natural Science." Honors students also must take at least one honors seminar; in 2004, these included "Madame Bovary's Ovaries: A Darwinian Look at Literature"; "Species Rhododendrons, Their Centers of Diversity in Southeast Asia and Rhododendron Evolutionary History"; and "Military History of the Second World War."

Although the honors curriculum looks promising on the surface, the reality is less impressive. The winter 2004 course offerings in the Western civilization sequence were "Social History of African Americans," "Thinking About Justice," and "The Middle Ages: Nexus of Love and War." The world civilization courses for the same term included "The Fetish as Agent in Agentless History"; the author of its course description claims that it "breaks free from the coercive imagination of social theories of integration, equilibrium, system, linearity, progress, rationality, civilization, and utopia.... The task, like the theory, texts, topic, even the instructor, is unstable.... Our focus is on the tools of negative space." The course includes "a final performance of individual knowledge-as-fetish."

One student in the program says, "Honors professors as a breed tend to be a little stranger and some are decidedly better than others." At least some of the courses are rigorous—especially the science courses, which are much better than the usual "science for non-science majors" fare. One student describes the honors program as "very intense, with only the most serious students." Unfortunately, the program does not extend outside the classroom; honors students share courses only, not extracurricular activities or residential facilities.

Another undergrad has unreserved praise for the program: "A student who is admitted into UW within its honors program and is thus entitled to attend honors courses (both in arts and in sciences) will have a much more agreeable experience. The university's policy is to appoint the professors with the most expertise to teach an honors section, allowing students who are genuinely interested in and committed to learning from the beginning to have the experience of instruction under the most knowledgeable and most qualified faculty members in the institution. My experience with the Honors Arts and Sciences courses was extremely positive. It was amazing to be permitted to use the resources and faculty of a large research institution in a classroom setting resembling a small private college."

Another optional program that does include housing options and adds structure to the curriculum while providing a smaller academic community is the Freshman Interest Group (FIG) program. In a typical FIG, 20 to 25 freshmen with similar academic interests share courses for the first term of college. Not all FIGs are based on shared academic interest. Others form around volunteer service or the participants' ethnicity. A student says that "I would

ACADEMIC REQUIREMENTS

In the absence of anything like a core curriculum, the University of Washington imposes some vague, unstructured general education requirements. Students must take the following:

- One course in English composition, and two other courses that involve writing.
- Three courses in a foreign language (or test out).
- One math or quantitative reasoning course.

Students also take 15 "areas of knowledge" courses, including four courses in each of the following three areas:

- Visual, literary, and performing arts. Options range from "Intellectual History of Classical Greece" to "Lesbian Lives and Culture" and even "Writing Hypertext for the Web."
- Individuals and society. A number of courses in religious studies and classics qualify; so do most courses in Chicano studies. As does just about any class in any social science.
- The natural world. Courses in epidemiology count; so does one dance class.

WEST

931

definitely recommend FIGs for any freshman, so that at least you can make a few friends in the sea of [39,000] people."

UW's philosophy department is solid. It emphasizes the philosophy of science, an area in which it has several eminent scholars. Undergraduate philosophy majors are required to take a course in logic, one in modern philosophy, and one in ancient philosophy, ancient political philosophy, or the history of ancient ethics. English majors concentrating in language and literature must take at least one course in each of several historical periods: medieval to Shakespeare, seventeenth- and eighteenth-century English literature, nineteenth-century English literature, American literature to 1917, and twentieth-century British and American literature. Courses focusing on these periods are generally traditional and include courses on Chaucer, Shakespeare, Milton, and one called "American Literature: The Colonial Period." Among the most respected faculty in the department are Paul Remley and Miceal Vaughan. The history department is said to be more committed to teaching than are some others. The department's best include Jon Bridgman (emeritus), James Felak, John Crump, Fred Levy, and R. Tracy McKenzie. Other good professors at UW include Gerald Baldasty and Patricia Moy in communication; Charles Barrack and Joe Voyles in Germanics; Keith Leffler in economics; Alicia Beckford Wassink and Richard Wright in linguistics; Galya Diment in Slavic studies; Patricia Conroy in the Scandinavian department; Parker MacCready in oceanography; Ramesh Gangolli in math and music; and Jonathan Mercer in political science. One upperclassman advises students to check online course evaluations before registering for courses; from these, students can often find out how past students have rated faculty.

As at so many schools, the political science department does not seem to be a hotbed of objectivity. According to one undergrad, "Unfortunately, most of my political science professors seem unable to contain their own opinions for 50 minutes to teach us factual material and usually end up 'lecturing' left-wing propaganda. . . . I feel that I dare not express my opinion in these classes for fear that I will be ridiculed or dismissed, not by other students, but by the professor in front of class."

Another student says of the political balance of professors that "any instructor worth his tenure will make his own opinions clear rather than trying to insinuate them within the course," but adds that that doesn't always happen. A professor says, "As at most schools, the faculty are overwhelmingly liberal-left, so that people of that persuasion feel more comfortable than the handful of conservatives." Students say that besides the ethnic studies programs and the women's studies department, political science and international studies—particularly Middle East studies—are especially leftist. A political science major professes himself "continually annoyed by the leanings of my colleagues." Economics and business are said to have less ideological faculties.

Every humanities department offers the usual trendy and trivial choices. An English professor says that his department is among the worst in this regard. In his department, students can, for example, take courses in "Introduction to Cultural Studies," "Contemporary American Indian Literature," "Women and the Literary Imagination," and "Gay and Lesbian Studies."

Oddly enough, a cultural and ethnic diversity course requirement has been proposed and rejected three times by UW faculty. An Arts and Sciences administrator says, "It's still in the works," and the director of the Task Force on Diversity in the Curriculum says she is "investigating how to enhance the number of courses on race, ethnicity, gender, class, etc. on campus," even without faculty backing.

Student Life: Smells like teen spirit

The university's setting in Seattle is probably the one factor that attracts students to this school more than any other; it is certainly an attribute that sets it apart from other large state schools. As one professor notes, "The best thing about UW is the location. Seattle is a wonderful town, and the campus, though in a city, is safe, has lots of greenery, and its buildings are readily accessible." On the weekends, Seattle offers a number of options for students eager to escape campus, including theaters, bars, and art galleries. Downtown Seattle is easily accessible via the U-PASS bus system (a great deal for students), and the Canadian border is less than two hours away by car. Seattle also boasts a number of local bands, including many of the grunge variety. Pike's Place Market, located on the pier in downtown Seattle, is a popular place to buy produce, fresh flowers, and crafts produced by local artists. UW has a large number of outdoor enthusiasts. Many students head out of town to go hiking, biking, skiing, and camping on the weekends. The Cascade Range is only minutes away; Mount Rainier is only an hour-and-a-half drive. And despite Seattle's reputation as a rainy city, students are quick to point out that, implausible as it sounds, both Boston and New York receive more rainfall each year than does the Emerald City. Visitors to Seattle are often struck by the beauty of the city as it shimmers in the sun after a morning shower.

The University of Washington's size makes it impossible to describe the typical student. Most students and faculty agree that when it comes to student types, UW is a truly diverse place, including a number of international students, fraternity and sorority members, arts aficionados, environmentalists, and athletes.

Housing on the UW campus is not guaranteed, even for freshmen. The student housing office attributes this policy to the high demand. Some claim that adequate housing is not a sufficiently important item on the administration's agenda: "UW has just finished its new Gates Law Building, which looks really nice. However, it seems to me that all of the money they spent on the HUB dining area and very expensive Intramural Activities Building could have been spent on something more important," one student says. The same person says, "Many of my friends have had to live in triple

SUGGESTED CORE
1. Classics 210, Greek and Roman Classics in English
2. Philosophy 320, Ancient Philosophy
3. Comparative Religion 220/240, Introduction to the New Testament / Introduction to the Hebrew Bible: Old Testament
4. Philosophy 321, Medieval Philosophy
5. Political Science 201A, Introduction to Political Theory
6. English 225, Shakespeare
7. History of the Americas 101, Survey of the History of the United States
8. History 207, Introduction to Intellectual History

WEST

933

rooms, where they stuff three people into two-person rooms. And the houses have increased security because of random people walking through the dorms. Now, those dorms require your ID card showing you're in that dorm to get in."

In fact, housing is difficult to find off campus, too, because Seattle's cost of living has been rising steadily over the past few years. The student housing office confesses that "UW is primarily not a residential campus"; fewer than a fifth of undergraduates live in the university's eight residence halls and off-campus apartments. A volunteer student group helps students find off-campus housing by posting listings of area apartments. Since most UW students live off campus, undergrads sometimes find it difficult to attain a sense of community. As one student reports in the freshman admission packet, "I can walk through the middle of campus and not necessarily see anyone I know." (We're not sure why this is considered bragging material.)

As a result, many students—roughly 3,400—opt to join one of UW's 44 residential fraternities or sororities. Although the Greek residences are private housing facilities, the administration has every fraternity and sorority sign a recognition agreement in which they submit to "certain well-defined rules," in particular, a pledge to keep residences alcohol free. Any Greek group that does not abide by the agreement is not officially recognized by the university. In any case, Greek life has kept some students from becoming just a number. "If I had to do it over again, I would have joined a fraternity," says an upperclassman. "They provide a sense of community." Alternative housing can be found in the many Christian houses around UW. Says a student resident of one such house, "I have lived all five years in the University Christian Union, in the middle of 'Greek Row,' and this experience alone would have justified my enrollment at UW. These houses range in size and affiliation, but I feel they present a superb alternative to the dorms, the apartments, or the Greek system."

Married couples and same-sex domestic partners are allowed to live together in UW's family housing buildings. In the residence halls, the university offers no single-sex dorm option for undergrads, but students can choose men-only or women-only floors. In many of the residence halls, men and women live next door to one another. However, there are no coed dorm rooms or bathrooms. That's good news, and so is this: the food court in the Husky Union Building won a 2003 grand prize in the large school category from the National Association of College and University Food Services.

Six years ago, Washington voters passed an initiative that prohibits preferential treatment based on race, sex, color, ethnicity, or national origin in public employment, education, and contracting. The Office of Minority Affairs has thus had to fall back on strategies more in line with what was originally meant by "affirmative action." UW recruits minority and economically disadvantaged students through its Educational Opportunity Program and also raises scholarship funds for minority students.

The 40 or so student organizations (out of about 550 total) devoted to political and social action can agree on one thing: they all want to end oppression. And if possible, they would like this to be accomplished quickly. Women, sweatshop workers, blacks, welfare recipients, Hispanics, gay/lesbian/transgender/questioning students, and animals—they all have vocal allies at UW. Currently, the most politically active groups are the Muslim Student Association, the Coalition against the War at the UW, the Student Action Network, and VOX (the Planned Parenthood chapter). Several multicultural student groups are actually components of the student government and are thus subsidized by it.

Conservatives make some noise, too. The College Republicans and some libertarian groups at UW have held "affirmative action bake sales," satires of student feminists' "wage gap" bake sales. At such events, cookies and brownies are sold at different prices depending on the buyer's race and sex. (White males and Asians pay more, favored minorities less.) At one of these affairs, two angry students opposed to the bake-sale protest threatened the participating students. They had to be restrained by police when they ripped down signs and threw cookies. A school official then told the College Republicans, the group holding the sale, to take down their table and disperse. "It sets a horrible precedent on campus, that if you want to stop someone's free speech, just get violent," said the president of the College Republicans club. Nevertheless, Jerry Grinstein, president of the University of Washington's Board of Regents, supported shutting down the bake sale and wrote in a letter to the student newspaper: "The 'statements' of the UW College Republicans in putting on a bake sale about affirmative action were tasteless and hurtful to many members of the university community. . . . We pledge our best efforts to foster a welcoming environment for a diverse university community." Just so long as all their ideas are the same.

Athletics are a fundamental element of student life at UW. Huskies football dominates the fall semester, and students can purchase season tickets for $90. In 2003, the athletics department was rocked by scandal when state health officials said a physician, Dr. William J. Scheyer, who had worked with the University of Washington's athletics department, had improperly prescribed thousands of doses of steroids, painkillers, and other drugs to athletes, trainers, and himself over a four-year period. A 2004 report by the school confirmed the abuses, according to the *Chronicle of Higher Education*. The doctor (nicknamed "the Candy Man" by team members) had his license suspended.

The Intramural Activities Building houses top-quality athletic facilities. Besides sports, the university also hosts all sorts of artistic and cultural performances in a 1,200-seat theater in the Meany Hall for the Performing Arts. The School of Drama stages productions in three smaller theaters.

There is an active chaplaincy program catering to a wide variety of faiths. Among the most active are the Episcopalian Canterbury group at Covenant House and the Catholic Newman Club. The latter is housed in the modernist Prince of Peace Chapel. Those looking for more traditional environs should seek out the liturgy offered at St. Joseph's Chapel in the Josephinum residence on Seattle's Second Avenue.

UW has a very safe campus, despite its large size and urban location. In 2003, the school reported only one forcible sex assault, one robbery, two aggravated assaults, and 74 burglaries on campus. However, the area surrounding UW is not as safe; according to a *Seattle Times* article, nearby University Way is one of the most crime-ridden areas in Seattle. A recent shooting in the University District (not officially part of the UW campus), in which a drunk and drugged felon walked into a coffeehouse with a gun, took students by surprise and increased fears. Another student was recently abducted and forced to withdraw money from an ATM, then released. The assailant was caught. Such events are rare and are generally limited to the area surrounding campus. The campus police, an accredited state police force, are regarded as efficient and committed to deterring campus crime. The school also offers several escort and shuttle services at night.

UW's in-state tuition in 2004–5 was only $4,458; nonresidents paid $15,661. Room and board cost $7,968. The university does practice need-blind admissions but does not guarantee to meet the full need of admitted students. About 47 percent of degree-seeking undergrads receive some aid from the school, and the average loan debt of a UW student upon graduation is $15,658.

WHITMAN COLLEGE

WALLA WALLA, WASHINGTON • WWW.WHITMAN.EDU

Not Walt

Whitman Seminary was founded as a coed secondary school in 1859 to honor not the bawdy poet Walt, but Marcus and Narcissa Whitman—missionaries to the Cayuse Indians and to the immigrants on the Oregon Trail. The Whitmans had been killed by Indians in 1847. In 1883, the seminary was chartered as a four-year college, and in 1913 it became the first U.S. college or university to have comprehensive exams for its majors. It was granted a Phi Beta Kappa chapter in 1919. Today, Whitman boasts the highest graduation rate and the largest endowment and trust funds per student of any school in the Pacific Northwest.

Whitman places a good deal of emphasis on the themes of environmental responsibility and multiculturalism, but at the same time the college continues to pay more than passing respect to Western classics and culture. The college forms a relationship with every student and provides a warm atmosphere for academic growth while demanding rigorous study and academic performance. A fairly radical left-leaning academic agenda sometimes stifles the free exchange of ideas in the classroom, but debate on the campus does exist—and it is sometimes bitter. In general, that's far better than sleepy complacency.

Academic Life: Be curious, not judgmental

Whitman continually ranks highly in several of the national college ranking lists, but lists aside, Whitman stands out. Its full-year freshman core curriculum of reading and writing on the great books is unusually rigorous and demanding. Also distinctive are the mandatory comprehensive examinations in students' majors and the "undergraduate conference," an option only a few years old, which is akin to the senior project demanded at other elite schools. Self-designed majors are an increasingly popular option at Whitman; in them, students cross disciplines to create their own programs. Overall, Whitman has lately put more emphasis on interdisciplinary study.

When a student enrolls at the college, he is assigned a faculty advisor (in the student's area of interest if he has specified one). During orientation week, students meet with their advisors to plan courses. They then meet with their advisors at least three more times throughout the first year. Student academic advisors (SAs) live in first-year residence hall sections and give advice on which professors to take, how to balance courseloads, and how to gain much-needed study skills. The SAs organize weekly study sessions for the first-year core class, and professors lead discussions in the residence halls.

A two-semester core class, "Antiquity and Modernity," is required of all first-year students. Students meet in small-group seminars of no more than 20 students and study under professors from a number of different disciplines; a biology professor may teach Shakespeare, and an English teacher might teach Darwin. Among the thinkers and texts studied in this year-long course are Homer's *Odyssey*, Sappho, Sophocles' *Antigone* and Euripides' *Medea*, Plato's *Symposium*, several Old and New Testament books, Virgil's *Aeneid*, Augustine's *Confessions*, and works by Galileo, Descartes, Shakespeare, Locke, Rousseau, Kant, Darwin, and Nietzsche.

A sophomore-level core course, "Critical and Alternative Voices," which explores voices that are "geographically non-Western as well as those excluded or subordinated by way of race, gender, or class within Europe and America," is (fortunately) optional. There is a common syllabus for all sections of the core courses. Although readings in the courses evolve a little from year to year, professors are restricted from altering course content significantly. "There is a reluctance to radically change the curriculum," says one professor. "Any changes mostly amount to one year reading the *Iliad* and the next year reading the *Odyssey*." A few students consider the core courses a bit of a burden, but for the most part, they realize the importance of them once they complete the

VITAL STATISTICS

Religious affiliation: none
Total enrollment: 1,405
Total undergraduates: 1,405
SAT/ACT midranges: SAT
  V: 620–710, M: 600–690;
  ACT: 27–31
Applicants: 2,143
Applicants accepted: 50%
*Accepted applicants who
  enrolled*: 31%
Tuition: $26,870
Room and board: $7,180
Freshman retention rate: 94%
Graduation rate: 75% (4 yrs.),
  85% (6 yrs.)
*Courses with fewer than 20
  students*: 70%
Student-faculty ratio: 10:1
*Courses taught by graduate
  TAs*: none
Most popular majors:
  English, psychology,
  sociology
Students living on campus:
  56%
*Guaranteed housing for four
  years?* no
Students in fraternities: 34%
  sororities: 32%

ACADEMIC REQUIREMENTS

Whitman requires an extremely abbreviated, but worthy, core course of all students: the two-course sequence "Antiquity and Modernity." In it, students encounter a sampling of the great works of Western literature and history. Beyond this, student must take two classes in each of the following areas:

- Social sciences. Choices range from "Argument in the Law and Politics" to "Introduction to Gender Studies."
- Humanities. Options include "Renaissance Art" and "Sexuality and Textuality."
- Fine arts. Choices here range from "Music History: Medieval through 1700" to "The Wardrobe Artist in the Theatre."
- Science (including one with a lab section).

courses. "The core courses create a built-in platform for dialogue in upper-level classes and outside the classroom. Students have a common ground," says one student. With so many great works in "Antiquity and Modernity," it's a shame that Whitman stops there—it imposes only a few distribution requirements apart from the demands of a major. And due to retirements and new faculty members, one professor says, "the emphasis has shifted from canonical writers and approaches to more emphasis on cultural studies and diversity perspectives. In the special topics courses, there is less consideration of major authors (e.g., James, Conrad, Faulkner, Pope, Dickens, Keats, Yeats, etc.) than in the past, in favor of multicultural themes and authors."

"Students *can* get a solid grounding in the liberal arts at Whitman, but merely meeting the requirements for graduation will not guarantee this," a professor says. "Students should discuss how to accomplish this with their premajor advisors as soon as they get to campus." A different teacher says, "It is possible to get a strong liberal arts education at Whitman, *if* the student chooses wisely from the potpourri of diverse offerings, and *if* the student gets solid direction from his/her advisor."

"The core does offer readings in substantial works in the Western tradition," one professor says, "but in some cases this is in snippets (the Bible), and a frequent complaint is that an insufficient amount of time is spent on individual texts." And while the core provides a good start for students, some departments don't reinforce it. "It cannot be said that the current English department offers a good survey of English literature," says one professor. Because of the many options open to students majoring in English literature, "it is possible for them to avoid hundreds of years of English lit., traditional major authors, and important periods," he says. However, if a student wants to encounter living authors, Whitman provides ample opportunities. The college offers the Walt Whitman Lecture, which has attracted major writers to read and speak, including Seamus Heaney, Robert Pinsky, Louise Gluck, Adrienne Rich, Derek Wolcott, Billy Collins, and Maya Angelou.

Students choose their majors during their second year. Whitman offers 42 majors and 34 minors. The most popular majors are English, psychology, and sociology. Once a student chooses a major, he also chooses a faculty advisor; he may select another advisor later for guidance in his thesis or research work for the undergraduate conference. Advising varies from student to student and from professor to professor.

"Some advisors take an active approach with pizza parties and such. Others let the students come to them, while encouraging them to speak to them if they need advice," says one student. Some majors are established departmental programs; others are amalgams, integrating work from two or more programs—many of these combine environmental studies with another discipline—or an individually devised plan of study. The last choice requires a good deal of extra work, including organizing a major committee, proposing the major, presenting its rationale, obtaining approval from the Board of Review, and getting the proposal approved by the Academic Council.

The college recently began inviting students to present their work at the Whitman Undergraduate Conference (also called the "major conference" or "major research conference"). The conference, scheduled near the end of the spring term, is a presentation and celebration of students' work, usually in their majors. Modeled partly on academic conferences, the event features studio art exhibits, original plays in the college theater, senior recitals, expository papers, and original scientific research. Whitman even cancels classes so students and faculty can pay full attention to the fruit of three (and sometimes more) years of intensive study.

The politics department claims that it has "earned a reputation of resisting the trend toward narrow specialization in classroom teaching." Now, just to mention this trend is admirable, but the department's courses don't always live up to its claim. They include "The Christian Right in the United States," "Welfare in America," "Capital Punishment," "Politics of Race, Ethnicity, and Religion," and several others concerning environmentalism. An overwhelming number of the politics courses—even those with innocuous titles like "Nations and Nationalism"—emphasize race, ethnicity, and gender. Still, some of them continue to use primary sources. For instance, in "Sexuality and Textuality," students read Plato, Sappho, and Shakespeare. Other comparatively strong departments are biology, chemistry, history, music, religion, and some of the foreign languages.

As Whitman is exclusively an undergraduate college, there are no graduate teaching assistants. However, "there are a significant number of adjuncts teaching regular courses at Whitman, especially in the first-year core," says a faculty member. Ninety percent of classes have fewer than 30 students; this allows students and faculty to interact closely. The school's student-faculty ratio is an outstanding 10 to 1. It is not unheard of for some classes to be taught at professors' homes, as most faculty members live within walking distance of campus. Students repeatedly praise the accessibility of professors, most of whom give students both their office and home phone numbers.

REQUIREMENTS (CONT'D)

- "Alternative voices." In addition to multi-culturalist classes, students can fulfill this requirement through upper-level language courses, history courses, or courses taken while studying abroad.

Every student must take one course in quantitative analysis. It can be fulfilled by any mathematics or computer science course or by various courses in different departments (including symbolic logic and advanced music theory).

Every student also faces a mandatory (and typically rigorous) comprehensive examination on the contents of his chosen major.

Professors and students often play intramurals, eat, and chat together around the small campus. The admissions department recounts how one mathematics professor, for instance, explained a difficult concept to a couple of students in the frozen juice section of a local grocery store. "I would have to say the best part of Whitman College is faculty-student relations," a religion major says. "I've always received help from my professors, and they sometimes go out of their way for me." One Whitman professor asserts that "excellent teaching is the top priority" at the school.

Students here are intellectual, but not as competitive as at some top schools in the Northeast. As one professor explains: "There is a cultural flavor here that you can notice in academic life. [The students] are more laid back about things, more well-rounded, and more cooperative in group projects. To generalize, they're not selfish about learning." Whitman students are mostly "bright and happy people with a lot of interests," says another professor.

One professor says that although her fellow faculty members are overwhelmingly liberal, "We don't wear our politics on our sleeves." One exception might be the politics department, which, as one student says, is "known for throwing its leftist views in your face."

"The political leaning of both the faculty and the student body is so liberal that conservatives like myself are . . . verbally attacked and affronted with regularity," one student says. "There are no right-leaning politics professors, and it is almost suicide to be a conservative politics major; the atmosphere of many courses is charged in this way, and it certainly influences the content of social science courses like history and politics." Another student says, "It would be hard to be a conservative here."

Whitman has a number of excellent professors. Students say the best teachers include Delbert Hutchison in biology; James Russo and Leroy G. "Skip" Wade in chemistry; Dana L. Burgess in classics; Jan Crouter in economics; John F. Desmond in English; Robert J. Carson in geology and environmental studies; David F. Schmitz in history; Bob Fontenot, Pat Keef (also the dean of the faculty), and Laura Schueller in mathematics; David Glenn and Susan Pickett in music; David Carey and Patrick Frierson in philosophy; Rogers Miles and Walter Wyman Jr. in religion; Robert Sickels in rhetoric and film studies; and Keith Farrington in sociology.

Whitman offers a strong study-abroad option, cosponsoring international programs in Sri Lanka, Scotland, New Zealand, China, Argentina, Spain, and dozens of other locations; 40 percent of juniors participate in one (or more) of them. Environmental interdisciplinary majors can take a "Semester in the West," an adventure term of field work with working environmentalists. Numerous opportunities to conduct and present original research are available to science (including premed) majors. Prelaw students can, with six years of study, combine a Whitman BA with a JD from Columbia University.

Four years ago, Whitman finished expanding and renovating its Penrose Memorial Library to accommodate its rapidly expanding collections. Currently, the college has more than 350,000 volumes. Whitman also participates in the SUMMIT system, which provides students access to more than three million volumes within 48 hours.

When classes are in session, the library is open 24 hours a day, allowing students to use study rooms and carrels and computers and printers. A cafe in the new addition is open in the evenings.

Whitman is thoroughly wired. Both PCs and Macs are available at all hours in the library and in computer labs. Laser printing is free for students, as are e-mail accounts and Internet access. All residence halls have Ethernet connections for students who bring computers, and about half do.

Student Life: To be with those I like is enough

Whitman College embodies the Green-and-granola lifestyle that permeates the Pacific Northwest, where the God-given landscape is so awe-inspiring, imposing, and noble that people seem keen not to wreck it. And so Whitman is the sort of place that uses 100 percent recycled paper for its course catalog—should you be so wasteful as to need to print what is available online. The school has a multitude of left-leaning student groups and two vaguely right-leaning ones. It shouldn't be surprising that the school is pretty darn liberal, politically.

> **SUGGESTED CORE**
>
> 1. Classics 130, Ancient Mythology
> 2. Philosophy 201, Ancient Philosophy
> 3. and 4. Religion 202, The New Testament and Early Christianity
> 5. Politics 222, Modern European Political Theory
> 6. English 351 and 352, Shakespeare
> 7. History 105, Development of the United States (1607–1877)
> 8. Philosophy 304, Kant and the Nineteenth Century

"There is no respect for open debate, and a true scrutiny of political issues is rare," says one conservative student, who laments a "lack of religious and political diversity" at the college. According to one professor, "both students and administrators have called for greater openness to Republicans, Christians, as well as the more usual minorities." The professor sees "more support for students all along the political spectrum than in the past" at Whitman.

Thomas E. Cronin, a fair-minded and popular figure who had served as president at Whitman since 1993, recently stepped down. His successor, George S. Bridges, comes from the University of Washington, where he was dean of undergraduate education and a professor of sociology. Bridges's scholarly research has been focused on problems of racial and ethnic minorities in the juvenile justice system. A professor, noting remarks Bridges has made about "diversity," says simply (and perhaps ominously), "Things will change."

In a student body of approximately 1,400, the College Republicans have almost 70 members, meet biweekly, and are trying to become more active and vocal on campus. Already, the group has made itself visible in the *Pioneer* (the student newspaper) and in somewhat vituperative discussions on the campus e-mail listserv.

Whitman's recent speakers have included Sister Helen Prejean (author of *Dead Man Walking*), physicist Amory Lovins, the solar-living guru John Shaeffer, historian and social activist Howard Zinn, Alix Olson (a feminist "slam" poet), Holocaust survivor and educator Alice Kern, Nobel Prize–winning economist Douglas North, civil rights

WEST

941

lawyer Morris Dees, Ralph Nader, and Christopher Hitchens. In spring 2004, speakers included environmentalist Helen Caldecott; conservative television personality Ben Stein; world-famous climber Lynn Hill; and Cornel West, activist and author, who was cosponsored by the Black Student Union.

Freshman orientation at Whitman is typical of most liberal arts colleges. In 2002, incoming first-years read and discussed *The Battle for God*, a book on religious fundamentalism by Karen Armstrong, and attended mandatory programs like "In One Room: Queer Conversations," a student-written, award-winning docudrama on "coming out, family, religion, politics, gender, and sexuality." A discussion followed, but it seems to have been more of a self-help, "my-experience-was" hour than an actual discussion and exchange of ideas. In 2003, the book was *The Things They Carried* by Tim O'Brien; there was also a multicultural student social and another performance of "In One Room."

Just over half of Whitman students live on campus; all students under 21 who haven't already lived on campus for four semesters are required to do so. But wherever students live, the college pledges that they "will be part of a close community that makes it easy to form lifelong friendships." The campus offers residence halls arranged in both traditional dormitory style and in suites. All dorms are coed, except for one that houses freshman women and some sorority members. Members of the four fraternities live in separate houses and enjoy separate dining services. Douglas Hall is a 24-hour quiet hall with a few single rooms and suites of eight students and is an option for upperclassmen. A housing official says that each year a handful of students opt for coed dorm rooms (they must have parental approval). Almost all dorm rooms, however, are single sex. Except for those in the "interest houses," all residence hall bathrooms are single sex.

Whitman's 11 interest houses include La Casa Hispana, La Maison Française, Tekisuijuku (Japanese House), Das Deutsche Haus, Asian Studies House, Outhouse (an environmental studies house), Fine Arts House, Community Service House, MECCA House (i.e., Multi-Ethnic Center for Cultural Affairs), Global Awareness House, and the Writing House.

Religious students who come to Whitman should "actively seek out a faith community on or off campus and become as active as possible," one professor says, noting that "only a minority of students are religiously active." Faith-based groups include Catholics on Campus, InterVarsity Christian Fellowship, and Shalom, a Jewish club. Interesting communities in Walla Walla include St. Silouan Greek Orthodox Church, which is composed mostly of former Episcopalians who worship in English using a modified Book of Common Prayer.

Whitman's campus is lovely. The administration plants dozens of trees every year, and a creek and duck pond further beautify the surroundings. Walla Walla, whose Main Street is within easy walking distance, is an agricultural center, but its downtown includes sidewalk cafes, restaurants, and art galleries.

Seattle is a four-hour drive and Spokane (home of Gonzaga University) is three hours away; in other words, Whitman students better get used to Walla Walla and its limited options. Students create their own entertainment with a good deal of help from the college. One of the country's top debate programs, active theater and music performance programs, a highly competitive ski program, and a highly rated student-run radio station are just some activities that "Whitties" enjoy. There are usually parties on weekends (and the days leading up to the weekends), guest lectures, and coffee-house music performances on Friday nights. One student says, "I know too many people who consider getting drunk a good way to spend their free time. But once the weekend ends, it is back to work." Half the student body spends time on community work, too. Whitman's Center for Community Services is the volunteer clearinghouse for the campus. Its on-campus volunteer programs include Whitman Mentors and a Cross-Cultural Outreach Program.

Placed in a stunning natural environment, Whitman offers lots of opportunities to enjoy the great outdoors. Students will find many options for outdoor activities nearby, including hiking in Rooks Park and in the Blue Mountains, skiing at Bluewood, skating at the Ice Chalet, fishing the South Fork of the Walla Walla River, camping in the Umatilla National Forest, whitewater rafting in northeastern Oregon, and even berry picking in the nearby mountains. Students say that everything in Walla Walla is bikeable, but many students have cars, which are helpful for escaping the immediate vicinity.

The Whitman Missionaries (really) compete on 20 intercollegiate varsity sports teams. Club sports for men and women include lacrosse and rugby, with coed leagues in fencing, volleyball, water polo, and ultimate Frisbee. There are also intramural sports. The physical education department teaches classes in basic fitness and sports. It also offers lifeguard training, self-defense, kayaking, swimming, rock climbing, snowboarding, and ice skating. A renovated athletic center accommodates most of these activities. The Outing Program activities (first-year students do the "Scrambles," a series of outdoor adventure trips in the Pacific Northwest) include cooperative wilderness trips, kayaking, fly fishing, survival classes, ski and bike clinics, and the like. If you go to Whitman, you should emerge physically fit.

The campus and the surrounding area are quite safe; on-campus crime statistics for the past three years total one burglary and one nonforcible and eight forcible sex offenses. However, six of those sex crimes took place in 2003.

Whitman's 2004–5 tuition rate of $26,870 and room and board cost of $7,180 are typical of prestigious liberal arts institutions. Admission, fortunately, is need-blind, with financial aid provided to 45 percent of undergraduates. The college spends approximately $10.6 million each year on financial aid.

Asking the Right Questions:
What You Need to Know to Choose the Right College

If you are like many readers of this college guide, you will soon be visiting various colleges and universities in an attempt to get a better feel for which institution is the best option for you—or for your son or daughter. In this section we offer some advice on how to make the most of these visits by doing some research of your own. Our hope is to alert you to some of the questions that you might wish to raise, and issues to which you will want to be sensitive, while visiting any campus, so that even if you are not visiting one of the institutions profiled here, you will be able to make a more informed choice.

The following questions, similar to those we asked in conducting our research for *Choosing the Right College*, are divided into three areas of inquiry: Academic Life, Student Life, and Political Atmosphere. The first two sections, Academic Life and Student Life, suggest questions to be asked of student tour guides, professors, and administrators. Each question is followed by a brief explanation of its importance.

A word of advice: Questioning on-campus representatives is a delicate matter that you should approach with savvy and tact. Don't assume that tour guides, in particular, will know the answers to some of the questions that follow. After all, they are often young students themselves and may have never thought about these issues. Therefore, you should be prepared to seek out professors and administrators, who will be better able to address your concerns. And of course, it is important to be polite, to size up each encounter individually, and to base your assessment on the totality of your on-campus experience.

The final section, Political Atmosphere, is intended to inform you of some widespread and often controversial issues affecting campus life. Raising such matters can be difficult, particularly in a group setting. The questioner in this instance risks appearing confrontational or overbearing when pressing student guides who might be leading a group of parents and students. Other official campus representatives are unlikely to acknowledge the existence of campus controversy. Being aware of the problems adverted to in this section, however, will allow you to identify trouble spots on any campus with confidence and ease.

I. ACADEMIC LIFE: KEY QUESTIONS

Question: *What percentage of classes is taught by teaching assistants (TAs)? Who is doing the grading?*

Explanation: At many schools, particularly large state universities and research institutions, both public and private, professors are recruited and retained by reducing (or even eliminating) their teaching loads. Therefore, undergraduates may be taught by graduate students in their twenties working their way toward a PhD rather than by the famous professors lauded in university literature. Pay particular attention to freshman and sophomore classes, where the use of TAs is greatest. And where tenure is decided primarily on the quantity of publications rather than the quality of a candidate's teaching, professors have a disincentive to pursue pedagogical excellence.

Question: *Is there a true core curriculum made up of required courses across the liberal arts and sciences that all students must take, or do you instead rely on distribution requirements that allow students to pick and choose from among numerous courses within a given discipline?*

Explanation: Most schools long ago abandoned their core curricula, which required each student to take a series of broadly informative courses that ensured that everyone emerged broadly educated in the arts and sciences regardless of his or her academic major. Many colleges falsely state that they have a core curriculum when that is not at all the case. If your sources answer this question affirmatively, ask them how many choices exist within each disciplinary requirement. If the answer is more than one or two, there is no core curriculum worthy of the name.

Question: *Must all students study Western history and literature?*

Explanation: When the core was abandoned, most schools still required students to take history and literature survey courses that exposed them to the broad sweep of our civilization's accomplishments. Today, however, an increasing number of schools have made these courses optional. Therefore, many students graduate without ever studying the history of Western civilization or its finest texts and thinkers. Students may often study cultures or works of literature that are either best left to more specialized studies or that do not merit serious academic attention.

Question: *Is a course on American history required for graduation?*

Explanation: The study of U.S. history has disappeared from many schools' graduation requirements in much the same way Western history has been removed from the required curriculum. While the absence of such courses from the required list does not mean that they are not available, it does reveal an administration lacking a commitment to foster in its students an understanding of our nation's past.

Question: *To what extent are students advised by faculty members? If faculty members are not advising students, who is carrying out this important task?*

Explanation: Many colleges assign students advisors or employ professional advisors, thus fulfilling, on paper, an important obligation. Yet these advisors often know little about the particular courses in which a student may be interested, or else are professional "educrats" with little qualification for the job. Professors, on the other hand, are best qualified to advise students on which courses and professors to take, as well as to offer insight into academic majors, internships, and postgraduate study. Of course, even assigning professors sometimes fails to guarantee access to good information. As documented in the *Chronicle of Higher Education*, some faculty members are often difficult to track down and hold infrequent office hours. Who your advisor is will impact your life during and after college. Choose wisely.

Question: *On average, how many years does it take to graduate?*
What percentage of freshmen graduate at all?

Explanation: Universities often fail to offer required courses in numbers sufficient to accommodate every student's needs. Courses fill up and leave students with no recourse but to spend additional semesters, and even a fifth or sixth year, fulfilling graduation requirements. Parents must pay more in tuition, while students postpone entry into the workplace and often assume additional debt. This administrative decision also increases the demand for teaching assistants, thus justifying universities' large doctoral programs while relieving professors of their obligation to teach. Everyone wins but the student (and parent).

II. STUDENT LIFE: INFORMATION TO GATHER

Question: *Can a student be assured of securing a room in a single-sex dorm if desired?*
Are bathrooms coed?

Explanation: Many colleges today offer only coed dorms. Some have single-sex floors within dorms, while others are single sex by room. Yet others have shared bathrooms—toilet areas and showers shared by both sexes.

Question: *Can a student be assured of living on campus each year if he or she so desires?*

Explanation: Living on campus is a very important element of the college experience. It places students in closer proximity to one another and to campus events and is therefore key to the development of a close-knit campus community. Dorm life also exposes students to others from varied backgrounds and with diverse interests.

Question: Are there substance-free dorms?

Explanation: Responding to demands from both students and parents, some schools have established special dorms, or floors, whose residents agree to abstain from alcohol, drugs, and tobacco. These areas provide a welcome relief for students seeking a more civil lifestyle in residence halls.

Question: Is there any mandatory student orientation that exposes students to sexually explicit material or graphic explanations of sexual practices?

Explanation: Films that most parents would consider pornographic are often shown during orientation. Practices that violate family morals may be presented in positive terms or even advocated.

Question: How much crime is there both on and adjacent to campus?

Explanation: Some schools engage in statistical high jinks in order to hide the true crime rate from parents, students, and donors. For example, schools often ignore crimes committed in areas immediately adjacent to campus—surely a distinction without a difference—in order to lower the apparent crime rate.

III. POLITICAL ATMOSPHERE: PROBLEMS TO CONSIDER

Issue: Speech codes operating under the guise of sexual harassment codes.

Explanation: During the late 1980s and early 1990s, many schools instituted speech codes that sought to intimidate into silence any students or professors who questioned the emerging politically correct orthodoxies. A public outcry ensued, colleges lost several important court challenges to the speech codes, and administrators publicly distanced themselves from speech codes in name if not always in practice. Today, the same degree of intimidation is sometimes achieved through so-called harassment (or sexual harassment) codes. While purporting to protect students, these codes can be used by schools to silence or punish those who disagree with politically correct mandates.

Issue: Ostracizing or punishing students for speaking their minds when they disagree with received academic opinion.

Explanation: Numerous examples exist of official harassment of students who voice dissenting opinions on matters ranging from the importance of feminist scholarship or the morality of affirmative action to questions of religious beliefs and sexual propriety. Beliefs associated with traditional virtues are sometimes ridiculed and even banned. Defending your beliefs in the face of criticism is part of the college experience; facing official sanction for voicing them is unacceptable.

Issue: The politicization of the curriculum. For example, literature courses that focus on topics other than great works of literature, such as colonialism, "marginalized voices," or popular culture, often conflate politics with scholarship.

Explanation: Remember that course titles can be misleading. For instance, a class titled "American Revolution" may present the causes of the Revolution, the search for constitutional order, or the founding generation in a relentlessly cynical light. Some professors will teach the entire period through the lenses of race, class, and gender, which allows them to condemn the Founders for failing to live up to the ideals of our own time. This type of approach is increasingly common among historians.

Issue: *The lack of intellectual diversity within academic departments. New faculty members are often expected to share the political opinions of their colleagues.*

Explanation: Radical faculty have consolidated their hold on many departments by gaining control of the hiring process for new professors. By hiring only those who share their politically correct views, they reduce opposition to their own schemes while persecuting dissenting colleagues, ridiculing religion, offering highly politicized courses, or harassing students who speak out against them. This is one of the most disturbing trends in higher education.

In addition to this college guide, there are other sources you should mine. Recruitment literature, college Web sites, and the university bookstore are especially important. Visit the school's Web site and look at course offerings in the departments of English and history, two bellwethers of a school's curricular trends. Many schools post syllabi on the Web, and you can learn much from perusing these sources. Look for classes that cast their subjects in the language of victimology. Course descriptions or readings that employ the terminology of race, class, gender, and other trendy academic categories usually indicate a high degree of politicization—the substitution of politics for genuine learning. In the campus bookstore, visit the course readings section. You may gauge the quality of departments by the number of politicized works assigned. Note titles that condemn America and the West, deconstruct literature, or celebrate political action over rigorous study. A preponderance of such books reveals a department run by professors who would rather indoctrinate than educate.

Additional Services from ISI

Choosing the Right College has been produced by the staff of the Intercollegiate Studies Institute (ISI), a nonprofit, nonpartisan educational organization. Since its founding in 1953, ISI has supported efforts to strengthen liberal arts curricula at colleges and universities nationwide. As we continue to mark our fiftieth anniversary, our programs and publications are stronger and more influential than ever.

ISI's Student Self-Reliance Project, of which *Choosing the Right College* is the foundation, is a comprehensive program designed to ensure that students have access to the intellectual tools they need to make the most of their education. The project consists of a broad selection of programs and publications that will help students navigate through their schools' academic, social, and political environments.

Students can turn first to *A Student's Guide to Liberal Learning*, by Georgetown University professor James V. Schall, for wise counsel on how to read well, mature intellectually, and gain insight into the nature of education. Mark Henrie's *Student's Guide to the Core Curriculum* will help them build a concrete foundation for their studies. It also demonstrates that, by choosing electives carefully, students can obtain the education they deserve even at schools that abolished their core curricula decades ago.

As students progress through their college years, they will find that our unique student guides will keep them ahead of the class. These brief essays by nationally known scholars on a number of topics and disciplines—including classics, psychology, U.S. history, economics, literature, philosophy, political philosophy, and the study of history—serve as superb introductions to the most important fields in the liberal arts. The text of each of these guides may be downloaded free of charge at www.isi.org. Forthcoming guides will treat the disciplines of law, natural science, religious studies, sociology, music, and American political thought.

Conferences, lectures, fellowships, books, and journals round out the services provided by ISI to tens of thousands of students and professors each year. ISI organizes conferences on important intellectual problems as well as career development seminars throughout the nation. Lecturers sponsored by ISI speak on more than two hundred college campuses annually on a vast array of topics. Graduate students in the sciences, social sciences, education, and humanities may apply for our prestigious fellowships. And ISI yearly publishes and distributes a range of scholarly and opinion journals, as well as nearly twenty serious books of nonfiction through its national trade imprint, ISI Books.

Whatever your stage of education—homeschool, high school, college, graduate school, or lifelong learner—ISI offers programs and publications designed to help you make the most of your talents. And whether you are a student or teacher, professor or parent, you can benefit from our resources and expertise.

To learn more about the Intercollegiate Studies Institute, a nonprofit 501(c)3 organization, or to make a donation to ISI, visit our Web site at www.isi.org or e-mail us at collegeguide@isi.org. You may also call us at (800) 526-7022 or mail us at: ISI, P.O. Box 4431, Wilmington, Delaware, 19807-0431. ISI Books titles—including the volumes mentioned above—may be ordered by calling (800) 621-2736 or by visiting the ISI Books Web site at www.isibooks.org.